Introduction to

LEGAL STUDIES

FIFTH EDITION

edited by

Stephen Tasson
Jane Dickson
Vincent Kazmierski
Betina Kuzmarov
Sebastien Malette

Department of Law and Legal Studies
Carleton University

CANADIAN LEGAL STUDIES SERIES

Captus Press

Canadian Legal Studies Series
Introduction to Legal Studies, Fifth Edition

This Selection Copyright © 2015 by the editors and Captus Press Inc.

First Captus Press edition, 1990
Fifth edition, 2015

Captus Press Inc.
Units 14 & 15
1600 Steeles Avenue West
Concord, ON   L4K 4M2
Telephone: (416) 736–5537
Fax: (416) 736–5793
Email: Info@captus.com
Internet: http://www.captus.com

Library and Archives Canada Cataloguing in Publication

Introduction to legal studies / edited by Stephen Tasson, Jane Dickson, Vincent Kazmierski, Betina Kuzmarov, and Sebastien Malette. -- Fifth edition.

(Canadian legal studies series)
Includes bibliographical references.
ISBN 978-1-55322-334-4

1. Law--Canada--Textbooks. 2. Sociological jurisprudence--Canada--Textbooks. 3. Sociological jurisprudence--Textbooks. I. Tasson, Stephen, editor II. Dickson, Jane (E. Jane), editor III. Kazmierski, Vincent, editor IV. Kuzmarov, Betina, editor V. Malette, Sébastien, editor VI. Series: Canadian legal studies series

KE442.I57 2015   349.71   C2015-905251-3
KF385.ZA2I57 2015

Canada

0 9 8 7 6 5 4 3 2 1
Printed and bound in Canada

Table of Contents

I

Law in Context

II
Looking at Law:
Different Lenses for Law and Legal Studies

III
Making Law:
Judicial Decisions and Legislation

IV
Law, the State, and Citizens

V
Law, Crime, and Social Order

VI
Law, Economy, and Society

VII
Dispute Resolution

VIII
Access to Justice

IX
The Personnel of Law

X
Law and Social Transformation

Preface

Introduction to Legal Studies has been designed as a course-book to support a full-year introductory course to the field of Legal Studies. Like its four predecessors, this fifth edition is structured to reflect the diversity of approaches and perspectives employed within Legal Studies. At the same time, the course-book and the field of study are unified by an underlying theme: that "law" cannot be understood simply as a set of formal rules, processes and institutions. Rather, law must be understood in its wider context, including the dynamic relations between "the written law", legal processes, and the political, cultural, social and economic forces within society. Thus any study of law must engage its subject reflexively and critically, rather than accept without question legal rules, processes and institutions as natural, fixed or given. For this reason, most of the material in this reader engages in critical reflection on the purposes, effects and operation of law, rather than provide empirical descriptions or narrow explanations. Readers may find that this course-book is usefully paired with a basic introductory text that outlines the pragmatic forms and structures of the Canadian legal system.

Many of the articles included in this new edition of *Introduction to Legal Studies* raise complex, and sometimes difficult, arguments that first-year university students may initially find difficult to fully appreciate. They are included to challenge students both academically and conceptually, and to acquaint them with many new and enduring debates in the field. It is our hope that the materials included in the course-book will encourage students to read and think more broadly, and critically, not only about what law is, but about the fundamental ambiguity of its roles, functions and even limits, in a wide range of societies.

This fifth edition of *Introduction to Legal Studies* builds upon the work of the many faculty members of the Department of Law and Legal Studies at Carleton University who contributed to the previous editions. The editors also wish to acknowledge the contributions of current faculty members who agreed to have their articles included in the course-book: Doris Buss, Stacy Douglas, Ummni Khan, Michael MacNeil, Dawn Moore, George Rigakos, Neil Sargent, and Christiane Wilke. Finally, the editors were greatly aided by research assistance provided by Alfredo Garcia, Hilary Rose, Marcus Sibley, and Andrew Tompkins, as well as by the editorial support provided by Pauline Lai and Lily Chu at Captus Press. Our thanks to you all.

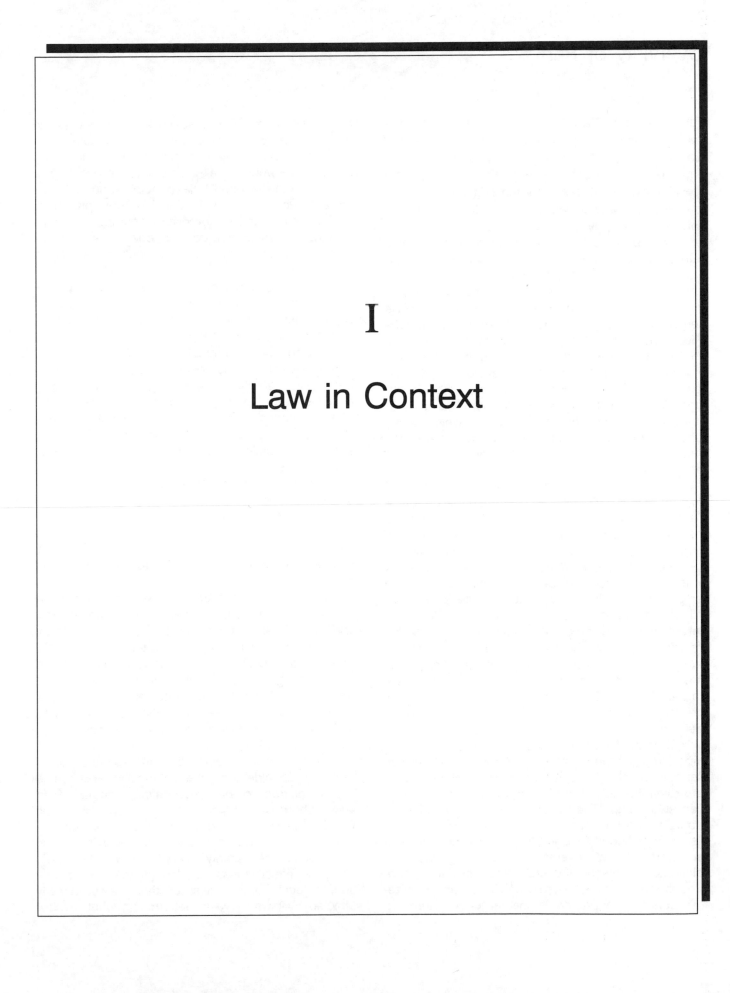

I

Law in Context

Overview of Part I

The readings in **Part I** have been selected to provide a foundation for understanding the broader context in which law operates both within Canada and globally. As such, the readings touch on both the role that law plays in organizing social behaviour and the way in which legal rules and institutions are themselves organized.

Chapter 1 considers law from a broadly social "functionalist" perspective: i.e., it advances the view that societies are complex systems with multiple parts that promote stability and innovation within those societies. In this view law generally fulfills certain necessary functions in most, if not all, societies. The chapter's readings identify different social functions that law fulfills, including serving as a mechanism that facilitates social control, dispute resolution and social change. However, these readings also suggest that existing formal legal rules or structures are not the only way in which these functions may be fulfilled, and that in some cases formal legal rules may inhibit desirable social interactions.

The readings in **Chapter 2** outline a number of different legal cultures that have shaped today's Canadian legal system. These legal cultures include the common law and civil law traditions imported from the United Kingdom and France, respectively. The readings explore the ways in which these legal traditions have shaped the contemporary Canadian legal system while also being influenced, shaped and modified by domestic political, ideological and social conditions. The piece by Borrows highlights the fact that aboriginal peoples had their own rich legal, cultural and political traditions prior to colonization. This crucial fact is rarely appreciated by Canadians and has been largely ignored or dismissed by Canadian governments in their ongoing negotiations with aboriginal peoples.

Chapter 3 includes excerpts from a number of important decisions of the Supreme Court of Canada, which identify the constitutional principles and rules that establish the framework for the Canadian state, e.g., "The Rule of Law". This framework regulates the relationship between the different levels of government in Canada and between the different branches of government. It also regulates the relationship between the state and individuals and groups. The article by Berger seeks to contextualize this Canadian approach in the larger literature on constitutionalism. Berger seeks to expose what he argues is the unique "architecture of Canadian constitutional culture" by exploring its basic founding tension: between "the universal", representing a basic faith in reasoned legal principle, and "the particular", which represents the everyday pragmatic political compromises of diverse communities like Canada. When compared with how other counties have approached their own difficult constitutions, Berger suggests that Canada's "constitutional culture" has balanced these tensions particularly well. Finally, the article by Douglas challenges the reader to consider the way in which "the Constitution" — both through its formal legal framework and its representation of communities — builds the basic framework for our democratic order and imagination, while necessarily remaining open to ongoing challenges to the way that representation occurs. She challenges us to consider the constitutive role of social institutions, like museums, in ongoing, socially and politically charged projects of "making communities".

Finally, **Chapter 4** includes a number of articles that explore Canadian law within a global context. Understanding the global context of law requires familiarity with the operation of rules of international law, including the way in which formal treaties and covenants may impact the actions of states in the international arena. However, it also requires an understanding of how international law may impact the creation, interpretation and application of domestic legal rules in Canada. The readings in this final chapter explore and critically question the relationship between international and domestic legal rules and institutions. Several of the articles emphasize the fundamental role of political decision-making processes in the negotiation and adoption (or otherwise) of important aspects of international law.

As you read through the articles included in this Part, consider how the perspectives expressed here differ from, or perhaps confirm, popularly held views about the origins, role, or scope of law in Canada. Does how we understand the basic history, functions, and composition of law in our, or in any, society necessarily affect how we view law's practical effectiveness or legitimacy? What role should local communities, or those most directly affected by laws, have in determining what the law is or ought to be; and how might we understand the place of international law in this regard? If Canadian law is ultimately the product of a complex federal system of intermingling, overlapping, and sometimes warring legal processes, traditions and cultures, does this challenge the unity or legitimacy of our law? Alternatively, might this dynamism be an important guarantee of democratic accessibility and accountability?

Social Context: Law in Social Life

(a) The Functions of Law†

Edward Adamson Hoebel

Law performs certain functions essential to the maintenance of all but the most simple societies.

The first is to define relationships among the members of a society, to assert what activities are permitted and what are ruled out, so as to maintain at least minimal integration between the activities of individuals and groups within the society.

The second is derived from the necessity of taming naked force and directing force to the maintenance of order. It is the allocation of authority and the determination of who may exercise physical coercion as a socially recognized privilege-right, along with the selection of the most effective forms of physical sanction to achieve the social ends that the law serves.

The third is the disposition of trouble cases as they arise.

The fourth is to redefine relations between individuals and groups as the conditions of life change. It is to maintain adaptability.

Purposive definition of personal relations is the primary law-job. Other aspects of culture likewise work to this end, and, indeed, the law derives its working principles (jural postulates) from postulates previously developed in the nonlegal spheres of action. However, the law's important contribution to the basic organization of society as a whole is that the law specifically and explicitly defines relations. It sets the expectancies of man to man and group to group so that each knows the focus and the limitations of its demand-rights on others, its duties to others, its privilege-rights and powers as against others, and its immunities and liabilities to the contemplated or attempted acts of others. This is the "bare-bones job", as Karl Llewellyn likes to call it. It is the ordering of the fundamentals of living together.

No culture has a specific starting point in time; yet in the operation of the first function it is as though men were getting together and saying to each other. "Look here! Let's have a little organization here or we'll never get anywhere with this mess! Let's have a clear understanding of who's who, what we are to do, and how we are going to do it!" In its essence it is what the social-contract theorists recognized as the foundation of social order.

The second function of the law — the allocation of authority to exercise coercive physical force — is something almost peculiar to things legal.

Custom has regularity, and so does law. Custom defines relationships, and so does law. Custom is sanctioned, and so is law. But the sanctions of law may involve physical coercion. Law is distinguished from mere customs in that it endows certain selected individuals with the privilege-right of applying the sanction of physical coercion, if need be. The legal, let it be repeated, has teeth that can bite. But the biting, if it is to be legal and not mere gangsterism, can be done only by those persons to whom the law

† Reprinted by permission of the publisher from THE LAW OF PRIMITIVE MAN: A STUDY IN COMPARATIVE LEGAL DYNAMICS by E. Adamson Hoebel, pp. 275–284, 287. Cambridge, Mass.: Harvard University Press. Copyright © 1954 by the President and Fellows of Harvard College. Copyright © renewed 1982 by Edward Adamson Hoebel. [Notes and/or references omitted.]

has allocated the privilege-right for the affair at hand.

We have seen that in primitive law authority is a shifting, temporary thing. Authority to enforce a norm resides (for private wrongs) with the wronged individual and his immediate kinsmen — but only for the duration of time necessary to follow through the procedural steps that lead to redress or punishment of the culprit. In primitive law the tendency is to allocate authority to the party who is directly injured. This is done in part out of convenience, for it is easier to let the wronged party assume the responsibility of legal action. It is also done because the primitive kinship group, having a more vital sense of entity, is naturally charged with a heavier emotional effect. In any event, when the community qua community acknowledges the exercise of force by a wronged person or his kinship group as correct and proper in a given situation, and so restrains the wrongdoer from striking back, then law prevails and order triumphs over violence.

We have also found in our studies of primitive societies that in a limited number of situations authority is directly exercised by the community on its own behalf. It takes the form of lynch law in some instances where clear procedures have not been set up in advance, as in the Comanche treatment of excessive sorcery and Shoshone treatment of cannibalism. Lynch law among primitives, however, is not a backsliding from, or detouring around, established formal law as it is with us. It is a first fitful step toward the emergence of criminal law in a situation in which the exercise of legal power has not yet been refined and allocated to specific persons. It is a blunt crude tool wielded by the gang hand of an outraged public.

Yet lynch law is rare among primitives. Even the simplest of them have crystallized standards as to what constitutes criminal behaviour, and the exercise of public authority is delegated to official functionaries — the chieftain, the council of chiefs, and the council of elders.

Power may sometimes be personal, as is the power of the bully in the society of small boys, and as was to some extent the power of William the Conqueror. But personal tyranny is a rare thing among primitives. Brute force of the individual does not prevail. Chiefs must have followers. Followers always impose limitations on their leaders. Enduring power is always institutionalized power. It is *transpersonalized*. It resides in the office, in the social status, rather than in the man. The constitutional structures of the several tribes examined in this book have all clearly revealed how political and legal authority are in each instance delimited and circumscribed.

This point is emphasized only to dispel any residue of the hoary political philosophies that assumed without basis in fact that primitive societies existed under the rule of fang and claw.

However, the personal still obtrudes. An "office" although culturally defined is, after all, exercised by an individual. And who that individual is at any moment certainly makes a difference. There is leeway in the exercise or non-exercise of power just as there are limits. A man may be skilled in finding the evidence and the truth in the cases he must judge and in formulating the norms to fit the case in hand — or he may be all thumbs. He may be one who thirsts for power and who will wield all he can while grasping for more. Or he may shrink from it. Power defined through allocation of legal authority is by its nature trans-personalized, yet by the nature of men it can never be wholly depersonalized. A Franklin Roosevelt is not a Warren Harding....

The third function of law calls for little additional comment.... Some trouble cases pose absolutely new problems for solution. In these cases the first and second functions may predominate. Yet this is not the situation in the instance of most legal clashes in which the problem is not the formulation of law to cover a new situation but rather the application of pre-existing law. These cases are disposed of in accordance with legal norms already set before the issue in question arises. The job is to clean the case up, to suppress or penalize the illegal behaviour and to bring the relations of the disputants back into balance, so that life may resume its normal course. This type of law-work has frequently been compared to work of the medical practitioner. It is family doctor stuff, essential to keeping the social body on its feet. In more homely terms, Llewellyn has called it, "garage-repair work on the general order of the group when that general order misses fire, or grinds gears, or even threatens a total breakdown." It is not ordinarily concerned with grand design, as is the first law-job. Nor is it concerned with redesign as is the fourth. It works to clean up all the little social messes (and the occasional big ones) that recurrently arise between the members of the society from day to day.

Most of the trouble cases do not, in a civilized society, of themselves loom large on the social scene, although in a small community even one can lead directly to a social explosion if not successfully cleaned up. Indeed, in a primitive society the individual case always holds the threat of a little civil war if procedure breaks down, for from its inception it sets kin group against kin group — and if it comes to fighting, the number of kinsmen who will be involved is almost always immediately enlarged. The fight may engulf a large part of the tribe in internecine throat-cutting. Relatively speaking, each run-of-the-mill trouble case in primitive law imposes a more pressing demand for settlement upon the legal system than is the case with us.

While system and integration are essential, flexibility and constant revision are no less so. Law is a dynamic process in which few solutions can be permanent. Hence, the fourth function of law: the redefinition of relations and the reorientation of expectancies.

Initiative with scope to work means new problems for the law. New inventions, new ideas, new behaviours keep creeping in. Especially do new behaviours creep in, nay, sweep in, when two unlike societies come newly into close contact. Then the law is called upon to decide what principles shall be applied to conflicts of claims rooted in disparate cultures. Do the new claims fit comfortably to the old postulates? Must the new realized ways of behaving be wholly rejected and legally suppressed because they are out of harmony with the old values? Or can they be modified here and altered there to gain legal acceptance? Or can the more difficult operations of altering or even junking old postulates to accommodate a new way be faced? Or can fictions be framed that can lull the mind into acceptance of the disparate new without the wrench of acknowledged junking of the old? What *is* that is wanted? The known and habitual, or the promise of the new and untested? Men may neglect to turn the law to the answer of such questions. But they do not for long. Trouble cases generated by the new keep marching in. And the fourth law-job presses for attention.

Recapitulation of just one Cheyenne case will throw the process into focus. The acquisition of horses greatly altered all Plains Indian cultures. One important Cheyenne basic postulate ran, "Except for land and tribal fetishes, all material goods are private property, but they should be generously shared with others." When it came to horses, this led some men to expect that they could freely borrow horses without even the courtesy of asking. For horse owners this got to the point of becoming a serious nuisance, as in the cases of Pawnee and Wolf Lies Down. Wolf Lies Down put his trouble case to the members of the Elk Soldier Society. They got his horse back for him with a handsome free-will offering of additional "damages" from the defendant to boot. The trouble case was neatly disposed of.

But the Elk Soldiers did not stop there. There was some preventive channeling of future behaviour to be done. Hence the "Now we shall make a new rule. There shall be no more borrowing of horses without asking. If any man takes another's goods without asking, we will go over and get them back for him. More than that, if the taker tries to keep them, we will give him a whipping." Here was the fourth function of law being performed. The lines for future conduct re horses were made clear.

Work under Function IV represents social planning brought into focus by the case of the instant and with an eye to the future.

The problem of reorienting conduct and redirecting it through the law when new issues emerge is always tied to the bare-bones demand of basic organization and the minimal maintenance of order and regularity. It may also shade over into work colored by a greater or lesser desire to achieve more than a minimum of smoothness in social relations. When this becomes an important aspect of law-work, a special aspect of law-ways activity may be recognized: the creation of techniques that efficiently and effectively solve the problems posed to all the other law-jobs so that the basic values of the society are realized through the law and not frustrated by it.

The doing of it has been called by Llewellyn "Juristic Method". It is the method not only of getting the law-jobs done but doing them with a sure touch for the net effect that results in smoothness in the doing and a harmonious wedding of what is aspired to by men and what is achieved through the law. It is the work not just of the craftsman but of the master craftsman....

. . . .

The very fact that the bulk of the substance and procedure of primitive law emerges through case action involving claim and counterclaim, pleading and counterpleading, tends to keep legal behaviour relatively close to the prevailing social values. Which way a new issue will go will depend not alone upon the facts but also upon the skill of the litigants in framing the issue and arguing the relevance of their respective positions to the prevailing social ideas of right conduct and group well-being — or upon persuasiveness in argument that a new orientation of values is in order to meet changed conditions, even though the tough man and his kinsman, though "wrong," may sometimes make his position stick with naked force. Thus, the wise claimant argues his case not in terms of "this is good for me" but rather by maintaining "this is what we all want and should do". If he is a primitive advocate, it is more likely than not that he will also insist, if he can, that this is the way it has been from time immemorial. But the past certainly has no inflexible grip on primitive law.

Fiction is one of the great devices of juristic method by means of which men fit new legal norms into old principles so as to reorient conduct without the need to junk long-standing postulates. Except for the universal practice of adoption, whereby outsiders are identified as *if* they are actually kinsmen, primitive men do not have to rely too heavily on the subterfuge of fiction to achieve legal change. Nevertheless, when the need is there many tribes have had recourse to its use.

An outstanding example may be found in adoptive marriage among the patrilineal groups of Indonesia. The important value for these people is to maintain the unbroken continuity of the paternal lineage. To do this, a family without sons adopts their daughter's husband as a "son" with the effect that her children remain within their clan and their inheritance will remain within their line. ...

. . . .

When the law-jobs get done, these norms inevitably become the common denominator of legal culture. But the functions of law, whatever the norms they may give rise to in any particular society, are what constitute the crucial universal elements of the law. Any one or half-hundred societies may select one rule of law and not another — the range is wide — but none can ignore the law-jobs. In the last analysis, that the law-jobs get done is more important than how they are done. Their minimal doing is an imperative of social existence. Their doing with juristic finesse is an achievement of high skill.

(b)   The Cheyenne Way†

Karl N. Llewellyn and E. Adamson Hoebel

A war party of eight Cheyennes, on its way south to take horses from the Kiowas, Comanches, or Apaches, was stopping at a large Arapaho camp. At the same time some Apaches came to visit Bull, an Arapaho leader. The Apaches told their host that the Kiowas and Comanches were seeking peace with the Arapahoes and Cheyennes. Bull took the opportunity to bring the eight Cheyennes together with the Apaches in his tipi; he filled his pipe and offered the smoke. The Cheyennes declined, Seven Bulls, the leader of the war party saying, "Friend, you know that we are not chiefs. We cannot smoke with these men, nor make peace with them. We have no authority; we can only carry the message. I have listened to what you say and tomorrow with my party I will start back [He has authority to call off his own raid.] to our Cheyenne village, and I will carry this word to the chiefs. It is for them to decide what must be done. We are young men and cannot say anything, but we will take your message back to the chiefs."

When Seven Bulls reached the Cheyenne camp with his companions, he told of the Kiowa-Comanche proposition. That night a crier went about the camp calling for the chiefs to convene the next day. The big double-sized chiefs' lodge was pitched and early the next morning the chiefs all gathered there. Seven Bulls and his companions were sent for to deliver their message officially. The proposal was then on the floor.

After the first speakers had sat down, it was evident that there was no ready agreement at hand within the Council, so the proposition was made and accepted that the Dog Soldier Society should be asked to render a decision to the Council on the question.

High Backed Wolf, who was the directing head chief of the Council, sent one of the door-servants to bring in White Antelope and Little Old Man, the bravest chiefs of the Dog Soldier Society. When these two had been greeted in the chiefs' lodge, High Backed Wolf told them

† From *The Cheyenne Way: Conflict and Case Law in Primitive Jurisprudence* by Karl N. Llewellyn & E. Adamson Hoebel, pp. 91–94, 127–28. Oklahoma: University of Oklahoma Press, 1941. Reproduced with permission of University of Oklahoma Press in the format Republish in a book via Copyright Clearance Center.

about the order of business, describing to them the state of opinion in the Council. "Now, my friends," he concluded, "you go and assemble your Dog Soldiers. Tell them about this matter and talk it over among them. Let us know what you think of it. Tell us what you think is best to be done."

When the Dog Soldiers had assembled, White Antelope laid the problem before them. "The chiefs are leaving this matter to us," he told his followers, "because we are the strongest of the military groups. It is my own thought that our chiefs are in favor of making peace. What do you all think about it?"

Said another of the Dog Soldier chiefs, "I think it best to leave the decision to you two, White Antelope and Little Old Man. Whatever you say will please us all." All the Dogs agreed to this with one assent.

The two men accepted it and declared for peace. Leaving their troop, they went back to where the Council was waiting for them, to tell the Council that they would make peace with the enemies. The chiefs all stood up at this and gladly said, "Thank you, thank you, Dog Soldiers."[20]

The procedure which has just been described is a typical handling of an important situation in the Cheyenne manner. The proposition, the reader will realize, was no simple one. The Cheyenne had become dependent upon the horse, and any warrior's path to glory and wealth lay most easily and quickly in raids upon the rich horse herders of the south, these same Kiowas and Comanches. Acceptance of the proposal meant that the young men would be blocked in one of their main and favorite avenues of activity. Hostility with the Kiowas and Comanches had been unceasing for at least half a century. The alternative values to the Cheyennes are not clear to us, unless they lay in some scheme for trading horses, on which we lack information. The soldier interest in the case is obvious; no less obvious is the fact that it had the favorable aspect of coinciding with the interests of the whole Cheyenne tribe. In the light of this one understands the diplomatic reluctance of the Council of Forty-Four to reach a decision by themselves. So smooth a delegation of an important decision, inverting the pyramid without any bickering, yet with the machinery at all points for the sensing of opinion in widening representative groups, is an act of social beauty. From the Council to the Dog Men, from the Dog Men to their two most outstanding warriors, to a momentous decision binding on the entire tribe! Nevertheless, the Council at no time gave up its authority; the decision, be it noted, was reported for announcement back to the

Council, which then discharged the Dog Soldiers with thanks. This is also a superb face-producing, as well as face-saving, procedure. The actual announcement of the decision for peace was made to the camp at large by the head priest-chief himself.

Such interaction between the Council and the military societies was not unusual; rather, whenever there was an important problem of tribal policy (new policy in general or in particular) to be decided, it was the ordinary thing to see the chiefs' and the soldiers' messengers moving back and forth between the meeting lodges, sensing, reporting, and subtly influencing the state of both "expert" and "lay" opinion until the decision was accomplished. In this way, the legislative knot was cut without resort to dictatorship or friction.

But what happened when there was an irreconcilable opposition within the body politic? Then the governmental authority could act with force. It acted also with tact. It moved sometimes in involution. Power was present, form was not always achieved. Note, however, the Cheyenne drive for form, if repetition of situation makes it possible, if time serves, if dramatic urge finds — even for a sole occasion — an inventive voice. Seven Bulls was called on for an "official" presentation of a proposal the camp had buzzed with for a night. Little Wolf was "required" to be present. Compare the careful staging of Pawnee's rehabilitation. It is not too much to argue that *drama* is a vital *line* of reconciliation hit on by the Cheyennes, between their urge toward form (pattern, ritual) and their urge toward individualizing self-glorification. If this be sound, it suggests a relation between aesthetic balance and soundness of working institution, or of the individual's work in and with an institution, which deserves inquiry.

.   .   .   .

While Wolf Lies Down was away, a friend took one of his horses to ride to war. This man had brought his bow and arrow and left them in the lodge of the horse's owner. When Wolf Lies Down returned, he knew by this token security who had his horse, so he said nothing.

A year passed without the horse's return, and then Wolf Lies Down invited the Elk Soldier chiefs to his lodge, because he was in their society. "There is this thing," he told them. "My friend borrowed my horse, leaving his bow and arrow; there they are yet. Now I want to know what to do. I want you to tell me the right thing. Will you go over and ask him his intentions?"

The borrower was in another camp well distant, yet the chiefs agreed. "We'll send a man to bring him in, get his word, or receive his presents," they promised.

The camp moved while the messenger was gone, but he knew of course where it would be on his return. The soldier returned with the borrower, who was leading two horses, "one spotted, one ear-tipped." He called for the four Elk chiefs on his arrival. The chiefs laid before him the story told by Wolf Lies Down.

"That is true," the man assented. "My friend is right. I left my bow and arrow here. I intended to return his horse, but I was gone longer than I expected. I have had good luck with that horse, though. I have treated it better than my own. However, when I got back to camp I found my folks there. Our camps were far apart and I just could not get away. I was waiting for his camp and mine to come together. Now, I always intended to do the right thing. I have brought two good horses with me. My friend can have his choice. In addition I give his own horse back, and further, I am leaving my bow and arrow."

Then up spoke Wolf Lies Down, "I am glad to hear my friend say these things. Now I feel better. I shall take one of those horses, but I am giving him that one he borrowed to keep. From now on we shall be bosom friends."

The chiefs declared, "Now we have settled this thing. Our man is a bosom friend of this man. Let it be that way among all of us. Our society and his shall be comrades. Whenever one of us has a present to give, we shall give it to a member of his soldier society.

"Now we shall make a new rule. There shall be no more borrowing of horses without asking. If any man takes another's goods without asking, we will go over and get them back for him.

More than that, if the taker tries to keep them, we will give him a whipping."

Thus was a situation fraught with possible friction brought to an amicable close through the good offices of the chiefs of the society of an aggrieved member.

Far more important, however, was the crystallization of a new social policy, the formulation of a law making it a crime henceforth to borrow an owner's horse without his expressed permission. The old custom of free utilization of another's goods, providing one left an identifying "security," was apparently creating friction as it came to be applied to horses. What between good friends could develop into a tense situation — as evidenced here by the resort to soldier chiefs as spokesmen of inquiry — could become immediately and actively disruptive if the concept "friend" were loosely interpreted by a borrower, or the horse not cared for, or if the unnotified borrowing broke in upon the owner's plans, or one owner became the recipient of too many such evidences of friendship. Pawnee's case of horse "borrowing" and its punishment (CASE 2) shows the degree of social irresponsibility which the older practice, left unguarded, could engender. Black Wolf stated that the soldiers, and even the tribal chiefs, had been for some time talking about means of putting a stop to the practice. The Elk Soldier chiefs on this occasion took the opportunity to make the step. After declaring the case at hand settled, they moved into general policy. They did not mix the two. Note also, as a soldier society moves into the very unfamiliar matter of legislation, their sound technical attention to what they shall do, if....

(c)   Conflicts as Property†

Nils Christie

Abstract

Conflicts are seen as important elements in society. Highly industrialised societies do not have too much internal conflict, they have too little. We have to organise social systems so that conflicts are both nurtured and made visible, and also see to it that professionals do not monopolize the handling of them. Victims of crime have in particular lost their rights to participate. A court procedure that restores the participants' rights to their own conflicts is outlined.

† (January 1977) 17 The British Journal of Criminology 1 at 1–5. Reproduced by permission of Oxford University Press. [Notes and/or references omitted.]

INTRODUCTION

Maybe we should not have any criminology. Maybe we should rather abolish institutes, not open them. Maybe the social consequences of criminology are more dubious than we like to think.

I think they are. And I think this relates to my topic. Conflicts as property. My suspicion is that criminology to some extent has amplified a process where conflicts have been taken away from the directly involved parties and thereby either disappeared or have become other people's property. In both cases a deplorable outcome. Conflicts ought to be used, not only left in erosion. And they ought to be used, and become useful, for those originally involved in the conflict. Conflicts *might* hurt individuals as well as social systems. That is what we learn in school. That is why we have officials. Without them, private vengeance and vendettas will blossom. We have learned this so solidly that we have lost track of the other side of the coin: our industrialised large-scale society is not one with too many internal conflicts. It is one with too little. Conflict might kill, but too little of it might paralyze. I will use this occasion to give a sketch of this situation. It can't be more than a sketch. This paper represents the beginning of the development of some ideas, not the polished end product.

ON HAPPENINGS AND NON-HAPPENINGS

Let us take our point of departure far away. Let us move to Tanzania. Let us approach our problem from the sunny hillside of the Arusha province. Here, inside a relatively large house in a very small village, a sort of happening took place. The house was overcrowded. Most grown-ups from the village and several from adjoining ones were there. It was a happy happening; fast talking, jokes, smiles, eager attention, not a sentence was to be lost. It was circus, it was drama. It was a court case.

The conflict this time was between a man and a woman. They had been engaged. He had invested a lot in the relationship through a long period, until she broke it off. Now he wanted it back. Gold and silver and money were easily decided on, but what about utilities already worn, and what about general expenses?

The outcome is of no interest in our context. But the framework for conflict solution is. Five elements ought to be particularly mentioned:

1. The parties, the former lovers, were in *the centre* of the room and in the centre of everyone's attention. They talked often and were eagerly listened to.
2. Close to them were relatives and friends who also took part. But they did not *take over*.
3. There was also participation from the general audience with short questions, information, or jokes.
4. The judges, three local party secretaries, were extremely inactive. They were obviously ignorant with regard to village matters. All the other people in the room were experts. They were experts on norms as well as actions. And they crystallized norms and clarified what had happened through participation in the procedure.
5. No reporters attended. They were all there.

My personal knowledge when it comes to British courts is limited indeed. I have some vague memories of juvenile courts, where I counted some 15 to 20 persons present, mostly social workers using the room for preparatory work or small conferences. A child or a young person must have attended, but except for the judge, or maybe it was the clerk, nobody seemed to pay any particular attention. The child or young person was most probably utterly confused as to who was who and for what, a fact confirmed in a small study by Peter Scott (1959). In the USA, Martha Baum (1968) has made similar observations. Recently, Bottoms and McClean (1976) have added another important observation: "There is one truth which is seldom revealed in the literature of the law or in studies of the administration of criminal justice. It is a truth which was made evident to all those involved in this research project as they sat through the cases which made up our sample. The truth is that, for the most part, the business of the criminal courts is dull, commonplace, ordinary and after a while downright tedious."

But let me keep quiet about your system, and instead concentrate on my own. And let me assure you: what goes on is no happening. It is all a negation of the Tanzanian case. What is striking in nearly all the Scandinavian cases is the greyness, the dullness, and the lack of any important audience. Courts are not central elements in the daily life of our citizens, but peripheral in four major ways:

1. They are situated in the administrative centre of the towns, outside the territories of ordinary people.
2. Within these centres they are often centralised within one or two large buildings of considerable complexity. Lawyers often complain that

they need months to find their way within these buildings. It does not demand much fantasy to imagine the situation of parties or public when they are trapped within these structures. A comparative study of court architecture might become equally relevant for the sociology of law as Oscar Newman's (1972) study of defensible space is for criminology. But even without any study, I feel it safe to say that both physical situation and architectural design are strong indicators that courts in Scandinavia belong to the administrators of law.

3. This impression is strengthened when you enter the courtroom itself — if you are lucky enough to find your way to it. Here again, the periphery of the parties is the striking observation. The parties are represented, and it is these representatives and the judge or judges who express the little activity that is activated within these rooms. Honoré Daumier's famous drawings from the courts are as representative for Scandinavia as they are for France.

   There are variations. In the small cities, or in the countryside, the courts are more easily reached than in the larger towns. And at the very lowest end of the court system — the so-called arbitration boards — the parties are sometimes less heavily represented through experts in law. But the symbol of the whole system is the Supreme Court where the directly involved parties do not even attend their own court cases.

4. I have not yet made any distinction between civil and criminal conflicts. But it was not by chance that the Tanzania case was a civil one. Full participation in your own conflict presupposes elements of civil law. The key element in a criminal proceeding is that the proceeding is converted from something between the concrete parties and into a conflict between one of the parties and the State. So, in a modern criminal trial, two important things have happened. First: the parties are being *represented*. Secondly: the one party that is represented by the State, namely the victim, is so thoroughly represented that she or he for most of the proceedings is pushed completely out of the arena, reduced to the triggerer-off of the whole thing. She or he is a sort of double loser. First vis-à-vis the offender, but secondly and often more cripplingly by being denied rights to full participation in what might have been one of the more important ritual encounters in life. The victim has lost its case to the State.

Professional Thieves

As we all know, there are many honourable as well as dishonourable reasons behind this development. The honourable ones have to do with the State's need for conflict reduction and certainly also its wishes for the protection of the victim. It is rather obvious. So is also the less honourable temptation for the State, or Emperor, or whoever is in power, to use the criminal case for personal gain. Offenders might pay for their sins. Authorities have back in time shown considerable willingness in representing the victim as receivers of the money or other property from the offender. Those days are gone. The crime control system is not run by profit. But they are also not gone. There are, in all banality, many interests at stake here, most of them related to professionalisation.

Lawyers are particularly good at stealing conflicts. They are trained for it. They are trained to prevent and solve conflicts. They are socialised into a sub-culture with a surprisingly high agreement concerning interpretation of norms, and regarding what sort of information can be accepted as relevant in each case. Many among us have, as laymen, experienced the sad moments of truth when our lawyers tell us that our best arguments in our fight against our neighbour are without any legal relevance whatsoever and that we for God's sake ought to keep quiet about them in court. Instead they pick out arguments we might find irrelevant or even wrong to use. My favourite example took place just after the war. One of my country's absolutely top defenders told with pride how he had just rescued a poor client. The client had collaborated with the Germans. The prosecutor claimed that the client had been one of the key people in the organisation of the Nazi movement. He had been one of the master-minds behind it all. The defender, however, saved his client. He saved him by pointing out to the jury how weak, how lacking in ability, how obviously deficient his client was, socially as well as organisationally. His client could simply not have been one of the organisers among the collaborators. He was without talents. And he won his case. His client got a very minor sentence as a very minor figure. The defender ended his story by telling me — with some indignation — that neither the accused, nor his wife, had ever thanked him, they had not even talked to him afterwards.

Conflicts become the property of lawyers. But lawyers don't hide that it is conflicts they handle. And the organisational framework of the courts underlines this point. The opposing parties, the judge, the ban against privileged communication within the court system, the lack of encouragement for specialisation — specialists cannot be internally controlled — it all underlines that this is an organisation for the handling of conflicts. *Treatment personnel* are in another position. They are more interested in *converting the image of the case from one of conflict into one of non-conflict*. The basic model of healers is not one of opposing parties, but one where one party has to be helped in the direction of one generally accepted goal: the preservation or restoration of health. They are not trained into a system where it is important that parties can control each other. There is, in the ideal case, nothing to control, because there is only one goal. Specialisation is encouraged. It increases the amount of available knowledge, and the loss of internal control is of no relevance. A conflict perspective creates unpleasant doubts with regard to the healer's suitability for the job. A non-conflict perspective is a precondition for defining crime as a legitimate target for treatment.

One way of reducing attention to the conflict is reduced attention given to the victim. Another is concentrated attention given to those attributes in the criminal's background which the healer is particularly trained to handle. Biological defects are per-fect. So are also personality defects when they are established far back in time — far away from the recent conflict. And so are also the whole row of explanatory variables that criminology might offer. We have, in criminology, to a large extent functioned as an auxiliary science for the professionals within the crime control system. We have focused on the offender, made her or him into an object for study, manipulation and control. We have added to all those forces that have reduced the victim to a non-entity and the offender to a thing. And this critique is perhaps not only relevant for the old criminology, but also for the new criminology. While the old one explained crime from personal defects or social handicaps, the new criminology explains crime as the result of broad economic conflicts. The old criminology loses the conflicts, the new one converts them from interpersonal conflicts to class conflicts. And they are. They are class conflicts — also. But by stressing this, the conflicts are again taken away from the directly involved parties. So, as a preliminary statements: Criminal conflicts have either become *other people's property* — primarily the property of lawyers — or it has been in other people's interests to *define conflicts away*.

Cultural Context: Legal Cultures in Canada

(a) The Environment of Canada's Judicial System†

Peter H. Russell

SOCIAL AND ECONOMIC DEVELOPMENT

As an industrialized and urbanized society, Canada has experienced, to a relatively high degree, what the political sociologists refer to as "modernization." This modernization has been accompanied by increased complexity in Canadian law and increased professionalization of Canada's legal institutions. For the judicial system this has meant, among other things, an increased insistence on the possession of professional legal credentials by those adjudicating disputes about the law. Thus in Canada we have witnessed nearly a complete repudiation of the lay person as judge and a tendency to regard juries as technically too incompetent to be reliable fact-finders. Growing professionalism has also been felt, although in a much more delayed fashion, in the administration of Canadian courts, where there is increasing recognition of the merit of applying specialized administrative skills and the techniques of the computer age to managing court case flows.

But the effects of the modernization of Canadian society on its judicial system have been more pervasive and profound than a tendency to specialization. As industrialization and urbanization weaken traditional social bonds of family and community, basic social attitudes and relations are altered. We become a society of strangers relying increasingly, each of us, on formal positive law to define our rights and obligations; as a consequence, we turn increasingly to formal adjudication to settle our differences.[2] This transformation of social relations from those based on custom and informal sources of authority to a system depending much more on legally defined rights and duties tends to expand the role of adjudicative agencies. This can be seen in fields as far apart as family law and federalism: as squabbling spouses and government turn to positive law as a guide to good conduct, they resort increasingly to courts to adjudicate conflict. Another facet of the social alienation accompanying modernity is increased reliance on enforcement of the criminal law rather than more informal communal sanctions as a means of maintaining social order. This, too, places increased burdens on Canadian courts, not so much to adjudicate disputes (few criminal charges produce not guilty pleas and formal court adjudication) but to provide a judicial presence in the processing of those selected by the police for criminal prosecution.

Socio-economic development does not affect the business of courts in industrialized societies in a uniform way. The impact is considerably influenced by the litigiousness of a people — that is to say, their general propensity to settle disputes by pressing claims to formal adjudication rather than negotiating settlements more informally. A litigious tendency may be present in a society quite independently of its level of modernization.[3] Among modern industrialized countries, England, New Zealand, and the United States have much higher civil case loads per

† From *The Judiciary in Canada* (Whitby, Ontario: McGraw-Hill Ryerson Limited, 1987) at 31–39. [Notes and/or references omitted.] Reproduced by permission.

capita than Italy, Japan, or Spain.[4] The preference of the Japanese for mediation and conciliation over adjudication is reflected in the small size of their legal profession: 1 lawyer for each 10,000 of population compared with a ratio of 1 to 400 in the United States.[5] No systematic research has been done on the litigiousness of Canadians, but the fact that on a per capita basis the Canadian judiciary and legal profession are roughly comparable in size to their American counterparts suggests that Canada is one of the more litigious of the industrialized and urbanized countries, perhaps only slightly less so than the United States. Canadian patterns may have been brought closer to American ones by the rapid expansion of the legal profession and legal aid programs over the past decade or so.[6] These developments, while not necessarily altering the general disposition of Canadians to litigate, have made the option of taking disputes to court more available to people of limited means.

Increases in the number and complexity of laws, in the number of lawyers, and even in the litigiousness of the population, do not necessarily lead to a mushrooming of court business and expansion of the courts. Much depends on the relative attractiveness of judicial institutions as dispute-settling mechanisms and the availability of alternatives.[7] The evidence in Canada suggests that very little of the increased need for adjudicative services generated by social change and industrial development has been taken care of by the general jurisdiction trial courts (i.e., the superior, district, and county courts of the provinces), which at the time of Confederation were regarded as the most important of Canada's judicial institutions.[8] These provincial courts, staffed by federally appointed judges — the original linchpins of Canada's judicial system — have scarcely expanded at all. Whereas the number of judges serving at this level was 2.52 per 100,000 of population in 1867, by 1975 the ratio had actually declined to 2.23 per 100,000.[9] Some of this increased demand for adjudication, especially in the field of criminal justice, has been met by the provincially appointed judges in the so-called lower courts of the provinces, and a little, on the civil side, by the major federally established trial court, the Federal Court of Canada.[10] But probably a great deal more has been taken care of outside the formal court system through private arbitration and administrative tribunals. Improvements in the administration of courts may begin to reverse this trend by reducing some of the delay and inconvenience which in the past drove business away from the courts. Another factor working in the same direction is the Canadian version of what in the United States is referred to as the "public law explosion."[11] On the one hand, the expanded use of the criminal sanction by the state; on the other hand, the expanded range of statutory and even constitutional rights that can be claimed by the individual or corporation against the state generate disputes which in our society must finally be settled by the courts.

POLITICAL BELIEFS AND IDEOLOGY

Here we encounter the second environmental influence on the judicial system: political beliefs and ideology. An increase in the degree of independence enjoyed by Canadian courts and their added capacity to serve as vehicles for challenging government has been closely related to a strengthening of support of liberalism in Canada's political culture. This growth in respect for liberal values — for the rights of individuals and the value of preventing excessive and illegal exercises of governmental authority — has not, to be sure, developed to the point of extinguishing strong conservative tendencies in Canada's political culture. Canada was founded by counter-revolutionaries suspicious of the excesses of American democracy.[12] The continued popularity of the national police force, the RCMP (despite the exposure of its infringements of the legal rights of Canadians and its intolerance of political dissent), as well as popular support for the invocation of the *War Measures Act* in the 1970 October crisis, point to the survival of this conservative strain. But liberal critics of these recent manifestations of Canadians' respect for authority and fear of disorder often fail to mark the liberalization of political attitudes that has been occurring in Canada.[13] Manifestations of moral outrage and the favourable treatment it receives in the popular media are, in themselves, an indication of this change.

A growing egalitarianism in Canadian society has fostered the extension of liberal values to all classes in society. This tendency has had important consequences for the functioning of the courts. Legal aid (the provision of publicly funded legal counsel to indigent persons) is, as we have noted, a leading example of this trend. Another is reform of the criminal justice system which has taken place over the last century.[14] The reduction of close ties between the criminal courts and the police, bail reform, and an upgrading of the qualifications of the judges who preside over the country's busiest criminal courts are part of this movement. These reforms are relatively modest; none goes as far as critics of the system might wish. But the direction of change is clearly liberal.

A further illustration of this liberalization of attitudes and its effect on the judicial system is the change which has taken place in the appeal system in criminal cases. Up until 1892 there was no right of appeal in criminal cases. When a right of appeal was included in the *Criminal Code*, it was typical of the mixture of values in Canadian society that not only was the accused given a right to appeal his conviction but the crown was also given a right to appeal the accused's acquittal, even if the verdict was rendered by a jury. The review of trial court decisions in criminal cases has become an increasingly important function of Canada's courts of appeal. We can get some idea of how much Canadian attitudes have changed by noting that in 1975 when the crown successfully appealed a jury's acquittal of Dr. Morgentaler, a Montreal physician who ran an abortion clinic, there was a sufficient public outcry to bring about an amendment of the *Criminal Code* removing the power of appeal courts to substitute a guilty verdict for an acquittal in a case heard by judge and jury.[15]

An egalitarian extension of legal rights has also affected the work of courts in non-criminal areas. New legal rights have been established for classes of persons whose bargaining position was relatively weak: for example, wives in relation to husbands, children in relation to parents, employees in relation to employers, students and professors in relation to university officials. The establishment of these rights means that disputes which might have been settled informally are now often litigated and go to court. Dispute settlement through informal negotiation becomes less acceptable when social and economic "underdogs" believe their interests will be better protected by claiming rights in court rather than counting on the benevolence of those in positions of power.

A similar reduction of trust in those exercising political authority has made Canadians more interested in the liberal notion of building checks and balances into their system of government. Canadians may continue to believe that the purpose of government is as much to provide for peace, order and good government as it is to protect the rights and liberties of the individual, but they have become increasingly apprehensive about the problems of controlling the governmental leviathan. Several generations of experience under big government have generated scepticism about the inherent good sense and self-restraint of those who govern. The nineteenth-century achievement of responsible government has proved to be no panacea for ensuring that government is accountable to the people. The decline of the legislature's significance in law-making and in its capacity for monitoring government operations has been evident for many years.[16] Cabinet government concentrates enormous power in the hands of a very few politicians and officials. There may be some dim recognition that the vitality of the division of powers and competition between federal and provincial governments in Canada by dispersing power enhances political liberty. Still, both provincial and federal governments are recognized as centres of power against whose arbitrary and unlawful activities citizens need further institutional protection.

Increasingly this liberal impulse looks to the judiciary for such protection. Where there is fear that government will abuse newly acquired powers, the judiciary is brought in to guard against this danger. A good example is the inclusion of a requirement for judicial warrants in the legislation that legalized electronic eavesdropping by the police.[17] More recently, in the debate over a federal *Access to Information Act*, distrust of the government forced the inclusion of a provision giving the courts, in most instances, the final word in deciding whether government refusals to provide information fall within statutory criteria.[18]

This tendency in the Canadian political system to rely on the judicial process as a means of preventing abuse of power and protecting rights may now be at a turning point. Canada's new constitutional *Charter of Rights and Freedoms* significantly expands expectations about the judiciary's capacity and inclination to check government. The apparent popularity of increasing the power of judges at the expense of the power of politicians and officials demonstrates the extent to which Canadians, at this point in their history, regard their judges as less tied to the interests of government; they are seen in a fundamental sense as being less political and more trustworthy than those holding executive and legislative positions. But, again, it is important to point out that this perception of the judiciary as the politically neutered branch of government may well be undermined by the political nature of the judiciary's responsibilities under the new Charter.

CANADA'S LEGAL CULTURE

The third and most direct of the environmental influences on the judicial system is a country's legal culture. The basic character of Canada's legal system, and hence of its judicial system, might be expected to reflect the legal cultures of the two European peoples, the English and the French, who founded Canada. But this expectation is not borne out by the facts. So dominant has the English common

15

law system been that it is misleading to think of Canada's legal culture as fundamentally dualistic. This is especially true of its judicial system, which has been even more thoroughly anglicized than the substantive law. As far as the legal culture of Canada's original inhabitants is concerned, it was totally ignored and for all practical purposes obliterated by the European settlers.[19] Thus, in legal terms, Canada today belongs essentially to the common law world although, as with all the common law countries, there are some distinctive wrinkles stemming from the country's particular circumstances.

There is a strong element of legal dualism in Quebec's history. Soon after the British conquest of New France, through the *Quebec Act* of 1774, the laws of the French Canadians were made the basis of the colony's civil law, while its criminal law was to be British. Despite this original dualism, French civil law was subjected to powerful common law influences. The principal vehicle for this process of anglicization was the judicial system. British governors selected the judges and for the most part they chose persons whose legal knowledge, if it existed at all, was based process on English experience.[20] Most importantly, the appeal process was dominated by English Canadians and British judges. Consequently the judicial method in both civil and criminal law became the common law method, with its emphasis on judicial precedent. These common law techniques were so firmly embedded by the time a *Civil Code* was adopted in Quebec that English-style judicial precedents rather than French civilian doctrine became the dominant force in interpreting the code. The anglicization of Quebec's civil law system is a testament to the quiet way in which power can flow through a judicial system, especially one with a powerful appeals hierarchy.

An essential part of the Confederation settlement in 1867 was that Quebec, as the province in which the French Canadians could maintain a majority, would be able to preserve the distinctive language, religion, and laws of the French-Canadian people. Section 92(13) of the *British North America Act* gave all the provinces jurisdiction over "property and civil rights" — a concept that embraces most of the subjects included in Quebec's *Civil Code* and *Code of Procedure*.[21] Thus Quebec has retained legislative jurisdiction over those matters which are central to the French civil law tradition. On particular points of substantive law and civil procedure Quebec civil law differs from the laws of the common law provinces, although under the impact of secularization and modern commerce these differences have narrowed and may not be more significant than dif-

ferences that exist in some areas of statutory law among the common law provinces. Since Confederation the highest court of appeal, whose opinions interpreting Quebec's civil law bind Quebec judges, has been, first, an imperial court, the Judicial Committee of the Privy Council, and then the Supreme Court of Canada. Although Quebec judges have always been in a minority position on the latter court,[22] more often than not they have been the dominant influence on the panels hearing civil law cases from Quebec.

For our purposes here the most important point is that the judicial institutions of Quebec, despite any residue of French civil law and procedure that survives, bear the essential features of English common law courts. A lawyer from English-speaking Canada, or for that matter from virtually any other part of the English-speaking world, who wished to practise in Quebec, would not have to adapt to an alien judicial system. It is only in very recent years that Quebec court reformers have begun to look to continental French institutions for inspiration — for instance, to the idea of a career judiciary based on a special legal education for judges.[23] So far, this application of Quebec nationalism to judicial institutions has not borne fruit in any concrete changes.

Some of the features of the common law tradition that have important consequences for the role of the judiciary in Canada (for example, the use of juries and the adversary system) have already been mentioned and will be referred to later in the text. In this introductory discussion of judicial power there are two features of common law systems that deserve special emphasis: the central importance of the judges, and the power of the legal profession.

In any legal system based on the common law tradition, the judge has a preeminent position as compared with other legal functionaries. Common law is indeed judge-made law. On many subjects of contemporary legislative interest, common law rules are dwarfed in importance by statutes enacted by the legislature, by delegated legislation or regulations enacted by the executive, and in Canada by the written Constitution. Long ago common law judges accepted their subordination to Parliament as a sovereign law maker, and in Canada they must accept the Constitution of Canada as the highest source of law.[24] Even so, judicial decisions applying and interpreting regulations, statutes, and the Constitution, as we have already stressed, can have a tremendous influence on the policies that are actually effected and the rights that are actually established through these other sources of law. It is true that the difference between the legislative role of the judge in the common law system as compared with the civil law system has been exaggerated. Modern scholarship on civil law systems has revealed the important role that judicial interpretation and judicial opinions play in applying civil law codes, despite the civil law system's theoretical denial of their importance. Nevertheless the fact remains that it is the common law system that openly accepts the judicial opinion with all its potential for law development as an integral part of the system.

The pre-eminence of the judge in the common law system extends beyond the judge's law-making role. It is also manifest in the social and political status of the judge.[25] In continental Europe the legal scholar has a high, if not a higher, status than the judge. This is certainly not the case in Canada. The lustre of the judicial position in Canada is reflected in the practice, already commented upon, of assigning judges major extra-judicial responsibilities, notably on royal commissions and commissions of inquiry, on matters of great public interest. A symbolic indication of the high status of the judicial office in Canada is that the chief justice of the country's highest court, the Supreme Court of Canada, in the absence or incapacity of the governor general, represents the head of state.[26] Whether or not there is validity in the generalization that Canadian judges are self-restrained or uncreative in the exercise of their judicial powers, the high status accorded them in the Canadian legal and political systems continues to be a significant political resource for the Canadian judiciary.

The prestige and power of judges in the common law system is closely related to the strength of the legal profession. It might even be said that the pre-eminent position of the bench within common law legal systems largely derives from the pre-eminent position of the bar within common law societies. Going back to the roots of the common law judicial system in England, it was the ability of a small guild of private legal practitioners centred in the Inns of Court in London — first the sergeants, then the barristers — to monopolize appointments to the Royal Courts of Justice that was decisive in ensuring that the common law judiciary would not develop in the continental fashion as a career branch of government service.[27] Instead, judicial positions in the higher courts would be awarded to persons who had distinguished themselves in private legal practice. The bench in Canada, even at its lowest levels, is recruited almost exclusively from the bar. Thus, in studying the forces that shape the Canadian judiciary it is essential to take into account the nature of the Canadian legal profession.[28] Access to that profes-

sion, its education system, and the characteristics of private practice will have a great deal to do with determining what kinds of men and women become judges in Canada.

In Canada the bar is considerably less elitist than in England. Instead of the English division between a small group of barristers who plead cases in court and a great mass of solicitors advising clients and transacting legal business out of court, or France's four or five separate legal professions (advocates, avoues, notaries, and judges), Canada has a fused and unified legal profession. There are specializations within this profession, but all Canadian lawyers belong to a single profession. Further, the Canadian bar is not concentrated in a single metropolitan centre but is dispersed across the country; there are centres of professional activity in every Canadian province. Thus the professional pool from which Canadian judges are recruited is much larger and more diverse than the tiny coterie of London-based barristers from which English judges are drawn. As a social interest group, geographical dispersal is more than compensated for by professional unity. The Canadian bar's ability to assert itself as a unified profession has few parallels in other countries.

Some lawyers might object to the suggestion that they belong to a private interest group. Formally, as members of the bar, they are "officers of the court," and in that sense belong to a public institution. Nevertheless, the profession has emphasized the need to maintain its independence of government. It has insisted, successfully, on its own self-government, on controlling the standards of professional education and in most provinces, on keeping private legal practitioners, rather than salaried lawyers, as the mainstay of publicly funded legal aid programs. The rationale for this commitment to the profession's independence has been fundamentally ideological: recognition of the value in a liberal state under the rule of law of ensuring that individuals and groups have access to legal counsel not controlled by the government.

If the press can be referred to as the fourth estate, the legal profession as a private organization providing an essential public service might be thought of as a fifth estate in Canada. The power of this fifth estate is exercised through its professional activities and advocacy, and also through the participation of so many of its members at the highest levels of the political branches of government. The private practice of law provides exceptional opportunities for those who wish to take their chances in electoral competition. No other profession or occupational group has been so well represented in legislatures and cabinets at both the federal and provincial levels.[29] Among other things, the political prominence of the profession means that the views of professional lawyers are paramount in shaping policies with regard to judicial institutions and judicial reform. No major changes in the structure or functioning of Canada's courts can take place without the approval of leaders of the bar.

It would be a mistake, however, to think of the bar as an unchanging monolithic force. The winds of change which affect all other important social institutions are beginning to bring about significant changes in the size and shape of Canada's legal profession. The last decade has seen a major transformation. The ranks of the profession have expanded so that on a per capita basis it approximates the size of the American profession. The dominant position of males and the charter ethnic groups has declined.[30] Most significantly, the political diversity of the profession would appear to have increased with the formation of radical breakaway organizations outside of the professional establishment. In the long run, all of this is likely to have profoundly important effects on the social and political orientation of the Canadian judiciary.

(b)   By Reason of Authority or By Authority of Reason†

The Honourable Madame Justice Claire L'Heureux-Dubé

Chief Justice Anglin once remarked that decisions by courts in civil law jurisprudence were determined by authority of reason rather than by reason of authority.[1] However, in his last year on the bench, he also wrote: "In my opinion, the doctrine of *stare decisis* must equally apply in the determination of any case before this court, whatever may be the province of its origin."[2]

These apparently contradictory statements, made by a Supreme Court Justice trained in the common law,[3] reflect a historical reality which, for the past century, has been the object of great controversy among Quebec jurists and scholars. Specifically, the Supreme Court of Canada is a national court of last resort and the majority of its judges are trained in common law, with its emphasis on precedent. However, this same Court has power to review and reverse the Quebec Court of Appeal even in cases governed by civil law, though the civilian tradition favours the spirit and content of civil legislation as well as doctrine over strict adherence to judicial precedents. In Quebec, the conjunction of these factors has long seemed to be a contradiction in terms.[4]

Given the function and composition of the Supreme Court of Canada, was Quebec's civil law not effectively destined to be shaped by reason of authority rather than authority of reason? What have been the consequences for Quebec's civilian tradition and the authority it confers upon previously decided cases?

While I could not realistically hope to resolve these questions in a definitive and exhaustive manner, I do hope to provide perspectives on these questions while introducing the essential characteristics of Quebec's civilian tradition.

.   .   .   .

Leaving aside for the moment the multiplicity of legal sources in Lower Canada prior to codification,[20] the unique nature of Quebec's system of private law can best be conveyed through an examination of the essential features of a civil code in the civilian legal system as a whole.

Although one author has remarked that "the characteristic features of a code are not easy to distil,"[21] every system of law has a primary organizing source, and so one can begin with a metaphor: the code is, first and foremost, the skeletal structure of the civilian legal system.[22] Non-codal legislation may be equal in authority, but it is the civil code which is the primary organizing source of law.[23] In that respect, Professor Brierley has compared the civil

---

† (1993) 27 U.B.C. L. Rev. 1 at 1–2, 6–18. [Notes and/or references omitted.] Reproduced with permission.

code's reservoir of concepts with the judicially-created English common law:

> ... [the Civil Code] has the status of a "common law" in its own right because of the scope of its regulation and the language in which it is expressed. It defines and sets out — it *constitutes* — the most fundamental categories and concepts that provide the *cadre* of Quebec legal thought in one of its main branches, the private law, and this mode of thought extends even beyond the private law to permeate other fields of legal regulation. The code in this regard has a role that is the functional equivalent of the accumulated work of the traditional (*i.e.,* judicially created) English common law in the shaping of private law concepts and relations. It provides, in this sphere, the first elements and the vocabulary of the law: what is a person (including a corporation), what is contract, inheritance, ownership, how property serves as security for debt and so on. In these respects, its language, whether English or French, acquires pre-eminent meaning. The Civil Code may even set the framework for the drawing of other large divisions of the law with which, however, it does not deal directly. It articulates therefore the basic concepts that are used and relied upon, or varied and extended, in other enactment that will moreover, when felicitously drafted, employ the same language and concepts.[24]

As the primary organizing source of law in private relations, the Civil Code enunciates its rules in a general fashion, in simple terms, and with an economy of words. The perfect example is Art. 1053 of the Quebec Civil Code, which reads:

> Art. 1053. Every person capable of discerning right from wrong is responsible for the damage caused by his fault to another, whether by positive act, imprudence, neglect or want of skill.

Although concepts such as "damage", "fault" and "another" will naturally have to be interpreted and adapted to a wide range of circumstances and factual situations, the general rule always remains the fundamental starting point in the civilian approach. In rendering a decision, the civilian judge is required to proceed by way of fundamental conceptual analysis. Because the law is deemed to be a coherent whole, civilian analysis is both systematic and rational. As Professors Smith and Kerby put it:

> In discovering the legislator's implied intention the civilian judge does not stop at adopting by *analogy* the rule laid down for some similar matter. He may formulate a rule by *deduction* from

a principle legislatively stated: this is how he arrived at the proportional allocation of blame in tort and it is what he does every time he adapts the law to new circumstances.[25]

Consistent with the basic premise that the law is complete, the civilian judge is obliged to decide every dispute. This fundamental obligation is expressed in Art. 11 of the Civil Code, which reads:

> 11. A judge cannot refuse to adjudicate under pretext of the silence, obscurity or insufficiency of the law.

Furthermore, in interpreting the rules in the Code, the civilian judge is to consider not only the letter, but equally the spirit of the law. Article 12 of the Quebec Civil Code states this principle and directs the judge to consider not only the language of the law, but also its purpose. It reads:

> 12. When a law is doubtful or ambiguous, it is to be interpreted so as to fulfil the intention of the legislature, and to attain the object for which it was passed.[26]

Beyond the language and the differing theoretical framework of a Code, the civilian tradition, in contrast to common law tradition, places a role of paramount importance on the doctrinal writings of legal scholars. The historical weight of *la doctrine* lies in its systematic and abstract articulation of the civil law.[27] Classical legal scholarship has played an important role by preceding, and allowing for, the codification movement of continental countries by way of its systematic and rational exposition of the private law; thus, scholarly opinion is traditionally viewed not simply as "writing *about* law," but is rather thought to be "fundamentally *constitutive* of law."[28] The great influence of academic writing is evidenced by Mignault J.'s description of the civilian adjudicative process. He observes:

> ... the civil law is a logical system, for from this it follows that the determination of controversies before the courts must proceed upon legal principles. The court is not bound to hunt up a case supporting the legal principle relied on, but it suffices that its decision conform to the dictates of reason as embodied in the maxims and principles of the civil law, or as taught by the jurists who have written on the law. The process whereby cases are decided, is the process of reasoning applied to the science of jurisprudence.[29]

This description, while illustrating the important function of civilian legal scholarship, also reveals the secondary role which is played by previously-decided cases. The classical function of the civilian judge is to interpret, not to create the law.[30] The natural flipside is that previously-decided cases are less important in the decision-making process and that the civilian judge is free to disregard precedent. The basic premise is inherent in the whole adjudicative process. As Planiol put it:

> Judicial interpretation is free in principle; each Court has the right of adopting the solution which seems to it the best and the most just: it is not bound either by decisions which it may have rendered previously in analogous cases, or by the decisions of another court though it be higher in rank.[31]

Therefore, through its conception of the judicial function, tradition civilian theory does not view judicial decisions as constituting, *per se*, binding sources of law.[32] This basic tenet of continental civil law tradition is illustrated in the French rule that a previous decision, even by a hierarchically superior court, is never binding;[33] the rationale being that in civil law, contrary to the common law, policy is for legislature, not for the courts. The courts interpret and apply the law. In common law, the courts determine policy as well.

It is against this background that one must consider the seemingly contradictory concepts of authority of reason and reason of authority. One can readily see that the language and theoretical framework of the Code, the traditional influence of legal scholarship and the restricted scope of previously-decided cases all point to a distinctive approach and a specific method of legal reasoning. The distinctive nature of the civilian legal system is not found too much in the solutions reached in particular cases. Rather, it is found in a reasoning process which favours a certain freedom and latitude in judicial interpretation. Thus, the very idea of a court of last resort laying down general principles through binding precedents seems, *a priori*, like the perfect antithesis of civilian theory.

When one considers the nature of the civilian legal system, and couples it with Lower Canada's reluctance concerning creation of the Supreme Court of Canada, one is forced to ask whether the Supreme Court's decisions in cases governed by the civil law were not effectively destined to be ignored within Quebec. What influence could a judicial hierarchy based on common law traditions possibly have on Quebec's civilian system?

As a starting point for the examination of these questions it is interesting to consider the early tendency of Quebec courts generally, and the Quebec Court of Appeal in particular, to ignore decisions of the Supreme Court of Canada in matters governed by the civil law. Although the principle of *stare decisis* was not expressly formulated by the Supreme Court of Canada until 1909,[34] Quebec courts demonstrated very early a reluctance to follow precedents laid down by Canada's court of last resort.[35] Despite Anglin C.J.'s statement that the principle of *stare decisis* also applied to cases governed by the civil law,[36] the Quebec Court of Appeal systematically contradicted certain Supreme Court of Canada decisions until the first half of this century.[37] Moreover, the authority of the Supreme Court of Canada in civil law matters suffered an additional setback as many Quebec scholars and practitioners severely criticized its judgments. Their main argument was that the integrity of civil law was at stake.[38]

Among the reasons put forward to explain this resistance, we find the Supreme Court's early tendency to unify certain aspects of Canadian private law.[39] In this regard, the case most frequently cited is *Canadian Pacific Railway v. Robinson*.[40] The issue was whether damages by way of *solatium doloris* could be claimed in an action under Art. 1056 of the Quebec Civil Code. The Supreme Court of Canada answered in the negative by referring to the English origin of Art. 1056. Taschereau J. wrote:

> It cannot have been intended by this legislation, that if a man was killed in Upper Canada, no *solatium* should be granted to his wife or legal representatives by way of damages, but that if he was killed in Lower Canada, such a *solatium* could be given. That in the present case, for instance, this plaintiff can get a *solatium* because her husband was killed in Lower Canada, whilst if he had been killed a few miles further west, in Upper Canada, none would be granted under the same statute....[41]

Justice Ritchie expressed a similar concern:

> I think it would be much to be regretted if we were compelled to hold that damages should be assessed by different rules in the different provinces through which the same railroad may run....[42]

This attempt to unify Canadian private law was criticized as ousting the civil law through a reasoning and interpretative process which was inspired by common law principles.[43] Further, the reasoning process in *Robinson* seemed to justify the application of common law principles to any civil law rules of English origin. By applying case law developed in common law jurisdictions, the Supreme Court of Canada risked importing principles without first addressing the question of whether these principles were even compatible with the recipient law. Although Quebec civil law embodies several rules of English origin in its Civil Code,[44] the reasoning of the Supreme Court was viewed as a threat to the integrity of the civil law. Under such conditions, it was feared that the interpretation of the Civil Code as a coherent and rational instrument would be hampered by the one-sided influence of the common law.[45]

The Supreme Court of Canada's early tendency towards unification of Canadian private law through reliance on common law judgments and authorities was, however, firmly halted by the influence of Mignault J. and his successors.[46] In the celebrated *Desrosiers*[47] decision in 1920, he argued forcefully against the use of common law precedents in civil law cases. In so doing, he distinguished the civil law from the common law on a systemic basis:

> ... With respect, it seems to me that it is time to react against the habit, in cases from the province of Quebec, of resorting to English common law precedents, on the ground that the Civil Code contains a rule which is in accordance with a rule of English law. On many points ... the Civil Code and the common law do have similar rules. However, the civil law is a complete system in itself and must be interpreted in accordance with its own rules. If, whenever the legal principles are the same, the courts can resort to English law in order to interpret French civil law, the monuments of French jurisprudence might equally be cited to throw light upon the rules of English law.[48]

The principle that each system of law should be administered through reference to authorities binding on that system alone has been reaffirmed very clearly by the Supreme Court of Canada ever since.[49] Illustrative of the Supreme Court of Canada's evolution on this question [is] Pigeon J.'s opinion in *Pantel v. Air Canada*.[50] Noting the English origin of Art. 1056 and recalling the Supreme Court's erroneous assumption in *Robinson, supra,* that the rule was to be interpreted following English authorities, Pigeon J. wrote:

> Art. 1056 C.C. must therefore be interpreted, not as reproducing a statute of English inspiration, but as a new provision forming part of a codification in which some fundamental principles are radically different from those of the common law, in terms of which *Lord Campbell's Act* was written.[51]

As mentioned earlier, the language and theoretical framework of a code, its internal coherence and its specific canons of interpretation are among the fundamental principles of civil law.[52] These basic tenets of civilian tradition were recently discussed, in the contexts of contempt of court and the compellability of parties to a civil action, in light of the *Code of Civil Procedure*.[53] The Quebec Court of Appeal's decision relied on common law precedents it considered binding. I have expressed a different view:

> There is nothing unusual about the fact that contempt of court is a concept borrowed from English law. Quebec private law includes a wealth of rules drawn from foreign sources. The common law principles cannot simply be applied to these rules, in my opinion, without first directly addressing the question of whether those principles are even compatible with the recipient law. Finally, such an approach seems particularly inappropriate where, as here, it is used in connection with provisions which form part of the general structure of a code [citations omitted].[54]

Since Mignault J., while upholding the reasoning and interpretative process inherent in each system of law, the Supreme Court of Canada has at the same time enhanced the authority of its decisions among Quebec judges, academics and practitioners. The scope of this *stare decisis* must then be considered against the background of two important factors.

First, in contrast to judges in France and other continental countries, Quebec judges administer a mixed system; private law matters are governed by the civil law, while public law matters are based on the foundation of the common law.[55] Beyond this strict duality in formal legal sources, the principles of judicial organization in Quebec private law itself are inspired from the common law.[56] As Jean-Louis Baudouin, now a judge of the Quebec Court of Appeal, explained, these organizational principles qualify one of the basic tenets of continental civil law tradition:

> In Quebec and Louisiana, the principle of the supremacy of legislation over other sources of law seems to be accepted as a premise. However, it would be futile to argue that this principle carries the same impact as it does in France, unless one forgets that both Quebec and Louisiana adopted the common-law procedure, most of the common-law rules of evidence, the common-law trial techniques, and, most important of all, the common-law respect and attitude towards the judiciary and the judicial function as a whole.[57]

This structural affinity with the common law judiciary could not but have an impact on the role played by previously-decided cases. Mignault J. himself recognized the impact of the hybrid character of Quebec's legal tradition on the role of judicial decisions:

> ... our civil law being French, our commercial law partly English and partly French, our procedure and mode of conducting trials a mixture of the two, and our criminal law entirely English — it is natural that, in so far as the authority of decided cases is concerned, we should be nearer to the English than to the French system.[58]

This Quebec legal tradition of mixed character has always tempered the theoretical freedom of the civilian judge to disregard precedent.[59] Some have even said that it is in greater danger of being mixed up. As the court of last resort in the judicial hierarchy, the Supreme Court of Canada itself is an integral part of this bi-systemic character of the Quebec legal tradition. This inevitably bears on the influence that the Court's decisions assume in the adjudicative process.

This being said, one cannot conclude that the doctrine of *stare decisis*, as understood and applied in common law jurisdictions, is the rationale of the present authority of the Supreme Court of Canada's decisions in cases governed by the civil law.[60] While precedent creates, to some degree, binding rules in common law jurisdictions, in the Quebec civil law system, precedent remains first and foremost a model.[61] Illustrative of this nuance is the Quebec Court of Appeal's position regarding its own precedents. It has always considered itself free to disregard a previous decision it later considers to be erroneous.[62] And so has the Supreme Court of Canada. As Laskin C.J. wrote in *Capital Cities Communications*, the Supreme Court of Canada "is not bound by judgments of the Privy Council any more than it is bound by its own judgments."[63] The authority which is given to the model cannot be separated from the model's respect for the content and spirit of codal legislation and the civilian tradition. It is in light of these constitutive elements that decisions of the Supreme Court of Canada in Quebec civil law may be thought to be "persuasive" in contrast to a strictly binding authority among Quebec courts. In reality, few, if any, today would dispute the authority of the Court's decisions in Quebec civil law.

In conclusion, the historical reluctance of Lower Canada concerning the Supreme Court of Canada should be seen against the background of the civilian tradition itself. Because this tradition reflects a distinctive approach and a specific method of legal reasoning, the authority of its decisions is indissociable from its endorsement of, and respect for, the basic tenets of the civil law. Through decisions which reflect these principles, the Court has affirmed its authority among Quebec judges and academics and has demonstrated that it could take up such a challenge. As Dickson C.J. recently said, before the International Academy of Comparative Law:

> The Supreme Court of Canada is fully conscious of its responsibility concerning the evolution of this dual heritage. Despite certain trends which at one time and particularly in certain areas, seemed to favour a policy of judicial unification of Canadian Private Law, it is now fully understood that each case before the Court must be dealt with according to and within the legal tradition from which it originated and in full respect for each of the two great legal traditions.[64]

This, of course, does not mean that comparative law has no place in Supreme Court of Canada decisions. While respecting two great legal traditions of the western world, it enjoys a privileged position. As political and economic systems seem to move irresistibly towards collaboration, cooperation and harmonization, a look at the forest may illuminate the trees. As my colleague Gonthier J. very aptly put it:

> Our two systems are legatees of the same foundation of Roman law, the subsequent evolution of each occurring at a time where communications were difficult. How much more simple, immediate and intimate are the communications and exchanges between societies of today, bringing new ideas, hopes and conceptions of law. Such an evolution is natural. We should not fear it as a menace to our identity. We need to remain conscious of the changes, and accept them as a necessary enrichment of the vitality of our law, of its capacity to respond to new demands, and to make a valuable contribution to the society of tomorrow, qualities which are, in short, the only true guarantees of the maintenance and integrity of the law.[65] [Translation]

These principles reflect nothing less, in my view, than reason itself.

(c)   Societal Norms Offer a Frame of Reference†

Gérard Bouchard and Charles Taylor

One of the key sources of anxiety mentioned during our consultations concerns the putative absence of guidelines to handle adjustment requests. Aside from the legal guidelines indicated in section III, Québec society has nonetheless adopted over the years an array of norms and guidelines that underpin its "common public culture." It is thus wrong to believe that there are no guidelines governing harmonization practices. However, this does not mean, either, that some facets of the guidelines would not benefit from clarification. Our approach comprises two stages. First, we will examine the existing guidelines, then, in keeping with the wish expressed by many interveners, we will seek to clarify the integration model and the system of secularism that seem most appropriate to Québec society.

A.   EXISTING GUIDELINES

1.   Québec's liberal democracy

Let us begin by noting that Québec's political system is both democratic and liberal. It is democratic insofar as political power ultimately resides with the people, who [delegate] such power to representatives who exercise it in the people's name for a given period of time. Our democracy is thus representative, but it is also liberal in that individual rights and freedoms are deemed to be fundamental and are thus confirmed and protected by the State.

We often lose sight of the extent to which the legitimacy of our political system centres on the complementarity of these two facets, i.e. its democratic and liberal nature. This system is democratic since, as we noted earlier, the people are sovereign. All citizens, who are deemed to be equal, are the ultimate holders of political power. All of them may in principle participate in political debate and take advantage of the right to vote. Since individuals often disagree about political questions and vote for different parties, a democracy is quite rightly subject to the rule of the majority.

Québec's democratic system is also liberal since it protects rights and freedoms from possible abuse by the majority. For example, no one would want a government, even a properly elected one, to flout the basic rights of a group of citizens in the name of the majority's interests. It is precisely to offer additional protection of the rights and freedoms guaranteed to all individuals that such rights and freedoms are enshrined in a charter, which imposes limits on the government's action and manages relations between citizens.

We cannot examine in detail here the Québec and Canadian charters. Let us simply note that both charters spell out a series of rights and freedoms from which all citizens may benefit, e.g. the right to life and equality, freedom of conscience and religion, freedom of expression and association, political rights and legal guarantees. They also prohibit several forms of discrimination, including discrimination based on sex, ethnic origin and religion. Everyone must be able to exercise these rights and freedoms since all human beings are deemed to be equal in dignity. The Preamble of the Québec Charter states that "all human beings are equal in worth and dignity, and are entitled to equal protection of the law."

It is also important to point out that the exercising of these rights and freedoms is not absolute and must respect the rights of others and the collective interest. When two rights come into conflict, the courts do not seek to determine which of the two is superior to the other, i.e. to organize rights along hierarchical lines, but endeavour to hand down a decision in which the level of infringement of the two rights is "minimal." This approach stems from the principle whereby basic rights are equally important. They form, to some extent, the links in the same chain. For this reason, the 1948 *Universal Declaration of Human Rights* does not establish a hierarchy of basic rights.

---

† From [Québec] Commission on Accomodation Practices Related to Cultural Differences, *Building The Future: A Time for Reconciliation*, Abridged Report (Quebec: Commission de consultation sur les pratiques d'accommodement reliées aux différences culturelle, 2008) Section IV. Reproduced with permission of Government of Québec. [Notes and/or references omitted.]

2. French as the common public language

In Québec, French is the official language. The *Charter of the French language* (Bill 101), adopted in 1977, stipulates that French is "the language of Government and the Law, as well as the normal and everyday language of work, instruction, communication, commerce and business." Québec's language policy therefore seeks to promote French as the common public language. However, Bill 101 does not cover the language that Quebecers use in the home or in their private lives. In keeping with the liberal nature of Québec society, the government has undertaken to promote French in a spirit of respect toward the linguistic minorities that live in Québec.

Through the provisions in Chapter VIII of the *Charter of the French language* covering the language of instruction, Québec French-language schools attended by students of different origins have become a hub for integration and learning to live together. The French language is the main medium that allows Quebecers of all origins to interact, get to know each other, cooperate and participate in the development of Québec society.

3. Québec's integration policy

It is widely acknowledged that the key directions in Québec's integration policy were defined in the *Policy Statement on Immigration and Integration* adopted in 1990. The policy statement stipulated the components of a "moral contract" that established, in a spirit of reciprocity, the respective commitments of the host society and newcomers. In particular, the policy statement stipulates that Québec is:

- a society in which French is the common language of public life;
- a democratic society that expects and encourages everyone to participate and contribute;
- pluralistic and open to outside contributions, within the limitations imposed by respect for basic democratic values and the need for inter-community exchange.

It notes that immigration is essential to the development of Québec society. As for cultural diversity, it is perceived as an asset inasmuch as its expression is guided by the charters of human rights and freedoms and it is achieved in a spirit of interaction rather than a spirit of division. Immigrants are encouraged to learn French and contribute to Québec society's cultural, economic and political vitality.

In return, the government undertakes to facilitate their integration.

Successive governments may interpret differently any of these policy directions. However, we have noted that the principles of the civil pact formulated in the policy statement have not been fundamentally altered since 1990.

The factors that we have just examined, i.e. the liberal democratic system, the charters of human rights and freedoms, the *Charter of the French language*, and the *Policy Statement on Immigration and Integration*, have made it possible to establish in Québec in recent decades a relatively harmonious group climate. However, debate on reasonable accommodation has revealed that certain aspects of the "common public culture" would benefit from broader dissemination or clarification.

B. INTEGRATION AND INTERCULTURALISM: A MODEL TO BE CLARIFIED

Often mentioned in academic papers, interculturalism as an integration policy has never been fully, officially defined by the Québec government although its key components were formulated long ago. This shortcoming should be overcome, all the more so as the Canadian multiculturalism model does not appear to be well suited to conditions in Québec, for four reasons: *a*) anxiety over language is not an important factor in English Canada; *b*) minority insecurity is not found there; *c*) there is no longer a majority ethnic group in Canada (citizens of British origin account for 34% of the population, while citizens of French-Canadian origin make up a strong majority of the population in Québec, i.e. roughly 77%); *d*) it follows that in English Canada, there is less concern for the preservation of a founding cultural tradition than for national cohesion.

Generally speaking, it is in the interests of any community to maintain a minimum of cohesion. It is through such cohesion that a community can adopt common orientations, ensure participation by citizens in public debate, create the feeling of solidarity required for an egalitarian society to function smoothly, mobilize the population in the event of a crisis, and take advantage of the enrichment that stems from ethnocultural diversity. For a small nation such as Québec, constantly concerned about its future as a cultural minority, integration also represents a condition for its development, and perhaps, for its survival.

That is why the integrative dimension is a key component of Québec interculturalism. According to the descriptions provided in scientific documentation, interculturalism seeks to reconcile ethnocultural diversity with the continuity of the French-speaking core and the preservation of the social link. It thus affords security to Quebecers of French-Canadian origin and to ethnocultural minorities and protects the rights of all in keeping with the liberal tradition. By instituting French as the common public language, it establishes a framework in society for communication and exchanges. It has the virtue of being flexible and receptive to negotiation, adaptation and innovation.

The 11 proposals below allow us to define Québec interculturalism even more precisely.

1. Québec as a nation, as recognized by all Québec political parties and the federal government, is the operational framework for interculturalism.
2. In a spirit of reciprocity, interculturalism strongly emphasizes interaction, in particular intercommunity action, with a view to overcoming stereotypes and defusing fear or rejection of the Other, taking advantage of the enrichment that stems from diversity, and benefiting from social cohesion.
3. Members of the majority ethnocultural group, i.e. Quebecers of French-Canadian origin, like the members of ethnocultural minorities, accept that their culture will be transformed sooner or later through interaction.
4. Cultural, and, in particular, religious differences need not be confined to the private domain. The following logic underpins this choice: it is healthier to display our differences and get to know those of the Other than to deny or marginalize them.
5. The principle of multiple identities is recognized, as is the right to maintain an affiliation with one's ethnic group.
6. For those citizens who so wish, it is desirable for initial affiliations to survive, since ethnic groups of origin often act as mediators between their members and society as a whole. A general phenomenon arises in this regard: almost without exception, each citizen integrates into society through a milieu or an institution that serves as a link, e.g. the family, a profession, a community group, a church, an association, and so on.
7. Multilingualism is encouraged at the same time as French as the common public language. The debate that opposes the language of identity and the common language (as a simple communication tool) is hardly promising. What is important, first and foremost, is the broadest possible dissemination of French, in whatever form.
8. To facilitate the integration of immigrants and their children, it is useful to provide them with the means to preserve their mother tongue, at least at the outset. This helps them to mitigate the shock of immigration by affording them a cultural anchor. It is also a means of preserving the enrichment that stems from cultural diversity.
9. Constant interaction between citizens of different origins leads to the development of a new identity and a new culture. This is what has been happening in Québec in recent decades without altering the cultural position of the majority group or infringing on the culture of minority groups.
10. Under a recent, highly promising orientation from the standpoint of pluralism, the groups present in Québec define themselves with reference to common, often universal, values stemming from their history rather than their ethnic traits. Québec is thus part of an international trend whereby societies choose to integrate diversity in light of shared values.
11. The civic and legal dimensions (and everything that concerns, in particular, non-discrimination) must be regarded as fundamental in interculturalism.

To summarize, we could say that Québec interculturalism *a)* institutes French as the common language of intercultural relations; *b)* cultivates a pluralistic orientation that is highly sensitive to the protection of rights; *c)* preserves the creative tension between diversity and the continuity of the French-speaking core and the social link; *d)* places special emphasis on integration; and *e)* advocates interaction.

As we noted earlier, we believe it would be useful for the Québec government to adopt an official text such as a statute, a policy statement or a declaration that broadly defines interculturalism. This text would thus constitute a key component of the social blueprint and would serve as a frame of reference for the elaboration of policies and programs. In addition to enhancing the coherence of the government's approach, it would offer all community interveners an official reference point.

C. A SECULAR REGIME FOR QUÉBEC

During the public consultation held in the fall of 2007, Quebecers massively espoused the concept of secularism, one of the most frequently mentioned themes, but sometimes with highly different meanings. We will first seek to clarify the meaning of this concept then will describe the type of secularism that we believe is best suited to Québec.

An initial ambiguity: the distinction between what is public and private

The argument that "religion must remain in the private sphere" was often cited by the proponents of secularism. While at first sight it seems clear, this statement is not quite as clear as we may think. Indeed, "public" can be understood in at least two separate ways. According to the first meaning, what is public relates to the State and its common institutions, i.e. "public institutions." According to the second meaning, what is public is open or accessible to everyone, i.e. "places of public use," for example, a "garden open to the public."

The first meaning concurs with the secular principle of the neutrality of the State with respect to religion. According to this first meaning, it is therefore accurate to confirm that religion must be "private." However, it does not go without saying that secularism demands of religion that it be absent from public space in the broad sense. In point of fact, religions already occupy this space and, pursuant to the charters, religious groups and the faithful have the freedom to publicly display their beliefs.

Confusion arises when these two ways of understanding the distinction between what is public and private intersect. This is true, for example, when we ask whether students and teachers may display their religious affiliation in the school. If a public institution must be neutral, are the individuals who frequent it subject to this obligation of neutrality?

A second ambiguity: State neutrality

The notion of neutrality is also more complex that it may seem. Thus, it is widely acknowledged that the secular State must be neutral in respect of all religions. To this we must add that the State must not take sides as regards religion and non-religion. It must maintain its position of neutrality when faced with all deep-seated moral convictions, whether they are religious or secular.

However, the secular, democratic State is based on a political moral code and on certain principles that are not negotiable. This is true of democracy, human rights and the equality of all citizens. When these principles come into play, the State may not remain neutral. Ideally, all citizens must share these same principles and political moral code, although their deep-seated convictions may differ.

For example, everyone may agree on the idea that we must defend the right to life, although individuals may do so in light of markedly different justifications: a Christian may confirm that human beings are created in God's image, while a secular philosopher might claim that a human being as a rational subject possesses a dignity that no one must infringe. Other deep-seated reasons might similarly be cited. The secular State defends certain principles but it does so without taking sides in respect of the deep-seated reasons that citizens may cite to justify their adherence.

Open secularism

Liberal democracies, including Québec, all adhere to the principle of secularism, which can nonetheless be embodied in different systems. Which system is best suited to Québec society, bearing in mind its history and the very foundations of secularism? To answer this question, it is useful to distinguish the four principles that underpin secularism. Two of them define its final purpose:

1. the moral equality of persons; and
2. freedom of conscience and religion.

The other two principles are expressed in institutional structures that make it possible to achieve these purposes:

3. the separation of Church and State; and
4. the neutrality of the State with respect to religions and deep-seated secular convictions.

Any secular system achieves some form of balance between these four principles. Certain systems impose fairly strict limits on freedom of religious expression. France, which has just adopted restrictive legislation governing the wearing of religious signs in the schools, is deemed to have this type of system, although in reality it is much more flexible that its reputation suggests. This type of system defines State neutrality very broadly, which leads to the exclusion of certain forms of religious expression in the public sphere.

We do not think that this is the best type of system. Since freedom of conscience and religion is one of the purposes of secularism (second principle), the neutrality of the State (fourth principle) should be designed so as to foster, not hinder, its expression. If such was the case in France, it is perhaps because a certain conception of the neutrality of the State, sanctioned by a national tradition, was raised to the level of an ultimate purpose. Recent debate in France, where secularism has often been presented as an essential component of the Republic's identity, illustrates this shift. Certain French republicans believe that the mission of secular schools must be to emancipate students from religion. Others believe that cultural and religious identities only impede social integration, which should be based on citizenship that excludes any particularism.

There are three reasons why we believe that this type of restrictive secularism is not appropriate for Québec: *a*) it does not truly link institutional structures to the purposes of secularism; *b*) the attribution to the school of an emancipatory mission directed against religion is not compatible with the principle of State neutrality in respect of religion and non-religion; *c*) the integration process in a diversified society is achieved through exchanges between citizens, who thus learn to get to know each other (that is the philosophy of Québec interculturalism), not by relegating identities to the background.

Open secularism, which we are advocating, seeks to develop the final purposes of secularism (first and second principles) by defining institutional structures (third and fourth principles) in light of this objective. This is the path that Québec has followed historically, as witnessed by the Proulx report, which also promotes open secularism.[4] Our position, once again, is in keeping with the path that Québec has followed.

The wearing by government employees of religious signs

Must a regime based on open secularism allow government employees to wear religious signs? Does the neutrality of public institutions demand the prohibition of such signs? To answer these questions, we must consider the type of neutrality that it is to be expected of the public service. We naturally hope that public servants will perform their duties loyally and impartially. Would they relinquish these qualities simply because they wear a religious sign? We do not think so.

By prohibiting the wearing in the public service of any religious sign, we would prevent the faithful from certain religions from engaging in careers in the public service, which would contravene freedom of conscience and religion (second principle) and would largely complicate the task of building a public service that reflects Québec's population, which is becoming increasingly diversified. This would also infringe the equality of citizens (first principle).

We do not believe that a general prohibition concerning the wearing by all government employees of religious signs is warranted. However, we acknowledge that certain duties may imply a duty of self-restraint. In the brief that it submitted to the Commission, the Bloc Québécois noted that certain functions "by their very nature embody the State and its essential neutrality." This is true, in particular, of judges, Crown prosecutors, police officers and the President of the National Assembly. Individuals who occupy these positions could be required to relinquish their right to display their religious affiliation in order to preserve the appearance of impartiality that their function requires.

Harmonization practices for religious reasons

In the course of our consultations, several interveners requested the adoption of legislation prohibiting any religious accommodation. This radical proposal cannot be adopted under a system based on open secularism, especially as it would require the amendment of the Québec *Charter of Human Rights and Freedoms*, which protects freedom of religion. Such an amendment would put Québec in an awkward position from the standpoint of the *Universal Declaration of Human Rights* and the numerous national charters based on it.

Furthermore, this proposal is incompatible with the principle of State neutrality. Since freedom of religion cannot be dissociated from freedom of conscience, the prohibition of religious accommodation would create inextricable legal problems. For example, let us consider the following case: a penitentiary offers a meat-based diet. Two inmates request a vegetarian meal, one because he is Hindu and the other (an atheist) because he believes it is immoral to kill animals for food. Should the first request be rejected under the pretence that it is motivated by religion and the second one accepted because it is not of a religious nature? How can we refuse requests related to freedom of religion without at the same time rejecting freedom of conscience? As we saw earlier, the neutrality of the State assumes that it does not take sides in favour of religion or non-religion.

According to another argument, the accommodation granted to the disabled should not be confused with religious accommodation because the disabled do not choose their disability, while a believer may decide to relinquish such and such a practice. This distinction, while it seems convincing, minimizes the fact that certain "religious choices" are actually experienced as non-optional. To infringe these choices of conscience would be tantamount to interfering with the individual's moral integrity and would entail relegating choices stemming from deep-seated convictions to the level of simple desires or whims. To no longer make a distinction between whims and deep-seated convictions, whether of a religious or a secular nature, would be to relinquish one of the most valuable established privileges of our civilization.

Religious heritage

Catholicism has left an indelible mark on Québec's history. Traces of it are all around us. Under the principle of the neutrality of the State, religious displays linked to the functioning of public institutions should be abandoned. Thus, we do not believe that the crucifix in the National Assembly and the prayers that precede municipal council meetings have their place in a secular State. In both instances, public institutions are associated with a single religious affiliation rather than addressing themselves to all citizens.

That being the case, it would be absurd to want to extend this rule of neutrality to all historic signs that no longer fulfil an obvious religious function, e.g. the cross on Mont-Royal or the crosses on old buildings converted to secular uses. The same is true of Québec toponymy, which is largely inspired by the calendar of the saints. Quebecers' common sense will surely prevail in this respect.

(d) Living Law on a Living Earth†

John Borrows

The Anishinabek Nation surrounds the North American Great Lakes. They are an Algonquian and (more recently) English speaking people who historically organized themselves in a loose confederacy of clans throughout the region. Anishinabek people possess laws pertaining to the earth. These laws have ancient roots but they are not stunted by time. They continue to grow and develop through observation, experience and interaction with other people's more recent presence within their territories. Anishinabek law is a living system of social order, developed through comparing, contrasting, accepting and rejecting legal standards from many sources. Anishinabek legal traditions do not lose their Indigenous status if they adopt viewpoints that address matters not encountered before European contact. Law is not solely a matter of history because it is reinterpreted and reapplied in every generation to remain relevant amidst changing circumstances.

The Anishinabek regard Michee-Makinakong on the narrows between Lake Huron and Michigan near Lake Superior as the world's centre; the place where the land above the water was formed. Michee-Makinakong was where Michabous (Nanabush) recre-ated the upper earth through breathing life into soil which was brought up from the ocean's depths by a muskrat. The earth grew as the soil was scattered around Michabous' raft and [trod] upon by this Great Being. The earth's ability to respond to Michabous' actions provided enough space for plants and animals to find a home. When these first animals died the first [Anishinabek] arose from their corpses. The Anishinabek take their identity and dodem or clan names from these ancestors. Professor Heidi Bohaker has observed that: "This sacred story is part of what Anishinaabe peoples call aadizoo-kaanag, or the grandfathers. Stories of this genre are set in time immemorial; they explain how the world came to have its present form and furnish embedded observations on how the beings who currently inhabit it should relate to one another." These stories contain law.

For the Anishinabek the earth's creation did not end with Michabous' experience on the raft. The earth grows and develops or dies and decays because it is a living being subject to many of the same forces as all other living creatures. Many Anishinabek people characterize the earth as a living

---

† From John Borrows and Leonard J. Rotman, *Aboriginal Legal Issues: Cases, Materials and Commentary*, 4th ed. (Markham: LexisNexis, 2012) at 184–89. [References omitted.] Reproduced with permission.

entity that has thoughts and feelings, can exercise agency by making choices, and is related to humans at the deepest generative levels of existence.

The subject of the earth's personality is a profound legal issue. Law is implicated in the earth's sentience because its life is considered sacred within most Anishinabek thought. Anishinabek people do not generally worship the earth as one would the Creator but she is regarded with great awe, respect and wonder because of her ability to live a good life and reproduce it in numerous forms. Anishinabek people believe in a Creator, Kitchee Manitou, who gave form and meaning to the earth following a vision. The first elements of Anishinabek creation stories explain how life came into being from a constellation of forces marshaled by the Creator. Later stories convey important spiritual insights by providing instruction about how the earth must be honoured and respected. Within these teachings there is a general recognition that the earth has a soul (chejauk) which animates her many moods and activities. Many believe the Creator, as the Great Master of Life, created a universal bond between all living things which placed the earth at the centre of a vast web of kinship relations. Great power can be attached to these relationships because of the spiritual energy that flows between, from and through them.

The land's sentience is a fundamental principle of Anishinabek law, one upon which many Anishinabek people attempt to build their societies and relationships. Of course, they have not always been successful in this regard; like most peoples, they often fall short of their highest ideals. That is why they developed law, to direct behavior towards [a] more peaceful, orderly, and respectful future.

The relationship between humans and rocks creates mutual obligations and entitlements that must be respected for this community to reproduce in a healthy manner. This legal structure requires humans to consult with [] the earth's Creator and to seek the earth's receptiveness before important decisions are undertaken. The Anishinabek will listen to the Creator and/or the earth through ceremonies or they will elect to understand the earth's requirements by observing its interactions with wind, water, fire and other beings to which she relates.

These obligations between Anishinabek and the earth have territorial aspects. At one level the political boundaries of Anishinabek relationships to the earth coincide with the totality of the planet's surface. An Anishinabemowin word that describes this relationship is aen-danee-yauk-kummikuak[,] which means the nature of the land's character from which

all derive sustenance. At this broadest level, we are all citizens with and of one land because we depend upon its total existence to survive.

At the same time this wider political ordering does not preclude Anishinabek or the land from being citizens of smaller polities: water-sheds, islands, valleys, countries, tribes, cities, reserves, etc. Anishinabek political community contemplates allegiances across global and smaller geographical units. The Anishinabemowin word for boundary is ani-ishkawaek-kummikauk meaning the place along the way of the land's end according to her character. Within Anishinabek thought there is an encouragement to determine the earth's character to make decisions about how to best divide ourselves in ways that are most respectful of her. The ability to relate to the earth on different scales feeds a multiplicity of citizenship rights and responsibilities for Anishinabek people and the earth. A person could be simultaneously a Clan (dodem) member, Anishinabek, Canadian, American, and a world citizen. Likewise, the earth can concurrently be a planet, geological plate, continent or small rock.

Rocks are animate or living in verb-oriented Algonkian languages, of which Anishnabemowin is one. The very way in which Anishinabek people conceive of the land as alive is hardwired through language. You cannot even describe the world without acknowledging this fact. Their active nature means rocks have an agency of their own which must be respected when Anishinabek people use them. As such it would be inappropriate to use rocks without their acquiescence and participation because such action could oppress their liberty in some circumstances. Using rocks without their consent could be considered akin to using another person against their will. Their enslavement could lead to great calamities for the earth and its people. Therefore, to ensure that rocks and land are appropriately used there are particular ceremonies, or legal permissions, needed to engage in such action.

Since Anishinabek law regards some rocks (or places on earth) as living they could not be owned or allocated if such ownership implied control of the earth without its involvement. However, a kind of ownership can occur if undertaken in accordance with appropriate Anishinabek principles. As such, the pipe ceremony is a particularly important certification-like process preceding the appropriate use or ownership of land. When one smokes the sacred pipe under the guidance of proper leaders, the earth's legal personality is acknowledged during this process. While the smoke is said to ascend to the Creator and demonstrate thankfulness for existence;

prayers of thanksgiving are expressed for the rocks, plants, animals and other humans as the smoke rises from the pipe. The pipe itself represents earth's different orders: "the earth, whose elemental substance was rock, made up the pipe; the plant, tobacco[,] was the sacrificial victim; the animal, symbolized by feathers and fur, was appended to the sacred pipe of rock; man was the celebrant." (Basil Johnston, Ojibway Heritage, Toronto: McClelland and Stewart, 1976 at 24–25)

The pipe's use is a token of peace between people and the land, and between peoples settling on the land. The earth was best used by celebrating her contributions and consulting with her Creator in this way. This is why, when treaties were signed, Anishinabek people often included non-Indigenous people in this relationship, and both would use the pipe to register their mutual agreement concerning her use. Anishinabek Elder Basil Johnston has observed that rocks are the elemental substance of life and must be continually acknowledged for their role in sustaining other orders of life. While plants, animals and humans all come to an end, the earth lives on. It is contrary to certain interpretations of Anishinabek law to claim to absolute ownership of the earth, which is called a mother because of her role in bringing forth life. In this vein Dr. Johnston has written:

> No man can own his mother. This principle extends even into the future. The unborn are entitled to the largess of the earth, no less than the living. During his life a man is but a trustee of his portion of the land and must pass on to his children what he inherited from his mother. At death, the dying leave behind the mantle that they occupied, taking nothing with them but a memory and a place for others still to come.

Thus, for many Anishinabek "ownership" is differently construed when compared with other Canadian legal traditions. The analogy of a trustee when explaining limitations concerning Anishinabek land use is somewhat helpful in understanding Anishinabek law. A trust in equity, as merged through the common law, is a right held by one person (the trustee) for the benefit of another person (the beneficiary). Under Anishinabek law, land is held by the present generation for future generations. Land does not ultimately belong to a person or people in the sense that they have absolute discretion and control; land is provisionally held for contemporary sustenance and for those unborn.

However, analogies to trust law can also create confusion in understanding Anishinabek legal tradi-

tions if carried too far. Under Anishinabek law, while the earth is somewhat dependent on other orders of life for its health and vitality[,] plants, animals and humans are much more reliant on the earth for their survival. In this sense, the earth could be considered the trustee for its beneficiaries (plants, animals and humans). This analogy may be a stretch for the common law legal imagination because of the legal personality the earth possesses under Anishinabek law as a living being. The common law does not generally regard the earth in this light. Nevertheless Anishinabek legal traditions recognize interdependence between rocks and humans because of their mutual agency. The concept of reciprocal obligations between rocks and humans is an important part of Anishinabek law. People are the beneficiaries of the earth's care, and under Anishinabek law this creates duties for the beneficiaries as well as for the earth (as the so-called trustee).

A contemporary applied example of these principles is demonstrated by the Anishinabek people of the Bruce Peninsula, who live between the waters of Lake Huron and Georgian Bay. Ten years ago the people of Neyashiingmiing, the Chippewas of the Nawash on the Cape Croker Indian Reserve, had to make a decision about moving the site of an annual summer festival on their reserve. Each August a powwow is held in their park, drawing thousands of people in a celebration of Anishinabek resilience and culture. A move was contemplated to accommodate the increasing number of park users during this annual event. One suggestion was to move the powwow to "the prairie", a broad, flat and largely treeless stretch of land lying below Jones Bluff just beyond the shores of Sydney Bay. The prairie had the advantage of being able to accommodate large crowds with easy access to the main road. The area affords beautiful views of the surrounding escarpments, lake and ever-changing skies. It is also easy to see from the park and other vantage points around the community. The idea to move the powwow to the prairie seemed to make sense by most principles of efficiency. To any casual observer the land looked empty in terms of human use, and did not seem to be productively used by most economic measures.

However, when it became apparent that a road would be built to facilitate access to the prairie a widespread community movement developed that drew upon Anishinabek legal principles. The land is host to a significant alvar, which is a rock-barren or natural pavement-like feature with little or no brush or tree cover. The alvar is a limestone plain composed of dolostone bedrock with a surface that is almost completely exposed to the air. The alvar is among the oldest exposed stone in Ontario, having an age in excess of four hundred and forty million years. For many Anishinabek the alvar is a story-teller that recounts the time when the land was younger and covered by shallow tropical seas. It is related to the surrounding limestone escarpments and fossil strewn beaches formed when the area once likely resembled the Great Barrier Reef of Australia's north-eastern coast. Furthermore, in those areas where a very thin layer of organic matter covers the alvar it accommodates a unique community of resilient mosses, lichens and plants which are very well adapted to extreme conditions of intense cold, heat, drought and flooding.

The alvar is also home to spiritually significant 'spirit trails' which wend their way through the area. Family stories amongst the Anishinabek speak of the place as having significant sacred power with accounts of bear-walkers, deceased relatives and supernatural transformers traversing over the area. Armed with this knowledge, there was consultation, debate, discussion, direct experience on the land, prayer and persuasion when making a decision about the alvar's use. Scientists and Anishinabek lawyers, band councillors, grandmothers, Elders, artists, medicine people, community employees and others participated in a process that drew most strongly on Anishinabek law respecting Anishinabek spiritual beliefs. Ceremonies were conducted and traditional teachings reviewed. This led to a decision to stop the prairie's development to respect and reverence the life force of what others might regard as barren rock.

This brief review of Anishinabek law demonstrates that Anishinabek Beliefs concerning the earth as a living being can be legally recognized and affirmed, within that legal system. It also shows how Anishinabek law can lead to land being accorded political citizenship with its other close relations. The attentiveness to land's character and the desire to respect significant sites where it manifests sacred power give the earth a place within this jurisprudential system.

Constitutional Context:
Law, the State, and the Constitution

(a) *Reference re Secession of Quebec†*

[THE COURT:]

I. INTRODUCTION

[1] This Reference requires us to consider momentous questions that go to the heart of our system of constitutional government. The observation we made more than a decade ago in *Reference re Manitoba Language Rights*, [1985] 1 S.C.R. 721 (*Manitoba Language Rights Reference*), at p. 728, applies with equal force here: as in that case, the present one "combines legal and constitutional questions of the utmost subtlety and complexity with political questions of great sensitivity". In our view, it is not possible to answer the questions that have been put to us without a consideration of a number of underlying principles. An exploration of the meaning and nature of these underlying principles is not merely of academic interest. On the contrary, such an exploration is of immense utility. Only once those underlying principles have been examined and delineated may a considered response to the questions we are required to answer emerge.

· · · ·

III. REFERENCE QUESTIONS

A. Question 1

Under the Constitution of Canada, can the National Assembly, legislature or government of Quebec effect the secession of Quebec from Canada unilaterally?

(1) Introduction

[32] As we confirmed in *Reference re Objection by Quebec to a Resolution to Amend the Constitution*, [1982] 2 S.C.R. 793, at p. 806, "The *Constitution Act, 1982* is now in force. Its legality is neither challenged nor assailable." The "Constitution of Canada" certainly includes the constitutional texts enumerated in s. 52(2) of the *Constitution Act, 1982*. Although these texts have a primary place in determining constitutional rules, they are not exhaustive. The Constitution also "embraces unwritten, as well as written rules", as we recently observed in the *Provincial Judges Reference, supra*, at para. 92. Finally, as was said in the *Patriation Reference, supra*, at p. 874, the Constitution of Canada includes

> the global system of rules and principles which govern the exercise of constitutional authority in the whole and in every part of the Canadian state.

These supporting principles and rules, which include constitutional conventions and the workings of Parliament, are a necessary part of our Constitution because problems or situations may arise which are not expressly dealt with by the text of the Constitution. In order to endure over time, a constitution must contain a comprehensive set of rules and principles which are capable of providing an exhaustive legal framework for our system of government. Such principles and rules emerge from an understanding of the constitutional text itself, the historical context, and previous judicial interpretations of constitutional meaning. In our view, there are four fundamental

---

† [1998] 2 S.C.R. 217 at paras. 1, 32, 49, 51–52, 43, 59, 61, 63–64, 66, 68, 70, 72, 76–77, 79, 81, 82..

and organizing principles of the Constitution which are relevant to addressing the question before us (although this enumeration is by no means exhaustive): federalism; democracy; constitutionalism and the rule of law; and respect for minorities. The foundation and substance of these principles are addressed in the following paragraphs. We will then turn to their specific application to the first reference question before us.

. . . .

(3) Analysis of the Constitutional Principles
(A) NATURE OF THE PRINCIPLES

[49] What are those underlying principles? Our Constitution is primarily a written one, the product of 131 years of evolution. Behind the written word is an historical lineage stretching back through the ages, which aids in the consideration of the underlying constitutional principles. These principles inform and sustain the constitutional text: they are the vital unstated assumptions upon which the text is based. The following discussion addresses the four foundational constitutional principles that are most germane for resolution of this Reference: federalism, democracy, constitutionalism and the rule of law, and respect for minority rights. These defining principles function in symbiosis. No single principle can be defined in isolation from the others, nor does any one principle trump or exclude the operation of any other.

. . . .

[51] Although these underlying principles are not explicitly made part of the Constitution by any written provision, other than in some respects by the oblique reference in the preamble to the *Constitution Act, 1867*, it would be impossible to conceive of our constitutional structure without them. The principles dictate major elements of the architecture of the Constitution itself and are as such its lifeblood.

[52] The principles assist in the interpretation of the text and the delineation of spheres of jurisdiction, the scope of rights and obligations, and the role of our political institutions. Equally important, observance of and respect for these principles is essential to the ongoing process of constitutional development and evolution of our Constitution as a "living tree", to invoke the famous description in *Edwards v. Attorney-General for Canada*, [1930] A.C. 123 (P.C.), at p. 136. As this Court indicated in *New Brunswick Broadcasting Co. v. Nova Scotia (Speaker of the House of Assembly)*, [1993] 1 S.C.R. 319, Canadians have long recognized the existence and importance of unwritten constitutional principles in our system of government.

(B) FEDERALISM

. . . .

[The Court discussed federalism in the context of Conferation earlier:]

[43] Federalism was a legal response to the underlying political and cultural realities that existed at Confederation and continue to exist today. At Confederation, political leaders told their respective communities that the Canadian union would be able to reconcile diversity with unity. It is pertinent, in the context of the present Reference, to mention the words of George-Etienne Cartier (cited in J. C. Bonenfant, "Les Canadiens francais et la naissance de la Confédération", [1952] C.H.A.R. 39, at p. 42):

> [TRANSLATION] When we are united, he said, we shall form a political nationality independent of the national origin or the religion of any individual. There are some who regretted that there was diversity of races and who expressed the hope that this distinctive character would disappear. The idea of unity of races is a utopia; it is an impossibility. A distinction of this nature will always exist, just as dissimilarity seems to be in the order of the physical, moral and political worlds. As to the objection based on this fact, that a large nation cannot be formed because Lower Canada is largely French and Catholic and Upper Canada is English and Protestant and the interior provinces are mixed, it constitutes, in my view, reasoning that is futile in the extreme.... In our own federation, we will have Catholics and Protestants, English, French, Irish and Scots and everyone, through his efforts and successes, will add to the prosperity and glory of the new confederation. We are of different races, not so that we can wage war on one another, but in order to work together for our well-being.

The federal–provincial division of powers was a legal recognition of the diversity that existed among the initial members of Confederation, and manifested a concern to accommodate that diversity within a single nation by granting significant powers to provincial governments. The *Constitution Act, 1867* was an act of nation-building. It was the first step in the transition from colonies separately dependent on the Imperial Parliament for their governance to a unified and independent political state in which different peoples could resolve their disagreements and work together toward common goals and a common interest. Federalism was the political mechanism by which diversity could be reconciled with unity.

. . . .

[59] The principle of federalism facilitates the pursuit of collective goals by cultural and linguistic minorities which form the majority within a particular province. This is the case in Quebec, where the majority of the population is French-speaking, and which possesses a distinct culture. This is not merely the result of chance. The social and demographic reality of Quebec explains the existence of the province of Quebec as a political unit and indeed, was one of the essential reasons for establishing a federal structure for the Canadian union in 1867. The experience of both Canada East and Canada West under the *Union Act, 1840* (U.K.), 3–4 Vict., c. 35, had not been satisfactory. The federal structure adopted at Confederation enabled French-speaking Canadians to form a numerical majority in the province of Quebec, and so exercise the considerable provincial powers conferred by the *Constitution Act, 1867* in such a way as to promote their language and culture. It also made provision for certain guaranteed representation within the federal Parliament itself.

. . . .

(C) DEMOCRACY

[61] Democracy is a fundamental value in our constitutional law and political culture. While it has both an institutional and an individual aspect, the democratic principle was also argued before us in the sense of the supremacy of the sovereign will of a people, in this case potentially to be expressed by Quebecers in support of unilateral secession. It is useful to explore in a summary way these different aspects of the democratic principle.

. . . .

[63] Democracy is commonly understood as being a political system of majority rule. It is essential to be clear what this means. The evolution of our democratic tradition can be traced back to the *Magna Carta* (1215) and before, through the long struggle for Parliamentary supremacy which culminated in the English *Bill of Rights* in 1688–89, the emergence of representative political institutions in the colonial era, the development of responsible government in the 19th century, and eventually, the achievement of Confederation itself in 1867. "[T]he Canadian tradi-

tion", the majority of this Court held in *Reference re Provincial Electoral Boundaries (Sask.)*, [1991] 2 S.C.R. 158, at p. 186, is "one of evolutionary democracy moving in uneven steps toward the goal of universal suffrage and more effective representation". Since Confederation, efforts to extend the franchise to those unjustly excluded from participation in our political system — such as women, minorities, and aboriginal peoples — have continued, with some success, to the present day.

[64] Democracy is not simply concerned with the process of government. On the contrary, as suggested in *Switzman v. Elbling, supra*, at p. 306, democracy is fundamentally connected to substantive goals, most importantly, the promotion of self-government. Democracy accommodates cultural and group identities: *Reference re Provincial Electoral Boundaries*, at p. 188. Put another way, a sovereign people exercises its right to self-government through the democratic process. In considering the scope and purpose of the *Charter*, the Court in *R. v. Oakes*, [1986] 1 S.C.R. 103, articulated some of the values inherent in the notion of democracy (at p. 136):

> The Court must be guided by the values and principles essential to a free and democratic society which I believe to embody, to name but a few, respect for the inherent dignity of the human person, commitment to social justice and equality, accommodation of a wide variety of beliefs, respect for cultural and group identity, and faith in social and political institutions which enhance the participation of individuals and groups in society.

. . . .

[66] It is, of course, true that democracy expresses the sovereign will of the people. Yet this expression, too, must be taken in the context of the other institutional values we have identified as pertinent to this Reference. The relationship between democracy and federalism means, for example, that in Canada there may be different and equally legitimate majorities in different provinces and territories and at the federal level. No one majority is more or less "legitimate" than the others as an expression of democratic opinion, although, of course, the consequences will vary with the subject matter. A federal system of government enables different provinces to pursue policies responsive to the particular concerns and interests of people in that province. At the same time, Canada as a whole is also a democratic community in which citizens construct and achieve goals on a national scale through a federal government acting within the

limits of its jurisdiction. The function of federalism is to enable citizens to participate concurrently in different collectivities and to pursue goals at both a provincial and a federal level.

. . . .

[68] Finally, we highlight that a functioning democracy requires a continuous process of discussion. The Constitution mandates government by democratic legislatures, and an executive accountable to them, "resting ultimately on public opinion reached by discussion and the interplay of ideas" (*Saumur v. City of Quebec, supra*, at p. 330). At both the federal and provincial level, by its very nature, the need to build majorities necessitates compromise, negotiation, and deliberation. No one has a monopoly on truth, and our system is predicated on the faith that in the marketplace of ideas, the best solutions to public problems will rise to the top. Inevitably, there will be dissenting voices. A democratic system of government is committed to considering those dissenting voices, and seeking to acknowledge and address those voices in the laws by which all in the community must live.

. . . .

(D) CONSTITUTIONALISM AND THE RULE OF LAW

[70] The principles of constitutionalism and the rule of law lie at the root of our system of government. The rule of law, as observed in *Roncarelli v. Duplessis*, [1959] S.C.R. 121, at p. 142, is "a fundamental postulate of our constitutional structure." As we noted in the *Patriation Reference, supra*, at pp. 805–6, "[t]he 'rule of law' is a highly textured expression, importing many things which are beyond the need of these reasons to explore but conveying, for example, a sense of orderliness, of subjection to known legal rules and of executive accountability to legal authority". At its most basic level, the rule of law vouchsafes to the citizens and residents of the country a stable, predictable and ordered society in which to conduct their affairs. It provides a shield for individuals from arbitrary state action.

. . . .

[72] The constitutionalism principle bears considerable similarity to the rule of law, although they are not identical. The essence of constitutionalism in Canada is embodied in s. 52(1) of the *Constitution Act, 1982*, which provides that "[t]he Constitution of Canada is the supreme law of Canada, and any law

that is inconsistent with the provisions of the Constitution is, to the extent of the inconsistency, of no force or effect." Simply put, the constitutionalism principle requires that all government action comply with the Constitution. The rule of law principle requires that all government action must comply with the law, including the Constitution. This Court has noted on several occasions that with the adoption of the *Charter*, the Canadian system of government was transformed to a significant extent from a system of Parliamentary supremacy to one of constitutional supremacy. The Constitution binds all governments, both federal and provincial, including the executive branch (*Operation Dismantle Inc. v. The Queen*, [1985] 1 S.C.R. 441, at p. 455). They may not transgress its provisions: indeed, their sole claim to exercise lawful authority rests in the powers allocated to them under the Constitution, and can come from no other source.

. . . .

[76] Canadians have never accepted that ours is a system of simple majority rule. Our principle of democracy, taken in conjunction with the other constitutional principles discussed here, is richer. Constitutional government is necessarily predicated on the idea that the political representatives of the people of a province have the capacity and the power to commit the province to be bound into the future by the constitutional rules being adopted. These rules are "binding" not in the sense of frustrating the will of a majority of a province, but as defining the majority which must be consulted in order to alter the fundamental balances of political power (including the spheres of autonomy guaranteed by the principle of federalism), individual rights, and minority rights in our society. Of course, those constitutional rules are themselves amenable to amendment, but only through a process of negotiation which ensures that there is an opportunity for the constitutionally defined rights of all the parties to be respected and reconciled.

[77] In this way, our belief in democracy may be harmonized with our belief in constitutionalism. Constitutional amendment often requires some form of substantial consensus precisely because the content of the underlying principles of our Constitution demand it. By requiring broad support in the form of an "enhanced majority" to achieve constitutional change, the Constitution ensures that minority interests must be addressed before proposed changes which would affect them may be enacted.

· · · ·

(E) PROTECTION OF MINORITIES

[79] The fourth underlying constitutional principle we address here concerns the protection of minorities. There are a number of specific constitutional provisions protecting minority language, religion and education rights. Some of those provisions are, as we have recognized on a number of occasions, the product of historical compromises. As this Court observed in *Reference re Bill 30, An Act to Amend the Education Act (Ont.)* [1987] 1 S.C.R. 1148, at p. 1173, and in *Reference re Education Act (Que.)*, [1993] 2 S.C.R. 511, at pp. 529–30, the protection of minority religious education rights was a central consideration in the negotiations leading to Confederation. In the absence of such protection, it was felt that the minorities in what was then Canada East and Canada West would be submerged and assimilated. See also *Greater Montreal Protestant School Board v. Quebec (Attorney General)*, [1989] 1 S.C.R. 377, at pp. 401–2, and *Adler v. Ontario*, [1996] 3 S.C.R. 609. Similar concerns animated the provisions protecting minority language rights, as noted in *Société des Acadiens du Nouveau-Brunswick Inc. v. Association of Parents for Fairness in Education*, [1986] 1 S.C.R. 549, at p. 564.

· · · ·

[81] The concern of our courts and governments to protect minorities has been prominent in recent years, particularly following the enactment of the *Charter*. Undoubtedly, one of the key considerations motivating the enactment of the *Charter*, and the process of constitutional judicial review that it entails, is the protection of minorities. However, it should not be forgotten that the protection of minority rights had a long history before the enactment of the *Charter*. Indeed, the protection of minority rights was clearly an essential consideration in the design of our constitutional structure even at the time of Confederation: *Senate Reference, supra*, at p. 71. Although Canada's record of upholding the rights of minorities is not a spotless one, that goal is one towards which Canadians have been striving since Confederation, and the process has not been without successes. The principle of protecting minority rights continues to exercise influence in the operation and interpretation of our Constitution.

[82] Consistent with this long tradition of respect for minorities, which is at least as old as Canada itself, the framers of the *Constitution Act, 1982* included in s. 35 explicit protection for existing aboriginal and treaty rights, and in s. 25, a non-derogation clause in favour of the rights of aboriginal peoples. The "promise" of s. 35, as it was termed in *R. v. Sparrow*, [1990] 1 S.C.R. 1075, at p. 1983, recognized not only the ancient occupation of land by aboriginal peoples, but their contribution to the building of Canada, and the special commitments made to them by successive governments. The protection of these rights, so recently and arduously achieved, whether looked at in their own right or as part of the larger concern with minorities, reflects an important underlying constitutional value.

(b) *Roncarelli v. Duplessis*†

[RAND J.:]

The material facts from which my conclusion is drawn are these. The appellant was the proprietor of a restaurant in a busy section of Montreal which in 1946 through its transmission to him from his father had been continuously licensed for the sale of liquor for approximately 34 years; he is of good education and repute and the restaurant was of a superior class. On December 4 of that year, while his application for annual renewal was before the Liquor Commission, the existing license was cancelled and his application for renewal rejected, to which was added a declaration by the respondent that no future license would ever issue to him. These primary facts took place in the following circumstances.

For some years the appellant had been an adherent of a rather militant Christian religious

---

† [1959] S.C.R. 121 at 131–34, 136–45.

sect known as the Witnesses of Jehovah. Their ideology condemns the established church institutions and stresses the absolute and exclusive personal relation of the individual to the Deity without human intermediation or intervention.

The first impact of their proselytizing zeal upon the Roman Catholic church and community in Quebec, as might be expected, produced a violent reaction. Meetings were forcibly broken up, property damaged, individuals ordered out of communities, in one case out of the province, and generally, within the cities and towns, bitter controversy aroused. The work of the Witnesses was carried on both by word of mouth and by the distribution of printed matter, the latter including two periodicals known as "The Watch Tower" and "Awake", sold at a small price.

In 1945 the provincial authorities began to take steps to bring an end to what was considered insulting and offensive to the religious beliefs and feelings of the Roman Catholic population. Large scale arrests were made of young men and women, by whom the publications mentioned were being held out for sale, under local by-laws requiring a licence for peddling any kind of wares. Altogether almost one thousand of such charges were laid. The penalty involved in Montreal, where most of the arrests took place, was a fine of $40, and as the Witnesses disputed liability, bail was in all cases resorted to.

The appellant, being a person of some means, was accepted by the Recorder's Court as bail without question, and up to November 12, 1946, he had gone security in about 380 cases, some of the accused being involved in repeated offences. Up to this time there had been no suggestion of impropriety; the security of the appellant was taken as so satisfactory that at times, to avoid delay when he was absent from the city, recognizances were signed by him in blank and kept ready for completion by the Court officials. The reason for the accumulation of charges was the doubt that they could be sustained in law. Apparently the legal officers of Montreal, acting in concert with those of the Province, had come to an agreement with the attorney for the Witnesses to have a test case proceeded with. Pending that, however, there was no stoppage of the sale of the tracts and this became the annoying circumstance that produced the volume of proceedings.

On or about November 12 it was decided to require bail in cash for Witnesses so arrested and the sum set ranged from $100 to $300. No such bail was furnished by the appellant; his connection with giving security ended with this change of practice; and in the result, all of the charges in relation to which he had become surety were dismissed.

At no time did he take any part in the distribution of the tracts: he was an adherent of the group but nothing more. It was shown that he had leased to another member premises in Sherbrooke which were used as a hall for carrying on religious meetings: but it is unnecessary to do more than mention that fact to reject it as having no bearing on the issues raised. Beyond the giving of bail and being an adherent, the appellant is free from any relation that could be tortured into a badge of character pertinent to his fitness or unfitness to hold a liquor licence.

The mounting resistance that stopped the surety bail sought other means of crushing the propagandist invasion and among the circumstances looked into was the situation of the appellant. Admittedly an adherent, he was enabling these protagonists to be at large to carry on their campaign of publishing what they believed to be the Christian truth as revealed by the Bible; he was also the holder of a liquor licence, a "privilege" granted by the Province, the profits from which, as it was seen by the authorities, he was using to promote the disturbance of settled beliefs and arouse community disaffection generally. Following discussions between the then Mr. Archambault, as the personality of the Liquor Commission, and the chief prosecuting officer in Montreal, the former, on or about November 21, telephoned to the respondent, advised him of those facts, and queried what should be done. Mr. Duplessis answered that the matter was serious and that the identity of the person furnishing bail and the liquor licensee should be put beyond doubt. A few days later, that identity being established through a private investigator, Mr. Archambault again communicated with the respondent and, as a result of what passed between them, the licence, as of December 4, 1946, was revoked.

In the meantime, about November 25, 1946, a blasting answer had come from the Witnesses. In an issue of one of the periodicals, under the heading "Quebec's Burning Hate", was a searing denunciation of what was alleged to be the savage persecution of Christian believers. Immediately instructions were sent out from the department of the Attorney-General ordering the confiscation of the issue and proceedings were taken against one Boucher charging him with publication of a seditious libel.

It is then wholly as a private citizen, an adherent of a religious group, holding a liquor licence and furnishing bail to arrested persons for no other purpose than to enable them to be released from detention pending the determination of the charges against them, and with no other relevant considerations to be taken into account, that he is involved in the issues of this controversy.

The complementary state of things is equally free from doubt. From the evidence of Mr. Duplessis and Mr. Archambault alone, it appears that the action taken by the latter as the general manager and sole member of the Commission was dictated by Mr. Duplessis as Attorney-General and Prime Minister of the province; that that step was taken as a means of bringing to a halt the activities of the Witnesses, to punish the appellant for the part he had played not only by revoking the existing licence but in declaring him barred from one "forever", and to warn others that they similarly would be stripped of provincial "privileges" if they persisted in any activity directly or indirectly related to the Witnesses and to the objectionable campaign. The respondent felt that action to be his duty, something which his conscience demanded of him; and as representing the provincial government his decision became automatically that of Mr. Archambault and the Commission. The following excerpts of evidence make this clear:

. . . .

LA COUR:

. . . .

D. Référant à l'article contenue dans la *Gazette* du 5 décembre, c'est-à-dire le jour suivant l'annulation du permis, vous trouvez là les mots en anglais :

In statement to the press yesterday, the Premier recalled that: "Two weeks ago, I pointed out that the Provincial Government had the firm intention to take the most rigorous and efficient measures possible to get rid of those who under the names of Witnesses of Jehovah, distribute circulars which in my opinion, are not only injurious for Quebec and its population, but which are of a very libellous and seditious character. The propaganda of the Witnesses of Jehovah cannot be tolerated and there are more than 400 of them now before the courts in Montreal, Quebec, Three Rivers and other centers."

"A certain Mr. Roncarelli has supplied bail for hundreds of witnesses of Jehovah. The sympathy which this man has shown for the Witnesses, in such an evident, repeated and audacious manner, is a provocation to public order, to the administration of justice and is definitely contrary to the aims of justice."

D. Je vous demande, monsieur le Premier Ministre, si ce sont les paroles presque exactes ou exactes que vous avez dites à la conférence de presse?

R. Que j'ai dit ici: "A certain Mr. Roncarelli has supplied bail for hundreds of witnesses of Jehovah. The Sympathy which this man has shown for the Witnesses, in such an evident, repeated and audacious manner, is a provocation to public order, to the administration of justice and is definitely contrary to the aims of justice." Je l'ai dit et je considère que c'est vrai.

...

M. ARCHAMBAULT:

D. Maintenant, ce jour-là où vous avez reçu une lettre, le 30 novembre 1946, avez-vous décidé, ce jour-là, d'enlever la licence?

R. Certainement, ce jour-là, j'avais appelé le Premier Ministre, en l'occurrence le procureur général, lui faisant part des constatations, c'est-à-dire des renseignements que je possédais, et de mon intention d'annuler le privilège, et le Premier Ministre m'a répondu de prendre mes précautions, de bien vérifier s'il s'agissait bien de la même personne, qu'il pouvait y avoir plusieurs Roncarelli, et [cetera]. Alors, quand j'ai eu la confirmation de Y3 à l'effet que c'était la même personne, j'ai rappelé le Premier Ministre pour l'assurer qu'il s'agissait bien de Frank Roncarelli, détenteur d'un permis de la Commission des Liqueurs; et, là, le Premier Ministre m'a autorisé, il m'a donné son consentement, son approbation, sa permission, et son ordre de procéder.

In these circumstances, when the *de facto* power of the Executive over its appointees at will to such a statutory public function is exercised deliberately and intentionally to destroy the vital business interests of a citizen, is there legal redress by him against the person so acting? This calls for an examination of the statutory provisions governing the issue, renewal and revocation of liquor licences and the scope of authority entrusted by law to the Attorney-General and the government in relation to the administration of the Act.

The liquor law is contained in R.S.Q. 1941, c. 255, entitled *An Act Respecting Alcoholic Liquor*. A Commission is created as a corporation, the only member of which is the general manager. By s. 5

The exercise of the functions, duties and powers of the Quebec Liquor Commission shall be vested in one person alone, named by the Lieutenant-Governor in Council, with the title of Manager. The remuneration of such person shall be determined by the Lieutenant-Governor in Council and be paid out of the revenues of the Liquor Commission. R.S. 1925, c. 37, s. 5; 1 Ed. VII (2), c. 14, es. 1 and 5; 1 Geo. VI, c. 22, es. 1 and 5.

The entire staff for carrying out the duties of the Commission are appointed by the general manager — here Mr. Archambault — who fixes salaries and assigns functions, the Lieutenant-Governor in Council reserving the right of approval of the salaries. Besides the general operation of buying and selling liquor throughout the province and doing all things necessary to that end, the Commission is authorized by s. 9 (e) to "grant, refuse or cancel permits for the sale of alcoholic liquors or other permits in regard thereto and to transfer the permit of any person deceased". By s. 12 suits against the general manager for acts done in the exercise of his duties require the authority of the Chief Justice of the province, and the Commission can be sued only with the consent of the Attorney-General. Every officer of the Commission is declared to be a public officer and by R.S.Q. 1941, c. 10, s. 2, holds office during pleasure. By s. 19 the Commission shall pay over to the Provincial Treasurer any moneys which the latter considers available and by s. 20 the Commission is to account to the Provincial Treasurer for its receipts, disbursements, assets and liabilities. Sections 30 and 32 provide for the issue of permits to sell; they are to be granted to individuals only, in their own names; by s. 34 the Commission "may refuse to grant any permit"; subs. (2) provides for permits in special cases of municipalities where prohibition of sale is revoked in whole or part by by-law; subs. (3) restricts or refuses the grant of permits in certain cities the Council of which so requests; but it is provided that

> ... If the fyling of such by-law takes place after the Commission has granted a permit in such city or town, the Commission shall be unable to give effect to the request before the first of May next after the date of fyling.

Subsection (4) deals with a refusal to issue permits in small cities unless requested by a by-law, approved by a majority vote of the electors. By subs. (6) special power is given the Commission to grant permits to hotels in summer resorts for five months only notwithstanding that requests under subss. (2) and (4) are not made. Section 35 prescribes the expiration of every permit on April 30 of each year. Dealing with cancellation, the section provides that the "Commission may cancel any permit at its discretion". Besides

the loss of the privilege and without the necessity of legal proceedings, cancellation entails loss of fees paid to obtain it and confiscation of the liquor in the possession of the holder and the receptacles containing it. If the cancellation is not followed by prosecution for an offence under the Act, compensation is provided for certain items of the forfeiture. Subsection (5) requires the Commission to cancel any permit made use of on behalf of a person other than the holder; s. 36 requires cancellation in specified cases. The sale of liquor is, by s. 42, forbidden to various persons. Section 148 places upon the Attorney-General the duty of

1. Assuring the observance of this Act and of the Alcoholic Liquor [Possession] and Transportation Act (Chap. 256), and investigating, preventing and suppressing the infringements of such acts, in every way authorized thereby;
2. Conducting the suits or prosecutions for infringements of this Act or of the said Alcoholic Liquor Possession and Transportation Act. R.S. 1925, c. 37, s. 78a; 24 Geo. V, c. 17, s. 17.

The provisions of the statute, which may be supplemented by detailed regulations, furnish a code for the complete administration of the sale and distribution of alcoholic liquors directed by the Commission as a public service, for all legitimate purposes of the populace. It recognizes the association of wines and liquors as embellishments of food and its ritual and as an interest of the public. As put in Macbeth, the "sauce to meat is ceremony", and so we have restaurants, cafés, hotels and other places of serving food, specifically provided for in that association.

At the same time the issue of permits has a complementary interest in those so catering to the public. The continuance of the permit over the years, as in this case, not only recognizes its virtual [necessity] to a superior class restaurant but also its [identification] with the business carried on. The provisions for assignment of the permit are to this most pertinent and they were exemplified in the continuity of the business here. As its exercise continues, the economic life of the holder becomes progressively more deeply implicated with the privilege while at the same time his vocation becomes correspondingly dependent on it.

The field of licensed occupations and businesses of this nature is steadily becoming of greater concern to citizens generally. It is a matter of vital importance that a public administration that can refuse to allow a person to enter or continue a calling which, in the absence of regulation, would be free and legitimate, should be conducted with complete impartiality and integrity; and that the grounds for refusing or cancelling a permit should unquestionably be such and such only as are incompatible with the purposes envisaged by the statute: the duty of a Commission is to serve those purposes and those only. A decision to deny or cancel such a privilege lies within the "discretion" of the Commission; but that means that decision is to be based upon a weighing of considerations pertinent to the object of the administration.

In public regulation of this sort there is no such thing as absolute and untrammelled "discretion", that is that action can be taken on any ground or for any reason that can be suggested to the mind of the administrator; no legislative Act can, without express language, be taken to contemplate an unlimited arbitrary power exercisable for any purpose, however capricious or irrelevant, regardless of the nature or purpose of the statute. Fraud and corruption in the Commission may not be mentioned in such statutes but they are always implied as exceptions. "Discretion" necessarily implies good faith in discharging public duty; there is always a perspective within which a statute is intended to operate; and any clear departure from its lines or objects is just as objectionable as fraud or corruption. Could an applicant be refused a permit because he had been born in another province, or because of the colour of his hair? The ordinary language of the legislature cannot be so distorted.

To deny or revoke a permit because a citizen exercises an unchallengeable right totally irrelevant to the sale of liquor in a restaurant is equally beyond the scope of the discretion conferred. There was here not only revocation of the existing permit but a declaration of a future, definitive disqualification of the appellant to obtain one: it was to be "forever". This purports to divest his citizenship status of its incident of membership in the class of those of the public to whom such a privilege could be extended. Under the statutory language here, that is not competent to the Commission and a fortiori to the government or the respondent: *McGillivray v. Kimber.* There is here an administrative tribunal which, in certain respects, is to act in a judicial manner; and even on the view of the dissenting justices in *McGillivray*, there is liability: what could be more malicious than to punish this licensee for having done what he had an absolute right to do in a matter utterly irrelevant to the *Liquor Act*? Malice in the proper sense is simply acting for a reason and purpose knowingly foreign to the administration, to

which was added here the element of intentional punishment by what was virtually vocation outlawry.

It may be difficult if not impossible in cases generally to demonstrate a breach of this public duty in the illegal purpose served; there may be no means, even if proceedings against the Commission were permitted by the Attorney-General, as here they were refused, of compelling the Commission to justify a refusal or revocation or to give reasons for its action; on these questions I make no observation; but in the case before us that difficulty is not present: the reasons are openly avowed.

The act of the respondent through the instrumentality of the Commission brought about a breach of an implied public statutory duty toward the appellant; it was a gross abuse of legal power expressly intended to punish him for an act wholly irrelevant to the statute, a punishment which inflicted on him, as it was intended to do, the destruction of his economic life as a restaurant keeper within the province. Whatever may be the immunity of the Commission or its member from an action for damages, there is none in the respondent. He was under no duty in relation to the appellant and his act was an [intrusion] upon the functions of a statutory body. The injury done by him was a fault engaging liability within the principles of the underlying public law of Quebec: *Mostyn v. Fabrigas*, and under art. 1053 of the *Civil Code*. That, in the presence of expanding administrative regulation of economic activities, such a step and its consequences are to be suffered by the victim without recourse or remedy, that an administration according to law is to be superseded by action dictated by and according to the arbitrary likes, dislikes and irrelevant purposes of public officers acting beyond their duty, would signalize the beginning of disintegration of the rule of law as a fundamental postulate of our constitutional structure. An administration of licences on the highest level of fair and impartial treatment to all may be forced to follow the practice of "first come, first served", which makes the strictest observance of equal responsibility to all of even greater importance; at this stage of developing government it would be a danger of high consequence to tolerate such a departure from good faith in executing the legislative purpose. It should be added, however, that that principle is not, by this language, intended to be extended to ordinary governmental employment: with that we are not here concerned.

It was urged by Mr. Beaulieu that the respondent, as the incumbent of an office of state, so long as he was proceeding in "good faith", was free to act in a matter of this kind virtually as he pleased. The office of Attorney-General traditionally and by statute carries duties that relate to advising the Executive, including here, administrative bodies, enforcing the public law and directing the administration of justice. In any decision of the statutory body in this case, he had no part to play beyond giving advice on legal questions arising. In that role his action should have been limited to advice on the validity of a revocation for such a reason or purpose and what that advice should have been does not seem to me to admit of any doubt. To pass from this limited scope of action to that of bringing about a step by the Commission beyond the bounds prescribed by the legislature for its exclusive action converted what was done into his personal act.

"Good faith" in this context, applicable both to the respondent and the general manager, means carrying out the statute according to its intent and for its purpose; it means good faith in acting with a rational appreciation of that intent and purpose and not with an improper intent and for an alien purpose; it does not mean for the purposes of punishing a person for exercising an unchallengeable right; it does not mean arbitrarily and illegally attempting to divest a citizen of an incident of his civil status.

I mention, in order to make clear that it has not been overlooked, the decision of the House of Lords in *Allen v. Flood*, in which the principle was laid down that an act of an individual otherwise not actionable does not become so because of the motive or reason for doing it, even maliciously to injure, as distinguished from an act done by two or more persons. No contention was made in the present case based on agreed action by the respondent and Mr. Archambault. In *Allen v. Flood*, the actor was a labour leader and the victims non-union workmen who were lawfully dismissed by their employer to avoid a strike involving no breach of contract or law. Here the act done was in relation to a public administration affecting the rights of a citizen to enjoy a public privilege, and a duty implied by the statute toward the victim was violated. The existing permit was an interest for which the appellant was entitled to protection against any unauthorized interference, and the illegal destruction of which gave rise to a remedy for the damages suffered. In *Allen v. Flood* there were no such elements.

Nor is it necessary to examine the question whether on the basis of an improper revocation the appellant could have compelled the issue of a new permit or whether the purported revocation was a void act. The revocation was *de facto*, it was intended to end the privilege and to bring about the consequences that followed. As against the respondent, the appellant was entitled to treat the breach of duty as effecting a revocation and to elect for damages.

Mr. Scott argued further that even if the revocation were within the scope of discretion and not a breach of duty, the intervention of the respondent in so using the Commission was equally a fault. The proposition generalized is this: where, by a statute restricting the ordinary activities of citizens, a privilege is conferred by an administrative body, the continuance of that enjoyment is to be free from the influence of third persons on that body for the purpose only of injuring the privilege holder. It is the application to such a privilege of the proposition urged but rejected in *Allen v. Flood* in the case of a private employment. The grounds of distinction between the two cases have been pointed out; but for the reasons given consideration of this ground is unnecessary and I express no opinion for or against it.

A subsidiary defence was that notice of action had not been given as required by art. 88 C.C.P. This provides generally that, without such notice, no public officer or person fulfilling any public function or duty is liable in damages "by reason of any act done by him in the exercise of his functions". Was the act here, then, done by the respondent in the course of that exercise? The basis of the claim, as I have found it, is that the act was quite beyond the scope of any function or duty committed to him, so far so that it was one done exclusively in a private capacity, however much in fact the influence of public office and power may have carried over into it. It would be only through an assumption of a general overriding power of executive direction in statutory administrative matters that any colour of propriety in the act could be found. But such an assumption would be in direct conflict with fundamental postulates of our provincial as well as dominion government; and in the actual circumstances there is not a shadow of justification for it in the statutory language.

The damages suffered involved the vocation of the appellant within the province. Any attempt at a precise computation or estimate must assume probabilities in an area of uncertainty and risk. The situation is one which the Court should approach as a jury would, in a view of its broad features; and in the best consideration I can give to them, the damages should be fixed at the sum of $25,000 plus that allowed by the trial court.

I would therefore allow the appeals, set aside the judgment of the Court of Queen's Bench and restore the judgment at trial modified by increasing the damages to the sum of $33,123.53. The appellant should have his costs in the Court of Queen's Bench and in this Court.

41

(c) *Reference re Firearms Act* (Can.)†

[THE COURT:]

I. INTRODUCTION

[1] In 1995, Parliament amended the *Criminal Code*, R.S.C., 1985, c. C-46, by enacting the *Firearms Act*, S.C. 1995, c. 39, commonly referred to as the gun control law, to require the holders of all firearms to obtain licences and register their guns. In 1996, the Province of Alberta challenged Parliament's power to pass the gun control law by a reference to the Alberta Court of Appeal. The Court of Appeal by a 3:2 majority upheld Parliament's power to pass the law. The Province of Alberta now appeals that decision to this Court.

[2] The issue before this Court is not whether gun control is good or bad, whether the law is fair or unfair to gun owners, or whether it will be effective or ineffective in reducing the harm caused by the misuse of firearms. The only issue is whether or not Parliament has the constitutional authority to enact the law.

[3] The answer to this question lies in the Canadian Constitution. The Constitution assigns some matters to Parliament and others to the provincial legislatures: *Constitution Act, 1867*. The federal government asserts that the gun control law falls under its criminal law power, s. 91(27), and under its general power to legislate for the "Peace, Order and good Government" of Canada. Alberta, on the other hand, says the law falls under its power over property and civil rights, s. 92(13). All agree that to resolve this dispute, the Court must first determine what the gun control law is really about — its "pith and substance" — and then ask which head or heads of power it most naturally falls within.

[4] We conclude that the gun control law comes within Parliament's jurisdiction over criminal law. The law in "pith and substance" is directed to enhancing public safety by controlling access to firearms through prohibitions and penalties. This brings it under the federal criminal law power. While the law has regulatory aspects, they are secondary to its primary criminal law purpose. The intrusion of the law into the provincial jurisdiction over property and

civil rights is not so excessive as to upset the balance of federalism.

II. REFERENCE QUESTIONS

[5] The formal questions put to the Alberta Court of Appeal by the Alberta government in 1996 are attached in Appendix A. Simply put, the issue before us is whether or not the licensing and registration provisions in the *Firearms Act*, as they relate to ordinary firearms, were validly enacted by Parliament. The impugned provisions of the Act are attached in Appendix B.

III. LEGISLATION

[6] For many years, the *Criminal Code* has restricted access to firearms, mainly automatic weapons and handguns, by classifying some as prohibited and some as restricted. The *Firearms Act* amendments extended this regulation to all firearms, including rifles and shotguns. As a result, s. 84 of the *Criminal Code* now controls three classes of firearms: (1) prohibited firearms (generally automatic weapons); (2) restricted firearms (generally handguns); and (3) all other firearms (generally rifles and shotguns). The third class of guns is variously referred to as "ordinary firearms", "long guns", and "unrestricted firearms". We will refer to this class as "ordinary firearms".

[7] The reference questions focus on the validity of the licensing and registration provisions for ordinary firearms introduced by the *Firearms Act*. The licensing sections of the Act provide that a person must be licensed in order to possess a firearm. Eligibility for a licence reflects safety interests. An applicant with a criminal record involving drug offences or violence, or a history of mental illness, may be denied a licence. An applicant who seeks to acquire a firearm must pass a safety course which requires a basic understanding of firearm safety and the legal responsibilities of firearm ownership. The chief firearms officer, who issues licences, may conduct a background check on the applicant in order to determine eligibility, and may attach conditions to a licence. Once issued, a licence is valid for five years, but it

---

† [2000] 1 S.C.R. 783 at paras. 1–61.

may be revoked for contravention of its conditions or for certain criminal convictions. A licence refusal or revocation may be appealed to a court.

[8] The registration provisions of the Act are more limited. A firearm cannot be registered unless the applicant is licensed to possess that type of firearm. Registration is generally done by reference to the serial number on the firearm. A registration certificate is valid as long as its holder owns the weapon. If ownership of a registered weapon is transferred, the new owner must register the weapon. In order to give gun owners time to register their weapons, people who owned ordinary firearms as of January 1, 1998 are deemed to hold registration certificates that are valid until January 1, 2003. Possession of an unregistered firearm of any type is an offence. All licences and registration certificates, along with imported, exported, lost and stolen guns, are recorded in the Canadian Firearms Registry, which is operated by a federal appointee.

IV. REASONS OF THE ALBERTA COURT OF APPEAL

[9] The Alberta Court of Appeal upheld the 1995 gun control law by a 3:2 majority: 1998 ABCA 306 (CanLII), (1998), 65 Alta. L.R. (3d) 1. The court wrote four judgments.

A. Majority

[10] Fraser C.J.A., in a comprehensive judgment, began by noting that guns may be regulated by both the federal and provincial governments for different purposes, and that the effectiveness of the law is irrelevant to its constitutional characterization. She found that Parliament's purpose in enacting the law was to enhance public safety. While guns preserve lives and serve as useful tools, they also wound and kill. The latter aspect of guns — their inherent dangerousness — is the focus of the impugned provisions of the Act. Parliament's aim was to reduce the misuse of guns in crime, including domestic violence, as well as to reduce suicides and accidents caused by the misuse of firearms. The licensing provisions, which require applicants to pass a safety course and undergo a criminal record check and background investigation, support this purpose. The registration system, by seeking to reduce smuggling, theft and illegal sales, also addresses misuse. The licensing and registration provisions are inextricably intertwined. While the provisions entail the regulation of property rights, this regulation is the means of the law, not its

end. On this basis, Fraser C.J.A. concluded that the Act is in pith and substance designed to protect public safety from the misuse of firearms.

[11] Fraser C.J.A. went on to the second step in the analysis: considering whether or not that pith and substance could be allocated to one of Parliament's heads of power under the *Constitution Act, 1867*. She held that the legislation falls under the criminal law power, s. 91(27), under either its "prevention" aspect or its "prohibition, penalty, and purpose" aspect. The law does not represent a "colourable" or improper intrusion into provincial jurisdiction.

[12] Berger and Hetherington JJ.A. wrote separate opinions agreeing with the Chief Justice. Hetherington J.A. held that any firearm, used improperly, is dangerous to human life and health. As a result, Parliament's purpose, in seeking to prevent crime and promote public safety by discouraging possession, is a valid criminal law purpose. The potential inefficacy of the law, highlighted by Alberta and the other provincial governments, is irrelevant unless it shows that Parliament had a different purpose — a colourable motive. Colourability has not been shown because the law genuinely attempts to improve firearms storage, reduce trafficking, and aid in tracking guns generally. While the law may affect property and civil rights, that does not prevent Parliament from enacting it. Hetherington J.A. concluded that the *Firearms Act* contains prohibitions accompanied by penal sanctions, enacted for criminal public purposes, and therefore it is a valid law under the test propounded by La Forest J. of this Court in *RJR-MacDonald Inc. v. Canada (Attorney General)*, 1995 CanLII 64 (S.C.C.), [1995] 3 S.C.R. 199, and *R. v. Hydro-Québec*, 1997 CanLII 318 (S.C.C.), [1997] 3 S.C.R. 213.

[13] Berger J.A. likewise noted that all guns are capable of causing death if misused. He held that Parliament's purpose in enacting the legislation was to ensure that firearms are only possessed by those qualified to use them. The licensing provisions identify those who are qualified. The registration system ensures that only qualified people can acquire firearms. As a prohibition backed by a penalty, for a public purpose, the law is a valid exercise of Parliament's criminal law power. The regulatory aspects of the law are merely the means to an end.

B. Minority

[14] Conrad J.A. dissented, Irving J.A. concurring. Conrad J.A. broadly defined the purpose of the law as regulating all aspects of the possession and use of firearms. While firearms and safety are subjects of

both federal and provincial concern, the criminal law power represents a "carve-out" from provincial jurisdiction. The regulation of ownership rather than use and the complexity of the regulations demonstrate that this legislation cannot be classified as valid criminal law. The *Criminal Code* generally prohibits acts, rather than regulating ownership. Possession itself is not dangerous; it is only misuse that is dangerous, and the law goes far beyond prohibiting misuse. This led Conrad J.A. to conclude that the *Firearms Act* represents a colourable intrusion into the provincial jurisdiction over property and civil rights, and is invalid as an exercise of Parliament's jurisdiction over criminal law or its peace, order and good government power. While she would have struck down the legislation entirely, she held that if the licensing scheme were deemed valid, the registration scheme could be severed from the licensing scheme.

V. ANALYSIS

[15] The issue before us is whether the licensing and registration provisions of the *Firearms Act* constitute a valid federal enactment pursuant to Parliament's jurisdiction over criminal law or its peace, order and good government power. In order to answer this question, we must engage in the division of powers analysis used so often by this Court, and most recently summarized in *Global Securities Corp. v. British Columbia (Securities Commission)*, 2000 SCC 21 (CanLII), [2000] 1 S.C.R. 494, 2000 SCC 21; see also *Whitbread v. Walley*, 1990 CanLII 33 (S.C.C.), [1990] 3 S.C.R. 1273, *R. v. Big M Drug Mart Ltd.*, 1985 CanLII 69 (S.C.C.), [1985] 1 S.C.R. 295, and *R. v. Morgentaler*, 1993 CanLII 74 (S.C.C.), [1993] 3 S.C.R. 463. There are two stages to this analysis. The first step is to determine the "pith and substance" or essential character of the law. The second step is to classify that essential character by reference to the heads of power under the *Constitution Act, 1867* in order to determine whether the law comes within the jurisdiction of the enacting government. If it does, then the law is valid.

A. Characterization: What Is the Pith and Substance of the Law?

[16] The first task is to determine the "pith and substance" of the legislation. To use the wording of ss. 91 and 92, what is the "matter" of the law? What is its true meaning or essential character, its core? To determine the pith and substance, two aspects of the law must be examined: the purpose of the enacting body, and the legal effect of the law.

[17] A law's purpose is often stated in the legislation, but it may also be ascertained by reference to extrinsic material such as Hansard and government publications: see *Morgentaler, supra*, at pp. 483–84. While such extrinsic material was at one time inadmissible to facilitate the determination of Parliament's purpose, it is now well accepted that the legislative history, Parliamentary debates, and similar material may be quite properly considered as long as it is relevant and reliable and is not assigned undue weight: see *Global Securities, supra*, at para. 25; *Rizzo & Rizzo Shoes Ltd. (Re)*, 1998 CanLII 837 (S.C.C.), [1998] 1 S.C.R. 27, at para. 35; and *Doré v. Verdun (City)*, 1997 CanLII 315 (S.C.C.), [1997] 2 S.C.R. 862, at para. 14. Purpose may also be ascertained by considering the "mischief" of the legislation — the problem which Parliament sought to remedy: see *Morgentaler, supra*, at pp. 483–84.

[18] Determining the legal effects of a law involves considering how the law will operate and how it will affect Canadians. The Attorney General of Alberta states that the law will not actually achieve its purpose. Where the legislative scheme is relevant to a criminal law purpose, he says, it will be ineffective (e.g., criminals will not register their guns); where it is effective it will not advance the fight against crime (e.g., burdening rural farmers with pointless red tape). These are concerns that were properly directed to and considered by Parliament. Within its constitutional sphere, Parliament is the judge of whether a measure is likely to achieve its intended purposes; efficaciousness is not relevant to the Court's division of powers analysis: *Morgentaler, supra*, at pp. 487–88, and *Reference re Anti-Inflation Act*, 1976 CanLII 16 (S.C.C.), [1976] 2 S.C.R. 373. Rather, the inquiry is directed to how the law sets out to achieve its purpose in order to better understand its "total meaning": W. R. Lederman, *Continuing Canadian Constitutional Dilemmas* (1981), at pp. 239–40. In some cases, the effects of the law may suggest a purpose other than that which is stated in the law: see *Morgentaler, supra*, at pp. 482–83; *Attorney-General for Alberta v. Attorney-General for Canada*, [1939] A.C. 117 (P.C.) (*Alberta Bank Taxation Reference*); and *Texada Mines Ltd. v. Attorney-General of British Columbia*, 1960 CanLII 43 (S.C.C.), [1960] S.C.R. 713; see generally P. W. Hogg, *Constitutional Law of Canada* (loose-leaf ed.), at pp. 15–14 to 15–16. In other words, a law may say that it intends to do one thing and actually do something else. Where the effects of the law diverge substantially from the stated aim, it is sometimes said to be "colourable".

[19] Against this background, we turn to the purpose of the *Firearms Act*. Section 4 states that the purpose of the Act is "to provide ... for the issuance of licences, registration certificates and authorizations under which persons may possess firearms" and "to authorize ... the manufacture of" and "transfer of" ordinary firearms. This is the language of property regulation. However, this regulatory language is directly tied to a purpose cast in the language of the criminal law. The licensing, registration and authorization provisions delineate the means by which people can own and transfer ordinary firearms "in circumstances that would otherwise constitute [a criminal] offence". Those who challenge the legislation point to the first part of the section and its regulatory focus. Those who seek to uphold the law point to the second part of the section and its criminal focus.

[20] The statements of the Honourable Allan Rock, Minister of Justice at the time, in his second-reading speech in the House of Commons, reveal that the federal government's purpose in proposing the law was to promote public safety. He stated: "The government suggests that the object of the regulation of firearms should be <u>the preservation of the safe, civilized and peaceful nature of Canada</u>" (*House of Commons Debates*, vol. 133, No. 154, 1st Sess., 35th Parl., February 16, 1995, at p. 9706 (emphasis added)). Mr. Rock went on to describe the contents of the bill in more detail (at p. 9707):

> First, tough measures to deal with the <u>criminal misuse of firearms</u>; second, specific <u>penalties to punish those who would smuggle illegal firearms</u>; and third, measures overall to provide a context in which the legitimate use of firearms can be carried on in a manner consistent with <u>public safety</u>. [Emphasis added.]
>
> (See also the judgment of Fraser C.J.A., at paras. 169–72.)

Later, the Minister referred to the problems of suicide, accidental shootings, and the use of guns in domestic violence, and detailed some of the shooting tragedies that had spurred public calls for gun control. Russell MacLellan, the Parliamentary Secretary of Justice at the time, underscored the government's concerns, noting that the Act pursues "three fundamental policies: the deterrence of the misuse of firearms, general controls on persons given access to firearms, and controls placed on specific types of firearms" ("Canada's firearms proposals" (1995), 37 *Can. J. Crim.* 163, at p. 163).

[21] Another way to determine the purpose of legislation is to look at the problems it is intended to address — the so-called "mischief" approach. The *Firearms Act* is aimed at a number of evils or "mischiefs". One is the illegal trade in guns, both within Canada and across the border with the United States: see *The Government's Action Plan on Firearms Control*, tabled in the House of Commons in 1994. Another is the link between guns and violent crime, suicide, and accidental deaths. In a paper commissioned by the Department of Justice in 1994, *The Impact of the Availability of Firearms on Violent Crime, Suicide, and Accidental Death: A Review of the Literature with Special Reference to the Canadian Situation*, Thomas Gabor found that all three causes of death may increase in jurisdictions where there are the fewest restrictions on guns. Whether or not one accepts Gabor's conclusions, his study indicates the problem which Parliament sought to address by enacting the legislation: the problem of the misuse of firearms and the threat it poses to public safety.

[22] Finally, there is a strong argument that the purpose of this legislation conforms with the historical public safety focus of all gun control laws. This reference challenges the licensing and registration provisions of the Act only as they relate to ordinary firearms. Alberta does not question the licensing and registration of restricted and prohibited weapons. It freely admits that the restrictions on those categories of weapons are constitutional. Indeed, Alberta would have difficulty alleging otherwise, as numerous courts have upheld the validity of different aspects of the federal gun control legislation that existed prior to the enactment of this Act: see *R. v. Schwartz*, 1988 CanLII 11 (S.C.C.), [1988] 2 S.C.R. 443; *McGuigan v. The Queen*, 1982 CanLII 41 (S.C.C.), [1982] 1 S.C.R. 284; and *Attorney General of Canada v. Pattison* (1981), 30 A.R. 83 (C.A.).

[23] More specifically, before the introduction of the *Firearms Act*, the registration of all restricted weapons was upheld by the British Columbia Court of Appeal in *Martinoff v. Dawson* reflex, (1990), 57 C.C.C. (3d) 482. Furthermore, the *Criminal Code* required anyone seeking to obtain <u>any kind</u> of firearm to apply for a firearms acquisition certificate. This requirement was upheld in *R. v. Northcott*, reflex, [1980] 5 W.W.R. 38 (B.C. Prov. Ct.). These cases upheld the previous gun control legislation on the basis that Parliament's purpose was to promote public safety. The *Firearms Act* extends that legislation in two respects: (1) it requires all guns to be registered, not just restricted and prohibited firearms; and (2) eventually all gun owners will be required to

be licensed, not just those who wish to acquire a firearm. These changes represent a continuation of Parliament's focus on safety concerns, and constitute a limited expansion of the pre-existing legislation. Given the general acceptance of the gun control legislation that has existed for the past hundred years, the constitutional validity of which has always been predicated on Parliament's concern for public safety, it is difficult to now impute a different purpose to Parliament. This supports the view that the law in pith and substance is about public safety.

[24] The effects of the scheme — how it impacts on the legal rights of Canadians — also support the conclusion that the 1995 gun control law is in pith and substance a public safety measure. The criteria for acquiring a licence are concerned with safety rather than the regulation of property. Criminal record checks and background investigations are designed to keep guns out of the hands of those incapable of using them safely. Safety courses ensure that gun owners are qualified. What the law does not require also shows that the operation of the scheme is limited to ensuring safety. For instance, the Act does not regulate the legitimate commercial market for guns. It makes no attempt to set labour standards or the price of weapons. There is no attempt to protect or regulate industries or businesses associated with guns (see *Pattison, supra*, at para. 22). Unlike provincial property registries, the registry established under the Act is not concerned with prior interests, and unlike some provincial motor vehicle schemes, the Act does not address insurance. In short, the effects of the law suggest that its essence is the promotion of public safety through the reduction of the misuse of firearms, and negate the proposition that Parliament was in fact attempting to achieve a different goal such as the total regulation of firearms production, trade, and ownership. We therefore conclude that, viewed from its purpose and effects, the *Firearms Act* is in "pith and substance" directed to public safety.

B. Classification: Does Parliament Have Jurisdiction to Enact the Law?

[25] Having assessed the pith and substance or matter of the law, the second step is to determine whether that matter comes within the jurisdiction of the enacting legislature. We must examine the heads of power under ss. 91 and 92 of the *Constitution Act, 1867* and determine what the matter is "in relation to". In this case, the question is whether the law falls under federal jurisdiction over criminal law or its peace, order and good government power; or under provincial jurisdiction over property and civil rights. The presumption of constitutionality means that Alberta, as the party challenging the legislation, is required to show that the Act does not fall within the jurisdiction of Parliament: see *Nova Scotia Board of Censors v. McNeil*, 1978 CanLII 6 (S.C.C.), [1978] 2 S.C.R. 662.

[26] The determination of which head of power a particular law falls under is not an exact science. In a federal system, each level of government can expect to have its jurisdiction affected by the other to a certain degree. As Dickson C.J. stated in *General Motors of Canada Ltd. v. City National Leasing*, 1989 CanLII 133 (S.C.C.), [1989] 1 S.C.R. 641, at p. 669, "overlap of legislation is to be expected and accommodated in a federal state". Laws mainly in relation to the jurisdiction of one level of government may overflow into, or have "incidental effects" upon, the jurisdiction of the other level of government. It is a matter of balance and of federalism: no one level of government is isolated from the other, nor can it usurp the functions of the other.

[27] As a general rule, legislation may be classified as criminal law if it possesses three prerequisites: a valid criminal law purpose backed by a prohibition and a penalty: *RJR-MacDonald, supra; Hydro-Québec, supra*; and *Reference re Validity of Section 5(a) of the Dairy Industry Act*, 1948 CanLII 2 (S.C.C.), [1949] S.C.R. 1 (the "*Margarine Reference*"). The Attorney General of Canada argues that the 1995 gun control law meets these three requirements, and points to commentary on this legislation which supports its position: D. Gibson, "The *Firearms Reference* in the Alberta Court of Appeal" (1999), 37 *Alta. L. Rev.* 1071; D. M. Beatty, "Gun Control and Judicial Anarchy" (1999), 10 *Constitutional Forum* 45; A. C. Hutchinson and D. Schneiderman, "Smoking Guns: The Federal Government Confronts The Tobacco and Gun Lobbies" (1995), 7 *Constitutional Forum* 16; and Peter W. Hogg's testimony before the Standing Senate Committee on Legal and Constitutional Affairs, October 26, 1995.

[28] Before determining whether the three criminal law criteria are met by this legislation, some general observations on the criminal law power may be apposite. Criminal law, as this Court has stated in numerous cases, constitutes a broad area of federal jurisdiction: *RJR-MacDonald, supra; Hydro-Québec, supra*; and *Margarine Reference, supra*. The criminal law stands on its own as federal jurisdiction. Although it often overlaps with provincial jurisdiction

over property and civil rights, it is not "carved out" from provincial jurisdiction, contrary to the view of Conrad J.A. It also includes the law of criminal procedure, which regulates many aspects of criminal law enforcement, such as arrest, search and seizure of evidence, the regulation of electronic surveillance and the forfeiture of stolen property.

[29] Not only is the criminal law a "stand-alone" jurisdiction, it also finds its expression in a broad range of legislation. The *Criminal Code* is the quintessential federal enactment under its criminal jurisdiction, but it is not the only one. The *Food and Drugs Act*, the *Hazardous Products Act*, the *Lord's Day Act*, and the *Tobacco Products Control Act* have all been held to be valid exercises of the criminal law power: see *Standard Sausage Co. v. Lee*, [1933] 4 D.L.R. 501 (B.C.C.A.); *R. v. Cosman's Furniture (1972) Ltd.* (1976), 73 D.L.R. (3d) 312 (Man. C.A.); *Big M Drug Mart*, *supra* (legislation struck down on other grounds); and *RJR-MacDonald*, *supra* (legislation struck down on other grounds), respectively. Thus the fact that some of the provisions of the *Firearms Act* are not contained within the *Criminal Code* has no significance for the purposes of constitutional classification.

[30] Although the criminal law power is broad, it is not unlimited. Some of the parties before us expressed the fear that the criminal law power might be illegitimately used to invade the provincial domain and usurp provincial power. A properly restrained understanding of the criminal law power guards against this possibility.

[31] Within this context, we return to the three criteria that a law must satisfy in order to be classified as criminal. The first step is to consider whether the law has a valid criminal law purpose. Rand J. listed some examples of valid purposes in the *Margarine Reference* at p. 50: "Public peace, order, security, health, morality: these are the ordinary though not exclusive ends served by [criminal] law". Earlier, we concluded that the gun control law in pith and substance is directed at public safety. This brings it clearly within the criminal law purposes of protecting public peace, order, security and health.

[32] In determining whether the purpose of a law constitutes a valid criminal law purpose, courts look at whether laws of this type have traditionally been held to be criminal law: see *Morgentaler*, *supra*, at p. 491, and *RJR-MacDonald*, *supra*, at para. 204; see also *Scowby v. Glendinning*, 1986 CanLII 30 (S.C.C.), [1986] 2 S.C.R. 226, *Westendorp v. The Queen*, 1983 CanLII 1 (S.C.C.), [1983] 1 S.C.R. 43, and *R. v.*

Zelensky, 1978 CanLII 8 (S.C.C.), [1978] 2 S.C.R. 940. Courts have repeatedly held that gun control comes within the criminal law sphere. As Fraser C.J.A. demonstrated in her judgment, gun control has been a matter of criminal law since before the enactment of the *Criminal Code* in 1892, and has continued since that date (see also E. M. Davies, "The 1995 Firearms Act: Canada's Public Relations Response to the Myth of Violence" (2000), 6 *Appeal* 44, and M. L. Friedland, *A Century of Criminal Justice* (1984), at pp. 125 ff.).

[33] Gun control has traditionally been considered valid criminal law because guns are dangerous and pose a risk to public safety. Section 2 of the *Criminal Code* (as amended by s. 138(2) of the *Firearms Act*) defines a "firearm" as "a barrelled weapon from which any shot, bullet or other projectile can be discharged and <u>that is capable of causing serious bodily injury or death to a person</u>" (emphasis added). This demonstrates that Parliament views firearms as dangerous and regulates their possession and use on that ground. The law is limited to restrictions which are directed at safety purposes. As such, the regulation of guns as dangerous products is a valid purpose within the criminal law power: see *R. v. Felawka*, 1993 CanLII 36 (S.C.C.), [1993] 4 S.C.R. 199; *RJR-MacDonald*, *supra*; *R. v. Wetmore*, 1983 CanLII 29 (S.C.C.), [1983] 2 S.C.R. 284; and *Cosman's Furniture*, *supra*.

[34] The finding of a valid criminal law purpose does not end the inquiry, however. In order to be classified as a valid criminal law, that purpose must be connected to a prohibition backed by a penalty. The 1995 gun control law satisfies these requirements. Section 112 of the *Firearms Act* prohibits the possession of a firearm without a registration certificate. Section 91 of the *Criminal Code* (as amended by s. 139 of the *Firearms Act*) prohibits the possession of a firearm without a licence and a registration certificate. These prohibitions are backed by penalties: see s. 115 of the *Firearms Act* and s. 91 of the *Code*.

[35] It thus appears that the 1995 gun control law possesses all three criteria required for a criminal law. However, Alberta and the provinces raised a number of objections to this classification which must be considered.

(1) Regulation or Criminal Prohibition?

[36] The first objection is that the *Firearms Act* is essentially regulatory rather than criminal legislation because of the complexity of the law and the discre-

tion it grants to the chief firearms officer. These aspects of the law, the provinces argue, are the hallmarks of regulatory legislation, not the criminal law: see Hogg, *supra*, at pp. 18–25 and 18–26.

[37] Despite its initial appeal, this argument fails to advance Alberta's case. The fact that the Act is complex does not necessarily detract from its criminal nature. Other legislation, such as the *Food and Drugs Act*, R.S.C., 1985, c. F-27, and the *Canadian Environmental Protection Act*, R.S.C., 1985, c. 16 (4th Supp.), are legitimate exercises of the criminal law power, yet highly complex. Nor does the Act give the chief firearms officer or Registrar undue discretion. The offences are not defined by an administrative body, avoiding the difficulty identified in the dissenting judgment in *Hydro-Québec*, *supra*. They are clearly stated in the Act and the *Criminal Code*: no one shall possess a firearm without a proper licence and registration. While the Act provides for discretion to refuse to issue an authorization to carry or transport under s. 68 or a registration certificate under s. 69, that discretion is restricted by the Act. A licence shall be refused if the applicant is not eligible to hold one: s. 68. Eligibility to hold a licence is delineated in the rest of the Act: a person is ineligible to hold a licence if the person has been convicted of certain offences (s. 5(2)) or is subject to a prohibition order (s. 6); s. 7 requires the applicant to complete a safety course. Discretion regarding registration is also bounded by the Act. A refusal by the chief firearms officer or the Registrar must be for "good and sufficient reason": ss. 68 and 69; the refusal must be in writing with reasons given (s. 72). These provisions demonstrate that the Act does not give the chief firearms officer or the Registrar undue discretion. Furthermore, the chief firearms officer and the Registrar are explicitly subject to the supervision of the courts. Refusal or revocation of a licence or a registration certificate may be referred to a provincial court judge: s. 74. The courts will interpret the words "good and sufficient reason" in ss. 68 and 69 in line with the public safety purpose of the Act, ensuring that the exercise of discretion by the chief firearms officer and the Registrar is always wed to that purpose.

[38] Furthermore, the law's prohibitions and penalties are not regulatory in nature. They are not confined to ensuring compliance with the scheme, as was the case in *Boggs v. The Queen*, 1981 CanLII 39 (S.C.C.), [1981] 1 S.C.R. 49, but stand on their own, independently serving the purpose of public safety. Nor are the prohibitions and penalties directed to the object of revenue generation. Parliament's inten-

tion was not to regulate property, but to ensure that only those who prove themselves qualified to hold a licence are permitted to possess firearms of any sort.

[39] Alberta and the supporting interveners argued that the only way Parliament could address gun control would be to prohibit ordinary firearms outright. With respect, this suggestion is not supported by either logic or jurisprudence. First, the jurisprudence establishes that Parliament may use indirect means to achieve its ends. A direct and total prohibition is not required: see *Reference re ss. 193 and 195.1(1)(c) of the Criminal Code (Man.)*, 1990 CanLII 105 (S.C.C.), [1990] 1 S.C.R. 1123, and *RJR-MacDonald*, *supra*. Second, exemptions from a law do not preclude it from being prohibitive and therefore criminal in nature: see *R. v. Furtney*, 1991 CanLII 30 (S.C.C.), [1991] 3 S.C.R. 89, *Morgentaler v. The Queen*, 1975 CanLII 8 (S.C.C.), [1976] 1 S.C.R. 616, and *Lord's Day Alliance of Canada v. Attorney General of British Columbia*, 1959 CanLII 42 (S.C.C.), [1959] S.C.R. 497. Third, as noted above, the prohibition in this case is not merely designed to enforce a fee payment or regulatory scheme separate from the essential safety focus of the law: by way of contrast, see *Boggs*, *supra*. Finally, if prohibition is not required to make handgun control constitutional, which no one suggests, why should it be required for ordinary firearms?

[40] In a related argument, some provincial interveners contended that if the purpose of the legislation is to reduce misuse, then the legislation should deal with misuse directly. On this view, Parliament could prohibit the careless or intentional misuse of guns, as it has in ss. 85–87 of the *Criminal Code*, but could not prohibit people from owning guns if they present risks to public safety or regulate how people store their guns. Again, the answer is that Parliament may use indirect means to further the end of public safety. The risks associated with ordinary firearms are not confined to the intentional or reckless conduct that might be deterred by a prohibition on misuse. The Attorney General of Canada argued, for example, that the suicide rate is increased by the availability of guns. A person contemplating suicide may be more likely to actually commit suicide if a gun is available, it was argued; therefore Parliament has a right to prevent people at risk, for example due to mental illness, from owning a gun. A prohibition on misuse is unlikely to deter a potential suicide; a prohibition on gun ownership may do so. Other examples where a prohibition on misuse falls short are not hard to envisage. A prohibition on misuse is unlikely to prevent the death of a child who

plays with a gun; a prohibition on irresponsible ownership or careless storage may do so. Again, reducing availability may have a greater impact on whether a robber uses a gun than a law forbidding him to use it. Whether the 1995 gun law actually achieves these ends is not at issue before us; what is at issue is whether Parliament, in targeting these dangers, strayed outside its criminal law power. In our view, it did not.

(2) Property and Civil Rights or Criminal Law?

[41] Alberta's second major objection to classifying the 1995 gun control scheme as criminal law is that it is indistinguishable from existing provincial property regulation schemes such as automobile and land title registries.

[42] This argument overlooks the different purposes behind the federal restrictions on firearms and the provincial regulation of other forms of property. Guns are restricted because they are dangerous. While cars are also dangerous, provincial legislatures regulate the possession and use of automobiles not as dangerous products but rather as items of property and as an exercise of civil rights, pursuant to the provinces' s. 92(13) jurisdiction: *Canadian Indemnity Co. v. Attorney-General of British Columbia*, 1976 CanLII 195 (S.C.C.), [1977] 2 S.C.R. 504; *Validity of Section 92(4) of the Vehicles Act, 1957 (Sask.)*, 1958 CanLII 61 (S.C.C.), [1958] S.C.R. 608; *Provincial Secretary of Prince Edward Island v. Egan*, 1941 CanLII 1 (S.C.C.), [1941] S.C.R. 396.

[43] The argument that the federal gun control scheme is no different from the provincial regulation of motor vehicles ignores the fact that there are significant distinctions between the roles of guns and cars in Canadian society. Both firearms and automobiles can be used for socially approved purposes. Likewise, both may cause death and injury. Yet their primary uses are fundamentally different. Cars are used mainly as means of transportation. Danger to the public is ordinarily unintended and incidental to that use. Guns, by contrast, pose a pressing safety risk in many if not all of their functions. Firearms are often used as weapons in violent crime, including domestic violence; cars generally are not. Thus Parliament views guns as particularly dangerous and has sought to combat that danger by extending its licensing and registration scheme to all classes of firearms. Parliament did not enact the *Firearms Act* to regulate guns as items of property. The Act does not address insurance or permissible locations of use.

Rather, the Act addresses those aspects of gun control which relate to the dangerous nature of firearms and the need to reduce misuse.

[44] In a variation on the theme of property and civil rights, the opponents of the 1995 gun control law argue that ordinary guns, like rifles and shotguns, are common property, not dangerous property. Ordinary firearms are different, they argue, from the automatic weapons and handguns that Parliament has regulated in the past. Ordinary guns are used mainly for lawful purposes in hunting, trapping and ranching. Automatic weapons and handguns, by contrast, have few uses outside crime or war. The fact that Parliament has the right under the criminal law power to control automatic weapons and handguns does not, they argue, mean that Parliament has the right to regulate ordinary guns.

[45] The difficulty with this argument is that while ordinary guns are often used for lawful purposes, they are also used for crime and suicide, and cause accidental death and injury. Guns cannot be divided neatly into two categories — those that are dangerous and those that are not dangerous. All guns are capable of being used in crime. All guns are capable of killing and maiming. It follows that all guns pose a threat to public safety. As such, their control falls within the criminal law power.

[46] In a further variation on this argument, the provinces of Ontario and Saskatchewan submitted that even if the licensing provisions of the law were valid criminal legislation, the registration provisions are mainly provincial property legislation and should be severed and struck out. The argument is that the registration portions of the Act simply amount to regulation, with little connection to the public safety purpose advanced by the federal government to justify the Act as a whole. Conrad J.A. agreed with this argument, finding that although the Act "cleverly intertwines" the licensing and registration provisions through "clever packaging", the registration provisions could be severed from the gun control law. As proof, she pointed to the fact that the pre-existing firearms acquisition certificate scheme, governing prohibited and restricted arms, applied to ordinary firearms without being connected to a registration system.

[47] We are not persuaded that the registration provisions can be severed from the rest of the Act, nor that they fail to serve Parliament's purpose in promoting public safety. The licensing provisions require everyone who possesses a gun to be licensed. The registration provisions require all guns to be regis-

tered. The combination of the two parts of the scheme is intended to ensure that when a firearm is transferred from one person to another, the recipient is licensed. Absent a registration system, this would be impossible to ascertain. If a gun is found in the possession of an unlicensed person, the registration system permits the government to determine where the gun originated. With a registration scheme in place, licensed owners can be held responsible for the transfer of their weapons. The registration system is also part of the general scheme of the law in reducing misuse. If someone is found guilty of a crime involving violence, or is prohibited from possessing a weapon, the registration scheme is expected to assist the police in determining whether the offender actually owns any guns and in confiscating them. The registration scheme is also intended to reduce smuggling and the illegal trade in guns. These interconnections demonstrate that the registration and licensing portions of the *Firearms Act* are both tightly linked to Parliament's goal in promoting safety by reducing the misuse of any and all firearms. Both portions are integral and necessary to the operation of the scheme. The government is not prevented from improving the system because the preexisting firearms acquisition certificate system was not connected to a registration system. Moreover, prior to this Act, the federal government had a registration system for handguns. It now seeks to extend it to all guns. Contrary to the suggestions of Conrad J.A., no improper purpose in including registration in the scheme has been demonstrated.

(3) Undue Intrusion into Provincial Powers?

[48] In a related argument, Alberta and the provincial interveners submit that this law inappropriately trenches on provincial powers and that upholding it as criminal law will upset the balance of federalism. In support of its submission, Alberta cites the work of D. M. Beatty, who suggests applying considerations of rationality and proportionality from the *Canadian Charter of Rights and Freedoms* s. 1 cases to questions of legislative competence: *Constitutional Law in Theory and Practice* (1995). It seems far from clear to us that it would be helpful to apply the technique of weighing benefits and detriments used in s. 1 jurisprudence to the quite different exercise of defining the scope of the powers set out in ss. 91 and 92 of the *Constitution Act, 1867*. This said, however, it is beyond debate that an appropriate balance must be maintained between the federal and provincial heads of power. A federal state depends for its very existence on a just and workable balance between the central and provincial levels of government, as this Court affirmed in *Reference re Secession of Quebec*, 1998 CanLII 793 (S.C.C.), [1998] 2 S.C.R. 217; see also *General Motors of Canada Ltd. v. City National Leasing*, *supra*. The courts, critically aware of the need to maintain this balance, have not hesitated to strike down legislation that does not conform with the requirements of the criminal law: see *Boggs*, *supra*, and the *Margarine Reference*, *supra*. The question is not whether such a balance is necessary, but whether the 1995 gun control law upsets that balance.

[49] The argument that the 1995 gun control law upsets the balance of Confederation may be seen as an argument that, viewed in terms of its effects, the law does not in pith and substance relate to public safety under the federal criminal law power but rather to the provincial power over property and civil rights. Put simply, the issue is whether the law is mainly in relation to criminal law. If it is, incidental effects in the provincial sphere are constitutionally irrelevant: see, e.g., *Consortium Developments (Clearwater) Ltd. v. Sarnia (City)*, 1998 CanLII 762 (S.C.C.), [1998] 3 S.C.R. 3, and *Mitchell v. Peguis Indian Band*, 1990 CanLII 117 (S.C.C.), [1990] 2 S.C.R. 85. On the other hand, if the effects of the law, considered with its purpose, go so far as to establish that it is mainly a law in relation to property and civil rights, then the law is *ultra vires* the federal government. In summary, the question is whether the "provincial" effects are incidental, in which case they are constitutionally irrelevant, or whether they are so substantial that they show that the law is mainly, or "in pith and substance", the regulation of property and civil rights.

[50] In our view, Alberta and the provinces have not established that the effects of the law on provincial matters are more than incidental. First, the mere fact that guns are property does not suffice to show that a gun control law is in pith and substance a provincial matter. Exercises of the criminal law power often affect property and civil rights to some degree: *Attorney-General for British Columbia v. Attorney-General for Canada*, [1937] A.C. 368 (P.C.). Such effects are almost unavoidable, as many aspects of the criminal law deal with property and its ownership. The fact that such effects are common does not lessen the need to examine them. It does suggest, however, that we cannot draw sharp lines between criminal law and property and civil rights. Food, drugs and obscene materials are all items of property and are all legitimate subjects of criminal laws. In order to determine the proper classification of this law, then, we must go beyond the simplistic proposition that

guns are property and thus any federal regulation of firearms is *prima facie* unconstitutional.

[51] Second, the Act does not significantly hinder the ability of the provinces to regulate the property and civil rights aspects of guns. Most provinces already have regulations dealing with hunting, discharge within municipal boundaries, and other aspects of firearm use, and these are legitimate subjects of provincial regulation: see *R. v. Chiasson* reflex, (1982), 66 C.C.C. (2d) 195 (N.B.C.A.), aff'd 1984 CanLII 136 (S.C.C.), [1984] 1 S.C.R. 266. The Act does not affect these laws.

[52] Third, the most important jurisdictional effect of this law is its elimination of the ability of the provinces to <u>not</u> have any regulations on the ownership of ordinary firearms. The provinces argue that it is in their power to choose whether or not to have such a law. By taking over the field, the federal government has deprived the provinces of that choice. Assuming (without deciding) that the provincial legislatures would have the jurisdiction to enact a law in relation to the property aspects of ordinary firearms, this does not prevent Parliament from addressing the safety aspects of ordinary firearms. The double aspect doctrine permits both levels of government to legislate in one jurisdictional field for two different purposes: *Egan, supra.*

[53] Fourth, as discussed above, this law does not precipitate the federal government's entry into a new field. Gun control has been the subject of federal law since Confederation. This law does not allow the federal government to significantly expand its jurisdictional powers to the detriment of the provinces. There is no colourable intrusion into provincial jurisdiction, either in the sense that Parliament has an improper motive or that it is taking over provincial powers under the guise of the criminal law. While we are sensitive to the concern of the provincial governments that the federal jurisdiction over criminal law not be permitted such an unlimited scope that it erodes the constitutional balance of powers, we do not believe that this legislation poses such a threat.

(4) Is Moral Content Required?

[54] Yet another argument is that the ownership of guns is not criminal law because it is not immoral to own an ordinary firearm. There are two difficulties with this argument. The first is that while the ownership of ordinary firearms is not in itself regarded by most Canadians as immoral, the problems associated with the misuse of firearms are firmly grounded in morality. Firearms may be misused to take human life and to assist in other immoral acts, like theft and terrorism. Preventing such misuse can be seen as an attempt to curb immoral acts. Viewed thus, gun control is directed at a moral evil.

[55] The second difficulty with the argument is that the criminal law is not confined to prohibiting immoral acts: see *Proprietary Articles Trade Association v. Attorney-General for Canada*, [1931] A.C. 310 (P.C.). While most criminal conduct is also regarded as immoral, Parliament can use the criminal law to prohibit activities which have little relation to public morality. For instance, the criminal law has been used to prohibit certain restrictions on market competition: see *Attorney-General for British Columbia v. Attorney-General for Canada, supra.* Therefore, even if gun control did not involve morality, it could still fall under the federal criminal law power.

(5) Other Concerns

[56] We recognize the concerns of northern, rural and aboriginal Canadians who fear that this law does not address their particular needs. They argue that it discriminates against them and violates treaty rights, and express concerns about their ability to access the scheme, which may be administered from a great distance. These apprehensions are genuine, but they do not go to the question before us — Parliament's jurisdiction to enact this law. Whether a law could have been designed better or whether the federal government should have engaged in more consultation before enacting the law has no bearing on the division of powers analysis applied by this Court. If the law violates a treaty or a provision of the *Charter*, those affected can bring their claims to Parliament or the courts in a separate case. The reference questions, and hence this judgment, are restricted to the issue of the division of powers.

[57] We also appreciate the concern of those who oppose this Act on the basis that it may not be effective or it may be too expensive. Criminals will not register their guns, Alberta argued. The only real effect of the law, it is suggested, is to burden law-abiding farmers and hunters with red tape. These concerns were properly directed to and considered by Parliament; they cannot affect the Court's decision. The efficacy of a law, or lack thereof, is not relevant to Parliament's ability to enact it under the division of powers analysis. Furthermore, the federal government points out that it is not only career criminals who are capable of misusing guns. Domestic violence often involves people who have no prior criminal record. Crimes are committed by first-time

offenders. Finally, accidents and suicides occur in the homes of law-abiding people, and guns are stolen from their homes. By requiring everyone to register their guns, Parliament seeks to reduce misuse by everyone and curtail the ability of criminals to acquire firearms. Where criminals have acquired guns and used them in the commission of offences, the registration system seeks to make those guns more traceable. The cost of the program, another criticism of the law, is equally irrelevant to our constitutional analysis.

VI.   CONCLUSION

[58] We conclude that the impugned sections of the *Firearms Act* contain prohibitions and penalties in support of a valid criminal law purpose. The legislation is in relation to criminal law pursuant to s. 91(27) of the *Constitution Act, 1867* and hence *intra vires* Parliament. It is not regulatory legislation and it does not take the federal government so far into provincial territory that the balance of federalism is threatened or the jurisdictional powers of the provinces are unduly impaired.

[59] Having determined that the legislation constitutes a valid exercise of Parliament's jurisdiction over criminal law, it is unnecessary to consider whether the legislation can also be justified as an exercise of its peace, order and good government power.

[60] We would dismiss the appeal. The licensing and registration provisions in the *Firearms Act* do not constitute an infringement of the jurisdiction of the Legislature of Alberta with respect to the regulation of property and civil rights pursuant to s. 92(13) of the *Constitution Act, 1867*. The Act is a valid exer-

cise of Parliament's jurisdiction over criminal law pursuant to s. 91(27).

[61] The answers to the reference questions are as follows:

[Question 2:

(1) Do the licensing provisions, insofar as they relate to an ordinary firearm, constitute an infringement of the jurisdiction of the Legislature of Alberta with respect to the regulation of property and civil rights pursuant to subsection 92(13) of the *Constitution Act, 1867*?

(2) If the answer to the question posed in subsection (1) is "yes", are the licensing provisions *ultra vires* the Parliament of Canada insofar as they regulate the possession or ownership of an ordinary firearm?]

    (1) No.
    (2) No.

[Question 3:

(1) Do the registration provisions, as they relate to an ordinary firearm, constitute an infringement of the jurisdiction of the Legislature of Alberta with respect to the regulation of property and civil rights pursuant to subsection 92(13) of the *Constitution Act, 1867*?

(2) If the answer to the question posed in subsection (1) is "yes", are the registration provisions *ultra vires* the Parliament of Canada insofar as they require registration of an ordinary firearm?

    (1) No.
    (2) No.

(d)   Judicial Review†

Benjamin L. Berger

The claim of this article has been that to understand contemporary Canadian constitutional culture, one has to grasp that Canadians are children of two dis-

tinct constitutional logics, the logic of the particular and that of the universal. When one finds points at which the local and particular are impervious to the

† "Children of Two Logics: A Way into Canadian Constitutional Culture" (2013) 11:2 ICON 319 at 327–332. [Notes and/or references omitted.] Reproduced by permission of Oxford University Press.

logic of the universal, we have our hands on something crucial to constitutional identity and culture. Debates regarding judicial review are another expression of this — an example of a prominent aspect of modern Canadian constitutional life that one cannot really understand absent an appreciation of the play of these logics.

The introduction of the Charter in 1982 inaugurated a debate on the legitimacy of judicial review, one that can fairly be said to have consumed Canadian constitutional theory and adjudication since that time. Of course, theoretical debates inquiring into the legitimacy of judicial review are in no way unique to Canada, serving as they have as a mainstay of constitutional theory in many jurisdictions. But the Canadian instantiation of these debates has certain unique contours and an intriguing history. After the introduction of the Charter, critics quickly emerged from the left, arguing that Courts lacked the legitimacy and competence to decide serious social policy questions.[24] These voices were matched and paralleled by commentators on the right who complained of "judicial activism" and the lack of judicial accountability.[25] Over time, the response to these critiques from those supporting the Charter took shape in a dialogic theory of judicial review, arguing that the judiciary's role was simply as one partner in a conversation about the meaning and application of the Charter, effectively defending judicial review by diminishing the sense of its finality. Debates over "dialogue theory" came not only to preoccupy (to the point of exhaustion, many would say) constitutional theory[26] but were eventually seized upon by the Supreme Court of Canada itself as an account of the legitimacy of its role.[27] Constitutionalism in Canada since 1982 has been shot through with contestation regarding the role and legitimacy of judicial review in the constitutional order.

One way of reading this fact of Canadian constitutionalism is simply as a democratic worry of the kind hashed about in the United States since the early nineteenth century,[28] delayed in its Canadian appearance owing to the late introduction of a constitutional bill of rights. On this reading, the story is essentially one about the democratic accountability of the judiciary. This is certainly part of the story in Canada and I do not suggest that this is a misreading. My argument, however, is that there is much more at play in this debate in Canada and that at its core is a tension between fundamental ways of imagining the role and function of a constitution, a tension made palpable and pronounced by the particularities of Canadian constitutional history and reflective of important dimensions of constitutional culture.

The dominant experience over constitutional history in Canada has been of a constitution as compact and political compromise. This is what I have called the consummately political constitution. From confederation in 1867 until 1982 the role of the courts in constitutional matters was one of sustaining the political. When they spoke in a constitutional idiom, the voice of the courts was not interpreting the governing truths of a constitutional text but, rather, using the constitution as a device in arbitrating as between political powers within the state. The courts were curating the political compact of confederation in a manner that left substantive matters to legislative will. When it spoke on constitutional matters, the Supreme Court of Canada was normally attempting to strike a balance as between provincial and federal legislative bodies, interpreting and applying the political bargain struck among provinces in the formation of the country. Substantive matters were left to political institutions with the courts umpiring the contest when the two sides wrestled over jurisdiction.[29]

The animating principle in this era of constitutionalism in Canada was that of the classic British constitution: parliamentary supremacy. The ethos of parliamentary supremacy elevates political will and interest. If a legislative act can be imagined, parliamentary supremacy in the Canadian federation begins with the proposition that one level of government or the other has the power to enact it.[30] There was a role for the courts in constitutional matters — an important one — but it was a role in "arbitrating will." The courts were tasked with maintaining a workable, balanced political compact within which interest and political preference remained supreme. One can see clearly the way in which this historic role for the courts matches the logic of the particular, as I have described it. On this logic, the Constitution is first and foremost about practical solutions to local problems of governance among multiple political communities. Judicial review was not a new issue with the Charter; courts suspended and declared invalid legislation for over a century before the Charter was instituted and yet Canadian constitutional theory did not bother much with the democratic legitimacy of judicial review. We were comfortable with judicial review because it was about curating the political, which, consistent with the logic of a consummately political constitution, remained responsible for substantive policy matters. For the first 115 years of Canadian constitutional history this is the principal role that courts played in Canadian constitutionalism.

One still finds this mode of constitutionalism, with its political and particular core, in modern federalism decisions. Yet perhaps the best expression of this constitutional logic from within the Supreme Court's own jurisprudence is found in the *Reference re Secession of Quebec*.[31] The question of whether Quebec could secede unilaterally from Canada was referred to the Supreme Court of Canada. This is the Ur-case of the courts curating the constitutional compact, tending to the local particulars of Canadian state history. The Court approached this question by articulating the foundational principles that animate the Canadian constitutional order (it named federalism, democracy, constitutionalism and the rule of law, and respect for minorities), setting the terrain on which political action would have to take place. The Court looked to Canadian history to catalogue the political conventions that form part of Canadian constitutionalism and ultimately held that political recognition and negotiation would be constitutionally required should a clear majority of Quebecers express the will to secede from Canada. In summarizing its role, the Court offered a passage that is perfectly emblematic of the first logic of constitutionalism — the logic of the particular, the local, and the political:

The task of the Court has been to clarify the legal framework within which political decisions are to be taken "under the Constitution," not to usurp the prerogatives of the political forces that operate within that framework. The obligations we have identified are binding obligations under the Constitution of Canada. However, it will be for the political actors to determine what constitutes "a clear majority on a clear question" in the circumstances under which a future referendum vote may be taken. Equally, in the event of demonstrated majority support for Quebec secession, the content and process of the negotiations will be for the political actors to settle. The reconciliation of the various legitimate constitutional interests is necessarily committed to the political rather than the judicial realm precisely because that reconciliation can only be achieved through the give and take of political negotiations. To the extent issues addressed in the course of negotiation are political, the courts, appreciating their proper role in the constitutional scheme, would have no supervisory role.[32]

This is the Court acting in execution of consummately constitutional duties but there is nothing universal, nothing based in general claims of right or reason, and everything contingent, local, and particular about its role. To be sure, in its decision the Court also reflected the Canadian constitutional commitment to broader norms, such as the protec-

tion of minorities. Again, these logics are not pure forms but, rather, pull on one another at all points. But the heart of the decision is deference to will rather than the assertion of universal claims of reason or right. It is the Court guiding procedurally while deferring substantively to the exigencies and force of political will. This is a judicial role consonant with one, venerable, logic of constitutionalism.

It is trite to observe that the Constitution Act 1982, and the Charter in particular, radically altered the role of the courts. More telling is the shift in constitutional logic that this change in role reflected. Rather than curating or sustaining the political, the Court's voice in constitutional matters would now involve limiting or containing the political. In its new role enforcing rights, the judiciary would now speak substantive truth in response to interest and will. The universals of rights and categorical claims of just state–citizen relations could and would now hollow out a space in the antecedent sphere of parliamentary (read political) supremacy into which no expression of will, no manifestation of political interest, could encroach. This is a familiar logic to US constitutional theory, that of courts as guardians of substantive limits on the political — the high priests of constitutionalism; but it was a fundamental shift in constitutional life in Canada.

With this shift, the ultimate word on substantive matters of policy would be spoken by courts in the idiom of rights and proportional limitations on rights. Means–ends proportionality is none other than the deployment of reason as a limit on political will.[33] Canadian courts were thus placed in the position of oracles of reason-based universals and, in this way, became part of a global conversation of constitutional courts. The universalist nature of rights discourse implies a convergence in method and reason, one that we have seen coalescing among contemporary supreme courts around the world. Met with an issue that turns on fundamental political or social rights, the tools, reasoning, and considerations ought not to differ much whether spoken by the Canadian, South African, or Israeli Supreme Courts or, for that matter, by the European Court of Justice or the UN Committee on Human Rights. Positions might differ but the language would be highly recognizable, maybe even portable. The introduction of the Charter was a rebalancing between political will as the expression of particular interest, and reason as the universal logic of rights; the new role for the courts reflected this shift in constitutional logics.

There is no shortage of Charter cases that [display] the judicial role incumbent on this second logic of constitutionalism. A sterling example is the

Court's unanimous decision in *United States v. Burns and Rafay*.[34] The question before the Court was whether it was constitutionally permissible to extradite two accused to Washington State to face three counts of aggravated first degree murder, where the potential penalties included capital punishment. The practice of capital punishment was abolished in Canada by act of Parliament in 1976, after years of political debate. The question in *Burns and Rafay* was, essentially, whether the Charter prohibited the Canadian government from exposing a citizen to capital punishment at all. The Court concluded that it would offend §7's guarantee of life, liberty and security of the person and offend the principles of fundamental justice to extradite without assurances that the death penalty would not be sought. In deciding this politically pregnant question, filled with issues of executive power and international relations, at every turn the Court's reasoning sounds in the register of constitutionalism as an expression of universal rights as limits on the political and on executive power. In its reasoning the Court invokes the International Covenant on Civil and Political Rights, various protocols under that covenant, the Convention on the Rights of the Child, various UN releases and reports, and European protocols, conventions, and court rulings as persuasive authority on the rights-offending nature of capital punishment. There is no sense of deference to the political process as the matter is cast entirely as one of fundamental and universal rights, albeit anchored in a Canadian context. Consistent with the underlying logic of rights-based constitutionalism, with some local color and legislative specifics extracted, the decision could have as easily been issued by the German Constitutional Court as by the Canadian Supreme Court. Now a Charter issue, the Court has the constitutional role and authority to conclusively settle a substantive question that was, prior to 1982, a matter determined exclusively by political will.

Contrasting the *Secession Reference* with *Burns and Rafay* draws into sharp focus my point that the nature of judicial review displays the extent to which Canadians are children of two constitutional logics. Read in this way, the pitched debate regarding judicial review is, amongst other things, an expression of the felt tension between a new sense of constitutionalism and an older way of thinking about the nature and function of constitutions. Indeed, the charge of judicial activism — a potent cry in Canada leveled equally by critical scholars on the left and conservatives on the right — can be heard as anxiety that the first constitutional logic is being eclipsed by the second. At core, we see in the Canadian practices of and debates about judicial review a contest of constitutional logics — one of managing political arrangements and finding working solutions among interests and another about declaring universal truth as found in rights and reason. Canadian constitutional life can't let go of a tradition in which judicial review fundamentally served the political, nor can it now turn its back on a newer role in which the courts honor the constitution by trumping interest with rights, will with reason, and the particular with the universal. This tension beats at the heart of constitutional life in Canada; but why is this tension so central? Of course, debates about the legitimacy of judicial review are found in constitutional systems around the world. Judicial review raises basic democratic questions, such as the legitimacy of an unelected judiciary and, at a deeper and more interesting level, the problem of a community governing itself over time.[35] Yet despite the substantial influence of US and international theory in Canadian debates on the legitimacy of judicial review, it is a mistake to reduce the anxiety about this issue in Canada to a shared concern with these structural issues. Scholars who draw easy equivalencies between the US and Canadian debates miss something important about Canadian constitutional culture. When we ask why this appearance of concern about the political and the particular continues to have such purchase in Canada despite the existence of an entrenched bill of rights, why the universal has not eclipsed the older logic of constitutionalism, the answer comes back to key narratives about Canadian constitutional identity. The British tradition, in which parliamentary supremacy is the particular expression of the priority of political will, is a deep part of constitutional self-understanding in Canada. It must be recalled that Canada is an anti-revolutionary constitutional culture, in some ways no less shaped by the American Revolution than its neighbor to the south. The preponderance of English inhabitants of what would become Canada were loyalists committed to the continuance of the British tradition in North America. The defeat of the Americans in the War of 1812 was the defence of political autonomy under this way of life, this form of governance. There is, thus, a deep way in which the claim about a kind of "Americanization" that comes with judicial review interacts with the narratives that help to shape Canadian political and constitutional identity.

But there is another narrative layer that helps to explain the distinctive purchase of the logic of the particular and, hence, the depth of anxiety around questions of judicial review. Over time, the British parliamentary tradition took on a particular inflection in Canada, becoming associated with the rise of social welfare. For much of Canadian history the most symbolically prized advances in social justice in Canada came through the legislatures, not the courts. *Brown v. Board of Education* was decided in 1954. The first iteration of national, universal healthcare was introduced by act of Parliament in 1957,[36] building on earlier provincial legislative innovations. What is often overlooked in discussions of the Canadian instantiation of the debate about judicial review is the way in which the parliamentary tradition has been imaginatively tethered to Canadian self-understanding as a social democracy committed to some version of a welfare state. This link between contests about judicial review and the social democratic identity of the country explains some of the deeper elements of the

public controversy — the trauma — that occurred when the Supreme Court used the Charter of Rights and Freedoms to invalidate a key aspect of the public health care scheme in Quebec.[37] This decision was not just an occasion for concern about the democratic nature of judicial review, but a site of overt conflict between two logics of constitutionalism, and a point at which the logic of the particular touched upon a key dimension of "who we are."

Limits on judicial review are limits that the particular imposes on the logic of the universal. Structurally, these limits are points at which constitutional culture privileges will over reason. In Canada, debates over these limits are also entwined with stories that shape constitutional identity and point to important dimensions of constitutional culture. ...

(e) Museums as Constitutions: A Commentary on Constitutions and Constitution Making†

Stacy Douglas

I. MUSEUMS AS CONSTITUTIONS

Museums function much like constitutions. Although they are not accorded the same juridical powers as the state-sanctioned constitution, nor are they recognized social contracts upon which the national juridical apparatus sits, they do operate as a site from which imaginations of political community are launched. Indeed, they are alike as both set the representation of political community as their task. Tony Bennett claims that museums "arrange their displays so as to simulate the organisation of the world — human and natural — outside the museum walls."[1] Similarly, Kevin Hetherington asserts that, "as spaces of political as much as scientific or aesthetic imagination, museums have always sought to articulate through both their archiving practices and their exhibition of artifacts an idea of society and of the subjects within it."[2] Constitutions too attempt to communicate an idea of society and of the subjects within it. Both attempt to tell a story of the world through their representational frameworks.

Moreover, both museums and constitutions are the subject of critique as a result of their representations of community. Indeed, critics of the museum take aim at the institution for its collections and memorializing practices that are built on legacies of colonialism and imperialism.[3] These collections, it is argued, often exclude or poorly represent particular groups of individuals and communities.[4] Detractors contend that, in order to address these violent histories, the museum must be reformed.[5] It is asserted that such reforms will make the museum a more democratic institution. Similarly, constitutions are often charged with failing to adequately represent communities. These arguments claim that, in doing so, the constitution leaves certain communities under-acknowledged and erases others entirely. Some critical constitutional scholars attempt to address the limits of the constitution by pairing it with reflexive politics.[6] For these authors, reflexive politics offer a tool for shaping the powers and possibilities of the constitution that can make up for the inadequacy of the representational structure of the institution. However, below I argue that the constitution cannot

---

† *Law, Culture and the Humanities*, 1743872113499226, first published on August 21, 2013 [Notes and/or references omitted.] Copyright © Stacy Douglas, 2013. Reprinted by permission of Sage Publications, Ltd.

accommodate these demands. Moreover, the museum and the constitution's common goal of achieving universal representation opens up both sites to an infinite critique for their failures. Drawing on insights from Michel Foucault, I suggest that both are also connected through their structurally insatiable claims to representation.

Lastly, museums and constitutional democracy share a common link with the advent of liberalism. For both, the revolutionary moment of secular statehood marks an organizational change, but one that allows sovereign hierarchies to persist. This moment is also characterized by Foucault as the untidy shift from sovereign to disciplinary power and can be seen in trends at large public museums as well as in other modes of contemporary governance.

This commentary elucidates these shared connections between museums and constitutions. These connections offer two related insights into the nature of constituting and constitution-making. Firstly, by drawing attention to the ways that museums can be thought of as constitutions, I hope to emphasize that constitutions are more than institutional documents. Rather, constitutions are made up of memorializing techniques that serve to help produce an idea of community. Secondly, by illuminating the role of museums in constituting a people, museums offer a challenge to constitutional thinkers that focus solely on the constitution in their attempts to constitute and reconstitute political community. Indeed, like constitutions, museums also function to demarcate and memorialize a people. While I do not dedicate space in this commentary to exploring the possibly productive pairings of museums and constitutions, I suggest that museums can offer a distinctive yet crucial role in constitutional deliberations, reconstructions, and theorizations.

II.   MUSEUMS AND THE PROBLEM OF REPRESENTATION

Didier Maleuvre explores the suffocation of ontological being at the museum. He argues that the museum employs repressive modes of identification through its creation and deployment of political constituencies that individual identities are then asked to comply with. For Maleuvre, any modes of identification are intrinsically limiting as they fundamentally collapse ontological primacy into identification to and through political constituencies. This compulsive identification denies the inherent relationality of the world.

As a result, Maleuvre also argues against what he sees as the limiting, confining, and ultimately oppressive practices of cultural essentialism posited by even the most well-meaning community-focused museums. He argues that museums that purport to be locally constituted and to have a voice "of the people" rely on discourses of authenticity that assimilate the individual into predetermined cultural or political communities. "By promoting 'roots' and identifying the individual with a folksy, contextualized, and meaningful culture, these museums advertise culture as compulsive identity formation."[7] According to Maleuvre this is a dangerous liaison with cultural essentialism that stifles difference.[8]

Donald Preziosi also explores practices in the museum that contribute to this sense of discernible coherence. Preziosi claims that the museum is entirely made up of anamorphic orientations — essentially, processes that give coherence to things that are otherwise distorted or conflictual. In this sense, he claims that "the disciplinary archive situates its users in [...] anamorphic positions from which the history of art may be seen as unfolding, on its own, almost magically, before one's eyes."[9] For Preziosi, the knowable, locatable, and explainable notion of the self in modernity is central to the foundations of the museum. Significantly then, visitors do not experience the potential loss of self at the museum; rather, through the unfolding of chronological time, they experience the putting-in place, or legibility, of themselves. Preziosi attributes this incessant fascination with order to the persistence of ancient Christian traditions in Enlightenment thought. According to Preziosi, "this is a practice aimed at forestalling the holy or divine terror, the *theios phobos* that Plato warned about as the destabilizing effect of the powers of art over the soul necessarily banished from his ideal polis [...]."[10]

Moreover, the opportunity to imagine a desirable, coherent self and attendant world offers visitors the chance to partake in a modern western European exercise of recording and archiving. The anamorphic orientations at work ensure that difference and messiness can be domesticated and tamed, in service of what Preziosi calls "the dream of a totally transparent society."[11] This desire to make the world legible and knowable is central to the modern museum as well as contemporary constitutionalism.

III.   CONSTITUTIONS AND THE PRODUCTION OF COMMUNITY

Constitutions produce an idea of community — "the people" — that they represent. According to Martin Loughlin and Neil Walker, "modern constitutional texts aspire not only to establish the forms of governmental authority (legally constituted power) but also to reconstitute the people in a particular way."[12] These conceptions of community rely on neat and stable categories that attempt to gloss over the messiness of the world. They forestall chaos by offering a manageable conception of community that is amenable to constitutional arrangements. Jean and John Comaroff comment on the custodial aspect of law. They claim that the constitution acts

> as an instrument of governance [that] allows the state to represent itself as the custodian of civility against disorder — and, therefore, as mandated to conjure moral community by exercising a monopoly over the construction of a commonwealth out of inimical diversities of interest.[13]

However, it may be argued that I am forwarding a concept of constitutions that is too static and unchanging. Indeed, scholars such as Jurgen Habermas contend that the constitution does not concretize community but changes with it. He claims that "a constitution can be thought of as an historical project that each generation of citizens continues to pursue."[14] While it is certainly true that the constitution is open to amendment and change, its principal function is the delimitation of community; the constitution bounds a body politic. Certainly a constitution can change over time to reflect the goals and aspirations of the people it represents; however, its central role is the production of political community through a representational framework. Indeed, many legal scholars share this concern with the limits of constitutionalism. Thinkers such as Martin Loughlin, Neil Walker, and Emilios Christodoulidis, admit to the restrictions of thinking political community through constitutional arrangements and, in light of said restrictions, attempt to draw a productive relationship between constitutionalism and politics. Specifically, these critical constitutional scholars attempt to address this issue by pairing the constitution with reflexive politics.[15]

For these authors, reflexive politics offer a tool for shaping the powers and possibilities of the constitution. Although each draws out a distinctly different conception of reflexivity, it is intended in all cases to provide for the maintenance of a constitutional structure while simultaneously allowing for that structure to be modified by political claims. Where Martin Loughlin is primarily concerned with elucidating a theory of public law that reveals the profound role of "right ordering" or *droit politique*,[16] Neil Walker is interested in thinking about the functioning of extra-state constitutionalism.[17] In contrast to both Loughlin

and Walker, Emilios Christodoulidis focuses on conceiving of a constitutional arrangement that incorporates disorganization and "dissensus" without assimilating it, usually in support of a broadly anti-capitalist, leftist politics.[18]

However, and importantly, Christodoulidis argues that constitutions cannot be asked to be radically reflexive.[19] What he means is that constitutions are institutional arrangements that represent a definite structure. As such, when constitutional thinkers attempt to stretch the constitution to include expansive conceptions of community, they fool themselves into thinking that such demands can be accommodated. He claims that you cannot ask a structure to defy itself.[20] Moreover, to put this demand on the constitution is to presume that it is the singular and central tool in the production of political community. Although Christodoulidis is partial to the task of reflexive politics, he argues that this cannot be done through the constitution itself. Rather, this reflexivity can only be achieved through the pairing of the constitution with the political activity of civil society.[21] Drawing on his own critical conception of systems theory, he contends that this activity has the potential to change the terms of the constitutional arrangement.[22]

Christodoulidis's critique illustrates three important facets of constitutionalism. Firstly, by drawing attention to the structural architecture of constitutions, he illuminates its central truth. The constitution is tasked with the delimitation of political community; it cannot do otherwise without undoing its core function. Moreover, as the constitution carries out its key function it necessarily excludes. This leads to a second central facet of constitutionalism. As this inherent exclusion is central to constitutionalism, it opens itself up to the incessant demand for enhanced and increased representation. Those who are excluded or feel inadequately represented subsequently make claims on constitutions that persist because the constitution perpetually creates an excluded audience that can demand inclusion. As long as the constitution strives to be inclusive, it will necessarily produce this indefatigable demand. Thirdly, Christodoulidis's critique of scholars' attempt to make constitutions reflexive also demonstrates the great attachment that these thinkers have to constitutions themselves. Indeed, the project of thinking about the limitations of constitutions and the dilemmas of political community are rarely considered at a distance from this juridical framework. While Gunther Teubner explores some of this work through what he calls "societal constitutionalism,"[23] his response to the "unitary bias" of constitutionalism is the "constitutionalization of a multiplicity of autonomous subsystems of world society."[24] Rather than attending to the problem of state-centric constitutionalism by advocating for the adoption of constitutions in the societal sphere, however, my project is to point to the shared techniques of memorialization used in the production of representations of political community at museums and constitutions. Indeed, museums are a site that can assist in illuminating the dynamic ways in which political community is produced and the limits of seeking its representation.

IV. REVOLUTIONS, MUSEUMS, AND THE PRODUCTION OF A CITIZENRY

Like modern constitutional democracy, the advent of the contemporary public museum descended from the revolutionary traditions of Western Europe. Its place as a public institution came largely as a result of anti-feudal demands that transformed political and cultural society, especially the private ownership of royal collections.[25] As monarchic supremacy declined in these states, museums came to be primarily public institutions funded and operated by the state. These collections were to be of service to the citizenry, displaying objects for the masses. For example, opening in 1759, the British Museum was free to enter for "all studious and curious Persons."[26] Alongside the British Museum, the Louvre is another example of one of the first large museums to be opened, funded, and operated by the state.[27] However, this further push towards more accessible collections did not necessarily disrupt the role of the sovereign. Rather, various scholars point to the ways in which the new, democratic institution envisioned by the revolutionaries, simply substituted the centrality of the monarch with the centrality of the state.[28] The revolutionaries' museum program perpetuated the paradigm whereby an individual's relationship to the collection was an extension of their relationship to the state mediated through the sovereign.[29]

Strikingly, the persistence of this sovereign paradigm has also been identified in the advent of the modern state. For example, launching a critique against the French revolutionaries' practical and theoretical program, Hannah Arendt asks poignantly, "what else did even Sieyès do but simply put the sovereignty of the nation into the place which had been vacated by a sovereign king?"[30] For skeptics, the museological and state revolutions did little to disrupt their fundamental hierarchical organizations. As Tony Bennett observes, the museum's objective was "to make a new conception of the state visible to the inspection of the citizen by redeploying expropriated royal treasures in a democratic public setting and thereby investing them with new meanings in embodying a public representativeness."[31] This new museum featured exhibitions aimed at displaying the transparency of the new democratic order, thereby validating the state and its rule. The shift functioned to interpellate the visitor, no longer as subject to the Lord but, as "citizen and therefore a shareholder in the state."[32] Under the new democratic organization, man was empowered to be the narrator of his own history, seeing for *himself* the objects of *his* state.[33]

Indeed, the civic trend at the museum was part of a larger social, political purging of the monarchy and its associated Christian religious institutions. According to Stuart Hall, the public character of the state emerged from the struggle against Absolutism during the transition from feudalism to capitalism. He claims that "in the modern conception, the state is not supposed to be a secret, private affair. It is something operating in the world, universally known and acknowledged, carrying the force of an established legal authority, established for all to see by public processes."[34] Hall argues that the rise of the conception of the individual as a naturally self-sufficient, self-interested unit, led to the burgeoning of the bourgeois public sphere and the masses' participation in it.[35] As with the processes at the museum, this new era of the supposedly transparent state centralized the role of the citizen.[36] As Paul Kahn claims, "by the modern era, the people have become the new absolute. The people as a single subject are the source of ultimate meanings in and for the Western state [...] The people have become the new god and their state founds the new world order."[37] Kahn's emphasis on the substitution of the religious monarch with that of "the people" at the helm of the liberal state resonates closely with Carl Schmitt's famous observation that "all significant concepts of the modern theory of the state are secularized theological concepts."[38] Schmitt intimates that, although the modern liberal state is often conceived of as antithetical to the traditions of religious monarchs that preceded it, the arrangements of power persist.[39] In short, the paradigm of transcendence endures, much like in the arrangements at the museum. Moreover, although the new era of democratic transparency is intended to make the people the authors of their own political communities, the result is their paradoxical positioning as both gods of the new state and subjects of its disciplinary power.

V. THE STATE AND THE MUSEUM THROUGH THREE EPISTEMES

Michel Foucault maps this transformation of political rationalities in Western culture through three consecutive epistemes — the Renaissance, Classical, and Modern — each with their attendant and divergent ways of seeing the world.[40] Where the systems of knowledge drawn on by Renaissance scientists emphasized the importance of items' myriad connections to the world,[41] the Classical episteme focused on drawing out unseen connections between objects, and rendering them legible through representation. This shift paved the way for the introduction of scientific taxonomy. In his book *The Order of Things*, Foucault notes that until the middle of the seventeenth century,

> history was the inextricable and completely unitary fabric of all that was visible of things and of the signs that had been discovered or lodged in them: to write the history of a plant or an animal was as much a matter of describing its elements or organs as of describing the resemblances that could be found in it, the virtues that it was thought to possess, the legends and stories with which it had been involved, its place in heraldry, the medicaments that were concocted from its substance, the foods it provided, what the ancients recorded of it, and what travellers might have said of it. The history of a living being was that being itself, within the whole semantic network that connected it to the world.[42]

However, according to Foucault, this form of historicism gave way under the influence of the botanist Carolus Linnaeus to a method that was less interested in compiling information on the object, and more focused on systematically synthesizing it.[43] This method was predicated on a newly emerging epistemological thrust that sought to uncover hidden relations in and between beings and was notably different from sixteenth and early seventeenth century conceptions of historical technique.[44] This shift led to the development of a classification system that allowed the "structure" of the objects to be "seen."[45] In other words, the semiotics of categorization became the primary form with which to convey meaning about the object. In so doing, the object of study became knowable as and through these categories. Whereas the previous method of classification compiled any and all information on the subject, Foucault argues that Linnaeus's procedure filtered this information into a visible structure.[46] What may have been a complex of networks of meaning for Renaissance naturalists, was thus tamed into a smooth, coherent and, importantly, *visible*, description of the object at hand.

Finally, the difference between the Classical and the Modern episteme is best characterized as one that shifts the importance from *taxonomic representations* of the object (e.g., natural history) to a concern with the object's properties of *biological life*. Foucault claims that the emergence of biological science in the Modern period brought along with it the notion of evolutionary thought and genealogical connection.[47] He claims that "up to the end of the eighteenth century, in fact, life does not exist: only living beings. These beings form one class, or rather several classes, in the series of all things in the world; and if it is possible to speak of life it is only as one character — in the taxonomic sense of that word — in the universal distribution of beings."[48] Significantly, this new attention to life processes and evolutionary thought also had repercussions in modes of governance. Foucault argues that this shift from the Classical to the Modern period brought along an attendant shift from sovereign to disciplinary power that resulted in what he famously terms "biopolitics."[49] Biopolitics refers to the management of life and populations (rather than individual bodies)[50] through capillary forms of power. These include techniques of normalization such as programs of monitoring and normalizing hygiene, as well as reproduction, birth, and mortality rates.[51] Foucault claims that this new technology of power emerged in the latter part of the eighteenth century and that it differed from the sovereign power that preceded it.[52]

Significantly, the emergence of evolutionary thought during the Modern episteme was a major influence on the organization of objects within the museum and, consequently, the relationship between object, visitor, and knowledge. Specifically, the evolutionary narratives found their way into museum exhibitionary practices not only in the arrangement of objects, but also in the framing of man as on a historical evolutionary path moving towards eventual flawlessness. According to Bennett,

> evolutionary thought allowed a revival of Enlightenment conceptions of human perfectibility. Precisely because of their secular nature — because they reflected an order that was to be made rather than one divinely pre-given — such conceptions allowed social life to be thought of as an object of techniques oriented to the progressive perfectibility of forms of thought, conduct and social interrelation.[53]

In the eighteenth century, relationships between visitors and the contents of the museum were no longer strictly officiated through religion or the monarch as they had been before. In their new conceptions, museums exhibited objects in relation to a scientific rationality that conferred new symbolic meanings on the objects, and importantly, the relationship *between* the objects.[54] According to Bennett, the new evolutionary narrative linked

> together the stories of the earth's formation, of the development of life on earth, of the evolution of human life out of animal life and its development from "primitive" to "civilized" forms, into a single narrative which posits modern Man (white, male, and middle class, as Catherine Hall (1992) would put it) as the outcome and, in some cases, telos of these processes.[55]

In other words, the visitor was to be seen as standing at the end of the history that lay before them at the museum. Moreover, this development of evolutionary thought subsequently paved the way for the program of education that would be the focus of the museum's agenda in the nineteenth and twentieth centuries.

Indeed, the nineteenth century public museum was seen as a place where working people could be reformed and brought up to the civilizational standards of the middle class. This was purported to occur by having the working classes attend the museum where they would see their esteemed compatriots acting in good manners and, subsequently, emulate the appropriate behavior.[56] In short, the middle class museum visitors were to set an example that the working class populations could follow.[57] These mid-nineteenth and early twentieth century plans for the museum were inscribed in its architecture, design, entrance policies, dress codes, as well as educational programming.[58]

VI. INDEFATIGABLE CLAIMS TO UNIVERSAL REPRESENTATION

What is significant about the advent of the museum as a tool for popular education is that it advances a conception of itself as part and parcel of a democratizing project, while simultaneously acting as a chief producer of public manners and civility.[59] In other words, the museum makes a doubled-sided assertion; it claims to universally represent while, at the same time, actively differentiating between populations both in how it grants (or does not grant) access to collections, as well as through the representations it provides in those collections. This double bind creates a paradox at the heart of the modern public museum, not dissimilar to that at the center of constitutional projects. The paradox is explained thusly: as the museum claims to tell a universal story of history, it necessarily opens itself to an endless chain of critiques from those who claim to be represented partially, poorly, or not at all. As Bennett points out, this was not the case with the collections and *studiolos* of Renaissance princes and naturalists who made no such claim to universality. It is only with the advent of this purportedly transparent and comprehensively inclusive institution that it is opened up to what Bennett calls "a constant discourse of reform as hitherto excluded constituencies seek inclusion."[60] In other words, the museum's claims to generality *produce* the onslaught of reformist strategies that animate museum studies today. Most importantly, these calls for reform and for better representation are *structurally insatiable* — the museum will never be able to satisfy them.[61]

VII. THE DESTINAL FIGURE OF COMMUNITY

The indefatigable project of attempting to reform the museum suffers from a misplaced understanding of its underlying political rationality. Rather than a site of universal inclusion, the museum differentiates between populations. Bennett draws on Foucault's observation about the persistent attempt to reform the prison to explain:

> The prison [...] has been endlessly subject to calls for reform to allow it to live up to its rehabilitative rhetoric. Yet, however ineffective such reforms prove, the viability of the prison is rarely put into question. Why? Because, Foucault argues, the political rationality of the prison lies elsewhere — less in its ability to genuinely reform behaviour than in its capacity to separate a manageable criminal sub-class from the rest of the population.[62]

As a result of this misplaced critique, calls for reform of the prison continue while the viability of the institution itself is never questioned. This dilemma also emerges in calls for reform of the museum and of the constitution. However, where Bennett claims that the missed rationality is the museum's biopolitical turn to the management of populations, this too misidentifies one of its primary political rationalities. Rather, both the call for the reform of the museum *and* the biopolitical critique miss the modern museum's concern with the destinal figure of community. In other words, it is not an over-emphasis on biological life that is the problem, but rather, the tenacious thinking of the sovereignty of community. As such, it is a critique of community, and not merely of biopolitics, that must be [sought].

To be sure, the civilizational discourses that undergird the museum's organizational and educative structure (explored above in Coombes and Bennett), as well as the colonialist and imperialist ties to much of the museum's contents, have brought the institution under heavy, and warranted[,] criticism in the past thirty years. These critiques call for better representations and pedagogical alterations. However, the critical aim of many of these reform strategies fails to address the problematic persistence of untroubled notions of community and democracy that circulate at the museum, a critique vocalized by museum scholars Maleuvre and Preziosi above.

In a recent article, Kevin Hetherington revisits Foucault's writing on museums, especially through his popular essay on heterotopias (originally given as a lecture in 1967)[63] but also in his essay, published one year earlier, exploring the work of Maurice Blanchot,[64] and his incomplete work on the French painter Édouard Manet.[65] Hetherington asserts that Foucault's thoughts on museums seek to elucidate what he termed the "outside of thought." Hetherington's reading is important because it emphasizes that Foucault's interest is not merely in explicating how the museum constitutes subjectivity but, significantly, how it renders the process of subjectivization apparent. According to Hetherington:

> What Foucault is suggesting is that visitors do not author the reception of culture/nature on display through their interior interpretation as Western thought has believed. Rather, the imagination that emerges though the discursive relationship between the objects constructs the viewer as a subject. Through this process of subjectification museums enact subjects who believe they then take possession of it through the process of imagination. However, what the museum reveals, after Manet, is the visibility of this process to itself.[66]

This last point is key. In the making visible of the process of subjectivization, Foucault finds the potential for the museum to be something other than a place that demands compulsive identity formation, as Maleuvre asserts. While the museum creates a visible apparatus that transforms the world into a place with discernible coherence, it also allows for the visibility of that transformation. The latter makes legible the *production* of the subject's interiority and, with it, affords the opportunity for recognition of the ontological primacy that precedes it.

Hetherington's insight emphasizes the potential that Foucault saw in the museum to unsettle its own

project. Indeed, Foucault was interested in sites that had "the curious property of being in relation with all the other sites, but in such a way as to suspect, neutralize, or invert the set of relations that they happen to designate, mirror, or reflect."[67] As such, the museum can possibly serve as a pivotal site from which to disrupt the suffocation of being introduced above via Maleuvre and Preziosi. However, this possibility does not come through claims for a more inclusive or otherwise reformed museum. Rather, it comes as a result of [] rendering visible the production of the subject. In this move, the museum lays bare this construction, troubling the myth of the "internally self-created agent."[68] This is also true for the constitution. As explored above, the aim of making the constitution entirely inclusive and representative subjects it to an indefatigable claim. Moreover, the constitution, like the museum, cannot attend to the ontological primacy of the world. Therefore, rather than attempt to force the constitution to map onto this dynamic, relational arena — a move criticized by Christodoulidis — we might think of the constitution as a site that can highlight the production of legal subjectivization and its limits. It is [] thinking through the museum and its theorizations that illuminates this potential.

VIII. CONCLUSION

Museums function like constitutions in their creation of a citizenry, shared experience of the shift from sovereign to disciplinary techniques, mutual commitment to the insatiable project of representation, and persistent concern with the creation of community. What these commonalities illuminate is that museums, like constitutions, also produce an idea of community. Indeed, both sites are places from which imaginations of political community are launched. What is significant about this insight is that it demonstrates that constitutions are more than stale documents that are amended or passed in houses of parliament. Rather, constitutions are made up of techniques that extend beyond the written word, and these techniques are also found in other sites, such as the museum. As such, the constitution is not the only device with which to navigate complex questions of politics and sociality. While constitutional negotiation may be able to provide some representational gains for groups seeking redress, the constitutional arrangement cannot attend to the vast possibilities for re-thinking politics and sociality in our dynamic world. Other sites such as the museum must also inform our constitutional deliberations, reconstructions, and theorizations.

Global Context:
The Transnational Influence of Law

(a) *Baker v. Canada (Minister of Citizenship and Immigration)*†

[L'HEUREUX-DUBÉ J., GONTHIER, MCLACHLIN, BASTARACHE and BINNIE JJ.:]

[1] Regulations made pursuant to s. 114(2) of the *Immigration Act*, R.S.C., 1985, c. I-2, empower the respondent Minister to facilitate the admission to Canada of a person where the Minister is satisfied, owing to humanitarian and compassionate considerations, that admission should be facilitated or an exemption from the regulations made under the Act should be granted. At the centre of this appeal is the approach to be taken by a court to judicial review of such decisions, both on procedural and substantive grounds. It also raises issues of reasonable apprehension of bias, the provision of written reasons as part of the duty of fairness, and the role of children's interests in reviewing decisions made pursuant to s. 114(2).

I.   FACTUAL BACKGROUND

[2] Mavis Baker is a citizen of Jamaica who entered Canada as a visitor in August of 1981 and has remained in Canada since then. She never received permanent resident status, but supported herself illegally as a live-in domestic worker for 11 years. She has had four children (who are all Canadian citizens) while living in Canada: Paul Brown, born in 1985, twins Patricia and Peter Robinson, born in 1989, and Desmond Robinson, born in 1992. After Desmond was born, Ms. Baker suffered from post-partum psychosis and was diagnosed with paranoid schizophrenia. She applied for welfare at that time. When she was first diagnosed with mental illness, two of her

children were placed in the care of their natural father, and the other two were placed in foster care. The two who were in foster care are now again under her care, since her condition has improved.

[3] The appellant was ordered deported in December 1992, after it was determined that she had worked illegally in Canada and had overstayed her visitor's visa. In 1993, Ms. Baker applied for an exemption from the requirement to apply for permanent residence outside Canada, based upon humanitarian and compassionate considerations, pursuant to s. 114(2) of the *Immigration Act*. She had the assistance of counsel in filing this application, and included, among other documentation, submissions from her lawyer, a letter from her doctor, and a letter from a social worker with the Children's Aid Society. The documentation provided indicated that, although she was still experiencing psychiatric problems, she was making progress. It also stated that she might become ill again if she were forced to return to Jamaica, since treatment might not be available for her there. Ms. Baker's submissions also clearly indicated that she was the sole caregiver for two of her Canadian-born children, and that the other two depended on her for emotional support and were in regular contact with her. The documentation suggested that she too would suffer emotional hardship if she were separated from them.

[4] The response to this request was contained in a letter dated April 18, 1994 and signed by Immigration Officer M. Caden, stating that a decision had been made that there were insufficient humanitarian and compassionate grounds to warrant process-

---

† [1999] 2 S.C.R. 817 at paras. 1–7, 51, 63–81.

ing Ms. Baker's application for permanent residence within Canada. This letter contained no reasons for the decision.

[5] Upon request of the appellant's counsel, she was provided with the notes made by Immigration Officer G. Lorenz, which were used by Officer Caden when making his decision. After a summary of the history of the case, Lorenz's notes read as follows:

> PC is unemployed — on Welfare. No income shown — no assets. Has four Cdn.-born children — four other children in Jamaica — HAS A TOTAL OF EIGHT CHILDREN
>
> Says only two children are in her "direct custody". (No info on who has ghe [*sic*] other two). There is nothing for her in Jamaica — hasn't been there in a long time — no longer close to her children there — no jobs there — she has no skills other than as a domestic — children would suffer — can't take them with her and can't leave them with anyone here. Says has suffered from a mental disorder since '81 — is now an outpatient and is improving. If sent back will have a relapse.
>
> Letter from Children's Aid — they say PC has been diagnosed as a paranoid schizophrenic. — children would suffer if returned
>
> Letter of Aug. '93 from psychiatrist from Ont. Govm't. Says PC had post-partum psychosis and had a brief episode of psychosis in Jam. when was 25 yrs. old. Is now an out-patient and is doing relatively well — deportation would be an extremely stressful experience.
>
> Lawyer says PS [*sic*] is sole caregiver and single parent of two Cdn born children. Pc's mental condition would suffer a setback if she is deported etc.
>
> This case is a catastrophy [*sic*]. It is also an indictment of our "system" that the client came as a visitor in Aug. '81, was not ordered deported until Dec. '92 and in APRIL '94 IS STILL HERE!
>
> The PC is a paranoid schizophrenic and on welfare. She has no qualifications other than as a domestic. She has FOUR CHILDREN IN JAMAICA AND ANOTHER FOUR BORN HERE. She will, of course, be a tremendous strain on our social welfare systems for (probably) the rest of her life. There are no H&C factors other than her FOUR CANADIAN-BORN CHILDREN. Do we let her stay because of that? I am of the opinion that Canada can no longer afford this type of generosity. However, because of the circumstances involved, there is a potential for adverse publicity. I recommend refusal but you may wish to clear this with someone at Region.

> There is also a potential for violence — see charge of "assault with a weapon" [Capitalization in original.]

[6] Following the refusal of her application, Ms. Baker was served, on May 27, 1994, with a direction to report to Pearson Airport on June 17 for removal from Canada. Her deportation has been stayed pending the result of this appeal.

II. RELEVANT STATUTORY PROVISIONS AND PROVISIONS OF INTERNATIONAL TREATIES

[7] *Immigration Act*, R.S.C., 1985, c. I-2

> **82.1**(1) An application for judicial review under the *Federal Court Act* with respect to any decision or order made, or any matter arising, under this Act or the rules or regulations thereunder may be commenced only with leave of a judge of the Federal Court — Trial Division.
>
> **83.**(1) A judgment of the Federal Court — Trial Division on an application for judicial review with respect to any decision or order made, or any matter arising, under this Act or the rules or regulations thereunder may be appealed to the Federal Court of Appeal only if the Federal Court — Trial Division has at the time of rendering judgment certified that a serious question of general importance is involved and has stated that question.
>
> **114.** ...
>
> (2) The Governor in Council may, by regulation, authorize the Minister to exempt any person from any regulation made under subsection (1) or otherwise facilitate the admission of any person where the Minister is satisfied that the person should be exempted from that regulation or that the person's admission should be facilitated owing to the existence of compassionate or humanitarian considerations.

Immigration Regulations, 1978, SOR/78-172, as amended by SOR/93-44

> 2.1 The Minister is hereby authorized to exempt any person from any regulation made under subsection 114(1) of the Act or otherwise facilitate the admission to Canada of any person where the Minister is satisfied that the person should be exempted from that regulation or that the person's admission should be facilitated owing to the existence of compassionate or humanitarian considerations.

Convention on the Rights of the Child, Can. T.S. 1992 No. 3

Article 3

1. In all actions concerning children, whether undertaken by public or private social welfare institutions, courts of law, administrative authorities or legislative bodies, the best interests of the child shall be a primary consideration.

2. States Parties undertake to ensure the child such protection and care as is necessary for his or her well-being, taking into account the rights and duties of his or her parents, legal guardians, or other individuals legally responsible for him or her, and, to this end, shall take all appropriate legislative and administrative measures.

Article 9

1. States Parties shall ensure that a child shall not be separated from his or her parents against their will, except when competent authorities subject to judicial review determine, in accordance with applicable law and procedures, that such separation is necessary for the best interests of the child. Such determination may be necessary in a particular case such as one involving abuse or neglect of the child by the parents, or one where the parents are living separately and a decision must be made as to the child's place of residence.

2. In any proceedings pursuant to paragraph 1 of the present article, all interested parties shall be given an opportunity to participate in the proceedings and make their views known.

3. States Parties shall respect the right of the child who is separated from one or both parents to maintain personal relations and direct contact with both parents on a regular basis, except if it is contrary to the child's best interests.

4. Where such separation results from any action initiated by a State Party, such as the detention, imprisonment, exile, deportation or death (including death arising from any cause while the person is in the custody of the State) of one or both parents or of the child, that State Party shall, upon request, provide the parents, the child or, if appropriate, another member of the family with the essential information concerning the whereabouts of the absent member(s) of the family unless the provision of the information would be detrimental to the well-being of the child. States Parties shall further ensure that the submission of such a request shall of itself entail no adverse consequences for the person(s) concerned.

Article 12

1. States Parties shall assure to the child who is capable of forming his or her own views the right to express those views freely in all matters affecting the child, the views of the child being given due weight in accordance with the age and maturity of the child.

2. For this purpose, the child shall in particular be provided the opportunity to be heard in any judicial and administrative proceedings affecting the child, either directly, or through a representative or an appropriate body, in a manner consistent with the procedural rules of national law.

V. ANALYSIS

. . . .

D. Review of the Exercise of the Minister's Discretion

. . . .

(1) The Approach to Review of Discretionary Decision-Making

[51] As stated earlier, the legislation and Regulations delegate considerable discretion to the Minister in deciding whether an exemption should be granted based upon humanitarian and compassionate considerations. The Regulations state that "[t]he Minister is ... authorized to" grant an exemption or otherwise facilitate the admission to Canada of any person "where the Minister is satisfied that" this should be done "owing to the existence of compassionate or humanitarian considerations". This language signals an intention to leave considerable choice to the Minister on the question of whether to grant an H & C application.

. . . .

(3) Was this Decision Unreasonable?

[63] I will next examine whether the decision in this case, and the immigration officer's interpretation of the scope of the discretion conferred upon him, were unreasonable in the sense contemplated in the judgment of Iacobucci J. in *Southam, supra,* at para. 56:

> An unreasonable decision is one that, in the main, is not supported by any reasons that can stand up to a somewhat probing examination. Accordingly, a court reviewing a conclusion on the reasonableness standard must look to see whether any reasons support it. The defect, if there is one, could presumably be in the evidentiary foundation itself or in the logical process

by which conclusions are sought to be drawn from it.

In particular, the examination of this question should focus on the issues arising from the "serious question of general importance" stated by Simpson J.: the question of the approach to be taken to the interests of children when reviewing an H & C decision.

[64] The notes of Officer Lorenz, in relation to the consideration of "H & C factors", read as follows:

> The PC is a paranoid schizophrenic and on welfare. She has no qualifications other than as a domestic. She has FOUR CHILDREN IN JAMAICA AND ANOTHER FOUR BORN HERE. She will, of course, be a tremendous strain on our social welfare systems for (probably) the rest of her life. There are no H&C factors other than her FOUR CANADIAN-BORN CHILDREN. Do we let her stay because of that? I am of the opinion that Canada can no longer afford this type of generosity.

[65] In my opinion, the approach taken to the children's interests shows that this decision was unreasonable in the sense contemplated in *Southam, supra*. The officer was completely dismissive of the interests of Ms. Baker's children. As I will outline in detail in the paragraphs that follow, I believe that the failure to give serious weight and consideration to the interests of the children constitutes an unreasonable exercise of the discretion conferred by the section, notwithstanding the important deference that should be given to the decision of the immigration officer. Professor Dyzenhaus has articulated the concept of "deference as respect" as follows:

> Deference as respect requires not submission but a respectful attention to the reasons offered or which could be offered in support of a decision.... (D. Dyzenhaus, "The Politics of Deference: Judicial Review and Democracy", in M. Taggart, ed., *The Province of Administrative Law* (1997), 279, at p. 286.)

The reasons of the immigration officer show that his decision was inconsistent with the values underlying the grant of discretion. They therefore cannot stand up to the somewhat probing examination required by the standard of reasonableness.

[66] The wording of s. 114(2) and of Regulation 2.1 requires that a decision-maker exercise the power based upon "compassionate or humanitarian considerations" (emphasis added). These words and their meaning must be central in determining whether an individual H & C decision was a reasonable exercise of the power conferred by Parliament. The legislation and regulations direct the Minister to determine whether the person's admission should be facilitated owing to the existence of such considerations. They show Parliament's intention that those exercising the discretion conferred by the statute act in a humanitarian and compassionate manner. This Court has found that it is necessary for the Minister to consider an H & C request when an application is made: *Jiminez-Perez, supra*. Similarly, when considering it, the request must be evaluated in a manner that is respectful of humanitarian and compassionate considerations.

[67] Determining whether the approach taken by the immigration officer was within the boundaries set out by the words of the statute and the values of administrative law requires a contextual approach, as is taken to statutory interpretation generally: see *R. v. Gladue*, 1999 CanLII 679 (S.C.C.), [1999] 1 S.C.R. 688; *Rizzo & Rizzo Shoes Ltd. (Re)*, 1998 CanLII 837 (S.C.C.), [1998] 1 S.C.R. 27, at paras. 20–23. In my opinion, a reasonable exercise of the power conferred by the section requires close attention to the interests and needs of children. Children's rights, and attention to their interests, are central humanitarian and compassionate values in Canadian society. Indications of children's interests as important considerations governing the manner in which H & C powers should be exercised may be found, for example, in the purposes of the Act, in international instruments, and in the guidelines for making H & C decisions published by the Minister herself.

(A) THE OBJECTIVES OF THE ACT

[68] The objectives of the Act include, in s. 3(c):

> to facilitate the reunion in Canada of Canadian citizens and permanent residents with their close relatives from abroad;

Although this provision speaks of Parliament's objective of reuniting citizens and permanent residents with their close relatives from abroad, it is consistent, in my opinion, with a large and liberal interpretation of the values underlying this legislation and its purposes to presume that Parliament also placed a high value on keeping citizens and permanent residents together with their close relatives who are already in Canada. The obligation to take seriously and place important weight on keeping children in contact with both parents, if possible, and maintaining connections between close family members is suggested by the objective articulated in s. 3(c).

(B) INTERNATIONAL LAW

[69] Another indicator of the importance of considering the interests of children when making a compassionate and humanitarian decision is the ratification by Canada of the *Convention on the Rights of the Child*, and the recognition of the importance of children's rights and the best interests of children in other international instruments ratified by Canada. International treaties and conventions are not part of Canadian law unless they have been implemented by statute: *Francis v. The Queen*, 1956 CanLII 79 (S.C.C.), [1956] S.C.R. 618, at p. 621; *Capital Cities Communications Inc. v. Canadian Radio-Television Commission*, 1977 CanLII 12 (S.C.C.), [1978] 2 S.C.R. 141, at pp. 172–73. I agree with the respondent and the Court of Appeal that the Convention has not been implemented by Parliament. Its provisions therefore have no direct application within Canadian law.

[70] Nevertheless, the values reflected in international human rights law may help inform the contextual approach to statutory interpretation and judicial review. As stated in R. Sullivan, *Driedger on the Construction of Statutes* (3rd ed. 1994), at p. 330:

> [T]he legislature is presumed to respect the values and principles enshrined in international law, both customary and conventional. These constitute a part of the legal context in which legislation is enacted and read. In so far as possible, therefore, interpretations that reflect these values and principles are preferred. [Emphasis added.]

The important role of international human rights law as an aid in interpreting domestic law has also been emphasized in other common law countries: see, for example, *Tavita v. Minister of Immigration*, [1994] 2 N.Z.L.R. 257 (C.A.), at p. 266; *Vishaka v. Rajasthan*, [1997] 3 L.R.C. 361 (S.C. India), at p. 367. It is also a critical influence on the interpretation of the scope of the rights included in the *Charter*: *Slaight Communications*, *supra*; *R. v. Keegstra*, 1990 CanLII 24 (S.C.C.), [1990] 3 S.C.R. 697.

[71] The values and principles of the Convention recognize the importance of being attentive to the rights and best interests of children when decisions are made that relate to and affect their future. In addition, the preamble, recalling the *Universal Declaration of Human Rights*, recognizes that "childhood is entitled to special care and assistance". A similar emphasis on the importance of placing considerable value on the protection of children and their needs and interests is also contained in other international instruments. The United Nations *Declaration of the Rights of the Child* (1959), in its preamble, states that the child "needs special safeguards and care". The principles of the Convention and other international instruments place special importance on protections for children and childhood, and on particular consideration of their interests, needs, and rights. They help show the values that are central in determining whether this decision was a reasonable exercise of the H & C power.

(C) THE MINISTERIAL GUIDELINES

[72] Third, the guidelines issued by the Minister to immigration officers recognize and reflect the values and approach discussed above and articulated in the Convention. As described above, immigration officers are expected to make the decision that a reasonable person would make, with special consideration of humanitarian values such as keeping connections between family members and avoiding hardship by sending people to places where they no longer have connections. The guidelines show what the Minister considers a humanitarian and compassionate decision, and they are of great assistance to the Court in determining whether the reasons of Officer Lorenz are supportable. They emphasize that the decision-maker should be alert to possible humanitarian grounds, should consider the hardship that a negative decision would impose upon the claimant or close family members, and should consider as an important factor the connections between family members. The guidelines are a useful indicator of what constitutes a reasonable interpretation of the power conferred by the section, and the fact that this decision was contrary to their directives is of great help in assessing whether the decision was an unreasonable exercise of the H & C power.

[73] The above factors indicate that emphasis on the rights, interests, and needs of children and special attention to childhood are important values that should be considered in reasonably interpreting the "humanitarian" and "compassionate" considerations that guide the exercise of the discretion. I conclude that because the reasons for this decision do not indicate that it was made in a manner which was alive, attentive, or sensitive to the interests of Ms. Baker's children, and did not consider them as an important factor in making the decision, it was an unreasonable exercise of the power conferred by the legislation, and must, therefore, be overturned. In addition, the reasons for decision failed to give sufficient weight or consideration to the hardship that a return to Jamaica might cause Ms. Baker, given the fact that she had been in Canada for 12 years, was

ill and might not be able to obtain treatment in Jamaica, and would necessarily be separated from at least some of her children.

[74] It follows that I disagree with the Federal Court of Appeal's holding in *Shah, supra*, at p. 239, that a s. 114(2) decision is "<u>wholly</u> a matter of judgment and discretion" (emphasis added). The wording of s. 114(2) and of the Regulations shows that the discretion granted is confined within certain boundaries. While I agree with the Court of Appeal that the Act gives the applicant no right to a particular outcome or to the application of a particular legal test, and that the doctrine of legitimate expectations does not mandate a result consistent with the wording of any international instruments, the decision must be made following an approach that respects humanitarian and compassionate values. Therefore, attentiveness and sensitivity to the importance of the rights of children, to their best interests, and to the hardship that may be caused to them by a negative decision is essential for an H & C decision to be made in a reasonable manner. While deference should be given to immigration officers on s. 114(2) judicial review applications, decisions cannot stand when the manner in which the decision was made and the approach taken are in conflict with humanitarian and compassionate values. The Minister's guidelines themselves reflect this approach. However, the decision here was inconsistent with it.

[75] The certified question asks whether the best interests of children must be <u>a</u> primary consideration when assessing an applicant under s. 114(2) and the Regulations. The principles discussed above indicate that, for the exercise of the discretion to fall within the standard of reasonableness, the decision-maker should consider children's best interests as an important factor, give them substantial weight, and be alert, alive and sensitive to them. That is not to say that children's best interests must always outweigh other considerations, or that there will not be other reasons for denying an H & C claim even when children's interests are given this consideration. However, where the interests of children are minimized, in a manner inconsistent with Canada's humanitarian and compassionate tradition and the Minister's guidelines, the decision will be unreasonable.

E.   Conclusions and Disposition

[76] Therefore, both because there was a violation of the principles of procedural fairness owing to a reasonable apprehension of bias, and because the exer-

cise of the H & C discretion was unreasonable, I would allow this appeal.

[77] The appellant requested that solicitor–client costs be awarded to her if she were successful in her appeal. The majority of this Court held as follows in *Young v. Young*, 1993 CanLII 34 (S.C.C.), [1993] 4 S.C.R. 3, at p. 134:

> Solicitor–client costs are generally awarded only where there has been reprehensible, scandalous or outrageous conduct on the part of one of the parties.

There has been no such conduct on the part of the Minister shown during this litigation, and I do not believe that this is one of the exceptional cases where solicitor–client costs should be awarded. I would allow the appeal, and set aside the decision of Officer Caden of April 18, 1994, with party-and-party costs throughout. The matter will be returned to the Minister for redetermination by a different immigration officer.

[IACOBUCCI J. (for Cory J. and himself):]

[78] I agree with L'Heureux-Dubé J.'s reasons and disposition of this appeal, except to the extent that my colleague addresses the effect of international law on the exercise of ministerial discretion pursuant to s. 114(2) of the *Immigration Act*, R.S.C., 1985, c. I-2. The certified question at issue in this appeal concerns whether federal immigration authorities must treat the best interests of the child as a primary consideration in assessing an application for humanitarian and compassionate consideration under s. 114(2) of the Act, given that the legislation does not implement the provisions contained in the *Convention on the Rights of the Child*, Can. T.S. 1992 No. 3, a multilateral convention to which Canada is party. In my opinion, the certified question should be answered in the negative.

[79] It is a matter of well-settled law that an international convention ratified by the executive branch of government is of no force or effect within the Canadian legal system until such time as its provisions have been incorporated into domestic law by way of implementing legislation: *Capital Cities Communications Inc. v. Canadian Radio-Television Commission*, 1977 CanLII 12 (S.C.C.), [1978] 2 S.C.R. 141. I do not agree with the approach adopted by my colleague, wherein reference is made to the underlying values of an unimplemented international treaty in the course of the contextual approach to statutory interpretation and administrative law,

because such an approach is not in accordance with the Court's jurisprudence concerning the status of international law within the domestic legal system.

[80] In my view, one should proceed with caution in deciding matters of this nature, lest we adversely affect the balance maintained by our Parliamentary tradition, or inadvertently grant the executive the power to bind citizens without the necessity of involving the legislative branch. I do not share my colleague's confidence that the Court's precedent in *Capital Cities*, *supra*, survives intact following the adoption of a principle of law which permits reference to an unincorporated convention during the process of statutory interpretation. Instead, the result will be that the appellant is able to achieve indirectly what cannot be achieved directly, namely, to give force and effect within the domestic legal system to international obligations undertaken by the executive alone that have yet to be subject to the democratic will of Parliament.

[81] The primacy accorded to the rights of children in the Convention, assuming for the sake of argument that the factual circumstances of this appeal are included within the scope of the relevant provisions, is irrelevant unless and until such provisions are the subject of legislation enacted by Parliament. In answering the certified question in the negative, I am mindful that the result may well have been different had my colleague concluded that the appellant's claim fell within the ambit of rights protected by the *Canadian Charter of Rights and Freedoms*. Had this been the case, the Court would have had an opportunity to consider the application of the interpretive presumption, established by the Court's decision in *Slaight Communications Inc. v. Davidson*, 1989 CanLII 92 (S.C.C.), [1989] 1 S.C.R. 1038, and confirmed in subsequent jurisprudence, that administrative discretion involving *Charter* rights be exercised in accordance with similar international human rights norms.

(b) Rethinking the Relationship Between International and Domestic Law†

Armand de Mestral and Evan Fox-Decent

INTRODUCTION

In light of the increased significance of public international law since 1945, the proliferation of international treaties, and the basic obligation of all states to perform their international legal obligations in good faith, states have good reason to seek a measure of congruence between their domestic legal orders and international law. This article argues that Canada has not yet struck the appropriate balance between domestic and international law. Canadian law views the two legal orders as fundamentally distinct and separate from one another. The result is that Canadian domestic law and its institutions have failed to articulate a persuasive account of the relationship between domestic and international law.

In this article we take stock of how this relationship is currently understood in Canada. We also make a series of recommendations that aim to recast the relationship between the two legal orders as a unity. The relationship between domestic and international law, properly understood, enables the two legal orders to complement one another as a unified and coherent set of legal rules and principles. This unity, we suggest, flows from the idea that all law, domestic and international alike, establishes norms and standards to which public bodies and private parties can be held publicly accountable. The unity of domestic and international law, in other words, follows from a shared and overarching commitment to public accountability.[1]

In Part I we provide background to the article's recommendations and outline several considerations relevant to the relationship between domestic and international law in Canada. We consider the impact

† (2008) 53 McGill L.J. 573 at 575–602. This article first appeared in the McGill Law Journal. Reproduced with permission. [Notes and/or references omitted.]

of international law on Canadian domestic law and the worry that a democratic deficit attends international law-making. Part II analyzes those elements of the relationship between domestic and international law in Canada that pose concerns. In particular, we survey the approaches Canada has adopted to the domestic reception of customary and treaty law. Part III prescribes measures intended to contribute to the unity of domestic and international law. These measures relate to (1) parliamentary participation in treaty making, (2) implementation of international law in Canada, (3) the role of judges and administrative decision makers (e.g., tribunals, agencies, frontline decision makers, ministers), and (4) the role of provinces.

One of our main recommendations is that Canada should adopt a *Canada Treaties Act* in order to support the participation of legislators in the treaty-making process and to formalize the modes through which treaties may be implemented and received into Canada's domestic law. At the core of our argument is a new and generous approach to treaty implementation. Contrary to prevailing judicial opinion in Canada, we argue that treaties should be viewed as "implemented" — and therefore as capable of producing domestic legal effects — if Canadian law at the time of ratification provides sufficient discretionary or rule-making power to enable public decision makers to comply with Canada's international obligations.

I. BACKGROUND: CANADA AND THE CHALLENGE OF INTERNATIONAL LAW

Which institutions in Canada determine the relationship of domestic and international law? In the broadest sense all three branches of government — the executive, the judiciary, and the legislatures — are responsible for the current legal situation. Both the executive, charged with international relations, and the judiciary, charged with the interpretation of law, have been increasingly active throughout the twentieth century. For various reasons, the legislative branch has been largely absent from the making and interpretation of international law. This absence may be the source of much of the uncertainty that currently exists concerning the relationship between domestic and international law in Canada. Parliament and provincial legislatures have passed a host of laws giving effect to international rules, but they have seldom sought to be part of the making of the rules themselves. Instead, presumably with the willing concurrence of their respective governments, they prefer

to leave it to the executive branch to negotiate treaties and conduct international affairs, on the assumption that the conduct of international relations is an executive function. But as we shall see below, the constitution of Canada is silent on the matter, the few laws dealing with foreign affairs provide little guidance, and domestic interpretation acts contain only a few provisions on the role of customary international law and treaty law. There is no general legislation governing interpretation of treaties or the place of international law in the domestic legal order.

The result of legislative inaction is that the courts have been left to deal with the relationship between international and domestic law without legislative guidance or even much assistance from the executive branch. This problem has been compounded by the often puzzling positions taken by officers of the various attorneys general at the federal and provincial levels in litigation before the courts. Winning the case by using any argument at hand sometimes seems to be more important than ensuring Canada's compliance with its international legal obligations. This tendency is especially unfortunate since Canada has clearly entered a period of history in which the courts are faced with an ever-increasing number of cases that raise issues of international law.

A. The Impact of International Law on Domestic Law-Making

Customary international law is a direct source of domestic legal rules unless a state takes explicit measures to ensure that a particular customary rule does not have the force of domestic law.[2] Failing any such step, the customary rule can be applied by courts in litigation between citizens. International customary law can also limit the exercise of public authority and may equally define the parameters within which a state may legitimately legislate. For example, it can define the limits of the jurisdiction of states over persons and territory.

Turning now to treaty law, international agreements frequently lead to the enactment of domestic legislation. International law may give rise to domestic law, for example, when UN specialized agencies, such as the International Civil Aviation Organization (ICAO), the International Maritime Organization (IMO), and the World Health Organization (WHO) adopt rules that bind their member states in accordance with their respective constitutional structures.[3] The same organizations sometimes adopt rules in the form of treaties that are negotiated in regular or special sessions.[4] They may range from the most general and comprehensive "law-making" treaties, such as the third *United Nations Convention on the Law of the Sea*,[5] or human rights treaties establishing rules for the protection of different categories of persons, such as the *Convention on the Rights of the Child*,[6] to much more specific treaties dealing, for example, with the regulation of the construction of ships, such as the *International Convention for the Safety of Life at Sea, 1979*,[7] or commercial matters, such as the *Convention on International Interests in Mobile Equipment*.[8] Moreover, virtually every type of intellectual property is now the object of an international convention that has given rise to implementing legislation.[9] International trade treaties — bilateral, regional or multilateral — have also required extensive legislative implementation in Canada.[10]

The domestic effects of treaty law-making do not end with implementation. An increasing number of treaties include provisions for compulsory dispute settlement. These proceedings can lead to rulings that require the losing state to change its legislation or reverse administrative decisions already taken.[11]

We estimate that roughly 40 per cent of federal statutes implement international rules in whole or in part. Examples include the *Canada Shipping Act, 2001*,[12] the *Aeronautics Act*,[13] the *Broadcasting Act*,[14] the *Special Import Measures Act*,[15] the *Special Economic Measures Act*,[16] the *Export and Import Permits Act*,[17] the *Customs Tariff*,[18] the *Customs Act*,[19] the *North American Free Trade Agreement Implementation Act*,[20] the *World Trade Organization Agreement Implementation Act*,[21] the *Oceans Act*,[22] and the *Remote Sensing Act*.[23] Other examples include the many double taxation acts,[24] as well as legislation concerning among other things Canada's membership in various international organizations,[25] international environmental protection,[26] the international protection of migratory species,[27] endangered species and wildlife,[28] heritage protection,[29] enforcement of chemical and biological weapons conventions,[30] enforcement of international humanitarian law,[31] enforcement of international human rights law,[32] and international arbitral procedure.[33]

This list represents an impressive body of law. The federal government, provincial governments, and even municipalities must enforce such legislation. Most of these statutes deal with both domestic and international issues, and it is frequently difficult to determine where one field stops and the other begins.

Given that international treaties play such an important role in the Canadian legislative process, it is important to understand where these treaties come from and the forces that have shaped them. If they condition the content of Canadian laws, it is important that Canada plays an appropriate part in their negotiation and drafting to ensure that they reflect Canadian values and protect Canadian interests.

B. The Democratic Principle

To be free and democratic, Canada must remain in control of its legislative processes at every level of government. No sovereign democracy can be subject to foreign control over the kind of laws it must adopt. Yet many issues have to be dealt with at the international level.

Canada is not alone in facing this dilemma: in different ways, all states must face it. The member states of the European Union must, in many respects, cope with an even greater dilemma than Canada. The majority of laws regulating business transactions in the twenty-seven member states are now made in Brussels. Some of these laws are automatically applicable in each member state, while others must be transposed into domestic law and applied by member states. Short of exiting the European Union, no choice is offered once these E.U. regulations and directives are adopted.[34]

This phenomenon is not limited to legislation in the economic sphere; it is now a daily fact of life for E.U.-member legislatures, governments, and courts.[35] The issues of ensuring respect for domestic democracy and constitutional integrity vis-à-vis the E.U. legislative process have arisen in every member state. Problems have been most acute in those member states that possess a written constitution and a formal constitutional charter of rights. In Germany, a federal state governed by a complex constitutional document that includes a charter of rights, challenges have been made to E.U. laws or governing treaty amendments on the ground that they threaten constitutional protections of fundamental freedoms or central principles, such as democracy, in the *Basic Law* of Germany, the state's constitutional document.[36] The Federal Constitutional Court of Germany has on every occasion determined that legitimate bounds were not crossed by the ratification of the law or treaty in question.[37] However, the court has categorically affirmed its right to review E.U. treaty commitments in light of German constitutional principles and, if necessary, to declare that an E.U. measure must give way before the *Basic Law*.[38]

The E.U. example is perhaps unique, yet it contains lessons for all states. Interestingly, these lessons even apply to the European Union itself, the European Court of Justice having recently ruled that E.U.

regulations pursuant to mandatory sanctions of the UN Security Council under chapter VII of the *Charter of the United Nations*[39] cannot violate fundamental human rights guaranteed by E.U. law.[40] The dilemmas of E.U. member states with respect to E.U. law can be resolved by political action and common policy making within the E.U. framework of supranational legislative processes. This type of resolution is virtually impossible at the international level: the international community does not possess the institutions necessary to reconcile the immense political differences that exist between the almost two hundred member states of the international community. Nonetheless, the degree of cooperation and interaction between states is increasing year by year. The result is an ever-growing body of treaty law that affects the domestic. decisions of states.

Canada, like all other states, faces the dilemma of preserving its democracy and democratic legislative practices while accommodating the legitimate demands of international cooperation. In *Reference Re Secession of Quebec*,[41] the Supreme Court of Canada affirmed that "democracy expresses the sovereign will of the people" and that democratic institutions must allow for participation and accountability.[42] Nevertheless, the Court was quick to add that the significance of democracy is not exhausted by majority rule. Democratic institutions must rest on a legal foundation, and that foundation is supplied by one of the other organizing principles identified by the Court: the rule of law.[43] The domestic reception of international law must respect all these principles.

Our contention is that a concern for democracy and the rule of law supports a much more generous approach to the domestic effect of international law than the one currently taken by Canada's judiciary. A key aspect of the separation of international and domestic legal orders often stressed by Canadian courts is that treaties are made by the executive arm of government without parliamentary direction or participation. It is then argued that international law has scant legitimacy in the Canadian legal order unless it is formally implemented by a legislative act. We have argued elsewhere that this objection is unconvincing because domestic courts routinely impose duties, such as procedural fairness, on administrative decision makers without the prompt of statute.[44] That being said, a changed view of the place of treaties in the domestic legal order would be all the more appropriate if Parliament and the provincial legislatures were to signal their desire to enhance legislative involvement in the treaty-making process. But Canadian courts have been strongly influenced by the fact that treaties are made exclusively by the executive branch. It will thus not be a simple task to displace the view that treaties cannot have the force of law in the Canadian legal order without express legislative intervention.

This "dualist" approach to international law — one that conceives of international and domestic law as operating in separate domains, can be seen to be motivated by a desire to protect Canadians from the unlicensed intrusion of international law. The dualist approach allows the Canadian legal system to pick and choose the bits of international law it wishes to receive into its domestic law through legislative implementation. Dualism thus appeals to the populist democratic ideal of contemporary liberal democracies according to which law is to be made by popularly elected legislators.

Many other countries adopt a dualist position with respect to treaties. Few countries adopt an entirely "monist" approach, which affirms that treaties always have direct domestic effect merely upon ratification. Nonetheless, as we shall discuss below, there may be no developed country that continues to maintain as thoroughgoing a dualism as Canada.

How should Canada balance dualist and monist principles? We suggest that the approach to be followed is one that facilitates harmony between Canadian and international law by taking international law seriously when Canadian statutes are interpreted and applied. First of all, we argue that because customary international law is now clearly part of Canadian law, the rules of customary law should be enforceable by courts at the behest of individuals, unless the relevant legislature has expressly stated in its legislation that a particular customary rule is of no effect. Secondly, we propose that treaties, duly ratified and implemented by Canada, should be recognized as part of a common normative order that treats international law and domestic law as a unity. In other words, ratified and implemented treaties should be regarded as fully legitimate sources of law in Canada, and they should be treated as capable of producing legal effects in the Canadian legal system.

While the dualist approach admits that implemented treaties can produce domestic effects, we shall see that the dominant judicial understanding of implementation is deeply impoverished. Far more treaties deserve to be recognized as "implemented" than the courts currently acknowledge. We claim that all branches of government — Parliament, the provincial legislatures, the courts, and the different elements of the executive — can take a variety of steps to accomplish this objective. As outlined below, such steps relate to treaty adoption and legislative participation in the treaty process. But they also call for a more generous understanding of implementation by courts and administrative agencies. It should be acknowledged that Canadian domestic law is in most cases already consistent with international treaties at the time they are ratified. As a consequence, the search for explicit *ex post* implementing legislation as a threshold test for whether international law can have domestic effects is misguided.

II. THE CURRENT RELATIONSHIP BETWEEN DOMESTIC AND INTERNATIONAL LAW IN CANADA

International law requires each state to respect and fulfill its international obligations, but leaves to states a large degree of latitude as to how they will achieve this goal. Some countries, such as the Netherlands, are on the monist side of the spectrum: international law is assumed to have direct force of law in the domestic legal order.[45] Other states, such as the United States, have a hybrid system that makes considerable room for international law, while retaining several techniques requiring its positive implementation before it can have the force of law in the domestic system.[46] As noted above, Canada is at the dualist end of the spectrum. The Canadian position is somewhat surprising given Canada's historic commitment to the United Nations and to an international legal system based on law rather than power.[47] One might reasonably expect to find Canada at the other end of the spectrum or at least in the middle. The fact that Canada continues to maintain an increasingly outmoded approach to the matter is the principal reason for this article.

A. Customary International Law in Canada

International customary law, unlike treaties, does not emanate from intergovernmental negotiations, although it is heavily influenced by the practice of states. Rather, it develops through the cumulative practice of states in accordance with what is perceived as a governing legal obligation (*opinio juris*). Historically, there has been considerable authority for the proposition that rules of customary international law have the force of law in Canada and that they may be invoked before the courts. As discussed at the end of this section, this view has been recently reaffirmed by the Supreme Court of Canada in *R. v. Hape*.[48]

Two theories exist with regard to how international law can be incorporated into domestic law. Adoption theory holds that international law is automatically part of domestic law, except in cases where it conflicts with domestic statutory laws or the common law. Transformation theory holds that international law can only become incorporated into domestic law when it has been integrated into domestic law by way of a legislative enactment.[49] Customary international law enters a legal system automatically by way of adoption.

The adoption approach means that customary international law is deemed to form part of the common law. As Gibran van Ert notes, "[t]he common law looks on customary international law as a facet of itself."[50] Thus, when a court is satisfied that a given proposition amounts to a rule of customary international law, it will apply it as a rule of common law. The adoption theory thus invites courts not only to render decisions that are consistent with international law, "but to adopt international custom as the rules upon which their adjudication is based."[51] As Ronald St. J. Macdonald observes in this regard, "customary rules of international law are adopted automatically into our law, amid a few caveats about sovereignty, and then directly applied unless they conflict with statute or some fundamental constitutional principle in which case legislation is required to enforce them."[52]

A conflict between customary international law and domestic legislation may arise if an international custom changes. A conflict may also be triggered by the "expansion of international custom beyond its former bounds and into spheres of law formerly reserved to domestic adjudication."[53] Nevertheless, incorporating international customary law into the common law does not depart from the principle of self-government because this process leaves the legislature with the authority to change or modify the common law through statutory action.[54] Similarly, a state that persistently objects to the emergence of an international custom cannot be bound by it.

Customary international law does pose special difficulties for those arguing for its adoption into the domestic legal framework.[55] The difficulty results from the fact that the use of customary international norms requires the party seeking their application to demonstrate the existence of "wide-sweeping objective and subjective evidence of the establishment of a custom."[56] This burden is often hard to discharge, as it can be daunting to determine what states believe as opposed to what they say.[57] Notwithstanding this difficulty, the rule holding that customary international law is genuinely part of domestic law appears to be firmly entrenched in Canada as well as in other democracies.

The rule was affirmed by eminent English jurists as early as the eighteenth century. In *Buvot v. Barbuit*, Lord Talbot stated that the law of nations to "its fullest extent was and formed Part of the law of England."[58] This dictum was reiterated in a case by Lord Mansfield.[59] Similarly, in *Heathfield v. Chilton*, Lord Mansfield affirmed that "the law of nations ... is part of the common law of England."[60] The unity of customary international law with the common law was also affirmed by Lord Langdale in *Charles Duke of Brunswick v. The King of Hanover*.[61]

Canadian jurisprudence suggests that customary international law is applicable in Canada so long as it does not conflict with existing Canadian law. The adoption doctrine was confirmed in early decisions such as *The Ship "North" v. R.*,[62] in which Justice Davies sanctioned the adoption approach taken by early English authorities. He declared that "[t]he right of hot pursuit ... being part of the law of nations was properly judicially taken notice of and acted upon by the learned judge ... "[63] A relatively recent example of this approach is provided by *Reference Re Newfoundland Continental Shelf*.[64] The Supreme Court of Canada unanimously identified a relevant rule of customary international law in determining whether Canada or Newfoundland had the right to seek and exploit natural resources of the continental shelf at the moment of Newfoundland's entry into Confederation. Unfortunately, as noted by Van Ert, "[t]he [C]ourt's consideration of customary international law, while not inconsistent with [adoption], did not clearly invoke it."[65] Similarly, in the *Secession Reference*, while the Court took into account some aspects of international law with regard to state secession, "nowhere did it make clear that those parts of the law which were customary in nature enjoyed direct effect in Canadian law via the doctrine of [adoption]."[66]

Canadian courts could well rely on the interpretative authority of international customary law to address a wide range of human rights questions.[67] But in the context of customary law, it is difficult to fully agree with Justice La Forest's observation that human rights norms "are applied consistently, with an international vision and on the basis of international experience. Thus our courts — and many other national courts — are truly becoming international courts in many areas involving the rule of law."[68] Applications of international customary law by Canadian courts have been inconsistent and at times half-hearted. A recent Supreme Court of Canada decision failed to acknowledge the peremptory status of a *jus cogens* norm of customary international law — the kind of norm from which no derogation is possible.[69] In

Suresh v. Canada (Minister of Citizenship and Immigration), the Court considered the peremptory norm of security against torture, but would recognize only that the norm "cannot be easily derogated from."[70] In *114957 Canada Ltée (Spraytech, Société d'arrosage) v. Hudson (Town of)*, the majority hastily affirmed the precautionary principle's status as a rule of customary international law without even examining the requirements of state practice and *opinio juris*.[71]

This situation has led Stephen Toope to go as far as stating that "[w]e know for certain that we *do not* know whether customary international law forms part of the law of Canada."[72] As Van Ert has accurately remarked, "[t]he cases do not deny [adoption], but neither do they engage with customary international law as the doctrine — and the related doctrine of judicial notice — require."[73] As we shall see now, the *Hape* decision — the Court's most recent pronouncement on the issue at the time of writing — provides some salutary clarification.[74]

In *Hape*, Justice LeBel for the Court reaffirmed the rule that international customary law is part of the common law. It may thus be pleaded before the courts unless it is in direct conflict with the constitution or with a legislative act. Justice LeBel stated:

> In my view, following the common law tradition, it appears that the doctrine of adoption operates in Canada such that prohibitive rules of customary international law should be incorporated into domestic law in the absence of conflicting legislation.[75]

Although the rules regarding the adoption of customary international law have been clarified by this decision, a number of questions still remain as to how the Supreme Court of Canada and lower courts will apply this holding. The dictum quoted above refers to prohibitive rules of customary international law. Many customary rules, however, empower states or confer rights to be exercised by their nationals, such as the rules governing navigation on the high seas.

Moreover, proof of custom is a thorny issue. How will the courts approach the issue of proof of a rule or custom? In particular, will the courts seek guidance from the minister of foreign affairs? Will the courts continue to be more comfortable with evidence from expert witnesses on matters that arguably should simply be pleaded as law? Many courts in recent years, when faced with pleadings based on customary international law, have allowed the parties to furnish expert evidence in writing and in testimony, which allows for cross-examination.[76] This approach to customary law is scarcely consonant with the idea that Canadian courts are dealing with part of the law of Canada. Justice LeBel has removed many ambiguities but only the future will tell where *Hape* will take the law.[77]

The approach in *Hape* is consistent with the approaches to customary international law adopted by courts in other jurisdictions, including the United Kingdom.[78] Also, the constitutions of a number of countries, notably South Africa,[79] Germany,[80] and the United States,[81] explicitly establish that customary international law is part of domestic law.

B. Treaty Law and Treaty Making in Canada

Contemporary international rule making is done largely by means of treaties to which states can commit themselves. Once the drafting stage has been completed and the text is formally adopted the treaty is subject to ratification, a process of formal acceptance by each state that takes place according to the state's domestic procedures and the ratification requirements established in the treaty. Through ratification the state indicates that it is both willing and able to fulfill its obligations under the treaty.

Having taken the decision to ratify, each state must consider how the provisions of the treaty will be respected. This process is generally called implementation. Implementation refers to a range of steps that a state can take to ensure its compliance with the treaty. Many states, such as Canada, have adopted a wide variety of implementation methods, each tailored to the treaty in question and to the shape of domestic law. Some states must adopt new legislation when implementation requires a change in domestic law, while others give direct effect in their domestic law to the very words of the treaty and thus require no legislative intervention.

Since there is no international executive power, virtually all decisions concerning implementation depend upon the willingness of states to take appropriate measures, separately and in concert with others, to ensure that a treaty is put into operation. States must provide the means of administering a treaty and must ensure that their laws and public institutions are in a position to give full effect to the policies enshrined in the treaty. International organizations play an important coordinating role with respect to the implementation of a number of treaties, and a growing number of international organizations are empowered to inquire into the adequacy of domestic implementation.[82] But the state remains the primary vehicle through which treaty obligations are (or are not) fulfilled.

Some see state implementation as a source of weakness in the international legal system. But given the nature of the contemporary international order, it cannot, and arguably should not, be otherwise. States are closer to their populations than any international organization could be in the foreseeable future. Unless governments turn to tyranny and authoritarianism, states enjoy a far greater degree of legitimacy with their populations than international organizations. In the modern international order, enforcement of treaties by states ensures a vital degree of both efficacy and legitimacy.

1. How Does Canada Enter into Treaties?

Much scholarship has been devoted to the subject of Canadian treaty making and related diplomatic practice.[83] Internationally, treaty making is governed by the *Vienna Convention on the Law of Treaties*, adopted in 1969 and ratified by Canada in 1994.[84] Treaty making relating to the creation of new international organizations or under the aegis of the United Nations or other leading international organizations demands the most formal procedures.[85] Many major treaties are negotiated at international conferences specially convened for the purpose.[86] Some treaty negotiations are led by one or more like-minded states, which seek to promote a policy and then convene an international conference when the time is ripe for the conclusion of a treaty.[87]

In almost all cases, the individuals principally charged with treaty negotiation are diplomats or officials of government departments specially accredited for the purpose of negotiating a treaty. But governments recognize that the inclusion of a broad-based group of individuals in a negotiation is often of assistance in ensuring that negotiations yield positive results.[88] For example, in recent years, it has become common for major treaty-making conferences to be attended by large numbers of representatives of non-governmental organizations (NGOs).[89]

Until only last year there was no general official description of Canadian treaty-making practice, although a statement of treaty practice, prepared by the legal adviser of the Department of Foreign Affairs and International Trade (DFAIT), is published annually in the Canadian Yearbook of International Law.[90] But in 2008, the Treaty Section of the DFAIT published on its website a *Policy on Tabling of Treaties in Parliament*,[91] which closely follows the Ponsonby Rule, a U.K. procedure whereby treaties are laid before Parliament for at least twenty-one sitting days before ratification.[92] The policy puts flesh on the government of Canada's announcement on 25 January 2008 that it henceforth intends to table treaties in the House of Commons prior to ratification.[93] Nonetheless, the federal government still takes the position that it alone is authorized to negotiate and ratify international treaties. This principle is enshrined in the *Department of Foreign Affairs and International Trade Act*, which vests the conduct of foreign affairs, including the negotiation and ratification of treaties, in the minister and deputy minister of foreign affairs and international trade.[94]

Various departmental and interdepartmental committees consider and discuss the need for a treaty. The actual decision to initiate or participate in a treaty negotiation may be incremental or very formal. When officials determine that a formal decision is required, a policy on the matter is usually worked out by several federal interdepartmental committees, though it is possible that the policy can be developed by only one department. Regardless of how the underlying policy is developed, it must be approved by the federal cabinet. In most cases, the policy will be put to the appropriate committees of cabinet for approval. Some major decisions, involving significant treaties, are referred to the full cabinet for approval.

In short, the policy-formation process relating to treaty negotiation is entirely in the hands of the federal public service, subject to political direction from the federal cabinet and other elected members of the federal government. In formal terms, provincial, territorial, and First Nations governments are not part of this process. They can be invited to participate, but the invitation is entirely subject to the discretion of the federal government and public service.

Once a formal decision has been taken to initiate or participate in treaty negotiations, the method of negotiation must be established. Negotiations may be as simple as a summit-meeting decision signed by heads of state. Similarly, expeditious negotiations may take the form of a telephone call between officials in Ottawa and their counterparts elsewhere, followed by correspondence and ultimately the exchange of letters duly signed by the responsible ministers. At the opposite end of the spectrum might be a very complex negotiation on a matter of high political significance and public interest, as in the case of the 1988 *Free Trade Agreement Between the Government of Canada and the Government of the United States.*[95]

The typical negotiation is conducted by federal officials. In the event of a strong provincial interest, particularly if the subject matter falls within provincial jurisdiction, there is in almost all cases intergovernmental discussion between officials and possibly ministers. Yet, there is little uniformity of approach, nor is there a general framework, for federal–provincial consultations.[96] Public participation in treaty negotiation (or prior policy formation) is even more driven by political choice and ad hoc decision making. In some sectors, particularly those involving environmental issues and human rights issues, many NGOs clamour for attention and inclusion in the planning and negotiation of treaties.[97] Whether they succeed is left to the discretion of federal officials and those elected members of the federal government who direct them.

In other sectors, particularly those involving economic matters, commercial and industrial associations have developed a pattern of consultations with federal officials before and during negotiations.[98] But these situations seldom involve requests to participate in negotiations as such. These same groups are often consulted on the question of implementation. A similar pattern exists where the focus of treaty negotiations concerns health care, a profession, or a mode of transportation. Interested professional groups often have a fairly close relationship to the federal officials responsible for such treaty negotiations. There is little or no tradition of consultation with outside groups on issues that are predominately of international intergovernmental interest.

Many practitioners of international treaty making are skeptical of wide public participation in the treaty-making process. Their case, however, is much harder to make when it comes to the ratification of a treaty. Ratification is the decision by which Canada declares itself bound by international law and assumes the obligation to do everything necessary to ensure respect for its obligations under the treaty. Notwithstanding the new and laudable *Treaty-Tabling Policy*, the position of the Canadian government at the present time is that ratification is strictly an executive matter, regardless of how many Canadians might be affected and no matter what the division of legislative jurisdiction might be.[99] As a result, the federal government can commit Canada internationally, without any form of legislative consent, to treaty obligations requiring changes to both federal and provincial laws. Very serious consequences for Canadian federalism would ensue were it not for the fact that the federal government, out of prudence, does not actually ratify treaties requiring legislative changes until these changes have been adopted by Parliament or the provincial legislatures, or until it is confident that such changes as are necessary will be forthcoming.

It is important to emphasize that as a general rule, at both levels of government, law officers of the Crown have been careful to ensure that legislation is in place before authorizing ratification. And now, under the *Treaty-Tabling Policy*, the cabinet document seeking authorization to ratify a treaty must state the legislation or regulatory power under which Canada can perform its international obligations with respect to the treaty in question.[100] This responsibility is shared by both the DFAIT, which is ultimately charged with ratification, and the Department of Justice, which is charged with ensuring that adequate legislation and regulatory authority is in place.[101]

Such a careful consideration of domestic law can have the effect of delaying ratification for a considerable period. A particularly striking example of this delay was the ratification process surrounding the *International Convention on the Settlement of Investment Disputes Between States and Nationals of Other States*.[102] Signed in 1965 and quickly ratified by many states, the *ICSID* presented problems in Canada, as provincial governments insisted that arbitration, even over international investment, fell within the provincial powers over administration of justice. Rather than face both legal and political challenges, and despite considerable pressure from Canadian foreign investors, the federal government delayed signature until after 2006. Also, in the face of continued opposition from two provincial governments, it postponed ratification yet again, despite the fact that by that time, federal jurisdiction over international trade and investment had been considerably strengthened, legislation had been adopted at the federal and provincial levels, and provincial governments supported the practice of international arbitration.[103] Despite the obvious frustrations that these delays may cause, the speed at which ratification occurs does ensure that only a very small number of treaties are ratified without adequate implementing legislation or regulatory authority, though some ratifications are delayed for strictly political reasons.[104]

2. *Where Did the Canadian Approach Come From and What Is Currently Driving It?*

A. SOURCES OF THE DUALIST APPROACH

The body of public law received from the United Kingdom as a result of British colonization of North America has been an influential factor in Canada's approach to treaties. This body of law vested the conduct of international relations and treaty making in the Crown.[105] It also established the principle that a treaty could not amend the positive law of the land unless the change received positive legislative endorsement.[106] As we have seen, however,

U.K. public law did admit the principle that customary international law was part of the law of the land and could be enforced by the courts as domestic law.[107]

A further contributing factor has been the constitution of Canada and the division of powers between the provincial legislatures and Parliament. In *Canada (A.G.) v. Ontario (A.G.)*, which was decided in 1937 and remains the leading decision on treaty implementation in Canada, the Judicial Committee of the Privy Council, although asked to rule on both executive and legislative powers in respect of certain conventions, ruled only that legislative jurisdiction necessary to implement a treaty followed the normal division of powers and was not vested exclusively in Parliament.[108]

The result of *Labour Conventions* has been to establish a rule that the federal division of legislative powers requires treaties to be implemented in accordance with the federal principle. In so doing, the Privy Council refused to accept the proposition that there existed a "treaty power" beyond that created by section 132 of the *Constitution Act, 1867* concerning "Empire" treaties made for Canada by the United Kingdom.[109] Since no Empire treaties have been made since the time of these decisions, that power serves only to renew federal legislation in respect of such treaties as still remain.[110]

Canadian federalism raises the question of the role of the provincial crowns in international relations. An equally important issue is the capacity of the provincial legislatures to legislate in respect of treaty implementation covering matters within provincial jurisdiction. We discuss a number of the issues that complicate provincial participation in international affairs in Part III.E, below.

Also relevant in determining the role of the federal and provincial crowns in foreign affairs and treaty making is the unwritten law of the Royal Prerogative.[111] Apart from section 132 of the *Constitution Act, 1867*, and more recently section 11(g) of the *Canadian Charter of Rights and Freedoms*,[112] the constitution of Canada is silent on treaty making and the place of international law in the Canadian legal order.[113] Given the relative silence of the constitution on the matter, it is largely the exercise of the Royal Prerogative that sustains the federal government's claim to the exclusive exercise of the foreign-affairs power. Various federal and provincial laws governing interpretation of statutes or particular treaties, some of which we discuss below, apply to the exercise of the foreign-affairs and treaty powers.[114] But the origin of these powers traces back to the Royal Prerogative.

The Canadian approach to treaties and treaty making is thus an amalgam of history, principles of public law, case law, administrative practice, and legislative direction. Not surprisingly, it has generated significant scholarship in recent years.[115] The division of powers provides an answer to the question of whether the federal or provincial legislatures (or both) have jurisdiction to implement treaties. The issue of the relationship between treaties and Canada's domestic legal order, however, has largely been left to administrative practice, political debate at the occasional federal–provincial conference, and numerous judicial decisions that, in the main, affirm a strong commitment to dualism.[116] These decisions, and the dualist approach that underlies them, have played a leading role in determining the principles of public law applicable to treaty implementation, the status of treaties, and the interpretation of treaties.

B. LEGISLATIVE INTERPRETATION AND THE PRINCIPLE OF CONFORMITY

To some extent the commitment to dualism is tempered by the interpretive presumption of conformity that calls on administrative officials and courts to interpret domestic law in a manner that respects Canada's international legal obligations.[117] In *Baker v. Canada (Minister of Immigration)*, the Supreme Court of Canada reviewed a minister's refusal to exercise his discretionary authority to stay a deportation on humanitarian and compassionate grounds in the case of a woman with Canadian-born dependent children.[118] In its analysis, the Court considered whether the *Convention on the Rights of the Child* could be used as an interpretative instrument in reviewing the exercise of the minister's discretion.[119] At issue was article 3 of the convention, which states that "[i]n all actions concerning children, whether undertaken by public or private social welfare institutions, courts of law, administrative authorities or legislative bodies, the best interests of the child shall be a primary consideration."[120] The convention had been ratified by Canada but, in the view of Justice L'Heureux-Dubé, had not yet been implemented and given effect under Canadian domestic law because no specific statute had been adopted whose purpose was implementation.[121] Nonetheless, the majority held that "the [concern for children's best interests] reflected in *international* human rights law may help inform the contextual approach to statutory interpretation and judicial review."[122]

In his remarkable book *Using International Law in Canadian Courts*, Gibran van Ert makes a powerful implicit case that many of the problems regarding the proper relationship of domestic and international law in Canada can be resolved by reference to the presumption of conformity.[123] In an earlier article, we have also noted the potential of the presumption of conformity to promote a more harmonious relationship between the two legal orders.[124] The presumption is further discussed at various points in this article. Nonetheless, we will argue below that legislative intervention and major policy changes to parliamentary practice are also desirable.

Since the adoption of the *Charter* the courts have been asked many times to determine the relevance of international human rights law to *Charter* interpretation, with the case law increasing almost exponentially.[125] In some decisions, however, the courts have put Canada in conflict with important ratified treaties or fundamental principles of public international law.[126]

The courts are thus dealing with arguments based on international treaty law on a routine basis. But they still lack clear guidance as to the approach they should adopt in different circumstances. Even the various interpretation acts have little to say to judges who are called upon to apply either treaties or laws based on treaties. The federal *Interpretation Act* states the following:

> 15(1) Definitions or rules of interpretation in an enactment apply to all the provisions of the enactment, including the provisions that contain those definitions or rules of interpretation.
>
> (2) Where an enactment contains an interpretation section or provision, it shall be read and construed
>
> (a) as being applicable only if a contrary intention does not appear; and
>
> (b) as being applicable to all other enactments relating to the same subject-matter unless a contrary intention appears.[127]

This section has been judicially considered on a number of occasions[128] but does not appear to have had a major influence on the interpretation of treaties. Its greatest influence may be to suggest, by its very brevity, that treaties play a very small role in statutory interpretation and that they must give way to statutes. Even less guidance is provided with respect to the place of customary international law.[129] Similarly, many provincial interpretation acts contain limited guidance on the place of treaty law.[130]

c. Treaty Approval

No Canadian statute contains specific provisions on the approval of treaties except the *Loi sur le ministère des Relations internationales*.[131] This act, which was first adopted by the National Assembly of

Quebec in 1988 and amended in 2002, gives the National Assembly an important role, along with the *ministre des relations internationales*, in the process of approval and implementation of treaties by the province of Quebec.[132] The law was adopted to regulate the process followed by Quebec in implementing treaties whose subject matter falls within provincial jurisdiction, and to clarify the role of the government of Quebec in the approval of all such treaties. While the government of Quebec has shown considerable interest in treaty approval, it has made less effort to clarify the status of rules of customary international law that fall within provincial jurisdiction. With the exception of possible implicit references in articles 2807 and 3155 to 3165 C.C.Q.,[133] the Civil Code of Quebec does not clarify the place of customary international law in the law of Quebec.

Some federal statutes contain indications of their relationship to treaties, as we discuss in Part III.C.1. But what is missing from federal implementing legislation is any sense of order or any governing principle. Each law appears to have been developed separately with very little regard to the development of a common approach to implementation.

One very striking absence from Canadian statutory texts is any reference to the *Vienna Convention*, although it is an important part of the *Treaty-Tabling Policy*.[134] The *Vienna Convention* is so widely adopted that many authorities have suggested that the convention is largely, if not entirely, declaratory of customary international law. The convention sets out two fundamental rules. Article 26 lays down the principle that states are obligated to fulfill their treaty commitments in good faith.[135] Article 27 stipulates that states, having made a treaty commitment, cannot plead internal legal or constitutional difficulties in mitigation of their treaty obligations.[136] In other words, the *Vienna Convention* requires states to fulfill their obligations and brooks few excuses by states for the failure to do so. It reinforces the legal duty incumbent upon Canada when a treaty commitment is made and should be a powerful message to Canadian judges called upon to rule, directly or indirectly, on a matter involving a treaty ratified by Canada. Sadly, no Canadian law deals with these principles and this important source has seldom been cited by the courts. At best, it can be argued that the rules of the *Vienna Convention* reflect customary international law and are thus part of the domestic law of Canada. Legislative affirmation of this fact would be a powerful message to the judiciary and might well embolden the courts to give treaties greater weight when deciding cases.[137]

It is encouraging that the government recently announced that it intends to bring Parliament back into the treaty-approval process. On 25 January 2008, the federal government announced that henceforth all treaties between Canada and other states or entities would be tabled in the House of Commons.[138] As noted above, this policy has been further developed in the *Treaty-Tabling Policy*.[139] Under this new procedure the government is required to table "all instruments governed by public international law, between Canada and other states or international organizations ... " in the House of Commons.[140] It must also observe a waiting period of twenty-one sitting days from the date of the tabling before taking any action to make the treaty binding upon Canada. When treaties require legislative amendment, the government will be bound to delay consideration of any implementing legislation until this twenty-one sitting-day period has passed.[141]

This initiative is welcome and long overdue. It will give parliamentarians an opportunity to debate the content of treaties that they consider worthy of scrutiny. But such a debate will only take place in time allotted to the opposition parties and at their behest. A further restriction is that, when Parliament reconvenes, parliamentarians may have to choose to debate many treaties within the twenty-one sitting days that have accumulated over the period of the parliamentary recess. As well, the minister of foreign affairs and international trade and lead ministers may request from the prime minister an exemption from the necessity of tabling.[142]

Nonetheless, other features further strengthen the policy's value. The policy requires that each treaty be accompanied on tabling in the House of Commons by an Explanatory Memorandum setting out considerable information on the objectives and impact of the treaty, including a statement on the chosen means of implementation.[143] In addition, the policy is also accompanied by instructions to departments of government on the process of seeking authorization from cabinet to negotiate a treaty, and it sets out the various stages of the participation of departments in the treaty-negotiation and approval process. It is in many respects a codification and will be of great utility to government departments and to the public in following the process.[144]

Yet, however well the new policy works, we suggest in Part III.B.3 that this initiative essentially reverts to the prevailing practice up to 1968, leaves unanswered many questions regarding the legal significance of parliamentary approval or disapproval, and comes much too late in the treaty-making process.

(c) Prosecuting Mass Rape: *Prosecutor v. Dragoljub Kunarac, Radomir Kovac and Zoran Vukovic*†

Doris Buss

INTRODUCTION

On February 22, 2001, the trial chamber of the International Tribunal for the former Yugoslavia (I.C.T.Y.)[1] delivered its decision in *Prosecutor v. Dragoljub Kunarac, Radomir Kovac and Zoran Vukovic*,[2] convicting the three male defendants of the rape, torture and enslavement of Muslim women in the municipality of Foca, Bosnia-Hercegovina. The decision is noteworthy in several respects. It is the first case solely to focus on the rape, torture and mistreatment of women during the armed conflict in Yugoslavia. It is the first case to prosecute successfully rape as a crime against humanity, and it is the first case to consider the phenomena of 'mass rape' in the context of Bosnia-Hercegovina.

For me personally, the decision is additionally important in light of my own scepticism about the I.C.T.Y.'s capacity to address rape and other wartime violence against women. In a 1998 article (Buss, 1998), I argued that the legal remit of the Tribunal reflected stereotypical constructions of women as 'victims', and left unchallenged discourses of war, militarism and nationalism that function to elide women's suffering with the suffering of the nation and, consequently, to marginalise women's experience of violence. Thus, as a long-awaited statement about how women's particular experiences during war are treated by the international community, *Kunarac* is an opportunity to take measure of the I.C.T.Y. and to consider if, in fact, it has lived 'up' to my low expectations.

In the following case comment, I aim to do three things. First, to provide an outline of the decision in *Kunarac*, exploring the significance of recognising rape as a crime against humanity. Second, I consider *Kunarac* in the context of earlier international developments in the area of rape and sexual violence, noting the several aspects of the decision which significantly advance international legal recognition of wartime violence against women. Third and finally, I evaluate *Kunarac* in light of my previous concerns about the I.C.T.Y. While concluding that the decision is important and contains a number of positive developments, I argue that there are aspects of the war crimes trial, as evidenced in *Kunarac*, which are still of concern for feminists seeking to secure greater international action on violence against women.

1. THE DECISION

In April 1992, the city and [municipality] of Foca were overtaken by Serb forces. Muslims living in Foca and the surrounding area[] were attacked, expelled from the region, and/or[] detained, with women, children and some older men taken to detention centres at the local high school and sports hall. Prior to the war in Bosnia-Hercegovina,[3] fifty-two per cent of the 40,513 inhabitants of the Foca Municipality were Muslim. After the conflict, approximately ten Muslims remained.[4] For the Muslims detained in Foca, conditions were extreme. The facilities were unhygienic, little food was available, and the prisoners were subject to beatings,[5] and, in the case of women and girls, repeated rapes.[6]

It is this latter development that concerns the judgement in *Kunarac*. Serb soldiers routinely raped the women and girls kept at the local school and sports hall. The three defendants were involved, in different capacities, with those rapes as well as with the removal of a group of women and girls, most of them ranging in age from twelve to twenty, from these centres to local houses/apartments, where they were raped by the defendants and other soldiers. Some of these women were detained for several months and were subject to constant rapes, taken as the 'property' of the individual defendants, and made to do housework, cleaning, and cooking.[7] After a period of time, some of these women/girls, including a twelve-year-old, were then sold to other soldiers. The twelve-year-old girl was never seen again.[8]

The three defendants were charged under the Statute of the Yugoslav Tribunal with various crimi-

---

† (October 2002) 10:3/4 Feminist Legal Studies 91–99. Reproduced with kind permission from Springer Science and Business Media. [Notes and/or references omitted.]

nal offences. The Yugoslav Tribunal has authority, from the United Nations Security Council,[9] to prosecute violations of the laws of war, grave breaches of the Geneva Conventions, crimes against humanity, and genocide committed within the territory of the former Yugoslavia. The Tribunal's statute — its constituting document — outlines the types of acts considered 'criminal' for the purposes of the Tribunal. It was drafted to reflect only the most settled areas of international humanitarian law, and to include, to the extent that this allowed, provisions that would cover crimes committed under a policy of 'ethnic cleansing.' As such, it is a curious balancing act between a conservative and reactive reading of international humanitarian law, and an innovative document, seeking to open up a new era of international adjudication of war 'crimes'. The result is a complex set of rules that aims to elaborate and condemn systematic persecution of groups, within a juridical system focused on the individual acts of individual defendants against specific members of the 'civilian' population.

The result is that indictments, such as those in *Kunarac*, are lengthy and convoluted, referring to individual acts and patterns of activity, and laying charges under multiple headings. In the context of *Kunarac*, the defendants were charged with rape as a crime against humanity (Article 5 (g) of the I.C.T.Y. statute) and as a violation of the laws of war (Article 3), and rape as torture, constituting both a crime against humanity (Article 5 (h)) and a violation of the laws of war (Article 3). In addition, the defendants were charged with enslavement as a crime against humanity (Article 5 (c)) and with outrages upon personal dignity (Article 3). In most cases, the multiple charges of rape (as a crime against humanity and as a violation of the laws of war) and torture (also as a crime against humanity and as a violation of the laws of war) are made in respect of the same incident. The reasons for this relate to the ad-hoc development of humanitarian law, the details of which are too lengthy for this comment.[10] However, the multiple charges are significant because they constitute the recognition that wartime rape occurs in different contexts, for different reasons, with various impacts.

For example, rape is specifically referred to in the I.C.T.Y. statute as a crime against humanity; an offence committed as part of an attack against a civilian population. Crimes against humanity evolved out of the Nuremberg tribunal as a means to criminalise the actions of the Nazi regime against particular communities such as the Jews. A crime against humanity is an act, such as rape, which is part of a larger attack on a group of people. The attack on the community must be "widespread or systematic", and the accused must have knowledge "of the wider context in which his acts occur".[11] In the Yugoslav context, charges of crimes against humanity are directed at the 'ethnic cleansing' — the forced removal, by various means, of whole populations from specific regions — that resulted in widespread, outrageous violations of humanitarian law.[12]

In *Kunarac*, the Tribunal found that individual acts of rape committed against Muslim women by the accused amounted to crimes against humanity, and were part of a larger policy to terrorise Muslims, evict them from the area, and convert the region into a Serb stronghold. For example, the Tribunal noted that in addition to substantial evidence of a Serb policy to "gain supremacy over the Muslims in the region" (para. 579), the defendant Kunarac made clear that "the rapes against the Muslim women were one of the many ways in which the Serbs could assert their superiority and victory over the Muslims" (para. 583). After raping one Muslim woman, Kunarac "told her that she should enjoy being 'fucked by a Serb' ... [adding] that she would now carry a Serb baby and would not know who the father would be" (*ibid.*).

Rape was also charged as a violation of the laws of war under Article 3 of the Tribunal's statute.[13] Under this provision, rape does not have to constitute an act against a population but it does have to occur in the context of an armed conflict and there must be a close nexus between the rape and the armed conflict.[14] Thus, rape as a crime against humanity and as a crime of war relate not so much to two distinct acts as distinct motivations or contexts. In *Kunarac*, the Tribunal found the accused guilty of acts of rape as both crimes against humanity and violations of the laws of war.

Like rape, torture was alleged to constitute a violation of the laws of war and a crime against humanity. Torture, in this context, refers to rape as a "means of punishing, intimidating, coercing or humiliating the victim, or obtaining information, or confession, from the victim or a third person".[15] The Tribunal found the accused guilty of torture as a crime against humanity and as a violation of the laws of war. The three defendants were also found guilty of enslavement (a crime against humanity) and of outrages upon personal dignity (violations of the laws of war).

2. *KUNARAC* IN CONTEXT

The mass rape of Muslim women in the war in Bosnia-Hercegovina was a headline grabbing event, shocking the (largely complacent) Western world,[16] and mobilizing feminist activists.[17] The decision to include rape in the Tribunal's statute and in subsequent indictments was a hard-fought battle by feminists against an implacable international community. The extent of the resistance to action against wartime violence against women is remarkable. Despite the widespread publicity of mass rape of women during the Yugoslav conflict and the inclusion of rape as a crime within the reach of both the Yugoslav and Rwandan tribunals, prosecutors have not always been willing to include rape in the indictments. For example, the first case before the Rwandan Tribunal, *The Prosecutor v. Akayesu*,[18] did not include references to rape, and indeed, the human rights investigators in Rwanda overlooked and failed to pursue lines of inquiry about rape.[19] It was not until Judge Navanethem Pillay, the only woman on the bench hearing *Akayesu*, pursued her own line of questions, that it emerged rape had been a significant part of the campaign against Rwandan Tutsis.[20]

Thus, the decision in *Kunarac* is an important development and a hard-won victory in gaining international recognition of the different ways in which women are vulnerable during armed conflict. It also sends a clear signal that wartime violence against women is being taken seriously and acted upon, at least at the level of ad-hoc criminal prosecutions. Aspects of the decision in *Kunarac* are also promising, particularly in the area of the legal definition of rape and enslavement. The Tribunal held that the definition of rape, first outlined in the *Prosecutor v. Furundžija*,[21] did not sufficiently address the factors that might "render an act of sexual penetration *non-consensual*" (para. 438, emphasis in original). The *Kunarac* tribunal ruled that in considering coercion, force, and lack of consent, the test should be if a victim's "sexual autonomy" has been violated (para. 457). The language of sexual autonomy allows the Tribunal to consider a broad range of factors and conditions that might negate consent. This was particularly relevant in *Kunarac* where two of the defendants alleged that some of the sexual activity between them and individual Muslim women was consensual. The Tribunal, after considering the overall pattern of conduct of the accused, and the relative position of the victims, refused to accept that consent had been given.[22]

In finding two of the defendants guilty of enslavement, the Tribunal provides some indication of how the law in this area is developing. While directing its comments to the particular facts before it, the Tribunal adopted a broad definition of enslavement as "the exercise of any or all of the

powers attached to the right of ownership over a person" (para. 540). Factors suggesting enslavement include:

> the control of someone's movement, control of physical environment, psychological control, measures taken to prevent or deter escape, forces, threat of force or coercion, duration, assertion of exclusivity, subjection to cruel treatment and abuse, control of sexuality and forced labour (para. 543).

While there was evidence of trafficking in Muslim women, the Tribunal held that this was not a requirement of enslavement. According to Regan Ralph, Human Rights Watch, this will form "the basis to prosecute others who enslave women around the world."[23]

3. *RETHINGING RAPE?*

Having been a skeptic of the I.C.T.Y. process, has the decision in *Kunarac* changed my mind? In some respects, it has. *Kunarac* is an important outcome in an international environment unreceptive to acting on women's human rights abuses. In addition to the intransigence of the I.C.T.R., attempts to include specific 'gender' crimes in the newly drafted statute of the International Criminal Court[] resulted in lengthy debates, and a reluctance to recognise crimes such as 'forced pregnancy'.[24] Thus, although there have been substantial expressions of international support for combating violence against women, it is difficult to translate that commitment into action. *Kunarac* may go a long way in securing substantive action on violence against women.

Second, the jurisprudence coming out of the I.C.T.Y. and I.C.T.R., in the context of violence against women, appears progressive on many levels. Witnesses are entitled to protection and can retain their anonymity, no corroboration of a victim's testimony in a sexual assault case is required, the Tribunal has established a victim and witness protection unit, and the Tribunal's rules of procedure include a 'rape shield' provision, limiting evidence of victims' sexual history.[25]

Despite these important developments, I retain some scepticism about the I.C.T.Y. and its capability to meaningfully address violence against women. The Tribunal's willingness to adopt a broad, flexible and arguably progressive approach to rape and women's 'sexual autonomy' is laudable, but arguably not that surprising in the context of the war in Yugoslavia. Wartime rape, perhaps more than any other, closely approximates what is popularly perceived as 'real rape' — stranger rape. It is the 'ideal' of rape, where an innocent, helpless woman is at the mercy of a brutal stranger. In this context, issues of consent and competing narratives of women's sexuality that dominate rape trials in Western domestic legal systems[26] are more easily marginalised. The evidence of ethnic cleansing, the detention of Muslim women and girls, and the overwhelming evidence of Serb brutality provide a, perhaps unshakeable, foundation for finding that rape occurred on a mass scale. I am not suggesting by this that the Tribunal's findings were somehow inevitable. Indeed, it is likely that the Tribunal's willingness to take a progressive approach to sexual violence is the result of hard work by feminist activists. My concern is that these developments may leave unchallenged dominant assumptions and constructions of women's sexuality and their role — as 'victims' — in wartime. The more difficult question is if violence against women, which does not fit so easily within the mold of 'stranger rape'[,] can be acted upon within the limits of the war crimes trial.

The model of the war crimes trial, based on an adversarial system, can be a limiting environment within which to bring cases of sexual abuse. The [decisions] in *Kunarac* and other cases[] have an air of unreality about them. The decisions relate horrible experiences of abuse and suffering, at the same time as those experiences are measured against convoluted and sometimes archaic rules of evidence and relevance. In *Kunarac*, for example, the decision runs to over 300 pages and contains masses of evidence and testimony on the experience of women raped and abused while in detention. In evaluating this evidence, the Tribunal details individual acts of abuse, noting times, places, supporting evidence. On a number of indictments, the Tribunal rules that there is insufficient evidence, or the indictment has not been properly drawn, to sustain a conviction. The result is bizarre. After reading pages and pages of witness evidence about the existence of what are, in effect, 'rape camps', the Tribunal then dismisses individual charges of rape for lack of evidence. Arguably, within a strict reading of criminal evidence and international law, the Tribunal is 'right' in its conclusion, but the very process of analysis feels particularly ill suited to the task of accounting for, and reconciling the experiences of[,] these women. What lesson do we take away from a Tribunal that can, on the one hand, find evidence of rape camps, and yet find that individual women are not to be believed in their accounts of rape and violence at those same camps? In this respect, the Yugoslav Tribunal reproduces many of the same problematic aspects of 'the rape trial' found in Western domestic legal systems. Does this mean that feminists and others should not seek to use this system to prosecute rape and sexual violence? Certainly not. But it does raise additional questions about the war crimes tribunal as a mechanism of reconciliation and resolution in a post-conflict situation.

(d) *Abdelrazik v. Canada (Foreign Affairs)*[†]

[ZINN J.:]

[1] Mr. Abdelrazik lives in the Canadian Embassy in Khartoum, Sudan, his country of citizenship by birth, fearing possible detention and torture should he leave this sanctuary, all the while wanting but being unable to return to Canada, his country of citizenship by choice. He lives by himself with strangers while his immediate family, his young children, are in Montreal. He is as much a victim of international terrorism as the innocent persons whose lives have been taken by recent barbaric acts of terrorists.

[2] Mr. Abdelrazik says that the government of Canada has engaged in a course of conduct designed to thwart his return to Canada and in so doing has breached his right as a citizen of Canada pursuant to section 6 of the *Canadian Charter of Rights and Freedoms* (the Charter) to enter or return to Canada. He describes the actions taken by Canada and its failure to act as "procrastination, evasiveness, obfuscation and general bad faith."

[3] Canada challenges that characterization of its conduct. It says that the impediment to Mr.

---

† [2009] F.C.J. No. 656, 2009 FC 580, at paras. 1–7, 45–57, 130–38, 148–69.

Abdelrazik's return is not of its making but is that of the United Nations Security Council 1267 Committee which has listed Mr. Abdelrazik as an associate of Al-Qaida, thus making him the subject of a global asset freeze, arms embargo and travel ban.

[4] There is a tension between the obligations of Canada as a member of the UN to implement and observe its resolutions, especially those that are designed to ensure security from international terrorism and the requirement that in so doing Canada conform to the rights and freedoms it guarantees to its citizens.

[5] In addition to the tension between Canada's international and national obligations, there is also a tension in this case between the roles of the executive and the judiciary. This is a positive tension; it results from the balancing necessary in a constitutional democracy that follows the rule of law. Lord Woolf[1] described this positive tension in the following manner:

> The tension ... is acceptable because it demonstrates that the courts are performing their role of ensuring that the actions of the Government of the day are being taken in accordance with the law. The tension is a necessary consequence of maintaining the balance of power between the legislature, the executive and the judiciary ...

[6] The rule of law provides that the Government and all who exercise power as a part of the Government are bound to exercise that power in compliance with existing laws. It is one of the "fundamental and organizing principles of the Constitution": *Reference re Secession of Québec*, 1998 CanLII 793 (S.C.C.), [1998] 2 S.C.R. 217 at para. 32. When the Government takes actions that are not in accordance with the law, and its actions affect a citizen, then that citizen is entitled to an effective remedy. Mr. Abdelrazik seeks such an effective remedy. He seeks an Order of this Court directing Canada to repatriate him to Canada "by any safe means at its disposal." The respondents submit that no such remedy is required as there has been no violation of Mr. Abdelrazik's rights by Canada and they further submit that in requesting such an Order the applicant is asking this Court to improperly tread on the rights and powers of the executive.

[7] I find that Mr. Abdelrazik's Charter right to enter Canada has been breached by the respondents. I do not find that Canada has engaged in a course of conduct and inaction that amounts to "procrastination, evasiveness, obfuscation and general bad faith." I do find, however, there has been a course of conduct and individual acts that constitute a breach of Mr. Abdelrazik's rights which the respondents have failed to justify. I find that Mr. Abdelrazik is entitled to an appropriate remedy which, in the unique circumstances of his situation, requires that the Canadian government take immediate action so that Mr. Abdelrazik is returned to Canada. Furthermore, as a consequence of the facts found establishing the breach and the unique circumstances of Mr. Abdelrazik's circumstances, the remedy requires that this Court retain jurisdiction to ensure that Mr. Abdelrazik is returned to Canada.

. . . .

LEGAL BACKGROUND

. . . .

Canada's International Obligations

[45] Article 24 of the *Charter of the United Nations* (the UN Charter) confers "primary responsibility for the maintenance of international peace and security" on the Security Council. Pursuant to Article 41 of the UN Charter, the Security Council may decide on measures to be employed to give effect to its decisions and call upon member nations to apply them.

[46] Article 25 of the UN Charter provides that "Members of the UN agree to accept and carry out the decisions of the Security Council in accordance with the present Charter." Canada is a member of the UN and in furtherance of its obligations has enacted the *United Nations Act*, R.S.C. 1985, c. U-2 which provides that the Governor in Council may make such orders and regulations as are "necessary or expedient" to effect decisions of the UN Security Council.

[47] In 1999, in response to the August 7, 1998 bombing of United States of America embassies in Nairobi, Kenya and Dar es Salaam, Tanzania, by Usama bin Laden and his associates, the UN Security Council passed Resolution 1267. Resolution 1267 was directed at the Taliban who were permitting their territory to be used by bin Laden and his associates. Section 4 of Resolution 1267 set out the measures the Security Council imposed on member nations. These were originally limited to a ban on Taliban aircraft landing or taking off from member states' territory, save for humanitarian purposes or for the performance of religious obligations such as the performance of the Hajj, and to a freeze on funds and financial resources of the Taliban. A

Committee of all members of the Security Council (the 1267 Committee) was established to implement Resolution 1267 and report back to the Council.

[48] The sanctions set out in Resolution 1267 has been modified and strengthened by subsequent resolutions, including resolutions 1333 (2000), 1390 (2002), 1455 (2003), 1526 (2004), 1617 (2005), 1735 (2006) and 1822 (2008) so that the sanctions now apply to designated individuals and entities associated with Al-Qaida, Usama bin Laden and the Taliban wherever located. Specifically, by Resolution 1390 adopted January 16, 2002, these measures were expanded to address the Al-Qaida network and other associated terrorist groups as a response to the attacks on the United States of America on September 11, 2001. Notwithstanding these further Resolutions, the oversight group continues to be known as the 1267 Committee. The most recent Resolution, and that which presently applies to Mr. Abdelrazik as a consequence of being listed, is Resolution 1822, adopted June 30, 2008.

[49] As noted, Mr. Abdelrazik was listed by the 1267 Committee as being associated with Al-Qaida. Section 2 of Resolution 1822 defines "associated with" as including, but not being restricted to the following:

(a) participating in the financing, planning, facilitating, preparing, or perpetrating of acts or activities by, in conjunction with, under the name of, on behalf of, or in support of;

(b) supplying, selling or transferring arms and related materiel to;

(c) recruiting for; or

(d) otherwise supporting acts or activities of;

Al-Qaida, Usama bin Laden or the Taliban, or any cell, affiliate, splinter group or derivative thereof.

[50] A Study commissioned by the United Nations Office of Legal Affairs, summarizes the lack of legal procedures available to persons listed by the 1267 Committee.[3]

> Targeted individuals and entities are not informed prior to their being listed, and accordingly do not have an opportunity to prevent their inclusion in a list by demonstrating that such an inclusion is unjustified under the terms of the respective Security Council resolution(s). There exist different de-listing procedures under the various sanctions regimes, but in no case are individuals or entities allowed directly to petition the respective Security Council committee for de-listing. Individuals or entities are not granted a hearing by the Council or a committee. The de-listing procedures presently being in force place great emphasis on the States particularly involved ("the original designating government" which proposed the listing, and "the petitioned government" to which a petition for de-listing was submitted by an individual or entity) resolving the matter by negotiation. Whether the respective committee, or the Security Council itself, grants a de-listing request is entirely within the committee's or the Council's discretion; no legal rules exist that would oblige the committee or the Council to grant a request if specific conditions are met.

> At the same time, no effective opportunity is provided for a listed individual or entity to challenge a listing before a national court or tribunal, as UN Member States are obliged, in accordance with Article 103 of the UN Charter, to comply with resolutions made by the Security Council under Chapter VII of the UN Charter. If, exceptionally, a domestic legal order allows an individual directly to take legal action against a Security Council resolution, the United Nations enjoys absolute immunity from every form of legal proceedings before national courts and authorities, as provided for in Article 105, paragraph 1, of the UN Charter, the General Convention on the Privileges and Immunities of the United Nations (General Assembly Resolution 1/22A of 13 February 1946) and other agreements.

> It has been argued by leading scholars of international law that the present situation amounts to a "denial of legal remedies" for the individuals and entities concerned, and is untenable under principles of international human rights law: "Everyone must be free to show that he or she has been justifiably placed under suspicion and that therefore [for instance] the freezing of his or her assets has no valid foundation." [footnotes and citations omitted]

[51] I add my name to those who view the 1267 Committee regime as a denial of basic legal remedies and as untenable under the principles of international human rights. There is nothing in the listing or de-listing procedure that recognizes the principles of natural justice or that provides for basic procedural fairness. Unlike the first Canadian security certificate scheme that was rejected by the Supreme Court in *Charkaoui v. Canada (Minister of Citizenship and Immigration)*, 2007 SCC 9 (CanLII), 2007 SCC 9; [2007] 1 S.C.R. 350, the 1267 Committee listing and de-listing processes do not even include a limited right to a hearing. It can hardly be said that the 1267 Committee process meets the requirement of independence and impartiality when, as appears may be the case involving Mr. Abdelrazik, the nation requesting the listing is one of the members of the

body that decides whether to list or, equally as important, to de-list a person. The accuser is also the judge.

[52] The 1267 Committee process has been amended since its inception to include a requirement that a narrative summary of the reasons for listing be included on the web site of the Consolidated Listing. Notwithstanding that Resolution 1822 provides that such information is also to be provided for those, such as Mr. Abdelrazik, who were previously listed, there is not yet any such narrative provided as regards the rationale for the listing of Mr. Abdelrazik.

[53] Originally de-listing requests could only be made by the individual's home State. Again, there has been an amendment to allow a listed individual to make an application personally to the 1267 Committee or to do so through his home State. The *Guidelines of the Committee for the Conduct of Its Work* provide that a petitioner seeking de-listing "should provide justification for the de-listing request by describing the basis for this request, including by explaining why he/she no longer meets the criteria described in paragraph 2 of resolution 1617 (2005)..." (emphasis added). Those criteria are the four criteria set out above in paragraph 49. For a person such as Mr. Abdelrazik who asserts that he never met the criteria and was wrongly listed in the first instance, it is difficult to see how he can provide the requested justification, particularly when he has no information as to the basis for the initial listing. Section 7(g)(iii) of the Guidelines further provide that if the request for de-listing is a repeat request and if it does not contain any information additional to that provided in the first request, it is to be returned to the petitioner without consideration. It is difficult to see what information any petitioner could provide to prove a negative, i.e. to prove that he or she is not associated with Al-Qaida. One cannot prove that fairies and goblins do not exist any more than Mr. Abdelrazik or any other person can prove that they are not an Al-Qaida associate. It is a fundamental principle of Canadian and international justice that the accused does not have the burden of proving his innocence, the accuser has the burden of proving guilt. In light of these shortcomings, it is disingenuous of the respondents to submit, as they did, that if he is wrongly listed the remedy is for Mr. Abdelrazik to apply to the 1267 Committee for de-listing and not to engage this Court. The 1267 Committee regime is, as I observed at the hearing, a situation for a listed person not unlike that of Josef K. in Kafka's *The Trial*, who awakens one morning and,

for reasons never revealed to him or the reader, is arrested and prosecuted for an unspecified crime.

[54] The UN Security Council itself has recognized the extreme difficulty persons listed have to obtain de-listing. In the Security Council Report *Update Report, April 21, 2008, No. 4* respecting the 1267 Committee it is stated:

> It is far easier for a nation to place an individual or entity on the list than to take them off. For example, the US last year wanted to remove Abdul Hakim Monib, a former Taliban minister who switched sides and until recently served as the governor of Afghanistan's Uruzgan province, working with US and NATO troops. But Russia blocked it. In other cases, the US has prevented removal of names and entities it has submitted for suspected involvement with Al-Qaida. (emphasis added)

I pause to comment that it is frightening to learn that a citizen of this or any other country might find himself on the 1267 Committee list, based only on suspicion.

[55] There are three general consequences set out in section 1 of Resolution 1822 that flow from being listed by the 1267 Committee: an asset freeze, a travel ban and an arms embargo. Only the first two are relevant for our purposes.

[56] The asset freeze set out in paragraph 1(a) requires member nations to freeze the assets of listed persons and requires that member nations ensure that neither the funds of the listed persons "nor any other funds, financial assets or economic resources are made available, directly or indirectly, for such persons' benefit..." The respondents submit that this measure prevents Canada, or anyone within Canada, from paying for transportation to Canada or providing such transportation for Mr. Abdelrazik. It was as a consequence of this measure that Canada sought an exemption from this restriction in order to provide Mr. Abdelrazik with the monthly loan it currently provides as well as the facilities it provides him in the Canadian Embassy in Khartoum.

[57] The travel ban set out in paragraph 1(b) requires member states to prevent the entry into or transit through their territories of listed individuals. There are three exceptions to the ban which the applicant submits would permit him to enter Canada. This submission will be considered in the Analysis section. The relevant provision reads as follows:

> 1(b) Prevent the entry into or transit through their territories of these individuals, provided

that nothing in this paragraph shall oblige any State to deny entry or require the departure from its territories of its own nationals and this paragraph shall not apply where entry or transit is necessary for the fulfilment of a judicial process or the Committee determines on a case-by-case basis only that entry or transit is justified;

. . . .

ISSUES

Whether Canada Violated Mr. Abdelrazik's Right to Enter Canada

. . . .

The flight scheduled for April 3, 2009

[130] In March 2009, Mr. Abdelrazik managed to obtain and pay for a flight from Khartoum to Montreal with a stop over in Abu Dhabi. He had been repeatedly assured for years that an emergency passport would be provided in that eventuality. Notwithstanding the numerous assurances given by Canada over a period of almost 5 years, and repeated as recently as December 23, 2008, on April 3, 2009 just two hours before the flight was to leave, the Minister of Foreign Affairs refused to issue that emergency passport on the basis that he was of the opinion, pursuant to Section 10.1 of the *Canadian Passport Order*, "that such action is necessary for the national security of Canada or another country."

[131] The respondents make a number of submissions urging this Court not to consider or examine this refusal as part of the applicant's Charter challenge. With the greatest of respect for these respondents and their counsel, I find that none of these submissions has merit. In light of the challenge the applicant has made asserting that his Charter rights have been violated, and in light of the evidence reviewed thus far, a failure of this Court to consider this refusal, in these circumstances, would bring the administration of justice into disrepute.

[132] The respondents firstly submit that because section 10.1 of the *Canadian Passport Order* has been found by the Federal Court of Appeal in *Canada (Attorney General) v. Kamel*, 2009 FCA 21 (CanLII), 2009 FCA 21, not to offend the Charter, it follows that decisions of the Minister made pursuant to the section likewise comply with the Charter. This submission is fundamentally contrary to the decision of the Supreme Court of Canada in *Eldridge v. British Columbia (Attorney General)*, 1997 CanLII 327 (S.C.C.), [1997] 3 S.C.R. 624. At paragraph 20 of

that decision, the Court said that the *Canadian Charter* can apply in two ways — to the legislation or to decisions made under the legislation.

> First, legislation may be found to be unconstitutional on its face because it violates a *Charter* right and is not saved by s. 1. In such cases, the legislation will be invalid and the Court compelled to declare it of no force or effect pursuant to s. 52(1) of the *Constitution Act, 1982*. Secondly, the *Charter* may be infringed, not by the legislation itself, but by the actions of a delegated decision-maker in applying it. In such cases, the legislation remains valid, but a remedy for the unconstitutional action may be sought pursuant to s. 24(1) of the *Charter*.

This view has more recently been affirmed by that Court in *Multani v. Commission scolaire Marguerite Bourgeoys*, 2006 SCC 6 (CanLII), 2006 SCC 6.

[133] Therefore, although there is no doubt that section 10.1 of the *Canadian Passport Order* has been found to be constitutionally valid by the Federal Court of Appeal in *Kamel*, it does not follow that every refusal of the Minister made pursuant to that section must necessarily also be constitutionally valid. The issue before the Federal Court of Appeal in *Kamel* was limited to whether section 10.1 violated section 6 of the Charter and, if it did, whether it was justified under section 1. In his judgment, Justice Décary was careful to note: "I will not comment on other aspects of this case, and nothing in my reasons shall be interpreted as having an impact on the decision the Minister will eventually make after reconsidering Mr. Kamel's passport application." In other words, while the section is valid, the decision made under it may not be.

[134] As is implied in section 4(3) of the *Canadian Passport Order*, the issuance or refusal to issue a passport is a matter of royal prerogative. The Supreme Court of Canada in *Operation Dismantle Inc. v. The Queen et al.*, 1985 CanLII 74 (S.C.C.), [1985] 1 S.C.R. 441 held that where the Crown prerogative violates an individual's rights provided in the Charter, then the exercise of the prerogative can be reviewed by the Court.

[135] The Federal Court of Appeal in *Veffer v. Canada (Minister of Foreign Affairs)*, 2007 FCA 247 (CanLII), 2007 FCA 247; [2008] 1 F.C.R. 641 at paragraph 23 has also specifically confirmed that the exercise of the royal prerogative in the issuance of passports is subject to examination for compliance with the Charter.

... [T]here is no question that the Passport Canada policy is subject to Charter scrutiny, even though the issuance of passports is a royal prerogative. As stated by Justice Laskin in *Black v. Canada (Prime Minister)* 2001 CanLII 8537 (ON C.A.), (2001), 54 O.R. (3d) 215 (C.A.), at paragraph 46:

> By s. 32(1)(*a*), the Charter applies to Parliament and the Government of Canada in respect of all matters within the authority of Parliament. The Crown prerogative lies within the authority of Parliament. Therefore, if an individual claims that the exercise of a prerogative power violates that individual's Charter rights, the court has a duty to decide the claim.

[136] The respondents submit that the validity of the Minister's decision of April 3, 2009 not to issue an emergency passport is not a matter that this Court may consider in the present application. It is argued that the proper course was for the applicant to file a judicial review application under section 18.1 of the *Federal Courts Act* challenging that decision. It is submitted that unless that course is taken, the Court does not have a proper evidentiary record before it on which to assess the validity of the decision.

[137] A similar submission was made by the Crown and rejected by this Court in *Khadr v. Canada (Attorney General)*, 2006 FC 727 (CanLII), [2007] 2 F.C.R. 218, 2006 FC 727. The Crown asked the Court not to decide the issue of whether the failure to issue a passport to Mr. Khadr was contrary to sections 6 and 7 of the Charter because of the inadequacy of the record. I adopt without reservation the following from paragraphs 57–59 of that decision of Justice Phelan:

> The respondent's concern for the record is two-fold. Firstly, the respondent acknowledges that the applicant was not treated fairly because he did not have a chance to address the new grounds for denial of a passport — national security. This assumes that the Minister had the right to create this new ground outside the bounds of the *Canadian Passport Order*. Secondly, the respondent says that it has not put forward sufficient section 1 Charter evidence to demonstrate that any breach of a Charter right is justified.
>
> The simple response to that is that the respondent cannot deprive the applicant of his rights to a proper determination because of the respondent's failure to put forward proper evidence. The applicant must take the record as it is — not the record it would like. So too, the respondent has to take the record it created — it

does not get a second chance to create a further and better record.

> With respect to section 1 evidence, the respondent gambled that the Charter arguments would be dismissed without the necessity of a section 1 analysis. Sometimes the gamble does not pay out.

[138] Justice Phelan ultimately determined that he would not decide the case on Charter grounds because, as stated in *Baker v. Canada (Minister of Citizenship and Immigration)*, 1999 CanLII 699 (S.C.C.), [1999] 2 S.C.R. 817, "courts should refrain from dealing with *Charter* issues raised in an application for judicial review where it is unnecessary to do so". In this case, the only claim raised by this applicant is his Charter claim; he has not raised the claim that the decision was procedurally unfair and contrary to the rules of natural justice. Accordingly, it is necessary in this case to determine the Charter issue raised with respect to the decision.

. . . .

[148] In my view, the submission that the applicant had not been denied entry into Canada by the Government of Canada was not accurate when made 6 days after the Minister had denied the applicant an emergency passport. Whether or not the Etihad Airways flight scheduled for April 3, 2009 would breach the travel ban set out in the 1822 Resolution, there is no evidence before the Court that had Mr. Abdelrazik been in possession of an emergency passport issued by Canada that he would not have been on that flight and now in Canada. I find that the only reason that Mr. Abdelrazik is not in Canada now is because of the actions of the Minister on April 3, 2009.

[149] The respondents submit that the right to enter Canada as provided for in subsection 6(1) of the Charter does not entail positive obligations on Canada. Their submission, to paraphrase Justice L'Heureux-Dubé in *Haig v. Canada*, 1993 CanLII 58 (S.C.C.), [1993] 2 S.C.R. 995, is that the freedom to enter Canada contained in subsection 6(1) prohibits Canada from refusing a citizen's entry into the country (subject to section 1) but does not compel Canada to take positive steps such as the issuance of a passport or the provision of an airplane to effect travel to Canada.

[150] In *Gosselin v. Quebec (Attorney General)*, 2002 SCC 84 (CanLII), 2002 SCC 84; [2002] 4 S.C.R. 429, a case involving section 7 of the Charter, the Supreme Court acknowledged that one day the Char-

ter may be interpreted to include positive obligations such that the failure to do the positive act will constitute a breach of the Charter. It was there stated:

> The question therefore is not whether s. 7 has ever been — or ever will be — recognized as creating positive rights. Rather, the question is whether the present circumstances warrant a novel application of s. 7 as the basis for a positive state obligation to guarantee adequate living standards.

[151] This Court and the Federal Court of Appeal in *Kamel* in the passage below noted the critical importance of a passport, not just to engage in travel, but for a citizen to enter Canada.[5] The fact that Mr. Abdelrazik had secured and paid for a flight for April 3, 2009 back to Canada but was prevented from flying only because he lacked the emergency passport previously promised by Canada, proves that importance.

> The appellant submits that subsection 6(1) of the Charter, which gives every Canadian citizen "the right to enter, remain in and leave Canada", does not impose a duty on the state to facilitate the international travel of Canadian citizens. The appellant also maintains that the respondent has not demonstrated that a passport is required to enter or leave Canada.
>
> At the hearing, we did not consider it useful to hear the respondent on this issue. In fact, we agree substantially with Justice Noël's remarks on this point. To determine that the refusal to issue a passport to a Canadian citizen does not infringe that citizen's right to enter or leave Canada would be to interpret the Charter in an unreal world. It is theoretically possible that a Canadian citizen can enter or leave Canada without a passport. In reality, however, there are very few countries that a Canadian citizen wishing to leave Canada may enter without a passport and very few countries that allow a Canadian citizen to return to Canada without a passport (A.B., Vol. 7, p. 1406, Thomas Affidavit). The fact that there is almost nowhere a Canadian citizen can go without a passport and that there is almost nowhere from which he or she can re-enter Canada without a passport are, on their face, restrictions on a Canadian citizen's right to enter or leave Canada, which is, of course, sufficient to engage Charter protection. Subsection 6(1) establishes a concrete right that must be assessed in the light of present-day political reality. What is the meaning of a right that, in practice, cannot be exercised?

[152] I agree with the Court of Appeal. In my view, where a citizen is outside Canada, the Government of Canada has a positive obligation to issue an emergency passport to that citizen to permit him or her to enter Canada; otherwise, the right guaranteed by the Government of Canada in subsection 6(1) of the Charter is illusory. Where the Government refuses to issue that emergency passport, it is a *prima facie* breach of the citizen's Charter rights unless the Government justifies its refusal pursuant to section 1 of the Charter. As noted in *Cotroni*, the Supreme Court held that such interference must be justified as being required to meet a reasonable state purpose. In *Kamel* the Federal Court of Appeal held that section 10.1 of the *Canadian Passport Order* was a reasonable state purpose; however, the respondent must still establish that the decisions made under section 10.1 are "justified" on a case by case basis.

[153] I find that the applicant's Charter right as a citizen of Canada to enter Canada has been breached by the respondents in failing to issue him an emergency passport. In my view, it is not necessary to decide whether that breach was done in bad faith; a breach, whether made in bad faith or good faith remains a breach and absent justification under section 1 of the Charter, the aggrieved party is entitled to a remedy. Had it been necessary to determine whether the breach was done in bad faith, I would have had no hesitation making that finding on the basis of the record before me. As I have noted throughout, there is evidence that supports the applicant's contention that the Government of Canada made a determination in and around the time of the listing by the 1267 Committee that Mr. Abdelrazik would not be permitted to return to Canada. The only legal way to accomplish that objective was by order made pursuant to section 10.1 of the *Canadian Passport Order*. Rather than instituting that process then, Canada put forward a number of explanations as to why he was not being provided with an emergency passport, only some of which were accurate: he is on a no-fly list and commercial air carriers will not board him; he has secured an itinerary but not paid for the flight; he is listed on the 1267 Committee list and cannot fly in the air space of Member States; and lastly, when he had managed to meet the last condition set by Canada that he have a paid ticket, the refusal is necessary for the national security of Canada or another country. This was an opinion the Minister was to make only after the process prescribed by his own department was followed, giving Mr. Abdelrazik an opportunity to know of and address concerns. Not only was that not done, the Minister waited until the very last minute before the flight was to depart to deny the emergency passport,

and although the basis of the refusal is indicated, he provides no explanation of the basis on which that determination was reached, no explanation as to what had changed while Mr. Abdelrazik resided in the Canadian embassy that warranted this sudden finding, and nothing to indicate whether the decision was based on him being a danger to the national security of Canada or on being a danger to another country. Further, there was no explanation offered as to whether Mr. Abdelrazik posed a security risk if returned to Canada, or a greater security risk[] than he did in Sudan. In my view, denying a citizen his right to enter his own country requires, at a minimum, that such increased risk must be established to justify a determination made under section 10.1 of the *Canadian Passport Order*. If he poses no greater risk, what justification can there be for breaching the Charter by refusing him to return home; especially where, as here, the alternative is to effectively exile the citizen to live the remainder of his life in the Canadian Embassy abroad. In short, the only basis for the denial of the passport was that the Minister had reached this opinion; there has been nothing offered and no attempt made to justify that opinion.

[154] The respondents have provided no evidence to support a section 1 defence to the *prima facie* breach of the Charter from refusing to issue the emergency passport. They simply submitted to the Court that there had been no breach. Having found a breach, the burden then shifted to the respondents to justify that breach. In the absence of any evidence, it has not been justified. Notwithstanding this, I have considered whether the Minister's determination that Mr. Abdelrazik posed a danger to national security or to the security of another country constitutes a section 1 defence in itself and have concluded that it does not.

[155] As previously noted, the guidelines of Passport Canada provide that whenever a citizen may be denied passport privileges, there is a mechanism in place that provides the citizen with procedural fairness and natural justice. It is fair to assume that the minister put these processes in place in his Department in recognition of a citizen's Charter rights and the special relationship that exists between a citizen and his country. There is no suggestion that the Minister followed this process. In fact, the Minister appears to have made the decision to deny the emergency passport with no input from Passport Canada. He had many years to render such a decision after following the processes set by his own department, if there was any basis to support his opinion. He did not. There is nothing in the report

of his decision to indicate that his decision is made based on recent information he has received. There is nothing to indicate the basis on which he reached his decision. Even if a decision such as his can be said to have been a decision prescribed by law as it is based on section 10.1 of the *Canadian Passport Order* the decision itself must also be shown to be justified as being required to meet a reasonable State purpose, as the Supreme Court stated in *Cotroni*. It is simply not sufficient for the Minister to say that he has reached this opinion and "trust me" — he must show more; he must establish that it was "required". While it is not the function of the judiciary to second guess or to substitute its opinion for that of the Minister, when no basis is provided for the opinion, the Court cannot find that the refusal was required and justified given the significant breach of the Charter that refusing a passport to a Canadian citizen entails. In this case, the refusal of the emergency passport effectively leaves Mr. Abdelrazik as a prisoner in a foreign land, consigned to live the remainder of his life in the Canadian Embassy or leave and risk detention and torture.

[156] I have found that Canada has engaged in a course of conduct and specific acts that constitute a breach of Mr. Abdelrazik's right to enter Canada. Specifically, I find:

(i) That CSIS was complicit in the detention of Mr. Abdelrazik by the Sudanese authorities in 2003;

(ii) That by mid 2004 Canadian authorities had determined that they would not take any active steps to assist Mr. Abdelrazik to return to Canada and, in spite of its numerous assurances to the contrary, would consider refusing him an emergency passport if that was required in order to ensure that he could not return to Canada;

(iii) That there is no impediment from the UN Resolution to Mr. Abdelrazik being repatriated to Canada — no permission of a foreign government is required to transit through its airspace — and the respondents' assertion to the contrary is a part of the conduct engaged in to ensure that Mr. Abdelrazik could not return to Canada; and

(iv) That Canada's denial of an emergency passport on April 3, 2009, after all of the pre-conditions for the issuance of an emergency passport previously set by Canada had been met, is a breach of his Charter right to enter Canada, and it has not been shown to be saved under section 1 of the Charter.

[157] Having found that the applicant's right as a citizen of Canada to enter this country has been breached by Canada, he is entitled to an effective remedy.

What is the effective remedy?

[158] I agree with the respondents that a Court should not go further than required when fashioning a remedy for a Charter breach: *Doucet-Boudreau v. Nova Scotia (Minister of Education)*, 2003 SCC 62 (CanLII), [2003] 3 S.C.R. 3. In this case, the applicant is entitled to be put back to the place he would have been but for the breach — in Montreal.

[159] In saying this, I am mindful of the international law principle that "reparation must, as far as possible, wipe-out all the consequences of the illegal act and re-establish the situation which would, in all probability, have existed if that act had not been committed," as it was put by the Permanent Court of International Arbitration in the *Chorzow Factory Case (Ger. v. Pol.)*, (1928) P.C.I.J., Sr. A, No.17, at 47 (September 13). To quote Chief Justice Dickson in the *Reference Re Public Service Employee Relations Act (Alta.)*, 1987 CanLII 88 (S.C.C.), [1987] 1 S.C.R. 313, at para. 57, "[t]he various sources of international human rights law — declarations, covenants, conventions, judicial and quasi-judicial decisions of international tribunals, customary norms — must, in my opinion, be relevant and persuasive sources for interpretation of the *Charter*'s provisions." Similarly, I am of the view that principles of international law are helpful where it is necessary to fashion a just and appropriate Charter remedy, as is the case here.

[160] Accordingly, at a minimum, the respondents are to be ordered to provide Mr. Abdelrazik with an emergency passport that will permit him to travel to and enter Canada. There is any number of ways available to him to return to Canada. He once secured an airline ticket and may be able to do so again. In the Court's view that would cure the breach and be the least intrusive on the role of the executive. If such travel is possible, and if funds or sufficient funds to pay for an air ticket are not available to the applicant from his April 3, 2009 unused ticket, then the respondents are to provide the airfare or additional airfare required because, but for the breach, he would not have to incur this expense.

[161] The applicant has asked that the respondents return him to Canada "by any safe means at its disposal." In my view, the manner of returning Mr.

Abdelrazik, at this time, is best left to the respondents in consultation with the applicant, subject to the Court's oversight, and subject to it being done promptly.

[162] The respondents may submit that they are unable to provide any financial assistance to permit Mr. Abdelrazik to return to Canada as Resolution 1822 prohibits it. As noted, an exception to the travel ban and asset freeze is the fulfilment of a "judicial process".

[163] "Process" is defined in the *Canadian Oxford Dictionary* (2nd ed.) to mean "a course of action or proceeding". *Black's Law Dictionary* (8th ed.) states that "process" means "the proceedings in any action or prosecution". A judicial process means the same as a judicial proceeding. The Supreme Court of Canada in *Markevich v. Canada*, 2003 SCC 9 (CanLII), [2003] 1 S.C.R. 94, 2003 SCC 9 discussed the meaning of the word "proceeding" as found in the *Crown Liability and Proceedings Act*, R.S.C. 1985, c. C-50 and found it to have a broad meaning. Its observations are equally applicable here.

> Although the word "proceeding" is often used in the context of an action in court, its definition is more expansive. The Manitoba Court of Appeal stated in *Royce v. MacDonald (Municipality)* (1909), 12 W.L.R. 347, at p. 350, that the "word 'proceeding' has a very wide meaning, and includes steps or measures which are not in any way connected with actions or suits". In *Black's Law Dictionary* (6th ed. 1990), at p. 1204, the definition of "proceeding" includes, *inter alia*, "an act necessary to be done in order to obtain a given end; a prescribed mode of action for carrying into effect a legal right

[164] Accordingly, a judicial process, for the purposes of the exemption from the asset freeze and travel ban, encompasses more than the issuance of a summons to appear as a witness before a Court as was submitted by the respondents. It includes all steps in the judicial process, including the steps required by Order of the Court as a part of the completion of the suit or application. This view is supported by the French language version of Security Council Resolution 1617 which uses the phrase "le présent paragraphe ne s'applique pas lorsque l'entrée ou le transit est nécessaire pour l'aboutissement d'une procédure judiciaire". On a plain meaning reading "aboutissement" means "outcome, result".[6] Thus it would include, in my view, measures required to be taken in execution or the completion of a Court order.

[165] In this case, any such assistance provided by Canada is in fulfilment of this judicial process and is not a violation of the UN Resolution.

[166] It is further required, in the Court's opinion that the respondents, at Canada's expense, provide an escort from Foreign Affairs to accompany Mr. Abdelrazik on his flight from Khartoum to Montreal, unless he waives the requirement for an escort. In my view, this is required to ensure that Mr. Abdelrazik is not stopped or delayed in his return to Canada while in transit or when laying-over at a foreign airport. The escort is to use his very best efforts to ensure that Mr. Abdelrazik returns to Canada unimpeded. To use the words of Foreign Affairs earlier — this is their contribution to ensure that he does return to Canada.

[167] It is further required, in the Court's judgment that the Court satisfy itself that Mr. Abdelrazik has in fact returned to Canada. Accordingly, in fulfilment of this judicial process, the Court requires that Mr. Abdelrazik attend before it at the time and date specified in the Judgment.

[168] The Court reserves the right to oversee the implementation of this Judgment and reserves the right to issue further Orders as may be required to safely return Mr. Abdelrazik to Canada.

[169] As agreed upon by the parties, costs are reserved. The applicant shall provide his submissions on costs to the respondents and file a copy with the Court, not exceeding 15 pages, within 15 days of this Judgment. The respondents shall serve and file their reply submissions, not exceeding 15 pages within a further 15 days. The applicant shall have a further 10 days to reply, not exceeding 10 pages.

JUDGMENT

THIS COURT ORDERS AND ADJUDGES that:

1. This application is allowed;
2. The applicant's right to enter Canada has been breached contrary to subsection 6(1) of the Charter;
3. The respondents are directed to issue the applicant an emergency passport in order that he may return to and enter Canada;
4. The respondents, after consultation with the applicant, are to arrange transportation for the applicant from Khartoum to Montreal, Canada such that he arrives in Canada no later than 30 days from the date hereof;
5. Should such travel arrangements not be in place within 15 days of the date hereof, the parties shall advise the Court and an immediate hearing shall be held at which time the Court reserves the right to issue such further Orders as are deemed necessary in order to ensure the transportation to and safe arrival of the applicant in Canada within 30 days of this Judgment, or such longer period as this Court then finds to be necessary in the circumstances;
6. In fulfilment of this judicial process, the applicant is ordered to appear before me at 2:00 o'clock in the afternoon on Tuesday, July 7, 2009, at the Federal Court at 30 McGill Street, Montreal, Quebec, Canada or, at the option of the applicant on five days advance notice to the Court and respondents, at 90 Sparks Street Ottawa, Ontario, or at such other location as is subsequently fixed by the Court, subject to an extension of that date on application by either party and upon the Court being satisfied that through no fault of the respondents it is not possible or practicable for the applicant to appear at the date and time set; and
7. Costs are reserved.

II

Looking at Law:
Different Lenses for Law
and Legal Studies

Overview of Part II

The readings in **Part II** invite readers into some of the seminal debates in Legal Studies and begin to sketch out some of the larger questions about the theoretical relationship between law and society, and our understanding of the symbolic power of law. As such, the chapters in this section should begin to challenge the reader to recognize the ambiguity and complexity of legal approaches to social problems, highlight some of the dangers of narrow unreflexive, understandings of "the law", and hint at the potential limits of using law to address social problems.

Chapter 5 introduces some enduring questions about the relationship between law and morality. How does law address moral questions? Should law be used to address moral issues, and what consequences follow from this decision? Can law avoid being moral? What constitutes the "harm" that justifies legal intervention? The articles and cases in this chapter demonstrate the practical difficulties that legal actors face when confronted with what are traditionally understood as "moral" issues or dilemmas: from a classic tale of shipwreck and survival on the high seas to a contemporary case of "compassionate homicide". These readings also serve to highlight potential disconnects between the purposes of law and the aspiration of fundamental justice.

The articles in **Chapter 6** challenge some of the foundational claims of classic political liberalism; most notably that the law offers a politically neutral framework to address social issues and maintain social order. What the articles and cases in this chapter demonstrate is that an overly narrow or rigid, formalized understanding of law and an unwavering belief in the law's "neutrality" may ultimately promote or reinforce the inequalities law aims to remedy. The articles in particular ask readers to consider the consequences of an uncritical faith in the law's guarantees of formal equality and the public/private divide that rests at the core of political liberalism. While both authors in this chapter are critical of the limits of law's traditional promise, each similarly points to the essential ambiguity of legal solutions and offers insight into how we might rethink the practical use and symbolic promise of law.

Chapter 7 serves as an important introduction to the many challenges of articulating the complex relationship between law and society. It offers the reader some insight into transformations that have taken place in legal education and scholarship in recent years. All the articles outline how different scholars — lawyers and social scientists — have tried to understand "the law" and its relationship to other social processes and also the relationship between legal scholarship and the social sciences more generally. While Menkel-Meadow highlights the dangers of ideological approaches to understanding law, Cotterrell reminds the reader that we cannot lose sight of law's role in structuring everyday practices and understandings of social life. Arthurs and Bunting specifically highlight the approach taken by Canadian scholars in this broad context — focusing on the historical tensions within the field between traditional legal scholarship and various interdisciplinary approaches. They discuss how legal education and research in Canada must change to meet contemporary challenges.

Each chapter in **Part II** highlights the importance of adopting broader approaches to the study of law; approaches willing to question the traditional assumptions and definitions of law, and approaches also willing to recognize the ambiguity and limits of legal solutions to complex social issues. These critical themes run throughout the remainder of the book and are taken up again more explicitly in the final Part on **Law and Social Transformation**.

As you read through the chapters that comprise **Part II** consider the broad implications of adopting alternative perspectives on what constitutes law or "the legal". How do the conceptual shifts described within the chapters force us to reconsider what comprises legal education and legal research in Canada? More broadly, how might the way we "know the law" force us to reconsider the broader role of law as a regulating force in liberal societies? Does conceptually breaking down the traditional boundaries between law and morality, or law and politics, or even law and the social sciences, make the processes of law-making and legal decision-making potentially more "accessible" or less "alienating", or do such changes render the law less certain, even less knowable, and so potentially more intrusive?

94

Law, Morality, and Justice

(a) Tragic Choices†

Patrick J. Fitzgerald

"You can't win 'em all," we say to console ourselves when things go wrong. What if they go so wrong that winning is impossible? What if life really puts us on the spot and confronts us with a tragic choice? Let's look at the following examples.

A pilot named Marten Hartwell crashed in the Northwest Territories in the early 70's. He was the only survivor. To stay alive until he was rescued he had to eat. His only source of food was the dead body of his companion, a young nurse. What should he have done — become a cannibal or starved to death? He chose to live.

In another case, some years ago, an international expedition set out to climb Mount Everest. One of the team, a man called Harsh, slipped and fell. He came to rest suspended upside down over an icefield. To get to him his companions would have had to venture across the extremely dangerous ice; and when they reached him there was no guarantee that they could bring him back alive. What should they have done — risked their lives with little hope of saving Harsh, or let him die? They let him die.

There are even worse situations. Two mountaineers were climbing in the Alps, roped together. On an isolated peak, one slipped and fell. Unable to move, he lay dangling at the end of the rope. The other climber couldn't lift his companion back up, nor could he himself move on without cutting the rope. What should he have done — cut the rope and sent his companion to his death, or stayed where he was till both died of exposure? He cut the rope.

1. What would you have done in Hartwell's place?
2. Do you think the Everest climbers ought to have risked their lives to save Harsh?
3. If you had been the climber in the Alps, would you have cut the rope?
4. Which would you put first — self-preservation or the maintenance of another human life?
5. Do you think the law should have the answers to these questions?

THE ONLY WAY

Sometimes the law is forced to deal with these tragic choices, as it did in the following nineteenth century English case. The case concerned three shipwrecked sailors and a cabin boy. The story was a grisly one. The facts were not in dispute. The only question was: had the law been broken? To answer this, the judges had to decide what the law was. And their decision, given almost a hundred years ago in England, still contains the law for Canada today.

For over twenty days three sailors and a cabin boy had drifted in an open boat a thousand miles from land. Their only food was two tins of turnips and a turtle they had caught, their only drink the rain collected in their oilskin capes. When this gave out, they stayed seven days without food and five without water. They couldn't have lived many more days unless they took the only course remaining. That course, said one of them, Captain Dudley, was

---

† From *This Law of Ours* (Scarborough, ON: Prentice-Hall of Canada, 1977) at 40–47, 49. Reproduced with permission.

to sacrifice one life to save the rest — kill one for the other three to eat.

Which one? The captain, who proposed this course? The sailor, Stephens, who agreed with him? The other sailor, Brooks, who disagreed? Or the seventeen-year-old cabin boy, prostrate from famine and drinking seawater? Which one should be the sacrificial victim?

1. Even if there is only one course, would they be right to take it?
2. If so, who should be the victim?
3. And how should they decide on the victim?

The Agony and the Argument

"If no help comes," said Dudley and Stephens, "We'll have to sacrifice one to save the rest." Brooks knew they meant the boy and didn't agree.

"Let's do it this way," said the captain the next day; "let's all draw lots to see which one to kill." It was the twentieth day when he made this suggestion to Brooks and Stephens. He never made it to the boy himself. But Brooks would not agree and lots were never drawn.

"We have families," said Dudley and Stephens, "and the boy has no one dependent on him. Better to kill him to save the rest of us. If no help comes tomorrow, we'll have to kill the boy."

Next day no help came. No ship appeared. The captain motioned to Stephens and to Brooks that they had better kill the boy, who lay helpless at the bottom of the boat. He would have died anyway before the other three. Once again Brooks would have no part of it.

1. Three possibilities of setting the question emerge from what the captain said. What are they?
2. Which is the best?
3. Who should decide?

The Ultimate Solution

The captain, a religious man, offered a prayer. He asked forgiveness for them all. Then he and Stephens told the boy his time had come. They put a knife to his throat and killed him.

For four days afterwards the three men fed upon his body and his blood. Had they not done so, they would all have died. On the fourth day a passing ship picked them up. All three were in the lowest state of prostration. Their rescuers brought them home to England, where the law took over.

The authorities investigated the incident and then launched a murder prosecution against two of the survivors — Dudley and Stephens. Brooks was never charged, but was a witness at the trial.

The trial took place before a jury which gave a special verdict. Instead of pronouncing the defendants guilty or not guilty, they merely decided what had happened. They decided that Dudley and Stephens had killed the boy, and that they had had no other chance of survival. They left it to the judge to say whether this was murder or not.

1. Do you think the sailors were justified in killing the cabin boy?
2. Can you think of any circumstances where killing is justified?
3. Do you think the case should have come to trial at all?
4. Was it fair that Brooks wasn't charged?
5. Only very exceptionally does a jury refuse to say "guilty" or "not guilty." Why do you think they did so in this case?
6. If you had been on the jury, would you have wanted to refuse to give a verdict?

The Judges' Verdict

Was the act of Dudley and Stephens justified? The jury left it to the judges to determine. This is what the judges said:

There remains to be considered the real question in the case — whether killing under the circumstances set forth in the verdict be or be not murder.

Now except for the purpose of testing how far the conservation of a man's own life is in all cases and under all circumstances, an absolute, unqualified, and paramount duty, we exclude from our consideration all the incidents of war. We are dealing with a case of private homicide, not one imposed upon men in the service of their Sovereign and in the defence of the country. Now it is admitted that the deliberate killing of this unoffending and unresisting boy was clearly murder, unless the killing can be justified by some well-recognized excuse admitted by the law. It is further admitted that there was in this case no such excuse, unless the killing was justified by what has been called "necessity." But the temptation to the act which existed here was not what the law has ever called necessity. Nor is this to be regretted. Though law and morality are not the same, and many things may be immoral which are not necessarily illegal, yet the absolute divorce of law from morality would be of fatal consequence; and such divorce would follow if the temptation to murder in this case were to be held by law an absolute defense of it. It is not so. To preserve one's life is generally speaking a duty, but it may be the plainest and the highest duty to sacrifice it. War is full of instances in which it is a man's duty not to live, but to die. The duty, in case of shipwreck, of a captain to his crew, of the crew to the passengers, of soldiers to women and children, these duties impose on men the moral necessity, not of the preservation, but of the sacrifice of their lives for others, from which in no country, least of all, it is to be hoped, in England, will men ever shrink, as indeed they have not shrunk. It is not correct, therefore, to say that there is any absolute or unqualified necessity to preserve one's life.

It is not needful to point out the awful danger of admitting the principle which has been contended for. Who is to be the judge of this sort of necessity? By what measure is the comparative value of lives to be measured? Is it to be strength, or intellect, or what? It is plain that the principle leaves to him who is to profit by it to determine the necessity which will justify him in deliberately taking another's life to save his own. In this case the weakest, the youngest, the most unresisting, was chosen. Was it more necessary to kill him than one of the grown men? The answer must be "No."

It is not suggested that in this particular case the deeds were "devilish," but it is quite plain that such a principle once admitted might be made the legal cloak for unbridled passion and atrocious crime. There is no safe path for judges to tread but to ascertain the law to the best of their ability and to declare it according to their judgment; and if in any case the law appears to be too severe on individuals, to leave it to the Sovereign to exercise that prerogative of mercy which the Constitution has entrusted to the hands fittest to dispense it.

It must not be supposed that in refusing to admit temptation to be an excuse for crime it is forgotten how terrible that temptation was; how awful the suffering; how hard in such trials to keep the judgment straight and the conduct pure. We are often compelled to set up standards we cannot reach ourselves, and to lay down rules which we could not ourselves satisfy. But a man has no right to declare temptation to be an excuse, though he might himself have yielded to it, nor allow compassion for the criminal to change or weaken in any manner the legal definition of the crime. It is therefore our duty to declare that the prisoners' act in this case was wilful murder, that the facts as stated in the verdict are no legal justification of the homicide; and to say that in our unanimous opinion the prisoners are upon this special verdict guilty of murder.

(R. v. Dudley & Stephens, 1884)

1. What is the argument put forward by the defence?
2. Why did the judges say it wasn't necessary to kill the cabin boy? Do you agree with them?
3. What did the judges say would be the consequences of accepting the argument put forward by the defence? Do you agree?
4. Do you think it was easier for the judges than it was for the jury to decide whether Dudley and Stephens were guilty? If so, why?
5. What do you think the consequence would have been if the judges, like the jury, had been unable to decide?

The Sentence of the Court

What Dudley and Stephens did was murder, said the judges. And murder was a capital offence in England at that time. The Lord Chief Justice sentenced them as follows:

The sentence of the court upon you is that you be taken from this place to a lawful prison and thence to a place of execution, and that you there suffer death by hanging; and that your body be afterwards buried within the precincts of the prison in which you shall have been confined before your execution. And may the Lord have mercy on your souls.

(R. v. Dudley & Stephens, 1884)

1. Was the death penalty justified in this case?
2. Is it ever justified? Does this alter your views on the sanctity of human life?
3. If they had had to decide, do you think the jury would have decided any differently than the judges did?

The Punishment

Dudley and Stephens were sentenced to death, but they were given a reprieve: the *royal prerogative of mercy* was exercised in their favor and the death sentence was commuted to one of life imprisonment. But this was not the end of it. The authorities exercised their discretion and released the prisoners after six months.

1. Should there be a royal prerogative of mercy? Why or why not?
2. Should the government be able to alter the sentences passed by the judges?
3. Should the law fix the sentence the judges must pass (as it does in murder cases)? Why not leave sentencing to the judges' discretion?

4. Do you think it was their knowledge of the penalty for murder that prevented the jury from saying Dudley and Stephens were guilty? If so, do you think the jury should have allowed that knowledge to prevent them?

THE MORAL DILEMMA

Murder, says the law, is intentionally killing a person without lawful justification. This is common sense, because in general we believe it is wrong to kill. However, we think it is justified in exceptional cases. When is it justified? The difficulty of this question can be seen from the following example, well known to legal textbook writers.

Two sailors, X and Y, are shipwrecked. Neither can swim. X reaches a floating plank and climbs onto it. Y reaches the plank and tries to climb onto it. The plank will hold only one person, so X prevents Y from getting onto it and Y drowns.

1. Is this situation exceptional enough to make X's act morally justified?
2. Suppose Y had climbed onto the plank and pushed X off, would Y's act have been morally justified?
3. Suppose the survivor in 1 or 2 had been charged in front of Dudley's and Stephens's judges with murder. What verdict do you think would have been given?
4. Suppose Y climbed onto the plank and X remained on it, and they both drowned. Would each have been justified in staying on the plank?

JETTISONING THE CARGO

"Necessity knows no law," it is often said. In other words, you can't be held legally liable for an act you had to do. From this point of view Dudley and Stephens would not be guilty of the murder of the cabin boy because their act was one which was necessary for their survival. But the judges in their case rejected the defendants' plea of necessity. As a result, it has been said that there is no defence of necessity in common law.

This is not true. Necessity can be a good defence, as in the 1608 *Mouse's* case.

A ship carrying a cargo of goods was overtaken by a storm. The captain feared that it would sink and that all aboard would be drowned, because it was already dangerously low in the water. To stop it from sinking further he ordered the crew to throw the cargo overboard. This lightened the vessel and enabled her to keep afloat, survive the storm, and come to safety.

The captain, so the court held at this trial, was within his rights in throwing the cargo overboard. He had to sacrifice the cargo for the greater good of saving human life.

1. Suppose the cargo had been a human one. Would the captain's act have been justified?
2. Suppose the open boat with the three men and the cabin boy had been sinking. Would Captain Dudley have been entitled to throw one of the passengers overboard to save the rest? If so, which one? If not, can you think of any circumstances where a captain might be morally justified in throwing a passenger overboard?
3. Saving human life is obviously more important than saving cargo. In Dudley's and Stephens's case was it equally obvious that saving the lives of the three sailors was more important than saving the cabin boy's life?
4. In such a case do three lives have three times the importance of one life?
5. Because the cabin boy would have died before they were rescued, was it more important to save the sailors' lives?
6. Do you think Dudley and Stephens would have been well-advised to put forward such arguments? Would they have answered the judges' points?
7. What light does this case throw on the notion of necessity? What do we mean by saying it was necessary for the captain to throw the cargo overboard? What did Dudley mean by saying it was necessary to kill the cabin boy?
8. There is a well-known story about Oscar Wilde in which a beggar, trying to convince Wilde to give him some money, says, "Man must live." Wilde answers, "I don't see the necessity." What point is Wilde making? Strictly speaking, is anything ever really necessary?

. . . .

ENEMIES IN WAR

. . . .

During the Second World War a British bomber pilot was shot down over Germany and taken prisoner. He escaped and on his way through Germany to neutral territory, he carried on his own private war effort: each day he killed one German soldier.

Back in England, he resumed his flying duties and ended the war with high rank and honors.

1. Do you think such killings are justified?
2. Are there any moral limits to the right to kill the enemy in war?
3. If Dudley and Stephens had been survivors of a warship torpedoed by the enemy, and the boy a survivor of the enemy submarine, would they have been justified in killing him simply as an enemy?
4. Would they have been justified in killing him for food?

THE ROMAN SOLDIER'S WAY OUT

So far we've discussed the taking of other people's lives. What about taking one's own life? Suicide has often been seen as an honorable way out. The Roman solider, if defeated, preferred death to dishonor. Rather than surrender and allow himself to be captured he would fall upon his sword and kill himself. We see this in the story of Brutus.

(b) *R. v. Dudley & Stephens*†

Indictment for the murder of Richard Parker on the high seas within the jurisdiction of the Admiralty.

At the trial before Huddleston, B., at the Devon and Cornwall Winter Assizes, November 7, 1884, the jury at the suggestion of the learned judge, found the facts of the case in a special verdict which stated "that on July 5, 1884, the prisoners, Thomas Dudley and Edward Stephens, with one Brooks, all able-bodied English seamen, and the deceased also an English boy, between seventeen and eighteen years of age, the crew of an English yacht, a registered English vessel, were cast away in a storm on the high seas 1,600 miles from the Cape of Good Hope, and were compelled to put into an open boat belonging to the said yacht. That in this boat they had no supply of water and no supply of food, except two 1 lb. tins of turnips, and for three days they had nothing else to subsist upon. That on the fourth day they caught a small turtle, upon which they subsisted for a few days, and this was the only food they had up to the twentieth day when the act now in question was committed. That on the twelfth day the remains of the turtle were entirely consumed, and for the next eight days they had nothing to eat. That they had no fresh water, except such rain as they from time to time caught in their oilskin capes. That the boat was drifting on the ocean, and

was probably more than 1000 miles away from land. That on the eighteenth day, when they had been seven days without food and five without water, the prisoners spoke to Brooks as to what should be done if no succour came, and suggested that some one should be sacrificed to save the rest, but Brooks dissented, and the boy, to whom they were understood to refer, was not consulted. That on the 24th of July, the day before the act now in question, the prisoner Dudley proposed to Stephens and Brooks that lots should be cast who should be put to death to save the rest, but Brooks refused to consent, and it was not put to the boy, and in point of fact there was no drawing of lots. That on that day the prisoners spoke of their having families, and suggested it would be better to kill the boy that their lives should be saved, and Dudley proposed that if there was no vessel in sight by the morrow morning the boy should be killed. That next day, the 25th of July, no vessel appearing, Dudley told Brooks that he had better go and have a sleep, and made signs to Stephens and Brooks that the boy had better be killed. The prisoner Stephens agreed to the act, but Brooks dissented from it. That the boy was then lying at the bottom of the boat quite helpless, and extremely weakened by famine and by drinking sea water, and unable to make any resistance nor did he ever assent to his being killed. The prisoner Dudley offered a prayer asking forgiveness for them all if

---

† (1884), 14 Q.B.D. 273 at 273–75, 279–88.

either of them should be tempted to commit a rash act, and that their souls might be saved. That Dudley, with the assent of Stephens, went to the boy, and telling him that his time was come, put a knife into his throat and killed him then and there; that the three men fed upon the body and blood of the boy for four days; that on the fourth day after the act had been committed the boat was picked up by a passing vessel, and the prisoners were rescued, still alive, but in the lowest state of prostration. That they were carried to the port of Falmouth, and committed for trial at Exeter. That if the men had not fed upon the body of the boy they would probably not have survived to be so picked up and rescued, but would within the four days have died of famine. That the boy, being in a much weaker condition, was likely to have died before them. That at the time of the act in question there was no sail in sight, nor any reasonable prospect of relief. That under these circumstances there appeared to the prisoners every probability that unless they then fed or very soon fed upon the boy or one of themselves they would die of starvation. That there was no appreciable chance of saving life except by killing some one for the others to eat. That assuming any necessity to kill anybody, there was no greater necessity for killing the boy than any of the other three men. But whether upon the whole matter by the jurors found the killing of Richard Parker by Dudley and Stephens be felony and murder the jurors are ignorant, and pray the advice of the Court thereupon, and if upon the whole matter the Court shall be of opinion that the killing of Richard Parker be felony and murder, then the jurors say that Dudley and Stephens were each guilty of felony and murder as alleged in the indictment."

. . . .

[LORD COLERIDGE C.J.:]

. . . .

...From these facts, stated with the cold precision of a special verdict, it appears sufficiently that the prisoners were subject to terrible temptation, to sufferings which might break down the bodily power of the strongest man, and try the conscience of the best. Other details yet more harrowing, facts still more loathsome and appalling, were presented to the jury, and are to be found recorded in my learned Brother's notes. But nevertheless this is clear, that the prisoners put to death a weak and unoffending boy upon the chance of preserving their own lives by feeding upon his flesh and blood after he was killed,

and with the certainty of depriving *him* of any possible chance of survival. The verdict finds in terms that "if the men had not fed upon the body of the boy they would *probably* not have survived," and that "the boy being in a much weaker condition was *likely* to have died before them." They might possibly have been picked up next day by a passing ship; they might possibly not have been picked up at all; in either case it is obvious that the killing of the boy would have been an unnecessary and profitless act. It is found by the verdict that the boy was incapable of resistance, and, in fact, made none; and it is not even suggested that his death was due to any violence on his part attempted against, or even so much as feared by, those who killed him. Under these circumstances the jury say that they are ignorant whether those who killed him were guilty of murder, and have referred it to this Court to determine what is the legal consequence which follows from the facts which they have found.

. . . .

There remains to be considered the real question in the case — whether killing under the circumstances set forth in the verdict be or be not murder. The contention that it could be anything else was, to the minds of us all, both new and strange, and we stopped the Attorney General in his negative argument in order that we might hear what could be said in support of a proposition which appeared to us to be at once dangerous, immoral, and opposed to all legal principle and analogy. All, no doubt, that can be said has been urged before us, and we are now to consider and determine what it amounts to. First it is said that it follows from various definitions of murder in books of authority, which definitions imply, if they do not state, the doctrine that in order to save your own life you may lawfully take away the life of another, when that other is neither attempting nor threatening yours, nor is guilty of any illegal act whatever towards you or any one else. But if these definitions be looked at they will not be found to sustain this contention. The earliest in point of date is the passage cited to us from Bracton, who lived in the reign of Henry III. ... But in the very passage as to necessity, on which reliance has been placed, it is clear that Bracton is speaking of necessity in the ordinary sense — the repelling by violence, violence justified so far as it was necessary for the object, any illegal violence used towards oneself....

It is, if possible, yet clearer that the doctrine contended for receives no support from the great authority of Lord Hale....

... For in the chapter in which he deals with the exemption created by compulsion or necessity he thus expresses himself: — "If a man be desperately assaulted and in peril of death, and cannot otherwise escape unless, to satisfy his assailant's fury, he will kill an innocent person then present, the fear and factual force will not acquit him of the crime and punishment of murder, if he commit the fact, for he ought rather to die himself than kill an innocent; but if he cannot otherwise save his own life the law permits him in his own defence to kill the assailant, for by the violence of the assault, and the offence committed upon him by the assailant himself, the law of nature, and necessity, hath made him his own protector *cum debito moderamino inculpatae tutelae.*" (*Hale's Pleas of the Crown*, vol. 1, 51.)

But, further still, Lord Hale in the following chapter deals with the position asserted by the casuists, and sanctioned, as he says, by Grotius and Puffendorf, that in a case of extreme necessity, either of hunger or clothing; "theft is no theft, or at least not punishable as theft, as some even of our own lawyers have asserted the same." "But," says Lord Hale, "I take it that here in England, that rule, at least by the laws of England, is false; and therefore, if a person being under necessity for want of victuals or clothes, shall upon that account clandestinely and *anima furandi* steal another man's goods, it is felony, and a crime by the laws of England punishable with death." (*Hale, Please of the Crown*, i, 54). If, therefore, Lord Hale is clear — as he is — that extreme necessity of hunger does not justify larceny, what would he have said to the doctrine that it justified murder?

· · · ·

Is there, then, any authority for the proposition which has been presented to us? Decided cases there are none. ... The American case cited by my Brother Stephen in his Digest, from Wharton on Homicide, in which it was decided, correctly indeed, that sailors had no right to throw passengers overboard to save themselves, but on the somewhat strange ground that the proper mode of determining who was to be sacrificed was to vote upon the subject by ballot, can hardly, as my Brother Stephen says, be an authority satisfactory to a court in this country....

The one real authority of former time is Lord Bacon, who, in his commentary on the maxim, "*necessitas inducit privilegium quoad jura privata,*" lays down the law as follows: — "Necessity carrieth a privilege in itself. Necessity is of three sorts — necessity of conservation of life, necessity of obedience, and necessity of the act of God or of a stranger. First of conservation of life, if a man steal viands to satisfy his present hunger, this is no felony nor larceny. So if divers be in danger of drowning by the casting away of some boat or barge, and one of them get to some plank, or on the boat's side to keep himself above water, and another to save his life thrust him from it, whereby he is drowned, this is neither *se defendendo* nor by misadventure, but justifiable." On this it is to be observed that Lord Bacon's proposition that stealing to satisfy hunger is no larceny is hardly supported by Staundforde, whom he cites for it, and is expressly contradicted by Lord Hale in the passage already cited. And for the proposition as to the plank or boat, it is said to be derived from the canonists. At any rate he cites no authority for it, and it must stand upon his own. Lord Bacon was great even as a lawyer; but it is permissible to much smaller men, relying upon principle and on the authority of others, the equals and even the superiors of Lord Bacon as lawyers, to question the soundness of his dictum. There are many conceivable states of things in which it might possibly be true, but if Lord Bacon meant to lay down the broad proposition that a man may save his life by killing, if necessary, an innocent and unoffending neighbour, it certainly is not law at the present day.

· · · ·

Now, except for the purpose of testing how far the conservation of a man's own life is in all cases and under all circumstances, an absolute, unqualified, and paramount duty, we exclude from our consideration all the incidents of war. We are dealing with a case of private homicide, not one imposed upon men in the service of their Sovereign and in the defence of their country. Now it is admitted that the deliberate killing of this unoffending and unresisting boy was clearly murder, unless the killing can be justified by some well-recognised excuse admitted by the law. It is further admitted that there was in this case no such excuse, unless the killing was justified by what has been called "necessity." But the temptation to the act which existed here was not what the law has ever called necessity. Nor is this to be regretted. Though law and morality are not the same, and many things may be immoral which are not necessarily illegal, yet the absolute divorce of law from morality would be of fatal consequence; and such divorce would follow if the temptation to murder in this case were to be held by law an absolute defence of it. It is not so. To preserve one's life is generally speaking a duty, but it may be the plainest and the highest duty to sacrifice it. War is full of instances in which it is a man's duty not to live, but to die. The duty in case of shipwreck, of a captain to his crew, of the crew to the passengers, of soldiers to women and children, as in the noble case of the *Birkenhead*; these duties impose on men the moral necessity, not of the preservation, but of the sacrifice of their lives for others, from which in no country, least of all, it is to be hoped, in England, will men ever shrink, as indeed, they have not shrunk. It is not correct, therefore, to say that there is any absolute or unqualified necessity to preserve one's life. *"Necesse est ut cam, no at vivam,"* is a saying of a Roman officer quoted by Lord Bacon himself with high eulogy in the very chapter on necessity to which so much reference has been made. It would be a very easy and cheap display of commonplace learning to quote from Greek and Latin authors, from Horace, from Juvenal, from Cicero, from Euripides, passage after passage, in which the duty of dying for others has been laid down in glowing and emphatic language as resulting from the principles of heathen ethics; it is enough in a Christian country to remind ourselves of the Great Example whom we profess to follow. It is not needful to point out the awful danger of admitting the principle which has been contended for. Who is to be the judge of this sort of necessity? By what measure is the comparative value of lives to be measured? Is it to be strength, or intellect, or what? It is plain that the principle leaves to him who is to profit by it to determine the necessity which will justify him in deliberately taking another's life to save his own. In this case the weakest, the youngest, the most unresisting, was chosen. Was it more necessary to kill him than one of the grown men? The answer must be "No" —

So spake the Fiend, and with necessity,
The tyrant's plea, excused his devilish deeds.

It is not suggested that in this particular case the deeds were "devilish," but it is quite plain that such a principle once admitted might be made the legal cloak for unbridled passion and atrocious crime. There is no safe path for judges to tread but to ascertain the law to the best of their ability and to declare it according to their judgment; and if in any case the law appears to be too severe on individuals, to leave it to the Sovereign to exercise that prerogative of mercy which the Constitution has intrusted to the hands fittest to dispense it.

It must not be supposed that in refusing to admit temptation to be an excuse for crime it is forgotten how terrible the temptation was; how awful the suffering; how hard in such trials to keep the judgment straight and the conduct pure. We are often compelled to set up standards we cannot reach ourselves, and to lay down rules which we could not ourselves satisfy. But a man has no right to declare temptation to be an excuse, though he might himself have yielded to it, nor allow compassion for the criminal to change or weaken in any manner the legal definition of the crime. It is therefore our duty to declare that the prisoners' act in this case was wilful murder, that the facts as stated in the verdict are no legal justification of the homicide; and to say that in our unanimous opinion the prisoners are upon this special verdict guilty of murder.

The Court then proceeded to pass sentence of death upon the prisoners.

(c) *R. v. Latimer*†

[TALLIS J.A. (Sherstobitoff J.A. concurring):]

INTRODUCTION

On November 16, 1994, following a jury trial for first degree murder, the appellant Robert Latimer was convicted of second degree murder for the killing of Tracy, his 12 year old daughter. The presiding judge imposed the mandatory sentence of life imprisonment without eligibility for parole for ten years.

Before dealing with the issues before this Court, we find it convenient to outline, in skeletal form,

---

† (1995), 125 D.L.R. (4th) 203 at 208–11, 232–35. [Notes and/or references omitted.]

the circumstances giving rise to this indictment for murder.

BACKGROUND

In October 1993, Tracy, who was 12 years old, suffered from severe cerebral palsy — a permanent condition caused by brain damage at birth. She was quadriplegic. Her physical handicaps of palsy and quadriplegia were such that she was bedridden for most of the time. Except for some slight head and facial movements she was immobile. She was physically helpless and unable to care for herself. She was in continual pain.

In undisputed testimony at trial, her mother described Tracy's day-to-day condition in this way. Tracy had five or six seizures every day, notwithstanding attempts to control her condition with prescribed drugs. She was unable to sit up on her own and could not communicate with her parents and siblings except to laugh or cry.

In February 1990 Tracy underwent surgery for the purpose of balancing the muscles around her pelvis. In August 1992 she underwent further surgery to reduce the abnormal curvature in her back. This surgery was successful but problems then developed in her right hip which became dislocated. This caused considerable pain.

Her attending physicians scheduled further surgery for November 19, 1993 to deal with the dislocated hip and thereby reduce the consequent pain. The recovery period for such surgery was estimated to be approximately one year.

Tracy had to be "spoon fed" in order to eat. Taking food was so difficult for her that she could not consume a sufficient amount of nutrients. Although her weight loss was not characterized as life threatening, it was a matter of concern.

Speaking generally, the Latimer family provided constant care for their daughter Tracy. During the period July to October 1993 she was placed in a group home in North Battleford to provide respite for the family particularly while Mrs. Latimer was pregnant.

After Tracy returned home, Kathleen Johnson, a Social Services worker, learned that an application for permanent placement at the group home had been received from the Latimer family. On October 12, 1993 she spoke to the appellant by phone to ascertain more details of the family's application and wishes. During this discussion the appellant advised her that it was not an urgent matter. If there was any immediate opening at the home he was not sure if they wanted a placement.

While in the appellant's care on Sunday, October 24, 1993 Tracy passed away at her family farm home near Wilkie. Her father remained at home to care for her while her mother and the other three children attended church. When they returned from church at about 1:30 p.m., Mrs. Latimer prepared lunch. Then she went to get Tracy up for lunch but found that she was dead.

At approximately 2:00 p.m. on the same day the appellant spoke to Constable Hartle of the Wilkie detachment of the Royal Canadian Mounted Police and advised him that Tracy had passed away in her sleep. Constable Hartle and the local coroner, Dr. Bhairo, attended at the Latimer farm. The appellant again stated that Tracy had passed away in her sleep. While at the farm Dr. Bhairo examined Tracy's body for any apparent cause of death. He found no evidence of vomit or mucous to suggest suffocation. Under the circumstances Dr. Bhairo arranged for an autopsy.

During his conversation with Constable Hartle the appellant said that Tracy was in pain and that he put her to bed at about 12:30 p.m. He said that he never checked her again. He also told the officer that he wanted Tracy to be cremated. Mrs. Latimer appeared shocked and shaken by such suggestion but after a private discussion with the appellant in their bedroom, she came out and advised the officer "Yes, we want her cremated." Tracy's body was removed by funeral home personnel.

Constable Hartle did not exclude homicide and conveyed his concern to the coroner. On October 25, 1993 Dr. Waghray, a pathologist, performed an autopsy. During this examination he found no pathological signs that would explain Tracy's death but he did find signs consistent with poisoning. Given these signs, samples of Tracy's blood were forwarded for analysis at the forensic laboratory in Regina. When examined this blood was found to be saturated with carbon monoxide.

Given this finding of death by carbon monoxide poisoning, members of the R.C.M.P. including Constable Hartle treated this matter as a homicide investigation.

On November 4, 1993 members of the R.C.M.P. arrived at the Latimer farm to execute a search warrant. They were accompanied by technicians from SaskPower for the purpose of checking the furnace and water heater in the house for any possible malfunction and consequent release of carbon monoxide. This possibility was excluded because no defects in the system were found.

With that, Sergeant Conlon and Corporal Lyons took the appellant into custody and returned to

North Battleford for the purpose of interviewing him. During this interview the appellant admitted his role in causing Tracy's death. Following a *voir dire*, his written statement (P-25) was admitted in evidence before the jury. In this statement the appellant describes how he removed Tracy from her bed and placed her in the cab of a pickup truck in a shed. He then hooked the hose to the exhaust and placed the other end through the back window of the cab. After he left Tracy exposed to carbon monoxide in the cab for a significant period of time, he determined that she was dead and then placed her back in her bed at the house.

Later the same day the appellant returned to his farm with the two interviewing officers and on a "walk through" he pointed out the truck, hoses, rags and other equipment that he used in terminating Tracy's life. This partial re-enactment of events was videotaped at the farm.

At the conclusion of this stage of the investigation the appellant was formally charged with first degree murder.

. . . .

GROUND 4 — FAILURE TO INSTRUCT JURY ON DEFENCE OF NECESSITY

The learned trial judge withdrew the defence of necessity from the jury. This was made clear in the following passage of his instructions:[7]

> ... Mr. Brayford made the argument that if you find that Mr. Latimer committed culpable homicide you should, nevertheless, excuse him and find him not guilty because it was done out of necessity. He says medical science had done everything possible for Tracy but that it was incapable of relieving her excruciating pain. The only humane option was to see her put to sleep. Well, that may be an attractive argument and while the doctrine of necessity can sometimes operate to excuse criminal misconduct, I must tell you as a matter of law that the doctrine does not apply in this case. The defence of necessity exists only where the perpetrator's decision to break the law is inescapable and unavoidable and necessary to avert some imminent risk of peril. It arises only in cases where there is no option, no other choice. That was not the situation here. There was an option, albeit not a particularly happy one. The option was to persevere in the attempts to make Tracy comfortable in her life, however disagreeable and heartwrenching those attempts might have been.

The controlling authority with respect to this defence is *Perka v. The Queen*, 1984 CanLII 23 (S.C.C.), [1984] 2 S.C.R. 232. In *Perka* the Supreme Court recognized necessity as a possible "excuse" in criminal law but emphasized the limitations placed on such defence. This is clearly articulated in the following passages of the judgment of Dickson J. (as he then was) at pp. 248–252:

> Conceptualized as an "excuse", however, the residual defence of necessity is, in my view, much less open to criticism. It rests on a realistic assessment of human weakness, recognizing that a liberal and humane criminal law cannot hold people to the strict obedience of laws in emergency situations where normal human instincts, whether of self-preservation or of altruism, overwhelmingly impel disobedience. The objectivity of the criminal law is preserved; such acts are still wrongful, but in the circumstances they are excusable. Praise is indeed not bestowed, but pardon is, when one does a wrongful act under pressure which, in the words of Aristotle in the *Nicomachean Ethics, supra*, at p.49, "overstrains human nature and which no one could withstand".
>
> ...
>
> Relating necessity to the principle that the law ought not to punish involuntary acts leads to a conceptualization of the defence that integrates it into the normal rules for criminal liability rather than constituting it as a *sui generis* exception and threatening to engulf large portions of the criminal law. Such a conceptualization accords with our traditional legal, moral and philosophic views as to what sorts of acts and what sorts of actors ought to be punished. In this formulation it is a defence which I do not hesitate to acknowledge and would not hesitate to apply to relevant facts capable of satisfying its necessary prerequisites.
>
> c) *Limitations on the Defence*
>
>   If the defence of necessity is to form a valid and consistent part of our criminal law it must, as has been universally recognized, be strictly controlled and scrupulously limited to situations that correspond to its underlying rationale. That rationale, as I have indicated, is the recognition that it is inappropriate to punish actions which are normatively "involuntary". The appropriate controls and limitations on the defence of necessity are, therefore, addressed to ensuring that the acts for which the benefit of the excuse of necessity is sought are truly "involuntary" in the requisite sense.
>
>   In *Morgentaler, supra*, I was of the view that any defence of necessity was restricted to instances of non-compliance "in urgent situations of clear and imminent peril when compliance

104

with the law is demonstrably impossible". In my opinion this restriction focuses directly on the "involuntariness" of the purportedly necessitous behaviour by providing a number of tests for determining whether the wrongful act was truly the only realistic reaction open to the actor or whether he was in fact making what in fairness could be called a choice. If he was making a choice, then the wrongful act cannot have been involuntary in the relevant sense.

The requirement that the situation be urgent and the peril be imminent, tests whether it was indeed unavoidable for the actor to act at all. In LaFave & Scott, *Criminal Law* (1972), at p.388, one reads:

> It is sometimes said that the defense of necessity does not apply except in an emergency — when the threatened harm is immediate, the threatened disaster imminent. Perhaps this is but a way of saying that, until the time comes when the threatened harm is immediate, there are generally options open to the defendant to avoid the harm, other than the option of disobeying the literal terms of the law — the rescue ship may appear, the storm may pass; and so the defendant must wait until that hope of survival disappears.

At a minimum the situation must be so emergent and the peril must be so pressing that normal human instincts cry out for action and make a counsel of patience unreasonable.

The requirement that compliance with the law be "demonstrably impossible" takes this assessment one step further. Given that the accused had to act, could he nevertheless realistically have acted to avoid the peril or prevent the harm, without breaking the law? *Was there a legal way out?* I think this is what Bracton means when he lists "necessity" as a defence, providing the wrongful act was not "avoidable". The question to be asked is whether the agent had any real choice: could he have done otherwise? If there is a reasonable legal alternative to disobeying the law, then the decision to disobey becomes a voluntary one, impelled by some consideration beyond the dictates of "necessity" and human instincts.

The importance of this requirement that there be no reasonable legal alternative cannot be overstressed.

Even if the requirements for urgency and "no legal way out" are met, there is clearly a further consideration. There must be some way of assuring proportionality. No rational criminal justice system, no matter how humane or liberal, could excuse the infliction of a greater harm to allow the actor to avert a lesser evil. In such circumstances we expect the individual to bear the harm and refrain from acting illegally. If he cannot control himself we will not excuse him.

Applying these controlling principles to the jury instructions under review, we must reject this ground of appeal. The trial judge was correct in finding that there was no factual foundation for this defence. In this case the appellant's life was not in peril. He was concerned with Tracy's quality of life. The evidence clearly established the bleak future that faced this little girl. Although her scheduled surgery involved a long recovery period, there was the prospect of some pain alleviation.

This is not a case of withholding potentially life-prolonging treatment to a seriously disabled person. It deals with the deliberate decision to terminate another's life rather than continue with the scheduled medical treatment and care. In such circumstances it is no defence for a parent to say because of a severe handicap, a child's life has such diminished value that the child should not live any longer. It does not advance the interest of the state or society to treat such a child as a person of lesser status or dignity than others.

In dealing with this aspect of the case learned counsel for the Crown stressed that Tracy's medical condition was not unique. She pointed to the many families that are visited with a similar type of misfortune. Dr. Snyder testified that one in 1,000 births involve children with cerebral palsy and ten percent of that unfortunate group have severe cerebral palsy. Dr. Dzus, a specialist in orthopaedic surgery limiting her practice mainly to children, testified that in her work at the Kinsmen Children's Centre in Saskatoon, she attended to many children with multiple handicaps similar to Tracy.

Although the appellant did not testify at trial, his statement to the investigating officers indicates how he set about the termination of Tracy's life. There is no evidence that his act in terminating her life was "involuntary" within the test articulated in *Perka*.

Furthermore the evidence is clear that the appellant and his family did have an option. If they could no longer bear the burden of caring for Tracy, there was the real prospect of permanent placement in a group home.

Accordingly this ground of appeal must fail.

(d) Law and Morality†

Lord Patrick Devlin

The relationship between law and morals has recently, in England and in the United States and also in Canada, received quite a considerable degree of interest. Of course, if one wants to go back to the very beginning, one must begin with John Stuart Mill in 1859 and the publication of his essay *On Liberty*, and his announcement of the famous principle which should govern, in his view, all law-making in relation to all subjects. That principle is, he said:

> ... the sole end for which mankind are warranted, individually or collectively, in interfering in the liberty of action of any of their number, is self-protection. That the only purpose for which power can be rightfully exercised over any member of a civilized community, against his will, is to prevent harm to others. His own good, either physical or moral, is not a sufficient warrant. He cannot rightfully be compelled to do or forbear because it will be better for him to do so, because it will make him happier, because in the opinions of others, to do so would be wise, or even right.[1]

This principle was attacked by Mr. Justice Stephen in the celebrated book, *Liberty, Equality, Fraternity*,[2] which he wrote in the 1870's. I think it is fair to say that the principle never got beyond academic discussion; nor had it ever been translated into practice. However, it was resurrected and translated into practice in 1957 in the report of the committee that was presided over by Sir John Wolfenden on the amendment of the laws on homosexuality and prostitution. There the principle was stated in this way:

> There must remain a realm of private morality and immorality which is, in brief and crude terms, not the law's business.

. . . .

The attraction of the doctrine, for undoubtedly it is attractive, to me lies in this: that it seems to be a logical extension from freedom of religion. We have now achieved, not without a great struggle, the sort of society in which a man's religion is his own affair. Ought not his morals to be his own affair too? Is there any greater need, we may ask ourselves, for a common morality than there is for a common religion? However, there is a distinction. The ordinary free thinker has no religion. He can doubt the existence of God as he does the existence of the Devil, and if society can accommodate people who have no personal religion and yet reckon them as good citizens, as so many of them are, then there is no need for a common religion. But it is one thing to doubt the existence of God and the Devil and another thing to doubt the existence of good and evil. God and the Devil is what religion is about; good and evil is what morals are about. Whether good and evil are properly personified in God and the Devil is a theological question upon which the man of faith, and the free thinker, can disagree, but there will be no disagreement, and can be no disagreement about whether good and evil exist.

Thus, while Mill, in common with most free thinkers, both of his century and of the present one, had no personal religion, and would deny the need for a common religion, he had a personal morality and he accepted the need for a common morality. Indeed, his opinion of what was virtuous did not substantially differ from that of his contemporaries, but no one, he felt, could be sure. In a free society, full scope must be given to individuality as one of the elements of well-being, and the individual must be free to question, to challenge, and to experiment. "The liberty of the individual", he wrote:

> must be thus far limited; he must not make himself a nuisance to other people. But if he refrains from molesting others in what concerns them, and merely acts according to his own inclination and judgment in things which concern himself, the same reasons which show that opinion should be free, prove also that he should be allowed, without molestation, to carry his opinions into practice at his own cost. That mankind is not infallible; that his truths, for the most part, are only half-truths; that unity of opinion, unless resulting from the fullest and freest comparison of opposite opinions, is not desirable, and diversity not an evil, but a good; until mankind is much more capable than at present of

† (1964) 3 Manitoba Law School Journal 243 at 243, 248–54. [Notes and/or references omitted.] (Based on material in *The Enforcement of Morals*, published by Oxford University Press, 1965.) Reproduced by permission of Oxford University Press.

recognizing all sides of the truth, are principles applicable to men's modes of action, not less than to their opinions. As it is useful that while mankind is imperfect there should be different opinions, so it is that there should be different experiments of living; that free scope should be given to varieties of character, short of injury to others; and that the worth of different modes of life should be proved practically, when anyone thinks fit to try them.[11]

You see, it is with freedom of opinion and discussion that Mill is primarily concerned. Freedom of action follows naturally on that. Men must be allowed to do what they are allowed to talk about doing. Evidently, what Mill visualizes is a number of people doing things he himself would disapprove of but doing them earnestly and openly after thought and discussion in an endeavour to find a way of life best suited to them as individuals.

This seems to me on the whole to be an idealistic picture. It has happened to some extent, say in the last couple of generations in the growth of free love outside marriage. Although for many it is just the indulgence of the flesh, for some it is a serious decision to break the constraint of chastity outside marriage. But in the area of morals that is touched by the law I find it difficult to think of any other example of high-mindedness. A man does not, as a rule, commit bigamy because he wants to experiment with two wives instead of one. He does not, as a rule, lie with his daughter or sister because he thinks that an incestuous relationship can be a good one, but because he finds in it a way of satisfying his lust in the home. He does not keep a brothel so as to prove the value of promiscuity, but so as to make money. There must be some homosexuals who believe theirs to be a good way of life, but many more who would like to get free of it if only they could. And certainly no one in his senses can think that habitual drunkenness or drugging leads to any good at all. But Mill believed, you see, that diversity in morals and the removal of restraint on what was traditionally held to be immorality (and held by him to be immorality) would liberate men to prove what they thought to be good. He would have been the last man to have advocated the removal of restraint so as to permit self-indulgence. He conceived of old morality being replaced by a new and perhaps better morality. He would not have approved of those who did not care whether there is any morality at all, but he never really grappled with the fact that along the paths that depart from traditional morals, pimps leading the weak astray far outnumber spiritual explorers at the head of the strong.

But let me return to the distinction I was drawing between freedom of religion and freedom in morals. The abolition of established religion is a relatively recent development. It is a feature of modern thought. It came with the Reformation, which is comparatively late in the history of civilization. Before that it would have been thought that a society could not exist without a common religion. The pluralist society in which we now live was not achieved without the complete destruction of medieval thought, and it involved a change of civilization which was comparable with the triumphs of Christianity over paganism. Mill records how the Emperor Marcus Aurelius, whom he considered to be one of the greatest of world rulers — tender, enlightened and humane — persecuted Christianity because existing society, as he saw it, was held together by belief in and reverence of the received divinities. The struggle more recently between received religion and freedom of conscience was of the same order, and entailed as much suffering.

But the removal of religion from the structure of society does not mean that a society can exist without faith. There is faith in moral belief as well as in religious belief, and although it is less precise and less demanding, moral belief is not necessarily less intense. In our society we believe in the advance of man towards a goal, and this belief is the mainspring of our morals. We believe that at some time in the history of mankind, whether on a sudden by divine stroke, or imperceptibly in evolutionary millennia, there was extracted from the chaos of the primeval mind, concepts of justice, benevolence, mercy, continence and others, that we call virtues. The distinction between virtue and vice, between good and evil as it affects our actions, is what morals [are] about. A common religious faith means that there is common agreement about the end of man; a common moral faith means that there is common agreement about the way he should go. A band of travellers can go forward together without knowing what they will find at the end of the journey, but they cannot keep in company if they do not journey in the same direction.

Keeping in company is what society is about.

Diversity in moral belief and practice would be no more injurious to a society which had no common morality than the like diversity in religious matters is to a society without a common religion. However, as I have said, Mill and his disciples do not conceive of a society without a common morality. If they did, if they wanted a society in which morality is as free as religion, they would indeed be faint-hearted in what they preached. They could not

107

then sensibly permit the law, as they do, to punish the corruption of youth or public acts of indecency. Where there is freedom of religion the conversion of a youth is not thought of as corruption. Men would have thought of it as that in the Middle Ages, just as we now think of the introduction of a youth to homosexual practices as corruption and not as conversion. Where there is true freedom of religion it would be thought intolerant to object to a religious ceremony in a public place on the ground that it was offensive to have brought to one's attention the exhibition of a faith which one thought false and pernicious. Why, then, do we object to the public exhibition of a false morality and call it indecency? If we thought that unrestricted indulgence in the sexual passions was as good a life as any other for those who liked it we should find nothing indecent in the practice of it either in public or in private. It would become no more indecent than kissing in public. Decency as an objective depends on the belief in continence as a virtue, a virtue which requires sexual activity to be kept within prescribed bounds.

These reflections show the gulf which separates the religious toleration we have achieved from the moral toleration that Mill wanted. The former is practicable, because while each man believes that his own religion, or the lack of it, is the truth or nearest to the truth, he looks upon the alternatives as lesser good and not as evil. What Mill demands is that we must tolerate what we know to be evil and what no one asserts to be good. He does not ask that in particular cases we should extend tolerance out of pity. He demands that we should cede it forever as a right. Because it is evil we can protect youth from corruption by it, but save for that we must allow it to spread unhindered by the law and infect the minds of those who are not strong enough to resist it. Why do ninety-nine of us have to grant this license to the other one? Because, the answer is, we are fallible; are all quite convinced that what we call vice is evil, but we may be mistaken. True it is that if the waters of toleration are poured upon the muck, bad men will wallow in the bog, but it may be (how can we tell otherwise?) that it is only in such a bog that seed may flourish that some day some good man may bring to fruit, and that otherwise the world would lose and be the poorer for it. That is the kernel of Mill's freedom; that is why we must not suppress vice. It is not because it is not evil; Mill thought that it was. It is not because legal suppression would be futile; some of Mill's followers advanced this argument, but he did not. Nor is it because Mill thought that virtue would be bound to triumph over vice without the aid of the law; in

some cogent passages he refuted that argument. When all this is stripped away, the kernel of Mill is just this: that he beseeches us to think it possible that we may be mistaken. Because of this possibility he demands almost absolute freedom for the individual to go his own way, the only function of society being to provide for him an ordered framework within which he might experiment in thought, and in action, secure from physical harm.

There is here, I believe, a flaw. Even assuming that we accept Mill's ideal, it is unacceptable to the lawmaker as a basis for action because it fails to distinguish sufficiently between freedom of thought and freedom of action. It may be a good thing for the man to keep an open mind about all his beliefs so that he will never claim for them absolute certainty and never dismiss entirely from his mind the thought that he may be wrong. But where there is a call for action he must act on what he believes to be true. The lawyer, who in this respect stands somewhere midway between the philosopher and the man of action, requires to be satisfied beyond a reasonable doubt. If he is so satisfied, he would then think it right to punish a man for breach of the law while acknowledging the possibility that he may be mistaken. Is there any difference, so far as the freedom of the individual is concerned, between punishing a man for an act which admittedly he did, and which we believe, perhaps erroneously, to be wrong, he denying that it is wrong; and punishing him for an act that is admittedly wrong, and which we honestly but perhaps erroneously believe that he did, he denying that he did it? Suppose you prosecute a man for bigamy. His defence might be, "I honestly believed that my first wife was dead". If that defense is rejected, it is rejected because there is no reasonable doubt in the minds of the jury that he did not honestly believe it. And yet they must say, "We might be mistaken; we are not required to have absolute certainty, but we must act on what we reasonably believe to be true". Well, then, if his defence were simply that: "I admit I married a second time but I honestly believe that bigamy is a good thing", must we not act in the same way? We must say, "Well, we have no reasonable doubt that bigamy is a bad thing; we can't be certain, we may be mistaken, but we must act upon our belief". Philosophers, after all, may philosophize under the shadow of perpetual doubt, but the governors of society cannot do their duty if they are not permitted to act upon what they believe.

I might now usefully return to what Mill said about Marcus Aurelius. He cited him as an example of the fallibility of even the best and wisest of men. Marcus Aurelius thought Christianity wholly unbelievable, and could see in it only a force that would cause the society he governed to fall into pieces. Mill certainly did not regard Christianity as an unmixed blessing, but it might have been a different thing, he thought, if it had been adopted under Marcus Aurelius instead of under Constantine. So, Mill urged, unless a man flatters himself that he is wiser than Marcus Aurelius, let him abstain from that assumption of joint infallibility of himself and the multitude which the great man made with such unfortunate results. The example is a perfectly fair one on the point of fallibility. If we were to be confronted with the creed today which taught that constraint was the only vice and the unlimited indulgence of the appetites of all sorts the only virtue worth cultivating, we should look at it without any comprehension at all. But I dare say that our contempt would not be greater than that of Marcus Aurelius for Christianity, or that of a medieval philosopher for the notion that heresy was something to be tolerated. The example is also a fair one on the point I am making. What else, one may ask, did Mill expect Marcus Aurelius to do? It is idle to lament that he did not forestall Constantine in accepting Christianity, for he could not accept what he disbelieved. In Mill's view, and probably in that of most of his disciples, Marcus Aurelius was right in rejecting the claims of Christianity. On this view the Emperor's mistake lay in his failure to realize that if he permitted the destruction of his society through the agency of a religion which he rightly concluded to be false, the successor civilization would be an improvement upon him. To put Mill's question again in another context, can any man, putting himself in the position of the great Emperor, flatter himself that he would have acted more wisely?

It is not feasible to require of any society that it should permit its own destruction by that which, whether rightly or wrongly, it honestly believes to be in error in case it may be mistaken. To admit that we are not infallible is not to admit that we are always wrong. What we believe to be evil may indeed be evil, and we cannot forever condemn ourselves to inactivity against evil because of the chance that we may by mistake destroy good.

For better or for worse, the lawmaker must act according to his lights, and he cannot, therefore, accept Mill's doctrine as practicable even if, as an ideal, he thought it desirable. But I must say that for my part I do not accept it even as an ideal. I accept it as an inspiration. What Mill taught about the value of freedom of inquiry and the dangers of intolerance has placed all free men forever in his debt. His admonitions were addressed to a society that was secure and strong and hidebound. Their repetition today is to a society much less solid. As a tract of the times, what Mill wrote was superb, but as dogma it has lost much of its appeal. I say dogma, for Mill's doctrine is just as dogmatic as any of those he repudiates. It is dogmatic to say that if only we were allowed to behave just as we liked so long as we did not injure each other the world would become a better place for all of us. There is no more evidence for this sort of utopia than there is evidence of the existence of heaven, and there is nothing to show that the one is any more easily attained than the other. We must not be bemused by words. If we are not entitled to call our society free unless we pursue freedom to an extremity that would make society intolerable for most of us, then let us stop short of the extreme and be content with some other name. The result may not be freedom unalloyed, but there are alloys which strengthen without corrupting.

(e)   *R. v. Butler*†

[SOPINKA J. (for Lamer C.J., La Forest, Cory, McLachlin, Stevenson, Iacobucci, JJ. and himself):]

This appeal calls into question the constitutionality of the obscenity provisions of the Criminal Code, R.S.C., 1985, c. C-46, s. 163. They are attacked on the ground that they contravene s. 2(b) of the Canadian Charter of Rights and Freedoms. The case requires the Court to address one of the most difficult and controversial of contemporary issues, that of

---

† [1992] 1 S.C.R. 452, 89 D.L.R. (4th) 449 at.

determining whether, and to what extent, Parliament may legitimately criminalize obscenity. I propose to begin with a review of the facts which gave rise to this appeal, as well of the proceedings in the lower courts.

1. FACTS AND PROCEEDINGS

In August 1987, the appellant, Donald Victor Butler, opened the Avenue Video Boutique located in Winnipeg, Manitoba. The shop sells and rents "hard core" videotapes and magazines as well as sexual paraphernalia. Outside the store is a sign which reads:

Avenue Video Boutique; a private members only adult video/visual club.

Notice: if sex oriented material offends you, please do not enter.

No admittance to persons under 18 years.

On August 21, 1987, the City of Winnipeg Police entered the appellant's store with a search warrant and seized all the inventory. The appellant was charged with 173 counts in the first indictment: three counts of selling obscene material contrary to s. 159(2)(a) of the Criminal Code, R.S.C. 1970, c. C-34 (now s. 163(2)(a)), 41 counts of possessing obscene material for the purpose of distribution contrary to s. 159(1)(a) (now s. 163(1)(a)) of the Criminal Code, 128 counts of possessing obscene material for the purpose of sale contrary to s. 159(2)(a) of the Criminal Code and one count of exposing obscene material to public view contrary to s. 159(2)(a) of the Criminal Code.

. . . .

The trial judge convicted the appellant on eight counts relating to eight films. Convictions were entered against the co-accused McCord with respect to two counts relating to two of the films. Fines of $1,000 per offence were imposed on the appellant. Acquittals were entered on the remaining charges.

The Crown appealed the 242 acquittals with respect to the appellant and the appellant cross-appealed the convictions. The majority of the Manitoba Court of Appeal allowed the appeal of the Crown and entered convictions for the appellant with respect to all of the counts, Twaddle and Helper JJ.A. dissenting.

. . . .

2. RELEVANT LEGISLATION

Criminal Code, R.S.C., 1985, c. C-46

163.(1) Every one commits an offence who,
(a) makes, prints, publishes, distributes, circulates, or has in his possession for the purpose of publication, distribution or circulation any obscene written matter, picture, model, phonograph record or other thing whatever; or
(b) makes, prints, publishes, distributes, sells or has in his possession for the purpose of publication, distribution or circulation a crime comic.

(2) Every one commits an offence who knowingly, without lawful justification or excuse,
(a) sells, exposes to public view or has in his possession for such a purpose any obscene written matter, picture, model, phonograph record or other thing whatever;
(b) publicly exhibits a disgusting object or an indecent show;
(c) offers to sell, advertises or publishes an advertisement of, or has for sale or disposal, any means, instructions, medicine, drug or article intended or represented as a method of causing abortion or miscarriage; or
(d) advertises or publishes an advertisement of any means, instructions, medicine, drug or article intended or represented as a method for restoring sexual virility or curing venereal diseases or diseases of the generative organs.

(3) No person shall be convicted of an offence under this section if he establishes that the public good was served by the acts that are alleged to constitute the offence and that the acts alleged did not extend beyond what served the public good.

(4) For the purposes of this section, it is a question of law whether an act served the public good and whether there is evidence that the act alleged went beyond what served the public good, [but] it is a question of fact whether the acts did or did not extend beyond what served the public good.

(5) For the purposes of this section, the motives of an accused are irrelevant.

(6) Where an accused is charged with an offence under subsection (1), the fact that the accused was ignorant of the nature or presence of the matter, picture, model, phonograph record, crime comic or other thing by means of or in relation to which the offence was committed is not a defence to the charge.

(7) In this section, "crime comic" means a magazine, periodical or book that exclusively or substantially comprises matter depicting pictorially

(a) the commission of crimes, real or fictitious; or

(b) events connected with the commission of crimes, real or fictitious, whether occurring before or after the commission of the crime.

(8) For the purposes of this Act, any publication a dominant characteristic of which is the undue exploitation of sex, or of sex and any one or more of the following subjects, namely, crime, horror, cruelty and violence, shall be deemed to be obscene.

3. ISSUES

The following constitutional questions are raised by this appeal:

1. Does s. 163 of the Criminal Code of Canada, R.S.C., 1985, c. C-46, violate s. 2(b) of the Canadian Charter of Rights and Freedoms?

2. If s. 163 of the Criminal Code of Canada, R.S.C., 1985, c. C-46, violates s. 2(b) of the Canadian Charter of Rights and Freedoms, can s. 163 of the Criminal Code of Canada be demonstrably justified under s. 1 of the Canadian Charter of Rights and Freedoms as a reasonable limit prescribed by law?

4. ANALYSIS

The constitutional questions, as stated, bring under scrutiny the entirety of s. 163. However, both lower courts as well as the parties have focused almost exclusively on the definition of obscenity found in s. 163(8). Other portions of the impugned provision, such as the reverse onus provision envisaged in s. 163(3) as well as the absolute liability offence created by s. 163(6), raise substantial Charter issues which should be left to be dealt with in proceedings specifically directed to these issues. In my view, in the circumstances, this appeal should be confined to the examination of the constitutional validity of s. 163(8) only.

. . . . .

(i) "Community Standard of Tolerance" Test

In Brodie, Judson J. accepted the view espoused notably by the Australian and New Zealand courts

that obscenity is to be measured against "community standards". He cited, at pp. 705–6, the following passage in the judgment of Fullager J. in *R. v. Close*, [1948] V.L.R. 445, at p. 465:

> There does exist in any community at all times — however the standard may vary from time to time — a general instinctive sense of what is decent and what is indecent, of what is clean and what is dirty, and when the distinction has to be drawn, I do not know that today there is any better tribunal than a jury to draw it ... I am very far from attempting to lay down a model direction, but a judge might perhaps, in the case of a novel, say something like this: "It would not be true to say that any publication dealing with sexual relations is obscene. The relations of the sexes are, of course, legitimate matters for discussion everywhere ... There are certain standards of decency which prevail in the community, and you are really called upon to try this case because you are regarded as representing, and capable of justly applying, those standards. What is obscene is something which offends against those standards."

The community standards test has been the subject of extensive judicial analysis. It is the standards of the community as a whole which must be considered and not the standards of a small segment of that community such as the university community where a film was shown (*R. v. Goldberg*, [1971] 3 O.R. 323 (C.A.)) or a city where a picture was exposed (*R. v. Kiverago* (1973), 11 C.C.C. (2d) 463 (Ont. C.A.)). The standard to be applied is a national one (*R. v. Cameron* (1966), 58 D.L.R. (2d) 486 (Ont. C.A.); *R. v. Duthie Books Ltd.* (1966), 58 D.L.R. (2d) 274 (B.C.C.A.); *R. v. Ariadne Developments Ltd.* (1974), 19 C.C.C. (2d) 49 (N.S.S.C., App. Div.), at p. 59). With respect to expert evidence, it is not necessary and is not a fact which the Crown is obliged to prove as part of its case (*R. v. Sudbury News Service Ltd.* (1978), 18 O.R. (2d) 428 (C.A.); *R. v. Prairie Schooner News Ltd.* (1970), 75 W.W.R. 585 (Man. C.A.); *R. v. Great West News Ltd.*, [1970] 4 C.C.C. 307 (Man. C.A.)). In *R. v. Dominion News & Gifts (1962) Ltd.*, [1963] 2 C.C.C. 103 (Man. C.A.), Freedman J.A. (dissenting) emphasized that the community standards test must necessarily respond to changing mores (at pp. 116–17):

> Community standards must be contemporary. Times change, and ideas change with them. Compared to the Victorian era this is a liberal age in which we live. One manifestation of it is the relative freedom with which the whole question of sex is discussed. In books, magazines, movies, television, and sometimes even in parlour

conversation, various aspects of sex are made the subject of comment, with a candour that in an earlier day would have been regarded as indecent and intolerable. We cannot and should not ignore these present-day attitudes when we face the question whether [the subject materials] are obscene according to our criminal law.

Our Court was called upon to elaborate the community standards test in *Towne Cinema Theatres Ltd.* v. *The Queen*, [1985] 1 S.C.R. 494. Dickson C.J. reviewed the case law and found (at pp. 508–9):

> The cases all emphasize that it is a standard of tolerance, not taste, that is relevant. What matters is not what Canadians think is right for themselves to see. What matters is what Canadians would not abide other Canadians seeing because it would be beyond the contemporary Canadian standard of tolerance to allow them to see it.
>
> Since the standard is tolerance, I think the audience to which the allegedly obscene material is targeted must be relevant. The operative standards are those of the Canadian community as a whole, but since what matters is what other people may see, it is quite conceivable that the Canadian community would tolerate varying degrees of explicitness depending upon the audience and the circumstances. [Emphasis in original.]

Therefore, the community standards test is concerned not with what Canadians would not tolerate being exposed to themselves, but what they would not tolerate other Canadians being exposed to. The minority view was that the tolerance level will vary depending on the manner, time and place in which the material is presented as well as the audience to whom it is directed. The majority opinion on this point was expressed by Wilson J. in the following passage, at p. 521:

> It is not, in my opinion, open to the courts under s. 159(8) of the Criminal Code to characterize a movie as obscene if shown to one constituency but not if shown to another.... In my view, a movie is either obscene under the Code based on a national community standard of tolerance or it is not. If it is not, it may still be the subject of provincial regulatory control.

(ii) "Degradation or Dehumanization" Test

There has been a growing recognition in recent cases that material which may be said to exploit sex in a "degrading or dehumanizing" manner will necessarily fail the community standards test....

. . . .

Among other things, degrading or dehumanizing materials place women (and sometimes men) in positions of subordination, servile submission or humiliation. They run against the principles of equality and dignity of all human beings. In the appreciation of whether material is degrading or dehumanizing, the appearance of consent is not necessarily determinative. Consent cannot save materials that otherwise contain degrading or dehumanizing scenes. Sometimes the very appearance of consent makes the depicted acts even more degrading or dehumanizing.

This type of material would, apparently, fail the community standards test not because it offends against morals but because it is perceived by public opinion to be harmful to society, particularly to women....

. . . .

(iv) The relationship of the tests to each other

. . . .

Pornography can be usefully divided into three categories: (1) explicit sex with violence, (2) explicit sex without violence but which subjects people to treatment that is degrading or dehumanizing, and (3) explicit sex without violence that is neither degrading nor dehumanizing. Violence in this context includes both actual physical violence and threats of physical violence. Relating these three categories to the terms of s. 163(8) of the Code, the first, explicit sex coupled with violence, is expressly mentioned. Sex coupled with crime, horror or cruelty will sometimes involve violence. Cruelty, for instance, will usually do so. But, even in the absence of violence, sex coupled with crime, horror or cruelty may fall within the second category. As for category (3), subject to the exception referred to below, it is not covered.

Some segments of society would consider that all three categories of pornography cause harm to society because they tend to undermine its moral fibre. Others would contend that none of the categories cause harm. Furthermore there is a range of opinion as to what is degrading or dehumanizing. See Pornography and Prostitution in Canada: Report of the Special Committee on Pornography and Prostitution (1985) (the Fraser Report), vol. 1, at p. 51. Because this is not a matter that is susceptible of proof in the traditional way and because we do not wish to leave it to the individual tastes of judges, we must have a norm that will serve as an arbiter in determining what amounts to an undue exploitation of sex. That arbiter is the community as a whole.

The courts must determine as best they can what the community would tolerate others being exposed to on the basis of the degree of harm that may flow from such exposure. Harm in this context means that it predisposes persons to act in an anti-social manner as, for example, the physical or mental mistreatment of women by men, or, what is perhaps debatable, the reverse. Anti-social conduct for this purpose is conduct which society formally recognizes as incompatible with its proper functioning. The stronger the inference of a risk of harm the lesser the likelihood of tolerance. The inference may be drawn from the material itself or from the material and other evidence. Similarly evidence as to the community standards is desirable but not essential.

In making this determination with respect to the three categories of pornography referred to above, the portrayal of sex coupled with violence will almost always constitute the undue exploitation of sex. Explicit sex which is degrading or dehumanizing may be undue if the risk of harm is substantial. Finally, explicit sex that is not violent and neither degrading nor dehumanizing is generally tolerated in our society and will not qualify as the undue exploitation of sex unless it employs children in its production.

If material is not obscene under this framework, it does not become so by reason of the person to whom it is or may be shown or exposed nor by reason of the place or manner in which it is shown. The availability of sexually explicit materials in theatres and other public places is subject to regulation by competent provincial legislation. Typically such legislation imposes restrictions on the material available to children. See *Nova Scotia Board of Censors* v. *McNeil*, [1978] 2 S.C.R. 662.

The foregoing deals with the interrelationship of the "community standards test" and "the degrading or dehumanizing" test. How does the "internal necessities" test fit into this scheme? The need to apply this test only arises if a work contains sexually explicit material that by itself would constitute the undue exploitation of sex. The portrayal of sex must then be viewed in context to determine whether that is the dominant theme of the work as a whole. Put another way, is undue exploitation of sex the main object of the work or is this portrayal of sex essential to a wider artistic, literary, or other similar purpose? Since the threshold determination must be made on the basis of community standards, that is, whether the sexually explicit aspect is undue, its impact when considered in context must be deter-

mined on the same basis. The court must determine whether the sexually explicit material when viewed in the context of the whole work would be tolerated by the community as a whole. Artistic expression rests at the heart of freedom of expression values and any doubt in this regard must be resolved in favour of freedom of expression.

. . . .

(a) Is s. 163 a Limit Prescribed by Law?

The appellant argues that the provision is so vague that it is impossible to apply it. Vagueness must be considered in relation to two issues in this appeal: (1) is the law so vague that it does not qualify as "a limit prescribed by law"; and (2) is it so imprecise that it is not a reasonable limit....

. . . .

Standards which escape precise technical definition, such as "undue", are an inevitable part of the law. The Criminal Code contains other such standards. Without commenting on their constitutional validity, I note that the terms "indecent", "immoral" or "scurrilous", found in ss. 167, 168, 173 and 175, are nowhere defined in the Code. It is within the role of the judiciary to attempt to interpret these terms. If such interpretation yields an intelligible standard, the threshold test for the application of s. 1 is met. In my opinion, the interpretation of s. 163(8) in prior judgments which I have reviewed, as supplemented by these reasons, provides an intelligible standard.

(b) Objective

The respondent argues that there are several pressing and substantial objectives which justify overriding the freedom to distribute obscene materials. Essentially, these objectives are the avoidance of harm resulting from antisocial attitudinal changes that exposure to obscene material causes and the public interest in maintaining a "decent society". On the other hand, the appellant argues that the objective of s. 163 is to have the state act as "moral custodian" in sexual matters and to impose subjective standards of morality.

. . . .

...To impose a certain standard of public and sexual morality, solely because it reflects the conventions of a given community, is inimical to the exercise and enjoyment of individual freedoms, which form the basis of our social contract. D. Dyzenhaus, "Obscenity and the Charter: Autonomy and Equality" (1991), 1 C.R. (4th) 367, at p. 370, refers to this as "legal moralism", of a majority deciding what values should inform individual lives and then coercively imposing those values on minorities. The prevention of "dirt for dirt's sake" is not a legitimate objective which would justify the violation of one of the most fundamental freedoms enshrined in the Charter.

On the other hand, I cannot agree with the suggestion of the appellant that Parliament does not have the right to legislate on the basis of some fundamental conception of morality for the purposes of safeguarding the values which are integral to a free and democratic society. As *Dyzenhaus, supra,* at p. 376, writes:

> Moral disapprobation is recognized as an appropriate response when it has its basis in Charter values.

As the respondent and many of the interveners have pointed out, much of the criminal law is based on moral conceptions of right and wrong and the mere fact that a law is grounded in morality does not automatically render it illegitimate. In this regard, criminalizing the proliferation of materials which undermine another basic Charter right may indeed be a legitimate objective.

In my view, however, the overriding objective of s. 163 is not moral disapprobation but the avoidance of harm to society. In Towne Cinema, Dickson C.J. stated, at p. 507:

> It is harm to society from undue exploitation that is aimed at by the section, not simply lapses in propriety or good taste.

The harm was described in the following way in the Report on Pornography by the Standing Committee on Justice and Legal Affairs (MacGuigan Report) (1978), at p. 18:4:

> The clear and unquestionable danger of this type of material is that it reinforces some unhealthy tendencies in Canadian society. The effect of this type of material is to reinforce male-female stereotypes to the detriment of both sexes. It attempts to make degradation, humiliation, victimization, and violence in human relationships appear normal and acceptable. A society which holds that egalitarianism, non-violence, consensualism, and mutuality are basic to any human interaction, whether sexual or other, is clearly justified in controlling and prohibiting any medium of depiction, description or advocacy which violates these principles.

. . . . .

This Court has thus recognized that the harm caused by the proliferation of materials which seriously offend the values fundamental to our society is a substantial concern which justifies restricting the otherwise full exercise of the freedom of expression. In my view, the harm sought to be avoided in the case of the dissemination of obscene materials is similar. In the words of Nemetz C.J.B.C. in *R.* v. *Red Hot Video Ltd.* (1985), 45 C.R. (3d) 36 (B.C.C.A.), there is a growing concern that the exploitation of women and children, depicted in publications and films, can, in certain circumstances, lead to "abject and servile victimization" (at pp. 43–44). As Anderson J.A. also noted in that same case, if true equality between male and female persons is to be achieved, we cannot ignore the threat to equality resulting from exposure to audiences of certain types of violent and degrading material. Materials portraying women as a class as objects for sexual exploitation and abuse have a negative impact on "the individual's sense of self-worth and acceptance".

. . . .

... I would therefore conclude that the objective of avoiding the harm associated with the dissemination of pornography in this case is sufficiently pressing and substantial to warrant some restriction on full exercise of the right to freedom of expression. The analysis of whether the measure is proportional to the objective must, in my view, be undertaken in light of the conclusion that the objective of the impugned section is valid only in so far as it relates to the harm to society associated with obscene materials. Indeed, the section as interpreted in previous decisions and in these reasons is fully consistent with that objective. The objective of maintaining conventional standards of propriety, independently of any harm to society, is no longer justified in light of the values of individual liberty which underlie the Charter. This, then, being the objective of s. 163, which I have found to be pressing and substantial, I must now determine whether the section is rationally connected and proportional to this objective....

. . . .

The values which underlie the protection of freedom of expression relate to the search for truth, participation in the political process, and individual self-fulfilment. The Attorney General for Ontario argues that of these, only "individual self-fulfilment", and only in its most base aspect, that of physical arousal, is engaged by pornography. On the other hand, the civil liberties groups argue that pornography forces us to question conventional notions of sexuality and thereby launches us into an inherently political discourse. In their factum, the B.C. Civil Liberties Association adopts a passage from R. West, "The Feminist-Conservative Anti-Pornography Alliance and the 1986 Attorney General's Commission on Pornography Report" (1987), 4 Am. Bar Found. Res. Jo. 681, at p. 696:

> Good pornography has value because it validates women's will to pleasure. It celebrates female nature. It validates a range of female sexuality that is wider and truer than that legitimated by the non-pornographic culture. Pornography (when it is good) celebrates both female pleasure and male rationality.

A proper application of the test should not suppress what West refers to as "good pornography". The objective of the impugned provision is not to inhibit the celebration of human sexuality. However, it cannot be ignored that the realities of the pornography industry are far from the picture which the B.C. Civil Liberties Association would have us paint. Shannon J., in *R. v. Wagner, supra,* described the materials more accurately when he observed, at p. 331:

> Women, particularly, are deprived of unique human character or identity and are depicted as sexual playthings, hysterically and instantly responsive to male sexual demands. They worship male genitals and their own value depends upon the quality of their genitals and breasts.

In my view, the kind of expression which is sought to be advanced does not stand on an equal footing with other kinds of expression which directly engage the "core" of the freedom of expression values.

This conclusion is further buttressed by the fact that the targeted material is expression which is motivated, in the overwhelming majority of cases, by economic profit. This Court held in *Rocket* v. *Royal College of Dental Surgeons of Ontario,* [1990] 2 S.C.R. 232, at p. 247, that an economic motive for expression means that restrictions on the expression might "be easier to justify than other infringements".

. . . .

I am in agreement with Twaddle J.A. who expressed the view that Parliament was entitled to have a "reasoned apprehension of harm" resulting from the desensitization of individuals exposed to materials which depict violence, cruelty, and dehumanization in sexual relations.

Accordingly, I am of the view that there is a sufficiently rational link between the criminal sanction, which demonstrates our community's disapproval of the dissemination of materials which potentially victimize women and which restricts the negative influence which such materials have on changes in attitudes and behaviour, and the objective.

. . . .

There are several factors which contribute to the finding that the provision minimally impairs the freedom which is infringed.

First, the impugned provision does not proscribe sexually explicit erotica without violence that is not degrading or dehumanizing. It is designed to catch material that creates a risk of harm to society. It might be suggested that proof of actual harm should be required. It is apparent from what I have said above that it is sufficient in this regard for Parliament to have a reasonable basis for concluding that harm will result and this requirement does not demand actual proof of harm.

Second, materials which have scientific, artistic or literary merit are not captured by the provision. As discussed above, the court must be generous in its application of the "artistic defence". For example, in certain cases, materials such as photographs, prints, books and films which may undoubtedly be produced with some motive for economic profit, may nonetheless claim the protection of the Charter in so far as their defining characteristic is that of aesthetic expression, and thus represent the artist's attempt at individual fulfilment. The existence of an accompanying economic motive does not, of itself, deprive a work of significance as an example of individual artistic or self-fulfilment.

Third, in considering whether the provision minimally impairs the freedom in question, it is legitimate for the court to take into account Parliament's past abortive attempts to replace the definition with one that is more explicit. In Irwin Toy, our Court recognized that it is legitimate to take into account the fact that earlier laws and proposed alternatives were thought to be less effective than the legislation that is presently being challenged. The attempt to provide exhaustive instances of obscenity has been shown to be destined to fail (Bill C-54, 2nd Sess., 33rd Parl.). It seems that the only practicable alternative is to strive towards a more abstract definition of obscenity which is contextually sensitive and responsive to progress in the knowledge and understanding of the phenomenon to which the legislation is directed. In my view, the standard of "undue exploitation" is therefore appropriate. The intractable nature of the problem and the impossibility of precisely defining a notion which is inherently elusive makes the possibility of a more explicit provision remote. In this light, it is appropriate to question whether, and at what cost, greater legislative precision can be demanded.

Fourth, while the discussion in this appeal has been limited to the definition portion of s. 163, I would note that the impugned section, with the possible exception of subs. 1, which is not in issue here, has been held by this Court not to extend its reach to the private use or viewing of obscene materials....

(f) R. v. Labaye: The Fogginess of "Increased" Causality in Obscenity Law†

Richard Jochelson

In 2005, the Supreme Court of Canada, in *R. v. Labaye*,[1] at long last retired the community standards of tolerance test for obscenity and indecency.[2] While the former community standards of tolerance test had a long and laboured history, its modern iteration melded the determination of "tolerance" with "undue exploitation of sex" (or "harm"). This later test was famously constituted in *R. v. Butler*,[3] where the majority of the Court considered the constitutionality of the obscenity provisions in the *Criminal Code* (which prohibit expression of unduly exploited sex)[4] and summarized the test succinctly as it applied to sexually explicit expression. The test was an objective assessment of the tolerance of Canadians (that is, whether the average Canadian would tolerate other Canadians being exposed to the impugned materials):

> [T]he portrayal of sex coupled with violence will almost always constitute the undue exploitation of sex [and therefore be intolerable to the average Canadian]. Explicit sex which is degrading or dehumanizing may be undue if the risk of harm is substantial. Finally, explicit sex that is not violent and neither degrading nor dehumanizing is generally tolerated in our society and will not qualify as the undue exploitation of sex unless it employs children in its production.[5]

In *Labaye*, the majority considered this *Butler* construction and reconstituted [it] to clarify the community standards of tolerance test as a harm test for obscenity and indecency. It did so in the context of

determining whether the appellant was keeping a "common bawdy-house" for the "practice of acts of indecency" under s. 210(1) of the *Criminal Code*.[6] The assessment of the Court took place in the context of a swingers' club operating in a Montreal apartment, which required members to pay dues, interviews prior to joining, and an opportunity for its members to engage in consensual sex with other members. Since "only those already disposed to this sort of sexual activity were allowed to participate and watch,"[7] "[n]o one was pressured to have sex, paid for sex, or treated as a mere sexual object for the gratification of others."[8] Further, there was no "physical or psychological harm to persons participating,"[9] and the majority could not find sufficient harm to trigger indecency. In reaching this decision, the majority, emphasizing more stringent causality between exposure to the activities and harm, reframed the new test for obscenity and indecency in the *Criminal Code*:

> Indecent criminal conduct [or obscenity] will be established where the Crown proves beyond a reasonable doubt the following two requirements:
>
> 1. That, by its *nature*, the conduct at issue causes harm or presents a significant risk of harm to individuals or society in a way that undermines or threatens to undermine a value reflected in and thus formally endorsed through the Constitution or similar fundamental laws by, for example:

---

† Alberta Law Review Online Supplement (June 9, 2010). [Notes and/or references omitted.] Reproduced with permission.

(a) confronting members of the public with conduct that significantly interferes with their autonomy and liberty; or

(b) predisposing others to anti-social behaviour; or

(c) physically or psychologically harming persons involved in the conduct, and

2. That the harm or risk of harm is of a *degree* that is incompatible with the proper functioning of society.[10]

The new test has profound implications for the application of obscenity law in Canada (and obviously indecency — a matter I shall leave for another day). Yet, we have not seen a profound application of the new test in lower courts in the context of sexually explicit expression, nor has much scholarly debate ensued. Few reported cases have, thus far, used the newly created test in the context of sexually explicit materials or in the freedom of expression context and the results of those cases do not provide ultimate clarity on the new approach.[11] For example, in *Latreille*, the Court found no harm in sadomasochistic photos relying on the notion that few members of the public would be exposed to the materials unwittingly. Despite the Court's emphasis on the lack of causality of harm, the Court curiously noted that the materials did not exceed the tolerance standards of members of the Canadian community — language from the old community standards of tolerance test.[12]

The new language of causality espoused by the Supreme Court of Canada in *Labaye* might give hope to those who believed that the community standards of tolerance test was "a judicial construct filling a legislative vacuum"[13] and that a test requiring more stringent causality would sufficiently fill the vacuum. There are at least three reasons to be cautiously pessimistic about the increased causal thrust of *Labaye*.

First, the majority in *Labaye* saw itself as merely restating the harm test. The majority expressed approval of the community standards of tolerance test as constructed in its preceding cases — most notably *Butler* and *Little Sisters Book and Art Emporium v. Canada (Minister of Justice)*:[14]

The shift to a harm-based rationale was completed by this Court's decisions in *R. v. Butler ...* and *Little Sisters*.[15]

...

The Court in *Little Sisters* confirmed that harm is an essential ingredient of obscenity. As Binnie J. pointed out, "the phrase 'degrading or dehumanizing' in *Butler* is qualified immediately by the words '*if* the risk of harm is substantial'.... This makes it clear that not all sexually explicit

erotica depicting adults engaged in conduct which is considered to be degrading or dehumanizing is obscene. *The material must also create a substantial risk of harm which exceeds the community's tolerance.*"[16]

If *Butler* and *Little Sisters* are examples of a harm test properly constructed, this risks undoing the Court's contention that harm is the ultimate arbiter of obscenity and indecency. This is a perplexing judicial turn because the Court in *Butler* all but conceded that harm due to exposure to sexually explicit material was virtually impossible to prove. The majority in *Butler* noted that "[w]hile a direct link between obscenity and harm to society may be difficult, if not impossible, to establish, it is reasonable to presume that exposure to images bears a causal relationship to changes in attitudes and beliefs."[17] This leads to a second observation. If the Court in *Labaye* is relying on *Butler* as the "gold standard" for a harm test, it surely must be concerned with something less than a true causal link between exposures to sexually explicit materials and harm than a strict reading of its reformulated test suggests. Indeed, a close reading of *Labaye* reveals that the majority has left plenty of open space in which to forgive a dearth of evidentiary causality. ... The Court concedes in a short paragraph, that actual harm is not required in all circumstances in order to found an obscenity or indecency charge.[19] Rather, the Crown could merely establish that there is a risk that exposure to the materials results in harm that is incompatible with the functioning of society.[20]

Most perplexingly, the Court in *Labaye* notes that "[t]he more extreme the nature of the harm, the lower the degree of risk that may be required to permit use of the ultimate sanction of criminal law. Sometimes, a small risk can be said to be incompatible with the proper functioning of society."[21] The majority then refers to a "terrorist" attack as emblematic of such an extreme nature of harm. Yet, one cannot help but feel the metaphor is inappropriate given that the Court is dealing with issues of obscenity and indecency, not national security. Given the lip service paid to the principled nature of the *Butler* and *Little Sisters* decisions, one cannot help but query whether the Court was musing that sexually explicit speech might be an area of analysis where the nature of the harm was severe enough so as to permit a low degree of risk to meet the causal threshold. ...

Lastly, the *Labaye* Court makes an interesting admission toward the end of its analysis. The majority, having swept the community standards of tolerance test into the dustbin of discarded precedent, embarks on an alternative argument. Having not found that the nature of harm was substantial enough to meet the level of indecency for the purposes of the "common bawdy-house" charge (effectively ending the analysis), the majority ponders whether the degree of harm might have hypothetically been severe enough for sanction had the nature of the harm been established. The majority argues that it was unlikely that the conduct at issue "rose to the level of incompatibility with the proper functioning of society."[25] The majority would have been wise to end the analysis there, for its next line will provide confusing fodder for lower courts to choke upon for years to come. The majority concluded by noting, "[c]onsensual conduct behind code-locked doors can *hardly be supposed to jeopardize a society as vigorous and tolerant as Canadian society.*"[26] Has the majority not just reinserted the community standards of toler-

ance test back into the analysis in this last line? Could a lower court not use this *obiter* to once again objectively evaluate what most Canadians would tolerate in our "vigorous" society? ...

It is no wonder that academic debate on obscenity law has slowed to a crawl in the wake of *Labaye*. The majority has issued a judgment which apparently reconstitutes the old community standards of tolerance test as a harm test. Yet, in doing so, the majority may have simply re-jigged the test such that all analyses of community standards, while subsisting, hide beneath the surface. This is an interesting idea to explore and I would urge those who have previously problematized the community standards of tolerance test to bring their collective expertise to this debate. I would urge them to give content to this new judicial vacuum — the harm test.

(a)   *Christie v. York Corp.*†

[RINFRET J. (for Duff C.J., Crocket and Kerwin JJ., and himself):]

The appellant, who is a negro, entered a tavern owned and operated by the respondent, in the city of Montreal, and asked to be served a glass of beer; but the waiters refused him for the sole reason that they had been instructed not to serve coloured persons. He claimed the sum of $200 for the humiliation he suffered.

The respondent alleged that in giving such instructions to its employees and in so refusing to serve the appellant it was well within its rights; that its business is a private enterprise for gain; and that, in acting as it did, the respondent was merely protecting its business interests.

It appears from the evidence that, in refusing to sell beer to the appellant, the respondent's employees did so quietly, politely and without causing any scene or commotion whatever. If any notice was attracted to the appellant on the occasion in question, it arose out of the fact that the appellant persisted in demanding beer after he had been so refused and went to the length of calling the police, which was entirely unwarranted by the circumstances.

The learned trial judge awarded the appellant the sum of $25 and costs of the action as brought. The only ground of the judgment was that the rule whereby the respondent refused to serve negroes in its tavern was "illegal," according to sections 19 and 33 of the *Quebec Licence Act* (Ch. 25 of R.S.P.Q., 1925).

The Court of King's Bench, however, was of opinion that the sections relied on by the Superior Court did not apply; and considering that, as a general rule, in the absence of any specific law, a merchant or trader is free to carry on his business in the manner he conceives to be best for that business, that Court (Galipeault, J., dissenting) reversed the judgment of the Superior Court and dismissed the appellant's action with costs [(1938) Q.R. 65 K.B. 104.]. The appeal here is by special leave, pursuant to sec. 41 of the *Supreme Court Act* [[1939] S.C.R. 50.].

In considering this case, we ought to start from the proposition that the general principle of the law of Quebec is that of complete freedom of commerce. Any merchant is free to deal as he may choose with any individual member of the public. It is not a question of motives or reasons for deciding to deal or not to deal; he is free to do either. The only restriction to this general principle would be the existence of a specific law, or, in the carrying out of the principle, the adoption of a rule contrary to good morals or public order. ...

. . . .

We will discuss later the effect of sec. 33 of the *Quebec Licence Act*, but for the moment it may be stated that, in this case, either under the law or upon the record, it cannot be argued that the rule adopted by the respondent in the conduct of its establishment was contrary to good morals or public order. Nor could it be said, as the law stood, that the sale of beer in the province of Quebec was either a monopoly or a privileged enterprise.

---

† [1940] S.C.R. 139.

The fact that a business cannot be conducted without a licence does not make the owner or the operator thereof a trader of a privileged class.

The license in this case is mainly for the purpose of raising revenue and also, to a certain extent, for allowing the Government to control the industry; but it does not prevent the operation of the tavern from being a private enterprise to be managed within the discretion of its proprietor.

The only point to be examined therefore is whether sec. 33 of the *Quebec Licence Act*, upon which the learned trial judge relied in maintaining the appellant's action, applies to the present case.

The view of the majority of the Court of King's Bench was that it did not; and we agree with that interpretation.

Section 33 reads:

> No licensee for a restaurant may refuse, without reasonable cause, to give food to travellers.

For the purpose of our decision, there are three words to be considered in that section: "restaurant," "food," and "travellers."

The word "restaurant" is defined in the Act (sec. 19-2):

> A "restaurant" is an establishment, provided with special space and accommodation, where, in consideration of payment, food (without lodging) is habitually furnished to travellers.

The word "traveller" is also defined in the same section as follows:

> A "traveller" is a person who, in consideration of a given price per day, or fraction of a day, on the American or European plan, or per meal, à table d'hôte or à la carte, is furnished by another person with food or lodging, or both.

With the aid of those two definitions in the Act, we think it must be decided that, in this case, the appellant was not a traveller who was asking to be furnished with food in a restaurant.

Perhaps, as stated by the learned trial judge, a glass of beer may, in certain cases, be considered as food. But we have no doubt that, in view of the definitions contained in the Act, the appellant was not a traveller asking for food in a restaurant within the meaning of the statute. In the Act respecting alcoholic liquor (ch. 37 of R.S.P.Q., 1925) we find the definition of the words "restaurant" and "traveller" in exactly the same terms as above. But, in addition, the words "meal" and "tavern" are also defined (Sec. 3, subs. 6 and 9).

Those definitions, so far as material here, are as follows:

> 6. The word "meal" means the consumption of food of a nature and quantity sufficient for the maintenance of the consumer, in one of the following places:
>
> ...
>
> (b) In the dining-room of a restaurant situated in a city or town, and equipped for the accommodation of fifty guests at one time, and which is not only licensed for the reception of travellers but where full meals are regularly served.
>
> 9. The word "tavern" means an establishment specially adapted for the sale by the glass and consumption on the premises of beer as hereinbefore defined, or, in a hotel or restaurant, the room specially adapted for such purpose.

It will be seen therefore that the appellant cannot be brought within the terms of sec. 33 of the *Quebec Licence Act*. He was not a traveller asking for a meal in a restaurant. According to the definitions, he was only a person asking for a glass of beer in a tavern.

As the case is not governed by any specific law or more particularly by sec. 33 of the *Quebec Licence Act*, it falls under the general principle of the freedom of commerce; and it must follow that, when refusing to serve the appellant, the respondent was strictly within its rights.

But perhaps it may be added that the Quebec statutes make a clear distinction between a hotel or a restaurant and a tavern. The Act (sec. 32) provides that "no licensee for a hotel may refuse without just cause to give lodging or food to travellers" and that (sec. 33) "No licensee for a restaurant may refuse without reasonable cause, to give food to travellers."

No similar provision is made for taverns; and, in our opinion, it would follow from the statute itself that the legislature designedly excluded tavern owners from the obligation imposed upon the hotel and restaurant owners.

For these reasons, the appeal ought to be dismissed with costs.

[DAVIS J. (dissenting):]

The appellant is a British subject residing in Verdun near the city of Montreal in the province of Quebec. He came from Jamaica and has been permanently resident in the said province for some twenty years. He is a coloured gentleman — his own words are "a negro" though counsel for the respondent, for what reason I do not know, told him during his examination for discovery that he wanted it on record that he is "not extraordinarily black." He appears to have a good position as a private chauffeur in Montreal. He was a season box subscriber to hockey matches held in the Forum in Montreal and in that building the respondent operates a beer tavern. Beer is sold by the glass for consumption on the premises. Food such as sandwiches is also served, being apparently purchased when required from nearby premises and resold to the customer. The appellant had often on prior occasions to the one in question, when attending the hockey matches dropped into the respondent's tavern and bought beer by the glass there. On the particular evening on which the complaint out of which these proceedings arose occurred, the appellant with two friends — he describes one as a white man and the other as coloured — just before the hockey game went into the respondent's premises in the ordinary course. The appellant put down fifty cents on the table and asked the waiter for three steins of light beer. The waiter declined to fill the order, stating that he was instructed not to serve coloured people. The appellant and his two friends then spoke to the bartender and to the manager, both of whom stated that the reason for refusal was that the appellant was a coloured person. The appellant then telephoned for the police. He says he did this because he wanted the police there to witness the refusal that had been made. The manager repeated to the police the refusal he had previously made. The appellant and his two friends then left the premises of their own accord. The appellant says that this was to his humiliation in the presence of some seventy customers who were sitting around and had heard what occurred.

The appellant then brought this action against the respondent for damages for breach of contract and damages in tort. No objection was taken to the suit having been brought both on contract and in tort on the same set of facts and I assume that this form of action is permissible under the Quebec practice and procedure. The appellant recovered $25 damages and costs at the trial. This judgment was set aside and the action was dismissed with costs upon an appeal to the Court of King's Bench (Appeal Side), Galipeault J. dissenting [(1938) Q.R. 65 K.B. 104.].

The learned trial judge found that the appellant had been humiliated by the refusal and was entitled to be compensated upon the ground that the tavern was a restaurant within the meaning of the *Quebec Licence Act*, R.S.Q. 1925, ch. 25, sec. 19, and that as such the respondent was forbidden by sec. 33 to refuse the appellant. By sec. 19(2) a restaurant is defined as

an establishment, provided with special space and accommodation, where, in consideration of payment, food (without lodging) is habitually furnished to travellers.

By sec. 33,

no licensee for a restaurant may refuse, without reasonable cause, to give food to travellers.

The Court of King's Bench did not consider the above statute, which deals with various licences granted by the government under the Act, applicable to the facts of this case, and, I think rightly, dealt with the case of the tavern under another statute, the *Alcoholic Liquor Act*, R.S.Q. 1925, ch. 37, and the majority of the Court took the view that "chaque propriétaire est maître chez lui" on the doctrine of freedom of commerce — "la liberté du commerce et de l'industrie." Pratte, J. ad hoc agreed with the conclusion of the majority but upon the single ground that the respondent's refusal was made under circumstances such that it could not cause any damage to the appellant. Galipeault, J. dissented upon the ground that the conduct of the respondent towards the appellant was contrary to good morals and the public order — "contre les bonnes moeurs, contre l'ordre public," and considered that under the special legislation in Quebec governing the sale of liquor the respondent was not entitled to the "freedom of commerce" applicable to ordinary merchants and places like theatres, etc. Galipeault, J. would have affirmed the trial judgment.

This Court gave special leave to the appellant to appeal to this Court from the judgment of the Court of King's Bench upon the ground that the matter in controversy in the appeal will involve "matters by which rights in future of the parties may be affected" within the meaning of sec. 41 of the *Supreme Court Act* and also because the matter in controversy is of such general importance that leave to appeal ought to be granted [[1939] S.C.R. 50.].

The question in issue is a narrow one but I regard it as a very important one. That is, Has a tavern keeper in the province of Quebec under the special legislation there in force the right to refuse to sell beer to any one of the public? There is no suggestion that in this case there was any conduct of a disorderly nature or any reason to prompt the refusal to serve the beer to the appellant other than the fact that he was a coloured gentleman.

The province of Quebec in 1921 adopted the policy of complete control within the province of the sale of alcoholic liquors. (The *Alcoholic Liquor Act*, 11 Geo. V, Quebec Statutes 1921, ch. 24, now

R.S.Q. 1925, ch. 37.) The words "alcoholic liquor" in the statute expressly include beer (sec. 3(5)). The word "tavern" means an establishment specially adapted for the sale by the glass and consumption on the premises of beer or, in a hotel or restaurant, the room specially adapted for such purpose (sec. 3(9)). The sale and delivery in the province of alcoholic liquor, with the exception of beer, is forbidden expressly, except that it may be sold or delivered to or by the Quebec Liquor Commission set up by the statute or by any person authorized by it, or in any case provided for by the statute (sec. 22). The sale of beer is specifically dealt with by sec. 25, which provides that

> The sale or delivery of beer is forbidden in the province, unless such sale or delivery be made by the Commission or by a brewer or other person authorized by the Commission under this Act, and in the manner hereinafter set forth.

The Commission is given power by sec. 9d to control the possession, sale and delivery of alcoholic liquor in accordance with the provisions of the statute and by sec. 9e to grant permits for the sale of alcoholic liquor. By sec. 33 the Commission may determine the manner in which a tavern must be furnished and equipped in order to allow the exercise therein of the "privilege conferred by the permit." Beer may be sold by any person in charge of a grocery or of a store where beer only is sold, on condition that no quantity of less than one bottle be sold, that such beer be not consumed in such store, and that a permit therefor be granted him by the Commission, and that such permit be in force (sec. 30(4)). Now as to the sale of beer by the glass, sec. 30(5) provides as follows:

> Any person in charge of a tavern, but in a city or town only, may sell therein beer by the glass, — provided that it be consumed on the premises, and provided that a permit to that effect be granted him by the Commission ... and that such permit be in force.

Section 30 further provides that in every such case the beer must have been bought directly by the holder of the permit from a brewer who is also the holder of a permit. Section 42(3) fixes the days and hours during which any holder of a permit for the sale of beer in a tavern may sell. Then by sec. 43, certain named classes of persons are forbidden to be sold any alcoholic liquor:

1. Any person who has not reached the age of eighteen years;
2. any interdicted person;
3. any keeper or inmate of a disorderly house;
4. any person already convicted of drunkenness or of any offence caused by drunkenness;
5. Any person who habitually drinks alcoholic liquor to excess, and to whom the Commission has, after investigation, decided to prohibit the sale of such liquor upon application to the Commission by the husband, wife, father, mother, brother, sister, curator, employer or other person depending upon or in charge of such person, or by the curé, pastor, or mayor of the place.

But no sale to any of the persons mentioned in 2, 3, 4 or 5 above shall constitute an offence by the vendor unless the Commission has informed him, by registered letter, that it is forbidden to sell to such person. Sec. 46 provides that no beer shall be transported in the province except as therein defined.

By a separate statute, the *Alcoholic Liquor Possession and Transportation Act*, 11 Geo. V (1921), ch. 25, now R.S.Q. 1925, ch. 38, which Act is stated to apply to the whole province, no alcoholic liquor as defined in the *Alcoholic Liquor Act* (which includes beer) shall be kept, possessed or transported in the province except as therein set forth. Subsection 3 of sec. 3 excepts:

> in the residence of any person, for personal consumption and not for sale, provided it has been acquired by and delivered to such person, in his residence, previous to the 1st of May, 1921, or has been acquired by him, since such date, from the Quebec Liquor Commission.

It is plain, then, that the province of Quebec, like most of the other provinces in Canada, took complete control of the sale of liquor in its own province. The permit system enables the public to purchase from either government stores or specially licensed vendors. A glass of beer can only be bought in the province from a person who has been granted by the Government Commission a permit (sec. 33 refers to it as a "privilege") to sell to the public beer in the glass for consumption on the premises. The respondent was a person to whom a permit had been granted. The sole question in this appeal then is whether the respondent, having been given under the statute the special privilege of selling beer in the glass to the public, had the right to pick and choose those of the public to whom he would sell. In this case the refusal was on the ground of the colour of the person. It might well have been on account of the racial antecedents or the religious faith of the person. The statute itself has definitely laid down, by sec. 43, certain classes of persons to whom a licensee must not sell. The question is, Has the licensee the right to set up his own particular code, or is he bound, as the custodian of a government permit to sell to the public, to sell to anyone who is ready to pay the regular price? Disorderly conduct on the premises of course does not enter into our discussion because there is no suggestion of that in this case. One approach to the problem is the application of the doctrine of "freedom of commerce." It was held by the majority in the Court below, in effect, that the licensee is in no different position from a grocer or other merchant who can sell his goods to whom he likes. The opposite view was taken by Galipeault, J. on the ground that the licensee has what is in the nature of a quasi monopolistic right which involves a corresponding duty to sell to the public except in those cases prohibited by statute. Pratte J., ad hoc, did not take either view; his decision rests solely upon the ground that the respondent's refusal was made under circumstances such that it could not cause any damage to the appellant.

. . . .

The question is one of difficulty, as the divergence of judicial opinion in the courts below indicates. My own view is that having regard to the special legislation in Quebec establishing complete governmental control of the sale of beer in the province and particularly the statutory provision which prohibits anyone of the public from buying beer in the glass from anyone but a person granted the special privilege of selling the same, a holder of such a permit from the government to sell beer in the glass to the public has not the right of an ordinary trader to pick and choose those to whom he will sell.

In the changed and changing social and economic conditions, different principles must necessarily be applied to the new conditions. It is not a question of creating a new principle but of applying a different but existing principle of the law. The doctrine that any merchant is free to deal with the public as he chooses had a very definite place in the older economy and still applies to the case of an ordinary merchant, but when the State enters the field and takes exclusive control of the sale to the public of such a commodity as liquor, then the old doctrine of the freedom of the merchant to do as he likes has in my view no application to a person to whom the State has given a special privilege to sell to the public.

If there is to be exclusion on the ground of colour or of race or of religious faith or on any other ground not already specifically provided for by the statute, it is for the legislature itself, in my view, to impose such prohibitions under the exclusive system of governmental control of the sale of liquor to the public which it has seen fit to enact.

The appellant sued for $200. The learned trial judge awarded him $25 damages. I would allow the appeal, set aside the judgment appealed from and restore the judgment at the trial with costs here and below.

Appeal dismissed with costs.

(b) *Delgamuukw v. B.C.*†

(2) **Application of General Principles**

(a) General Comments

The general principle of appellate non-interference applies with particular force in this appeal. The trial was lengthy and very complex. There were 318 days of testimony. There were a large number of witnesses, lay and expert. The volume of evidence is enormous. To quote the trial judge at pp. 116–17:

A total of 61 witnesses gave evidence at trial, many using translators from their native Gitksan or Wet'suwet'en language; "word spellers" to assist the official reporters were required for many witnesses; a further 15 witnesses gave their evidence on commission; 53 territorial affidavits were filed; 30 deponents were cross-examined out of court; there are 23,503 pages of transcript evidence at trial; 5898 pages of transcript of argument; 3,039 pages of commission evidence and 2,553 pages of cross-examination on affidavits (all evidence and oral arguments are conveniently preserved in hard copy and on diskettes); about 9,200 exhibits were filed at trial compris-

---

† [1997] 3 S.C.R. 1010 at 1070–79, per Lamer C.J.

ing, I estimate, well over 50,000 pages; the plaintiffs' draft outline of argument comprises 3,250 pages, the province's 1,975 pages, and Canada's over 1,000 pages; there are 5,977 pages of transcript of argument in hard copy and on diskettes. All parties filed some excerpts from the exhibits they referred to in argument. The province alone submitted 28 huge binders of such documents. At least 15 binders of reply argument were left with me during that stage of the trial.

The result was a judgment of over 400 pages in length.

It is not open to the appellants to challenge the trial judge's findings of fact merely because they disagree with them. I fear that a significant number of the appellants' objections fall into this category. Those objections are too numerous to list in their entirety. The bulk of these objections, at best, relate to alleged instances of misapprehension or oversight of material evidence by the trial judge. However, the respondents have established that, in most situations, there was *some* contradictory evidence that supported the trial judge's conclusion. The question, ultimately, was one of weight, and the appellants have failed to demonstrate that the trial judge erred in this respect.

One objection that I would like to mention specifically, albeit in passing, is the trial judge's refusal to accept the testimony of two anthropologists who were brought in as expert witnesses by the appellants. This aspect of the trial judge's reasons was hotly contested by the appellants in their written submissions. However, I need only reiterate what I have stated above, that findings of credibility, including the credibility of expert witnesses, are for the trial judge to make, and should warrant considerable deference from appellate courts.

On the other hand, the appellants have alleged that the trial judge made a number of serious errors relating to the treatment of the oral histories of the appellants. Those oral histories were expressed in three different forms: (i) the adaawk of the Gitksan, and the kungax of the Wet'suwet'en; (ii) the personal recollections of members of the appellant nations, and (iii) the territorial affidavits filed by the heads of the individual houses within each nation. The trial judge ruled on both the admissibility of, and the weight to be given to, these various forms of oral history without the benefit of my reasons in *Van der Peet*, as will become evident in the discussion that follows.

(b) Adaawk and Kungax

The adaawk and kungax of the Gitksan and Wet'suwet'en nations, respectively, are oral histories of a special kind. They were described by the trial judge, at p. 164, as a "sacred 'official' litany, or history, or recital of the most important laws, history, traditions and traditional territory of a House". The content of these special oral histories includes its physical representation totem poles, crests and blankets. The importance of the adaawk and kungax is underlined by the fact that they are "repeated, performed and authenticated at important feasts" (at p. 164). At those feasts, dissenters have the opportunity to object if they question any detail and, in this way, help ensure the authenticity of the adaawk and kungax. Although they serve largely the same role, the trial judge found that there are some differences in both the form and content of the adaawk and the kungax. For example, the latter is "in the nature of a song ... which is intended to represent the special authority and responsibilities of a chief...." However, these differences are not legally relevant for the purposes of the issue at hand.

It is apparent that the adaawk and kungax are of integral importance to the distinctive cultures of the appellant nations. At trial, they were relied on for two distinct purposes. First, the adaawk was relied on as a component of and, therefore, as proof of the existence of a system of land tenure law internal to the Gitksan, which covered the whole territory claimed by that appellant. In other words, it was offered as evidence of the Gitksan's historical use and occupation of that territory. For the Wet'suwet'en, the kungax was offered as proof of the central significance of the claimed lands to their distinctive culture. As I shall explain later in these reasons, both use and occupation, and the central significance of the lands occupied, are relevant to proof of aboriginal title.

The admissibility of the adaawk and kungax was the subject of a general decision of the trial judge handed down during the course of the trial regarding the admissibility of all oral histories (incorrectly indexed as *Uukw v. R.*, [1987] 6 W.W.R. 155 (B.C.S.C.)). Although the trial judge recognized that the evidence at issue was a form of hearsay, he ruled it admissible on the basis of the recognized exception that declarations made by deceased persons could be given in evidence by witnesses as proof of public or general rights: see Michael N. Howard, Peter Crane and Daniel A. Hochberg, *Phipson on Evidence* (14th ed. 1990), at p. 736. He affirmed that earlier ruling in his trial judgment, correctly in my view, by stating, at p. 180, that the adaawk and kungax were admissible "out of necessity as exceptions to the hearsay rule" because there was no other way to prove the history of the Gitksan and Wet'suwet'en nations.

The trial judge, however, went on to give these oral histories no independent weight at all. He held, at p. 180, that they were only admissible as "direct evidence of facts in issue ... in a few cases where they could constitute confirmatory proof of early presence in the territory". His central concern [was] that the adaawk and kungax could not serve "as evidence of detailed history, or land ownership, use or occupation". I disagree with some of the reasons he relied on in support of this conclusion.

Although he had earlier recognized, when making his ruling on admissibility, that it was impossible to make an easy distinction between the mythological and "real" aspects of these oral histories, he discounted the adaawk and kungax because they were not "literally true", confounded "what is fact and what is belief", "included some material which might be classified as mythology", and projected a "romantic view" of the history of the appellants. He also cast doubt on the authenticity of these special oral histories (at p. 181) because, *inter alia*, "the verifying group is so small that they cannot safely be regarded as expressing the reputation of even the Indian community, let alone the larger community whose opportunity to dispute territorial claims would be essential to weight". Finally, he questioned (at p. 181) the utility of the adaawk and kungax to demonstrate use and occupation because they were "seriously lacking in detail about the specific lands to which they are said to relate".

Although he framed his ruling on weight in terms of the specific oral histories before him, in my respectful opinion, the trial judge in reality based his decision on some general concerns with the use of oral histories as evidence in aboriginal rights cases. In summary, the trial judge gave no independent weight to these special oral histories because they did not accurately convey historical truth, because knowledge about those oral histories was confined to the communities whose histories they were and because those oral histories were insufficiently detailed. However, as I mentioned earlier, these are features, to a greater or lesser extent, of all oral histories, not just the adaawk and kungax. The implication of the trial judge's reasoning is that oral histories should never be given any independent weight and are only useful as confirmatory evidence in aboriginal rights litigation. I fear that if this reasoning were followed, the oral histories of aboriginal peoples would be consistently and systematically undervalued by the Canadian legal system, in contradiction of the express instruction to the contrary in Van der Peet that trial courts interpret the evidence of aboriginal peoples in light of the difficulties inherent in adjudicating aboriginal claims.

(c) Recollections of Aboriginal Life

The trial judge also erred when he discounted the "recollections of aboriginal life" offered by various members of the appellant nations. I take that term to be a reference to testimony about personal and family history that is not part of an adaawk or a kungax. That evidence consisted of the personal knowledge of the witnesses and declarations of witnesses' ancestors as to land use. This history had been adduced by the appellants in order to establish the requisite degree of use and occupation to make out a claim to ownership and, for the same reason as the adaawk and kungax, is material to the proof of aboriginal title.

The trial judge limited the uses to which the evidence could be put. He reasoned, at p. 177, that this evidence, at most, established "without question, that the plaintiff's immediate ancestors, for the past 100 years or so" had used land in the claimed territory for aboriginal purposes. However, the evidence was insufficiently precise to demonstrate that the more distant ancestors of the witnesses had engaged in specific enough land use "far enough back in time to permit the plaintiffs to succeed on issues such as internal boundaries". In the language of *Van der Peet*, the trial judge effectively held that this evidence did not demonstrate the requisite continuity between present occupation and past occupation in order to ground a claim for aboriginal title.

In my opinion, the trial judge expected too much of the oral history of the appellants, as expressed in the recollections of aboriginal life of members of the appellant nations. He expected that evidence to provide definitive and precise evidence of pre-contact aboriginal activities on the territory in question. However, as I held in *Van der Peer*, this will be almost an impossible burden to meet. Rather, if oral history cannot conclusively establish pre-sovereignty (after this decision) occupation of land, it may still be relevant to demonstrate that current occupation has its origins prior to sovereignty. This is exactly what the appellants sought to do.

(d) Territorial Affidavits

Finally, the trial judge also erred in his treatment of the territorial affidavits filed by the appellant chiefs. Those affidavits were declarations of the territorial holdings of each of the Gitksan and Wet'suwet'en houses and, at trial, were introduced for the purposes of establishing each House's ownership of its specific territory. Before this Court, the appellants tried to amalgamate these individual claims into collective claims on behalf of each nation and the relevance of the affidavits changed accordingly. I have already held that it is not open to the appellants to alter fundamentally the nature of their claim in this way on appeal. Nevertheless, the treatment of the affidavits is important because they will be relevant at a new trial to the existence and nature of the land tenure system within each nation and, therefore, material to the proof of title.

The affidavits rely heavily on the declarations of deceased persons of use or ownership of the lands, which are a form of oral history. But those declarations are a kind of hearsay and the appellants therefore argued that the affidavits should be admitted through the reputation exception to the hearsay rule. Although he recognized, at p. 438, that the territorial affidavits were "the best evidence [the appellants] could adduce on this question of internal boundaries", the trial judge held that this exception did not apply and refused to admit the declarations contained in the affidavits.

I am concerned by the specific reasons the trial judge gave for refusing to apply the reputation exception. He questioned the degree to which the declarations amounted to a reputation because they were largely confined to the appellants' communities. The trial judge asserted that neighbouring aboriginal groups whose territorial claims conflicted with those of the appellants, as well as non-aboriginals who potentially possessed a legal interest in the claimed territory, were unaware of the content of the alleged reputation at all. Furthermore, the trial judge reasoned that since the subject-matter of the affidavits was disputed, its reliability was doubtful. Finally, the trial judge questioned, at p. 441, "the independence and objectivity" of the information contained in the affidavits, because the appellants and their ancestors (at p. 440) "have been actively discussing land claims for many years".

Although he regretted this finding, the trial judge felt bound to apply the rules of evidence because it did not appear to him (at p. 442) "that the Supreme Court of Canada has decided that the ordinary rules of evidence do not apply to this kind of case". The trial judge arrived at this conclusion, however, without the benefit of *Van der Peet*, where I held that the ordinary rules of evidence must be approached and adapted in light of the evidentiary difficulties inherent in adjudicating aboriginal claims.

Many of the reasons relied on by the trial judge for excluding the evidence contained in the territorial affidavits are problematic because they run against this fundamental principle. The requirement that a reputation be known in the general community, for example, ignores the fact that oral histories, as noted by the Royal Commission on Aboriginal Peoples, generally relate to particular locations, and refer to particular families and communities and may, as a result, be unknown outside of that community, even to other aboriginal nations. Excluding the territorial affidavits because the claims to which they relate are disputed does not acknowledge that claims to aboriginal rights, and aboriginal title in particular, are almost always disputed and contested. Indeed, if those claims were uncontroversial, there would be no need to bring them to the courts for resolution. Casting doubt on the reliability of the territorial affidavits because land claims had been actively discussed for many years also fails to take account of the special context surrounding aboriginal claims, in two ways. First, those claims have been discussed for so long because of British Columbia's persistent refusal to acknowledge the existence of aboriginal title in that province until relatively recently, largely as a direct result of the decision of this Court in *Calder*, supra. It would be perverse, to say the least, to use the refusal of the province to acknowledge the rights of its aboriginal inhabitants as a reason for excluding evidence which may prove the existence of those rights. Second, this rationale for exclusion places aboriginal claimants whose societies record their past through oral history in a grave dilemma. In order for the oral history of a community to amount to a form of reputation, and to be admissible in court, it must remain alive through the discussions of members of that community; those discussions are the very basis of that reputation. But if those histories are discussed too much, and too close to the date of litigation, they may be discounted as being suspect, and may be held to be inadmissible. The net effect may be that a society with such an oral tradition would never be able to establish a historical claim through the use of oral history in court.

(e) Conclusion

The trial judge's treatment of the various kinds of oral histories did not satisfy the principles I laid down in *Van der Peet*. These errors are particularly worrisome because oral histories were of critical importance to the appellants' case. They used those histories in an attempt to establish their occupation and use of the disputed territory, an essential requirement for aboriginal title. The trial judge, after refusing to admit, or giving no independent weight to these oral histories, reached the conclusion that the appellants had not demonstrated the requisite degree of occupation for "ownership". Had the trial judge assessed the oral histories correctly, his conclusions on these issues of fact might have been very different.

In the circumstances, the factual findings cannot stand. However, given the enormous complexity of the factual issues at hand, it would be impossible for the Court to do justice to the parties by sifting through the record itself and making new factual findings. A new trial is warranted, at which the evidence may be considered in light of the principles laid down in *Van der Peet* and elaborated upon here. In applying these principles, the new trial judge might well share some or all of the findings of fact of McEachern C.J.

(c) Racially Based Jury Nullification: Black Power in the Criminal Justice System†

Paul Butler

INTRODUCTION

I was a Special Assistant United States Attorney in the District of Columbia in 1990. I prosecuted people accused of misdemeanor crimes, mainly the drug and gun cases that overwhelm the local courts of most American cities.[3] As a federal prosecutor, I represented the United States of America and used that power to put people, mainly African-American men, in prison. I am also an African-American man. While at the U.S. Attorney's office, I made two discoveries that profoundly changed the way I viewed my work as a prosecutor and my responsibilities as a black person.

The first discovery occurred during a training session for new Assistants conducted by experienced prosecutors. We rookies were informed that we would lose many of our cases, despite having persuaded a jury beyond a reasonable doubt that the defendant was guilty. We would lose because some black jurors would refuse to convict black defendants who they knew were guilty.

The second discovery was related to the first, but was even more unsettling. It occurred during the trial of Marion Barry, then the second-term mayor of the District of Columbia. Barry was being prosecuted by my office for drug possession and perjury. I learned, to my surprise, that some of my fellow African-American prosecutors hoped that the mayor would be acquitted, despite the fact that he was obviously guilty of at least one of the charges — he had smoked cocaine on FBI videotape.[4] These black prosecutors wanted their office to lose its case because they believed that the prosecution of Barry was racist.

Federal prosecutors in the nation's capital hear many rumors about prominent officials engaging in illegal conduct, including drug use. Some African-American prosecutors wondered why, of all those people, the government chose to "set up" the most famous black politician in Washington, D.C.[5] They also asked themselves why, if crack is so dangerous, the FBI had allowed the mayor to smoke it. Some members of the predominantly black jury must have had similar concerns: They convicted the mayor of only one count of a fourteen-count indictment, despite the trial judge's assessment that he had "'never seen a stronger government case.'"[6] Some African-American prosecutors thought that the jury, in rendering its verdict, jabbed its black thumb in the face of a racist prosecution, and that idea made those prosecutors glad.

As such reactions suggest, lawyers and judges increasingly perceive that some African-American jurors vote to acquit black defendants for racial reasons,[7] a decision sometimes expressed as the juror's desire not to send yet another black man to jail.[8] This Essay examines the question of what role race should play in black jurors' decisions to acquit defendants in criminal cases. Specifically, I consider trials

† (1995) 105 Yale L.J. 677 at 678–80, 690–701, 705–14, 725. Reproduced by permission of Paul Butler and The Yale Law Journal Company, Inc. [Notes and/or references omitted.]

that include both African-American defendants and African-American jurors. I argue that the race of a black defendant is sometimes a legally and morally appropriate factor for jurors to consider in reaching a verdict of not guilty or for an individual juror to consider in refusing to vote for conviction.[9]

My thesis is that, for pragmatic and political reasons, the black community is better off when some nonviolent lawbreakers remain in the community rather than go to prison. The decision as to what kind of conduct by African-Americans ought to be punished is better made by African-Americans themselves, based on the costs and benefits to their community, than by the traditional criminal justice process, which is controlled by white lawmakers and white law enforcers. Legally, the doctrine of jury nullification gives the power to make this decision to African-American jurors who sit in judgment of African-American defendants. Considering the costs of law enforcement to the black community and the failure of white lawmakers to devise significant nonincarcerative responses to black antisocial conduct, it is the moral responsibility of black jurors to emancipate some guilty black outlaws.

. . . . .

My goal is the subversion of American criminal justice, at least as it now exists. Through jury nullification, I want to dismantle the master's house with the master's tools.[10] My intent, however, is not purely destructive; this project is also constructive, because I hope that the destruction of the status quo will not lead to anarchy, but rather to the implementation of certain noncriminal ways of addressing antisocial conduct. Criminal conduct among African-Americans is often a predictable reaction to oppression. Sometimes black crime is a symptom of internalized white supremacy; other times it is a reasonable response to the racial and economic subordination every African-American faces every day. Punishing black people for the fruits of racism is wrong if that punishment is premised on the idea that it is the black criminal's "just desert." Hence, the new paradigm of justice that I suggest in Part III rejects punishment for the sake of retribution and endorses it, with qualifications, for the ends of deterrence and incapacitation.

In a sense, this Essay simply may argue for the return of rehabilitation as the purpose of American criminal justice, but a rehabilitation that begins with the white-supremacist beliefs that poison the minds of us all — you, me, and the black criminal. I wish that black people had the power to end racial oppression right now. African-Americans can prevent the application of one particularly destructive instrument of white supremacy — American criminal justice — to some African-American people, and this they can do immediately. I hope that this Essay makes the case for why and how they should.[11]

. . . . .

II. "JUSTICE OUTSIDE THE FORMAL RULES OF LAW"[71]

Why would a black juror vote to let a guilty person go free? Assuming that the juror is a rational actor, she must believe that she and her community are, in some way, better off with the defendant out of prison than in prison. But how could any rational person believe that about a criminal? The following section describes racial critiques of the American criminal justice system. I then examine the evolution of the doctrine of jury nullification and argue that its practice by African-Americans is, in many cases, consistent with the Anglo-American tradition and, moreover, is legally and morally right.

A. The Criminal Law and African-Americans: Justice or "Just us"?[72]

Imagine a country in which more than half of the young male citizens are under the supervision of the criminal justice system, either awaiting trial, in prison, or on probation or parole.[73] Imagine a country in which two-thirds of the men can anticipate being arrested before they reach age thirty.[74] Imagine a country in which there are more young men in prison than in college.[75] Now give the citizens of the country the key to the prison. Should they use it?

Such a country bears some resemblance to a police state. When we criticize a police state, we think that the problem lies not with the citizens of the state, but rather with the form of government or law, or with the powerful elites and petty bureaucrats whose interests the state serves. Similarly, racial critics of American criminal justice locate the problem not so much with the black prisoners as with the state and its actors and beneficiaries. As evidence, they cite their own experiences and other people's stories,[76] African-American history, understanding gained from social science research on the power and pervasiveness of white supremacy, and ugly statistics like those in the preceding paragraph.

For analytical purposes, I will create a false dichotomy among racial critics by dividing them into two camps: liberal critics and radical critics. Those are not names that the critics have given themselves or that they would necessarily accept, and there would undoubtedly be disagreement within each camp and theoretical overlap between the camps. Nonetheless, for the purposes of a brief explication of racial critiques, my oversimplification may be useful.

1. The Liberal Critique

According to this critique, American criminal justice is racist because it is controlled primarily by white people, who are unable to escape the culture's dominant message of white supremacy, and who are therefore inevitably, even if unintentionally, prejudiced.[77] These white actors include legislators, police, prosecutors, judges, and jurors. They exercise their discretion to make and enforce the criminal law in a discriminatory fashion.[78] Sometimes the discrimination is overt, as in the case of Mark Fuhrman, the police officer in the O.J. Simpson case who, in interviews, used racist language and boasted of his own brutality,[79] and sometimes it is unintentional, as with a hypothetical white juror who invariably credits the testimony of a white witness over that of a black witness.

The problem with the liberal critique is that it does not adequately explain the extent of the difference between the incidence of black and white crime, especially violent crime. For example, in 1991, blacks constituted about fifty-five percent of the 18,096 people arrested for murder and non-negligent manslaughter in the United States (9924 people).[80] One explanation the liberal critique offers for this unfortunate statistic is that the police pursue black murder suspects more aggressively than they do white murder suspects. In other words, but for discrimination, the percentage of blacks arrested for murder would be closer to their percentage of the population, roughly twelve percent.[81] The liberal critique would attribute some portion of the additional forty-three percent of non-negligent homicide arrestees (in 1991, approximately 7781 people[82]) to race prejudice. Ultimately, however, those assumptions strain credulity, not because many police officers are not racist, but because there is no evidence that there is a crisis of that magnitude in criminal justice. In fact, for all the faults of American law enforcement, catching the bad guys seems to be something it does rather well. The liberal critique fails to account convincingly for the incidence of black crime.

2. The Radical Critique

The radical critique does not discount the role of discrimination in accounting for some of the racial disparity in crime rates, but it also does not, in contrast to the liberal critique, attribute all or even most of the differential to police and prosecutor prejudice. The radical critique offers a more fundamental, structural explanation.

It suggests that criminal law is racist[83] because, like other American law, it is an instrument of white supremacy.[84] Law is made by white elites to protect their interests and, especially, to preserve the economic status quo, which benefits those elites at the expense of blacks, among others.[85] Due to discrimination and segregation, the majority of African-Americans receive few meaningful educational and employment opportunities and, accordingly, are unable to succeed, at least in the terms of the capitalist ideal.[86] Some property crimes committed by blacks may be understood as an inevitable result of the tension between the dominant societal message equating possession of material resources with success and happiness and the power of white supremacy to prevent most African-Americans from acquiring "enough" of those resources in a legal manner. "Black-on-black" violent crime, and even "victimless" crime like drug offenses, can be attributed to internalized racism, which causes some African-Americans to devalue black lives — either those of others or their own. The political process does not allow for the creation or implementation of effective "legal" solutions to this plight,[87] and the criminal law punishes predictable reactions to it.[88]

I am persuaded by the radical critique when I wonder about the roots of the ugly truth that blacks commit many crimes at substantially higher rates than whites. Most white Americans, especially liberals, would publicly offer an environmental, as opposed to genetic, explanation for this fact.[89] They would probably concede that racism, historical and current, plays a major role in creating an environment that breeds criminal conduct. From this premise, the radical critic deduces that but for the (racist) environment, the African-American criminal would not be a criminal. In other words, racism creates and sustains the criminal breeding ground, which produces the black criminal. Thus, when many African-Americans are locked up, it is because of a situation that white supremacy created.

Obviously, most blacks are not criminals, even if every black is exposed to racism. To the radical critics, however, the law-abiding conduct of the majority of African-Americans does not mean that racism does not create black criminals. Not everyone exposed to a virus will become sick, but that does not mean that the virus does not cause the illness of the people who do.

The radical racial critique of criminal justice is premised as much on the criminal law's *effect* as on its intent. The system is discriminatory, in part, because of the disparate impact law enforcement has on the black community.[90] This unjust effect is measured in terms of the costs to the black community of having so many African-Americans, particularly males, incarcerated or otherwise involved in the criminal justice system. These costs are social and economic, and include the perceived dearth of men "eligible" for marriage,[91] the large percentage of black children who live in female-headed households,[92] the lack of male "role models" for black children, especially boys,[93] the absence of wealth in the black community,[94] and the large unemployment rate among black men.[95]

3. Examples of Racism in Criminal Justice

Examples commonly cited by both liberal and radical critics as evidence of racism in criminal justice include: the Scottsboro case;[96] the history of the criminalization of drug use;[97] past and contemporary administration of the death penalty;[98] the use of imagery linking crime to race in the 1988 presidential campaign[99] and other political campaigns;[100] the beating of Rodney King and the acquittal of his police assailants;[101] disparities between punishments for white-collar crimes and punishments for other crimes;[102] more severe penalties for crack cocaine users than for powder cocaine users;[103] the Charles Murray and Susan Smith cases;[104] police corruption scandals in minority neighborhoods in New York and Philadelphia;[105] the O.J. Simpson case, including the extraordinary public and media fascination with it,[106] the racist police officer who was the prosecution's star witness,[107] and the response of many white people to the jury's verdict of acquittal;[108] and, cited most frequently, the extraordinary rate of incarceration of African-American men.[109]

4. Law Enforcement Enthusiasts

Of course, the idea that the criminal justice system is racist and oppressive is not without dissent, and among the dissenters are some African-Americans. Randall Kennedy succinctly poses the counterargument:

> Although the administration of criminal justice has, at times, been used as an instrument of racial oppression, the principal problem facing African-Americans in the context of criminal justice today is not over-enforcement but under-enforcement of the laws. The most lethal danger facing African-Americans in their day-to-day lives is not white, racist officials of the state, but private, violent criminals (typically black) who attack those most vulnerable to them without regard to racial identity.[110]

According to these theorists, whom I will call law enforcement enthusiasts, the criminal law may have a disproportionate impact on the black community, but this is not a moral or racial issue because the disproportionate impact is the law's effect, not its intent. For law enforcement enthusiasts, intent is the most appropriate barometer of governmental racism.[111] Because law enforcement is a public good, it is in the best interest of the black community to have more, rather than less, of it. Allowing criminals to live unfettered in the community would harm, in particular, the black poor, who are disproportionately the victims of violent crime. Indeed, the logical conclusion of the enthusiasts' argument is that African-Americans would be better off with more, not fewer, black criminals behind bars.

To my mind, the enthusiasts embrace law enforcement too uncritically: They are blind to its opportunity costs. I agree that criminal law enforcement constitutes a public good for African-Americans when it serves the social protection goals that Professor Kennedy highlights. In other words, when locking up black men means that "violent criminals ... who attack those most vulnerable"[112] are off the streets, most people — including most law enforcement critics — would endorse the incarceration. But what about when locking up a black man has no or little net effect on public safety, when, for example, the crime with which he was charged is victimless?[113] Putting aside for a moment the legal implications, couldn't an analysis of the costs and benefits to the African-American community present an argument against incarceration? I argue "yes," in light of the substantial costs to the community of law enforcement. I accept that other reasonable people may disagree. But the law enforcement enthusiasts seldom acknowledge that racial critics even weigh the costs and benefits; their assumption seems to be that the racial critics are foolish or blinded by history or motivated by their own ethnocentrism.[114]

5. The Body Politic and the Racial Critiques

I suspect that many white people would agree with the racial critics' analysis, even if most whites would not support a solution involving the emancipation of black criminals. I write this Essay, however, out of concern for African-Americans and how they can use the power they have now to create change. The important practicability question is how many African-Americans embrace racial critiques of the criminal justice system and how many are law enforcement enthusiasts?

According to a recent *USA Today/CNN/Gallup* poll, sixty-six percent of blacks believe that the criminal justice system is racist and only thirty-two percent believe it is not racist.[115] Interestingly, other polls suggest that blacks also tend to be more worried about crime than whites;[116] this seems logical when one considers that blacks are more likely to be the victims of crime.[117] This enhanced concern, however, does not appear to translate into endorsement of tougher enforcement of traditional criminal law. For example, substantially fewer blacks than whites support the death penalty,[118] and many more blacks than whites were concerned with the potential racial consequences of the strict provisions of the Crime Bill of 1994.[119] While polls are not, perhaps, the most reliable means of measuring sentiment in the African-American community, the polls, along with significant evidence from popular culture,[120] suggest that a substantial portion of the African-American community sympathizes with racial critiques of the criminal justice system.

African-American jurors who endorse these critiques are in a unique position to act on their beliefs when they sit in judgment of a black defendant. As jurors, they have the power to convict the defendant or to set him free. May the responsible exercise of that power include voting to free a black defendant who the juror believes is guilty? The next section suggests that, based on legal doctrine concerning the role of juries in general, and the role of black jurors in particular, the answer to this question is "yes."

B. Jury Nullification

When a jury disregards evidence presented at trial and acquits an otherwise guilty defendant, because the jury objects to the law that the defendant violated or to the application of the law to that defendant, it has practiced jury nullification. In this section, I describe the evolution of this doctrine and consider its applicability to African-Americans. I then examine Supreme Court cases that discuss the role of black people on juries. In light of judicial rulings in these areas, I argue that it is both lawful and morally right that black jurors consider race in reaching verdicts in criminal cases.

1. What Is Jury Nullification?

Jury nullification occurs when a jury acquits a defendant who it believes is guilty of the crime with which he is charged. In finding the defendant not guilty, the jury refuses to be bound by the facts of the case or the judge's instructions regarding the law. Instead, the jury votes its conscience. In the United States, the doctrine of jury nullification originally was based on the common law idea that the function of a jury was, broadly, to decide justice, which included judging the law as well as the facts.[121] If jurors believed that applying a law would lead to an unjust conviction, they were not compelled to convict someone who had broken that law.[122] Although most American courts now disapprove of a jury's deciding anything other than the "facts," the Double Jeopardy Clause of the Fifth Amendment prohibits appellate reversal of a jury's decision to acquit, regardless of the reason for the acquittal.[123] Thus, even when a trial judge thinks that a jury's acquittal directly contradicts the evidence, the jury's verdict must be accepted as final.[124] The jurors, in judging the law, function as an important and necessary check on government power.[125]

. . . .

C. The Moral Case for Jury Nullification by African-Americans

Any juror legally may vote for nullification in any case, but, certainly, jurors should not do so without some principled basis. The reason that some historical examples of nullification are viewed approvingly is that most of us now believe that the jurors in those cases did the morally right thing; it would have been unconscionable, for example, to punish those slaves who committed the crime of escaping to the North for their freedom. It is true that nullification later would be used as a means of racial subordination by some Southern jurors,[155] but that does not mean that nullification in the approved cases was wrong. It only means that those Southern jurors erred in their calculus of justice. I distinguish racially based nullification by African-Americans from recent right-wing proposals for jury nullification[156] on the ground that the former is sometimes morally right and the latter is not.

The question of how to assign the power of moral choice is a difficult one. Yet we should not allow that difficulty to obscure the fact that legal resolutions involve moral decisions, judgments of right and wrong. The fullness of time permits us to judge the fugitive slave case differently than the Southern pro-white-violence case. One day we will be able to distinguish between racially based nullification and that proposed by certain right-wing activist groups.[157] We should remember that the morality of the historically approved cases was not so clear when those brave jurors acted. After all, the fugitive slave law was enacted through the democratic process, and those jurors who disregarded it subverted the rule of law. Presumably, they were harshly criticized by those whose interests the slave law protected. Then, as now, it is difficult to see the picture when you are inside the frame.

In this section, I explain why African-Americans have the moral right to practice nullification in particular cases.[158] I do so by responding to the traditional moral critiques of jury nullification.

1. African-Americans and the "Betrayal" of Democracy

There is no question that jury nullification is subversive of the rule of law. It appears to be the antithesis of the view that courts apply settled, standing laws and do not "dispense justice in some ad hoc, case-by-case basis."[159] To borrow a phrase from the D.C. Circuit, jury nullification "betrays rather than furthers the assumptions of viable democracy."[160] Because the Double Jeopardy Clause makes this power part-and-parcel of the jury system, the issue becomes whether black jurors have any moral right to "betray democracy" in this sense. I believe that they do for two reasons that I borrow from the jurisprudence of legal realism and critical race theory: First, the idea of "the rule of law" is more mythological than real, and second, "democracy," as practiced in the United States, has betrayed African-Americans far more than they could ever betray it. Explication of these theories has consumed legal scholars for years, and is well beyond the scope of this Essay. I describe the theories below not to persuade the reader of their rightness, but rather to make the case that a reasonable juror might hold such beliefs, and thus be morally justified in subverting democracy through nullification.

2. The Rule of Law as Myth

The idea that "any result can be derived from the preexisting legal doctrine" either in every case or many cases,[161] is a fundamental principle of legal realism (and, now, critical legal theory). The argument, in brief, is that law is indeterminate and incapable of neutral interpretation.[162] When judges "decide" cases, they "choose" legal principles to determine particular outcomes. Even if a judge wants to be neutral, she cannot, because, ultimately, she is vulnerable to an array of personal and cultural biases and influences; she is only human. In an implicit endorsement of the doctrine of jury nullification,

legal realists also suggest that, even if neutrality were possible, it would not be desirable, because no general principle of law can lead to justice in every case.[163]

It is difficult for an African-American knowledgeable of the history of her people in the United States not to profess, at minimum, sympathy for legal realism.[164] Most blacks are aware of countless historical examples in which African-Americans were not afforded the benefit of the rule of law: Think, for example, of the existence of slavery in a republic purportedly dedicated to the proposition that all men are created equal, or the law's support of state-sponsored segregation even after the Fourteenth Amendment guaranteed blacks equal protection. That the rule of law ultimately corrected some of the large holes in the American fabric is evidence more of its malleability than of its virtue; the rule of law had, in the first instance, justified the holes.[165]

The Supreme Court's decisions in the major "race" cases of the last term underscore the continuing failure of the rule of law to protect African-Americans through consistent application. Dissenting in a school desegregation case,[166] four Justices stated that "[t]he Court's process of orderly adjudication has broken down in this case."[167] The dissent noted that the majority opinion "effectively ... overrule[d] a unanimous constitutional precedent of 20 years standing, which was not even addressed in argument, was mentioned merely in passing by one of the parties, and discussed by another of them only in a misleading way."[168] Similarly, in a voting rights case,[169] Justice Stevens, in dissent, described the majority opinion as a "law-changing decision."[170] And in an affirmative action case,[171] Justice Stevens began his dissent by declaring that, "[i]nstead of deciding this case in accordance with controlling precedent, the Court today delivers a disconcerting lecture about the evils of governmental racial classifications."[172] At the end of his dissent, Stevens argued that "the majority's concept of *stare decisis* ignores the force of binding precedent."[173]

If the rule of law is a myth, or at least is not applicable to African-Americans, the criticism that jury nullification undermines it loses force. The black juror is simply another actor in the system, using her power to fashion a particular outcome; the juror's act of nullification — like the act of the citizen who dials 911 to report Ricky but not Bob, or the police officer who arrests Lisa but not Mary, or the prosecutor who charges Kwame but not Brad, or the judge who finds that Nancy was illegally entrapped but Verna was not — exposes the indeterminacy of law, but does not create it.

3. The Moral Obligation to Disobey Unjust Laws

For the reader who is unwilling to concede the mythology of the rule of law, I offer another response to the concern about violating it. Assuming, for the purposes of argument, that the rule of law exists, there still is no moral obligation to follow an unjust law.[174] This principle is familiar to many African-Americans who practiced civil disobedience during the civil rights protests of the 1950s and 1960s. Indeed, Martin Luther King suggested that morality requires that unjust laws not be obeyed.[175] As I state above,[176] the difficulty of determining which laws are unjust should not obscure the need to make that determination.

Radical critics believe that the criminal law is unjust when applied to some antisocial conduct by African-Americans: The law uses punishment to treat social problems that are the result of racism and that should be addressed by other means such as medical care or the redistribution of wealth. Later, I suggest a utilitarian justification for why African-Americans should obey most criminal law: It protects them.[177] I concede, however, that this limitation is not *morally* required if one accepts the radical critique, which applies to all criminal law.

4. Democratic Domination

Related to the "undermining the law" critique is the charge that jury nullification is antidemocratic. The trial judge in the *Barry* case, for example, in remarks made after the conclusion of the trial, expressed this criticism of the jury's verdict: " 'The jury is not a mini-democracy, or a mini-legislature.... They are not to go back and do right as they see fit. That's anarchy. They are supposed to follow the law.' "[178] A jury that nullifies "betrays rather than furthers the assumptions of viable democracy." In a sense, the argument suggests that the jurors are not playing fair: The citizenry made the rules, so the jurors, as citizens, ought to follow them.

What does "viable democracy" assume about the power of an unpopular minority group to make the laws that affect them? It assumes that the group has the power to influence legislation. The American majority-rule electoral system is premised on the hope that the majority will not tyrannize the minority, but rather represent the minority's interests. Indeed, in creating the Constitution, the Framers attempted to guard against the oppression of the minority by the majority.[179] Unfortunately, these attempts were expressed more in theory than in actual constitutional guarantees, a point made by some legal scholars, particularly critical race theorists.

The implication of the failure to protect blacks from the tyrannical majority is that the majority rule of whites over African-Americans is, morally speaking, illegitimate. Lani Guinier suggests that the moral legitimacy of majority rule hinges on two assumptions: 1) that majorities are not fixed; and 2) that minorities will be able to become members of some majorities.[180] Racial prejudice "to such a degree that the majority consistently excludes the minority, or refuses to inform itself about the relative merit of the minority's preferences," defeats both assumptions.[181] Similarly, Owen Fiss has given three reasons for the failure of blacks to prosper through American democracy: They are a numerical minority, they have low economic status, and, "as a 'discrete and insular' minority, they are the object of 'prejudice' — that is, the subject of fear, hatred, and distaste that make it particularly difficult for them to form coalitions with others (such as the white poor)."[182]

According to both theories, blacks are unable to achieve substantial progress through regular electoral politics.[183] Their only "democratic" route to success — coalition building with similarly situated groups — is blocked because other groups resist the stigma of the association. The stigma is powerful enough to prevent alignment with African-Americans even when a group — like low income whites — has similar interests.

In addition to individual white citizens, legislative bodies experience the Negrophobia described above. Professor Guinier defines such legislative racism as

> a pattern of actions [that] persistently disadvantag[es] a fixed, legislative minority and encompasses conscious exclusion as well as marginalization that results from "a lack of interracial empathy." It means that where a prejudiced majority rules, its representatives are American minority.[184]

Such racism excludes blacks from the governing legislative coalitions. A permanent, homogeneous majority emerges, which effectively marginalizes minority interests and "transform[s] majority rule into majority tyranny."[185] Derrick Bell calls this condition "democratic domination."[186]

Democratic domination undermines the basis of political stability, which depends on the inducement of "losers to continue to play the political game, to continue to work within the system rather than to try to overthrow it."[187] Resistance by minorities to the operation of majority rule may take several forms, including "overt compliance and secret rejection of the legitimacy of the political order."[188] I suggest that another form of this resistance is racially based jury nullification.

If African-Americans believe that democratic domination exists (and the 1994 congressional elections seem to provide compelling recent support for such a belief[189]), they should not back away from lawful self-help measures, like jury nullification, on the ground that the self-help is antidemocratic.[190] African-Americans are not a numerical majority in any of the fifty states, which are the primary sources of criminal law.[191] In addition, they are not even proportionally represented in the U.S. House of Representatives or in the Senate.[192] As a result, African-Americans wield little influence over criminal law, state or federal. African-Americans should embrace the antidemocratic nature of jury nullification because it provides them with the power to determine justice in a way that majority rule does not.

D. "[J]ustice must satisfy the appearance of justice":[193] The Symbolic Function of Black Jurors

A second distinction one might draw between the traditionally approved examples of jury nullification and its practice by contemporary African-Americans is that, in the case of the former, jurors refused to apply a particular law, e.g., a fugitive slave law, on the grounds that it was unfair, while in the case of the latter, jurors are not so much judging discrete statutes as they are refusing to apply those statutes to members of their own race. This application of race consciousness by jurors may appear to be antithetical to the American ideal of equality under the law.

This critique, however, like the "betraying democracy" critique, begs the question of whether the ideal actually applies to African-Americans. As stated above, racial critics answer this question in the negative.[194] They, especially the liberal critics, argue that the criminal law is applied in a discriminatory fashion.[195] Furthermore, on several occasions, the Supreme Court has referred to the usefulness of black jurors to the rule of law in the United States.[196] In essence, black jurors symbolize the fairness and impartiality of the law. Here I examine this rhetoric and suggest that, if the presence of black jurors sends a political message, it is right that these jurors use their power to control or negate the meaning of that message.

As a result of the ugly history of discrimination against African-Americans in the criminal justice system,[197] the Supreme Court has had numerous opportunities to consider the significance of black jurors.[198]

In so doing, the Court has suggested that these jurors perform a symbolic function, especially when they sit on cases involving African-American defendants,[199] and the Court has typically made these suggestions in the form of rhetoric about the social harm caused by the exclusion of blacks from jury service.[200] I will refer to this role of black jurors as the "legitimization function."

The legitimization function stems from every jury's political function of providing American citizens with "the security ... that they, as jurors actual or possible, being part of the judicial system of the country can prevent its arbitrary use or abuse."[201] In addition to, and perhaps more important than, seeking the truth, the purpose of the jury system is "to impress upon the criminal defendant and the community as a whole that a verdict of conviction or acquittal is given in accordance with the law by persons who are fair."[202] This purpose is consistent with the original purpose of the constitutional right to a jury trial, which was "to prevent oppression by the Government."[203]

When blacks are excluded from juries, beyond any harm done to the juror who suffers the discrimination or to the defendant, the social injury of the exclusion is that it "undermine[s] ... public confidence — as well [it] should."[204] Because the United States is both a democracy and a pluralist society, it is important that diverse groups appear to have a voice in the laws that govern them. Allowing black people to serve on juries strengthens "public respect for our criminal justice system and the rule of law.[205]

The Supreme Court has found that the legitimization function is particularly valuable in cases involving "race-related" crimes.[206] According to the Court, in these cases, "emotions in the affected community [are] inevitably ... heated and volatile."[207] The potential presence of black people on the jury in a "race-related" case calms the natives, which is especially important in this type of case because "[p]ublic confidence in the integrity of the criminal justice system is essential for preserving community peace."[208] The very fact that a black person can be on a jury is evidence that the criminal justice system is one in which black people should have confidence, and one that they should respect.

But what of the black juror who endorses racial critiques of American criminal justice? Such a person holds no "confidence in the integrity of the criminal justice system." If she is cognizant of the implicit message that the Supreme Court believes her presence sends, she might not want her presence to be the vehicle for that message. Let us assume that there is a black defendant who, the evidence suggests, is guilty of the crime with which he has been charged, and a black juror who thinks that there are too many black men in prison. The black juror has two choices: She can vote for conviction, thus sending another black man to prison and implicitly allowing her presence to support public confidence in the system that puts him there, or she can vote "not guilty," thereby acquitting the defendant, or at least causing a mistrial. In choosing the latter, the juror makes a decision not to be a passive symbol of support for a system for which she has no respect. Rather than signaling her displeasure with the system by breaching "community peace," the black juror invokes the political nature of her role in the criminal justice system and votes "no." In a sense, the black juror engages in an act of civil disobedience, except that her choice is better than civil disobedience because it is lawful.[209] Is the black juror's race-conscious act moral? Absolutely. It would be farcical for her to be the sole color-blind actor in the criminal process, especially when it is her blackness that advertises the system's fairness.[210]

At this point, every African-American should ask herself whether the operation of the criminal law in the United States advances the interests of black people. If it does not, the doctrine of jury nullification affords African-American jurors the opportunity to control the authority of the law over some African-American criminal defendants. In essence, black people can "opt out" of American criminal law.

How far should they go? Completely to anarchy? Or is there some place between here and there, safer than both? The next part describes such a place, and how to get there.

. . . .

CONCLUSION

This Essay's proposal raises other concerns, such as the problem of providing jurors with information relevant to their decision within the restrictive evidentiary confines of a trial. Some of these issues can be resolved through creative lawyering.[237] Other policy questions are not as easily answered, including the issue of how long (years, decades, centuries?) black jurors would need to pursue racially based jury nullification. I think this concern is related to the issue of the appropriate time span of other race-conscious remedies, including affirmative action. Perhaps, when policymakers acknowledge that race matters in criminal justice, the criminal law can benefit from the successes and failures of race consciousness in other areas of the law. I fear, however, that this day of acknowledgement will be long in coming. Until then, I expect that many black jurors will perceive the necessity of employing the self-help measures prescribed here.

I concede that the justice my proposal achieves is rough because it is as susceptible to human foibles as the jury system. I am sufficiently optimistic to hope that my proposal will be only an intermediate plan, a stopping point between the status quo and real justice. I hope that this Essay will encourage African-Americans to use responsibly the power they already have. To get criminal justice past the middle point, I hope that the Essay will facilitate a dialogue among all Americans in which the significance of race will not be dismissed or feared, but addressed. The most dangerous "forbidden" message is that it is better to ignore the truth than to face it.

(d) Perpetuating the Cycle of Abuse: Feminist (Mis)use of the Public/Private Dichotomy in the Case of Nixon v. Rape Relief[†]

Ummni Khan

OPENING REMARKS

The enshrined common law maxim, "a man's home is his castle",[1] has long stood for the principle

of man's freedom and autonomy in private spaces. Though he must conform to legal codes and rules in public areas, man becomes the supreme ruler when

---

† (June, 2007) 23 W.R.L.S.I. 27 at 28–31, 32–45, 49–53. [Notes and/or references omitted.] Reproduced with permission.

nestled in his home. I use the words "man", "he", and "his" purposefully here, not as gender-neutral terms, but rather to foreshadow the feminist engagement with this legal principle. In this regard, feminist legal scholarship has argued that the notion of a man's home-cum-castle perpetuates a public/private dichotomy where men enjoy freedom and women suffer servitude in spaces designated as "private."

Tracing the public/private divide back to Aristotle,[2] feminists have argued that this ordering of society allowed "private" sites to become havens of legal impunity. For example, in the quintessential private space — the hallowed home — "man" (and here man operates metonymically for husband and father) can control, abuse, rape and exploit his wife and children without significant legal intervention, or with a mitigated punishment.[3] By analyzing family, criminal, employment, administrative and virtually every other aspect of law, feminists demonstrated that the carving off of certain spaces as "private" has often worked to the disadvantage of women and children. Harms and inequalities in these so-called private spaces were rendered invisible, irrelevant or inevitable. On this view, feminists posited that the separation of the public and the private in law was not an empirical observation of a natural division, but rather an ideological operation serving the status quo of patriarchy.

This article examines how the public/private divide was exploited to support the status quo, not of patriarchy, but of feminism, in the human rights case between Kimberly Nixon and Vancouver Rape Relief and Women's Shelter ("Rape Relief").[4] This high-profile case involved Kimberly Nixon, a transsexual woman[5] who filed a human rights complaint against Rape Relief, an all-woman collective that rejected Nixon as a potential peer counsellor. Rape Relief's refusal of Nixon was based on the claim that she was not born a woman, and therefore, had not been assigned the "historically subordinate status assigned to women", nor treated exclusively as a girl and woman. Based on this, Nixon did not qualify as a peer in Rape Relief's regard. A subsidiary justification offered by Rape Relief was that Nixon's appearance might cause discomfort to the clients who seek counselling and services from their organization.

The crux of my argument is that Rape Relief relied on a regressive understanding of law's proper role in regulating harmful behaviour, by capitalizing on the hegemonic concept of the public/private divide, in order to escape legal accountability for its members' discriminatory conduct. Further, Rape Relief's position on the contestability of Nixon's

womanness, which was accepted by the appellate courts, relied on the larger implication of the public/private divide by re-entrenching that what matters for the law happens in the public sphere, and what does not matter for the law happens in the private and personal sphere. By framing the case as one centering on the autonomy interests of Rape Relief and the privacy interests of their clients, Rape Relief portrayed itself as the proverbial castle, with the women who run the organization as the ruling "queens." What will hopefully become evident throughout this paper is the irony of a purportedly feminist organization dichotomizing the public and the private spheres in order to discount the experiences and identities of one of the most marginalized subcategories of women: transsexual women.

As is obvious from the previous paragraph, I take it as a given that Kimberly Nixon is a woman. The purpose of this paper is not to advocate this viewpoint. Whether one subscribes to this position or not, I believe we need to be suspicious of the ways that Rape Relief exploited the governing assumptions of the public/private dichotomy in order to justify its behaviour. The arguments put forth by Rape Relief can be seen as highly problematic from a feminist perspective, even accepting its right to define who qualifies as a "woman" for the purposes of their volunteer program. As my title implies, I believe that Rape Relief's arguments could be understood as perpetuating a cycle of abuse: by deploying the public/private dichotomy as a cloaking and sanitizing measure, Rape Relief perpetuated the legitimacy of a legal principle that has consistently been used to the disadvantage of all women in society.

· · · ·

The body of this article proceeds in two parts. The first part provides a background of the material facts of the case and its adjudicative progression. In the second part, I demonstrate how Rape Relief relied on the public/private divide to claim that Nixon's complaint was unjustified and should be dismissed. I explore five dimensions of the public/private dichotomy in play during the litigation of the human rights complaint. First, I examine Rape Relief's restrictive interpretation of the term "sex" as a prohibited ground of discrimination. Second, I critique their assertion that volunteering should not be considered an employment. Third, I deconstruct their rhetorical manipulation of their clients' privacy interests. Fourth, I turn to the reasoning of Justice Edwards of the British Columbia Supreme Court to examine how his concurrence with Rape Relief's position was built upon the problematic assumptions of the public/private dichotomy. Fifth, I deconstruct how the portrayal of Nixon's private identification as a girl and woman as materially irrelevant, [which] is premised on a privileging of the public sphere, over the private sphere, as the space that demands judicial notice.

Ultimately, this paper takes issue with the hegemonic conception of the public/ private dichotomy perpetuated by Rape Relief, and how this worked against the interests of both non-transsexual women as well as transsexual and transgendered women.

PART I: BACKGROUND FACTS AND CASE HISTORY[10]

In August of 1995, Nixon responded to an advertisement from Rape Relief calling for volunteers who wished to be trained as peer counsellors for victims of male violence. Nixon herself had suffered male violence in multiple forms, including relationship violence, sexual assault, and street harassment. She had previously received counselling from Battered Women's Support Services (BWSS), an all-woman collective designed to assist women who have experienced violence and sexual assault. From this empowering experience, Nixon was inspired to give back to other women the kind of positive support she had received. Because BWSS had a policy against former clients volunteering immediately after having received counselling from them, Nixon turned to Rape Relief as an ideal venue to support women who, like her, had suffered from male violence.

Rape Relief has a pre-screening process for their training program, the goal of which is to ensure that potential volunteers adhere to the group's listed political beliefs, which are:

1. Violence is never a woman's fault;[11]
2. Women have the right to choose to have an abortion;
3. Women have the right to choose who their sexual partners are; and
4. Volunteers agree to work on an on-going basis on their existing prejudices, including racism.

At this pre-screening interview, Nixon accepted these four principles and was invited to begin her training at the next scheduled session, beginning the following week. At the first training session, Cormier, a facilitator for the workshop, visually identified Nixon as someone who may not belong. During a break, Cormier asked Nixon about her sex status.[12] When Nixon confirmed she was a transsexual woman, Cormier asked her to leave.

In response to this exclusion, Nixon filed a human rights complaint alleging that Rape Relief had discriminated against her by refusing her employment and by denying her a service on the basis of sex.[13] On judicial review, Rape Relief questioned the British Columbia Human Rights Tribunal decision to hear the case on the basis that the Tribunal lacked jurisdiction, primarily relying on the argument that freedom from discrimination on the basis of "sex" under the Code does not protect against discrimination based on transsexualism.[14] Rape Relief's challenge was unsuccessful and the complaint proceeded with a full evidentiary hearing in front of the Human Rights Tribunal in 2001. Tribunal member Heather MacNaughton found that Rape Relief breached the *Code* by discriminating against Nixon on the basis of sex, and held no statutory defences applied to its' members' conduct.

Rape Relief applied for judicial review of the Tribunal's decision. Justice Edwards of the British Columbia Supreme Court agreed that the Tribunal had erred and quashed the decision on the basis of two findings. First, he concluded that Rape Relief's refusal of transsexual women was allowed based on s. 41 of the *Code*, dubbed the "groups' rights exemption." This section provides a defence to a *prima facie* case of discrimination for a non-profit organization provided: its primary purpose is the promotion of an identifiable group of persons, characterized by sex (among other grounds); and the organization is granting a preference to members of that identifiable group of persons. Although he held this finding was dispositive of the case, Justice Edwards nevertheless applied the *Law* framework to the facts of the case. Using a mixed subjective–objective test, he concluded that Nixon did not satisfy the legal test for discrimination because she had failed to show an objective impact on her human dignity.

Though Nixon's appeal of this decision was unsuccessful, she was vindicated to a degree by the Court of Appeal's reasoning. Justice Saunders held that the *Law* framework was not applicable to the test for discrimination in the present case. Through this reasoning, it was established that Rape Relief had committed an act of *prima facie* discrimination. However, Justice Saunders agreed with Justice Edwards that Rape Relief's conduct was legally justified by the groups' rights exemption pursuant to s. 41 of the *Code*.

PART II: WORKING THE PUBLIC/PRIVATE DIVIDE TO ERASE THE HARMS OF GENDER ESSENTIALISM

A. Taking the Sex out of Transsexualism

As discussed above, Rape Relief first challenged Nixon's complaint by an application for judicial review, contesting the jurisdiction of the Human Rights Tribunal to hear the case. Rape Relief argued it was not the legislature's intention to "alter the ground 'sex' to encompass transsexualism or 'gender identity'".[15] Rape Relief submitted that sex discrimination refers exclusively to conduct that disadvantages a person based on their status as a man or a woman, or based on associations to a person's maleness or femaleness. It relied on earlier case law holding that the ground "sex" in human rights legislation did not include discrimination based on sexual orientation. Finally, Rape Relief argued that three previous decisions of the Tribunal, finding sex did include transsexualism, were wrongly decided.[16]

Had Rape Relief been successful in their argument to restrict the meaning of "sex" to address male and female inequality exclusively, transsexuals and transgendered people would have faced serious barriers to access human rights protection in *any* kind of employment, service or housing relationship, not just women-only spaces. In consequence, transgendered and transsexual individuals would either have been completely excluded from protection from discrimination, or they would have been forced to self-construct as suffering from a disability.[17] Leaving transgendered and transsexual people with no protection would clearly be contrary to their human rights, as studies have shown that transgendered and transsexual people are acutely vulnerable to discrimination in all areas of life.[18] Though some transsexual persons have argued that discrimination has occurred on the basis of "disability" as well as "sex", other claimants object to what they perceive to be the medicalisation of their sex status.[19] In addition, this ground may not be available to transgendered claimants who have chosen not to undergo sex reassignment surgery. Though Rape Relief's main focus of concern regards women who were assigned the female sex at birth, I believe that as a feminist and justice seeking equality group, it betrayed its own principles. Rape Relief chose to pursue arguments that potentially had devastating repercussions on transgendered people, a group, which Rape Relief itself did not contest, is a minority group, is marginalized and is disadvantaged in Canadian society.

Beyond their harmful effects for transgendered people, Rape Relief's arguments further entrenched the public/private divide. In attempting to ground "sex" in a (bio)logical[20] discourse of female and male, Rape Relief needed to sever the connections of sexuality and gender from the category of sex. The logic of a public/private dichotomy lurks behind this reasoning and has the effect of rendering the private identifications of one's gender and/or one's sexual desires to be legally irrelevant. On Rape Reliefs analysis, what counts for law is the public assignment and recognition of coherent sexed subjects without the gender imperatives that attach to one's sex.

This erasure of the gender components of sex is reflected in the rhetoric used by Rape Relief. According to the decision, Rape Relief submitted that "the issue is not what the term 'sex' might mean in the abstract, or in some other legislative or semantic context, but rather what it means in the context of the legal concept of sex discrimination."[21] In this argument, the use of the terms "abstract" and "semantic" work to dematerialize the issues of gender, implying that gender has less corporeality than sex, and that it primarily exists in the world of language and ideas, and not in the concrete world of "male" and "female". This concrete world is construed by Rape Relief as a "male dominated society" in which "sex discrimination" in law is meant to deal solely with issues of inequality between men and women. The inequality between transsexual women and non-transsexual women becomes an irrelevant issue within this binary thinking. Gender expression and identity are rendered epiphenomenal private choices and not public issues of inequality.

Discrimination based on sexual orientation is also deemed by Rape Relief to be outside of the scope of "sex." Relying on case law that predated the inclusion of sexual orientation as its own ground in human rights legislation, Rape Relief sought to demonstrate that these cases gave a restrictive meaning to "sex" that did not include sexual preference. By presenting these cases as part of their legal strategy to delimit "sex", Rape Relief further underscored the category of sex as something that is ontologically fixed, and not something that is policed through the regulation of sex roles. And yet, as Catharine MacKinnon argues, "[s]ame-sex discrimination is sex discrimination ... sex roles are socially enacted in part through sexual expression and sexual identity."[22] By citing jurisprudence that denies the [imbrications] of sexuality with sex, Rape Relief tacitly approved of the ways sexuality is coded as private within legal reasoning, and therefore outside of law's scrutiny.[23]

B. Disavowing the Dignity Issues in Volunteering

Rape Relief's second argument, concerning the nature of volunteering, also attempted to exploit the governing assumptions of the public/private divide. Rape Relief argued before the Tribunal that volunteering does not constitute "employment" under the *Code*, and that the Tribunal therefore lacked jurisdiction with regards to the complaint. In support of this proposition, Rape Relief submitted that performing paid work provides dignity in a way that volunteering does not, and that the denial of the opportunity to engage in paid work therefore harms dignity in a way that denial of the opportunity to volunteer does not. Rape Relief further argued that volunteering does not raise the same concerns regarding the power imbalance as are involved in paid relationships.

Rape Relief's strategy of bracketing volunteer work as work that does not implicate legally relevant dignity contributes to the patriarchal undervaluation of women's unpaid or underpaid work.[24] Although men and women tend to volunteer about the same amount of time, there is a stark gender gap regarding the kinds of volunteer activities they perform and the significance it holds in their lives. According to a government sponsored research brief, men are more likely to occupy prestigious positions in the volunteer sector, such as serving on boards of directors, and women are more likely to be delivering hands-on services, such as care giving.[25] As such, men tend to have more supervisory roles, while women will have less power and less control over their volunteer work. Male volunteers are also more likely than women to have paid employment alongside their volunteer activity.[26] Women, who are systemically excluded from waged work, will often turn to volunteering to obtain skills and gain valuable experience in order to increase their chances of acquiring paid work.[27] For women, volunteering is also noted as a means to feel connected to the community and gain self-confidence.[28]

Had Rape Relief been successful in its bid to legally immunize volunteering from discrimination law, women — who have less power in their volunteer jobs and who rely on such work to upgrade skills, to connect with their community and to improve their self-esteem — would have been disproportionately affected. The non-profit volunteer-driven organization would become overdetermined as

a private sphere that can escape accountability for harmful treatment because money is not exchanged.

Rape Relief's view that the dignity of work is inextricably tied to the value of money was reflected in its final argument that volunteering does not implicate the same power imbalance as paid work, presumably because being denied such work does not directly affect one's financial status. Yet, feminists have argued that the domestic sphere, where women continue to perform most of the unpaid work, involves stark power imbalances between parties that need to be addressed in law and economic policy.[29] In other words, feminists have argued that the fact that labour is unpaid, whether in the community or at home, should not indicate that such work is performed under fair or equal conditions.

In sum, Rape Relief's attempt to preclude Nixon's complaint by distinguishing volunteer work from paid work, premised on purported differential dignity and power issues, recalled the problematic ways the state has traditionally ignored the harms and inequality that occur when unremunerated work is performed, most often by women, in spaces designated as private.

C. Using the 'Best Interests of the Clients' Rhetoric to Justify Discrimination

Rape Relief argued before the Tribunal that even if *prima facie* discrimination was established, it was still not liable for a breach of the law because it was a *bona fide* occupational requirement that volunteers have lived their whole lives as girls and women. A substantial part of this alleged justification rested on the purported privacy and dignity interests of their clients. In [its] evidence, Rape Relief called on Edith Swain, a former client of the organization. Swain testified that she would not have confided her story to someone she believed was a man or had grown up as a man.

In [its] oral argument to the Tribunal, Rape Relief cited Supreme Court of Canada jurisprudence protecting the privacy of sexual assault victim records. Rape Relief then sought to draw an analogy between the privacy interests of those victims and the privacy interests of its clients. Rape Relief submitted:

> Women who have suffered male violence should be entitled to maintain the privacy of their stories and *to choose* to whom they tell their stories. Women like Ms. Swain cannot be honestly reassured that a transgendered person has lived as a woman.[30] [emphasis added]

Using Swain's discomfort as evidence, Rape Relief suggested that to accept a transgendered or transsexual woman as a volunteer would violate the right to privacy for victims of sexual assault.

The nexus, however, between a sexual assault victim's privacy interests and a transsexual woman counsellor is not elaborated upon. The mere fact that Swain would have felt uncomfortable with Nixon as a counsellor does not establish an invasion of privacy, and instead shows little more than the fact that Swain prefers certain types of women as counsellors over others. Interestingly, Rape Relief does not allow other types of stated client preferences to govern the choice of counsellor. For example, imagine a woman from a socially conservative background who requests a different counsellor because she is not comfortable disclosing sexual abuse to a woman who appears to be a lesbian. Rape Relief's policy is to refuse such requests, despite evidence from its own expert witness, Dr. Pacey, who testified under cross-examination that in her view, "the sexual orientation of a peer counselor could be an issue for a victim of sexual assault because the issues following a sexual assault sometimes differ for heterosexual and lesbian women."[31]

It is therefore clear that despite Rape Relief's claim that a woman's right to privacy entitles her "to choose" to whom she will confide with [regard] to her history of sexual abuse, the organization does not attempt to accommodate all such client requests, even if this may disturb or upset the client. Apparently, "privacy" interests are not at stake when a client suffers discomfort in the presence of a lesbian woman. Nixon, on the other hand, because of her transsexualism, is constructed as an invasive presence that would violate the privacy of clients who are not comfortable with transsexual women.

This perspective reflects a version of the public/private dichotomy, specifically the one that genders the public as male and the private as female.[32] Part of Rape Relief's semantic strategy was to emphasize Nixon's sex-designation at birth by continually referring to Nixon as a "male-to-female transsexual" and never as a transsexual woman. Counsel for Rape Relief sought to discursively bind Nixon to that temporal place of "maleness" in order to overdetermine her as "public" within a patriarchal framework. Thus, Rape Relief capitalizes on the underlying gendered nature of the public-man/private-woman dichotomy to couch an argument about client discomfort within the terms of a right to privacy.[33] The inconsistency in analysis — that discomfort with a transsexual counsellor violates one's right to privacy, while discom-

fort with a lesbian counsellor does not — is never addressed by Rape Relief.

Boyle maintained this strategy of using a client's discomfort with transsexualism in her academic article, arguing that a substantive approach to discrimination would take into consideration third party interests.[34] As part of her evidence, she cites a European Court of Human Rights decision, *X, Y, and Z v. United Kingdom*, which upheld a British law prohibiting a transsexual man from registering as the father of his partner's child, conceived through artificial insemination.[35] Boyle quotes the court, which stated, "'it is not clear that it [registration] would necessarily be to the advantage of the children' and 'might have undesirable or unforeseen ramifications for the children in Z's position.'"[36] Thus, Boyle borrowed rhetoric from the "best interest of the child" doctrine to forward the notion of the "best interest of the client".

Yet, feminists and other critical scholars have argued that the notion of "best interest of the child" is indeterminate and often manipulated by judges to justify their own prejudices or stereotypes.[37] For example, William Eskridge has argued that despite the fact that judges have replaced discourses of immorality with the discourse of best interests of the child, gay men and lesbians are still often disadvantaged because of homophobic conceptions of the capacities of gay and lesbian parents and assumptions regarding what a "healthy" and "normal" childhood should entail.[38]

Along the same lines, the majority decision-makers in *X, Y, and Z* cite no evidence in support of their suspicion that registration of the transsexual parent as father might "not be to the advantage" of the child, nor ever elaborate on their assertion that "undesirable or unforeseen ramifications" might flow from the registration.[39] Instead, the majority simply assumes that the mere fact of transsexuality is enough to justify the British government's decision to treat transsexual men differently from non-transsexual men where children are involved. In contrast to this perspective, the dissenting opinion of Judge Gotchev found that the best interest of the child standard would be best served by treating transsexual parents equally to non-transsexual parents; by drawing baseless distinctions between these groups, the British law violated the right of respect for one's private and family life.[40]

The same indeterminacy that plagues the "best interest of the child" analysis exists with respect to Rape Relief's arguments concerning the "best interest of the client". Based on evidence of merely one former client, who was already aware of Nixon's status as a transsexual, Boyle homogenizes and reifies Rape Relief's client base to support its anti-transsexual stance. She sets up false distinctions that inherently portray the use of transsexual women counsellors as being contrary to the best interests of sexual assault victims.

For example, Boyle argues, "[o]ne way of stating the issue is how to be attentive to the human rights of both [sic] transgendered persons, raped and beaten women seeking help from women-only space, and women with the life experience of being treated as women who want to combat male violence."[41] By framing the issue in this manner, Boyle suggests that the interests of transgendered women are necessarily in contradistinction to "raped and beaten" women and non-transgendered women. Yet, transgendered women could very well be the "raped and beaten" women that Boyle and Rape Relief seek to protect. Indeed, Nixon herself was a "raped and beaten" woman who sought services in a women-only space and Rape Relief members testified that the organization had, on at least two occasions, assisted transsexual or transgendered women.[42] Boyle's framework disavows the intersectional oppression that occurs when transsexual or transgendered women suffer sexual abuse. These victims of male violence get erased and their possible interests are occluded from Rape Relief's analysis.

Further, even with non-transsexual women victims of male violence, Rape Relief and Boyle presented only inconclusive opinion evidence to support their argument that it was in the best interest of their clients not to have a transsexual woman counsellor. In this regard, expert witness Dr. Pacey hypothesized that a transsexual woman would not be appropriate as a peer counsellor. However, Dr. Pacey also testified that she had no experience with transgendered people in women's shelters or in peer counselling situations, either as members or as facilitators.[43] Under cross-examination, she further conceded that a transgendered woman may be an effective counsellor.[44] Edith Swain's evidence was similarly speculative, as she had never encountered a transsexual woman herself when seeking services and instead testified about how she would have felt had this situation occurred. By contrast, Nixon adduced uncontroverted evidence that she had been a successful counsellor at two women's shelters, BWSS and Peggy's Place.[45] Based on this evidence, it appears that the human rights and interests of Rape Relief's clients would have been best served by the organization enrolling Nixon into the volunteer training program, since she had already proven herself to be an effective counsellor for victims of male violence. In

rushing to label Nixon as a volunteer who is contrary to its clients' best interests, Rape Relief ignored the direct evidence of her past accomplishments as a counsellor.

Boyle's "best interests of the client" framework also sets up an inherent antagonism between transsexual women and non-transsexual women — even though both groups of women may have as their goal the eradication of male violence. Indeed, many women-only organizations that advocate for the end of violence against women include both transsexual women and non-transsexual women.[46] Rather, the conflict of interest lies between transsexual women who seek inclusion, and non-transsexual women who seek to exclude transsexual women. Casting non-transsexual women's interests in the altruistic "best interests of the client" rhetoric obscures their self-interested desires of exclusion. Much like a parent who seeks exclusive custody of a child over her gay ex-spouse using the "best interest of the child" rhetoric to justify her own homophobia, Rape Relief sought to exclude Nixon partly using a "best (privacy) interest of the client" rhetoric to justify its own stereotypes and assumptions concerning the capacities of transsexual women.

. . . .

E. Transsexual Bodies that Do Not Matter

As was stated earlier, the Court of Appeal invalidated Justice Edwards' reasoning with [regard] to the applicability of the *Law* framework and found that Nixon had established a *prima facie* case of discrimination.[58] The Court of Appeal did find, however, that the exemption provision in s.41 of the *Code* was a valid defence for Rape Relief. It is not my purpose in this section to mount an argument against this finding, but instead to highlight how the hegemony of the public/ private divide was utilized in the Court's reasoning.

Justice Saunders, who wrote the main decision for the Court of Appeal, based her interpretation of s. 41 on the Supreme Court of Canada's reasoning in *Caldwell et al. v. Stuart et. al.*[59] In that case, the Court held that a Catholic school could legitimately refuse to rehire a Catholic teacher who had married a divorced man, contrary to the organization's own interpretation of church dogma. Relying on this reasoning, Justice Saunders determined that she need only inquire if Rape Relief's exclusionary practice was rationally connected to its work and done in good faith.

In the course of analyzing Rape Relief's arguments about *bona fide* occupational requirements, Tribunal member MacNaughton found that Rape Relief met both of these conditions; nevertheless the requirement that a volunteer counsellor must have been treated as female her whole life could not stand because it was not reasonably necessary.[60] Taking these findings, Justice Saunders concluded that for the purposes of a s. 41 exemption, so long as a rational connection and good faith were established, Rape Relief "... was entitled to exercise an internal preference in the group served, to prefer to train women who had never been treated as anything but female."[61] This assessment echoed Rape Relief's unwavering contention that Nixon did not fit their definition of "woman" because she did not have the life-long experience of having been treated exclusively as a girl and a woman.

This perspective imposes on Nixon a gender identity constituted by the public sphere, depoliticizing her personal experiences as a girl and a woman who has struggled against a patriarchal system that imposes and polices a rigid sex/ gender binary. By accepting Rape Relief's assertion — that volunteers must have been treated by others as female for their entire lives — as rational and in good faith, Justice Saunders places paramount importance on how other people defined and treated Nixon. It should be recalled that in *Caldwell*, the appellant, Caldwell, was treated differently because it was perceived that she had contravened Catholic doctrine by marrying a divorced man in a civil ceremony. This was something she *did*. Nixon did not *do* anything to contravene Rape Relief's beliefs, and in fact had concurred with their list of stated political beliefs in her pre-interview with the organization. She was excluded simply because of the way others perceived and reacted to her, i.e. what *other* people did. This difference was immaterial in the eyes of the law, which found that the public sphere holds the trump card. It did not matter that Nixon had, her whole life, understood and treated herself as female. Ultimately, by rendering the public the final arbiter of Nixon's femaleness, the Court of Appeal reinscribed the public/private dichotomy by making Nixon's conviction from childhood that she was female irrelevant; something that does not matter.

When I say that the law accepted Rape Relief's contention that Nixon's self-identification as female does not matter, I want to exploit the overlapping double-meaning of "matter" as both physicality and as a subject of importance by recalling Judith Butler's useful reformulation of the materiality of the body in her book, *Bodies That Matter*.[62] Butler argues that the matter of bodies, and particularly the sex of the body, comes about through an effect of power, of coercive regulatory systems and of violent reiterative processes that materialize the sexed subject into intelligibility, as someone who matters in society. Rape Relief insists that Nixon's childhood, because she was iterated and reiterated as a boy, has thus now irrevocably made her into something other than a woman.

The rejection of Nixon from Rape Relief's "club-like sisterhood" continues this violent reiterative process by arguing that the truth of Kimberly Nixon lies in the gaze of others. Her own truth — that of a girl who was (mis)taken for a boy, who had to remain fearfully vigilant about hiding her true sex (knowing that publicly expressing herself would mean confronting violent opposition) and who sought assistance in order for her body to conform to her visceral sex identity — this truth does not matter. Nixon's ordeals — experiences of patriarchal oppression, including domestic violence, sexual assault and street harassment — these ordeals did not matter. By accepting Rape Relief's standards of womanhood for their volunteer program as rational and in good faith, Justice Saunders dematerializes both Ms. Nixon's own experiential truth and her life-long subordination under a patriarchal system. Once again, what matters for the law happens in public, what does not matter, happens in private.

CONCLUDING REMARKS

This paper has disclosed how the law and Rape Relief relied upon the governing principles of the public/private dichotomy in order to minimize, trivialize and neutralize the discriminatory nature of Rape Relief's policy against transsexual women volunteers. The fact that Rape Relief is a non-profit, equality-seeking feminist organization should not absolve or justify their complicity in naturalizing this divide. It is not only ironic, but also tragic, that a feminist organization exploited the public/private divide as part of its legal strategy to defend its policy, since this man-made divide has historically obscured the harms that women suffer in "private" spaces.

This is reflected in Rape Relief's arguments concerning the restrictive meaning of sex and the significance of volunteering that worked against the interests of all women. Indeed, arguments seeking to interpret the ground "sex" in a restrictive way have historically been used in attempts to deny legal recourse to women who suffered sexual harassment, who were victims of stalking, who suffered discrimination on the basis of pregnancy, who refused to conform to stereotypes of femininity in the workplace, and who came out as lesbian or bisexual. Positioning volunteer work outside the scope of human rights protections would have left many women vulnerable to discrimination and harassment in an area that can be crucial to their livelihood, self-esteem, sense of community and future prospects. On a symbolic level, evacuating the dignity interests and disavowing the power imbalances present in many volunteer relationships would have continued the patriarchal tradition of devaluing the work that women do in spaces designated as "private".

Although Rape Relief failed in its attempt to restrict the scope of the "sex" and "employment" categories, its appropriation of the language of "privacy" rights found some support in the reviewing courts. Meanwhile, Nixon's struggle to be recognized and respected as the woman she has always known herself to be was construed as private business that did not ultimately matter to Rape Relief or for the proceeding. Thus, marginalized women like Kimberly Nixon, who suffer from the intersectional oppression of being female and transsexual, find themselves further isolated from the women's community and from social services. Ultimately, the case proceeded in a manner that further marginalized transgendered and transsexual people and furthered the inequality between non-transsexual women and transsexual women, while ignoring the history of prejudice and stigmatization continually faced by transsexual women in both public and private spaces and in both mainstream and feminist circles.[63]

(a) Taking Law and _____ Really Seriously: Before, During and After "The Law"†

Carrie Menkel-Meadow

I. INTRODUCTION: THREE THOUGHT EXPERIMENTS ABOUT LAW AND LEGAL EDUCATION

A. What is "Law" as a Field?

Any consideration of what legal education should consist of must begin with the question of what "law," as a field of study, is. Whether a study of "the law" is science, philosophy, political science, or a field unto itself, or is more like a social science study of the norms and behaviors that human beings create and enforce for their self-governance, what the field is should have something to do with how it is studied.

So, one can ask, what is the object of study when one studies "the law"? Court decisions and interpretations (doctrine) and statutes and regulations (the rules) are "the substantive law" one could study. Or, one could study law's processes ("adjectival" law): procedure; constitutionalism (as in separation of powers, limited and specified authority, and federalism); institutional competence; law-making (legislation, administrative regulation, lobbying, advocacy); or enforcement and compliance (the "law in action"). Then there are the hermeneutics, or interpretative study, of law's meaning(s). To get at more root matters, one could study why there is law and what its purpose is (or should be) — the jurisprudence or theory of law.

Even after defining the field of law one would still have to ask whether this field has a particular method of study that qualifies it to be called a discipline. Is law the study of the particular method of legal reasoning,[1] which relies on precedents and rules of cases, differentiation of facts, policy analysis, and use of analogical reason to arrive at statements of what the law is? Does one treat law as the study of texts (as a humanistic discipline)? As the study of predictions or principles of social allocation (law and economics)? Or as predictions or descriptions of the actions of social institutions, legal actors, or the acted upon (socio-legal studies)?

Or is law merely a practice or activity, without any particular disciplinary or field boundaries? Law would then be simply all that lawyers *do*.[2] Or, in Holmesian terms, the law would be only what the law does to those who violate it — the sanctions imposed on "bad men."[3]

Or, as this paper will suggest, perhaps there is no one way to see and study this elephant.[4] Rather, the study of law is itself necessarily a multi-disciplinary enterprise, borrowing from or using the insights, methods, and canons of other fields to tell us about how we govern ourselves. As one sociologist of law has urged, when admonishing us to consider law and legal institutions from outside the categories that lawyers make: "[L]aw is to be understood in terms of social theory. Legal theory is to be seen as a particular branch or application of social theory."[5]

Law is created by human beings to govern themselves, to create order and social control, and,

---

† (2007) 60:2 Vanderbilt L. Rev. 555 at 556–560. [Notes and/or references omitted.] Reproduced with permission.

at its best, to provide justice. So, in my view, to study how law is made, interpreted, complied with, enforced, or resisted, is to study how law is experienced — by those who make and interpret law, by those who use it and advise others how to use it, and by those who are acted upon by law. To study experience we need not only logic (apologies to Oliver Wendell Holmes, Jr.[6]) but also social science, including statistics (numbers), narrative (words), and empathic understanding, as well as all of their constituent field, requiring study of other disciplines that provide methods and ideas with which to understand and evaluate it.[7]

B. What "Ideas" Has Law Generated as a Field[8]?

If law claims to be a field, what ideas has it uniquely or originally contributed to human knowledge? Do "due process," or "rules of evidence and proof," or "the rule against perpetuities," or "American Constitutionalism" (separation of powers, judicial review, federalism), or even basic notions of fairness, constitute original insights of law as a discipline?[9] Or are all of these ideas derivative of political philosophy? Certainly, transaction costs (the Coase theorem), efficiency, and the deterrence effects of sanctions are all derived from economics or sociology. Has law, as a field, contributed anything new to what we know? Can you think of any new ideas that are peculiarly legal?[10] Does a field have to generate ideas to be a discipline?[11] Must it have a distinctive method of inquiry? Of validation?

If law is rather a practice or activity — a way of organizing human behavior in furtherance of some important human goals, like justice, peace, or order — has it created particular forms or ideas of practice, for example, the trial, the contract, the interrogatory? As an arena of professional practice, one can ask is law more or less a field than medicine or engineering or architecture (which are practices based on the derivative teachings of science) or ministry (which is a practice based on the derivative teachings of theology)? Is law as a practice a "creative art," like other forms of performance? Is making a good argument the equivalent of composing a symphony, or more like successfully completing a difficult *pas de deux*?

C. What is the Purpose of Legal Education in Relation to the Above?

If law does generate its own ideas and observations about human behavior and practices, then at least one purpose of legal education is the production of knowledge about law and its practice through study and research into "new" ideas about law. How should legal education be structured to bring out the best (most accurate or robust) ideas about law? How does one do "research" in the new ideas of law? How does one combine the transmittal of known ideas and practices with the development of new ones?

If law is not a discipline unto itself, but merely transmits the relevant knowledge required for its use or practice, how should that knowledge regarding law itself be transmitted: by Langdellian induction of principles through reading cases;[12] by parsing of statutes according to the canons of statutory construction; by simulated experiences of lawyers doing client advising, advocacy, negotiating, or lobbying? What forms of training or teaching are appropriate for students to learn how to "think," "act," or "do" like a lawyer, or as one sage commentator has noted, how to think about doing?[13]

Is there such a thing, in the modern world, as acting or thinking like "a" lawyer? Aren't there too many different forms of legal practice to construct a generalizable or uniform idea of "a" lawyer for educational purposes?

How is law used in modern society? Is legal education only for practicing lawyers, judges, or theorizing legal academics, or should legal education be thought of more broadly (as in many non-American settings) as basic civic knowledge or education about the rules and institutions that govern one's life? And what should would-be lawyers learn about the impact of law and legal institutions on society? What difference do law, legal institutions, and lawyers make?

However you have answered these questions or thought about these issues, I want to suggest that the modern and rigorous study of law and legal institutions must take seriously the ideas and empirical findings of many other disciplines outside of law, because law is not an entirely autonomous discipline. Legal doctrine is derived from policy considerations (which are in turn based on empirical claims about the condition of the world and normative claims about how it might be changed), as well as the facts of disputed individual cases. Law, in turn, affects and influences how people behave toward each other and the policies that are in turn made by both public and private parties as they deploy the law in their interactions. What law is made and how it is experienced are determined by factors exogenous to "simple" doctrinal legal logic.

(b) Subverting Orthodoxy, Making Law Central: A View of Sociolegal Studies†

Roger Cotterrell

INTRODUCTION

... Everyone seriously concerned with sociolegal scholarship has a view of its potential, a view coloured by ambitions or dissatisfactions that first led to involvement with sociolegal work. Institutional work location also affects the nature of each person's ongoing involvement. An important reason for the vitality of the sociolegal community in Britain, as of the law and society community in the United States of America, has surely been its rich, almost anarchic heterogeneity and its consistent openness to many different aims, outlooks, and disciplinary backgrounds.[1] Perhaps it is undesirable to argue that such a field should tilt in any particular direction. At the very least, anyone expressing general views about the sociolegal enterprise should surely reveal the conditioning background factors that provide a context and perhaps a partial explanation for those views.

Here, briefly, are some of those factors. With many other legal academics, what this writer initially sought from sociolegal work was a set of new perspectives on law to allow a breakout from the claustrophobic world of legal scholarship and education, as previously encountered. Most legal study ... seemed to focus on technicality as an end in itself and was unconcerned with fundamental questions about law's nature, sources, and consequences as a social phenomenon or about its moral groundings. Value-judgements pervading legal studies cried out for theoretical examination but were routinely treated as obviously correct or simply unrecognized. Policy argument, the 'unruly horse'[2] that judges were sometimes forced to ride, was not considered to be 'real' legal reasoning and so not given serious attention in the law school, legal study being seen as confined to interpreting rules and analysing their logical or plausible interrelations. Moral argument was to be disposed of quickly so that sophisticated legal thinking could begin. Legislation, an unfortunate necessity, was often presented as a salutary warning about the results of amateur (non-lawyers') dabbling in law-making. To draw seriously on knowledge-fields beyond the contents of the law reports was suspect and the fortress walls of law-as-discipline were well guarded, perhaps because of mute suspicions about their ultimate fragility and law's still unsure intellectual place in the academy. The common law judge was the intellectual centre of the legal world; and thinking like a lawyer meant, as it seemed, being condemned to a professional state of intellectual tunnel-vision and moral and political impotence.

In those conditions, social science was a flag to nail to the mast, something to proclaim adherence to in trying to navigate an intellectually credible route beyond the world of orthodox doctrinal legal commentary and debate. The effort especially to apply sociological perspectives to law was not a matter of swearing adherence to sociology as a distinct discipline but of rejecting the boundary claims of academic disciplines, including those of law and sociology. It seemed important to approach legal study as an empirical, systematic study of a field of social experience. That did not necessarily demand that every legal academic must conduct empirical research on behaviour in legal contexts but it demanded that as a legal scholar one should become well informed about such research being done and about the resources social science could offer legal studies. It involved finding how best to incorporate social scientific insights and perspectives into one's own legal scholarship, and supporting and cooperating with sociolegal empirical research initiatives.

Though sociology appeared initially as a special, relatively distinct intellectual field, miraculously provided to save legal scholarship from itself, it later seemed more appropriate to view it as a compendium of methods, approaches, traditions, and aspirations which could be contributed to by many of the so-called separate academic disciplines and by work not easily fitted into any of them.[3] Using these resources one could gain distance from doctrinal legal scholarship and so develop different perspectives on it but one could also hope to participate in this scholarship in new ways, bringing a fresh outlook to bear on old problems.

Because legal theory had long had an indefinite licence to range beyond lawyers' immediate practical concerns with legal doctrine, it always seemed potentially to be a vehicle for developing an understanding of important general aspects of law that traditional legal study ignored. But this depended on jurisprudence as a taught law school subject and legal theory as a research field being infused with social scientific insight. Although sociolegal scholarship had a vital role in studying the social effects of behaviour in legal contexts, understandings of legal doctrine and reasoning also needed altering. On this view, the theoretical study of legal ideas should not be left to legal philosophers but pursued as an empirical inquiry about the conditions, significance, consequences, and potential of those ideas in particular historical conditions. So the fields of speculation that legal philosophy had monopolized, as the theoretical self-awareness of lawyers, should also be a central concern of sociolegal research. In this way sociolegal studies would not merely be juxtaposed with traditional legal scholarship but would invade it and begin to reshape it in ways that renewed its vital engagement with the currents of change in society that social scientists studied.

It would be dishonest to pretend that the ideas expressed above were fully developed from the time sociolegal studies first began to seem important to this particular academic lawyer in company with many others. But they indicate long-held convictions about what sociolegal scholarship could offer, and they colour all the suggestions to be made in the rest of this paper about directions in which it might be desirable for the sociolegal field to tilt to some degree.

THE USES OF THEORY

Phil Thomas has recently written that sociolegal studies should not be ennobled with the title of 'discipline' because to do so risks marginalizing sociolegal scholarship in the legal academy and defusing its 'growing challenges to orthodox legal pedagogy, traditional research areas and methods'[4] by setting it apart. The temptation to seek status by building disciplinary walls is strong, particularly for new fields of scholarly practice unsure of their identity and overshadowed by powerful, competing knowledge-fields. But the instinct to avoid disciplinary demarcations is

likely to be felt strongly by those who took up sociolegal studies as a tool to break open the claustrophobic discipline of law. As sociolegal perspectives seep into virtually all areas of legal scholarship many researchers have stopped worrying about the intellectual criteria of law-as-discipline. Legal scholarship is not weakened by this lack of concern but strengthened and enriched. The same is true for sociolegal studies as they extend their reach, drawing new insights about the legal from whatever intellectual sources seem appropriate.

These views imply no lack of interest in the integrity of the sociolegal field. Strengthening that integrity depends on both an increased sensitivity to its intellectual foundations in classic writings and a sustained effort to develop new sociolegal theory. Sensitivity to intellectual traditions lends perspective to the research culture but the classic sociolegal theorists are still too little valued in the sociolegal enterprise and considered too arbitrarily and marginally. Weber, Marx, and Durkheim receive habitual acknowledgement in current sociolegal scholarship but Georges Gurvitch, Leon Petrazycki, Eugen Ehrlich, Marcel Mauss, Emmanuel Lévy[5] and other important contributors are not celebrated as sources of intellectual tradition in the way that, for example, Kelsen, Bentham or Austin are in legal philosophy. If sociolegal scholarship is to transform the legal academy, its scholarly traditions need to be strongly present in the pantheon of markers of the progress of thought about law. ...

Beyond a sense of tradition, sociolegal scholarship needs more theory addressing the nature of contemporary law. It needs theory to map and organize the sociolegal realm. Again, a comparison with legal philosophy is instructive. Legal philosophy has not obviously contributed directly to the disciplinary self-consciousness of legal practice but it has elaborated [on] lawyers' perspectives on law and ordered and legitimized general concerns that legal scholars take up. It has reinforced and clarified ideas about the nature of law that lawyers often assume. If sociolegal scholarship is properly unconcerned with disciplinary status it cannot be unconcerned with clarifying its object of study, described conventionally (but, I shall suggest, inadequately) as 'law and society' or 'law in society'. Sociolegal scholarship needs theories appropriate to this task but legal philosophy has not usually produced ideas about the nature of law that take serious account of and are designed to facilitate empirical research on law as a social phenomenon. Indeed, the idea of 'the social' and its empirical variability has been largely absent from legal philosophy but it is this idea that needs most centrality in sociolegal theory. Sociolegal theory has the job of bringing the social as an object of rigorous inquiry into the study of law.[6]

Many people argue for less theory, not more, in legal and sociolegal scholarship and some reasons for this are understandable. 'Grand narratives'[7] of classic sociolegal theories — their broadest agendas and central unifying themes — seem exhausted. For example, Marx's and Engels's vision of a trajectory of world history culminating in the withering away of law and the state no longer seems credible. The concept of formal legal rationality, the primary legal expression of Weber's great thesis of the rationalization of the modern world, seems unable now to capture the vast diversity of regulatory practices of contemporary law and governance,[8] evoking instead a (partly mythical) modern age of 'pure' legal formality that has passed. And few accept solidarity as a master concept to characterize the structure of societies in the optimistic way Durkheim proposed. If postmodernist and post-structuralist writing has been too uninterested in the projects of empirical sociolegal research,[9] it has nevertheless performed an important service in linking together many scattered, accumulating doubts about modern approaches to social explanation. Emphasizing the indeterminacy, complexity, fragmentation, and fluidity of social life, postmodernists have shown that across the whole sweep of social theory the main traditions of ambitious schematization of social change no longer resonate with contemporary experience. This does not remove the need for theory, or for the centrality of social theory in sociolegal studies. Theory provides perspective in a complex, diverse field. But distrust of grand narratives leads to a more modest view of what can be asked of social theory. For example, recent literature on governmentality,[10] inspired by Foucault's work, offers no general theory of the social. But it promises new ways of conceptualizing the diversity of regulation in some contemporary societies. It addresses the complex interrelations between, on the one hand, actions of state agencies at many levels as legal-administrative regulators and, on the other, the 'quasi-governmental' and 'private' disciplinary strategies and normalizing practices that pervade social life. In reconceptualizing regulation, it avoids the increasingly implausible public/private dichotomy in social and legal thought.[11] Theory focused on the diversity of contemporary regulation also allows an escape from legal philosophy's 'What is law?' conundrums and potentially highlights regulation's fluidity, ubiquity, and varied consequences, making it possible to locate whatever we choose to designate as law in

a continuum, network or web[12] of regulatory practices and techniques.

Sociolegal theory needs to specify a realm of the legal but not necessarily in categorical fashion. Identifying the legal merely means enabling sociolegal scholarship to determine its own scope rather than to have that scope given by policy-makers. As many sociolegal scholars recognize, legal pluralist writings provide a partial means to this end.[13] ... Leaving aside legal anthropology's work on colonial and post-colonial societies, modern sociolegal scholarship has still not fully explored the potential and problems of legal pluralist theory, perhaps because the pressure to treat as law whatever lawyers and policy makers recognize as such has been almost overwhelming. Yet a legal pluralist approach does not usually entail denying lawyers' or policy makers' views of law but more often supplementing, expanding, interpreting, and explaining them in a broader social scientific context.

A legal pluralist approach does not, for example, force us to say that rules of clubs, schools, factories, and hospitals are law, though it might be interesting to think of them in that way for some analytical purposes. But it enables us to look for phenomena sufficiently like state law in some respects to make comparison illuminating. It also highlights the possibility that some types of regulation whose formal origins or primary bases of practical authority do not lie in the state are becoming so important that to ignore their interpenetration with or consequences for state law is impermissible. Most importantly, a legal pluralist approach raises the question of where law's ultimate authority resides and whether simple positivist tests adequately explain legal validity. Law's authority might depend on how far it corresponds with, or meets, felt needs for regulation of social relations. If social sources of law, located in different kinds of community life, are diverse, law itself will be diverse in meaning or effect, coloured by the varied moral expectations and responsibilities attached to it.

LAW AS ROUTINE STRUCTURING

In another area, theory in sociolegal studies may have a crucial task to perform. Nearly a century ago, Ehrlich complained[14] that lawyers overemphasize disputes and conflicts, the pathology of social life, and so distort the social significance of law. Still today, law is probably often thought of in popular consciousness mainly as criminal law (state action against social disorder) or litigation (private conflict pursued through courts). Lawyers have been criticized for seeing international law as a response to crisis rather than 'issues of structural justice that underpin everyday life'.[15] And where legal education is strongly oriented to case-law it mainly presents law as a product of dispute and disorder.

A major role of law is to repress disorder and to process disputes, but to present it entirely in these terms is to present law and lawyers' work as essentially parasitic on social pathology, the breakdown of social relations of community. Some sociolegal writing reinforces this image: Donald Black declares bluntly that law flourishes as community declines.[16] Yet, much sociolegal scholarship, operating in research settings far removed from courts (in lawyers' offices, administrative and regulatory agencies, corporate legal departments, neighbourhoods, organizations, and so on) tells a different story: of law used (with varying degrees of success and failure) to guide and structure social relations, engineer deals and understandings, define lines of authority, make provision for future contingencies, facilitate projects, distribute resources, promote security, limit risks, and encourage trust. Images (whether or not empirically-based) of common law adversarial processes as ritual tournaments, of the excesses of rights culture and of 'litigation explosions'[17] reinforce a view of law and lawyers as part of social pathology. Sociolegal scholarship gives a more balanced view through studies of law's contributions to the routine structuring of social relations, as well as its responses to social breakdown.

This is not an invitation to complacency because sociolegal research often shows how poorly law succeeds in that routine structuring, and this critique is among its most important contributions. But countering the image of law as purely a response to social pathology is part of a wider project of showing law's social centrality and hence the centrality of the sociolegal enterprise. In the image of law as routine structuring, law appears ubiquitous, not socially marginal.[18] The strength of Foucault's work for legal scholarship has been to emphasize the ubiquity of power and its necessity in structuring social relations. As Foucault revolutionized views of power, sociolegal scholarship should revolutionize views of law: from an image of exceptionality and pathology to one of normality and pervasiveness. Law, like power, should be seen as a resource operating routinely in innumerable social sites and settings. Work on law as constitutive of social institutions, practices, ideas, and identities, on law's ideological significance and rootedness in culture, on legal consciousness and on images of law in everyday life all point in this direction.[19]

. . . .

LEGAL AUTHORITY AND TRANSNATIONAL LAW

The significance of these ideas lies in two directions. One is towards recovering a concern in sociolegal studies and legal scholarship more generally with moral foundations of law. Durkheim stressed law's rootedness in the diverse moral milieux of social life, but he did not follow the matter far enough and made obviously unjustifiable assumptions about the moral cohesion of modern societies. He made law central as a concern for social science by stressing its necessary moral resonance (its rootedness in everyday values and understandings of social relations) and its corresponding emptiness if that moral resonance were absent. From a Durkheimian standpoint, a contemporary task of legal scholarship guided by sociolegal perspectives is to rediscover this moral resonance of law, reinterpreting it in terms of the diversity and fluidity of social relations in contemporary society.[20] Crucially, the old Durkheimian 'grand narrative' of an overarching solidarity of modern society needs to be replaced with more modest talk of diverse types of community life and their legal needs and expressions.

... Sociolegal identification of law's failures in representing and reconciling these conflicting demands provides a basis for powerful moral critique of law.

A view of law as a structuring of social relations of community also points in a second direction. This is towards new perspectives on the familiar claim that the state monopoly of the making, interpreting, and enforcing of law is slowly ending. ... In particular it is now widely recognized that 'society', taken to mean the realm of the social marked by the boundaries of the nation-state, can no longer be treated sociologically as a self-contained totality. Social relations of many kinds (for example, commercial or financial links and interdependencies, bonds of religious, ethnic or ideological solidarity, kinship and friendship ties, security alliances, and political movements) now routinely escape limitation by the political boundaries of states.

If relations of community operate extensively on transnational bases as well as reflecting the fluidity of social relations in nation states, it should be unsurprising that new regulatory forms are being shaped to frame these kinds of relations. Sociolegal scholarship is already extensively mapping and analysing these new forms of regulation[24] in environmental, commercial, human rights, information technology, and many other fields. But much legal scholarship and legal education still implies that nation state law and traditional international law, focused on relations between states, define the essential nature of the legal. Sociolegal studies can help to redraw the legal map, emphasizing how and why the changing character of the social in transnational and intranational contexts forces change in structures of regulation; change which will eventually demand from legal theory entirely new conceptions of law. ...

. . . .

A consequence of all the developments discussed above is that both limbs of 'law and society' — the traditional object of sociolegal scholarship — are now deeply problematic. On the one hand, the social is no longer merely 'society' as classical sociology defined it: co-existent with the territorial reach of the nation state. On the other hand, 'law' now must be rethought as a diversity of regulatory strategies and forms, evolving from many different social sources in and beyond nation states. Sociolegal scholarship, I suggest, should lead legal studies forward by providing new frameworks for understanding these fundamental developments which make many older views of law and society redundant.

LAW, POWER, COMMUNITY

If, as suggested earlier, social science was a flag to fly in trying to escape the unsatisfactory character of traditional legal education and scholarship, what has been achieved through empirical sociolegal scholarship in Britain in the past thirty years suggests that the flag was a good one to adopt. ...

The heart of the enterprise in this sense has surely been its consistent focus on power. No concept is more important for sociolegal studies. Most sociolegal work explores the power of law: how it is structured and organized, its consequences and sources, and the way people and organizations seek to harness it, have differential access to it or find themselves differentially affected by it. Traditional legal scholarship has often largely ignored these aspects of the power of law. Instead, where it has considered power, it has typically seen it as external and opposed to law. Law has usually been seen as a control of power, above all of the directive and

police power of the state; generally less attention has been paid to law's relation to economic power. The very idea of law as a control of state power indicates the incoherence and naivety of traditional legal scholarship's view of power: law being seen bizarrely as created by the state with the object of controlling the state. Sociolegal scholarship, by contrast, has shown how law as institutionalized doctrine formalizes and channels power rather than controlling it, often making its effects more predictable and precise and its exercise more orderly.

Whatever directions sociolegal scholarship takes in future, surely this emphasis on power should remain. ... [It is also] important somehow to keep a firm attachment to the idea of law as a *communal* rather than individual or private resource for channelling power. Law addresses stable social relations of all kinds, which can be thought of as relations of community. Indeed, viewed in this way, law has no valid reason for existence except as an expression and support of community. Major traditions of sociolegal writing stretching back to the beginnings of modern sociology of law ... [emphasize] its social roots in a way that traditional legal scholarship has invariably failed to do.

But, if such a view is taken, certain consequences follow. To see law as an expression of community is to value it as a shared resource before asking how far and in what ways it fails as such an expression. Such an approach bases critique of actual law on a celebration of the idea of law as a communal resource, a vital part of the definition of communal solidarity. What sociolegal theory requires law to be according to this view, provides a measure of how far law fails in particular contexts. ...

My suggestion for tilting the sociolegal field is thus to reassert links between law and morality, viewing morality sociologically as the varied normative conditions of solidarity necessary to the diverse kinds of relations of community that comprise the social. Relations of community and relations between networks of community are power relations but power, like law, pervades social life. It is not to be regretted but analysed, shaped, and channelled. ... We may hope that, from positions such as these, sociolegal scholarship will be able to show how central its researches are for the whole range of legal studies and in addressing many of social science's most fundamental concerns.

(c)   Socio-legal Scholarship in Canada: A Review of the Field†

Harry Arthurs and Annie Bunting

INTRODUCTION: DEFINING THE FIELD — WHAT DO WE MEAN BY SOCIO-LEGAL SCHOLARSHIP?

Legal academics tend to define socio-legal scholarship negatively — scholarship that is not doctrinal. However, this definition tells us more about sectarianism within the legal academy than about the field itself. Social scientists and humanists, by contrast, are likely to adopt a more positive definition: socio-legal research investigates legal institutions, processes, cultures, texts, experiences, and outcomes from a variety of external perspectives. Undergraduate and graduate programmes in law and society in Canada, for example, define themselves more explicitly as programmes for the interdisciplinary study of law — though interdisciplinarity is far from a settled concept. And importantly, the Canadian Law and Society Association (CLSA) describes itself inclusively as 'a group of scholars from many disciplines who are interested in the place of law in social, political, economic and cultural life'.[1] ... In our survey of the field, we define law and society scholarship as that which has legal institutions, practices, and meanings as its objects of study but is not only a doctrinal study of law; we include interdisciplinary scholarship but also that derived from distinct sub-disciplines such as legal anthropology, geography, history, sociology, and so on.

... As a consequence, we have to acknowledge that the boundaries of our study remain porous, and our description of the state of the field in Canada impressionistic. Part of this impression of the field in Canada is concerned with the relationship between law schools and socio-legal research as well as the evolution of the field over the past thirty years. ...

... As in other jurisdictions, law and society research in Canada emerged in the 1960s as a challenge to narrow vocational understandings of law. Some of the early critical work in Canada was conducted by faculty in law schools with interests in social justice, feminism, legal history, and anti-racism and faculty in social sciences and the humanities concerned with similar questions. However, as a site of socio-legal research, Canada was distinctive for a number of reasons including its federal legal structure, its bilingual and multi-juridical system (conventionally understood as bi-juridical with civil and common law traditions, but in fact multi-juridical with Indigenous and other non-state legal systems), and its proximity to the United States and the American Law and Society Association (LSA). Whereas in the late 1980s and early 1990s, Canadian law and society scholarship could be characterized as predominantly national, historical, and policy-oriented, current socio-legal research tends to be more international, interdisciplinary, and theoretical.

Progress has been neither linear nor inevitable. ... The centre of gravity of socio-legal research has shifted from the legal academy to social science- and humanities-based programmes and back again. And it has fallen in and out of favour with funding agencies and its relevant others in professional, academic, and policy communities. However, a significant cohort of Canadian socio-legal researchers has emerged (including some legal academics with graduate degrees in other disciplines); the CLSA is a vibrant intellectual community; graduate and undergraduate teaching programmes in the field have proliferated and grown to maturity; book series and journals dedicated to socio-legal themes have become far more numerous; and ambitious socio-legal research projects have multiplied, some funded by research-granting agencies, others by law reform commissions or by bodies such as the Canadian Institute for Advanced Research. And thirty years on, even relatively conservative faculties of law and their learned journals seem to have accepted interdisciplinary teaching and scholarship as legitimate, if not yet indispensable or even mainstream. That at least is what our research suggests.

A BRIEF PRE-HISTORY OF SOCIO-LEGAL SCHOLARSHIP IN CANADA

The history of socio-legal scholarship is closely interwoven with the history of university faculties of

† (2014) 41:4 Journal of Law and Society 487–99. [Notes and/or references omitted.] © 2014, Harry Arthurs and Annie Bunting. Journal of Law and Society © 2014 Cardiff University of Law School. Reprinted with permission of John Wiley and Sons via Rightslink.

social science and law. In general, the social sciences developed somewhat later in Canada than in the United States, and Canadian professional associations and scholarly journals emerged rather slowly, ... As for the legal academy, university law faculties emerged in the late nineteenth and early twentieth centuries in several common law provinces,[6] in Québec (a civil law province) somewhat earlier,[7] and in British Columbia and Ontario (two of the largest common law jurisdictions) much later — after the Second World War.[8] Until the 1960s, most law teaching was undertaken by part-time practitioner-lecturers,[9] and focused largely on the analysis of legal texts, rather than on law's causes and consequences.[10] There were few full-time legal academics in Canada — only 44 in 1948, still only 66 in 1956[11] — and no forum for the exchange of scholarly ideas and opinions until 1951 when the Canadian Association of Law Teachers was formally established.[12] Not surprisingly, relatively little scholarly research of any description was published, and even less that could be described as 'socio-legal'.[13]

Despite the underdeveloped state of these and other relevant disciplines, what might be described as pioneering or proto–socio-legal scholarship began to appear during the inter-war years. It was inspired in part by the emergence of sociological jurisprudence and the legal realist movement in the United States and developments in European social science, in part by the upheavals in legal and social ordering triggered by the Great War and the Great Depression.[14] Several contributors to this early scholarship had backgrounds in law and/or political science;[15] others were associated with nascent movements in sociology, anthropology, and criminology in both French and English Canada.

The picture began to change rapidly in the 1960s, as the social sciences came into their own in Canadian universities, and as Canadian law schools began to enlarge their enrolments, faculty complements, and intellectual ambitions. ...

... [F]rom the 1960s onwards, non-lawyer social scientists began to analyse subjects as diverse as the effect of legal frameworks on industrial relations,[18] the legislative regulation of narcotics,[19] and the work of the Supreme Court of Canada.[20] By the 1970s and 1980s, socio-legal scholars in Canada — scholars with backgrounds in law and/or the social sciences and humanities — had begun to develop a significant body of work in legal theory and history, the sociology of the legal profession, family and gender studies, the justice system, criminology, and other fields.

This increase in the number of scholars involved in socio-legal research was in part cause, in part

effect, of several institutional initiatives. These included the establishment of undergraduate Law and Society programmes at several universities leading to the emergence of a cadre of socio-legal scholars;[21] the commissioning of socio-legal research by the Law Reform Commission of Canada and its provincial counterparts;[22] the increased use of socio-legal evidence in litigation following the introduction of the Canadian Charter of Rights and Freedoms in 1982;[23] and (as mentioned above) enhanced interest by the SSHRC in the impoverished state of legal research.

. . . .

THE FUTURE

Whether one takes an optimistic or a pessimistic view of progress to date, it would be unwise to assume that socio-legal scholarship will follow the same trajectory in the next ten or twenty years that it has in the recent past. Too much is changing too rapidly. Increased interest in interdisciplinarity across all academic disciplines, the emergence of transnational and trans-systemic legal systems and practices, and the trend towards the multi- and post-professional practice of law would all seem to argue for a bright future for socio-legal research. If indeed these trends prevail, the Canadian socio-legal community is ready to respond to the new opportunities they will bring. It comprises a critical mass of scholars in a variety of disciplines; it has constructed a fairly stable foundation of undergraduate and graduate teaching programmes, professional networks, research centres and journals; and its confidence has grown along with its capacities.

On the other hand, a scan of the political economy of socio-legal research reveals some disturbing developments as well. Under the influence of globalization and technology, Canada's economy has been going through a prolonged period of restructuring; governments of all stripes have been reducing taxes and regulation; tectonic shifts are taking place in the market for legal services and in the organization of legal practice; the costs of a law school education have risen while the job prospects for law graduates are deteriorating. The resulting crises in legal education and research are not (yet) as dire in Canada as in the United States, but socio-legal scholarship is likely to face a number of challenges as a result.

The first is the return of legal fundamentalism — a reassertion by the profession of its control over law faculties in order to ensure that graduating students are educated in 'the basics' and have mastered designated 'competencies'. Given the profession's current obsession with producing 'practice-ready lawyers', under its tight grip, law faculties are likely to be persuaded or forced to stick to their 'core mission' and to reduce their investment in 'frills' such as research and graduate studies. This pressure will in turn reignite and reinforce suspicion and resentment of non-doctrinal research which is accurately perceived to be a destabilizing influence on legal knowledge, practice, and culture. Of course, the profession uses socio-legal research when it must, for example, in presenting evidence of systemic discrimination in Charter litigation or in making the case for more (or less) intrusive regulation of the securities industry or labour markets. That said, it is one thing to treat socio-legal scholarship as an occasional useful supplement to 'real' legal knowledge, another to treat it as indispensable to all thinking about legal regimes and relations. Unfortunately, much of the bar and significant elements of the legal academy tend to the former view. So too does Canada's neo-liberal government which is inclined to disparage all the social sciences — except economics.

The second is a long-term trend away from the era of activist government that in Canada was closely associated with projects of law reform, broadly defined. Such projects — ranging from the adoption of a constitutional Charter of Rights and Freedoms to the decriminalization of abortion and the legalization of gay marriage to the reform of criminal, employment, consumer, and environmental laws — depended heavily on socio-legal research for both their inspiration and their implementation. And they offered socio-legal researchers more than challenging and well-funded professional opportunities; they conferred on them a degree of political legitimacy and legal-professional salience they would not

otherwise have enjoyed. In the new era of passive government, socio-legal researchers will have to find all of these elsewhere.

And finally, within the university sector, changes are in prospect. The rise of socio-legal scholarship largely coincided with, and was made possible by, an expansionary era in Canadian academe — albeit one punctuated by periods of constraint. Now the long-term prospects of our universities seem less optimistic and, therefore, so do the prospects for socio-legal research. General government support for higher education is likely to be curtailed, as part of a drive for lower taxes and balanced budgets; student enrolments in the humanities and social sciences have been declining over the long term (though 'applied' programmes — including law and society — have so far resisted this trend); and while the aggregate funding provided by Canada's national research-granting agencies has increased in recent years, increases have been targeted at science-based research, especially research produced through industry–university partnerships. Whether this amounts to full-scale 'corporatization' of Canadian universities, the least that can be said is that these developments offer little encouragement to those contemplating careers as socio-legal researchers, and little prospect of support for research which is perceived to be neither 'real' science nor business-friendly.

On balance, we suspect, the future of socio-legal scholarship will less and less be determined inside the legal academy, more and more elsewhere in the university. But we are confident that it will survive the looming threats we have identified, and over the long term, will make increasingly important and varied contributions both to an understanding of law and to its practical improvement.

153

III

Making Law:
Judicial Decisions and Legislation

Overview of Part III

Part III focuses on issues related to two formal processes of "law-making" in common law legal systems.

The articles in **Chapter 8** discuss the basic elements of the process by which judges make common law rules through judicial decisions. These decisions become precedents that are meant to "bind" other judges. The excerpt from Morton's book provides a brief introduction to the classic distinctions between law-making through judicial precedents and law-making through legislation, and also introduces some of the important critiques of judicial discretion raised by Legal Realists. Atiyah provides a more in-depth discussion of the way in which certain decisions become identified as "precedents" that must be followed according to the rule of *stare decisis* — which requires us to "stand by the decided case". Llewellyn revisits these basic elements of *stare decisis* by exploring the ways in which lawyers and judges necessarily use interpretation of precedents to suit their interests. Llewellyn thus stresses the ambiguity and essential flexibility of the system of precedent. The system of precedent, then, is neither determinative nor completely without structure.

Chapter 9 includes two case excerpts that highlight the Supreme Court of Canada's approach to interpreting legislation. *Re Rizzo & Rizzo Shoes Ltd.* is a leading Supreme Court decision on statu-tory interpretation and outlines the Court's "modern approach" to interpreting laws made by legislatures. *R. v. Mills* illustrates the Supreme Court's understanding of the relationship between the legislature and the judiciary and outlines many of the factors the Court considers when evaluating legislation that responds to judicial decisions. The excerpt by Fish forcefully challenges the traditional divide between "textual" and "contextual" approaches to interpretation. Through his playful discussion of *Re Soper's Estate*, Fish demonstrates the way in which the interpretive process in legal decision-making ultimately serves to stabilize a version of legal formalism and legal authority.

As you read through this Part, ask yourself: in what ways might our view of the law-making process be shaped by the different theoretical approaches to understanding law discussed in both **Part I** and **Part II**? In light of the important role of judicial decisions in the process of interpreting and making law, is the law ever static and knowable, or is it always contingent and fundamentally uncertain? Is law-making by legislatures more desirable or legitimate than law-making by judges? If so, why? How do discretionary decisions by administrators or enforcement personnel shape the implementation of legal rules? Is this another form of 'law-making'?

8 Judicial Decisions and the Common Law

(a) Precedents, Statutes and Legal Reasoning†

F.L. Morton

One of the most distinctive characteristics of the judicial process is its formalized method of reasoning. Because their authority flows from the public perception that they are "merely" applying pre-existing rules to resolve new disputes, judges are not permitted the broad prerogative enjoyed by the legislative and the executive branches. Unlike the latter, courts are not supposed to create new policies to deal with new problems. In their oral or written judgments, judges must explain where and how they derived the "rule" used to settle a case. There are three principal sources for these "rules": a written constitution, legislative statutes (including administrative regulations), and prior judicial decisions, known as precedents. Constitutional interpretation is the subject of the following two chapters. This chapter is concerned with the role of precedent and statutory interpretation in judicial reasoning.

Until the middle of the nineteenth century, most internal or domestic law in English-speaking societies was common law. Common law originated in the judicial recognition and enforcement of traditional usages and customs of the Anglo-Saxon and later Norman peoples in the British Isles. As these judicial decisions were made, they in turn became part of the common law. The common law in contemporary Canadian society consists of all previous judicial decisions by Canadian and British courts, as they are recorded in the case reports of these nations. The common law system is distinguished from the civil law system by its basis in precedent rather than legislative enactment. The civil law system originated in ancient Roman law, developed on the European continent, and was imported into Quebec by the French. It is based on a single, comprehensive code, enacted by the legislature.

The law of precedent, or *stare decisis*, is a self-imposed judicial rule that "like cases be decided alike." As Gordon Post explains, the law of precedent is essentially a formalization of the common sense use of past experience as a guide to present conduct. The value of judicial adherence to *stare decisis* is two-fold. First, continuity and certainty in the law is a prerequisite of civilized human activity. If there is no reasonable guarantee that what is valid law today will still be valid law tomorrow, personal, economic, and political intercourse would grind to a halt. In each of these spheres of human activity, present-day decisions and activities are predicated on expectations about the future. Ensuring a high degree of predictability and continuity between the present and the future is one of the primary purposes of a political regime. As the institutions charged with interpreting and adapting the laws over time, the courts are responsible for maintaining continuity and certainty. As Dicey said, "A law which was not certain would in reality be no law at all." Adherence to the rule of precedent — "deciding like cases alike" — is the mechanism that provides this certainty.

The rule of precedent also contributes to guaranteeing the "rule of law, not of men." One of the

† From *Law, Politics and the Judicial Process in Canada* (Calgary: University of Calgary Press, 1984) at 185–89. [Notes and/or references omitted.] Reproduced with permission.

ideals of the Western tradition's conception of justice is that the laws be applied equally and impartially to all persons. This ideal precludes any *ad hoc* application of the laws, and demands instead that laws be applied uniformly, or that any deviation from the rule be justified on principle — that is, by another rule. The idiosyncrasies or personal preferences of a judge are not permissible grounds for judicial decisions. This would re-introduce the "rule of men" rather than the "rule of law." By minimizing the discretion or freedom of individual judges, *stare decisis* preserves the "rule of law."

It should be emphasized that *stare decisis* minimizes but does not eliminate the element of judicial discretion or creativity. While legal reasoning presents itself as a deductive process, the reality is a more subtle blend of both inductive and deductive reasoning. Legal reasoning is accurately described as "reasoning by example."[1] The judges are essentially asking, "Whether the present case resembles the plain case 'sufficiently' and in the 'relevant' aspects."[2] In determining what is "sufficient" and what is "relevant," the judge must ultimately make certain choices. Because of this element of choice, a judge is responsible for striking the balance between continuity and innovation. The central thrust of the theory of legal realism has been to emphasize this element of choice and judicial discretion, and the ensuing responsibility of the judge for his choice.

Weiler's analysis of the Supreme Court's responsibility for the development of tort law is based on this legal realist perspective. Weiler argues that judges can no longer claim that precedent "dictates" nonsensical or patently unfair legal conclusions. Judges must be critical in their use of precedent, and go beyond the surface "rule" to discover the animating "principle." The proper function of the common law judge, according to Weiler, is to derive specific rules from more general principles, as the situation demands. Since situations change, rules must change also. While the "cattle trespass" exemption to normal tort law responsibility may have been appropriate to the rural, agricultural society of eighteenth century England, it had become a dangerous anachronism in twentieth century Canada. Similarly in *Boucher v. The King*, the Court was faced with a conflict between the definition of "seditious libel" developed in nineteenth century, homogeneous, protestant Britain, and the norms of freedom of religion and speech in twentieth century, pluralistic Canada. Appeal court judges have a duty, says Weiler, to adapt the common law to the changing needs and circumstances of contemporary society.

Strict adherence to *stare decisis* is yet another aspect of the "adjudication of disputes" function of courts that poses problems for judicial policy-making. Refusal to disavow or change past decisions plays no constructive role in a policy-making institution, as the examples of legislative and executive practice make clear. While certainty and continuity are legal virtues, adaptability and innovation are more important in the policy-making process. The case for abandoning a strict adherence to precedent is especially strong in constitutional law. Not only is policy-impact more probable, but constitutional law lacks the flexibility of common law and statutes. If the courts make a "mistake" in the latter areas, it can be corrected by remedial legislation. But if the Supreme Court makes a constitutional decision with undesirable policy consequences, the only direct way to correct the damage is through formal constitutional amendment, an extremely cumbersome and difficult process.[3] Predictably, the U.S. Supreme Court was the first court of appeal in a common law nation to abandon *stare decisis* as an absolute requirement. The demotion of *stare decisis* from a binding rule to a guiding principle is another index of a court's evolution toward a greater policy-making role.

The recent advent of judicial realism in Canadian jurisprudence has brought with it a decline in the status of the rule of *stare decisis*. Long after the American Supreme Court had abandoned absolute adherence to precedent, the Canadian Supreme Court continued to perceive itself as bound to adhere not only to its own previous decisions but those of the British House of Lords as well. This latter restriction is attributable to the role of the Judicial Committee of the Privy Council as Canada's final court of appeal until 1949. Ten years after the abolition of that role, the Supreme Court declared its independence from British precedents as well. In 1966 the British House of Lords officially declared that, when appropriate, it would no longer follow its own prior decisions. However, the Supreme Court of Canada continued to profess strict adherence to its prior decisions until the 1970's. Under the leadership of Bora Laskin, the Canadian Supreme Court began to move in the same direction. In 1972, before his appointment as chief justice, Laskin had written that *stare decisis* was "no longer an article of faith in the Supreme Court of Canada, but it still remains a cogent principle."[4] Speaking as the new Chief Justice at the Centennial Symposium of the Supreme Court in 1975, Laskin repeated that *stare decisis* was no longer "an inexorable rule," but rather, simply an important element of the judicial process, a necessary consideration which should give pause to any but the most sober conclusion that a previous decision or line of authority is wrong and ought to be changed.[5]

Practising what he preached, Laskin led the Supreme Court to overturn three precedents during the next three years, including an old Privy Council decision dealing with the federal division of powers.[6] The abandoning of strict adherence to *stare decisis* is yet another indicator of the Supreme Court's institutional evolution toward more of a policy-making court.

The second principal source of law is legislative statutes. Beginning in the nineteenth century, legislatures in Great Britain, Canada, and the United States began to codify large portions of the common law. In large part this was a democratic reaction against the perceived elitism of the "judge-made" character of the common law. By reducing the confusing maze of common law precedent to clearly worded, legislative statutes, it was thought that the law would be made easier for "the people" to understand, and that the democratic authority of "government by consent" would be enhanced.

In 1892 the Canadian Parliament abolished all criminal offenses at common law, and replaced them with a comprehensive statute, the *Criminal Code*. In so doing, Parliament hoped to reap the alleged advantages of codification mentioned above, including restricting judicial discretion in the criminal law. Since crimes were now clearly and authoritatively defined, judges would simply apply the law as Parliament had written it. It would no longer be necessary to refer to a vast and confusing system of precedent to apply the criminal law, or so it was hoped.

In fact, precedent and *stare decisis* quickly found their way back into the criminal law. Perhaps, as Parker has suggested, it was (and still is) impossible for judges and lawyers trained in the common law tradition to properly construe a code of law.[7] More likely the common law "habit" simply compounds a more serious problem — the ultimate ambiguity of statutory terminology itself. Try as they might, legislators will never be able to draft statutes that anticipate and encompass all possible future situations. This is due in part to the inherent tension between the generality of words and the specificity of reality, and in part to human ignorance of the future. As new situations inevitably arise, the applicability of the original wording of statutes becomes increasingly questionable....

The preceding argument notwithstanding, judicial discretion in interpreting statutes, including the *Criminal Code*, is much more circumscribed than in interpreting the common law. As Weiler says, judges can develop new torts, but not new crimes, and there are sound reasons for preferring this arrangement. As issues of tort law are rarely the subject of partisan political controversy, an innovative court cannot be accused of usurping the legislative function. The controversies over capital punishment and abortion show that the same is not true of the criminal law. In the area of tort law, judicial expertise is very high, relative to other policy-making institutions. Finally, judicial initiatives in substantive criminal law would pose the threat of punishing innocent persons. No comparable problem of "due process" arises in tort law.

While codification and statutes clearly circumscribe the limits of judicial law-making, there is still the element of judicial "choice" and its accompanying responsibility. This is especially true of the *Criminal Code*, which authorizes the continued use of common law defenses such as *mens rea*. Once again, Weiler argues that judges should go beyond superficial resemblances of wording of facts and grasp the principles that animate this area of law. The examples used appear to be contradictory decisions concerning the availability of the *mens rea* defense. Weiler suggests that these can be reconciled by reference to the underlying competition between the "crime control" and "due process" principles of criminal law. Different judges could reasonably reach different conclusions in these two cases. The essential point from Weiler's perspective is not so much what a judge decides, but how he decides the case. A final appellate court should explicitly ground its decision in the underlying principles, and explain why the particular circumstances of this case dictated favouring one over the other. Failure to do so is a failure to live up to the standards of judicial craftsmanship that can reasonably be expected from a final appellate court in an age of legal realism.

(b)   The Doctrine of Precedent†

Patrick Atiyah

There are, of course, rules about law-making by courts, rules laid down by the courts themselves. Not everything said by a judge makes law. In the first place, decisions on pure questions of fact clearly do not create precedents. The fact that X shot Y may make him guilty of murder but is of no relevance to another case in which Z is the accused. Even evaluative decisions, such as a decision that a certain piece of conduct constitutes negligence, are not regarded as decisions on points of law which can constitute precedents. To take a simple example, if a judge says that a defendant in a civil action was driving his car at 80 mph in a public street, and that he was therefore guilty of negligence, that is no precedent for holding that it is negligence for another driver in a subsequent case to have driven at the same speed (even on the same road). This is partly because (as is commonly said) evaluative decisions like this must depend on all the circumstances of the case, and so it is impossible to be sure that the relevant facts in the first decision were in all respects the same as in the second. But it also seems pretty clear that one reason why decisions of this kind are not treated as precedents is simply that the courts do not want to make their every decision suffocated under the weight of previous cases. If every case of this kind became a precedent, the volume of case law would become enormous, the argument of simple cases would become inordinately complicated, as each side would support its case with a mountainous pile of precedents, and judges would find it increasingly difficult to explain why and how decision Z was consistent with decisions A, B, C ... in favour of one side, and not inconsistent with decisions M, N, O ... in favour of the other side. So judicial decisions would inevitably appear inconsistent, and this is disliked by judges. Decisions on discretionary matters are also not decisions which can constitute precedents, although the guiding principles on which discretions are to be exercised are treated as questions of law.

The doctrine of precedent, then, is largely concerned with pure questions of law. A decision on a point of law constitutes a precedent which can in principle *bind* other courts to follow it. But before we can say that a decision constitutes a binding precedent two further qualifications need to be made. First, it must indeed be a *decision*, and not merely an *obiter dictum*, that is, a statement made by the way, an aside. In principle the distinction between the binding part of the decision (the *ratio decidendi*) and an *obiter dictum* is clear, but in practice it is not always easy to distinguish between them. Sometimes judges give several reasons for a decision: are they all binding, or is there one binding reason, the others being merely *dicta*? Or again, there may be several different judgements given in an appeal court, and the reasons given by all the judges may not wholly coincide, so what is the *ratio decidendi* then? In any event, the question of *ratio* or *dictum* may be less important than the weight of the remarks in their context, and the tribunal from which they emanate. Fully considered *dicta* in the House of Lords are usually treated as more weighty than the *ratio* of a judge at first instance in the High Court. So the whole distinction is more blurred than it might seem. Further, the distinction often does not matter at all. It does not matter basically when the second court agrees with the decision (or *dicta*) in the previous case, and would arrive at the same conclusion anyhow; it does not matter even when the second court might, if it were to go into the issue in depth, have doubts about the first decision (or *dicta*) but feel disinclined to reopen the issue for any one of a number of possible reasons. Nor does the distinction between *ratio* and *dicta* matter if the second court disagrees so strongly with what was said in the earlier case that it is not prepared to follow it, even if in theory some lawyers might regard the prior case as a binding precedent. Where this happens, the second court may 'distinguish' the first decision by finding some relevant fact to be decisive of the second case which was not present in the first. Every lawyer knows that fine distinctions are sometimes seized upon to justify departing from a prior decision with-

† From *Law and Modern Society* (London, U.K.: Oxford University Press, 1983) at 134–37. Reproduced by permission of Oxford University Press.

out an apparent breach with the rules of binding precedent.

The second qualification that needs to be made to the binding nature of the doctrine of precedent is that the strictly binding feature of the doctrine depends on the relative status of the courts concerned. Decisions of the House of Lords bind all lower courts, and are normally treated as binding by the House itself. Since 1966 the House has claimed the right to overrule previous decisions in exceptional cases, but it has so far been very sparing in its willingness to exercise this power. Decisions of the Court of Appeal bind lower courts, and also in principle bind the Court of Appeal itself. But there is much controversy on this and practice varies. Lord Denning, who as Master of the Rolls presides over the Court of Appeal, has frequently expressed his belief that that court ought to have the same freedom to depart from its own prior decisions as the House of Lords now claims; some of his colleagues appear to agree with him, but a majority do not. Furthermore, while most of those who agree with Lord Denning are generally prepared to accept the majority view that the Court of Appeal should remain bound by its own decisions, Lord Denning himself (and occasionally, it would seem, one or two others) are not. There are, in any event, a number of established exceptions to the rule that that court is bound by its own decisions, but their limits are somewhat ill-defined, so in practice it is really quite rare that the court must seriously face the question whether it is absolutely bound by one of its own decisions.

Decisions of Divisional Courts bind all lower courts, and even decisions of a single High Court judge are treated as binding on magistrates and tribunals, and generally by lawyers in the public service. Decisions of judges below the level of the High Court are not regarded as binding on anyone, and there is no systematic method of reporting such decisions.

The above account of the doctrine of precedent may well give a misleading impression of the importance of single binding decisions. Undoubtedly there are some situations where such decisions settle the law on a clear, simple point. In the interpretation of a statute, for instance, a simple ambiguity may be found which gives two alternative meanings to a section: the choice may be stark and straight-forward, even though the resolution of the ambiguity may be quite difficult. In such a case, a single decision may settle the issue, particularly if it is in the Court of Appeal or the House of Lords. But much more commonly, it is clusters of decisions which are important for the development of the law. Usually it is found that areas of doubt and uncertainty in the law, as well as newly developing areas, give rise to more litigation than other areas: this occurs for the obvious reason that lawyers are unable to advise their clients with the same degree of confidence in these areas, and the prospects of successful appeals may well be higher in such cases. So it quite often happens that a whole series of new cases arises in a relatively short period of time. When this happens, it also often becomes clear that new vistas are opening up, and, perhaps, that new problems, hitherto unsuspected, have been thrown up. Such a cluster of cases may well trigger off academic writing, which in turn may influence counsel in arguing subsequent cases. After a while matters may settle down again, and a new bit of law is, as it were, digested by the law and lawyers. This sort of development does not necessarily raise serious issues about the binding force of particular precedents, though such a development is occasionally triggered off by a loosening-up of the effect of an earlier series of precedents.

One recent illustration of this process, of some general interest, concerns the liability of barristers and solicitors for negligence in handling their clients' affairs. Until the early 1960s the law was taken to be settled that (1) a solicitor was liable for negligence on the same footing as any other professional adviser, but (2) that a barrister was not so liable because a barrister did not have a direct contract with his client — the client being compelled to approach the barrister through the solicitor with whom he contracted. Then in 1964 the House of Lords decided the famous *Hedley Byrne* case [1964] AC 465 which had nothing at all to do with the liability of barristers or solicitors, but which recognized for the first time that liability for negligent professional advice might arise *in tort*, that is, even between parties not in a contractual relationship. Barristers, of course, were quick to appreciate that their own traditional immunities might now be called in question, and in two subsequent decisions the House of Lords has begun to explore this possibility. These two decisions have laid down a new framework of law, much of which remains to be filled in by later decisions. Barristers remain immune from negligence liability in respect of the actual conduct of a case in court and in respect of advisory work which is so closely connected with the conduct of the case that it is in effect preparatory work for the trial, but they are no longer immune in respect of purely advisory work. Further, although none of these cases has so far actually involved the liability of a solicitor, it is pretty clear from *dicta* in them, that a solicitor's liability will now be equated with a barrister's, and he will share the barrister's immunity in respect of the actual conduct of a case in court — and cases in lower courts often are handled by solicitors. What is now likely to happen is that there will be a number of cases defining somewhat more clearly the line between purely advisory work and preparation for actual litigation.

This series of cases (and I have omitted some of the less significant) illustrates the way in which the common law can still develop, step by step, almost as though it were an organic growth. We now have a number of judgments in several cases, each of which offers arguments and opinions in favour of this or that development. Hypothetical examples may also be given, some of the arguments in one judgment may be rebutted in another judgment, and so on. Then for a while, the issues may move into the public domain, particularly where, as in this case, there is a public interest in the legal rules being developed. There may be academic articles and notes, media discussion, perhaps anecdotal evidence of past injustices, and possibly even a parliamentary debate. All this may indirectly feed into the next round of developments, and so the process continues.

(c)   This Case System: Precedent†

Karl Llewellyn

We turn first to what I may call the orthodox doctrine of precedent, with which, in its essence, you are already familiar. Every case lays down a rule, the rule of the case. The express ratio decidendi is prima facie the rule of the case, since it is the ground upon which the court chose to rest its decision. But a later court can reexamine the case and can invoke the canon that no judge has power to decide what is not before him, can, through examination of the facts or of the procedural issue, narrow the picture of what was actually before the court and can hold that the ruling made requires to be understood as thus restricted. In the extreme form this results in what is known as expressly "confining the case to its particular facts." This rule holds only of redheaded Walpoles in pale magenta Buick cars. And when you find this said of a past case you know that in effect it has been overruled. Only a convention, a somewhat absurd convention, prevents flat overruling in such instances. It seems to be felt as definitely improper to state that the court in a prior case was wrong, peculiarly so if that case was in the same court which is speaking now. It seems to be felt that this would undermine the dogma of the infallibility of courts. So lip service is done to that dogma, while the rule which the prior court laid down is disembowelled. The execution proceeds with due respect, with mandarin courtesy.

Now this orthodox view of the authority of precedent — which I shall call the *strict* view — is but *one of two views* which seem to me wholly contradictory to each other. It is in practice the dogma which is applied to *unwelcome* precedents. It is the recognized, legitimate, honorable technique for whittling precedents away, for making the lawyer, in his argument, and the court, in its decision, free of them. It is a surgeon's knife.

It is orthodox, I think, because it has been more discussed than is the other. Consider the situation. It is not easy thus to carve a case to pieces. It takes thought, it takes conscious thought, it takes analysis. There is no great art and no great difficulty in merely looking at a case, reading its language, and then applying some sentence which is there expressly stated. But there is difficulty in going underneath what is said, in making a keen reexamination of the case that stood before the court, in showing that the language used was quite beside the point, as the point is revealed under the lens of leisured microscopic refinement. Hence the technique of distinguishing cases has given rise to the closest of scrutiny. The technique of arguing for a distinction has become systematized. And when men start talking of authority, or of the doctrine of precedent, they turn naturally to that part of their minds which has been *consciously* devoted to the problem; they call up the

† From Karl Llewellyn, *The Bramble Bush: On Our Law and Its Study* (New York: Oceana Publications, Inc., 1960) at 66–69. Reproduced by permission of Oxford University Press.

cases, the analyses, the arguments, which have been made under such conditions. They put this together, and call this "*the* doctrine". I suspect there is still another reason for the orthodoxy. That is that only finer minds, minds with sharp mental scalpels, can do this work, and that it is the finer minds — the minds with a sharp cutting edge — which write about it and which thus set up the tradition of the books. To them it must seem that what blunt minds can do as well as they is poor; but that which they alone can do is good. They hit in this on a truth in part: you can pass with ease from this strict doctrine of precedent to the other. If you can handle this, then you can handle both. Not vice versa. The strict doctrine, then, is the technique to be learned. *But not to be mistaken for the whole.*

For when you turn to the actual operations of the courts, or, indeed, to the arguments of lawyers, you will find a totally different view of precedent at work beside this first one. That I shall call, to give it a name, the *loose view* of precedent. That is the view that a court has decided, and decided authoritatively, *any* point or all points on which it chose to rest a case, or on which it chose, after due argument, to pass. No matter how broad the statement, no matter how unnecessary on the facts or the procedural issues, if that was the rule the court laid down, then that the court has held. Indeed, this view carries over often into dicta, and even into dicta which are grandly obiter. In its extreme form this results in thinking and arguing exclusively from *language* that is found in past opinions, and in citing and working with that language wholly without reference to the facts of the case which called the language forth.

Now it is obvious that this is a device not for cutting past opinions away from judges' feet, but for using them as a springboard when they are found convenient. This is a device for *capitalizing welcome precedents.* And both the lawyers and the judges use it so. And judged by the *practice* of the most respected courts, as of the courts of ordinary stature, this doctrine of precedent is like the other, recognized, legitimate, honorable.

What I wish to sink deep into your minds about the doctrine of precedent, therefore, is that it is two-headed. It is Janus-faced. That it is not one doctrine, nor one line of doctrine, but two, and two which, *applied at the same time to the same precedent, are contradictory of each other.* That there is one doctrine for getting rid of precedents deemed troublesome and one doctrine for making use of precedents that seem helpful. That these two doctrines exist side by side. That the same lawyer in the same brief, the same judge in the same opinion, may be using the one doctrine, the technically strict one, to cut down half the older cases that he deals with, and using the other doctrine, the loose one, for building with the other half. Until you realize this you do not see how it is possible for law to change and to develop, and yet to stand on the past. You do not see how it is possible to avoid the past mistakes of courts, and yet to make use of every happy insight for which a judge in writing may have found expression. Indeed it seems to me that here we may have part of the answer to the problem as to whether precedent is not as bad as good — supporting a weak judge with the labors of strong predecessors, but binding a strong judge by the errors of the weak. For look again at this matter of the *difficulty* of the doctrine. The strict view — that view that cuts the past away — is *hard* to use. An ignorant, an unskilful judge will find it hard to use: the past will bind him. But the skilful judge — he whom we would make free — *is* thus made free. He has the knife in hand; and he can free himself.

Nor, until you see this double aspect of the doctrine-in-action, do you appreciate how little, in detail, you can predict *out of the rules alone*; how much you must turn, for purposes of prediction, to the reactions of the judges to the facts and to the life around them. Think again in this connection of an English court, all the judges unanimous upon the conclusion, all the judges in disagreement as to what rule the outcome should be rested on.

Applying this two-faced doctrine of precedent to your work in a case class you get, it seems to me, some such result as this: You read each case from the angle of its *maximum* value as a precedent, at least from the angle of its maximum value as a precedent *of the first water.* You will recall that I recommended taking down the ratio decidendi in substantially the court's own words. You see now what I had in mind. Contrariwise, you will also read each case for its *minimum* value as a precedent, to set against the maximum. In doing this you have your eyes out for the narrow issue in the case, the narrower the better. The first question is, how much can this case fairly be made to stand for by a later court to whom the precedent is welcome? You may well add — though this will be slightly flawed authority — the dicta which appear to have been well considered. The second question is, how much is there in this case that cannot be got around, even by a later court that wishes to avoid it?

You have now the tools for arguing from that case as counsel on *either* side of a new case. You turn them to the problem of prediction. Which view will this same court, on a later case on slightly different facts, take: will it choose the narrow or the loose? Which use will be made of this case by one of the other courts whose opinions are before you? Here you will call to your aid the matter of attitude that I have been discussing. Here you will use all that you know of individual judges, or of the trends in specific courts, or, indeed, of the trend in the line of business, or in the situation, or in the times at large — in anything which you may expect to become apparent and important to the court in later cases. But always and always, you will bear in mind that each precedent has not one value, but two, and that the two are wide apart, and that whichever value a later court assigns to it, such assignment will be respectable, traditionally sound, dogmatically correct. Above all, as you turn this information to your own training you will, I hope, come to see that in most doubtful cases the precedents *must* speak ambigu-

ously until the court has made up its mind whether each one of them is welcome or unwelcome. And that the job of persuasion which falls upon you will call, therefore, not only for providing a technical ladder to reach on authority the result that you contend for, but even more, if you are to have *your* use of the precedents made as *you* propose it, the job calls for you, on the facts, to persuade the court your case is sound.

People — and they are curiously many — who think that precedent produces or ever did produce a certainty that did not involve matters of judgment and of persuasion, or who think that what I have described involves improper equivocation by the courts or departure from the court — ways of some golden age — such people simply do not know our system of precedent in which they live.

Interpreting Legislation

(a) *Re Rizzo & Rizzo Shoes Ltd.*†

[Iacobucci J. for the Court:]

[1] This is an appeal by the former employees of a now bankrupt employer from an order disallowing their claims for termination pay (including vacation pay thereon) and severance pay. The case turns on an issue of statutory interpretation. Specifically, the appeal decides whether, under the relevant legislation in effect at the time of the bankruptcy, employees are entitled to claim termination and severance payments where their employment has been terminated by reason of their employer's bankruptcy.

. . . .

2. RELEVANT STATUTORY PROVISIONS

[6] The relevant versions of the *Bankruptcy Act* (now the *Bankruptcy and Insolvency Act*) and the *Employment Standards Act* for the purposes of this appeal are R.S.C., 1985, c. B-3 (the "*BA*"), and R.S.O. 1980, c. 137, as amended to April 14, 1989 (the "*ESA*") respectively.

Employment Standards Act, R.S.O. 1980, c. 137, as amended:

> 7. ...
>
> > (5) Every contract of employment shall be deemed to include the following provision:
> >
> > > All severance pay and termination pay become payable and shall be paid by the employer to the employee in two weekly instalments beginning with the first full week following termination of employment and shall be allocated to such weeks accordingly. This provision

does not apply to severance pay if the employee has elected to maintain a right of recall as provided in subsection 40a (7) of the *Employment Standards Act*.

> 40.(1) No employer shall terminate the employment of an employee who has been employed for three months or more unless the employee gives,
> (a) one weeks notice in writing to the employee if his or her period of employment is less than one year;
> (b) two weeks notice in writing to the employee if his or her period of employment is one year or more but less than three years;
> (c) three weeks notice in writing to the employee if his or her period of employment is three years or more but less than four years;
> (d) four weeks notice in writing to the employee if his or her period of employment is four years or more but less than five years;
> (e) five weeks notice in writing to the employee if his or her period of employment is five years or more but less than six years;
> (f) six weeks notice in writing to the employee if his or her period of employment is six years or more but less than seven years;
> (g) seven weeks notice in writing to the employee if his or her period of employment is seven years or more but less than eight years;
> (h) eight weeks notice in writing to the employee if his or her period of employment is eight years or more, and such notice has expired.
>
> ...
>
> > (7) Where the employment of an employee is terminated contrary to this section,

---

† [1998] 1 S.C.R. 27 at paras. 1, 6, 17–43.

(a) the employer shall pay termination pay in an amount equal to the wages that the employee would have been entitled to receive at his regular rate for a regular non-overtime work week for the period of notice prescribed by subsection (1) or (2), and any wages to which he is entitled;

...

40a ...

(1a) Where,

(a) fifty or more employees have their employment terminated by an employer in a period of six months or less and the terminations are caused by the permanent discontinuance of all or part of the business of the employer at an establishment; or

(b) one or more employees have their employment terminated by an employer with a payroll of $2.5 million or more,

the employer shall pay severance pay to each employee whose employment has been terminated and who has been employed by the employer for five or more years.

Employment Standards Amendment Act, 1981, S.O. 1981, c. 22

2.(1) Part XII of the said Act is amended by adding thereto the following section:

...

(3) Section 40a of the said Act does not apply to an employer who became a bankrupt or an insolvent person within the meaning of the *Bankruptcy Act* (Canada) and whose assets have been distributed among his creditors or to an employer whose proposal within the meaning of the *Bankruptcy Act* (Canada) has been accepted by his creditors in the period from and including the 1st day of January, 1981, to and including the day immediately before the day this Act receives Royal Assent.

Bankruptcy Act, R.S.C., 1985, c. B-3

121.(1) All debts and liabilities, present or future, to which the bankrupt is subject at the date of the bankruptcy or to which he may become subject before his discharge by reason of any obligation incurred before the date of the bankruptcy shall be deemed to be claims provable in proceedings under this Act.

Interpretation Act, R.S.O. 1990, c. I.11

10. Every Act shall be deemed to be remedial, whether its immediate purport is to direct the doing of anything that the Legislature deems to be for the public good or to prevent or punish the doing of any thing that it deems to be contrary to the public good, and shall accordingly receive such fair, large and liberal construction and interpretation as will best ensure the attainment of the object of the Act according to its true intent, meaning and spirit.

...

17. The repeal or amendment of an Act shall be deemed not to be or to involve any declaration as to the previous state of the law.

. . . .

4. ISSUES

[17] This appeal raises one issue: does the termination of employment caused by the bankruptcy of an employer give rise to a claim provable in bankruptcy for termination pay and severance pay in accordance with the provisions of the *ESA*?

5. ANALYSIS

[18] The statutory obligation upon employers to provide both termination pay and severance pay is governed by ss. 40 and 40a of the *ESA*, respectively. The Court of Appeal noted that the plain language of those provisions suggests that termination pay and severance pay are payable only when the employer terminates the employment. For example, the opening words of s. 40(1) are: "No employer shall terminate the employment of an employee...." Similarly, s. 40a(1a) begins with the words, "Where ... fifty or more employees have their employment terminated by an employer...." Therefore, the question on which this appeal turns is whether, when bankruptcy occurs, the employment can be said to be terminated "by an employer".

[19] The Court of Appeal answered this question in the negative, holding that, where an employer is petitioned into bankruptcy by a creditor, the employment of its employees is not terminated "by an employer", but rather by operation of law. Thus, the Court of Appeal reasoned that, in the circumstances of the present case, the *ESA* termination pay and severance pay provisions were not applicable and no obligations arose. In answer, the appellants submit that the phrase "terminated by an employer" is best interpreted as reflecting a distinction between involuntary and voluntary termination of employment. It is their position that this language was intended to relieve employers of their obligation to pay termination and severance pay when employees leave their jobs voluntarily. However, the appellants maintain that where an employee's employment is involuntarily terminated by reason of their employer's bankruptcy, this constitutes termination "by an employer" for the

purpose of triggering entitlement to termination and severance pay under the *ESA*.

[20] At the heart of this conflict is an issue of statutory interpretation. Consistent with the findings of the Court of Appeal, the plain meaning of the words of the provisions here in question appears to restrict the obligation to pay termination and severance pay to those employers who have actively terminated the employment of their employees. At first blush, bankruptcy does not fit comfortably into this interpretation. However, with respect, I believe this analysis is incomplete.

[21] Although much has been written about the interpretation of legislation (see, e.g., Ruth Sullivan, *Statutory Interpretation* (1997); Ruth Sullivan, *Driedger on the Construction of Statutes* (3rd ed. 1994) (hereinafter "*Construction of Statutes*"); Pierre-André Côté, *The Interpretation of Legislation in Canada* (2nd ed. 1991)), Elmer Driedger in *Construction of Statutes* (2nd ed. 1983) best encapsulates the approach upon which I prefer to rely. He recognizes that statutory interpretation cannot be founded on the wording of the legislation alone. At p. 87 he states:

> Today there is only one principle or approach, namely, the words of an Act are to be read in their entire context and in their grammatical and ordinary sense harmoniously with the scheme of the Act, the object of the Act, and the intention of Parliament.

Recent cases which have cited the above passage with approval include: *R. v. Hydro-Québec*, [1997] 3 S.C.R. 213**; *Royal Bank of Canada v. Sparrow Electric Corp.*, [1997] 1 S.C.R. 411; *Verdun v. Toronto-Dominion Bank*, [1996] 3 S.C.R. 550; *Friesen v. Canada*, [1995] 3 S.C.R. 103.

[22] I also rely upon s. 10 of the *Interpretation Act*, R.S.O. 1980, c. 219, which provides that every Act "shall be deemed to be remedial" and directs that every Act shall "receive such fair, large and liberal construction and interpretation as will best ensure the attainment of the object of the Act according to its true intent, meaning and spirit".

[23] Although the Court of Appeal looked to the plain meaning of the specific provisions in question in the present case, with respect, I believe that the court did not pay sufficient attention to the scheme of the *ESA*, its object or the intention of the legislature; nor was the context of the words in issue appropriately recognized. I now turn to a discussion of these issues.

[24] In *Machtinger v. HOJ Industries Ltd.*, [1992] 1 S.C.R. 986, at p. 1002, the majority of this Court recognized the importance that our society accords to employment and the fundamental role that it has assumed in the life of the individual. The manner in which employment can be terminated was said to be equally important (see also *Wallace v. United Grain Growers Ltd.*, [1997] 3 S.C.R. 701). It was in this context that the majority in *Machtinger* described, at p. 1003, the object of the *ESA* as being the protection of "... the interests of employees by requiring employers to comply with certain minimum standards, including minimum periods of notice of termination". Accordingly, the majority concluded, at p. 1003, that, "... an interpretation of the Act which encourages employers to comply with the minimum requirements of the Act, and so extends its protections to as many employees as possible, is to be favoured over one that does not".

[25] The objects of the termination and severance pay provisions themselves are also broadly premised upon the need to protect employees. Section 40 of the *ESA* requires employers to give their employees reasonable notice of termination based upon length of service. One of the primary purposes of this notice period is to provide employees with an opportunity to take preparatory measures and seek alternative employment. It follows that s. 40(7)(a), which provides for termination pay in lieu of notice when an employer has failed to give the required statutory notice, is intended to "cushion" employees against the adverse effects of economic dislocation likely to follow from the absence of an opportunity to search for alternative employment. (Innis Christie, Geoffrey England and Brent Cotter, *Employment Law in Canada* (2nd ed. 1993), at pp. 572–81.)

[26] Similarly, s. 40a, which provides for severance pay, acts to compensate long-serving employees for their years of service and investment in the employer's business and for the special losses they suffer when their employment terminates. In *R. v. TNT Canada Inc.* (1996), 27 O.R. (3d) 546, Robins J.A. quoted with approval at pp. 556–57 from the words of D. D. Carter in the course of an employment standards determination in *Re Telegram Publishing Co. v. Zwelling* (1972), 1 L.A.C. (2d) 1 (Ont.), at p. 19, wherein he described the role of severance pay as follows:

> Severance pay recognizes that an employee does make an investment in his employer's business — the extent of this investment being directly related to the length of the employee's service. This investment is the seniority that the

employee builds up during his years of service.... Upon termination of the employment relationship, this investment of years of service is lost, and the employee must start to rebuild seniority at another place of work. The severance pay, based on length of service, is some compensation for this loss of investment.

[27] In my opinion, the consequences or effects which result from the Court of Appeal's interpretation of ss. 40 and 40*a* of the *ESA* are incompatible with both the object of the Act and with the object of the termination and severance pay provisions themselves. It is a well established principle of statutory interpretation that the legislature does not intend to produce absurd consequences. According to Côté, *supra*, an interpretation can be considered absurd if it leads to ridiculous or frivolous consequences, if it is extremely unreasonable or inequitable, if it is illogical or incoherent, or if it is incompatible with other provisions or with the object of the legislative enactment (at pp. 378–80). Sullivan echoes these comments noting that a label of absurdity can be attached to interpretations which defeat the purpose of a statute or render some aspect of it pointless or futile (Sullivan, *Construction of Statutes*, *supra*, at p. 88).

[28] The trial judge properly noted that, if the *ESA* termination and severance pay provisions do not apply in circumstances of bankruptcy, those employees "fortunate" enough to have been dismissed the day before a bankruptcy would be entitled to such payments, but those terminated on the day the bankruptcy becomes final would not be so entitled. In my view, the absurdity of this consequence is particularly evident in a unionized workplace where seniority is a factor in determining the order of lay-off. The more senior the employee, the larger the investment he or she has made in the employer and the greater the entitlement to termination and severance pay. However, it is the more senior personnel who are likely to be employed up until the time of the bankruptcy and who would thereby lose their entitlements to these payments.

[29] If the Court of Appeal's interpretation of the termination and severance pay provisions is correct, it would be acceptable to distinguish between employees merely on the basis of the timing of their dismissal. It seems to me that such a result would arbitrarily deprive some employees of a means to cope with the economic dislocation caused by unemployment. In this way the protections of the *ESA* would be limited rather than extended, thereby defeating the intended working of the legislation. In my opinion, this is an unreasonable result.

[30] In addition to the termination and severance pay provisions, both the appellants and the respondent relied upon various other sections of the *ESA* to advance their arguments regarding the intention of the legislature. In my view, although the majority of these sections offer little interpretive assistance, one transitional provision is particularly instructive. In 1981, s. 2(1) of the *ESAA* introduced s. 40*a*, the severance pay provision, to the *ESA*. Section 2(2) deemed that provision to come into force on January 1, 1981. Section 2(3), the transitional provision in question[,] provided as follows:

> 2. ...
>
> (3) Section 40*a* of the said Act does not apply to an employer who became a bankrupt or an insolvent person within the meaning of the *Bankruptcy Act* (Canada) and whose assets have been distributed among his creditors or to an employer whose proposal within the meaning of the *Bankruptcy Act* (Canada) has been accepted by his creditors in the period from and including the 1st day of January, 1981, to and including the day immediately before the day this Act receives Royal Assent.

[31] The Court of Appeal found that it was neither necessary nor appropriate to determine the intention of the legislature in enacting this provisional subsection. Nevertheless, the court took the position that the intention of the legislature as evidenced by the introductory words of ss. 40 and 40*a* was clear, namely, that termination by reason of a bankruptcy will not trigger the severance and termination pay obligations of the *ESA*. The court held that this intention remained unchanged by the introduction of the transitional provision. With respect, I do not agree with either of these findings. Firstly, in my opinion, the use of legislative history as a tool for determining the intention of the legislature is an entirely appropriate exercise and one which has often been employed by this Court (see, e.g., *R. v. Vasil*, [1981] 1 S.C.R. 469, at p. 487; *Paul v. The Queen*, [1982] 1 S.C.R. 621, at pp. 635, 653 and 660). Secondly, I believe that the transitional provision indicates that the Legislature intended that termination and severance pay obligations should arise upon an employers' bankruptcy.

[32] In my view, by extending an exemption to employers who became bankrupt and lost control of their assets between the coming into force of the amendment and its receipt of royal assent, s. 2(3) necessarily implies that the severance pay obligation

does in fact extend to bankrupt employers. It seems to me that, if this were not the case, no readily apparent purpose would be served by this transitional provision.

[33] I find support for my conclusion in the decision of Saunders J. in *Royal Dressed Meats Inc., supra*. Having reviewed s. 2(3) of the *ESAA*, he commented as follows (at p. 89):

> ... any doubt about the intention of the Ontario Legislature has been put to rest, in my opinion, by the transitional provision which introduced severance payments into the E.S.A. ... it seems to me an inescapable inference that the legislature intended liability for severance payments to arise on a bankruptcy. That intention would, in my opinion, extend to termination payments which are similar in character.

[34] This interpretation is also consistent with statements made by the Minister of Labour at the time he introduced the 1981 amendments to the *ESA*. With regard to the new severance pay provision he stated:

> The circumstances surrounding a closure will govern the applicability of the severance pay legislation in some defined situations. For example, a bankrupt or insolvent firm will still be required to pay severance pay to employees to the extent that assets are available to satisfy their claims.
>
> ...
>
> ... the proposed severance pay measures will, as I indicated earlier, be retroactive to January 1 of this year. That retroactive provision, however, will not apply in those cases of bankruptcy and insolvency where the assets have already been distributed or where an agreement on a proposal to creditors has already been reached.
>
> (*Legislature of Ontario Debates*, 1st sess., 32nd Parl., June 4, 1981, at pp. 1236–37.)

Moreover, in the legislative debates regarding the proposed amendments the Minister stated:

> For purposes of retroactivity, severance pay will not apply to bankruptcies under the Bankruptcy Act where assets have been distributed. However, once this act receives royal assent, employees in bankruptcy closures will be covered by the severance pay provisions.
>
> (*Legislature of Ontario Debates*, 1st sess., 32nd Parl., June 16, 1981, at p. 1699.)

[35] Although the frailties of Hansard evidence are many, this Court has recognized that it can play a limited role in the interpretation of legislation. Writing for the Court in *R. v. Morgentaler*, [1993] 3 S.C.R. 463, at p. 484, Sopinka J. stated:

> ... until recently the courts have balked at admitting evidence of legislative debates and speeches.... The main criticism of such evidence has been that it cannot represent the "intent" of the legislature, an incorporeal body, but that is equally true of other forms of legislative history. Provided that the court remains mindful of the limited reliability and weight of Hansard evidence, it should be admitted as relevant to both the background and the purpose of legislation.

[36] Finally, with regard to the scheme of the legislation, since the *ESA* is a mechanism for providing minimum benefits and standards to protect the interests of employees, it can be characterized as benefits-conferring legislation. As such, according to several decisions of this Court, it ought to be interpreted in a broad and generous manner. Any doubt arising from difficulties of language should be resolved in favour of the claimant (see, e.g., *Abrahams v. Attorney General of Canada*, [1983] 1 S.C.R. 2, at p. 10; *Hills v. Canada (Attorney General)*, [1988] 1 S.C.R. 513, at p. 537). It seems to me that, by limiting its analysis to the plain meaning of ss. 40 and 40*a* of the *ESA*, the Court of Appeal adopted an overly restrictive approach that is inconsistent with the scheme of the Act.

[37] The Court of Appeal's reasons relied heavily upon the decision in *Malone Lynch, supra*. In *Malone Lynch*, Houlden J. held that s. 13, the group termination provision of the former *ESA*, R.S.O. 1970, c. 147, and the predecessor to s. 40 at issue in the present case, was not applicable where termination resulted from the bankruptcy of the employer. Section 13(2) of the *ESA* then in force provided that, if an employer wishes to terminate the employment of 50 or more employees, the employer must give notice of termination for the period prescribed in the regulations, "and until the expiry of such notice the terminations shall not take effect". Houlden J. reasoned that termination of employment through bankruptcy could not trigger the termination payment provision, as employees in this situation had not received the written notice required by the statute, and therefore could not be said to have been terminated in accordance with the Act.

[38] Two years after *Malone Lynch* was decided, the 1970 *ESA* termination pay provisions were amended by *The Employment Standards Act, 1974*, S.O. 1974, c. 112. As amended, s. 40(7) of the 1974 *ESA* eliminated the requirement that notice be given before termination can take effect. This provision makes it clear that termination pay is owing where an employer fails to give notice of termination and that

employment terminates irrespective of whether or not proper notice has been given. Therefore, in my opinion it is clear that the *Malone Lynch* decision turned on statutory provisions which are materially different from those applicable in the instant case. It seems to me that Houlden J.'s holding goes no further than to say that the provisions of the 1970 *ESA* have no application to a bankrupt employer. For this reason, I do not accept the *Malone Lynch* decision as persuasive authority for the Court of Appeal's findings. I note that the courts in *Royal Dressed Meats, supra*, and *British Columbia (Director of Employment Standards) v. Eland Distributors Ltd. (Trustee of)* (1996), 40 C.B.R. (3d) 25 (B.C.S.C.), declined to rely upon *Malone Lynch* based upon similar reasoning.

[39] The Court of Appeal also relied upon *Re Kemp Products Ltd., supra*, for the proposition that although the employment relationship will terminate upon an employer's bankruptcy, this does not constitute a "dismissal". I note that this case did not arise under the provisions of the *ESA*. Rather, it turned on the interpretation of the term "dismissal" in what the complainant alleged to be an employment contract. As such, I do not accept it as authoritative jurisprudence in the circumstances of this case. For the reasons discussed above, I also disagree with the Court of Appeal's reliance on *Mills-Hughes v. Raynor* (1988), 63 O.R. (2d) 343 (C.A.), which cited the decision in *Malone Lynch, supra*, with approval.

[40] As I see the matter, when the express words of ss. 40 and 40*a* of the *ESA* are examined in their entire context, there is ample support for the conclusion that the words "terminated by the employer" must be interpreted to include termination resulting from the bankruptcy of the employer. Using the broad and generous approach to interpretation appropriate for benefits-conferring legislation, I believe that these words can reasonably bear that construction (see *R. v. Z. (D.A.)*, [1992] 2 S.C.R. 1025). I also note that the intention of the Legislature as evidenced in s. 2(3) of the *ESAA*, clearly favours this interpretation. Further, in my opinion, to deny employees the right to claim *ESA* termination and severance pay where their termination has resulted from their employer's bankruptcy, would be inconsistent with the purpose of the termination and severance pay provisions and would undermine the object of the *ESA*, namely, to protect the interests of as many employees as possible.

[41] In my view, the impetus behind the termination of employment has no bearing upon the ability of the dismissed employee to cope with the sudden economic dislocation caused by unemployment. As all dismissed employees are equally in need of the protections provided by the *ESA*, any distinction between employees whose termination resulted from the bankruptcy of their employer and those who have been terminated for some other reason would be arbitrary and inequitable. Further, I believe that such an interpretation would defeat the true meaning, intent and spirit of the *ESA*. Therefore, I conclude that termination as a result of an employer's bankruptcy does give rise to an unsecured claim provable in bankruptcy pursuant to s. 121 of the *BA* for termination and severance pay in accordance with ss. 40 and 40*a* of the *ESA*. Because of this conclusion, I do not find it necessary to address the alternative finding of the trial judge as to the applicability of s. 7(5) of the *ESA*.

[42] I note that subsequent to the Rizzo bankruptcy, the termination and severance pay provisions of the *ESA* underwent another amendment. Sections 74(1) and 75(1) of the *Labour Relations and Employment Statute Law Amendment Act, 1995*, S.O. 1995, c. 1, amend those provisions so that they now expressly provide that where employment is terminated by operation of law as a result of the bankruptcy of the employer, the employer will be deemed to have terminated the employment. However, s. 17 of the *Interpretation Act* directs that, "[t]he repeal or amendment of an Act shall be deemed not to be or to involve any declaration as to the previous state of the law". As a result, I note that the subsequent change in the legislation has played no role in determining the present appeal.

6. DISPOSITION AND COSTS

[43] I would allow the appeal and set aside paragraph 1 of the order of the Court of Appeal. In lieu thereof, I would substitute an order declaring that Rizzo's former employees are entitled to make claims for termination pay (including vacation pay due thereon) and severance pay as unsecured creditors. As to costs, the Ministry of Labour led no evidence regarding what effort it made in notifying or securing the consent of the Rizzo employees before it discontinued its application for leave to appeal to this Court on their behalf. In light of these circumstances, I would order that the costs in this Court be paid to the appellant by the Ministry on a party-and-party basis. I would not disturb the orders of the courts below with respect to costs.

(b) *R. v. Mills*†

[McLACHLIN AND IACOBUCCI JJ. and L'Heureux-Dubé, Gonthier, Major, Bastarache and Binnie JJ.:]

I. INTRODUCTION

[17] The question of when accused persons should have access to private records of complainants and witnesses in sexual assault trials is a vexed one. This Court addressed this issue in *R. v. O'Connor*, [1995] 4 S.C.R. 411. Following this decision, and a lengthy consultation process, Parliament reviewed the issue and drafted Bill C-46, (now S.C. 1997, c. 30) which came into force on May 12, 1997 and amended the *Criminal Code*, R.S.C., 1985, c. C-46. The issue in the present appeal is whether Bill C-46 is constitutional. The resolution of this appeal requires understanding how to define competing rights, avoiding the hierarchical approach rejected by this Court in *Dagenais v. Canadian Broadcasting Corp.*, [1994] 3 S.C.R. 835, at p. 877. On the one hand stands the accused's right to make full answer and defence. On the other hand stands the complainant's and witness's right to privacy. Neither right may be defined in such a way as to negate the other and both sets of rights are informed by the equality rights at play in this context. Underlying this question is the relationship between the courts and Parliament when Parliament alters a judicially created common law procedure that already embodies *Charter* standards.

II. SUMMARY

[18] This appeal presents an apparent conflict among the rights to full answer and defence, privacy, and equality, all of which are protected by the *Canadian Charter of Rights and Freedoms* (ss. 7 and 11(d), s. 8, and s. 15, respectively). The underlying issue is what is required by the "principles of fundamental justice" protected by s. 7. Bill C-46 reflects Parliament's effort at balancing these rights. Our task is to decide whether Parliament's balance is a constitutional one.

[19] As a preliminary matter, we conclude that this appeal is not premature. While it is true that the accused did not actually make an application for records under Bill C-46, this does not deprive the Court of a sufficient basis to decide the issues raised in the appeal.

[20] As noted above, this Court has previously addressed the issue of disclosure of third party records in sexual assault proceedings: see *O'Connor*, *supra*. However, it is important to keep in mind that the decision in *O'Connor* is not necessarily the last word on the subject. The law develops through dialogue between courts and legislatures: see *Vriend v. Alberta*, [1998] 1 S.C.R. 493. Against the backdrop of *O'Connor*, Parliament was free to craft its own solution to the problem consistent with the *Charter*.

[21] As this Court's decision in *Dagenais*, *supra*, makes clear, *Charter* rights must be examined in a contextual manner to resolve conflicts between them. Therefore, unlike s. 1 balancing, where societal interests are sometimes allowed to override *Charter* rights, under s. 7 rights must be defined so that they do not conflict with each other. The rights of full answer and defence, and privacy, must be defined in light of each other, and both must be defined in light of the equality provisions of s. 15.

[22] Turning to the legislation at issue in this appeal, we find it constitutional. It is undisputed that there are several important respects in which Bill C-46 differs from the regime set out in *O'Connor*. However, these differences are not fatal because Bill C-46 provides sufficient protection for all relevant *Charter* rights. There are, admittedly, several provisions in the Bill that are subject to differing interpretations. However, in such situations we will interpret the legislation in a constitutional manner where possible: see *Slaight Communications Inc. v. Davidson*, [1989] 1 S.C.R. 1038, at p. 1078. By so doing, we conclude that Bill C-46 is a constitutional response to the problem of production of records of complainants or witnesses in sexual assault proceedings.

. . . .

VI. ANALYSIS

. . . .

† [1999] 3 S.C.R. 668 at paras. 17–22, 43–60, 94, [1999] S.C.J. No. 68.

C. Background Considerations

(1) The O'Connor Regime and Bill C-46

[43] The respondent in this appeal and several interveners argued that the provisions of Bill C-46 are unconstitutional to the extent that they are inconsistent with the reasons of the majority of this Court in *O'Connor, supra*. Belzil J., for the court below, similarly held that Bill C-46 is unconstitutional because it alters the constitutional balance achieved in *O'Connor*. Before addressing these arguments, we will briefly review the production regimes at issue.

(A) THE *O'CONNOR* REGIME

[44] This Court's decision in *O'Connor* concerned the common law procedure to be followed by an accused seeking production of therapeutic records in the hands of third parties. As a preliminary matter, Lamer C.J. and Sopinka J., for the majority on the issue of production, also discussed the issue of disclosure of therapeutic records in the hands of the Crown. In their opinion, the Crown's obligation to disclose records in its possession or control, as established in *Stinchcombe, supra*, is unaltered by the confidential nature of therapeutic records where the records have been shared with the Crown or "confidentiality has been waived for the purpose of proceeding against the accused" (para. 9). Even if privileged, these records must be disclosed to the accused where "clearly relevant and important to the ability of the accused to raise a defence" (para. 11).

[45] In the context of ordering production of records that are in the hands of third parties, Lamer C.J. and Sopinka J. outlined a two-stage process. At the first stage, the issue is whether the document sought by the accused ought to be produced to the judge; at the second stage, the trial judge must balance the competing interests to decide whether to order production to the accused. At the first stage, the onus is on the accused to establish that the information in question is "likely to be relevant" (para. 19 (emphasis in original)). Unlike in the Crown disclosure context, where relevance is understood to mean "may be useful to the defence", the threshold of likely relevance in this context requires that the presiding judge be satisfied "that there is a reasonable possibility that the information is logically probative to an issue at trial or the competence of a witness to testify" (para. 22 (emphasis in original)). This shift in onus and the higher threshold, as compared to when records are in the possession of the Crown, was necessitated by the fact that the information in question is not part of the state's "case to meet",

the state has not been given access to it, and third parties are under no obligation to assist the defence.

[46] Lamer C.J. and Sopinka J. held that the threshold of likely relevance at this first stage is not a significant or onerous burden. It is meant to prevent requests for production that are "speculative, fanciful, disruptive, unmeritorious, obstructive and time-consuming" (para. 24). Although Lamer C.J. and Sopinka J. disagreed with L'Heureux-Dubé J. that therapeutic records are rarely relevant to the accused, they declined to set out "categories of relevance" (para. 27).

[47] If the first stage is passed, the record is disclosed to the court and the application for production moves onto the second stage where the judge determines whether the record should be produced to the accused. At this second stage, Lamer C.J. and Sopinka J. require the trial judge to balance the competing interests in order to determine whether a non-production order would be a reasonable limit on the accused's ability to make full answer and defence. They list a series of factors that trial judges should consider in making this determination (at para. 31):

> (1) the extent to which the record is necessary for the accused to make full answer and defence; (2) the probative value of the record in question; (3) the nature and extent of the reasonable expectation of privacy vested in that record; (4) whether production of the record would be premised upon any discriminatory belief or bias; and (5) the potential prejudice to the complainant's dignity, privacy or security of the person that would be occasioned by production of the record in question.

Although L'Heureux-Dubé J., for the minority on this issue, outlined the same five factors as the majority, she also included two additional factors: the integrity of the trial process and the societal interest in reporting sexual crimes. Lamer C.J. and Sopinka J. held that the former is better dealt with when determining admissibility of the evidence and that the latter, while a relevant factor, was "not a paramount consideration" as there are many other avenues open to the trial judge to protect this interest than declining production (at paras. 32 and 33).

(B) BILL C-46

[48] On May 12, 1997, approximately 17 months after this Court released its decision in *O'Connor*, Bill C-46 came into force. Bill C-46 sets out a pro-

cess to govern the production of the private records of complainants and witnesses in sexual assault trials in place of the common law regime this Court established in *O'Connor*. The preamble to the Bill indicates that Parliament was concerned about the incidence of sexual violence and abuse in Canadian society, its prevalence against women and children, and its "particularly disadvantageous impact on the equal participation of women and children in society and on the rights of women and children to security of the person, privacy and equal benefit of the law as guaranteed by sections 7, 8, 15 and 28 of the [*Charter*]". The preamble expressly declares that Parliament seeks to provide a framework of laws that are fair to and protect the rights of both accused persons and complainants.

[49] While the Bill retains the two-stage structure set out in *O'Connor*, there are significant differences between the two regimes. Many of these are uncontentious. In the following overview of the Bill, we expound on only the provisions brought under review in this appeal.

[50] Bill C-46 begins by defining the records to which it applies: "any form of record that contains personal information for which there is a reasonable expectation of privacy", excluding investigatory or prosecutorial records: s. 278.1. It goes on to define the types of offences that will trigger its application: s. 278.2(1). Generally, these are sexual assault and similar sexual offences. Section 278.2(1) states that an accused person charged with these offences cannot obtain the records relating to complainants or witnesses covered by s. 278.1, except in accordance with the process set out by the Bill.

[51] A third preliminary section, s. 278.2(2), states that the Bill applies to records in the possession or control of any person, including the Crown prosecutor, unless the complainant or witness "has expressly waived the application of [the Bill]". Absent waiver, documents in the possession of the prosecution are treated in the same manner as documents in the hands of a private individual or organization and therefore are subject to disclosure pursuant to the Bill's procedures.

[52] Yet another preliminary provision sets out "assertions" that are "not sufficient on their own" on an application for production to establish that a record is "likely relevant to an issue at trial or to the competence of a witness to testify": s. 278.3(4).

[53] This brings us to the heart of the Bill — the process established to govern the production of pri-

vate records to an accused person in sexual offence proceedings. Like *O'Connor*, Parliament has set up a two-stage process: (1) disclosure to the judge; and (2) production to the accused. At the first stage, the accused must establish that the record sought is "likely relevant to an issue at trial or to the competence of a witness to testify" and that "the production of the record is necessary in the interests of justice" (s. 278.5(1)). Bill C-46 diverges from *O'Connor* by directing the trial judge to consider the salutary and deleterious effects of production to the court on the accused's right to full answer and defence and the complainant's or witness's right to privacy and equality. A series of factors is listed that the trial judge is directed to take into account in deciding whether the document should be produced to the court (s. 278.5(2)):

(a) the extent to which the record is necessary for the accused to make a full answer and defence;

(b) the probative value of the record;

(c) the nature and extent of the reasonable expectation of privacy with respect to the record;

(d) whether production of the record is based on a discriminatory belief or bias;

(e) the potential prejudice to the personal dignity and right to privacy of any person to whom the record relates;

(f) society's interest in encouraging the reporting of sexual offences;

(g) society's interest in encouraging the obtaining of treatment by complainants of sexual offences; and

(h) the effect of the determination on the integrity of the trial process.

[54] If the requirements of this first stage are met, the record will be ordered produced to the trial judge. At the second stage, the judge looks at the record in the absence of the parties (s. 278.6(1)), holds a hearing if necessary (s. 278.6(2)), and determines whether the record should be produced on the basis that it is "likely relevant to an issue at trial or to the competence of a witness to testify" and that its production is "necessary in the interests of justice" (s. 278.7). Again at this stage, the judge must consider the salutary and deleterious effects on the accused's right to make full answer and defence and on the right to privacy and equality of the complainant or witness, and is directed to "take into account" the factors set out at s. 278.5(2): s. 278.7(2). When ordering production, the judge may impose conditions on production: s. 278.7(3).

[55] The respondent and several supporting interveners argue that Bill C-46 is unconstitutional to the extent that it establishes a regime for production that differs from or is inconsistent with that established by the majority in *O'Connor*. However, it does not follow from the fact that a law passed by Parliament differs from a regime envisaged by the Court in the absence of a statutory scheme, that Parliament's law is unconstitutional. Parliament may build on the Court's decision, and develop a different scheme as long as it remains constitutional. Just as Parliament must respect the Court's rulings, so the Court must respect Parliament's determination that the judicial scheme can be improved. To insist on slavish conformity would belie the mutual respect that underpins the relationship between the courts and legislature that is so essential to our constitutional democracy: *Vriend, supra*. We turn now to a brief discussion of that relationship.

(2) Relationship Between the Courts and the Legislature Generally

[56] A posture of respect towards Parliament was endorsed by this Court in *Slaight Communications, supra*, at p. 1078, where we held that if legislation is amenable to two interpretations, a court should choose the interpretation that upholds the legislation as constitutional. Thus courts must presume that Parliament intended to enact constitutional legislation and strive, where possible, to give effect to this intention.

[57] This Court has also discussed the relationship between the courts and the legislature in terms of a dialogue, and emphasized its importance to the democratic process. In *Vriend, supra*, at para. 139, Iacobucci J. stated:

> To my mind, a great value of judicial review and this dialogue among the branches is that each of the branches is made somewhat accountable to the other. The work of the legislature is reviewed by the courts and the work of the court in its decisions can be reacted to by the legislature in the passing of new legislation (or even overarching laws under s. 33 of the *Charter*). This dialogue between and accountability of each of the branches have the effect of enhancing the democratic process, not denying it.

See also P. W. Hogg and A. A. Bushell, "The *Charter* Dialogue Between Courts and Legislatures" (1997), 35 *Osgoode Hall L.J.* 75. If the common law were to be taken as establishing the only possible constitutional regime, then we could not speak of a dialogue with the legislature. Such a situation could only undermine rather than enhance democracy. Legislative change and the development of the common law are different. As this Court noted in *R. v. Salituro*, [1991] 3 S.C.R. 654, at p. 666, the common law changes incrementally, "while complex changes to the law with uncertain ramifications should be left to the legislature". While this dialogue obviously is of a somewhat different nature when the common law rule involves interpretation of the *Charter*, as in *O'Connor*, it remains a dialogue nonetheless.

[58] Moreover, in this Court's recent decision *Reference re Secession of Quebec*, [1998] 2 S.C.R. 217, we affirmed the proposition that constitutionalism can facilitate democracy rather than undermine it, and that one way in which it does this is by ensuring that fundamental human rights and individual freedoms are given due regard and protection (at paras. 74–78). Courts do not hold a monopoly on the protection and promotion of rights and freedoms; Parliament also plays a role in this regard and is often able to act as a significant ally for vulnerable groups. This is especially important to recognize in the context of sexual violence. The history of the treatment of sexual assault complainants by our society and our legal system is an unfortunate one. Important change has occurred through legislation aimed at both recognizing the rights and interests of complainants in criminal proceedings, and debunking the stereotypes that have been so damaging to women and children, but the treatment of sexual assault complainants remains an ongoing problem. If constitutional democracy is meant to ensure that due regard is given to the voices of those vulnerable to being overlooked by the majority, then this court has an obligation to consider respectfully Parliament's attempt to respond to such voices.

[59] Parliament has enacted this legislation after a long consultation process that included a consideration of the constitutional standards outlined by this Court in *O'Connor*. While it is the role of the courts to specify such standards, there may be a range of permissible regimes that can meet these standards. It goes without saying that this range is not confined to the specific rule adopted by the Court pursuant to its competence in the common law. In the present case, Parliament decided that legislation was necessary in order to address the issue of third party records more comprehensively. As is evident from the language of the preamble to Bill C-46, Parliament also sought to recognize the prevalence of sexual violence against women and children and its disadvantageous impact on their rights, to encourage the reporting of incidents of sexual violence, to rec-

ognize the impact of the production of personal information on the efficacy of treatment, and to reconcile fairness to complainants with the rights of the accused. Many of these concerns involve policy decisions regarding criminal procedure and its relationship to the community at large. Parliament may also be understood to be recognizing "horizontal" equality concerns, where women's inequality results from the acts of other individuals and groups rather than the state, but which nonetheless may have many consequences for the criminal justice system. It is perfectly

reasonable that these many concerns may lead to a procedure that is different from the common law

position but that nonetheless meets the required constitutional standards.

[60] We cannot presume that the legislation is unconstitutional simply because it is different from the common law position. The question before us is not whether Parliament can amend the common law; it clearly can. The question before us is whether in doing so Parliament has nonetheless outlined a constitutionally acceptable procedure for the production of private records of complainants in sexual assault trials. This question is considered at length below, following the discussion of the constitutional rights at stake in this appeal.

(c)   The Law Wishes to Have a Formal Existence†

Stanley Fish

ACHIEVING PLAIN AND CLEAR MEANINGS

The law wishes to have a formal existence. That means, first of all, that the law does not wish to be absorbed by, or declared subordinate to, some other — nonlegal — structure of concern; the law wishes, in a word, to be distinct, not something else. And second, the law wishes in its distinctness to be perspicuous; that is, it desires that the components of its autonomous existence be self-declaring and not be in need of piecing out by some supplementary discourse; for were it necessary for the law to have recourse to a supplementary discourse at crucial points, that discourse would be in the business of specifying what the law is, and, consequently, its autonomy would have been compromised indirectly. It matters little whether one simply announces that the principles and mechanisms of the law exist ready-made in the articulations of another system or allows those principles and mechanisms to be determined by something they do not contain; in either case, the law as something independent and self-identifying will have disappeared.

In its long history, the law has perceived many threats to its autonomy, but two seem perennial:

morality and interpretation. The dangers these two pose are, at least at first glance, different. Morality is something to which the law wishes to be related, but not too closely; a legal system whose conclusions clashed with our moral intuitions at every point so that the categories *legally valid* and *morally right* never (or almost never) coincided would immediately be suspect; but a legal system whose judgments perfectly meshed with our moral intuitions would be thereby rendered superfluous. The point is made concisely by the Supreme Court of Utah in a case where it was argued that the gratuitous payment by one party of the other party's mortgage legally obligated the beneficiary to repay. The court rejected the argument, saying "that if a mere moral, as distinguished from a legal, obligation were recognized as valid consideration for a contract that would practically erode to the vanishing point the necessity for finding a consideration."[1] That is to say, if one can infer directly from one's moral obligation in a situation to one's legal obligation, there is no work for the legal system to do; the system of morality has already done it. Although it might seem (as it does to many natural law theorists) that such a collapsing of categories recommends itself if only on the basis of efficiency (why have two systems when you can

† Excerpt from Austin Sarat and Thomas R. Kearns, eds., *The Fate of Law* (Ann Arbor, MI: University of Michigan, 1993) at 159–62, 173–79. [Notes and/or references omitted.]

make do with one?), the defender of a distinctly legal realm will quickly answer that since moral intuitions are notoriously various and contested, the identification of law with morality would leave every individual his or her own judge; in place of a single abiding standard to which disputing parties might have recourse, we would have many standards with no way adjudicating between them. In short, many moralities would make many laws, and the law would lack its most saliently desirable properties, generality and stability.

It is here that the danger posed by morality to law, or, more precisely, to the rule (in two senses) of law intersects with the danger posed by interpretation. The link is to be found in the desire to identify a perspective larger and more stable than the perspective of local and individual concerns. Morality frustrates that desire because, in a world of more than one church, recourse to morality will always be recourse to someone's or some group's challengeable moral vision. Interpretation frustrates that desire because, in the pejorative sense it usually bears in these discussions, interpretation is the name for what happens when the meanings embedded in an object or text are set aside in favor of the meanings demanded by some angled, partisan object. Interpretation, in this view, is the effort of a morality, of a particular, interested agenda, to extend itself into the world by inscribing its message on every available space. It follows then that, in order to check the imperial ambitions of particular moralities, some point of resistance to interpretation must be found, and that is why the doctrine of formalism has proved so attractive. Formalism is the thesis that it is possible to put down marks so self-sufficiently perspicuous that they repel interpretation; it is the thesis that one can write sentences of such precision and simplicity that their meanings leap off the page in a way no one — no matter what his or her situation or point of view — can ignore; it is the thesis that one can devise procedures that are self-executing in the sense that their unfolding is independent of the differences between the agents who might set them in motion. ...

Obviously then, formalism's appeal is a function of the number of problems it solves, or at least appears to solve: it provides the law with a palpable manifestation of its basic claim to be perdurable and general; that is, not shifting and changing, but standing as a point of reference in relation to which change can be assessed and controlled; it enables the law to hold contending substantive agendas at bay by establishing threshold requirements of procedure that force those agendas to assume a shape the system

will recognize. The idea is that once a question has been posed as a *legal* question — has been put into the proper *form* — the answer to it will be generated by relations of entailment between that form and other forms in the system. As Hans Kelsen put it in a book aptly named *The Pure Theory of Law*,

> The law is an order, and therefore all legal problems must be set and solved as order problems. In this way legal theory becomes an exact structural analysis of positive law, free of all ethical-political value judgments.[2]

Kelsen's last clause says it all: the realms of the ethical, the political, and of value in general are the threats to the law's integrity. They are what must be kept out if the law is to be something more than a misnomer for the local (and illegitimate) triumph of some particular point of view.

There are at least two strong responses to this conception of law. The first, which we might call the "humanistic" response, objects that a legal system so conceived is impoverished, and that once you have severed procedures from value, it will prove enormously difficult, if not impossible, to relink them in particular cases. Since the answers generated by a purely formal system will be empty of content (that, after all, is the formalist claim), the reintroduction of content will always be arbitrary. The second response, which we might call "radical" or "critical," would simply declare that a purely formal system is not a possibility, and that any system pretending to that status is already informed by that which it purports to exclude. Value, of both an ethical and political kind, is already inside the gate, and the adherents of the system are either ignorant of its sources or are engaged in a political effort to obscure them in the course of laying claim to a spurious purity. In what follows, I shall be elaborating a version of the second response, and arguing that however much the law wishes to have a formal existence, it cannot succeed in doing so, because — at any level from the most highly abstract to the most particular and detailed — any specification of what the law is will already be infected by interpretation and will therefore be challengeable. Nevertheless, my conclusion will not be that the law fails to have a formal existence but that, in a sense I shall explain, it always succeeds, although the nature of that success — it is a political/rhetorical achievement — renders it bitter to the formalist taste.

. . . .

In short, the parol evidence rule is of more service to the law's wish to have a formal existence than one might think from these examples. The service it provides, however, is not (as is sometimes claimed) the service of safeguarding a formalism already in place, but the weaker (although more exacting) service of laying down the route by which a formalism can be fashioned. I am aware, of course, that this notion of the formal will seem strange to those for whom a formalism is what is "given" as opposed to something that is made. But, in fact, efficacious formalisms — marks and sounds that declare meanings to which all relevant parties attest — are always the product of the forces — desire, will, intentions, circumstances, interpretation — they are meant to hold in check. No one has seen this more clearly than Arthur Corbin who, noting that "sometimes it is said that 'the courts will not disregard the plain language of a contract or interpolate something not contained in it,'"[41] offers for that dictum this substitute.

. . . .

Consider, for example, ... [a] famous case in legal interpretation, *In Re Soper's Estate*. The facts are the stuff of soap opera. After ten years of marriage, Ira Soper faked his suicide and resurfaced in another state under the name of John Young. There he married a widow who died three years later, whereupon he married another widow with whom he lived for five years when he again committed suicide, but this time for real. The litigation turns on an agreement Soper-Young made with a business partner according to which, upon the death of either, the proceeds of the insurance on the life of the deceased would be delivered to his wife. The question of course is who is the wife, Mrs. Young or the long-since deserted Mrs. Soper, who, to the surprise of everyone, appeared to claim her rightful inheritance. The majority finds for the second wife, Gertrude, while a strong dissent is registered on behalf of the abandoned Adeline. There is a tendency in both opinions to present the case as if it were a textbook illustration of a classic conflict in contract law between the view (usually associated with Williston) that determinations of the degree of integration and of the meaning of an agreement are to be made by looking to the agreement itself and the view (later to be associated with Corbin) that such issues can only be decided by ascertaining the intentions of the drafting parties, that is, by going outside the agreement to something not in it but in the light of which it is to be read. But, in fact, what the case illustrates is the impossibility of this very distinction. It is the minority that raises the banner of literalism,

arguing that since a man can have only one lawful wife and since Adeline was, at the time of the agreement "the only wife of Soper then living,"[45] the word *wife* must refer to her. The majority replies that by the same standard of literalism, the agreement contains no mention of a Mr. Soper, referring only to a Mr. Young whose only possible wife was a lady named Gertrude; and indeed, observes Justice Olson, the document can only be read as referring to Adeline by bringing in the same kind of oral evidence her lawyers (and the dissent) now wish to exclude. An inquirer merely looking at the document might well conclude "that two different men are involved," for after all,

> in what manner may either establish relationship to the decedent as his "wife" except by means of oral testimony.... Adeline, to establish her relationship, was necessarily required to and did furnish proof, principally oral, that her husband, Ira Collins Soper, was in fact the same individual as John W. Young, [and] Gertrude by similar means sought to establish her claim.[46]

The moral is clear even though the court does not quite draw it: rather than a dispute between a reading confining itself to the document and one that goes outside it to the circumstances from which it emerged, this is a dispute between two opposing accounts of the circumstances. Depending on which of these accounts is the more persuasive — that is, on which of the two stories about the world, responsibility, and wives is firmly in place — the document will acquire one of the two literal meanings being proposed for it. The majority finds itself persuaded by Gertrude's story and thus can quite sincerely declare that the "agreement points to no one else than Gertrude as Young's 'wife,'"[47] and Justice Olsen with an *e* ... can declare with equal sincerity that "I am unable to construe this word to mean anyone else than the only wife of Soper then living."[48] Indeed he is unable, since as someone who subscribes to the moral vision that underlies Adeline's claims — a vision in which responsibilities once entered into cannot be weakened by obligations subsequently incurred — *wife* can only refer to the first in what is, for him, a nonseries; just as, for Justice Olson with an *o* — in whose morality obligations in force at the time of agreement take precedence over obligations recognized by a legal formalism — *wife* can only refer to the person "all friends and acquaintances ... recognized ... as his wife."[49] The majority says that the "question is not just what words mean literally but how they are intended to operate practically on the subject matter,"[50] but its own arguments show that words *never* mean literally except in the context of the intention they are presumed to be effecting, and that rather than being determined by the meanings the words already (by right) have, the intentional context — established when one or the other party succeeds in being convincing — determines the meaning of the words. In short, the issue is not nor could ever be the supposed choice between literal and contextual reading, but the relative persuasiveness of alternative contexts as they are set out in ideologically charged narratives. That is why it is no surprise to find Justice Olsen's [confident] declaration of linguistic clarity ("I am unable to construe") preceded by a rehearsal of the moralizing story that produces that clarity.

> Much is said in the opinion as to the wrong done to the innocent woman whom he purported to marry. Nothing is said about the wrong done to the lawful wife. To have her husband abandon her and then purport to marry another, and live in cohabitation with such other, was about as great a wrong as any man could inflict upon his wife.[51]

The majority thinks that something else ... is the greater wrong and therefore thinks, like the minority, that the meaning of the agreement is obvious and inescapable. Again, my point is not to discredit the reasoning of either party nor to dismiss the claim of each to have pointed to a formal linguistic fact; rather, I wish only to observe once again that such formal facts are always "achieved" and that they are achieved by the very means — the partisan urging of some ideological vision — to which they are then rhetorically (and not unreasonably) opposed.

CONTRACT'S TWO STORIES

That is to say — and in so saying I rehearse the essence of my argument — the law is continually creating and recreating itself out of the very materials and forces it is obliged, by the desire to be law, to push away. The result is a spectacle that could be described (as members of the critical legal studies movement tend to do) as farce, but I would describe it differently, as a signal example of the way in which human beings are able to construct the roadway on which they are traveling, even to the extent of "demonstrating" in the course of building it that it was there all the while. ... Not only does the law forge its identity out of the stuff it disdains, it does so in public.

178

IV

Law, the State, and Citizens

Overview of Part IV

Part IV explores the ways in which law shapes and mediates the relationship between the state and the individuals and groups within it.

Chapter 10 considers the way in which law can be used to either extend or restrict the recognition of groups and individuals as "citizens" within a state. Here the term "citizen" is applied not just to those who qualify as formal citizens (e.g. those with the right to hold a passport and vote in national elections), but also to those accorded the fullest rights of participation within society. The excerpt from the famous "Persons Case" (*Henrietta Muir Edwards v. Canada (A.G.)*) provides a historical example of how the status and rights of an entire social group may be affected by the decisions of a handful of judges and their preference for narrow or broad approaches to constitutional interpretation.

The article by Revi evaluates the ongoing impact and relevance of T.H. Marshall's seminal essay "Citizenship and Social Class" and, particularly, his theory of "social rights". Revi argues that Marshall's highly influential, expanded conception of citizenship, emphasizing the right to substantive equality and to participation in the "shared social heritage" of one's community, still serves as a powerful normative challenge to contemporary neo-liberalism; which has (also) failed to solve the inherent tensions between 'civil' and 'social rights'.

The article that follows, by Bauder, examines a similar set of issues using a different, though equally critical, conceptual framework. Drawing on the highly influential work of Pierre Bourdieu, Bauder discusses the idea of citizenship as a form of strategically produced "capital". He highlights the way in which 'legal citizenship' is not synonymous with 'social citizenship' by examining the position of a growing population of migrant workers in Canada. Like all the authors included in this chapter, Bauder notes that narrow distinctions between migrant and non-migrant labour enable particular forms of precarity and exploitation.

Finally, Wilke and Willis employ a multi-dimensional understanding of citizenship to analyze the Supreme Court of Canada's decision in *Charkaoui*. Their article explores the vulnerability of non-citizens, particularly in the face of governments focused on issues of state security. The authors emphasize the dynamic ways in which the vulnera- bility of non-citizens may be exacerbated when they are caught between their lack of formal citizenship and their lack of belonging within their national community.

Chapter 11 considers a number of different ways in which rights may be protected through law — ranging from non-constitutional to constitutional rights protection — and raises questions about the effectiveness of law in protecting rights.

First, the *Somerset Case* provides an historical example of both the potential and limits of the common law as a source of rights protection. In that case, Justice Mansfield found that the British common law would not allow an American slave-owner to force his slave to leave England against his will. At the same time, Justice Mansfield recognized that legislation could still legalize "chattel slavery" even if the common law would not.

The *Baker v. Canada* case (initially introduced in **Chapter 4**), where Justice L'Heureux-Dubé used administrative law principles (among others) to prevent the deportation of a mother with Canadian born children, provides a more contemporary example of non-constitutional rights protection.

The chapter then shifts to consider a series of debates concerning the utility of entrenching rights in a constitutional bill of rights, namely the *Canadian Charter of Rights and Freedoms*. Prime Minister Pierre Trudeau, one of the chief architects of the *Charter*, identifies the core liberal notion supporting constitutional entrenchment of individual rights protections as constitutive of the dignity of human beings. Justice L'Heureux-Dubé's article traces both the challenges and triumphs of protecting women's equality rights both before and after the entrenchment of the *Charter*.

Finally, more critically, Turpel's article identifies the ways in which the conception of rights underlying the *Charter* conflicts with aboriginal culture and traditions. She goes on to advance an alternative approach: First Nations Human Rights and Responsibilities Laws.

As you read through the articles and cases selected for **Part IV**, ask yourself the following questions: What is the role of law in shaping the relationship between the state and citizens? What does full citizenship require? How do we choose who gets to participate fully within a political community? Which rights should be protected, and how best can they be protected? How should the culture, traditions and rights of aboriginal peoples be recognized within or by the Canadian state? Can issues of accommodation and the recognition of cultural diversity within contemporary societies like Canada be addressed through rights? Do rights provide an adequate framework for community belonging?

(a) *Henrietta Muir Edwards et al. v. Canada (A.G.)*[†]

[LORD SANKEY L.C.:]

By s. 24 of the *British North America Act, 1867*, it is provided that "The Governor General shall from time to time, in the Queen's name, by instrument under the Great Seal of Canada, summon qualified persons to the Senate; and, subject to the provisions of this Act, every person so summoned shall become and be a member of the Senate and a senator."

The question at issue in this appeal is whether the words "qualified persons" in that section include a woman, and consequently whether women are eligible to be summoned to and become members of the Senate of Canada.

Of the appellants, Henrietta Muir Edwards is the Vice-President for the Province of Alberta of the National Council of Women for Canada; Nellie L. McClung and Louise C. McKinney were for several years members of the Legislative Assembly of the said Province; Emily F. Murphy is a police magistrate in and for the said Province; and Irene Parlby is a member of the Legislative Assembly of the said Province and a member of the Executive Council thereof.

On August 29, 1927, the appellants petitioned the Governor General in Council to refer to the Supreme Court certain questions touching the powers of the Governor General to summon female persons to the Senate, and upon October 19, 1927, the Governor General in Council referred to the Supreme Court the aforesaid question. The case was heard before Anglin C.J., Duff, Mignault, Lamont, and Smith JJ., and upon April 24, 1928, the Court answered the question in the negative; the question

being understood to be "Are women eligible for appointment to the Senate of Canada."

The Chief Justice, whose judgment was concurred in by Lamont and Smith JJ., and substantially by Mignault J., came to this conclusion upon broad lines mainly because of the common law disability of women to hold public office and from a consideration of various cases which [have] been decided under different statutes as to their right to vote for a member of Parliament.

Duff J., on the other hand, did not agree with this view. He came to the conclusion that women are not eligible for appointment to the Senate upon the narrower ground that upon a close examination of the *British North America Act 1867*, the word "persons" in s. 24 is restricted to members of the male sex. The result therefore of the decision was that the Supreme Court was unanimously of opinion that the word "persons" did not include female persons, and that women are not eligible to be summoned to the Senate.

Their Lordships are of opinion that the word "persons" in s. 24 does include women, and that women are eligible to be summoned to and become members of the Senate of Canada.

. . . .

The exclusion of women from all public offices is a relic of days more barbarous than ours, but it must be remembered that the necessity of the times often forced on man customs, which in later years were not necessary. Such exclusion is probably due to the fact that the deliberative assemblies of

[†] [1930] A.C. 124 (J.C.P.C.) at 126–31, 135–38, 140–143. [Notes and/or references omitted.]

the early tribes were attended by men under arms, and women did not bear arms. *"Nihil autem neque publicae neque privatae rei, nisi armati, agunt"*: Tac. Germ., c. 13. Yet the tribes did not despise the advice of women. *"Inessequin etiam sanctum et providum putant, nec aut consilia earum aspernantura ut responsa neglegunt"*: Germ., c. 8. The likelihood of attack rendered such a proceeding unavoidable, and after all what is necessary at any period is a question for the times upon which opinion grounded on experience may move one way or another in different circumstances. This exclusion of women found its way into the opinions of the Roman jurists, Ulpian (A.D. 211) laying it down. *"Feminae ab omnibus offiis civilibus vel publicis remotae sunt"*: Dig. 1.16.195. The barbarian tribes who settled in the Roman Empire, and were exposed to constant dangers, naturally preserved and continued the tradition.

In England no woman under the degree of a Queen or a Regent, married or unmarried, could take part in the government of the State. A woman was under a legal incapacity to be elected to serve in Parliament and even if a peeress in her own right she was not, nor is, entitled as an incident of peerage to receive a writ of summons to the House of Lords.

Various authorities are cited in the recent case of *Viscountess Rhondda's Claim*, where it was held that a woman was not entitled to sit in the House of Lords. Women were, moreover, subject to a legal incapacity to vote at the election of members of Parliament: Coke, 4 *Inst.*, p. 5; *Chorlton v. Lings*; or of town councillor: *Reg. v. Harrald*; or to be elected members of a County Council: *Beresford-Hope v. Sandhurst*. They were excluded by the common law from taking part in the administration of justice either as judges or as jurors, with the single exception of inquiries by a jury of matrons upon a suggestion of pregnancy: Coke, 2 *Inst.* 119, 3 Bl. Comm. 362. Other instances are referred to in the learned judgment of Willes J. in *Chorlton v. Lings*.

No doubt in the course of centuries there may be found cases of exceptional women and exceptional instances, but as Lord Esher M.R. said in *De Souza v. Cobden*: "By the common law of England women are not in general deemed capable of exercising public functions, though there are certain exceptional cases where a well recognised custom to the contrary has become established." An instance may be referred to in the case of women being entitled to act as churchwardens and as sextons, the latter being put upon the ground that a sexton's duty was in the nature of a private trust: *Olive v. Ingram*. Also of being appointed as overseer of the poor: *Rex v. Stubbs*. The tradition existed till quite modern times: see *Bebb v. Law Society*, where it was held by the Court of Appeal that by inveterate usage women were under a disability by reason of their sex to become attorneys or solicitors.

The passing of *Lord Brougham's Act* in 1850 does not appear to have greatly affected the current of authority. Sect. 4 provided that in all acts words importing the masculine gender shall be deemed and taken to include female unless the contrary as to gender is expressly provided.

The application and purview of that *Act* came up for consideration in *Chorlton v. Lings*, where the Court of Common Pleas was required to construe a statute passed in 1861, which conferred the parliamentary franchise on every man possessing certain qualifications and registered as a voter. The chief question discussed was whether by virtue of *Lord Brougham's Act* the words "every man" included women. Bovill C.J., having regard to the subject-matter of the statute and its general scope and language and to the important and striking nature of the departure from the common law involved in extending the franchise to women, declined to accept the view that Parliament had made that change by using the term "man" and held that the word was intentionally used expressly to designate the male sex. Willes J. said: "It is not easy to conceive that the framer of that Act, when he used the word 'expressly,' meant to suggest that what is necessarily or properly implied by language is not expressed by such language."

Great reliance was placed by the respondents to this appeal upon that decision, but in our view it is clearly distinguishable. The case was decided on the language of the *Representation of the People Act, 1867*, which provided that "every man" with certain qualifications and "not subject to any legal incapacity" should be entitled to be registered as a voter. Legal incapacity was not defined by the Act, and consequently reference was necessary to the common law disabilities of women.

A similar result was reached in the case of *Nairn v. University of St. Andrews*, where it was held under s. 27 of the *Representation of the People (Scotland) Act, 1868*, which provided that every person whose name is for the time being on the register of the general council of such university shall, being of full age and not subject to any legal incapacity, be entitled to vote in the election of a member to serve in any future Parliament for such university, that the word "person" did not include women, but the Lord Chancellor, Lord Loreburn, referred to the position of women at common law, and pointed out that they were subject to a legal incapacity. Both in this case and in the case of the Viscountess Rhondda the various judgments emphasize the fact that the legislature in dealing with the matter cannot be taken to have departed from the usage of centuries, or to have employed loose and ambiguous words to carry out so momentous and fundamental a change.

The judgment of the Chief Justice in the Supreme Court of Canada refers to and relies upon these cases, but their Lordships think that there is great force in the view taken by Duff J. with regard to them, when he says that s. 24 of the *British North America Act, 1867*, must not be treated as an independent enactment. The Senate, he proceeds, is part of a parliamentary system, and in order to test the contention based upon this principle that women are excluded from participating in working the Senate or any other institution set up by the Act one is bound to consider the Act as a whole and its bearings on this subject of the exclusion of women from public office and place.

．．．．

The communities included within the Britannic system embrace countries and peoples in every stage of social, political and economic development and undergoing a continuous process of evolution. His Majesty the King in Council is the final Court of Appeal from all these communities, and this Board must take great care therefore not to interpret legislation meant to apply to one community by a rigid adherence to the customs and traditions of another. Canada had its difficulties both at home and with the mother country, but soon discovered that union was strength. Delegates from the three maritime Provinces met in Charlottetown on September 1, 1864, to discuss proposals for a maritime union. A delegation from the coalition government of that day proceeded to Charlottetown and placed before the maritime delegates their schemes for a union embracing the Canadian Provinces. As a result the Quebec conference assembled on October 10, continued in session till October 28, and framed a number of resolutions. These resolutions as revised by the delegates from the different Provinces in London in 1866 were based upon a consideration of the rights of others and expressed in a compromise which will remain a lasting monument to the political genius of Canadian statesmen. Upon those resolutions the *British North America Act of 1867* was framed and passed by the Imperial legislature. The Quebec resolutions dealing with the Legislative Council — namely, Nos. 6–24 — even if their Lordships are entitled to look at them, do not shed any light on the subject

under discussion. They refer generally to the "members" of the Legislative Council.

The *British North America Act* planted in Canada a living tree capable of growth and expansion within its natural limits. The object of the Act was to grant a Constitution to Canada. "Like all written constitutions it has been subject to development through usage and convention": *Canadian Constitutional Studies*, Sir Robert Borden (1922), p. 55.

Their Lordships do not conceive it to be the duty of this Board — it is certainly not their desire — to cut down the provisions of the Act by a narrow and technical construction, but rather to give it a large and liberal interpretation so that the Dominion to a great extent, but within certain fixed limits, may be mistress in her own house, as the Provinces to a great extent, but within certain fixed limits, are mistresses in theirs. "The Privy Council, indeed, has laid down that Courts of law must treat the provisions of the *British North America Act* by the same methods of construction and exposition which they apply to other statutes. But there are statutes and *statutes*; and the strict construction deemed proper in the case, for example, of a penal or taxing statute or one passed to regulate the affairs of an English parish, would be often subversive of Parliament's real intent if applied to an Act passed to ensure the peace, order and good government of a British Colony": see Clement's *Canadian Constitution*, 3rd ed., p. 347.

The learned author of that treatise quotes from the argument of Mr. Mowat and Mr. Edward Blake before the Privy Council in *St. Catherine's Milling and Lumber Co. v. The Queen*: "That Act should be on all occasions interpreted in a large, liberal and comprehensive spirit, considering the magnitude of the subjects with which it purports to deal in very few words." With that their Lordships agree, but as was said by the Lord Chancellor in *Brophy v. Attorney-General of Manitoba*, the question is not what may be supposed to have been intended, but what has been said.

It must be remembered, too, that their Lordships are not here considering the question of the legislative competence either of the Dominion or its Provinces which arise under ss. 91 and 92 of the Act providing for the distribution of legislative powers and assigning to the Dominion and its Provinces their respective spheres of Government. Their Lordships are concerned with the interpretation of an Imperial Act, but an Imperial Act which creates a constitution for a new country. Nor are their Lordships deciding any question as to the rights of women but only a question as to their eligibility for a particular position. No one, either male or female, has a right to be summoned to the Senate. The real point at issue is whether the Governor General has a right to summon women to the Senate.

The Act consists of a number of separate heads.

The preamble states that the Provinces of Canada, Nova Scotia and New Brunswick have expressed their desire to be federally united into one Dominion under the Crown of the United Kingdom of Great Britain and Ireland with a constitution similar in principle to that of the United Kingdom.

. . . . .

The word "person" as above mentioned, may include members of both sexes, and to those who ask why the word should include females the obvious answer is why should it not? In these circumstances the burden is upon those who deny that the word includes women to make out their case.

. . . . .

Their Lordships do not think it possible to interpret the word "persons" by speculating whether the framer of the *British North America Act* purposely followed the system of Legislative Councils enacted in the *Acts of 1791* and *1840* rather than that which prevailed in the maritime Province for the model on which the Senate was to be formed, neither do they think that either of these sub-sections is sufficient to rebut the presumption that the word "persons" includes women. Looking at the sections which deal with the Senate as a whole (ss. 21–36) their Lordships are unable to say that there is anything in those sections themselves upon which the Court could come to a definite conclusion that women are to be excluded from the Senate.

So far with regard to the sections dealing especially with the Senate — are there any other sections in the Act which shed light upon the meaning of the word "persons"?

Their Lordships think that there are. For example, s. 41 refers to the qualifications and disqualifications of persons to be elected or to sit or vote as members of the House of Assembly or Legislative Assembly, and by a proviso it is said that until the Parliament of Canada otherwise provides at any election for a member of the House of Commons for the district of Algoma in addition to persons qualified by the law of the Province of Canada to vote every male British subject aged twenty-one or upwards being a householder shall have a vote. This section shows a distinction between "persons" and "males." If persons excluded females it would only have been necessary to say every person who is a British subject aged twenty-one years or upwards shall have a vote.

Again in s. 84, referring to Ontario and Quebec, a similar proviso is found stating that every male British subject in contradistinction to "person" shall have a vote.

Again in s. 133 it is provided that either the English or the French language may be used by any person or in any pleadings in or issuing from any court of Canada established under this Act and in or from all of any of the courts of Quebec. The word "person" there must include females, as it can hardly have been supposed that a man might use either the English or the French language but a woman might not.

If Parliament had intended to limit the word "persons" in s. 24 to male persons it would surely have manifested such intention by an express limitation, as it has done in ss. 41 and 84. The fact that certain qualifications are set out in s. 23 is not an argument in favour of further limiting the class, but is an argument to the contrary, because it must be presumed that Parliament has set out in s. 23 all the qualifications deemed necessary for a senator, and it does not state that one of the qualifications is that he must be a member of the male sex.

. . . . .

The history of these sections and their interpretation in Canada is not without interest and significance.

From confederation to date both the Dominion Parliament and the Provincial legislatures have interpreted the word "persons" in ss. 41 and 84 of the *British North America Act* as including female persons, and have legislated either for the inclusion or exclusion of women from the class of persons entitled to vote and to sit in the Parliament and Legislature respectively, and this interpretation has never been questioned.

From confederation up to 1916 women were excluded from the class of persons entitled to vote in both Federal and Provincial elections. From 1916 to 1922 various Dominion and Provincial Acts were passed to admit women to the franchise and to the right to sit as members in both Dominion and Provincial legislative bodies. At the present time women are entitled to vote and to be candidates:

1. At all Dominion elections on the same basis as men.
2. At all Provincial elections save in the Province of Quebec.

From the date of the enactment of the *Interpretation Acts* in the Province of Canada, Nova Scotia and New Brunswick prior to confederation and in the Dominion of Canada since confederation and until the franchise was extended, women have been excluded by express enactment from the right to vote.

Neither is it without interest to record that when upon May 20, 1867, the *Representation of the People Bill* came before a Committee of the House of Commons, John Stuart Mill moved an amendment to secure women's suffrage, and the amendment proposed was to leave out the word "man" in order to insert the word "person" instead thereof: see *Hansard*, 3rd series, vol. clxxxvii., col. 817.

A heavy burden lies on an appellant who seeks to set aside a unanimous judgment of the Supreme Court, and this Board will only set aside such a decision after convincing argument and anxious consideration, but having regard:

1. To the object of the Act — namely, to provide a constitution for Canada, a responsible and developing State;
2. That the word "person" is ambiguous, and may include members of either sex;
3. That there are sections in the Act above referred to which show that in some cases the word "person" must include females;
4. That in some sections the words "male persons" are expressly used when it is desired to confine the matter in issue to males;
5. To the provisions of the *Interpretation Act*;

their Lordships have come to the conclusion that the word "persons" in s. 24 includes members both of the male and female sex, and that, therefore, the question propounded by the Governor General should be answered in the affirmative, and that women are eligible to be summoned to and become members of the Senate of Canada, and they will humbly advise His Majesty accordingly.

(b)   T.H. Marshall and His Critics: Reappraising 'Social Citizenship' in the Twenty-first Century†

Ben Revi

INTRODUCTION

In his 1949 lecture, 'Citizenship and Social Class', T.H. Marshall argued that Britain had developed a closed, rights-based system of social welfare, which he called 'social citizenship'. The system was closed in the sense that social welfare was provided only to British citizens; it was rights-based in the sense that services were provided to Britons as rights of citizenship. A British passport entitled its holder to a suite of services in housing, education, health and more. These were not human rights, but 'social' rights, which promised to allow citizens full participation in British society.

In recent decades, this rights-based model has been challenged by neoliberalism, which argues that state welfare undermines self-reliance. At the same time, Marshall's thesis has also been challenged by

contemporary research into citizenship and identity incorporating the perspectives of migrants, women, indigenous peoples and cultural groups.

Yet, the present moment, with rising inequality, global recession and social protest, suggests a chance to reassess whether a rights-based model could again successfully increase social participation. A reappraisal of Marshall's work could serve as a first step towards a new social citizenship, with new tools to address social tensions.

The importance of Marshall's lecture is not to be understated. It remains the foundational text for studies of citizenship and social policy (Hoxsey 2011; Turner 2009). Many recent studies pay homage to Marshall's pioneering work, even when observing its contradictions, flaws and false predictions. Some accounts have suggested that Marshall's work is irrelevant to a changed world, incompatible with civil

† (2014) 18:3-4 Citizenship Studies, 452–64. [Notes and/or references omitted.] Reprinted by permission of the publisher (Taylor & Francis Ltd, http://www.tandfonline.com).

liberty or insufficient to address inequalities based upon sex, migration, cultural affiliation and group differentiation. However, Marshall himself was acutely aware of these problems. Indeed, he made these contradictions a focus of his study. The key insight of Marshall's lecture is that the post-war welfare state in Britain created a new definition and practice of citizenship. Yet, citizenship can, to Marshall, be the 'architect of legitimate social inequality' (1992, p. 39). Social provision based on accepted social practices can exclude alternatives. Marshall anticipated this critique, although his work does not completely resolve it.

The aim of this article is to reconcile the object of Marshall's study — a suite of social services provided as a right of community membership — with its critics, as a first step towards a contemporary social rights model. The article begins by outlining the tensions Marshall himself found in social citizenship, before addressing a sample of Marshall's direct critics. Some space will then be given to broader recent studies of citizenship, which have added to understandings of social tensions and rights. By opening rights to marginalised groups — even to non-citizens — social citizenship can be reclaimed as a means of social progress.

MARSHALL'S TENSIONS

Marshall's work has positive and normative elements. On the positive side, Marshall argued the post-war welfare system in Britain constituted a new, 'social' citizenship. On the normative side, Marshall believed this was a good thing. Marshall's critics often concentrate on one or the other — either his analysis was wrong, or his ideals were misguided.

Context is important here. After World War II, a suite of new public services were initiated rapidly; state-based services quickly became the norm across the developed world. Previously, social services were provided mostly through charitable or commercial organisations, and the poor were stigmatised as service recipients, not respected as citizens.

... State-based social insurance found its blueprint in William Beveridge's *Social Insurance and Allied Services* report, published during the war, in 1942 (Beveridge 1942; Klausen 1995, 246). The war effort had increased the role of government in the economy. This had proved the viability of state intervention, and its extension into peacetime was easily promoted as an aid to an effective social and economic recovery (Macintyre 1999).

. . . . .

The idea of a social citizenship, though not expressed as such, informs Beveridge's report:

> There is no longer an admitted claim of the individual citizen to share in national insurance and yet to stand outside it, keeping the advantage of his individual lower risk whether of unemployment or of disease or accident. (1942, 13)

The Beveridge report inspired Britain to build what is commonly known as the 'welfare state'. Education was the first to be implemented; in 1944, the 'all-age' elementary school system was replaced with free specialised secondary schooling offered to all Britons until the age of 15. Between 1945 and 1948, legislation was passed in Britain establishing the National Health Service, the short-lived Central Land Board, national insurance against illness and unemployment, and a full employment policy (Lowe 1990).

The implementation of the Beveridge reforms was underpinned by an equally radical development: the economics of John Maynard Keynes. Keynes argued that the Great Depression of the 1930s had been caused by a drop in aggregate demand, which could have been prevented by an increase in government borrowing and investment ([1936] 1949). Under Keynes' intellectual guidance, increasing state spending was promoted not just for the development of British citizens, but also for the health of the British economy. It is little surprise that Marshall saw this as an entirely new form of citizenship. The British government was now actively transforming British citizens, to eradicate poverty and create a mass middle class. As Marshall quotes the (unrelated) economist Alfred Marshall:

> the question ... is not whether all men will ultimately be equal — that they certainly will not — but whether progress may not go on steadily, if slowly, till, by occupation at least, every man is a gentleman. I hold that it may, and that it will. (1992, 5)

Later critics of Marshall have argued that this goal situated the male breadwinner model at the heart of the British social economy; others argue its outcomes favoured ethnic British citizens at the expense of migrants; yet still others argue that social rights are essentially illiberal. Each of these critiques rests on a misinterpretation of Marshall's thesis and intent.

MARSHALL'S ANALYSIS OF CITIZENSHIP

Marshall develops a typology of citizenship, dividing British political history in three: civil, political and social citizenship.

Civil rights comprised those liberties, such as speech and association, which are 'necessary for individual freedom' (Marshall 1992, 8). Political rights are based on the free and fair exercise of suffrage. *Social* rights incorporate

> the whole range from the right to a modicum of economic welfare and security to the right to share to the full in the social heritage and to live the life of a civilised being according to the standards prevailing in the society. (Marshall 1992, 8)

Marshall did not necessarily see these as distinct and separate; rather, he saw each as intertwined and overlapping, as one generated the next. Once all citizens possess civil rights and are equal under the law, a claim can be naturally made for political rights, to give all a voice in shaping laws. Upon being granted suffrage, citizens have the political power to successfully push for legislated social rights.

As Roche argues, Marshall 'presupposes ... *an ontology of the citizen*' (1987, 371). This historical view led Marshall to the perhaps optimistic conclusion that Britain was by 1949 'a frankly socialist system' with a limited market (1992, 7).

By 1972, Marshall had tightened his analysis to show that social citizenship was not 'frankly socialist', but was rather a component of a 'hyphenated society', called 'democratic-welfare-capitalism' (1972, 1981). Here, Marshall admitted citizenship was not socialism (defined as the nationalisation of industry); rather, it was a means by which capitalism and democracy, two systems in natural tension, could coexist. Put another way, social rights were a necessary result of the competition between civil and political rights.

Marshall took great pains to show how his three spheres of citizenship overlap. For example, to ensure citizens are sufficiently well informed to exercise a meaningful vote, the government is required to provide schooling. Therefore, political rights require, and are in turn supported by, social rights (Marshall 1992, 16). Indeed, Marshall saw education as having

> a direct bearing on citizenship, and, when the state guarantees that all children shall be educated, it has the requirements and the nature of citizenship definitely in mind. It is trying to stimulate the growth of citizens in the making. (1992, 16)

When the state 'grows', the citizen, the citizen's civil liberties, are curtailed to the extent that the state chooses the paths available to the individual. To some, this is an unacceptable intervention. Marshall, again, was aware of the potential for this conflict:

social rights in their modern form imply an invasion of contract by status, the subordination of market price to social justice, the replacement of the free bargain by the declaration of rights (1992, 40).

However Marshall's response that social rights are 'entrenched within the contract system itself' (1992, 40) is unsatisfying. Later scholars have tried to reassess how social and civil rights can be reconciled. This will be explored in the next section.

Marshall was also aware of the conflict between rights and duties. He outlines the kind of rights-and-duties system Turner calls 'contributory rights' (2009, 71). To Marshall, the demands of social rights 'do not require a man to sacrifice his individual liberty ... but they do require that his acts should be inspired by a lively sense of responsibility towards the welfare of the community' (1992, 41). He also claims that 'the incentive that responds to social rights is that of public duty ... the citizen is urged to respond to the call of duty by allowing some scope to the motive of individual self-interest' (1992, 43). So, if the citizen would only realise that his or her self-interest lies in the performance of duties corresponding to social rights, then Marshall's system will not impinge on civil rights. If social services are accepted as being in the citizen's self-interest, then taxes to provide these services will be viable. This invites the question: what would result if support for the system were to decline?

This conflict has played out in recent debates on welfare and work. Mead (1997) has claimed that social citizenship is compatible with 'mutual obligation' schemes that require citizens to work (a duty) to receive welfare (a right), just as Marshall considered education to be a 'public duty' (1992, 16). Lister (2005), on the other hand, argues that any work-for-welfare scheme would not qualify, as the work involved is punitive, and not in itself a right that a citizen has any duty to exercise. Marshall held that rights should promote an 'equality of status', an equality that does not require equal outcomes. Crucially, to Marshall, 'equality of status is more important than equality of income' (1992, 33). Klausen (1995, 252) argues that this amounts to middle-class welfare; and it is true that universal provision of social services, without means-testing, enables the middle classes to receive government benefits. But to Marshall this universality is in fact a key goal, to bring citizens into an equal social category. To Marshall, equality of status would provide

> a general enrichment of the concrete substance of civilised life, a general reduction of risk and

insecurity, an equalisation between the more and the less fortunate at all levels — between the healthy and the sick, the employed and the unemployed, the old and the active, the bachelor and the father of a large family. (1992, 33)

Means-testing, on the other hand, creates a new exclusive status reserved for the lower classes. The Poor Laws that had preceded the twentieth-century reforms created an exclusive category of paupers, which targeted social services but created a second-class citizenship. The poor were simply not entitled to participate in the 'concrete substance of civilised life'. The social citizenship of the Beveridge plan would, instead, bring all British citizens into the same social space.

... This is how citizenship can become the 'architect of legitimate social inequality' (Marshall 1992, 39). This striking phrase is open to interpretation. Marshall himself leaves it only partially defined, vague and contestable.

It could be that under an equal category of citizenship there can remain 'legitimate' social inequality, as determined by the shared preferences of equal citizens. In other words, as long as we all share equality of status and can participate in the 'substance of civilised life', we can choose how much economic inequality we consider acceptable.

The second suggestion is that a meritocracy can provide some 'legitimate social inequality'. ... To Marshall, then, the key aim of social citizenship is to create a social stratification on the basis of merit within each generation; so one cannot inherit wealth, but must earn it, and all are offered an equality of status at birth that allows equal competition for resources.

The obvious retort is that a meritocracy allows those enriched by merit to bequeath their gains — financial gains, and other less tangible gains such as personal networks and academic support. Marshall does not address this in his 1949 essay. In a later essay (1953), he admits that children from privileged backgrounds are more likely to win places in selective state schools, and thus 'status' will accrue disproportionately to the middle class. To this, Marshall only offers, 'it is fortunate that the selection net has some pretty big holes in it' (92).

MARSHALL'S EMPIRICAL CRITICS

There have been many critics of Marshall's empirical analysis who have missed his commentary on the tension between civil and social rights, and thus between equality and liberty. For example, Harris argues,

contrary to Marshall's vision of citizenship, the State's operationalization of social rights in bureau-professional regimes had the potential to infringe civil and political rights. (1999, 918)

He goes on to suggest that Marshall 'never faced the empirical evidence that the interests of the state ... were sometimes in opposition to those of ordinary citizens' (Harris 1999, 929).

Roche goes even further, arguing,

Marshall seems to have assumed that not only were there no particularly important and noteworthy logical connections between the three elements of his concept, as we have already seen, but also that there was little in the way of ultimate normative conflicts of value and principle between them either. (1987, 372)

These claims are quite startling, considering the lengths taken by Marshall to underline the clear links between the three spheres of citizenship, as well as his acknowledgement that social rights imply an 'invasion of contract by status'.

Moreover, both Harris and Roche argue that neoliberalism has rendered social citizenship obsolete. To Roche, it is neoliberalism that first uncovered the conflict between social and other rights:

New Right Conservative and neo-liberal political philosophy, in the light of the post-war development of the welfare state and of social rights, have argued that there is a conflict of principle between civil and social rights, and in general between social equality and freedom as competing political aims and ideals. (1987, 372)

Harris in turn invokes a 'consumer-citizen' who should be 'seen as capable of entering into responsible relations with the state's structured social services ... services were to be made more responsible to their users' (1999, 923). Harris believes that a political consensus has formed in support of consumer-citizenship; in his view, 'the Left has sought to distance citizens' social entitlements to welfare from unpopular statism and has articulated a new concern with the individual citizen as a reaction to the bureau-professional regimes of welfare state bureaucracies' (1999, 924).

Roche is certainly right to argue that neoliberal thought undermined the social citizenship project, and Harris is certainly right to identify a shift in the mechanics of social provision. During the 1970s, neoliberalism redefined the Beveridge programme as 'statist', arguing that it set the state and its citizens as adversaries rather than seeing all citizens as equals. To neoliberals, there was an outright opposition between civil and social rights. The universal aims of the welfare state contradicted the individual aims of each citizen. To neoliberalism, the most important equality of status is legal, provided by civil citizenship alone.

The Blair Government, elected in 1997, sought to distinguish its platform from the Beveridge model. It promoted deregulation, privatisation and competition for social service contracts. New Public Management (Niskanen 1994; Lane 2000), which stresses decentralisation and contractualism, gained traction. The neoliberal critique of government-funded welfare programmes, that they create an underclass of dependent citizens, remained largely in tact.

So Roche and Harris are correct to argue that liberal individualism represents a strong challenge to social citizenship. However, Roche and Harris err in arguing that this is empirically grounded, as though a philosophically neutral *discovery* of liberal individualism has undermined the Marshall project. Surely, individualism is as much a normative ideal as social citizenship. Individualism also has its critics. ... It is not enough to disregard Marshall on the basis of normative trends. One must persuasively argue that Marshall's normative project falls short of serving the public good.

Other scholars have worked to amend some of Marshall's empirical shortcomings. Lister argues that Marshall offers more than a teleology of citizenship ending with social citizenship rights ... (2005, 485). Instead, Marshall's categories of citizenship can be fluid and unfinished:

> citizenship appears, on the one hand, to be underpinned by the same principle and on the other, riven with contradictions. I believe that these two accounts can be reconciled. Marshall notes that there is no universal principle which determines citizenship rights and obligations, but rather that there are ideal images which societies progress towards. As such, the precise meaning of equality of status is unknown. (Lister 2005, 482)

Furthermore, she notes that 'equality of status in the civil sphere promotes different ideas of equality of status in the social and political spheres' (Lister 2005, 482). To Lister, Marshall's work is best used as a study of citizenship, which can be developed and extended as the meaning and application of citizenship rights changes over time. 'Equality of status' is therefore malleable. It not defined by a single set of objectives, but can be redeveloped over time to suit the changing needs of the population.

... There remains, as well, the question of how to engage Marshallian equal status with the structural inequality found in recent accounts of citizenship. King and Waldron offer one way to address this, building on social rights to develop a theory of social justice. King and Waldron use arguments derived from John Rawls, offering citizenship as a mechanism for social justice requiring state intervention.

. . . .

... According to King and Waldron, any citizen whose social rights were not protected would not willingly enter this contract. Therefore, no state is legitimate, from this contractarian perspective, unless it works to guarantee social rights, by ensuring financial security and full cultural participation for its citizens (King and Waldron 1988, 433).

This goes some way towards strengthening the social citizenship argument, beyond Marshall's weak contention that social rights have always been 'entrenched within the contract system itself' (1992, 40). It helps to define Marshall's argument in more precise terms — that justice can be advanced through social policy to support a broadly agreed 'equality of status'. This, in turn, provides a solid foundation to respond to Marshall's normative critics, who argue that social citizenship is variously illiberal, elitist, exclusive or unjust.

IDENTITY AS A CHALLENGE TO SOCIAL RIGHTS

Recent studies of identity and citizenship have expanded upon Marshall's idea that citizenship can be 'the architect of legitimate social inequality'. Fraser and Gordon's influential study of women's rights, Brubaker's study of migration, Kymlicka's work on group rights and Soysal's idea of a 'universal personhood' all challenge the inclusive, but monocultural, character of social citizenship. Each of these studies has contributed greatly to the study of identity politics. They should be used not to cast Marshall aside, but to reform his work into something new. As King and Waldron used novel accounts of justice to resolve Marshall's contention between civil and social rights, so too can we use novel studies of identity to give a more precise definition to citizenship as a category of equality.

Even 18 years prior to the publication of Marshall's essay, R.H. Tawney warned that a citizenship characterised by membership of a single culture may lead to exclusive and unjust ends. ... [Marshall] committed this error by wishing for the British to be 'civilised'.

... [This view reflected] a strain of social thinking influential in Britain during the nineteenth and twentieth centuries. British socialism was heavily influenced by the utopianism of Robert Owen, an industrialist who provided not only wages, but also housing, goods and services for his workers. Owen believed that men were mostly the product of social influences, and that education, not merely for knowledge but for character, was the key to a fully functional society (Jarman 1972, 122; Hinton 1983, 100–107). Owen's experiments were designed to transform the whole of the working class into 'gentlemen'.

. . . .

Marshall's (1939) promotion of gentlemen dates at least to an early essay on the professions. Keynes (1930), too, considered the purpose of economics to be an increase in the amount and quality of leisure time in all classes, to allow citizens to cultivate civilised tastes. There seems to be a whole strain of British economics whose goal is the adoption, by the working classes, of the characteristics of their supposed social superiors.

This goal of course only extended to working-class men. Fraser and Gordon argue that, although women were able to claim the title of citizen, its benefits were never fully conferred upon them. Indeed,

> *contra* Marshall's assumption, the exclusion of married women from civil citizenship was no mere archaic vestige destined to fade as citizenship evolved. Rather, women's subsumption in coverture was the other face and enabling ground of modern civil citizenship. The two mutually defined one another. (Fraser and Gordon 1992, 55)

In this way, citizenship has been built on gender inequality. Despite the existence of a broad interventionist social policy, women were for most of the twentieth century excluded from any meaningful equality of status. Many rights were accorded to heads of households rather than individuals, so civil rights 'belonged instead to male property owners and family heads, often by virtue of their responsibility for "dependents"' (Fraser and Gordon 1992, 56). As social policy was bestowing social rights on male citizens, whole groups were excluded from equal participation:

> the widespread fear that 'welfare' recipients are 'getting something for nothing' is an understand-ably embittered response from those who work hard and get little ... such responses are of course exacerbated when the poor are represented as female, sexually immoral, and/or racially 'other'. (Fraser and Gordon 1992, 64)

. . . .

Large numbers of non-citizens, along with citizens from diverse backgrounds, present new challenges to Marshall's citizenship. If social citizenship aimed to allow universal access to participate in the society around them, the existence of multiple, plural societies — side by side and intertwining — threatens to overcomplicate Marshall's premise. If citizenship can no longer be tied to a shared social identity, it becomes more difficult to speak of citizenship in terms of agreed rights and responsibilities.

Recent issues such as the banning of the burqa in France speak to the struggle to maintain a single national citizenship within plural societies. Furthermore, where a significant percentage of the workforce is unable to access citizenship, such as migrants on work visas, or Europeans travelling within the European Union, this further complicates the idea of a single equality of status. Working migrants participate in the economic life of a country through adding value and paying taxes, but are not entitled to access the full suite of social rights which stem from legal membership of the civic community. To the challenge of plural cultures within one nation, one can advocate in favour of plural citizenships. In a later essay, Marshall (1969) acknowledged that rights to participate in the existing, unequal society may not suffice to give equal power to marginalised groups; social movements may demand radical changes to the structure of society. Women, gays, indigenous communities and the elderly are just some of the existing groups whose needs are not captured within the existing social structure (Young 1989). If a liberal society should allow each individual to pursue a range of cultural and economic practices, then states encompassing different distinct cultures must accommodate different cultural needs. Any set of rules dictated by the majority — including standards of dress, public religious holidays, legal frameworks and relationships — can infringe on the rights of citizens from marginal cultures. The answer may be a 'differentiated citizenship', which Kymlicka defines as 'the adoption of group-specific polyethnic, representation, or self-government rights' (1995, 174). This could include the ability of defined cultural groups to vote for their own representative in parliament, a right given to the Māori people of New Zealand, or of a bounded area of self-determination within the state, such as given to the Inuit people of Canada. Rights to communicate in minority languages, practice minority religions fully and gain access to culturally relevant services in education and care can also be included.

Kymlicka makes a strong argument that such a multicultural citizenship can be reconciled with liberalism if there are no 'internal restrictions ... that is, the demand by a minority culture to restrict the basic civil or political liberties of its own members'. Therefore, one should not find any rights restricted once identifying as a member of a defined cultural group. However, there should be some 'external protections ... which reduce a minority's vulnerability to the decisions of the larger society' (Kymlicka 1995, 152).

Another way to expand citizenship is to decouple it from nationality entirely. The European Union is a contemporary example, with an identity based not on national culture but on an idealised civic space, with a membership beyond national bounds. Old ideas of citizenship are being replaced with a 'personhood' derived from the discourse of human rights (Soysal 1994). Neoliberalism in Europe has encouraged these non-national forms of belonging, as the responsibility for promoting social inclusion has shifted from the state to the individual.

The disappearance of a discourse of citizenship rights limits the state's ability to bring diverse groups into a common civic community. Tensions between migrant and majority populations have recently increased ... While this 'ethnic conflict' view has had some unpleasant echoes, it could inspire a movement towards social rights and differential citizenship. Instead, the current neoliberal approach is limited [to] empowering marginalised individuals to take advantage of market opportunities (Soysal 2011). Here, citizenship is a legal, but no longer a social status. Australia, Canada and New Zealand offer forms of differentiated citizenship to fit Kymlicka's model, whereas Europe follows a universal model closer to Soysal's view. In no case has a differentiated model of citizenship been reconciled with Marshall's objective of an 'equality of status'.

A NEW SOCIAL CITIZENSHIP

Marshall's view of aligning the provision of social rights with the category of citizenship was indeed based on a narrow understanding of social needs and an outdated analysis of population trends. Welfare provisions in post-war Britain directly discriminated against women who, after marriage, had their contributions and benefits determined by the circumstances

of their husbands (Pascall 1997, 121). The alignment of citizenship with the characteristics of the 'civilised', or the 'gentleman', conferred social rights upon an exclusive economic group. The intention of the social rights was to bring previously excluded groups of working men into this inclusive, but also exclusive, status; to allow, but also compel, them to adopt a set of social behaviours. Migrants, who were legally excluded from the category of citizenship, were excluded from the provision of social rights entirely. Marshall's equal citizenship limited the possibility of plural citizenships, and plural understandings of social and economic behaviour. Marshall's framework is by no means perfect. And while Marshall anticipated some of these problems, he was either not able, or willing, to address them.

Among the most persuasive critiques is that the conflict between civil and social rights may have made social rights unsustainable. Marshall himself argued this with some prescience:

> it may be that some of the conflicts within our social system are becoming too sharp for the compromise [mixed economy] to achieve its purpose much longer ... [but] we must ... realise the profound and disturbing effects which would be produced by any hasty attempt to reverse present and recent trends. (1992, 49)

The trend towards providing social service as a matter of right has been reversed. The neoliberal challenge to the economic logic of public investment and the social logic of collective responsibility has been powerful, assisted (perhaps ironically) by strong and important claims to pluralistic, differentiated citizenship on behalf of women, migrants, and cultural, indigenous, LGBTI and other groups. Social citizenship has not survived these challenges. ... By reducing people to economic units, neoliberalism creates a space for socially marginalised citizens to be valued for economic productivity.

However, neoliberalism is not without its own tensions, and the welfare model has not been destroyed. Indeed, throughout the years of the proudly neoliberal Thatcher government, public spending actually increased (Pierson 1994). Although Britain has taken many steps to break the model of social rights as a condition of citizenship, many expensive programmes such as the National Health Service remain popular.

Neoliberalism's promotion of individual responsibility has come into conflict with the contemporary experience of material deprivation and an increasingly unequal distribution of wealth (Feinstein 1996; Irvin 2011). The 2011 England riots and the Occupy movement can be seen as the result of a neoliberal crisis. The Global Financial Crisis has disproportionately affected low-income earners, who have protested to secure a more equal distribution of social benefits (Angel 2012; Slater 2011). The same problem of inequality that led to the first instance of social rights may now lead to its revival.

The present challenges to neoliberalism open up a space to restate the claim for social rights. This need not be 'citizenship', *per se* — there is no reason why migrants, who contribute both socially and economically to the societies they live in, should be excluded from the benefits of their participation. There is certainly no reason why women or LGBTI groups should be treated unequally as members of this broad community. There is also no compelling reason to prevent pluralistic approaches to law, land ownership and political engagement, which support the cultural practices of marginal groups. Social rights emerged in conjunction with social practices, which favoured working white men; however, a more inclusive rights agenda can be developed to suit new circumstances and understandings. Through member-

ship of a broad community — like citizenship, if not citizenship itself — we can legitimise the claim to make social contributions and receive social benefits. ... The 'welfare state' has not disappeared, even though many of its functions have been privatised either to the corporation or the individual. The tension between social and civil rights has not been resolved by neoliberalism. The promotion of civil rights over social rights has amplified inequalities, leading to radical, sometimes violent reaction by marginalised groups hoping to again achieve some 'equality of status'.

Revisiting Marshall's work offers the potential to help resolve these tensions. The formation of an inclusive category with differentiated options could form the basis for a revised social rights model. If citizenship is to be the 'architect of legitimate social inequality', contemporary critiques can reduce that inequality by promoting shared, plural understandings of social needs. It is possible to develop a more inclusive social rights system. The challenge is there for the taking.

(c) The Exploitation of Vulnerability: Dimensions of Citizenship and Rightlessness in Canada's Security Certificate Legislation[†]

Christine Wilke and Paula Willis

. . . .

I. INTRODUCTION

That the majority on occasion must be checked when proceeding against a minority of its fellow citizens is inevitable and probably salutary; but that the majority must be checked in proceedings against hostile aliens by a judge, simply because he doesn't think deportation is a good idea, is intolerable.[1]

Non-citizens are often the first to be targeted by policies that are implemented in the name of

national security: they easily appear to be "hostile aliens" about whom Rehnquist complained, as noted above. How are ideas of national security translated into policies that exclusively target non-citizens as security risks? And how do courts engage with the ideas of security, foreignness and risk on which these policies are based? This article examines the Canadian Supreme Court's *Charkaoui* decision's engagement with the politics of belonging, foreignness, and risk. *Charkaoui* invalidated portions of the security certificate mechanism that facilitated the long-term detention of non-nations deemed to pose a threat to Canadian security.[2] This mechanism has parallels in

---

† (2008) 26 Windsor Y.B. Access Just. 25 at 25–31, 33, 37–40, 42–44, 50–51. [Notes and/or references omitted.] Reproduced with permission.

the immigration legislation of other countries, notably the United Kingdom and the United States.[3] Since 2004, the highest courts in these countries have reviewed and partially challenged the legal framework underpinning the detention of non-citizens.[4] Some of these detentions, such as the ones complained about in *Charkaoui* and the British *Belmarsh* case,[5] have no clear end in sight. These cases raise the issue of indefinite detention: the application of immigration law mandates that the "strangers" who suddenly appear threatening to the body politic are detained to be sent home,[6] but they lack a home to which they can return without fear of torture or mistreatment. Indefinite detention arises at this intersection between immigration detention for the purpose of deportation and the presence of severe legal, moral or practical concerns about deportation.[7]

We examine the Canadian Supreme Court's *Charkaoui* decision on the security certificate procedure through the lens of citizenship and belonging and its opposites — statelessness and rightlessness. Our analysis of citizenship and rightlessness is based on a re-reading of Hannah Arendt's discussion of human rights in *The Origins of Totalitarianism*[8] through the lens of recent accounts that conceptualize citizenship and subordination as multidimensional and disaggregated practices and statuses. Which understandings of security and citizenship underpin these policies and the courts' responses to them? How do the legal challenges to such measures reconfigure the imaginations of rights, membership, and security? We argue that *Charkaoui* does not recognize but instead exploits the security certificate detainees' substantive rightlessness.

The security certificate process has the ostensible purpose of facilitating the speedy deportation of non-citizens deemed threats to Canadian security. As of February 2008, six persons are subject to security certificates: Mohamed Harkat, a refugee from Algeria; Hassan Almrei, a refugee from Syria; Mahmoud Jaballah and Mohammed Mahjoub, Egyptian citizens; Adil Charkaoui, a Moroccan citizen and permanent resident of Canada; and Manickavasagam Suresh, citizen of Sri Lanka.[9] The cases of Harkat, Charkaoui, Mahjoub, Jaballah, and Almrei have attracted special public attention since the certificates against them coincide with the wider post-9/11 securitization of Muslim men in North America and beyond. The "Security Certificate Five" are considered to be dangerous in Canada, but the *Charter* and human rights instruments halts their deportation due to the risk of torture in their countries of citizenship. Four of the detainees have been released into supervised house

arrest. Family members and communities have been enlisted in the control of the detainees. Hassan Almrei, who has no family in Canada, remains in detention.[10] We propose to interpret this regime of detention, supervised release and threat of deportation not as a specific human rights violation. Rather, we follow Hannah Arendt in conceptualizing the detainees' situation as a denial of the more fundamental "right to have rights" or the right to be treated as a person to whom the human rights envisioned in national constitutions and international law apply as a matter of right, not of discretion or charity.[11] While the detainees are not treated as non-persons without any rights whatsoever, the rights that they are granted appear as *grants* arising from the state's discretion and the commitment to the rule of law as procedural justice, not as rights inherent in the human status of the detainees.

In February 2007, the *Charkaoui* invalidated parts of the security certificate scheme but left the overall framework in place. In the media, the *Charkaoui* decision was hailed as "not just a ruling, [but] a statement"[12] in favour of reconciling competing legal values without jeopardizing security. Some commentators praised the Court for having "found a fair and pragmatic way to resolve the moral dilemma of the age of terror.[13] Yet in parliamentary committee hearings on a bill designed to render the partially invalidated legislation compatible with the *Charter*, a member of parliament cautioned against amendments that would grant detainees substantively more rights, remarking that "[t]he Supreme Court has upheld almost the entire security certificate regime, except for the part about the special advocate."[14] The complacent tone of the debate and Parliament's very moderate pace and scope of reforming the security certificate mechanism hint at serious limitations of *Charkaoui* as far as the rights of the detainees are concerned. Here, we scrutinize the decision for its theoretical underpinnings, its language, its silences, and its limits. We ask why certain non-citizens remain extremely vulnerable to harsh security measures and show how rightlessness persists alongside a robust commitment to human rights.

. . . .

II. DISPLACING INSECURITY: SECURITY CERTIFICATES IN CANADA

Security certificates are used when information surfaces indicating that a person who is lawfully present in Canada might nevertheless be "inadmissible". Inadmissibility on security grounds is stipulated in section 34 of the *Immigration and Refugee Protection Act* (2002) [IRPA] as follows:

(1) A permanent resident or a foreign national is inadmissible on security grounds for:
   (a) engaging in an act of espionage or an act of subversion against a democratic government, institution or process as they are understood in Canada;
   (b) engaging in or instigating the subversion by force of any government;
   (c) engaging in terrorism;
   (d) being a danger to the security of Canada;
   (e) engaging in acts of violence that would or might endanger the lives or safety of persons in Canada; or
   (f) being a member of an organization that there are reasonable grounds to believe engages, has engaged or will engage in acts referred to in paragraph (a), (b) or (c).

Security certificates are issued by the Minister of Citizenship and Immigration and the Minister of Public Safety on the advice of the Canadian Security Intelligence Service [CSIS]. Upon the signature by the ministers, the certificate is automatically referred to a designated Federal Court judge who has to assess the "reasonableness" of the certificate.[17] The reasonableness test asks the Federal Court judge to decide whether there are "reasonable grounds to believe" that the evidence presented by the government establishes inadmissibility on security grounds. The designated judge merely needs "a *bona fide* belief in a serious possibility based on credible evidence," which is "more than a flimsy suspicion, but less than the civil test of balance of probabilities."[18] The threshold is much lower than the standard of proof beyond reasonable doubt required by criminal law.

Since 1991, twenty-eight security certificates have been issued, twenty of which were upheld.[19] Membership in a terrorist organization[20] has been the most common reason for the issuance of a security certificate. Yet, three suspected spies from Russia and two members of Yasser Arafat's secret security force were also deported under certificates.[21] Of the twenty-eight certificates, five have named women. The current detainees have been subjected to detention or subject to supervised house arrest since 2000, 2001, 2002, and 2003, respectively. They have been held on certificates for much longer than had been the custom prior to 9/11: in twelve out of the fifteen pre-9/11 cases, the persons named in the certificate were deported (occasionally to a third state) within two years; the large majority of them within one year. Security certificates were designed to speed up

the deportation of non-citizens who are inadmissible on security grounds, and they largely accomplished this goal prior to 9/11. In current practice, however, they facilitate indefinite detention instead of speedy removal. This shift in the practical application of pre-existing rules poses new moral and legal questions.

Under the old IRPA security certificate process, the Minister of Citizenship and Immigration may present *ex parte* evidence to the Federal Court judge *in camera* (in secret) if the disclosure of evidence to the individual, their legal counsel or the general public could jeopardize national security or the safety of any person. The designated judge reviews the file prepared by CSIS which may include evidence that would be inadmissible in criminal proceedings.[22] The judge provides a summary of the evidence to the individual named under a certificate to the extent that the information may be disclosed. Additionally, IRPA guarantees the 'opportunity to be heard' for the individual named to respond to the summary of evidence. Depending on the nature of such a summary, individuals named in a security certificate might be unaware of the evidence presented against them and thus in no position to counter it. This procedure has gained the IRPA security certificate process the nickname "secret trials" and caused considerable uneasiness for participants in the process, including some of the "designated judges".[23] The *Charkaoui* decision has invalidated this part of the IRPA as a violation of the "fundamental justice" guarantee contained in section 7 of the *Canadian Charter of Rights and Freedoms*,[24] but has suspended the effect of the invalidation until February 23, 2008. Parliament is tasked with devising a new procedure that gives more weight to the detainees' right to see and meet the case against them, and that provides for an "independent agent at the stage of judicial review"[25] to enable limited advocacy on behalf of the detainees. Drafts and committee deliberations indicate that Parliament intends to introduce the British special advocate system without, however, giving much weight to the criticisms of this system voiced by special advocates, British courts, and analysts.

How does the security certificate process facilitate potentially indefinite detention? The practical effects of the security certificate scheme result from the interaction between legislative framework, administrative practice, and political context. First, all non-residents and most permanent residents who are subject to a security certificate are detained. The detention review process before *Charkaoui* varied depending on a person's residence status in Canada:

if the individual named under the certificate is a permanent resident of Canada, she is entitled to a review of her case every six months until the certificate is either found reasonable or quashed. At each review, the person named in the certificate has the opportunity to present new evidence concerning the threat they pose to Canadian society. Under the old framework, non-resident foreign nations were only entitled to a review 120 days after the certificate has been found reasonable. In *Charkaoui*, the Supreme Court found this disparity of procedural rights according to immigration status unjustifiable and mandated that all persons subject to security certificates should have equal access to judicial review of the reasonableness of their detention.[26] Second, if a security certificate is upheld, the ruling immediately becomes a deportation order that is not subject to appeal. The final recourse is a Pre-Removal Risk Assessment [PRRA] which, if successful, classifies the individual as a "person in need of protection" and disallows deportation to the individual's country of origin[27]. This can be the case, for example, if the detainee would be at risk of torture in their country of citizenship. Under the *Convention against Torture*, states are not allowed to "expel, return ('refouler') or extradite a person to another State where there are substantial grounds for believing that he would be in danger of being subject to torture."[28] Since deportation is the only option envisioned in the security certificate mechanism for individuals deemed 'dangerous', but is disallowed by a different body of law, those caught between the regimes of security and immigration law and human rights are subsequently left in detention with no specific endpoint in sight.

. . . .

We now turn from the overview of the security certificate scheme to a contextual analysis of the social and legal vulnerabilities of the security certificate detainees that helps to see why certain people are more likely to be caught in a limbo between detention, supervised house arrest, and the threat of deportation to torture. The security certificate detainees belong to a population that is vulnerable along several axes: they are perceived as culturally foreign and even threatening to the country, they do not hold Canadian passports, and they have few other sources of rights and protection available to them. The confluence of these conditions fixes the specific status of these detainees in a particular zone of rightlessness. Attention to the multiple axes of rights and membership claims helps us to position the

detainees in relationship to, for example, Canadian citizens who were caught in the web of Canadian or U.S. anti-terrorism policies.

. . . .

IV.   *CHARKAOUI*: DEALING IN RIGHTLESSNESS

The security certificate detainees largely lack the three dimensions of citizenship that would enable their rights claims to resonate with the Canadian public and the legal system. They are mostly perceived as foreign and threatening, outside of the realm of effective belonging. They are not Canadian citizens and therefore outside of the realm of full legal protection under Canadian laws. And they cannot rely on the protection of their countries of citizenship for any other rights claims. To the contrary, their formal citizenship becomes a liability because it raises the threat of deportation to torture. How does *Charkaoui* deal with these vulnerabilities? In the remainder of this article, we show that the *Charkaoui* ruling exploits each of these sources of rightlessness without fully acknowledging their effects on the status and experiences of the detainees. In short, *Charkaoui* presumes that the detainees effectively do not belong to the Canadian demos, it stresses the privileges of formal citizenship in order to counter allegations of discrimination against non-citizens, and it fails to recognize the detainees' lack of options for exit due to their lack of effective citizenship elsewhere.

A.   Our Security, Their Insecurity: Effective Belonging

How does *Charkaoui* map the place of the detainees in relationship to the "imagined community"[65] of Canada? Although *Charkaoui* gestures towards the humanity and individuality of the security certificate detainees, the Court sees them as fundamentally alien to Canada. Not only do they not belong to the nation whose security is encompassed by the ubiquitous term "national security" — even worse, the detainees are deemed to threaten this, "our" security. They are positioned as clearly distinguishable from Canadian society, as irreducibly alien. The legal remedies suggested by the Court barely conceal this abyss.

Analyses of previous certificate decisions have noted that the Federal Courts have relied on "profiles" of terrorists based on travel patterns and ideology. Once a person is marched with a "profile", they have little room for disputing their designation as dangerous to Canadian security.[66] On a more fundamental level, the language of process, law, evidence and innocence obscures the nature of the accusations at the heart of the certificates: security certificates can be issued for people who are members of organizations that *might* engage in terrorism in the future.[67] Thus, the certificate is to a significant degree based on predictions of future conduct and on assessments of inner dispositions that might not have surfaced in material actions. But how is a person to prove that they will not engage in terrorism? Given the folk knowledge voiced in court rooms that terrorism is connected to certain Islamic fundamentalist ideologies that are acquired or nourished by visits to "the region", and that someone "hooked" on these ideologies will remain committed to them,[68] it is illusionary to expect someone who fits the terrorist profile to be able to prove that they are not dangerous. The speculative questions about a person's likely future associations, actions, and commitments have to be assessed by the Federal Court with the low standard of "reasonable grounds to believe" that favours the government's characterization of the case. The setup of the security certificate process encourages the translation of societal threat perceptions into legal exclusion orders.

In contemporary nation-states, the "imagined community" of the nation usually extends only to fellow citizens or nationals. The shape of the Canadian imagined community, expressed and shaped through institutionalized policies of multiculturalism and bilingualism, is elusive and widely debated.[69] What it means to be Canadian is rarely explicitly attributed to immutable characteristics such as ethnicity, common language or shared history. Canadian-ness is most often described in terms of commonality in beliefs (in diversity, tolerance and liberalism) underlined by the assumption of (at least) residency and family ties in Canada. These beliefs, in turn, are more readily attributed to some demographic groups and more easily disputed for other groups. The culturally dominant or "original citizens"[70] who derive their citizenship from ancestry and membership in a major cultural and language group have a firmer social standing than those who are relative "newcomers" and members of minority language and cultural groups. The Canadian *National Security Policy*, for example, begins by defining Canadian-ness by the moral (as opposed to legal or geographic) boundaries of the country. The "Canadian" of the *National Security Policy* is defined not by citizenship but through reference to Canadian values:

> Canadians stand together in reaffirming that the use of violence to pursue political, religious or ideological goals is an affront to our values ... No one better appreciates the need to protect our society than those who chose this country as a place to build a better life or who fled the consequences of instability and intolerance in other parts of the world.[71]

Some immigrants, and [...] particularly those who "chose" Canada for themselves, are readily embraced in the Canadian demos. Yet, "somewhere between the people who 'chose' Canada and the homogenous 'Canadians' opposed to violence, is the insertion of some non-Canadian 'other' (in a legal or national sense)."[72] The "foreignness" of those whose alleged values do not fit the *National Security Policy's* vision of Canadian-ness is not given fact.[73] Rather, it is established through this policy and other government pronouncements. Foreignness, as Bonnie Honing puts it, is "a symbolic marker that the nation attaches to the people we want to disavow, deport, or detain because we experience them as a threat."[74] It is therefore not reducible to the lack of formal citizenship. In the context of terrorism threats, foreignness becomes an attribute of the threat as well as of persons associated with the threat.

In *Charkaoui*, the detainees' foreignness is presumed and affirmed from the opening paragraph on. The judgment situates itself by describing "a tension that lies at the heart of modern democratic governance":

> One of the most fundamental responsibilities of a government is to ensure the *security of its citizens*. This may require it to act on information that it cannot disclose and to *detain people who threaten national security*. Yet in a constitutional democracy, governments must act accountably and in conformity with the Constitution and the rights and liberties it guarantees.[75]

The government's mandate is to ensure the security of "its citizens" and to "detain people who threaten national security." These two groups presumably do not overlap: people who threaten national security are not part of the nation to be secured. The "citizens" are different from the "people who threaten national security" whom the government "may" be required to detain. "People who threaten national security" are implicitly associated with foreignness through contrasting them with "citizens". In framing the case as a balancing act between liberty and security, the Court slides towards balancing the citizens' security against the liberty (and security) of the detainees ("people who threaten national security"), keeping the desires and interests of these two groups strictly separated. *Charkaoui* does not contemplate, for example, that people who appear suspect share everyone else's vulnerability to acts of violence; or that "citizens" as well as non-citizens might see their personal security threatened by anti-terrorism policies. Such considerations could have helped to blur the line between the stipulated interests of the citizens and the "others".

. . . .

B. Citizens, Residents, Foreign Nationals: Formal Citizenship

Charkaoui engages with the formal meaning of citizenship by affirming that non-citizens suspected of being threats to national security are subject to a legal framework that citizens are never subject to: immigration law. By insisting that *Charkaoui* is an immigration matter, the Court evades arguments about the unequal treatment of citizens and non-citizens in terrorism-related matters. In addition, the Court asks Parliament to devise a new security certificate procedure. Yet democratic institutions are often complicit in establishing different sets of rights for citizens and non-citizens because only citizens' interests are systematically (though imperfectly) represented in such bodies.

Charkaoui highlights the distinction between citizens and non-citizens by disallowing comparisons between the treatment of citizen terrorism suspects and the non-citizen security certificate detainees. The treatment of the non-citizen terrorism suspects raises the question of discrimination since Canadian citizens, irrespective of their dangerousness or intention to engage in terrorism, cannot be detained unless as part of criminal proceedings against them. Discrimination, however, presumes that two groups of persons who share relevant characteristics are treated unequally on the basis of irrelevant traits. The Court found that the security certificate process does not constitute discrimination because the mobility and residence rights of s. 6 of the Charter "specifically allow ... for differential treatment of citizens and non-citizens in deportation matters: only citizens are accorded the right to enter, remain in and leave Canada."[88] The discrimination framework is unavailable as long as the case is treated as a deportation matter. The Court, relying on the *Suresh* exception that renders deportation never completely impossible, found that "the record on which we must rely does not establish that the detentions at issue have become unhinged from the state's purpose of deportation."[89] Indeed, the availability of an ongoing "effective review process that permits the judge

to consider all matters relevant to the detention" ensures that detention will continue only as long as it is connected to deportation.[90] The procedural justice of ongoing review brings the detention closer to the principles of the rule of law and thereby normalizes it.[91] Yet it silences the underlying questions about the nature and effects of the detention that depend on the substantive rightlessness of the circumscribed group of non-citizens.

The Court raises two allegedly hypothetical constellations in which the security certificate detention scheme might be discriminatory: "[f]irst, detention may become indefinite as deportation is put off or becomes impossible, for example because there is no country to which the person can be deported."[92] This situation, however, is already present: the five men have been held for prolonged periods of time. In the case of Mahmoud Jaballah, deportation to Egypt was specifically prohibited by a Federal Court. It is not clear, then, how his continued detention and supervised release are meaningfully connected to the attempt to deport him, let alone deport him speedily. The indefinite character of this detention and surveillance is not seen by the courts.

The logic of *Charkaoui* hinges on the distinction between, on the one hand, "lengthy and indeterminate" detention, which is conceded for the cases at hand,[93] and, on the other hand, "indefinite detention", which is unconstitutional and allegedly not present in the current cases. *Charkaoui* affirms that "the IRPA ... does not authorize indefinite detention."[94] This statement is only plausible if "indefinite" is read to mean "endless", not if it means "lasting for an unknown or unstated length of time." The latter, however, is the *Oxford English Dictionary's* definition of "indefinite."[95] If the court had taken this definition of the term as its point of departure, it could have conceded that the combination of immigration legislation, administrative practice, and the protection against torture have created a constellation of indefinite immigration detention in Canada. By using a particular understanding of "indefinite" and insisting on the theoretical possibility of deportation even in the absence of strong evidence of governmental will or feasibility, *Charkaoui* upholds the fiction that security certificate detention is "lengthy"[96] but not "indefinite." These fine distinctions were lost on some commentators: a *Globe & Mail* editorial summarized *Charkaoui* as ruling that "the indefinite jailing of non-citizens suspected of being terrorists is legitimate, as long as their detention is subject to meaningful and regular review."[97] This is decidedly not what the Court intended to say, but the editorial might unwittingly have provided a perceptive account of the decision's effects.

The Court envisioned a second case in which, potentially, the detention would be unconstitutional: "the government could conceivably use the IRPA not for the purpose of deportation, but to detain the person on security grounds."[98] This scenario can also be seen as a description of the current situation. After all, security and immigration have become intertwined as policy matters in the post-9/11 period. The Court started the *Charkaoui* judgment with a meditation on the tension between security and liberty, not a discussion of immigration law. The deportations that are ostensibly sought are not very likely to materialize. Ultimately, none of the persons named by a security certificate who fit the "profile" of a transnational Islamic terrorist have been deported after 9/11. Detention on security grounds is at least a convenient side effect, if not the intended goal of the current administrative practice of issuing security certificates.

.   .   .   .   .

V.   CONCLUSION

The *Charkaoui* ruling is an attempt to assimilate anti-terrorism policies to the rule of law. Yet the decision exploits rather than acknowledges the vulnerabilities of the people for whom being subject to security certificates means indefinite detention. The treatment of the non-citizens who are subject to security certificates does not hinge on their guilt or innocence as established in legal proceedings. Instead, security certificates are based on assessments of dangerousness. Dangerousness, in turn, is established on the basis of untested evidence and assumptions about future behaviour and associations. Persons who are subject to security certificates are judged according to what they *did*. Yet the security certificate process is often described in terms borrowed from criminal law in ways that suggest suspicions about specific individual culpability that are in fact absent in these cases. Even the criticism of "secret trials" fails to capture that the proceedings, however deficient they might be, do not adjudicate guilt or innocence and do not amount to trials at all. The conjunction of rightlessness and the irrelevance of legal innocence in this context leads us back to consider Arendt's observation on the treatment of stateless people in interwar Europe: "Jurists are so used to thinking of law in terms of punishment, which indeed always deprives us of certain rights, that they may find it even more difficult

than the layman to recognize that the deprivation of legality, *i.e.* of all rights, no longer has a connection with specific crimes."[129] The aspiration to being "judged by one's actions and opinions,"[130] in turn, can only be fulfilled if one belongs to a political community that recognizes one's distinctiveness and humanity, Arendt concluded. Security certificates do not adjudicate guilt or innocence in relationship to specific crimes, but a person's abstract dangerousness based on their "profile."

Security certificates exploit the rightlessness of some non-citizens by subjecting them to a process in which not their actions and opinions but their physical appearance, place of birth, and formal citizenship determine their fate. The Security Certificate Five are non-citizens of Canada who share additional vulnerabilities: they are perceived as alien and threatening to the national community, and their citizenships in Algeria, Morocco, Syria and Egypt operate as further liabilities rather than supplementary sources of rights. The Supreme Court's response to the detainees' claims adopted the language of constitutional rights rather than human rights. It addressed some concerns but upheld the fundamental distinction between citizens and non-citizens in the context of anti-terrorism policies.

Since the detainees' particular form of rightlessness results from a combination of their lack of formal citizenship, lack of effective belonging and the quality of their citizenships elsewhere, attempts to include them (and others) within the framework of ordinary legality need to pay attention to the intersecting sources of rightlessness. A proposal to follow the Law Lords' reasoning that citizens and non-citizens cannot be treated differently in anti-terrorism policies, for example, should take into account that the *Belmarsh* decision led to legislation that allows house arrest and extensive surveillance of citizens *and* non citizens who are seen as foreign and threatening to national security. This alternative route of normalized surveillance is no less exclusionary than the attempt to secure security on the backs of non-citizens. In the end, foreignness is not a natural attribute but a product of decisions about the shape of the nation whose security is to be protected; it is "not exhausted nor even finally defined by working papers, skin color, ethnicity, or citizenship. Indeed, it is not an empirical line at all; it is a symbolic one, used for political purposes."[131] As a result, the lines of foreignness drawn in national security policies and public rhetoric need to be challenged, not just redrawn. Finally, the threat of deportation despite the risk of torture holds the detainees hostage to their formal citizenships. The

Suresh exception that enables the continued detention fails to acknowledge that for some people who allegedly don't belong "here," there is no other place to go. Nurturing the mistaken and unethical hope of deporting all those who are deemed threats to Canadian security fails to recognize that for a number of them, Canada is the only home they have. They, too, should have the rights, meaning the right to belong "to a community willing and able to guarantee ... rights."[132] Respecting the detainees' right to have rights requires judging them by their actions.[133] The current regime, in contrast, judges them by their asserted dangerousness — a dangerousness that is first constructed and then invoked in order to balance "their" rights against "our" security from the threat they are seen to pose.

(d) Citizenship as Capital: The Distinction of Migrant Labor†

Harald Bauder

Industrialized economies have become structurally dependent on the availability and continual supply of [migrant] labor.[1] In this article, I draw on Pierre Bourdieu's ideas of capital to argue that citizenship functions as a key mechanism of distinction that renders migrants vulnerable and exploitable, and therefore particularly valuable to the economies of the global North. Citizenship as a culturally produced category manifests itself in formal (legal and institutional) as well as informal (practiced and cultural) forms. I suggest that both aspects of citizenship function as a form of capital and a mechanism of distinction.

This view of citizenship corresponds to the treatment of citizenship as strategic concept not only in association with constructions of identity and belonging, struggles over recognition, and the politics of participation and contribution,[2] but also in relation to regulating access to scarce resources and institutionalizing difference.[3] In this article, I develop a perspective of citizenship that integrates processes of inclusion and exclusion under the logic of distinction and reproduction.

As a form of capital, citizenship serves as a strategy of accumulation[4] that is deliberately deployed and can be exchanged into other forms of capital. But rather than constituting an overarching cultural logic of capitalism, citizenship, as I develop it here, follows the wider logic of distinction. For Bourdieu, capital is about the reproduction of social order. In this context, social reproduction cannot be neatly separated into contexts of home, work, and politics.[5] The coexistence of interchangeable economic, social, and cultural forms of capital reflects the interlocking nature of processes of production, social practices, and cultural identities in the perpetuation of inequality and the reproduction of capitalist society.[6]

Labor markets are important sites for the reproduction of social order: They operate at the intersection of economic, political, social, and cultural processes, and they are politically, socially and culturally regulated.[7] International migrants serve as an illustrative example of the significance of non–market-driven processes of labor-market regulation through citizenship. Instead of gaining access to occupations that reflect their education and training once they upgrade their language skills — as human capital theory would predict[8] — many migrants categorically lack access to the upper labor-market segments or to the formal labor market altogether. The legal status and cultural meanings associated with citizenship play a key role in rendering many migrants into a labor force that is particularly vulnerable and exploitable. In industrialized countries, citizenship is an ordering principle of labor markets.

The view of citizenship as a form of capital offers not only valuable insights into the concrete labor-market segmentation of international migrants but also permits integrating political, cultural, and geographical processes of inclusion and exclusion into a conceptual framework that locates the strategic

---

† (2008) 33 *Alternatives* 315 at 316–27. [Notes and/or references omitted.] Copyright © 2008 SAGE Publications. Reprinted by permission of SAGE Publications, Ltd.

nature of citizenship with the motivations of distinction and reproduction. Although citizenship is a historically and politically constructed concept that changes over time and space,[9] the process of distinction and reproduction may constitute an underlying logic of its construction and transformation. ...

The remainder of this article is divided into three sections. First, I discuss the concepts of capital and distinction with particular reference to migrant labor. Second, I develop the notion of citizenship as a form of capital and a mechanism of labor regulation. By presenting evidence from Canada, a traditional immigration country, and Germany, a country that until recently held to policies of being a nonimmigrant country,[11] I illustrate the international and transcontinental relevance of the idea of citizenship as capital. Third, I conclude by addressing some implications regarding contemporary perspectives of citizenship and geographical scale that emerge from this discussion.

CAPITAL AND DISTINCTION

The notion of capital assumes variable meanings throughout the social sciences. Orthodox economists tend to emphasize the economic and monetary forms of capital, but they also speak of, for example, human capital, referring to the educational and skill characteristics of labor. Karl Marx and Friedrich Engels offered other interpretations of capital, including estate capital, associated with landholdings,[12] and variable capital, referring to labor.[13] Bourdieu[14] also endorsed this multidimensional character of capital. He identified various "species of capital" in his writing, including political, military, scientific, and technological capital, symbolic capital,[15] and cultural capital, which he further subdivided into objectified, embodied, and institutionalized cultural capital.[16] Expanding the definition of capital from its purely monetary form[,] to include the social and the cultural, permits an integrated perspective of society and the processes of production.[17] While Marx, however, saw the concept of capital primarily as a "means of exploitation and domination,"[18] Bourdieu emphasized the role of capital in the reproduction of society.

The various complementary forms of capital coexist, and people and social groups who possess the necessary "competence"[19] can transfer resources from one form of capital to another to achieve distinction and reproduction. This perspective of capital stresses human agency. Individuals and social groups do not simply respond to market forces but, rather, strategically create, valorize, and endorse different forms of capital. Capital is a way to actively construct difference and express distinction. People who possess it use it to distinguish themselves from nonowners and thereby elevate their status and congeal their privilege, while people who lack access to it can be excluded and subordinated.

For example, based on empirical work on the practices of distinction in France, Bourdieu suggests that the members of an elite social group may signify their status through embodied cultural capital in the form of subtle "gestures or the apparently most insignificant techniques of the body — ways of walking or blowing one's nose, ways of eating or talking."[20] In this case, people who do not possess the code to read or enact these cultural performances lack access to important symbols of status. Another process of distinction exists in the form of institutionalized cultural capital represented by educational diplomas, certificates, or other types of institutional acknowledgment. ...

Such constructions and expressions of capital regulate labor markets. For example, gender performances inscribed onto workers' bodies[22] shape workplace expectations and career trajectories in occupations as diverse as corporate banking and shop-floor manufacturing.[23] In the cases of migrants, lack of access to embodied cultural capital that is expected by employers can lead to the denial of job opportunities in professional occupations.[24] Similarly, the nonrecognition of foreign credentials often constitutes a barrier for international migrants to gain access to professional jobs. Licensing bodies and government regulators may seek to protect well-paying and prestigious jobs by mobilizing institutional cultural capital that is inaccessible to migrants.[25] Unable to practice in their occupations of training, migrants often take low-status, manual, or informal jobs as janitors, maids, restaurant helpers, or other employment at the margins of the labor market.

. . . .

The attractiveness of Bourdieu's approach to explain the labor-market situation of migrants lies in the geographical nature of the production of capital. Systems of creating, valorizing, and exchanging capital are place-contingent: in different places different systems exist. For example, similar social practices — such as withdrawing from the labor market and the ability to "idle," — signify social status in some places, such as rural areas of India,[30] but symbolize social pathology in the capitalist market economies of the global North.[31] Such geographical differences affect migrants who move between places and who, as a result, often experience social dislocation.[32] In addition, the nonmigrant population may strategically create and invest in forms of capital that are inaccessible to migrants for the very purpose of distinction between the migrant population and itself. Citizenship, I will show in the next section, is a particularly powerful place-bound mechanism of distinction that facilitates the exclusion of migrants and the subordination of their labor.

CITIZENSHIP AS CAPITAL

Citizenship is a mechanism of distinction between migrants and nonmigrants based on associations with place, origin, and national community. It is important to recognize at this point that the definition of migrant and "citizen" may overlap, but they are not synonymous. The work by Yasmine Soysal[33] on migrants in Berlin, for example, illustrates that migrants can acquire "postnational" citizenship rights, enabling them to "participate in Berlin's public institutions and make claims to its authority structures"[34] without carrying a German passport. ... Nevertheless, the association between citizenship and geographical territory enables the distinction and exclusion of large numbers and proportions of migrants who cross from one territory to another. The lack of citizenship defines some migrants as legal and cultural outsiders. Below, I discuss formal and informal aspects of citizenship[37] as a mechanism of legal and cultural distinction and exclusion. I am particularly interested in the manner in which these two aspects facilitate the reproduction of labor-market privilege.

Formal Citizenship

Formal citizenship is a legal category that is strategically created, endorsed, and valorized by the collective membership of a national community or the political elites that claim to represent them. The rules that guide formal citizenship cater to the particular historical context, political agendas, and economic needs of nation-states. For example, territorial (*jus soli*) and origin (*jus sanguinis*) principles of citizenship emphasize either birthplace or ancestry as criteria for membership. In immigration countries, such as Canada, which have historically depended on the influx of newcomers to sustain territorial expansion, demographic growth, and economic development, the jus soli principle and a regular naturalization process have granted formal citizenship privileges to first- and second-generation immigrants. ... Most countries pursue a combination of jus soli, jus sanguinis, and naturalization practices, depending on strategic objectives to include and exclude population groups.

Not only the members of a national community use citizenship as a tool of collective inclusion and exclusion, but also individuals and families acquire and deploy formal citizenship strategically for purposes of distinction, reproduction, and accumulation. For example, wealthy East Asian families have used Canadian immigration policy — in particular the Business Immigration Program — to obtain immigrant status and subsequently citizenship in exchange for economic capital investments of 400,000 Canadian dollars in Canadian businesses or the establishment of a new business in Canada.[41] The possession of multiple passports can, in turn, be converted into other forms of capital, including monetary capital through expanded possibilities for international business transactions, social capital through establishing multinational personal and professional contacts and communities, and cultural capital through the acquisition of language capacity, education, and professional credentials.[42] ... Formal citizenship, in this case, functions as a form of capital in the sense intended by Bourdieu. It is a strategically deployed category that can be exchanged with other forms of capital and serves the aim of accumulation and reproduction.

The strategies of citizenship pursued by individuals or families and national communities often pursue different objectives. For example, over the last decades many Lebanese refugees have acquired Canadian citizenship because it carries value by enabling mobility and providing political security when the family returns to Lebanon. Such a strategic use of citizenship, however, was never intended by the Canadian state. Accordingly, public outcry was large when the Canadian government evacuated fifteen thousand Lebanese Canadians from Lebanon in the wake of the 2006 Israeli invasion. Critics alleged that these citizens, many of whom were naturalized immigrants, "want all the benefits of being Canadian, but none of the burden" and suggested that citizenship policy be reviewed to better "serve Canada's interests."[44] This public debate arose because migrants and the collective national community — represented by the Canadian state — pursue their own strategic interests and agendas of reproduction as they assume and grant formal citizenship. In this case, the cost of evacuating thousands of citizens from Lebanon was not matched by the perceived economic benefits to Canada created when these migrants became Canadian citizens.

In the context of setting economic agendas, national communities use citizenship to extend or withdraw economic rights[45] and to "cheapen the labour power"[46] of migrant workers. Citizens usually have unconstrained access to the national labor market and enjoy social and economic rights. For many noncitizens, labor-market access is either denied or conditional on permits, special legal status, or international agreements. ... In the sense that formal citizenship permits the denial of economic rights, formal citizenship (or lack thereof) is a legal mechanism of labor-market inclusion and exclusion.

When noncitizens receive only conditional labor-market access, the lack of formal citizenship often functions as a mechanism of subordination. ... The alternative to unattainable work in the formal labor market is employment in the informal sector, where wages are low, abuse is rampant, and employers make no contributions to heath, employment, and social insurances.[52]

[In] Canada citizenship subordinates workers who are formally "classified as non-citizens."[53] Nonstatus immigrants are particularly vulnerable as workers who "are denied basic social and health services,"[54] although many of them pay taxes. If the lack of status denies work in the formal economy, many migrants are pushed into the informal economy, where labor standards are not formally controlled.

Labor-market institutions tend to reproduce distinctions based on citizenship. For example, the nonrecognition of foreign credentials is a common barrier to employment of migrants in high-skill occupations. ...

The use of formal citizenship as a mechanism of distinction and the subordination of labor is particularly apparent in the context of temporary foreign labor. ... Canada issued 165,198 permits to noncitizen migrant workers in 2007 under its Temporary Foreign Worker programs.[58] Severely restricted circumstances deny these workers the choice of employer or occupation and effectively render them "unfree labour."[59] New regulations have increased the period these workers are available to Canadian employers (from one year to two years) and signify the [intention] to expand, rather than reduce, this vulnerable labor force of noncitizens.[60] The lack of formal citizenship relegates these migrant workers to the lowest segments of the labor market and ensures that nonmigrants obtain privileged access to upper–labor-market segments. It distinguishes migrants from nonmigrants and reproduces economic privilege.

Informal Citizenship

Informal citizenship is a dimension of membership in a national community related to practices of identity and belonging. This substantive dimension of

citizenship complements formal citizenship as a mechanism of distinction and applies to migrants who "are not considered 'to belong' to the nation state community, even if formally they are entitled to."[61] This dimension of citizenship affects the labor-market situation of many migrants and reproduces the economic privileges of nonmigrants.

Although migrants and nonmigrants often share a range of common principles of social and economic participation, they are not on equal footing in the labor market. For example, although the foreign permanent residents with Turkish citizenship in Berlin, Germany, have acquired postnational rights,[62] these rights do not equate with social and economic inclusion. The Turkish population of Berlin and other German cities has continued to experience major disadvantages in the labor market. Their unemployment rates are soaring compared with that of the German population, and those workers who do have jobs typically bring home earnings far below the national and local averages. Research involving German youth in Berlin indicates that popular constructions of citizenship continue to hinge on notions of origin, birthplace, and "culture." This research rejects "the notion that national citizenship is declining in importance in favour of post-national forms of citizenship."[63] Constructions of identity and practices of distinction associated with informal citizenship help produce and reproduce labor market inequality.

Informal citizenship cannot be entirely separated from "race." In fact, racial markers often signify cultural nonbelonging.[64] When "racial" markers are measured, statistics indicate that persons belonging to "racial" minority groups suffer from labor-market disadvantages, independent of formal citizenship.[65] However, the idea of informal citizenship as a category of distinction and exclusion can be applied in a more territorial manner than the category of race. In some places in Canada, so-called visible minorities are increasingly represented as belonging. For example, cities, such as Toronto and Vancouver, assume a distinctly "multicultural" identity. In this case, a person's belonging may not be defined so much by "racial" markers as by having access to territorially defined cultural codes and conventions and by being able to enact place-particular habitual performances. My use of the term *informal citizenship* captures this territorial idea of belonging.

This idea of informal citizenship defines cultural membership in national communities.[66] These communities are "imagined" because members do not personally know each other and therefore produce collective systems of identity and difference.[67] National communities and their boundaries are creations of cultural and political processes of inclusion and exclusion and distinction between "us and them," citizens and noncitizens.[68] Nonmigrants often express identities of belonging through citizenship. ... This commitment correlates with the entitlement of citizens to the social, cultural, and economic resources controlled by the national community. The commitment to imagined national behavioral norms, attitudes, and cultural conventions distinguishes citizens from those migrants who are unable to express belonging in this way and who can therefore be denied entitlement to these resources.

Throughout the global North, and particularly in Europe, the demand of immigrants to express their loyalty to the nation-state, to embrace the cultural identity of their country of settlement and demonstrate their willingness to adapt to an imagined national habitus and associated national "values," have been on the rise, rather than in decline.[71] In Canada ... the acquisition of formal citizenship hinges on the internalization of some of these informal markers of citizenship, such as the ability to speak English/French ... or, in the case of Canada, the successful completion of a citizenship test that demands knowledge of national history, geography, and "Canadian values."[72] Through this implication in formal citizenship, informal citizenship links back to the formal processes of distinction and labor-market exclusion described in the preceding section.

Informal citizenship distinctions associated with belonging and entitlement also shape the labor-market situation of migrants in a more direct manner. For example, migrants are often unable to give the cultural performances expected from the members of an imagined national community. They may speak with an accent rather than "proper" standardized language or accepted national dialect or they project embodied images or institutionalized symbols of nonbelonging. The judgments of such performances of nonbelonging can motivate, for example, staff in Canadian employment and settlement agencies to place South Asian immigrants into occupations at the lower end of the job market, with more prestigious and better paying positions being reserved for workers who project the images of national belonging. In fact, that these markers of unbelonging often facilitate and legitimate employment in multicultural institutions and settlement agencies illustrates the currency that these markers possess in the context of occupational inclusion and exclusion.[73]

Media reporting reflect such processes of distinction associated with informal citizenship. For example, seasonal agricultural work in Canada is seen as too dangerous, physically strenuous, and demeaning for Canadian workers, but not for foreign migrant workers from Mexico and the Caribbean.[74] Popular media narratives mobilize the category of citizenship to create a double standard that distinguishes between the nonmigrants, who are entitled to certain labor standards and social and economic protection, and migrants, who can be denied these entitlements.[75] This double standard became particularly apparent in 1999 when the media discussed a proposal by the government of the province of Ontario to replace seasonal "offshore" workers with Canadian unemployed welfare recipients. This proposal met fierce opposition in the press. Newspaper reports lamented that Canadian workers would not learn any valuable skills through farm labor, compared this proposal with forced-labor camps, and complained that the harvesting jobs were too strenuous, dangerous, and low-paying to be acceptable to Canadians.[76] The voices of Canadian labor advocates and civil-rights activists opposed the infringement on the economic and social entitlements of fellow citizens. However, neither the newspapers nor the labor advocates expressed the same degree of solidarity with foreign migrant workers.[77] The lack of access to the identity and entitlements associated with citizenship apparently devalues the labor of noncitizens, legitimating their exploitation.

* * *

... I have illustrated how citizenship can function as a form of capital. Formal citizenship implicates legal and institutional processes; informal citizenship involves cultural practices and constructions of identities. Both of these aspects of citizenship reflect processes and practices of inclusion and exclusion that Bourdieu associates with the concept of capital and that follow the logic of distinction and reproduction. Informal citizenship can even be converted into formal citizenship through the requirement of cultural citizenship competencies as a condition for naturalization.

In the national labor market, formal and informal aspects of citizenship can further be translated into economic and other forms of capital. In this context, of course, citizenship is not independent from class, race, gender, and other categories of distinction. Rather, it constitutes one element in a complex system of globally, nationally, and locally interlocking processes of reproduction. ...

Conceiving of citizenship as capital and a mechanism of distinction and reproduction contributes to an explanation of why "European countries have been reluctant to give citizenship status to migrants"[78] and why immigrant countries, such as Canada, maintain a "permanent" workforce of temporary foreign workers.[79] As politically and culturally excluded noncitizens, many migrants do not compete on a level playing field for the resources of the welfare state. By denying these migrants citizenship rights and access to a shared identity, national communities and their nation-states ensure that these migrant workers remain in positions in which they are vulnerable and contribute disproportionately to the economies of industrialized countries.[80] In the context of the regulation of labor markets, citizenship is a strategy for the accumulation of monetary capital.

. . . .

By integrating citizenship into Bourdieu's larger framework of capital, the strategic nature of citizenship can be located with motivations of distinction and reproduction. The idea that the vulnerability of many migrants and their sometimes appalling employment situations are the inevitable outcome of self-regulating labor markets and side-effects of globalization must be rejected. Rather, their vulnerability and labor-market circumstances are strategically produced through the deployment and denial of formal and informal citizenship.

This perspective of citizenship as a form of capital paints a rather pessimistic picture of the potential of migrants exercising their agency and subverting meanings and practices of citizenship to their benefit. Powerful social, economic, and political elites continuously redefine the contents and value of variable forms of capital before underprivileged groups figure out how to obtain it.[81] Unfortunately for migrants, this principle may apply to both formal and informal aspects of citizenship. Not only legal bodies but also "ordinary" citizens "imagine and re-imagine"[82] citizenship in a variety of ways and thereby articulate ever-changing systems of distinction and exclusion. Recognizing the underlying motivations of distinction and reproduction, however, is a critical step toward improving the economic and political situation of migrants.[83]

The underlying motivations of distinction and reproduction affirm the material basis of the construction of citizenship.[84] With material change, the concept of citizenship is also likely to transform. ...

Protecting Rights: Inside and Outside the Constitution

(a) The *Somerset* Case†

U.K. National Archive

548. THE CASE OF JAMES SOMMERSETT, A NEGRO, ON A HABEAS CORPUS,* KING'S-BENCH: 12 GEORGE III. A.D. 1771–72.

Of this Case only a Statement of the Facts, and Mr. Hargrave's learned Argument were inserted in the former edition of this Work. I have here added the other Arguments, and the Judgment of the Court, from Lofft's Reports, in which is a Note of the Case under the name of Sommersett against Stewart.

On the 3d of December 1771, affidavits were made by Thomas Walklin, Elizabeth Cade, and John Marlow, that James Sommersett, a negro, was confined in irons on board a ship called the Ann and Mary, John Knowles commander, lying in the Thames, and bound for Jamaica; and lord Mansfield, on an application supported by these affidavits, allowed a write of Habeas Corpus, directed to Mr. Knowles, and requiring him to return the body of Sommersett before his lordship, with the cause of detainer.

Mr. Knowles on the 9th of December produced the body of Sommersett before lord Mansfield, and returned for cause of detainer, that Sommersett was the negro slave of Charles Steuart, esq. who had delivered Sommersett into Mr. Knowles's custody, in order to carry him to Jamaica, and there sell him as a slave. Affidavits were also made by Mr. Steuart and two other gentlemen, to prove that Mr. Steuart had purchased Sommersett as a slave in Virginia, and had afterwards brought him into England, where

he left his master's service; and that his refusing to return, was the occasion of his being carried on board Mr. Knowles's ship.

Lord *Mansfield* chusing to refer the matter to the determination of the court of King's-bench, Sommersett with sureties was bound in a recognizance for his appearance there on the second day of the next Hilary term; and his lordship allowed till that day for settling the form of the return to the Habeas Corpus. ...

. . . .

Lord Mansfield: The question is, if the owner had a right to detain the slave, for the sending of him over to be sold in Jamaica. In five or six cases of this nature, I have known it to be accommodated by agreement between the parties: on its first coming before me, I strongly recommended it here. But if the parties will have it decided, we must give our opinion. Compassion will not, on the one hand, nor inconvenience on the other, be to decide; but the law: in which the difficulty will be principally from the inconvenience on both sides. Contract for sale of a slave is good here; the sale is a matter to which the law properly and readily attaches, and will maintain the price according to the agreement. But here the person of the slave himself is immediately the object of enquiry; which makes a very material difference. The now question is, Whether any dominion, authority or coercion can be exercised in this country, on a slave according to the American

† From the U.K. National Archive website: <www.nationalarchives.gov.uk/pathways/blackhistory/rights/transcripts/somerset_case.htm>. Originally published in *Howell's State Trials*, vol. 20 (London: T.C. Hansard) at cols 1–6, 79–82.

laws? The difficulty of adopting the relation, without adopting it in all its consequences, is indeed extreme; and yet, many of those consequences are absolutely contrary to the municipal law of England. We have no authority to regulate the conditions in which law shall operate. On the other hand, should we think the coercive power cannot be exercised: it is now about 50 years since the opinion given by two of the greatest men of their own or any times, (since which no contract has been brought to trial, between the masters and slaves;) the service performed by the slaves without wages, is a clear indication they did not think themselves free by coming hither. The setting 14,000 or 15,000 men at once loose by a solemn opinion, is very disagreeable in the effects it threatens. There is a case in Hobart, (Coventry and Woodfall,) where a man had contracted to go as a mariner: but the now case will not come within that decision. Mr. Steuart advances no claims on contract; he rests his whole demand on a right to the negro as slave, and mentions the purpose of detainure to be the sending of him over to be sold in Jamaica. If the parties will have judgment, 'fiat justitia, ruat coelum;' let justice be done whatever be the consequence. 50*l.* a-head may not be a high price; then a loss follows to the proprietors of above 700,000*l.* sterling. How would the law stand with respect to their settlement; their wages? How many actions for any slight coercion by the master? We cannot in any of these points direct the law; the law must rule us. In these particulars, it may be matter of weighty consideration, what provisions are made or set by law. Mr. Steuart may end the question, by discharging or giving freedom to the negro. I did think at first to put the matter to a more solemn way of argument: but if my brothers agree, there seems no occasion. I do not imagine, after the point has been discussed on both sides so extremely well, any new light could be thrown on the subject. If the parties chuse to refer it to the Common Pleas, they can give themselves that satisfaction whenever they think fit. An application to parliament, if the merchants think the question of great commercial concern, is the best, and perhaps the only method of settling the point for the future. The Court is greatly obliged to the gentlemen of the bar who have spoke on the subject; and by whose care and abilities so much has been effected, that the rule of decision will be reduced to a very easy compass. I cannot omit to express particular happiness in seeing young men, just called to the bar, have been able so much to profit by their reading. I think it is right the matter should stand over; and if we are called on for a decision, proper notice shall be given. [The hearing was adjourned until June 22, 1771.]

Trinity Term, June 22, 1772.

Lord Mansfield: On the part of Sommersett, the case which we gave notice should be decided this day, the Court now proceeds to give its opinion. I shall recite the return to the writ of Habeas Corpus, as the ground of our determination; omitting only words of form. The captain of the ship on board of which the negro was taken, makes his return to the writ in terms signifying that there have been, and still are, slaves to a great number in Africa; and that the trade in them is authorized by the laws and opinions of Virginia and Jamaica; that they are goods and chattels; and, as such, saleable and sold. That James Sommersett is a negro of Africa, and long before the return of the king's writ was brought to be sold, and was sold to Charles Steuart, esq. then in Jamaica, and has not been manumitted since; that Mr. Steuart, having occasion to transact business, came over hither, with an intention to return; and brought Sommersett to attend and abide with him, and to carry him back as soon as the business should be transacted. That such intention has been, and still continues; and that the negro did remain till the time of his departure in the service of his master Mr. Steuart, and quitted it without his consent; and thereupon, before the return of the king's writ, the said Charles Steuart did commit the slave on board the Anne and Mary, to safe custody, to be kept till he should set sail, and then to be taken with him to Jamaica, and there sold as a slave. And this is the cause why he, captain Knowles, who was then and now is, commander of the above vessel, then and now lying in the river of Thames, did the said negro, committed to his custody, detain; and on which he now renders him to the orders of the Court. We pay all due attention to the opinion of sir Philip Yorke, and lord chancellor Talbot, whereby they pledged themselves to the British planters, for all the legal consequences of slaves coming over to this kingdom or being baptized, recognized by lord Hardwicke, sitting as chancellor on the 19th of October, 1749, that trover would lie: that a notion had prevailed, if a negro came over, or became a Christian, he was emancipated, but no ground in law: that he and lord Talbot, when attorney and solicitor-general, were of opinion, that no such claim for freedom was valid; that though the statute of tenures had abolished villeins regardant to a manor, yet he did not conceive but that a man might still become a villein in gross, by confessing himself such in open court. We are so well agreed, that we think there is no occasion of having it argued (as I intimated an intention at first,) before all the judges, as is usual, for obvious reasons, on a return to Habeas Corpus. The only question before us is, whether the cause on the return is sufficient? If it is, the negro must be remanded; if it is not, he must be discharged. Accordingly, the return states, that the slave departed and refused to serve; whereupon he was kept, to be sold abroad. So high an act of dominion must be recognized by the law of the country where it is used. The power of a master over his slave has

been extremely different, in different countries. The state of slavery is of such a nature, that it is incapable of being introduced on any reasons, moral or political, but only by positive law, which preserves its force long after the reasons, occasion, and time itself from whence it was created, is erased from memory. It is so odious, that nothing can be suffered to support it, but positive law. Whatever inconveniences, therefore, may follow from the decision, I cannot say this case is allowed or approved by the law of England; and therefore the black must be discharged.

(b) *Baker v. Canada (Minister of Citizenship and Immigration)* [Revisited]†

[L'HEUREUX-DUBÉ J. (for Gonthier, McLachlin, Bastarache, Binnie JJ, and himself).:]

[1] Regulations made pursuant to s. 114(2) of the *Immigration Act*, R.S.C., 1985, c. I-2, empower the respondent Minister to facilitate the admission to Canada of a person where the Minister is satisfied, owing to humanitarian and compassionate considerations, that admission should be facilitated or an exemption from the regulations made under the Act should be granted. At the centre of this appeal is the approach to be taken by a court to judicial review of such decisions, both on procedural and substantive grounds. It also raises issues of reasonable apprehension of bias, the provision of written reasons as part of the duty of fairness, and the role of children's interests in reviewing decisions made pursuant to s. 114(2).

. . . .

IV.   ISSUES

[11] Because, in my view, the issues raised can be resolved under the principles of administrative law and statutory interpretation, I find it unnecessary to consider the various *Charter* issues raised by the appellant and the interveners who supported her position. The issues raised by this appeal are therefore as follows:

(1) What is the legal effect of a stated question under s. 83(1) of the *Immigration Act* on the scope of appellate review?

(2) Were the principles of procedural fairness violated in this case?

　(i) Were the participatory rights accorded consistent with the duty of procedural fairness?

　(ii) Did the failure of Officer Caden to provide his own reasons violate the principles of procedural fairness?

　(iii) Was there a reasonable apprehension of bias in the making of this decision?

(3) Was this discretion improperly exercised because of the approach taken to the interests of Ms. Baker's children?

I note that it is the third issue that raises directly the issues contained in the certified question of general importance stated by Simpson J.

V.   ANALYSIS

. . . .

B.   The Statutory Scheme and the Nature of the Decision

[13] Before examining the various grounds for judicial review, it is appropriate to discuss briefly the

---

† [1999] 2 S.C.R. 817, [1999] S.C.J. No. 39, at paras 1, 11, 13–28, 30–40, 43–48, 76. See paras. 2–7, in Chapter 4(c), for a summary of the facts in the case.

nature of the decision made under s. 114(2) of the *Immigration Act*, the role of this decision in the statutory scheme, and the guidelines given by the Minister to immigration officers in relation to it.

[14] Section 114(2) itself authorizes the Governor in Council to authorize the Minister to exempt a person from a regulation made under the Act, or to facilitate the admission to Canada of any person. The Minister's power to grant an exemption based on humanitarian and compassionate (H & C) considerations arises from s. 2.1 of the *Immigration Regulations*, which I reproduce for convenience:

> The Minister is hereby authorized to exempt any person from any regulation made under subsection 114(1) of the Act or otherwise facilitate the admission to Canada of any person where the Minister is satisfied that the person should be exempted from that regulation or that the person's admission should be facilitated owing to the existence of compassionate or humanitarian considerations.

For the purpose of clarity, I will refer throughout these reasons to decisions made pursuant to the combination of s. 114(2) of the Act and s. 2.1 of the Regulations as "H & C decisions".

[15] Applications for permanent residence must, as a general rule, be made from outside Canada, pursuant to s. 9(1) of the Act. One of the exceptions to this is when admission is facilitated owing to the existence of compassionate or humanitarian considerations. In law, pursuant to the Act and the Regulations, an H & C decision is made by the Minister, though in practice, this decision is dealt with in the name of the Minister by immigration officers: see, for example, *Minister of Employment and Immigration v. Jiminez-Perez*, [1984] 2 S.C.R. 565, at p. 569. In addition, while in law, the H & C decision is one that provides for an <u>exemption</u> from regulations or from the Act, in practice, it is one that, in cases like this one, determines whether a person who has been in Canada but does not have status can stay in the country or will be required to leave a place where he or she has become established. It is an important decision that affects in a fundamental manner the future of individuals' lives. In addition, it may also have an important impact on the lives of any Canadian children of the person whose humanitarian and compassionate application is being considered, since they may be separated from one of their parents and/or uprooted from their country of citizenship, where they have settled and have connections.

[16] Immigration officers who make H & C decisions are provided with a set of guidelines, contained in chapter 9 of the *Immigration Manual: Examination and Enforcement*. The guidelines constitute instructions to immigration officers about how to exercise the discretion delegated to them. These guidelines are also available to the public. A number of statements in the guidelines are relevant to Ms. Baker's application. Guideline 9.05 emphasizes that officers have a duty to decide which cases should be given a favourable recommendation, by carefully considering all aspects of the case, using their best judgment and asking themselves what a reasonable person would do in such a situation. It also states that although officers are not expected to "delve into areas which are not presented during examination or interviews, they should attempt to clarify possible humanitarian grounds and public policy considerations even if these are not well articulated".

[17] The guidelines also set out the bases upon which the discretion conferred by s. 114(2) and the Regulations should be exercised. Two different types of criteria that may lead to a positive s. 114(2) decision are outlined — public policy considerations and humanitarian and compassionate grounds. Immigration officers are instructed, under guideline 9.07, to assure themselves, first, whether a public policy consideration is present, and if there is none, whether humanitarian and compassionate circumstances exist. Public policy reasons include marriage to a Canadian resident, the fact that the person has lived in Canada, has become established, and has become an "illegal de facto resident", and the fact that the person may be a long-term holder of employment authorization or has worked as a foreign domestic. Guideline 9.07 states that humanitarian and compassionate grounds will exist if "unusual, undeserved or disproportionate hardship would be caused to the person seeking consideration if he or she had to leave Canada". The guidelines also directly address situations involving family dependency, and emphasize that the requirement that a person leave Canada to apply from abroad may result in hardship for close family members of a Canadian resident, whether parents, children, or others who are close to the claimant, but not related by blood. They note that in such cases, the reasons why the person did not apply from abroad and the existence of family or other support in the person's home country should also be considered.

C. Procedural Fairness

[18] The first ground upon which the appellant challenges the decision made by Officer Caden is the allegation that she was not accorded procedural fairness. She suggests that the following procedures are required by the duty of fairness when parents have Canadian children and they make an H & C application: an oral interview before the decision-maker, notice to her children and the other parent of that interview, a right for the children and the other parent to make submissions at that interview, and notice to the other parent of the interview and of that person's right to have counsel present. She also alleges that procedural fairness requires the provision of reasons by the decision-maker, Officer Caden, and that the notes of Officer Lorenz give rise to a reasonable apprehension of bias.

[19] In addressing the fairness issues, I will consider first the principles relevant to the determination of the content of the duty of procedural fairness, and then address Ms. Baker's arguments that she was accorded insufficient participatory rights, that a duty to give reasons existed, and that there was a reasonable apprehension of bias.

[20] Both parties agree that a duty of procedural fairness applies to H & C decisions. The fact that a decision is administrative and affects "the rights, privileges or interests of an individual" is sufficient to trigger the application of the duty of fairness: *Cardinal v. Director of Kent Institution*, [1985] 2 S.C.R. 643, at p. 653. Clearly, the determination of whether an applicant will be exempted from the requirements of the Act falls within this category, and it has been long recognized that the duty of fairness applies to H & C decisions: *Sobrie v. Canada (Minister of Employment and Immigration)* (1987), 3 Imm. L.R. (2d) 81 (F.C.T.D.), at p. 88; *Said v. Canada (Minister of Employment and Immigration)* (1992), 6 Admin. L.R. (2d) 23 (F.C.T.D.); *Shah v. Minister of Employment and Immigration* (1994), 170 N.R. 238 (F.C.A.).

(1) Factors Affecting the Content of the Duty of Fairness

[21] The existence of a duty of fairness, however, does not determine what requirements will be applicable in a given set of circumstances. As I wrote in *Knight v. Indian Head School Division No. 19*, [1990] 1 S.C.R. 653, at p. 682, "the concept of procedural fairness is eminently variable and its content is to be decided in the specific context of each case". All of the circumstances must be considered in order

to determine the content of the duty of procedural fairness: *Knight*, at pp. 682–83; *Cardinal, supra*, at p. 654; *Old St. Boniface Residents Assn. Inc. v. Winnipeg (City)*, [1990] 3 S.C.R. 1170, *per* Sopinka J.

[22] Although the duty of fairness is flexible and variable, and depends on an appreciation of the context of the particular statute and the rights affected, it is helpful to review the criteria that should be used in determining what procedural rights the duty of fairness requires in a given set of circumstances. I emphasize that underlying all these factors is the notion that the purpose of the participatory rights contained within the duty of procedural fairness is to ensure that administrative decisions are made using a fair and open procedure, appropriate to the decision being made and its statutory, institutional, and social context, with an opportunity for those affected by the decision to put forward their views and evidence fully and have them considered by the decision-maker.

[23] Several factors have been recognized in the jurisprudence as relevant to determining what is required by the common law duty of procedural fairness in a given set of circumstances. One important consideration is the nature of the decision being made and the process followed in making it. In *Knight, supra*, at p. 683, it was held that "the closeness of the administrative process to the judicial process should indicate how much of those governing principles should be imported into the realm of administrative decision making". The more the process provided for, the function of the tribunal, the nature of the decision-making body, and the determinations that must be made to reach a decision resemble judicial decision making, the more likely it is that procedural protections closer to the trial model will be required by the duty of fairness. See also *Old St. Boniface, supra*, at p. 1191; *Russell v. Duke of Norfolk*, [1949] 1 All E.R. 109 (C.A.), at p. 118; *Syndicat des employés de production du Québec et de l'Acadie v. Canada (Canadian Human Rights Commission)*, [1989] 2 S.C.R. 879, at p. 896, *per* Sopinka J.

[24] A second factor is the nature of the statutory scheme and the "terms of the statute pursuant to which the body operates": *Old St. Boniface, supra*, at p. 1191. The role of the particular decision within the statutory scheme and other surrounding indications in the statute help determine the content of the duty of fairness owed when a particular administrative decision is made. Greater procedural protections, for example, will be required when no appeal proce-

dure is provided within the statute, or when the decision is determinative of the issue and further requests cannot be submitted: see D. J. M. Brown and J. M. Evans, *Judicial Review of Administrative Action in Canada* (loose-leaf), at pp. 7-66 to 7-67.

[25] A third factor in determining the nature and extent of the duty of fairness owed is the importance of the decision to the individual or individuals affected. The more important the decision is to the lives of those affected and the greater its impact on that person or those persons, the more stringent the procedural protections that will be mandated. This was expressed, for example, by Dickson J. (as he then was) in *Kane v. Board of Governors of the University of British Columbia*, [1980] 1 S.C.R. 1105, at p. 1113:

> A high standard of justice is required when the right to continue in one's profession or employment is at stake.... A disciplinary suspension can have grave and permanent consequences upon a professional career.

As Sedley J. (now Sedley L.J.) stated in *R. v. Higher Education Funding Council, ex parte Institute of Dental Surgery*, [1994] 1 All E.R. 651 (Q.B.), at p. 667:

> In the modern state the decisions of administrative bodies can have a more immediate and profound impact on people's lives than the decisions of courts, and public law has since *Ridge v. Baldwin* [1963] 2 All E.R. 66, [1964] A.C. 40 been alive to that fact. While the judicial character of a function may elevate the practical requirements of fairness above what they would otherwise be, for example by requiring contentious evidence to be given and tested orally, what makes it "judicial" in this sense is principally the nature of the issue it has to determine, not the formal status of the deciding body.

The importance of a decision to the individuals affected, therefore, constitutes a significant factor affecting the content of the duty of procedural fairness.

[26] Fourth, the legitimate expectations of the person challenging the decision may also determine what procedures the duty of fairness requires in given circumstances. Our Court has held that, in Canada, this doctrine is part of the doctrine of fairness or natural justice, and that it does not create substantive rights: *Old St. Boniface, supra*, at p. 1204; *Reference re Canada Assistance Plan (B.C.)*, [1991] 2 S.C.R. 525, at p. 557. As applied in Canada, if a legitimate expectation is found to exist, this will affect the content of the duty of fairness owed to the individual or individuals affected by the decision. If the claimant has a legitimate expectation that a certain procedure will be followed, this procedure will be required by the duty of fairness: *Qi v. Canada (Minister of Citizenship and Immigration)* (1995), 33 Imm. L.R. (2d) 57 (F.C.T.D.); *Mercier-Néron v. Canada (Minister of National Health and Welfare)* (1995), 98 F.T.R. 36; *Bendahmane v. Canada (Minister of Employment and Immigration)*, [1989] 3 F.C. 16 (C.A.). Similarly, if a claimant has a legitimate expectation that a certain result will be reached in his or her case, fairness may require more extensive procedural rights than would otherwise be accorded: D. J. Mullan, *Administrative Law* (3rd ed. 1996), at pp. 214–15; D. Shapiro, "Legitimate Expectation and its Application to Canadian Immigration Law" (1992), 8 *J.L. & Social Pol'y* 282, at p. 297; *Canada (Attorney General) v. Human Rights Tribunal Panel (Canada)* (1994), 76 F.T.R. 1. Nevertheless, the doctrine of legitimate expectations cannot lead to substantive rights outside the procedural domain. This doctrine, as applied in Canada, is based on the principle that the "circumstances" affecting procedural fairness take into account the promises or regular practices of administrative decision-makers, and that it will generally be unfair for them to act in contravention of representations as to procedure, or to backtrack on substantive promises without according significant procedural rights.

[27] Fifth, the analysis of what procedures the duty of fairness requires should also take into account and respect the choices of procedure made by the agency itself, particularly when the statute leaves to the decision-maker the ability to choose its own procedures, or when the agency has an expertise in determining what procedures are appropriate in the circumstances: Brown and Evans, *supra*, at pp. 7-66 to 7-70. While this, of course, is not determinative, important weight must be given to the choice of procedures made by the agency itself and its institutional constraints: *IWA v. Consolidated-Bathurst Packaging Ltd.*, [1990] 1 S.C.R. 282, *per* Gonthier J.

[28] I should note that this list of factors is not exhaustive. These principles all help a court determine whether the procedures that were followed respected the duty of fairness. Other factors may also be important, particularly when considering aspects of the duty of fairness unrelated to participatory rights. The values underlying the duty of procedural fairness relate to the principle that the individual or individuals affected should have the opportunity to present their case fully and fairly, and have decisions affecting their rights, interests, or

privileges made using a fair, impartial, and open process, appropriate to the statutory, institutional, and social context of the decision.

. . . . .

(3) Participatory Rights

[30] The next issue is whether, taking into account the other factors related to the determination of the content of the duty of fairness, the failure to accord an oral hearing and give notice to Ms. Baker or her children was inconsistent with the participatory rights required by the duty of fairness in these circumstances. At the heart of this analysis is whether, considering all the circumstances, those whose interests were affected had a meaningful opportunity to present their case fully and fairly. The procedure in this case consisted of a written application with supporting documentation, which was summarized by the junior officer (Lorenz), with a recommendation being made by that officer. The summary, recommendation, and material was then considered by the senior officer (Caden), who made the decision.

[31] Several of the factors described above enter into the determination of the type of participatory rights the duty of procedural fairness requires in the circumstances. First, an H & C decision is very different from a judicial decision, since it involves the exercise of considerable discretion and requires the consideration of multiple factors. Second, its role is also, within the statutory scheme, as an exception to the general principles of Canadian immigration law. These factors militate in favour of more relaxed requirements under the duty of fairness. On the other hand, there is no appeal procedure, although judicial review may be applied for with leave of the Federal Court — Trial Division. In addition, considering the third factor, this is a decision that in practice has exceptional importance to the lives of those with an interest in its result — the claimant and his or her close family members — and this leads to the content of the duty of fairness being more extensive. Finally, applying the fifth factor described above, the statute accords considerable flexibility to the Minister to decide on the proper procedure, and immigration officers, as a matter of practice, do not conduct interviews in all cases. The institutional practices and choices made by the Minister are significant, though of course not determinative factors to be considered in the analysis. Thus, it can be seen that although some of the factors suggest stricter requirements under the duty of fairness, others suggest more relaxed requirements further from the judicial model.

[32] Balancing these factors, I disagree with the holding of the Federal Court of Appeal in *Shah, supra*, at p. 239, that the duty of fairness owed in these circumstances is simply "minimal". Rather, the circumstances require a full and fair consideration of the issues, and the claimant and others whose important interests are affected by the decision in a fundamental way must have a meaningful opportunity to present the various types of evidence relevant to their case and have it fully and fairly considered.

[33] However, it also cannot be said that an oral hearing is always necessary to ensure a fair hearing and consideration of the issues involved. The flexible nature of the duty of fairness recognizes that meaningful participation can occur in different ways in different situations. The Federal Court has held that procedural fairness does not require an oral hearing in these circumstances: see, for example, *Said, supra*, at p. 30.

[34] I agree that an oral hearing is not a general requirement for H & C decisions. An interview is not essential for the information relevant to an H & C application to be put before an immigration officer, so that the humanitarian and compassionate considerations presented may be considered in their entirety and in a fair manner. In this case, the appellant had the opportunity to put forward, in written form through her lawyer, information about her situation, her children and their emotional dependence on her, and documentation in support of her application from a social worker at the Children's Aid Society and from her psychiatrist. These documents were before the decision-makers, and they contained the information relevant to making this decision. Taking all the factors relevant to determining the content of the duty of fairness into account, the lack of an oral hearing or notice of such a hearing did not, in my opinion, constitute a violation of the requirements of procedural fairness to which Ms. Baker was entitled in the circumstances, particularly given the fact that several of the factors point toward a more relaxed standard. The opportunity, which was accorded, for the appellant or her children to produce full and complete written documentation in relation to all aspects of her application satisfied the requirements of the participatory rights required by the duty of fairness in this case.

(4) The Provision of Reasons

[35] The appellant also submits that the duty of fairness, in these circumstances, requires that reasons be given by the decision-maker. She argues either that

the notes of Officer Lorenz should be considered the reasons for the decision, or that it should be held that the failure of Officer Caden to give written reasons for his decision or a subsequent affidavit explaining them should be taken to be a breach of the principles of fairness.

[36] This issue has been addressed in several cases of judicial review of humanitarian and compassionate applications. The Federal Court of Appeal has held that reasons are unnecessary: *Shah*, *supra*, at pp. 239–40. It has also been held that the case history notes prepared by a subordinate officer are not to be considered the decision-maker's reasons: see *Tylo v. Minister of Employment and Immigration* (1995), 90 F.T.R. 157, at pp. 159–60. In *Gheorlan v. Canada (Secretary of State)* (1995), 26 Imm. L.R. (2d) 170 (F.C.T.D.), and *Chan v. Canada (Minister of Citizenship and Immigration)* (1994), 87 F.T.R. 62, it was held that the notes of the reviewing officer should not be taken to be the reasons for decision, but may help in determining whether a reviewable error exists. In *Marques v. Canada (Minister of Citizenship and Immigration) (No. 1)* (1995), 116 F.T.R. 241, an H & C decision was set aside because the decision-making officer failed to provide reasons or an affidavit explaining the reasons for his decision.

[37] More generally, the traditional position at common law has been that the duty of fairness does not require, as a general rule, that reasons be provided for administrative decisions: *Northwestern Utilities Ltd. v. City of Edmonton*, [1979] 1 S.C.R. 684; *Supermarchés Jean Labrecque Inc. v. Flamand*, [1987] 2 S.C.R. 219, at p. 233; *Public Service Board of New South Wales v. Osmond* (1986), 159 C.L.R. 656 (H.C.A.), at pp. 665–66.

[38] Courts and commentators have, however, often emphasized the usefulness of reasons in ensuring fair and transparent decision-making. Though *Northwestern Utilities* dealt with a statutory obligation to give reasons, Estey J. held as follows, at p. 706, referring to the desirability of a common law reasons requirement:

> This obligation is a salutary one. It reduces to a considerable degree the chances of arbitrary or capricious decisions, reinforces public confidence in the judgment and fairness of administrative tribunals, and affords parties to administrative proceedings an opportunity to assess the question of appeal....

The importance of reasons was recently reemphasized by this Court in *Reference re Remuneration of Judges of the Provincial Court of Prince Edward Island*, [1997] 3 S.C.R. 3, at paras. 180–81.

[39] Reasons, it has been argued, foster better decision making by ensuring that issues and reasoning are well articulated and, therefore, more carefully thought out. The process of writing reasons for decision by itself may be a guarantee of a better decision. Reasons also allow parties to see that the applicable issues have been carefully considered, and are invaluable if a decision is to be appealed, questioned, or considered on judicial review: R. A. Macdonald and D. Lametti, "Reasons for Decision in Administrative Law" (1990), 3 *C.J.A.L.P.* 123, at p. 146; *Williams v. Canada (Minister of Citizenship and Immigration)*, [1997] 2 F.C. 646 (C.A.), at para. 38. Those affected may be more likely to feel they were treated fairly and appropriately if reasons are given: de Smith, Woolf, & Jowell, *Judicial Review of Administrative Action* (5th ed. 1995), at pp. 459–60. I agree that these are significant benefits of written reasons.

[40] Others have expressed concerns about the desirability of a written reasons requirement at common law. In *Osmond*, *supra*, Gibbs C.J. articulated, at p. 668, the concern that a reasons requirement may lead to an inappropriate burden being imposed on administrative decision-makers, that it may lead to increased cost and delay, and that it "might in some cases induce a lack of candour on the part of the administrative officers concerned". Macdonald and Lametti, *supra*, though they agree that fairness should require the provision of reasons in certain circumstances, caution against a requirement of "archival" reasons associated with court judgments, and note that the special nature of agency decision-making in different contexts should be considered in evaluating reasons requirements. In my view, however, these concerns can be accommodated by ensuring that any reasons requirement under the duty of fairness leaves sufficient flexibility to decision-makers by accepting various types of written explanations for the decision as sufficient.

. . . .

[43] In my opinion, it is now appropriate to recognize that, in certain circumstances, the duty of procedural fairness will require the provision of a written explanation for a decision. The strong arguments demonstrating the advantages of written reasons suggest that, in cases such as this where the decision has important significance for the individual, when there is a statutory right of appeal, or in other

circumstances, some form of reasons should be required. This requirement has been developing in the common law elsewhere. The circumstances of the case at bar, in my opinion, constitute one of the situations where reasons are necessary. The profound importance of an H & C decision to those affected, as with those at issue in *Orlowski*, *Cunningham*, and *Doody*, militates in favour of a requirement that reasons be provided. It would be unfair for a person subject to a decision such as this one which is so critical to their future not to be told why the result was reached.

[44] In my view, however, the reasons requirement was fulfilled in this case since the appellant was provided with the notes of Officer Lorenz. The notes were given to Ms. Baker when her counsel asked for reasons. Because of this, and because there is no other record of the reasons for making the decision, the notes of the subordinate reviewing officer should be taken, by inference, to be the reasons for decision. Accepting documents such as these notes as sufficient reasons is part of the flexibility that is necessary, as emphasized by Macdonald and Lametti, *supra*, when courts evaluate the requirements of the duty of fairness with recognition of the day-to-day realities of administrative agencies and the many ways in which the values underlying the principles of procedural fairness can be assured. It upholds the principle that individuals are entitled to fair procedures and open decision-making, but recognizes that in the administrative context, this transparency may take place in various ways. I conclude that the notes of Officer Lorenz satisfy the requirement for reasons under the duty of procedural fairness in this case, and they will be taken to be the reasons for decision.

(5) Reasonable Apprehension of Bias

[45] Procedural fairness also requires that decisions be made free from a reasonable apprehension of bias by an impartial decision-maker. The respondent argues that Simpson J. was correct to find that the notes of Officer Lorenz cannot be considered to give rise to a reasonable apprehension of bias because it was Officer Caden who was the actual decision-maker, who was simply reviewing the recommendation prepared by his subordinate. In my opinion, the duty to act fairly and therefore in a manner that does not give rise to a reasonable apprehension of bias applies to all immigration officers who play a significant role in the making of decisions, whether they are subordinate reviewing officers, or those who make the final decision. The subordinate officer

plays an important part in the process, and if a person with such a central role does not act impartially, the decision itself cannot be said to have been made in an impartial manner. In addition, as discussed in the previous section, the notes of Officer Lorenz constitute the reasons for the decision, and if they give rise to a reasonable apprehension of bias, this taints the decision itself.

[46] The test for reasonable apprehension of bias was set out by de Grandpré J., writing in dissent, in *Committee for Justice and Liberty v. National Energy Board*, [1978] 1 S.C.R. 369, at p. 394:

> ... the apprehension of bias must be a reasonable one, held by reasonable and right minded persons, applying themselves to the question and obtaining thereon the required information ... [T]hat test is "what would an informed person, viewing the matter realistically and practically — and having thought the matter through — conclude. Would he think that it is more likely than not that [the decision-maker], whether consciously or unconsciously, would not decide fairly."

This expression of the test has often been endorsed by this Court, most recently in *R. v. S. (R.D.)*, [1997] 3 S.C.R. 484, at para. 11, *per* Major J.; at para. 31, *per* L'Heureux-Dubé and McLachlin JJ.; and at para. 111, *per* Cory J.

[47] It has been held that the standards for reasonable apprehension of bias may vary, like other aspects of procedural fairness, depending on the context and the type of function performed by the administrative decision-maker involved: *Newfoundland Telephone Co. v. Newfoundland (Board of Commissioners of Public Utilities)*, [1992] 1 S.C.R. 623; *Old St. Boniface, supra*, at p. 1192. The context here is one where immigration officers must regularly make decisions that have great importance to the individuals affected by them, but are also often critical to the interests of Canada as a country. They are individualized, rather than decisions of a general nature. They also require special sensitivity. Canada is a nation made up largely of people whose families migrated here in recent centuries. Our history is one that shows the importance of immigration, and our society shows the benefits of having a diversity of people whose origins are in a multitude of places around the world. Because they necessarily relate to people of diverse backgrounds, from different cultures, races, and continents, immigration decisions demand sensitivity and understanding by those making them. They require a recognition of diversity, an understanding of others, and an openness to difference.

[48] In my opinion, the well-informed member of the community would perceive bias when reading Officer Lorenz's comments. His notes, and the manner in which they are written, do not disclose the existence of an open mind or a weighing of the particular circumstances of the case free from stereotypes. Most unfortunate is the fact that they seem to make a link between Ms. Baker's mental illness, her training as a domestic worker, the fact that she has several children, and the conclusion that she would therefore be a strain on our social welfare system for the rest of her life. In addition, the conclusion drawn was contrary to the psychiatrist's letter, which stated that, with treatment, Ms. Baker could remain well and return to being a productive member of society. Whether they were intended in this manner or not, these statements give the impression that Officer Lorenz may have been drawing conclusions based not on the evidence before him, but on the fact that Ms. Baker was a single mother with several children, and had been diagnosed with a psychiatric illness. His use of capitals to highlight the number of Ms. Baker's children may also suggest to a reader that this was a reason to deny her status. Reading his comments, I do not believe that a reasonable and well-informed member of the community would conclude that he had approached this case with the impartiality appropriate to a decision made by an immigration officer. It would appear to a reasonable observer that his own frustration with the "system" interfered with his duty to consider impartially whether the appellant's admission should be facilitated owing to humanitarian or compassionate considerations. I conclude that the notes of Officer Lorenz demonstrate a reasonable apprehension of bias.

. . . .

E.   Conclusions and Disposition

[76] Therefore, both because there was a violation of the principles of procedural fairness owing to a reasonable apprehension of bias, and because the exercise of the H & C discretion was unreasonable, I would allow this appeal.

(c)   The Concept of Human Dignity†

Pierre Elliott Trudeau

The very adoption of a constitutional charter is in keeping with the purest liberalism, according to which all members of a civil society enjoy certain fundamental, inalienable rights and cannot be deprived of them by any collectivity (state or government) or on behalf of any collectivity (nation, ethnic group, religious group, or other). To use Maritain's phrase, they are "human personalities," they are beings of a moral order — that is, free and equal among themselves, each having absolute dignity and infinite value. As such, they transcend the accidents of place and time, and partake in the essence of universal Humanity. They are therefore not coercible by any ancestral tradition, being vassals neither of their race, nor to their religion, nor to their condition of birth, nor to their collective history.

† From *The Essential Trudeau / Pierre Elliott Trudeau* edited by Ron Graham (Toronto: McClelland and Stewart, 1998) at 80. © by Pierre Elliott Trudeau. Used with the permission of the publisher.

(d) It Takes A Vision: The Constitutionalization of Equality in Canada[†]

The Honorable Claire L'Heureux-Dubé

Combining paid work with motherhood and accommodating the childbearing needs of working women are ever-increasing imperatives. That those who bear children and benefit society as a whole thereby should not be economically or socially disadvantaged seems to bespeak the obvious. It is only women who bear children; no man can become pregnant.... it is unfair to impose all of the costs of pregnancy upon one half of the population.[1]

I. INTRODUCTION

With these ringing words, in 1988 the Supreme Court of Canada overturned its prior jurisprudence on women's equality rights. The author was Chief Justice Brian Dickson, a person I consider to have been one of Canada's great feminists. After all, you know you've made a good deal of progress toward equality when your male Chief Justice is citing Catharine MacKinnon on sexual harassment in the workplace![2]

I am a great believer in the positive impact of Canada's constitutional guarantee of equality, found in section 15 of our Canadian Charter of Rights and Freedoms, which guarantees the right to be "equal before and under the law" and "to the equal protection and equal benefit of the law without discrimination and, in particular, without discrimination based on race, national or ethnic origin, color, religion, sex, age or mental or physical disability."[3] While the Canadian model cannot and should not simply be transposed into other contexts, exploring how and why section 15 came into being in Canada provides valuable insight into the positive effects that constitutionalizing equality may bring. Specifically, I will outline how and why Canadian women contributed to the adoption of section 15 of the Charter, as well as show how their vision has helped to bring about greater justice for all through a major transformation of Canadian law.

II. BACKGROUND TO THE CONSTITUTIONALIZATION OF EQUALITY IN CANADA

But first, a little background. In 1867, Canada became a country.[4] We had a written constitution, but it contained no express guarantee of human rights or civil liberties. This did not stop five women from going to the courts in 1929 to ask a rather fundamental question: Are women persons? They needed to know in order to be appointed to Canada's Senate, among other things. In 1928, the Supreme Court of Canada said "no", women are not persons.[5] In 1929, the Law Lords of the British Privy Council, then our highest court of appeal, overturned that decision and held that women were persons, at least within the meaning of certain sections of the Canadian Constitution.[6] Lord Sankey took care to note, however, that "No doubt in any code where women were expressly excluded from public office, the problem would present no difficulty."[7] Clearly, Canadian women were still a long way from a constitutional right to equality!

The struggle continued, however, and gradually some of the most blatant limitations on women's rights to work and to own property were removed due to political pressures. Then, in 1960, Canadians got a Bill of Rights,[8] which recognized every individual's right to equality before the law and the equal protection of the law. The Bill of Rights had an important limitation, however: While it stated that it could invalidate another federal law, it was only an ordinary law itself, not a constitutional document.

Perhaps for this reason, courts interpreted the equality guarantee narrowly, as a formal and procedural right rather than a substantive one. In other words, if like people were treated the same, the treatment would not be subject to scrutiny on equality grounds, even though differing social groups were not accorded equal treatment. Thus, to give one of the most infamous examples, in the 1979 decision in *Bliss v. Canada*,[9] the Court decided that the denial of benefits on the basis of pregnancy did not consti-

---

† (2002) 14 Yale J.L. & Feminism 363 at 363–68, 370–75. [Notes and/or references omitted.] Reproduced with permission.

tute sex discrimination, finding instead that: "If section 46 treats unemployed pregnant women differently from other unemployed persons, be they male or female, it is ... because they are pregnant and not because they are women."[10] Needless to say, women quickly realized that the Bill of Rights had not provided them with an effective tool for achieving greater equality.

At the same time, however, some judges were beginning to take a more "enlightened" view of women's role in society, particularly in the context of family law. In 1975, for instance, Justice Laskin, later to become Chief Justice of the Supreme Court, wrote in a dissenting judgment:

> No doubt, legislative action may be the better way to lay down policies and prescribe conditions under which and the extent to which spouses should share in property acquired by either or both during marriage. But the better way is not the only way; and if the exercise of a traditional jurisdiction by the Courts can conduce to equitable sharing, it should not be withheld merely because [of] difficulties in particular cases....[11]

By 1978, his views on the need for a doctrine of equitable sharing upon the breakdown of marriage had the support of two other Supreme Court judges and had influenced the other judges to a significant extent.[12]

Not surprisingly, each of these contradictory trends in Canada's Supreme Court jurisprudence inspired women to make concerted efforts in the political sphere to obtain greater recognition of their rights. The time was right: In the late 1970s, Prime Minister Pierre Trudeau opened the door to a process of constitutional renewal in Canada. Although the initiative was partly to secure the final and total independence of Canada from Great Britain, the focal point of the renewal was the proposed Charter of Rights and Freedoms.

As a bit of an aside, I note that the initial drafts of the Charter presented to the public in 1980 made it clear that the government of the day was using the framework set out in international human rights conventions as its model,[13] rather than the civil liberties model found in the American Bill of Rights.[14] As Madam Justice Rosalie Abella has observed, the key insight of the human rights approach is that human beings should not only be free from the intrusive state but should also be treated with dignity and should have the means necessary for full and equal participation in society. Since human dignity and equal participation encompass both individual and collective aspects of the

human experience, the human rights approach requires balancing the rights of individuals, the recognition that historically disadvantaged or minority groups may need special protection, and the collective social interest. Fundamentally, the human rights approach requires that society be free from discrimination.[15]

Thus, while the Charter's initial drafters may not have been aware of it, their selection of the human rights model set the stage for a uniquely Canadian approach to equality, shaped in large part by women, as well as by advocates for the disabled and other disadvantaged groups in Canadian society.

At this historic moment, women were more organized than ever before, with a publicly funded lobby group providing strong leadership in the constitutional process.[16] With great perseverance, they pursued three key demands with respect to the draft Charter: first, the language of the equality guarantee had to be *broader* than that of the Bill of Rights; second, distinctions based on sex had to be subject to a *stringent review* by the courts; and third, the *Charter* had to include a *general statement of equality* between men and women.

Women were obviously sensitive to the language of the draft provision, given their experience with the Bill of Rights. They therefore lobbied for the addition of the words "equal *under* the law" and "equal *benefit* of the law" to the equality guarantee, to ensure that the provision would be more broadly interpreted than the Bill of Rights had been.[17] Their proposed wording was accepted and now forms part of section 15(1) of the Charter.

Canadian women were also aware of the struggle by American women to have the United States Supreme Court accord at least an intermediate level of scrutiny to sex-based distinctions under the Fourteenth Amendment. Some groups therefore sought to have an explicit statement in the Charter guaranteeing the strictest level of scrutiny for distinctions based on "sex." Other groups felt that there should be a uniquely Canadian approach to equality and that the levels of scrutiny approach ought to be avoided. Ultimately, the United States model was rejected by the government. The very fact that a debate took place on the issue, however, led to a public record of government statements favoring a strict test for distinctions on the basis of sex.[18]

Finally, at the eleventh hour, the Ad Hoc Conference on Women and the Constitution, a broadbased women's lobby group, secured the inclusion in the Charter of an overarching equality guarantee to women and men from which there could be no derogation, either in the name of preserving Canada's multicultural heritage, or under the government's temporary legislative "opt-out" from the Charter's application.[19] This is now section 28 of our Charter, which reads: "Notwithstanding anything in this Charter, the rights and freedoms referred to in it are guaranteed equally to male and female persons."

As you can see, Canadian women, and particularly women lawyers, had a significant influence in shaping the discourse surrounding, and the content of, Canada's constitutional equality guarantees. This constitutes one of the most unique aspects of the Canadian guarantee, as its origins both are modem and relatively inclusive.

Just as crucial, however, is the fact that the vision of the women who negotiated section 15 did not end with the adoption of the Charter in 1982. Based in part on consultations with their American counterparts, who had much to share given their long experience with anti-discrimination legislation, these women understood that they would need to follow up with a multifaceted "Charter-watching" strategy.[20] Thus, the Women's Legal Education and Action Fund, or "LEAF," was born.

III. TOWARD SUBSTANTIVE EQUALITY

The Charter-watching strategy included launching test cases, engaging in public education campaigns and producing academic texts on equality.[21] There was also a comprehensive audit of federal and provincial legislation to determine whether it complied with section 15.[22] Above all, however, it was understood that the first case heard by the Supreme Court on the issue would be crucial in determining whether a broader interpretation would be given to section 15 than had been given to the Bill of Rights equality guarantee. For all of these reasons, many of the same women who led the constitutional negotiation efforts formed LEAF specifically for the purpose of ensuring that women's voices would be heard wherever equality issues arose in the courts.

This was an important strategic tactic, particularly since *Andrews v. Law Society of British Columbia*,[23] the first section 15 case to come before the Supreme Court, involved a white, male lawyer from England who argued that his equality rights had been infringed under the Charter because, as a non-citizen, he wasn't able to practice law in the province of British Columbia. Not exactly the ideal test case for women's equality! Nevertheless, LEAF sought and was granted intervenor status in the appeal, along with a number of other groups, in order to ensure that the Supreme Court had before it impor-

tant reminders of all that was at stake when it decided *Andrews*.

In *Andrews*, the Court essentially adopted the purposive approach to section 15 put forth by LEAF, thereby overturning the decisions of the lower courts, which had taken a "similarly situated" approach to equality. Both Justices Bertha Wilson and William McIntyre made it clear in *Andrews* that they understood the purpose of section 15 to be the protection and promotion of what we in Canada call "substantive equality,"[24] meaning equality of opportunity and of result, not just similar treatment for those similarly situated. They did so based on the link made in section 15 between equality and discrimination, which led them to find that the *Charter's* equality provisions had a "large remedial component" requiring the legislature to take positive measures to improve the status of disadvantaged groups. Thus, the Court *broadened* the scope of the equality guarantee.

. . . .

IV. PLACING EQUALITY AT THE HEART OF THE LAW

Convincing the courts to adopt a substantive definition of equality in the abstract is only half the battle, as women and other equality-seekers well know. To be meaningful and effective, a constitutional equality guarantee must not only lie at the heart of the law, it must become its very life-blood.[34] In Canada, it is clear that despite some setbacks, the efforts of women and other equality-seeking groups over the past fifteen years have begun to bring about this necessary transformation in areas such as criminal, family, employment and tort law. Similarly, Canadian courts have increasingly recognized that all decisions must be consistent with the philosophy of substantive equality, even if the parties are not bringing a direct constitutional challenge to the law or state action in question on the basis of their constitutional equality rights.[35]

To give some concrete examples of how the permeation of the law by equality principles may occur, years of dialogue between Parliament and the courts recently culminated in the upholding of significant changes to the manner in which sexual offences are prosecuted. In 1999, our new Chief Justice Beverley McLachlin, writing with Justice Iacobucci, upheld legislation which protects the complainant's therapeutic records from disclosure by the defense, where the evidence is of marginal or no relevance and could lead the trier of fact to make impermissible inferences based on stereotypes about women and discriminatory reasoning.[36] In so finding, the Court balanced the complainant's rights to dignity, privacy and equality with the accused's right to a full answer and defense. Similarly, the Court has recognized that the criminal law must be applied in a manner consistent with equality and therefore that the justice system must understand women's experience.[37]

In family law, equality principles have continued to inform and strengthen doctrines of equitable sharing of the economic consequences of marriage or its breakdown.[38] Somewhat ironically, however, where direct constitutional challenges were brought to income tax legislation relating to the taxation of child care expenses and child support payments, women have not had as much success in court.[39] Parliament has since bowed somewhat, however, to women's demands on this front.[40]

In employment law, the equality guarantees provided by anti-discrimination legislation have proven the most significant means of ensuring that substantive equality applies even in the absence of direct government action. Even though the Charter does not itself apply to most workplaces, it has led to the reinterpretation of this anti-discrimination legislation[41] and has therefore had an important, if indirect, effect on equality rights in the employment context.[42] Post-Charter decisions of the Supreme Court and of human rights commissions have reminded us, for example, that when sexual harassment occurs,[43] when there is systemic discrimination within a workplace,[44] or when rules of the workplace have a negative impact on members of certain groups,[45] discrimination has occurred. In addition, the Supreme Court has recently emphasized the need to ensure that the two streams of statutory and constitutional human rights jurisprudence are consistent in their respect for the principle of substantive equality.[46]

The principle of substantive equality has also begun to permeate certain aspects of the common law. The Supreme Court has held that common law rules must develop "in accordance with 'Charter values,'" including substantive equality.[47] In tort law, the Court has therefore recognized that even though constitutional rights may not be directly in issue, the principle of substantive equality requires that the law take into account women's experiences where they have been ignored or excluded in the course of the law's development, such as with respect to limitation periods and the specific problems they cause in relation to the reasonable discovery of childhood sexual assault.[48] The Court has also recognized the power imbalance which may exist between a male doctor and his female patient.[49]

V. CONCLUSION

Overall, there is no question that section 15 of the Charter has brought about a major and ongoing transformation in many areas of Canadian law. Recognizing that my views are informed by this Canadian experience, in all of its social, historical and political specificity, I hope nevertheless that this overview of why women fought to constitutionalize equality and how they brought it about, may provide some insight as to how such guarantees have the potential to achieve greater justice for all.

But please do not think me naive: I would be the first to admit that on its own, a formal constitutional guarantee of equality does not go very far toward achieving justice. The word "equality" is notoriously indeterminate[30] and, depending on the meaning ascribed to it, has the potential to lead to justice or injustice, inclusion or exclusion, substantive change or maintenance of the *status quo*.[51] Indeed, this is the very reason Canadian women mobilized to ensure a rich definitional content of the guarantee prior to its constitutionalization, and to watch over its interpretation subsequent to 1982.

Moreover, a meaningful statutory, constitutional or international guarantee of equality requires much more than a good definition. Those who need its protection must have the means to ensure it is put into practice. For, as one of America's great female leaders, Eleanor Roosevelt, expressed so eloquently:

> Where, after all, do universal human rights begin? In small places, close to home — so close and so small that they cannot be seen on any map of the world.... Such are the places where every man, woman or child seeks equal justice, equal opportunity, equal dignity, without discrimination. Unless these rights have meaning there, they have little meaning anywhere.[52]

The deplorable situation of women in Afghanistan today, as well as recent gross violations of human rights in Yugoslavia, Rwanda and East Timor[,] demonstrate in the clearest manner possible that all the human rights treaties in the world, drafted and interpreted to give the most meaningful protections possible, cannot achieve justice on their own.

There are no easy answers to these problems. I put it to you, however, that part of the solution is for each of us to *envision* all possible means of ensuring that guarantees of equality, whether they be statutory, constitutional or international, penetrate every aspect of state conduct and, ultimately, of human behavior. This brings me back to the passage I quoted from Chief Justice Brian Dickson at the beginning of this paper. My observation that he was one of the greatest Canadian feminists was made half in jest, half in great seriousness. For it is only when men as well as women become open to women's experience and perspectives, that we know that we are well on our way to transforming attitudes and behavior. In Canada, thanks in large part to the vision and strategy of women's groups, the constitutionalization of equality has played a large part in bringing about such a transformation.

Furthermore, the Canadian experience suggests that when women help to forge and shape the development of constitutional guarantees of equality, these norms have the potential to provide one of the most powerful means available for making equality a reality for all. Taking hope and inspiration from this experience, and from our professional and personal aspirations as jurists, we must therefore re-dedicate ourselves to the achievement of equality in all aspects of the law. For it is my firm belief that justice without equality is no justice at all.

(e) Aboriginal Peoples and the Canadian Charter of Rights and Freedoms: Contradictions and Challenges†

Aki-Kwe/Mary Ellen Turpel

Whereas Canada is founded upon principles that recognize the supremacy of God and the rule of law ...

> Preamble to Part I, *Canadian Charter of Rights and Freedoms).*

Your religion was written upon tables of stone by the iron finger of your God so that you could not forget. The Red Aboriginal people could never comprehend nor remember it. Our religion is the traditions of our ancestors — the dreams of our old men, given them in solemn hours of night by the Great Spirit; and the visitations of our sachems: and it is written in the hearts of our people

> (Chief Seattle to the Governor of Washington Territory, 1854).

When anthropologists, government officials, and churchmen have argued that our ways have been lost to us, they are fulfilling one of their own tribal rituals — wish fulfilment.

> (Chief George Manuel, *The Fourth World*).

The contemporary world of aboriginal politics is inhabited by discussions about rights — the right to self-government, the right to title of land, the right to equality, the right to social services, and the right

to practice spiritual beliefs. None of this is very new, nor is it surprising, given that non-aboriginal people have been writing on behalf of the "rights" of aboriginal people since the 16th century.

The earliest of these works were concerned primarily with how the colonial powers (Spain) should treat the "uncivilized" and savage peoples discovered in America (see, for instance de Las Casa, 1656 and de Victorio, 1917). Many would argue that there have been no real advances in "rights" for aboriginal people in America since the 16th century, but to seek advances in "rights" presupposes the acceptance of terminology. It strikes me that when aboriginal people discuss rights and borrow the rhetoric of human rights in contemporary struggle, we are using the paradigm of human rights, both nationally and internationally, as an instrument for the recognition of historic claims — and in many cases as the "only" resort. Is that really buying into the distinctly western and liberal vision of human rights concepts?

Underlying the use of human rights terminology is a plea for recognition of a different way of life, a different idea of community, of politics, of spirituality — ideas which have existed since time immemorial, but which have been cast as differences to be repressed and discouraged since colonization. In ask-

---

† From Elizabeth Comack and Stephen Brickey (eds.), *The Social Basis of Law*, 2d ed. (Halifax: Garamond Press, 1991) at 223–36. [Notes and/or references omitted.] This article was originally published in (1989) 10:2 and 10:3 *Canadian Women Studies*. Reproduced by permission of Mary Ellen Turpel Lafond.

ing for recognition by another culture of the existence of your own, and for toleration of, and respect for, the practical difference that it brings with it, there seems to be something at stake which is larger than human rights, and certainly larger than the texts of particular documents which guarantee human rights, such as the *Canadian Charter of Rights and Freedoms*: a more basic request — the request to be recognized as peoples. I believe that from early colonization up to the present, no government or monarch has ever recognized aboriginal peoples as distinct peoples with cultures different from their own, in other words, as peoples whose ways of life should be tolerated and respected, even though certain customs may challenge the cultural assumptions of the newcomers.

I also believe that one reason for this, aside from the obvious one of the assertion of government power and the quest for economic dominance, is that aboriginal ways have been and still are presumed to be primitive, in the sense of "lesser" states of development. This presumption denies genuine differences by presuming that another culture is the same, just not quite as "civilized" yet. Hence, it is important for the colonial governments to take jurisdiction over aboriginal peoples in order to guide them to a more reasoned state where they can become just like them (it is not surprising that the church was usually the state's best ally).

No government has ever dealt with aboriginal peoples on an equal basis — without seeing us as means to an economic goal (settlement and development), as noble savages, the pagans without civilization, or as specimens for anthropological investigation and scientific collection.[1] Genuinely recognizing another people as another culture is more than recognizing rights of certain persons. It is not simply recognizing peoples of another colour, translated in European terms as "race," nor is it recognizing the presence of a minority because the minority is always defined by and in subordination to the majority. Placing the emphasis on race or minority (and consequently on rights) has the effect of covering over the differences at work to the majority's advantage. Aboriginal cultures are not simply different "races" — a difference explained in terms of biology (or colour): aboriginal cultures are the manifestations of a different human (collective) imagination.

To borrow the words of a non-aboriginal writer, [aboriginal] cultures "are oriented as wholes in different directions. They are travelling along different roads in pursuit of different ends, and these ends and these means in one society cannot be judged in terms of those of another society because essentially they are incommensurable ..." (Benedict, 1935). While it seems that, in the Canadian context, aboriginal peoples and non-aboriginal persons have some understanding and recognition of each other, it also seems that aboriginal peoples have been the ones who have had to suffer for tolerance (even by force and imprisonment).[2]

It is true that there have been treaties between aboriginal peoples and the British Crown. However, these do not amount, in my view, to a genuine recognition of diverse indigenous cultures; they were really Western-style (written in a highly legalistic form in most cases) methods to make way for progress, with "progress" defined according to the standards of the newcomers. After all, signing treaties was the British practice in almost all of the colonies, irrespective of cultural differences among those they "discovered" or "conquered." It is no wonder, then, that in studying the law of treaties, we quickly learn that, according to Anglo-Canadian legal standards, treaties (even before Confederation) are not seen as agreements between sovereign peoples or nations. When we inquire as to why treaties are not viewed as agreements between two (or more) sovereign peoples, we are generally led to the theory that aboriginal people (either at the time of treaty-making or now) were not sufficiently "civilized" and organized to qualify as "sovereign" peoples, or that they had already "lost" their sovereignty through some predestined and mysterious process (for example, by virtue of being "discovered").

Of course, there is no compelling reason, according to the doctrines and principles of international law, to view treaties between aboriginal peoples and the Crown as anything other than treaties between sovereigns, or *international* treaties. Nor does there seem to be any compelling reason for continuing to pretend that aboriginal peoples do not have distinct cultures, cultures which are deserving of recognition by the dominant (European) one which has been imposed in Canada. Why is it, then, that aboriginal peoples, and aboriginal claims, must be "fit-in" to the categories and concepts of a dominant culture, in some form of equivalence, in order to be acknowledged? There appears to be a contradiction at work in areas like human rights, that is, a contradiction between pretending, on the one hand to accept aboriginal peoples as distinct peoples and, on the other, of accepting something called aboriginal peoples' rights. This contradiction, which I explore briefly in the following pages, has led to a great deal of misunderstanding and has given the dominant culture (as represented by the government of Canada) plenty of scope in which to maneuvre, while avoiding a difference-based approach to aboriginal peoples as equals or as sovereigns.

"Aboriginal rights" is a category, primarily a category of law, in which most discussions about our historic claims and cultural differences are carried out in Canadian society. It is a category with severe limitations politically and legally — limitations which have been set, whether or not intentionally, by those who thought up the category — mostly non-aboriginal people. It is a realm in which discussions focusing on strange expressions like "title," "usufructory rights," "mere premises," "status," "referential incorporation," "extinguishment," and "existing" take on enormous significance, even though they do not seem to have anything to do with the everyday lives of aboriginal people. A frightening and frustrating thing about the centrality of these expressions is that they were thought up by the same non-aboriginal people that brought us the "rights" category; they seem incompatible with aboriginal ideas about land, family, social life, and spirituality. Yet, somehow, they are supposed to be helping us out, assisting in our struggle to continue to practice our cultures. Could it be that they just serve to limit the possibilities for genuine acknowledgement of the existence of aboriginal peoples as distinct cultures and political communities possessing the ability to live without external regulation and control?

I chose the first two quotations prefacing this article to illustrate the contradiction here. A *Charter* based on the supremacy of a foreign God and the (Anglo-American) rule of law just doesn't seem to be the kind of constitution that aboriginal peoples can get too excited about. Rather, it is the kind of constitution which we can get rather angry about because it has the effect of excluding aboriginal vision(s) and (diverse) views about the land and the society now called Canada. Clearly, as an historical document, it represents only one story of Canada — that is, the story of the colonialists. As a document held out to be the "supreme law of Canada" (according to Section 52 of the *Constitution Act*, 1982), it represents an act of ethnocentrism and domination, acknowledging at no point The Great Law of customary laws of the First Peoples of this territory (except unless through wish-fulfilment Section 35 is read in this way).[3]

Could aboriginal spirituality ever be represented by the likes of the preamble to the *Canadian Charter of Rights and Freedoms*? Do Chief Seattle's words render this impossible? Are we travelling along a different road, one which does not need formal written declarations to convince ourselves of what kinds of societies we are? Should we even try to do things

this way? Who are we trying to please in doing so? Is it inevitable that aboriginal traditions and customs have to take the form of "rights" which are brought to courts, proven to exist, and then enforced? Is not the fundamental problem here the fact that everything has to be adjusted to fit the terms of the dominant system?

I view the problems of the aboriginal peoples — human rights area [—] as further evidence of the fact that the dominant culture has never recognized aboriginal peoples as distinct peoples and cultures. I suppose that the exclusion or repression of the "aboriginal fact" of Canada in the present *Constitution Act* in a strange way bolsters the idea that aboriginal peoples are sovereign and distinct (yet entrapped) nations. Unless there was a conscious strategy of "ignore them and they'll go away," one would presume more ink would have been spilt on setting out the nature of the relationship between the Crown and the First Peoples of Canada; or at least on mentioning it more directly than in two perfunctory sections in the *Constitution Act*.

Larger questions loom over all of these problems. What does it mean for aboriginal peoples to advance claims enveloped in the rhetoric of human rights? While there is no question that there are serious human problems in aboriginal communities which seem to warrant redress as "human rights" violations, are such claims too piecemeal? Is there a difference between having discrete "rights" incrementally recognized, and being recognized as a people? What alternatives to rights-based claims are available? In the very pragmatic-oriented work of human rights lawyers and activists in Canada — a discourse about litigation strategies and legal doctrines — there hardly seems to be an opportunity to stop and consider these kinds of questions about aboriginal rights and the *Canadian Charter of Rights and Freedoms*. I wonder to what extent those who support struggles for the recognition of aboriginal rights have really considered these issues?

Generally, we have never really had to address these problems during the first five years of the *Charter* because we were too preoccupied with negotiations to recognize (both within the *Charter* and within another specific section of the *Constitution Act*) the "right to self-government."[4] When these negotiations failed miserably at the final meeting of the First Ministers in 1987 — a failure which was something of a foregone conclusion given that the aboriginal peoples were never seen as equal parties in the negotiation process from the beginning (instead we were given special "observer" status) — people returned to the *Charter* and the vague provision on the aboriginal rights in section 35 of the *Constitution Act, 1982* to consider legal challenges and claims based upon these provisions. It is my belief that questions regarding *which* forums and laws are especially urgent now. Such questions can hardly be avoided any longer, especially in light of the fact that aboriginal peoples are turning more to the *Charter* for recognition of their rights *vis-à-vis* the Canadian Crown, and perhaps more disturbingly, turning to the *Charter* to fight out internal battles in communities.

I would like to explore some of the layers of contradiction or conflict which are raised in the context of aboriginal peoples' claims and the *Charter*, and describe briefly an effort to meet one aspect of these contradictions which has been made by aboriginal women through the Native Women's Association of Canada. The views put forward here are my own, many of which have been developed in the course of advising the Native Women's Association of Canada on human rights matters in recent years. I have been greatly influenced in these questions by situations facing the Association and its constituents, and by both my mixed education and ancestry.[5] I do not propose to consider in any detail traditional and customary practices of specific aboriginal peoples, both for reasons of the limits of space here and because I have reservations about the extent to which knowledge about these matters can be transmitted in such a medium.[6]

THE ORIGINS OF HUMAN RIGHTS

While it might seem obvious that human rights and the *Canadian Charter of Rights and Freedoms* are incompatible with aboriginal culture and traditions, it is helpful to trace the origin of the idea of human rights in the modern era in order to locate the differences here. The Anglo-American concept of rights was set out, for the most part, by two 17th century English political theorists, Thomas Hobbes (1651) and John Locke (1690). Locke is the more famous of the two on these matters. He developed a theory of "natural rights" — later "human" came to be substituted for "natural," after the recognition (post-Holocaust) that peoples are capable of barbaric actions in the name of what is "natural." Locke's theory of natural rights was based around his idea that every *man* (and emphasis should be on *man* because Locke is famous for his theory that society was naturally patriarchal) possesses a right to private property, or the right to own property. This right, he suggested, flowed from the fact that human beings are God's property ("God" as in the preamble to the

Canadian Charter). He argued that people enter into "civil society" for the central, and negatively conceived, purpose of protecting their right to private property against random attack.

The idea of the absolute right to property, as an exclusive zone of ownership capable of being transmitted through the family (through males according to a doctrine called "primogenitor"), is the cornerstone of the idea of rights — the idea that there is a zone of absolute human right where the individual can do what he chooses: "The right is a loaded gun that the right holder may shoot at will in his corner of town" (Unger, 1986). It does not take much of a stretch of the imagination to see where slavery and the subordination of women found legitimacy in the Anglo-American tradition — with the absolute ownership of property, and autonomous domains, "naturally" rights will extend "even to another person's body" (Hobbes, 1651).

Although there is no pan-aboriginal culture of iron-clad system of beliefs, this notion of rights based on individual ownership is antithetical to the widely-shared understanding of creation and stewardship responsibilities of First Nations peoples for the land, or for Mother Earth. Moreover, to my knowledge, there are no notions among aboriginal Nations of living together for the purposes of protecting an individual interest in property. Aboriginal life has been set out in stories handed down through generations and in customary laws sometimes represented by wampum belts, sacred pipes, medicine bundles, and rock paintings. For example, the teachings of the Four Directions [are] that life is based on four principles: trust, kindness, sharing and strength. While these are responsibilities which each person owes to others, they represent the larger function of social life, that is, to honour and respect Mother Earth. There is no equivalent of "rights" here because there is no equivalent to the ownership of private property. The collective or communal bases of aboriginal life [do] not really have a parallel to individual rights; they are incommensurable. To try to explain to an Elder that, under Canadian law, there are carefully worked-over doctrines pertaining to who owns every inch of the country, the sky, the ocean, and even the moon, would provide disbelief and profound sadness.

THE STRUCTURE OF THE *CANADIAN CHARTER*

Nevertheless, the Canadian human rights system, having been distanced in time and space somewhat from its origin and conceptual basis in the theories about the right to individual ownership to property, seems little less foreign, especially since so much is said of aboriginal matters in the context of human rights. Some writers even argue that, in Canada, the *Charter* recognized certain collective rights, such as aboriginal rights, and not merely individual rights. However, my reading of the law leads me to believe that the individual property basis of human rights is revealed clearly in the text of the *Canadian Charter*, as well as in recent cases which have been decided under the *Charter*. The language of the *Charter* refers to human rights enjoyed by "every citizen of Canada," "every individual," "any person," etc. The section of the *Charter* on enforcement applies to "[a]ny *one* whose rights or freedoms ... have been infringed," permitting them to apply to court for the order the court considers appropriate in the circumstances — almost always the singular subject.

The extent to which a human rights law set out in such individualist terms could ever either (i) be interpreted as including a collective understanding of rights, or (ii) lead to judges acknowledging that other peoples might not base their social relations on these individual "rights" notions, is highly questionable. There is nothing strong enough in the *Charter* to allow for either a collectivist idea of rights (or responsibilities), if such a theory is conceivable, or toleration of a community organized around collective values. When cases involving aboriginal peoples come before the courts, it is doubtful that different standards of legal analysis will be applied. Already the case law has taken a disturbing course from the viewpoint of aboriginal peoples.

With shades of private property notions in mind, the Supreme Court of Canada in the recent *Morgentaler* case on abortion suggested that "the rights guaranteed in the *Charter* erect around each individual, metaphorically speaking, an invisible fence over which the state will not be allowed to trespass. The role of the courts is to map out, piece by piece, the parameters of the fence."[7] In an earlier decision, one involving aboriginal persons, the Federal Court of Canada took the view that "in the absence of legal provisions to the contrary, the interests of individual persons will be deemed to have precedence over collective rights. In the absence of law to the contrary, this must be as true of Indian Canadians as of others."[8]

Even in the area of language rights — an area said to be a cornerstone of collective rights in the *Charter* — the Supreme Court of Canada in the recent case involving Québec's former *Bill 101* has indicated that this right is somehow both an individual and a collective one: "Language itself indicates a means by which a people may express its cultural identity. It is also the means by which the individual expresses his or her personal identity and sense of individuality."[9] How to go about reconciling these two aspects when they conflict is no easy task, and the Court gives little guidance here on its view of collective rights, except to say that the right to speak their language must be protected at law against the community's prohibition of it.

Even in the area of equality rights, as recognized in section 15 of the *Charter*, the text applies to "every individual." This provision has been interpreted by the courts not as a general recognition of the idea of equality (which, if read as "sameness," would be deeply disturbing to aboriginal people), but simply as a principle in relating to the application of given laws. In a recent equality case, the Supreme Court of Canada stated that section 15 "is not a general guarantee of equality, it does not provide for equality between individuals or groups within society in a general or abstract sense, nor does it impose on individuals or groups an obligation to accord equality treatment to others. *It is concerned with the application of the law.*"[10] The scope for aboriginal rights claims under section 15 is limited, even if such a course was seen as desirable by aboriginal leaders.

Moreover, we can begin to see the broader implications of these cases for aboriginal peoples or aboriginal claims. It is difficult to move in a certain direction as a people if individuals can challenge collective decisions based on infringement of their individual rights and if collective goals will not be understood or prioritized. Some people may view this as the triumph of democracy, but it makes the preservation of a different culture and the pursuit of collective political goals almost impossible.

In aboriginal communities where customary political and spiritual institutions are the guiding force (even alongside the imposed *Indian Act* system of Band Councils), such as the Haudenosaunee of the Iroquois Confederates, recourse to an individual-rights based law like the *Charter* could result in further weakening of the cultural identity of the community. This could take one of two forms: either a member of the community would challenge aboriginal laws based on individual rights protections in the *Charter* arguing that they have not been respected by their government (an internal challenge); or a non-aboriginal person could challenge the laws of an aboriginal government on the basis that they do not conform with *Charter* standards (an external challenge).

In the case of an external challenge, for example, on the basis of voting or candidacy rights where a non-aboriginal complainant argued that they could not vote or stand for elections in an aboriginal community because of cultural restrictions, the court would be given the authority to decide on an important part of the future of an aboriginal community. It would have to consider the protections of aboriginal rights in the *Charter* and weigh these against the individual right to vote recognized in section 3. Should Canadian courts (and non-aboriginal judges) have authority in these cases? Given the highly individualistic basis of the *Charter*, and of the history of human rights, would the collective aboriginal right stand a chance? I doubt it. As the Assembly of First Nations argued before the Parliamentary Committee on Aboriginal Affairs in 1982:

> [as] Indian people we cannot afford to have individual rights override collective rights. Our societies have never been structured that way, unlike yours, and that is where the clash comes ... If you isolate the individual rights from the collective rights, then you are heading down another path that is even more discriminatory ... The *Canadian Charter of Rights* is in conflict with our philosophy and culture ...[11]

The other possible challenge, the internal challenge, where a member of an aboriginal community felt dissatisfied with a particular course of action the aboriginal government was taking and turned to the *Charter* for the recognition of a right, is equally if not more worrisome. This kind of challenge would be a dangerous opening for a Canadian court to rule on individual versus collective rights *vis-a-vis* aboriginal peoples; it would also break down community methods of dispute-resolution and restoration. Here, the example of the *Indian Civil Rights Act*[12] in the United States is instructive. This act, based on the idea that protections for the *American Bill of Rights* should be extended to aboriginal communities, along with the establishment of tribal courts which would have the same function as American courts generally, has been greatly criticized by aboriginal people as imposing alien ways of life. As two noted scholars suggest:

> In philosophical terms, it is much easier to describe the impact of the ... Act. Traditional Indian society understood itself as a complex of responsibilities and duties. The [Act] merely transposed this belief into a society based on rights against government and eliminated any sense of responsibility that people might have felt for one another. Granted that many of the customs that made duties and responsibilities a serious matter of individual action had eroded badly in the decades since the tribes had agreed

to move to the reservations, the impact of the [Act] was to make these responsibilities impossible to perform because the Act inserted the trial court as an institution between the people and their responsibilities. People did not have to confront one another before their community and resolve their problems; they had only to file suit in tribal court (Deloria and Lytle, 1984).

The lessons of the *American Indian Civil Rights Act* and of the establishment of tribal courts are important ones in light of the *Charter*. If internal disputes are brought before Canadian courts, it will seriously undermine the aboriginal system of government based on responsibility (like the Four Directions) and interpose a system of individual-based rights. It also has the effect of encouraging people to go outside the community, and outside of custom, to settle disputes in formal courts — instead of having to deal with a problem within a community.

This might sound like a hard line to take, especially when one considers the extent to which customs and traditional methods of governance and dispute-resolution have been dislodged in aboriginal communities after more than a century of life under the *Indian Act*. The experience of gender-based discrimination was employed as a technique of assimilation up until the 1985 amendments to the *Indian Act* (many see the gender-based discriminatory provisions as having continuing effect despite the amendments), and scarred many aboriginal communities as male-dominated Band councils frequently sided against women and with the Canadian government in the belief that to do otherwise would undermine the Crown's responsibility for aboriginal peoples.

As a consequence, women were forced to go outside the community to resolve the injustices of gender discrimination, so cases were brought under the *Canadian Bill of Rights* and eventually under the *United Nations Covenant on Civil and Political Rights*. Changes were made to the *Indian Act*, but many of the after-effects of gender discrimination still plague aboriginal communities, including problems associated with women returning to communities and being able to take up residence, educate their children, share in social services, and receive per capita payments from resource exploitation on aboriginal lands.

Communities have been slow to address questions related to the aftermath of gender discrimination in the *Indian Act*, and the mechanisms available to resolve disputes according to customary practices are not necessarily available. This places a great deal of pressure on aboriginal communities, which could lead to cases being taken to Canadian courts pursuant to the *Charter* for recognition of rights against aboriginal governments. As a result of concern over what this could lead to, in light of the individual-based notions of rights under Canadian law, and in light of lessons derived from the United States experience with the *Indian Civil Rights Act*, aboriginal women have been working on projects to encourage the development of First Nations laws in areas like "citizenship" and human rights and responsibilities — laws based, as far as possible, on inherent First Nation jurisdiction and customary practices.

AN ALTERNATIVE APPROACH: FIRST NATIONS HUMAN RIGHTS AND RESPONSIBILITIES LAWS

The Native Women's Association of Canada has addressed questions relating to gender discrimination in the *Indian Act* and related problems in aboriginal communities since the late 1970s. In 1985, when amendments to the *Indian Act* aimed at eliminating gender discrimination were finally passed, the Native Women's Association took the position that, while aboriginal women could support the end of unfair bias against women, they could not simply support the Federal government's efforts to "improve" the *Indian Act* and the extension of legislative control over the lives of aboriginal peoples through its paternalistic provisions. Consequently, the Association turned its attention to the development of a "First Nation Citizenship Code," or a model law which would address the issues of membership or citizenship in a First Nation, but would base its principles and jurisdiction not on Canadian law, but on the inherent jurisdiction of First Nations to regulate citizenship as practices since time immemorial.

The model code was distributed to every aboriginal community in Canada with a letter encouraging communities to take a First Nations approach to citizenship (and not an *Indian Act* approach) and to set up local mechanisms based, as much as possible, on customary principles for settling disputes, so that problems regarding citizenship could be addressed in the community itself and not in the Canadian courts. As it became clear that citizenship was not the only area of concern in communities (although the issue of Indian status was by far the most divisive), it was evident that some other efforts would need to be expended to discourage internal challenges of aboriginal government actions getting into Canadian courts under the *Charter*. In 1986, the Native Women's Association of Canada began to consider the development of another model law,

parallel to the Citizenship Code, which would be a First Nations human rights and responsibilities law.

It appears that this Code (which at the time of writing is still in the draft stages) will be based on the inherent jurisdiction of First Nations to make laws for their peoples. It will include a very loosely and generously worded part on human rights and responsibilities, corresponding to the four groups of rights and responsibilities which come from the teachings of the Four Directions. Hence, there are the following responsibilities and rights:

(i) *kindness* — social rights
(ii) *honesty* — political and civil rights
(iii) *sharing* — economic rights, and
(iv) *strength* — cultural rights.

For example, the responsibility and rights category of strength / cultural rights would include provisions on the right to pursue traditional occupations, the right to education in aboriginal languages, the right to customary marriage and adoptions, the right to participate in ceremonies according to laws and traditions of the Nation, and, most importantly, the recognition of the fundamental importance of Elders and spiritual leaders in the preservation of ancestral and customary law and in the health and well-being of the community as a whole.

The provisions on the model law developed by the Native Women's Association on dispute-resolution provide options for a particular community to consider creating a law which fits within its customs and aspirations. These include mediation, the establishment of a Human Rights Committee, and a Council of Elders. Also included are options for setting up methods to deal with conflicts on a regional basis (for example, an Iroquois or Ojibway council of Elders). It is hoped that the work of the Association will contribute to the development of community laws and less formal community solutions to reduce the possibilities that individual members of the First Nations communities will have to go outside their communities (to foreign courts) for redress of grievances. It appears that the development of community codes is the best available solution to the problems in communities and to the threat of the (further) imposition of a Western individualistic human rights system on aboriginal communities.

FUTURE CHALLENGES

The work of the Native Women's Association of Canada really only addresses the problem of internal challenges based on the *Charter* by members of First

Nations communities. It does not attempt to deal with other areas of concern, such as external challenges or claims brought by non-aboriginal peoples pursuant to the *Charter*, calling into question the collective basis of aboriginal communities.[13] Even claims brought by aboriginal communities against the Federal Government based on provisions of the *Charter* seem to present a dangerous opportunity for the court to take a restrictive view of collective-based community goals. Any case which presents a Canadian court with the opportunity to balance or weigh an individual right against a collective understanding of community will be an opportunity to delimit the recognition of aboriginal peoples as distinct cultures.

This is something quite different from dealing on an equal footing with aboriginal peoples about historic claims and cultural differences which have to be addressed and settled. These cases permit the court to say, "Yes, we do have jurisdiction over you, and we will decide what is best for you under Canadian law." It is not that different from the imposed system of rule under the *Indian Act*, except in the *Charter* cases, the court can cloak its decision in the rhetoric of democratic freedom, emancipation, multiculturalism and human rights for "all Canadians." The only way to really consider the political and cultural differences between aboriginal peoples and the Canadian state is through discussions which are quasi-international, so that the respective "sovereignty" of the parties will be respected.

Aboriginal peoples have been trying to pursue this (international) course during the past decade. The United Nations has established a special Working Group on Indigenous Populations to consider the human rights violations (really historic claims under international law) of indigenous peoples from around the globe. During the past seven years, there have been six meetings of the Working Group, and recently efforts have been directed at the development of a United Nations [Declaration] on Indigenous Rights. Although aboriginal peoples have been participating quite actively in this process of development of a United Nations Declaration, once again, we are really on the outside of the United Nations system. Nevertheless, certain States which are part of the United Nations structure have been willing to advocate for the recognition of indigenous rights in a declaration.[14]

The matters dealt with in the proceedings of the Working Group and in the Draft Declaration can hardly be ignored, especially when one considers the extent to which they are present in all areas of the globe. As one noted international scholar has suggested, "[t]he peoples of entrapped nations are a sleeping giant in the workings of power politics" (Falk, 1987). A cornerstone of an eventual declaration would have to be, from the aboriginal perspective, a recognition and explicit extension of self-determination to indigenous peoples under international law. There are persuasive arguments that, even without a specific declaration, international law already recognizes the right of all peoples (including aboriginal peoples) to self-determination.

Self-determination is something different than self-government, although it could include the latter. Self-government (which has been the pinnacle of all human rights discussions in the Canadian context) implies that aboriginal peoples were not previously able to govern themselves because they were not at an advanced enough stage of civilization, but can now take on some responsibility for their own affairs.[15] Very few people make a distinction between self-government and self-determination. In a recent (1988) report by the Canadian Bar Association Special Committee on Native Justice, the idea of self-government is used throughout without any distinction as to its historical context or political implications. On this point, aboriginal women in Canada, through the voice of the Native Women's Association, have again made their position in support of self-determination over self-government quite clear.[16]

In the international context, the draft declaration on indigenous rights is silent on the issue of self-determination. It contains many disturbing provisions on lesser notions like "autonomy ... in local affairs" and the "right to exist." While these might seem progressive in some situations where the very life of aboriginal people is systematically threatened on a daily basis, the provisions do not go far enough in recognizing aboriginal people as distinct cultures and political entities, equally as capable of governing and making decisions as European sovereigns, except with different political and cultural goals.

A great deal more work will have to be done in the next few years to ensure that the text of the draft declaration is one which will recognize indigenous people as legitimate, though different, governments and cultures. The only way to do this, in international law, is through a recognition of self-determination. Realizing this goal will require broad-based support from international society, manifested in the work of non-government organizations, women's movements, and sympathetic States. The Canadian government and Canadian people could do much to assist the international process if the government would simply recognize aboriginal peoples as distinct peoples with different but equally legitimate cultures and ways of life. This cannot be done through Canadian courts and in the rhetoric of Canadian human rights — it has to be done through a joint aboriginal-Canadian discussion process where, unlike the series of discussions held on Canadian constitutional amendments, aboriginal peoples are equal participants in the process, along with the Prime Minister and perhaps Provincial Premiers.

In the meantime, aboriginal women will continue to do what can be done to ensure that aboriginal communities are governed by customary laws and practices, through the development of First Nations laws, and through the political and spiritual voice of the Native Women's Association of Canada as guided by its Elders and affiliated women's organizations.

V

Law, Crime, and Social Order

Overview of Part V

The readings in **Part V** explore and critique the way that law may be used as a broader mechanism of social order and social control. In particular, the readings in this part focus on the creation, enforcement and impact of criminal law. The articles consider not only the strict legal rules, but also the actors, processes, and even "cultures", that constitute and interact within what we broadly identify as the "criminal justice system".

The articles in **Chapter 12** question the motivations behind the use of criminal law to prohibit some activities but not others. In particular, Hunt explores the ways in which criminal law, like other forms of law, may be used as a tool of class domination. This domination occurs not only through law's exercise of coercive control over individuals, but also in the way law reinforces and legitimizes unequal social relationships through processes of "ideological domination".

In a similar critical vein, the article by Adam *et al.* explores the impact of criminal law on those diagnosed with HIV/AIDS. The authors explore the effects of criminalization of an illness, and ask the reader to consider the way in which the criminal law might further marginalize already marginal groups. The article highlights the effects of the Supreme Court's controversial decision in *Cuerrier* on the lives of those living with HIV/AIDS and suggests that explicit attempts to minimize "risky" sexual conduct using Canadian criminal law may ultimately only serve to exacerbate the issues it has sought to mitigate.

The reports and articles included in **Chapter 13** focus on a range of longstanding, long-identified problems within the criminal justice system. Building on themes identified in the previous chapter, this chapter provides readers with a foundation for discussing some of the most widely acknowledged failings of our criminal justice system. Among the problems discussed are the ways in which institutionally entrenched issues, and the discretionary decisions of individual actors within the system (e.g. police, Crown attorneys, judges, etc.), connect to contribute to the overrepresentation of racial minorities in the criminal justice system (Commission on Systemic Racism in the Ontario Justice System), and at times, the wrongful conviction of members of these groups (Royal Commission on the Donald Marshall Jr. Prosecution) and others.

Following the reports, the article by Green focuses explicitly on the complex factors that lead to wrongful convictions, more generally. He underscores the potential negative impacts of prosecutorial discretion and a "Crown culture" marked by contradiction, competition, and, crucially, a reluctance to acknowledge error. Green argues that effective reform requires prosecutors to first admit fallibility, while broader institutional reforms must simultaneously blend both incentives and disincentives to re-orient the practice of prosecutorial power. (Some of the core themes explored by Green are also taken up in **Chapter 17** by Roach in his critique of the adversarial model of adjudication)

Several of the articles in this chapter also explore ways in which the criminal justice system might be improved by providing more meaningful participation for victims of crime, and by adopting restorative justice approaches. First, the shift in the way the criminal law understands and addresses victims of crime is examined in the article by Barrett. Barrett notes the various "gains" made by victims in recent decades, but challenges the reader to consider what have been the real impact of these reforms. She suggests that a number of high profile initiatives, including so-called "victims' rights" legislation, may ultimately only create "false hope" for many victims of crime, and not address what she calls "the lingering dissatisfaction of victims with the criminal justice system". Finally, Daly considers the effectiveness of restorative justice initiatives within the context of youth criminal justice cases. She does so by identifying the limits of both criminal and restorative justice approaches within a framework that recognizes that justice itself is an ideal that we can never fully achieve.

As you read through the articles selected for this section consider some of the following questions: What exactly is "crime"? What broader functions does crime, or the criminal law, play in society? How do we choose which behaviours or actors to discipline through criminal law? Exactly what "order" (or "orders") does criminal law maintain? What role does violence play in the enforcement of criminal law? If many of the issues within the criminal justice system remain stubbornly tied to larger social issues such as racism, sexism, homophobia, etc., can we successfully address them within the criminal justice system in isolation?

Finally, if, as all the selected articles and reports reinforce, the criminal justice system's failures are the result of practically complex personal and institutional relations — and so require equally complex solutions — how should we greet simplistic or ideologically driven initiatives to address these failures?

What Is Crime?

(a) Law, State, and Class Struggle†

Alan Hunt

INTRODUCTION

This chapter sets out to examine the way in which law operates to maintain class domination. The argument that is developed shows that law should not simply be regarded as part of the coercive armoury of the state; but also must be understood as making a major contribution to what will be called "ideological domination." Ideological domination consists of those processes that produce and reaffirm the existing social order and thereby legitimize class domination. The processes involved in creating and reproducing ideological domination play a major part in ensuring the continuation of capitalist social relations.

There has been relatively little attention paid by Marxists to law. This absence of discussion has resulted in a tendency for the more obvious repressive characteristics to be stressed; and as a consequence the more pervasive contribution of law to the maintenance of capitalist society has not been sufficiently explored. The analysis of law in this wider context is of considerable political importance. Marxists are increasingly being forced to come to grips with the fact that modern capitalism has exhibited very considerable "staying power." In the period since the Second World War capitalism in Western Europe has shown what may be best described as relative stability; that is to suggest that despite the occurrence of very deep economic, social and political crises the capitalist social order in the major Western European states has survived substantially

intact. This chapter examines the extent and the manner in which legal systems contribute to the perpetuation of capitalist systems.

STATE AND LAW

In class societies the economic and social dominance of an exploiting class does not sustain itself automatically. The exploiting class always strives to turn itself into a ruling class by means of an institutional structure, the state, which operates to sustain and to reproduce that position. While the state is a product of class antagonism it takes on the appearance of being an entity which stands above society and which embodies the interests of the community as a whole. This apparently *universal* quality is especially significant with reference to legal systems:

> Right, law, etc. are merely the symptom, the expression of *other* relations upon which State power rests.... These actual relations are in no way created by the State power; on the contrary they are the power creating it. The individuals who rule in these conditions, besides having to constitute their power in the form of the *State*, have to give their will, which is determined by these definite conditions, a universal expression as the will of the state, as law. (Marx/Engels 1968: 366)

The distinctive feature then of legal systems of class societies is the fact that they embody the material interests of the ruling class in a universal form,

---

† From *Explorations in Law and Society: Towards a Constitutive Theory of Law* (London: Routledge, 1993) at 17–35. Originally from (1976) 20 *Marxism Today* at 178–87. Reproduced with permission of Martin Jacques. [Notes and/or references omitted.]

and thus present law as the embodiment of the interests of the community as a whole:

> In a modern state, law must not only correspond to the general economic condition and be its expression, but must also be an *internally coherent* expression which does not[,] owing to inner contradictions, reduce itself to nought. And in order to achieve this, the faithful reflection of economic conditions suffers increasingly. All the more so the more rarely it happens that a code of law is the blunt, unmitigated, unadulterated expression of domination of a class — this in itself would offend the "conception of right".
> (Engels 1890: 504)

This striving of "internal coherence," in which law comes to be seen as the embodiment of universal notions of "justice" and "right," needs to be explored. At the hands of bourgeois legal and political theorists it has been used to provide an ideological dogma, important in bourgeois political and legal theory, of the doctrine of the "separation of powers." The essence of this view is that the character of the democratic state is defined as one in which there exists a separation between the major components of the state. Specifically it is argued that not only is there, but also that there ought to be, a separation between the legislature, which makes the laws, and the judiciary, which apply those laws.

The doctrine of the separation of powers has played, and continues to play a central part in bourgeois theory of the law and the state. There has been a tendency of Marxists in seeking to expose the ideological character of this doctrine to react against it by asserting the identity of the state and law. Thus the legal system has been presented simply as the direct and totally subservient agent of the state. Such a position is too simple, but more importantly it obscures the real class character of the legal system as a mechanism whereby the existing form of class domination is perpetuated and reproduced.

We need to start by asking, how does it come about that a separation appears to exist between law and state? Engels provides a useful starting point:

> But once the state has become an independent power *vis-à-vis* society, it produces forthwith a further ideology. It is indeed among professional politicians, theorists of public law and jurists of private law that the connection with economic facts gets lost for fair [*sic*]. Since in each particular case the economic facts must assume the form of juristic motives in order to receive legal sanction; and since, in so doing, consideration of course has to be given to the whole legal system already in operation, the

juristic form is, in consequence, made everything and the economic content nothing. (Engels 1958: 396–97)

If these ideological functions are to be fulfilled they cannot operate exclusively as ideological forces, they must find some expression in the actual practice embodied within the legal system. As a consequence the legal system operates in a manner which cannot be explained exclusively by reference to the dictates of the state as a whole.

The doctrine of the separation of powers appeals to the independence of the judiciary. Yet this independence is clearly very restricted. Judicial appointments are made by the highest representatives of the political apparatus of the state.[1]

But what does need to be stressed is that even the relative degree of autonomy sets up stresses and contradictions within the state as a whole. Decisions by courts do not always please the holders of state power. The protracted struggle between the courts and Nixon throughout the "Watergate affair" is perhaps the most important recent example of such a tension in operation, in which the conflict between court and state contributed in no small measure to the downfall of Nixon.

But the tension between courts and state may also have advantages for the holders of state power. The institutional complexity of the English legal system allowed the government to brush the cobwebs off the Official solicitor whose intervention facilitated the release of the "Pentonville 5" in 1972 when faced with the prospect of a General Strike. Frequently it serves as a convenient smoke-screen behind which to hide; Roy Jenkins, as Home Secretary, consistently used the excuse of separation between government and courts to refuse to intervene and secure the release of the Shrewsbury pickets.

This discussion points toward the general conclusion that the relationship between the state and the legal system must always be a matter for concrete examination. While the general dependence of the law on the state as a whole is an important proposition within Marxist theory, this must not be treated as if it suggested a complete identity between law and state.

DOMINATION AND HEGEMONY

Domination is a universal feature of class society. It consists in the subjection of one or more classes to another class (or grouping of classes) in such a way that exploitative relations are perpetuated. But the form that domination takes varies with the form of the exploitative class relations; thus the domination of slave by slaveholder differs from the employer's domination of the factory worker. Domination must be viewed not as a single act but as a process that reproduces the conditions for exploitative social relations.

Domination can only be based for very short periods of time on direct physical coercion. Even the most barbarous and coercive systems do not rely exclusively upon coercive violence. Direct coercion will often play a major part in the establishment of a new system of class power, but, however much it continues to depend on physical repression, it will strive to promote other means of consolidating its domination.

An extremely fruitful approach to the discussion of domination is provided by the early leader of the Italian Communist Party, Antonio Gramsci, who made use of the concept of "hegemony." He used it to identify the processes that create

> the "spontaneous" consent given by the great mass of the population to the general direction imposed on social life by the dominant fundamental group (i.e., the ruling class). (Gramsci 1971: 12)

The vital characteristic of "hegemony" is that it is an active process; it is concerned not only with the *fact* of consent, but focuses on the creation and the mobilization of that consent. One major facet of the class struggle that takes place within capitalist societies is the continual struggle for influence over the ideas, perceptions, and values of members of the different classes. The maintenance of capitalism would be impossible unless the capitalist class was able to decisively influence the ideas, attitudes and consciousness of the working class.

It is important to stress that the ideological struggle is not simply concerned with the conflict between general theories of society. It is concerned with every aspect of the way in which people think about, react to, and interpret their position in class society.

COERCIVE AND IDEOLOGICAL DOMINATION

In examining the part that is played by law in the class struggle it is useful to distinguish between two different aspects. Law plays an important role in sustaining the domination of the ruling class because it operates both as a form of *coercive domination* and of *ideological domination*. It will also be necessary to stress that they are not simple alternatives. I hope to show the way in which these two elements are closely

bound together and as such contribute to the special effectiveness of law as a mechanism of social order.

Let us first consider the coercive character of law. The legal system is able to call upon the organized power of the state. This repression operates both through specific institutions, which range from the courts themselves to the prison system, probation service, etc. In addition it also operates more generally through the police system that operates with wide-ranging powers, sanctioned by law, but able to act with a very considerable degree of autonomy.

Legal coercion operates at a number of different levels. Of greatest importance is the application of coercion to protect the *general conditions* of the capitalist order. First and foremost coercion is applied to protect and reinforce the property relations of capitalist society. There exists an increasingly complex body of "offences against property" that are concerned with the defense of private property. First they are important in demarcating the "lawful" from the "unlawful"; they differentiate between the unlawful appropriation of property, the acts of the "criminals," and the lawful forms of appropriation that are the hallmark of the capitalist system. Just how close is the dividing line between lawful and unlawful appropriation has been clearly revealed by recent bribery and corruption cases. But second, it is not only the offender that is coerced, but all members of society because the coercion of the offender reinforces the values, attitudes, and behavior associated with the existence of private property. It is for this reason that it was stressed above that the coercive and ideological functions of law are closely related.

While the criminal law protects the property interests of the capitalist class it operates more generally to protect the "private property" of all members of society. Indeed it is important to recognise that the vast majority of "property offences" are committed, not against the property of the capitalist class, but rather against the property of noncapitalists. Property offences are usually directed against the privately owned consumption goods of working people.

Another way in which legal coercion is applied to defend the *general* conditions of capitalist society is with respect to "offences against the person." Again this area of the criminal law does not merely act against offences against members of the capitalist class. The significance of this type of legal coercion is that some level of general social order is a necessary precondition for the maintenance of its specifically capitalist content.

One of the most important manifestations of legal coercion is the application of law for the direct protection of the state itself. The state has at its disposal a veritable armory of measures that are ready to be invoked to defend the existing political order. These range from a number of traditional offences such as treason, treachery, and sedition (which have been invoked fairly infrequently in the recent past), through such legislation as the *Official Secrets Act* of 1911 and 1920 and the *Incitement to Disaffection Act* 1934, to the wide ranging emergency powers that the ruling class has gradually accumulated. *The Emergency Powers Acts* of 1920 and 1964 give very extensive powers to the civil and military authorities to intervene in the class struggle. These powers have been used on no less than eight occasions since the War; on four of these occasions by the Heath government against dockers, power supply workers, and the miners; Labour Governments have not shrunk from invoking them.

In the recent past Northern Ireland has been a fertile source of emergency regulations. *The Northern Ireland (Emergency Provisions) Act* 1973 and the *Prevention of Terrorism (Emergency Powers) Act* 1974 have aided the British government's struggle against the Irish people and their scope has been extended to the mainland.[2]

The ruling class also has at its disposal a wide range of legal devices that can be used against offences against public order. These range through riot, affray, unlawful assembly and breach of the peace. Of particular importance is the *Public Order Act* 1936, supposedly introduced to curb the Fascists, but used systematically against the Left. It is interesting to observe the skill of the police and courts in making use of "appropriate" legal mechanisms. A good example has been the recent resuscitation of the *Conspiracy and Protection of Property Act* 1875.

In protecting the existing political order the law does not only have at its disposal the wide ranging powers contained in the legislation discussed above. The general principles of criminal law offer not only ample scope, but also special advantage. It is often in the interest of the ruling class to seek to depoliticize the class struggle. One of the means that is frequently invoked is to charge the "political offender" with ordinary crimes. This can be achieved by using a charge that is incidental to the main social or political issue involved; the most favored police strategy being to invoke charges involving or implying violence. A very good example of this technique is to be seen in the trial of the Shrewsbury pickets. The use of such charges allows the political issues to be ignored while branding the defendants as "common criminals," a tactic favored by Roy Jenkins and Frank Chapple in their attacks on the Shrewsbury pickets.

A related prosecution strategy is to use blanket charges; much in favor in the recent past has been the use of conspiracy charges. These are not only significant in that they allow the prosecution to evade some of the restrictions with regard to the evidence and procedure that normally apply. But in addition, through the orchestration by the mass media, to create impressions of the existence of an unspecified "threat to law and order."

The legal order has at its disposal this powerful armoury of techniques of legal coercion that enable it to directly intervene in the class struggle to defend the interest of the existing order. This direct intervention in the class struggle stands out most sharply in the case of industrial and trade union laws.[3] The history of trade union law, from the *Combination Act* 1800 to the *Industrial Relations Act* 1971, is testimony to the attempt to provide a legal framework favorable to the interests of capital as opposed to those of labor. Yet it is also testimony to the extent of the resistance that over the period as a whole has not only forced tactical retreats, but has also witnessed significant advances in the legal positions of trade unions. I will return later to take up this question of law as an arena of class struggle.

What stands out in sharp relief is the extent to which the ruling class utilizes a legal framework for sustaining and buttressing their class interests. But a certain degree of care is needed in drawing conclusions from this common ground. The argument is frequently advanced that in periods of crisis the capitalist class resort to an increasingly repressive strategy and embark on major attacks on civil liberties. This type of analysis is very clearly presented in John Hostettler's article "Trends to Authoritarian Rule in Britain" (*Marxism Today*, Dec. 1973). This line of argument is sometimes presented in such a way that it obscures important contradictory dimensions, which if correctly considered throw much light on the specific role of law within capitalist society.

The lurch of legal authoritarianism is checked by an equally strong need on the part of the ruling class to maintain the legitimacy of their class rule. This contradiction is not an interaction between two equal forces that smoothly balance each other out; hence there are periods in which there are major shifts toward authoritarianism, but equally there are periods of movement toward more liberal and less coercive forms. The particular result at any point in time is a complex result of the level of class struggle itself.

There is a more general, and possibly more fundamental, political point that underlies this discussion that needs to be more fully discussed. Lenin was correct when he argued that

> bourgeois states are most varied in form, but their essence is the same; all these states, whatever their form in the final analysis are inevitably the dictatorship of the bourgeoisie. (CW 25: 413).

Yet there has been a tendency (which is present in Lenin as well as in others) to regard bourgeois democracy as simply a sham or fraud designed to conceal the class character of the rule of the bourgeoisie. Capitalism has been in existence long enough to demonstrate that its most persistent, stable and "successful" form has proved to be the *bourgeois democratic* political form. Thus for the bourgeoisie whatever pressures manifest themselves toward the "authoritarian solution" there is at the same time a profound concern to sustain the legitimacy of the capitalist order.

This analysis does not lead to the conclusion that the resort by the ruling class to fascism or to military coup is impossible. The tragic example of Chile is too urgent to allow such a naive conclusion. But this analysis does insist that the resort to fascism is not the automatic response of a capitalist class in crisis. We should have no illusions about the fact that the capitalist class has been prepared, in the final analysis, to abandon bourgeois democracy. But we should be equally insistent that the interests of the bourgeoisie have been best served where they have been able to sustain their class rule within the bourgeois democratic form and that the ruling class itself has an interest in the preservation of bourgeois democracy.

The legal order plays a central role within bourgeois democracy. Thus while the coercive role of the legal order has been emphasized in the first half of this article it is now necessary to draw attention to and to examine the contribution made by the legal system to sustaining the legitimacy of the bourgeois democratic order. In other words it is necessary to discuss law as a method of ideological domination.

LAW AS IDEOLOGICAL DOMINATION

Repressive and ideological domination are in no sense alternatives. On the contrary they are interdependent; they interact and reinforce each other. While the coercion of the criminal law is directed against those it punishes, its ideological effects are directed much wider. For example, the jailing of the Shrewsbury pickets was legal violence against the accused which was concerned with more than "deterring" others; it was an ideological offence against the strategy of the "flying picket" developed by the miners and applied so effectively by building workers.

Ideological domination describes those activities and processes whereby the assent to the existing social order is produced and mobilized. The notion of assent embraces both the idea of legitimacy as active assent and also acceptance as the passive form. The means by which assent is produced are ideological in that it involves the production and dissemination of ideas that affect social practice through the determination of the social consciousness of individuals, groups, and classes. This process is one of domination in that it involves two elements; first, a differential ability of groups and classes in society to produce, communicate, and disseminate ideas, and second, these ideas, directly or indirectly, have consequences for the maintenance of the existing social order.

Law is ideological in that it conveys or transmits a complex set of attitudes, values, and theories about aspects of society. Its ideological content forms part of the dominant ideology because these attitudes, values, etc. are ones that reinforce and legitimize the existing social order.

The most pervasive ideological effect of law is to be found in the fact that legal rules and their application give effect to existing social relations. The rules of law affirm the social and economic relations that exist within capitalist society. Thus the law of property is not only based on the inequality of property ownership but it reinforces it by allowing and facilitating the owners of property to make use of that property as capital. The complex of legal rules relating to mortgages, trusts, leases, etc. not only allows but also enables property to be used as capital. The law relating to contracts and commercial activity gives effect to the mechanisms of the market.

Similarly labor law facilitates the capitalist form of the relationship between labor and capital; it gives effect to the economic fact of the dependence of the majority on the sale of their labor power. It embodies the economic power of capital over labor by granting to the employer rights regarding not only the control of labor but also over hiring and firing of labor.

Rules of law impinge on almost every form of social relations. For example, family law, despite the reforms of the past decades, incorporates the fact of the dominant role of the husband over the wife, of the parents over the children. Likewise the law of landlord and tenant underlines the power of landlords over tenants in regard to the supply of housing. It is important to stress that the legal rules do not *create* the social relations that make up capitalist society. But by stating them as principles and by enforcing them the law operates not only to reinforce these relations but also to legitimize them in their existing form. This function is further advanced by the role of law in conferring authority upon officials such as the police, magistrates, etc.

The rules of law not only define social relations but confer rights and powers on certain categories of individuals. Thus, for example, landlord and tenant law not only incorporates the economic fact of the monopolization of housing by private interests, but it also legitimizes that economic power by granting rights to landlords to extract rent, to impose conditions, and to evict tenants. The legal system not only reinforces existing social and economic relations, but in addition it confers authority on dominant social interests.

One important aspect that should not be overlooked is the extent to which law operates to regulate the mutual interests of the bourgeoisie. It provides a mechanism for the resolution of disputes and conflicts that arise *between* capitalist interests:

> The administration of ... civil justice is concerned almost exclusively with conflicts over property and hence affects almost exclusively the possessing classes. (Marx 1958: II, 34)

Company law, for example, is concerned in the main with the respective interests of shareholders and directors. Much commercial law is likewise concerned with the interests of merchants, middlemen, and dealers.

The law regulating the interests of the propertied classes is detailed and complex, but it has a significant common core. The operation of capitalistic functions is facilitated where the law provides a degree of certainty and predictability. What bourgeois legal theory fails to recognize is that it is only that element of law that regulates the mutual interests of the bourgeoisie, and not the whole of law in a capitalist society that exhibits this quest for certainty.

It is necessary to consider more closely the nature of the correspondence between legal rules and the social relations to which they relate. Legal rules do not simply "reflect" social relations. The rules of law have an added ideological dimension. To explain this it is important to recall that a central feature of capitalist society is that its essential features are obscured or concealed by the very nature of the operation of the capitalist economy. Marx insisted on the need to distinguish between how

things appear (the "appearance" or "phenomenal form") and how they really are ("real substratum" or "essence").

The "real" relations that exist find themselves expressed in legal rules in a distorted or truncated form because the law gives effect to only the appearance ("phenomenal form") of social relations. This theoretical point could be taken further by applying the argument developed by Marx in the famous section on "the fetishism of commodities" in *Capital* Vol. I in which he shows how our comprehension of commodities embodies not the real social relations of production which create them, but simply as things; and as a result what are relations between people come to be seen as relations between things.

So legal rules appear abstracted from social relations, and are therefore a "fetishistic" expression of social relations. Legal rules are further divorced from the social relations to which they refer because they (like the state itself) appear separated, independent of society; they seem to have an independent origin and life of their own. Thus as ideological forms of social relations legal rules are doubly removed from the real world.

Legal rules express the appearance of social relations:

> This phenomenal form, which makes the actual relations invisible ... forms the basis of all the juridical notions of both labourer and capitalist, of all the mystifications of the capitalist mode of production, of all its illusions as to liberty. (Marx 1961: I, 540)

Marx showed how our initial perception of the capitalist economy focuses on the process of circulation and exchange, and thus ignores the production process itself. It is significant to note that legal rules follow this pattern and reduce social relations to a system of exchanges. The key legal concept of bourgeois law is that of *contract*. All the most important relations within capitalist society are moulded into the form of contractual relations.

By treating social relations as "contracts" bourgeois law strips them of their most important characteristics. Perhaps the most important example is in the labor relationship between employers and workers. At law the labor relation is a contract between individual employer and individual employee; they are therefore presumed to bargain over the terms of the contract. This individualizing of the contract of employment by focusing on it as an individual exchange excludes the social character of the relation between capital and labor. It is incapable of embracing the increasingly collective determination of labor relations through negotiations between trade unions and employers' federations. English law has reduced itself to great confusion in attempting to preserve the "individual contract" while taking some note of the real "collective contract."

It is not only economic relations that are reduced to contractual form. A wide range of other social relations is similarly treated. Thus, for example, the social institution of marriage is enshrined in law as a contract within which the "parties" have obligations that derive from the contract, and the "breach" of which can result in the contract being terminated, i.e., in divorce. Yet by expressing the marriage relationship in contractual form the law inadvertently exposes something of the real economic basis on which the bourgeois marriage is based, founded on the economic dependence of women.

The principles of contract have been so pervasive that they have been developed into a contractual ideology which continues to have wider ranging influences. Contractual ideology leans heavily on the notions of freedom and equality. But the "freedom" and "equality" to which it refers is purely *formal*; that is individuals are regarded as free if there is no legal bar to them entering into a contract, and are therefore deemed to be equal. It is a notion of equality brilliantly captured by Anatole France:

> The law in its majestic impartiality forbids rich and poor alike to sleep under bridges, to beg in the streets and steal bread (1927: 91)

These formal notions of freedom and equality are characteristic of bourgeois legal and political theory. They do violence to social reality because they are incapable of grasping the real inequality and lack of freedom that results from the dependence of all workers on the sale of their labor.

This discussion has focused on the way in which the rules of law, far from being pure or independent creations, are but a distorted expression of the existing social relations which are thereby reinforced and legitimised. This ideological character of legal rules is extended by two further considerations.

One of the difficulties in penetrating the ideological form of bourgeois law stems from the fact that it operates by abstracting the cases that come before the courts from their social and class context. They are thereby reduced to the status of being pure *technical* issues, apparently divorced from any political or ideological overtones. If, for example, a householder inquires why it is that tax relief is granted on mortgage payments but not on rent, the law replies that it is not a question of relief on mortgage or rent, but on interest repayments. By focusing on a technical distinction the law thereby obscures the social and economic reality.

Second, the law further depoliticizes social issues through the universal form of many legal rules. The fact that rules of criminal law protect the person and property of all members of society not only hides the fundamental class differences, but it also treats the capital of the employer and the personal belongings of the worker as if they were the same. The ideological significance is that it induces the view that all classes in society have a common interest in the protection of private property. Thereby the legal system is aided in fulfilling the ideological function of asserting the unity of interests of all classes. The ideology of the "rule of law" operates to assert and reinforce, and even seeks to celebrate, a social unity and cohesion in the face of the manifest class differentiation of capitalist society.

There is one further facet of the ideological character of law. It is directly ideological in the sense that the legal system propagates a range of views about the nature of the social and political system. This general ideological character of law is contained in what I will call "bourgeois legal ideology."

Bourgeois legal ideology is the fundamental component of the justification of the bourgeois democratic state; many of its elements directly enter into the consciousness of wide sections of the population. The central element of this ideology is the doctrine of "the rule of law." Its classic expression is to be found in Dicey:

> When we speak of the "rule of law" as a characteristic of our country we mean, not only that with us no man is above the law, but (what is a different thing) that every man, whatever be his rank or condition, is subject to the ordinary law of the realm.... With us every official, from the Prime Minister down to a constable ... is under the same responsibility for every act done without legal justification as any other citizen. (1967: 193)

The fundamental tenet is that both the ruled and the rulers are equally subject to a common system of the law. The "law" itself is thus viewed as something separate from the interests of classes. As such it plays a central role in the legitimation of the bourgeois democratic political order.

One particularly interesting feature of bourgeois legal ideology in the context of English law is the way in which it holds itself out as the protector of the individual against the incursions of the state. This antithesis between individual and state has a lengthy history in bourgeois legal thought. Its roots were in the historical alliance between the common law judges and the bourgeois interests against the absolutism of the Stuarts. It became more fully elaborated during the nineteenth century as the legal reflex of laissez-faire ideology. And in the twentieth century it has been used as the basis of antistate attitudes that characterize one element of the conservative reaction to the growth of the Welfare State.

In addition to explicit constitutional principles bourgeois legal ideology consists of a range of important background or implicit assumptions. The intention is only to roughly sketch some of these assumptions, but at the same time to argue that the more the "law and order" debate moves into the center of the political stage the more important it becomes to develop a systematic critique of bourgeois legal ideology.

Almost all discussion about law is based on the assumption that the existence of law is an inevitable or natural feature of social life. Hence law becomes identified with "civilization"; the absence of law is seen as synonymous with the absence of civilization. The classic expression of this assumption is the equation of the absence of law with anarchy; in its classical form in the political philosophy of Hobbes the absence of law implies a condition of "the war of all against all." The whole of society is presumed to have an interest in the existence of law, and is therefore closely connected with the "universalism" of law discussed above.

A closely associated assumption insists on the inherent rationality of law. The existence of rules of social life brought together or codified as law is presented as socially desirable in that it makes social life more certain and predictable. Social life is viewed as if it were a game or a sport in which it is essential that all the "players" adhere to the same rules; without this common set of rules social life would revert to anarchy. Such an attitude places stress on the desirability of rules *as such*, and hence leaves unquestioned the content of those rules and any questions concerning the social and economic interests that are embodied in the rules.

Flowing directly from the insistence on the naturalness and rationality of law is the insistence that adherence to law is natural, and as a corollary, that nonadherence to law is unnatural or deviant. The very existence of a state is treated as a sufficient condition to make obedience to law obligatory for all citizens. The assumption is made that the offender who violates the law is a deviant whose deviation stems from some pathological condition. While the nature of the pathology appealed to has varied, from the genetic inferiority of the "lower orders" to deficiencies in "socialization," the same assumption

of the naturalness of obedience to law persists. It is interesting to note that in the recent past this essentially conservative tradition has come under increasing attack from criminologists, and that radical theories of crime are being developed which draw upon Marxism (Taylor, Walton, and Young 1972).

These interrelated attitudes and assumptions about law are not usually expressed in a coherent form: they are a cluster of ideas, but they add up to an assertion of the "sanctity of law" that forms the heart of the pervasive and powerful "law and order" ideology. This ideology finds expression not only in the moralizing editorials of the *Times*, but also forms an important part of widespread and diffuse social attitudes. The essential substance of these views is that they appeal to the sanctity of law, elevated above social life itself, and thereby ignore the class content of law and its role in legitimising the existing forms of class domination.

There is one final aspect of the ideological character of law that needs to be mentioned. The most formal and systematic expression of legal ideology is provided by jurisprudence or legal theory. The history of jurisprudence consists in successive attempts to provide a justification for obedience to law. The central concern has been to provide a socially persuasive account of the legitimacy of the existing legal order, and through that of the social order itself. However, a very interesting development has occurred within jurisprudence which is worth noting. Increasingly a number of liberal academics have been afflicted with growing self-doubt and disillusionment with the whole edifice of law, and are increasingly aware of a very real decline in the legitimacy of the existing legal order (Rostow 1970; Wolff 1971).

The operation of law is, therefore, not confined to simply giving effect to the direct and immediate interests of the ruling class. It must be understood as having an ideological function of an extensive character. Within capitalist society the legal system not only provides substantial ideological underpinnings to the existing capitalist organization of society. It also provides a consistent and coherent legitimation of a multitude of key institutions and principles that are central to the smooth operation of a system of capitalist social relations.

It is this ability to integrate two critical functions, on the one hand to give practical effect to the interests of the dominant class, and, at the same time, to provide a justification or legitimation for these interests in terms of some higher and apparently universal interest of all classes that demonstrates the real power and influence of law in capitalist society.

239

LAW AND CLASS STRUGGLE

Our attention has been focused on the part that law plays in the process of reproducing capitalist social order. Yet law is not simply an instrument which can be wielded at will by an omnipotent ruling class. Precisely because it is an active element in the class struggle, it is at the same time affected by and involved in the class struggle. The law and the legal system form part of the context within which the class struggle takes place, and it is itself an arena in which that struggle occurs. To recognize that class struggle occurs *within* the legal system is not to suggest that the legal system is some neutral territory over which the class struggle wrestles for control. As a major component of the state law is necessarily part of the process through which the ruling class seeks to preserve its domination.

To argue that class struggle occurs within law is only the first step in examining the way in which class struggle makes itself evident within law. It has been argued above that law plays a central part in bourgeois democratic society, not only in theory but also in practice. The form taken by the class struggle has its boundaries broadly defined by the existing law. Thus, for example, trade union activity in Britain is pursued by forms of struggle that are recognized as being lawful. Some of the most important stages in the history of British trade unionism have been periods when struggle has occurred around attempts by the ruling class to narrow or restrict this lawful sphere of operations. The struggle against the *Industrial Relations Act* was a classic example of this type of struggle.

While law plays this important part of defining the parameters of class struggle, it also needs to be recognized that it does not necessarily stay confined within this framework. Indeed a change in this boundary or its breach will normally mark a critical phase in the class struggle. For example, a very important stage of the struggle against the *Industrial Relations Act* occurred in the months after it had been put on the statute book. The right-wing inside the Labour Movement argued that despite the objection they had to the Act it was now "law" and had to be accepted. The critical phase was the decisions made in the individual unions and within the TUC (Croydon and Blackpool Congresses 1971) as to whether they would "register" under the Act, and thus come within "the law," or whether to remain unregistered and to conduct trade union activity without the forms of protection that had been established since the beginning of the century.

Not only does law play an important part in defining the parameters of the class struggle, but many important stages in the class struggle take place around demands for legislative reforms. Marx himself gave considerable attention to one very important example of such struggles, the early *Factory Acts* (in particular the *Factories Regulation Act* of 1833). His chapter in *Capital* Volume I, on "The Working-Day" is a classic study of the interrelation and interaction of class forces in a struggle for legislative control of working hours.

> The creation of a normal working-day is, therefore, the product of a protracted civil war, more or less dissembled, between the capitalist class and the working-class. (1961: I, 231–302)

Elsewhere he summarized the significance of the victory underlying the Act in the following terms:

> it was the first time that in broad daylight the political economy of the middle class succumbed to the political economy of the working class. (1958: I, 383)

His analysis makes clear that the Factory Acts were not simply the direct result of class struggle between the capitalist and working classes. Two particular features of the analysis are worth drawing attention to. The first concerns the relationship between the state and the capitalist class. The advent of machinery and industrial production in the textile industry gives rise to a veritable orgy of exploitation in which the working-day is extended to such lengths that a real threat is posed to the survival of the work force. At this stage the state represents the collective interests of capital, as distinct from the interests of individual capitalists.

Second, he stresses the divisions between the various sections of the capitalist class. Not only is there the division between the landed and industrial capitalists, which led the Tories as representatives of landed capital, to support factory legislation. But more important are the divisions between the more advanced sections of industrial capital and the smaller, more traditional employers. The passage of the factory acts represented a victory not only for the working class, but also for the more advanced sections of capital, who triumphed over their less efficient rivals. The overall analysis therefore brings out with great sharpness the way in which the development of the productive forces, in association with the more or less conscious struggle of various classes, finds its expression in legislation.

In his discussion of factory legislation Marx showed clearly how each legislative victory was only partial; while each was a major practical and ideological victory, the employers, with the direct complicity of the magistrates and judges, impeded the effective enforcement of the provisions of the statutes.

CONCLUSION

In this chapter I have stressed the importance of law in capitalist society, and as a consequence argued that it is a question that requires a more thorough analysis by Marxists. While this chapter does not complete that task, it has sought to raise a number of questions, and to stress a number of areas for discussion. Some of these have been of a general nature that revolve around an assertion of law as an important agency in the maintenance of capitalist social relations. In particular I have argued the need to understand the significance of law as a system of ideological-coercive domination. It is through this emphasis on this combined process, rather than as two distinct or separate processes, that we can achieve a better understanding of the specific functioning of law within capitalist society, and is also of assistance in achieving a fuller theoretical treatment of the capitalist state.

The legal system within the bourgeois democratic state operates in such a way as to legitimize the class rule of the bourgeoisie. This legitimation involves not only the recognition and reinforcement of the social and economic relations of capitalism. It also encompasses the reification of law (through which law appears to be a power above and outside society) in which the social and political relations of capitalist society are presented as natural and universal. Law then operates to provide ideological reinforcement to those processes that make the reality of class and class power less visible.

The really difficult question is posed by the fact that bourgeois democratic society is not entirely a facade and a fraud. If it were its veils and deceits would have been stripped away long ago. Its strength and persistence result from the fact that in varying degrees it has successfully combined the continued social, political and economic dominance of the capitalist class with, at the same time, a significant level of involvement of the exploited classes sufficient to ensure a relatively high level of acceptance of, and even commitment to, the existing order.

Within the bourgeois democratic state law provides, alongside those aspects that reinforce the domination of the ruling class, an important set of rights, protections, and powers that in varying degrees incorporate certain class interests of the nonruling classes. The most obvious examples of these are such things as the right to vote, to form trade unions, to take strike action, etc.

It is important to recognize that most of these have been secured as the result of class struggle. But these facts should not lead us to view them simply as concessions wrung from the capitalist. Once granted they become woven into the fabric of bourgeois democracy. It should also be noted that we need to recognize that the range of legal rights that may be used to the advantage of the working class extends beyond the range of the more obvious "political" rights mentioned. The law confers rights and protections on all classes as "citizens" in bourgeois democracy. It is of course important to stress the inequality of their application and the inequality of access to legal redress. Yet this does not negate their political and ideological importance. Their very existence plays a significant part in securing the acceptance of, and allegiance to, the existing capitalist social order.

(b) Impacts of Criminalization on the Everyday Lives of People Living with HIV in Canada†

Barry D. Adam, Richard Elliott, Patrice Corriveau, and Ken English

As part of a study on the social consequences of the criminal justice system on people living with HIV or AIDS (PHAs) in Canada, this article focuses on how heightened public identification of HIV with criminal

† (2014) 11 Sex Res Soc Policy 39 at 39–45, 47–48. [Notes and/or references omitted.] Copyright © 2013, Springer Science+Business Media New York. With kind permission from Springer Science and Business Media.

matters is having wide ranging effects on perceived personal security and in particular on negotiating potential romantic and sexual interactions. As articulated by the Supreme Court of Canada, the courts have been enforcing a requirement that HIV-positive people disclose their serostatus to prospective partners, relying on the notion that "through deterrence it [the Criminal Code] will protect and serve to encourage honesty, frankness and safer sexual practices." Nevertheless an accumulating set of evidence in the social and health sciences is pointing toward the difficulties of carrying out this directive in everyday life and toward the ways in which the application of law creates counter-productive or unanticipated consequences that can run contrary to the ostensible objective of discouraging behaviour likely to transmit HIV.

THE SOCIO-LEGAL CONTEXT

In recent years, the judicial system has become an increasingly prominent player in the public policy response to HIV. Eighty-four percent of criminal prosecutions for alleged HIV non-disclosure to sexual partners have occurred in the 6 years from 2004 to 2010 in Ontario though HIV was identified more than 30 years ago (Mykhalovskiy and Betteridge 2012). The rising number of prosecutions has been accompanied by media attention bringing criminalization increasingly to the fore in HIV coverage. The treatment of HIV (non)disclosure within a criminal law framework shows a particular gender and racial pattern. Sixty-nine percent of the criminal cases in this period have involved men who have been charged with failing to disclose their serostatus to female sex partners, and half of these cases have involved men from black Caribbean or African communities (Mykhalovskiy and Betteridge 2012, 40–41; Larcher and Symington 2010), a pattern that has also been observed in Britain and Australia (Weait 2007; Persson and Newman 2008). The media have extensively covered the cases with greatest potential for public scandal, turning them into high-profile instances of HIV criminalization, potentially shaping perceptions of HIV transmission for many members of society including institutional actors, people at risk and people living with HIV.

Much of the increased judicial attention to HIV follows on the 1998 decision of the Supreme Court of Canada in *R. v. Cuerrier*, [1998] 2 S.C.R. 371, which established a requirement that HIV-positive people disclose their serostatus in situations of "significant risk of serious bodily harm" (Elliott 1999; Symington 2009). The Court ruled that not disclosing in such circumstances could constitute fraud that vitiates consent to the sexual activity, therefore turning it into an assault as a matter of law under the country's *Criminal Code* and indeed, the charge most frequently laid in subsequent years has been *aggravated sexual assault*, the most serious of the three categories of sexual assault, which includes any assault that "endangers the life of the complainant." The elevation of disclosure as a primary consideration in criminal cases and the publicizing of these cases by the media have made disclosure a leading part of public discourse on HIV and have resulted in the courts becoming significant actors in the definition of HIV as a public problem. The general absence of legislative action in this area and the low visibility of AIDS service organizations and public health in the public sphere (apart from a few organizations with a specifically legal mandate), have created a striking case study in the *governmentality* of health and disease. In other words, the accumulation of case law, occurring through the actions of individual complainants, police authorities, prosecutors, judges and juries in a range of lower courts has created an uneven accretion of decisions that have been constituting public policy in the absence of defined legislative parameters on the subject.

In February 2012, HIV non-disclosure returned to the Supreme Court of Canada in the cases of *R. v. Mabior* and *R. v. D.C.*, in which the Attorneys General of Manitoba and Alberta (and more ambiguously, the Attorney General of Quebec) argued for obligatory disclosure of HIV status in any sexual encounter regardless of the degree of risk of transmission (Canadian HIV/AIDS Legal Network 2012; Elliott and Symington 2012a, b). The Ontario Attorney General also originally sought to advance this position, subsequently withdrew its request for intervener status at the Supreme Court, but reinstated it in materials filed in other prosecutions before the Ontario Court of Appeal in June of 2012. Striking the "significant risk" qualification from the legal test for conviction and from prosecutorial policy would have elevated the question of whether there has been disclosure to the status of the single, overriding consideration in the application of the criminal law to HIV. In its paired rulings in the *Mabior* and *D.C.* cases, released in October 2012, the Supreme Court of Canada did not, strictly speaking, go as far as was urged by the attorneys-general. The Court did not impose a blanket obligation to disclose (known) HIV-positive status, and instead asserted that it was maintaining the "significant risk of serious bodily harm" test from its earlier ruling[;] however, the Court ruled that there is a "significant risk" if there is a "realistic possibility" of HIV transmission[,] declaring that, at least in the case of penile–vaginal sex (the activity that was before the Court on the facts of the two cases), only if there had been *both* the use of latex condom *and* the HIV-positive partner had a "low" viral load (under 1,500 copies/mL) at the time of the encounter would there to be no "realistic possibility" of transmission. By deciding that there is a duty to disclose before vaginal sex unless both a condom is used *and* a person's viral load is low, the Court effectively decided that anything greater than this very strict measure of risk could trigger a duty to disclose. This approach was at odds with the suggestion by a majority of the Court in its earlier *Cuerrier* ruling that protected sex (i.e. using a condom) should or might not attract criminal liability, a proposition that had been explicitly or implicitly adopted in the bulk of the subsequent lower court rulings after *Cuerrier*.

The courts, then, have become actors in the field of HIV prevention. Indeed, on behalf of the majority of the Supreme Court of Canada in the 1998 *Cuerrier* decision, Justice Cory opined:

> If ever there was a place for the deterrence provided by criminal sanctions it is present in these circumstances. It may well have the desired effect of ensuring that there is disclosure of the risk and that appropriate precautions are taken.... It is true that all members of society should be aware of the danger and take steps to avoid the risk. However, the primary responsibility for making the disclosure must rest upon those who are aware they are infected. I would hope that every member of society no matter how "marginalized" would be sufficiently responsible that they would advise their partner of risks. In these circumstances it is, I trust, not too much to expect that the infected person would advise his partner of his infection. That responsibility cannot be lightly shifted to unknowing members of society who are wooed, pursued and encouraged by infected individuals to become their sexual partners.... Yet the *Criminal Code* does have a role to play. Through deterrence it will protect and serve to encourage honesty, frankness and safer sexual practices. (paras. 142, 144, 147)

The court-mandated requirement for disclosure of HIV status flows from a particular model of human behaviour that holds that: (a) HIV-positive people can and should assume the responsibility of warning others of the potential for infection, and (b) prospective partners, once informed of that potential, will act appropriately to avoid infection. It is a model of human behaviour that grounds a good deal of law in liberal, democratic societies: people are conceived as autonomous, rational makers of contracts. Indeed, the Supreme Court of Canada's interpretation and application of the criminal law of assault to the circumstance of alleged HIV non-disclosure in *Cuerrier* explicitly rests on adapting established principles from the domain of fraud in the context of commercial contracts. The question arises, however, how well this model of human behaviour works in everyday instances of sexual encounter to bring about the objective of HIV prevention as enunciated by the Court.

DISCLOSURE IN PRACTICE

The research record, however, shows just how problematic a reliance on disclosure can be in managing HIV risk (Simoni and Pantalone 2004; Adam 2006; Race 2012). The relationship between disclosure and HIV risk is complex at best. Research on gay and bisexual men shows that the consistent practice of safer sex usually does not require discussion and typically happens without it (Henriksson and Månsson 1995). In fact, those who decide from encounter to encounter whether to disclose or not, and who then disclose inconsistently, have higher rates of unprotected sex than either those who disclose consistently or those who do not disclose (Hart et al. 2005; Mao et al. 2006; Holt et al. 2011; St de Lore et al. 2012). While some studies have found an association between disclosure and condom use, more have found no relationship (Galletly and Pinkerton 2006). Indeed, John de Wit et al. (2009, 105) conclude, "using a condom with casual sexual partners is more likely if there is *no* disclosure, suggesting that for many men disclosure signals the possibility of not using condoms." This indicates a tacit norm, shared by gay men of different serostatuses, that presumes that disclosure is unnecessary if safe sex is practised (Heaphy 2001, 127).

Disclosure poses a range of challenges in everyday social situations. The demand to disclose essentially requires HIV-positive people to place themselves in a situation to be rejected or stigmatized (Galletly and Dickson-Gomez 2009), a situation exacerbated in a climate of rising prosecution and media attention. Michael Stirratt's (2005, 103) interviews with HIV-positive people found that "rejection from partners following disclosure took many forms, including refusal to have sex, unwillingness to engage in particular sex practices, emotional distancing, abrupt or longer-term relationship dissolution and even (although rarely) acts of violence." A publication of the National Association of People Living with HIV/AIDS in Australia explains it this way,

"Most people experience several episodes of rejection if they are upfront with every sex partner about their status, and some find it difficult to get the confidence to disclose until they have been HIV-positive for some time. Any kind of sexual rejection can be crushing to the ego and to self-esteem, and for quite a few, disclosing every time takes considerable courage and bravery" (Menadue 2009, 147).

In practice, disclosure proves to be particularly difficult for people (often women) in a relationship of dependency (Siegel et al. 2005) or those who feel disadvantaged by age, attractiveness or ethno-cultural background (Adam 2005). Disclosure occurs more often with partners in an ongoing relationship; less often with new acquaintances (Bairan et al. 2007; Driskell et al. 2008). Though disclosure may often be presumed to be a communication between two people in private, once disclosure has happened, the confidentiality of that information is dependent on the trustworthiness and thoughtfulness of the recipient who can easily break confidence or disclose to more people in potentially damaging ways. Criminalization may in fact *discourage* people from disclosing as they may decide that it is better to let "sleeping dogs lie" rather than risk being placed in a position of vulnerability by a potentially vindictive partner (Adam et al. 2008; Galletly and Dickson-Gomez 2009). Criminalization heightens the sense of HIV as a stigmatized status making it more difficult to live openly as HIV-positive (Dodds and Keogh 2006).

This conflict of exigencies can heighten the tension between approach and avoidant coping strategies (Chaudoir et al. 2011) resulting in protracted or indirect disclosure where HIV-positive people feel out interlocutors or test the waters to gauge the receptiveness of potential audiences (Welch Cline and McKenzie 2000). For example, some refer to receiving disability payments, working in HIV-related organizations, living in an HIV residence, having symptoms that could be construed as HIV disease or taking medication as methods of incremental disclosure (Stirratt 2005; Adam 2005; Serovich et al. 2005; Adam et al. 2008).

Ultimately reliance on disclosure makes sense as an HIV prevention measure only if both partners are certain of their serostatus, though epidemiologists point out that significant percentages of people who are HIV-positive do not know they are. In Canada, an estimated 26% of people infected with HIV are unaware of this fact (Public Health Agency of Canada 2010). Indeed some researchers contend that transmission by those unaware of their infection accounts for a significant portion of new infections (Brenner et al. 2007). Criminal prosecutions for non-disclosure encourage at-risk persons to rely on prospective sex partners to disclose their HIV status, if positive, and to assume that there is no or minimal risk in the absence of positive serostatus disclosure, evident in complainants' testimony at trial in such cases. Serostatus disclosure laws may thus foster a false sense of security among HIV-negative persons who may default to forgoing safer sex unless notified of their partners' HIV-positive status (Galletly and Pinkerton 2006). Reliance on disclosure, then, is a shaky foundation for HIV avoidance. By absolving people of responsibility for practising safer sex, it may even *increase* vulnerability to infection.

Disclosure, then, is often challenging to accomplish in everyday life and the research evidence shows that disclosure is far from reliable as a method of avoiding HIV. The accumulation and consolidation of a body of legal doctrine that rests primarily on an obligation to disclose by those who know they are HIV-positive raises a number of problems in the pursuit of effective public policy in HIV prevention. This study sets out to examine how the court obligation to disclose plays out in negotiating potential romantic and sexual interactions in everyday life in the contemporary legal climate in Canada.

. . . .

IMPACTS OF CRIMINALIZATION ON EVERYDAY LIFE

Focus groups with PHAs in Britain and Canada concerning criminalization have shown responses ranging from no personal impact to heightened anxiety, including both increased and decreased disclosure in the face of increased stigma (Dodds et al. 2009; Mykhalovskiy et al. 2010). A focus group of 31 Michigan PHAs showed that many "perceived vulnerability to unwanted secondary disclosure by a prospective partner to whom they disclosed in compliance with the law" (Galletly and Dickson-Gomez 2009, 615). They worried about "being falsely accused [as] there is likely to be little evidence with which to prove that the HIV-positive person indeed disclosed" and that the criminal justice system "went beyond biased attitudes to include frank discrimination."

The rising tide of prosecutions for non-disclosure and exposure to HIV in Ontario has a wide range of effects on people living with HIV. The largest number of respondents believe that criminalization has unfairly shifted the burden of proof so that PHAs are held to be guilty until proven innocent and that: (a) PHAs are now caught in a difficult he-said/(s)he-said situation of having to justify their actions, (b) disgruntled partners now have a legal weapon to wield against them regardless of the facts and (c) the onus now falls on women whose male partners could ignore their wishes regarding safer sex. In terms of general impact, many respondents report: (a) a heightened sense of uncertainty, fear or vulnerability, but others feel that (b) the climate of acceptance is still better than in the early days of the epidemic or that (c) the prosecution of the high profile cases is justified and these PHAs are giving all PHAs a bad name.

A sizeable contingent of study participants feels unaffected because they: (a) always disclose their serostatus in sexual encounters, (b) openly negotiate serostatus often preferring sero-concordant partners, (c) feel that disclosure of serostatus is the morally right thing to do regardless of the law or (d) are not having sex anyway. It is worth bearing in mind that the best represented age group, both in the HIV prevalence numbers and among participants in this study, is people in their 40s and 50s. Many are in long-term relationships and others report not having sex in recent months[,] meaning that disclosure in sexual relationships may not be seen as immediately relevant to their lives.

Other PHAs take a more situational or conditional strategy, believing that disclosure is unnecessary if safe sex is practised[;] assess how safe they feel before disclosing or disclose only if a relationship has potential to be more than casual.

CRIMINALIZATION AND HEIGHTENED VULNERABILITY

The rising number of criminal cases results in many respondents reporting a heightened sense of fear and vulnerability. In response to the question, *How do you feel the current public climate around HIV and the law is affecting HIV-positive people?* The most common narrative theme centred on anxiety:

> I mean I get nervous. I get scared. I feel like a loner. I'm afraid that if I do anything, am I going to be charged? (012, bisexual, male, 40s)

> I was scared. I was scared to make a disclosure. I was scared to have unsafe sex. I was scared if I have sex with a stranger, if the condom broke, I might be going to go to jail. I was scared to disclose my status at work, to my friends, to anybody because what else. They will keep an eye on me. As soon as I do anything I will be jailed. You feel unsafe.... I'm afraid of stigma. I'm afraid of discrimination. I'm afraid of rejection. We [are] all afraid to be rejected, men and women. I'm protecting myself emotionally and morally. I'm saving

myself the humiliation but I'm taking all the precautions. Accidents happen. What am I supposed to do? (029, bisexual, male, 40s)

For some, criminalization has made the already difficult area of pursuing intimate relationships an even more treacherous undertaking. In the context of discussing media coverage of HIV criminalization, these study participants remark,

> I'm human and I also need a partner or a friend. But then because of this HIV status, I'm so scared and I just keep it to myself. (035, heterosexual, female, 40s)

> Since I have it, I can't sleep with nobody. I'm now totally virgin. (036, heterosexual, male, 40s)

> It's almost getting to a point where an HIV person like myself is almost feeling that they can't have sex again. They can't be intimate with anybody again or else they're going to risk being in trouble with the law, perhaps even looking at jail time, having your name run through in the paper or whatever. So that's frightening because I mean now you become more insular. (056, gay, male, 40s)

Even before the increasing prominence of criminalization of HIV in the public eye, many PHAs felt stigma and challenges in negotiating new relationships; criminalization appears to have amplified a sense of personal insecurity and uncertainty for many.

Shifted Burden of Proof

A predominant theme was that criminalization has unfairly shifted the burden of proof so that PHAs are held to be guilty until proven innocent.

> The whole premise of the charge that puts all the responsibility on the HIV-positive person to not only disclose but to ensure safer sex practices are used, I think it's a bit unfair. I mean it scares me. (006, gay, male, 40s)

> The thing is that if I was put in to that situation myself, I would think I haven't got a hope in hell. I'm guilty before I've even gone to court. (025, gay, male, 60s)

> Even before you [are] found guilty, you will be [in the] public consciousness. You're guilty. You haven't anything to prove. Wherever they caught you, you will be on the news, before you go to court. (030, heterosexual, male, 30s)

The Court's explicit admonition that the "primary responsibility for making the disclosure must rest upon those who are aware they are infected" is not lost on PHAs. They, nevertheless, wonder about how disclosure is to be proven if worse comes to worst and a defence has to be mounted in court.

> I guess what I would be anxious about is that even doing stuff which I feel is legally and ethically sound, I still find myself vulnerable. Because I'm positive and because the way these cases are being treated is that I basically have to prove that I'm innocent. The onus of proof is on me. It [criminalization] makes many people see or think of people with HIV as somehow dangerous to the rest of the community. It puts the onus completely on people with HIV in terms of transmission. (059, gay, male, 50s)

A number of PHAs express a sense of feeling themselves under siege, finding themselves caught in a difficult he-said/(s)he-said situation of having to justify their actions.

> The concern is that even if I have protected sex, which is what I practise, then it would be somebody else's word against mine. (045, gay, male, 40s)

> Let's say you're out for a night and then somebody says, "You know what? You never told me," and it's my word against their word. It really bothers me. It scares me. (012, bisexual, male, 40s)

> What if I don't have sex with somebody and they get pissed off and then they go to the police and say he had sex with me in the baths? I mean here I am you know. It's his word against mine.... I could still end up with my picture in the [paper] ... that everybody who's ever had any contact with should call the police, right? That kind of trial by media is not something anybody would look forward to. So yeah, it makes me kind of anxious. (059, gay, male, 50s)

Disgruntled partners now have a legal weapon to wield regardless of the facts. Some had experienced precisely that scenario:

> So you come here, you are in a marital relationship or somebody is promising to marry you and he's your legal status and they infect you. Then you fear calling the police because this person is your breadwinner and he's almost like your everything. I went out with a guy who was HIV negative. I let him know my status but when we broke up, he started telling me how he's going to go to the police and tell the police. (067, heterosexual, female, 30s)

> It's more of a moral issue [for] the other person and I don't think the media has the right to put that person's name or picture and flash it all over the news. Ten years ago when I lived in BC, I had a partner and he knew, and things went sour in the friendship and he got angry and

he threatened to have me charged for not telling him that I was HIV-positive which was not true. (071, gay, male, 40s)

Like other stigmatized peoples, people living with HIV may come to feel that police and public officials will not provide them the protection accorded to other citizens but will presume that they are automatically suspect.

> Someone within my home that I had [intended to have] sex with was trying to rob me. I called the police. He told the police that we'd had sex, which he hadn't, and they arrested me and charged with me aggravated assault.... I went to court, repeated appearances, this guy disappeared. He had a criminal record already.... He disappeared after 4 months of court appearances. The crown finally withdrew all charges. (022, gay, male, 40s)

> I've had an incident myself where someone's tried to go after me.... Thank god for MSN and saving chats. The police showed up, I showed them the chat logs and pretty much that was it. (O27, gay, male, 30s)

This study participant did have charges laid against him in a situation where exposure to HIV was scarcely at issue. Only after many months were the charges dropped by the prosecutor before trial.

> I was seeing a man I met online. I think he liked me a little too much. I was going away. He didn't want me to go away. It seemed like he wanted to get me a job where he was working and living with him and I was like, I don't think so.... He got scared I guess without realizing the sex we had is totally insignificant risk or low risk.... This other guy kept emailing me. He emailed me saying, 'Do you do bareback sex?' 'Do you do bareback sex?' 'Do you do bareback sex?' and we found out that it was the same person who charged me. He was putting fake profiles to try and entrap me.... It makes you feel embarrassed. It makes you feel dirty and it makes you feel like you're not human. It makes me feel they should just slap on a pink triangle[1] of the poz and negative on people. It really does. It's really fearful. (063, gay, male, 30s)

Many others worry that just that kind of scenario could happen to them:

> We had agreed to have unprotected sex. I went over to his place and I could tell that there was a financial difference in terms of our lives.... What came into my head was, is he going to see this as an opportunity in the future? ... You know, he had lost his job, he had to go on welfare, all these kinds of things ... Is he going to see this as an opportunity to get some money? I

was afraid in that situation because we had agreed to unsafe sex. (006, gay, male, 40s)

Even if you tell people, they could turn around and say you never told them, you know, out of spite. (038, gay, male, 40s)

Criminalization can compound other inequalities that already place an HIV-positive person in a vulnerable position reinforcing, for example, the difficulty that some women experience as their male partners are able to ignore their wishes.

We could break up, like we could have an argument or we could quarrel and then he could use that as an excuse. He's Canadian and he has everything. I just came to Canada. I just had my refugee claim accepted. (088, heterosexual, female, 40s)

When you're married in our culture, you are supposed to submit. You know, the man is the head of the house. Like he wanted a child and I didn't want to have a child. I wanted him to use a condom and he didn't want to use a condom. So I'm not protected. (044, heterosexual, female, 40s)

As criminal justice logic tends to start with the notion of autonomous individuals entering into voluntary contracts, in these instances, it pushes aside women's capability to assert the kind of responsibility demanded by legal precepts. In doing so, it reinforces gender inequality by holding women who feel subordinate in domestic relationships to the same standard as men who have greater power to assert themselves in the household.

. . . .

DISCUSSION

HIV litigation in Canada has become increasingly centred on the question of nondisclosure of HIV status to prospective sexual partners regardless of whether HIV transmission occurs or not. The increasing number of criminal prosecutions over the last decade and accompanying media attention have created a social climate perceived by many PHAs as one where they face peremptory judgment by the courts and public opinion. The result is widespread apprehensiveness, a heightened sense of vulnerability and considerable uncertainty about how to conduct oneself in a way that avoids unnecessary risk and balances multiple risks of prosecution, of adverse reactions to disclosure or of further loss of confidentiality through onward secondary disclosure.

This accretion of case law has created de facto public policy, ostensibly with a view to HIV preven-

tion, but it is policy premised on a rational, contractual model of human interaction that does not necessarily or clearly advance that objective. The public enforcement of a norm of disclosure, through the penalty of possible criminal prosecution and imprisonment, generates potential double binds and disincentives to successful HIV avoidance in everyday life. By amplifying a sense of stigma and vulnerability, disclosure comes to feel even more difficult in a public climate of legal retribution. The expectation that disclosure will happen consistently is undermined by a heightened sense of insecurity increased by the legal climate.

Strong reliance on, and enforcement of, a norm of disclosure proves to be a shaky foundation for HIV prevention in day-to-day practice. Increasing emphasis on disclosure undermines the message promoted by HIV prevention agencies that everyone must take responsibility to practise protected sex in order to avoid HIV, as it replaces a safe sex ethic with the presumption that unprotected sex is an acceptable default approach *unless* there is disclosure of sero-positive status by a partner, upon whom the obligation to disclose is placed despite the shadow of criminal prosecution creating a climate more hostile to disclosure. This normative shift creates a self-negating prophecy where vulnerability is heightened through the encouragement of unsafe sex.

CONCLUSION

The dominance of a legal discourse of full disclosure and rational contract-making in sexual interaction, then, proves to be difficult to carry out and is experienced as rife with ambiguities and tensions by those charged with realizing it in their everyday lives. While conceived as a regulation to improve HIV prevention, it is a judicial policy that may undermine a long history of messaging by AIDS service organizations and public health that encourages consistent safer sex practice as the most reliable way to avoid HIV transmission. More than a decade of experience with legal regulation in this area raises the question of whether people living with HIV are being held to an exceptional and unnecessarily strict standard of conduct when compared to people with other kinds of transmissible diseases. The current legal situation permits charges to be laid for failure to disclose even when risk of transmission is slight or negligible.

The experiences of people living with HIV in the current legal climate point to a need for prosecutorial guidelines to curb excessive and arbitrary laying of charges and for a better articulation of public health, community-based organizations, and the criminal justice system to divert genuine cases of problematic conduct toward more supportive models of case management. Fewer charges and diversion could, in turn, significantly decrease the tendency of police and media to construct images of demon infectors for public consumption, even before people facing charges have had a chance to be heard in court. Moves in this direction would be consistent with an emerging international consensus that "law enforcement authorities must not prosecute people in cases of HIV non-disclosure or exposure where no intentional or malicious HIV transmission has been proven to take place" (Global Commission on HIV and the Law 2012, 97) and likely place public policy on firmer footing regarding the exigencies of everyday life.

(a) The [Nova Scotia] Royal Commission on the Donald Marshall, Jr., Prosecution†

Royal Commission on the Donald Marshall, Jr., Prosecution

FACTUAL FINDINGS

Introduction

We find:

- That the criminal justice system failed Donald Marshall, Jr. at virtually every turn from his arrest and conviction in 1971 up to — and even beyond — his acquittal by the Supreme Court of Nova Scotia (Appeal Division) in 1983.
- That this miscarriage of justice could have and should have been prevented if persons involved in the criminal justice system had carried out their duties in a professional and/or competent manner.
- That Marshall was not the author of his own misfortune.
- That the miscarriage of justice was real and not simply apparent.
- That the fact that Marshall was a Native was a factor in his wrongful conviction and imprisonment.

On May 28, 1971, four people came together in a brief, unplanned nighttime encounter in Wentworth Park in Sydney, Nova Scotia. One of them, a 17-year-old black youth named Sandford (Sandy) William Seale, was killed. Another, a 17-year-old Micmac Indian named Donald Marshal, Jr., was wrongfully convicted of his murder, and was sentenced to life imprisonment in November 1971.

Eleven years later, after Marshall's lawyer, Stephen Aronson, brought forward information suggesting Marshall did not commit the murder, the RCMP reinvestigated the case for a second time. After that investigation confirmed that Marshall did not kill Seale, he was released on parole and subsequently acquitted by the Supreme Court of Nova Scotia (Appeal Division) in May 1983. A third man, Roy Newman Ebsary, who was one of the four people who had come together in Wentworth Park that night, was charged with killing Seale and was convicted of manslaughter following three trials. He was sentenced to three years in prison. In 1986, the Court of Appeal reduced his sentence to one year. He died in 1988.

The events that took place in Wentworth Park in those few moments on that spring night in 1971 have spawned numerous official inquiries and proceedings, including three formal police investigations, two preliminary inquiries, four trials, three appeals to the Supreme Court of Nova Scotia (Appeal Division), a Reference to the Court of Appeal and two Royal Commissions, including this one. The cost in dollars has been tremendous. The toll in human anguish has been incalculable.

The principal task of this Royal Commission has been to determine why Donald Marshall, Jr. was wrongfully convicted and to make recommendations

---

† Nova Scotia, *Report of the Royal Commission on the Donald Marshall, Jr., Prosecution*: Findings and Recommendations, Vol. 1 (Halifax, N.S.: The Commission, 1989) at 15–18 (Chair: T. Alexander Hickman). Copyrighted by the Province of Nova Scotia. [Notes and/or references omitted.]

to ensure that such a miscarriage of justice does not happen again.

First, what did go wrong? Although we will examine in detail each of the relevant events of the Marshall case from its beginning on May 28, 1971, to our appointment on October 28, 1986, we can begin with the following general conclusions that flow from our consideration of all of the evidence.

The criminal justice system failed Donald Marshall, Jr. at virtually every turn, from his arrest and wrongful conviction in 1971 up to — and even beyond — his acquittal by the Court of Appeal in 1983. The tragedy of this failure is compounded by the evidence that this miscarriage of justice could have — and should have — been prevented, or at least corrected quickly, if those involved in the system had carried out their duties in a professional and/or competent manner.

If, for example, the Sergeant of Detectives of the Sydney City Police Department had not prematurely concluded — on the basis of no supporting evidence and in the face of compelling contradictory evidence — that Donald Marshall, Jr. was responsible for the death of Sandy Seale, Marshall would almost certainly never have been charged with the crime. If the Crown prosecutor had provided full disclosure to Marshall's lawyers of the conflicting statements provided by alleged eyewitnesses; if Marshall's lawyers had conducted a more thorough defence, including pressing for such disclosure and conducting their own investigations into the killing; if the judge in the case had not made critical errors in law; Marshall would almost certainly not have been convicted.

Even after he was convicted and sent to prison, however, there were numerous other occasions when this miscarriage of justice should have been discovered and rectified, but was not.

For example, when the Crown received evidence shortly after Marshall's conviction suggesting Roy Ebsary might have been involved in the killing, it did not disclose this information to Marshall's counsel. When the RCMP reinvestigated the murder as a result of that new evidence, it did so in such an entirely inadequate and unprofessional manner that it prevented his wrongful conviction from being discovered. During Marshall's appeal of his conviction, his lawyers failed to identify and argue critical errors of law which occurred during the trial. Similarly, the Court of Appeal failed to identify these errors.

When Marshall's wrongful conviction was finally discovered in the early 1980s, the Court of Appeal compounded the miscarriage of justice by describing Marshall as having contributed in large measure to his own conviction and by stating that any miscar-

riage of justice in the case was more apparent than real.

This Commission has concluded that Donald Marshall, Jr. was not to blame for his own conviction and that the miscarriage of justice against him was real.

That is the inescapable, and inescapably distressing, conclusion we have reached after listening to 113 witnesses during 93 days of public hearings in Halifax and Sydney in 1987 and 1988 and after sifting through 176 exhibits submitted in evidence during those hearings.

But concluding that Donald Marshall, Jr. was the victim of a miscarriage of justice does not answer the complex question of why Marshall came to be wrongfully convicted and imprisoned in the first place. Was it because he was a Native? Was it because he was poor?

To answer those admittedly difficult questions, this Commission has looked not only at how the criminal justice system in Nova Scotia operated in the Marshall case, but it has also compared the handling of the Marshall case with the way in which the system dealt with cases involving powerful and prominent public officials. At the same time, we commissioned independent research studies to find out how Natives and Blacks are treated in the criminal justice system.

From all of that, the evidence is once again persuasive and the conclusion inescapable that Donald Marshall, Jr. was convicted and sent to prison, in part at least, because he was a Native person. We will look at these issues in more detail in our section on visible minorities in the justice system later in this volume.

Having reached these conclusions, we take the next logical step in fulfilling our mandate and ask what can and should be done to make sure that the criminal justice system lives up to this promise of equal justice for all? That too is a question we will deal with later in this volume of our Report.

There are certain issues, however, that we will not be addressing in our Report. For example, this Royal Commission is not recommending that criminal charges be laid against any specific individuals arising out of the findings of fact we will make. Although some counsel urged us to do so during their final arguments to the Royal Commission, it is our opinion that a decision on whether or not any charges should be laid is one that should be taken by the appropriate authorities after due consideration of all relevant factors. We agree with the sentiments expressed by the Attorney General of Ontario when establishing the Grange Commission, sentiments which were concurred in by the Ontario Court of Appeal in *Re Nelles et al. and Grange et al.* (1984), 9 D.L.R. (4th) 79 at p. 84:

> The purpose of a public inquiry is not to attach criminal culpability. It is not a forum to put individuals on trial. The just and proper place to make and defend allegations of crime or civil liability is in a court of law.
>
> In this context, I am reminded of the remarks of an eminent Ontario jurist, Mr. Justice Riddell of the Ontario Court of Appeal, whose observations almost 50 years ago are equally applicable today.
>
> A Royal Commission is not for the purpose of trying a case or a charge against anyone, any person or any institution — but for the purpose of informing the people concerning the facts of the matter to be enquired into. The object of a Royal Commission is to determine facts, not try individuals or institutions, and this consideration is sufficient to guide the Commissioner in the performance of his duty.

The Court went on to say:

> A public inquiry is not the means by which investigations are carried out with respect to the commission of particular crimes.... Such an inquiry is a coercive procedure and is quite incompatible with our notion of justice in the investigation of a particular crime and the determination of actual or probable criminal or civil responsibility.

We share this view.

Further, we are not — as some have also urged us to do — specifically recommending that Donald Marshall, Jr. receive additional compensation. The Commission accepted that a settlement had been negotiated, and accordingly, heard no evidence on the amount of compensation that may have otherwise been appropriate. However, the Commission did examine the process by which compensation was ultimately negotiated and paid. We have concluded that the negotiations were strongly influenced by factors which, in our view, were either wrong or inappropriate, and that as a result the compensation process was so seriously flawed that the amount paid should be re-evaluated.

(b) Understanding Over-representation†

Commission on Systemic Racism in the Ontario Criminal Justice System

Why are black people over-represented among prison admissions? What explains the dramatic increase in the imprisonment of black women and men since 1986/87? Why is there such a large difference in imprisonment rates of black and white people for some offences and much smaller differences, or even under-representation of black people, for other offences?

A superficial answer might be that the data "prove" that black people are inherently criminal. This explanation does not fit the facts. Equally superficial — and equally unconvincing — is the conclusion that all white police officers, lawyers and judges are blatantly racist and deliberately criminalize black people.

Consider the superficial view that race determines criminal behaviour, and that racial inequality in prison admissions merely reflects black people's inherent criminality.

How could race cause people to commit criminal offences? Is the answer in biology — could a gene related to dark skin, curly hair and broad noses cause people to commit crimes? Would this gene lead black people to specialize in drug trafficking? Does a gene cause white people to drive after drinking alcohol? Does pale skin and straight hair, or a gene related to these characteristics, prevent people from obstructing justice?

Consider also the dramatic increase in prison admissions of black people. How could a biological

---

† From the *Report of the Commission on Systemic Racism in the Ontario Criminal Justice System* (Toronto: Queen's Printer, 1995) at 95–105. [Notes and/or references omitted.] © Queen's Printer for Ontario, 1995. Reproduced with permission.

link between race and crime explain this? Surely the genetic make-up of black Ontarians did not suddenly change during the late 1980s and early 1990s.

Most important, if biology causes criminality, why are only a small percentage of black Ontarians in conflict with the law? Even if each prison admission represented one individual (which is not the case), 96 percent of black people were not admitted to prison in 1992/93. If a "race gene" caused black people to commit crimes, then most of Ontario's black residents, and few or no white Ontarians, would be in jail.

Such questions are absurd, as is the belief that biology explains criminal behaviour. There is no such thing as a criminality gene, nor, more fundamentally, is there any scientific evidence of a race gene. As Stephen Jay Gould states:

> Intense studies ... have detected not a single "race gene" — that is a gene present in all members of one group and none of another. Frequencies vary, often considerably, among groups, but all human races are much of a muchness.... [T]he great preponderance of human variation occurs within groups, not in the differences between them....
>
> Human groups do vary strikingly in a few highly visible characteristics (skin colour, hair form) — and these external differences may fool us into thinking that overall divergence must be great. But we know now that our usual metaphor of superficiality — skin deep — is literally accurate.[19]

Clearly then, the dark skins and curly hair of black people do not cause criminal behaviour. Nor does some other genetic difference lead black people to commit crimes. Since biology is not destiny, the explanation of racial inequalities in prison admissions must lie elsewhere.

Some people who rightly reject biological explanations of criminal activity find cultural ones persuasive. Recognizing that racial appearance cannot determine behaviour, they may think, nonetheless, that culture does. Are cultural propensities to criminality, violence or lack of respect for law and authority the reasons for racial differentials in admissions to Ontario's prisons?

If all or some black cultures are inherently criminal, but white cultures are not, why are the vast majority of prison admissions people from white cultures? Why are most black people (like most white people) not in conflict with the law? If black culture causes criminality, what explains the relatively low proportions of black admissions in 1986/87 and the massive increase since then?

Finally, how do cultural explanations of criminality account for what John Pitts calls "one of the few things we know with any certainty about the relationship between race and crime" — the evidence, documented in many countries, that crime rates among immigrants are lower than among persons born in the country?[20] Crime rates among descendants of immigrants, however, tend to be the same as or higher than crime rates of the dominant culture.[21] If culture explains crime, why are members of the immigrant generation, who presumably have the allegedly criminal tendencies of an "alien" culture in its strongest form, less likely to commit offences than their children and grandchildren raised in the culture of the new society?

The answer, of course, is that cultural characteristics do not explain the evidence. As Pitts states,

> Crime rates are neither a simple product of the proclivities of individuals nor of the cultural penchant of particular ethnic groups but, rather, a product of the chances, choices and solutions available within the milieu they enter. The rise in crime rate among the second and subsequent generations of an immigrant group is a product of ... [the] process whereby people make an accommodation with, and establish ways of being within, a new social environment. In the process some "incoming" young people will adopt the strategies and behaviours of the established social group [where they live].[22]

Cultures may be real and enriching forces in people's lives, but they are not "timeless and inexorable determinants of behaviour."[23] They do not, in other words, dictate what people do. Culture cannot cause people to commit crimes or account for racial inequalities in prison admissions. Far from explaining anything, beliefs that some cultures are inherently violent, criminal, anti-social or disrespectful of law are stereotypes that racialize others. They promote constructions of races as real, different and unequal, and allow people to act as if such constructions were true.

Cultural characteristics of specific racialized groups or minority groups in general clearly cannot explain racial differentials in prison admissions. So how do we explain these differentials in Ontario prisons? In jurisdictions where disproportionate imprisonment of black people has been openly recognized for years, research suggests two general explanations, which may overlap. One explanation emphasizes the influence of social and economic inequality on behaviour; the other points to differential enforcement of the criminal law, including racial discrimination in the administration of justice.

SOCIAL AND ECONOMIC INEQUALITY

Some studies of differential imprisonment emphasize failures to integrate black and other racialized people into the wider society. They draw on evidence of disproportionately high rates of unemployment and dead-end jobs among racialized people, particularly young adults. They also cite poor housing conditions and lack of educational opportunities. These studies make the important point that social and economic opportunities are racialized. That is, members of racialized groups are much more likely than members of non-racialized groups to have limited opportunities. Since people with limited social and economic opportunities are most likely to be policed, prosecuted and punished as criminals,[24] racialized people are more likely than white people to be in conflict with the law. Thus they are over-represented at all stages of the criminal justice process, including prisons.

Three important elements of this explanation are worth emphasizing. First, those who adopt it may generally accept that racialized people are over-represented in prison populations, at least in part, because of greater participation in some criminal activities.[25] They do not accept, however, that biology or culture is the reason for higher rates of participation. Nor do they always see racism in the wider society as the only contributing factor.

According to this view, the social and economic conditions of people's lives are crucial to their participation in criminal activity. The criminality rate should be the same for racialized and non-racialized people where these conditions are the same. If, on the other hand, opportunities are unequally distributed, members of the socially disadvantaged groups are likely to commit a higher proportion of crimes than others. If a higher proportion of a particular racialized group has limited opportunities, compared with other groups, then the average crime rate for this group is likely to be higher.

Second, according to this approach sub-groups with similar life opportunities — in racialized and non-racialized communities alike — are likely to display similar levels of criminality. Young, unemployed white men living in areas of social stress and economic deprivation, for example, would be [as] likely to commit crimes as their young, male, unemployed black neighbours. Conversely, as Pitts noted of the British context, "...the amount of street crime perpetrated by 28-year-old, male, British Afro-Caribbean chartered accountants is the same as that perpetrated by 28-year-old, male, British Caucasian chartered accountants, namely 0.0 per cent."[26] The point is that any difference in street crime rates of British Afro-Caribbean men and British Caucasian men arises because fewer of the former have opportunities for economic advancement.

Finally, this viewpoint does not imply that lack of opportunities or social inequality causes individuals — whether white or racialized — to commit crimes. It does say, rather, that people with limited life-chances may be more likely to view some forms of criminal activity as more attractive or exciting than their other choices.[27] They may see crime as a means to acquire material goods otherwise unobtainable. They may fail to respect the rules of a society that excludes them from its benefits. They may feel they have much to gain and little to lose from criminal activity. Crime may make them feel powerful. It may add excitement to, or provide a means of escape from otherwise dreary lives. Crime, in short, may be a rational choice.

Experts who make these observations do not, of course, excuse or condone the actions of any individual who harms others. They recognize that crime is a serious social problem, hurting immediate victims and the families and friends of victims and perpetrators. They know that fear of crime may severely restrict people's lives. But since imprisonment does not appear to deter or in any other way significantly to reduce crime, it is important to develop strategies likely to work rather than to continue with those known to fail. More emphasis on or investment in crime prevention, as opposed to punishment, is their answer.

DIFFERENTIAL ENFORCEMENT

Other explanations of racialized patterns in prison admissions also stress social and economic conditions, but from a different perspective. These conditions are seen as explanations of who is caught, not who commits crimes.[28] Enforcement practices, rather than offending behaviours, are key.

People who hold this view argue that involvement in criminal activity is not limited to an identifiable group of anti-social and marginal individuals. Criminality is instead a widespread social phenomenon in which many ordinary and apparently respectable people participate. Drawing on studies of employers, employees, taxpayers, retailers and service suppliers, police officers, university students, youths and drug users, and women and children abused by men, these experts conclude that with regard to crime "everybody does it" at least occasionally.[29]

If criminal activity is indeed widespread among the population, the explanation for racial inequality in prison admissions cannot be attributed mainly to disproportionate involvement in crime. Studies in Canada and elsewhere consistently show, for example, that more than 90 percent of young men say they have committed criminal offences.[30] This indicates that variations in offending rates by race or economic class may be small. Variations in enforcement practices likely make the difference.

Law enforcement is not the only possible response to crime, nor is it always desirable. Many studies suggest that law enforcement is costly, blunt and not very effective in reducing crime.[31] Since law enforcement resources are finite, priorities must be established and variations in enforcement practices are inevitable. The critical question is what criteria are used to decide which offenders and which offences the criminal justice system should select.

Formal and informal selection criteria are used in law enforcement. Experts suggest that these criteria make black and other racialized people particularly vulnerable. They point, first, to poverty. Study after study shows that offences by those at the bottom of social and economic hierarchies are more likely to be policed, prosecuted and punished severely than offences committed by wealthier people.[32] The implication is clear: a society that allows racialization to influence people's economic opportunities is likely to produce racial inequality in its prison populations.

Even if criminal activity is widespread, patterns of offending behaviour differ according to the opportunities available. Those with access to other people's money through their employment or profession, for example, are much more likely to embezzle funds than to sell drugs on a street corner. They are also less likely to be caught. Crimes committed in the privacy of corporate offices tend to be more difficult to detect and prosecute than street crimes because of their low visibility, and because the law generally shelters these private spaces from state officials.

Enforcement practices clearly vary with the seriousness of offences committed, and also with factors such as whether and how offences are reported, ease of identification and apprehension, and likelihood of conviction. Racialization in the wider society may also influence law enforcement practices. The criminal justice system requires police officers, lawyers, justices of the peace and judges to make judgments about individuals and their behaviour. Though the law provides a general framework for these judgments, it seldom specifies fixed rules that dictate outcomes. Instead, the law sets out broad standards that allow considerable scope for interpretation of the standards, the individual and the (alleged) offence.

For example, when deciding if someone should be imprisoned before trial, judges or justices of the peace are expected to predict whether the accused, if released, will fail to appear for trial or is substantially likely to commit a criminal offence before the trial. Rarely does a judge or justice of the peace have much information about the accused relevant to such a prediction.* Consequently their decisions must draw more heavily on intuition and what lawyers responding to our survey describe as "empathy." This in turn increases subjectivity in decision-making. It creates conditions under which lack of familiarity with racialized communities may lead a decision-maker to rely subconsciously on stereotypes.

Because the processes leading to discretionary choices in the criminal justice system are subtle and complex, studies of racial discrimination in this system use an approach that is now well established in human rights law. They begin with evidence of adverse impact — such as our findings of racial disproportion in prison admissions — and investigate how far legitimate non-discriminatory factors explain the adverse impact. Racial inequalities that remain after these factors have been taken into account are then treated as evidence of racial discrimination that is tolerated by the criminal justice system.

Using this approach, studies in many jurisdictions have documented direct and indirect discrimination that results in over-representation of black or other racialized people in prisons.[33] Later in this Report we document the Commission's findings that racial discrimination in policing, bail hearings and sentencing decisions affects Ontario prison admissions. The remainder of this chapter presents a brief overview of the various stages where the exercise of discretionary authority may be susceptible to the introduction of racialization.

DECISIONS THAT PRODUCE IMPRISONMENT: AN OVERVIEW

The criminal justice process involves a great deal of interaction among different people with different roles. Decisions made at one stage affect those made later. It is essential to view the system as a whole. Imprisonment is always ordered by a particular judge or justice of the peace, but that decision results from the cumulative choices made by police officers, crown attorneys, defence counsel and probation officers.

Entry into the Criminal Justice Process

In general, accused persons are drawn into the criminal justice system in two ways. Reports of crime may come from victims or observers. In addition, accused persons may be identified by proactive policing.

Victims are an important source of information about violent offences and property crimes. Their decision about whether to report a crime is crucial. Surveys in Canada and elsewhere show that large proportions of individuals harmed by criminal offences do not report them to the police.[34]

These surveys raised the question of whether racialization influences people in selectively reporting offences. As yet, no Canadian data deal with this question, and evidence from other jurisdictions is mixed. Some studies indicate racial inequalities result from victim reporting;[35] others do not show such patterns.[36]

Offences may also be identified through planned and systematic police work. Police may seek evidence of specific offences or focus their attention on specific geographic areas or particular communities. Police may also initiate encounters, such as stopping vehicles and people on the street during routine patrols. Whether or not it is planned, such proactive policing is highly discretionary.

Much evidence from other jurisdictions indicates that this type of policing disproportionately pulls black people into the criminal justice system.[37] Officers working on "gut feelings" or popular stereotypes may stop black people more than others, and may question them more aggressively. Hostile encounters may not only uncover offences but also produce them.

Police Discretion to Charge

Once the police have information identifying a person with an alleged criminal offence, they must decide whether to charge the suspect. Police officers are not legally or professionally obligated to lay charges, even if they believe they have enough grounds (evidence) to meet the test. They may instead do nothing, simply caution suspects, or advise victims how to lay charges themselves.

The scope of police officers' discretion in laying charges is extremely broad. For example, an 18-year-old who shoves another and runs off with the other's baseball cap could be charged with robbery (punishable by up to life imprisonment), theft (two years), assault (five years) or possession of stolen property (two years). As an alternative to laying charges, the police could instead talk with the teenager, per-

haps in the presence of family members. This range of choices provides considerable scope for police officers' personal attitudes, perceptions and stereotypes to influence their decision. Even when an officer is acting with conscious fairness and objectivity, subtle influences may arise such as, in this example, whether the teenager comes from what the officer perceives to be a "good" or "stable" family. This assessment might lead to the conclusion that a black youth should be subjected to the criminal justice process, whereas a white youth could be dealt with adequately in the home.

Studies of the extent to which racialization influences police discretion over charging tend to concentrate on outcomes because police interpretations of alleged criminal incidents and their classification are not open to scrutiny. Formal records of officers' conclusions on whether and what to charge are available and may be studied, but the process by which officers arrive at these conclusions is not always obvious. Evidence from some jurisdictions, such as Britain, clearly shows that police discretion not to charge has racialized outcomes, at least with regard to youths. Canadian studies document class and other biases in police practices, particularly in their processing of Aboriginal people.[38]

Imprisonment before Trial

Once a charge is laid, the next critical set of decisions concern whether to hold accused persons in prison or to seek other controls on them during the period before trial. *Criminal Code* provisions suggest that once the accused have been processed by police and told of their duty to appear in court to answer the charges against them, the vast majority of accused persons should be set free.

However, a judge or justice of the peace may order imprisonment before trial if it is necessary to ensure that the accused person will attend court for trial. The accused may also be detained if it is necessary to protect the public. The decision to detain or free the accused takes into account the seriousness of the charges and accused's criminal record as well as criteria such as "ties to the community,"[39] employment status and mental health.

Racialization may influence police decisions about whether to release accused persons, and may affect the bail process through information the police supply to crown attorneys. Racialization may also be introduced through the criteria used to predict whether the accused will fail to appear at trial or is "substantially likely" to commit a criminal offence before trial. There is little Canadian research on imprisonment before trial. Some studies conducted in other jurisdictions have found evidence that racialization influences pre-trial release decisions;[40] others are inconclusive.[41] Chapter 5 reports our findings that racial inequalities do appear in the outcomes of bail decisions.

Processing Charges

Once charges have been laid, crown attorneys assume responsibility for how they are processed. Crown attorneys have a professional duty to scrutinize charges and decide whether some or all should be withdrawn because of lack of evidence or because prosecution would not be in the public interest. They may also engage in resolution discussions with defence counsel to see if charges can be disposed of without a contested trial. This may also be an important step for the exercise of crown discretion.

Since crown attorneys make these decisions mostly on the basis of written material rather than interaction with accused persons, there seems to be little scope for racialization to influence their choices. Nonetheless, research in other jurisdictions suggests that the possibility cannot be dismissed.[42] Much of the information available to crown attorneys is supplied by police officers who have met the accused and may have formed racialized judgments. For example, clues to accused persons' racial origin may be recorded on paper. Their names, countries of birth and physical descriptions are all normally included in the information available to crown attorneys. Moreover, some residential areas are identified with racialized communities, so that even an address may be taken to indicate the race of an accused. The exercise of crown discretion is discussed later in this Report (see chapters 5, 6 and 7).

Court Resolutions

Even if charges have been resolved through plea discussions, the accused person still appears in court. This appearance is a public announcement of the conviction and sentence. If the crown attorney and defence counsel have agreed on sentence before the court appearance, they present their agreement to the judge. Judges always have discretion to decide on an appropriate sentence, but they generally accept joint proposals. Consequently, in cases with a guilty plea, potential for racial inequality in sentencing may arise from the resolution discussions that led to the plea and from judges' responses to sentencing proposals.

An accused who contests the charge(s) appears in court for a trial at which verdicts and any punishment are determined. These are adversarial processes in which crown attorneys and defence lawyers compete to influence decision-makers (judges and juries). If there is any possibility that decision-makers may be swayed by racialization, one side or the other may use it (see Chapter 7).

This risk has been raised concerning jury trials of white police officers charged with shooting black persons.[43] It has also been addressed concerning jury trials of black and other racialized accused. In *R. v. Parks*, the Ontario Court of Appeal specifically acknowledged that anti-black racism may influence potential jurors in criminal trials.[44] Sentencing is highly discretionary. The *Criminal Code* sets out maximum sentences for each offence, but offers judges little further guidance about the appropriate penalty for a typical offender who commits a routine offence. Although appellate decisions provide a framework for sentencing, the trial judge retains a broad discretion to determine sentence.

Concerns about inconsistency in sentencing decisions in Canada and other jurisdictions are longstanding. Research has identified "extraordinary discrepancies in almost all aspects of sentencing"[45] and noted that "disparity between courts in sentencing practices ... is an established fact."[46] In this connection the prison admissions data presented earlier in this chapter raises the question of how far the disparity reflects racialization in the criminal justice system.

There are clearly strong and widespread perceptions that judges discriminate against accused people from racialized groups.* Evidence concerning sentencing practices in Canada and other jurisdictions is mixed. Many studies show racial inequalities in sentencing practices;[47] others do not or are inconclusive.[48] In Chapter 8 we report the Commission's findings that racial inequalities do appear in sentencing decisions.

CONCLUSION

> There can be few more significant interventions by the public into the private than imprisoning someone ... the decision to imprison a person, to take away their capacity to act in private society and to subject them constantly and totally to the supervision of the state, stands therefore in need of particularly clear justification by law.[49]

Imprisonment is society's most vivid and extreme form of exclusion. The dramatic findings presented in this chapter show that black women, men and youth in Ontario disproportionately experience imprisonment, and that this massive inequality in Ontario prison admissions is a relatively recent occurrence. Ontario simply must not continue to admit black people to prisons at the current rates.†

These findings simply cannot be rationalized by suggesting that black people are inherently more criminal than others. Nor can they be rationalized as reflecting a criminal justice system consisting of officials who are driven by racial hatred.

However, racialization in Canadian society is a recognized fact both inside and outside the criminal justice system. Wherever broad discretion exists, racialization can influence decisions and produce racial inequality.

The criminal justice system operates through a series of highly discretionary decision-making stages. Discretion is exercised in subtle, complex and interactive ways, which leave considerable scope for racialization to influence practices and decisions, and for bias to be transmitted from one stage of the process to others.

In the remainder of this Report we document evidence of the influence of racialization on criminal justice practices, and evidence that this influence is tolerated — evidence of systemic racism. We also make recommendations for securing racial equality in the criminal justice system.

(c) Crown Culture and Wrongful Convictions: A Beginning†

Melvyn Green

A. INTRODUCTION

Wrongful murder convictions no longer shock the conscience of the legal community. Still, the occurrence of three such convictions in less than a decade in the Province of Newfoundland and Labrador was, by any measure, a disturbing development. Greg Parsons, one of the three wronged men, was convicted of the 1991 killing his mother. On appeal, a new trial was ordered. Parsons was later exonerated through DNA testing. The Crown's efforts to resolve the matter by way of a stay of proceedings was opposed by the defence. In the end, the Crown agreed to enter no evidence and Parsons was acquitted. Subsequently, another man confessed to and was convicted of the murder for which Parson was wrongly convicted. Randy Druken's fate was less fortunate. Like Parsons, the Court of Appeal reversed his 1995 conviction for murder and the new trial it ordered was never prosecuted. Unlike Parsons, the Crown entered a stay of proceedings. That stay has long dissolved, but the Province has steadfastly refused to recognize the widely-held and well-founded belief that Druken was factually innocent

of his girlfriend's demise. The third man, Ronald Dalton, was convicted in 1998 of killing his wife. It took eight years for the Court of Appeal to hear Dalton's appeal, and almost no time for the Court to order a new trial on the basis of fresh evidence demonstrating that there was no murder: the death was accidental. A jury agreed, acquitting Dalton at his second trial. The Province has thus far refused to recognize the acquittal as a finding of factual innocence.

The Province did strike a public inquiry, headed by the former Chief Justice of Canada, Antonio Lamer, to look into the events surrounding these three miscarriages of justice. In Dalton's case, the terms of reference restricted the inquiry to questions bearing on the appellate delay. The scope of inquiry in the other two cases was much broader, including all "practices or systemic issues" that may have contributed to these wrongful convictions. Police ineptitude undoubtedly played a part, as did a judicial failure to adequately protect against the risk of erroneous conviction. Prosecutorial conduct was also implicated and, in a rare departure for such inquiries, subject to modest institutional scrutiny.

† (2005) 29 Criminal Reports (6th) 262. [Notes and/or references omitted.] Published by Carswell, a Thomson Reuters Business. Reproduced with permission.

B. THE SYSTEMIC NATURE OF WRONGFUL CONVICTIONS

The phenomenon of wrongful convictions, and particularly the recent frequency of their disclosure in Canada, the United Kingdom and the USA, have discredited forever the suggestion that their occurrence is the aberrant product of a few maverick actors within an otherwise healthy criminal justice system. It is now roundly recognized that the causes of wrongful convictions are fundamentally systemic, and that the remedies, to prove effective, must be of the same order.

Wrongful convictions are best understood as the product of multiple system failures. Each presents its own constellation of factors that contribute to the miscarriage of justice. But there is a disheartening familiarity about them: in-custody informants, non-disclosure, mistaken identification, false confessions, "junk science", the mishandling of alibi witnesses and, of course, "tunnel vision".

Institutional elements also play a role. Indeed, the police, forensic facilities, trial and appellate courts and even provincial legal aid plans have all had their turn under the microscopes of social scientists and public inquiries. There are two conspicuous exceptions to this wide-ranging review: the defence bar and the office of the Crown prosecutor. This paper addresses the latter area of institutional neglect.[1]

Certainly, the conduct of individual Crown attorneys has been scrutinized — and, on occasion, found wanting — at several public inquiries into wrongful convictions. The risk that prosecutors, like the police, may succumb to "tunnel vision" has frequently been noted. And senior Crown attorneys have recently acknowledged, if only theoretically, that prosecutorial attitudes and practices may have a role in the genesis of wrongful convictions.[2] What is still missing is any critical analysis of the *institution* of "the prosecutor" — of those interdependent roles and functions that make up the Crown law office irrespective of the particular inhabitants of those roles at any given moment — and of how that institution contributes to the manufacture of wrongful convictions.

C. CROWN CULTURE

Individual prosecutors come and go. There are some things, however, about the very office of the Crown that both shape the behaviour of individual prosecutors and persist over time. It is at this level — elevated from the conduct of individual office holders — that one can speak of *systemic* factors that con-

tributed to the occurrence of factually wrongful convictions. In the words of the *Morin Report*, these are factors "which transcend the particular case and speak generally to the administration of criminal justice."[3]

Social science research has long recognized the existence of a "police culture," a set of beliefs and attitudes that influence the thinking, loyalties and conduct of individual officers. Crown counsel are no more immune than the police to the laws of social dynamics. They too share a belief system that arises from their institutional mandate — in short, a "Crown culture." The phrase itself is neutral. That prosecutors share values and norms is of no necessary concern to the administration of justice. What is of concern is a Crown culture that places paramount value on winning, that confuses its functions with those of the police, and that stubbornly resists the prospect of factual error. It is this historical concentration of attitudes, practices and beliefs that gives rise to the tunnel vision, blinkered exercise of discretion and institutional tenacity that contributes to both wrongful convictions and their perpetuation.

While police culture has attracted considerable study, the culture of the Canadian prosecutor's office lies virtually unexplored. There have, of course, been learned studies of the powers and responsibilities of officers of the Crown.[4] There are ample policy manuals and much jurisprudence on the norms governing prosecutors' conduct. What is missing is a contemporary sociology of Crown law officers, a social anthropology of how legal norms and policy are translated into the conduct of everyday prosecutorial life and, *in particular*, the part these institutional and cultural features play in the creation and perseverance of factually wrongful convictions.[5]

D. THE POWER OF THE CROWN

This would all be of purely academic interest but for the central role of the Crown in any prosecution. As Wayne Gorman, then Director of Public Prosecutions (DPP) for Newfoundland and Labrador, observed, "[n]o other participant in the Canadian criminal trial process wields such immense power."[6] This power flows from the immense discretion exercised by the Crown at every stage of a prosecution. These decisions are critical to the life-cycle of most prosecutions and, where factually innocent persons are involved, crucial to both the occurrence and endurance of their wrongful convictions. As the Supreme Court noted in *R. v. Beare* (1988), 45 C.C.C. (3d) 57, 66 C.R. (3d) 97, at 76 [C.C.C.], "[prosecutorial] discretion is an essential feature of the criminal justice system." The exercise of this discretion is almost always institutionally informed.

E. THE CONTRIBUTION OF PUBLIC INQUIRIES

But for rare instances, Canadian wrongful convictions have been generally free of the conscious corruption and deliberate perversions of justice that characterize some notorious American and British cases. The role of the Crown in Canadian disasters of justice, like that of the police, appears more attributable to institutionally-rooted failings or defects than any conscious malice. Commissions of inquiry into Canadian wrongful homicide convictions have enjoyed broad mandates that expressly direct the Commission's attention to these systemic issues. Their published reports recognize, if subtly, that Crown culture may contribute to the genesis and perseverance of wrongful convictions. The recent report of the FPT and the paper "Convicting the Innocent" by Bruce MacFarlane, the Deputy Attorney General of Manitoba, reinforce this view.

The lessons learned through public inquiries are a particularly valuable resource. They help to identify systemic problems, provide a framework for their analysis, and craft recommendations for institutional reform. The issue of "disclosure" affords one obvious example. Every Canadian historical wrongful conviction is attributable, at least in part, to the Crown's failure to provide full disclosure to the defence. The patent non-disclosure in all these cases was not a product of coincidence. It did not just happen that the prosecuting counsel in each case was corrupt or incompetent. Material non-disclosure happened because adversarial advantage was more highly valued than was the risk of injustice and, as a result, disclosure was treated as a matter of tactical discretion. It took the Marshall Inquiry[7] — its reporting of the close nexus between non-disclosure and that terrible miscarriage of justice, and its recommendations for wholesale reform in this area of the law — to launch a national debate about full disclosure that, ultimately, found constitutional purchase in the Supreme Court's judgment in *R. v. Stinchcombe* (1991), 8 C.R. (4th) 277. Subsequent public inquiries — Morin in Ontario, Sophonow in Manitoba and, now, Milgaard in Saskatchewan — have revealed a similar practice of non-disclosure, and, thus, the same institutionally-ingrained, historical vulnerability to injustice. Non-disclosure, in short, was a system-wide problem rooted in the culture of the Crown prosecutor.

F. THE ROLE OF THE CROWN: THE NORMATIVE MODEL v. INSTITUTIONAL PRACTICE

Normative descriptions of the role of Crown counsel make clear the push-pull tension that defines the office. As set out in Justice Rand's oft-cited passage in the seminal case of *R. v. Boucher* (1954), 110 C.C.C. 263, 20 C.R. 1 (S.C.C.) at 270 [C.C.C.]:

> It cannot be over-emphasized that the purpose of criminal prosecution is not to obtain a conviction; it is to lay before a jury what the Crown considers to be credible evidence relevant to what is alleged to be a crime. Counsel have a duty to see that all available legal proof of the facts is presented; it should be done firmly and pressed to its legitimate strength but it also must be done fairly. The role of the prosecutor excludes any notion of winning or losing; his function is a matter of public duty than which in civil life there can be none charged with greater personal responsibility. It is to be efficiently performed with an ingrained sense of the dignity, the seriousness and the justness of judicial proceedings.[8]

This model of prosecutorial conduct — that of a quasi-minister of justice — contains inherent contradictions. It is also fundamentally at odds with the adversarial nature of the criminal justice system. As a guide to prosecutorial conduct, it requires a delicate balancing. In practice, the duty to pursue seemingly inconsistent goals too often, perhaps routinely, yields to a simpler *modus operandi*, one consonant with a more basic adversarialism. Gross misconduct and unfairness is kept in check, but the obligation to positively protect innocence is abandoned, left exclusively to "the defence." The first line of protection from wrongful convictions, that borne by the Crown, thus evaporates. Fairness replaces justice as a Crown normative imperative, and let the chips fall where they may. Inevitably, innocence suffers.

Doctrinal architecture aside, there are a number of institutional impediments to the fulfillment of the *Boucherian* ideal. A comprehensive inventory awaits further research. Nonetheless, any tentative typology of those cultural features of "the prosecutor" that contribute to the manufacture of wrongful convictions and the institutional resistance to their remedy must include the linkage of "winning" to career advancement, professional self-selection and adherence to a law enforcement ideology.

The first of these institutional concerns focuses on prosecutorial success as the essential measure of professional performance. Daniel S. Medwed, an

American legal scholar, has observed that the evaluation and career advancement of prosecutors in the United States is largely a product of their conviction rates, thus "placing a premium on 'winning' ... [and] encourag[ing] prosecutors to secure convictions in each and every trial, a dangerous concept considering oftentimes the strongest cases against defendants result in plea bargains and [only the] weaker ones go to trial."[9] While there are no parallel studies of Canadian prosecutors, it would be naïve to believe that trial performance, particularly in difficult or notorious cases, is not employed as a barometer of professional success. Further, once having secured a conviction, the individual prosecutor and his office may become vested in the integrity of the conviction. These two realities, says Medwed, "have arguably led to an organizational 'conviction psychology,' an environment where convictions are prized above all and the minister of justice concept becomes a myth."[10]

The prosecutorial environment may be less skewed in Canada, but the view that the performance of Crown counsel is assessed, at least in part, on the basis of courtroom success, and the notion that there exists an institutional investment in conviction maintenance, both seem sound propositions to anyone immersed in Canadian criminal practice. And both are inherently inimical with the model of the Crown as vigilant guardian of innocence.

A second class of institutional resistance to innocence-protection relates more to psychological or personal characteristics. These include certain self-selecting features of the prosecutorial personality: a commitment to public service and protection; personal morality; a "gung ho," "macho" or "crime fighter" persona — a personality profile familiar to any member of the Canadian criminal bar.

For many prosecutors there is, as well, an ideological identification with law enforcement. The interpersonal relations that accompany the work of a prosecutor reinforce these sentiments, including reliance on the police, the teamwork essential to any substantial prosecution and, naturally enough, sympathy for the victims of crime, particularly those most traumatized by their experiences. Further, a prosecutor's perspective is inevitably distorted by his or her professional circumstances. As S.Z. Fisher has observed, prosecutors are

> constantly exposed to victims, police officers, civilian witnesses, probation officers and others who can graphically establish that the defendant deserves punishment, and who have no reason to be concerned with competing values of justice. [Whereas] the prosecutor is normally isolated from those — the defendant his family and

friends, and often, his witnesses — who might arouse the prosecutor's empathy or stimulate concern for treating him fairly.[11]

These sets of factors have broad impact, whether conscious or otherwise, on the mindset, forensic orientation and decision-making of any North American prosecutor. They influence both the pre-trial and post-conviction assessment of a case. Having secured a hard-won conviction, there is little psychological or institutional incentive on the part of the prosecution team to question the sanctity of the verdict.

G.   TUNNEL VISION AND THE CROWN DUTY TO PREVENT INJUSTICE

Tunnel vision is a large part of the problem. It filters out information inconsistent with the prosecution theory, or compels the Crown to strain to rationalize it in ways that often test both credulity and common sense. It leads to prosecutorial overreach and overzealousness. Wrongful conviction cases are particularly vulnerable to these prosecutorial sins. Unlike most homicide prosecutions, those involving persons ultimately recognized as factually innocent almost always rest on the most infirm of evidence: suspect confessions, inherently unreliable and self-interested informants, fleeting eye-witness identification of strangers, the thinnest of circumstantial evidence, uncertain motive and, often enough, plausible "other suspects." Once locked into their theory of the case, and faced with credible forensic challenges, it is hardly surprising that the police sometimes fall victim to the "noble cause corruption" that leads, by way of more benign examples, to such practices as "assisting" identifying witnesses and discouraging those prepared to support an alibi.

Crown counsel fall prey to similar temptations in order to shore-up a weak case. Too often, they uncritically inherit the police brief. Rather than exercising scepticism, they compensate for the evidentiary infirmities by pushing the limits, thereby risking a wrongful conviction. The prosecutions of Milgaard, Morin and Sophonow well illustrate the proposition that the weaker the case, the greater the incentive to overreach. Indeed, this is exactly what must be assiduously guarded against.

Increasingly, Canadian courts have recognized that the Crown is duty-bound to ask tough questions and to conduct its own investigations in cases involving inherently suspect evidence. In a cautionary guide to Crown counsel,[12] Robert Frater, a senior prosecutor with the federal Department of Justice, observed that this evolving jurisprudence[13] is a further attempt to bring home to the Crown one of the primary lessons of the Morin Commission: the Crown must be ever vigilant to guard against "tunnel vision" — whether our own or that of the police. The Crown may have to poke and prod the investigators, to ensure that they were not afflicted by tunnel vision. Hard questions must be asked, and firm measures taken to ensure the integrity of the administration of justice.

There appears to be little basis to conclude that Crown counsel applied these critical faculties to their prosecution of Greg Parsons and Randy Druken, the two most recent wrongful homicide convictions to be submitted to the retrospective scrutiny of a public inquiry. Instead, faced with a frail case, they strove to extend the goalposts of admissibility in Parsons and, in both prosecutions, tendered inherently unreliable evidence that had little value other than prejudice. These were institutional failings, the product of a Crown culture driven to compensate for the evidentiary frailties of its case by risking the fairness of the trial process and, thereby, inviting the wrongful convictions that followed.

H. POST-CONVICTION TUNNEL VISION

(a) The Crown Power to Stay Prosecutions

A similar overzealousness infected the Crown's approach at the post-conviction stages in Parsons and Druken. There appears to have been no immediate effort to independently re-assess the evidence or take seriously the early defence claims of factual innocence. The possibility that the juries' verdicts were founded on unreliable evidence and cumulative prejudice never appears to have been seriously considered at any pre-terminal stage of the appeal or re-trial proceedings.

One practice in the course of wrongful conviction prosecutions that has thus far escaped investigation at public inquiries is the use of the Crown power to stay proceedings.[14] This power serves various purposes, including (as in the cases reviewed at the Lamer Inquiry) the termination of criminal proceedings without conceding either factual innocence or prosecutorial error.

Three points need be made about the use of a prosecutorial stay. First, it is a peremptory power. But for manifest impropriety, its exercise is unreviewable by the courts. It is a residual Crown prerogative, an exercise of executive power that defies both judicial review and any other form of accountability. It is, arguably, both undemocratic and contrary to post-*Charter* public understandings of the rule of law. It is the Crown saying, "I am the Crown. I can do what I want. I don't have to answer to anyone."

Second, as just suggested, the privilege of the stay is such that the Crown never has to say it's sorry — or, for that matter, anything at all. Subject to the rarely exercised power to revive within one year, a stay permanently terminates a prosecution. While some defendants undoubtedly welcome this resolution, others — in particular, those who have endured a false accusation — want something more: failing an apology, at least some meaningful words of explanation.[15] Typically, there are none. Some empty phrases might accompany the entry of a stay — the invocation of an "ongoing investigation," the earnest "after careful consideration," the ever-handy "public interest" — but rarely anything of substance. The Crown, in short, never has to publicly justify its use of the power to stay proceedings.

All of which relates to the third facet of a Crown stay: its grey-zone message. A stay, it is clear, is not an exoneration. There is no admission here of a misconceived or ill-executed prosecution. The defendant is left in a legal — and very public — limbo: no longer an accused but forever shrouded in a cloud of officially induced suspicion. This is a conscious and likely deliberate consequence of a Crown decision to enter a stay of proceedings in cases informed by claims of factual innocence. It preserves, if barely, the propriety of the initial prosecution while indelibly tarnishing the defendant. For the innocent accused, it is a resolution far closer to purgatory than redemption. Indeed, the public appreciation of the pejorative meaning of a Crown stay of prosecution was recently reinforced by the federal Minister of Justice. In explaining why he had referred the Steven Truscott case to the Ontario Court of Appeal rather than a trial court following his Department's review of Truscott's s. 696.1 application, the Minister observed that the latter remedy would, on account of the case's antiquity, likely result in the entry of a Crown stay of proceedings. If, the Minister continued, Truscott sought exoneration, his best hope rested in a referral to the Court of Appeal where justice — rather than the ambiguity flowing from the exercise of a Crown stay — would prevail.[16]

(b) Crown Resistance to Acknowledging Error

The entry of terminal stays is but one means by which the Crown contributes to the perpetuation of wrongful convictions. In Sophonow, the Attorney

General of Manitoba sought leave, unsuccessfully, to reverse the "technical" acquittal entered by the Court of Appeal and, thereby, conduct a fourth trial of a factually innocent man whose conviction the Court came within a hair's breath of describing as perverse. In Morin, the Ontario Attorney General persuaded the Court of Appeal, and then the Supreme Court of Canada, to set aside the accused's jury acquittal in a case in which it knew (but the appellate courts did not) that suppressed disclosure (respecting, for example, the defendant's window of opportunity, the unreliability of two jailhouse informants and the results of various forensic experiments) only buttressed the defence claim of innocence. In Milgaard, the Saskatchewan Attorney General resorted to a stay of proceedings rather than permit either a retrial or an acquittal; Milgaard was not publicly cleared until years later when DNA testing both excluded Milgaard and positively identified Larry Fisher, the now-obvious culprit who had been tunnel-visioned off the police and Crown radar screens. The post-conviction treatment of Parsons and Druken in Newfoundland and Labrador mirrored this cultural temperament.

Prosecutorial resistance to righting wrongful convictions is deeply ingrained. There is a profound reluctance to acknowledge even the possibility of error, and an equally profound reluctance to admit any responsibility for a miscarriage of justice once incontrovertibly exposed. This posture is an endemic form of institutional denial that inhibits the reforms necessary to eliminate further wrongful convictions.

I. SUGGESTIONS FOR REFORM

(a) Acknowledging Error: Ethos and Practice

Students of wrongful convictions have learned that the most effective prophylactic is institutional reform: the acknowledgement by police and prosecuting authorities of their vulnerabilities, and the sincere resolve of these authorities to institute those measures necessary to identify and inoculate themselves against the risk of error. It is a matter of accountability and essential to public confidence. It is also the justice and fairness side of the *Boucher* injunction.

Acknowledgement of the risk of wrongful conviction means recognizing that there are unexposed miscarriages of justice, and that there is an institutional responsibility to identify and remedy them. As James Lockyer, the co-founder of AIDWYC, noted in accepting the G. Arthur Martin award in Toronto in October, 2004:[17]

Prosecutors then need to become far less reluctant to acknowledge that a wrongful conviction may have taken place. The adversarial system has its place, but the consequences of its use in cases which do not merit its use are profound, as wrongly convicted people have to wait years and years in agony and fear as they try to establish their innocence.

(b) Areas of Institutional Reform

Several remedial suggestions of a general nature commend themselves. They flow from the cultural and institutional impediments to wrongful conviction recognition and correction identified earlier in this paper. As put by Medwed[18], they are intended to "rehabilitate the ideal that prosecutors are obliged to do justice."

Education is a trite but effective starting point in any effort to liberate Crown counsel from a "conviction psychology." Training must be continuous. It must be anchored in the reality of wrongful convictions. It must encourage reflection. And it must enjoy the sanction and support of the most senior and respected members of the prosecution service. The FPT has lent its endorsement to Crown-directed education programs, recommending that, "Regular training for Crowns and police on the dangers and prevention of tunnel vision should be implemented."[19]

A blend of *incentives and disincentives* could also re-orient prosecuting counsel. Performance evaluations that rewarded prosecutors for identifying, and endeavouring to rectify, police misconduct would go some way to reducing the risk of miscarriages of justice, as would encouragement of post-conviction innocence-review initiatives. At the same time, prosecutorial misconduct that contributes to wrongful convictions should result in discipline proceedings and, where proven, public sanction. It is a constant source of discouragement that no Canadian prosecutor — or police officer or forensic scientist, for that matter — has ever been held accountable for his or her misdeeds (including continuing instances of material non-disclosure) in the course of a wrongful conviction prosecution.

Provincial Crown law offices should create special units to *investigate claims of* **factual** innocence. Their personnel should never include those who prosecuted the cases under review. These "innocence units" would inevitably generate an expertise in identifying sources of wrongful conviction and, in time, would develop a less adversarial relationship with defence counsel championing claims of miscarriage of justice. Thus far, only Manitoba, through the creation of a forensic committee that has been examining convictions founded, at least in part, on a now-discredited hair comparison methodology, has initiated such an agenda. These fledgling efforts warrant nation-wide support and replication.

Finally (if more radically), each province should consider *outsourcing* a portion of *the prosecution* caseload to private counsel. The result, as exemplified by the English criminal bar, would be a far less partisan or adversarial process than that which characterizes the Canadian public prosecutor model. It would also reduce the insularity and, on occasion, fortress mentality of the Crown. At minimum, counsel freed of any ideological commitment to obtaining or maintaining convictions would be introduced into the prosecutorial process. British Columbia is the only province where criminal "barristers" routinely practice on both sides of the prosecutorial divide. Perhaps coincidentally, it is also one of the very few provinces without a recognized case of wrongful homicide conviction.

(d) Expanding Victims' Rights in the Charter Era and Beyond†

Joan Barrett

I. OVERVIEW

The role and importance of victims of crime to the criminal justice system was aptly described by the Honourable Mr. Justice Martin in his Report to the Attorney General as follows:

> The victim of crime is uniquely placed among members of the public to assess how effectively the administration of criminal justice responds to the fact of a crime having been committed. No one, with the possible exception of the offender, is closer to the criminal act, and thus, generally speaking, more interested in the response of the criminal justice system to that act. Therefore, satisfying the interests and needs of victims, is, along with treating the accused fairly, one of the criminal justice system's most important objectives.[1]

Ironically, while there can be little doubt that the victim is the person most directly affected by the commission of a criminal offence, traditionally our adversarial system failed to accommodate the interests of anyone other than the state and the accused.[2] This flowed from the concept that crimes were committed against the state and prosecutions were undertaken in the name of Her Majesty the Queen. The result was that the criminal trial was viewed as "a contest between the state and the accused",[3] thereby barring the consideration of the rights or interests of any third party.

Hence, while the criminal justice system expected much from victims of crime in terms of reporting offences and cooperating as required in the investigation and any subsequent prosecution, it provided little in return. Rather, once a crime was reported, victims were largely ignored and relegated to the role of silent bystanders despite the fact that their privacy, security and safety interests could be at risk. Moreover, in some circumstances, the criminal process itself exacerbated the loss of autonomy and trauma experienced by victims.

In the late 20th century, the plight of victims and the need to safeguard their interests hit the political radar. By the time the *Canadian Charter of Rights and Freedoms*[4] was proclaimed in force on April 17, 1982, the victims' rights movement had gained momentum throughout North America. Compensation schemes were established for victims of crime, other support services were developed to assist victims through the criminal process, and efforts were made to reduce the risk of secondary victimization arising from some of the discriminatory evidentiary and procedural rules of the criminal process. The Charter assisted this movement by offering

---

† From J. Cameron and J. Stribopoulos, eds., The Charter and Criminal Justice: Twenty-Five Years Later (Markham, Ont.: LexisNexis Canada, 2008) (also (2008) 40 Supreme Court Law Review (2d) 627–653. [Notes and/or references omitted.] Reprinted with permission of author and LexisNexis Canada.

the means by which persons other than the accused and the Crown could assert rights in criminal proceedings. The Charter also provided the basis upon which the Supreme Court would ultimately find that the rights of complainants and witnesses are entitled to equal protection.

Not long after the Charter's enactment, its influence on legislative initiatives was readily apparent. Parliament embraced Charter principles in enacting legislation designed to advance the procedural, substantive and welfare rights of victims. Indeed, since the early 1990s the Charter has been expressly referenced in several amendments to the *Criminal Code*[5] that are aimed at facilitating the testimony of children and sexual assault complainants as well as the protection of privacy interests in third party records. As a result of this legislative reform, victims have gained greater recognition as well as a greater role in the criminal process. For instance, prior to the proclamation of the Charter in April of 1982, any form of victim participation in criminal proceedings was non-existent. Now, victims have statutory rights of participation at various stages of the criminal process. In addition, the evidentiary and procedural rules governing criminal proceedings have undergone significant reform in an attempt to reduce the risk of secondary victimization. Also, as a result of legislative reform by provincial and territorial governments, victims' rights legislation has been enacted in all Canadian jurisdictions. Most jurisdictions also offer some form of compensation for victims of crime. Consequently, victims of crime now enjoy more procedural, substantive and welfare rights. In short, the evolution of the role of victims during the 1980s and 1990s transformed the legal landscape.

This paper focuses on the gains that victims have made over the last 25 years predominately through legislative reform and the related Charter jurisprudence. It then questions whether these gains have resulted in increased victim satisfaction or whether the Charter, and the numerous legislative initiatives designed to address victims' interests, including the enactment of victims' bills of rights, merely created false hopes. Finally, it considers some of the remaining challenges and whether there are other viable measures to address the lingering dissatisfaction of victims with the criminal justice system.

II. LEGISLATIVE REFORM DURING THE CHARTER ERA

The concept of some degree of victim participation in criminal proceedings and the need for greater evidentiary and procedural protections to guard against the risk of secondary victimization took hold in the late 1980s and continued with vigour well into the 1990s. This evolution in the role of the victim and the need to safeguard victims' interests is evident in the introduction of victims' rights legislation, the numerous amendments to the *Criminal Code*[6] and other legislative initiatives during this period which are discussed herein.

1. Victims' Bills of "Rights": A Misnomer

Starting in 1986 with the enactment of Manitoba's *Victims' Bill of Rights*,[7] every province and territory throughout Canada has enacted some form of victims' rights legislation. While the bills vary to some extent, at a minimum they all provide that, upon request, victims are entitled to receive information about the status of the investigation and the progress of the proceedings. This formal recognition that victims are entitled to certain basic information about the proceedings is significant. Indeed, it is a critical first step in allowing for greater victim involvement in and understanding of the criminal process.

Prior to the enactment of victims' rights legislation, criticism was often voiced that victims were being forgotten and ignored by the criminal justice system. Following the laying of a charge, the victim heard nothing more of the case unless and until required as a witness. In cases of a plea or where the victim was not required as a witness, the victim sometimes heard nothing more of the matter and was left guessing as to the ultimate disposition of the case. Even in cases of notoriety, victims would learn of developments in the case such as an offender's release on bail, plea agreements and sentencing dispositions through the media, through members of their community, or through first-hand observations if they subsequently encountered the offender.[8] Consequently, the enactment of victims' rights legislation was an essential development in the evolution of the victim's role in the criminal process. By recognizing that victims are entitled to basic information about the criminal process, legislatures have provided the necessary foundation for victims to become aware of their role, of the support services that may be available, and of any rights of participation that may exist.

The Charter's influence on the enactment of victim rights legislation is evident. For instance, prior to the enactment of the Ontario *Victims' Bill of Rights, 1995*,[9] there were calls for a victim-centred and

Charter-driven review of the criminal process in Ontario to ensure that victims were afforded "equal protection and benefit" of the law and "security of the person" as guaranteed by the Charter.[10] Also, in 1992, the coroner's jury at the Jonathan Yeo inquest went so far as to recommend a "Charter of Rights for victims" in order to "stop victims from being re-victimized".[11] Following on the heels of the Yeo jury recommendations, CAVEAT,[12] a victims' rights non-profit organization founded by Priscilla de Villiers, the mother of one of Yeo's murder victims, lobbied for the enactment of a victims' bill of rights to help protect the victim and inject more accountability into the justice system.

Further, the Canadian Statement of Basic Principles of Justice for Victims of Crime, which serves as a guide to the federal and all provincial and territorial governments in the development of policies, programs and legislation related to victims of crime, expressly recognizes that "all persons have the full protection of rights guaranteed by the Canadian Charter of Rights and Freedoms ..." and that the "rights of victims and offenders need to be balanced".

Accordingly, the Charter has assisted in shaping provincial and territorial legislation designed to assist victims and witnesses in the criminal process. The enactment of victims' bills of rights has provided a recognized standard of treatment for victims of crime which includes the right to receive information about the process. The provision of information is an essential first step towards ensuring that the system is more accountable and that victims have the opportunity to become more involved if they so choose.

While the enactment of victims' rights legislation is significant as it recognizes the need to keep victims apprised of developments in the proceedings, it unrealistically heightened the expectations of some victims. This is likely due to the fact that the very title of most bills, *"Victims' Bill of Rights"*, is misleading in that it suggests something that does not exist: rights. Indeed, any hope that victims' bills of rights provided enforceable statutory rights vanished soon after their enactment. Within three years of the enactment of Ontario's *Victims' Bill of Rights, 1995*,[13] the decision of *Vanscoy v. Ontario*[14] found that the *Victims' Bill of Rights* conferred no rights at all and was nothing more than "a statement of governmental policy wrapped in the language of legislation".[15]

In *Vanscoy*,[16] the victims in two separate cases relied upon the *Victims' Bill of Rights, 1995*[17] to request declaratory relief after the Crown proceeded with pleas over their objection. One applicant, Ms. Vanscoy, was the mother of a 14-year-old girl who was shot to death by a young person. Ms. Vanscoy challenged the Crown's decision to accept a plea to manslaughter and proceed with a joint submission for a two-year custodial disposition over her objection. The second applicant, Ms. Even, objected to the Crown accepting a plea to aggravated assault from the original charge of attempt murder. In dismissing the applications, the Court unequivocally rejected the assertion that the pleas violated any of the victims' "rights" under the Ontario *Victims' Bill of Rights* or that the failure to be kept informed violated their section 7 Charter rights. Rather, the Court held that the *Victims' Bill of Rights, 1995* was merely "a statement of principle and social policy, beguilingly clothed in the language of legislation"[18] and therefore did not confer any "rights".

As a result of the *Vanscoy*[19] decision, victims' rights legislation has been criticized as lacking teeth and giving rise to false expectations.[20] In addition to the lack of any enforceable "rights", the bills suffer from other weaknesses. For instance, the standards of treatment set out in victims' bills of rights are often reliant upon victim initiative, silent as to the particular person or group responsible for providing the "right", and are couched heavily in language that conveys broad discretion to justice system participants as to how and when information and other services are to be provided. Indeed, while all bills recognize that victims are entitled, upon request, to information about the status of the investigation and the proceedings, they do not state who is responsible for providing this information — whether it is the Crown, the police, the victim/witness assistance program or some other justice system participant. In addition, with the exception of Manitoba and British Columbia, there is no formal complaint process to deal with alleged violations and most bills of rights expressly state that no remedy exists for violations.[21]

As noted by Professor David Paciocco,[22] the purely symbolic nature of "victims' rights" is clearly deliberate on the part of legislatures. Indeed, had the legislatures intended anything more substantive, remedial and enforcement provisions could have been included as is found in the victims' rights legislation of other jurisdictions. For instance, in the United States, the *Crime Victims' Rights Act*,[23] enacted in October 2004 as part of the federal Code of Service, expressly provides that victims may apply for a writ of *mandamus* and may also motion the court to re-open a plea or sentence in certain circumstances.[24] Further, to ensure compliance, the Act requires the Attorney General to promulgate regulations containing "disciplinary sanctions, including suspension or termination from employment" for Department of Justice employees who "willfully or wantonly" fail to comply with federal law as it relates to the treatment of crime victims. The victims' rights legislation of the United Kingdom also contains remedial provisions. As of April 2006, the *Code of Practice* for Victims of Crime provides a binding set of policies on all criminal justice agencies in England and Wales in respect of how victims of crime are to be treated. Although a breach does not give rise to criminal or civil liability, violations may be investigated by the parliamentary ombudsman and may be taken into account by courts in determining a question in the proceedings.[25]

While most Canadian victims' bills of rights lack remedial provisions and are largely symbolic in nature, this does not strip them of value. Indeed, the enactment of victims' rights legislation has been significant in that the bills establish standards for the treatment of victims, which includes the provision of information. The very existence of such legislation also serves to increase the general awareness of victims in the criminal process. In fact, victims' rights legislation has had a direct impact on the policies governing Crown prosecutors in their treatment of victims.[26] Further, the victims' rights legislation has influenced the development of support services such as the Victim/Witness Assistance Program, which provides support and information for victims of crime through the criminal process.

Accordingly, victims today are better informed of the process and their role in the system than they have been in the past. Information enables victims to assert their rights and thereby exercise more control. However, due to the purely administrative nature of victims' rights legislation, it is limited in scope. Consequently, legislative reform aimed at providing victims and witnesses with increased procedural and participatory rights has also been essential in the evolution of victims' rights. As with the victim rights legislation, the Charter's influence in the reform of the procedural and substantive rules governing criminal proceedings is readily apparent.

2. Procedural Rights: Creating a Fairer Process

A common complaint of victims of crime is the lack of control over the criminal process. Upon the reporting of a crime, victims are thrust involuntarily into an unknown entity: the criminal justice system. Further, in some circumstances, the criminal process poses a risk of secondary victimization, particularly in respect of child witnesses and sexual assault complainants.

The Supreme Court recognized the hardships endured by child witnesses in its early Charter jurisprudence. In the decision of *R. v. Levogiannis*,[27] L'Heureux-Dubé J., on behalf of a unanimous Supreme Court, recognized that the criminal justice system was failing children and that it was necessary to consider this context when determining whether the accused's Charter rights were violated by section 486(2.1) (now 486.2) of the *Criminal Code*,[28] which allowed for children to testify from outside of the courtroom or from behind a screen:

> The examination of whether an accused's rights are infringed encompasses multifaceted considerations, such as the rights of witnesses, in this case children, the rights of accused and courts' duties to ascertain the truth. ... one cannot ignore the fact that, in many instances, the court process is failing children, especially those who have been victims of abuse, who are then subjected to further trauma as participants in the justice process.[29]

Applying this contextual analysis, the Court upheld the constitutionality of section 486(2.1) and found that the Charter required the protection of child witnesses from emotional harm during criminal proceedings.

The fact that the criminal justice system was equally failing sexual assault complainants also did not escape notice.[30] Consequently, in an effort to protect vulnerable witnesses from the risk of secondary victimization, in 1988 Parliament completely overhauled the procedural and evidentiary rules applicable in respect of sexual offence proceedings and children's testimony through a series of amendments designed to: allow for the use of various testimonial aids including screens, closed-circuit television, videotaped evidence and support persons; abolish the former statutory requirement of corroboration in respect of the unsworn evidence of children; and create a statutory presumption against the admission of a complainant's sexual history.[31]

As with section 486(2.1) of the *Criminal Code*,[32] it was only a question of time before these other provisions were challenged on the basis that they violated the right to a fair trial and the right to full answer and defence. Indeed, in *R. v. L. (D.O.)*,[33] the Supreme Court considered the validity of section 715.1 of the Code, which allows for the admission of prior videotaped statements of children in certain circumstances. In upholding the validity of this provision, the Supreme Court again adopted a contextual analysis and considered the rights of the accused alongside the rights of complainants and witnesses.

As stated by L'Heureux-Dubé J., in a concurring judgment:

> I suggest that the *Charter* requires that we bring these multiple considerations foremost in our mind, as truth cannot be attained in a vacuum. Children require special treatment to facilitate the attainment of truth in a judicial proceeding in which they are involved.
>
> .....
>
> ... in the determination of what is fair, one must bear in mind the rights and capabilities of children ...[34]

As evidenced by these statements, almost immediately following the enactment of the Charter, the Supreme Court of Canada used Charter principles to recognize that the rights of complainants and witnesses must be considered at the initial stage of defining the actual scope of an accused's Charter rights, rather than under section 1 of the Charter.[35]

Through the 1988 amendments to the Code the risk of secondary victimization at the hands of the adversarial process was highlighted and statutory measures were implemented to minimize it. While these amendments were aimed at reducing the risk of secondary victimization and eradicating discriminatory beliefs and practices that were prevalent under the pre-Charter regime, Parliament did not expressly cite Charter principles as the underlying objective when enacting the legislation. Rather, the first substantive recognition of victims' rights by Parliament came in August 1992, just over 10 years after the enactment of the Charter, with Bill C-49.[36] Bill C-49 was enacted in response to the Supreme Court of Canada's decision of *R. v. Seaboyer*.[37] In that case, although the Supreme Court recognized the need to prohibit cross-examination of sexual assault complainants on their prior sexual history, the Court struck down the former section 276 on the basis that a blanket prohibition, irrespective of the circumstances of the case, was unreasonable.[38]

Significantly, the preamble of Bill C-49[39] specifically recognizes the need to consider and accommodate the Charter rights of complainants as well as the accused by providing, in part, as follows:

> ... Whereas the Parliament of Canada intends to promote and help to ensure the full protection of the rights guaranteed under sections 7 and 15 of the *Canadian Charter of Rights and Freedoms*;
>
> Whereas the Parliament of Canada wishes to encourage the reporting of incidents of sexual violence or abuse, and to provide for the prosecution of offences within a framework of laws that are consistent with the principles of funda-

mental justice and that are fair to complainants as well as to accused persons ...

Since the enactment of Bill C-49[40] in 1992, Parliament has continued to cite Charter principles, particularly sections 7 and 15, as its underlying objective when enacting other amendments to the *Criminal Code*[41] aimed at enhancing and protecting victims' interests. For instance, in creating the regime governing the production of third party records, as set out in sections 278.1–278.91 of the *Criminal Code*, Parliament expressly stated that its objective behind Bill C-46 was to help "ensure the full protection of the rights guaranteed by the *Canadian Charter of Rights and Freedoms* for all". The preamble to Bill C-46 also provides that since Charter rights "are guaranteed equally to all", in cases of a conflict, Charter rights "are to be accommodated and reconciled to the greatest extent possible".[42] Similar language is also found in the preamble to Bill C-79, which, in part, expanded the use and availability of testimonial aids to more vulnerable witnesses and also expanded the term "victim" to allow for the increased use of victim impact statements.[43]

Most recently, as of January 2, 2006,[44] the former age restrictions on the availability of testimonial aids and publication bans have been lifted entirely, thereby extending the use of these supports and procedural protections to all witnesses and complainants provided certain criteria are met. In addition, the former discretionary nature of these orders in respect of young witnesses testifying in proceedings of enumerated offences has been replaced with orders that are mandatory in any proceedings whenever the witness is under the age of 18 years or has a disability that impairs the witness's ability to communicate the evidence. Consequently, the new provisions effectively create a presumption that children or disabled persons can testify with testimonial aids upon request subject only to a limited right of refusal where the court is of the view that this will interfere with the proper administration of justice.

The expanded availability and use of testimonial aids in criminal proceedings is significant as it gives effect to the Charter principles of equality and security of the person by creating a process designed to ensure that the testimony of all persons is given equal treatment regardless of age, disability or other vulnerability that may affect their ability to testify.[45] Further, as the eradication of discriminatory beliefs and practices enhances the ultimate fairness of trial and the search for the truth, these developments do not violate the Charter rights of accused persons.

3. Participatory Rights: Gaining a Voice in Criminal Proceedings

(a) Sentencing and Other Disposition Proceedings

The road to acquiring participatory rights in the criminal justice system for victims has been long and arduous. Prior to 1988, victims were forced to assume the role of silent bystanders who were entirely dependent upon the prosecutor to determine what, if any, evidence of victim impact to adduce in the sentencing proceedings. In fact, some early attempts by victims to adduce direct evidence of the impact that the offence had on them were quickly dismissed by courts.[46]

Given this history, the introduction of victim impact statements arising from the proclamation of Bill C-89 on October 1, 1988,[47] was an unprecedented breakthrough for victims of crime. For the first time in the history of the *Canadian* criminal justice system, victims were given a voice in the criminal process, albeit a limited one which was subject to the court's discretion.[48]

It took a further eight years before the concept of victim participation in sentencing proceedings became a statutory right of victims, rather than one subject to the court's discretion.[49] Since then, the Code has undergone further amendments, each one further entrenching the concept of victim participation in the criminal process. For instance, in an effort to give victims greater participatory rights at the time of sentencing, the victim impact provisions of the Code were amended on December 1, 1999.[50] The 1999 amendments expanded the term "victim" to allow for multiple victim impact statements,[51] created a duty of inquiry on sentencing courts, and provided victims with the option of reading their impact statements in court.[52] The duty of inquiry requires sentencing courts to inquire as to whether or not the victim has been advised of the opportunity to prepare an impact statement and allows the court to adjourn the proceedings to allow for the preparation, filing and presentation of a victim impact statement.[53]

Despite the mandatory language of the new duty of inquiry found in the Code, in practice sentencing courts do not invariably make the required inquiry. The failure to make the required inquiry has been found not to affect the validity of the proceedings.[54] Hence, although the creation of a duty of inquiry implicitly recognizes that the existence of the right to submit a victim impact statement is meaningless absent knowledge that this right exists, whether this will ultimately increase the use of victim impact statements remains to be seen as it is highly depend-

ent upon compliance by justice system participants. What is evident is that as a result of the December 1999 amendments, the admission of victim impact statements from multiple persons who are affected by the commission of the offence is now not uncommon.[55] In addition, victims are availing themselves of the opportunity to read their impact statements at sentencing hearings.

Significantly, the right to adduce evidence of victim impact does not start and end with sentencing proceedings. Rather, this right has been extended to other proceedings including faint-hope hearings,[56] hearings before the National Parole Board[57] and hearings before the Review Board in respect of offenders who are found not criminally responsible on account of mental disorder.[58] Of these extensions, the most controversial is the right to file and present victim impact statements in Review Board disposition hearings since the objectives of such hearings differ significantly from those of sentencing hearings. Specifically, while the acknowledgment of, and reparation for, harm done to victims are express statutory objectives of sentencing,[59] the same is not true of disposition hearings in which the primary issue is whether the accused poses a significant risk of harm to public safety.[60] Also interesting is the unprecedented duty of notification imposed on the Review Board. Pursuant to section 672.5(13.2) of the Code, upon receipt of an assessment report which reflects a change in the accused's mental condition which may provide grounds for a discharge, the Review Board must "notify every victim of the offence" that they are entitled to file a victim impact statement.[61] The introduction of a notification duty in respect of disposition hearings is interesting as it goes well beyond the duty of inquiry imposed on sentencing courts but is silent as to what, if any, remedy exists for a failure to comply. Presumably, as with a failure by a sentencing court to comply with its duty of inquiry, a failure by the Review Board to comply with the duty of notification will not be fatal to the validity of the proceedings.[62]

While victim participation is now firmly entrenched in sentencing and other disposition proceedings as a result of legislative reform, courts are vigilant in guarding against a "runaway model for victim participation". Consequently, courts resist any suggestion that the right to prepare and submit evidence of victim impact is a general right of standing in the proceedings.[63] The lack of a general right of standing in sentencing proceedings is evident in the ability of courts to limit the number of statements filed and exclude statements that are not in the prescribed form or that attempt to speak to the actual length of the sentence.[64] Given these controls, in order to guard against victims developing unrealistic expectations as to their role in sentencing or other disposition proceedings, clear guidelines at the very outset of the process are required as to the use and limits of victim impact statements. Absent such guidelines, any subsequent limitations that are placed on the admission and use of this evidence will surely leave victims feeling cheated by the system.

(b) Participatory Rights in the Trial Process

Although the concept of victim participation originated in the sentencing phase, through the Charter and statutory reform based on Charter principles, it has now extended to parts of the trial stage. While criminal proceedings are far from tripartite in nature, victims now have statutory rights of standing in respect of defence applications for the production of their private records,[65] requests for publication bans[66] as well as requests for the use of testimonial aids such as a support person,[67] screens and closed-circuit television.[68]

Through this extensive legislative reform, Parliament has expressly recognized the need to encourage and facilitate participation by all victims and witnesses in the criminal justice system. The creation of limited participatory rights at various stages of the criminal process is not only laudable social policy but is essential in circumstances where the Charter rights of victims or other third parties are at stake.[69] Indeed, the enactment of the Charter expanded the focus of criminal proceedings such that the criminal trial is no longer exclusively concerned with determinations of guilt or innocence, but may also be used by the accused to challenge the conduct of the police, as well as by third parties to assert their Charter rights to the extent their rights are affected.

Although the Charter offered the means by which courts could allow direct participation by victims, victim participation has predominantly been based upon statutory rights expressly set out in the *Criminal Code*.[70] Also, while courts recognize the need to consider and balance victims' rights with those of the accused for purposes of resolving conflicts, they are reluctant to recognize any general common law rights of participation. For instance, in *R. v. O'Connor*,[71] the Supreme Court created a regime for the production and disclosure of private records in the hands of third parties. While this regime required that notice be given to third parties, the Court was silent as to whether or not the third parties were entitled to make legal submissions at the hearing of the application.[72] It was only through the enactment of sections 278.1–278.91 of the Code

in May 1997,[73] that third parties, including the record holder, the subject of the records and any other person to whom the records relate, acquired statutory rights of standing for purposes of making legal submissions at the hearing.

In circumstances where there is no statutory right to make submissions, requests for standing fall within the court's discretionary powers and are dealt with on a case-by-case basis.[74] Such requests have met with mixed success. For instance, the decision of *Vanscoy v. Ontario*[75] established that victims have no standing to challenge pleas entered into by the Crown. Also, while victims now have statutory rights to provide evidence of victim impact, attempts to expand this into a right to speak to or challenge the actual sentence imposed have failed.[76]

By refusing requests for participatory rights in the resolution of charges and by limiting the nature and scope of victim participation at the sentencing phase to that which is expressly provided for in the *Criminal Code*,[77] courts recognize that the basic concept underlying our criminal justice system is that crimes are offences against society as a whole. Therefore, the exercise of prosecutorial discretion and issues of sentencing must serve the public interest, not private interests. Consequently, to the extent that victim participation is sought in matters falling within prosecutorial discretion or for purposes of speaking to the severity of the sentence, it will most likely be denied.

However, in circumstances where victims have sought standing in respect of matters that do not impinge on prosecutorial discretion or do not concern the actual sentence imposed, courts have been more receptive. Indeed, in the criminal proceedings against Paul Bernardo and the related proceedings against his accomplice, Karla Teale, the families of two murder victims obtained limited rights of standing at both the trial and appellate stage. At the trial stage,[78] the families were granted intervenor status for purposes of making submissions on an application for an order excluding the public from the courtroom during the playing of a videotape depicting their deceased daughters. In that case, the families argued that their rights under sections 7 and 12 of the Charter would be violated if the videotapes were played in open court as it would have a serious detrimental effect on their emotional and physical well-being. In granting standing, Le Sage A.C.J.O. found that the families had a unique and different perspective to offer from the Crown, but also noted that intervenor status for victims "will be rare".[79] At the appellate stage, in separate proceedings relating to an appeal of a section 810.2 recognizance which was ordered in respect of Karla Teale upon her release from prison, the two families were again granted intervenor status to make submissions on one of four grounds of appeal.[80] The standing granted to the French and Mahaffy families in the proceedings against Paul Bernardo and Karla Teale serves as an excellent example of how victims may play a direct role in criminal proceedings without compromising the fair trial rights of the accused.

While the very nature of our adversarial system will always impede the expansion of participatory rights for victims in the criminal process — since the state as the singular antagonist against the accused is inconsistent with criminal proceedings becoming tripartite in nature — this does not necessarily preclude any further expansion of victim participation.[81] Rather, the focus should now be on the ways in which the Charter may be used to allow for increased victim participation while maintaining the fair trial rights of the accused.

In determining whether or not to allow direct victim participation in criminal proceedings, factors that courts ought to consider include the nature of the issue (*e.g.*, whether it is a matter falling within prosecutorial discretion),[82] the interests at stake, the risk of prejudice to the accused, whether the victims can offer a unique perspective that may be useful to the court in resolving the matter in dispute and whether the granting of intervention will result in any delay in the proceedings. With respect to concerns regarding delays in the proceedings, consideration should also be given to the extent to which increased participation can realistically be accommodated in an already overburdened system that is on the brink of collapse.[83] Hence, although some participation by victims in the criminal process can co-exist with the fair trial rights of an accused, given the need to ensure that criminal charges are not in jeopardy of being stayed on account of unreasonable delay, it may be that any increased participatory rights of victims can be better accommodated at the appellate stage. For instance, in the section 810.2 proceedings in respect of Karla Teale, the French and Mahaffy families sought direct involvement in the proceedings before the trial court but were persuaded to maintain only a "watching brief" at that stage. However, on appeal they were granted intervenor status in respect of one issue.[84]

The extent to which courts are willing to grant standing to interest groups at the appellate stage also offers some guidance as to when and how the system can best accommodate increased third party participation. While public interest groups do not represent the victim of the offence, they often share common interests. For instance, in *R. v. Latimer*,[85] following the accused's conviction for murdering his severely disabled daughter, groups representing disabled persons were granted intervenor status on appeal for purposes of advancing the rights of disabled persons. Also, in *R. v. Ahenakew*,[86] B'nai Brith was granted intervenor status on the issue of the *mens rea* for the offence of wilful promotion of hatred and the meaning of the word "wilfully" in the realm of hate speech and its effects on minorities. While standing was granted in these cases at the appellate stage, it is unlikely it would have been granted at the trial stage given the increased risk of prejudice to the accused, the risk of delay and the need to avoid adding to the complexity of the trial proceedings. Indeed, in *Canadian Foundation for Children, Youth and the Law v. Canada*,[87] the Foundation was granted standing on appeal for purposes of advocating on behalf of children and children's rights. However, the Court rejected the claim that children should have the right to independent legal representation at the trial stage or that the failure to provide for this violated children's rights to due process under section 7 of the Charter. These decisions demonstrate the greater flexibility of the appellate stage to allow for the direct participation of third parties.

4. Welfare Rights of Victims: Restitution and Criminal Injuries Compensation Schemes

In addition to the increased procedural and substantive rights of victims, there has also been an increase in the welfare rights of victims over the last 25 years. This increase is most evident in the creation and growth of support services designed to assist victims of crime through the criminal process and in the increased availability of restitution for loss suffered as a result of the commission of the offence. Victims now have the support of the Victim/Witness Assistance Program, toll-free government information lines and an increased number of community-based services.

With regards to the issue of compensation, there is no doubt that in many circumstances crime victims suffer financial loss as a result of the offence. The financial loss may arise from various factors such as the loss of, or damage to, property, the loss of income or support in circumstances where the commission of the crime affects the victim's earning capacity, or it may be due to expenses incurred for a funeral, counselling or medical treatment. While some form of compensation for victims of crime has always been available, whether under the *Criminal*

Code[88] or some other legislative provision, compensation for victims of crime remains woefully inadequate.

From the inception of the *Criminal Code* in 1892,[89] provision was made for some degree of compensation. However, the difficulty with these provisions was that it required the victim to bring the application and it was also closely tied to the property values underlying the Code such that it compensated for loss of or damage to property but made no provision for the loss of income or other forms of financial harm. This changed with the proclamation of Bill C-41 on September 3, 1996, which created a new Part XXIII of the *Criminal Code*.[90] Bill C-41 repealed the former compensation provisions of the Code and replaced them with new provisions allowing for restitution orders that were not dependent upon an application by the aggrieved party and which were available to cover pecuniary damages such as loss of income.[91] Consequently, the availability of restitution was significantly expanded.

The availability of restitution under the *Criminal Code* is important as the civil process is not readily accessible to all victims of crime for a myriad of reasons, including a lack of financial resources as well as the time and emotional stamina required to pursue the matter in civil courts. Accordingly, the making of a restitution order spares the victim the civil process yet achieves the same result since the order may be filed and enforced as a judgment of the civil court.[92]

Interestingly, one of the more controversial restitution orders made in recent years was the order made in favour of Louise Russo, who was rendered a paraplegic when hit by a stray bullet during a botched contract killing. In that case, a number of accused were charged and pleaded guilty to various offences including attempt murder, conspiracy to commit murder and weapon offences.[93] As part of the plea agreement, Ms. Russo received $2 million in restitution from the convicted offenders to assist with the costs of her future care. Although all of the offenders also received fairly lengthy and entirely fit jail sentences, the substantial restitution was the subject of much controversy. Many questioned whether the offenders had bought a "get out of jail early" card. The controversy surrounding the making of this restitution order crystallizes how society's interest in punishing offenders is not the mirror image of the victim's interest and can be more punitive.

The availability of restitution orders under the *Criminal Code*[94] is an important tool for victims seeking financial redress, but its availability is limited. Indeed, it is dependent upon many variables including, most of all, a conviction. It is also dependent upon the discretion of the sentencing court,[95] the offender's ability to pay,[96] the amount of the loss being readily ascertainable[97] and the general principles of sentencing. Given these variables, it is easy to see why many victims who have suffered financial loss do not receive any restitution. Consequently, the availability of other avenues of financial redress and particularly victim compensation schemes is crucial. However, victims have been ill served by the compensation schemes in existence throughout the country.

Commencing in 1973, the federal government started to fund criminal injuries compensation schemes. However, federal funding ceased in 1992 with the introduction of the victim fine surcharge scheme instituted under the *Criminal Code*.[98] Since then, the funding and operation of criminal injuries compensation schemes has fallen to provincial and territorial governments. The lack of a national scheme gives rise to inequality of treatment. Some jurisdictions offer no compensation for victims of crime, while others that do offer compensation subject victims to a highly cumbersome and bureaucratic process or lack measures designed to ensure that victims are made aware of its availability. Hence, it is not surprising that over the years many criticisms have been voiced concerning the criminal injuries compensation programs.[99]

By far the most damning criticism of any provincial criminal injuries compensation scheme came in February 2007, with the release of the Ontario Ombudsman's Report *Adding Insult to Injury*.[100] In his Report, the Ombudsman found that rather than supporting and helping victims of crime, the Ontario Criminal Injuries Compensation Board greeted victims with "bureaucratic indifference and suspicion". The Report also found that the Board "trades in technicality and embraces delay" rather than "giving steadfast and urgent assistance". Throughout his scathing Report, the Ombudsman cites several examples of shockingly poor treatment by the Board of victims of violent crime. The Ombudsman also found that in many instances, rather than offering a helping hand, the Board was guilty of inflicting secondary victimization by operating in a manner that invites and encourages victims to fail in their attempt to obtain compensation. Moreover, in addition to making the application process extremely lengthy and unnecessarily complicated, the Board attempts to "fly under the radar" such that only one in every 40 victims of violent crime even tries to apply for compensation.[101] As a result of reviewing several files which had been the subject of complaint, the Ombudsman concluded as follows:

The obvious conclusion is that the Criminal Injuries Compensation Board functions, even in the unimpressive way it does, by flying under the radar so that only a miniscule number of entitled claimants ever come forward. It creates hyper-technical hurdles that discourage applicants and stockpiles the claims made by those who are uncommonly persistent. This is a shocking state of affairs. The Criminal Injuries Compensation Board is not an institution to be celebrated. It is an embarrassment.[102]

While the Ombudsman's Report highlighted the many problems with the Ontario Criminal Injuries Compensation Board, the Boards of other provinces are not without criticism. Rather, all criminal injuries compensation schemes may be criticized for their restrictive eligibility criteria and their lack of out-reach programs to increase awareness and encourage applications. Further, they are all saddled with over-bureaucratized processes. What is clear is that the money raised through the imposition of victim fine surcharges pursuant to section 737 of the *Criminal Code*[103] is not reaching the intended beneficiaries: victims. Renewed efforts must be made to ensure that the millions of dollars raised each year through the imposition of victim fine surcharges is actually used to fund programs designed to assist victims of crime at all stages of the criminal process. Further, outreach programs are necessary to ensure that victims are aware of the availability of compensation and offered assistance in the application process.

In response to the Ombudsman's Report con-demning the Ontario Criminal Injuries Compensation Board, on March 2, 2007, the Attorney General announced the appointment of former Chief Justice McMurtry, who is "to forge a new framework for victim support and compensation" following broad-based consultations with both victims' organizations and communities.[104] Hopefully this review will address the problems with the current program and develop a new framework for victim support and compensation. Such a new framework should focus on the needs and interests of victims and be driven by Charter principles, including the right to security of the person, privacy and the right to equal protec-tion and benefit of the law.

III. CONCLUSION

There is no doubt that victims of crime have made significant gains over the last 25 years. There is also no doubt that the Charter has contributed greatly to these gains and will continue to influence the devel-opment of victims' rights in the coming years.

Indeed, the media, another traditional outsider to the criminal process, has used section 2 of the Char-ter to acquire recognized rights of standing in respect of restrictions that are placed on the right to access or disseminate information filed or heard in court proceedings. Interestingly, the media, through its continuous efforts, appear to have made greater gains under section 2 of the Charter than victims have obtained through sections 7, 8 and 15 of the Charter. In fact, as a result of the Supreme Court's decision of *Dagenais v. Canadian Broadcasting Corp.*,[105] the media gained a common law right of standing in criminal trial proceedings prior to vic-tims. There are several possible explanations for this apparent disparity. First, unlike victims, who are not mentioned in the Charter, "freedom of the press" is expressly recognized in section 2 of the Charter. Further, the media have significantly greater resources and are capable of advancing more coordi-nated and focused challenges to restrictions on their ability to access and disseminate information to the pubic. Media conglomerates have highly skilled in-house counsel who are capable of effectively responding in short order to any such restrictions. In contrast, crime victims do not constitute one collec-tive group with a shared common interest, they do not have counsel on retainer and they often do not know or fully understand their rights within the sys-tem. Also, one of the key obstacles faced by victims is a lack of financial resources needed to participate in the process for purposes of advancing their own interests. In this regard, it is noteworthy that of all the victims' bills of rights, only Manitoba's and Brit-ish Columbia's expressly provide for legal represen-tation for victims in respect of third party record applications. In other provinces, legal aid assistance may be available for such applications.[106] However, there is no available funding in respect of the many other issues that may impact on victims' rights and interests.

Accordingly, while the role of victims in the criminal process has evolved significantly over the last 25 years, there are lingering concerns.[107] The Charter offers a mechanism for addressing these concerns. Since the Charter is a "living tree", victims can continue to use the Charter to further entrench their role and rights of participation in the criminal process. The Charter should also be used to ensure an equitable balance between victims' rights and the rights of the accused in individual cases. Indeed, the Supreme Court's leading decisions of *R. v. O'Connor*[108] and *R. v. Mills*[109] recognize that victims' rights are deserving of equal protection. No doubt, the concept of equal protection and equal rights will

272

continue to influence all cases in which there is a conflict of rights. In this regard, the words of La Forest J., in *R. v. Lyons* offer some guidance: "... s. 7 of the Charter entitles the appellant to a fair hearing; it does not entitle him to the most favourable procedures that could possibly be imagined".[110] Also, as stated by McLachlin J. (as she then was) and Iacobucci J. in *R. v. Mills*: "fundamental justice embraces more than the rights of the accused."[111]

Finally, it remains to be seen whether the appointment of an Ombudsman for Victims of Crime

by the federal government in 2007 will assist in the further development of victims' rights. What is clear, however, is that victims have moved from the sidelines and are no longer silent passive observers in the criminal process. Accordingly, efforts must be made to accommodate their interests in a manner that also preserves the fundamental right of an accused to a fair trial. The Charter has [served] and will continue to serve as a key instrument by which these goals can be accomplished, through both statutory reform and developments in the common law.

(e) The Limits of Restorative Justice[†]

Kathleen Daly

Restorative justice (RJ) is a set of ideals about justice that assumes a generous, empathetic, supportive, and rational human spirit. It assumes that victims can be generous to those who have harmed them, that offenders can be apologetic and contrite for their behaviour, that their respective 'communities of care' can take an active role of support and assistance, and that a facilitator can guide rational discussion and encourage consensual decision-making between parties with antagonistic interests. Any one of these elements may be missing and thus potentially weaken an RJ process. The ideals of RJ can also be in tension. For example, it may not be possible to have equity or proportionality across RJ outcomes, when outcomes are supposed to be fashioned from the particular sensibilities of those in an RJ encounter.

Achieving justice — whether RJ or any other form — is a fraught and incomplete enterprise. This is because justice cannot be achieved, although it is important to reach for it. Rather, drawing from Derrida, justice is an 'experience of the impossible' (Pavlich 1996: 37), 'an ideal, an aspiration, which is supremely important and worth striving for constantly and tirelessly' (Hudson 2003: 192).

This chapter addresses a selected set of limits of RJ, those concerning its scope and its practices. My discussion is selective and limited. I do not consider the discursive limits of liberal legality as these are

viewed through a postmodern lens (Arrigo 2004), nor do I consider related problems when nation states or communities cannot imagine particular offences or understand 'ultra-Others' (see Hudson 2003: 212–13). My focus instead is on the limits of current RJ practices, when applied to youth justice cases in common law jurisdictions. There are other contexts where RJ can be applied, including adult criminal cases; non-criminal contexts (school disputes and conflicts, workplace disputes and conflicts, and child welfare); and responding to broader political conflict or as a form of transitional justice practice, among other potential sites (see Braithwaite 2002). I focus on RJ in youth justice cases because it currently has a large body of empirical evidence. However, as RJ is increasingly being applied in adult cases and in different contexts (pre- or post-sentence advice, for example, as is now the case in England and New Zealand), we might expect to see different kinds of limits emerging.

THE SCOPE OF RJ

Limit (1): there is no agreed-upon definition of RJ

There is robust discussion on what RJ is or should be, and there is no consensus on what practices should be included within its reach. One axis of

---

† From Dennis Sullivan and Larry Tifft (eds.), *Handbook of Restorative Justice* (Oxon, UK: Routledge, 2006), pp.134–45. [Notes and/or references omitted.] Copyright c2006 Routledge, reproduced with permission of Taylor & Francis Books UK.

disagreement is whether RJ should be viewed as a process or an outcome (Crawford and Newburn 2003). A second is what kinds of practices are authentic forms of RJ, what kinds are not, and what is in between (McCold and Wachtel 2002; *Contemporary Justice Review* 2004). A third is whether RJ should be viewed principally as a set of justice values, rather than a process or set of practices (compare, e.g. Braithwaite 2003 and Johnstone 2002, with von Hirsch *et al.* 2003), or whether it should include both (Roche 2003). Finally, there is debate on how RJ can or should articulate with established criminal justice (CJ).

A lack of agreement on definition means that RJ has not one but many identities and referents; and this can create theoretical, empirical, and policy confusion. Commentators, both advocates and critics, are often not talking about or imagining the same thing. Although the lack of a common understanding of RJ creates confusion, especially for those new to RJ, it reflects a diversity of interests and ideologies that people bring to the table when ideas of justice are discussed. A similar problem occurred with the rise of informal justice in the late 1970s. Informal justice could not be defined except by what it was not, i.e. it was not established forms of criminal justice (Abel 1982). An inability to define RJ, or justice more generally, is not fatal. Indeed, it is a logical and defensible position: there can be no 'fixed definition of justice' because justice has 'no unchanging nature' and 'it is beyond definition' (Hudson 2003: 201, characterizing the ideas of Lyotard and Derrida).

Gerry Johnstone (2004) suggests that the RJ advocates have too narrowly focused their efforts on promoting RJ by claiming its positive effects in reducing re-offending and increasing victim satisfaction. Instead of taking this instrumental and technical tack, Johnstone argues that we should see RJ as a set of ideas that challenge established CJ in fundamental ways. There is much to commend in having this more expansive vision of RJ as a long-term political project for changing the ways we think about 'crime,' 'being a victim,' 'responding to offenders,' among other categories nominated by Johnstone. However, I restrict my use of the term to a set of core elements in RJ practices. I do so not to limit the potential applicability of RJ to other domains or as a political project for social change but rather to conceptualize justice practices in concrete terms, not as aspirations or values. As RJ takes shape and evolves, it is important that we have images of the social interactions being proposed. I identify these core elements of RJ:

It deals with the penalty (or post-penalty) not fact-finding phase of the criminal process.

It normally involves a face-to-face meeting with an admitted offender and victim and their supporters, although it may also take indirect forms.

It envisions a more active role for victim participation in justice decisions.

It is an informal process that draws on the knowledge and active participation of lay persons (typically those most affected by an offence), but there are rules circumscribing the behavior of meeting members and limits on what they can decide in setting a penalty.

It aims to hold offenders accountable for their behavior, while at the same time not stigmatizing them, and in this way it is hoped that there will be a reduction in future offending.

It aims to assist victims in recovering from crime.

As we shall see, some (or all) of these elements may not be realized in RJ practices. For example, an RJ process aims to assist victims in recovering from crime, but this may be possible for some victims more than others. And although it is hoped that an RJ process will shift admitted offenders toward a law-abiding future, this too may occur for some, but not others. It should be emphasized that victims are not forced to meet an admitted offender in an RJ process. There can be other ways in which victims may engage an RJ process, including through the use of victim representatives or material brought into the meeting itself. In fact, some have proposed that victims have access to RJ processes when a suspect has not been caught for (or admitted to) an offence.

Limit (2): RJ deals with the penalty not fact-finding phase of the criminal process

There is some debate over whether RJ processes could be used in fact-finding, but virtually all the examples cited are of dispute resolution mechanisms in pre-modern societies, which rely on particular sets of 'meso-social structures' that are tied to kinship, geography, and political power (see discussion below by Bottoms 2003; see also Johnstone 2002). When we consider the typical forms of RJ practices, such as family group conferences (in New Zealand), family or community conferences (in Australia), police restorative cautioning schemes (in selected jurisdictions in England and North America), circles and sentencing circles (North America), or enhanced forms of victim offender mediation (North America and some European countries), we see that all are concerned with what a justice practice should be *after* a person has admitted committing an offence. RJ does not address whether a 'crime' occurred or not, or whether a suspect is 'guilty' of a crime or not. Rather, it focuses on 'what shall we do?' after a person admits that s/he has committed an offence.

Ultimately, as I shall argue, we should view this limit as a strength of RJ. The reason is that it bypasses the many disabling features of the adversarial process, both for those accused of crime and for victim complainants. Without a fact-finding or investigating mechanism, however, RJ cannot replace established CJ. To do so, it must have a method of adjudication, and currently it does not. However, RJ can make inroads into methods of penalty setting (in the context of court diversion or pre-sentence advice to judicial officers), and it may be effective in providing assurances of safety to individual victims and communities when offenders complete their sentences (in the context of post-sentence uses of RJ), but all of these activities occur only after a person has admitted committing an offence.

Several commentators point out that RJ differs from established CJ in that it is participatory and consensually based, not adversarial. However, this muddles things greatly. The reason that established CJ is adversarial is that its adjudication process rests on a fundamental right of those accused to say they did not commit an offence[2] and to defend themselves against the state's allegations of wrong-doing. There may well be better methods of adjudicating crime, and a troubling feature of established CJ is how long it takes for cases to be adjudicated and disposed; but surely, no one would wish to dispense with the right of citizens to defend themselves against the state's power to prosecute and punish alleged crime.

The focus of RJ on the penalty (or post-penalty) phase can be viewed as a strength. It enables us to be more imaginative in conceptualizing what is the 'right response' to offending behavior, and it opens up potential lines of communication and understanding between offenders, victims, and those close to them, when this is desirable (and it may not always be desirable). Communication and interaction are especially important elements because many victims want answers to questions: for example, about why *their* car was stolen, and not another person's car. They may be concerned about their security and seek reassurances from an offender not to victimize them again (although this may not stop an offender from victimizing others). There can be positive sources of connection between the supporters

of offenders (say, a mother or father) and victims or their supporters. All of this is possible because RJ processes seek a conversational and dialogic approach to responding to crime. Decisions are not made by a distant magistrate or judge and an overworked duty solicitor and prosecutor with many files to process. In established CJ processes, research shows that in the courtroom, a defendant is typically mute and a victim is not present. State actors do all the work of handling and processing crime. The actual parties to a crime (the persons charged and victim-complainants) are bystanders or absent.

Some victim advocates who are critical of RJ think that it is 'outside' or not part of established CJ. Although a common perception, it is inaccurate. In all jurisdictions where RJ has been legislated in response to crime, it is very much 'inside' the established CJ process, as the police or courts make a decision about how to handle a case.

RJ IDEALS AND PRACTICES

There is a gap between the ideals or aspirations for RJ and actual practices. This gap should not surprise us because the ideals for RJ are set very high, and perhaps too high. Advocates have made astonishing claims for what RJ can achieve and what it can do for victims, offenders, their family members, and communities. Thus, a gap arises, in part from inflated expectations for what RJ can achieve. There are deeper reasons for the gap, however.

First, as Bottoms (2003: 109) argues, the 'social mechanisms of RJ' rest on an assumption that 'adequate meso-social structures exist to support RJ-type approaches.' By 'meso-social structures,' Bottoms refers to ordered sets of relationships that are part of pre-modern societies (for example, residence, kinship, or lineage). These relationships embed elements of 'intra-societal power' and coercion, which make dispute settlement possible (see also Merry 1982). A second feature of relationships in premodern societies is that disputants are 'part of the same moral/social community.' They live in close proximity to one another or are related to one another, and typically wish to continue living in the community. These meso-social structures and 'thick' social ties, which are commonly associated with premodern (or *gemeinschaft*) societies,[3] are not present in modern urban contemporary societies. Thus, as Bottoms (2003: 110) suggests, 'a "blanket" delivery of RJ ... is always likely to achieve modest or patchy results in contemporary societies.'

Second, as I suggest elsewhere (Daly 2003: 200), gaps emerge because those participating in an RJ process may not know what is supposed to happen, how they are supposed to act, nor what an optimal result could be. Participants may have an idea of what 'their day in court' might be like, but they have little idea of what 'their day in an RJ conference' would be like. Moreover, effective participation requires a degree of moral maturity and empathetic concern that many people, and especially young people, may not possess. Finally, we know from the history of established CJ that organizational routines, administrative efficiency, and professional interests often trump justice ideals (Daly 2003: 232). RJ is no exception. It takes time and great effort to create the appropriate contexts for RJ processes to work effectively, including a facilitator's contacting and preparing participants, identifying who should be present, coordinating the right time for everyone, running the meeting, and following up after it is over.

Some commentators argue that it is more appropriate to compare 'what restorative justice has achieved and may still achieve with what conventional justice systems have to offer' (Morris 2002: 601). This is a valid and important point. We know that substantial gaps exist between the ideals and practices of established CJ. Thus, for example, it would be relevant to compare the effects of the court's sentencing practices on victims, offenders, and others with their participation in penalty discussions in RJ meetings. Although court-conference comparative research can be illuminating and helpful, there is also a value to observing and understanding what happens in an RJ process itself, including the variable degree to which the aims of RJ are achieved. When we do that, several limits of RJ are apparent. It is important to bear in mind that these limits are not necessarily peculiar to RJ; they may have their analogy in established CJ as well. I draw from my research on youth justice conference in South Australia (the South Australia Juvenile Justice [SAJJ] project, Daly 2000, 2001a, 2002, 2003, 2005; see Daly *et al.* 1998, Daly 2001b for SAJJ technical reports), along with other research, to elucidate these limits.

Limit (3): it is easier to achieve fairness than restorativeness in an RJ process

Studies of RJ in Australia, New Zealand, and England often examine whether the observer-researcher, offender, and victim perceive the process and outcome as fair. All published studies find high levels of perceived fairness, or procedural justice, in the process and outcome (see review in Daly 2001a for Australian and New Zealand research; see

also Hoyle *et al.* 2002; Crawford and Newburn 2003). For example, to questions such as 'Were you treated fairly?' 'Were you treated with respect?' 'Did people listen to you?' among other questions, a very high percentage of participants (80 per cent or more) say that they were. In addition, studies show that offenders and victims are actively involved in fashioning the outcome, which is indicative that laypeople are exercising decision-making power. Overall, RJ practices in the jurisdictions studies definitely conform to the ideals of procedural justice.

Compared to these very high levels of procedural justice, there appears to be relatively less evidence of 'restorativeness.' The measures of restorativeness used in the SAJJ project include the degree to which the offender was remorseful, spontaneously apologized to the victim, and understood the impact of the crime on the victim; the degree to which victims understood the offender's situation; and the extent of positive movement between the offender, victim, or their supporters. Depending on the variable, restorativeness was present in 30 to 60 per cent of the youth justice conferences studied.[4] Thus, RJ conferences receive high marks for procedural fairness and victim and offender participation, but it may be more difficult for victims and offenders to resolve their differences or to find common ground in an RJ meeting (Daly 2001a, 2003).

Why is fairness easier to achieve than restorativeness? Fairness is largely, although not exclusively, a measure of the behavior of the professional(s) (the facilitator and, depending on the jurisdiction, a police officer). As the professionals, they are polite, they listen, and they establish ground rules of respect for others and civility in the conference process. Whereas fairness is established in the relationship between the professionals and participants, restorativeness emerges in the relationships between a victim, an offender, and their supporters. Being polite is easier to do than saying you are sorry; listening to someone tell their story of victimization is easier to do when you are not the offender. Indeed, understanding or taking the perspective of the other may be easier when you are not the actual victim or the offender in the justice encounter.

Restorativeness requires a degree of empathic concern and perspective-taking; and as measured by psychologists' scales, these qualities are more frequently evinced for adults than adolescents. For example, from interviews with youthful offenders, the SAJJ project found that over half had not thought *at all* about what they would say to the victim. Most did not think in terms of what they might *offer victims*, but rather what they would be *made to do by others.* It is possible that many adolescents may not yet have the capacity to think empathetically, to take the role of the other (Frankenberger 2000); they may be expected to act as if they had the moral reasoning of adults when they do not (Van Voorhis 1985). And, at the same time, as we shall see in limits (4) and (5), victims may have high expectations for an offender's behavior in the conference process which cannot be realized, or victims' distress may be so great that the conference process can do little to aid in their recovery.

Limit (4): a 'sincere apology' is difficult to achieve

It is said that in the aftermath of crime, what victims want most is 'symbolic reparation, primarily an apology' (Strang 2002: 55, drawing from Marshall and Merry 1990). Perhaps for some offences and some victims this may be true, but I suspect that most victims want more than an apology. Fundamentally, victims want a sense of vindication for the wrong done to them and they want the offender to stop harming and hurting them or other people. A sincere apology may be a useful starting point,[5] but we might expect most victims to want more. In research on violent offences, for example, Cretney and Davis (1995: 178) suggest that a 'victim has an interest in punishment,' not just restitution or reparation, because punishment 'can reassure the victim that he or she has public recognition and support.'

Let us assume, for the sake of argument, that a sincere apology is what victims mainly desire. What are the elements of a sincere apology and how often might we expect this to occur in an RJ process?

Drawing from Tavuchis' work on the sociology of apology (1991) Bottoms (2003: 94–8) distils the 'experiential dynamics' of an 'ideal-typical apology':[6]

> In the fully-accomplished apology ... we have first a *call* for an apology from the person(s) who regard themselves as wronged, or from someone speaking on their behalf; then the *apology* itself; and finally an expression of *forgiveness* from the wronged to the wrongdoer.
>
> (p. 94, emphasis in original)

Bottoms then says that 'each of these moves' in the fully accomplished (or ideal-typical) apology 'can be emotionally fraught' such that 'the whole apologetic discourse is (on both sides) "a delicate and precarious transaction"' (quoting Tavuchis 1991: vii).

It is important to distinguish between two types of apologies: an 'ideal-typical apology,' where there is an expression of forgiveness from a victim to an offender, and a 'sincere apology,' where there is a mutual understanding between the parties that the offender is really sorry but there is no assumption of forgiveness. I make this distinction because we might expect a 'sincere apology' to occur in an RJ process but we should not expect a victim to forgive an offender. In fact, I wonder if Tavuchis' formulation may be unrealistic in the context of a victim's response to crime. Tavuchis analyzes a range of harmful or hurtful behavior, not just crime; and I suspect that forgiveness may arise more often in non-criminal than in criminal contexts.

There is surprisingly little research on the character of apologies in RJ processes. From the RISE project, we learn that conference victims rated the offender's apology as 'sincere' (41 per cent), and a further 36 per cent rated it 'somewhat sincere' (Strang 2002: 115; 2004). Hayes's (2004) summary of RISE observational and interview data on the apology process concludes that 'the ideal of reconciliation and repair was achieved in less than half of all cases.'

The SAJJ project explored the apology process in detail (see Daly 2003: 224–5). When we asked the youth why they decided to say sorry to victims, 27 per cent said they did not feel sorry but thought they'd get off more easily, 39 per cent said to make their family feel better, and a similar per cent said they felt pushed into it. However, when asked what was the *main reason* for saying sorry, most (61 per cent) said they really were sorry. When we asked victims about the apology process, most believed that the youth's motives for apologizing were insincere. To the item, 'The youth wasn't sorry, but thought they would get off more easily if they said sorry,' 36 per cent of victims said 'Yes, definitely,' and another 36 per cent said 'Yes, a little.' A slim majority of victims believed that the youth said sorry either to get off more easily (30 per cent) or because they were pushed into it (25 per cent). Just 27 per cent of victims believed that the main reason that they youth apologized was because s/he really was sorry.[7]

This mismatch of perception between victims and offenders was explored further, by drawing on conference observations, interview material, and police incident reports to make inferences about the apology process for all eighty-nine conferences in the SAJJ sample (Daly 2005). The results reinforce the findings above: they reveal that communication failure and mixed signals are present when apologies are made and received. Such communication gaps are overlaid by the variable degree to which offenders are in fact sorry for what they have done. In 34 per cent of cases, the offenders and victims agreed (or were in partial agreement) that the offender was sorry,[8] and in 27 per cent, the offenders and victims definitely agreed that the offender was not sorry. For 30 per cent, there was a perceptual mismatch: the offenders were not sorry, but the victims thought they were (12 per cent); or the offenders were sorry, but the victims did not think so (18 per cent). For the remaining 9 per cent, it was not possible to determine. The findings show that a sincere apology may be difficult to achieve because offenders are not really sorry for what they have done, victims wish offenders would display more contrite behavior, and there are misreadings of what the other is saying.

Hayes (2004) proposes an added reason for why sincere apologies are difficult to achieve. He suggests that there are 'competing demands' placed on youthful offenders in the conference process: they are asked both to explain what happened (or provide an 'account') and to apologize for what they did. Hayes surmises that 'offenders' speech acts ... may drift from apologetic discourse to mitigating accounts and back again.' Victims may interpret what is said (and not said) as being insincere.

Limit (5): the conference process can help some victims recover from crime, but this is contingent on the degree of distress they experienced

One of the major aims of a RJ process is to assist victims in recovering from the disabling effects of crime. This central feature of RJ has not been explored in any systematic way. The SAJJ data offer insights on this complex process, and here I distil from a study of the impact of crime on victims for their likelihood of recovery a year later (see Daly 2005).

An important finding, although typically not discussed in the RJ literature, is that victims experience crime differently: some are only lightly touched, whereas others experience many disabling effects such as health problems, sleeplessness, loss of self-confidence, among others. To describe this variability, I created a measure of 'victim distress,' which was derived from a set of questions about the effects of crime.[9] Initially, I identified four categories of victims: no distress (28 per cent), low distress (12.5 per cent), moderate distress (36.5), and high distress (23 per cent). For ease of analysis, I then collapsed the four groups into two, combining the no/low dis-

tress (40.5 per cent) and the moderate/high distress (59.5 per cent), which, for convenience, I will refer to as the 'low' and 'high' distress victims, respectively.

Some important findings emerged. The high distress group was significantly more likely to be composed of female victims, personal crime victims (including those victimized in their occupational role or at their organizational workplace), violent offences, and victims and offenders who were family members or well known to each other. The offences most likely to cause victims distress were assaults on family members or teachers (89 per cent in the high distress group); adolescent punch-ups (76 per cent); and breaking into, stealing, or damaging personal property (75 per cent). By comparison, the offences least likely to cause victims distress were breaking into, stealing, or damaging organizational property (19 per cent) and stranger assault (33 per cent). Theft of bikes or cars was midway (55 per cent of victims were in the high distress group).

Victims' distress was significantly linked to their attitude toward offenders and their interest to find common ground during the conference. For example, while 43 per cent of high distress victims had negative attitudes toward the offender after the conference, this was the case for just 8 per cent of low distress victims. Most high distress victims said it was more important for them to be treated fairly (67 per cent) than to find common ground with the offender, whereas most low distress victims (71 per cent) said it was more important to find common ground. This is a key finding: what crime victims hope to achieve from an RJ process — that is, whether to seek mutual understanding with offenders (other-regarding victims) or to be treated well as individuals (self-regarding) — is related to the character and experience of the victimization. Organizational and stranger assault victims were most likely to be other-regarding — that is, to want to find common ground; personal property crime victims were least likely to be other-regarding; and adolescent, family, and teacher assault victims fell in between.

In general and in the context of youth justice, victims who are only lightly touched by a crime orient themselves more readily to restorative behaviors. Compared to high distress victims, it was easier for the low distress group to be other-regarding because the wrong had not affected them deeply. After a conference ended, the high distress victims were far more likely to remain angry and fearful of offenders, and to be negative toward them, than the low distress victims. This result anticipates findings on victim recovery a year later.

In 1999, the SAJJ researchers re-interviewed the victims and asked them, 'Which of the following two statements better describes how you're feeling about the incident today? Would you say that it is all behind you, you are fully recovered from it; or it is partly behind you, there are still some things that bother you, you are not fully recovered from it?' Two-thirds said that they had recovered from the offence and it was all behind them. Thus, most victims had recovered from the offence a year later, but which ones? And did the conference process assist in their recovery?

When comparing victim distress in 1998 with their recovery a year later, there were startling results. Whereas 63 per cent of the moderate, 78 per cent of the low, and 95 per cent of the no distress victims had recovered in 1999, 71 per cent of the high distress victims had *not* recovered. Thus, for the most highly distressed victims, an RJ process may be of little help in recovering from crime. In 1999, we also asked victims, 'Would you say that your ability to get the offence behind you was aided more by your participation in the justice process or things that only you could do for yourself?' Half (49 per cent) said their participation in the justice process, and 40 per cent, only things they could do for themselves; 11 per cent said both were of equal importance. The recovered victims were more likely to say participation in the justice process (72 per cent) than the non-recovered victims (38 per cent). Likewise, the low distress victims were more likely to say participation in the justice process (77 per cent) than the high distress victims (49 per cent).

Non- (or partly) recovered victims held more negative views of the offender and how their case was handled compared to the recovered victims. They were significantly more likely to see the offender as a 'bad' person rather than a 'good' person who had done a bad thing, less satisfied by how their case was handled, and more likely to say they wished their case had gone to court. When asked what was the most important thing hindering their recovery, 74 per cent of the non- (or partly) recovered victims cited financial losses, injuries, and emotional harms arising from the offence.

These findings on victim distress and recovery pose significant challenges to the RJ field. They invite reflection on the variable effects of victimization for the ways in which victims orient themselves to a restorative process. For the high distress victims, it was harder to act restoratively at the conference, and it was more difficult to be generous to offenders. The effects of victimization did not end with the conference but continued to linger for a long time.

A process like RJ, and indeed any legal process (such as court), may do little to assist victims who have been deeply affected by crime. Improving practices by conference facilitators may help at the edges but this too is unlikely to have a major impact. Victims who are affected negatively and deeply by crime need more than RJ (or court) to recover from their victimization.

Limit (6): we should expect modest results, not the nirvana story of RJ

The nirvana story of RJ is illustrated by Jim Consedine (1995: 9), who opens his book by excerpting from a 1993 New Zealand news story:

> The families of two South Auckland boys, killed by a car, welcomed the accused driver yesterday with open arms and forgiveness. The young man, who gave himself up to the police yesterday morning, apologised to the families and was ceremonially reunited with the Tongan and Samoan communities at a special service last night.

> The 20-year-old Samoan visited the Tongan families after his court appearance to apologise for the deaths of the two children ... The Tongan and Samoan communities ... later gathered at the Tongan Methodist Church in a service of reconciliation. The young man sat at the feast table flanked by the mothers of the dead boys.

Later, in discussing the case, Consedine sees it as

> Ample evidence of the power that healing and forgiveness can play in our daily lives ... The grieving Tongan and Samoan communities simply embraced the young driver ... and forgave him. His deep shame, his fear, his sorrow, his alienation from the community was resolved.
> (Consedine 1995: 162)

This nirvana story of RJ contains elements that are not likely to be present in most RJ encounters: it was composed of members of racial-ethnic minority groups, who were drawn together with a shared experience of church, and there appeared to be 'meso-social structures' and 'thick' social ties between the families and kin of the offender and victims. These *gemeinschaft* qualities are atypical in modern urban life, and thus we should expect 'modest and patchy results' (Bottoms 2003: 110) to be the norm, not the exception. Much depends on the capacities and orientations of offenders and victims to be empathetic or to understand the other's situation, and on the degree to which offenders are genuinely sorry for what they have done and can communicate their remorse effectively. It also depends on the character of the victimization itself and how deeply it affects victims. All of these elements are largely outside the control of facilitators or other professionals, who are in a position only to coordinate, guide, or encourage such processes. We must also recognize the limits of time and resources that can be put to RJ processes. Some propose, for example, that with better preparation, RJ conferences will go more smoothly and achieve intended results. This may well be true, but it sets up a policy question: does one put a lot of resources (including more time in preparation) in a fewer number of RJ encounters, or does one attempt to apply RJ as widely and broadly as possible? We should not assume that the nirvana story of RJ is typical, nor that it can be achieved often.[10] This sets up RJ to fail with unrealistic and too high expectations.

CONCLUSION

That there exist limits on what RJ can achieve should not be grounds for dispensing with it, nor for being disillusioned, once again, with a new justice idea. My reading of the evidence is that face-to-face encounters between victims and offenders and their supporters *is* a practice worth maintaining, and perhaps enlarging, although we cannot expect it to deliver strong stories of repair and goodwill most of the time.

In the penalty phase of the criminal process, both RJ and the established court process have limits. RJ is limited by the abilities and interests of offenders and victims to think and act in ways we may define as restorative. Established CJ is limited by the inability of formal legality to listen to the accounts of crime and their effects by those most directly involved. Legal professionals do the talking, and what is legally or administratively relevant takes precedence.

By recognizing the limits of both RJ and established CJ in the penalty (or post-penalty) phase of the criminal process, we more effectively grasp the nettle of justice as a promise, as something that may be partly but never fully realized. As such, we see that all justice practices, including RJ, are limited.

VI

Law, Economy, and Society

Overview of Part VI

The readings in **Part VI** further explore the role of law in regulating particular types of relationships between individuals and groups in society, including relationships that arise through our economic activities, through our actions (or failures to act) and through our personal lives.

The articles and cases in **Chapter 14** focus on the ways in which private law rules (particularly those relating to contracts) may be used to shape relationships. Trubek's article provides a summary of Max Weber's view that laws of contract were developed in order to provide certainty in the exchange relationships that emerged in early capitalist society. By imposing penalties on parties who broke the terms of their agreements, the legal rules of contract increased the confidence of the parties that agreements that were recognized as 'contracts' would be kept and thereby increased their willingness to enter into such agreements. As demonstrated in the *Rudder v. Microsoft* decision, we continue to develop the basic rules of contract to define enforceable agreements in a modern economy. Indeed, Conklin's article highlights how 'e-commerce' contracts that we enter into online (such as browsewrap and clickwrap contracts) can make commercial transactions easier or more uncertain, depending on how courts define the rules for these contracts. Finally, Mac Neil considers the broader challenges to legal regulation posed by the Internet in his analysis of the use of French law to prevent access to Yahoo! sites auctioning Nazi memorabilia. Drawing on the work of Lessig, Mac Neil notes that some of the architectural features of the Internet, and the increased concentration of private service providers, may actually facilitate both legal regulation and allow for a diversity of legal approaches in different jurisdictions. Thus, a forum that was once thought to escape legal regulation, the Internet, remains subject to legal regulation, if in different ways.

Regulation of capitalist economic relationships is only one of the many conjunctions that the law attempts to define and regulate. **Chapter 15** provides a brief introduction to two other areas where the law defines relationships among private individuals within society. The classic case of *Donoghue v. Stevenson* included in this chapter was the first case to clearly define the legal duty of care that flows between individuals under the law of negligence, a category of tort law. While the law of contract can be used to enforce agreements between individuals, tort law is used to enforce duties governing how individuals act towards one another. These duties extend to many different contexts of our daily lives. The *Childs v. Desormeaux* decision provides an example of how Canadian courts have approached the issue of that duty of care in the more contemporary social context of a house party. Finally, the excerpt from the *Petkus v. Becker* case shows the way in which courts can creatively apply legal doctrines to enforce obligations within intimate personal relationships in an attempt to avoid inequalities that are sometimes reinforced by, or result from, the application of formal legal rules. Tragically, the *Petkus v. Becker* case is also an example of the limits of law and how much may be lost in the translation of law into the practical, day-to-day relationships that define our lives (as will be explored in **Chapter 21**).

As you read this section, consider again the choice we make in employing law to order, stabilize, or legitimize certain relationships or remedy social problems. Why are certain types of relationships, agreements, or behaviours favoured over others? Is law always the best option for ordering relationships? How does law regulate in relation to other regulators of behaviour? As the Mac Neil article emphasizes, the Internet is a critical case to consider: first, because social relationships are increasingly mediated by evolving technologies — e.g. Facebook, Twitter, etc.; and second, because contrary to those who might still imagine the Internet as a new Wild West, behaviour on the Internet is still regulated. However, as MacNeil notes, traditional legal approaches are necessarily supplemented or even superseded by regulation through the very architecture of the Internet. What implications might follow from this?

(a)   Max Weber on Law and the Rise of Capitalism†

David M. Trubek

III.   LEGALISM AND CAPITALISM: A RECONSTRUCTION OF WEBER'S THEORY OF LAW IN ECONOMIC LIFE

We now have most of the elements needed to understand Weber's theory of the relationship between the rise of modern law and capitalism. We have examined his legal sociology, which identifies distinctive types of legal systems, and his political sociology, which shows that the structure of power determines to some degree the type of legal order that can exist. We have seen why Weber thought legalism developed in Europe. Now we must turn to his economic sociology, in which the dynamics of the market are developed. This analysis will show why capitalism and legalism are intimately related.

In his economic sociology, Weber stressed the importance for capitalist development of two aspects of law: (1) its relative degree of *calculability*, and (2) its capacity to develop *substantive* provisions — principally those relating to freedom of contract — necessary to the functioning of the market system.

The former reason was the more important of the two. Weber asserted that capitalism required a highly calculable normative order. His survey of types of law indicated that only modern, rational law, or logically formal rationality, could provide the necessary calculability. Legalism supported the development of capitalism by providing a stable and predictable atmosphere; capitalism encouraged legalism because the bourgeoisie were aware of their own need for this type of governmental structure.[38]

Legalism is the only way to provide the degree of certainty necessary for the operation of the capitalist system. Weber stated that capitalism "could not continue if its control of resources were not upheld by the legal compulsion of the state; if its formally 'legal' rights were not upheld by the threat of force."[39] He further specified that: "[T]he rationalization and systematization of the law in general and ... the increasing calculability of the functioning of the legal process in particular, constituted one of the most important conditions for the existence of ... capitalistic enterprise, which cannot do without legal security."[40]

Weber never worked out in detail a model of capitalist production which might explain why legal calculability was so important to capitalist development. I have developed such a model,[41] and I believe that underlying Weber's repeated emphasis on legal calculability is a vision similar to this latter-day ideal type.

The essence of the model is the conflict of egoistic wills, which is an inherent part of competitive capitalism. In pure market capitalism of the type idealized in micro-economics texts, each participant is driven to further his own interests at the expense of all other participants in the market. Theoretically, the profit motive is insatiable, and is unconstrained by any ethical or moral force. Thus, each actor is unconcerned with the ramifications of his actions on the economic well-being of others.

† (1972) Wisconsin L. Rev. 720 at 739–45, 748–50. [Notes and/or references omitted.] Copyright 1972 by The Board of Regents of the University of Wisconsin System. Reproduced by permission of the Wisconsin Law Review.

At the same time, however, economic actors in this system are necessarily interdependent. No market participant can achieve his goals unless he secures power over the actions of others. It does little good, for example, for the owner of a textile plant to act egocentrically to further his interests if at the same time he cannot be sure that other actors will supply him with the necessary inputs for production and consume his product. If suppliers do not provide promised raw materials, if workers refuse to work, if customers fail to pay for goods delivered, all the ruthless, rational self-interest in the world will be of little value to the textile producer in his striving for profits.

Now if all the other actors were nice, cooperative fellows, our textile manufacturer might not have to worry. Others would play their roles in the scheme and he would come out all right. But this may not always happen because they are, by hypothesis, as selfish as he is. Thus, they, too, will do whatever leads to the highest profit; if this means failing to perform some agreement, so be it. And since one can assume that there will frequently be opportunities for other actors to better themselves at the expense of providing him with some service or product necessary to the success of his enterprise, our hypothetical businessman lives in a world of radical uncertainty.

Yet, as Weber constantly stressed, uncertainty of this type is seriously prejudicial to the smooth functioning of the modern economy. How can the capitalist economic actor in a world of similarly selfish profitseekers reduce the uncertainty that threatens to rob the capitalist system of its otherwise great productive power? What will permit the economic actor to predict with relative certainty how other actors will behave over time? What controls the tendency toward instability?

In order to answer these questions, Weber moved to the level of sociological analysis. The problem of the conflict between the self-interest of individuals and social stability — what Parsons calls "the Hobbesian problem of order"[42] — is one of the fundamental problems of sociology, and, to deal with it, Weber constructed his basic schemes of social action.[43] Weber recognized that predictable uniformities of social action can be "guaranteed" in various ways and that all of these methods of social control may influence economic activities. Actors may internalize normative standards, thus fulfilling social expectations "voluntarily." Or they may be subjected to some form of "external effect" if they deviate from expectations. These external guarantees may derive from some informal sanctioning system or may involve organized coercion. Law is one form of organized coercion. All types of control may be involved in guaranteeing stable power over economic resources; factual control of this type, Weber observed, may be due to custom, to the play of interests, to convention, or to law.[44]

As I have indicated, however, Weber believed that the organized coercion of *law* was necessary in modern, capitalist economies. While internalization and conventional sanctions may be able to eliminate or resolve most conflict in simpler societies, it is incapable of serving this function in a way that satisfies the needs of the modern exchange economy. For this function, law, in the sense of organized coercion, was necessary. Weber stated:

> [T]hough it is not necessarily true of every economic system, certainly the modern economic order under modern conditions could not continue if its control of resources were not upheld by the legal compulsion of the state; that is, if its formally "legal" rights were not upheld by the threat of force.[45]

Why is coercion necessary in a market system? And why must this coercion take legal form? Finally, when we speak of *legal* coercion, do we mean state power, regardless of how it is exercised, or do we mean power governed by rules, or legalism? Weber gives no clear-cut answer to these questions. The discussion suggests answers but the issues are not fully developed. And the most crucial question, the interrelationship between the need for coercion and the model of legalism, is barely discussed at all. However, I think answers to the questions can be given which fit coherently with other aspects of his analysis.

Coercion is necessary because of the egoistic conflict I have identified above. While Weber never clearly identified this conflict, he himself was aware of it. Some principle of behavior other than short term self-interest is necessary for a market system. Tradition cannot function to constrain egoistic behavior because the market destroys the social and cultural bases of tradition. Similarly, the emerging market economy erodes the social groupings which could serve as the foci for enforcement of conventional standards. Indeed, the fact that the type of conflict I have described comes into existence is evidence of the decline of tradition and custom. Only law is left to fill the normative vacuum; legal coercion is essential because no other form is available.

A second reason why the necessary coercion must be legal is tied to the pace of economic activity and the type of rationalistic calculation characteristic of the market economy. It is not enough for the capitalist to have a general idea that someone else will more likely than not deliver more or less the performance agreed upon on or about the time stipulated. He must know exactly what and when, and he must be highly certain that the precise performance will be forthcoming. He wants to be able to predict with certainty that the other units will perform. But given the potential conflict between their self-interests and their obligations, he also wants to predict with certainty that coercion will be applied to the recalcitrant. The predictability of performance is intimately linked to the certainty that coercive instruments can be invoked in the event of nonperformance.

In this context, it becomes clear why a calculable legal system offers the most reliable way to combine coercion and predictability. Here the model of legalism and the model of capitalist dynamics merge. A system of government through rules seems inherently more predictable than any other method for structuring coercion. Convention is inherently too diffuse, and, like custom, was historically unavailable given the market-driven erosion of the groups and structures necessary for effective constraint of egoism. Like Balzac, Weber saw how the decline of family, guild, and Church unleashed unbridled egoism. Pure *power*, on the other hand, is available in the sense that the state is increasingly armed with coercive instruments. But untrammeled power is unpredictable; wielders of power, unconstrained by rules, will tend not to act in stable and predictable ways. Legalism offers the optimum combination of coercion and predictability.

It is here that the significance of legal autonomy can be seen. Autonomy is intimately linked to the problem of predictability. The autonomous legal system in a legalistic society is an institutional complex organized to apply coercion only in accordance with general rules through logical or purely cognitive processes. To the extent that it truly functions in the purely logical and, consequently, mechanical manner Weber presented, its results will be highly predictable. If it is constantly subject to interference by forces which seek to apply coercion for purposes inconsistent with the rules, it loses its predictable quality. Thus Weber observed that authoritarian rulers (and democratic despots) may refuse to be bound by formal rules since:

> They are all confronted by the inevitable conflict between an abstract formalism of legal certainty and their desire to realize substantive goals. Juridical formalism enables the legal system to operate like a technically rational machine. Thus

it guarantees to individuals and groups within the system a relative maximum of freedom, and greatly increases for them the possibility of predicting the legal consequences of their actions.[46]

Of course, the idea of legal autonomy is a much more complex one than this simplified model suggests. In Weber's work, the emergence of the autonomous legal order is correlated with other important phenomena. An autonomous legal order was essential if certain norms of a certain type were to emerge. Neither theocratic nor patrimonial rulers would allow the development of the substantive norms of economic autonomy contained in the idea of freedom of contract. Only an independent structure of normative order could guarantee these, and only a universal and supreme structure could guarantee that these norms would be adhered to. Thus the legal system had to be autonomous of other sources of normative order on the one hand, and of pure power on the other, and simultaneously control the adverse effects of both for capitalism. At least some areas of social life had to be freed of the bonds of kinship, religion, and other foci of traditional authority, and, at the same time, insulated from the arbitrary action of the state. This required that the state, as legal order, be strengthened, so that it superseded other sources of social control, and at the same time be limited, so that it did not encroach upon areas of economic action. The state was to provide a formal order, or facilitative framework within which free economic actors could operate.[47] Contained in the idea of an autonomous legal order are fundamental paradoxes of the 19th-century idea of the liberal state.[48]

. . . .

V. LEGALISM AND THE LEGITIMIZATION OF CLASS DOMINATION

Up to this point, "capitalism" has been presented as a vague abstraction. While Weber thought that capitalism was in some ways the most rational possible economic system,[60] he was no apologist for it. He could be scathingly critical of the moral effects of this system. These criticisms can be seen in several points; they emerge clearly in another part of the sociology of law where Weber takes up an issue raised by Marx: the role of legalism in legitimizing capitalist domination.

Legalism served more than purely economic functions under capitalism. Weber showed how the idea of an autonomous legal system dispensing formal justice legitimizes the political structure of capitalist society.

Legalism legitimizes the domination of workers by capitalists. The relationships between law, the state, and the market are complex. Legalism, while seeming to constrain the state, really strengthens it, and while the system guaranteed formal equality, it also legitimized class domination. Legalism strengthens the state by apparently constraining it, for the commitment to a system of rules increases the legitimacy of the modern state and thus its authority or effective power. And as the liberal state grows stronger, it reduces the hold of other forces on the development of the market. This strengthens the position of those who control property, since market organization increases the effective power of those individuals and organizations that control economic resources. "[B]y virtue of the principle of formal legal equality ... the propertied classes ... obtain a sort of factual 'autonomy'...," Weber observed.[61]

He believed that these effects of legalism stem from the fundamental antinomy between formal and material criteria of justice, and the negative aspects of purely formal administration of justice under modern conditions. Formal justice is advantageous to those with economic power; not only is it calculable but, by stressing formal as opposed to substantive criteria for decisionmaking, it discourages the use of the law as an instrument of social justice. In a passage reminiscent of Anatole France's famous quip that the law forbids both rich and poor to sleep under the bridges of Paris, Weber observed:

> Formal justice guarantees the maximum freedom for the interested parties to represent their formal legal interests. But because of the unequal distribution of economic power, *which the system of formal justice legalizes*, this very freedom must time and again produce consequences which are contrary to ... religious ethics or ... political expediency.[62]

Formal justice not only is repugnant to authoritarian powers and arbitrary rulers; it also is opposed to democratic interests. Formal justice, necessarily abstract, cannot consider the ethical issues raised by such interests; such abstention, however, reduces the possibility of realizing substantive policies advocated by popular groups.[63] Thus, certain democratic values and types of social justice could only be achieved at the cost of sacrificing strict legalism.[64] Weber also pointed out that formal legalism could stultify legal creativity, and that legal autonomy could lead to results opposed to both popular and capitalist values.

(b) *Rudder v. Microsoft Corp.*†

[WINKLER J.:]

[1] This is a motion by the defendant Microsoft for a permanent stay of this intended class proceeding. The motion is based on two alternative grounds, first that the parties have agreed to the exclusive jurisdiction, and venue, of the courts, in King County in the State of Washington in respect of any litigation between them, and secondly, that in any event, Ontario is not the appropriate forum for the conduct of this proceeding and that the service ex juris of the Statement of Claim ought to be set aside.

[2] The Microsoft Network ("MSN"), is an online service, providing, inter alia, information and services including Internet access to its members. The service is provided to members, around the world, from a "gateway" located in the State of Washington through computer connections most often made over standard telephone lines.

[3] The proposed representative plaintiffs in this action were subscriber members of MSN. Both are law school graduates, one of whom is admitted to the Bar in Ontario while the other worked as a legal researcher. They were associated with the law firm which originally represented the intended class. The plaintiffs claim under the Class Proceedings Act, 1992, S.O., C.6 on behalf of a Canada-wide class defined as:

---

† [1999] O.J. No. 3778 (Ont. Sup. Ct.).

All persons resident in Canada who subscribed for the provision of Internet access or information or services from or through MSN, The Microsoft Network, since September 1, 1995. This class is estimated to contain some 89,000 MSN members across Canada.

[4] The plaintiffs claim damages for breach of contract, breach of fiduciary duty, misappropriation and punitive damages in the total amount of $75,000,000.00 together with an accounting and injunctive relief. The plaintiffs allege that Microsoft has charged members of MSN and taken payment from their credit cards in breach of contract and that Microsoft has failed to provide reasonable or accurate information concerning accounts. The Statement of Claim was served on Microsoft at its offices in Redmond, Washington on January 5, 1998.

[5] The contract which the plaintiffs allege to have been breached is identified by MSN as a "Member Agreement". Potential members of MSN are required to electronically execute this agreement prior to receiving the services provided by the company. Each Member Agreement contains the following provision:

> 15.1 This Agreement is governed by the laws of the State of Washington, U.S.A., and you consent to the exclusive jurisdiction and venue of courts in King County, Washington, in all disputes arising out of or relating to your use of MSN or your MSN membership. The defendant relies on this clause in support of its assertion that the intended class proceeding should be permanently stayed.

[6] Although the plaintiffs rely on the contract as the basis for their causes of action, they submit that the court ought not to give credence to the "forum selection clause" contained within. It is stated in support of this contention that the representative plaintiffs read only portions of the Member Agreement and thus had no notice of the forum selection clause. Alternatively, the plaintiffs contend, in any event, that the Washington courts are not appropriate for the conduct of this lawsuit.

[7] I cannot accede to these submissions. In my view, the forum selection clause is dispositive and there is nothing in the factual record which persuades me that I should exercise my discretion so as to permit the plaintiffs to avoid the effect of the contractual provision. Accordingly, an order will go granting the relief sought by the defendant. My reasons follow.

ANALYSIS AND DISPOSITION

[8] Forum selection clauses are generally treated with a measure of deference by Canadian courts. Madam Justice Huddart, writing for the court in *Sarabia v. "Oceanic Mindoro"* (1996), 4 C.P.C. (4th) 11 (B.C.C.A.), leave to appeal denied [1997] S.C.C.A. No. 69, adopts the view that forum selection clauses should be treated the same as arbitration agreements. She states at 20:

> Since forum selection clauses are fundamentally similar to arbitration agreements, ... there is no reason for forum selection clauses not to be treated in a manner consistent with the deference shown to arbitration agreements. Such deference to forum selection clauses achieves greater international commercial certainty, shows respect for the agreements that the parties have signed, and is consistent with the principle of international comity. (Emphasis added.)

[9] Huddart J.A. further states at 21 that "a court is not bound to give effect to an exclusive jurisdiction clause" but that the choice of the parties should be respected unless "there is strong cause to override the agreement." The burden for a showing of a "strong cause" rests with the plaintiff and the threshold to be surpassed is beyond the mere "balance of convenience". The approach taken by Huddart J.A. is consistent with that adopted by courts in Ontario. (See *Holo-Deck Adventures Ltd. v. Orbotron Inc.* (1996), 8 C.P.C. (4th) 376 (Gen. Div.); *Mithras Management Ltd. v. New Visions Entertainment Corp.* (1992), 90 D.L.R. (4th) 726 (Ont. Gen. Div.)).

[10] The plaintiffs contend, first, that regardless of the deference to be shown to forum selection clauses, no effect should be given to the particular clause at issue in this case because it does not represent the true agreement of the parties. It is the plaintiffs submission that the form in which the Member Agreement is provided to potential members of MSN is such that it obscures the forum selection clause. Therefore, the plaintiffs argue, the clause should be treated as if it were the fine print in a contract which must be brought specifically to the attention of the party accepting the terms. Since there was no specific notice given, in the plaintiffs' view, the forum selection clause should be severed from the Agreement which they otherwise seek to enforce.

[11] The argument advanced by the plaintiffs relies heavily on the alleged deficiencies in the technological aspects of electronic formats for presenting the terms of agreements. In other words, the plaintiffs

contend that because only a portion of the Agreement was presented on the screen at one time, the terms of the Agreement which were not on the screen are essentially "fine print".

[12] I disagree. The Member Agreement is provided to potential members of MSN in a computer readable form through either individual computer disks or via the Internet at the MSN website. In this case, the plaintiff Rudder, whose affidavit was filed on the motion, received a computer disk as part of a promotion by MSN. The disk contained the operating software for MSN and included a multi-media sign up procedure for persons who wished to obtain the MSN service. As part of the sign-up routine, potential members of MSN were required to acknowledge their acceptance of the terms of the Member Agreement by clicking on an "I Agree" button presented on the computer screen at the same time as the terms of the Member Agreement were displayed.

[13] Rudder admitted in cross-examination on his affidavit that the entire agreement was readily viewable by using the scrolling function on the portion of the computer screen where the Membership Agreement was presented. Moreover, Rudder acknowledged that he "scanned" through part of the Agreement looking for "costs" that would be charged by MSN. He further admitted that once he had found the provisions relating to costs, he did not read the rest of the Agreement. An excerpt from the transcript of Rudder's cross-examination is illustrative:

> Q. 314. I will now take you down to another section. I am now looking at heading 15, which is entitled "General", and immediately underneath that is subsection 15.1. Now, do I take it, when you were scanning, you would have actually scanned past this, and you would have at least seen there was a heading that said "General"? Is that fair? Or did you not even scan all the way through?
> A. I did not go all the way down, I can honestly say. Once I found out what it would cost me, that is where I would stop.
>
> Q. 315. So, I take it that you did not read 15.1?
> A. No, I definitely did not read this, no.
>
> Q. 316. I now have 15.4 on the screen, and presumably you did not read that either?
> A. No, I did not.
>
> Q. 317. I take it, during the whole signup process that you did, you did the whole thing online on the computer ...
> A. Yes.

> Q. 318. ... using the disk? And we will come to the connection. You did not have any voice communication with MSN?
> A. No.
>
> Q. 319. Or with Microsoft Corporation?
> A. No.
>
> Q. 320. You did not have any written correspondence with them at the time of signup?
> A. No.
>
> Q. 321. All right. Now, I take it that, after doing the review of this that you did do, you clicked, "I agree"? Is that what you did?
> A. After I was satisfied with what it was going to cost me, I agreed. (Emphasis added.)

[14] I have viewed the Member Agreement as it was presented to Rudder during the sign up procedure. All of the terms of the Agreement are displayed in the same format. Although, there are certain terms of the Agreement displayed entirely in upper-case letters, there are no physical differences which make a particular term of the agreement more difficult to read than any other term. In other words, there is no fine print as that term would be defined in a written document. The terms are set out in plain language, absent words that are commonly referred to as "legalese". Admittedly, the entire Agreement cannot be displayed at once on the computer screen, but this is not materially different from a multi-page written document which requires a party to turn the pages. Furthermore, the structure of the sign-up procedure is such that the potential member is presented with the terms of membership twice during the process and must signify acceptance each time. Each time the potential member is provided with the option of disagreeing which terminates the process. The second time the terms are displayed occurs during the online portion of the process and at that time, the potential member is advised via a clear notice on the computer screen of the following:

> ... The membership agreement includes terms that govern how information about you and your membership may be used. To become a MSN Premier member, you must select "I Agree" to acknowledge your consent to the terms of the membership agreement. If you click "I Agree" without reading the membership agreement, you are still agreeing to be bound by all of the terms of the membership agreement, without limitation ....

[15] On cross-examination, Rudder admitted to having seen the screen containing the notice. In order to replicate the conditions, portions of the cross-examination were conducted while Rudder was being

led through an actual sign-up process including the online connection portion. While online, and after having been shown the notice posted above, Rudder responded to questioning as follows:

> Q. 372. All right. You see immediately below the printing that we have just read, a rectangular box that says, "MSN Premier Membership Rules"?
>
> A. Yes.
>
> Q. 373. And, below that, a larger white box that says, "Please click MSN Membership Rules and read the membership agreement"?
>
> A. Yes.
>
> Q. 374. Did you read the phrase that I just stated in the big white box?
>
> A. No. What I probably did ... I can't say for sure ... is I probably just went to "I Agree", and then "Next".
>
> Q. 375. Did you understand, when you clicked "I Agree" on this occasion, that [what] you were agreeing to was something that was going to govern your legal relationship surrounding your use of MSN?
>
> A. If you are asking me if I made a mental note, or if I had knowledge of that, no, I did not really pay attention to that. That is a common practice when I sign up on anything. Like I said, my main concern is what the costs are.

[16] It is plain and obvious that there is no factual foundation for the plaintiffs' assertion that any term of the Membership Agreement was analogous to "fine print" in a written contract. What is equally clear is that the plaintiffs seek to avoid the consequences of specific terms of their agreement while at the same time seeking to have others enforced. Neither the form of this contract nor its manner of presentation to potential members are so aberrant as to lead to such an anomalous result. To give effect to the plaintiffs' argument would, rather than advancing the goal of "commercial certainty", to adopt the words of Huddart J.A. in Sarabia, move this type of electronic transaction into the realm of commercial absurdity. It would lead to chaos in the marketplace, render ineffectual electronic commerce and undermine the integrity of any agreement entered into through this medium.

[17] On the present facts, the Membership Agreement must be afforded the sanctity that must be given to any agreement in writing. The position of selectivity advanced by the plaintiffs runs contrary to this stated approach, both in principle and on the evidence, and must be rejected. Moreover, given that both of the representative plaintiffs are graduates of law schools and have a professed familiarity with Internet services, their position is particularly indefensible.

[18] Having found that the terms of the Member Agreement, including the forum selection clause, bind the plaintiffs, I turn to a consideration of whether it is appropriate to exercise my discretion to override the forum clause agreed to by the parties. In my view, the submissions made by the defendant are compelling. On the facts of this case, it would not be appropriate for this court to permit the plaintiff to continue this action in Ontario contrary to the forum selection clause.

[19] Simply put, I find that the plaintiffs have not met the burden of showing a "strong cause" as to why the forum selection clause should not be determinative. In Sarabia, Huddart J.A. referred to the English case, *"Eleftheria" (The) (Cargo Owners) v. "Eleftheria" (The)*, [1969] 2 All E.R. 641, as the decision most often followed in Canada in setting out the factors that a court will consider in determining whether it should exercise its discretion and refuse to enforce a forum selection clause in an agreement.

[20] The factors to consider may be paraphrased as follows:

1. in which jurisdiction is the evidence on issues of fact situated, and the effect of that on the convenience and expense of trial in either jurisdiction;
2. whether the law of the foreign country applies and its differences from the domestic law in any respect;
3. the strength of the jurisdictional connections of the parties;
4. whether the defendants desire to enforce the forum selection clause is genuine or merely an attempt to obtain a procedural advantage;
5. whether the plaintiffs will suffer prejudice by bringing their claim in a foreign court because they will be
   (a) deprived of security for the claim; or
   (b) be unable to enforce any judgment obtained; or
   (c) be faced with a time-bar not applicable in the domestic court; or
   (d) unlikely to receive a fair trial.

[21] When these factors are applied within the factual matrix of this case, it is apparent that the plaintiffs cannot meet the threshold of a "strong cause".

Most of the activities associated with the provision of services pursuant to the Member Agreements that are the subject of the allegations in the Statement of Claim are carried out in King County, Washington. This includes the business management of accounts of MSN members, member authentication, policy-making regarding member accounts, billing and customer service. All of the computers in which MSN content and information are contained are located in King County. The sheer size of the intended class means that there is a potential that voluminous amounts of billing statements and related information, which is most likely to be located in Washington, will be required as evidence. Furthermore, the MSN witnesses are located at the company's center of operations in King County.

[22] Since I have found that the forum selection clause applies in this case, by operation of that clause the choice of law agreed to by the parties is the law of the State of Washington. Regardless of whether this action [were] tried in Ontario or elsewhere, the law to be applied would remain the same.

[23] Microsoft has demonstrated substantial connection to the State of Washington, and in particular to King County. The plaintiffs, on the other hand, propose to represent a Canada-wide class whose connections to Ontario are not readily apparent on the evidence before the court. Class proceedings may be conducted under both the federal and state court systems in the State of Washington and while the test for certification may be somewhat more advantageous to the plaintiffs in Ontario, it is not sufficiently so as to permit me to ignore the other factors which clearly favour the defendant in this case. Moreover, in the interests of international comity, and in the absence of any evidence to the contrary, there is nothing to suggest that the plaintiffs would not receive a fair trial in the State of Washington. Indeed, considering that the defendant is resident there, it would be more advantageous to the plaintiffs, in respect of enforcement, if a judgment were obtained from a court in that jurisdiction.

[24] I note in passing that this forum selection clause has been upheld on appeal in an intended class proceeding in the State of New Jersey. (*Caspi v. The Microsoft Network*, L.L.C., 732 A.2d 528 (N.J. App. 1999).

[25] In view of my disposition on the first point, it is unnecessary to deal with the forum non conveniens and service ex juris arguments.

[26] The defendant shall have the relief requested. The action brought by the plaintiffs in Ontario is permanently stayed. The defendant shall have its costs of this motion, which, by agreement of the parties will be fixed by the court and payable forthwith. Counsel may make brief written submissions with respect to costs within two weeks of the date of release of these reasons.

(c) Be Careful What You Click for: An Analysis of Online Contracting†

Rachel S. Conklin

I. INTRODUCTION

Thanks to the Internet, a shopper in Chicago can make a purchase from a seller in Shanghai, any time of the day or night, with nothing more than a click of the mouse.[1] That click will form an agreement which differs from the traditional 'sign-on-the-dotted-line' format in how it satisfies the traditional requirements of a contract. ... While online shopping has broad appeal, the majority of online consumers have at one time or another abandoned a transaction over uncertainty or distrust of the website.[3] Consumer distrust arises primarily out of concerns over safety and security of the website[4] and a lack of confidence with the parameters of the bargain itself[5] — an issue directly impacted by the clarity of the contract formed online.

---

† (2008) 20:3 Loyola Consumer Law Review 325 at 325–32, 346–47. [Notes and/or references omitted.] Reproduced with permission.

Online contracting encompasses more than the final click of a purchase or download. During a typical online session, an Internet user may unknowingly form numerous contracts, just by visiting a particular website.[6] For instance, the terms and conditions of the use of a website may be listed in small print along the bottom of the site, or alternatively, on a separate page accessed only by clicking a link.[7] Even if the site never presents its terms and conditions to the user, those terms and conditions may be legally binding.[8] In a recent article, Michelle Slatalla, a frequent contributor to the *New York Times*, described noticing a ten dollar charge on her credit card from an unfamiliar source.[9] Slatalla deduced that after purchasing movie tickets online, her husband entered his e-mail address in a pop-up on the site to receive promotions in the future, unaware that the promotion program cost ten dollars per month.[10] Slatalla eventually discovered that she and her husband had been members of the program for sixteen months.[11]

Online contracts must comply with the customary legal requirements of offer and acceptance, but these prerequisites can exist in non-traditional ways in the realm of the Internet.[12] The two main forms of online contracts are clickwrap and browsewrap.[13] Clickwrap agreements require the user to make some manifestation of his or her intent to be bound by a contract after being presented with that contract's terms, for instance by clicking a button labeled "I Agree" after viewing the terms.[14] On the other hand, the terms of a browsewrap contract are often inconspicuous or even unavailable to a consumer online; a contract is accepted by performance as the consumer continues to navigate the website or uses a product or service found on the site.[15] Slatalla's article does not mention whether her husband was presented with the terms of the ten-dollar-per-month promotion program.[16] If not, Slatalla's husband likely accepted a browsewrap contract for the program when he typed his email address into the pop-up even though he was never presented with the program's details, including the price.

. . . .

II. CONTRACT THEORY

A. Fundamentals

The traditional legal theory of bargains identifies three conditions required to form a contract: offer, acceptance, and consideration. When these conditions are met, a contract is binding and enforceable.[19] If the bargain is fair, the value of the bargain is proportional to the value of the consideration for each party, regardless of how small or large that consideration may be.[20]

The most beneficial effect of a contract is to facilitate deferred exchanges.[21] Typically when a bargain is struck, the parties do not simultaneously perform their promises.[22] Without a contract, the party that is scheduled to perform second would have an incentive against performance because she could acquire the benefit of the first party's promise without doing anything in return.[23] This in turn creates an incentive for the first party to refrain from making the promise at all, since he knows the second party will likely breach.[24] Thus, without a contract to insure future performance, parties would rarely strike bargains for deferred exchange.[25] Alternatively, when a contract makes both promises enforceable, the second party will not be able to appropriate the benefit of the first party's performance without paying compensatory damages.[26] The second party will have an incentive to perform, and the first party will be willing to enter into the bargain.[27]

B. Fundamentals Online

An agreement formed online must fulfill the traditional requirements to be considered an enforceable contract; however, the principles of offer and acceptance operate in somewhat novel ways.[28] Clickwrap agreements require the user to make some manifestation of their intent to be bound by the contract.[29] This can include clicking a button labeled, "I Accept," typing those same words into a box, or checking one of two boxes marked "Accept" and "Decline."[30] The website's performance of the contract is conditioned on the user's manifesting consent by clicking the proper button.[31]

Browsewrap agreements are generally passive presentations of contract terms; the terms may be listed at the bottom of a webpage, accessible by clicking on a link which directs the user to a separate webpage, or even found in an email which is sent to the user after the contract has been formed.[32] Internet users may not realize the terms of a browsewrap contract are available to them if they do not notice or actively seek out the terms.[33] Whereas express manifestation of acceptance is required to form a clickwrap agreement, browsewrap agreements are generally accepted implicitly through continued use of the site, or use of the site's products, services or information.[34]

The contents of online contracts for goods and services typically mirror paper contracts for goods and services. Online and paper contracts often specify procedures the user must comply with, such as arbitration in the case of conflict.[35] These contracts also explain the user's rights and restrictions regarding the bargained-for good or information.[36] Finally, the contract discloses what the user gives up in the exchange and what rights the user gains against the website.[37]

C. Transaction Costs

In a perfect world, parties wishing to form contracts would be able to find each other and negotiate mutually beneficial bargains without burdens or inefficiencies.[38] In the real world, many circumstances hinder the process of bargaining for a contract. Some examples include parties over or undervaluing the exchange, agreements in which one side has more information than the other, and high costs associated with finding and negotiating with bargaining partners.[39] These hindrances to efficient contracts, known as transaction costs,[40] burden the bargaining process because parties must factor them into the price that they are willing to pay for an exchange.[41]

One of the most notable characteristics of the Internet is the possibility for almost instant gratification. For example, after a bargain has been struck for a song online, the buyer can immediately download and play that song in his own home. This reduces transaction costs by eliminating the difficulty in finding a bargaining partner and reducing the time needed to perform.[42] Speed and efficiency are particular advantages of browsewrap. The user can form a binding contract without spending any time proceeding through multiple screens or acknowledging contract terms. This is particularly useful if the Internet user is familiar and comfortable with a website. If a consumer makes frequent purchases on a particular website, she may prefer not to scroll through the same terms and conditions before each purchase.

However, online contracts can increase transaction costs as well, primarily in the form of uncertainty.[43] If an Internet user is wary of inadvertently accepting a hidden contract, or if the user knows contract terms are available but has difficulty finding them, the added outlay of time and effort could actually exceed that of driving to a store and forming a paper contract for a good or service. Asymmetric information between the parties also adds to transaction costs.[44] This situation occurs when one party has significantly more information than the other, or when one party does not understand the information presented to it by the other party.[45] If a consumer is unaware he is forming a contract, the website has superior knowledge regarding the terms of that contract and consequently, the parties have

asymmetric information. Browsewrap contracts can create situations where the parties are not equally informed about the terms and conditions, including one party remaining unaware that a contract has been formed. If consumers are uneasy with the situation, they may find themselves with an incentive to refrain from online contracting.

D. Uncertainty and E-commerce

Consumers have overwhelmingly demonstrated their approval of e-commerce with their dollars; U.S. shoppers are expected to spend $157.4 billion online this year.[46] However, consumers have repeatedly indicated that they are very concerned with the presence of uncertainty in e-commerce: eighty-four percent of online shoppers have at least some doubts about the trustworthiness of e-retailers.[47] Consumers fear they may be putting themselves at risk by agreeing to provisions of the website that they are not aware of or comfortable with[;][48] this can include misuse of personal information, constraints on future behavior,[49] and adverse financial effects.[50]

The burden of uncertainty has concrete effects in ecommerce: sixty-five percent of online consumers have failed to complete a transaction due to a lack of trust in a website.[51] Browsewrap contracts can augment this uncertainty; the browsewrap-related cases that have made it to court generally involve internet users feeling misled by browsewrap.[52] Any uncertainty that browsewrap adds to a transaction also increases the burden of transaction costs in that contract.

. . . .

VII. CONCLUSION

Over the past few decades, agreements between buyers and sellers have evolved to satisfy the requirements of a contract in novel ways. Some of these new formations, such as shrinkwrap and clickwrap, have come into widespread use and make bargaining quick and easy for all parties. The traditional requirements of a contract, including offer and acceptance, must still be met for these agreements to be legally binding. Browsewrap may be the most efficient type of contract created so far. A consumer generally is not presented with the terms of a browsewrap bargain and does not need to alter his or her behavior to indicate acceptance. The price of this efficiency is that the consumer may be unaware of the terms he or she has agreed to, or may be unaware that a contract has been formed at all. The U.S. judiciary should use case law to clarify when browsewrap does and does not constitute a binding contract. If restriction on the practice is deemed necessary, rather than hindering e-commerce, the overall number of contracts formed online may actually increase. Boundaries outlining the acceptable uses of browsewrap would give websites an incentive to present contracts to consumers in a more upfront and clear manner. This should reduce the uncertainty many consumers feel when proceeding with transactions online. If consumers' increased confidence is great enough, it will lead to an overall increase in the number of contracts formed online, a result that will leave both buyers and sellers in a better position. ... The courts have an opportunity to create a stronger forum for buyers and sellers on the Internet; they should not miss the chance.

(d) Law, Cyberspace and the Role of Nation States†

Michael Mac Neil

The development of the Internet and the growth of cyberspace pose new challenges for nation states seeking to regulate citizen conduct and to protect citizens from external threats. States typically apply legal rules and sanctions to regulate behaviour. Law is one of a number of tools used to both shape norms of conduct and to legitimize the imposition of coercive measures to induce compliance. The effectiveness of law as a tool rests in part on states' ability to employ legal institutions and policing mechanisms which operate directly on the individuals whose behaviour they are seeking to control. These direct effects depend on states having control over people or property within the political territory over which they assert their sovereignty. Johnson and Post[1] argue that there is a strong logical nexus between sovereignty, law, and territoriality, based on four factors. First, effective law making depends on exerting physical control over potential law violators. Second, there is a congruence between physical boundaries and the effects of particular behaviour. Third, democratic participation, enhancing the legitimacy of law, is facilitated by sovereignty within political boundaries. Fourth, boundaries serve to provide notice of the ambit of legal rules.

The question is whether the emergence of cyberspace fundamentally alters the ability of state sovereigns to exercise their authority to control behaviour. Johnson and Post contend that the old rules no longer apply, because cyberspace activity is untied from physical location. Individuals engage in social, political, and economic relations in cyberspace without regard to political boundaries. The technology and the architecture of the Internet facilitate global communication and global transactions, so that the behaviour of individuals is no longer easily subjected to physical control by a particular sovereign state, is no longer local in effect, and is no longer confined to a geographically based community. In the face of this, there are both practical and normative limitations on the ability and legitimacy of regulation of cyberspace activity by nation states. For Johnson and Post, the natural consequence is to develop both practical and normative models that rely on the unique features of cyberspace, allowing for a great deal more self-regulation within constantly reconfigured cyberspace communities from which exit is an easy option for those who do not accept the legitimacy of the rules being imposed in a particular community.

However, there is a considerable amount of evidence to belie the powerlessness of the nation state in the face of an emerging cyberspace. There may be less of a nexus between law and territory than Post and Johnson suppose. The emergence of international human rights norms, the development of cooperative international approaches to defining and enforcing acceptable rules of conduct, and some of the very features of cyberspace architecture which mark it as unique may also facilitate an ongoing role for nation states. It is on this last feature that I wish to concentrate.

---

† A corrected version of original published in (2001) 2:1 McGill International Review 24–26. [Notes and/or references omitted.] Reproduced with permission.

There are a number of elements of Internet architecture which lead some to believe that there is likely to be a great deal more chaos or anarchy in cyberspace than exists in "real" space. The decentralized, non-hierarchical, global structure of the Internet appears, on the face of it, to enable individuals to easily route around state imposed restrictions on their conduct. However, recent trends towards concentration of ownership, combined with more sophisticated surveillance and monitoring techniques, may facilitate the ability of a single state to impose its will on activity which originates beyond its physical boundaries. The consequences for both our conceptions of governance and the future of cyberspace remain to be determined, but [it] is by no means certain that the emergence of cyberspace will lead to the decline of the nation state.

The recent decision[2] by a French court to apply French law prohibiting the display of Nazi memorabilia demonstrates these themes. In this case, several groups initiated an action against Yahoo, an American based web portal which also operates a companion portal, Yahoo France, specifically designed for French Internet users. Yahoo sponsors an auction web site, in which numerous Nazi artifacts were being made available for sale. The server hosting the auction site was located in the United States. The Yahoo France web site did not contain a direct link to the auction site, but there was nothing preventing a French user who originally connected to the Yahoo France site from browsing to the general Yahoo site and from thence to the auction site. The French court ordered Yahoo to implement measures which would prevent French users from gaining access to the auction site, with the threat of 100,000 franc per day fine in the event that Yahoo failed to implement appropriate measures. Is this merely an example of an ineffectual attempt by a national court to overreach the territorial boundaries within which its laws normally apply, or is it a sign of a wave of such actions which will entrench the power of nation states to protect their own culture and values from the libertarian imposition of individual choices?

It is probably too early to answer the preceding question, but there are a number of features of the case that deserve further reflection. First, it demonstrates that there continues to be a clash of values despite the forces which may otherwise be leading to considerable harmonization of laws. The choice of the French government (not alone on this score) to regulate forms of expression which may be considered hateful and thus harmful to minority groups stands in stark contrast to the claim made by Yahoo, that American law with its strong constitutional commitment to free speech should apply. If nation states can successfully regulate actions which are taking place outside their borders but which contravene the legal values which they have enacted to protect their citizens, the ability of cybercitizens to build communities governed by rules which do not defer to state laws and geographic boundaries is considerably attenuated.

Second, the case raises significant questions about how law can regulate. Earlier, I argued that the effectiveness of state-based regulation depends to a considerable extent on the ability of the nation state to impose coercive sanctions directly on those whose behaviour it seeks to control. However, cyberspace gives a great deal more scope for indirect action by law. Rather than seeking to directly regulate the behaviour of individuals who display Nazi memorabilia, the French court is seeking to apply law indirectly by taking advantage of the very architecture of cyberspace. Yahoo was ordered to develop filters which could be used to identify and deny access to French cyberspace browsers seeking to view the Yahoo auction site. In real space, a merchant may be able to control who is able to view its merchandise, e.g. by excluding minors, or by setting up shop in a trendy district. This succeeds in real space because the merchant is able to monitor and assess the clientele entering the store, or take advantage of geographic location to cater to a particular clientele. At first blush, it appears that such control is precluded by the architecture of cyberspace which enabled individuals to engage in cyberspace activity on an anonymous basis. However, the commercialization of the Internet has led to the development of ever more sophisticated monitoring tools, motivated in part by the desire to gather more accurate data about consumers and provide more targeted marketing schemes. That very same technology has the potential to enable nation states to erect virtual boundaries which emulate political-geographic boundaries. If major portals are able to identify who is seeking to view particular web pages, and if it is possible to selectively refuse "admittance" to the site on the basis of the geographical location of the browser, then the scope for control by nation states is considerably enhanced.

This enhancement, however, depends not only on the existence of monitoring and control technology, but also on the ability of the state to impose its will, by coercive sanctions, on those who control the communications routes of the Internet. This leads to a third point — the concentration of ownership and control, with a small number of large corporate actors who are actively engaged in a global enterprise, facilitates the ability of any one state to [significantly] impose its laws directly on those actors, and hence indirectly on all Internet users.

Lessig[3] writes about the ability of the state to regulate intermediaries — companies like Yahoo through whom cyberspace users must connect to the Internet. These intermediaries are more regulable because they are fewer, their interests are usually commercial and they are ordinarily pliant targets of regulation. On the face of it, the commercialization and privatization of provision of Internet services may appear antithetical to the ability of the state to govern cyberspace activity in the public interest.[4] The state is no longer directly involved as the provider of services nor is it typically the owner of the Internet infrastructure. These developments certainly make it more difficult for the government to directly achieve its goals, whether of expanding accessibility, fostering community, or monitoring cyberspace activity. Nevertheless, they may allow governments to employ law indirectly. This indirect regulation of intermediaries will be effective only if a nation state can actually impose their decisions on the intermediaries. That is becoming increasingly possible as a result of many of the giant global Internet service providers maintaining computer servers, offices and local sites in other countries, making them more vulnerable to enforcement action.[5] That is precisely what Yahoo has done in setting up Yahoo France, and it is Yahoo's French presence that makes the French court's threat of sanctions credible.

It would be imprudent to unduly stress the ability of [nation] states to harness the architectural features of the Internet to their own quest for maintaining control both over the actions of their own citizens and over content to which their citizens may be exposed. There is an inherent tension in the architecture of the Internet between its decentralizing features and the tendency towards centralization of power and control. Monitoring technology may not be sufficiently sophisticated to allow completely precise identification of browsers. Individuals can engage in a variety of actions, (e.g. use of encryption, anonymizers or long distance access), which makes it difficult to determine their geographic location, [let alone] their precise identity. Which of the trends towards decentralization or centralization will win out remains to be seen, but certainly there is potential for individual nation states to exploit some features of cyberspace architecture in an attempt to continue using law as a tool for regulation of behaviour.

Having concluded that it may be possible for states to retain a measure of control over cyberspace activity through the indirect application of law to modify the code or architecture of cyberspace, I do not wish to be seen as endorsing this as a necessarily positive development. There are many problems with a future in which a multiplicity of states each attempt to regulate Internet code in a way to ensure that local values prevail. One of the positive boons of the Internet is the potential it [offers] for open communication, the facilitation of community development, and the promotion of democratic practices and human rights. If individual states can effectively build virtual borders that preclude or hamper these developments, much of the positive value of communicative freedom in cyberspace may be jeopardized.

Furthermore, not all states will be equal in their ability to shape cyberspace code and architecture. Because of the history of Internet development, much of the crucial architecture may be subject to greater control by the United States than by other countries. The domain name root servers for the Internet are housed in the United States, and continue to be under the control of the United States government. It is, for example, the United States which was able to play a dominant role in establishing the governing institutions for domain name policy, namely the Internet Corporation for Assigned Names and Numbers (ICANN). There is still considerable reluctance in the United States to accept that the Internet may have grown into something which is beyond the competence of the United States government to legitimately control and dominate.[6]

The Internet is a new technology hailed by some as revolutionary in a way that undermines the ability of sovereign states to maintain their sovereignty. However, the Internet is not the first technology to which sovereign states have responded in innovative ways to maintain their central role in the schemes of governance. The difficulties of employing law in traditional ways as a tool of governance of cyberspace activity undoubtedly [challenge] the state to develop new techniques and approaches to regulation. However, the challenges posed by cyberspace technology may be met with technologies which facilitate [government's] ability to engage in monitoring and to achieve indirectly that [] it may no longer be able to do directly.

(a) *Donoghue v. Stevenson*

The defendant was the manufacturer of a well-known brand of ginger-beer which was sold in opaque bottles. The plaintiff consumed part of a bottle of the defendant's ginger-beer in which she found the remains of a decomposed snail. The bottle had been purchased by the plaintiff's friend at a railway café.

The defendants denied liability on the basis that as a manufacturer it owed no duty of care to the plaintiff consumer.

[LORD ATKIN:]

The sole question for determination in this case is legal: Do the averments made by the pursuer in her pleading, if true, disclose a cause of action? I need not re-state the particular facts. The question is whether the manufacturer of an article of drink sold by him to a distributor in circumstances which prevent the distributor or the ultimate purchaser or consumer from discovering by inspection any defect is under any legal duty to the ultimate purchaser or consumer to take reasonable care that the article is free from defect likely to cause injury to health. I do not think a more important problem has occupied your Lordships in your judicial capacity, important both because of its bearing on public health and because of the practical test which it applies to the system of law under which it arises. The case has to be determined in accordance with Scots law, but it has been a matter of agreement between the experienced counsel who argued this case, and it appears to be the basis of the judgments of the learned judges of the Court of Session, that for the purposes

of determining this problem the laws of Scotland and the law of England are the same. I speak with little authority on this point, but my own research, such as it is, satisfies me that the principles of the law of Scotland on such a question as the present are identical with those of English law, and I discuss the issue on that footing. The law of both countries appears to be that in order to support an action for damages for negligence the complainant has to show that he has been injured by the breach of a duty owed to him in the circumstances by the defendant to take reasonable care to avoid such injury. In the present case we are not concerned with the breach of the duty; if a duty exists, that would be a question of fact which is sufficiently averred and for the present purposes must be assumed. We are solely concerned with the question whether as a matter of law in the circumstances alleged the defender owed any duty to the pursuer to take care.

It is remarkable how difficult it is to find in the English authorities statements of general application defining the relations between parties that give rise to the duty. The courts are concerned with the particular relations which come before them in actual litigation, and it is sufficient to say whether the duty exists in those circumstances. The result is that the courts have been engaged upon an elaborate classification of duties as they exist in respect of property, whether real or personal, with further divisions as to ownership, occupation or control, and distinctions based on the particular relations of the one side or the other, whether manufacturer, salesman or landlord, customer, tenant, stranger, and so on. In this way it can be ascertained at any time

---

† [1932] All E.R. 1 at 10–13, 20. (H.L.)

whether the law recognises a duty, but only where the case can be referred to some particular species which has been examined and classified. And yet the duty which is common to all the cases where liability is established must logically be based upon some element common to the cases where it is found to exist. To exist a complete logical definition of the general principle is probably to go beyond the function of the judge, for, the more general the definition, the more likely it is to omit essentials or introduce non-essentials. The attempt was made by Lord Esher in *Heaven v. Pender* in a definition to which I will later refer. As framed it was demonstrably too wide, though it appears to me, if properly limited, to be capable of affording a valuable practical guide.

At present I content myself with pointing out that in English law there must be and is some general conception of relations giving rise to a duty of care, of which the particular cases found in the books are but instances. The liability for negligence, whether you style it such or treat it as in other systems as a species of "culpa," is no doubt based upon a general public sentiment of moral wrongdoing for which the offender must pay. But acts or omissions which any moral code would censure cannot in a practical world be treated so as to give a right to every person injured by them to demand relief. In this way rules of law arise which limit the range of complainants and the extent of their remedy. The rule that you are to love your neighbour becomes in law: You must not injure your neighbour, and the lawyers' question: Who is my neighbour? receives a restricted reply. You must take reasonable care to avoid acts or omissions which you can reasonably foresee would be likely to injure your neighbour. Who then, in law, is my neighbour? The answer seems to be persons who are so closely and directly affected by my act that I ought reasonably to have them in contemplation as being so affected when I am directing my mind to the acts or omissions which are called in question. This appears to me to be the doctrine of *Heaven v. Pender* as laid down by Lord Esher when it is limited by the notion of proximity introduced by Lord Esher himself and A.L. Smith, L.J., in *Le Lievre and another* v. *Gould*. Lord Esher, M.R., says ([1893] 1 Q.B. at p. 497):

> That case established that, under certain circumstances, one man may owe a duty to another, even though there is no contract between them. If one man is near to another, or is near to the property of another, a duty lies upon him not to do that which may cause a personal injury to that other, or may injure his property.

So A.L. Smith, L.J., says ([1893] 1 Q.B. at p. 504):

> The decision of *Heaven* v. *Pender* was founded upon the principle that a duty to take due care did arise when the person or property of one was in such proximity to the person or property of another that, if due care was not taken damage might be done by the one to the other.

I think that this sufficiently states the truth if proximity be not confined to mere physical proximity, but be used, as I think it was intended, to extend to such close and direct relations that the act complained of directly affects a person whom the person alleged to be bound to take care would know would be directly affected by his careless act. That this is the sense in which nearness or "proximity" was intended by Lord Esher is obvious from his own illustration in *Heaven* v. *Pender* (11 Q.B.D. at p. 510) of the application of his doctrine to the sale of goods.

> This [*i.e.*, the rule he has just formulated] includes the case of goods, [etc.], supplied to be used immediately by a particular person or persons, or one of a class of persons, where it would be obvious to the person supplying, if he thought, that the goods would in all probability be used at once by such persons before a reasonable opportunity for discovering any defect which might exist, and where the thing supplied would be of such a nature that a neglect of ordinary care or skill as to its condition or the manner of supplying it would probably cause danger to the person or property of the person for whose use it was supplied, and who was about to use it. It would exclude a case in which the goods are supplied under circumstances in which it would be a chance by whom they would be used, or whether they would be used or not, or whether they would be used before there would probably be means of observing any defect, or where the goods would be of such a nature that a want of care or skill as to their condition or the manner of supplying them would not probably produce danger of injury to person or property.

I draw particular attention to the fact that Lord Esher emphasises the necessity of goods having to be "used immediately" and "used at once before a reasonable opportunity of inspection." This is obviously to exclude the possibility of goods having their condition altered by lapse of time, and to call attention to the proximate relationship, which may be too remote where inspection even by the person using, certainly by an intermediate person, may reasonably be interposed. With this necessary qualification of proximate relationship, as explained in *Le Lievre* v. *Gould*, I think the judgment of Lord Esher expresses the law of England. Without the qualification, I think that the majority of the court in *Heaven* v. *Pender* was justified in thinking that the principle was expressed in too general terms. There will, no doubt, arise cases where it will be difficult to determine whether the contemplated relationship is so close that the duty arises. But in the class of case now before the court I cannot conceive any difficulty to arise. A manufacturer puts up an article of food in a container which he knows will be opened by the actual consumer. There can be no inspection by any purchaser and no reasonable preliminary inspection by the consumer. Negligently in the course of preparation he allows the contents to be mixed with poison. It is said that the law of England and Scotland is that the poisoned consumer has no remedy against the negligent manufacturer. If this were the result of the authorities, I should consider the result a grave defect in the law and so contrary to principle that I should hesitate long before following any decision to that effect which had not the authority of this House. I would point out that in the assumed state of the authorities not only would the consumer have no remedy against the manufacturer, he would have none against anyone else, for in the circumstances alleged there would be no evidence of negligence against anyone other than the manufacturer, and except in the case of a consumer who was also a purchaser no contract and no warranty of fitness, and in the case of the purchase of a specific article under its patent or trade name, which might well be the case in the purchase of some articles of food or drink, no warranty protecting even the purchaser-consumer. There are other instances than of articles of food and drink where goods are sold intended to be used immediately by the consumer, such as many forms of goods sold for cleaning purposes, when the same liability must exist. The

doctrine supported by the decision below would not only deny a remedy to the consumer who was injured by consuming bottled beer or chocolates poisoned by the negligence of the manufacturer, but also to the user of what should be a harmless proprietary medicine, an ointment, a soap, a cleaning fluid or cleaning powder. I confine myself to articles of common household use, where everyone, including the manufacturer, knows that the articles will be used by persons other than the actual ultimate purchaser — namely, by members of his family and his servants, and, in some cases, his guests. I do not think so ill of our jurisprudence as to suppose that its principles are so remote from the ordinary needs of civilized society and the ordinary claims which it makes upon its members as to deny a legal remedy where there is so obviously a social wrong.

. . . .

If your Lordships accept the view that the appellant's pleading discloses a relevant cause of action, you will be affirming the proposition that by Scots and English law alike a manufacturer of products which he sells in such a form as to show that he intends them to reach the ultimate consumer in the form in which they left him, with no reasonable possibility of intermediate examination, and with the knowledge that the absence of reasonable care in the preparation or putting up of the products will result in injury to the consumer's life or property, owes a duty to the consumer to take that reasonable care.

It is a proposition that I venture to say no one in Scotland or England who was not a lawyer would for one moment doubt. It will be an advantage to make it clear that the law in this matter, as in most others, is in accordance with sound common sense. I think that this appeal should be allowed.

(b) *Childs v. Desormeaux*†

[McLACHLIN C.J. for the Court:]

1. INTRODUCTION

[1] A person hosts a party. Guests drink alcohol. An inebriated guest drives away and causes an accident

in which another person is injured. Is the host liable to the person injured? I conclude that as a general rule, a social host does not owe a duty of care to a person injured by a guest who has consumed alcohol and that the courts below correctly dismissed the appellants' action.

---

† 2006 SCC 18, [2006] 1 S.C.R. 643 at paras. 1–11, 24–49.

2. FACTS

[2] This case arises from a tragic car accident in Ottawa in the early hours of January 1, 1999. At 1:30 a.m., after leaving a party hosted by Dwight Courrier and Julie Zimmerman, Desmond Desormeaux drove his vehicle into oncoming traffic and collided head-on with a vehicle driven by Patricia Hadden. One of the passengers in Ms. Hadden's car was killed and three others seriously injured, including Zoe Childs, who was then a teenager. Ms. Childs' spine was severed and she has since been paralyzed from the waist down. Mr. Desormeaux and the two passengers in his car were also injured.

[3] Mr. Desormeaux was impaired at the time of the accident. The trial judge found that he had probably consumed 12 beers at the party over two and a half hours, producing a blood-alcohol concentration of approximately 235 mg per 100 ml when he left the party and 225 mg per 100 ml at the time of the accident — concentrations well over the legal limit for driving of 80 mg per 100 ml. Mr. Desormeaux pleaded guilty to a series of criminal charges arising from these events and received a 10-year sentence.

[4] The party hosted by Dwight Courrier and Julie Zimmerman at their home was a "BYOB" (Bring Your Own Booze) event. The only alcohol served by the hosts was three-quarters of a bottle of champagne in small glasses at midnight. Mr. Desormeaux was known to his hosts to be a heavy drinker. The trial judge heard evidence that when Mr. Desormeaux walked to his car to leave, Mr. Courrier accompanied him and asked, "Are you okay, brother?" Mr. Desormeaux responded "No problem", got behind the wheel and drove away with two passengers.

[5] The trial judge found that a reasonable person in the position of Mr. Courrier and Ms. Zimmerman would have foreseen that Mr. Desormeaux might cause an accident and injure someone else. However, the *prima facie* duty of care this gave rise to was negatived, in his view, by policy considerations involving the social and legal consequences of imposing a duty of care on social hosts to third parties injured by their guests, government regulation of alcohol sale and use and the preferability of a legislative, rather than a judicial, solution. Accordingly, the trial judge dismissed the action ((2002), 217 D.L.R. (4th) 217).

[6] The Court of Appeal for Ontario dismissed Ms. Childs' appeal. In its view, the circumstances did not disclose even a *prima facie* duty of care. Unless social hosts are actively implicated in creating the risk that gives rise to the accident, they cannot be found liable. Here, the social hosts "did not assume control over the supply or service of alcohol, nor did they serve alcohol to [Mr.] Desormeaux when he was visibly impaired" ((2004), 71 O.R. (3d) 195, at para. 75). Unlike commercial hosts, they were under no statutory duty to monitor the consumption of alcohol or to control the premises where alcohol was served, nor did anyone rely on them to do so. The court, *per* Weiler J.A., concluded (at para. 75):

> ... I cannot accept the proposition that by merely supplying the venue of a BYOB party, a host assumes legal responsibility to third party users of the road for monitoring the alcohol consumed by guests, ... It would not be just and fair in the circumstances to impose a duty of care.

[7] Ms. Childs appeals to this Court and asks that we reverse the courts below and conclude that Mr. Courrier and Ms. Zimmerman, as social hosts of the party where Mr. Desormeaux was drinking, are liable for the injuries she suffered.

[8] The central legal issue raised by this appeal is whether social hosts who invite guests to an event where alcohol is served owe a legal duty of care to third parties who may be injured by intoxicated guests. It is clear that commercial hosts, like bars or clubs, may be under such a duty. This is the first time, however, that this Court has considered the duty owed by social hosts to plaintiffs like Ms. Childs.

3. ANALYSIS

3.1 The General Test for a Duty of Care

[9] Before the decision of the House of Lords in *Donoghue v. Stevenson*, [1932] A.C. 562, the law governing tort liability for wrongs to others was a complex of categories derived from cases decided over the centuries. In *Donoghue v. Stevenson*, the House of Lords replaced the category approach with a principled approach. It recognized the existence of a "general conception of relations giving rise to a duty of care, of which the particular cases found in the books are but instances" (p. 580, *per* Lord Atkin). The general concept of a duty owed to those whom one might injure proved both powerful and practical. However, it brought with it a question — a question we wrestle with to this day. How do we define the persons to whom the duty is owed?

[10] Lord Atkin recognized this problem in *Donoghue v. Stevenson*. He accepted that negligence is based on a "general public sentiment of moral wrongdoing for which the offender must pay", but distinguished legal duties from moral obligation: "... acts or omissions which any moral code would censure cannot in a practical world be treated so as to give a right to every person injured by them to demand relief" (p. 580). My legal duty, he said, extends to my "neighbour". Legal neighbourhood is "restricted" to "persons who are so closely and directly affected by my act that I ought reasonably to have them in contemplation as being so affected when I am directing my mind to the acts or omissions which are called in question" (p. 580). This concept, sometimes referred to as proximity, remains the foundation of the modern law of negligence.

[11] In *Anns v. Merton London Borough Council*, [1978] A.C. 728 (H.L.), Lord Wilberforce proposed a two-part test for determining whether a duty of care arises. The first stage focuses on the relationship between the plaintiff and the defendant, and asks whether it is close or "proximate" enough to give rise to a duty of care (p. 742). The second stage asks whether there are countervailing policy considerations that negative the duty of care. The two-stage approach of *Anns* was adopted by this Court in *Kamloops (City of) v. Nielsen*, [1984] 2 S.C.R. 2, at pp. 10–11, and recast as follows:

(1) is there "a sufficiently close relationship between the parties" or "proximity" to justify imposition of a duty and, if so,

(2) are there policy considerations which ought to negative or limit the scope of the duty, the class of persons to whom it is owed or the damages to which breach may give rise?

. . . . .

3.3 Stage One: A Prima Facie Duty?

[24] Applying the first stage of the *Anns* test requires, as noted above, an examination of the relationship between the parties to determine if it meets the requirement of sufficient proximity. The question is: What, if anything, links party hosts to third-party users of the highway?

[25] The law of negligence not only considers the plaintiff's loss, but explains why it is just and fair to impose the cost of that loss on the particular defendant before the court. The proximity requirement captures this two-sided face of negligence.

[26] I conclude that the necessary proximity has not been established and, consequently, that social hosts of parties where alcohol is served do not owe a duty of care to public users of highways. First, the injury to Ms. Childs was not reasonably foreseeable on the facts found by the trial judge. Second, even if foreseeability were established, no duty would arise because the wrong alleged is a failure to act or nonfeasance in circumstances where there was no positive duty to act.

3.3.1 Foreseeability

[27] Ms. Childs argues that the parties are linked by the foreseeability of physical harm due to the manner in which the party hosts exercised "control or influence over" the party at which Mr. Desormeaux was drinking.

[28] The question of foreseeability is complicated by ambiguity in the findings of the trial judge. The trial judge found that Mr. Desormeaux would be showing "obvious signs of impairment" (para. 73), but did not find that the hosts in the circumstances knew, or ought to have known, that Mr. Desormeaux was too drunk to drive. The risks of impaired driving, and their consequences for motorists and their passengers, are well known. However, if there is no finding that the hosts *knew*, or ought to have known, that the guest who was about to drive was impaired, how can it be said that they should have foreseen that allowing him to drive might result in injury to other motorists?

[29] Instead of finding that the hosts ought reasonably to have been aware that Mr. Desormeaux was too drunk to drive, the trial judge based his finding that the hosts should have foreseen injury to motorists on the road on problematic reasoning. He noted that the hosts knew that Mr. Desormeaux had gotten drunk in the past and then driven. He inferred from this that they should have foreseen that unless Mr. Desormeaux's drinking at the party was monitored, he would become drunk, get into his car and drive onto the highway. The problem with this reasoning is that a history of alcohol consumption and impaired driving does not make impaired driving, and the consequent risk to other motorists, reasonably foreseeable. The inferential chain from drinking and driving in the past to reasonable foreseeability that this will happen again is too weak to support the legal conclusion of reasonable foreseeability — even in the case of commercial hosts, liability has not been extended by such a frail hypothesis.

[30] Ms. Childs points to the findings relating to the considerable amount of alcohol Mr. Desormeaux had consumed and his high blood-alcohol rating, coupled with the fact that Mr. Courrier accompanied Mr. Desormeaux to his car before he drove away, and asks us to make the finding of knowledge of inebriation that the trial judge failed to make. The problem here is the absence of any evidence that Mr. Desormeaux displayed signs of intoxication during this brief encounter. Given the absence of evidence that the hosts in this case in fact knew of Mr. Desormeaux's intoxication and the fact that the experienced trial judge himself declined to make such a finding, it would not be proper for us to change the factual basis of this case by supplementing the facts on this critical point. I conclude that the injury was not reasonably foreseeable on the facts established in this case.

3.3.2 Failure to Act: Nonfeasance Versus Misfeasance

[31] Foreseeability is not the only hurdle Ms. Childs' argument for a duty of care must surmount. "Foreseeability does not of itself, and automatically, lead to the conclusion that there is a duty of care": G. H. L. Fridman, *The Law of Torts in Canada* (2nd ed. 2002), at p. 320. Foreseeability without more *may* establish a duty of care. This is usually the case, for example, where an *overt act of the defendant* has *directly caused foreseeable physical harm* to the plaintiff: see *Cooper*. However, where the conduct alleged against the defendant is a *failure to act*, foreseeability alone may not establish a duty of care. In the absence of an overt act on the part of the defendant, the nature of the relationship must be examined to determine whether there is a nexus between the parties. Although there is no doubt that an omission may be negligent, as a general principle, the common law is a jealous guardian of individual autonomy. Duties to take positive action in the face of risk or danger are not free-standing. Generally, the mere fact that a person faces danger, or has become a danger to others, does not itself impose any kind of duty on those in a position to become involved.

[32] In this case, we are concerned not with an overt act of the social hosts, but with their alleged failure to act. The case put against them is that they should have interfered with the autonomy of Mr. Desormeaux by preventing him from drinking and driving. It follows that foreseeability alone would not establish a duty of care in this case.

[33] The appellants' argument that Mr. Courrier and Ms. Zimmerman committed positive acts that created, or contributed to, the risk cannot be sustained. It is argued that they *facilitated* the consumption of alcohol by organizing a social event where alcohol was consumed on their premises. But this is not an act that creates risk to users of public roads. The real complaint is that having organized the party, the hosts permitted their guest to drink and then take the wheel of an automobile.

[34] A positive duty of care may exist if foreseeability of harm is present *and* if other aspects of the relationship between the plaintiff and the defendant establish a special link or proximity. Three such situations have been identified by the courts. They function not as strict legal categories, but rather to elucidate factors that can lead to positive duties to act. These factors, or features of the relationship, bring parties who would otherwise be legal strangers into proximity and impose positive duties on defendants that would not otherwise exist.

[35] The first situation where courts have imposed a positive duty to act is where a defendant intentionally attracts and invites third parties to an inherent and obvious risk that he or she has created or controls: *Hendricks v. The Queen*, [1970] S.C.R. 237; *Horsley v. MacLaren*, [1972] S.C.R. 441; *Arnold v. Teno*, [1978] 2 S.C.R. 287; and *Crocker v. Sundance Northwest Resorts Ltd.*, [1988] 1 S.C.R. 1186. For example, it has been held that a boat captain owes a duty to take reasonable care to rescue a passenger who falls overboard (*Horsley*) and that the operator of a dangerous inner-tube sliding competition owes a duty to exclude people who cannot safely participate (*Crocker*). These cases turn on the defendant's causal relationship to the origin of the risk of injury faced by the plaintiff or on steps taken to invite others to subject themselves to a risk under the defendant's control. If the defendant creates a risky situation and invites others into it, failure to act thereafter does not immunize the defendant from the consequences of its acts. These cases are akin to the positive and *continuing* duty of manufacturers or transferors of goods to warn of inherently dangerous products or dangerous uses of safe products: *Lambert v. Lastoplex Chemicals Co.*, [1972] S.C.R. 569; *Hollis v. Dow Corning Corp.*, [1995] 4 S.C.R. 634.

[36] The second situation where a positive duty of care has been held to exist concerns paternalistic relationships of supervision and control, such as those of parent–child or teacher–student: *Dziwenka v. The Queen in right of Alberta*, [1972] S.C.R. 419;

Bain v. Board of Education (Calgary) (1993), 146 A.R. 321 (Q.B.). The duty in these cases rests on the special vulnerability of the plaintiffs and the formal position of power of the defendants. The law recognizes that the autonomy of some persons may be permissibly violated or restricted, but, in turn, requires that those with power exercise it in light of special duties. In the words of Virtue J. in *Bain*, in the context of a teacher–student relationship, "[t]hat right of control carries with it a corresponding duty to take care for the safety of, and to properly supervise the student, whether he or she is a child, an adolescent or an adult" (para. 38).

[37] The third situation where a duty of care may include the need to take positive steps concerns defendants who either exercise a public function or engage in a commercial enterprise that includes implied responsibilities to the public at large: *Dunn v. Dominion Atlantic Railway Co.* (1920), 60 S.C.R. 310; *Jordan House Ltd. v. Menow*, [1974] S.C.R. 239; *Doe v. Metropolitan Toronto (Municipality) Commissioners of Police* (1998), 39 O.R. (3d) 487 (Gen. Div.). In these cases, the defendants offer a service to the general public that includes attendant responsibilities to act with special care to reduce risk. Where a defendant assumes a public role, or benefits from offering a service to the public at large, special duties arise. The duty of a commercial host who serves alcohol to guests to act to prevent foreseeable harm to third-party users of the highway falls into this category: *Stewart v. Pettie*.

[38] Running through all of these situations is the defendant's material implication in the creation of risk or his or her control of a risk to which others have been invited. The operator of a dangerous sporting competition creates or enhances the risk by inviting and enabling people to participate in an inherently risky activity. It follows that the operator must take special steps to protect against the risk materializing. In the example of the parent or teacher who has assumed control of a vulnerable person, the vulnerability of the person and its subjection to the control of the defendant creates a situation where the latter has an enhanced responsibility to safeguard against risk. The public provider of services undertakes a public service, and must do so in a way that appropriately minimizes associated risks to the public.

[39] Also running through the examples is a concern for the autonomy of the persons affected by the positive action proposed. The law does not impose a duty to eliminate risk. It accepts that competent people have the right to engage in risky activities. Conversely, it permits third parties witnessing risk to decide not to become rescuers or otherwise intervene. It is only when these third parties have a special relationship to the person in danger or a material role in the creation or management of the risk that the law may impinge on autonomy. Thus, the operator of a risky sporting activity may be required to prevent a person who is unfit to perform a sport safely from participating or, when a risk materializes, to attempt a rescue. Similarly, the publican may be required to refuse to serve an inebriated patron who may drive, or a teacher be required to take positive action to protect a child who lacks the right or power to make decisions for itself. The autonomy of risk takers or putative rescuers is not absolutely protected, but, at common law, it is always respected.

[40] Finally, the theme of reasonable reliance unites examples in all three categories. A person who creates or invites others into a dangerous situation, like the high-risk sports operator, may reasonably expect that those taking up the invitation will rely on the operator to ensure that the risk is a reasonable one or to take appropriate rescue action if the risk materializes. Similarly, a teacher will understand that the child or the child's parents rely on the teacher to avoid and minimize risk. Finally, there is a reasonable expectation on the part of the public that a person providing public services, often under licence, will take reasonable precautions to reduce the risk of the activity, not merely to immediate clients, but to the general public.

[41] Does the situation of the social host who serves alcohol to guests fall within the three categories just discussed or represent an appropriate extension of them having regard to the factors of risk-control and reasonable preservation of autonomy that animate them? I conclude that it does not.

[42] The first category concerns defendants who have created or invited others to participate in highly risky activities. Holding a house party where alcohol is served is not such an activity. Risks may ensue, to be sure, from what guests choose to do or not do at the party. But hosting a party is a far cry from inviting participation in a high-risk sport or taking people out on a boating party. A party where alcohol is served is a common occurrence, not one associated with unusual risks demanding special precautions. The second category of paternalistic relationships of supervision or control is equally inapplicable. Party hosts do not enjoy a paternalistic relationship with

their guests, nor are their guests in a position of reduced autonomy that invites control. Finally, private social hosts are not acting in a public capacity and, hence, do not incur duties of a public nature.

[43] More broadly, do the themes that animate the cases imposing positive duties to act — risk enhancement and control, autonomy and reasonable reliance — suggest that the social hosts in this case owed a duty of care to third-party users of the highway, to take reasonable steps to prevent what happened? Again, the answer is that they do not.

[44] Holding a private party at which alcohol is served — the bare facts of this case — is insufficient to implicate the host in the creation of a risk sufficient to give rise to a duty of care to third parties who may be subsequently injured by the conduct of a guest. The host creates a place where people can meet, visit and imbibe alcohol, whether served on the premises or supplied by the guest. All this falls within accepted parameters of non-dangerous conduct. More is required to establish a danger or risk that requires positive action. It might be argued that a host who continues to serve alcohol to a visibly inebriated person knowing that he or she will be driving home has become implicated in the creation or enhancement of a risk sufficient to give rise to a *prima facie* duty of care to third parties, which would be subject to contrary policy considerations at the second stage of the *Anns* test. This position has been taken in some states in the U.S.A.: N.J. Stat. Ann. §§ 2A:15-5.5 to 2A:15-5.8 (West 2000). We need not decide that question here. Suffice it to say that hosting a party where alcohol is served, without more, does not suggest the creation or exacerbation of risk of the level required to impose a duty of care on the host to members of the public who may be affected by a guest's conduct.

[45] Nor does the autonomy of the individual support the case for a duty to take action to protect highway users in the case at bar. As discussed, the implication of a duty of care depends on the relationships involved. The relationship between social host and guest at a house party is part of this equation. A person who accepts an invitation to attend a private party does not park his autonomy at the door. The guest remains responsible for his or her conduct. Short of active implication in the creation or enhancement of the risk, a host is entitled to respect the autonomy of a guest. The consumption of alcohol, and the assumption of the risks of impaired judgment, is in almost all cases a personal choice and an inherently personal activity. Absent the special

considerations that may apply in the commercial context, when such a choice is made by an adult, there is no reason why others should be made to bear its costs. The conduct of a hostess who confiscated all guests' car keys and froze them in ice as people arrived at her party, releasing them only as she deemed appropriate, was cited to us as exemplary. This hostess was evidently prepared to make considerable incursions on the autonomy of her guests. The law of tort, however, has not yet gone so far.

[46] This brings us to the factor of reasonable reliance. There is no evidence that anyone relied on the hosts in this case to monitor guests' intake of alcohol or prevent intoxicated guests from driving. This represents an important distinction between the situation of a private host, as here, and a public host. The public host provides alcohol to members of the public, under a strict regulatory regime. It is reasonable to expect that the public provider will act to protect the public interest. There is public reliance that he will comply with the rules that prohibit serving too much alcohol to a patron and that if this should occur and the patron seeks to drive, that the public host will take reasonable steps to prevent the person from driving. The same cannot be said of the private social host, who neither undertakes nor is expected to monitor the conduct of guests on behalf of the public.

[47] I conclude that hosting a party at which alcohol is served does not, without more, establish the degree of proximity required to give rise to a duty of care on the hosts to third-party highway users who may be injured by an intoxicated guest. The injury here was not shown to be foreseeable on the facts as found by the trial judge. Even if it had been, this is at best a case of nonfeasance. No duty to monitor guests' drinking or to prevent them from driving can be imposed having regard to the relevant cases and legal principles. A social host at a party where alcohol is served is not under a duty of care to members of the public who may be injured by a guest's actions, unless the host's conduct implicates him or her in the creation or exacerbation of the risk. On the facts of this case, I agree with the Court of Appeal, at para. 75, *per* Weiler J.A.:

> The person sought to be held liable must be implicated in the creation of the risk.... The social hosts had no statutory duty to monitor the consumption of alcohol or to control the structure of the atmosphere in which alcohol was served. There is no evidence that anyone relied on them to do so.... I cannot accept the proposition that by merely supplying the venue of a

BYOB party, a host assumes legal responsibility to third party users of the road for monitoring the alcohol consumed by guests, ... It would not be just and fair in the circumstances to impose a duty of care.

[48] Having concluded that a *prima facie* duty of care has not been established, I find it unnecessary to consider whether any duty would be negated by policy considerations at the second stage of the *Anns* test.

4.   CONCLUSION

[49] I would dismiss the appeal with costs.

Appeal dismissed with costs.

(c)   *Pettkus v. Becker*†

[DICKSON J., Laskin C.J. and Estey, McIntyre, Chouinard, and Lamer JJ. (Martland and Ritchie JJ concurring, with different reasons):]

The appellant, Lothar Pettkus, through toil and thrift, developed over the years a successful beekeeping business. He now owns two rural Ontario properties, where the business is conducted, and he has the proceeds from the sale, in 1974, of a third property, located in the Province of Quebec. It is not to his efforts alone, however, that success can be attributed. The respondent, Rosa Becker, through her labour and earnings, contributed substantially to the good fortune of the common enterprise. She lived with Mr. Pettkus from 1955 to 1974, save for a separation in 1972. They were never married. When the relationship sundered in late 1974, Miss Becker commenced this action, in which she sought a declaration of entitlement to a one-half interest in the lands and a share in the beekeeping business.

I   THE FACTS

Mr. Pettkus and Miss Becker came to Canada from central Europe, separately, as immigrants, in 1954. He had $17 upon arrival. They met in Montreal in 1955. Shortly thereafter, Mr. Pettkus moved in with Miss Becker, on her invitation. She was thirty years old and he was twenty-five. He was earning $75 per week; she was earning $25 to $28 per week, later increased to $67 per week.

A short time after they began living together, Miss Becker expressed the desire that they be married. Mr. Pettkus replied that he might consider marriage after they knew each other better. Thereafter, the question of marriage was not raised, though within a few years Mr. Pettkus began to introduce Miss Becker as his wife and to claim her as such for income tax purposes.

From 1955 to 1960 both parties worked for others. Mr. Pettkus supplemented his income by repairing and restoring motor vehicles. Throughout the period Miss Becker paid the rent. She bought the food and clothing and looked after other living expenses. This enabled Mr. Pettkus to save his entire income, which he regularly deposited in a bank account in his name. There was no agreement at any time to share either monies or property placed in his name. The parties lived frugally. Due to their husbandry and parsimonious lifestyle, $12,000 had been saved by 1960 and deposited in Mr. Pettkus' bank account.

The two travelled to Western Canada in June 1960. Expenses were shared. One of the reasons for the trip was to locate a suitable farm at which to start a beekeeping business. They spent some time working at a beekeeper's farm.

They returned to Montreal, however, in the early autumn of 1960. Miss Becker continued to pay the apartment rent out of her income until October 1960. From then until May 1961, Mr. Pettkus paid rent and household expenses, Miss Becker being jobless. In April 1961, she fell sick and required hospitalization.

In April 1961, they decided to buy a farm at Franklin Centre, Quebec, for $5,000. The purchase money came out of the bank account of Mr. Pettkus. Title was taken in his name. The floor and roof of

---

† [1980] 2 S.C.R. 834 at 839–40, 847–51, 852–53, 854.

the farmhouse were in need of repair. Miss Becker used her money to purchase flooring materials and she assisted in laying the floor and installing a bathroom.

For about six months during 1961 Miss Becker received unemployment insurance cheques, the proceeds of which were used to defray household expenses. Through two successive winters she lived in Montreal and earned approximately $100 per month as a babysitter. These earnings also went toward household expenses.

After purchasing the farm at Franklin Centre the parties established a beekeeping business. Both worked in the business, making frames for the hives, moving the bees to the orchards of neighbouring farmers in the spring, checking the hives during the summer, bringing in the frames for honey extraction during July and August, and the bees for winter storage in autumn. Receipts from sales of honey were handled by Mr. Pettkus; payments for purchases of bee hives and equipment were made from his bank account.

The physical participation by Miss Becker in the bee operation continued over a period of about fourteen years. She ran the extracting process. She also, for a time, raised a few chickens, pheasants and geese. In 1968, and later, the parties hired others to assist in moving the bees and bringing in the honey. Most of the honey was sold to wholesalers, though Miss Becker sold some from door to door.

In August 1971, with a view to expanding the business a vacant property was purchased in East Hawkesbury, Ontario, at a price of $1,300. The purchase monies were derived from the Franklin Centre honey operation. Funds to complete the purchase were withdrawn from the bank account of Mr. Pettkus. Title to the newly acquired property was taken in his name.

In 1973 a further property was purchased, in West Hawkesbury, Ontario, in the name of Mr. Pettkus. The price was $5,500. The purchase monies came from the Franklin Centre operation, together with a $1,900 contribution made by Miss Becker, to which I will again later refer. Nineteen seventy-three was a prosperous year, yielding some 65,000 pounds of honey, producing net revenue in excess of $30,000.

In the early 1970's the relationship between the parties began to deteriorate. In 1972 Miss Becker left Mr. Pettkus, allegedly because of mistreatment. She was away for three months. At her departure, Mr. Pettkus threw $3,000 on the floor. He told her to take the money, a 1966 Volkswagon, forty beehives containing bees, and "get lost". The beehives

represented less than ten percent of the total number of hives then in the business.

Soon thereafter, Mr. Pettkus asked Miss Becker to return. In January, 1973, she agreed, on condition he see a marriage counselor, make a will in her favor and provide her with $500 per year so long as she stayed with him. It was also agreed that Mr. Pettkus would establish a joint bank account for household expenses, in which receipts from retail sales of honey would be deposited. Miss Becker returned; she brought back the car and $1,900 remaining out of the $3,000 she had earlier received. The $1,900 was deposited in Mr. Pettkus' account. She also brought the forty bee hives but the bees had died in the interim.

In February 1974 the parties moved into a house on the West Hawkesbury property, built in part by them and in part by contractors. The money needed for construction came from the honey business, with minimal purchases of materials by Miss Becker.

The relationship continued to deteriorate and on October 4, 1974 Miss Becker [again] left, this time permanently, after an incident in which she alleged that she had been beaten and otherwise abused. She took the car and approximately $2,600 in cash, from honey sales. Shortly thereafter the present action was launched.

At trial, Miss Becker was awarded forty beehives, without bees, together with $1,500, representing earnings from those hives for 1973 and 1974.

The Ontario Court of Appeal varied the judgment at trial by awarding Miss Becker a one-half interest in the lands owned by Mr. Pettkus and in the beekeeping business.

. . . . .

III   CONSTRUCTIVE TRUST

The principle of unjust enrichment lies at the heart of the constructive trust. "Unjust enrichment" has played a role in Anglo-American legal writing for centuries. Lord Mansfield, in the case of *Moses v. Macferlan*[7] put the matter in these words: "... the gist of this kind of action is, that the defendant, upon the circumstances of the case, is *obliged by the ties of natural justice and equity to refund* the money". It would be undesirable, and indeed impossible, to attempt to define all the circumstances in which an unjust enrichment might arise. (See A.W. Scott, "Constructive Trusts", (1955), 71 L.Q.R. 39; Leonard Pollock, "Matrimonial Property and Trusts: The Situation from Murdoch to Rathwell", (1978), 16 Alberta

Law Review 357). The great advantage of ancient principles of equity is their flexibility: the judiciary is thus able to shape these malleable principles so as to accommodate the changing needs and mores of society, in order to achieve justice. The constructive trust has proven to be a useful tool in the judicial armoury. See *Babrociak v. Babrociak*[8]; *Re Spears and Levy et al.*[9]; *Douglas v. Guaranty Trust Company of Canada*[10]; *Armstrong v. Armstrong.*[11]

How then does one approach the question of unjust enrichment in matrimonial causes? In *Rathwell* I ventured to suggest there are three requirements to be satisfied before an unjust enrichment can be said to exist: an enrichment, a corresponding deprivation and absence of any juristic reason for the enrichment. This approach, it seems to me, is supported by general principles of equity that have been fashioned by the courts for centuries, though, admittedly, not in the context of matrimonial property controversies.

The common law has never been willing to compensate a plaintiff on the sole basis that his actions have benefited another. Lord Halsbury scotched this heresy in the case of *The Ruabon Steamship Company, Limited v. London Assurance*[12] with these words: "... I cannot understand how it can be asserted that it is part of the common law that where one person gets some advantage from the act of another a right of contribution towards the expense from that act arises on behalf of the person who has done it." (p. 10) Lord Macnaghten, in the same case, put it this way: "there is no principle of law which requires that a person should contribute to an outlay merely because he has derived a material benefit from it". (p. 15) It is not enough for the court simply to determine that one spouse has benefited at the hands of another and then to require restitution. It must, in addition, be evident that the retention of the benefit would be "unjust" in the circumstances of the case.

Miss Becker supported Mr. Pettkus for 5 years. She then worked on the farm for about 14 years. The compelling inference from the facts is that she believed she had some interest in the farm and that that expectation was reasonable in the circumstances. Mr. Pettkus would seem to have recognized in Miss Becker some property interest, through the payment to her of compensation, however modest. There is no evidence to indicate that he ever informed her that all her work performed over the nineteen years was being performed on a gratuitous basis. He freely accepted the benefits conferred upon him through her financial support and her labour.

On these facts, the first two requirements laid down in *Rathwell* have clearly been satisfied:

Mr. Pettkus has had the benefit of nineteen years of unpaid labour, while Miss Becker has received little or nothing in return. As for the third requirement, I hold that where one person in a relationship tantamount to spousal prejudices herself in the reasonable expectation of receiving an interest in property and the other person in the relationship freely accepts benefits conferred by the first person in circumstances where he knows or ought to have known of that reasonable expectation, it would be unjust to allow the recipient of the benefit to retain it.

I conclude, consonant with the judgment of the Court of Appeal, that this is a case for the application of constructive trust. As Madam Justice Wilson noted, "the parties lived together as husband and wife, although unmarried for almost twenty years during which period she not only made possible the acquisition of their first property in Franklin Centre during the lean years, but worked side by side with him for fourteen years building up the beekeeping operation which was their main source of livelihood".

Madam Justice Wilson had no difficulty in finding that a constructive trust arose in favour of the respondent by virtue of "joint effort" and "teamwork", as a result of which Mr. Pettkus was able to acquire the Franklin Centre property, and subsequently the East Hawkesbury and West Hawkesbury properties. The Ontario Court of Appeal imposed the constructive trust in the interests of justice and, with respect, I would do the same.

IV   THE "COMMON LAW" RELATIONSHIP

One question which must be addressed is whether a constructive trust can be established having regard to what is frequently, and euphemistically, referred to as a "common law" relationship. The purpose of constructive trust is to redress situations which would otherwise denote unjust enrichment. In principle, there is no reason not to apply the doctrine to common law relationships. It is worth noting that counsel for Mr. Pettkus, and I think correctly, did not, in this Court, raise the common law relationship in defence of the claim of Miss Becker, otherwise than by reference to *The Family Law Reform Act, 1978*, 1978 (Ont.) c. 2.

Courts in other jurisdictions have not regarded the absence of a marital bond as any problem. See *Cooke v. Head*[13]; *Eves v. Eves*[14]; *Spears v. Levy, supra*; and in the United States, *Marvin v. Marvin*[15] and a comment thereon (1977), 90 Harv. L.R. 1708. In *Marvin* the Supreme Court of California stated that constructive trust was available to give effect to the reasonable expectations of the parties, and to the notion that unmarried co-habitants intend to deal fairly with each other.

I see no basis for any distinction, in dividing property and assets, between marital relationships and those more informal relationships which subsist for a lengthy period. This was not an economic partnership nor a mere business relationship, nor a casual encounter. Mr. Pettkus and Miss Becker lived as man and wife for almost twenty years. Their lives and their economic well-being were fully integrated. The equitable principle on which the remedy of constructive trust rests is broad and general; its purpose is to prevent unjust enrichment in whatever circumstances it occurs.

In recent years, there has been much statutory reform in the area of family law and matrimonial property. Counsel for Mr. Pettkus correctly points out that *The Family Law Reform Act, 1978*, of Ontario, enacted after the present litigation was initiated, does not extend the presumption of equal sharing, which now applies between married persons, to common law spouses. The argument is made that the courts should not develop equitable remedies that are 'contrary to current legislative intent'. The rejoinder is that legislation was unnecessary to cover these facts, for a remedy was always available in equity for property division between unmarried individuals contributing to the acquisition of assets. The effect of the legislation is to divide 'family assets' equally, regardless of contribution, as a matter of course. The Court is not here creating a presumption of equal shares. There is a great difference between directing that there be equal shares for common law spouses, and awarding Miss Becker a share equivalent to the money or money's worth she contributed over some nineteen years. The fact there is no statutory regime directing equal division of assets acquired by common law spouses is no bar to the availability of an equitable remedy in the present circumstances.

. . . .

VII RESPECTIVE PROPORTIONS

Although equity is said to favour equality, as stated in *Rathwell* it is not every contribution which will entitle a spouse to a one-half interest in the property. The extent of the interest must be proportionate to the contribution, direct or indirect, of the claimant. Where the contributions are unequal, the shares will be unequal.

It could be argued that Mr. Pettkus contributed somewhat more to the material fortunes of the joint enterprise than Miss Becker but it must be recognized that each started with nothing; each worked continuously, unremittingly and sedulously in the joint effort. Physically, Miss Becker pulled her fair share of the load; weighing only 87 pounds, she assisted in moving hives weighing 80 pounds. Any difference in quality or quantum of contribution was small. The Ontario Court of Appeal in its discretion favoured an even division and I would not alter that disposition, other than to note that in any accounting regard should be had to the $2,600, and the car, which Miss Becker received on separation in 1974.

. . . .

I would dismiss the appeal with costs to the respondent.

VII

Dispute Resolution

Overview of Part VII

The articles in **Part VII** consider the ways in which the traditional processes of formal legal decision-making may or may not adequately fulfill the function of dispute resolution in our society (one of the four key functions of law posited by Hoebel in **Chapter 1**). They identify and evaluate ways in which disputes might be resolved using alternatives to formal legal adjudication, and also examine ways in which processes of formal legal adjudication (e.g. courts and trials) have been transformed, or could be transformed, to make them less insular, more responsive, and thus more effective and legitimate.

The articles in **Chapter 16** discuss how and why parties who may be entitled to rely on formal adjudication may choose to rely instead on informal negotiations or alternative dispute resolution (ADR) processes to resolve their disputes. Macaulay's influential article discusses the incentives for businesses to avoid formal litigation in order to maintain long-term commercial relationships. He argues that, contrary to popular opinion, formal contracts are rarely enforced in the courts but usefully provide normative frameworks for informal negotiation and compromise between the contracting parties. Robert Mnookin similarly argues that divorce law, like contracts, should provide a formal framework for spouses to negotiate their own determinations of rights and responsibilities — through a process he calls "private ordering" — rather than having those determinations imposed by an external authority such as a judge. Mnookin asks us to seriously consider what role, if any, the courts ought to have in the dissolution of marriages and redistribution of marital property and children.

Both authors emphasize law's role in establishing informal norms of conduct that take place, as Mnookin says, "in the shadow of law" rather than within law's formal frameworks. They explore some of the advantages and disadvantages of informal, or alternative, dispute resolution practices and remind the reader that law's impact need not be *direct* in order for it to have measurable consequences. Mnookin, specifically, emphasizes the importance of understanding informal individual bargaining in the shadow of law beyond his narrower focus on family law. Given that the vast majority of all legal disputes — from "plea bargaining" in criminal law to "consent agreements" in administrative law — increasingly result in negotiated settlements and not in authoritative determinations by a court, understanding the complex relationship between formal legal frameworks and informal decision-making by disputants is a necessary step to understanding how most people practically *experience* "the law".

The articles in **Chapter 17** critically explore the key characteristics and assumptions of the formal adjudication process in most common law countries. Neil Brooks surveys the ideological and practical justifications for the current adversarial system of adjudication. In highlighting the system's virtues and potential failings, Brooks suggests that traditionally detached, passive judges may be required to take a more active role in the trial process to mitigate against inequalities exasperated by the adversarial nature of the system.

The excerpt by Sanders explores the basic issue of how the legal system produces "truth" by contrasting it with the scientific process. For Sanders the basic tension between these two systems is embodied in the figure of the expert witness within the courtroom. Sanders argues that within the adversarial system scientific expertise is too often reduced to a partisan resource, which may limit and ultimately undermine its probative value. Similarly, he argues that expert witnesses too often fail to recognize the necessity that the justice system produce definitive answers to complex questions.

The similarly critical article that follows, by Roach, highlights the troubling connection between the adversarial nature of our adjudicative process and wrongful convictions. Echoing many of the issues raised by Green in **Chapter 13**, Roach challenges the reader to recognize that the adversarial nature of the current system may undermine its ability to get to the "truth" and achieve just outcomes. Roach points to "inquisitorial" systems as an alternative to a strictly adversarial process. While he recognizes flaws in this alternative, he also highlights the relative merits of inquisitorial systems in other jurisdictions and asks readers to consider the possibility of an explicitly "hybrid" system of legal fact-finding; one that considers the practical strengths and weaknesses of both systems, and not just their ideological foundations.

Finally, the excerpt "In the Cathedral" from Kafka's *The Trial* raises two related concerns. First, in the context of Kafka's fictionalized account of an accused caught in a system he cannot comprehend, the reader is forced — through the eyes of Kafka's protagonist, Josef K. — to confront the adjudication process as many people actually experience it: as something that is at once distant and impenetrable, while also being intrusive and inescapable. Kafka provokes his readers to consider the basic structure of a legal system that has become so procedurally driven and bureaucratized that it has lost any aspiration to provide just outcomes to those of us who arrive "from the country". How does Kafka's image of Law, or the alienating properties of the adjudication process, challenge us to understand the basic structure of our own legal system?

Chapter 18, then, explores alternatives to formal adjudication. These alternatives include the use of mediation and arbitration as alternatives to the trial process, but also include the use of these alternatives within the context of ongoing litigation. The chapter includes articles on newer forms of litigation that try to reduce the negative impacts of traditional adversarial litigation (outlined in the articles in **Chapter 17**). In particular, Moore's article discusses whether the multi-disciplinary approach adopted in "drug treatment courts" can address issues of addiction more effectively than traditional criminal courts. Wiegers and Keet discuss whether "collaborative lawyering" may allow for a less adversarial method of settling family law disputes.

Lastly, Dickson and Malette critically investigate the rationale, intent, and implementation of "Gladue rights" established in the Supreme Court's decision in *Gladue* to address the justice system's ongoing failure to deal with Indigenous overrepresentation and over-incarceration at all levels in the system. Their blistering assessment is that, while initially full of possibility, the implementation of Gladue rights, particularly in the context of ongoing systemic discrimination and underfunding, has meant their impact has been minimal at best. The pair contend that *Gladue* offered an opportunity for system actors at all levels to confront the embodied impact of colonialism through the offenders caught up in

the criminal justice system. But in failing to make good on *Gladue*'s promise, Dickson and Malette see yet another broken promise between the Canadian state and Canada's First Nations.

Finally, **Chapter 19** outlines some of the more theoretically oriented debates concerning the use of alternative dispute resolution (ADR) processes. McThenia and Shaffer provide a useful rebuttal to the first article by Fiss, who argues that the turn toward ADR (or "settlement") at the expense of authoritative pronouncements of "right and wrong" by the court (or "judgement") risks reducing the social function of the court. McThenia and Shaffer challenge this assessment and offer an alternative foundation on which to assess the effectiveness of different dispute resolution processes. Ultimately they suggest that the real difference between their position and the one offered by Fiss is that they are founded on two different theories of justice: one that equates justice with law, or with a definitive outcome (Fiss), and the other that understands justice as emerging in the processes of negotiation in, and between, the parties to a dispute. The final article by Sargent reinforces that the debates surrounding the utility and effectiveness of ADR often arise from very different conceptions of the role and function of law in contemporary society.

As you read the wide-ranging articles comprising **Part VII**, ask yourself some of the following questions: How effective are courts at resolving disputes? Can litigation and formal adjudication ultimately help resolve the problems at the root of legal conflicts? Might alternatives both within, and "outside", current formal adjudication processes achieve more effective outcomes? How much do positive outcomes depend on stable long-term funding of alternatives? Do the "outside" alternatives to adjudication provide sufficient protection of vulnerable, less powerful parties? How might guarantees of formal equality and "just outcomes" in disputes be assured outside of the publicity offered by the current processes of formal adjudication, i.e. courts? Do alternatives to formal processes help address the alienation emphasized in Kafka's parable or by Christie in **Chapter 1**? How do we practically balance rights with interests, or "healing" processes with "just" results?

(a)   Non-Contractual Relationships in Business: A Preliminary Study†

Stewart Macaulay

TENTATIVE FINDINGS

. . . .

The Adjustment of Exchange Relationships and the Settling of Disputes

While a significant amount of creating business exchanges is done on a fairly noncontractual basis, the creation of exchanges usually is far more contractual than the adjustment of such relationships and the settlement of disputes. Exchanges are adjusted when the obligations of one or both parties are modified by agreement during the life of the relationship. For example, the buyer may be allowed to cancel all or part of the goods he has ordered because he no longer needs them; the seller may be paid more than the usual contract price by the buyer because of unusual changed circumstances. Dispute settlement involves determining whether or not a party has performed as agreed and, if he has not, doing something about it. For example, a court may have to interpret the meaning of a contract, determine what the alleged defaulting party has done and determine what, if any, remedy the aggrieved party is entitled to. Or one party may assert that the other is in default, refuse to proceed with performing the contract and refuse to deal ever again with the alleged defaulter. If the alleged defaulter, who in fact may not be in default, takes no action, the dispute is then "settled."

Business exchanges in non-speculative areas are usually adjusted without dispute. Under the law of contracts, if B orders 1,000 widgets from S at $1.00 each, B must take all 1,000 widgets or be in breach of contract and liable to pay S his expenses up to the time of the breach plus his lost anticipated profit. Yet all ten of the purchasing agents asked about cancellation of orders once placed indicated that they expected to be able to cancel orders freely subject to only an obligation to pay for the seller's major expenses such as scrapped steel.[6] All 17 sales personnel asked reported that they often had to accept cancellation. One said, "You can't ask a man to eat paper [the firm's product] when he has no use for it." A lawyer with many large industrial clients said,

> Often businessmen do not feel they have "a contract" — rather they have "an order." They speak of "cancelling the order" rather than "breaching our contract." When I began practice I referred to order cancellations as breaches of contract, but my clients objected since they do not think of cancellation as wrong. Most clients, in heavy industry at least, believe that there is a right to cancel as part of the buyer-seller relationship. There is a widespread attitude that one can back out of any deal within some very vague limits. Lawyers are often surprised by this attitude.

Disputes are frequently settled without reference to the contract or potential or actual legal sanctions. There is a hesitancy to speak of legal rights or to

---

† (1963) 28:1 *American Sociological Review* 55 at 60–67. [Notes and/or references omitted.] Reproduced with permission.

threaten to sue in these negotiations. Even where the parties have a detailed and carefully planned agreement which indicates what is to happen if, say, the seller fails to deliver on time, often they will never refer to the agreement but will negotiate a solution when the problem arises apparently as if there had never been any original contract. One purchasing agent expressed a common business attitude when he said,

> if something comes up, you get the other man on the telephone and deal with the problem. You don't read legalistic contract clauses at each other if you ever want to do business again. One doesn't run to lawyers if he wants to stay in business because one must behave decently.

Or as one businessman put it, "You can settle any dispute if you keep the lawyers and accountants out of it. They just do not understand the give-and-take needed in business." All of the house counsel interviewed indicated that they are called into the dispute settlement process only after the businessmen have failed to settle matters in their own way. Two indicated that after being called in house counsel at first will only advise the purchasing agent, sales manager or other official involved; not even the house counsel's letterhead is used on communications with the other side until all hope for a peaceful resolution is gone.

Law suits for breach of contract appear to be rare. Only five of the 12 purchasing agents had ever been involved in even a negotiation concerning a contract dispute where both sides were represented by lawyers; only two of ten sales managers had ever gone this far. None had been involved in a case that went through trial. A law firm with more than 40 lawyers and a large commercial practice handles in a year only about six trials concerned with contract problems. Less than 10 per cent of the time of this office is devoted to any type of work related to contracts disputes. Corporations big enough to do business in more than one state tend to sue and be sued in the federal courts. Yet only 2,779 out of 58,293 civil actions filed in the United States District Courts in fiscal year 1961 involved private contracts.[7] During the same period only 3,447 of the 61,138 civil cases filed in the principal trial courts of New York State involved private contracts.[8] The same picture emerges from a review of appellate cases.[9] Mentschikoff has suggested that commercial cases are not brought to the courts either in periods of business prosperity (because buyers unjustifiably reject goods only when prices drop and they can get similar goods elsewhere at less than the contract price) or in periods of deep depression (because people are unable to come to court or have insufficient assets to satisfy any judgment that might be obtained). Apparently, she adds, it is necessary to have "a kind of middle-sized depression" to bring large numbers of commercial cases to the courts. However, there is little evidence that in even "a kind of middle-sized depression" today's businessmen would use the courts to settle disputes.[10]

At times relatively contractual methods are used to make adjustments in ongoing transactions and to settle disputes. Demands of one side which are deemed unreasonable by the other occasionally are blocked by reference to the terms of the agreement between the parties. The legal position of the parties can influence negotiations even though legal rights or litigation are never mentioned in their discussions; it makes a difference if one is demanding what both concede to be a right or begging for a favour. Now and then a firm may threaten to turn matters over to its attorneys, threaten to sue, commence a suit or even litigate and carry an appeal to the highest court which will hear the matter. Thus, legal sanctions, while not an everyday affair, are not unknown in business.

One can conclude that while detailed planning and legal sanctions play a significant role in some exchanges between businesses, in many business exchanges their role is small.

TENTATIVE EXPLANATIONS

Two questions need to be answered: (A) How can business successfully operate exchange relationships with relatively so little attention to detailed planning or to legal sanctions, and (B) Why does business ever use contract in light of its success without it?

Why Are Relatively Non-Contractual Practices So Common?

In most situations contract is not needed.[11] Often its functions are served by other devices. Most problems are avoided without resort to detailed planning or legal sanctions because usually there is little room for honest misunderstandings or good faith differences of opinion about the nature and quality of a seller's performance. Although the parties fail to cover all foreseeable contingencies, they will exercise care to see that both understand the primary obligation on each side. Either products are standardized with an accepted description or specifications are written calling for production to certain tolerances or results. Those who write and read specifications are experienced professionals who will know the customs of their industry and those of the industries with which they deal. Consequently, these customs can fill gaps in the express agreements of the parties. Finally, most products can be tested to see if they are what was ordered; typically in the manufacturing industry we are not dealing with questions of taste or judgment where people can differ in good faith.

When defaults occur they are not likely to be disastrous because of techniques of risk avoidance or risk spreading. One can deal with firms of good reputation or he may be able to get some form of security to guarantee performance. One can insure against many breaches of contract where the risks justify the costs. Sellers set up reserves for bad debts on their books and can sell some of their accounts receivable. Buyers can place orders with two or more suppliers of the same item so that a default by one will not stop the buyer's assembly lines.

Moreover, contract and contract law are often thought unnecessary because there are many effective non-legal sanctions. Two norms are widely accepted. (1) Commitments are to be honored in almost all situations; one does not welsh on a deal. (2) One ought to produce a good product and stand behind it. Then, too, business units are organized to perform commitments, and internal sanctions will induce performance. For example, sales personnel must face angry customers when there has been a late or defective performance. The salesmen do not enjoy this and will put pressure on the production personnel responsible for the default. If the production personnel default too often, they will be fired. At all levels of the two business units personal relationships across the boundaries of the two organizations exert pressures for conformity to expectations. Salesmen often know purchasing agents well. The same two individuals occupying these roles may have dealt with each other from five to 25 years. Each has something to give the other. Salesmen have gossip about competitors, shortages and price increases to give purchasing agents who treat them well. Salesmen take purchasing agents to dinner, and they give purchasing agents Christmas gifts hoping to improve the chances of making a sale. The buyer's engineering staff may work with the seller's engineering staff to solve problems jointly. The seller's engineers may render great assistance, and the buyer's engineers may desire to return the favour by drafting specifications which only the seller can meet. The top executives of the two firms may know each other. They may sit together on government or trade committees. They may know each other socially and even belong to the same country club. The interrelationships may

be more formal. Sellers may hold stock in corporations which are important customers; buyers may hold stock in important suppliers. Both buyer and seller may share common directors on their boards. They may share a common financial institution which has financed both units.

The final type of non-legal sanction is the most obvious. Both business units involved in the exchange desire to continue successfully in business and will avoid conduct which might interfere with attaining this goal. One is concerned with both the reaction of the other party in the particular exchange and with his own general business reputation. Obviously, the buyer gains sanctions insofar as the seller wants the particular exchange to be completed. Buyers can withhold part or all of their payments until sellers have performed to their satisfaction. If a seller has a great deal of money tied up in his performance which he must recover quickly, he will go a long way to please the buyer in order to be paid. Moreover, buyers who are dissatisfied may cancel and cause sellers to lose the cost of what they have done up to cancellation. Furthermore, sellers hope for repeats for orders, and one gets few of these from unhappy customers. Some industrial buyers go so far as to formalize this sanction by issuing "report cards" rating the performance of each supplier. The supplier rating goes to the top management of the seller organization, and these men can apply internal sanctions to salesmen, production supervisors or product designers if there are too many "D's" or "F's" on the report card.

While it is generally assumed that the customer is always right, the seller may have some counterbalancing sanctions against the buyer. The seller may have obtained a large downpayment from the buyer which he will want to protect. The seller may have an exclusive process which the buyer needs. The seller may be one of the few firms which has the skill to make the item to the tolerances set by the buyer's engineers and within the time available. There are costs and delays involved in turning from a supplier one has dealt with in the past to a new supplier. Then, too, market conditions can change so that a buyer is faced with shortages of critical items. The most extreme example is the post World War II gray market conditions when sellers were rationing goods rather than selling them. Buyers must build up some reserve of good will with suppliers if they face the risk of such shortage and desire good treatment when they occur. Finally, there is reciprocity in buying and selling. A buyer cannot push a supplier too far if that supplier also buys significant quantities of the product made by the buyer.

Not only do the particular business units in a given exchange want to deal with each other again, they also want to deal with other business units in the future. And the way one behaves in a particular transaction, or a series of transactions, will colour his general business reputation. Blacklisting can be formal or informal. Buyers who fail to pay their bills on time risk a bad report in credit rating services such as Dun and Bradstreet. Sellers who do not satisfy their customers become the subject of discussion in the gossip exchanged by purchasing agents and salesmen, at meetings of purchasing agents' associations and trade associations, or even at country clubs or social gatherings where members of top management meet. The American male's habit of debating the merits of new cars carries over to industrial items. Obviously, a poor reputation does not help a firm make sales and may force it to offer great price discounts or added services to remain in business. Furthermore, the habits of unusually demanding buyers become known, and they tend to get no more than they can coerce out of suppliers who choose to deal with them. Thus, often contract is not needed as there are alternatives.

Not only are contract and contract law not needed in many situations, their use may have, or may be thought to have, undesirable consequences. Detailed negotiated contracts can get in the way of creating good exchange relationships between business units. If one side insists on a detailed plan, there will be delay while letters are exchanged as the parties try to agree on what should happen if a remote and unlikely contingency occurs. In some cases they may not be able to agree at all on such matters and as a result a sale may be lost to the seller and the buyer may have to search elsewhere for an acceptable supplier. Many businessmen would react by thinking that, had no one raised the series of remote and unlikely contingencies, all this wasted effort could have been avoided.

Even where agreement can be reached at the negotiation stage, carefully planned arrangements may create undesirable exchange relationships between business units. Some businessmen object that in such a carefully worked out relationship one gets performance only to the letter of the contract. Such planning indicates a lack of trust and blunts the demands of friendship, turning a cooperative venture into an antagonistic horse trade. Yet the greater danger perceived by some businessmen is that one would have to perform his side of the bargain to its letter and thus lose what is called "flexibility." Businessmen may welcome a measure of vagueness in the obligations they assume so that they may negotiate matters in light of the actual circumstances.

Adjustment of exchange relationships and dispute settlement by litigation or the threat of it also has many costs. The gain anticipated from using this form of coercion often fails to outweigh these costs, which are both monetary and non-monetary. Threatening to turn matters over to an attorney may cost no more money than postage or a telephone call; yet few are so skilled in making such a threat that it will not cost some deterioration of the relationship between the firms. One businessman said that customers had better not rely on legal rights or threaten to bring a breach of contract law suit against him since he "would not be treated like a criminal" and would fight back with every means available. Clearly actual litigation is even more costly than making threats. Lawyers demand substantial fees from larger business units. A firm's executives often will have to be transported and maintained in another city during the proceedings if, as often is the case, the trial must be held away from the home office. Top management does not travel by Greyhound and stay at the Y.M.C.A. Moreover, there will be the cost of diverting top management, engineers, and others in the organization from their normal activities. The firm may lose many days work from several key people. The non-monetary costs may be large too. A breach of contract law suit may settle a particular dispute, but such an action often results in a "divorce" ending the "marriage" between the two businesses, since a contract action is likely to carry charges with at least overtones of bad faith. Many executives, moreover, dislike the prospect of being cross-examined in public. Some executives may dislike losing control of a situation by turning the decision-making power over to lawyers. Finally, the law of contract damages may not provide an adequate remedy even if the firm wins the suit; one may get vindication but not much money.

Why Do Relatively Contractual Practices Ever Exist?

Although contract is not needed and actually may have negative consequences, businessmen do make some carefully planned contracts, negotiate settlements influenced by their legal rights and commence and defend some breach of contract law suits or arbitration proceedings. In view of the findings and explanation presented to this point, one may ask why. Exchanges are carefully planned when it is thought that planning and a potential legal sanction will have more advantages than disadvantages. Such a judgment may be reached when contract planning serves the internal needs of an organization involved in a business exchange. For example, a fairly detailed contract can serve as a communication device within a large corporation. While the corporation's sales manager and house counsel may work out all the provisions with the customer, its production manager will have to make the product. He must be told what to do and how to handle at least the most obvious contingencies. Moreover, the sales manager may want to remove certain issues from future negotiation by his subordinates. If he puts the matter in the written contract, he may be able to keep his salesmen from making concessions to the customer without first consulting the sales manager. Then the sales manager may be aided in his battles with his firm's financial or engineering departments if the contract calls for certain practices which the sales manager advocates but which the other departments resist. Now the corporation is obligated to a customer to do what the sales manager wants to do; how can the financial or engineering departments insist on anything else?

Also one tends to find a judgment that the gains of contract outweigh the costs where there is a likelihood that significant problems will arise. One factor leading to this conclusion is complexity of the agreed performance over a long period. Another factor is whether or not the degree of injury in case of default is thought to be potentially great. This factor cuts two ways. First, a buyer may want to commit a seller to a detailed and legally binding contract, where the consequence of a default by the seller would seriously injure the buyer. For example, the airlines are subject to law suits from the survivors of passengers and to great adverse publicity as a result of crashes. One would expect the airlines to bargain for carefully defined and legally enforceable obligations on the part of the airframe manufacturers when they purchase aircraft. Second, a seller may want to limit his liability for a buyer's damages by a provision in their contract. For example, a manufacturer of air conditioning may deal with motels in the South and Southwest. If this equipment fails in the hot summer months, a motel may lose a great deal of business. The manufacturer may wish to avoid any liability for this type of injury to his customers and may want a contract with a clear disclaimer clause.

Similarly, one uses or threatens to use legal sanctions to settle disputes when other devices will not work and when the gains are thought to outweigh the costs. For example, perhaps the most common type of business contracts case fought all the way through the appellate courts today is an action

for an alleged wrongful termination of a dealer's franchise by a manufacturer. Since the franchise has been terminated, factors such as personal relationships and the desire for future business will have little effect; the cancellation of the franchise indicates they have already failed to maintain the relationship. Nor will a complaining dealer worry about creating a hostile relationship between himself and the manufacturer. Often the dealer has suffered a great financial loss both as to his investment in building and equipment and as to his anticipated future profits. A cancelled automobile dealer's lease on his showroom and shop will continue to run, and his tools for servicing, say, Plymouths cannot be used to service other makes of cars. Moreover, he will have no more new Plymouths to sell. Today there is some chance of winning a law suit for terminating a franchise in bad faith in many states and in the federal courts. Thus, often the dealer chooses to risk the cost of a lawyer's fee because of the chance that he may recover some compensation for his losses.

An "irrational" factor may exert some influence on the decision to use legal sanctions. The man who controls a firm may feel that he or his organization has been made to appear foolish or has been the victim of fraud or bad faith. The law suit may be seen as a vehicle "to get even" although the potential gains, as viewed by an objective observer, are outweighed by the potential costs.

The decision whether or not to use contract — whether the gain exceeds the costs — will be made by the person within the business unit with the power to make it, and it tends to make a difference who he is. People in a sales department oppose contract. Contractual negotiations are just one more hurdle in the way of a sale. Holding a customer to the letter of a contract is bad for "customer relations." Suing a customer who is not bankrupt and might order again is poor strategy. Purchasing agents and their buyers are less hostile to contracts but regard attention devoted to such matters as a waste of time. In contrast, the financial control department — the treasurer, controller or auditor — leans toward more contractual dealings. Contract is viewed by these people as an organizing tool to control operations in a large organization. It tends to define precisely and to minimize the risks to which the firm is exposed. Outside lawyers — those with many clients — may share this enthusiasm for a more contractual method of dealing. These lawyers are concerned with preventive law — avoiding any possible legal difficulty. They see many unstable and unsuccessful exchange transactions, and so they are aware of, and perhaps overly concerned with, all of the things which can go wrong.

Moreover, their job of settling disputes with legal sanctions is much easier if their client has not been overly casual about transaction planning. The inside lawyer, or house counsel, is harder to classify. He is likely to have some sympathy with a more contractual method of dealing. He shares the outside lawyer's "craft urge" to see exchange transactions neat and tidy from a legal standpoint. Since he is more concerned with avoiding and settling disputes than selling goods, he is likely to be less willing to rely on a man's word as the sole sanction than is a salesman. Yet the house counsel is more a part of the organization and more aware of its goals and subject to its internal sanctions. If the potential risks are not too great, he may hesitate to suggest a more contractual procedure to the sales department. He must sell his services to the operating departments, and he must hoard what power he has, expending it on only what he sees as significant issues.

The power to decide that a more contractual method of creating relationships and settling disputes shall be used will be held by different people at different times in different organizations. In most firms the sales department and the purchasing department have a great deal of power to resist contractual procedures or to ignore them if they are formally adopted and to handle disputes their own way. Yet in larger organizations the treasurer and the controller have increasing power to demand both systems and compliance. Occasionally, the house counsel must arbitrate the conflicting positions of these departments; in giving "legal advice" he may make the business judgment necessary regarding the use of contract. At times he may ask for an opinion from an outside law firm to reinforce his own position with the outside firm's prestige.

Obviously, there are other significant variables which influence the degree that contract is used. One is the relative bargaining power or skill of the two business units. Even if the controller of a small supplier succeeds within the firm and creates a contractual system of dealing, there will be no contract if the firm's large customer prefers not to be bound to anything. Firms that supply General Motors deal as General Motors wants to do business, for the most part. Yet bargaining power is not size or share of the market alone. Even a General Motors may need a particular supplier, at least temporarily. Furthermore, bargaining power may shift as an exchange relationship is first created and then continues. Even a giant firm can find itself bound to a small supplier once production of an essential item begins for there may not be time to turn to another supplier. Also, all of the factors discussed in this paper can be viewed as *components* of bargaining power — for example, the personal relationship between the presidents of the buyer and the seller firms may give a sales manager great power over a purchasing agent who has been instructed to give the seller "every consideration." Another variable relevant to the use of contract is the influence of third parties. The federal government, or a lender of money, may insist that a contract be made in a particular transaction or may influence the decision to assert one's legal rights under a contract.

Contract, then, often plays an important role in business, but other factors are significant. To understand the functions of contract the whole system of conducting exchanges must be explored fully. More types of business communities must be studied, contract litigation must be analyzed to see why the nonlegal sanctions fail to prevent the use of legal sanctions and all of the variables suggested in this paper must be classified more systematically.

(b) Bargaining in the Shadow of the Law: The Case of Divorce†

Robert H. Mnookin

I wish to suggest a new way of thinking about the role of law at the time of divorce. It is concerned primarily with the impact of the legal system on negotiations and bargaining that occurs *outside* of

† (1979) 32 Current Legal Problems 65 at 65–70, 93–95, 96–102. [Notes and/or references omitted.] Reproduced by permission of Thomson Reuters (Professional) UK Limited.

court. Rather than regard order as imposed from above, I see the primary function of contemporary divorce law as providing a framework for divorcing couples themselves to determine their respective rights and responsibilities after dissolution. This process, by which parties to a marriage are empowered to create their own legally enforceable commitments, I shall call *"private ordering."*[2]

Available evidence concerning how divorce proceedings actually work suggests that a re-examination from the perspective of private ordering is long overdue. "Typically the parties do not go to court at all until they have worked matters out and are ready for the rubber stamp."[3] Both in the United States and England the overwhelming majority of divorcing couples resolve or settle the distributional questions concerning marital property, alimony, child support, and custody without bringing any contested issue to the court for adjudication.[4]

This new perspective and the use of the term "private ordering" [are] not meant to suggest an absence of important social interests in how this process works, or in the fairness of the outcomes. The implicit policy questions are ones of emphasis and degree: to what extent should law permit and encourage divorcing couples to work out their own arrangements? Within what limits should parties be empowered to make their own law that they bring into existence by their agreement? What procedural or substantive safeguards are necessary because of various social interests? Nor is this new perspective meant to imply that the law and the legal system are unimportant. For divorcing spouses and their children, family law is inescapably relevant. The legal system affects *when* a divorce may occur; *how* a divorce must be procured; and *what happens* as a consequence of divorce. The primary purpose of this paper is to develop a framework for thinking about how the legal rules and procedures used in court for adjudicating disputes affect the bargaining process that occurs between divorcing couples *outside* the courtroom.

Before setting out together, let me provide you with a road map of where we are going. Our first stop involves an examination of the degree to which the law today authorises private ordering at the time of divorce. In other words, to what extent can a divorcing couple create their own legally enforceable commitments? In this context, I will also explain why I think the legal system should provide divorcing couples broad power through agreement to resolve the various questions that arise.

Secondly, against this background, I present a simple bargaining model to suggest how the legal

system affects negotiations between spouses and their representatives at the time of divorce.

Finally, I will apply this framework to several issues that have dominated much of the academic discussion concerning family law during recent years:

1. The advantages and disadvantages of discretion conferring legal standards for child custody;
2. Goldstein, Freud and Solnit's proposed standard for visitation;
3. The role of lawyers in the divorce process; and
4. The role of courts in "undisputed" divorces.

Let us now turn to the question of the extent to which the law today sanctions private ordering. At the outset it is important to recall that a legal system might allow varying degrees of private ordering upon the dissolution of marriage. Until the no-fault revolution, the law concerning divorce did reflect a highly regulatory model that attempted to restrict private ordering. Couples had no formal power to end their marriage by mutual agreement. Divorce was granted only after an official inquiry by a judge, who had to determine whether there were "appropriate grounds," which were themselves very narrowly defined in terms of marital offences. If a divorce were granted, the State asserted broad power to impose distributional consequences, and to have continuing regulatory jurisdiction over the children and their relationship to their parents. Doctrines such as collusion, connivance and condonation were meant to curtail the degree to which parties themselves could through agreement bring about a divorce; and the procedural requirements reflected the view, in R.M. Jackson's words, that both the petitioner and the respondent were "suspicious characters."[5] Obviously, the marital offence regime — even at its most restrictive — could not entirely eliminate collusion. Some divorcing spouses worked things out for themselves and then (with the help of their lawyers) staged a carefully rehearsed and jointly produced play for the court.[6] Nonetheless, the legal system was structured to minimise private ordering.

Dramatic changes in divorce law during the past decade now permit a substantial degree of private ordering. The "no fault revolution" has made the fundamental decision of whether there shall be divorce largely a matter of private concern. Parties to a marriage can now explicitly create circumstances that will allow divorce. Indeed, the reality is that agreement between spouses is not even necessary — either spouse can unilaterally create the grounds for dissolution simply by separation for a sufficient period of time.[7]

What about the parties' power to decide for themselves the consequences of divorce? Here the presence of children makes an important difference. Where the divorcing couple has no children, the law both in England and the United States largely recognises the power of the parties upon separation or divorce to make their own arrangements concerning marital property and alimony.[8] A spousal agreement may be subject to some sort of judicial proceeding — or submission to a Registrar — but on both sides of the Atlantic the official review appears to be largely perfunctory.[9] In some American states, a couple may if they choose make their agreement binding and final — i.e., not subject to later modification by a court after the divorce.[10] In England, strictly speaking, this probably is not possible.[11] Nonetheless, English courts are very slow after a divorce is granted to modify an agreement intended to be binding or an order issued with the consent of the parties.[12]

Where there are minor children, existing law imposes substantial doctrinal constraints. For those allocational decisions that directly affect children — that is, child support, custody and visitation — parents lack the formal power "to make their own law." The court, exercising the state's *parens patrine* power, is said to have responsibility to determine who should have custody and on what conditions. Private agreements concerning these matters are possible, and common, but these agreements cannot bind the court which is said to have an independent responsibility for determining what arrangements best serve the child's welfare.[13] Thus, the court has the power to reject a parental agreement, and order some other level of child support or some other custodial arrangement, if that is thought more desirable.[14] Moreover, even if the parties' initial agreement is accepted by the court, the parties entirely lack the power to provide for finality. A court may at any time during the child's minority reopen and modify the initial decree in light of any subsequent change in circumstances.[15] The parties entirely lack the power to deprive the court of this jurisdiction.

These limitations on parental power reflect a variety of policy concerns. They may acknowledge the fact that the child, although profoundly affected by the bargain, is not normally a meaningful participant in the negotiating process. A parental agreement concerning custody, visitation or support may not reflect the child's interests but instead the interests of the parents.[16] A parent eager to escape an unhappy marriage may agree to custodial arrangements and levels of support that are less advantageous to the child than some feasible alternative. Judicial scrutiny and continual supervision of the ele-

ments of the separation agreement concerning the child might therefore be seen as a safeguard of the child's interests.

Available evidence concerning how the legal system in fact processes undisputed divorce cases involving minor children suggests that in fact parents have very broad powers to make their own deals. Typically separation agreements are rubber stamped even in cases involving children. A study of custody here in England suggests, for example, that courts rarely set aside an arrangement acceptable to the parents. Anecdotal evidence in America suggests that the same is true in the U.S.

That the legal system in fact gives parents broad discretion is less than surprising when one considers a number of factors. First, getting information is difficult when there is no dispute. There are usually very limited resources for a thorough or an independent investigation of the family's circumstances. Secondly, the applicable legal standards are extremely vague and give registrars or judges very little guidance as to what circumstances justify overriding a parental decision.[17] Finally, there are obvious limitations on a court's practical power to control parental behaviour once they leave the courtroom. For all these reasons, it is not surprising that most courts behave as if their function in the divorce process is dispute settlement. Where there is no dispute, busy judges or registrars are typically quite willing to rubber stamp a private agreement, thus conserving resources for disputed cases.

Before proceeding, I should make clear the reasons I think law should give divorcing spouses broad powers to make their own agreement. When a couple can resolve distributional consequences of divorce without resort to court for adjudication, there are obvious and substantial savings. The cost of litigation, both private and public, is minimised. The pain of an adversarial proceeding is avoided. Recent findings from psychological studies suggest the desirability from a child's perspective in having parents agree on custodial arrangements. Moreover, through a negotiated agreement the parties can often avoid the risks and uncertainties of litigation which sometimes involve all or nothing consequences. Given the substantial delays that often characterise contested judicial proceedings, an agreement can often provide significant time-savings for the parties, thus allowing the spouses to proceed with their lives. Finally, a solution agreed to by the parties seems more likely to be consistent with their own preferences and accepted by them over time than a result that is simply imposed by a court.

319

For divorces where there are no minor children, divorcing couples should have very broad powers to make their own arrangements; significant limitations are inconsistent with the premises of no fault divorce. After all, who can better evaluate the comparative advantages of alternative arrangements than the parties themselves? In John Stuart Mill's words, each spouse "is the person most interested in his own well-being ... with respect to his own feelings and circumstances, the most ordinary man or woman has means of knowledge immeasurably surpassing those that can be possessed by anyone else."[18] Courts should not, of course, enforce agreements that reflect fraud or overreaching. Nor do I wish to minimise the importance of appropriate standards for alimony and marital property for, in ways that I will describe shortly, these standards very much affect negotiated outcomes. Nonetheless, against a backdrop of fair standards, parties should be encouraged to settle for themselves these economic issues. The state should provide an efficient and fair mechanism for enforcing such agreements, and for settling disputes when the parties are unable to agree.

Where there are minor children, the state obviously has broader interests than simply dispute settlement. The state also has a responsibility for *child protection*. To acknowledge this responsibility, however, is not to define its limits. Indeed the critical questions concern the proper scope of the child protection function at the time of divorce, and the mechanisms that best achieve this goal.

For reasons I have spelled out at length elsewhere,[19] the actual determination of what is in fact in a child's best interest is ordinarily quite indeterminate: it requires predictions beyond the capacity of the behavioural sciences. It also involves the imposition of values about which there appears to be little consensus in our societies today. Thus the fundamental question is: who decides on behalf of the child? To what extent should the child's parents be given the freedom to decide between themselves how responsibility for their children is to be allocated following divorce? I believe divorcing parents should be given considerable freedom to decide custody matters — subject only to the same minimum standards for child protection that the State imposes on *all* families with respect to neglect and abuse. A negotiated resolution is desirable from the child's perspective for several reasons. Since a child's social and psychological relationships with *both* parents ordinarily continue after the divorce, a process that leads to agreement between the parents is preferable to one that necessarily has a winner and a loser. A child's future relationship with each of his parents may be better maintained and his existing relationship less damaged by a negotiated settlement than by one imposed by a court after an adversarial proceeding. Moreover, the parents will know more about the child than the judge, since they have better access to information about the child's circumstances and desires. Indeed, given the basic indeterminacy of anyone knowing what is best for the child, having a privately negotiated solution by those who will be responsible for care after the divorce seems much more likely to match the parents' capacities and desires with the child's needs. These advantages suggest that courts should not second-guess parental agreements unless judicial intervention is required by the strict child-protection standard implicit in neglect laws.

If parents have the authority to decide, there can be no doubt that some parents will make mistakes. But so do judges. Parents (not the state) are primarily responsible for their children after divorce. Part of this responsibility involves attempting, themselves, to agree upon some allocation of responsibilities in the future. This is not to suggest that the State does not have an important responsibility to inform parents concerning the child's needs during and after divorce; nor does it mean that the State does not have an important interest in facilitating parental agreement. Nevertheless, the law in action (which acknowledges substantial parental power) strikes me as preferable to existing doctrine (which imposes substantial restrictions on parental power to decide for themselves).

Everyone may not share these premises concerning the desirability of private ordering. But no matter what one's thinking on these questions, the fact that most divorcing couples do not bring disputes to court for adjudication suggests the appropriateness of analysing how the legal system affects the bargaining behaviour of divorcing couples.

. . . .

An Evaluation of the Lawyer's Role

If one accepts the proposition that the primary function of the legal system should be to facilitate private ordering and dispute resolution, then several important questions come into sharp focus. To what extent does the participation of lawyers facilitate dispute resolution? Are there alternative procedures (in which lawyers play a lesser role) that are less costly and more fair? Many observers are very critical of the way some lawyers behave in divorce negotiations. Lawyers may "heat up" the process, make negotiations more adversarial and painful than they would otherwise be, and make it more difficult and costly for the spouses to reach agreement. Indeed, it may well be that lawyers more than lay people are prepared to adopt negotiating strategies involving threats, and the strategic misrepresentation of their client's true preferences in order to reach a more favourable settlement for the client. Ivan Illich has recently suggested that a broad range of illnesses are in fact "iatrogenic,"[33] i.e., induced and created by medical treatment and the health industry. The same charge might be laid on the legal profession. The participation of lawyers in the divorce process may on balance lead to more disputes and higher costs without improving the fairness of the outcomes.

There are also arguments that lawyers facilitate dispute settlement. The participation of lawyers may make negotiations more rational, may minimise the number of disputes, may increase the opportunities for resolution out of court, and may insure that the outcomes reflect the applicable legal norms. Professor Eisenberg has suggested how a pair of lawyers — each acting for his client — may make the process of negotiation in dispute settlement very much like adjudication, i.e., a process where "rules, precedents, and reasoned elaboration — may be expanded to determine outcome ..."[34] Where each spouse has a lawyer, the lawyers

> are likely to find themselves allied with each other as well as with the disputants, because of their relative emotional detachment, their interest in resolving the dispute, and, in some cases, their shared professional values. Each therefore tends to take on a Janus-like role, facing the other as an advocate of that which is reasonable in the other's position.... Because a lawyer is both a personal advisor and a technical expert, each actor-disputant is likely to accept a settlement his lawyer recommends. Because of their training and the fact that typically they become involved only when formal litigation is contemplated, lawyers are likely to negotiate on the basis of *legal* principles, rules, and precedents. When these two elements are combined, the result is that paired legal affiliates typically function as a coupled unit which is strikingly similar to a formal adjudicative unit in terms of both input and output. Indeed, in terms of sheer number of dispute-settlements effected, the most significant legal dispute-settlement institution is typically not the bench, but the bar.[35]

The perspective of private ordering exposes these various roles and raises the obvious question: what in fact do lawyers do in the process? Lawyers may serve various functions, and yet we know very little about how in fact lawyers behave. Obviously, lawyers are not of all one piece. Their styles differ. Some lawyers may prefer (and be more effective at) certain roles. Some lawyers are known within the profession as negotiators who strive to find middle ground acceptable to both sides; others are fighters, who love the courtroom battle. Research could usefully explore how much specialisation there is, and the extent to which clients (when they are choosing a lawyer at the time of divorce) have any notion at all of their lawyers' skills or tastes for these various roles. More generally, systematic empirical research might illustrate how often (and in what circumstances) lawyers facilitate dispute settlement at the time of divorce, and how often (and in what circumstances) they hurt.

This framework also suggests how timely it is to re-examine the question of why the legal profession should have a monopoly with respect to these roles, and the extent to which it does in fact have such a monopoly. How well are lawyers trained to perform these various roles? Other professionals or para-professionals might serve some of these functions as well as lawyers at a substantially lower cost. This is most obviously the case where there is no dispute, and the attorney's role is essentially that of "clerk." A recent study in Connecticut suggests that in most uncontested divorces, clients believe their lawyer did no more than fill out the necessary forms (a complaint, a claim for a hearing, and a decree) and made an appearance at a *pro forma* hearing. Moreover, the same study suggests that because the forms and procedures are complicated, do-it-yourself "divorce dissolution kits" (without additional lay assistance) pose rather little threat to the monopoly of the organised bar.[36] Most people lack the time, confidence, or ability to navigate through the legal shoals themselves — even where they have no dispute with their spouse. This suggests that procedural reform aimed at simplifying the procedure for uncontested divorce could substantially reduce transaction costs in many cases.

. . . .

THE ROLE OF COURTS

Let us consider the role of courts in the divorce process from the perspective of private ordering. Obviously, the judicial system provides a mechanism for dispute settlement through adjudication where the parties have not been able to agree. But courts also play a role in a much larger number of cases than those where the dispute is adjudicated. Because each party knows the other can invoke the court's power to settle their differences, the presence of the judiciary exerts considerable pressure towards settlement. Indeed, anecdotal evidence suggests that courts often put pressure on the parties in disputed cases "to settle their own differences" through private negotiations, thus avoiding the need for adjudication.

One striking feature of the present day system, however, is the requirement that undisputed cases pass through court. With a narrow exception recently enacted in California, every American state requires a judicial proceeding to secure a divorce in all cases. From a historical perspective, this requirement is not surprising: it represented a regulatory mechanism to ensure that divorces were only granted in narrowly defined circumstances. Before the no-fault revolution, dispute settlement was not the primary function of divorce proceedings.

The no-fault revolution has now empowered either spouse unilaterally to create the circumstances for divorce. The state no longer purports to have an interest preventing re-marriage where either spouse wants to dissolve an earlier marriage. Ironically, however, the shell of the same administrative and regulatory mechanisms has been preserved. Indeed, this analysis suggests a policy question of substantial importance: where there is no dispute between the divorcing spouses concerning the allocation implications of their divorce, why should a judicial proceeding be required? Absent a dispute, why should a court have any role? Why require a costly legal transaction in court when the questions can be resolved by negotiations?

It would not be difficult to imagine the elimination of a judicial proceeding in undisputed divorce cases. Getting married obviously does not require judicial proceedings. Why should getting a divorce?[42] The requirement of a judicial proceeding probably imposes significant transaction costs, both public and private. Because even uncontested divorces must go through court, parties may end up hiring a lawyer, even where the lawyer's function is basically that of a clerk. An appearance by a lawyer in court takes time — time for which the parties are charged. Moreover a judicial proceeding requires the use of judicial resources as well as the time of the parties themselves. Some countries have largely eliminated the requirement that undisputed divorces go through court; it certainly seems timely to examine the justifications for the requirement, and to ask whether there might not be alternatives that are preferable which cost less.

While the analysis that follows is necessarily preliminary, it is useful to identify and examine four arguments in defence of a judicial proceeding, in uncontested divorce cases.

Ceremonial Function

A judicial proceeding might be thought to serve a ceremonial function that re-confirms, both for the divorcing parties and the general public, the seriousness with which the state takes marriage and divorce. Rituals are important, and the court proceeding can be seen as a socially imposed divorce ritual. But as a ritual, the court proceeding for uncontested divorces[] seems peculiar. The marriage ceremony itself is, after all, extremely simple, and does not require lawyers and a judge. Moreover, in most states, the parties themselves are not usually required to appear in court in order to procure a divorce. Their lawyers, instead, can appear for them. If the ritual were for the benefit of the parties, presumably their presence would be required. In all events, one can ask how well the existing requirement serves the ceremonial function? Is the purpose of the requirement ceremonial? Or is it more like a civil fine, imposed on a divorcing couple; a fine payable not to the treasury but to the divorce bar?

Review Ensures Fair Outcomes:
Fairness between the Spouses

The requirement of judicial approval of post-marital agreements might be justified on the ground that the state has an interest in ensuring that the results of the bargaining process are fair, as between the spouses. A judicial proceeding might protect people from their own ignorance, and might also be thought to prevent unfair results arising from unequal bargaining capacity between the spouses. These arguments have a plausible air, but the reality of the present day system might suggest that they mean very little in practice. Courts typically rubber stamp an agreement reached between the parties. Moreover, there are reasons to doubt that the requirement of judicial review is very often necessary for these purposes. There may well be cases where one spouse (presumably the husband) is highly sophisticated in business matters, while the other spouse (the wife) is an innocent lamb being led to the slaughter. But typically married couples generally have similar educational and cultural backgrounds. Moreover, most individuals perceive very well their own financial interests and needs at the time of divorce.

If there are systematic biases in the process, a more appropriate safeguard would be to change the *substantive standards* concerning who gets what. For example, if it is thought that husbands systematically provide their wives with an insufficient share of the family's assets, or with inadequate alimony, after marriages of long duration where the wife has not worked, the *legal standards* can be changed to provide greater claims for the wife. Moreover, procedural mechanisms can then be developed that require review and a hearing only in those cases where the spousal agreement falls outside the norm (e.g., where marital property was divided very unequally, or where alimony claims were being waived). In practice today, I suspect judges or registrars attempt to identify such cases for intensive examination. At the present time, however, cases falling within the normal range must also pass through a judicial proceeding, with its attendant costs. A system where the state defines reasonable norms, and then permits couples to reach agreement outside the norms provided there were additional procedural safeguards, would seem both more effective and less costly.

Effect on Out-of-Court Settlements

It might be thought that the requirement that undisputed cases go to court[] improves the private settlement process outside of court. Knowing that they will have to display their agreement to a judge, the parties (and their attorneys) may deal with each other in a fairer way and be more likely to reach an agreement reflecting the appropriate social norms. Behavioural scientists have suggested that the presence of an "audience" can affect bargaining.[43] With respect to out-of-court negotiations, the judge represents both an "actual" audience and "abstract" audience. He is an actual audience in that parties know that eventually they may have to explain their agreement to a judge. This may mitigate extreme claims. The judge also represents an abstract audience as well, which symbolically represents the social interests in the child and various notions of honour, reputation, and history.

It is extremely difficult to evaluate this argument, and to know how the requirement of judicial proceedings in undisputed cases affects negotiations in such cases. A requirement that disputed cases alone would go before a court might be sufficient to bring the "audience" benefits to the process of negotiation. Moreover, it is possible that the requirement of judicial approval makes dispute settlement more not less difficult. For one thing, the requirement probably means that lawyers are more often involved in the process than would otherwise be the case. As earlier noted, it at least seems an open question whether having lawyers in the process facilitates dispute resolution in those case where the parties might otherwise reach agreement anyway. Moreover, there is always the possibility that in the occasional case where the judge does upset the agreement reached by the parties, the eventual outcome may on balance be no more desirable (or even less desirable) than would otherwise be the case.

Child Protection

Where a divorcing couple has minor children, the state has an important interest in child protection. The requirement of court review of private agreements relating to custody or child support might be justified on this ground. For one thing, from the child's perspective, the quality of negotiated agreements may be improved. Some parents might otherwise engage in divorce bargaining on the basis of preferences that reflected narrowly selfish interests, rather than concern for the child. The review requirement might serve as an important reminder to the parents of the social concern for their children, and may somehow constrain otherwise selfish behaviour. Even a selfish spouse may be more concerned about his reputation as a parent if there is some sort of public process. Especially in cases where there are children, the judge may represent an important "audience" whose unseen presence affects bargaining behaviour. Finally, although most parental agreements are approved after only superficial examination by the judge, some agreements are in fact disapproved: to the extent courts succeed in identifying arrangements that are disadvantageous to a child in a particular case and in imposing some better alternative, the child's welfare is obviously improved.

A variety of arguments can be made on the other side, however. For one thing, what evidence we have suggests that in operation courts rarely overturn parental agreements. Given the resources that are devoted to this task there is little reason to believe that the process today in fact operates as much of a safeguard where there is no parental dispute. Moreover, the process itself probably imposes not insubstantial transaction costs — both public (in terms of traditional resources expended) and private (in terms of the cost to the parties, the legal fees and time). These extra transaction costs might otherwise enure (at least in part) to the benefit of the children.

There are also reasons to think that, in the vast majority of cases, this review may well be unnecessary. For one thing, the custodial spouse will typically perceive very clearly the economic consequences for the child of any support arrangement that he or she agrees to. There is after all, considerable joint consumption between the custodial parent and the child. Moreover, child support payments (like alimony and the earnings of the custodial spouse) typically go into a single economic pot that supports both the custodial parent and the child. In other words, the economic interests of the child and the economic interests of the custodial parent substantially coincide.

A second safeguard — banal as it sounds — is that most parents care deeply for their children. No court proceeding can of course require parents to love their children, and prevent selfish calculation by a divorcing parent. Nevertheless, to the extent that divorcing parents do love their children there is every reason to think that they will in fact themselves be very concerned with making arrangements that are beneficial to the child. Perhaps there are good reasons not to trust parents with child-rearing responsibilities on or after divorce. That was certainly the implicit attitude during the heyday of the marital offence regime. But is it really appropriate today? Indeed, it is interesting to compare the review requirements imposed by law if the child's family is disrupted by divorce with the review requirements imposed if the family is disrupted by the death of one of the parents. American law permits a parent to disinherit his minor children. A decedent cannot, however, disinherit his spouse and in effect present day law trusts the surviving parent with child-rearing responsibility in the light of existing economic resources. With respect to any inheritance of any surviving spouse, there is no supervision imposed by operation of law on how he or she spends the inheritance, and there is no examination of what portion is spent on the child. Instead, the surviving parent is trusted to look after the child, subject of course to the minimum limitations imposed by the child neglect laws which apply to all parents.

The review requirement may, ironically, send an inappropriate set of signals to parents at the time of divorce: it may suggest to them that because of the divorce they are no longer trusted to be adequate parents, and that the state will now assume special responsibility for their children. Indeed, court review might conceivably induce more selfish behaviour on the part of parents who take the attitude that it is the court's job, not their own responsibility, to be concerned with the interests of their children. In fact, the state does not and cannot assume a broad role for child-rearing responsibility after divorce.

CONCLUSION

Viewing the process of dissolution from the perspective of private ordering does not make previously intractable family law problems disappear. If anything, the world seems even more complex, for analysis involves the examination of the effects of alternative rules and procedures on informal and formal bargaining outside of court about which we have little understanding. There is little existing theory to inform the enquiry. There now exists no bargaining theory that can yield accurate predictions of the expected outcomes, assuming different legal rules where rational self-interested parties are negotiating over money issues. Where there are minor children involved, the parents are not simply bargaining over money; they also must be necessarily concerned with allocating child-rearing responsibilities in the future. We have tried to suggest how the variability of parental preferences with respect to custody makes the task of analysing bargaining especially difficult. Furthermore, rational bargaining may be in short supply when a family is in the process of breaking up. Some divorcing spouses seem motivated by spite or envy, more than a careful assessment of self-interest in the light of available alternatives. Where bargaining is motivated by emotional drives, the assessment of the effects of alternative legal rules seems even more speculative. Finally, it must sadly be reported that there has been little empirical work which has involved the systematic observation of how the process of private ordering in fact works today.

Given the absence of powerful theory or systematic data, this essay makes no claims at being definitive. It instead has suggested a theoretical perspective that permits a broader analysis of the probable consequences of family law rules and procedures. It also more sharply exposes a set of questions of enormous social importance. If one accepts the proposition that disputes settlement should be the primary goal of the legal system, the analysis does not imply that the state should simply withdraw all resources from the process, and leave it to the divorcing spouses to work things out on their own, unassisted by any professional help. Instead, this inquiry should underline the desirability of learning more about how alternative procedural mechanisms might facilitate dispute resolution during a typically difficult and painful time in the lives of parents and children alike.

The perspective certainly has implications far broader than family law. In a wide variety of contexts, individuals bargain in the shadow of the law. Few automobile accident claims are ever tried; most are settled out of court. Criminal prosecutions are typically resolved by a plea bargain, not an adjudication of guilt. Most administrative proceedings result in consent agreements not trials. In each of these contexts, the preferences of the parties, the entitlements created by law, transaction costs, and attitudes towards risk, will presumably substantially affect the negotiated outcomes. Indeed, I hope this essay will stimulate and encourage further work by others in a variety of contexts. Theoretical and empirical research concerning how people bargain in the shadow of law should provide us with a richer understanding of how the legal system affects behaviour, and allow a better appraisal of the consequences of reform proposals.

(a) The Judge and the Adversary System†

Neil Brooks

THE ROLE OF THE JUDGE IN THE ADVERSARY SYSTEM

A thorough discussion of this subject would require an examination of the judge's role at each stage of the litigation process: at the pre-trial investigative stage;[1] at the pre-trial procedural stages;[2] at the trial; at the sentencing hearing;[3] and at the hearing to determine law and policy.[4] While the same principles may be applicable to each stage, the discussion in this paper will focus on the role of the trial judge in the conduct of the trial. The trial has a first claim on our attention since it is at this stage of the litigation process that all aspects of the adversary system bear most directly on the judge's role. Moreover, restricting the discussion in this way will permit, in the time available, a more detailed development of the central theoretical themes of the subject.[5]

In determining the precise role that he will assume in discharging his responsibilities at trial, a judge will undoubtedly consider a wide range of factors: the peculiarities of his own temperament and abilities, the significance of the particular case to the parties and to the public,[6] the complexity of the factual and legal issues raised by the case, and the effectiveness of the parties or their counsel in presenting the case. However, whatever other factors a judge might consider in defining the precise nature of the role he will play, the fact that he is an arbiter in an adjudicative proceeding that is adversarial in nature necessarily prescribes for him the parameters of his involvement in the proceeding. In this paper I

will develop this theme by speculating about the justifications which have been or might be advanced supporting the adversary system, and then exploring the limitations that these justifications impose on the judge's role in conducting a judicial trial.

. . . .

Definition of "Adversary System"

The greatest impediment to clear thinking about the judge's role in the adversary system is the variety of meanings that are often assigned to the concept of the adversary system. Therefore, before examining the premises underlying the adversary system let me make clear the sense in which that concept is used in this paper by distinguishing it from various senses in which it is often misleadingly used.

The term is being used in this paper to refer generally to a procedural system in which the parties and not the judge have the primary responsibility for defining the issues in dispute and for carrying the dispute forward through the system. Thus, it should not be confused with what might more accurately be referred to as the adjudicative process. Adjudication is a method of settling disputes that is commonly contrasted with other methods of dispute resolution such as mediation, negotiation and conciliation. Used in this context, it refers characteristically to a means of resolving disputes in which some general principle or rule of law is applied to the facts that gave rise to the dispute and in which the parties involved are

---

† From Allen Linden, ed., *The Canadian Judiciary* (Toronto: Osgoode Hall Law School, 1976) at 89–118. [Notes and/or references omitted.] Reproduced with permission.

able to participate by presenting proofs and reasoned argument.[9]

Professor Lon Fuller, who in a series of essays clarified the tasks for which adjudication because of its institutional framework was well-suited as a means of social ordering,[10] argued that an adversary presentation is essential to adjudication.[11] He postulated that the fundamental characteristic of adjudication is the opportunity it provides for the affected parties to participate in the decision-making by presenting proofs and arguments. He concluded that only the adversary system is capable of affording this requisite degree of participation. Whether or not these two concepts need to be so closely wed,[12] it remains useful in analysing the judge's role to distinguish between them.

. . . .

[I]t is sometimes argued that the adversary system is deficient because it presents an all-or-nothing proposition — there are always winners and losers — and, as a consequence, the total satisfaction of the parties is often reduced.[16] This is particularly the case in areas such as family law, labour law, or criminal law where the parties are part of a close social or economic relationship. Again the adversary system is here a victim because of its close association with adjudication. The attempt at the outset to adjudicate this kind of claim is more properly criticized.[17]

. . . .

The adversary system, as that term is used by many proceduralists and as it will be used in this paper, embodies two distinct principles.[24] The issues resolved by these two principles raise the two most basic questions that confront any adjudicative procedural system. The first issue is what should the respective functions of the parties and the judge be with reference to the initiation and content of the adjudication. The adversary system rests on the principle of party-autonomy. That is to say, that the parties have the right to pursue or dispose of their legal rights and remedies as they wish. The second issue is what should the respective functions of the parties and the judge be with reference to the progress of a dispute through the procedural system once initiated and defined. The adversary system rests on the principle of party-prosecution. This principle holds that the parties have the primary responsibility to choose without interference from the judge the manner in which they will go forward with their case and the proofs they will present for the judge's consideration in adjudicating the dispute.

Party-Autonomy

In defining the judge's role in the conduct of the trial it is, of course, the principle of party-prosecution that requires careful analysis. However, to place that examination in perspective, the principle of party-autonomy must be briefly examined. The principle of party-autonomy has two aspects. First, it limits the judge's function to disputes which have been presented to him. A judge plays a role only when a conflict has arisen between two or more parties, and at least one of them seeks the assistance of the judge in resolving the dispute. John Chipman Gray, in defining a judge, summarized this principle: "A judge of an organized body is a man appointed by that body to determine duties and the corresponding rights upon the application of persons claiming those rights."[25] The authors of a casebook on civil procedure described the principle more prosaically: "Courts ought not to function as self-propelled vehicles of justice and right like King Arthur's knights in Good Humor trucks."[26] Lon Fuller quotes a socialist critic of bourgeois law who caricatured this premise of the adversary system by asserting that courts in such a system "are like defective clocks; they have to be shaken to set them going". Fuller noted that, "[h]e of course added the point that the shaking costs money".[27]

The second aspect of party-autonomy is that the parties have the sole responsibility for defining the dispute that they would like adjudicated. Thus, if the parties want the judge to decide one dispute, he will not insist on resolving another even though he perceives the other issue to be the real cause of the conflict between the parties.

Both aspects of party-autonomy are subject to qualifications. While the judge cannot initiate proceedings, he can prevent the parties from initiating certain proceedings. The courts have an important social function to perform by resolving disputes. Thus the judge can prevent parties from using the litigation process to resolve hypothetical or moot problems. He can judicially notice all facts that he considers beyond reasonable dispute and thus prevent the parties from consuming the time of the court by presenting evidence on clear factual issues. He can also prevent misuses of the process by a judicial screening of cases, he can give judgment on the pleadings or give a summary judgment. Indeed he is assisted in controlling the use of the court's process by counsel for the parties. Lawyers have a professional responsibility to ensure the claims and defences they put forward have merit and are related to a real conflict.

In criminal cases, the judge's role in controlling the issues disputed is even greater than his responsibility in civil cases.[28] While the judge cannot control the criminal cases to reach his docket, nor find the accused guilty of a crime he is not charged with, nor insist that the Crown amend the indictment to add charges, he does not permit the accused or the Crown complete autonomy in defining the issues contested. For instance, he can prevent the Crown from initiating the case if he concludes that the Crown is abusing the process. There is also an increasing recognition of the judge's responsibility to examine the factual basis of a plea of guilty. In the United States a Presidential Commission has recently recommended that the guilty plea be abolished entirely because, among other things, it leaves too much of the public interest to the parties.[29]

The limits of the principle of party-autonomy can, of course, only be defined by reference to the reasons why it is regarded as being an essential principle of the Anglo-American procedural system. Two justifications sometimes put forward fail to appreciate that party-autonomy is only a principle which defines the respective roles of the parties and the judge. In civil cases, it has been said that the principle of party-autonomy — that the judge only operates when the parties present him with a dispute to resolve — rests on the judgment that "the social interest in securing general observance of the rules of private law is sufficiently served by leaving their enforcement to the self-interest of the parties more or less directly affected".[30] However, while this reason might explain why the state need not become involved in the enforcement of the civil law, it does not go directly to the issue of the roles of the parties and the judge in initiating actions. In many areas where there is an important public interest in the enforcement of the civil law, as in the enforcement of the criminal law, the state, through an administrative agency, might initiate actions enforcing the law.[31] And yet, since it is not the judge who initiates such actions, the principle of party-autonomy would be satisfied.

Others have suggested that the principle of party-autonomy reflects a political ideology. Thurman Arnold asserted, "...the civil trial dramatizes the moral beauty of the noninterference of government in private affairs.... The whole ideology, and procedural organization of the civil trial is designed to insulate the court and the government from taking the initiative in enforcing or even protecting the civil rights of individuals".[32] Thurman Arnold was at the time decrying the resistance to the New Deal and exploring its causes. He went on, "[t]his role of the civil trial as a symbol of individual freedom

from active interference by the government makes it a most important factor in preserving conservative traditions in the face of new legislation". While party-autonomy may reflect a *laissez-faire* philosophy, Arnold's point goes to the role of the government generally in the enforcement of the civil law.[33]

. . . . .

Party-Prosecution

The second major premise of the adversary system, as that term is used by most proceduralists, is the principle of party-prosecution. This principle holds that the parties have the right and the responsibility to choose the manner in which they will go forward with their case and the proof they will present to support it. The judge's role is to passively evaluate the merits of the case as and when it is presented to him.

In the remainder of this paper I will explore the reasons why the principle of party-prosecution is adhered to at trial, and offer some general comments on the parameters that these reasons place upon the judge's intervention in the conduct of the case. The conclusion that I reach is that viewed in this way the adversary system does not impose as severe restraints on the judge's intervention as is often assumed, and that in appropriate cases the judge should, if he deems it necessary, play a much larger role in the conduct of the case. My argument will be a plea for more judicial activism in controlling the conduct of the trial.

The principle of party-prosecution at trial rests, in the main, upon two broad empirical assumptions. Firstly, that the legitimacy of adjudication as a means of social ordering is enhanced if it is conducted according to an adversarial presentation. Secondly, that more accurate fact-finding is likely to result if parties motivated by self-interest are given the responsibilities of investigating facts and presenting arguments, and if the decision-maker remains passive.

The Adversary System Increases the Acceptability of Adjudication

Every means of social ordering used by the state must be acceptable not only to those immediately affected by its particular sanctions but also to all those governed by the state. This need for legitimacy is particularly paramount in a free society with respect to adjudication since a judge's decision might be perceived, in some sense at least, to be undemocratic.

Legitimacy or acceptability is a derivative value. That is to say, a decision-making process will be acceptable to the extent that it meets all the criteria that people expect of that decision-making process. With respect to adjudication these expectations undoubtedly include such considerations as expediency, finality, inexpensiveness, and the protection of privacy and other social values. To the extent that the adversary system furthers these values it will render the adjudicative process more acceptable than would some other procedural device for finding the facts. But aside from these considerations, which are necessary attributes of any acceptable adjudicative proceeding, it is often argued that the adversary system has unique characteristics which render it in judicial trials a more acceptable procedure in our society than other methods of fact-finding. The reasons for the acceptability of the adversary system, if indeed it is more acceptable than other methods of fact-finding, must rest ultimately upon complex questions of political theory and psychology. I can only be suggestive here, in part repeating what others have speculated. Four reasons might be given as to why the adversary system is a more acceptable method of fact-finding in judicial trials than any other method.

Relationship to the Prevalent Political and Economic Theory

The adversary system yields greater satisfaction to the litigants and others because it is a procedure that is consistent with the prevalent social and political ideology of western society. An assertion made in the editorial page of a bar association journal illustrates this argument: "If you believe in the Anglo-Saxon common law tradition, that the individual is the important unit of our society, and the state exists to serve him, then it seems that the adversary system is preferable. If you hold a corporate view of society, that is to say, that the community is the important unit, and that the citizen must be primarily considered as a part of the corporate unit, then it seems you should champion the inquisitorial system...."[36]

Jerome Frank is well known for linking the adversary system with economic theory. In his writings he repeatedly associated it with classic, *laissez-faire*, economic theory and unbridled individualism.[37] Surprisingly, however, only recently has scholarship emerged in the English language which attempts to seriously study the influence of political and economic theory on judicial procedure. Naively, perhaps, the assumption has been made that procedure is value-free. Scholars who have turned their attention to this question in recent years seem to agree that at least at a very general and theoretical level there are connections between ideology and procedural choices.[38] The connection may not be direct, nor empirically demonstrable.[39] However, at least arguably, the adversary system can be seen as reflecting the political and economic ideology of classic English liberalism in three ways: by its emphasis upon self-interest and individual initiative; by its apparent distrust of the state; and, by the significance it attaches to the participation of the parties.

The adversary system legitimizes, indeed necessitates, a self-interested role for the parties. Thus one of its premises would appear to be consistent with the premise of the capitalist system of economic organization that if each individual strives to promote his self-interest an optimum allocation of resources will result. As Professors Neef and Nagel note, "...at the base of the adversary proceeding we encounter the old *laissez-faire* notion that each party will (or indeed can) bring out all the evidence favorable to his own side, and that if the accused is innocent (if his is the best case) he can act to 'out-produce' the presentation made by his competitors".[40] With this competitive individualism at its base, if the party with the better case — that is the case that is correct on the facts — were to lose, that result would be satisfactory in an adversary system because he, not the system, would be the author of his defeat. Initiative is rightly rewarded, laziness or ignorance penalized. This justification for the adversary system is illustrated in a statement made in a commentary on the Japan *Code of Civil Procedure* that was enacted after World War II when Japan adopted the adversary system.

> [S]ince civil litigation is essentially a dispute concerning private rights, as a matter of course, the responsibility and duty to present proof rests with the parties; it is neither the responsibility nor the duty of the court.... When the necessary facts to maintain the allegation of a party cannot be proven, the disadvantage should be borne by such party, and it is sufficient grounds for the court to issue him an unfavorable determination. The disadvantage is a consequence invited by the party himself, over and beyond which the court should neither assist a party on one side nor interfere.[41]

If this is one of the justifications for the adversary system then not many people today would likely perceive [...] it as placing very serious constraints on the judge's intervention in the trial. *Laissez-faire* theory is no longer taken as being determinative in the economic and social fields. It would be incongruous if its basic postulate was still the premise used to define the respective roles of the parties and the judge in a judicial trial.[42]

A basic socialist value is a strong emphasis on collectivism. The interests of the state and the individual are assumed to coincide, state power is not distrusted. On the other hand, liberal political philosophy is premised on a distrust of the state and public officials. The adversary system can thus be viewed in a liberal state as a means of decentralizing power, and as an attempt to prevent abuses of political power.[43] This view finds some support in the fact that the genesis of at least some rules of procedure and evidence can also be explained on the basis of a felt concern to decentralize power. Professor Friedman in his recent text, a *History of American Law*, notes that the law of evidence "... was founded in a world of mistrust and suspicion of institutions; it liked nothing better than constant checks and balances...".[44] This concern in an adversary system to decentralize power was illustrated during the period of Jacksonian democracy in the United States when a serious effort was initiated to take many rights from the judge including not only the right to comment upon the evidence but also the right to summarize the evidence to the jury.[45]

. . . .

Finally, the adversary system can be seen as being consistent with our prevalent political philosophy because it affords the parties the opportunity to participate in the making of decisions that affect their interests. Both psychological and theoretical literature in political philosophy support the view that the most acceptable type of decision in a democracy is personal choice. However, since it is clearly impossible to realize personal choice in many situations the best alternative is a system that assures to those affected by the decision some participation in the decisional process.[46] A procedural system in which the judge assumes the primary responsibility for eliciting the proof, but permits the parties to assist in the proof-taking, would provide the parties a measure of participation in the decision-making process. However, Fuller argues that the adversary system "heightens the significance of ... participation" and thus "lifts adjudication toward its optimum expression".[47] For this reason, he concludes that the adversary system is an essential characteristic of the adjudicative process.[48]

The extent to which the judge's intervention in the trial, either in clarifying evidence or in calling for new evidence, impairs the parties' sense of participation is obviously an extremely complex question

that cannot be explored in any detail here.[49] In some instances, however, it might clearly be a consideration that leads the judge to the conclusion that he should not intervene. But in other situations his intervention in the form of asking questions might actually increase the meaningfulness of the parties' participation. Everyone has different cognitive needs and if the judge makes these needs known to the parties then it will make their participation more meaningful — obviously their participation will be meaningless unless the judge's understanding of the case is the meaning that they are attempting to convey to him.[50] Also, even if the judge were to call additional proof, so long as he gives the parties the opportunity to test such proof and call rebutting proof their participation in the decision-making process would appear to remain meaningful.

Cathartic Effect

Particularly in civil suits the adversary system might be a more acceptable procedure for fact-finding than the inquisitorial system because it satisfies the psychology of the litigants by legitimizing a courtroom duel which is a sublimation of more direct forms of hostile aggression. It has been suggested that there are psychological benefits in the "battle atmosphere" of adversary litigation.[51] Charles Curtis in his book *It's Your Law* summarized this argument. He said:

> The law takes the position that we ought to be satisfied if the parties are; and it believes that the best way to get this done is to encourage them to fight it out, and dissolve their differences in dissention. We are still a combative people not yet so civilized and sophisticated as to forget that combat is one way to justice.[52]

The use of the adversary system to satisfy the primeval competitive urges of the litigants might be suggested by its genealogy. The ancestry of the trial is of course the blood feud, trial by battle and individual or class acts of revenge.[53] The justification for the adversary system is also apparent in the frequent analogy of the judicial trial to a sporting event.[54] It leads lawyers to talk of tactics and strategy and to refer to the judge as an umpire. This view of the adversary process is most clearly perceived if the trial is regarded as a "game", using that word in the sense that it is used by game theorists. The "sporting theory of justice" describes the rules of the game. There has been a social disturbance and the game is played only to gain some relief or satisfaction.[55]

The adversary system viewed as part of a game perhaps explains the system's acceptance of the result when a party loses on a technicality, even if his loss was due to a violation of one of the technical rules of evidence of procedure which regulate the game.[55] If Justice is equated to the satisfaction of the litigants then the adversary system, which is directly responsible for this satisfaction, becomes an end in itself. The true facts of the case are less important than how well the parties play the game. Reasoning from this premise, Charles Curtis concluded:

> Justice is something larger and more intimate than truth. Truth is only one of the ingredients of justice. Its whole is the satisfaction of those concerned.... The administration of justice is no more designed to elicit truth than the scientific approach is designed to extract justice from the atom.[57]

If this justification for the adversary system is correct then the judge's role in the trial would be a limited one. However, the basic premise of the argument is disputable. As one author posed the question: "Is the battle atmosphere of trial proceedings truly cathartic, in the sense of relieving tensions and aggressions that would otherwise find more destructive outlets, or does it instill an aggressive approach to problems that is incompatible with the need to compromise and co-operate in the vast majority of interpersonal contacts?"[58] Unfortunately, no serious effort has been made to resolve this question by asking the ultimate consumers of the system — the litigants. Basing a judgement on common experience, however, most people would probably agree with Professor Garlan who wrote at the height of the legal realist movement, referring to the jurisprudential theory of what he called "sporting fairness":

> The game has become too brutal, too destructive of human life, too exhaustive to those who win, and too fatal for those who lose. Living begins to look more like a struggle, than a game. The participant's sense of humor and sense of balance are worn, and the sporting morale is breaking up into a fighting morale. The sides are too unequal for successful competition, and, in the eyes of the defeated, the game looks more like exploitation than competition.[59]

While we know very little about the psychology of litigants, I suspect that most of them do not view social conflicts as social events. They come to court expecting justice, and unless the rules of substantive law are perverse, that means they expect their dispute to be resolved according to the law.[60] A theory about the judge's role that begins by assuming that rules of evidence and procedure are simply rules of competition is therefore deficient.[61]

Role of Counsel

A third aspect of the adversary system that might render it more acceptable than the inquisitorial system is the role played by counsel. It has been hypothesized that "[i]f parties perceive their adversary attorneys as having interests convergent with their own, they may begin to experience the comforting strength of belonging to a coalition the total purpose of which is to gain a favorable verdict at the expense of the opposing party".[62] Also the lawyer will be a person who, in some sense, shares in the litigant's defeat. Certain institutional characteristics of the adversary system might encourage this coalition and the apparent identity of interest between the adversary lawyer and his client. However, assuming this to be true, intervention in the trial proceedings by the trial judge is unlikely to destroy in any way this coalition or this sense of shared purpose.

Appearance of Impartiality

Finally, the adversary system might be more acceptable than an inquisitorial system because it gives the tribunal the appearance of impartiality.[63] Proponents of the Anglo-American procedural system attach great importance to the appearance of impartiality.[64] While its importance cannot be denied,[65] the intelligent control of the conduct of the trial need not leave a judge open to the charge of partiality. The possible appearance of impartiality is a matter a judge should consider when intervening, and to that extent it limits his intervention. For instance, if a judge calls a witness he must ensure that the parties have an opportunity to test the testimony of the witness and to call rebutting evidence or he might be open to the charge that he is shaping the record. If a witness is evasive in answering questions the judge must ensure that he does not appear hostile towards the witness.[66] However, if the judge intervenes in a fair and dispassionate manner this consideration should not seriously impair his ability to intervene when he thinks it is necessary.

The Adversary System Increases the Accuracy of Fact-Finding

A second justification given for the adversary system is that it is a better fact-finding mechanism than the inquisitorial system. That is to say, given all the interests that must be balanced in a procedural system more accurate factual judgments about past events are likely to be achieved using the adversary system than using some other system. This justification rests, in turn, upon two premises. The first premise is that the adversary system will result in a more thorough investigation of the facts than the inquisitorial system. The second premise is that under the adversarial system the trier of fact is more likely to reach the correct decision because during the proceedings he will not acquire a bias towards one conclusion or the other. He will be able to remain completely disinterested in the outcome until all the proof has been elicited and the arguments made. In order to define the role of the judge in the adversary system these two premises must be explored in detail.

Parties Motivated by Self-Interest Are Likely to Be Most Diligent in Presenting and Critically Evaluating All the Evidence

The first premise of this justification for the adversary system is that in an adversary proceeding the judge will, when he makes his decision, be more informed as to the facts than a similarly situated judge in an inquisitorial system. This is so, it is argued, because parties who are given a free hand in pursuing their perceived self-interest are more likely than an official motivated only by official duty to transmit to the judge all evidence favorable to their case and to critically test all unfavourable evidence presented to him.[67] Empirical studies have attempted to test whether this premise is correct.[68] However, for purposes of defining the judge's role in the adversary system the premise must be accepted as true.

The parties do not have complete control over the presentation and testing of proof and this premise of the adversary system does not require them to have such control. Control is given to the parties to promote accurate fact-finding and to further achieve this end the parties are constrained in the conduct of their case by rules of procedure and evidence. The need for these rules arises because if this premise of the adversary system is to achieve its objective a number of factors must be present in the litigation of particular disputes. The rules are intended, in part, to ensure that these factors are present. If these factors are not present in a particular case the adversary system will not achieve its goal of accurate fact-finding; or if it is to achieve this end in their absence the judge may have to regulate his conduct accordingly. Thus the judge, in defining his role must be sensitive to the presence or absence of these factors. For purposes of clarity I will discuss these factors as assumptions of the premise that the adversary system is an accurate fact-finding mechanism because parties motivated by self-interest will present and critically test all relevant evidence.

ASSUMPTION 1: THE PARTIES ARE INITIALLY MOTIVATED

The first assumption that this premise of the adversary system makes is that the parties are initially motivated to seek out all the evidence favorable to their case. This obviously depends upon both parties being equally interested in the outcome of the case, that is, equally interested in pursuing their respective rights and remedies and in opposing the rights of the other party.[69] If this is not the case, if one of the parties is not motivated to oppose the other party's case, the requisite factual investigation and presentation of proof will not take place. By way of illustration, one area where the parties may not be sufficiently interested in defending their legal rights, and in which, therefore, the adversary system breaks down, is in the area of divorce. A divorce cannot be granted under the *Divorce Act* unless the judge is satisfied that there has been no condonation or connivance on the part of the petitioner.[70] But since both parties in a particular case may want to be divorced, neither will be motivated to bring such evidence forward. In England, in recognition of the lack of motivation on the part of the parties in a divorce case, and of the state's interest in ensuring that divorces are only granted where the law authorizes them, an officer called the Queen's Proctor has been appointed.[71] His duty is to intervene in divorce cases and ferret out facts that might suggest a collusive divorce. In Canada, while a Queen's Proctor has been officially appointed in some provinces, he is seldom called upon to discharge his duties. However, section 9 of the *Divorce Act* would appear on a literal reading to require the judge to embark on his own investigation of the possibility of condonation or connivance in the undefended divorce cases.[72]

ASSUMPTION 2: THE PARTIES WILL SUSTAIN THEIR MOTIVATION

A second assumption of this premise of the adversary system is that throughout the proceedings both parties will sustain their motivation to present all the evidence. A number of rules of evidence have been developed to encourage parties to diligently pursue all the evidence favorable to their side; at least these rules can, in part, be understood by reference to this need. The privilege against self-incrimination, for instance, is sometimes justified on this basis. By denying the police the right to compel the accused to incriminate himself the rule forces them to seek more reliable evidence.[73] In the same way rules requiring the corroboration of certain witnesses who are generally assumed to be unreliable might be justified on the basis that they compel the Crown to search for additional independent evidence. It is interesting to note that these rules apply in the main against the prosecution in criminal cases — they encourage the police to seek additional evidence. Perhaps this is so because there is a fear that, at least in some cases, the prosecution motivated only by official duty, may not otherwise display the diligence in pursuing evidence that the adversary system demands.

A further rule of evidence that has the effect of encouraging the parties to independently investigate all evidence in their favour is the solicitor-client privilege — at least that part of it that the Americans call the work product rule. This rule, in general, prevents one lawyer or litigant from demanding disclosure, particularly before trial, of the other litigant's trial briefs, witness statements and related materials prepared or collected for use in the litigation. If a litigant could compel such disclosure there would be a great temptation for each litigant to rely on the other to do the investigations and to gather the necessary information. Eventually, litigants would become more and more reluctant to make an independent effort to collect information and to prepare arguments for trial. Thus, the rule contributes to the efficiency of the adversary scheme of litigation. Professor Maguire observed, "so long as we depend upon thorough advanced preparation by opposing trial counsel to accumulate the necessary information about law, fact and evidence, we must not let the drones sponge upon the busy bees. Otherwise it would not be long before all lawyers become drones".[74]

As well as forming the basis of a number of rules of evidence and procedure this assumption of party-prosecution has a more direct implication in defining the judge's role. In a system that relies on party prosecution the judge cannot intervene to such an extent in the trial that the parties begin to rely upon him to search out the facts favourable to their case and thus become less diligent themselves in seeking out the facts. There is some evidence that this attitude on the part of litigants results when the court assumes a large responsibility for proof-taking. At least it is a concern that has been expressed in countries in which the judge assumes such a role.[75] For example, in Japan, when the adversarial system was adopted in 1948 the commentators on the new *Code of Civil Procedure* noted that, "[e]xcessive interference by the Court dampens the zeal of the parties and instead — it being entirely impossible under the present trial system for the court completely to gather all evidence *ex officio* — produces a result which is accidental in nature. This is the reason why we thoroughly follow the doctrine of party presenta-

tion under the new constitution, in which the freedom and responsibility of the individual is made a fundamental principle."[76]

In some cases a judge might justifiably be unwilling to intervene to correct an oversight or to call further proof in order to discipline a prosecutor in a criminal case for the inefficient presentation of a case. However, within the framework of the present Anglo-American trial increased intervention by the judge would likely have little impact on the parties' presentation of their case. The stakes in most cases are too high to risk leaving important proof-taking to the judge's initiative. Even if increased judicial intervention did not have the effect in some cases of weakening the parties' presentation of proof, there is the further question of "whether in the long run this is outweighed by benefits, such as helping the party represented by an ineffective lawyer".[77]

ASSUMPTION 3: THE PARTIES HAVE EQUAL CAPACITY, SKILL AND RESOURCES

Party-prosecution, as a principle of the adversary system, rests on a third assumption: that each party has the ability, skill, and resources to search out the evidence favorable to his case and to present it to the court. Do the parties always have the capacity or ability to obtain access to all facts favourable to their case? The adversary system encourages parties to assume a self-interested role. While casting the parties into this role [...] ensures that they will be diligent in presenting evidence favorable to their cause, it also legitimizes or at least would appear to sanction their suppressing evidence that is unfavorable to their case. This temptation laid before the parties is regarded by many as the greatest obstacle to accurate fact-finding in the adversary system. Professor Brett argued that because "...neither of the rival theorists ... [is] bound to put forward all the data in his possession — indeed ... each ... [regards] it as proper to suppress any 'inconvenient' or inconsistent observations of whose existence he ... [knows,] 'the adversary system' must be regarded as basically unscientific in approach, and unsound".[78] He further asserted that Macaulay's justification of the adversary system that "we obtain the fairest decision when two men argue, as unfairly as possible, on opposite sides, for then it is certain that no important consideration will altogether escape notice", confuses an incentive to obtain contradictory evidence with the capacity or ability to obtain it.[79] Jerome Frank also noted, in supporting his contention that the "fight" theory of litigation does not coincide with the "truth" theory, that "frequently the partisanship of the opposing lawyers blocks the uncovering of vital evidence or leads to a presentation of vital testimony in a way that distorts it".[80] There is little a judge in any system can do to prevent the parties from suppressing or falsifying evidence.[81] A number of rules of evidence and procedure, however, attempt to provide both parties with access to as much evidence as possible. While these rules do not bear directly on the judge's role they are important in increasing our understanding of the adversary system and thus at least indirectly the judge's role in it.

First, rules of pre-trial discovery assist the parties in obtaining evidence. In civil cases, these rules generally permit a party to question the other prior to the trial about his knowledge of the facts in the case.[82] It has been argued that pre-trial discovery is inconsistent with the adversary system. However, this argument confuses means with ends. If one begins the analysis by looking at the reasons for the adversary system, the better view would appear to be that of Professor Goldstein who concluded the discovery "has as its object the harnessing of the full creative potential of the adversary process, bringing each party to trial as aware of what he must meet as his finances and his lawyer's energy and intelligence permit".[83]

Another device used both by the common law and by the legislatures to overcome the danger that the parties will suppress evidence and thus render the adversary system self-defeating is the presumption. While presumptions are sometimes created for reasons of social policy, or in order to expedite proof-taking, many presumptions operate against the party who has the superior access to the proof with respect to a particular fact. Thus it forces him to come forward with evidence that his opponent would have difficulty obtaining.[84] A simple illustration is the presumption that arises if a bailor proves that he delivered property to a bailee in good condition and that the property was returned to him in a damaged condition. Because the bailor is not likely to have access to evidence relating to the bailee's negligence the damage will be presumed, at common law, to have been caused by the negligence of the bailee. Thus the bailee will have to come forward with sufficient evidence to prove that the damage was not caused by his negligence.[85] In another situation a higher than normal standard of proof is placed on a party because he has control over the proof. The prosecutor must prove beyond a reasonable doubt that a confession is voluntary before the confession is admissible in evidence. At least one justification for imposing this high standard of proof is that the accused's adversary, the prosecution, has the ability, to some extent, to control the proof that relates to

the voluntariness of a confession. The police can usually take statements under circumstances in which there can be no doubt as to their voluntariness. The accused, if the burden were placed on him to prove involuntariness, would likely be able to produce only his own testimony as proof. If the burden on the Crown were to prove voluntariness only on the balance of probability, the confession would usually be admitted since the issue would resolve itself into the question of who is likely to be more credible, the police or the accused.[86]

To assist a party in gaining access to all the evidence favorable to his case an adverse inference is drawn against a party who fails to disclose to the court evidence which is within his power to produce.[87] This inference rests on the assumption that an "honest and fearless claimant" will produce all the evidence favorable to his case and over which he has control. Therefore if he fails to produce evidence over which he has control, it can be inferred that the evidence is unfavourable to his cause.[88] As well as drawing an adverse inference against a party who fails to produce evidence over which he has control, conduct by a party which renders it difficult or impossible for the other party to produce certain evidence will be regarded by the court as an admission of guilt or liability against that party. "Spoliation" admissions might include such things as the destruction or concealment of relevant documents or objects, intimidation, or the fabrication of evidence.[89]

Finally, to ensure that the party's strong sense of self-interest and stake in the trial [do] not result in the degeneration of the trial into fraud and deceit, interposed between the litigant and the process is a lawyer; a person who will, to a large extent, conduct the proceedings and who has a responsibility not only to the litigant, his client, but also to the process. While the exact nature of the lawyer's responsibility to the process is the subject of dispute, there is agreement that he has a responsibility in most cases to protect the process from evidence he knows to be falsified.[90]

For this assumption of the adversary system to be operative both parties must also have equal resources to investigate and collect facts favorable to their case, and both must be of equal skill in presenting these facts and in testing the facts presented that are unfavorable to their case. If the adversaries do not have equal representation — if for instance the accused in a criminal trial is unable to avail himself of effective counsel — this premise, upon which the adversary system rests, will be impaired. But even when both parties are represented by counsel, the quality of the representation will obviously seldom be equal. What is the role of the judge if one party is not represented or if his representation is inadequate? In such a situation the adversary system will fail to achieve its objective. The judge should not hesitate to intervene. Whatever dangers arise when a judge intervenes in such a situation, they are outweighed by the serious danger that is present if he does not intervene. Professor Fleming James noted that[91] "[a]nything that the law of procedure or the judge's role can do to equalize opportunity and to put a faulty presentation on the right track so that disputes are more likely to be settled on their merits, will in the long run bolster up rather than destroy the adversary system, and will increase the moral force of the decisions." Judge Breitel, in an article on judicial ethics, describes how, when he first went to the bench, he tried to be detached and disciplined in his conduct of the case — which he believed to reflect the ideal role of a judge in the adversary process. After several months, however, and after seeing numerous cases where the lawyers were not equal or were unequal to their task, he began, he says, "to feel revulsion and pangs of conscience". He concluded, "[p]assivity and silence in such a situation ceased to be an acceptable role. Indeed, it made the function and responsibility of being an umpire judge a distortion, an intolerable distortion of the whole process of the administration of justice".[92] Canadian case authorities would appear to support the proposition that when the parties' representation is unequal, the judge has a responsibility to intervene to a greater extent than he otherwise would.[93]

In many inquisitorial systems one of the principal justifications given for increasing the authority of the judge is the need to equalize the parties. The major innovation of the Austrian *Code of Civil Procedure* of 1895, which has had a great influence upon the legislation of many other European countries, was "...its emphasis on a more active role for the judge in both expediting the proceedings and of promoting the social aim of effective quality of the parties".[94] Socialist scholars have contended that there is a reluctance in bourgeois jurisprudence to give the judge a stronger role precisely so that the weaker party can be manoeuvred by the system into a disadvantaged position.[95]

A final aspect of this assumption of the adversary system is the necessity that both parties have the resources to carry out a thorough investigation of the facts. This, of course, is seldom the case. Jerome Frank suggested that in all cases there should be some kind of government intervention to help an impecunious litigant obtain evidence.[96] In criminal cases the state's facilities for investigation are obviously far superior to those of the ordinary defendant. It might be possible to reduce this disparity by providing legal aid programs with the resources necessary to locate and investigate evidence favorable to the accused. A more efficient remedy, since it does not involve the costly duplication of investigative efforts, would be to place the results of government investigations in the hands of the defence. In the United States a rule of procedure that will have this result is emerging.[97] Clearly if we do not wish to be accused of continuing to tolerate a system whose operations negate the reason for having it we will have to continue to move in this direction.

In some areas the adversary system might have to be completely abandoned because the potential parties are not likely to have sufficient resources to pursue their remedies. Where one spouse has been deserted, for instance, we assume that he or she will bring an action for maintenance. But because of the lack of resources this remedy is seldom pursued. The adversary system is simply not an adequate means of protecting civil rights in this area. Judicial intervention obviously cannot overcome this problem, and resort may be needed to administrative investigative bodies.[98]

ASSUMPTION 4: THE PARTIES WILL BE GIVEN THE OPPORTUNITY TO TEST ADVERSE EVIDENCE

Party-prosecution assumes that each party will have the opportunity and the ability to thoroughly test the evidence unfavorable to his case. It assumes, also, that this testing of adverse evidence must be done by an adversary cross-examination as opposed to a dispassionate inquisitorial examination. Opinions on the utility of cross-examination are sharply divided.[99] However, a judge presiding over an adversary proceeding must, to some extent at least, assume its efficacy. Numerous rules of evidence, the hearsay rule, the best evidence rule, and the opinion evidence rule, attempt to ensure that the parties will be given the opportunity to confront and cross-examine as effectively as possible the evidence that is introduced against them.[100] But whatever the value of cross-examination in revealing and in testing evidence, it can present grave dangers to the process. In some cases it will have the effect of misleading the trier of fact. Cross-examination, even with the best of intentions on the part of the cross-examiner, may make reliable testimony look debatable, and clear information look confused.[101] Witnesses on the witness stand, in a strange setting, compelled to give their testimony in an unnatural manner, and under the threat of a rigorous cross-examination, can very easily be led to say things that do not accurately represent their recollections. But more seriously, counsel might well use techniques in questioning a witness by which he deliberately attempts to force the witness to narrate his testimony in a way that gives a misleading impression as to his honest recollections.

Cross-examination has other costs of equal or greater significance, costs in terms of human dignity. Cross-examination sometimes results in the total humiliation and destruction of a witness without any corresponding benefits. But I have introduced here a value extrinsic to the adversary system, and I wish to discuss the judge's role only in terms of the assumptions of that system. The point is that if cross-examination is to achieve its purpose in the adversary system, the judge must ensure that it is not used as an instrument to distort and obscure testimony. That is not abandoning his role in the adversary system, it is assuming the responsibility of his role. Eliciting the testimony of children is an area, for instance, where there might be a need for strong intervention by the judge, perhaps to the point where all the questions directed to the child are asked through the judge. Harsh and critical cross-examination techniques can confuse the child to the point where he is unable to give intelligible answers.[102]

The judge is also in a dilemma when cross-examination has proved to be ineffective, or when counsel declines to cross-examine a witness about whose perception of the event described, for instance, the judge is in serious doubt. Should he ask questions, the answer to which he feels might assist him in evaluating the witness's perception? The answer would appear obvious. While certain dangers arise when the judge asks questions, these dangers are overridden by the fact that if the questions are not asked, the adversary system will have failed to achieve its objective.

ASSUMPTION 5: ALL INTERESTS AFFECTED ARE REPRESENTED

Finally, the principle of party-prosecution assumes that all interests affected by the adjudication are represented by the parties. The adversary system depends upon the parties to bring forward the information upon which the judge will rely in reaching his decision. In reaching a decision the judge must reconcile all the competing interests affected by his decision. If he does not receive information about some of these interests because they are interests of no immediate concern to the parties before him the adversary system will be a defective method of fact-finding for that decision. The importance of this assumption can be illustrated by reference to two

areas. In a custody proceeding the adversaries are commonly seen to be the parents of the child, both of whom will supply the court with information as to why they should take custody of the child. Both will obviously be arguing in their own perceived best interest. However, the real issue in the case is the best interest of the child. In such a situation it is possible that facts relevant to the real issue in the case will not be presented to the judge by the parties and if he is to reach a decision based on all relevant information, he will have to intervene in the fact-finding.[103]

Another area in which the adversaries will not represent all the interests might be described broadly, if not with some circularity, as being the area of public interest law, such as environmental, consumer protection law. Again, in these areas, the wise judge might well call upon the intervention of third parties to represent those interests not represented by the immediate parties to the particular dispute. At the appellant level this is commonly done by means of asking for or inviting *amicus curiae* factums. Justice Thurgood Marshall of the United States Supreme Court recently called upon the organized bar to finance public interest law on the grounds that the practice of public interest law is a vital function of the adversary system since that system presupposes representation of all interests affected.[104]

The Adversary System Counteracts Bias in Decision-Making

The second reason often given as to why the adversary system leads to more accurate fact-finding than an inquisitorial system is that the adversary system permits the judge to remain unbiased as between the parties throughout the proceedings.[105] Bias is a word used in a wide variety of senses, many of which shade into each other.[106] In this context, where important consequences are being drawn from the concept, it is particularly important to be clear about its meaning.

Bias in this context does not mean, as it commonly means in other contexts, a preconceived point of view about issues of law or policy, a personal prejudice against certain types of parties, or bias in the sense of being personally interested in the outcome of the case. No fact-finding mechanism can remove these types of biases. It refers to a bias or prejudgment that is acquired by a decision-maker because of the mechanism of fact-finding used. If the judge takes an active part in proof-taking, it could be argued that he might acquire a bias towards one party or the other for one of the following reasons:

1. If the judge questions a witness and the witness is evasive, disrespectful, hostile, or in some way does not live up to the expectations of the judge, the judge may become antagonistic towards the witness and therefore tend to discredit his testimony.

2. If the judge in proof-taking is responsible for having some important evidence revealed, he may tend to give too much weight to that evidence, either because he is overly impressed with the skilful manner in which the evidence was presented, or because it is important to him that his intervention is seen to have served a useful purpose.

3. The judge may, in his investigation, become so concerned about a detail of the case that the balance of the evidence will escape his careful attention. This is perhaps the kind of consideration that judges are concerned about when they assert that their ability to evaluate the credibility of a witness is impaired if they themselves become too involved in examining a witness. That is to say, as an investigator preoccupied with his own line of thought, the judge may unconsciously fail to explore important points, may amass so much detail that obvious truths are obscured, or may not carefully observe all of the diverse matters, such as demeanor evidence, that he should take into consideration in evaluating the probative value of testimonial proof.

4. A fourth source of bias that is not present in the adversary system, but which one might argue is present in the inquisitorial system, is the bias that is acquired when the judge is presented with a file of the evidence before the case is heard by him. In an inquisitorial system the judge will of course have had to study the documents contained in the file with some care if he is to be effective in carrying out the proof-taking at trial. There is an obvious danger that the information supplied in the file will bias the judge towards one side or the other. As Glanville Williams noted, "Our reaction to the French system is that it creates a danger that the point of view of the prosecution will communicate itself to the judge before the case has been heard."[107]

5. Finally, it has been contended that the adversary system is an unbiasing fact-finding technique because it counteracts what psychologists call decision-maker bias. Decision-maker bias is acquired when a decision-maker himself investigates the facts upon which he is to rest his

judgement.[108] It arises because of the need when one begins to investigate facts to form certain tentative hypotheses about the reality that one is called upon to reconstruct. More or less imperceptively, these preconceptions influence the course of the investigation. As well, facts which confirm the original hypothesis will make a strong imprint upon the mind, while facts that run counter to it are received with diverted attention. This bias, which arises from the process of fact-finding, is avoided in the adversary system, it is argued. It is avoided because, in the adversary system, the judge, since he is not responsible for the investigation, is able to avoid any judgment of the case until he has heard all the evidence.

While all of these kinds of bias may be present in an adversary proceeding, none of them should limit to any great extent, within the framework of our present trial, the judge's intelligent intervention in the case. A recognition of their presence should permit the judge to conduct the proceedings in a fashion that minimizes the dangers that might arise.

Conclusion

I suggested at the outset of this paper that the role of the judge, at least the limits of his intervention in the conduct of the trial, must be established by a careful reference to the premises of the adversary system. However, in some sense, that is only a starting point in defining his role. The adversary system is not a moral axiom. We do [not] maintain it for its own sake, and the values that we seek by use of the adversary system — the acceptability of the process, and accuracy in fact-finding — are only two of the process values that must be pursued in any system of adjudication. As well as these values, any procedural system designed to resolve disputes must strike a balance among many other process values such as finality, expedition, administrative efficiency, and the protection of the dignity of the participants. Interests extrinsic to the process must also be considered, for instance, the protection of important relationships, the control of governmental power, and the protection of the innocent in criminal cases. This is not the place to expand on these interests and their implications, I merely mention them, and the fact that they must be considered by the judge in defining his role in particular situations, in order to place the discussion in this paper in its larger context.

I do not intend to explore the specific instances where a judge might be called upon to intervene in a trial. However, I will make reference to one such instance to illustrate how the premises of the adversary system could form the guidelines upon which the judge relies in defining the extent of his intervention. If a judge decided that a person, whom neither party had called, could perhaps give relevant testimony, the following dangers, in terms of the adversary system, might arise if he called that person as a witness himself: it could weaken the motivating force of the parties in calling all evidence favorable to their case, they might become careless about calling evidence knowing that if they do not call the evidence the judge will, or they might not call a witness hoping that the judge will and thus give a witness favorable to them the appearance of objectivity; it might bias the trier of fact in favour of that witness's testimony, the judge might acquire a commitment to the witness's credibility because of his interest in making his efforts appear worthwhile, the jury might give a witness called by the judge undue weight because of the witness's apparent objectivity; it could give the judge the appearance of partiality, if the witness gives testimony adverse to the accused, for instance, the judge, who called the witness, might appear to be biased against the accused; it could render the judge's ultimate decision less acceptable to the parties, if they view his intervention as an unjustified intrusion in their private fight; or, it could lead to inaccurate fact-finding if the judge called the witness at a time which made it difficult for one of the parties to lead evidence rebutting the testimony, or at a time when it had the effect of weakening the persuasive force of one of the parties' case. As well as these considerations, when the judge calls a witness a number of purely pragmatic procedural considerations arise: who can examine, cross-examine and impeach the witness; if the judge questions the witness, how do the parties effectively object to any improper questions or other

procedural errors; and, how does the judge, who does not likely have any detailed or even perhaps general knowledge about the proof in the case until it unfolds before him, know that his intervention is not going to simply waste time.

While I do not have time to explore each of these dangers, and others that might rise in specific contexts, in detail, it should be clear that they provide the judge a wide latitude in which to call witnesses in appropriate cases. A similar analysis could be done for each specific instance where a judge might intervene in a trial. Giving due considerations to the dangers that might be present in specific instances, if the judge thinks in a particular case it would be helpful, I see no reason why he should hesitate, for instance, to call his own witnesses, to question witnesses both to clarify and to develop additional evidence, to invite witnesses to give a narrative account of their testimony, to invite perhaps three or four witnesses to be sworn and take their evidence in a conference-room style, to intervene to protect witnesses from harassment and confusing questions, or to advise the parties in the presentation of their case so that they do not commit procedural errors.

In conclusion, there is undoubtedly considerable experience and knowledge of human nature captured in the adversary system. What I have attempted to do is re-examine the assumptions of the adversary system and review the judge's role in light of these assumptions. My conclusion is that the adversary system imposes on the judge as well as the parties an important and active role in the conduct of the trial.[109] The adversary system is not an end in itself; it is a procedural device which we have adopted in the pursuit of more ultimate process values. The judge has responsibility not only to arrive at a decision but also to ensure that these process values are attained.

(b)   Science, Law, and the Expert Witness†

Joseph Sanders

[S]cientific inquiry is by nature tentative and thoroughly fallibilist; it focuses on the general law or principle rather than the particular case; its core values are intellectual honesty and willingness to share evidence.... So it is hardly surprising that the legal system has had trouble

† (2009) 1 Law and Contemporary Problems 63 at 63–71, 73–80, 88–90. [Notes and/or references omitted.] Reproduced with permission.

handling scientific testimony, for the legal culture could hardly be more different: adversarial; focused on the specific case; formally procedurally anchored; valuing promptness and finality....[1]

I. INTRODUCTION

... [T]he central issue was how legal conventions and scientific conventions differ, and, insofar as they do differ, what impact this has on the behavior of individuals at the interface of law and science.[2] This article addresses one aspect of that question: how these conventions affect the behavior of expert witnesses when they appear in court in both civil and criminal cases. Expert witnessing is a particularly useful place to observe the clash of legal and scientific conventions because it is here that one group of people (scientific experts) who are integrated into one set of conventions are challenged by the expectations of a different set of conventions.

Section II of this article reviews differences in scientific and legal conventions as they apply to expert knowledge. Section III discusses two central reasons for these differences: adversarialism and closure. Section IV focuses on expert testimony. It indicates how differences in legal and scientific conventions caused by adversarialism and the law's need for closure create role conflicts for experts, as well as uncertainty about the level of justification an expert should have before expressing an opinion in court.[3] The article concludes with some thoughts about the appropriate accommodation between scientific and legal conventions.

II   SCIENTIFIC AND LEGAL CONVENTIONS CONCERNING EXPERT KNOWLEDGE

A.   Scientific Conventions

What are the conventions surrounding scientific expert knowledge?[4] Most people who study the "doing of science" would agree that there is no special "scientific method" that is different from and better than other ways of understanding the world.[5] The successes of the natural sciences over the last few centuries are not the result of a special way of going about the production of knowledge.[6]

But methods are a core part of scientific conventions. Each corner of the scientific enterprise is chock full of methodological prescriptions. A substantial part of having what passes for scientific expertise in a field is an ability to use the tools of the trade and an appreciation of the nuances of the

methods of investigation commonly employed in the discipline. Susan Haack divides these aids to understanding into three categories: "helps" to the senses, "helps" to reasoning, and "helps" to evidence-sharing and intellectual honesty.[7]

. . . .

This article focuses on the second and third set of aids: aids to reasoning and aids to evidence-sharing and intellectual honesty. The common mathematical and logical aids to reasoning are designed to facilitate not simply inquiry, but inquiry of a certain type: inquiry into general laws or principles. This does not mean that scientists are uninterested in the particular case; many scientists and individuals in fields such as engineering that rely on science may devote most of their energy to specific situations. But the heroes of science are those who are able to put forth explanations in terms of general laws that explain myriad particular observations.

This interest in the general and the generalizable leads to a second component of scientific conventions concerning knowledge — the lack of a timetable. An inquiry takes as long as it takes and, with respect to many questions, the answer experts are most comfortable with is, "We don't know." "We don't know" does not necessarily mean that we don't have a guess. Often it means we do not have enough evidence of the kind we find persuasive to support a conclusion.[10]

Aids to evidence-sharing and intellectual honesty are central components of the ethical culture of the scientific enterprise. They are part of what Merton described as a "norm of communism" — calls for the sharing of data and results.[11] Peer review and publication are also part of this set of aids. Although these latter devices may play a small role in detecting intellectual dishonesty, most studies that have explored the peer-review process agree that it is better suited to evidence-sharing than to ferreting out deception.[12] As Kitcher notes, scientific communication and cooperation within the scientific community usually are based on the risky assumption that scientists can trust one another to tell the truth as they understand it.[13] Scientists rarely prepare for deception and betrayal. Except when specifically warranted by circumstances, attacks that imply less than honest communication are out of bounds.[14] This is one reason the peer-review process often appears to fall short when asked to perform the role of assessing the truth of assertions made in a manuscript. Were scientists to turn the peer-review process into a search for deception, they would perhaps prevent a few cases of scientific fraud, but only at the cost of an enormous amount of investigator time and of undermining the scientific culture of trust.

In the long run, the failure of others to replicate one's alleged findings may act as a counterweight to fabricated results; but in the short run, the culture of honesty is the primary bulwark against deception. At the core of this culture are norms calling on individuals to be honest with themselves and others about what the evidence is, and to adopt what Merton called "a posture of disinterestedness."[15] Intellectual honesty and disinterestedness are threatened by the pressures that test the commitment to any such norms: reputation, money, job security, et cetera. These pressures come from all sides — from businesses that fund one's research, from the need to publish significant results in order to obtain future grants, from lawyers prepared to offer substantial remuneration to testify in court, and insidiously, from one's own political and social values that cause one to assess evidence somewhat differently when it appears to affect those values. What is most noteworthy, perhaps, is not that individuals succumb to such pressures, but that so often they do not, a fact that is a testament to the internalization of this scientific convention.

How then should we summarize the conventions of expert (scientific) knowledge? Four components are particularly relevant to this discussion. Scientific conventions involve: (1) searching for the general and theoretical, (2) employing the methods and techniques accepted by one's field, (3) an attitude of agnosticism that encourages waiting for persuasive evidence before making up one's mind, and (4) a commitment to sharing data, intellectual honesty, and disinterestedness. How do these stack up against legal conventions concerning expert knowledge?

B. Legal Conventions

In his article in this symposium, Professor Kritzer notes that legal conventions differ from scientific conventions in at least three ways relevant to the preceding discussion: differences in data sources, differences in mindset toward drawing conclusions, and differences in the approach to evidence.[16] A word about each of these is in order.

If scientific conventions focus on systematic and general knowledge, legal inquiry, at least in the context of most trials, focuses on experience and specific events. To be sure, law is often concerned with general questions, such as, "Does drug X cause injury to Y?" However, law is nearly always also concerned with what happened to a specific person at a particular point in time.

The second difference is what Professor Kritzer calls mindset. He quotes a comment from an engineer who had never appeared in court before, concerning one of his first preparation sessions with a trial attorney named Bill:

> Bill asked me a question about whether the belt was on or not, the lap belt. And I said, "Well, could have been. But then, it may not have been." Woo, rockets went off. "What do you mean? You're my expert in this case, and you say it 'could be' or 'couldn't be?' Look, I'm going to tell you. The other side doesn't waffle. They pick one view. And they will push that view. And they will make their case in front of a jury. And there will be no misunderstanding. There will be no gray area. They will take a position one way or the other and make it stick. Now, they don't have any other course of action. That's their life. They make their living going in front of juries and making statements, whether they have facts to back them up or not. Now you, you can go back to designing cars. You have another career. They don't. You better start thinking like they do.[17]

In this passage, the expert's initial position reflects the scientific convention that values caution and a "wait and see" attitude. It runs headlong into the legal convention that pushes the witness to make a decision and to do so with a reasonable degree of certainty.[18]

The legal preference for certainty is related to a third difference. Expert knowledge in law is a partisan resource. Each party gets to choose which experts to present and to shape its presentation in the way that puts the party's case in the best possible light. There is no obligation to take a critical, disinterested look at all the evidence and, as Kritzer notes, it is part of the partisan nature of the process that an advocate is expected to do everything possible to cast doubt on opposing testimony, even when the advocate knows that the testimony is accurate.[19] It goes without saying that this approach is contrary to scientific conventions of data sharing, intellectual honesty, and disinterestedness.

Professors Kritzer and Haack are quick to observe that this distinction describes an ideal. On the one hand, scientists are not always disinterested. They often become advocates for their preferred hypothesis or theory. Moreover, all of us, scientists included, are prone to what psychologists call confirmation bias.[20] On the other hand, the legal system places limits on partisanship. Witnesses are sworn to tell the "whole truth." But if it is important to avoid the trap of a false dichotomy, it is equally important to eschew an attitude that science and law are the same. There are real differences. The norm among scientists is to take a critical approach to evidence. That norm is not always followed. But it is different from the legal arena where the norm is to adopt a partisan approach to evidence.

III REASONS FOR THE DIFFERENT APPROACHES TO EXPERT KNOWLEDGE

Two factors explain much of the difference in legal and scientific approaches to expert knowledge. They are the U.S. adversarial system and a legal system's need for prompt closure. Understanding how each of these factors influences legal conventions is necessary if we are to find an appropriate accommodation when science enters the courtroom.

A. Adversarialism

One source of differences between legal and scientific conventions is the U.S. legal system's commitment to adversarial processes — most importantly, the partisan use of expert knowledge. Adversarial processes are a part of a larger commitment to what Robert Kagan terms "adversarial legalism."[21] Oscar Chase focuses on four components that define U.S. adversarial processes: (1) the civil jury, (2) the use of party-controlled pretrial investigation, (3) the relatively passive role of the judge at the trial or hearing, and (4) the method of obtaining and using expert opinions (that is, parties hire and prepare experts).[22] Note that three of these components — party-controlled, pretrial investigation, passive judiciary, and party selection and employment of experts — are directly tied to the idea that expert knowledge is a partisan resource. Moreover, the features interact with each other to heighten the overall level of adversarialism. Party control of pretrial investigations and a relatively passive judiciary both enhance the effect of the party selection of witnesses.

. . . . .

Although a commitment to adversarial procedures is an important source of differences between legal and scientific conventions concerning evidence, one should not lose sight of the fact that this commitment is an incidental feature of a legal system.[27] To claim that our strong commitment to adversarial procedures is an incidental feature may sound heretical to a large portion of the U.S. legal community that has little knowledge [of] or interest in other legal systems and whose members have been steeped in adversarial ideology since law school. From a wider international perspective, however, our commitment to the party selection of experts is unusual and, judging by the operation of other legal systems, unnecessary.

B. Closure

The second source of differences in legal and scientific conventions is the law's need for closure. Both science and law deal with controversy, and both, therefore, must be concerned with how controversies come to an end. The end of a controversy may be influenced by both epistemic and nonepistemic factors. Epistemic factors are those that people involved in the controversy regard as knowledge-based and therefore internal to the very understanding of the problem. Nonepistemic factors are those factors external to the undertaking of the issue as an endeavor of rational, empirical investigation.[28]

Controversies may conclude in a number of ways. Two types of closure are particularly relevant to this discussion: closure by way of *resolution* and by way of *termination*.[29] A controversy is resolved when agreement is reached on the merits of the case. The factors involved are necessarily epistemic. Termination occurs when nonepistemic factors, such as an authoritative ruling by some official agency, brings an end to a controversy. These two types of closure are not mutually exclusive. Closure is often accomplished by a combination of these processes. However, both empirically and normatively, different arenas assign different weights to methods of closure. The conventions of science value resolution as a proper way to resolve questions. And in one sense, science lives up to this idea. Closure without substantial resolution is very rare in science. ...

The problem with resolution as a strategy to end controversies is that it is open-ended. Science's commitment to resolution produces the attitude of agnosticism that values doubt and encourages waiting for persuasive evidence before making up one's mind. Given that a central objective of courts is to bring controversies to an end in reasonably prompt fashion, it is not surprising that the legal system is rarely willing to wait for an issue to be resolved before concluding litigation. Instead, courts usually rely on termination, that is, an authoritative ruling by the court, to bring an end to a controversy.

This does not mean that courts are indifferent to achieving the factually (and legally) correct outcome. They would prefer to get it right, and thus resolution is a goal, but one to be achieved within

341

the boundaries of the court's obligation to resolve disputes in a timely fashion. Reopening a case that has been decided is a rare phenomenon.[31]

. . . .

In sum, closure is a more fundamental issue than adversarialism. Unless we are prepared to craft a tort system that is indifferent to questions of causation, the law's need for relatively prompt closure stands in direct conflict with the scientific convention that closure should only occur when a consensus forms, however long that might be. Moreover, closure requires the fact finder to address specific questions concerning the parties before it, questions that scientists may be relatively less prepared to answer.

IV ADVERSARIALISM, CLOSURE AND EXPERT WITNESSES

Given these reasons for the differences between legal and scientific conventions, how do they affect our understanding of expert witnessing? The question can be divided into two parts: the *role* the expert should assume and the *justification* an expert should require before making an assertion.

A. Role

From the point of view of many experts, the most troublesome aspect of expert witnessing is balancing the scientific conventions of data-sharing, intellectual honesty, and disinterestedness with legal conventions that treat expert knowledge as a partisan resource. This, ultimately, translates into a question of the expert's proper role. One vision is of the expert as an educator.[50] The expert is someone who conveys the knowledge of her field in a way that permits the fact finder to understand the strengths and weaknesses of the parties' arguments. A different vision is the expert as part of the team that hired her, a party's advocate.[51] The tension between the two is something felt by many experts. The following comment is typical:

> I always experience a certain amount of tension in the process of testifying. The conflict is between whether I am testifying for the people who hired me or whether I am a servant of the court, and am simply supposed to answer questions and however the questions come up, the answers fall where they will.[52]

Note that this tension is not between the ideal expressed in scientific conventions and the ideal embodied in the law. The legal ideal is identical to the scientific convention. It conceives of the expert witness as a source of independent and disinterested information.[53] The expert is a witness, not an advocate, and as a witness the expert takes the typical oath promising to tell "the truth, the whole truth, and nothing but the truth." This is a promise not only not to lie, but not to engage in half-truths and withheld truths.[54] It is the legal system's commitment to adversarialism in the form of party control of expert witnesses that creates substantial pressures on experts to adopt a more party-oriented point of view.

What evidence we have suggests that adversarial procedures do indeed take their toll. Indeed, in one survey of experts, seventy-seven percent agreed with the statement that lawyers manipulate their experts to weaken unfavorable testimony and to strengthen favorable testimony, and fifty-seven percent agree that lawyers urge their experts to be less tentative.[55] Judges, too, complain about expert-witness bias. ...

... When federal judges are asked about problems they encounter with expert testimony, the most-frequently mentioned problem is that experts abandon objectivity and become advocates for the side that hired them.[57]

. . . .

... Some research on witnesses confirms this effect. In one study, Shepard and Vidmar conducted an experiment in which undergraduates viewed a slide show and heard an audio tape depicting a fight.[61] The "witnesses" then were interviewed by either an adversary or a nonadversary lawyer and a week later testified about what they saw.[62] Witnesses interviewed by the adversary lawyer biased their testimony in favor of the lawyer's client, and this bias affected impressions of the factual evidence and responsibility judgments of "naive" adjudicators — those unaware of who had interviewed the witness.[63]

Several studies of accountants affirm this result. Bazerman and colleagues have explored what they call a "self-serving bias."[64] They gave undergraduate and business students a complex set of information about a potential sale of a fictional company and asked them to estimate its value. The subjects were assigned different roles — buyer, seller, buyer's auditor, and seller's auditor. Most relevant for purposes of showing that expert bias is a byproduct of an adversarial system is the comparison of those subjects asked to play the two auditor roles. Their valuations were biased in their client's favor in both a public statement about the company's worth and in private communication to their client. At the end of the experiment, the subjects were asked to estimate the company's "true value" and were told that they would be rewarded according to how close their private judgments were to those of impartial experts. Even with this incentive, subjects asked to play the role of the buyer's auditor produced estimates that were on average thirty percent higher than the estimates of the subjects asked to play the role of the seller's auditor.[65]

. . . .

One must be careful in drawing conclusions from studies that are so different from the actual expert-witnessing experience. However, the results do suggest that very weak role manipulations can produce biasing effects even among witnesses who themselves have no psychological or economic interest in a given outcome. In general, these studies suggest that experts are more likely to come to the stand with "hot biases."[68] Such biases are not necessarily intentional, but they are directionally motivated. The experts are more likely to want a certain outcome to prevail.[69]

Party control over the selection of experts produces bias not only by pushing experts to a more one-sided view than the individual expert might express if placed in a different role; it produces bias in the selection process itself. Witnesses are chosen because they prefer a point of view, and the very choice of experts clouds the degree of consensus that may surround a topic. Other aspects of the adversarial trial produce similar effects. ...

Given the many shortcomings of the present arrangement, complaints about the use of expert witnesses have a long history, beginning shortly after party control of experts became the norm,[71] and continuing to the present time.[72] These concerns have [led] to many proposals designed to lessen the adversarial nature of expert testimony. They include expert panels, neutral experts, court-appointed experts, and science courts. None of the proposals has met with much success, although many of them would be an improvement over the status quo. A less-adversarial selection of experts would assist juries by giving them a more balanced view of the scientific issues at stake.

These proposals are resisted precisely because they interfere with attorney control and, more fundamentally, they challenge adversarial procedures that are, as Kessler notes, far more than a legal technique and instead encompass an entire political image of justice.[73] In light of this ideology, substantial movements away from party-witness experts seems unlikely.[74]

. . . .

... If we are unwilling to move away from party selection as the primary method of witness selection, we can at least better arm experts to resist efforts by their attorneys to have them adopt a more partisan stance. Many professional associations have codes of ethical conduct that call upon experts to adopt a disinterested, educator posture,[82] but except for the oath taken when sworn in to testify, courts do not systematically reinforce that this is how the law wishes experts to behave as well. ...

. . . .

The underlying purposes of the code are to inform experts that their duty is to the court and to reinforce the ideal of a disinterested, educator role for experts. Even if the code of conduct is only hortatory, without any sanctions for its violation, it underlines that both the court and the professional organization expect an expert to adopt a neutral, educator role when testifying and that just because one of the parties engaged the expert should not present an ethical role conflict. At the very least, such a code provides some ammunition to the conscientious expert when dealing with her attorney. ...

B.   Justification

. . . .

5.   *Summary*

The question of what constitutes sufficient justification poses more serious intellectual and ethical issues than does the question of what role an expert should adopt. Our choices are either to endorse the level of justification routinely employed by experts in a field, or to endorse some lesser standard. In my judgment, the "same intellectual rigor" standard or something like it is the most appropriate benchmark for judging justificatory sufficiency, but this standard must be understood against the backdrop of the law's need for closure. The standard should be no more restrictive than the standard an expert might use in other contexts in which closure is needed. What this implies is a shrinkage of the "let's wait and see" category of responses. Ideally, it also implies that the expert would acknowledge this fact in his testimony.[119] Unfortunately, this latter hope is likely to be dashed on the rocks of the adversarial selection of experts, which pushes not simply for an opinion, but for an opinion that is expressed with a substantial degree of certainty.

V CONCLUSION: ACCOMMODATING LEGAL AND SCIENTIFIC CONVENTIONS

Nearly everyone agrees that there are several important differences between legal and scientific conventions toward knowledge. As Professors Haack and Kritzer note, scientific inquiry involves (1) searching for the general and theoretical, (2) doing so by employing the methods and techniques accepted by one's field, (3) an attitude of agnosticism that encourages waiting for persuasive evidence before making up one's mind, and (4) a commitment to sharing data, intellectual honesty, and disinterestedness.[120] In contrast, legal inquiry (1) focuses more on experience and specific events, (2) desires certainty in expert judgments, and (3) views expert knowledge as a partisan resource.[121]

A central question is why we observe these differences. There are two central causes: the adversarial nature of U.S. trials and the need for closure. ... A key component of U.S. adversarialism is the party selection of experts. Closure is also a central component of our legal system, but a component for which there seems to be no reasonable alternative as long as we believe that a key purpose of a legal system is to permit people to resolve disputes peaceably.

Both of these factors influence all of the differences between scientific and legal conventions, but each has its greatest effect on one of them, by subtly, and sometimes not so subtly altering the role experts play in court. Adversarialism has its greatest impact on the last difference between legal and scientific conventions: science's commitment to sharing data, intellectual honesty, and disinterestedness versus law's view of expert knowledge as a partisan resource. Closure has its greatest impact on the second difference: science's attitude of agnosticism versus law's desire for greater willingness on the part of an expert to express an opinion.

If one accepts the above analysis, it leads to a few conclusions about how law ought to accommodate scientific conventions in the context of expert witnesses. First, as to role, the law should take substantial steps to adopt scientific conventions on the role experts play in court. Abandoning party selection of experts in favor of a European-style, court-appointed–experts system seems to be beyond our reach, but other steps could move law in the direction of science. I particularly favor trying something like what is done in New South Wales, where each expert is given a code of conduct that makes clear the fact that the experts' obligation is to the court

and not the party who engaged them. Such steps not only move the law-in-practice toward the scientific norm, they actually move the law toward its own ideal.

Such a move has a number of potential advantages. It may help jurors understand cases better by helping them to understand the many things scientists agree upon, as well as those things that are legitimately in controversy. Second, it may increase the willingness of a number of experts who currently refuse to participate in the role of expert to offer their expertise to the courts. Third, it may improve the opinion each side has of the other. The very process of forcing experts into the role of advocate has the perverse effect of causing the legal profession to look down on experts as hired guns and causes many experts to view law as a place where the search for truth is absent. Procedures that make expert witnessing less adversarial may ameliorate this mutual condescension.

If law should give way to scientific conventions concerning the expert's role, science must make some concessions to law when it comes to justification. Scientific agnosticism concerning the truth of a causal assertion or a theory must be moderated to accommodate the law's need for closure. It is important to note the contours of this accommodation. First, it is not a requirement that scientists become more "certain" of their judgment. The law's interest in certainty is more a result of adversarialism than of a need for closure. What closure does require is that experts be willing to abandon a "wait and see" response when in possession of probative, but limited, evidence on some point. Moreover, this is not a request unique to legal proceedings. There are many affairs of life in which a need for a decision causes us to ask experts for their best guess.

Finally, a word about law's focus on the specific versus science's focus on the general: Here, scientific communities will perform a great service to law when they develop methods that allow experts to say more with more certainty about a particular case. Any advances in science that give experts a better purchase on the questions of specific causation will find immediate application in the law, as the history of DNA testing has so clearly demonstrated over the last couple of decades. The emerging field of toxiogenomics offers to have a similar impact on the area of toxic torts in the future.[122] Law's need for this information demonstrates a fundamental point that can easily be lost in discussions about the differences between legal and scientific conventions: Law and science share many conventions. Most important, both would prefer as much as possible that controversies end by resolution — an agreement, based on the evidence, that the proper outcome has been reached. This may not be possible with respect to the litigants themselves, but it is possible with respect to the rest of us who would prefer that in both science and in law [] we do our best to "get it right."

(c) Wrongful Convictions: Adversarial and Inquisitorial Themes†

Kent Roach

I. INTRODUCTION

The discovery of wrongful convictions in Anglo-American systems over the last twenty years has shaken confidence in the adversarial[1] system of criminal justice. In the United States, commentators have identified 340 exonerations between 1989 and 2003,[2] including 245 DNA exonerations since the first such exoneration in 1989.[3] In the United Kingdom, the Criminal Cases Review Commission (CCRC) has, from the start of its work in 1997, ordered 444 cases referred back to the Court of Appeal because of suspected miscarriages of justice.[4] Convictions have been quashed in 290 of those cases.[5] In Canada, growing awareness of wrongful convictions, including a number of high-profile wrongful convictions, led the Supreme Court in 2001 to overrule 1991 precedents and to hold that the risk of wrongful convictions made it unconstitutional to extradite fugitives without assurances that the death penalty would not be applied.[6] No fewer than six commissions of inquiry in Canada have recommended that the government create a permanent criminal case review commission to investigate claims of wrongful convictions with a number of the inquiries defending such commissions as inquisitorial and non-adversarial.[7]

All around the common-law world, criminal justice systems have produced wrongful convictions in which innocent people have been convicted or in which serious doubts have been placed on the reliability of results produced by adversarial criminal trials. Although most of the attention has been devoted to the immediate causes of wrongful convictions such as faulty eyewitness identification, police tunnel vision, false confessions, and faulty scientific evidence, commentators have begun to ask whether the significant numbers of wrongful convictions may not be a symptom of flaws in the adversarial system and, in particular, its qualified commitment to the discovery of truth.[8]

There is nothing new in the argument that the adversarial system contributes to wrongful convictions. In 1932, Edwin Borchard wrote a pioneering book detailing sixty-five miscarriages of justice.[9] He identified almost all of the immediate causes that are associated with wrongful convictions today. Moreover, he hinted that the adversarial system was frequently to blame in the sense that convictions were often regarded "as a personal victory calculated to enhance the prestige of the prosecutor"[10] while "the inability to engage competent attorneys makes it often impossible for the accused to establish his innocence."[11] Professor Borchard looked to Europe for answers, particularly with regard to the ability in many continental systems to obtain indemnity for errors committed by prosecutors and even judges.[12] He appealed to inquisitorial ideals when he recommended the creation of "an independent public investigating committee," believing that "the haphazard investigations now often instigated are hardly adequate or efficient."[13]

In 1957, Jerome and Barbara Frank related wrongful convictions to the idea that the criminal trial was "a sort of game or sporting event."[14] They noted that the defense was often mismatched in such a game and looked to Scandinavia as an example where there was not only public legal aid, but where defense counsel "can call on government officials, at government expense, to make all necessary investigations (including searches for witnesses and documents) and to supply analyses of handwriting as well as expert testimony on behalf of the defendant."[15]

---

† (2010) 35 N.C. J. INT'L L. & COM. REG. 387 at 388–91, 424–28, 431–39, 444–46. [Notes and/or references omitted.] Reproduced with permission.

They also criticized plea-bargaining as a potential source of wrongful convictions and compared restrictions on the introduction of new evidence on appeal to the idea "that a criminal trial is a sort of prize fight."[16] They criticized the jury as an amateur trier of fact compared to "well-trained, experienced trial judges."[17] Prosecutors, in their view, should be trained professionals on the European model[18] with disclosure and discovery obligations.[19] Finally, they argued that the criminal trial "should not be a game; it should be a diligent search for the truth."[20] There is nothing particularly new to the idea that inquisitorial systems might be better suited than adversarial systems in preventing wrongful convictions, and such conclusions have been reached by some of the best minds that have examined the phenomena of wrongful convictions.[21]

It should not be assumed that wrongful convictions do not occur in inquisitorial systems. One of the main findings about wrongful convictions in Anglo-American systems, namely that they are often the product of a phenomenon affecting police, prosecutors, and courts known as tunnel vision or confirmation bias, seems intuitively to be even more prevalent in inquisitorial rather than adversarial systems. In other words, tunnel vision — a process in which evidence is wrongly interpreted or discarded so as to confirm a suspect's guilt and the investigator's cognitive biases — seems even more likely to occur in official investigations conducted by prosecutors or judges in inquisitorial trials than in an adversary system. Wrongful convictions provide an excellent and timely context to reflect on the comparative strengths and weaknesses of adversarial and inquisitorial systems, including what each system can learn from the other and the potential for creative hybrids between the two systems.[22]

. . . .

IV. SOME INQUISITORIALLY-INSPIRED REMEDIES FOR WRONGFUL CONVICTIONS

This section will outline some inquisitorially inspired reforms that might help prevent or remedy wrongful convictions. There are some common analytical features to inquisitorially inspired reforms. They rely on a more proactive stance by the judge and the state in ensuring that criminal cases are resolved in a manner that discovers the truth of the allegation. Inquisitorial features generally place less reliance on party presentation of the evidence and the strategic decision-making of the parties in resolving the case.

The idea in this section is not to suggest that features of inquisitorial systems could simply be transplanted or even borrowed by adversarial systems. The end result of any reform will inevitably be shaped by the particular legal and political cultures of each jurisdiction. Moreover, there would be differences in how different adversarial systems would adapt to inquisitorially inspired reforms.[182] For example, the United States, with its deep commitments to the adversary and jury systems, might be more resistant to some inquisitorially inspired reforms than the United Kingdom or Canada, where judges already play a greater role in instructing juries about the facts.[183] The danger that adversary systems may resist reforms if they are presented in explicitly inquisitorial terms, however, can be overstated. In 2002, Barry Scheck and Peter Neufeld stopped short of recommending the creation of [an] American criminal cases review commission patterned after the British Criminal Cases Review Commission.[184] This was in part because they feared that such proposals "could be too easily, albeit unfairly, attacked as requiring large government bureaucracies based on un-American notions of an inquisitorial justice system that would squander precious law enforcement funds on prisoners making frivolous claims."[185] Even at the time, however, other American commentators advocated the adoption of such an institution.[186] In 2006, North Carolina became the first North American jurisdiction to create such a body when it created the North Carolina Innocence Inquiry Commission.[187] This Commission has robust powers to investigate claims of factual innocence and to refer suspected wrongful convictions back to the courts.[188] Both adversarial and inquisitorial systems have proven able to accept reforms inspired by the other systems in part because the differences between the two systems can be overstated and in part because each system will place its own stamp on reforms drawn from the other system. Contemporary concerns about wrongful convictions have the potential to allow both adversary and inquisitorial systems to adopt reforms inspired by the other system.

A. An Increased Role of Judges in Preventing Wrongful Convictions

One remedy that could assist in preventing wrongful convictions is to have the judge take a more active role at various junctures of the trial process. George Thomas III has recently recommended radical changes to American criminal procedure that are inspired from continental procedures.[189] He recommends that judicial officials or "magistrates" be involved in ensuring the reliability of identifications, confessions, and any jailhouse informers who may testify.[190] He also recommends that such judicial officials supervise disclosure and plea bargaining and that they conduct a more robust pre-screening of cases before the cases go to trial.[191]

As described above, a recent Ontario inquiry has suggested that judges should be more active in determining the threshold reliability of expert forensic evidence.[192] Although concerns have been raised that stricter *Daubert* standards may frequently result in the exclusion of expert evidence called by the accused than the prosecutor,[193] they have the potential to prevent the prosecutor from relying on forensic evidence of dubious reliability.[194] It is also important for judges to go beyond binary decisions about the admissibility or inadmissibility of expert evidence and to evaluate whether the language used by the expert is appropriate given the evidence and the scientific theory. Such enhanced judicial controls could address the dangers of overstating the science, but they will require trial judges to abandon a passive role and to become more knowledgeable about the scientific evidence in question.[195]

One limit on the ability of the judge to assume a more active role in the adversary system is the idea that the jury should have a monopoly on making factual and credibility determinations. In his report on three wrongful convictions in Newfoundland, the late Antonio Lamer, the former Chief Justice of Canada, recommended that trial judges have an increased role in taking weak cases away from juries.[196] He made these comments in a case where a man had been wrongfully convicted of murdering his mother in part on the basis of post-offense conduct and footprint evidence.[197] ... He recommended that the trial judge be allowed, on his or her own motion, to take a case away from the jury in instances where the evidence was manifestly unreliable on any essential element of the offense, including cases where the only evidence of identification was circumstantial evidence of motive or opportunity.[199] Although such an approach has not yet been implemented in Canada, it demonstrates a willingness to inject reforms that require judges to be more active in assessing the reliability of evidence and of a conviction. Such reforms are a way of introducing inquisitorial elements into the adversary jury trial that has traditionally reserved all findings about the credibility and sufficiency of the evidence to the jury.

Another example of increased judicial participation is the use of judicial warnings to juries about suspect forms of evidence. ... Judicial warnings on issues such as the frailties of identification evidence and the dangers that accomplices may give false testimony are seen in Canada as a means by which amateur juries can benefit from the accumulated experience of the professional judge.[201] Given the reluctance of trial judges to exclude evidence on reliability grounds, judicial warnings to juries may be seen as a second best strategy that draws on the knowledge and expertise of a professional judiciary in a jury system.

. . . . .

Judges can in some cases also conduct their own inquiries. Judicial inquiries into suspected wrongful convictions are available in the Australian state of New South Wales. The judges heading such inquiries can be appointed either by the government or by the Supreme Court itself. The inquiries are conducted under general legislation providing for royal commissions that provide judges with investigative powers.[219] Judicial use of such inquisitorial powers has led to convictions being quashed in New South Wales.[220]

The fact that Courts of Appeal in Canada, England, and Australia can order other bodies to conduct investigations for them indicates that appellate courts in adversarial systems can draw on some of the investigative powers and resources that are typically associated with inquisitorial systems. In the United States, a judge was appointed to inquire into misconduct relating to forensic evidence given by Fred Zain. The judge was assisted by a court-ordered investigation of Zain's work by other forensic experts. After finding gross and systemic misconduct by Zain, the judge ordered that Zain's testimony should be deemed invalid and unreliable in any subsequent habeas corpus proceeding.[221] This represents a proactive judicial investigation and audit of a category of cases that would not normally be expected in a party-initiated adversary system where judges are thought to play a passive role. All of these examples suggest that when necessary judges[] in adversary systems can take on a proactive role to discover and prevent wrongful convictions.

B. Innocence Procedures

. . . .

Another commentator has proposed that accused should be able to plead innocence in addition to the traditional plea of not guilty.[223] In innocence cases, it is proposed that the accused would have to waive both the right to silence and the right to solicitor–client privilege.[224] The police would not be obliged to investigate the accused's claim of innocence, but adverse inferences could be drawn from their failure to do so.[225] Although this proposal is presented as inquisitorial, it does not examine any continental procedure. Even a cursory examination of such systems would indicate that it is possible to require the police and prosecutors to follow lines of investigation proposed by the accused and that such procedures do not necessarily have to result in waivers of the right to silence or right to counsel. It is important to avoid stereotyped and archaic notions that see inquisitorial systems as incompatible with rights protection.

Another type of innocence procedure would be innocence hearings to provide a person with the opportunity to go beyond a not guilty verdict and to obtain some official declaration of innocence. Writing in 1932, Edwin Borchard praised European countries for providing indemnity for innocent people who had been wrongfully convicted, sometimes even in cases where the conviction was overturned on the first appeal. He wrote:

> In Europe, the opportunity to assert and prove innocence is practically always available before the courts, on a petition for revision of the sentence. It is therefore appropriate that the court which finds the innocence of the accused and which has all the evidence before it, shall at the same time determine whether he merits an indemnity from the state.[226]

Borchard clearly saw European systems as more concerned about truth and innocence than Anglo-American adversary systems.

Concerns have been raised in Canada about the practice of prosecutors entering stays of proceedings in cases of suspected miscarriages of justice which hold the prosecution in abeyance and deprive the wrongfully convicted of a not guilty verdict. A Manitoba Commission of Inquiry in 2007 disapproved of the use of prosecutorial stays in miscarriage of justice cases on the basis that they deprive the previously convicted person of a verdict.[227] In most cases, the appropriate procedure would be for the prosecutor to call no evidence so that the accused received the benefit of a not guilty verdict. If a stay is used, it should be approved by the Attorney General and generally replaced by a not guilty verdict if new evidence justifying a new trial is not discovered [within] a year. This recommendation appeals to the notion that the prosecutor is not a pure adversary but rather is concerned that justice be done.[228]

The Commission also recommended that the desirability of innocence hearings be further studied in conjunction with issues of compensation for the convicted person.[229] Compensation in Canada gener-

ally requires a finding of innocence beyond a not guilty verdict.[230] Subsequently, criminal appeal courts in Canada have found that they do not have jurisdiction to make official declarations of innocence.[231] Although there are serious concerns that innocence procedures might devalue the meaning of the not guilty verdict, the lack of such procedures is a testament to a lack of official concern about innocence.[232]

C. Continental Appeal and Revision Proceedings on the Facts

Although common law systems differ in their receptiveness of fact-based appeals,[233] appeals are generally oriented towards revealing mistakes of law.[234] In contrast, many continental systems allow generous fact-based appeals or retrials. The apparent willingness of continental systems to reconsider factual findings may indicate the primacy that they accord to the discovery of the truth, over the final settlement of disputes and ensuring respect for legal rights which seem to be the major concerns of adversarial systems.[235] In the wrongful conviction context, fact-based appeals and reviews seem promising in light of studies which suggest that appeals on questions of law, including questions of constitutional violations, have generally been ineffective in correcting cases that have later turned out to be wrongful convictions.[236]

. . . .

In many adversarial systems, a likely objection to the introduction of broad appeals on facts or trial de novo would be that they have the potential to swamp the courts in appeals. Indeed, many adversarial systems already struggle with their limited capacity for trials given their high volume caseloads. Many continental systems make more sparing use of the criminal sanction than the United States and even the United Kingdom and Canada.[242] These differences are related to cultural and political factors,[243] but they may also be related to the more limited capacity of inquisitorial trial and appeal systems to accommodate high volumes of cases.

In France, there is a formal procedure that allows for revisions of serious criminal convictions in cases where these robust appeal rights have been exhausted. The Minister of Justice or the accused can apply to a five judge commission of revision which has the ability to refer the case to a revision court on limited grounds, with the most important being that a new fact has occurred or has been discovered after conviction which is liable to raise doubts about the conviction.[244] Both the revision commission and the revision court have powers to conduct appropriate inquiries and investigations in addition to hearing representations from the accused and the prosecutor before deciding whether to quash the conviction, and if necessary, to require a new trial.[245]

Although the French power of revisions looks strong on paper, it is rarely exercised. One commentator has observed that over 2,000 demands have been filed with the commission of revision since the enactment of the law in 1989, but only fifty-four have been transferred to the commission with thirty-two verdicts being repealed and six reviewed trials resulting in an acquittal.[246] ... These facts provide a timely reminder not to romanticize or overestimate the ability of inquisitorial systems to prevent or remedy wrongful convictions. Nevertheless, the French revision procedure at least provides the judiciary an ability to engage in self-correction on factual matters after appeals have been exhausted.

D. Investigative Innocence Commissions

Another reform that is in part inspired by inquisitorial procedures is the appointment of commissions with powers to investigate allegations of wrongful convictions. ...

In Canada, six different commissions of inquiry have addressed the benefits of the British CCRC, with some specifically recommending the creation of an independent commission patterned after the CCRC to investigate claims of wrongful convictions.[251] The Canadian government has not followed these recommendations, so the federal Minister of Justice still makes the decision to order new trials or new appeals if there is a reasonable basis to believe that a miscarriage of justice occurred.[252] In part because of this high standard for re-opening convictions, both the numbers of applications for review and the number of actual referrals are far less than in the United Kingdom, even when Canada's smaller population is considered.[253]

The Canadian procedure was changed in 2002 to give both the Minister and a person delegated by the Minister the same investigative powers as a Canadian commission of inquiry.[254] ... These investigative powers mean that the Minister's delegate has full powers to subpoena documents and compel the attendance of witnesses.[256] These powers are in law stronger than those available to the CCRC because they extend to the compulsion of private persons. They represent a willingness to use inquisitorial powers of investigations within an adversary system to investigate claims of wrongful convictions. That said, complaints are frequently made in Canada that the

wrongfully convicted have to assemble new evidence before the Minister of Justice decides to use the investigative powers.[257] ...

The expectation that the applicant be able, independent of subsequent investigation by the Minister or his delegates, to present new evidence is found in section 696.4 of the Canadian Criminal Code, which directs the Minister of Justice to consider "whether the application is supported by new matters of significance that were not considered by the courts [and] the relevance and reliability of information that is presented in connection with the application."[259] This sends a clear signal that the initial application needs to contain decisive new evidence even before it is amplified by the Minister's investigations. ...

. . . . .

IV. CONCLUSION

Recent widespread revelations of wrongful convictions provide an excellent opportunity to re-evaluate the strengths and weaknesses of the adversary system. Some of the causes of wrongful convictions, particularly those relating to inadequate defense counsel and the entry of guilty pleas, are directly related to the weaknesses of adversary systems. Compared to continental systems, the adversary system places less of a premium on the discovery of truth about allegations of criminality and more on resolving disputes in a manner where parties have a formal opportunity to present their case and make decisions in their own self-interest. Many of the reforms advocated to respond to wrongful convictions, particularly the creation of commissions to investigate claims of wrongful convictions, would add inquisitorial features to adversarial systems. The acceptance of such commissions in England and North Carolina [suggests] that adversary systems have the ability to accommodate inquisitorially inspired reforms. That said, adversary systems are likely to be more resistant to more fundamental reforms such as limiting guilty pleas or keeping evidence of contested reliability away from the jury.

Before the inquisitorial system is accepted as the answer to the wrongful conviction problem, however, attention should be paid to the limits of the continental system. Indeed those concerned about wrongful convictions in countries such as the Netherlands have bemoaned "the lack of adversary debate at trial, which would force judges to listen to the other side of the story and to consider possible alternatives to the defendant's guilt."[278] Countries such as France have had to broaden their procedures to reconsider cases that may be miscarriages of justice. In continental systems, the same premium is placed on finding new evidence as in adversary systems. Few legal systems will abandon the concern about finality that makes it so difficult to obtain post-conviction remedies for the wrongfully convicted. The operation of Norway's Criminal Cases Review Commission has revealed a significant number of cases where people have been wrongly convicted in that country which employs an inquisitorial system.[279] In addition, that Norwegian Commission stresses its independence from the courts and it frequently appoints defense counsel to assist in the investigation of applications to re-open convictions. Wrongful convictions occur in inquisitorial systems and many in those systems look to adversarial-inspired reforms as a mean of both preventing and remedying wrongful convictions.

Some of the lessons of wrongful convictions in Anglo-American systems can in fact signal caution about relying on official investigations, whether they are conducted in adversarial or continental systems. The process of tunnel vision or confirmation bias, in which police and prosecutors single-mindedly focus on one suspect, would seem to be an equal or greater risk in inquisitorial systems given the centrality of official investigations. Similarly, the danger of reliance on faulty expert evidence would seem to be greater in a system that relies on court appointed experts. Both systems in this respect could benefit by facilitating adversarial challenges to official inquiries.

At the same time, however, police, prosecutors, and governmental scientists in adversary systems could benefit from a greater internalization of the idea that they are impartial seekers of the truth,[280] a principle found in at least the official ideology of many continental systems. Accused people should be able to request re-investigation by the police, prosecutors, and government scientists without the fear that their theory will be investigated in an adversarial

manner designed to shore up the prosecution's case. Inquisitorial ideals can play a role in inspiring greater professionalism and commitment to the discovery of the truth. Nevertheless, attention should also be paid to the hypothesis that the high volume of cases that are processed through many Anglo-American justice systems encourages shortcuts and adversarial habits that diminish respect for truth-seeking.

Some have argued that adversary systems devote too much attention to ensuring respect for legal rights and not enough attention to the factual accuracy of the verdicts.[281] Nevertheless, the inquisitorial systems of continental Europe abide by a fairly robust set of due process rights under the European Convention on Human Rights.[282] The choice between rights and reliability may be a false one. ...

There is a fundamental ambivalence about adversary and inquisitorial systems when it comes to wrongful convictions. The grass looks greener from both sides of any fence that divides the two systems, and for good reasons. There are obvious weaknesses in the adversary system that help produce wrongful convictions, and a growing number of cases in those systems have recognized wrongful convictions. On the other hand, complete reliance on state investigations also seems dangerous, given the flaws in police, prosecutorial, and forensic expert conduct that have produced many wrongful convictions in the first place.

In the end, the optimal criminal justice system to prevent and remedy wrongful convictions is likely to combine elements of adversarial and inquisitorial procedures. Such a system should be built in recognition that each system has its own vulnerabilities when its underlying assumptions and strengths break down.[283] In recognition of these weak spots, each system should incorporate fail-safe mechanisms, drawn from the other system, to counteract its particular weaknesses. ...

(d) In the Cathedral†

Franz Kafka

K. waited for him at the foot of the steps. While he was still on one of the higher steps as he came down them the priest reached out his hand for K. to shake. "Can you spare me a little of your time?"

† From *The Trial*, Dover Thrift Editions, translated by David Wyllie (Mineola, NY: Dover Publications, 2009 [2003]) at 153–60. [Edited.] Reproduced with permission.

asked K. "As much time as you need," said the priest, and passed him the little lamp for him to carry. Even at close distance the priest did not lose a certain solemnity that seemed to be part of his character. "You are very friendly towards me," said K., as they walked up and down beside each other in the darkness of one of the side naves. "That makes you an exception among all those who belong to the court. I can trust you more than any of the others I've seen. I can speak openly with you." "Don't fool yourself," said the priest. "How would I be fooling myself?" asked K. "You fool yourself in the court," said the priest, "it talks about this self-deceit in the opening paragraphs to the law. In front of the law there is a doorkeeper. A man from the countryside comes up to the door and asks for entry. But the doorkeeper says he can't let him in to the law right now. The man thinks about this, and then he asks if he'll be able to go in later on. 'That's possible,' says the doorkeeper, 'but not now'. The gateway to the law is open as it always is, and the doorkeeper has stepped to one side, so the man bends over to try and see in. When the doorkeeper notices this he laughs and says, 'If you're tempted give it [to] a try, try and go in even though I say you can't. Careful though: I'm powerful. And I'm only the lowliest of all the doormen. But there's a doorkeeper for each of the rooms and each of them is more powerful than the last. It's more than I can stand just to look at the third one.' The man from the country had not expected difficulties like this, the law was supposed to be accessible for anyone at any time, he thinks, but now he looks more closely at the doorkeeper in his fur coat, sees his big hooked nose, his long thin tartar-beard, and he decides it's better to wait until he has permission to enter. The doorkeeper gives him a stool and lets him sit down to one side of the gate. He sits there for days and years. He tries to be allowed in time and again and tires the doorkeeper with his requests. The doorkeeper often questions him, asking about where he's from and many other things, but these are disinterested questions such as great men ask, and he always ends up by telling him he still can't let him in. The man had come well equipped for his journey, and uses everything, however valuable, to bribe the doorkeeper. He accepts everything, but as he does so he says, 'I'll only accept this so that you don't think there's anything you've failed to do'. Over many years, the man watches the doorkeeper almost without a break. He forgets about the other doormen, and begins to think this one is the only thing stopping him from gaining access to the law. Over the first few years he curses his unhappy condition out loud, but later, as he becomes old, he just grumbles to himself. He becomes senile, and as he has come to know even the fleas in the doorkeeper's fur collar over the years that he has been studying him he even asks them to help him and change the doorkeeper's mind. Finally his eyes grow dim, and he no longer knows whether it's really getting darker or just his eyes that are deceiving him. But he seems now to see an inextinguishable light begin to shine from the darkness behind the door. He doesn't have long to live now. Just before he dies, he brings together all his experience from all this time into one question which he has still never put to the doorkeeper. He beckons to him, as he's no longer able to raise his stiff body. The doorkeeper has to bend over deeply as the difference in their sizes has changed very much to the disadvantage of the man. 'What is it you want to know now?' asks the doorkeeper, 'You're insatiable.' 'Everyone wants access to the law,' says the man, 'how come, over all these years, [no one] but me has asked to be let in?' The doorkeeper can see the man's come to his end, his hearing has faded, and so, so that he can be heard, he shouts to him: 'Nobody else could have got in this way, as this entrance was meant only for you. Now I'll go and close it'."

"So the doorkeeper cheated the man," said K. immediately, who had been captivated by the story. "Don't be too quick," said the priest, "don't take somebody else's opinion without checking it. I told you the story exactly as it was written. There's nothing in there about cheating." "But it's quite clear," said K., "and your first interpretation of it was quite correct. The doorkeeper gave him the information that would release him only when it could be of no more use." "He didn't ask him before that," said the priest, "and don't forget he was only a doorkeeper, and as doorkeeper he did his duty." "What makes you think he did his duty?" asked K., "He didn't. It might have been his duty to keep everyone else away, but this man is who the door was intended for and he ought to have let him in." "You're not paying enough attention to what was written and you're changing the story," said the priest. "According to the story, there are two important things that the doorkeeper explains about access to the law, one at the beginning, one at the end. At one place he says he can't allow him in now, and at the other he says this entrance was intended for him alone. If one of the statements contradicted the other you would be right and the doorkeeper would have cheated the man from the country. But there is no contradiction. On the contrary, the first statement even hints at the second. You could almost say the doorkeeper went beyond his duty in that he offered the man some prospect of being admitted in the future. Throughout the story, his duty seems to have been merely to turn the man away, and there are many commentators who are surprised that the doorkeeper offered this hint at all, as he seems to love exactitude and keeps strict guard over his position. He stays at his post for many years and doesn't close the gate until the very end, he's very conscious of the importance of his service, as he says, 'I'm powerful,' he has respect for his superiors, as he says, 'I'm only the lowliest of the doormen', he's not talkative, as through all these years the only questions he asks are 'disinterested', he's not corruptible, as when he's offered a gift he says, 'I'll only accept this so that you don't think there's anything you've failed to do,' as far as fulfilling his duty goes he can be neither ruffled nor begged, as it says about the man that, 'he tires the doorkeeper with his requests', even his external appearance suggests a pedantic character, the big hooked nose and the long, thin, black tartar-beard. How could any doorkeeper be more faithful to his duty? But in the doorkeeper's character there are also other features which might be very useful for those who seek entry to the law, and when he hinted at some possibility in the future it always seemed to make it clear that he might even go beyond his duty. There's no denying he's a little simple minded, and that makes him a little conceited. Even if all he said about his power and the power of the other doorkeepers and how not even he could bear the sight of them[,] I say even if all these assertions are right, the way he makes them shows that he's too simple and arrogant to understand properly. The commentators say about this that, 'correct understanding of a matter and a misunderstanding of the same matter are not mutually exclusive'. Whether they're right or not, you have to concede that his simplicity and arrogance, however little they show, do weaken his function of guarding the entrance, they are defects in the doorkeeper's character. You also have to consider that the doorkeeper seems to be friendly by nature, he isn't always just an official. He makes a joke right at the beginning, in that he invites the man to enter at the same time as maintaining the ban on his entering, and then he doesn't send him away but gives him, as it says in the text, a stool to sit on and lets him stay by the side of the door. The patience with which he puts up with the man's requests through all these years, the little questioning sessions, accepting the gifts, his politeness when he puts up with the man cursing his fate even though it was the doorkeeper who caused that fate[,] all these things seem to want to arouse

our sympathy. Not every doorkeeper would have behaved in the same way. And finally, he lets the man beckon him[,] and he bends deep down to him so that he can put his last question. There's no more than some slight impatience. [T]he doorkeeper knows everything's come to its end[,] shown in the words, 'You're insatiable'. There are many commentators who go even further in explaining it in this way and think the words, 'you're insatiable'[,] are an expression of friendly admiration, albeit with some condescension. However you look at it the figure of the doorkeeper comes out differently from how you might think."

"You know the story better than I do and you've known it for longer," said K. They were silent for a while. And then K. said, "So you think the man was not cheated, do you?" "Don't get me wrong," said the priest, "I'm just pointing out the different opinions about it. You shouldn't pay too much attention to people's opinions. The text cannot be altered, and the various opinions are often no more than an expression of despair over it. There's even one opinion which says it's the doorkeeper who's been cheated." "That does seem to take things too far," said K. "How can they argue the doorkeeper has been cheated?" "Their argument," answered the priest, "is based on the simplicity of the doorkeeper. They say the doorkeeper doesn't know the inside of the law, only the way into it where he just walks up and down. They see his ideas of what's inside the law as rather childish, and suppose he's afraid himself of what he wants to make the man frightened of. Yes, he's more afraid of it than the man, as the man wants nothing but to go inside the law, even after he's heard about the terrible doormen there, in contrast to the doorkeeper who doesn't want to go in, or at least we don't hear anything about it. On the other hand, there are those who say he must have already been inside the law as he has been taken on into its service and that could only have been done inside. That can be countered by supposing he could have been given the job of doorkeeper by somebody calling out from inside, and that he can't have gone very far inside[,] as he couldn't bear the sight of the third doorkeeper. Nor, through all those years, does the story say the doorkeeper told the man anything about the inside, other than his comment about the other doorkeepers. He could have been forbidden to do so, but he hasn't said anything about that either. All this seems to show he doesn't know anything about what the inside looks like or what it means, and that that's why he's being deceived. But he's also being deceived by the man from the country[,] as he's this man's subordinate and doesn't know it. There's a lot to indicate that he treats the man as his subordinate, I expect you remember, but those who hold this view would say it's very clear that he really is his subordinate. Above all, the free man is superior to the man who has to serve another. Now, the man really is free, he can go wherever he wants, the only thing forbidden to him is entry into the law and, what's more, there's only one man forbidding him to do so — the doorkeeper. If he takes the stool and sits down beside the door and stays there all his life[,] he does this of his own free will[, and] there's nothing in the story to say he was forced to do it. On the other hand, the doorkeeper is kept to his post by his employment[;] he's not allowed to go away from it[,] and it seems he's not allowed to go inside either, not even if he wanted to. Also, although he's in the service of the law he's only there for this one entrance, therefore he's there only in the service of this one man who the door's intended for. This is another way in which he's his subordinate. We can take it that he's been performing this somewhat empty service for many years, through the whole of a man's life, as it says that a man will come, that means someone old enough to be a man. That means the doorkeeper will have to wait a long time before his function is fulfilled, he will have to wait for as long as the man liked, who came to the door of his own free will. Even the end of the doorkeeper's service is determined by when the man's life ends, so the doorkeeper remains his subordinate right to the end. And it's pointed out repeatedly that the doorkeeper seems to know nothing of any of this, although this is not seen as anything remarkable, as those who hold this view see the doorkeeper as deluded in a way that's far worse, a way that's to do with his service. At the end, speaking about the entrance he says, 'Now I'll go and close it', although at the beginning of the story it says the door to the law is open as it always is[;] but if it's always open[,] always that means it's open independently of the lifespan of the man it's intended for, and not even the doorkeeper will be able to close it. There are various opinions about this, some say the doorkeeper was only answering a question or showing his devotion to duty or, just when the man was in his last moments, the doorkeeper wanted to cause him regret and sorrow. There are many who agree that he wouldn't be able to close the door. They even believe, at the end at least, the doorkeeper is aware, deep down, that he's the man's subordinate, as the man sees the light that shines out of the entry to the law[,] whereas the doorkeeper would probably have his back to it and says nothing at all to show there's been any change."

"That is well substantiated," said K., who had been repeating some parts of the priest's explanation to himself in a whisper. "It is well substantiated, and now I too think the doorkeeper must have been deceived. Although that does not mean I've abandoned what I thought earlier as the two versions are, to some extent, not incompatible. It's not clear whether the doorkeeper sees clearly or is deceived. I said the man had been cheated. If the doorkeeper understands clearly, then there could be some doubt about it, but if the doorkeeper has been deceived then the man is bound to believe the same thing. That would mean the doorkeeper is not a cheat but so simple-minded that he ought to be dismissed from his job immediately; if the doorkeeper is mistaken[,] it will do him no harm but the man will be harmed immensely." "There you've found another opinion," said the priest, "as there are many who say the story doesn't give anyone the right to judge the doorkeeper. However[,] he might seem to us he is still in the service of the law, so he belongs to the law, so he's beyond what man has a right to judge. In this case we can't believe the doorkeeper is the man's subordinate. Even if he has to stay at the entrance into the law[,] his service makes him incomparably more than if he lived freely in the world. The man has come to the law for the first time[,] and the doorkeeper is already there. He's been given his position by the law[;] to doubt his worth would be to doubt the law." "I can't say I'm in complete agreement with this view," said K. shaking his head, "as if you accept it you'll have to accept that everything said by the doorkeeper is true. But you've already explained very fully that that's not possible." "No," said the priest, "you don't need to accept everything as true, you only have to accept it as necessary." "Depressing view," said K. "The lie made into the rule of the world."

K. said that as if it were his final word[,] but it was not his conclusion. He was too tired to think about all the ramifications of the story, and the sort of thoughts they led him into were not familiar to him — unrealistic things, things better suited for officials of the court to discuss than for him. The simple story had lost its shape[;] he wanted to shake it off, and the priest who now felt quite compassionate allowed this and accepted K.'s remarks without comment, even though his view was certainly very different from K.'s.

In silence, they carried on walking for some time[;] K. stayed close beside the priest without[,] knowing where he was. The lamp in his hand had long since gone out. Once, just in front of him, he thought he could see the statue of a saint by the glitter of the silver on it, although it quickly disappeared back into the darkness. So that he would not remain entirely dependent on the priest, K. asked him, "We're now near the main entrance, are we?" "No," said the priest, "we're a long way from it. Do you already want to go?" K. had not thought of going until then, but he immediately said, "Yes, certainly, I have to go. I'm the chief clerk in a bank and there are people waiting for me, I only came here to show a foreign business contact round the cathedral." "Alright," said the priest offering him his hand, "go then." "But I can't find my way round in this darkness by myself," said K. "Go to your left as far as the wall," said the priest, "then continue alongside the wall without leaving it and you'll find a way out." The priest had only gone a few paces from him, but K. was already shouting loudly, "Please, wait!" "I'm waiting," said the priest. "Is there anything else you want from me?" asked K. "No," said the priest. "You were so friendly to me earlier on," said K., "and you explained everything, but now you abandon me as if I were nothing to you." "You have to go," said the priest. "Well, yes," said K., "you need to understand that." "First, you need to understand who I am," said the priest. "You're the prison chaplain," said K., and went closer to the priest[;] it was not so important for him to go straight back to the bank as he had made out, he could very well stay where he was. "So that means I belong to the court," said the priest. "So why would I want anything from you? [T]he court doesn't want anything from you. It accepts you when you come[,] and it lets you go when you leave."

Alternatives to Adjudication/ Alternatives within Adjudication

(a)   The Mediator and the Judge[†]

Torstein Eckhoff

Mediation consists of influencing the parties to come to agreement by appealing to their own interest. The mediator may make use of various means to attain this goal. He may work on the parties' ideas of what serves them best, for instance, in such a way that he gets them to consider their common interests as more essential than they did previously, or their competing interests as less essential. He may also look for possibilities of resolution which the parties themselves have not discovered and try to convince them that both will be well served with his suggestion. The very fact that a suggestion is proposed by an impartial third party may also, in certain cases, be sufficient for the parties to accept it (*cf.* Schelling, 1960, pp. 62, 63, 71 and 143 ff.). The mediator also has the possibility of using promises or threats. He may, for instance, promise the parties help or support in the future if they become reconciled or he may threaten to ally himself with one of them if the other does not give in. A mediator does not necessarily have to go in for compromise solutions, but for many reasons he will, as a rule, do so. The compromise is often the way of least resistance for one who shall get the parties to agree to an arrangement. As pointed out by Aubert (1963, p. 39) it may also contribute to the mediator's own prestige that he promotes intermediate solutions. Therewith he appears as the moderate and reasonable person with ability to see the problem from different angles — in contrast to the parties who will easily be suspected of having been onesided and quarrelsome since they have not managed to resolve the conflict on their own.

In order that both parties should have confidence in the mediator and be willing to co-operate with him and listen to his advice, it is important that they consider him impartial. This gives him an extra reason to follow the line of compromise (Aubert, 1963, p. 39, and Eckhoff, 1965, pp. 13–14). For, by giving both parties some support, he shows that the interests of one lie as close to his heart as those of the other. Regard for impartiality carries with it the consequence that the mediator sometimes must display caution in pressing the parties too hard. That the mediator, for instance, makes a threat to one of the parties to ally himself with the opponent unless compliance is forthcoming, may be an effective means of exerting pressure, but will easily endanger confidence in his impartiality. This can reduce his possibilities for getting the conflict resolved if threats do not work and it can weaken his future prestige as a mediator.

The conditions for a mediator are best in cases where both parties are interested in having the conflict resolved. The stronger this common interest is, the greater reason they have for bringing the conflict before a third party, and the more motivated they will be for co-operating actively with him in finding a solution, and for adjusting their demands in such a way that solution can be reached.

If the parties, or one of them, is, to begin with, not motivated for having the conflict resolved, or in any case not motivated to agree to any compromise, such motives must be *created* in him, for instance with the help of threats or sanctions. Cases may occur where the parties (or the unwilling one of them), may have a mediator forced upon them, and under pressure of persuasion from him or from the environment agree to an arrangement. But mediation under such circumstances presents difficulties, among other reasons, because it demands a balancing between the regard for impartiality and the regard for exertion of sufficient pressure. If the conditions for resolving the conflict by a judgement or administrative decision exist these will, as a rule, be more effective procedures than mediation in the cases described here.

That normative factors are considered relevant for the solution[] can in certain cases be helpful during mediation. By referring to a norm (e.g., concerning what is right and wrong) the mediator may get the parties to renounce unreasonable demands so that their points of view approach each other. Even if the parties do not feel bound by the norms, it is conceivable that others consider it important that they be followed and that the mediator can therefore argue that a party will be exposed to disapproval if he does not accommodate.

The norms will be of special support for the mediator if the parties are generally in agreement on their content and are willing to submit to them, so that the reason that there is a conflict at all can be traced back to the fact that the norms do not cover all aspects of the difference. The remainder which is not covered will then have the features of a fairly pure conflict of interests where the norms have brought the points of departure nearer one another than they would otherwise have been.

If, however, the parties consider the norms as giving answers to the questions being disputed, but disagree on what the answers are, the possibilities for mediation will, as a rule, be weakened. In the first place, the probability that the conflict will at all be made the object of mediation is reduced, among other reasons, because bringing it before a judge will often be possible and more likely in these cases. Secondly, mediation which has been begun may be made difficult because of the parties' disagreement concerning the norms or the relevant facts. This is the more true the more inflexibly the opinions are opposed to each other and the more value-laden they are. The parties' resistance to compromising on questions of rights or truth makes itself felt also when the mediator appears in the arena. Perhaps the presence of a third party will make the parties even more set on asserting their rights than they otherwise would have been. The mediator can try to 'de-ideologize' the dispute by arguing that it is not always wise to 'stand on one's right' and that one should not 'push things to extremes', but go the 'golden middle road'.[1] Sometimes he succeeds in this and manages to concentrate attention on the interest-aspects, so that the usual mediation arguments will have an effect. But it may also go the other way. The mediator lets himself be influenced by the parties to see the normative aspects as the most important, and ends up by judging instead of mediating. And even if he does not go so far, his opinions concerning norms and facts may inhibit his eagerness to mediate. In any case, it may be distasteful for him to work for a compromise if he has made up his mind that one of the parties is completely right and the other wrong.

Hoebel's survey (1954) of conflict-resolution in various primitive cultures confirms the impression that conditions are, generally speaking, less favourable for mediation than for other forms of conflict-resolution when the conflicts are characterized by disagreements about normative factors. Most of the third party institutions he describes have more in common with what I in this article call judgemental and administrative activity than with mediation. The only example in Hoebel's book of the development of a pure mediation institution for the resolution of disputes[,] which have a strongly normative element, is found among the Ifugao-people in the northern part of Luzon in the Philippines. This is an agricultural people without any kind of state-form but with well developed rules governing property rights, sale, mortgage, social status (which is conditional on how much one owns), family relations, violation of rights, etc. Conflicts concerning these relations occur often. If the parties do not manage to solve them on their own they are regularly left to a mediator, who is called a *mokalun*. This is not a permanent office that belongs to certain persons but a task to which the person is appointed for the particular case. In practice the *mokalun* is always a person of high rank and generally someone who has won esteem as a head-hunter. He is chosen by the plaintiff, but is regarded as an impartial intermediary, not as a representative for a party. The parties are obligated to keep peace so long as mediation is in progress and they may not have any direct contact with each other during this period. The *mokalun* visits them alternately. He brings offers of conciliation and replies to these offers, and he tries, with the help of persuasion, and also generally with threats, to push through a conciliation. If he attains this he will receive good pay and increased prestige. If the mediation is not successful the conflict will remain unresolved and will perhaps result in homicide and blood feuds, for the *mokalun* has no authority to make decisions which are binding on the parties.

It is easy to point to features in the Ifugao culture which can have favoured the growth of such a method of conflict-resolution. On the one hand, there has obviously been a strong need to avoid open struggle within the local society, among other reasons, because the people were resident farmers who had put generations of work into terraces and irrigation works. On the other hand, there was no political leadership and no organized restraining power, and the conditions were therefore not favourable for conflict-resolution by judgement or coercive power. Nevertheless, it is noteworthy that the mediation arrangement functioned so well as it did, considering that it was applied to conflicts where divergent opinions of right and wrong were pitted against each other. It is natural to make a comparison with our present international conflicts, where the conditions are parallel to the extent that the danger for combat actions and the absence of other kinds of third party institutions create a strong need for mediation, but where the mediation institutions so far developed have been far less effective.

The *judge* is distinguished from the mediator in that his activity is related to the level of norms rather than to the level of interests. His task is not to try to reconcile the parties but to reach a decision about which of them is right. This leads to several important differences between the two methods of conflict-resolution. The mediator should preferably look forward, toward the consequences which may follow from the various alternative solutions, and he must work on the parties to get them to accept a solution. The judge, on the other hand, looks back to the events which have taken place (e.g., agreements which the parties have entered into, violations which one has inflicted on the other, etc.) and to the norms concerning acquisition of rights, responsibilities, etc. which are connected with these events. When he has taken his standpoint on this basis, his task is finished. The judge, therefore, does not have to be an adaptable negotiator with ability to convince and to find constructive solutions, as the mediator preferably should be. But he must be able to speak with authority on the existing questions of norms and facts in order to be an effective resolver of conflicts.

The possibility for judging in a dispute presupposes that the norms are considered relevant to the solution. The norms may be more or less structures. They may consist in a formal set of rules (e.g., a judicial system, the by-laws of an organization or the rules of a game), in customs or only in vague notions of what is right and just. The normative frame of reference in which a decision is placed does not have to be the same — and does not even have to exist — for all those who have something to do with the conflict. What one person perceives as a judgement another may perceive as an arbitrary command. If, however, *none* of those involved (the parties, the third party, the environment) applies normative considerations to the relationship because all consider it a pure conflict of interests, decision by judgement is excluded.

A decision may be a 'judgement' (in the sense in which the term is used here) even if the parties do not comply with it. But the greater the possibility that a judgement will be lived up to, the more suitable judgement will be as a method for conflict-resolution, and the better reason will the person who desires a solution have for preferring that procedure. It is therefore of significance to map out the factors which promote and hinder compliance to judgements.

The parties' interests in the outcome play an important role in this connexion. If the main thing for them is to have the dispute settled, and it is of secondary importance what the content of the solution is, it will require very little for them to comply with the judgement. If, on the other hand, there are strong and competing interests connected with the outcome, so that submission to the judgement implies a great sacrifice for one or both of the parties, the question of compliance is more precarious.

That one party (voluntarily or by force) submits to a judgement in spite of the sacrifice it means for him[] may be due in part to norms and in part to the authority of the judge. There may be many reasons for the parties' respect for those *norms* on which the judge bases his decision; for instance, they may be internalized, or one fears gods' or people's punishment if one violates them, or one finds it profitable in the long run to follow them (e.g., because it creates confidence in one's business activities if one gains a reputation for law-abidance or because it makes the game more fun if the rules are followed). If the parties are sufficiently motivated to comply with the norms and give exhaustive answers to the question under dispute, then relatively modest demands are made on the judge's authority. If he is regarded as having knowledge of the norms and as having ability to find the facts, this will be sufficient to assure that his judgements are respected. Sometimes this is a simple assignment which many can fulfill. We may, for instance, take the case of two chess players who have not yet completely learned the rules of the game and who disagree as to whether it is permissible to castle in the present position. They ask a more experienced player who is present and comply without question to his decision because they consider it obvious that the rules should be followed and know that he is acquainted with them. But there are also cases where insight into norms, and perhaps also ability to clarify the factual relations in the matter, presuppose special expertise which only a few have. The kind of expertise required varies with the nature of the normative ideas. It may be, for instance, that contact with supernatural powers is considered to provide special prerequisites for finding out what is true and right, or it may be life-experience or professional studies. Monopolizing of insight may be a natural consequence of the fact that a norm system is large and cannot be taken in at a glance, but there are also many examples of systematic endeavours on the part of experts to prevent intruders from acquiring their knowledge.

If the parties are not sufficiently strongly motivated to comply with the norms which regulate their mutual rights and duties, or if they do not regard these as giving exhaustive answers to the matter of dispute, the judgement must appear as something more than a conveyance of information in order to command respect. The parties must, in one way or another, be bound or forced to adhere to it. One condition which may contribute to this is that, in addition to the primary norms which define the parties' mutual rights and obligations, there is also a set of secondary norms of adjudication which single out the judge as the proper person to settle the dispute and which possibly also impose upon the parties the duty to abide by his decision. That the judge is in this way equipped with *authority* is in many cases sufficient reason for the parties to consider themselves bound to live up to his decisions. But the establishment of authority often presupposes power, and even if the authority-relationship is established, it may sometimes be necessary to press through a decision by force. The power can reside with the judge, with someone he represents (e.g., the state) or with others who are interested in the decision being respected (e.g., the winning party or his relatives or friends). And it can have various bases: physical or military strength, control of resources on which the

parties are dependent, powers of sorcery, etc. How *much* power is necessary depends partly on what other factors promote and hinder compliance, and partly upon the relative strength of the enforcing authority and the disobedient party.

That the parties and others have confidence in the judge's impartiality promotes compliance [with] judgements. It strengthens the belief that the decisions he makes are right and it facilitates enforcement by making the application of force more legitimate. As mentioned before, it is also important for the mediator to appear impartial, but the manner of showing impartiality is different for the two kinds of third parties.[2] To a certain extent the judge can display that he gives equal consideration to both parties, for instance, by giving both the same possibilities for arguing and for presenting evidence. But he cannot, like the mediator, systematically endeavour to reach compromises, because the norms sometimes demand decision in favour of one of the parties. If he finds that one party is completely right he must judge in his favour, and the outcome of the case will not in itself be a testimony to his giving equal consideration to both.

But the judge has other possibilities for appearing impartial. Sometimes his person gives sufficient guarantee. He is, for instance, because of his high rank, his contact with supernatural powers or his recognized wisdom and strength of character regarded as infallible, or at least freed from suspicion of partisanship. The privilege of the judge to assume a retired position during the proceedings and not to engage in argumentation with the parties makes it easier to ascribe such qualities to him than to the mediator. Another significant factor is that there are, as a rule, small possibilities for checking the rightness of a judgement because this presupposes knowledge of both the system of norms and the facts of the particular case. To maintain a belief that certain persons are infallible can, nevertheless, present difficulties, especially in cultures characterized by democratization and secularization. To reduce or conceal the human factor in decision-making will therefore often be better suited to strengthening confidence in the decisions. Letting the judge appear as a 'mouthpiece of the law', who cannot himself exert any influence worth mentioning on the outcome of the cases, tends to remove the fear that his own interests, prejudices, sympathies and antipathies may have impact on his rulings.

Tendencies to overestimate the influence of the norms and underestimate the influence of the judge may also have other functions than strengthening confidence in the judge's impartiality. Firstly, these tendencies contribute to the transmission of authority from the norm system to the individual decisions. Secondly, the conditions are favourable for a gradual and often almost unnoticeable development of a norm system through court practice, so that the resistance to change is reduced. And thirdly, the judge will be less exposed to criticism and self-reproach when he (both in his own and others' eyes) avoids appearing as personally responsible for his decisions. This is important because it might otherwise involve great strain to make decisions in disputes where the parties' contentions are strongly opposed to each other, where there are perhaps great interests at stake for both, and where it may be extremely doubtful who is right (*cf.* Eckhoff and Jacobsen, 1960, especially pp. 37 ff.). It is therefore not surprising that many techniques have been used in the various judicial systems for the purpose of eliminating, limiting or concealing the influence of the judge. The use of ordeals and drawing of lots in the administration of justice (*cf.* Eckhoff, 1965, pp. 16–17; and Wedberg, 1935) may be mentioned as examples of this, and the same is true for the technique of judicial argumentation which gives the decisions the appearance of being the products of knowledge and logic, and not of evaluation and choice.

Judicial activity and formation of norms serve to support each other mutually. On the one hand, the judge is dependent on normative premises on which he can base his decisions. The greater the relevance attributed to them, and the stronger the ideological anchoring of the norm system, the more favourable are the conditions for conflict-resolution by judgement. On the other hand, the activity of judges can contribute to the spreading of knowledge about norms, to their increased recognition and authority, and to a gradual extension of the norm system to cover new types of conflict situations.

The activity of judging is in these respects quite different from the activity of mediating. As mentioned before, the task of the mediator becomes more difficult the more emphasis the parties place on the normative aspects of the conflict (presupposing that there is disagreement about these, as there usually will be in conflict situations). The mediator, therefore, must try to 'de-ideologize' the conflict, for instance, by stressing that interests are more important than the question of who is right and who is wrong, or by arguing that one ought to be reasonable and willing to compromise. The use of mediation in certain types of disputes may tend to create

or reinforce the norm that willingness to compromise is the proper behaviour in conflict situations, and thereby to reduce the significance of such norms as judges base their decisions on.

The contrasts between the two types of third-party intervention make it difficult to combine the role of the judge and the role of the mediator in a satisfactory way. Indeed it does happen that a third party first tries to mediate between the parties and if that does not succeed, passes judgement.[3] Also the reverse is conceivable: that a third party first passes judgement and then proceeds to mediate when he sees that the judgement will not be respected. But in both cases attempts to use one method may place hindrances in the way of the other. By mediating one may weaken the normative basis for a later judgement and perhaps also undermine confidence in one's impartiality as a judge; and by judging first one will easily reduce the willingness to compromise of the party who was supported in the judgement, and will be met with suspicion of partiality by the other.

When the establishment of new third-party institutions is sought, for instance, by a legislator who is looking for new ways of settling labour conflicts, or by those who are working for the peaceful adjustment of international conflicts, there may be a dilemma about which way to go. Should one go in for building up the norm system, and for strengthening the normative engagement with the aim of having as many conflicts as possible decided by judgement? Or ought one rather [to] rely on 'de-ideologization' and mediation? In considering such questions it is important not to let oneself be led by superficial analogies but to take account of all the relevant factors. Regarding international conflicts, for instance, one must consider that there is no superior instance which is powerful enough to force a powerful state to obedience. This has the consequence that courts can hardly be effective organs for the resolution of conflicts where substantial interests are at stake. Mediation also presents difficulties, among other reasons because the parties often place great emphasis on the moral and legal aspects of the conflict, and have strongly divergent opinions concerning both norms and (perhaps especially) the relevant facts. But there is good reason to believe that the difficulties in mediation are, after all, easier to overcome and that endeavours should therefore go in the direction of reducing the normative engagement.

(b) Translating Justice and Therapy: *The Drug Treatment Court Networks*[†]

Dawn Moore

INTRODUCTION

The judge calls the drug treatment court (DTC) to attention. He is addressing a specific client but makes it clear he wants the entire court to listen. He proceeds to reiterate the goals of the treatment court, concluding that 'the purpose of this court is to cure addiction, the closer he (the client) or anyone is brought to cure the better'. The promotional video produced in 1999 for this same court (Toronto Drug Treatment Court) illuminates this goal. Both the judge and the Crown attorney explain that the mandate of this court is to 'close the revolving door on crime' by treating drug addicts. Drug treatment courts are meant to cure those who come before them through the direct supervision of the court and, quite literally, within the walls of the courtroom. The project formalizes and amplifies extant crossovers between law and therapy in order to translate the courtroom into a curative realm. This paper maps these crossovers by looking at the circulation of disciplinary knowledges and actors. Borrowing analytic tools from Actor Network Theory (Latour 1987; Law 1999), I show how the DTCs are legal spaces deliberately set up for knowledge exchanges. These exchanges are effected by the uncoupling of psy and legal knowledges from their respective actors. Through a series of translations, knowledges circulate in the court and both the therapeutic and legal actors realign themselves, their goals and interests, to ally with the broader goal of curing the offender.

Drug treatment courts are part of a broader phenomenon born out of a theoretical movement called therapeutic jurisprudence (TJ). Coined by David Wexler and Bruce Winnick (1996: xvii), TJ is:

> ... the study of the role of law as a therapeutic agent. It is an interdisciplinary enterprise designed to produce scholarship that is particularly useful for law reform. Therapeutic Jurisprudence proposes the exploration of ways in which, consistent with principles of justice, the knowledge, theories and insights of the mental health and related disciplines can help shape the development of the law.

The notion of TJ emerged from the observed need to provide extra support to individuals in conflict with the law who also have mental health problems. The movement rapidly expanded to encompass all kinds of issues, including drug use, domestic violence, labour conflicts, youth crime and sex offenses. The expansion of the ideal of TJ is so profound that a search on any university data base of the terms 'Therapeutic Jurisprudence' reveals hundreds of hits.[1]

TJ, as it is written about in the fecund literature, is not limited solely to advocating for the establishing of special courts organized around addressing therapeutic issues. Instead, TJ is applied to all kinds of legal practices in which a crossover between law and therapy is possible. The most definitive text on TJ, Wexler and Winnick's (1996) edited collection, *Law in a Therapeutic Key*, features debates on long-standing legal doctrine, including the insanity defense (Perlin 1996), the tort doctrine of standard of care[2] (Shuman 1996) and the court's *in loco parenti* responsibility to underage participants (as either litigants, victims or accused) (Shiff and Wexler 1996). Those aspects of TJ that do centre on the courtroom, however, offer accounts of courtroom dynamics and reforms to legal processes that mandate the interplay of legal and psy knowledges. Courts focusing on issues of mental health, family violence and drugs all work through formal crossovers between law and treatment. The DTC arm of TJ enjoys giddy popularity throughout the United States and is expanding globally. The first DTC opened in Miami in 1989 (Goldkamp *et al.* 2001). Now, there are over 600 DTCs in the United States, and more operating and slated to begin operations in Australia, Great Britain, Guam, the Cayman Islands, Puerto Rico and Scotland (Anderson 2001; Belenko 1999). Through the application of TJ, the DTCs bring

---

† (2007) 47 Brit. J. Criminol. 42 at 42–45, 47–51, 53–57. [Notes and/or references omitted.] Reproduced by permission of Oxford University Press.

together therapeutic and legal actors in the court-room, reorienting them around the unified goal of curing the offender.

The interplay between law and other forms of knowledge is not innovative. Law, as both an episte-mology and a discipline, has never been pure. This is what the law and society project and the legal realist movement have been teaching us for the better part of a century (Tomlins 2000). Noting the ways in which the social seeps into legal arenas, legal philosophers such as Pound (1921) were quick to point out that law is not only driven by legal knowledges or processes. Instead, social factors (including knowledges) are firmly fixed within law. In the earlier realist tradition, the project tended toward normativity and positivism with an eye to re-imagining the juridical project as deeply sociologi-cal. More recent incantations gesture toward the descriptive and genealogical, looking at the role of law in society and society in law (see Ewick *et al.* 1999).

Psy disciplines, actors, knowledges and prac-tices (coming from psychiatry, psychology and social work), in particular, are stock features of Western penal systems (Arrigo 2002). Prisoners and proba-tioners are actuarially assessed and managed through psychologically based risk-prediction tools and offered cognitive–behavioural programming to target criminogenic factors (see Andrews and Bonta 1998; Mair 2004). The advent of the conditional sen-tence in Canada introduced psy interventions into the courtroom by way of allowing judges to place treatment orders on offenders as part of sentencing (Chiodo 2002; Fisher *et al.* 2002). In the broader realm of addictions, Canadian law continues to be used as a means to force people into treatment (Fisher *et al.* 2002).

Social scientists and socio-legal scholars have been quick to interrogate these developments. Some of the best work here arises out of concerns about the application of psy interventions to women in conflict with the law, revealing the gendered and discriminatory nature of these initiatives (Hannah-Moffat 2001; Kendall 2000; 2005). Other work lays open these programmes as culturally insensitive and empirically ineffective (Shaw and Hannah-Moffat 2004; Doob and Webster 2004). The rise of psy interventions, although often held up as an indicator of the humanization of punishment, is also arguably a punitive wolf in a benevolent sheep's clothing, with the potential for exerting and justifying extensive and harsh punishments (Moore and Hannah-Moffat 2005). The DTCs have not escaped this criticism. A growing body of scholars (Anderson 2001; Fisher *et*

al. 2002; Nolan 2001) raise doubts about the effec-tiveness of these initiatives and share concerns with those writing in the realm of punishment about the humaneness of forced or legally supervised treat-ment. We know, then, that even as they are com-monplace, these intersections between law and psy are cause for concern. The extant literature focuses on the outcomes of these initiatives. I am interested in their processes. Specifically, I focus on the kinetics of legal and psy knowledges and actors within the DTCs.

This paper maps out the knowledge exchanges between law and psy in the two operating Canadian DTCs (Toronto and Vancouver). From 2003 to 2006, I conducted courtroom observations in both courts. During this time, I also conducted interviews with key practitioners in both settings (judges, lawyers, therapists, court advocates and liaisons). Exploring movements of knowledge is important because ways of knowing are also ways of governing (Foucault 1980). Thus, exploring knowledge exchanges has something to tell us about practices of rule. The DTCs are likely spaces in which to conduct such a study because the knowledge crossovers in these courts are so explicit and the actors involved define their own work as markedly different from the work done in traditional criminal courts. At the open-ing of the Ottawa Drug Treatment Court, Deputy Attorney General for Ontario, Murray Segal,[3] makes this point quite plain in stating that the DTCs 'sit outside the traditional punitive paradigm ... by embracing multidisciplinary, interdisciplinary and col-laborative work'. The courts mandate a collective enterprise, drawing on the same actors and the same set of knowledges, marking their uniqueness through the particular collection of knowledges and actors found in these courts.

Taking my cue from Latour's (1987) work on the Actor-Network and Rose's (1998) study of psy knowledges, I show how expert knowledges are freed from expert actors. This uncoupling allows for the translation of the goals and interests of legal and therapeutic actors involved in the court. Translations influence the ways in which both justice and therapy are imagined in these settings. These developments have concerning implications for questions of due process and the ethical treatment of court clients as they explicitly erase fundamental protections against abuse of power in the realms of both therapy and justice (Boldt 2002). These erasures are allowable, even desirable, in the assuredly benevolent quest to cure the offender.

I begin with an overview of the ways in which knowledges are theorized with an eye to legal settings. Through this, I explain why some Actor Network Theory tools are useful in developing an understanding of the knowledge dynamics of the DTCs. I then offer a descriptive map of the knowledge exchanges in the courtrooms, drawing on court observations. Here I pay careful attention to the ways in which court actors affect translations of their actions such that legal actions like sanctioning serve therapeutic purposes and therapeutic acts such as assessing an individual's motivations become justifications for legal decisions. From here, I consider the role of the 'team' structure of the court as a primary means of facilitating the translations that occur. Within this team structure, I am also interested in how the team members themselves reorient their own personal goals and interests to align with the broader goals of the DTC. These translations have particular implications for the legal notion of due process on the one hand and the therapeutic ethic of care on the other. In the final section of this paper, I explore how actors redefine these notions as part of participating in the DTC network.

. . . .

TREATMENT COURTS IN CANADA

The first DTC opened in Toronto in 1997, the second in Vancouver in 2001. In 2006 four more courts opened in Edmonton, Ottawa, Regina and Winnipeg. The Toronto and Vancouver courts function similarly, although there are notable differences between the two. Both courts are mandated to deal with people convicted of non-violent crimes for which they would otherwise receive custodial sentences. Accused persons wanting to apply to the court programmes must undergo an assessment to show that they have an addiction of at least three months' duration to either heroin, crystal methamphetamine or crack/cocaine. Potential 'clients' are also evaluated for violent histories, mental health issues and levels of motivation to actively engage in an addiction treatment programme. Once accepted to the programme, successful court clients cascade down through levels of supervision as indicated by frequency of court appearances and participation in treatment. Through their time in the programme, clients are placed on a special bail[5] specific to the treatment courts. They also must sign a waiver acknowledging that sentencing will be delayed and quitting a number of other rights and protections (they must agree to participate in a random urine screen programme, have their therapeutic experiences discussed in open court and accept their inability to fully participate in legal

processes, described in more detail below). Clients considered to be of higher risk must enter a guilty plea to be admitted to the court programme. Those who successfully complete the programme are guaranteed non-custodial sentence. The courts follow a system of sanctions and rewards. The sanctioning systems in the two courts are quite different and discussed independently below. In both courts, clients are rewarded for consistent attendance and showing progress in their treatment (as defined by periods of abstinence or decreased drug use). Rewards include easing up on bail restrictions, decreasing court appearances and praise from the judge and the court.

The differences between the courts are as considerable as their similarities. Most primary here is the location of the courts in the different cultures of drug use from which they emerge. Vancouver boasts one of the largest and most visible drug-using populations in the world. The acuity of Vancouver's drug scene indicates that responses to drug use there are tailored to fit the surroundings. Vancouver is the first Canadian city to host a safe injection site, needle exchange programme and harm-reduction hotel. The drug scene in Vancouver has a huge influence on policing in the downtown core, rendering the area a de facto decriminalized zone for small-scale drug possession and sex trade work. At least one marijuana café operates in the Downtown Eastside without much reported police intervention.

The Vancouver DTC (VDTC) is shaped to fit the contours of its surroundings. The court itself is located in the heart of the Downtown Eastside, placing court clients in the thick of the drug trade on a regular basis. The court programme tempers this by offering a 'one stop shopping' day treatment centre for court clients deliberately located outside of the Hastings and Main neighbourhood. Clients are either encouraged or mandated (depending on their status in the court) to attend the treatment centre daily, especially at the start of their participation in the programme. The centre offers addiction-related programming, social programmes, individual therapy, a methadone clinic and a breakfast and lunch programme. Clients also have access to a physician, nurse, housing and child custody support services through the centre. The court and some treatment centre programmes are gender-segregated — an initiative which attempts to alleviate the gendered exploitation and victimization often faced by street-involved women. Largely because of *de facto* decriminalization, the court does not, for the most part, deal with simple possession charges.

Instead, almost all the clients in the court are facing possession for the purpose of trafficking charges or property offences. Sanctions in the VDTC are typically placed on clients who fail to appear either in court or at the treatment centre. The sanctions most commonly used in this court include issuing a warrant unique to the VDTC that mandates treatment centre attendance, placing clients in custody or altering bail conditions such that clients are mandated to attend a residential treatment facility. Finally, the VDTC does not demand total abstinence from all substances in order to graduate. Clients need only test negative for six months for the three mandated substances.

The drug scene in Toronto lacks the truculence of Vancouver, although, as a large urban centre, Toronto hosts a considerable amount of drug trafficking and use. Crack, cocaine, crystal methamphetamine and, to a lesser extent, opiates are all common in the city. The scene in Toronto is geographically dispersed, lacking the dramatic, palpable concentration found in Vancouver. The city has a needle exchange programme, methadone clinics and, alongside Vancouver and Montreal, is one of the sites for the current prescription heroin trials. The Toronto DTC (TDTC) does not have gender-specific programming or a comprehensive treatment centre (although the Centre for Addiction and Mental Health — part of a downtown hospital — does serve as a hub for the treatment programme). Abstinence is a requirement for graduation in Toronto and the court tends to take a harder line in general on drug use. In the Toronto court, there are two kinds of sanctions available: community service orders (CSOs), through which the individual is mandated to perform a set number of hours of community service (ranging from working at a homeless shelter to tearing posters off of phone poles), and bail revocation, referred to in this court as 'therapeutic remand'. CSOs are given far more often than therapeutic remands. These orders are assigned to clients who miss treatment groups and urine analyses, and do not 'process' relapses well.

EXCHANGING KNOWLEDGES

The positioning of actors in the courts is instructive. In Vancouver, a liaison from the treatment team holds a permanent position in the witness box and several other treatment team members are present in the courtroom, moving back and forth across the Bar. In Toronto, a probation officer and two therapists sit along side the duty counsel at the Bar. The presence of treatment people in a courtroom is not particularly curious; certainly, therapists, psychologists and psychiatrists are called into court on a regular basis to provide testimony, report on assessments and offer support to victims. The DTC treatment people are not, however, invited into the courts as witnesses or to offer court support. Instead, flagging the oddity of these courts, treatment people participate directly in legal processes. In this venue, legal knowledges and actors do not serve as filters for other kinds of expert knowledges (Jasanoff 1995). Instead, legal knowledges share space with clinical (mainly psy) knowledges and experts.

In both treatment courts, each of the clients has to go before the judge to report in. On one occasion in the Toronto court, a man is called up who has been on methadone maintenance for a few weeks. When the judge asks him whether he has any drug use to report, he admits that he has been using heroin fairly regularly for the last week. The judge thanks him for his honesty, as he always does, and asks the man why he used. The man responds that he was craving heroin and had been unable to overcome those cravings. The judge refuses to accept this response, relying on clinical knowledge to justify his position. The judge says, 'Look, the whole purpose of methadone is to stop you from having cravings. That's why you're on methadone is so you don't feel that need to use the heroin anymore. That's how methadone works.' The judge goes on to explain that the court encourages heroin users to get on methadone so that they can stabilize their lives, learn and practise coping mechanisms. 'And,' he concludes, 'it's dangerous to mix methadone and heroin.' Here, the judge takes up clinical knowledge in considering the pharmacological properties and clinical purposes of methadone as well as the psychological techniques of addressing and attempting to remedy drug addiction (in talking about cravings and coping mechanisms).

The judges in both courts not only engage in clinical–medical assessments, but also take up psychological treatment knowledges in dealing with clients. After listening to a client named Paulo[6] explain his reasons for wanting to be admitted to the VDTC, the judge offers an assessment of his level of motivation to actually change his drug-using behaviours. The judge says:

> I think you are very sincere about wanting to get treatment and wanting to get clean but I am not convinced by your plan so far. I want you to go to develop a tight plan that will get you into a recovery house.[7] Come back and show me you've done this and that will show me your commitment.

Here, the judge is referring to the body of knowledge around addiction recovery on which the court programme is based. Motivation-based psychology holds that before you can expect someone to change a set of behaviours, s/he has to be motivated to change those behaviours (Prochaska et al., 1988). Programming can start to foster those motivations by using external forces such as the sanction and reward system followed by the court. At a point, as the theory goes, the individual begins to internalize motivations and programming no longer needs to rely on external incentives to get an individual to want to change.

The judge's ability to bring her own psy knowledge into the courtroom does not merely serve the purpose of lectures directed at clients. It also justifies legal actions against clients. If a client shows a pattern of absence from or late arrival to the treatment centre, the judge typically reads this behaviour as a sign of the client's waning motivation to participate in the programme (and, ultimately, to become drug-free). In the Vancouver court, on reaching this diagnosis, the judge often offers the remedy of adding the client's name to the warrant list, thus making attendance at the treatment centre part of her bail conditions and giving police reason to arrest her if she does not attend the treatment centre. The judge's rationale for placing a client on the warrant list draws on therapeutic principles. For example, in responding to Carrie's admission that she is having a hard time getting to the treatment centre, the judge suggests that perhaps being added to the warrant list would help Carrie with this problem. When Carrie agrees, the judge confirms the decision by saying 'I'll give you that motivating factor then'.

In the treatment court, the notion of punishment is translated into the therapeutic goal of motivation. Increasing surveillance and the possibility of arrest and incarceration are decidedly punitive, akin to sanctioning through heightened probation conditions. Here, however, the punitive act is translated into a therapeutic one. Exercising a warrant in the DTC becomes the therapeutic application of external motivating forces described above. The act itself remains unaltered but its purpose is modified by rationalizing it through therapeutic rather than legal knowledges. This is similar to Hannah-Moffat's (2005) conclusions about risk assessments in prisons. Hannah-Moffat shows how, in the name of rehabilitation, prisoners are rated higher-risk and placed under amplified security. While the results (increased security) are clearly punitive, the risk/need assessment is justified, in part, through the therapeutic desire to meet women's needs.

Crowns and duty counsel also use clinical knowledges. This is made most clear when an individual is facing expulsion from the programme. Lying to the judge, breaching bail conditions, dealing drugs to other programme participants and having new criminal charges are all grounds for expulsion from either DTC. Clients can also be ejected from the programmes if they consistently show a lack of motivation to change their drug-using behaviours. While ejection does not arise that often, when it does happen, it is typically on the grounds of lacking motivation. For example, Karen — a client in the TDTC — faced ejection. Karen was consistently using heroin. The Crown takes her repeated use as evidence of her low motivation. The Crown's submission claims '[Karen] has shown poor quality and quantity of effort in her own recovery and clearly doesn't want to be here'. The duty counsel submits that Karen can complete her recovery and should be able to remain in the programme. Karen, she argues, simply needs time in detox to sort herself out. Again, engaging in translation, the Crown is not concerned with legal issues such as Karen's threat to public safety or criminal culpability. Karen's failure to comply with directions set out by a criminal court is not evidence of her dangerousness or blameworthiness. Instead, her actions speak to her status as a viable recipient of addiction treatment. Ejecting Karen from the programme is not presented as a punitive measure but rather as the clinical best practice for a therapeutically non-responsive client.

The treatment team plays a significant role in the court and also participates in knowledge exchanges and translations. Often, their role is supportive, offering comments to the judge on a client's progress, and on-the-spot counselling for those in crisis in the court. But treatment team members use legal knowledges and participate in legal actions as well. Frequently, treatment providers are positioned to make recommendations and, in some cases, legal decisions regarding clients. The most typical here is to see treatment team members advising the court on sanctions against clients.

An exchange around a client shows not only how treatment uses legal knowledges, but also how therapeutic knowledge is taken up by the legal actors. This passage comes from my research notes on the TDTC.

Sam is next to be called before the judge. I have never seen Sam fail to report drug use in the court and today is no different. Sam is new to the programme so his continued drug use has always been excused and he has typically been commended for being forthright about having used. Today, though, Sam also admits that he missed a treatment group and a drug screen. A member of the treatment team stands immediately to speak. She indicates that the treatment team is concerned about Sam's missing a group and that his case management officer has recommended that he do four hours of community service in order to make up for the group. She adds that the treatment team feels that it is very important for Sam to learn how important it is to attend groups. The Crown is next to speak and argues that in fact Sam's continued use coupled with his failure to attend groups calls into question Sam's motivation to be in the programme. The Crown calls for a revocation of Sam's bail in order to have him think about his motivation. The defence argues that it is still early days for Sam and that he has been up-front with the court about his use as well as his failure to attend groups. The judge decides to revoke Sam's bail, taking the [Crown's] position that Sam needs to show greater motivation and that perhaps having a strong external motivation like being placed in custody will help him to commit to the programme. Sam is taken into custody and led away.

Here, a therapeutic actor takes up the legal practice of sanctioning, not directly to achieve therapeutic ends but rather to serve a deterrent function of encouraging both Sam as well as the other court participants not to miss groups. On the other hand, the Crown takes up a therapeutic discourse about Sam's levels of motivation to voice his concerns, not about Sam's status as a law breaker, but rather about Sam's level of commitment to change his substance-using habits. Just as therapeutic actions and knowledges need not be altered in order to be marshalled by legal actors, punitiveness can translate into therapeutic practice without need of removing itself from even the most literal place of punishment — a prison.

. . . .

TRANSLATING ACTORS

. . . .

The DTC, then, is not only a venue with the purpose of curing addiction. Through the exchange of knowledges and the realignment of goals, the DTC is also a locale in which social justice is created, public safety protected, access to social services facilitated and punishment carried out effectively. In helping legal actors and institutions to redefine their goals and see their interests represented in different ways and in liberating knowledges from their perceived bonds to disciplines and disciplinary actors, the DTC network takes both law and psy from their imagined positions as pure disciplines and makes them utterly impure through varying relationships to diverse actors, interests and goals.

But what does this overt sullying of law and therapy mean for each of these disciplines? We have a society which holds out for the promises of due process on the one hand and ethical therapy on the other (even if no one knows what those terms mean and we are hard pressed to find pure examples of the application of these principles). These principles are meant to shield vulnerable people from huge power imbalances and potential for abuse and exploitation inherent to the practices of both therapy and law (Banks 2003; Roach *et al.* 2004). The goals of actors working under each of these paradigms are realigned through the network such that they fit with the network's goal of curing addiction while still being able to maintain pre-existing individual and organizational goals. In these shifts, it is clear the mythology of the purity of the discipline vanishes. This being the case, how do the actors within these networks understand this realignment vis-à-vis the principles of their respective disciplines? I want to explore this question with respect to law's promise of procedural fairness and psy's ethic of caring for clients.

PROCEDURAL FAIRNESS

Boldt (2002) argues that the adversarial mode of decision making favoured in the common law system runs counterintuitive to therapeutic practices. The adversarial system is based on the premise that fairness is ensured by having opposing 'sides' in a hearing and appointing someone to act only on behalf and in the interest of the client. One of the goals of structuring in this opposition is to offer procedural protections and assurances of fairness to those who come before the law. In Canadian criminal law, the adversarial system is meant to enshrine notions of procedural fairness — rules that are supposed to protect the most vulnerable from the overarching power of the law. These protections are laid out in the codes of professional conduct for most Bar Associations (cf. Law Society of Upper Canada 2000). Boldt suggests that when therapeutic ends are injected into the adversarial system, the principles of fairness are compromised to serve the emergent therapeutic goals.

These compromises are apparent in the DTCs. Clients enrolled in the DTCs are asked to sign a waiver giving up the right to [plead] not guilty, the right to a swift and determinate sentence (which in most cases would amount to less time in custody than the time that clients are expected to participate in the DTC programme) and the right to confidentiality (from both attorney and therapist). Clients also give up, through their agreement to participate in the urine screen, protections against unreasonable search and seizure. Clients must participate in a random drug-screening programme in which they have to produce a urine sample for testing at least once a week.

The actors within the DTC are aware that these aspects of the programme compromise legal protections. However, the importance of safeguards (and their subsequent promise of justice) is eclipsed through the broader court goal of curing addiction. The duty counsel for the Toronto court speaks to this issue:

> You know, it's probably the biggest thing that comes up is the whole issue are you acting in your client's best interest? If you're acting in a program where you're representing the clients but you're also part of this whole realm then how do you balance that? ... But I don't actually see it as a problem because basically what I say to people is that my role hasn't changed.... When it comes down to it, I'm not going to do what the team wants me to do. I'm going to talk to my client and I'm going to do what the client wants me to.[13]

Here, the duty counsel privileges the interests of her client over those of the court. Earlier on in this same interview, however, she defines her own notion of the client's best interest as getting the client into the programme and keeping her there. This definition is closely aligned with the interests of the court (to get an individual to stop using drugs) and assumes that all people in conflict with the law who also use drugs are best served through efforts to arrest their drug use.

Justice Bentley (2000), penning an early description of the TDTC programme, argues that the DTC is structured to make the role of defence counsel near irrelevant. He (2000: 268) writes that 'unless the judge is considering a revocation of bail or expulsion from the program, defence counsel does not attend court and duty counsel contributes simply as a member of the team'. The constitution of the duty counsel as 'simply a member of the team' indicates a formal breakdown of the traditional adversarial roles taken by Crown and defence. Here, the defence counsel's goal of working solely in the interest and on behalf of her client is translated

through team membership. The defence counsel now works as part of a larger whole within the network rather than (as is the intent in the adversarial system) an independent representative of the accused. Importantly, the defence counsel does not understand her own translation that way. Her role as client advocate has not changed in her eyes. She still works in the best interest of her client. It is those best interests that are translated. Thus, the best possible outcome in the DTC is to have the client become drug-free — not to have the client be acquitted of criminal charges.

THE ETHIC OF CARE

The changes in goals and interests made through the DTC networks are not exclusive to the realm of law. Those involved in the DTC teams as psy actors are also engaged in a process of realignment. Traditionally, therapeutic initiatives work directly with and for the individual and have their own procedural safeguards and ethical best practices (see O'Donohue and Ferguson 2003; Samuels 2002). Paramount are guarantees of client confidentiality and the idea that the therapist (like the lawyer) works in the best interests and under the direction of the client.

The majority of therapists working in the DTCs are either psychologists or social workers, bound by Codes of Ethics set out by professional colleges and governing bodies.[14] Their locations within the DTCs effect a realignment of these therapeutic operatives. I show above that therapists often participate in making legal decisions about their clients, including, from time to time, recommending sanctions. Like the lawyers involved in the court, the therapists are also keenly aware of the ways in which their participation in the DTC team indicates a shift in their professional practices.

One therapist observes that her role changed considerably since joining the DTC. She reasons that presenting a 'united front' to clients is vital to her ability to do her job well — a practice that she did not have to engage in before coming to the DTC. She explains that even if she disagrees with the way in which a client is handled in court, she will not directly advocate for her client in the courtroom.[15] Her practice, instead, is to take her dissatisfaction back to the DTC team for discussion. 'We make decisions as a team and only as a team,' she explains.[16] This therapist's phraseology is itself informative. United fronts are united fronts because there is an enemy whose presence warrants collective and strategic action in order to win (and thereby to ensure that the enemy loses) (Sontag 1978). In an interesting role reversal, the role of a therapist for this person changes from assistive to adversarial and the therapeutic process becomes akin to war, not care.

Another therapist recalls the first few times she watched a client of hers taken into custody based on her recommendation. She felt 'awful' but learned to accept this part of the client's therapy (spending up to five nights in a detention centre) and now has few reservations[17] about participating in the DTC process. The head of the treatment team in Vancouver maintains that 'the only time you should sanction is to engage people in treatment'.[18] She justifies this approach to dealing with drug addicts by saying that coercion must be used in addiction treatment programmes outside the court as well. She explains that people are always coerced on some level, whether the coercion comes from a partner who vows to leave, a child protection worker who threatens to take children away or a police officer who promises arrest if the user does not get help.

Involvement in the network has notable procedural effects for those involved. Consistently, narratives of the DTC practitioners, both therapeutic and legal, reveal rationalizations of their participation that allow them to change their practices while maintaining, according to their own account, their original goals. This is not to suggest, however, that the actions of any of these actors preceding their involvement with the DTC were necessarily any more closely aligned with maintaining the traditional goals of their respective disciplines. Promises of procedural fairness and ethical care do not themselves translate into guaranteed real actions or protections. If they did, we would have little need for appeals courts or disciplinary bodies set up to police professional conduct. And even if there were some absolute way of ensuring that these promises were carried out in the DTCs or indeed in any courtroom or therapist's office, there is good reason to resist normative claims that these promises somehow translate into 'fairness', 'ethical treatment' or 'justice', as these notions themselves are loaded with ambiguity. This flags the wide gap between formal and substantive equality (cf. Ontario 1995; Manfredi 2004).

CONCLUSION

In the DTCs, knowledges and goals are redefined and the boundaries surrounding knowledges are blurred. These courts are assembled networks in which therapeutic and legal knowledges are exchanged among the different personnel rendering the courts, at the same time and often in the

same breath, spaces of both justice and therapy. Members of the network undergo processes of translation whereby their goals and interests shift. Translation, however, does not indicate the erasure of individual goals and interests which pre-exist DTC involvement. Rather, participation in the network allows the actors to maintain their old interests but redefine them so as to have them met through the technologies and practices of the DTC.

Latour (1993) claims 'we have never been modern'. The purity of disciplines and knowledges never existed. If we have never been modern, then neither law nor psy has ever been pure. A broader consideration of justice bears this out. Law and psy are well met in other facets of the criminal justice system. In actuality, the criminal law routinely blends knowledges as a matter of codification (think of how important mental capacity is to a criminal proceeding) (Sarat et al. 2003). The same court house that hosts the TDTC is also home to courts designed specifically to address mental health, family violence and Aboriginal peoples in conflict with the law. The growing movement of collaborative family law in Canada sees lawyers trained by psychologists and social workers to assist in assuaging family conflicts.

I emphasize the point of contamination here to caution against the possibility of hailing fictional juxtapositions to the treatment courts that come in the form of 'pure' therapy or 'pure' law. That is, I want to avoid concluding that the arrangement of expert actors and knowledges in the DTC is somehow unique as compared to what we might call 'traditional' assemblies of law and psy in which each discipline is imagined to be bounded and untainted. The DTCs might be best understood not as revolutions in the practices of either law or therapy, but as markers of a more explicit turn toward abandoning the suggestion of purity and formalizing governing practice that rely on the convergence of expertise and expert actors and, with these, the broader project of modernity. Beyond these rather tentative attempts to predict the future, the DTCs also give us a handy window on the present. Because the intersections between law and psy are so clear in this space, the courts lend themselves to attempts to further understand these interactions as governing strategies.

Through translation in the DTCs, cure and control become synonymous. This stylized murkiness reimagines justice. The courts are recruited in the progressive project of curing addiction. In the face of the, at times, dark and ugly side of habitual drug use, the frustratingly apparent futility of imprisonment, the disasters of the war on drugs and the reality that decriminalization is a far distant possibility (Bourgeoise 2003; Erickson and Smart 1988; Marez 2004; Mauer 1999), it is hard to argue against an initiative that directs people out of the penal system, offers them rarified social services and health care and attempts to rid them of what, in actuality, can be a debilitating problem. Still, despite their very real and apparent appeal, DTCs maintain the same old practices of justice and punishment, only now they are known by different names. Detention translates into therapy, a warrant is now an incentive and appearance in a criminal court a chance to process a drug-use relapse. Translating these practices into a network with a broader curative goal does not erase their punitive, disciplinary intentions or effects. This does not make the treatment courts inherently good or bad. Instead, it reveals the rather complicated assemblages of power/knowledge through which they are formed.

(c) Collaborative Family Law and Gender Inequalities: Balancing Risks and Opportunities†

Wanda Wiegers and Michaela Keet

[1] The vast majority of family law disputes in Canada are settled rather than adjudicated.[1] Restricted legal aid coverage, high litigation costs, and mounting institutional pressures[2] combine to render settlement the most viable option for most family law clients.[3] In negotiating these settlements, the stakes are high since agreements negotiated with legal counsel are difficult to overturn and are likely to affect clients in profound ways long into the future.[4] Against this backdrop, lawyers and clients continue to search for more effective ways to enhance the settlement process. Dissatisfied with both litigation and mediation, many lawyers have recently turned to Collaborative Law (CL) as their process of choice.[5]

[2] In this article, we examine whether and how the distinctive features of CL affect the impact and salience of gender inequalities in the negotiation of family law disputes. First developed by lawyers in the United States, the emergence of CL has been described as a "paradigm shift" in legal practice.[6] One of the key distinguishing features of CL is the role lawyers play in the settlement process. CL seeks to realize the benefits of client participation and interest-based negotiation through the active involvement of lawyers as both facilitators and advocates. Unlike in traditional negotiation or litigation, CL lawyers commit to a set of transparent values that emphasizes the importance of the emotional and participatory needs of their clients, the possibility of creative outcomes, and the interdependence of the parties.[7] In another departure from most settlement processes, CL requires that both lawyers and clients work together in open four-way sessions toward the resolution of their dispute.

[3] The CL process is also typically structured according to rules of engagement and disengagement that are set out in agreements entered into by both clients and their lawyers. The content of these agreements varies between provinces and/or regions, but generally these agreements require open disclosure of all material information within the four-way session and demand that lawyers cease representing their clients if the process fails to generate a settlement. To date, the CL process, in both Canada and the United States, has been restricted largely to the family law area.[8]

[4] The impact of CL on gendered inequalities in bargaining power in family disputes has, as of yet, been largely unexplored. In an earlier article, we documented the results of a small-scale qualitative study that examined the experience of eight clients and twelve lawyers in CL.[9] We explored variables affecting client engagement inside the process and identified gendered power imbalances as one factor that led to varying, and often problematic, results. Given the same sample size of this study, our results

---

† (2008) 46 Osgoode Hall L.J. 733–72 at paras. 1–27, 32–36, 29–51, 54–56, 64–67. [Notes and/or references omitted.] Reproduced with permission.

could not be generalized to the client population at large. In the present article, we undertake a more comprehensive analysis of CL's potential to alleviate gendered differences in bargaining power between family law clients. We focus specifically on gender inequalities and draw to a greater extent on our lawyer interviews[10] to shed further light on the role of the lawyer in CL and on the effect of various procedural norms or constraints unique to the CL process. We also draw more broadly on the academic literature in the dispute resolution field, to the extent that this literature provides a critical lens into the potential risks and dangers of CL for the client population as a whole.

[5] The results of our qualitative study are consistent with established correlations between gender inequalities and well-recognized sources of unequal bargaining power in the context of separation.[11] Much higher rates of spousal abuse have been reported in past or previous relationships than in subsisting ones.[12] In intimate relationships generally, women are more likely than men to experience repeated incidents and more serious forms of physical violence[13] — including a higher risk of lethal violence after separation[14] — and are more likely to confront a climate of coercive control.[15]

[6] Women's disproportionate responsibility for childcare[16] and lower earning potential also function as sources of power imbalance. Women are more likely to have both a stronger preference for custody and a greater need for support than men. Economically, women are more likely than men to have lower and often untested earning power[17] and less access to income-generating assets of the marriage. They may also have less accurate information regarding assets and future earning potential, and be more concerned about the cost of prolonged negotiation and litigation.[18]

[7] Gender role socialization further suggests that women might perceive themselves, or be perceived by others, as having less credibility or status in asserting their needs or interests,[19] might tend to prefer co-operation to conflict or strategic negotiation, and might compromise their claims to obtain better interpersonal relations in the longer run.[20] Finally, men are more likely than women to benefit from the difficulty of reliably predicting or quantifying legal entitlements in the area of family or divorce law.[21] These sources of power imbalance can render women in heterosexual relationships particularly vulnerable to settlement pressures and may not be fully offset or muted by other individualized variables.[22]

[8] There are inevitable limits on the extent to which any dispute resolution process can address inequalities in bargaining power that are rooted in social structures and relations external to the bargaining process. In the private dispute resolution context, critics worry that processes such as mediation will both obscure inequitable outcomes[23] and legitimize them as a product of voluntary consent.[24] Adjudication, however, can similarly reinforce social inequalities. Adjudication can provide a public record, provide a check on the quality of legal representation, and has the potential to generate new substantive norms, but it is also highly constrained in its ability to address poverty and inequality.[25] Not only is litigation dependent on the resources of the disputants, but many judges also remain insensitive to the impact of systemic inequalities[26] and to a host of process-based shortcomings that plague female litigants. These limitations include litigation's tendency to escalate hostilities and delay a resolution, clients' lack of control or understanding of the proceedings, high financial costs, and use of the process to harass and control.[27]

[9] No dispute resolution method will provide a panacea, but processes may well differ in their potential to mitigate the impact of inequalities and offer other benefits to clients. Advocates of CL have argued that the more extensive involvement of lawyers, among other features, has the potential to deal more effectively with vulnerable clients than current forms of either litigation or family mediation.[28] We agree that CL's potential in managing gender inequalities flows largely from the integration of lawyers in the process because counsel can facilitate the provision of more thorough legal advice and more individualized negotiating support. This potential, however, will not be fully realized unless lawyers demonstrate high levels of sensitivity to imbalances, utilize effective screening strategies, provide timely and specific legal advice, and work at achieving deeper and more effective client–lawyer communication. In particular, we raise serious concerns regarding the risks arising from the use of the standard disqualification provision (DP), which heightens the importance of building adequate screening into the process.

[10] Given the limitations in current research on the specific impact of CL, the analysis we provide is by necessity speculative or exploratory in nature and is limited to the variables we identify. In Part I, we examine the common goals and background norms of mediation and CL, and provide a summary of the extensive literature on gender imbalances in the context of mediation. In Part II, the potential risks we

identify are evaluated in light of the unique structural features of the CL process.

I. EVIDENCE OF OUTCOMES AND BACKGROUND NORMS

[11] Although CL agreements vary across communities of practice, the background norms and goals of CL closely mirror those of family mediation.[29] Both processes follow the basic stages of an interest-based model: identifying issues, exploring interests, generating options, and reaching agreement.[30] Both CL and family mediation strive to return ownership of the problem — and the solution — to the clients and, through future-oriented, co-operative frameworks, seek to avoid strategic positional bargaining, improve communication, and facilitate emotional healing.[31] Proponents of both processes claim similar benefits: psychological empowerment, emotional healing, durable agreements, and, in the best of cases, personal transformation.[32]

[12] Researchers have had more opportunity to evaluate the outcomes of mediation given its long-established use in the family law field; yet, even in this context, alleged benefits have not been conclusively established or universally acknowledged. Connie Beck and Bruce Sales, for example, question the extent to which existing studies of mediation use sound methodologies[33] and point out that, when separated by gender, the results of empirical studies of satisfaction rates are mixed.[34] Empirical assessments of substantive outcomes are sparse, likely due to the difficulty of controlling for all salient variables — and again the results are mixed.[35] Research also overlooks the effect of mediation on distinctive groups of women, such as racialized women or homosexual women.[36]

[13] Drawing on the largest longitudinal study of mediation conducted in Canada, Desmond Ellis and Noreen Stuckless found that women in a voluntary, publicly-funded mediation sample were more likely to be satisfied with child support alone, but women in the lawyer negotiation sample, funded through legal aid tariffs, more often obtained sole legal custody.[37] They also found that differences in income, or the experience of abuse, did not significantly correlate with outcomes, which considered access, custody or property division, and levels of child support among wives in both samples.[38] It is important to note that couples with "power imbalances great enough to adversely influence the bargaining capacity of the partners" were screened out of the mediation sample at intake and that abusive behavior was consistently monitored by trained mediators throughout the process.[39] Ellis and Stuckless also did not assess the impact of either process on spousal support. It is unclear with what specificity they examined property division because the economic differences between parties did not appear to have been great in either sample. In a subsequent article, Desmond Ellis and Laurie Wight note that available evidence "strongly suggests" that "[economic] resources ought to be included in a theory of interpersonal power in divorce mediation."[40]

[14] In its findings on the question of custody, the Ellis and Stuckless study is consistent with others that suggest a tendency among mediators to favour joint custody or shared parenting.[41] Critics have complained that this tendency reflects a bias on the part of mediators who present their primary concerns as emotional healing, equal participation, and minimal conflict, and are insensitive both to the impact of the primary care role performed disproportionately by women and to issues of abuse.[42] In 1988, Martha Fineman argued that the use of family mediation and the growing influence of social workers and psychologists had precipitated a shift in substantive norms toward shared parenting and had dramatically reallocated power between mothers and fathers.[43] While this emphasis on contact and joint custody has since become increasingly evident in all legal modes of dispute resolution, including lawyer-to-lawyer negotiations, pre-trial conferences, and adjudicated outcomes, it is likely intensified through the collaborative frame of mediation.

[15] Early research into CL has shown high settlement rates[44] but has also raised red flags about a similar "harmony agenda"[45] that is linked to a specific conception of what "healthy family transitions" entail.[46] Prominent CL authors, such as Nancy Cameron and Pauline Tesler, emphasize the importance of deescalating conflict and acrimony for the sake of the children, promote the importance of contact with each parent through the restructuring of the post-divorce family, and portray the adversarial system largely as a catalyst for increased hostilities.[47] Within such a normative vision, the parties' interests are focused on maintaining a good relationship between parents, promoting future co-operation, and settling promptly without protracted debate.[48]

[16] In some respects, CL goes further than mediation to de-emphasize adversarial tendencies and defuse conflict. In addition to the DP, which intensifies the commitment to settlement, CL requires a more overt commitment to the concept of teamwork:

"the lawyers and clients work together as a team of equals, all pulling together on the same side of the problem."[49] The commitment of each party's lawyer to these ideals has the potential to reinforce the collaborative framework to a greater extent than typically occurs in mediation.

[17] This "harmony agenda" can also affect women differently than men. On the one hand, CL's value orientation may strongly validate negotiation behaviour or an "ethic of care" that, some argue, is more common to women, both as clients and lawyers.[50] To the extent that they do prefer collaborative negotiation, CL might provide some comfort to women and simultaneously influence or put pressure on men to adopt a more co-operative, conciliatory style.[51] Ultimately, the magnitude of this benefit depends on how successful the CL process is in encouraging men to abandon strategic, adversarial bargaining. While CL's formalized collaborative approach may be more successful in this respect than mediation, if unsuccessful, the process may simply induce a false sense of security in women. As Trina Grillo indicates in relation to mediation: "[i]f she is easily persuaded to be co-operative, but her partner is not, she can only lose."[52]

[18] The emphasis on familial welfare can also pressure weaker parties, typically mothers, to abandon legitimate claims to reduce conflict and obtain closure.[53] The emphasis on harmony may be particularly problematic for victims in abusive relationships since it can compound an abused spouse's reluctance or impaired ability to communicate.[54] Linda Neilson's New Brunswick study[55] found evidence that both mediators and lawyers failed to recognize abuse and pressured clients to accept generic settlements. Case studies of mediation in England also suggest that allegations of violence, even if identified through screening instruments, can often be sidelined, marginalized, and eventually discounted.[56] In her study of CL, Julie Macfarlane notes one instance where a client could not admit, in the joint four-way meeting, that she was afraid to go home that night because the parties were cohabiting.[57]

[19] As is common in mediation, the Collaborative Law Contract in Saskatchewan specifies that "unnecessary discussions of past events are to be avoided."[58] This exclusive orientation toward the future can suppress not only the disclosure of past domestic violence or abuse,[59] but also the expression of negative feelings that may be necessary for empowerment or healing.[60] Although collaborative strategies typically acknowledge emotions, critics argue that they

can discourage the expression of anger, which, in the context of abuse or violence, can silence a spouse who should otherwise be speaking out.[61] Tesler, a leading proponent of CL, suggests that lawyers should help clients avoid their "shadow states," which are described as "the temporary upwelling(s) of intense and primitive emotions such as fear, rage, grief, or shame."[62] In an effort to preserve the ideal of the "higher self," CL lawyers may thus inadvertently suppress their clients' anger and other intense emotions that can legitimately arise from abuse.

[20] Given these substantive and co-operative norms, CL can be expected to generate concerns regarding gender-based power imbalances that are similar to those cited in the mediation context. The question, to be examined in the next part of this article, is how effectively the unique procedural framework of CL can address or moderate the impact of such power imbalances.

II. STRUCTURAL FEATURES OF COLLABORATIVE LAW

A. Entrenchment of Lawyers into the Process

[21] In family mediation, clients typically consult lawyers only on a periodic basis, outside sessions or after a tentative agreement has been reached.[63] In CL, by contrast, the lawyers of each client are actively involved and jointly part of the process from the outset. One of the principal arguments advanced by scholars,[64] lawyers,[65] and clients[66] who favour CL is that the ongoing involvement of lawyers can effectively address power imbalances. In the mediation context, Jane Murphy and Robert Rubinson similarly argue that legal advocates can act as "power enhancers and equalizers," as "they can speak on behalf of clients, evaluate proposed solutions in light of applicable legal norms and the specific experiences of the client, and, if necessary, suggest opting out of the mediation itself if it is not serving the interests of the client."[67]

[22] It is not entirely clear why family mediation has developed without the continuous presence of legal advocates. The emphasis on therapeutic intervention in the divorce context[68] and the lack of a functional role for lawyers inside the mediation process may have had some impact.[69] From a practical standpoint, family mediators may not have encouraged lawyer participation since lawyers who lack significant training in dispute resolution and have not internalized co-operative norms can critically undermine the pos-

sibility of collaboration. Perhaps one of the most influential factors weighing against lawyer participation has been the cost to clients.

[23] CL can also increase costs relative to the cost of a single mediator. William Schwab's survey in the United States produced a profile for CL clients that was largely "white, middle-aged, well-educated and affluent."[70] Surveys conducted by collaborative organizations also suggest that CL is significantly more costly than mediation.[71] These studies, however, do not indicate whether the costs of legal advice have been factored into the mediation tab, nor do they control for factors such as degrees of conflict or complexity.

[24] The recruitment of lawyers into the heart of the dispute resolution process in CL would appear to increase protection for vulnerable clients. However, a number of assumptions underlie this conclusion: that lawyers can effectively determine whether and how clients ought to participate in collaborative processes, that lawyer involvement increases the client's access to legal information, and that lawyers can provide clients with the right balance of self-determination and negotiation support. The following discussion explores the extent to which these assumptions are likely to be true in the CL context.

1. Screening for Power Imbalances and Abuse

[25] Despite the development of protocols and screening tools, there are still no clear criteria among mediators for determining "what a power difference is and when it is occurring."[72] Mediation literature addresses power differentials caused by abuse and individual incapacity but does not adequately acknowledge inequalities arising from socialized gender roles, differences in earning power, and contributions to domestic labour that affect the bargaining process.[73] Mediators largely agree that allegations of domestic violence require "special treatment"[74] and support the screening out of cases involving systematic patterns of control — physical, emotional, or economic abuse — particularly where women victims are fearful or abusive partners seek to hide, deny, or minimize abuse.[75] Although academic discussion suggests that mediators have a fairly high level of consciousness of domestic violence, empirical research suggests that mediators in practice often fail to screen for it.[76] Critics argue that mediators underestimate the frequency and impact of power imbalances and rely too heavily on "quick-fix power balancing techniques."[77]

[26] Available research suggests that lawyers are not necessarily more conscious of unequal power or more prepared to deal with screening than mediators. Neilson's extensive research of case law, court files, and interview data in New Brunswick in 2001 revealed that evidence of abuse was siphoned off continuously throughout the legal process, possibly because lawyers either failed to detect abuse or underestimated or discounted its existence.[78]

[27] In the CL literature, issues of power and abuse are only beginning to be acknowledged. Collaborative Family Law includes only a few paragraphs on power issues;[79] Collaborative Practice: Deepening the Dialogue devotes more attention to these issues but acknowledges that the comments offer only a "starting point."[80] Basic CL training sessions may also pay little attention to screening issues, providing no template or systematic screening checklist and no training on how to conduct a screening interview.[81]

. . . .

[32] The task of screening for domestic violence or emotional abuse — whether in mediation or in CL — is inherently difficult and requires specialized knowledge of the nature and dynamics of spousal abuse and its long-term effects on children and victims. Women may raise allegations in indirect and tentative ways, often to test whether it is safe to provide more extensive disclosure.[97] Lesbian, immigrant, and Aboriginal women are less apt to report violence to authorities for fear of child protection proceedings, deportation, or loss of status in their communities, and these fears may inhibit disclosure even in more private negotiations.[98] After establishing a basis for trust, lawyers need to screen using specific questions while also paying attention to behavioural cues, such as unexplained injuries, absences from work, unusual fear, and avoidance of conflict.[99] Faced with ambiguity, lawyers, like mediators, may tend too often to reformulate the victim's story to conform to the presumptions of equality that underpin collaborative processes.[100]

[33] The potential for abuse or violence to remain hidden suggests that lawyers require specific training not only to identify its existence, but also to assess the type of violence and the magnitude of risks clients may face.[101] Standard screening protocols should be used to help lawyers recognize the continuum of abuse and respond in different ways, such as by declining to proceed, recommending against the process, or proceeding with safety or other supportive measures clearly in place. Abusive spouses may con-

test allegations of abuse, and they may be highly skilled in presenting themselves. To identify spousal abuse and distinguish it from claims of mutual abuse, a lawyer must examine the history of the relationship and consider both the context in which the violence or abuse occurs and its consequences. Third party verification of claims and counter-claims may also need to be explored.[102]

[34] Relationships involving a history of escalating acts or threats of harm against spouses or children (or threats of, or attempted suicide), along with a pattern of domination, control, or obsessive jealousy can particularly pose a serious risk to the well-being of victims and children, and to the possibility of an agreement that meets the parties' needs.[103] In such circumstances, conventional advocacy, rather than CL or mediation, could result in more ready access to restraining or protective orders, less direct exposure to the abusive party, and less risk that the victim's substantive claims will be devalued.

[35] Assumptions that power imbalances can be easily managed, even through the joint action of lawyers, belies the complexity of these issues. While screening is essential for mediation, it is even more important in CL, given the heightened costs of terminating the process and the inevitability of face-to-face encounters through the use of four-way meetings.[104]

2. Ambiguity Over the Influence of Legal Norms

[36] To the extent that legal entitlements provide a defence against the impact of power imbalances, the ongoing presence of lawyers in the CL process could render legal advice more accessible and help to ensure that a client's legal entitlements are respected. Studies to date, however, find significant variations between CL lawyers in how much legal advice they give, when they give it, and how specific it is to the client's situation.[105] These differences in practice reflect differences in the weight lawyers themselves place on legal entitlements relative to the "interests" identified by clients in the negotiation process. As with mediation, CL acknowledges that both parties' interests can be fully met outside the bounds of legal norms.[106] Indeed, proponents of CL argue that legal positions easily get in the way of creative problem solving. Instead, clients should feel "free to compromise and substitute their own standards of acceptability and reasonableness for the legal standard,"[107] and lawyers should avoid "premature advice-giving [that] may put a chill on the negotiations."[108]

[39] Unfortunately, our lawyer and client interviews suggest that some CL lawyers are divesting themselves of the protective role advocated by Murphy and Robinson in mediation.[114] This is problematic because less powerful clients may be losing access to legal standards that have evolved over time precisely to protect their interests. These standards are especially significant in family cases, given the social devaluation of women's domestic labour and the prevalence of abuse. In this context, legal norms remain an important benchmark against which a client can assess her interests.

3. Traditional Advocacy and Emotional Support

[40] In its emphasis on client self-determination and control as a central norm of the process,[115] CL calls for a reformulation of the lawyer–client relationship and a redefinition of lawyer advocacy. In line with this objective, CL agreements typically provide that each client is expected to assert his or her own interests, and lawyers attempt to avoid reinforcing feelings of dependency or treating the client as simply a passive recipient of terms or entitlements. However, feedback from our study suggests that vulnerable clients may still depend heavily on their lawyers as a source of emotional support.[116] Clients who complained of abuse in their relationships objected to their lawyers' "hands-off" approach; they felt they needed an advocate to "back [them] up,"[117] to respond to harassment and put-downs, and to help them "stand up to"[118] their spouse. CL lawyers must therefore navigate not only a tension between "zealous advocacy" and "peace-making,"[119] but also a tension between client autonomy and protective support and representation.

[41] Are lawyers adequately equipped to fulfill these complex expectations given the emotional intensity of such negotiations, the manipulative dynamics of long-standing abusive relationships, and the limits of conventional legal training?[120] For economically privileged clients, many of these concerns may be mitigated by the involvement of other counsellors, such as mental health professionals who work separately with clients; however, this Cadillac version of CL is not widely accessible.

[42] Managing these issues requires intensive lawyer–client communication such as open, ongoing feedback from the client to the lawyer through initial screening and preparatory interviews. Relative to a single mediator, CL lawyers are in a position to provide

more individualized negotiating support. Lawyers can also try to work as a team in order to challenge rather than reinforce power imbalances between the parties.[121] While engaging the efforts of both lawyers is a creative and no doubt helpful response, there are also limits to this strategy. In the context of longstanding abusive relationships, these strategies may simply be unable to alter the dynamics.[122] Lawyers for an abusive spouse can only go so far to contain the abuse because of their professional duty to represent their individual client. Without adequate support, professional teamwork can leave the abused client feeling isolated, unprotected, or abandoned.[123] These limitations again underline the importance of careful screening.

[43] In summary, the integration of lawyers into CL can provide a number of significant potential benefits for clients through the integration of legal advice, the opportunity to develop deeper, more supportive solicitor–client relationships, and the opportunity to work jointly with other counsel to facilitate and preserve respectful communication on the part of both parties. However, as with screening, these potential benefits are also subject to limitations, such as insensitivity to the existence of power differentials and their implications for the bargaining process, formal rules discouraging lawyers from providing legal advice at appropriate stages of the process, and limited skill sets in dealing with problems of abuse.

B. Disclosure, Good Faith Bargaining, and Limits on Communication

[44] In addition to the extent to which it integrates lawyers into the problem-solving process, CL differs from mediation in its allegiance to particular rules of engagement — its "choreography."[124] Both mediation and CL agreements include a range of commitments that require the parties to negotiate with openness, co-operation, integrity, and in good faith. Since lawyers are signatories to the CL agreement and are, relative to mediation, more actively involved in the process, these commitments can come to life in a more meaningful way in CL. Whereas the mediation process is flexible and is designed in accordance with the guidance and preferences of the mediator,[125] the CL process imposes unique procedural norms and limitations on communications between lawyers and clients.

[45] First, CL lawyers are active participants in the commitments to full disclosure of all relevant information and rectification of any mistakes,[126] and they must typically withdraw from the process if they know such commitments are not being fulfilled.[127] In mediation, only the parties themselves agree to disclosure and lawyers are not usually witness to the exchange of information. Through the lawyers' contractual commitments and their ability to monitor disclosure, the promise of openness can be enforced more consistently in CL than in mediation.

[46] Nonetheless, CL lawyers, like mediators, must ultimately depend on their clients' veracity and good faith and on assumptions that may be ill-founded.[128] While any settlement may be explicitly premised on full disclosure, redress for the failure to disclose will also generally require court action. Clients may request that statements making full and final disclosure be sworn; however, not all lawyers use or recommend sworn statements.[129] Whether such assumptions of honesty are warranted is questionable and, in part, depends on whether lawyers have adequately screened for basic levels of trust, prior levels of financial disclosure, and the particular dynamics of the parties' relationship.

[47] The CL process imposes additional constraints through the inclusion of a DP that prohibits lawyers from acting for their clients in any contested court proceeding.[130] Unless clients specifically agree in advance to formal discovery procedures, they give up their right to access formal discovery procedures during CL. As well, where a client takes "unfair advantage" of the process by non-disclosure or bad faith bargaining to the knowledge of his or her lawyer, the lawyer must withdraw, bringing the CL process to an end.[131] In effect, the party acting in bad faith is able to force the discharge of the other party's lawyer, increasing the costs for that party.[132]

[48] The requirement that information exchange and negotiation occur primarily in four-way open sessions with both lawyers and clients[133] can also be of mixed benefit to clients affected by power imbalances. Four-way meetings are intended to help achieve openness and transparency, and avoid the strategic positioning or tactical maneuvering that can accompany traditional advocacy. Collaborative law proponents believe that these goals are more easily achieved if "all important conversations are ... experienced directly by each participant."[134] Lawyers and clients are encouraged to debrief between CL sessions,[135] but according to some agreements, full discussion of the substantive issues and exchange of information about the law should occur only in the four-way and not in private lawyer–client meetings.[136] These explicit constraints represent a significant change from both lawyer-led negotiations, where

most communication would occur in two-way meetings between the lawyer and client and be subject to solicitor–client privilege, with follow up negotiation between the two lawyers — and from family mediation, where most mediators would ask the parties to seek information about their legal rights and obligations outside of the sessions.

[49] This emphasis on four-way communication can negatively affect spouses in abusive situations by discouraging lawyers from caucusing separately with their clients and fully discussing the matters in dispute. Private dialogue between lawyer and client may often be necessary to effectively manage the process, to ensure that the client fully understands his or her legal position, and to support his or her participation in the process. Providing information or advice privately is not per se being adversarial or positional. Where there are power imbalances and, particularly, patterns of control and abuse, open disclosure of concerns to the other party can in some circumstances impede the recovery process, undermine the client's coping strategies, or even put her in danger. While separate caucusing with the client may produce tension, under abusive or unequal conditions it may in fact work to advance the goals of openness and transparency. In our exploratory study, the four clients dealing with abuse or power imbalances all indicated a need for more intensive management and support beyond the four-way meetings.[137]

[50] Thus, while the CL structure may encourage more open and transparent communication between the parties, it can also disadvantage parties in unequal or abusive relationships. An undue emphasis on the four-way model as a primary mode of negotiation can restrict access to the verification tools of the discovery process, and restrict the advice and independent support for vulnerable clients. Where an abusive party bargains in bad faith or does not fully disclose, the DP will operate to penalize the innocent spouse through the loss of his or her counsel.

C. Disqualification Provision (DP)

[51] The DP is the key distinguishing feature in CL, and many lawyers[138] view it as essential.[139] Most CL agreements require the parties not to threaten or commence court action during the process and to compromise if necessary to reach a settlement. The DP further provides that contracting lawyers are disqualified from representing their clients in any contested court proceeding involving the parties.[140] This clause is broad enough to be triggered by a number of events leading to court action, including the fail-

ure to reach an agreement; the need for a restraining order to protect a client; the reliance on formal discovery methods in order to obtain full disclosure; or the need for an order to prohibit the disposition of family property, to compel enforcement after reaching a settlement, or to vary the terms of the initial agreement.[141]

. . . .

[54] There is significant academic controversy in the United States as to whether the DP is consistent with ethical rules of professional conduct.[148] Nine state ethics committees have considered collaborative agreements in relation to their professional codes of conduct and all but one have upheld their use.[149] Three states have passed statutes authorizing the use of CL. Although DPs might be seen as analogous to agreements allowing for the withdrawal of one's lawyer — and which are enforceable in Canada[150] — there is a key difference in that the loss of one's lawyer under the DP can be triggered by the conduct of either party, and not only the lawyer's own client. Some writers have argued that parties might be better served by a different process, especially where the parties' economic resources and the merits of their legal positions differ significantly.[151] An alternative process is Co-operative Law, which includes a Co-operative Agreement that incorporates the co-operative norms of CL but excludes the DP.[152] According to Hilary Linton, in circumstances of financial and legal inequality, the DP will unfairly compromise the power of the party with the superior legal claim and deny a legitimate source of leverage.[153]

[55] Although the DP is gender neutral in form, it is likely to have a disparate impact on female clients and place them at greater risk of relative disadvantage. Since women are most often the claimants in family disputes, legal entitlements are more apt to operate as a source of power for them.[154] Upon separation, it is women who more often lack access to an adequate income stream or marital assets or who may have superior claims to custody through their disproportionate role as primary caregivers.[155] To the extent that the DP raises the financial and emotional costs of litigation, it can increase the pressure to accept agreements that meet neither womens' identified interests nor their legal entitlements.

[56] Because both parties must share the eventual cost of litigation, the risk of being undermined in this way is most significant where trust is lacking, economic resources are unequal, and clients are

affected by abusive and controlling dynamics. By increasing the cost of litigation as an alternative, the DP affords one more lever for manipulation and control.[156] Unequal, abusive, and controlling dynamics can also have a far more negative emotional impact where clients have high expectations and are encouraged to engage, from the outset, in co-operative rather than adversarial negotiation.[157]

. . . .

III. CONCLUSION

[64] Access to justice has been identified as a key concern in family law.[173] The future significance of collaborative family law for women will depend on the extent to which it addresses existing barriers to access to justice, including its accessibility and cost-effectiveness, and its response to underlying inequalities in the bargaining process. The intense involvement of legal advocates in CL provides an opportunity not only to enhance the problem-solving experience for women in the family law system but also to contribute, through a resocialization of lawyers, to more lasting systemic change. CL has given lawyers, both male and female, permission to talk about negative aspects of the image of the litigious lawyer.[174] Although many such accounts still rely on "simplistic dichotomous images" and a "generic horror story,"[175] the obvious passion, commitment, and "ethic of care"[176] that many CL lawyers bring to their work highlight what may be too often missing in the adversarial system. In this sense, the turn to CL from mediation is more than an appropriation of similar rhetoric or a power grab in a professional turf war.

[65] CL could ultimately do more than mediation to change the legal culture.[177] Although mediation has been institutionalized to a greater degree and extended to other areas of law, its impact has been limited by the peripheral and uncertain role lawyers have played in its development. The excitement that many lawyers have for CL likely flows precisely from the discovery of a "functional role model" within an alternative dispute resolution process — accompanied by a new, still rule-oriented, procedural structure and ethical framework. The fact that many lawyers practising CL continue to include litigation in their family practice also suggests that rather than polarizing the practice of family law, the co-operative norms and values of CL may "spill over" into traditional negotiations and litigation.

[66] CL may also have a unique capacity to raise lawyers' sensitivity to power differentials through the organizational structures the movement has spawned among practising lawyers. Whereas mediation practice groups and policy debates tend to exclude lawyers who are not also professional mediators, CL can draw on professional associations and community groups that have formed across the country to provide information to the public as well as training and support for lawyers.[178] Through training and collective discussion, these groups have the potential to increase sensitivities and work through new approaches.

[67] Under current social conditions, the fundamental conflict of interest between the men and women who ultimately finance the provision of CL will inevitably limit the extent of this influence. Gendered inequalities are also difficult issues for a movement still struggling for legitimacy in a conservative profession to confront, particularly in times of political reaction and resistance to feminist discourse and initiatives.[179] However, heightened attention to the existence of gendered power differentials, the exploration of variations in the "meaning of co-operation" by screening clients into different processes,[180] timely and specific legal advice, and deeper and more effective lawyer–client communication could provide meaningful ways of improving the experience of female clients in the family law justice system. While not a radical challenge to systemic inequality, the adoption of such measures could at least mitigate the damage that can otherwise result when power differentials are obscured for the sake of family harmony.

(d)   The Indigenous Peoples of Canada: Over-Representation, and the Colonization of *Gladue*†

Jane Dickson and Sebastien Malette

All communities, no matter how prosperous, positive or proud, experience crime and disorder. The latter are inevitable facts of life and part of a larger balance that informs all our lived experiences. Yet for many Indigenous communities, balance can be difficult to locate — centuries of settler colonialism focused on eradication of Indigenous cultures and societies have shifted the balance heavily on the side of high rates of crime and disorder that both reflect and reinforce a lack of wellness. This is captured starkly by statistics: although Indigenous people constitute roughly 4.3% of the population of Canada, they are grossly over-represented on almost every indicator of poor health or well-being (Anaya, 2014). Indigenous children are more likely than their non-Aboriginal counterparts to be raised in poverty, endure early exposure to violence and substance abuse in their homes, leave school, and experience foster care and early contact with the criminal justice system (Weatherburn, Fitzgerald & Hua, 2004; Dickson-Gilmore & LaPrairie, 2005). As a result of exposure to such pathologies, these children are also far more likely to experience conflict with the law and the intervention of police, courts and corrections over much of their lives.

The magnitude of Indigenous involvement with the criminal justice system has long been a focus of deep concern on the part of Indigenous leaders and communities, and those who stand with them. It is also a problem which is steadily and consistently worsening. In 1991/2, Indigenous people constituted 11% of the federal prison population; by 1997/8 that number had risen to 17% (Canadian Centre for Justice Statistics, 2000); it continues to rise to this day. The Canadian Centre for Justice Statistics reports that in 2013, Indigenous people constituted one-quarter of all admissions to federal, provincial and territorial prisons (Correctional Services Program, 2015a). This means that the number of Indigenous people in prison was *five-times their population in Canada* generally. This startling statistic masks much worse ones. For example, the Office of the Correctional Investigator reported that, in 2013, one in every three federally-sentenced women was Indigenous (Office of the Correctional Investigator, 2013/2014), and their sisters comprised 41% of women held in provincial jails (Urquijo & Milan, 2011). Indigenous youth are equally over-represented in the criminal justice and correctional systems. In 2014 Statistics Canada reported that Aboriginal youth constituted 7% of the youth population of Canada, but accounted for 41% of all youth custody admissions. Within this population, the male–female disparity in the adult correctional system is replicated, but is far more polarized: Aboriginal girls accounted for 53% of female youth admitted to the corrections system, whereas 38% of males admitted were Aboriginal youth (Correctional Services Program, 2015b).

Once in prison, Aboriginal people face remarkable levels of disadvantage, often fuelled by systemic ignorance and prejudice. Almost without exception, Indigenous offenders in the federal prison system in particular are routinely classified as higher risk and higher need, which results in them being placed in higher security facilities. This classification matters because it can impact access to programs and to culturally-appropriate interventions. For example, the Healing Lodges created by Correctional Services Canada to house Indigenous offenders are deemed to be minimum security facilities, thus roughly 90% of Aboriginal offenders do not qualify for admission to institutions created entirely to serve Indigenous inmates (Office of the Correctional Investigator, 2012). Routinely placed in maximum and medium security facilities, Indigenous inmates are more likely to be involved in violent altercations and manifest higher incidents of prison self-injury (Office of the Correctional Investigator, 2012). At least in part because of their higher security classification and the problems they encounter in medium/maximum institutions, Indigenous inmates are less likely to receive parole and are consistently released later in their sentence; in fact, most leave prison on their Statutory Release or Warrant Expiry dates (Office of the Correctional Investigator, 2012).

---

† This article was written specifically for this text.

To date, our efforts to undermine over-incarceration have failed utterly. Despite the rise of restorative justice and increased awareness of the challenges facing Indigenous people, decades of policy and program initiatives have had little to no impact on the steadily rising number of Aboriginal people drawn into the criminal justice system. Initially motivated by a belief that systemic racism was the reason behind over-incarceration rates, early efforts reflected a commitment to 'indigenizing' the system by trying to entice greater numbers of Indigenous people to become police officers, lawyers and correctional, probation and parole officers. These efforts had limited impact, as many of those who took up the challenge experienced racism and discrimination in the workplace, leading to high rates of attrition and, as word spread, difficulty recruiting (Roman, 2009; Orenstein, 2010; Hutchins, 2013; Martel et al, 2011). Indigenization having availed little (McMillan, 2011), policy attention shifted to encouraging Indigenous communities to become 'responsibilized' and assume ever-greater control over conflict and disorder in their own communities. Thus, we saw the rise of such initiatives as Sentencing Advisory Panels, Elder Panels, and Sentencing Circles, all of which were directed to increasing community involvement in community and criminal justice services. Evaluation of many of these programs has been inadequate and, in many cases, fraught with methodological problems (Dickson-Gilmore & LaPrairie, 2005), with the result that we are unable to say with any certainty whether 'community justice' has had a significant impact on over-representation of Indigenous people (Fitzgerald, 2008; Dickson-Gilmore & LaPrarie, 2005) — although the numbers alone suggest minimal impact.

While many Indigenous communities have long sought greater control over the management of conflict and crime, such measures were given a notable boost in 1996 with changes to the federal sentencing rules contained in Bill C-41. In that year, amendments were made to the sentencing provisions of the Canadian *Criminal Code*, requiring judges to alter the sentencing process and focus when dealing with Indigenous offenders. Specifically, s. 718.2(e) directed that

> ... A court that imposes a sentence shall also take into consideration the following principles:
> ...
> (e) All available sanctions other than imprisonment that are reasonable under the circumstances should be considered for all offenders, with particular attention to the circumstances of aboriginal offenders.

These changes translated into two notable alterations to judicial practices when sentencing Indigenous offenders. Courts were now required to not only entertain different *processes* for determining an appropriate sentence, but also the *nature of the sentence* itself, which now must be informed by judicial awareness of the unique background and circumstances of Aboriginal offenders.

In 1999, s. 718.2(e) received full explication in the Supreme Court of Canada's decision in *R. v. Gladue*, [1999] 1 S.C.R. 688 [*Gladue*]. This decision marked the establishment of *Gladue* rights, and '*Gladue* reports' became a central element of all criminal cases where an Indigenous person was facing a sentence of incarceration. Intended to be the 'magic bullet' ending over-representation, *Gladue* shows little result in this regard, as evidenced in the continued and dramatic rise in the Indigenous prison population since 1999. While there are undoubtedly a range of reasons for the neutered effects of *Gladue*, we believe that these can be explained at least in part by evident problems in the state's approach to the implementation and support of *Gladue* rights, especially in contexts such as bail and show cause hearings. In the discussion which follows, we will trace the rationale, implementation and intent of *Gladue*. We will consider the logic behind *Gladue* reports and discuss the myriad problems which have arisen across Canada with the implementation of *Gladue*. Our analysis leads to the conclusion that, while the top court may affirm rights, insofar as it falls to the state and its agencies to respect and realize *Gladue* rights, these rights will always be vulnerable to the agendas and inertia of state actors.

WHAT IS *GLADUE*?

In 1995, Jamie Tanis Gladue, a Cree person from Alberta, was charged with the murder of her fiancé Reuben Beaver, a man whom she had known for some time and had been living with since 1993 (*Gladue*, para. 2). The couple had a daughter, Tanita, and at the time of the offence, Jamie was five months pregnant with their second child, a boy who would be named after his father (*Gladue*, para. 2). Jamie and Reuben's relationship was unstable and fraught; Jamie had experienced intimate partner violence and infidelity by Reuben, and she also struggled with ongoing medical conditions which impacted her mood.

The murder happened on Jamie's nineteenth birthday, following the couple's attendance at her birthday celebration. There was considerable drinking at the party and both Jamie and Reuben had become deeply intoxicated. At one point, Jamie observed her sister Tara and Reuben in a situation which reinforced Jamie's long-held beliefs that Reuben was having an affair with Tara. Drunk and feeling provoked, Jamie confronted Reuben, and their conversation quickly became heated and violent:

> During the argument, the appellant confronted him with his infidelity and he told her that she was fat and ugly and not as good as the others. A neighbour, Mr. Gretchin, who lived next door was awakened by some banging and shouting and a female voice saying "I'm sick and tired of you fooling around with other women." ... Mr. Gretchin saw the appellant run toward Beaver with a large knife in her hand and, as she approached him, she told him that he had better run. Mr. Gretchin heard Beaver shriek in pain and saw him collapse in a pool of blood. The appellant had stabbed Beaver once in the left chest, and the knife had penetrated his heart. As the appellant went by on her return to her apartment, Mr. Gretchin heard her say, "I got you, you fucking bastard." The appellant was described as jumping up and down as if she had tagged someone. Mr. Gretchin said she did not appear to realize what she had done. At the time of the stabbing, the appellant had a blood-alcohol content of between 155 and 165 milligrams of alcohol in 100 millilitres of blood. (*Gladue*, *supra*, at paras. 5–6)

Jamie was charged with manslaughter, and pled guilty; her sentencing took place 17 months after her trial. When the court accepted submissions on sentence, Jamie's legal counsel did not inform the court she was an Indigenous person despite his knowledge of such and the clear relevance of s. 718.2(e) to the case. When the judge enquired if Jamie was Aboriginal, her lawyer confirmed she was, in fact, Cree, but was from a "regular community" rather than a reserve. The court seized upon this distinction, dispensed with Jamie's *Gladue* rights, and sentenced her to three years' imprisonment and a ten-year weapons prohibition. At sentencing,

> [t]he trial judge noted that both the appellant and the deceased were aboriginal, but stated that they were living in an urban area off-reserve and not "within the aboriginal community as such". He found that there were not any special circumstances arising from their aboriginal status that he should take into consideration. (*Gladue*, *supra*, at para. 18)

Jamie appealed her sentence to the British Columbia Court of Appeal, and ultimately to the Supreme Court of Canada, where the court took up the opportunity to determine the proper interpretation and application of s. 718.2(e). In so doing, the Court pronounced that the section is meant to be remedial, that is, it is intended to 'remedy' the problem of over-incarceration of Indigenous people, and that this is to be achieved by requiring "judges to undertake the process of sentencing aboriginal offenders differently, in order to endeavor to achieve a truly fit and proper sentence in the particular case" (*Gladue*, *supra*, at para. 33). Key to the remedial approach and the crafting of a fit sentence is a requirement that judges consider:

> (a) The unique background and circumstances which may have played a part in bringing the particular aboriginal offender before the courts; and
> (b) The types of sentencing procedures and sanctions which may be appropriate in the circumstances for the offender because of his or her particular aboriginal heritage or connection. (*Gladue*, *supra*, at para. 66)

In elaborating on these requirements the Court expressed that, while background and circumstances are also important considerations in sentencing non-Aboriginal offenders,

> it must be recognized that the circumstances of aboriginal offenders differ from those of the majority because many aboriginal people are victims of systemic and direct discrimination, many suffer the legacy of dislocation, and many are substantially affected by poor social and economic conditions. Moreover, as has been emphasized repeatedly in studies and commission reports, aboriginal offenders are, as a result of these unique systemic and background factors, more adversely affected by incarceration and less likely to be "rehabilitated" thereby, because the internment milieu is often culturally inappropriate and regrettably discrimination towards them is so often rampant in penal institutions. (*Gladue*, *supra*, at para. 68)

The court in *Gladue* clearly advocated for an approach to sentencing that respects both Indigenous histories of colonization and state-imposed marginalization, and the individual experiences of the Indigenous offender. Thus, while lower courts were directed that they may "take judicial notice of [these] systemic or background factors" (*Gladue*, *supra*, at para. 83), it was also clear that these factors provide a backdrop against which the individual offender's unique background and circumstances must be considered.

Reflecting on Jamie Gladue's case, the Court expressed clearly that the fact of her residence off-reserve did not render her 'less Indian' and therefore less entitled to her *Gladue* rights: As an Aboriginal person her *Gladue* rights attached to her notwithstanding where or how she lived, and hence must be respected by the courts. The court stated that s. 718.2(e) "applies to all aboriginal offenders wherever they reside, whether on- or off-reserve, in a large city or a rural area" and that "[f]or all purposes, the term "community" must be defined broadly so as to include any network of support and interaction that might be available" (*Gladue, supra,* paras. 91, 92). In short, although approximately 71% of Aboriginal people currently reside off-reserve (Dickson-Gilmore & LaPrairie, 2005: 24), this reality does not diminish their culture or heritage, nor does it separate the history of colonization they have endured to the present day. Key here is the Supreme Court's direction that, while the immediate experiences of an Indigenous offender matter and must be considered in crafting sentence, these experiences transpire within a larger set of social and historical forces that have deeply impacted Indigenous people generally within Canada.

The changes to the sentencing provisions in the Criminal Code, and the interpretation given to them by the Court in *Gladue*, set a new bar for judges in determining sentences for Indigenous offenders. After 1999, Aboriginal history and the unique background and circumstances of an Indigenous offender became mandatory considerations in crafting fit sentences for Indigenous offenders, as did the consideration of any reasonable alternatives to incarceration. It is important to recognize, however, that although the Court required judges to change the way they sentence Indigenous offenders, *Gladue* did not provide, as some critics have maintained (Stenning & Roberts, 2001, p. 67), a 'race-based discount' to Aboriginal offenders, nor would *Gladue* lead to an "<u>automatic</u> reduction of a sentence, or a remission of a <u>warranted</u> period of incarceration, simply because the offender is aboriginal" (*Gladue, supra,* at para. 88; emphasis in the original). Indeed, the Court was clear that "it will generally be the case as a practical matter that particularly violent and serious offences will result in imprisonment for aboriginal offenders as often as for non-aboriginal offenders" (*Gladue, supra,* at para. 33, cited in *R. v. Wells* 2000 SCC 10, [2000] 1 S.C.R. 207 [*Wells*], at para. 44).

Subsequent decisions in the wake of *Gladue* reinforced the importance of the Court's directions, but also appear to have contributed to an increasingly limited and inconsistent application of s. 718.2(e). Commentators have observed that the Supreme Court's failure to address how courts may best balance the 718.2(e) requirements with other legally relevant sentencing considerations, such as deterrence and denunciation, has fostered inconsistency in the use of *Gladue* as well as the rise of a number of practical problems in sentencing. The Court's decision in *Wells,* for example, seemed to place courts on a path which elevates deterrence and denunciation over the remedial approach of *Gladue.* This has led to a situation whereby "judges may find that conditional sentences and other alternatives to incarceration may be inappropriate for Aboriginal and other offenders who commit the most serious crimes" (Welsh & Ogloff, 2008, p. 494). Given that Indigenous people appear to commit a disproportionate number of serious crimes against the person (Dickson-Gilmore & LaPrairie, 2005, pp. 53–54; Welsh & Ogloff, 2008, p. 494), this decision appears to place the remedial direction provided in *Gladue* in direct conflict with other, technically equally important, sentencing requirements (Welsh & Ogloff, 2008, p. 494). These and other difficulties with *Gladue* have arisen, including, but not limited to, uncertainty in the courts regarding who qualifies as "Aboriginal" for purposes of a *Gladue* report, when reports should be ordered, and an ongoing confusion over the proper tone and content of these reports (Pfefferle, 2006/08; Jeffries & Stenning, 2014, pp. 453–454).

In 2013, the Supreme Court revisited *R. v. Gladue* in *R. v. Ipeelee* (2012 SCC 13, [2012] 1 S.C.R. 433 [*Ipeelee*]). This case was heard and decided along with the case of *R. v. Ladue,* which like *Ipeelee,* involved an Inuit offender charged with breaching a Long Term Supervision Order under s. 752(1) of the Criminal Code. *Ipeelee* provided the Court with an opportunity to clarify and confirm their directions in *Gladue,* and to comment upon Aboriginal sentencing practices in the wake of *Gladue.* The result is a careful judgement which reiterates the *Gladue* principles and reinforces the absence of judicial discretion whether to apply those principles in the sentencing of Indigenous offenders. Focusing upon what they perceived as the lack of progress in remedying over-incarceration since their decision in *Gladue,* the Court observed that "statistics indicate that the overrepresentation and alienation of Aboriginal peoples in the criminal justice system has only worsened" (*Ipeelee, supra* at para. 62), and that "[t]here is some indication ... that the failure can be attributed to some extent to a fundamental misunderstanding and misapplication of both s. 718.2(*e*) and this Court's decision in *Gladue*"

(Ipeelee, supra, at para. 63). Taking up the latter, the Court not only clarified its decision in *Gladue,* but went further than they had in *Gladue,* asserting that:

> The sentencing judge has a *statutory duty,* imposed by s. 718.2(*e*) of the Criminal Code, to consider the unique circumstances of Aboriginal offenders. Failure to apply *Gladue* in any case involving an Aboriginal offender runs afoul of this statutory obligation. As these reasons have explained, such a failure would also result in a sentence that was not fit and was not consistent with the fundamental principle of proportionality. Therefore, application of the *Gladue* principles is required *in every case involving an Aboriginal offender,* including breach of an LTSO, and *a failure to do so constitutes an error justifying appellate intervention (Ipeelee, supra,* at para. 87; emphasis is ours).

Ipeelee thus underscored the mandatory nature and remedial intent of *Gladue,* and elevated this with a promise that a failure by courts to respect *Gladue* rights of Aboriginal offenders will automatically convey a right of appeal. As such, the Court was sending a clear message to courts and counsel that they have an legal obligation to treat Indigenous offenders fairly and in a manner which respects Aboriginal culture and history, and that a failure to do so will not be tolerated.

WHAT HAS *GLADUE* WROUGHT?

There is little doubt that, when it directed courts to be mindful of the life paths and larger histories of Indigenous offenders in crafting proper sentences, the Supreme Court understood that there are limits to the law's ability to achieve social change. The Court acknowledged that *Gladue,* while an important leveller, is not a "panacea" (*Ipeelee, supra,* at para. 63), and that remedying the over-representation of Indigenous people at every level of the criminal justice system would require much larger sociopolitical and economic change. That said, it is also clear that too many Indigenous people are in jail because judges send them there, and thus the courts have a clear role to play in the overall effort to reduce the over-incarceration of Indigenous people. The question, however, is whether judges required the push of s. 718.2(c) and *Gladue* to attend to over-representation, and whether that push would send them in the remedial direction intended by the Supreme Court.

Around the time of the changes to the Criminal Code, over-representation rates were troublingly high: In 1995–1996, Indigenous people comprised approximately 3.7% of the Canadian population, and 12% of the federal prison population and 16% of the provincial population (Pelletier, 2001, p. 471). Today, nearly two decades after the amendments to the Code, and 16 years after *Gladue,* Indigenous people constitute 4.3% of the Canadian population, but 21.5% of federal prison inmates and, in provinces such as Saskatchewan, 81% of those admitted to custody (Office of the Correctional Investigator, 2014/15). Put another way, in 2013/2014, 1 in every 4 admissions to federal and provincial correctional facilities was Indigenous (Canadian Centre for Justice Statistics, 2013/14). The problem is especially dire for Indigenous women, whose incarceration rates have exploded to the point where 1 in every 3 federally-sentenced women is Indigenous (Office of the Correctional Investigator, 2014/15).

How is it that, in the wake of the remedial approach imposed on courts by *Gladue,* the situation could have gotten so much worse for Indigenous offenders? There is undoubtedly a range of reasons for the neutered effects of *Gladue,* but given the limited parameters of this brief paper, we will narrow our focus to concentrate on what we believe can be best described as the 'colonization of *Gladue*' by the Canadian state. The term 'colonization' describes here the manner in which non-Indigenous governments and elites have chosen to administer *Gladue* rights, which not only impedes the ability of Indigenous offenders to vindicate that right, but also undermines the remedial intentions of *Gladue* — as confirmed by the Supreme Court most recently in its decision in *Ipeelee.* This approach to *Gladue* reveals not only the limited imagination of non-Indigenous governments in supporting Indigenous rights, but more obviously the difficulty they are experiencing in stepping away from colonialist arrogating attitudes and actions.

THE COLONIZATION OF *GLADUE:* COURTS, REPORTS AND THE CHALLENGES OF LEGAL AID

While as yet no researcher has knuckled down and attempted to document with precision the actual frequency with which courts actively incorporate *Gladue* into their sentencing of Indigenous offenders, what seems clear is that *Gladue* has been an inconsistent and often incomprehensible addition to sentencing deliberations (Pfefferle, 2006/08; Jeffries & Stenning, 2014, pp. 453–454; Welsh & Ogloff, 2008, p. 494; Pelletier, 2001, pp. 469–489; Roach, 2014, pp. 566–595). In their 2013 canvass of "Gladue

Practices in The Provinces and Territories", the federal Department of Justice documented that virtually all 11 jurisdictions included in the study had "initiatives and programs that comply with the *Gladue* decision (April & Orsi, 2013, p. 4). The most common approach seems to be the creation of *Gladue* Courts, which are essentially a hybrid of old approaches to Aboriginal justice, including incorporating indigenization where possible and combining this with a roster of non-Indigenous court officials who have received training in *Gladue* practices as well as some 'cultural awareness' or 'cultural sensitivity' training. The result is a series of 19 courts where Indigenous offenders can be heard in a less formal setting by a court consisting of both Indigenous and non-Indigenous officials schooled in, and committed to, *Gladue* principles (April & Orsi, 2013, p. 4).

It is also apparent that most Canadian jurisdictions have endeavored to provide *Gladue* training to judges, probation officers, courtworkers and duty counsel. This training is important, as it remains the case that most *Gladue* reports are not really full reports, but are more commonly 1–2 paragraphs or pages attached to a standard pre-sentence report compiled by a probation/parole officer. Unfortunately, as important as this training may be, indications are that it is often inadequate: Probation officers involved in the Department of Justice study lamented that the training rarely comes from "community people" who can provide important insight and context for those writing reports, few of whom are actually Aboriginal (April & Orsi, 2013, p. 8). There were also complaints that "the training offered to probation officers is very limited" (April & Orsi, 2013, p. 8) and that "the Aboriginal component is very small" (April & Orsi, 2013, p. 8).

Judges also seem unhappy with their *Gladue* education. At least one judge criticized the training provided to the judiciary as of dubious quality, and most felt the term 'training' over-stated the matter, indicating that what they received was more in the nature of an 'information session' (April & Orsi, 2013, p. 6). And while most acknowledged receiving some *Gladue* training, judges in Nunavut, the Yukon and New Brunswick expressed concern that they receive no education in Indigenous culture and history (April & Orsi, 2013, p.7) — a remarkable omission given that such knowledge is integral to respecting the spirit and intent of *Gladue*. Perhaps most troublingly of all, judges in the Yukon, Northwest Territories and Nunavut received no training whatsoever, on the logic that they "are faced with cases involving Aboriginal persons every day. As a result they are very familiar with the *Gladue* princi-

ples and thus no "formal" training is necessary" (April & Orsi, 2013, p. 6).

This statement is completely at odds with the directive reaffirmed by the Supreme Court of Canada in *Ipeelee*, insofar as we would argue that full respect for the spirit and intent of *Gladue* requires knowledge not only of the history of communities and cultures of offenders, but also of an individual's specific story. It is not clear how sitting in judgement of 'Indigenous others' day after day can automatically convey the meaningful connections between their personal stories or those of their communities and nations. The continued, apparently inexorable rise of over-incarceration of Indigenous people would seem to confirm these suspicions, and reinforces just how limited the "informal training" of day-to-day legal work is for communicating Indigenous stories to the courts. Furthermore, an abundance of anecdotal evidence speaks of Indigenous defendants who have sat quietly in courtrooms whilst non-Indigenous judges, lawyers and Crowns have debated whether the offender is 'sufficiently Aboriginal' to warrant a *Gladue* report — that 'white elites' should arrogate the right to decide Indigeneity is deeply offensive, and serves to reminds us that the colonial headspace is alive and well (Pfefferle, 2006/08, pp. 126–129). Such behaviour is also deeply hurtful to Indigenous people and communities, and serves to reinforce the historic traumas experienced by Aboriginal survivors — traumas recently defined as a "cultural genocide" by Justice Murray Sinclair and confirmed by Supreme Court Chief Justice Beverley McLachlin. Clearly, there is a deep and compelling need for structured and mandatory *Gladue* and cultural awareness training for all judges and officers of the court.

In his analysis of court debates and definitions of Indigeneity, Pfefferle laments the challenges of determining whether *Gladue* applies "particularly where offenders do not appear "culturally" or visibly "Aboriginal", and reports on cases where

> ... the Crown had disputed the Aboriginal status of the accused and later argued that although the accused was Aboriginal, he "did not come before the courts as a result of any Aboriginal-specific or 'unique systemic or background factors' ... Counsel for the defense in *R. v. J.R.* conceded that, although the offender had a somewhat troubled past, he had not been affected by the common features defining many Aboriginal offenders, including poverty, racism, family or community breakdown, or substance abuse in his community ... (Pfefferle, 2006/08, pp. 127–128)

While there is certainly a strong case to be made that acknowledging the factors noted above is a central intention of *Gladue*, at the same time this focus also suggests a troubling stereotype of Indigenous people that endures in many court rooms. In other words, any offender who is, for example, Indigenous but not poor and addicted, is likely to be seen by the courts and its officers as somehow 'not really Indian'. This is deeply problematic in at least two ways. First, it utterly fails to respect the fact that, while some Indigenous people and communities fared better and evince greater resilience than others in coping with the historic trauma and historic trauma cffccts visited upon them by, for example, Indian Residential Schools, this should in no way be taken as meaning those traumas had no impact and thus has no explanatory or contextual value in understanding the actions and choices of individual Indigenous people in conflict with the law. We would argue further that such a position speaks to an ingrained prejudice within the system which renders it blind to Aboriginal people who, as in the lower court in *Gladue*, do not live on reserves, or as in *R. v. R.J.*, are not poor, addicted or from a 'broken family'. This prejudice not only greatly impoverishes Indigenous histories and realities, but also makes much easier the much-lamented elevation of 'deterrence and denunciation' over the s. 718.2(e) factors as evinced in *Wells* (see above) (Pelletier, 2001, pp. 481–489), whereby those Indigenous people who 'fit' the stereotype cannot benefit from *Gladue* precisely *because they fit the stereotype* and thus present too difficult risk/need profiles, whilst those who do not fit the stereotype cannot benefit from their *Gladue* rights because *they don't fit the stereotype and are thus somehow 'not really Indian.'* Clearly, the colonial headspace remains alive and well, and reinforces the vital need for *Gladue* reports to not only tell the offender's story, but to do so in a way which teaches the courts about Indigenous histories, cultures and communities, and resists racist and essentialist understandings of what it is to be Indigenous.

This teaching is important because while many Canadians, both within and outside the courts, appear more aware of the challenges which have been visited upon Indigenous people due to such high-profile entities as the Truth and Reconciliation Commission (2015), there is much to suggest that this awareness is not supported by deep knowledge or understanding of those challenges. Indeed, it is precisely such an 'awareness–knowledge' disconnect that enables predominantly non-Indigenous judges to simultaneously 'respect' *Gladue* rights and take it upon themselves to decide what measure of 'Indigeneity' will trigger the right. When courts and counsel argue that an Indigenous person can be severed from their past and culture, and thus from any consideration of these things in the crafting of a fit sentence, it is clear how far we still have to go to educate non-Indigenous society about how and why history matters not just to Aboriginal people in conflict with the law, but to all Indigenous people as the source of Aboriginal identity, power and self-esteem.

While control over Indigenous identity is an important power restraining the penetration of *Gladue* into the courts, equally important in this regard is off-loading of the administration of those rights to pre-existing bureaucracies, mostly notably Legal Aid Programs or Probation and Parole services. The Department of Justice report has much positive stuff to say about the province of Ontario, which like British Columbia, has taken a lead in the provision of *Gladue* services. As a general trend, these provinces provide funding for *Gladue* reports through their Legal Aid organizations, with the result that provision of *Gladue* services, like virtually all Legal Aid services, are deeply influenced by the chronic underfunding of Legal Aid programs.

In Ontario, the ongoing funding squeeze has led to a number of problems directly impacting access to *Gladue* reports. For example, while Indigenous people are more likely to be held awaiting trial and sentencing (Hamilton & Sinclair, 1991), Legal Aid Ontario will not generally provide funding for a *Gladue* report that can inform a bail or show cause hearing. Although the LAO website states that they will provide 5 hours of funding to the Aboriginal defendant's legal counsel to "prepare submissions on *Gladue* principles for an Aboriginal client at bail hearing or sentencing under the Criminal Code or the YJCA" <http://www.legalaid.on.ca/en/news/newsarchive/0907-03_gladueextension.asp>), there are in fact in general "few or no submissions of Gladue principles at bail hearings" (Toronto: Legal Aid Ontario, 2008, p. 32). In our experience, where such submissions are made in regard to bail, they usually amount to little more than a lawyer making some basic remarks about their client's Indigenous heritage; only rarely are suggestions made as to alternatives to remand, for cxample accessing structured healing services or, in appropriate cases, placement in a residential treatment program, which could keep a defendant out of jail awaiting trial. Insofar as the latter would seem to be one of the essential goals of *Gladue*, and pre-trial release may be one part of the larger solution to over-incarceration, it is strange indeed that there would not be more attention paid to this situation.

Why does the limited involvement of *Gladue* in bail and show cause hearings matter? In Canadian law, pre-trial incarceration is primarily intended to achieve two ends: to ensure that the accused attends at trial, and to reduce any "substantial" risks he or she may present to the public while awaiting trial and sentencing (Webster et al, 2009, p. 82). As a general rule, the default position is release, however, it is also the case that this default does not seem to kick in very often, and on any given day, more people are held in provincial jails in Canada awaiting trial and sentencing than those who are serving sentences (Webster et al, 2009, p. 82). It probably goes without saying that, at the most basic level, imprisoning people who have yet to be proven guilty constitutes a "fundamental denial of their freedom" (Webster et al, 2009, p. 82) and profound intrusion into their liberty. What makes matters worse, however, is that pre-trial detention has a 'domino' effect that can trigger a number of other events, including a greater likelihood an accused will enter a guilty plea or be found guilty (Kellough & Wortley, 2002, pp. 187–188). People who are held in remand are also more likely to face a custodial sentence following a determination of guilt (Kellough & Wortley, 2002, pp. 187–188). Not surprisingly then, the reason why attention to *Gladue* rights matter as much at the point of bail as at sentence, can be explained by the simple fact that *Indigenous defendants are more likely to be denied bail and thus more vulnerable to all the domino effects this implies* (Kellough & Wortley, 2002, p. 187). Why are they more likely to be denied bail? Again, there are many reasons, and they are similar to the factors which go some distance to explaining why so many Indigenous people receive custodial sentences. As a general rule, most Indigenous defendants have much longer criminal records reflecting a consistent escalation in the nature and severity of the charges. They are also much more likely to have records marked by high incidents of 'breaches', including failures to appear and/or to comply with orders of the court. Insofar as decisions to release are very much exercises in risk management (Kellough & Wortley, 2002, p. 187), long records and a documented history of failing whilst on release communicate risk to courts tasked with deciding whether to release someone. While this may make it easier to understand higher levels of pretrial detention among Indigenous defendants, it also speaks to the great necessity of a *Gladue* report which can not only provide options for release, but also a larger context to assist the court in understanding an Aboriginal defendant's personal and offending history. Given the impacts of pre-trial detention and the greater likelihood Indigenous defendants will be held pending trial, *Gladue* would seem imperative at this early stage.

CONCLUSION

Although LAO announced an expansion of their support for LAO clients at bail hearings on June 8, 2015, it is not clear from their publicly available information whether or in what way this support might extend to *Gladue* reports and those who require them. (It is interesting to note that, in their 2008 publication outlining their Aboriginal Justice Strategy (Toronto: Legal Aid Ontario, 2008, p. 32), LAO included the concern about *Gladue* at bail hearings expressed by those they serve; there does not appear to be any explicit statement in that report of how this important problem will be tackled. It may be that this matter will be attended to more explicitly now that LAO has announced the extended funding for *Gladue* at bail hearings.) Regrettably, however, it is likely that LAO will be hamstrung here, as in other locations, by limitations in the funding they can put toward funding *Gladue* rights and reports. That said, despite funding and related challenges, Legal Aid Ontario is nonetheless a clear leader in the provision of *Gladue* reports within Canada. Other provinces, including British Columbia, which through its Legal Services Society has set a standard of exemplary practices in *Gladue*, have also experienced problems. As observed by a retired B.C. provincial judge and practising lawyer, "many Aboriginal people never get a *Gladue* report in B.C.":

> Only in exceptional cases will legal aid be able to fund a *Gladue* report, which is about $1,000 a report. So lawyers like myself only ever ask for them in very serious or exceptional cases. We know it's not even worth our time," he said. We're going to get rejected for them if we apply on a routine basis. So in other words, judges do not have the information that they need and should have to render a fair and just sentence". (Jackson, 2015)

As indicated by the Department of Justice study, most Canadian jurisdictions have made efforts to educate and train court personnel in the meaning and purpose of *Gladue*. At the same time, however, it appears that their ability (and commitment?) to implement the provision of actual *Gladue* reports appears piecemeal, uneven and quite probably inconsistent with the spirit and intent of *Gladue*. In our experience, the commitment to *Gladue* as a legal principle has trumped its role as an Indigenous right, leading to a situation where *Gladue* has too often become little more than a 'box to be ticked' in sentencing an Indigenous person, rather than a means for conveying a story and teaching the court, and by implication all Canadians, about the history and impact of colonization. Because at base, this is what *Gladue* is really about — the story of one person's path within their nation's larger journey through and beyond colonization. That story is not only integral in crafting a fit sentence for an Indigenous offender; each *Gladue* story is, or should be, a piece of truth which can assist in the reconciliation of our nations.

Clearly, there must be a better way to support Indigenous peoples' *Gladue* rights than is evident in current Canadian practices. Given the persistent and remarkable rise in the rates of over-incarceration of Indigenous people in federal and provincial correctional systems, and their over-representation at every level of the criminal justice system, we believe that a full and complete attention to *Gladue* rights is a matter of the "Honour of the Crown". We also believe that dual failure of the state both to adequately fund *Gladue* and to resolve those larger socioeconomic and structural issues which reduce the human potential of Indigenous people and place too many on paths to conflict with the law, constitute a failure of the Crown to respect its fiduciary obligations to the First People of Canada. Until the state takes up the full challenges of building communities and supporting *Gladue* rights, it is unlikely that we will undermine over-representation and over-incarceration one bit. And that is not only legally problematic, but also constitutes a compelling ethical failure on the part of the Canadian state in its pursuit of a genuine reconciliation with the Indigenous peoples of Canada.

References

April, Sébastien, and Myléne Magrinelli Orsi, *Gladue Practices in the Provinces and Territories* (Ottawa: Department of Justice Canada, Research and Statistics Division, 2013).

Anaya, James, *Report of the Special Rapporteur on the rights of Indigenous peoples*, Addendum: The situation of indigenous peoples in Canada (United Nations General Assembly, Human Rights Council, Twenty-seventh session, 4 July 2014). Online at: <http://unsr.jamesanaya.org/docs/countries/2014-report-canada-a-hrc-27-52-add-2-en.pdf>.

Canadian Centre for Justice Statistics, *The Over-Representation of Aboriginal People in the Criminal Justice System* (Ottawa: Statistics Canada, 2000).

Correctional Services Program, "Adult Correctional Statistics in Canada 2013/14", Jurisdat Bulletin (Ottawa: Statistics Canada, 22 April 22 2015). Online at: <http://www.statcan.gc.ca/pub/85-002-x/2015001/article/14163-eng.htm#a8>.

Correctional Services Program, "Youth Correctional Statistics in Canada 2013/14", Jurisdat Bulletin (Ottawa: Statistics Canada, 22 April 2015). Online at: <http://www.statcan.gc.ca/pub/85-002-x/2015001/article/14164-eng.htm#a6>.

Dickson-Gilmore, Jane, and Carol LaPrairie, *Will the Circle be Unbroken? Aboriginal Communities, Restorative Justice, and the Challenges of Conflict and Change* (Toronto: University of Toronto Press, 2005).

Fine, Sean, "Chief Justice says Canada attempted 'cultural genocide' on aboriginals", *The Globe and Mail* (29 May 2015). Online at: <http://www.theglobeandmail.com/news/national/chief-justice-says-canada-attempted-cultural-genocide-on-aboriginals/article24688854/>

Fitzgerald, Jacqueline, "Does circle sentencing reduce Aboriginal offending?" *Crime and Justice Bulletin* No. 115, May 2008.

Hamilton, A.C., and C.M. Sinclair, *Report of the Aboriginal Justice Inquiry of Manitoba* (Winnipeg: Government of Manitoba, 1991).

Hutchins, Hope, Canadian Centre for Justice Statistics, "Police Resources in Canada, 2013", Jurisdat Bulletin (Ottawa: Statistics Canada, 2013). Online at: <http://www.statcan.gc.ca/pub/85-002-x/2014001/article/11914-eng.pdf>

Jackson, Kenneth, "Aboriginal man uses experience behind bars to help offenders tell their 'Gladue' story", *APTN National News* (9 February 2015). Online at: <http://aptn.ca/news/2015/02/09/aboriginal-man-uses-experience-behind-bars-to-help-offenders-tell-their-gladue-story/>.

Jeffries, Samantha, and Philip Stenning, "Sentencing Aboriginal Offenders: Law, Policy and Practice in Three Countries", *Canadian Journal of Criminology and Criminal Justice* (2014) 56(4): 447–494.

Kellough, Gail, and Scot Wortley, "Remand for Plea: Bail Decisions and Plea Bargaining as Commensurate Decisions", *British Journal of Criminology* (2002) 42: 186–210.

Legal Aid Ontario, *The Development of Legal Aid Ontario's Aboriginal Strategy* (Toronto: Legal Aid Ontario, 2008).

Legal Aid Ontario, "Sentencing and bail submissions eligible for Gladue Certificate Extension". Posted on "Newsroom": Friday, July 3/09 at *Hot Bytes*, <http://www.legalaid.on.ca/en/news/newsarchive/0907-03_gladueextension.asp>.

Legal Aid Ontario, "Legal Aid Eligibility Increase Backgrounder: Certificates for Previously Ineligible Legal Criminal Matters" (8 June 2015). Online at: <http://www.legalaid.on.ca/en/info/backgrounders/eligibilityexpansion/Certificates%20for%20previously%20ineligible%20legal%20criminal%20matters_lawyers.pdf?t=1434386628660>.

Martel, Joane, Renée Brassard, and Myléne Jaccoud, "When two worlds collide: Aboriginal risk management in Canadian Corrections", *British Journal of Criminology* (2011) 51: 235–255.

McMillan, L. Jane, "Colonial Traditions, Co-optations, and *Mi'kmaq* Legal Consciousness", *Law & Social Inquiry* (2011) 36(1): 171–200.

Office of the Correctional Investigator, *Spirit Matters: Aboriginal People and the Corrections and Conditional Release Act* (Final Report, October 22, 2012). Online at: <http://www.oci-bec.gc.ca/cnt/rpt/oth-aut/oth-aut20121022-eng.aspx>.

Office of the Correctional Investigator, *Annual Report, 2013–2014*. Online at: <http://www.oci-bec.gc.ca/cnt/rpt/pdf/annrpt/annrpt20132014-eng.pdf>.

Orenstein, *Michael, Racialization and Gender of Lawyers in Ontario. Report for the Law Society of Upper Canada.* Report prepared for the Law Society of Upper Canada, April 2010 (Toronto: Law Society of Upper Canada, 2010). Online at: <http://www.lsuc.on.ca/media/convapril10_ornstein.pdf>

Pelletier, Renée, "The Nullification of Section 718.2(e): Aggravating Aboriginal Over-Representation in Canadian Prisons", *Osgoode Hall Law Journal* (2001) 39(2&3): 469–489.

Pfefferle, Brian R., "Gladue Sentencings: Uneasy Answers to the Hard Problem of Aboriginal Over-Incarceration", *Manitoba Law Journal* (2006–2008) 32(2): 113–143.

Roach, Kent, "Blaming the Victim: Canadian Law, Causation, and Residential Schools", *University of Toronto Law Journal* (2014) 64: 566–595.

Roman, Marisa, *Final Report: Aboriginal Bar Consultation.* (Toronto: Law Society of Upper Canada, Equity Initiatives Department, 29 January 2009). Online at:

<http://www.lsuc.on.ca/WorkArea/DownloadAsset.aspx?id=2147487118).

Stenning, Philip, and J.V. Roberts, "Empty Promises: Parliament, The Supreme Court, and the Sentencing of Aboriginal Offenders" (2001) 64 *Sask. L. Rev.* 137.

Truth and Reconciliation Commission of Canada, *Honouring the Truth, Reconciling for the Future: Summary of the Final Report of the Truth and Reconciliation Commission of Canada* (Winnipeg, MB: Truth and Reconciliation Commission of Canada, 2015). Online at: <www.trc.ca/websites/trcinstitution/index.php?p=893>.

Urquijo, Covadonga Robles, and Anne Milan, "Female Population", *Women in Canada: A Gender-based Statistical Report*, Catalogue no. 89-503-X (Ottawa: Statistics Canada, July 2011). Online at: <http://www.statcan.gc.ca/pub/89-503-x/2010001/article/11475-eng.pdf>.

Weatherburn, Don, Jackie Fitzgerald, and Jiuzhao Hua, "Reducing Aboriginal Over-Representation in Prison", *Australian Journal of Public Administration* (2004) 62(3): 65–73.

Webster, Cheryl Marie, Anthony N. Doob, and Nicole M. Myers, "The Parable of Ms. Baker: Understanding Pre-Trial Detention in Canada" *Current Issues in Criminal Justice* (July 2009) 21(1): 80–102.

Welsh, Andrew, and James R.P. Ogloff, "Progressive Reforms or Maintaining the Status Quo? An Empirical Evaluation of the Judicial Consideration of Aboriginal Status in Sentencing Decisions", *Canadian Journal of Criminology and Criminal Justice* (July 2008) 50(4): 491–517.

The Debate over Use of Settlement-based Dispute Resolution Processes

(a)   Against Settlement†

Owen M. Fiss

In a recent report to the Harvard Overseers, Derek Bok called for a new direction in legal education.[1] He decried "the familiar tilt in the law curriculum toward preparing students for legal combat," and asked instead that law schools train their students "for the gentler arts of reconciliation and accommodation."[2] He sought to turn our attention from the courts to "new voluntary mechanisms"[3] for resolving disputes. In doing so, Bok echoed themes that have long been associated with the Chief Justice,[4] and that have become a rallying point for the organized bar and the source of a new movement in the law. This movement is the subject of a new professional journal,[5] a newly formed section of the American Association of Law Schools, and several well-funded institutes. It has even received its own acronym — ADR (Alternative Dispute Resolution).

The movement promises to reduce the amount of litigation initiated, and accordingly the bulk of its proposals are devoted to negotiation and mediation prior to suit. But the interest in the so-called "gentler arts" has not been so confined. It extends to ongoing litigation as well, and the advocates of ADR have sought new ways to facilitate and perhaps even pressure parties into settling pending cases. Just last year, Rule 16 of the Federal Rules of Civil Procedure was amended to strengthen the hand of the trial judge in brokering settlements: The "facilitation of settlement" became an explicit purpose of pre-trial conferences, and participants were officially invited, if that is the proper word, to consider "the possibility of settlement or the use of extrajudicial procedures to resolve the dispute."[5] Now the Advisory Committee on Civil Rules is proposing to amend Rule 68 to sharpen the incentives for settlement: Under this amendment, a party who rejects a settlement offer and then receives a judgment less favorable than that offer must pay the attorney's fees of the other party.[7] This amendment would effect a major change in the traditional American rule, under which each party pays his or her own attorney's fees.[8] It would also be at odds with a number of statutes that seek to facilitate certain types of civil litigation by providing attorney's fees to plaintiffs if they win, without imposing liability for the attorney's fees of their adversaries if they lose.[9]

The advocates of ADR are led to support such measures and to exalt the idea of settlement more generally because they view adjudication as a process to resolve disputes. They act as though courts arose to resolve quarrels between neighbors who had reached an impasse and turned to a stranger for help.[10] Courts are seen as an institutionalization of the stranger and adjudication is viewed as the process by which the stranger exercises power. The very fact that the neighbors have turned to someone else to resolve their dispute signifies a breakdown in their social relations; the advocates of ADR acknowledge this, but nonetheless hope that the neighbors will be able to reach agreement before the stranger renders judgment. Settlement is that agreement. It is a truce more than a true reconciliation, but it seems preferable to judgment because it rests on the consent of both parties and avoids the cost of a lengthy trial.

---

† (1984) 93 Yale L. J. 1073 at 1073–78, 1082–90. [Notes and/or references omitted.] Reproduced with permission.

In my view, however, this account of adjudication and the case for settlement rest on questionable premises. I do not believe that settlement as a generic practice is preferable to judgment or should be institutionalized on a wholesale and indiscriminate basis. It should be treated instead as a highly problematic technique for streamlining dockets. Settlement is for me the civil analogue of plea bargaining: Consent is often coerced; the bargain may be struck by someone without authority; the absence of a trial and judgment renders subsequent judicial involvement troublesome; and although dockets are trimmed, justice may not be done. Like plea bargaining, settlement is a capitulation to the conditions of mass society and should be neither encouraged nor praised.

THE IMBALANCE OF POWER

By viewing the lawsuit as a quarrel between two neighbors, the dispute-resolution story that underlies ADR implicitly asks us to assume a rough equality between the contending parties. It treats settlement as the anticipation of the outcome of trial and assumes that the terms of settlement are simply a product of the parties' predictions of that outcome.[11] In truth, however, settlement is also a function of the resources available to each party to finance the litigation, and those resources are frequently distributed unequally. Many lawsuits do not involve a property dispute between two neighbors, or between AT&T and the government (to update the story), but rather concern a struggle between a member of a racial minority and a municipal police department over alleged brutality, or a claim by a worker against a large corporation over work-related injuries. In these cases, the distribution of financial resources, or the ability of one party to pass along its costs, will invariably infect the bargaining process and the settlement will be at odds with a conception of justice that seeks to make the wealth of the parties irrelevant.

The disparities in resources between the parties can influence the settlement in three ways. First, the poorer party may be less able to amass and analyze the information needed to predict the outcome of the litigation, and thus be disadvantaged in the bargaining process. Second, he may need the damages he seeks immediately and thus be induced to settle as a way of accelerating payment, even though he realizes he would get less now than he might if he awaited judgment. All plaintiffs want their damages immediately, but an indigent plaintiff may be exploited by a rich defendant because his need is so great that the defendant can force him to accept

a sum that is less than the ordinary present value of the judgment. Third, the poorer party might be forced to settle because he does not have the resources to finance the litigation, to cover either his own projected expenses, such as his lawyer's time, or the expenses his opponent can impose through the manipulation of procedural mechanisms such as discovery. It might seem that settlement benefits the plaintiff by allowing him to avoid the costs of litigation, but this is not so. The defendant can anticipate the plaintiff's costs if the case were to be tried fully and decrease his offer by that amount. The indigent plaintiff is a victim of the costs of litigation even if he settles.[12]

There are exceptions. Seemingly rich defendants may sometimes be subject to financial pressures that make them as anxious to settle as indigent plaintiffs. But I doubt that these circumstances occur with any great frequency. I also doubt that institutional arrangements such as contingent fees or the provision of legal services to the poor will in fact equalize resources between contending parties: The contingent fee does not equalize resources; it only makes an indigent plaintiff vulnerable to the willingness of the private bar to invest in his case. In effect, the ability to exploit the plaintiff's lack of resources has been transferred from rich defendants to lawyers who insist upon a hefty slice of the plaintiff's recovery as their fee. These lawyers, moreover, will only work for contingent fees in certain kinds of cases, such as personal-injury suits. And the contingent fee is of no avail when the defendant is the disadvantaged party. Governmental subsidies for legal services have a broader potential, but in the civil domain the battle for these subsidies was hard-fought, and they are in fact extremely limited, especially when it comes to cases that seek systemic reform of government practices.[13]

Of course, imbalances of power can distort judgment as well: Resources influence the quality of presentation, which in turn has an important bearing on who wins and the terms of victory. We count, however, on the guiding presence of the judge, who can employ a number of measures to lessen the impact of distributional inequalities. He can, for example, supplement the parties' presentations by asking questions, calling his own witnesses, and inviting other persons and institutions to participate as amici.[14] These measures are likely to make only a small contribution toward moderating the influence of distributional inequalities, but should not be ignored for that reason. Not even these small steps are possible with settlement. There is, moreover, a critical difference between a process like settlement, which is based on bargaining and accepts inequalities of wealth as an integral and legitimate component of the process, and a process like judgment, which knowingly struggles against those inequalities. Judgment aspires to an autonomy from distributional inequalities, and it gathers much of its appeal from this aspiration.

. . . .

THE LACK OF A FOUNDATION FOR CONTINUING JUDICIAL INVOLVEMENT

The dispute-resolution story trivializes the remedial dimensions of lawsuits and mistakenly assumes judgment to be the end of the process. It supposes that the judge's duty is to declare which neighbor is right and which wrong, and that this declaration will end the judge's involvement (save in that most exceptional situation where it is also necessary for him to issue a writ directing the sheriff to execute the declaration). Under these assumptions, settlement appears as an almost perfect substitute for judgment, for it too can declare the parties' rights. Often, however, judgment is not the end of a lawsuit but only the beginning. The involvement of the court may continue almost indefinitely. In these cases, settlement cannot provide an adequate basis for that necessary continuing involvement, and thus is no substitute for judgment.

The parties may sometimes be locked in combat with one another and view the lawsuit as only one phase in a long continuing struggle. The entry of judgment will then not end the struggle, but rather change its terms and the balance of power. One of the parties will invariably return to the court and again ask for its assistance, not so much because conditions have changed, but because the conditions that preceded the lawsuit have unfortunately not changed. This often occurs in domestic-relations cases, where the divorce decree represents only the opening salvo in an endless series of skirmishes over custody and support.[26]

The structural reform cases that play such a prominent role on the federal docket provide another occasion for continuing judicial involvement. In these cases, courts seek to safeguard public values by restructuring large-scale bureaucratic organizations.[27] The task is enormous, and our knowledge of how to restructure on-going bureaucratic organizations is limited. As a consequence, courts must oversee and manage the remedial process for a long time — maybe forever. This, I fear, is true of most school desegregation cases, some of which have been pend-ing for twenty or thirty years.[28] It is also true of antitrust cases that seek divestiture or reorganization of an industry.[29]

The drive for settlement knows no bounds and can result in a consent decree even in the kinds of cases I have just mentioned, that is, even when a court finds itself embroiled in a continuing struggle between the parties or must reform a bureaucratic organization. The parties may be ignorant of the difficulties ahead or optimistic about the future, or they may simply believe that they can get more favorable terms through a bargained-for agreement. Soon, however, the inevitable happens: One party returns to court and asks the judge to modify the decree, either to make it more effective or less stringent. But the judge is at a loss: He has no basis for assessing the request. He cannot, to use Cardozo's somewhat melodramatic formula, easily decide whether the "dangers, once substantial, have become attenuated to a shadow,"[30] because, by definition, he never knew the dangers.

The allure of settlement in large part derives from the fact that it avoids the need for a trial. Settlement must thus occur before the trial is complete and the judge has entered findings of fact and conclusions of law. As a consequence, the judge confronted with a request for modification of a consent decree must retrospectively reconstruct the situation as it existed at the time the decree was entered, and decide whether conditions today have sufficiently changed to warrant a modification in that decree. In the Meat Packers litigation, for example, where a consent decree governed the industry for almost half a century, the judge confronted with a request for modification in 1960 had to reconstruct the "danger" that had existed at the time of the entry of the decree in 1920 in order to determine whether the danger had in fact become a "shadow."[31] Such an inquiry borders on the absurd, and is likely to dissipate whatever savings in judicial resources the initial settlement may have produced.

Settlement also impedes vigorous enforcement, which sometimes requires use of the contempt power. As a formal matter, contempt is available to punish violations of a consent decree.[32] But courts hesitate to use that power to enforce decrees that rest solely on consent, especially when enforcement is aimed at high public officials, as became evident in the Willowbrook deinstitutionalization case[33] and the recent Chicago desegregation case.[34] Courts do not see a mere bargain between the parties as a sufficient foundation for the exercise of their coercive powers.

Sometimes the agreement between the parties extends beyond the terms of the decree and includes stipulated "findings of fact" and "conclusions of law," but even then an adequate foundation for a strong use of the judicial power is lacking. Given the underlying purpose of settlement — to avoid trial — the so-called "findings" and "conclusions" are necessarily the products of a bargain between the parties rather than of a trial and an independent judicial judgment. Of course, a plaintiff is free to drop a lawsuit altogether (provided that the interests of certain other persons are not compromised), and a defendant can offer something in return, but that bargained-for arrangement more closely resembles a contract than an injunction. It raises a question which has already been answered whenever an injunction is issued, namely, whether the judicial power should be used to enforce it. Even assuming that the consent is freely given and authoritative, the bargain is at best contractual and does not contain the kind of enforcement commitment already embodied in a decree that is the product of a trial and the judgment of a court.

JUSTICE RATHER THAN PEACE

The dispute-resolution story makes settlement appear as a perfect substitute for judgment, as we just saw, by trivializing the remedial dimensions of a lawsuit, and also by reducing the social function of the lawsuit to one of resolving private disputes: In that story, settlement appears to achieve exactly the same purpose as judgment — peace between the parties — but at considerably less expense to society. The two quarrelling neighbors turn to a court in order to resolve their dispute, and society makes courts available because it wants to aid in the achievement of their private ends or to secure the peace.

In my view, however, the purpose of adjudication should be understood in broader terms. Adjudication uses public resources, and employs not strangers chosen by the parties but public officials chosen by a process in which the public participates. These officials, like members of the legislative and executive branches, possess a power that has been defined and conferred by public law, not by private agreement. Their job is not to maximize the ends of private parties, nor simply to secure the peace, but to explicate and give force to the values embodied in authoritative texts such as the Constitution and statutes: to interpret those values and to bring reality into accord with them. This duty is not discharged when the parties settle.

In our political system, courts are reactive institutions. They do not search out interpretive occasions, but instead wait for others to bring matters to their attention. They also rely for the most part on others to investigate and present the law and facts. A settlement will thereby deprive a court of the occasion, and perhaps even the ability, to render an interpretation. A court cannot proceed (or not proceed very far) in the face of a settlement. To be against settlement is not to urge that parties be "forced" to litigate, since that would interfere with their autonomy and distort the adjudicative process; the parties will be inclined to make the court believe that their bargain is justice. To be against settlement is only to suggest that when the parties settle, society gets less than what appears, and for a price it does not know it is paying. Parties might settle while leaving justice undone. The settlement of a school suit might secure the peace, but not racial equality. Although the parties are prepared to live under the terms they bargained for, and although such peaceful coexistence may be a necessary precondition of justice,[35] and itself a state of affairs to be valued, it is not justice itself. To settle for something means to accept less than some ideal.

I recognize that judges often announce settlements not with a sense of frustration or disappointment, as my account of adjudication might suggest, but with a sigh of relief. But this sigh should be seen for precisely what it is: It is not a recognition that a job is done, nor an acknowledgment that a job need not be done because justice has been secured. It is instead based on another sentiment altogether, namely, that another case has been "moved along," which is true whether or not justice has been done or even needs to be done. Or the sigh might be based on the fact that the agony of judgment has been avoided.

There is, of course, sometimes a value to avoidance, not just to the judge, who is thereby relieved of the need to make or enforce a hard decision, but also to society, which sometimes thrives by masking its basic contradictions. But will settlement result in avoidance when it is most appropriate? Other familiar avoidance devices, such as certiorari,[36] at least promise a devotion to public ends, but settlement is controlled by the litigants, and is subject to their private motivations and all the vagaries of the bargaining process. There are also dangers to avoidance, and these may well outweigh any imagined benefits. Partisans of ADR — Chief Justice Berger, or even President Bok — may begin with a certain satisfaction with the status quo. But when one sees injustices that cry out for correction — as Congress did when it endorsed the concept of the private attorney general[37] and as the Court of another era did when it sought to enhance access to the courts[38] — the value of avoidance diminishes and the agony of judgment becomes a necessity. Someone has to confront the betrayal of our deepest ideals and be prepared to turn the world upside down to bring those ideals to fruition.

THE REAL DIVIDE

To all this, one can readily imagine a simple response by way of confession and avoidance: We are not talking about *those* lawsuits. Advocates of ADR might insist that my account of adjudication, in contrast to the one implied by the dispute-resolution story, focuses on a rather narrow category of lawsuits. They could argue that while settlement may have only the most limited appeal with respect to those cases, I have not spoken to the "typical" cases. My response is twofold.

First, even as a purely quantitative matter, I doubt that the number of cases I am referring to is trivial. My universe includes those cases in which there are significant distributional inequalities; those in which it is difficult to generate authoritative consent because organizations or social groups are parties or because the power to settle is vested in autonomous agents; those in which the court must continue to supervise the parties after judgment; and those in which justice needs to be done, or to put it more modestly, where there is a genuine social need for an authoritative interpretation of law. I imagine that the number of cases that satisfy one of these four criteria is considerable; in contrast to the kind of case portrayed in the dispute-resolution story, they probably dominate the docket of a modern court system.

Second, it demands a certain kind of myopia to be concerned only with the number of cases, as though all cases are equal simply because the clerk of the court assigns each a single docket number. All cases are not equal. The Los Angeles desegregation case,[39] to take one example, is not equal to the allegedly more typical suit involving a property dispute or an automobile accident. The desegregation suit consumes more resources, affects more people, and provokes far greater challenges to the judicial power. The settlement movement must introduce a qualitative perspective; it must speak to these more "significant" cases, and demonstrate the propriety of settling them. Otherwise it will soon be seen as an irrelevance, dealing with trivia rather than responding to the very conditions that give the movement its greatest sway and saliency.

Nor would sorting cases into "two tracks," one for settlement, and another for judgment, avoid my objections. Settling automobile cases and leaving discrimination or antitrust cases for judgment might remove a large number of cases from the dockets, but the dockets will nevertheless remain burdened with the cases that consume the most judicial resources and represent the most controversial exercises of the judicial power. A "two track" strategy would drain the argument for settlement of much of its appeal. I also doubt whether the "two track" strategy can be sensibly implemented. It is impossible to formulate adequate criteria for prospectively sorting cases. The problems of settlement are not tied to the subject matter of the suit, but instead stem from factors that are harder to identify, such as the wealth of the parties, the likely post-judgment history of the suit, or the need for an authoritative interpretation of law. The authors of the amendment to Rule 68 make a gesture toward a "two track" strategy by exempting class actions and shareholder derivative suits, and by allowing the judge to refrain from awarding attorney's fees when it is "unjustified under all of the circumstances."[40] But these gestures are cramped and ill-conceived, and are likely to increase the workload of the courts by giving rise to yet another set of issues to litigate.[41] It is, moreover, hard to see how these problems can be avoided. Many of the factors that lead a society to bring social relationships that otherwise seem wholly private (e.g., marriage) within the jurisdiction of a court, such as imbalances of power or the interests of third parties, are also likely to make settlement problematic. Settlement is a poor substitute for judgement; it is an even poorer substitute for the withdrawal of jurisdiction.

For these reasons, I remain highly skeptical of a "two track" strategy, and would resist it. But the more important point to note is that the draftsmen of Rule 68 are the exception. There is no hint of a "two track" strategy in Rule 16. In fact, most ADR advocates make no effort to distinguish between different types of cases or to suggest that "the gentler arts of reconciliation and accommodation" might be particularly appropriate for one type of case but not for another. They lump all cases together. This suggests that what divides me from the partisans of ADR is not that we are concerned with different universes of cases [and] that Derek Bok, for example, focuses on boundary quarrels while I see only desegregation suits. I suspect instead that what divides us is much deeper and stems from our understanding of the purpose of the civil law suit and its place in society. It is a difference in outlook.

Someone like Bok sees adjudication in essentially private terms: The purpose of lawsuits and the civil courts is to resolve disputes, and the amount of litigation we encounter is evidence of the needlessly combative and quarrelsome character of Americans. Or as Bok put it, using a more diplomatic idiom: "At bottom, ours is a society built on individualism, competition, and success."[42] I, on the other hand, see adjudication in more public terms: Civil litigation is an institutional arrangement for using state power to bring a recalcitrant reality closer to our chosen ideas. We turn to the courts because we need to, not because of some quirk in our personalities. We train our students in the tougher arts so that they may help secure all that the law promises, not because

we want them to become gladiators or because we take a special pleasure in combat.

To conceive of the civil lawsuit in public terms as America does might be unique. I am willing to assume that no other country — including Japan, Bok's new paragon[43] — has a case like *Brown v. Board of Education*[44] in which the judicial power is used to eradicate the caste structure. I am willing to assume that no other country conceives of law and uses law in quite the way we do. But this should be a source of pride rather than shame. What is unique is not the problem, that we live short of our ideals, but that we alone among the nations of the world seem willing to do something about it. Adjudication American-style is not a reflection of our combativeness but rather a tribute to our inventiveness and perhaps even more to our commitment.

(b)   For Reconciliation†

Andrew W. McThenia and Thomas L. Shaffer

Professor Owen Fiss, in his recent comment, *Against Settlement*,[1] weighs in against the Alternative Dispute Resolution (ADR) movement. He brings to the discussion his often stated preference for adjudication, which he views as "a tribute to our inventiveness,"[2] to be encouraged because it is a forum for the articulation of important public values. Fiss argues that the entire movement for alternatives to litigation is misplaced. He understands that the movement's claim to legitimacy turns on the inefficiency of the legal system and on popular dissatisfaction with law as a means for maintaining order,[3] and he challenges this claim.

Fiss attacks a straw man. In our view, the models he has created for argument in other circumstances[4] have become mechanisms of self-deception not only for him but for most of those who write about alternatives to litigation. His understanding that the plea of ADR advocates is based on efficiency reduces the entire question to one of procedures. Fiss's argument rests on the faith that justice — and he uses the word — is usually something people get from the government. He comes close to

arguing that the branch of government that resolves disputes, the courts, is the principal source of justice in fragmented modern American society.[5]

Fiss's view that the claims of ADR advocates arise from a popular dissatisfaction with law reduces the issue to one of order.[6] As his first stated understanding reduces justice to statism, this understanding reduces justice (or, if you like, peace) to a tolerably minimum level of violence in the community. In our view, an appropriate engagement of the Fiss attack on ADR must go all the way back to these two characterizations in his argument against ADR and in favor of court-dominated dispute resolution. We are not willing to let him frame the issue.

Certain themes recur in the ADR literature. Many advocates of ADR make efficiency-based claims. And a plea for ending the so-called litigation explosion, and for returning to law and order, runs through the rules-of-procedure branch of the ADR literature.[7] But the movement, if it is even appropriate to call it a single movement, is too varied for Fiss's description. Rather than focusing on the substance of claims made for ADR, Fiss has created a

---

† (1985) 94 Yale L.J. 1660. [Notes and/or references omitted.] Reproduced with permission.

view of the function of courts that he can comfortably oppose.

In an earlier and provocative article, Fiss called for both a recognition and an affirmation of the expanded role of courts in modern America.[8] He urged an explicit recognition that "[a]djudication is the social process by which judges give meaning to our public values."[9] Further, he argued that a new form of adjudication, "structural reform," be celebrated as "a central — maybe the central — mode of constitutional adjudication."[10] To develop his thesis and to meet Professor Lon Fuller's arguments on the limits of adjudication,[11] Fiss resorted to modelling. He contrasted his preferred view of adjudication, "structural reform," with what he described as a "traditional" model of adjudication. Although it is not clear whether he understood the *substance* of the two types of adjudication to be fundamentally different,[12] he clearly viewed the *form* of structural reform litigation as "breathtakingly different"[13] from the "dispute resolution" or "traditional" model of adjudication.

While Fiss was initially content to construct contrasting models of adjudication simply in order to accentuate his position and argue against Fuller's, he has in more recent writings asserted that one of these models, that of traditional dispute resolution, has a life of its own, a life that has "long dominated the literature and our thinking."[14] In fact, Fiss's later positive description of structural reform continues to flower, while his negative description of traditional adjudication has become abstract and lifeless. Fiss's response to the imperfections of life that lay bare the difficulties with his model of structural reform has been, it seems to us, to provide a shrill description of traditional judicial dispute resolution.[15]

Fiss's description of traditional dispute resolution is a story of two neighbors "in a state of nature" who each claim a single piece of property and who, when they cannot agree, turn to "a stranger" to resolve their dispute.[16] He asserts that traditional dispute resolution depicts a sociologically impoverished universe,[17] operates in a state of nature where there are no public values or goals[18] except a supposed "natural harmony" of the status quo,[19] and calls on the exercise of power by a stranger.[20] That was never Fuller's position. Nor do we find much support in the literature or in reality for such a view of traditional adjudication. If there ever was such a world we expect it was "nasty, brutish and short." However, we don't really believe that traditional adjudication ever bore much resemblance to that story. Yet this is the view of the world that Fiss attributes to the advocates of ADR; his attack on ADR is premised on that notion.[21]

Models are, of course, human creations. The good ones contain elements of the creator's perception of the world and of the reality he seeks to perceive.[22] They are designed to invite conversation and to appeal to the reader in a search for understanding. They are abstractions; but to be effective, they must have some connection either with the creator's view of reality or with what he wants the world to be like. Fiss's model of structural reform is, in this way, an effective model.[23] While it may not depict the world that many of us observe, it does reflect his view of the world he wishes he could find. It reflects, we suspect, more his hope than his actual belief. We honor that. The model is rich. It leads to conversation and debate.

But Fiss's model of traditional dispute resolution is flat; it is only an abstraction, and is therefore also a caricature. It has no relation to the world as it is; it does not appeal to the reader as a convincing way to understand adjudication or its alternatives. It does not permit one to express hope in alternatives to adjudication.

In any event, after setting up his "state of nature" model of dispute resolution, Fiss attributes that view of the world to the advocates of ADR. He understands pleas to consider alternatives to current means of resolving disputes as turning on the inefficiency of traditional adjudication (his negative model), and popular dissatisfaction with it. He equates the ADR movement with those who urge settlement more than judgment and who seek a "truce more than a true reconciliation."[24] He argues that settlement is "a capitulation to the conditions of mass society," a capitulation that "should be neither encouraged nor praised."[25] He assumes that the ADR movement is one that wants peace at any price and treats settlement as "the anticipation of the outcome of trial,"[26] that is, trial in his stranger-judge, negative model of adjudication.

Fiss is against settlement because he views the matters that come before courts in America, and that are inappropriate for ADR, as including cases in which: (1) there are distributional inequities; (2) securing authoritative consent or settlement is difficult; (3) continued supervision following judgment is necessary; and (4) there is a genuine need for an authoritative interpretation of law.[27] Fiss characterizes disputes in this limited way — as arguments between two neighbors, one of whom has vastly superior bargaining power over the other. It is then easy for him to prefer litigation to settlement, because litigation is a way to equalize bargaining power.

The soundest and deepest part of the ADR movement does not rest on Fiss's two-neighbors model. It rests on values — of religion, community, and work place — that are more vigorous than Fiss thinks. In many, in fact most, of the cultural traditions that argue for ADR, settlement is neither an avoidance mechanism nor a truce. Settlement is a process of reconciliation in which the anger of broken relationships is to be confronted rather than avoided, and in which healing demands not a truce but confrontation. Instead of "trivializing the remedial process,"[28] settlement exalts that process. Instead of "reducing the social function ... to one of resolving private disputes,"[29] settlement calls on substantive community values. Settlement is sometimes a beginning, and is sometimes a postscript, but it is not the essence of the enterprise of dispute resolution. The essence of the enterprise is more like the structural injunction, about which Fiss has written so eloquently, than like an alternative to the resolution-by-stranger described by his negative model.[30]

The "real divide"[31] between us and Fiss may not be our differing views of the sorts of cases that now wind their way into American courts, but, more fundamentally, it may be our different views of justice. Fiss comes close to equating justice with law. He includes among the cases unsuited for settlement "those in which justice needs to be done, or to put it more modestly, where there is a genuine social need for an authoritative interpretation of law."[32] We do not believe that law and justice are synonymous. We see the deepest and soundest of ADR arguments as in agreement with us: Justice is not usually something people get from the government. And courts (which are not, in any case, strangers) are not the only or even the most important places that dispense justice.[33]

Many advocates of ADR can well be taken to have asked about the law's response to disputes, and alternatives to that response, not in order to reform the law but in order to locate alternative views of what a dispute is. Such alternatives would likely advance or assume understandings of justice (or, if you like, peace) that are also radically different from justice as something lawyers *administer*, or peace as the absence of violence. They assume not that justice is something people get from the government but that it is something people give to one another. These advocates seek an understanding of justice in the way Socrates and Thrasymachus did in the *Republic*: Justice is not the will of the stronger; it is not efficiency in government; it is not the reduction of violence; Justice is what we discover — you and I, Socrates said — when we walk together, listen together, and even love one another, in our curiosity about what justice is and where justice comes from.

Most of us who have gone to college know something about Socrates. Many more of us who grew up in the United States know something about Moses and Jesus. It is from Torah and Gospel, more than from Plato, that we are most likely to be able to sketch out radical alternatives to the law's response to disputes. As a matter of fact, our religious culture contains both a theoretical basis for these alternatives and a way to apply theory to disputes.

In the Hebraic tradition (as in the Islamic), scripture is normative. Judaism, for example, does not merely seek to follow Torah; it loves Torah, it finds life in Torah, it celebrates Torah as one might celebrate the presence of a lover, or of a loving parent, or of a community that nourishes peace — commitment to common well being, and even a feeling of being well. (Salvation is not too strong a word for it.) Justice is the way one defines a righteous life; justice does involve according other persons their due but, more radically, in the Hebraic view, it involves loving them. Such a justice is the product of piety, to be sure, but not piety alone; it is the product of study, of reason, and of attending to the wise and learning from them how to be virtuous.[34] *Quare fidem intellectum.*[35]

The Christian side of the Hebraic tradition has, or should have, all of this. It also has a unique procedure established in St. Matthew's Gospel — a *system* backed up by stern condemnation of Christians who turn from the Gospel and seek instead the law's response to disputes. In this system — as well as Judaism[36] — the religious community claims authority to resolve disputes and even to coerce obedience. The procedure involves, first, conversation; if that fails, it involves mediation; if mediation fails, it involves airing the dispute before representatives of the community. If the dispute goes so far as judgment, the system — as is also the case in Judaism — permits pressure: "[I]f he refuses to listen to the community, treat him like a pagan or a tax collector. I tell you solemnly, whatever you bind on earth shall be considered bound in heaven; whatever you loose on earth shall be considered loosed in heaven."[37]

Thus, the procedure gives priority to restoring the relationship. Hebraic theology puts primary emphasis on relationships, a priority that is political and even ontological, as well as ethical, and therefore legal.[38] And so, most radically, the religious tradition seeks not *resolution* (which connotes the sort of doctrinal integrity in the law that seems to us to be Fiss's highest priority) but *reconciliation* of brother to brother, sister to sister, sister to brother, child to parent, neighbor to neighbor, buyer to seller, defendant to plaintiff, *and judge to both*. (The Judge is also an I and a Thou.) This view of what a dispute is, and of what third parties seek when they intervene in disputes between others, provides an existing, traditional, common alternative to the law's response. The fact seems to be that this alternative has both a vigorous modern history and a studiable contemporary vitality (Jerrold Auerbach[39] to the contrary notwithstanding).

Contemporary manifestations of the Hebraic tradition claim adherence to a moral authority that is more important than the government.[40] The Torah is the wisdom of God, the Gospel is the good news that promises a peace the world cannot give. From one perspective, theology makes such religious views of dispute and resolution seem peripheral. That impression is deceptive, though: In the aggregate these views of what a dispute is are consistent with one another and, as such, consistent with the moral commitments of most people in America. The numbers of people in this country who might find them so is not declining; it is increasing. "In the aggregate" is an appropriate consideration, as one assays radical alternatives to the law's response to disputes, because there is substantial commonality among the practitioners of this radical Hebraic alternative. Religious systems of reconciliation rest on a substantively common theology and on a substantively common argument that, contrary to the implications of Fiss's view of justice, the government is not as important as it thinks it is.

Professor David Trubek ends a recent and pessimistic essay on alternative dispute resolution[41] with a paradox: "[N]o one," he says, "really seems to believe in law any more."[42] The "elites" who complain of a litigation explosion — Chief Justice Warren Burger and others "who champion alternatives"[43] — "question the law's efficacy."[44] But so do those who criticize the law as political and oppressive, most notably scholars in the Critical Legal Studies movement. The elites exalt an informalism they don't believe in, Trubek says; and the radicals exalt a formalist they distrust. Apparently the new legal-process school — or at least one of its eloquent spokesmen, Owen Fiss — still believes in law. Fiss's writing on structural reform is powerful. It may not reflect the way the world actually is, but it is a statement of hope. And that is important in an age of nihilism. But we suspect those who believe in law and in nothing else; we hope Fiss is not among them. Informalism of the Chief Justice's formulation[45] may deserve distrust. But informalism has some contemporary manifestations — many of them resting on the most ancient and deepest of our traditions — that deserve trust and even celebration. These manifestations too are statements of hope. Suggestions for alternatives to litigation need to be critically examined — no doubt many of them are hollow. What they do not need, and what the legal community does not need, is an argument that reduces these alternatives to a caricature.

(c) Understanding the Critiques of Mediation: What Is All the Fuss About?[†]

Neil Sargent

The essential claim I am making in this paper is that it is difficult, if not impossible, to discuss the topic of 'critical perspectives on mediation' in any coherent way as if there is a comprehensive set of critiques of mediation which can be talked about in the same breath, or listed in one extended paragraph. Instead, I argue that there is a range of critiques of media-

tion which start from very different theoretical positions, which view the role and functioning of the formal justice system from quite different perspectives, and which have very different implications for the development of mediation theory and practice.

On the one hand, there is a strong liberal consensus critique of mediation which critiques the

---

† Unpublished. [Notes and/or references omitted.] Reproduced with permission.

advocates of mediation for their supposed emphasis on the quantity of justice over the quality of justice. Within this liberal consensus critique, mediation and other forms of Alternative Dispute Resolution, or ADR, are often described as offering, at best, a commitment to 'second class justice'.[1] It may be, according to even some of the liberal critics of mediation and ADR, that there is a place for mediation and informal justice in relation to some types of disputes for which mediation might be appropriate. But, according to this liberal critique, we must never lose sight of the fact that the formal justice system, with its commitment to the rule of law, the requirements of due process, and the adversarial trial process, provides the only true measure of justice within the liberal, democratic state.[2]

It is worth observing that even many advocates for an increased role for mediation and other ADR initiatives articulate their support for this position in terms which are not inconsistent with this liberal critique of mediation.[3] In other words, the liberal critique always insists that a clear hierarchy of the forms of justice be drawn, with mediation and other ADR initiatives being seen as supplements to the existing formal justice system, but never as a substitute or alternative to the formal justice system. In consequence, here the language of mediation existing "in the shadow of the law", as Mnookin and Kornhauser put it, is very clearly articulated.[4]

In addition to the liberal consensus critique of settlement and mediation there is an equally strong contingent of critics of mediation who frame their critique of mediation and informal justice from within a conflict perspective which differs radically from the liberal consensus critique in its view of the ideological function of law within liberal democracy. Rather than viewing the formal justice system as a reflection of a shared liberal democratic value system, the conflict perspective begins from the assumption that conflict, rather than consensus, characterizes the structured inequalities of social, economic and political relations within capitalist societies. Consequently, here the emphasis of the critique of mediation is not so much the liberal consensus view of the inadequate promise of mediation as it is with what a conflict theorist might refer to as the false promise of mediation.

Thus, critics such as Richard Abel and Laura Nader have pointed to the insidious nature of the state sponsored community justice movement, which seems to provide a means of empowerment for communities which have been traditionally marginalized by the formal justice system. They warn that the promise of increased community control over the

forms of justice is a trojan horse, by means of which the liberal state seeks to gain entrance within the walls of those very communities which are capable of providing sites of resistance to capitalist liberal hegemony, precisely because they have been so marginalized. Community justice models, which provide a means by which such communities will effectively police themselves according to standards and values established outside their own milieu, offer a very powerful mechanism of informal social control to the liberal state, which is all the more effective because it is voluntary, and thus avoids the social, economic and political costs of more direct, coercive forms of social control.

A primary concern in much of this literature is that the ideology of mediation and informal justice operate to neutralize social conflict by privatizing and individualizing conflict and making it appear that all conflicts can be resolved through consensual processes such as mediation, rather than through more confrontational forms of political action. Nader argues that the 'harmony ideology' associated with mediation and other forms of alternative dispute resolution functions to suppress legitimate social conflict.[7] According to Nader, the theory of harmony justice which undergirds the alternative dispute resolution movement views conflict as "dysfunctional and threatening to the social order".[8] For Nader, however, social conflict is rational and to be expected in a society in which access to economic, legal and political power is unevenly distributed. Indeed, social conflict may be a way to expose inequalities and make claims to social justice.[9] In this context, Nader views official expressions of state support for harmony justice models with suspicion, as part of a legitimizing ideology which is aimed at defusing and depoliticizing forms of societal conflict which otherwise have the potential to challenge the status quo.[10]

In some respects it seems as if the conflict critique of community mediation and harmony ideology provides an inverted mirror image of the liberal consensus critique of mediation and ADR. Different sides of the same coin, neither critique seems to recognize mediation as a form of justice having any identity, any history, or any integrity in its own right. Thus, conflict theorists like Auerbach and Harrington also tend to see the informal justice system as existing 'in the shadow of the law'.[11] But here that shadow is a more ominous presence. The formal legal system retains all of its power and authority, while the informal justice system looks after the minor dispute processing; all the while reinforcing, rather than challenging, the legitimacy of the existing set of power relations within capitalist society.

Alongside the liberal and conflict critiques of mediation there is also a significant camp of feminist critics of mediation, who raise the question whether mediation (and by implication other forms of alternative dispute resolution) is capable of addressing imbalances of power between the participants in mediation. The focus of much of this feminist critique of mediation has been directed to the particular context of divorce mediation;[12] although there has also been a significant degree of concern expressed in the feminist literature over attempts to promote mediation as an alternative to formal criminal proceedings in the context of violence against women.[13]

In its concern with the family as a site of oppression against women, the feminist critique of mediation differs from both of the preceding liberal and conflict positions. And yet, at the same time, the feminist critique of mediation also has affinities with each of the above critiques. Thus, many feminist commentators have pointed to the lack of due process safeguards for women in mediation; as well as to a risk that women's hard won substantive legal rights in the area of family property and support entitlements may be sacrificed within the mediation process in the interest of reaching a 'consensual' mediated agreement between participants who are often in very unequal bargaining positions.[14] In this sense, the feminist critique of divorce mediation bears more than a passing resemblance to the liberal critique of settlement as an inadequate alternative to the formal justice system, one that is less concerned with protecting the legal rights and procedural interests of the participants than is the adversarial trial process.

At the same time, feminist critics have also pointed to the ideological dimensions of the divorce mediation movement in suppressing and depoliticizing conflicts over systemic gender inequalities within 'the family'. Thus, Pickett argues that the 'familial ideology' of divorce mediation constructs the 'private' emotional nature of family disputes as being illfitted to the adversarial forum of the court system; thereby succeeding in transforming feminist struggles over the legal norms governing property and custody entitlements on family breakdown into individualized

disputes which are suited to therapeutic treatment by divorce mediators.[15] In this context, Pickett's critique of the ideological function of divorce mediation in legitimizing the existing 'gendered' structure of power relations within the nuclear family bears an obvious relation to many conflict theorists' critique of 'harmony justice'. Divorce mediation is presented as a trojan horse which women accept at their peril.

In conclusion, two themes seem to emerge out of this brief discussion of the critiques of mediation. We could categorize them as emphasizing on the one hand, the inadequate promise of mediation, and on the other the false promise of mediation. Both themes are concerned with the problem of power. However, they appear to address the problem of power in very different ways. The liberal critique of mediation assumes that the procedural requirements of due process within the formal justice system provide an appropriate (and sufficient) mechanism for redressing imbalances of power between litigants. Indeed, within the liberal conception of justice, law occupies a privileged institutional position as a protector of the interests of the weak against those of the strong.

However, seen from a conflict perspective, (and from many feminists' perspective) the liberal ideal of justice is just that, an ideal, which operates to legitimize the unequal structure of class, gender and race relations within capitalist and patriarchal society. From this critical perspective, mediation also functions to legitimize the status quo, rather than to pose any real challenge to it. However, in some respects mediation is seen as being even more ideologically 'dangerous' than the formal justice system, because it appears to hold out the promise of individual 'empowerment' to those who feel disempowered by the formal justice system. As a result, many conflict and feminist critics of mediation are forced into the position of becoming reluctant defenders of the formal justice system as the 'least worst alternative' available for pursuing claims to social justice. It is one of the ironies of this field of study that from a certain distance it is hard to tell the liberal and the conflict and the feminist critics of mediation apart.

VIII

Access to Justice

Overview of Part VIII

The readings in **Part VIII** explore issues concerning access to justice from a number of different perspectives.

Chapter 20 includes articles that highlight two traditional approaches to increasing access to justice for persons living in poverty. R.J. Gathercole's article is a classic discussion of the benefits and detriments of two models of providing legal aid services. The Executive Summary of Buckley's Research Paper for the CBA sets out a number of challenges for ensuring that legal aid services provide true access to justice for Canadians in a more contemporary context. Similarly, McGill's article examines a number of different approaches to designing and reforming small claims courts across Canada and the ways in which small claims courts may serve as effective and efficient mechanisms for providing access to justice for individuals with lower incomes. Are these methods of improving access to justice effective? Are they sufficient?

The articles in **Chapter 21** consider other impediments to access to justice that are more closely tied to procedural aspects of the legal system. Chief Justice McLachlin of the Supreme Court of Canada discusses the challenges posed by the high cost of litigation, long trials, delays in the justice system, and endemic social problems. Her comments are important because they emphasize that issues of access are not only faced by low-income Canadians but increasingly by the middle class as well; those whose options she says "are grim". The executive summary of the Action Committee on Access to Justice in Civil and Family Matters, headed by Justice Cromwell of the Supreme Court of Canada, notes the importance of viewing access to justice in the broader context of how a lack of access to justice impacts the everyday lives of Canadians. The Committee's report

points to the need for a culture of reform in order to achieve truly accessible justice in Canada. In turn, Justice Winkler's article describes the specific, sometimes unsuccessful, measures implemented to limit delays within the Ontario justice system. The Ontario example highlights the fact that sometimes well-intentioned procedural reforms actually exacerbate existing problems. For her part, Mathen identifies additional impediments to access to justice that arise when individuals and groups are prevented from raising *Charter* issues due to changes in rules of "standing" and the retraction of government support for initiatives like the Court Challenges Program, which funded test-case litigation. Finally, Marsden's report on the tragic story of Rosa Becker (recall the *Petkus v. Becker* decision from **Chapter 15**) provides a chilling reminder that success in court does not always translate to financial or personal victory outside the court. Sometimes when you "win" you still lose.

As you read these articles, ask yourself: what does access to justice really mean? Can access to justice be defined by measures of "affordability" or "efficiency" alone, or do we require some other more substantive measure of the "quality" of the result(s) offered by the process? In the context of questions about whether law can or should be used for social transformation (see **Part X**), can we still ask this question without acknowledging that access to justice is, for most Canadians, an ideal more than the reality?

Kafka's story-within-a-story of a man who comes seeking entrance to "the law" (included in Chapter 17) is often read as a tragic lesson in the inaccessibility and cold indifference of "the law". Does the story told to K., or his subsequent interactions with the priest, offer any insights into the issues of access raised in this Part?

Access to Justice: Income Issues

(a) Legal Services and the Poor†

R.J. Gathercole

Justice is open to all — like the Ritz Hotel.[1]

Making legal services accessible to the poor[2] is an issue that has long confronted the legal profession, although significant developments in legal aid have taken place only in the last two decades.[3] There had been relatively little discussion of whether the poor really are in dire need of lawyers' services; rather lawyers assume that the poor, like the rest of society, need these services almost as much as food, clothing, shelter and medical attention.

Nor have lawyers been modest about what legal services — as provided by lawyers[4] — can accomplish for the poor. Reginald Heber Smith in his classic work, *Justice and the Poor*, published in 1919 and generally regarded as the motivating force of the American legal aid movement, wrote "In vast tracts of the civil law and in all of the criminal law related to the more severe crimes, equality in the administration of justice can be had only by supplying attorneys to the poor."[5] If more legal aid offices were opened and existing staff increased, "that part of the denial of justice which is traceable solely to the inability of the poor to employ counsel will be completely overcome."[6]

Forty-six years later, E. Clinton Bamberger Jr., a young Baltimore attorney who attended an A.B.A. conference to learn about the new neighbourhood legal offices being established in the United States and found himself recruited as the first Director of Legal Services in the Office of Economic Opportu-nity (O.E.O.) — the central office of the "War on Poverty"[7] — went even further than Smith.

> We cannot be content with the creation of systems rendering free legal assistance to all the people who need it but cannot afford a lawyer's advice. Our responsibility is to marshal the forces of law and the strength of lawyers to combat the causes and effects of poverty. Lawyers must uncover the legal causes of poverty, remodel the systems which generate the cycle of poverty, and design new social, legal and political tools and vehicles to move poor people from deprivation, depression and despair to opportunity, hope and ambition.[8]

These high expectations of what lawyers could accomplish for the poor were not restricted to the United States. In a 1971 study prepared for the National Council of Welfare, a leading Canadian legal aid activist wrote:[9]

> At the lowest level of abstraction, a legal services programme can at least assist in mitigating the surface attributes of poverty. As a service provided to the poor at no cost, it has a redistributive effect. The nature of the day-to-day legal care provided would lessen at least the effect of poverty. Illegal evictions, consumer fraud, and abuses of official discretion, all wrongs to which the poor are particularly vulnerable, could be vigilantly monitored and often remedied. As well, efforts directed at law reform might succeed in gaining even more widespread relief.

† From Robert G. Evans and Michael J. Trebilcock (eds.), *Lawyers and the Consumer Interest: Regulating the Market for Legal Services* (Toronto: Butterworth & Co. (Canada) Ltd., 1982) 407 at 407–18, 423, 426–29. [Notes and/or references omitted.] Reproduced with permission.

...

The lawyer's business is to assist his client in analysing alternatives. He is expected to be partial, to act as the advocate of those with interests to pursue. This work, carried on in a way which encouraged the participation of the individual and the group in the work involved in the pursuit of grievances could offer the poor an opportunity to come to grips, perhaps for the first time, with problems heretofore beyond reach.

...

At first, through their lawyers, but later with progressively less and less assistance, the poor could make articulate and knowledgeable inputs into decision-making processes which affect their lives. This new access to the levers of policy-making might be an important first step in the efforts of the poor to gain some control of their own lives. The degree to which this control can be achieved is the degree to which a legal services programme can contribute to the alteration of the structure of poverty in this country.

It is almost 15 years since these goals of the legal aid movement were articulated. During that time virtually every Canadian province that did not already have one[] has developed a legal aid program to provide at least the services envisioned by Smith.[10] A Legal Services Corporation has been established in the United States as an outgrowth of the legal services work started in the O.E.O.[11] and the United Kingdom has made some significant, if somewhat overdue improvements in its legal aid services.[12] Nevertheless, the poor in each of these countries are at best only marginally better off for all of these efforts and even the relatively limited goals articulated by Reginald Heber Smith 60 years ago have not been achieved. It is doubtful that they will be in the foreseeable future.

What went wrong? Although the leaders of the legal aid movement in Canada, and elsewhere, were motivated by the best intentions and a genuine desire to help alleviate the problems of the poor, they did not and perhaps could not fully understand their problems. Contrary to their expectations, the fundamental problems of the poor are not susceptible to traditional legal solutions. They are not the traditional middle class legal problems that lawyers are familiar with. As Bernard Veney, Executive Director of the National Clients' Council in the United States put it:[13]

The problems of low-income people are different from the problems of other people; and their cases must be handled differently. Most attorneys in private practice do not have, as a matter of

routine, the skills necessary to practice law for poor people ... low-income people have lives of constant crisis. What may be a casual matter for someone who has options is a life and death matter for a low-income person because one of the characteristics of poverty is the *absolute lack of options*. That lack of options may mean that to meet one crisis, people do something that is going to cause another crisis further down the line.

So it is not enough just to handle the legal matter that is there on the surface. Unless you are skilled at recognizing this problem, and skilled at recognizing what the possible remedies are, skilled enough to resolve the initial crisis but also take care of the longer-range crisis, you haven't done anything for low-income people.

Most legal aid programs, even if not so designed originally, have tended to develop according to the interests and priorities of lawyers providing the services rather than those of their clients. Legal services are traditionally provided on a one-to-one, private enterprise basis. The legal profession is generally identified with, and identifies itself with the *status quo*. Lawyers cannot accept the fact that the problems of the poor can only be solved through a fundamental restructuring of traditional institutions, not by suing someone in a court of law. While the motivations ascribed by one observer to the early development of legal aid in the United Kingdom (that "[it] was produced to justify ideologically the operations of the legal system, which was primarily concerned with property interests, by giving the appearance of making equal access to the legal system available to the lower classes")[14] may not be applicable to recent developments in legal aid, the fact remains that the legal profession remains identified in the minds of the poor with the source of their problems rather than with the solution. An equally important consideration is that governments have consistently underfunded legal services, partly because the poor are not a powerful political constituency[15] but also because government departments and agencies are prime targets of legal aid lawyers. Both of these factors will be discussed more fully later. First, a brief history of the development of legal aid is necessary.

JUDICARE VERSUS LEGAL SERVICES

Civil legal aid has generally followed one of the two models — Judicare or legal services.[16] The Judicare model utilizes members of the private bar as the prime deliverers of legal services. They are paid on a fee-for-service basis, usually in accordance with a specified tariff. The administrative responsibility for most Judicare plans is assigned to the legal profession. The underlying philosophy of Judicare is to provide the poor with access to the same services as are available to the rest of society. Judicare plans tend to concentrate on providing legal assistance for serious criminal offences and for civil actions in superior courts. For example, 41% of the Ontario legal aid budget in 1978 was spent on criminal offences and 27% on divorce and other civil matters.[17] There were only 184 small claims and 578 review board cases out of a total of more than 24,000 civil cases.[18] There were insufficient welfare, landlord-tenant, or unemployment insurance cases to justify a separate heading in the annual report.[19] Judicare's emphasis on litigation stresses a "problem solving" rather than "problem preventing" approach. The emphasis is on ensuring that the poor are accorded their "day in court" rather than on substantive reform of existing laws and institutions.

The legal services model did not become a significant alternative to Judicare until the 1960s and early 1970s. This model stresses the use of full-time salaried lawyers and non-legal personnel operating from offices located in low-income communities, generally of the "storefront" variety. Emphasis is placed on providing legal services in areas of prime concern to the poor — welfare, housing, unemployment insurance, workers' compensation, small claims, domestic disputes — providing assistance to groups and organizations in the community, education programs and law reform activities such as lobbying and test case litigation.

The stated philosophy of the legal services movement is that the goal of legal aid should be nothing less than the eradication of poverty.[20] Poverty is a question of power — or, more particularly, lack of it — and the role of the lawyer is to assist the poor person to gain the power to change the institutions, both private and public, which contribute to his poverty and control his life. Case-by-case legal services must be provided but only within this overall framework. In jurisdictions that have adopted the legal services model, administration of legal aid is generally the responsibility of an independent board or commission rather than the legal profession.

For years proponents of the two models carried on a sometimes heated debate over their respective merits.[21] Questions of cost-effectiveness, the efficacy of professional control and whether lawyers had any role to play in social change were argued at great length. Generally, the traditional bar and most politicians tended to support the development of Judicare, professional administrative control and limitations on

law reform and lobbying activities by legal aid lawyers.[22] Legal services lawyers criticized Judicare for its adherence to traditional legal solutions and its failure to deal with the "real" problems of the poor.

However, it became apparent that neither approach had all the answers and both had important strengths and weaknesses. As a result, most jurisdictions have developed mixed civil legal aid systems, albeit with the emphasis on one of the two models.

. . . .

Canada, as it often does, has borrowed extensively from both the United States and the United Kingdom. Legal aid in Canada falls within provincial constitutional jurisdiction as part of the administration of justice, although the federal government does provide financial assistance to the provinces for legal aid in criminal matters based on a negotiated formula which can vary from province to province. All provinces, with the exception of Prince Edward Island and New Brunswick, have well-developed legal aid programs. Most have a mixed Judicare and legal services system. Quebec, Saskatchewan and Nova Scotia have adopted legal services as the basic model with a limited Judicare component. The other provinces have adopted the Judicare model.

Both the Manitoba and British Columbia plans have a legal services component. Ontario has a fairly extensive network of legal services offices (approximately 40 throughout the province as of September 1980).[49] They initially developed outside the Ontario Legal Aid Plan, are not referred to in the *Legal Aid Act*[50] and have, at best, only the grudging support of the Law Society of Upper Canada.[51] Funding of these offices is now provided for by regulation, amounting to $4.75 million for the 1980–81 fiscal year,[52] and they now are part of the Ontario Legal Aid Plan under the general supervision of the Clinical Funding Committee which allocates their funding and closely monitors their operations. For example, it is empowered by regulation to require a clinic to employ a solicitor and to train personnel to an approved standard.[53]

The Ontario Legal Aid Plan arose from the report of a joint committee of the Law Society and the government of Ontario released in March 1965.[54] This report drew heavily on the English experience in recommending a Judicare plan to be operated by the Law Society and made no reference at all to the American experience. On the other hand, the Quebec Plan, established in 1972[55] and the Saskatchewan Plan, established in 1974[56] adopted the American legal services model which by then was well established. Service under both plans is provided primarily by full-time salaried lawyers. However, the Quebec plan has a more significant Judicare component,[57] and is less community based than the Saskatchewan plan. The boards of directors of the Quebec offices (or "bureaux") are appointed by the Commission de Services Juridiques which administers the plan while boards of the Saskatchewan clinics are elected by the communities for which they operate. The Saskatchewan Plan also has a specific mandate to undertake law reform and related activities.[58] Other provinces have drawn from the Ontario, Quebec and Saskatchewan plans for inspiration depending upon the political views of each provincial government and its susceptibility to the pressures of the provincial bar.

The legal services offices established in Ontario, British Columbia and Manitoba[] also imitated the American experience. The first such office in Ontario, Parkdale Community Legal Services, located in a low income area of Toronto, was one of four such offices funded by the federal Department of Health and Welfare on the basis of a study which strongly supported the American approach.[59] Parkdale also received funding from the Council for Legal Education in Professional Responsibility, a branch of the Ford Foundation, which also funded a number of legal services offices in the United States affiliated with law schools as Parkdale was with Osgoode Hall Law School of York University.

The early development of legal aid in Canada produced some tension between the proponents of Judicare and the supporters of the legal services movement. This was particularly true in Ontario, where Judicare was well established and the Law Society was particularly powerful. After a decade or more of relatively peaceful co-existence, however, the clear consensus is that both models are needed. The traditional bar has overcome its initial paranoia about legal services offices, in part because the fundamental social changes that they feared and legal services lawyers hoped for have not materialized, and in part because legal services offices have created work for private lawyers, both through direct referral and through bringing legal action against their clients. Legal services lawyers, on the other hand, have come to accept that the private bar has a role to play in legal aid, both because of its special expertise and its ability to take cases where legal services lawyers might have conflicts of interest.

THE INADEQUACIES OF LEGAL AID

"Comprehensive" legal aid plans have existed for a decade or more, but the fact remains that the poor still have, at best, only limited access to legal services. One main reason is that legal aid is funded from public monies and governments have failed to provide more than minimal funding. This is partly because the poor do not constitute an effective political constituency, but also because the most effective legal aid programs are continually engaged in fighting government agencies. Accordingly, politicians react with, at best, grudging support and, at worst, outright hostility.

. . . .

A recent Canadian example is the decision of the Saskatchewan government in June 1978 to require the legal services offices in that province to cease their practice of referring criminal cases to private lawyers under the Judicare component of the Saskatchewan plan, while concentrating themselves on the provision of the civil legal aid. The legal services lawyers felt that the demands for services could best be met by utilizing the experience of the private bar in criminal matters and developing their own expertise in civil matters, such as housing and welfare. The government, however, stated that budgetary restraints were necessary and money could be saved if the offices did the criminal work themselves because using private lawyers cost more. This, of course, meant that legal services lawyers would be spending most of their time on criminal matters and would have to neglect what they considered to be the more important civil cases. It was not clear whether the government was motivated solely by financial concerns or whether it wanted to limit the effectiveness of legal services offices. After the Saskatoon Legal Assistance Clinic threatened to close rather than comply with the government's directive, the government backed down and agreed to conduct a review of the province's legal aid system.[66] However, the government appears to have succeeded in the end. The 1979–80 *Annual Report* of the Saskatchewan Community Legal Services Commission showed that the number of criminal cases completed by the private bar in the fiscal year dropped to 505 from 2,562 the previous fiscal year. Private bar civil cases also were reduced from 281 to 120.[67]

Governments continue to refuse to fund legal aid adequately. In 1977 Clinton Bamberger claimed that it would cost $500 million to provide basic minimum legal services to the poor in the United States.

This represented 5 lawyers for every 10,000 poor people, compared to the ratio in the general population of 14 lawyers for every 10,000 persons.[68] This year, after years of inflation the Legal Services Corporation budget is still under $300 million, with no chance of any increase in the next few years.[69]

In Canada the situation is no better. In Ontario, legal aid is funded through the Ministry of the Attorney General. The Ministry's entire budget represents less than 1% of the provincial budget ($165.5 million out of $17.1 billion in 1980–81).[70] The legal aid component is $43.3 million or about 26% of that total,[71] but a portion of that amount (about $8 million)[72] is received from the federal government as a contribution towards the provision of criminal legal aid. In other words 1/4 of 1% of the provincial budget is allocated to legal aid. The legal aid expenditure in Quebec ($32 million in the 1978–79 fiscal year)[73] has not increased significantly in the past few years. New Brunswick continues to refuse to establish a civil legal aid program mainly for financial reasons.[74] Similar situations exist in other provinces.

Even with adequate funding however, there are inherent weaknesses in existing legal aid programs which result in seriously inadequate access of the poor to legal services. The main weakness is the emphasis on individual case service. This results in a curative rather than a preventive approach to legal problems. It also means that available legal aid resources cannot begin to cope with the potential caseload let alone undertake effective law reform, lobbying or other group-oriented activities.

The emphasis on case-by-case service of both Judicare and legal services plans results from different factors. The Judicare approach is predicated on this type of service delivery. The legal profession is organized on a free enterprise, single lawyer, single client basis and Judicare seeks to apply this approach in delivering legal services to the poor. Legal services offices, however, have to some extent been forced to emphasize individual cases by funding agencies. While lawyers' training and interests and client demand are also important factors, the requirements of funding agencies that individual services be stressed is the predominant reason for the "caseload crisis" faced by most legal services offices. The evaluation of a legal services office is based on its caseload. This is easier to measure than more nebulous factors such as acceptance in the community, long-term interests of clients and law reform. It is also easier to persuade politicians that public money is being properly used if something concrete,

e.g., a thousand cases handled, has resulted from the expenditure.

There are other inadequacies in both legal aid models which have to be considered. Judicare suffers from the underlying assumption that all the poor need is access to the same services that lawyers traditionally provide. Not only does this ignore the specific legal problems of the poor, most of which are substantively different than those of the middle class, but reliance on the private bar also creates particular problems. Most law offices are physically and psychologically inaccessible to the poor. They are located some distance from most poor communities and are designed to appeal to traditional clients. Most poor people find this a completely foreign environment, adding to the pressures of dealing with lawyers. The poor person also identifies the private bar with the "other side" — landlords, finance companies, government agencies — that represent the source of his problem.

The private lawyer lacks expertise in the legal problems of the poor. The intricacies of social welfare legislation, for example, are not easily grasped by handling one or two such cases a year. Conflicts of interest can and do arise between the poor and other existing or potential clients of the lawyer (for example in landlord-tenant and debtor-creditor cases). There is an inability to identify patterns and to organize strategies to deal with underlying problems. Most Judicare plans lack effective research components resulting in a great deal of duplication of effort, as individual lawyers continue to re-invent the wheel. The Ontario Legal Aid plan, in existence for some 13 years, has only recently created a research facility and then only because it was one of the conditions imposed by the provincial Attorney General for his support of a tariff increase.[75]

The method of payment — fee for service, usually in accordance with an established tariff — also limits the coverage which can be provided by Judicare. It is not acceptable politically or economically to expend $500 of public funds in an attempt to recover $50 in unpaid welfare benefits, to sue for $200 in Small Claims Court or to force a landlord to effect small but necessary repairs or to cease harassing tenants. Legal aid assistance is therefore given only in very special cases. In Ontario, for example, clients are entitled to legal aid services for indictable criminal matters and for civil cases brought in the "higher" courts.[76] In other civil cases the test is whether a person of modest means would retain a lawyer in the circumstances. Given the present level of legal fees, the answer is usually negative. The result is that Judicare plans tend to concentrate on providing services for serious criminal cases, traditional civil lawsuits (e.g., motor vehicle accidents, collections) and divorce and other family matters. The Ontario Legal Aid Plan, a representative Judicare plan, shows a very high proportion of certificates granted for these types of cases.[77] In his oft-quoted article "Practicing law for Poor People,"[78] Stephen Wexler pointed out that "poor people are not just like rich people without money. Poor people do not have legal problems like those of private plaintiffs and defendants in law school casebooks."[79] Judicare plans are premised on the opposite assumption and limit themselves to providing services for those "casebook" problems.

Outside of the United States, most legal services programs came into being because of the deficiencies of Judicare and were specifically tailored to deal with the particular problems of the poor. The salaried lawyers employed in these offices were expected to — and did — develop an expertise in these areas.[80] In jurisdictions where legal services were the basic delivery model, such as the United States and Quebec, provision was made for a substantial research component to assist lawyers in the field and to identify particular problem areas which might require collective action. Emphasis was also supposed to be placed on law reform activities, both judicial and legislative.

However, as noted above, the emphasis in legal services programs as in their Judicare counterparts has been on the provision of individual case services. Although the type of case emphasized has been somewhat different than in Judicare programs, the fact remains that the essential service provided is the same — problem-solving on a one-to-one basis rather than preventive services on a collective basis as was the hope of many of the early proponents of the legal services movement.[81]

. . . .

If the legal profession as presently structured, even if supplemented by trained non-legal personnel, cannot adequately deal with the problems of the poor, what is the answer? The assumption is that increased access to lawyers and traditional legal services will benefit the poor. In fact that is not the case. The poor need services which will assist them in dealing effectively with their problems; this cannot be done on a case-by-case basis. While there is, and will continue to be, a huge demand for individual case service, the resources do not presently exist to fill that demand and alternative approaches must be considered.

. . . .

Community organization must also be a priority. An effective tenants' organization prepared to utilize techniques such as rent strikes is more effective in enforcing a landlord's repair obligations than any number of individual court cases, particularly given the problems of enforcement. The welfare bureaucracy is more likely to respond to the immediate pressure of an organized welfare group than to the strictures of a court. When a welfare cheque is not forthcoming on time, this type of pressure, unlike a time-consuming application to a court, can bring quick results. In 1972 Stephen Wexler argued that only effective community organizing could give the poor power to effect change.[115] The passage of time has only proven the validity of this argument.

New methods of dispute resolution are also required. Traditional methods are slow, costly and ineffective. Too much emphasis is placed on due process rather than on effective decision-making. Procedures need to be streamlined and simplified so that individuals can effectively represent themselves. More emphasis should be placed on providing official assistance to persons appearing before tribunals. This would reduce the need for lawyers and allow more effective participation by the individuals concerned.[116]

These changes would have serious ramifications for the legal profession. Lawyers are not necessarily the most effective lobbyists and they are certainly not trained to be organizers. They are trained to provide specific services to individual clients. This means that the lawyer's role in providing services to the poor is limited. Most bar associations and professional governing bodies have opposed any developments along these lines, suggesting that the profession could not operate effectively in the type of service system.

The provision of legal services to the poor should be the responsibility of persons, both lawyers and non-lawyers, specifically trained for that purpose. How should they be trained? There is no scope in this chapter for a discussion of the problems in legal education but there is no doubt that law schools have a dismal record of training lawyers to serve the poor. Law school curricula emphasize traditional legal subjects, with the special legal problems of the poor being dealt with in one or two courses with such titles as "Poverty Law" and "Law and the Poor", a phenomenon that caused Wexler to remark that "[these courses] serve a useful function by making it crystal clear that the remainder of the curriculum deals with law and the rich; they do little, however, to change the law schools' treatment of legal problems, or their perception of the proper roles and concerns of a lawyer."[117] The calendar of the People's Law School of Los Angeles, California, a law school whose aim is "the development and training of lawyers dedicated to the struggle for social change in the communities of oppressed peoples",[118] puts it more graphically:[119]

> In the past, traditional legal institutions have mass-produced lawyers whose concept of lawyering consisted of joining an elite organization dedicated to maintaining the national socio-economic *status quo*, as well as the lawyer's superior position in it, by serving the rich or acting as legal functionaries of the state.... Existing law schools, at their worst, destroy the development of socially-conscious students, and at their best allow only a limited development of skills by a highly motivated and often select group. Traditional legal education almost uniformly teaches the skills which are required to serve the establishment; the non-establishment student, if not an outcast, is nevertheless segregated with a small group concerned with what are institutionally considered the marginal interests of society: the areas of poverty, civil rights, labour and criminal law.

Specially trained people are needed to serve the interests of the poor. If the law schools are not prepared to meet this challenge, other institutions will, and the law schools will be limited to providing training to a limited portion of the legal services community.

In any legal aid system it is crucial that the poor have some control over the nature of the services to be provided. Most legal services plans recognize this and provide for representation of the client community on the board of directors of each legal services clinic. Invariably, however, client representation is limited to one-half or less. Sometimes express provision is made for lawyers and legal staff to form a majority of the board of directors; sometimes the client representation is specifically restricted, but, in either case, the poor are allowed only to participate in, but not control, the decision-making process. Given lawyers' ability and propensity to control meetings, it is unlikely that lawyers' influence would be seriously diminished even if non-lawyers had a majority on any board.

. . . .

Codes of Professional Conduct also support lawyer control. A lawyer is responsible for the conduct of any case he undertakes; he must take instructions from his individual client. Any attempt by outsiders, such as boards of directors, to interfere in a case must be resisted. Additionally, a lawyer is under a duty of confidentiality. He cannot disclose details of any case to outsiders without the express consent of the client or in other very limited circumstances. Therefore any attempt by a client-controlled board of directors to determine what cases should or should not be undertaken by lawyers in its employ, or how a particular case should be handled (e.g., whether it should be settled in the interest of the individual client or carried through to litigation in the hope of obtaining a favourable decision which might benefit a broader community) must, under the present Codes, be resisted by a lawyer. Meaningful client input into the determination of the services to be provided and the manner of their provision seems possible by non-legal personnel not subject to the same professional constraints. This is not to say that these constraints are necessarily wrong in every case; only that they do militate against effective client control of legal services.

In the final analysis, whether the poor are to receive effective services from the legal profession either through the provision of traditional services by the established bar or through a more sophisticated and responsive model, depends on whether governments and the people they represent are prepared to make that commitment. Even if the legal profession were to change fundamentally its outlook on legal aid and itself make a profound commitment to providing adequate services to the poor (an admittedly unlikely development) this would not be enough. To date, few, if any, governments or societies have shown any such inclination. There are too many vested interests to overcome. Governments, the economically and politically powerful, and the legal profession, have no immediate interest in alleviating the plight of the poor. Until we are prepared to accept that fundamental changes are required, we will continue to provide, always grudgingly, inadequate legal assistance. The underlying problems will continue to be ignored. The poor, it seems, will always be with us and justice will continue to be identified with the Ritz Hotel.

(b) Moving Forward on Legal Aid — Executive Summary†

Vicki Schmolka

I. INTRODUCTION

This is a summary of an extensive research paper prepared by Melina Buckley, LL.B., Ph.D., for the Canadian Bar Association.

Moving Forward on Legal Aid: Research on Needs and Innovative Approaches presents new research findings, profiles innovations in legal aid service delivery in Canada and elsewhere and suggests future directions to improve legal aid and access to justice generally.

This summary highlights key elements of [ ] Dr. Buckley's research and analysis. Please refer to the paper for the details.

II. THE ROUGH ROAD TO HERE

Publicly-funded legal aid programs started in Canada almost 40 years ago. Their purpose was to provide the poorest residents with access to a lawyer and the justice system. It was generally recognized that Canada could not claim to be a fair and just society if some of its members were denied an opportunity to seek justice.

Early ideals have, however, given way to ever tightening budget realities. Legal aid programs do not enjoy the same public profile as government-run health care or education programs. As a result, shrinking government support for legal aid has been largely a "silent crisis." The people most deeply affected by the shrinkage in legal aid services are low-income and disadvantaged people who have no political clout. And only those within the justice system are seeing the negative effects of the growing number of unrepresented litigants in civil and criminal courts.

The Canadian Bar Association (CBA) has a long history of unwavering support for a legal aid system that provides publicly-funded legal services for essential criminal and civil matters. It has directed resources to advocacy work but has seen little positive change from these sustained national and local efforts.

Canada is not alone among more economically developed countries struggling to balance the financing of legal services for low-income people with ensuring fairness in a justice system that is supposed to be accessible to everyone. In some jurisdictions a renewed emphasis on social policy goals, such as combating social exclusion and increasing social equality, is driving a regeneration of legal aid policy. Innovative approaches to service delivery and strategies to expand efforts beyond direct legal services are also being put in place. The following sections profile this work.

III. THE JUSTICE GAP: IDENTIFYING THE GAP BETWEEN THE NEED FOR AND THE AVAILABILITY OF LEGAL SERVICES FOR LOW-INCOME PEOPLE

1. Civil law poblems

Several jurisdictions have undertaken studies to find out more about low-income citizens who have legal problems related to civil law matters. The studies all come to remarkably similar conclusions. A majority of low-income people experience one or more serious legal problems that make their day-to-day lives more difficult.

These legal problems usually exist in context with related social problems: economic vulnerability, mental health, physical health, safety and security issues, discrimination, and language barriers. As a result, unresolved legal issues can have a cascading negative effect in people's lives, causing significant economic, social, and health consequences, particularly additional stress. Physical and mental illnesses have been directly attributed to unresolved legal problems among low-income people.[2]

Members of vulnerable groups, such as, for example, aboriginal people, immigrants, and people with less than a high school education, may have difficulty identifying the legal issue in their situation. Furthermore, they may fail to take action to resolve their legal problems because of a perceived or actual barrier to getting assistance. Having a legal problem

---

† Executive Summary for Melina Buckley, *Moving Forward on Legal Aid: Research on Needs and Innovative Approaches*, Research Paper for the Canadian Bar Association. [Notes and/or references omitted.] Reprinted with permission of the Canadian Bar Association.

often generates a negative attitude to the law and the justice system, regardless of the outcome.

British studies have also documented "referral fatigue." People are exhausted by the required "Herculean efforts to be seen by an advisor." This is unfortunate as a major study found that people who get legal advice fare substantially better than those who try to get advice and do not.[3]

Finally, there is often a recognizable pattern to the legal problems experienced by low-income people and a direct consequence — social exclusion. When legal problems related to, for example, poor housing, family breakdown, and unemployment remain unresolved there is a perpetuation of disadvantage and a greater likelihood of increased detachment from the mainstream. Rather than categorize social exclusion as a "condition", it is now be seen as a "dynamic process" exacerbated by a lack of access to needed legal services.

2. Criminal law problems

Legal aid advice, usually provided through duty counsel, must be made available to a person who cannot afford a lawyer at the time of arrest, as a result of the Supreme Court of Canada's 1990 decision in the *Brydges* case. After that initial contact, however, regardless of the accused's low-income level, legal aid is often limited to situations in which a conviction would result in a loss of livelihood or incarceration.

The coverage criteria currently in place generally deny legal representation to low-income accused who have been charged with minor offences even though the impact of a criminal record would be extremely serious for them.

As well, basing eligibility for legal aid on the consequences of conviction fails to address the real needs of many accused. Studies show that unrepresented accused are often vulnerable and disadvantaged due to their personal characteristics, low levels of education and literacy, and higher rates of drug and alcohol addiction. Regardless of the seriousness of the charges against them, these individuals cannot adequately advocate for themselves. Many of them end up in prison as a result.

Given these findings, Canadian studies have recommended that legal aid policy take a more client-centred approach when determining eligibility for legal aid in criminal matters. This would mean looking to the accused's personal circumstances such as any disabilities; linguistic, social and cultural characteristics; overlapping legal problems; and needs related to systemic social factors.

3. Unmet needs for legal services

A major United States study looked at the civil legal needs of low-income individuals and families and concluded that there is a significant "Justice Gap."[4]

In British Columbia and Alberta, mapping projects have correlated the presence of legal services — information, advice, and representation — with an assessment of the legal needs of low-income citizens. The biggest gaps are in rural and remote areas, in delays in accessing services, and in the ways services are provided. People with low levels of education, for example, prefer face-to-face assistance and find using the telephone or Internet to access services a frustrating barrier.

In Canada, legal aid funding has dropped by 10%, although, overall, funding for health care and education has risen. For example, between 1996 and 2006, Ontario saw an increase of 33% in health spending and 20% in education spending.

The gap between the need for and the availability of legal aid services continues to grow not only because of the general decline in funding for legal aid programs but also because of factors such as the increasing number of working poor and changing government policies leading to, for example, more criminal charges and increasingly complex income support programs. The Legal Services Commission in England and Wales has recommended that when government policies can be expected to result in an increased need for legal aid services, there should be an accompanying increase in the legal aid budget.

In its 2006–07 *Business Plan*, Legal Aid Ontario quantified some of the ways in which legal aid services can reduce the costs of other government programs, particularly in the social services sector. Dr. Buckley concludes that more research to identify the complete social and economic costs of inadequate legal aid programs and to support the business case for adequate legal aid services would be useful.

IV. POLICY OBJECTIVES: EVOLVING LEGAL AID SERVICES

1. In the beginning ... 40 years ago

Canadian legal aid programs began during the 1960s, an era of strong public commitment to social justice and a shared belief in the benefits of equal access to justice. Funding for legal aid programs, delivered by the provinces and territories, came from both the federal and provincial governments, with the federal government setting policy goals in its funding agreements. These policy goals focused on the types of situations (case coverage) and the financial needs (thresholds for eligibility) that legal aid programs should address.

Today, federal funding for provincially-delivered civil legal aid is part of a general social services transfer payment with no strings attached. A national policy perspective has been lost and, as a result, access to civil legal aid varies widely across the country. In some provinces, for example, legal assistance is available for child protection cases where a parent risks losing custody of a child but not for most family law matters. The very limited access to legal assistance and the disparities in the availability of legal aid services experienced across the country point to the need to re-think and re-establish a national policy for legal aid services.

2.   A shift in policy objectives

Some provinces have identified new policy objectives as they work to address unmet legal service needs and assist clients. British Columbia has re-oriented its legal aid policy to a needs-based problem-solving approach from one based on statutory entitlement. In 2007, the *Legal Services Society Act* broadened the mandate of the Legal Services Society beyond providing an effective and efficient legal aid program to helping people to solve their legal problems and facilitating access to justice. More is being done to integrate legal aid services with other social services and to help clients to reach positive, long-lasting solutions to their legal problems.

A report commissioned for Legal Aid Ontario[5] proposed a similar approach — focusing on prevention and early resolution of legal problems and promoting a greater integration of legal aid services with other social services.

In the criminal justice field, policy papers are looking past the strictly legal issues of the right to counsel when liberty is in jeopardy to social objectives. Some American legal aid programs have "preventing crime" as part of their mandate.

Recognizing the links between poor health, poverty, and inadequate access to justice at least one author has suggested that to measure the success of legal aid services one should ask "have lives and life chances been improved?"[6]

In the United Kingdom, the lack of access to legal assistance is identified as a factor in social exclusion. *An Action Plan on Social Exclusion*, overseen by a Cabinet Minister for Social Exclusion, is guided by five principles: early intervention; systematic identification of what works; better co-ordination of the many separate agencies; personal rights and responsibilities; and intolerance of poor performance. The Plan emphasizes the need for legal aid service delivery approaches that respect the dynamics of social exclusion.[7]

Australia's National Legal Aid organization, which links the country's eight legal aid commissions, has proposed a new legal aid policy grounded in a human rights framework and providing service based on priority areas of need rather than jurisdictional sources of laws. Three of the six priority areas are tied to social exclusion. The policy objective is "to ensure that all disadvantaged Australians are able to have recourse to the law for the preservation and enforcement of their legal rights."[8]

3.   Thresholds for eligibility

Increases in the cost of living without a parallel increase in the minimum wage or social assistance benefits and pensions mean that more people are living in poverty or on the edge of poverty. For the most part, eligibility levels for legal aid have not changed[,] leaving more people without access to legal services.

Quebec and Manitoba have expanded eligibility for legal aid by having clients whose incomes are just above the eligibility threshold pay for some of the services provided.

In the United Kingdom and Australia work is underway to develop national means tests to establish a national eligibility standard.

4.   Legal arguments for legal aid services

Frustrations over the deficiencies in legal aid services and governments' refusals to increase funding to improve the situation have led to court actions.

The CBA published a set of legal opinions on the constitutional right to civil legal aid in 2002[9] and then launched a public interest test case on the issue. However, the case was dismissed at the pre-trial stage and appeals, up to the Supreme Court of Canada, were unsuccessful.[10]

In the United States, a 1981 Supreme Court decision[11] held that there is a presumption against appointing counsel in civil cases where no threat of incarceration exists and that the presumption can only be overcome in exceptional circumstances. This has led the National Coalition for a Civil Right to Counsel[12] to bring right to [counsel] cases in several states.

In 2006, the American Bar Association passed a resolution that federal, state, and territorial governments provide "legal counsel as a matter of right at public expense to low-income persons in those categories of adversarial proceedings where basic human needs are at stake, such as those involving shelter, sustenance, safety, health or child custody."[13]

Model laws are designed to provide a starting point for a state considering legislating a right to counsel. To encourage progress, the California Model Statute Task Force drafted a *State Equal Justice Act* and a *State Basic Access to Justice Act*, which provides a right to counsel for certain high priority basic needs such as shelter, sustenance, safety, health, and child custody.[14]

Despite lobbying and litigation efforts, there have been no significant systemic improvements in access to justice in Canada during the last four decades.

V.   INNOVATIONS: IMPROVING ELEMENTS OF LEGAL AID SERVICES

Historically, Canadian provinces have used one of three ways to provide legal aid representation to eligible clients — through staff legal aid lawyers, lawyers practicing in the community and paid by legal aid, and a mixed system that offers both.

Over the years, tight budget constraints and narrowly-focused government agendas have not provided many opportunities for creative programming strategies and innovation. Instead, legal aid services have become desperate to find more efficient ways to provide services to more people within their limited budgets.

The main trend in service delivery has been to shift the onus onto individuals to navigate the justice system on their own. Legal aid services have been unbundled. By offering legal information, advice, and representation at different stages, legal aid providers are able to assist more people. Under the new self-help model, clients do not usually benefit from ongoing representation — an all-inclusive service relationship with a lawyer — but must figure out how the legal information they have received applies to them and advocate for themselves much of the time.

Some developments in legal aid service delivery have become the subject of research and evaluations.

1.   Mechanisms for providing legal information and advice

Legal information was traditionally provided in pamphlets or small booklets. Today, legal information is increasingly available through many different multi-lingual media including:

- Web sites
- Touch-screen services available at kiosks in shopping malls and public places (for example, to file Earned Income Tax Credits in the United States)
- Telephone messages (for example, dial-a-law programs which offer recorded scripts on legal topics)
- Videos
- Video conferencing

In the United Kingdom, free, case-specific, legal advice is now available from a lawyer through community-based telephone help lines and "ask us" web sites.[15]

In Canada, lawyer referral services run by the law societies give the name of a lawyer who will provide a free half-hour consultation.

2.   The role of paralegals and other legal aid personnel

The expansion of the team of legal aid personnel to include more non-lawyers is another innovation. Legal information outreach workers, family resource facilitators, and counsellors do not replace lawyers but can assist clients by taking time to discuss information with them and helping them to access other services.

3.   Outreach programs

Outreach programs, usually connected to a hub office, bring legal aid services to communities that are too far from the legal aid office and to people who may not otherwise visit the office.

In the United Kingdom, outreach advice sessions are held at neighbourhood centres, day centres, residential homes, youth centres, doctors' offices, hospitals, community colleges, and community centres. The Citizens Advice Bureaux offers outreach information or advice in over 1000 health settings, giving people access to legal services in a place with which they are familiar and are likely to feel comfortable.

A 2002 analysis of poverty law services in Canada concluded that to be successful outreach services must be linked to community networks that offer ancillary services and have local credibility.[16]

4.   Point of entry services

Several access to justice and civil justice reform reports have recommended that services be provided at a single point of entry to the courts so that members of the public can receive assistance directly and easily.[17]

British Columbia has, for example, established the Supreme Court Self-Help Information Centre, located in the Vancouver Law Courts, and the Nanaimo Justice Access Centre.

Ontario has Family Law Information Centres at family courts throughout the province. These centres are stocked with information materials and have staff available to answer questions during designated hours. Lawyers provide advice to legal [aid-eligible] centre visitors.

Concerns have been raised about the usefulness of self-help centres to, for example, people with low literacy skills, people who cannot get to a centre during regular working hours, and people in rural and remote communities. Using a rigid means test to determine service eligibility also results in frustration for centre visitors who do not qualify and may not get legal advice. More flexible financial eligibility criteria have been recommended.[18]

5. The expanded role of duty counsel

Duty counsel are the emergency room professionals of the court system.[19] They keep the courts running by providing unrepresented litigants with immediate help. Duty counsel offer legal advice at a critical moment in the legal process but their advice is, of necessity, quick and cursory, and may sometimes be limited by a lack of time to accumulate necessary information.

The last decade has seen an expansion in duty counsel programs. While the service model was originally developed for a small range of criminal matters, duty counsel now assists with more criminal as well as family law matters. In some jurisdictions specialized duty counsel are also available in youth, domestic violence, mental health, aboriginal, and drug treatment courts.

Evaluations of duty counsel programs have found many positive attributes including better working relationships among justice system participants (Crown, court and support services, client, etc.), improved file and lawyer continuity, and increased efficiency due to the duty counsel's knowledge of the law, the system, and support services. There were fewer delays and adjournments, and more matters were resolved without going to trial. Shortcomings were related to workload and scheduling.

In the United Kingdom the duty counsel role has been expanded beyond criminal and family law cases to include other civil law matters, such as housing evictions.

Duty counsel are especially helpful to people who are less likely to access legal advice before coming to court because of alienation from the legal process generally or mental health, literacy, or language challenges.

Duty counsel are not seen as replacing the need for full legal representation at a trial.

6. Legal aid offices

In some jurisdictions, staffed legal aid offices have been part of legal aid service delivery since the beginning. Other jurisdictions have chosen to give legal aid certificates to clients who can then ask a private practice lawyer to take on the work at the legal aid rate. Some jurisdictions offer a combination of both systems.

Manitoba recently reviewed its mixed legal aid approach to assess cost differences. The Manitoba research concluded that a complete staff system would cost more than a mixed system but noted that the conclusion is a function of the tariff paid to private bar lawyers, the cost of staff, and the productivity of staff and that these factors all vary over time.[20]

Ontario and Alberta have piloted and evaluated staff offices for criminal and family law matters. Research on the pilot Criminal Law Offices in Ontario found that they provided a valuable service to address a significant previously-unmet need. Cost comparisons between staff and private bar legal aid services were considered misleading because of the different work realities including: the private bar does not receive a fixed salary, staff lawyers do; the private bar can take on or refuse any type of case, staff lawyers are restricted and must handle more difficult cases without additional compensation or assistance; the private bar can hire or [lay off] staff depending on workload, staff offices cannot.[21]

7. Community-based legal clinics

The community clinic model is multi-disciplinary, and includes a mandate for community education and development, and law reform. These community-based clinics were established to provide poverty law services not only to alleviate an individual's legal problem but also with the goal of eliminating the systemic causes of poverty. In practice, however, community clinics are often overwhelmed by individual casework[,] and the strategic, long-term actions and test cases to shape law and protect rights may not take place.

A few community-based legal clinics are managing to fulfil their original mandate. For example, the Manitoba Public Interest Law Centre, a division of Legal Aid Manitoba, focuses on strategic litigation on behalf of disadvantaged groups. Calgary Legal Guidance enjoys grassroots and legal community support, is free of government interference, and operates with staff (lawyers and social workers) and volunteers, including law students. Legal Aid Ontario funds 17 speciality legal aid clinics for, for example, people with disabilities, the elderly, injured workers, and African-Canadians.

The 2002 analysis of Canadian poverty law services found that the capacity to launch *Charter of Rights and Freedoms* litigation is crucial to poverty law lawyers but requires more funding than is currently provided to public interest advocacy organizations. The report also recommended that one constitutional law specialist be part of any group of poverty law lawyers, providing some capacity for test case litigation and being available as a resource for others seeking to understand the application of the *Charter* to administrative regulations.[22]

8. Law school legal aid programs

Law school clinic programs have been an important component of legal aid services to low-income people over the last decades [*sic*]. In the 2006–07 fiscal year almost 1000 Ontario law students — 25% of the enrolment in the six Ontario law faculties — participated in the Student Legal Aid Service Societies program. A significant number of students are doing work that is currently not integrated with other legal aid services.

A study of American law school clinics[23] found that although there has been a steady increase in the number of law school clinics there has been a narrowing of service goals and a reduction in the number of clients served. The study compares law school legal aid clinics to teaching hospitals and suggests that the clinics should become research sites developing and testing service delivery models, providing access to researchers interested in the relationship between law and legal services to conditions of poverty and disadvantage, and making comparative assessments of differing methods for teaching about the practice of law.

9. A more holistic approach to legal aid service delivery

A few jurisdictions have gone beyond small legal aid innovations and have taken a bigger step "out of the box" towards comprehensive and integrated legal aid service delivery. There are three main approaches.

i. **Multidisciplinary practices** bring together legal, social, and health services giving clients the ability to access the services they need in one place and eliminating referral fatigue. Being part of an integrated service means that lawyers can smoothly transfer clients needing counselling to other professionals and can focus on legal issues. Other professionals may give legal staff a useful perspective on a client's circumstances. "Well-planned inter-professional collaboration that leads to seamless client services has no downside" concludes one report,[24] although it does require sensitivity to professional obligations such as solicitor–client privilege.

Community Legal Advice Centres, piloted by the United Kingdom Legal Services Commission, are one-stop-shop services delivering combined social and welfare legal services, including community care, debt counselling, housing support, employment assistance, and welfare advice. The Centres are designed to serve clients from initial diagnosis and information provision to advice, support, and legal representation in court.

ii. **Increased coordination among agencies serving the low-income community** yields advantages for both clients and service providers. In the United Kingdom the emphasis has been on "joined up" work between government agencies as a means to assist disadvantaged individuals and communities and to combat social exclusion. Community Legal Service is a key partner.

iii. **A holistic approach to criminal legal aid services** has only been discussed in Canada[25] but has been put in practice in a handful of American projects. The objectives of these projects go beyond high quality defence services for accused clients. Holistic advocacy means providing broad client-focused services that address underlying problems such as poverty, mental illness, alcoholism, substance abuse, post-traumatic stress disorder, and family dysfunction with a view to preventing future crimes. The social service orientation is collaborative, intensive, and long-term.[26]

The Bronx Defenders, for example, has social workers, criminal defence lawyers, civil lawyers specializing in child welfare, housing and immigration workers, and youth and community outreach staff working together out of the same building.[27]

Inter-disciplinary working groups reflect the interconnectedness of the issues facing low-income clients and can best meet their overall needs. Instead of solving a legal problem and often seeing the client continue in the situation that gave rise to the problem, a holistic approach holds the promise of a more fundamental and permanent change in circumstances.

Services for underserved communities

Various reports have stressed that the legal aid system fails to adequately address the needs of specific disadvantaged communities. Projects are underway in some jurisdictions to better meet the unique needs of, for example:

* Aboriginal communities
* inmates in federal institutions, and
* single young mothers who find themselves in trouble with the law.

All these innovative strategies may improve some element of a legal aid service or service delivery generally. None of them have yet become entrenched in legal aid programs across Canada as part of a national access to justice vision.

VI. ENHANCEMENTS: PUTTING IN PLACE MECHANISMS TO INCREASE ACCESS TO LEGAL SERVICES

Dr. Buckley's paper presents two mechanisms for enhancing access to legal services that are related to but separate from legal aid reform: access to justice communities and *pro bono* work.

1. Access to justice communities

In the United States access to civil justice communities [is] in place in most states to create a comprehensive, integrated, and state-wide legal assistance service. Organized under Access to Justice Commissions, these communities bring together the federally-funded Legal Services Corporation and non-Legal Services Corporation providers, other service providers, including social service providers, *pro bono* programs, initiatives supporting unrepresented litigants, law school clinics, and key private bar and state judicial system elements.

The main goals of access to justice communities are to:

* create a single point of entry to legal assistance for low-income clients

* integrate all institutional and individual providers and partners
* allocate resources among providers to ensure that representation can occur in all forums for all low-income persons, and
* provide access to a range of services for all eligible clients no matter where they live, what language they speak, or the ethnic or cultural group to which they belong.

Although Canadian legal aid programs have experimented with elements of this approach, no jurisdiction has set up a permanent collaborative structure similar to the American Access to Justice Commissions. A recent review of legal aid in New Brunswick did propose approaching the other Atlantic Provinces to explore the benefits of a joint delivery model for legal aid services[28], which could perhaps lead to an Atlantic Access to Justice Commission.

2. *Pro bono* work

Lawyers have always taken on a few clients at greatly reduced rates or for free. Cutbacks in government support for legal aid programs has led to a substantial increase in *pro bono* activity in many countries and a move toward greater organization and integration of *pro bono* efforts within legal aid programs and the court system itself. There has also been a move to quantify the amount of *pro bono* work being done with some American states making it mandatory for attorneys to report on *pro bono* activities.

A roundtable discussion on the relationship between legal aid and *pro bono* legal services by the Victoria Law Foundation, Australia[29] raises the concern that *pro bono* work is being substituted for adequate government-funding of legal aid services. Participants noted that the private legal profession has subsidized and supported legal aid since legal aid began but worried that *pro bono* work is now being required to handle legal aid overflow cases, civil cases that were previously funded. Unlike legal aid[,] which is a matter of right, lawyers take on *pro bono* cases as a matter of charity and professionalism and there is no entitlement to receive it. It was recognized that a significant amount of unmet need for legal services cannot be filled by *pro bono* efforts.

In Canada, lawyers continue to offer *pro bono* services[,] although the tensions at the juncture between legal aid and *pro bono* services still need to be resolved. It has been suggested that the bar use a formal commitment to *pro bono* work as a *quid* pro quo for governments to reinvest in legal aid systems.[30]

In addition to access to justice communities and *pro bono* work, the paper mentions a few other mechanisms that could make legal services more widely accessible to middle and lower income Canadians. These include:

- prepaid legal services plans (legal expense insurance)
- contingency legal aid funds (successful legal aid litigants must reimburse a portion of their settlement)
- contingency fees (where lawyers are paid depending on the success of their efforts)
- tax deductions for legal expenses, and
- low-cost information and summary advice services.

VII. SUGGESTIONS FOR ACTION: FULFILLING THE CBA'S ROLE AS AN ADVOCATE FOR EQUAL JUSTICE

The CBA has consistently maintained that governments must accept the primary responsibility to ensure equal access to justice through the provision of legal aid services. The CBA has also promoted the legal profession's responsibility to contribute to access to justice by assisting in the delivery of government-funded legal aid and by providing *pro bono*

services. CBA members have adopted numerous resolutions on legal aid improvements, supported lobbying campaigns across Canada, and contributed to a national public relations campaign to raise public awareness about the inadequacies of the Canadian legal aid system. The CBA has been the only consistent advocate for legal aid reform at the national level, although there are important allies in the anti-poverty and social justice movements.

The CBA has a five-point platform on legal aid reform:

- Legal aid should be recognized as an essential public service, like health care.
- Public funding should be confirmed as necessary to ensure access to justice for low-income people.
- Public funding for legal aid must be increased.
- National standards for criminal and civil legal aid coverage and eligibility criteria are required.
- The federal government should revitalize its commitment to legal aid.

Dr. Buckley notes that despite all its efforts to improve legal aid funding and services, the CBA's advocacy efforts to date have not been successful. The paper suggests several possible approaches for the CBA to refresh its commitment to improved civil and criminal legal aid services in Canada. Justice demands it.

(c) Small Claims Court Identity Crisis: A Review of Recent Reform Measures†

Shelley McGill

I. INTRODUCTION

The small claims court is a very active forum with over 63,000 claims issued annually in Ontario alone.[1] It is the only court many people will ever experience and millions more will know only its television incarnation. As a cornerstone in the catalogue of reality-based programming,[2] the television version mocks the process. Litigants are dismissed with lightning speed

and a condescending lecture. Sadly, this image shapes the public's perception of the actual small claims court.[3]

Unfortunately, television parody is not the court's only identity crisis. Despite decades of reform, the small claims court still struggles to fulfill its promise. Long described as an access to justice initiative dedicated to the resolution of monetarily minor disputes, critics have questioned its contribu-

† (2010) 49 Canadian Business Law Journal 213 at 213–23 (sections I–III), 248–51 (sections V and VI). [Notes and/or references omitted.] Extracts reproduced by permission of Canadian Business Law Journal Inc., and Canada Law Book, a division of Thomson Reuters Canada Limited.

tion in this area.[4] Is it a forum for particular disputes or particular disputants? What should it offer to users, the public, the justice system, the government, and society as a whole? These are just a few of the questions contributing to an identity crisis for the small claims court.

A variety of strategic approaches and reforms all profess to "improve access to justice" as if it were a one-dimensional concept with a single objective. This article considers the small claims court's place in access to justice theory and evaluates the express expectations placed on the court. In addition, it identifies other less publicized objectives. It examines the compatibility of recent Canadian reforms and proposals with the stated and unstated objectives of the court. It concludes that multiple conflicting objectives have led to the adoption of counterproductive strategies and an unclear mandate for Canadian small claims courts. Features within individual systems conflict and undermine the intended results. Wide jurisdictional variations in policy approaches compound the small claims court identity crisis. Some times [sic] a forum for business, sometimes a haven for the self-represented, some times [sic] capacity within an overburdened system, and sometimes an alternative to that same system, the small claims court struggles to fulfill all of the conflicting expectations.

II. ACCESS TO JUSTICE

The small claims court is a legislative initiative pledged to promote access to justice, a long-recognized fundamental right.[5] Justice has been defined as the "vindication of state determined legal rights through the adjudicative institution that administers and enforces them."[6] Applying this definition, the small claims court would seem to offer justice. However, this definition is now considered by many to be far too narrow.[7]

Access to justice has evolved over time into a broad interdisciplinary concept, not confined to legal rights, remedies and institutions.[8] Current models and theories transcend law and non-law realms.[9] Despite criticism that legal reality and structure continue to dominate the models and limit their universality,[10] it seems clear that access to justice lies not exclusively in state sponsored legal institutions but with society generally.[11] Reflective of this evolution is the distinction commentators draw between access to justice and access to the courts.[12] However, recognizing this distinction does not make access to the courts irrelevant; rather it is an acknowledgement of the pluralistic nature of access to justice.[13]

Initiatives developed in waves beginning with improved access to lawyers and court systems, expanding to include entrenched substantive rights and Alternate Dispute Resolution (ADR) processes, and culminating with the incorporation of social, community, and political mechanisms.[14] The result is a multi-faceted approach in which each component remains relevant and contributes to the overall goal; no new approach "leaves behind the initiatives of the earlier waves; rather the strategies evolve and build on each other."[15] The rule of law and the justice system remain an integral part of access to justice.[16] One commentator defends the justice system's role as follows:

> Ultimately, while the formal justice system may not deliver perfect justice in every instance, it offers the hope of realizing some aspiration of piecemeal and even systemic justice through the entrenchment of rights and effective remedial enforcement.[17]

In this light, access to the courts may be characterized as one component in a multi-dimensional strategy to promote access to justice. Reducing barriers to the court system furthers the larger goal. Although there are certainly others, the cost of litigation is a recognized barrier to accessing the court system.[18] This barrier is enlarged when the means of the disputant are modest, the relative means of the parties divergent, or the value of the dispute small. Justice system initiatives targeting the cost barrier include legal aid, class actions and the small claims court.[19]

Some research challenges the effectiveness of the small claims court as a means of improving access to justice for the poor or disengaged, while still acknowledging some value to the overall legal system.[20] Other studies find it efficient[21] and report user satisfaction with the process.[22] Diverse findings stem from the varying expectations placed on the court.[23]

III. SMALL CLAIMS COURT OBJECTIVES

Articulating the court's objectives is more complicated than would first appear. As noted, access to justice is the professed objective of and rationale for the small claims court. Access and justice are two separate but interrelated elements; access focusing on barriers to use and justice addressing fairness.[24] The objectives of the small claims court are clarified by general and seemingly simple expectations. Common components of the standard description are:

- *quick*
- *easy*
- *informal*
- *inexpensive* (and)
- *fair*
- *resolution (of)*
- small disputes.[25]

Consideration of each of these components suggests an access-over-justice emphasis or more specifically, cost-over-fairness. Ontario Superior Court Chief Justice Heather Smith listed the priorities for Ontario's small claims court as cost reduction, and then, enhanced access to justice through simplicity, efficiency and effectiveness.[26] The British Columbia Ministry of the Attorney General emphasized that systemic delay and expense render the justice system inaccessible.[27] Although some lament the apparent emphasis on access and cost, they dominate the "Small Claims Court Cant."[28]

Quick, *easy*, *informal* and *inexpensive* processes reduce the cost of litigation.[29] Time is money and a quick resolution means less money wasted. Easy informal processes encourage self-represented litigants to function without legal representation — a cost-saving necessary when the value of the dispute does not justify the expense of legal fees or the means of the disputant are modest. Inexpensive is a broad parameter, overtly targeting the fees and costs levied on users. Measures adopted in furtherance of the access objectives generally relax the fees and *eliminate* some formal procedural requirements associated with traditional litigation.[30]

Fairness and *resolution* are expectations that reference justice rather than access. They speak to the process, the outcome and enforcement. Perceptions of fairness are influenced by factors relating to both the substance of the decision and the decision-making process; consistency, neutrality, accuracy of decisions together with transparency and [appealability] are features of a fair decision-making model.[31] Measures adopted in furtherance of the justice objective generally *add* procedural requirements to the litigation process; in this context access and justice can be characterized as conflicting objectives.

Informality may also promote the fairness objective. When viewed as a means of leveling the playing field, informality discourages the dependence on legal tools and embraces the language of the public.[32] This leads to *relaxing* traditional procedural justice components. As a result, there is uncertainty about what fairness should look like in the small claims court context. Should procedural requirements be added or

removed? A 2009 Evaluation of the Nova Scotia Small Claims Court[33] described the dilemma saying:

> While the absence of many procedural rules in small claims courts is meant to facilitate access to justice, it is possible that the lack of formality actually interferes with fairness ... [T]here is a fine balance between small claims courts' objectives of rapid, informal access to justice, and inequities that may arise from their inherent procedural flexibility.[34]

Policy-makers must weigh the compromises made to the fairness of the process against the potential cost benefits. It becomes an assessment of what justice sacrifices are acceptable in the interests of access.[35] Irrespective of the apparent priority of the access objective, inexpensive availability of an unfair process is not access to justice.[36] Minimum standards of fairness must qualify the access initiatives.

Although access through cost reduction is a connecting (although not [the] sole) theme of the stated objectives, it too is multi-dimensional. Cost assessment is a relative concept that begs the question: Compared to what?[37] There are a variety of standards against which small claims court costs are measured:

- Traditional litigation: Obviously small claims court compares favorably to the fees and costs associated with traditional litigation; an approach taken by the Ontario Superior Court and British Columbia Attorney General.[38] One might expect this to be the minimum standard.
- Other ADR processes: Results are less clear when compared with other processes such as consumer arbitration.[39] Conflicting reports characterize consumer arbitration as both economical and expensive. Dispute and disputant characteristics may be more important than cost when comparing these forums.
- Means of the disputant: Cost relative to the means of the disputants focuses on access for the poor and the reported under-representation of poor plaintiffs.[40] However, under-representation may have less to do with cost than other social, cultural, and political realities of society.[41]
- Value of the dispute: Research contains repeated reference to disputes "worth pursuing."[42] Cost relative to the value of the dispute requires maintaining a *meaningful* spread between the potential recovery and the cost of proceeding; arguably the most relevant [criterion] for a forum defined by dispute value.

Attempting to satisfy the multiple-cost [criterion] further complicates the small claims court mandate.

Other objectives, although understated, also affect strategic decisions. As the court most likely to be experienced by the general public, small claims court shapes the public's impression of the entire justice system.[43] A justice system that does not provide a forum for small disputes may be seen as incomplete, class-based or out of touch. A court that is expensive, slow, complicated or unfair will reflect . negatively on the administration of justice as a whole.[44] However, a court that provides a positive experience for users[] should foster confidence and trust in the entire system.[45]

Another understated objective relates to funding of the justice system. The efficiency goal may include realizing cost savings in the justice system. It is neither cynical nor surprising to acknowledge that a government charged with the responsibility of providing an accessible justice system must consider available cost efficiencies in its delivery.[46] One policy analyst for the British Columbia Attorney General put it this way:

> [W]e balance the interests of justice with cost-effectiveness in order to increase access to justice ... The concept applies both to the amount of procedure the parties are allowed to invoke and to the amount of judicial management and resources the court must devote to a case.[47]

An unusually overt focus on this objective is contained in a study of the California Small Claims Court.[48] The Ventura County court was found to be efficient because it processed 5,000 cases in one year using a single courtroom and temporary judges at substantially less expense to the state than standard civil cases.[49] Unfortunately efficiency initiatives will inevitably conflict with other objectives; the introduction of user-friendly and fairness reforms are likely to increase (rather than reduce) costs to government.[50] One would hope that the cost efficiencies objective, although valid, would not become the dominant strategic criterion.

Finally, a European Union proposal for a common small claims court describes a less publicized business/economic objective.[51] It suggests that inconsistent availability of effective debt collection forums in member states leads to an unfair economic advantage for businesses in particular states and has "significant negative macroeconomic impacts on the proper functioning of the internal market."[52] At first glance such a business-based focus seems at odds with the notion of the peoples' court but it is consistent with the court's historic roots.

In 1791, the small claims court debuted in its first stand alone configuration in Upper Canada, as the Court of Requests.[53] Its formation responded to the need of the fledgling merchant community for a quick, easy and inexpensive debt collection process.[54] Similarly, American small claims courts developed, at least in part, to assist small business with the collection of outstanding accounts.[55] However[,] over time, some researchers and legislators began to view debt collection by business as a negative, resulting in measures that discourage the practice.[56] One wonders how the exclusion of business debt collection improves the lot of the individual debtor, now facing an unchallengeable blight on their credit record or a lawsuit in a slower, more technical and expensive court. The intended beneficiary of the restriction may end up worse off.[57]

The expectations and objectives for small claims court are numerous and conflicting. Designing a system that fulfills all expectations and accommodates their interdependency is a utopian task. Compromises and sacrifices are inevitable[,] and attempting to address all objectives without an overriding priority leads to conflicting measures that obscure the intended results. Differing jurisdictional approaches contribute to an unclear purpose and identity for the small claims court.

. . . .

V. MOVING FORWARD

The prerequisite for successful re-design of the small claims court is clarification of the court's mandate. Clear objectives are also fundamental to the fair evaluation of the court's performance. Policy makers must expressly prioritize among the varied objectives before embarking upon reform. The identified priority should be used to weigh the relative merits of particular features and ensure a consistent approach to system design and compatibility among features within the given system. Proceeding otherwise leads to a mass of conflicting features and an unclear mandate for the court.

Neither the design nor the mandate of the small claims court can be developed in a vacuum; the court is one component in a strategy to improve access to the courts — the existence of other initiatives within the jurisdiction[,] such as higher court simplified procedures or paralegals regulation[,] must be considered. The small claims court must fit within the structure of the overall system.

Arguably Québec and New Brunswick have already identified their priorities — and they are polar opposites. New Brunswick promotes government cost efficiency in the management of system backlogs as the rationale for both creating and eliminating its small claims court. Québec prioritizes the informal non-business character of the court and offers a forum for individuals, a people's court. To advance this mandate it sets a relatively low monetary value and excludes most businesses, corporations, debt collectors and lawyers. Judges are specialized and appeals are restricted. Neither position has a national following; a uniform mandate across the country remains illusory.

Cost relative to the value of the dispute is the most commonly referenced objective and is deserving of priority. The court's initial access to justice mandate was to reduce cost barriers for any party wishing to access the courts. With uncharacteristic uniformity all jurisdictions use the value of the dispute as the primary criterion defining eligibility for the court. Combining these two dominant components, cost and value of the dispute, reveals the natural priority for system design: cost of proceedings relative to the value of dispute. Some features and system design that would reflect this priority include:

- monetary values set to maintain a meaningful spread;
- graduated fees set to maintain a meaningful spread between dispute value and cost of proceeding across the entire monetary jurisdiction;
- elimination of the loser-pays principle to avoid cross-over consequences of other initiatives such as frequent user fees;
- removal of counsel or representation fees so that personal choices about representation are not passed over to other parties;
- elimination of cost-related settlement incentives so litigants are not punished for improperly valuing their claims;
- allowing a single right of appeal within the small claims system so cost of appeals [does] not become an access barrier; and
- creation of a state-driven model of enforcement to provide cost-effective collection.

Even if a uniform national mandate is unattainable, consistency among features within any given system is a necessity and is an **impossibility** without an explicit priority.

VI.   CONCLUSION

The small claims court has a place in access to justice strategy. However, the objectives and expectations for this court are not one-dimensional; they are numerous, diverse and conflicting. The cliché justification of every reform proposal captures neither the pluralism of access to justice nor the complexity of the small claims court mandate. It is not a forum seeking only to resolve access issues for particular disputants; instead its stakeholders include users, nonusers, business, non-business, the public, the government, and the justice system. Its express objectives target access barriers of cost, formality, complexity and delay, and justice issues of fairness, finality and compliance. Government cost efficiencies and the effective functioning of the business markets are less publicized but no less relevant objectives. In addition to all of these, it bears the responsibility of maintaining public trust in the entire civil justice system. The result is an impossible list of conflicting expectations which sabotage system design.

Wide variation between jurisdictions reveals differing priorities among the multiple objectives and fuels the small claims court identity crisis. Some jurisdictions embrace business while others exclude it; some jurisdictions reward lawyers while others discourage them, and some jurisdictions adjudicate while others offer to mediate. Differing combinations and permutations result in a wide range of possible identities for the small claims court.

This review of recent reform measures also identifies multiple conflicting objectives within individual jurisdictions. Well-intentioned attempts to meet all expectations have led to inconsistency among features within any given system. User-friendly service conflicts with strong enforcement, high limits attract lawyers, settlement incentives conflict with low fees, and mediation lengthens the abbreviated process. A mass of conflicting features work at cross purposes. As British Columbia's multi-track pilot project demonstrates, one design cannot possibly meet all of these objectives.

Ultimately resolving the identity crisis will require deliberate and transparent choices of priority and proportionality. However, resolution begins by acknowledging the diverse and conflicting nature of the stated and unstated objectives placed on the small claims court.

(a)   The Challenges We Face†

Right Honourable Beverley McLachlin, P.C.

Mr. President, distinguished guests, thank you for that welcome. I am delighted to be here again to address the Empire Club. More than a quarter century ago, a Canadian Justice Minister, Pierre Elliott Trudeau, challenged Canadians to build "the just society". In the ensuing years, thousands of Canadians have worked to establish their visions of a just society. The centrepiece of Prime Minister Trudeau's vision of the just society was the *Charter of Rights and Freedoms*, adopted in 1982, and whose 25th anniversary we will celebrate on April 17, 2007. Whatever our political persuasion or our particular conception of justice, there can be no doubt that Canadians today expect a just society. They expect just laws and practices. And they expect justice in their courts. Today, I would like to share with you my perspective on justice in our courts and the challenges we face in assuring Canadian men, women and children a just and efficacious justice process. Let me begin by asserting that Canada has a strong and healthy justice system. Indeed, our courts and justice system are looked to by many countries as exemplary. We have well-appointed courtrooms, presided over by highly qualified judges. Our judges are independent and deliver impartial justice, free of fear and favour. The Canadian Judicial Council, which I head, recently issued an information note on the judicial appointments process in which it affirmed these long-standing principles on which our justice system is based. Canadians can have confidence that judges are committed to rendering judg-

ment in accordance with the law and based on the evidence. Corruption and partisanship are non-issues. In all these things, we are fortunate indeed. Yet, like every other human institutional endeavour, justice is an ongoing process. It is never done, never fully achieved. Each decade, each year, each month, indeed each day, brings new challenges. Canadian society is changing more rapidly than ever before. So is the technology by which we manage these changes. Thus it should not come as a surprise that Canada's justice system, in 2007, faces challenges. Some represent familiar problems with which we have yet to come to grips. Others arise from new developments, and require new answers. In my comments today I will touch on four such challenges:

* the challenge of access to justice,
* the challenge of long trials,
* the challenge of delays in the justice system, and
* the challenge of dealing with deeply rooted, endemic social problems.

THE CHALLENGE OF ACCESS TO JUSTICE

The most advanced justice system in the world is a failure if it does not provide justice to the people it is meant to serve. Access to justice is therefore critical. Unfortunately, many Canadian men and women find themselves unable, mainly for financial reasons, to access the Canadian justice system. Some of them decide to become their own lawyers. Our courtrooms today are filled with litigants who are not repre-

---

† Remarks presented at the Empire Club of Canada, Toronto, March 8, 2007. [Notes and/or references omitted.] Reproduced with the permission of the Supreme Court of Canada.

sented by counsel, trying to navigate the sometimes complex demands of law and procedure. Others simply give up. Recently, the Chief Justice of Ontario stated that access to justice is the most important issue facing the legal system.[1]

The Canadian legal system is sometimes said to be open to two groups — the wealthy and corporations at one end of the spectrum, and those charged with serious crimes at the other. The first have access to the courts and justice because they have deep pockets and can afford them. The second have access because, by and large, and with some notable deficiencies, legal aid is available to the poor who face serious charges that may lead to imprisonment. To the second group should be added people involved in serious family problems, where the welfare of children is at stake; in such cases the Supreme Court has ruled that legal aid may be a constitutional requirement.[2]

It is obvious that these two groups leave out many Canadians. Hard hit are average middle-class Canadians. They have some income. They may have a few assets, perhaps a modest home. This makes them ineligible for legal aid. But at the same time, they quite reasonably may be unwilling to put a second mortgage on the house or gamble with their child's college education or their retirement savings to pursue justice in the courts. Their options are grim: use up the family assets in litigation; become their own lawyers; or give up. The result may be injustice. A person injured by the wrongful act of another may decide not to pursue compensation. A parent seeking custody of or access to the children of a broken relationship may decide he or she cannot afford to carry on the struggle — sometimes to the detriment not only of the parent but the children. When couples split up, assets that should go to the care of the children are used up in litigation; the family's financial resources are dissipated. Such outcomes can only with great difficulty be called "just". To add to this, unrepresented litigants — or self-represented litigants as they are sometimes called — impose a burden on courts and work their own special forms of injustice. Trials and motions in court are conducted on the adversary system, under which each party presents its case and the judge acts as impartial decider. An unrepresented litigant may not know how to present his or her case. Putting the facts and the law before the court may be an insurmountable hurdle. The trial judge may try to assist, but this raises the possibility that the judge may be seen as "helping", or partial to, one of the parties. The proceedings adjourn or stretch out, adding to the public cost of running the court. In some

courts, more than 44 per cent of cases involve a self-represented litigant.[3] Different, sometimes desperate, responses to the phenomenon of the self-represented litigant have emerged. Self-help clinics are set up. Legal services may be "unbundled", allowing people to hire lawyers for some of the work and do the rest themselves. The Associate Chief Justice of the British Columbia Provincial Court is quoted as saying this is "absurd", not unlike allowing a medical patient to administer their own anaesthetic.[4]

It is not only the unrepresented litigants who are prejudiced. Lawyers on the other side may find the difficulty of their task greatly increased, driving up the costs to their clients. Judges are stressed and burned out, putting further pressures on the justice system. And so it goes.

The bar and the bench are attempting to improve the situation. Some modest progress is being made. Lawyers are organizing themselves to give free, or *pro bono*, service to needy clients. Clinics have been set up by governments, NGOs and legal groups to help self-represented litigants. Rule changes to permit contingency fees — the lawyer is paid out of the proceeds of the litigation, if any — and class actions provide ways for people of modest means to litigate some tort and consumer actions. Thought is being given to coverage for legal services within specified limits as an endorsement to home insurance policies. Justice groups are working to simplify procedures and thus reduce costs or assist the unrepresented litigant.

All this is good. Yet much more needs to be done if access to justice is to become a reality for ordinary Canadians.

THE CHALLENGE OF LONG TRIALS

A second challenge is the challenge of long trials, an increasingly urgent problem both in civil and criminal litigation. Not too many years ago, it was not uncommon for murder trials to be over in five to seven days. Now, they last five to seven months. Some go on for years.[5] The length of civil trials is also increasing. For example, in 1996, the average length of a trial at the Vancouver Law Courts was 12.9 hours. Six years later, the average length of a trial had doubled, to 25.7 hours.[6] This trend is consistent with developments in other jurisdictions throughout Canada.

There are a number of reasons why trials seem to have taken on a life of their own. On the criminal side, the *Canadian Charter of Rights and Freedoms* has had a significant impact on the criminal trial process. *Charter* pre-trial motions regularly last two to three times longer than the trial itself.[7] Changes in the law of evidence have also increased litigation and lengthened trials.[8]

On the civil side, there are also a number of reasons why trials have become longer. Although Canadian rules of procedure impose limits on examinations for discovery, some argue that they are still too broad, allowing parties to canvass issues that are not relevant and material to the issues in the litigation. This results in longer, and more expensive discoveries, and a larger volume of evidence being placed before the trier of fact at trial. The expanded use of expert witnesses has also lengthened trials.

Efforts at reform are underway. On the criminal side, a recent report by the Ontario Superior Court of Justice makes a number of recommendations to improve the efficacy and effectiveness of judicial pre-trial conferences with a view to improving the efficiency of criminal trials.[9] The Ontario government recently launched a process to suggest reforms to the province's civil justice system.[10] A similar review is underway in British Columbia.[11]

THE CHALLENGE OF DELAYS IN THE JUSTICE SYSTEM

A third and related challenge is the problem of delays in the processing of cases. Here again, the problem afflicts both criminal and civil cases. On the criminal side, delays in proceedings may result in serious cases being stayed, since the *Charter* guarantees a trial within a reasonable time. Delays may also result in lengthy periods of incarceration for the accused person prior to trial. Even where the accused is out on bail, the stress of the ongoing proceedings and the upcoming, ever-deferred trial may be considerable. Witnesses are less likely to be reliable when testifying to events that transpired many months, or even years, before trial. Not only is there an erosion of the witnesses' memories with the passage of time, but there is an increased risk that a witness may not be available to testify through ordinary occurrences of sickness or death. As the delay increases, swift, predictable justice, which is the most powerful deterrent of crime, vanishes. The personal and social costs are incalculable. On the civil side, different but similar problems arise. Whether the litigation has to do with a business dispute or a family matter, people need prompt resolution so they can get on with their lives. Often, they cannot wait for years for an answer. When delay becomes too great, the courts are no longer an option. People look for other alternatives. Or they simply give up on justice.

Courts have been promoting various forms of out-of-court mediation and arbitration as a more effective way of achieving settlement and dealing with many civil cases. This is good. But the fact is, some cases should go to court. They raise legal issues that should be considered by the courts for the good of the litigants and the development of the law.

I do not want to give the impression that all is bleak. Ten years ago, in Ontario, civil appeals were taking two to three years from the date of perfection to be heard. Criminal appeals were not much better. They were being heard one and a half to two years from the date of perfection.[12] Today, the time required for bringing appeals on for hearing has been greatly reduced.

In a recent speech, Ontario Court of Appeal Justice Michael Moldaver noted that the solution to delays in the justice system was not to hire more judges, but for the court to take control of the process from the litigants and put it back in the hands of the judges. This is what happened in Ontario. Within a space of 18 months, the backlog was gone. Civil appeals in Ontario are now being heard within nine to 12 months of perfection. Criminal appeals are being heard within six to nine months.

THE CHALLENGE PRESENTED BY ENDEMIC SOCIAL PROBLEMS

The final justice challenge I wish to discuss is the challenge presented by intractable, endemic social problems, including drug addiction and mental illness.

A few years ago, I found myself at a dinner at government house. Next to me sat the chief of one of Toronto's downtown precincts. I asked him what his biggest problem was. I thought he would say the *Charter* and "all those judges who pronounce on rights". But he surprised me. "Mental illness", was his reply. He then told me a sad story, one I have heard throughout the country in the years since. Every night, his jails would fill up with minor offenders or persons who had created a nuisance — not because they are criminals, but because they are mentally ill. They would be kept overnight or for a few days, only to be released — the cycle inevitably to repeat itself.

Such people are not true criminals, not real wrong-doers in the traditional sense of those words. They become involved with the law because they are mentally ill, addicted or both. Today, a growing awareness of the extent and nature of mental illness and addiction is helping sensitize the public and those involved in the justice system. This sensitization and knowledge is leading to new, more appropriate responses to the problem.

One response has been the development of specialized courts — such as mental health courts and drug courts. As Brian Lennox, Chief Justice of the Ontario Court of Justice, said recently at the opening of the Mental Health Court in Ottawa:

> The Ottawa Mental Health Court is an example of a progressive movement within criminal justice systems in North America and elsewhere in the world to create "problem-solving courts". These courts, with collaborative interdisciplinary teams of professionals and community agencies, attempt to identify and to deal with some of the underlying factors contributing to criminal activity, which have often not been very well-addressed by the conventional criminal justice process. The goal is to satisfy the traditional criminal law function of protection of the public by addressing in individual cases the real rather than the apparent causes that lead to conflict with the law.

Mental health courts have opened in Ontario, New Brunswick and Newfoundland.[13] Many other jurisdictions, including British Columbia, Manitoba, Nunavut and Yukon, are in various stages of developing these courts. These courts can do much to alleviate the problems.

Other problem-solving courts within the Ontario Court of Justice include drug treatment courts and *Gladue* courts, the latter dealing with aboriginal

offenders. Such courts are also being used in other Canadian jurisdictions.

This is just the beginning. I could go on. The point is this. In a variety of ways, throughout Canada we are adapting our criminal law court procedures to better meet the realities of endemic social problems and better serve the public.

CONCLUSION

I have shared with you four challenges faced by Canada's justice system in 2007 — challenges close to my heart, and that of justice workers, including judges, throughout Canada. I have also described the efforts which are being made to alleviate the problems and ultimately, with luck, perhaps solve them.

Let me close on this note. Nothing is more important than justice and the just society. It is essential to [the] flourishing of men, women and children and to maintaining social stability and security. You need only open your newspaper to the international section to read about countries where the rule of law does not prevail, where the justice system is failing or non-existent.

In this country, we realize that without justice, we have no rights, no peace, no prosperity. We realize that, once lost, justice is difficult to reinstate. We in Canada are the inheritors of a good justice system, one that is the envy of the world. Let us face our challenges squarely and thus ensure that our justice system remains strong and effective.

(b) Access to Civil & Family Justice: A Roadmap for Change†

Action Committee on Access to Justice in Civil and Family Matters

PART 1
ACCESS TO CIVIL AND FAMILY JUSTICE: URGENT NEED FOR CHANGE

OVERVIEW

There is a serious access to justice problem in Canada. The civil and family justice system is too complex, too slow and too expensive. It is too often incapable of producing just outcomes that are pro-

portional to the problems brought to it or reflective of the needs of the people it is meant to serve.[2] While there are many dedicated people trying hard to make it work and there have been many reform efforts, the system continues to lack coherent leadership, institutional structures that can design and implement change, and appropriate coordination to ensure consistent and cost effective reform. Major change is needed.

---

† The final report of the Action Committee on Access to Justice in Civil and Family Matters. Released in October 2013. [Notes and/or references omitted.] Reproduced with permission.

PURPOSE

This report has three purposes: (in part 1) to promote a broad understanding of what we mean by access to justice and of the access to justice problem facing our civil and family justice system; (in part 2) to identify and promote a new way of thinking — a culture shift — to guide our approach to reform; and (in part 3) to provide an access to justice roadmap for real improvement. The report does not set out to provide detailed, line-item guidance on how to improve all aspects of the civil and family justice system across Canada's ten provinces and three territories. That needs to come largely from the ground up, through strong mechanisms and institutions developed locally. Local service providers, justice system stakeholders and individual champions must be the change makers. This report can, however, help fill the need for a coordinated and collaborative national voice — a change agent — providing a multi-party justice system vision and an overall goal-based roadmap for change. The ways of the past — often working in silos and reinventing wheels — are not sustainable. A coordinated, although not centralized, national reform effort is needed. Put simply, we should "think systemically and act locally."[3] Innovative thinking at all levels will be critical for success.

ACCESS TO JUSTICE: AN EXPANSIVE VISION

When thinking about access to justice, the starting point and consistent focus of the Action Committee is on the broad range of legal problems experienced by the public — not just those that are adjudicated by courts.[4] Key to this understanding of the justice system is that it looks at everyday legal problems from the point of view of the people experiencing them. Historically, access to justice has been a concept that centered on the formal justice system (courts, tribunals, lawyers and judges) and its procedures.[5] The formal system is, of course, important. But a more expansive, user-centered vision of an accessible civil and family justice system is required. We need a system that provides the necessary institutions, knowledge, resources and services to avoid, manage and resolve civil and family legal problems and disputes. That system must be able to do so in ways that are as timely, efficient, effective, proportional and just as possible:

- by preventing disputes and by early management of legal issues;
- through negotiation and informal dispute resolution services; and

- where necessary, through formal dispute resolution by tribunals and courts.

Important elements of this vision include:

- public awareness of rights, entitlements, obligations and responsibilities;
- public awareness of ways to avoid or prevent legal problems;
- ability to participate effectively in negotiations to achieve a just outcome;
- ability to effectively utilize non-court and court dispute resolution procedures; and
- institutions and mechanisms designed to implement accessible civil and family justice reforms.

CURRENT GAPS IN ACCESS TO JUSTICE — THE PROBLEM

1. Everyday Legal Problems

Civil justice problems are "pervasive in the lives of Canadians" and frequently have negative impacts on them.[6]

- **Many People Have Everyday Legal Problems.** Nearly 12 million Canadians will experience at least 1 legal problem in a given 3 year period.[7] In the area of family law alone, annual averages indicate that approximately 40% of marriages will end in divorce.[8] These are the problems of everyday people in everyday life.[9]
- **The Poor and the Vulnerable are Particularly Prone to Legal Problems.** Individuals with lower incomes and members of vulnerable groups experience more legal problems than higher income earners and members of more secure groups.[10] For example, people who self-identify as disabled are more than 4 times more likely to experience social assistance problems and 3 times more likely to experience housing related problems, and people who self-identify as aboriginal are nearly 4 times more likely to experience social assistance problems.[11]
- **Problems Multiply.** One kind of legal problem (for example, domestic violence) often leads to, or is aggravated by, others (such as relationship breakdown, child education issues, etc.).[12] Legal problems also have momentum: the more legal problems an individual experiences, the greater the likelihood that she or he will experience others.[13] Legal problems also tend to lead to other problems of other types. For example, almost 40% of people with one or more legal problems reported having other social or health related

424

problems that they directly attributed to a justiciable problem.[14]

- **Legal Problems Have Social and Economic Costs.** Unresolved legal problems adversely affect people's lives, their finances and the public purse. They of course tend to make people's lives difficult.[15] Unresolved problems relating (for example) to debt, housing, and social services lead to social exclusion, which may in turn lead to a dependency on government assistance.[16] One recent U.K. study reported that unresolved legal problems cost individuals and the public £13 billion over a 3.5 year period.[17]

2. Importance Of Accessible Justice

To address these problems, we need a stronger and more effective civil and family justice system that is viewed and experienced as such by the public. This is critically important for the daily lives of people and for the social, political and economic well-being of society. For the system to be strong and effective, people must have meaningful access to it.[18]

3. The Current System Has Serious Gaps In Access

According to a wide range of justice system indicators and stakeholders, Canada is facing major access to justice challenges. For example, in the area of access to civil justice Canada ranked 13th out of 29 high-income countries in 2012–2013 and 16th out of 23 high-income countries in 2011.[19] According to the 2011 study, Canada's ranking was "partially explained by shortcomings in the affordability of legal advice and representation, and the lengthy duration of civil cases."[20]

These international indicators tell us two things. First, Canada has a functioning justice system that is well regarded by many countries in the world. Second, improvement is urgently needed. There is a major gap between what legal services cost and what the vast majority of Canadians can afford. Some cost indicators are:

- **Legal Aid Funding and Coverage is Not Available for Most People and Problems**. Legal aid funding is available only for those of extremely modest means. For example in Ontario, legal aid funding is generally only available for individuals with a gross annual salary of less than $18,000, or for a family of 4 with a total gross annual salary of $37,000.[21] In Alberta, legal aid funding is generally only available for individuals with a net annual salary of approximately $16,000, or for a

family of 4 with a total net annual salary of approximately $30,000.[22] In Manitoba[23] and Saskatchewan,[24] the eligibility levels for individuals and families of 4 are, respectively, gross annual salaries of $14,000 and $27,000 and net annual salaries of $11,800 and $22,800. Even within these financial eligibility ranges, legal aid covers only a limited number of areas of legal services.[25] For example, in Ontario, but for some civil matters covered by community, specialty and student clinics, legal aid coverage for civil matters does not exist.[26]

- **The Cost of Legal Services and Length of Proceedings is Increasing**. Legal fees in Canada vary significantly; however, one recent report provides a rough range of national average hourly rates from approximately $195 (for lawyers called in 2012) to $380 (for lawyers called in 1992 and earlier).[27] Rates can vary from this range significantly depending on jurisdiction, type of case, seniority and experience. The cost of civil and family matters also varies significantly. For example, national ranges of legal fees are recently reported to be $13,561–$37,229 for a civil action up to trial (2 days), $23,083–$79,750 for a civil action up to trial (5 days), $38,296–$124,574 for a civil action up to trial (7 days), and $12,333–$36,750 for a civil action appeal.[28] The length and cost of legal matters have continued to increase.[29]

4. Unmet Legal Needs

Most people earn too much money to qualify for legal aid, but too little to afford the legal services necessary to meaningfully address any significant legal problem. The system is essentially inaccessible for all of these people.[30] Below are some of the indicators.

- **Unmet Legal Needs**. According to one recent American study, as much as 70%–90% of legal needs in society go unmet.[31] This statistic is particularly troubling given what we know about the negative impacts of justiciable problems, particularly those that go unresolved.[32] In Canada, over 20% of the population take no meaningful action with respect to their legal problems, and over 65% think that nothing can be done, are uncertain about their rights, do not know what to do, think it will take too much time, cost too much money or are simply afraid.[33]
- **Cost is a Major Factor.** Of those who do not seek legal assistance, recent reports indicate that between 42% and 90% identified cost — or at least perceived cost — as the reason for not doing

so.[34] An important result of the inaccessibility of legal services and the fact that many people do nothing to address their legal problems is that a proportion of legal problems that could be resolved relatively easily at an earlier stage escalate and shift to ones that require expensive legal services and court time down the road.[35]

- **Self-Representation.** As a result of the inaccessibility of early assistance, legal services and dispute resolution assistance, as well as the complexity and length of formal procedures, approximately 50% of people try to solve their problems on their own with no or minimal legal or authoritative non-legal assistance.[36] Many people — often well over 50% (depending on the court and jurisdiction) — represent themselves in judicial proceedings (usually not by choice).[37] The number is equally — and often more — significant and troubling in family court proceedings.[38] And statistics indicate that individuals who receive legal assistance are between 17% and 1,380% more likely to receive better results than those who do not.[39]

Not surprisingly, people's attitudes towards the system reflect this reality. According to a recent study of self-represented litigants in the Canadian court system, various court workers were of the view that the "civil system [is] ... very much open to abuse by those with more money at their disposal"; and the "general public has no idea about court procedures, requirements, the language, who or where to go for help".[40]

Further, according to a recent study, people expressed similar concerns about access to justice, including the following:

- "I don't have much faith in the lawyers and the system";
- the "language of justice tends to be ... foreign to most people";
- "[p]eople with money have access to more justice than people without";
- "I think there are a lot of people who don't ... understand what the justice system is or how to use it — struggling to earn a living, dealing with addictions..."; and
- the justice system "should be equally important as our health care system...."[41]

5. What is Needed?

There are clearly major access to justice gaps in Canada.[42] The current system, which is inaccessible to so many and unable to respond adequately to the problem, is unsustainable.[43] Two things are urgently needed.

- **First,** a new way of thinking — a culture shift — is required to move away from old patterns and old approaches. We offer six guiding principles for change reflecting this culture shift in part 2 of this report.
- **Second,** a specific action plan — a goal-oriented access to justice roadmap — is urgently needed. That roadmap, which is set out in part 3 of this report, proposes goals relating to innovation, institutions and structures, and research and funding.

Taken together, what is needed is major, sustained and collaborative system-wide change — in the form of cultural and institutional innovation, research and funding-based reform.

PART 2
MOVING FORWARD: SIX GUIDING PRINCIPLES FOR CHANGE

CULTURE SHIFT

Many dedicated people in our civil and family justice system do their best to make the system work and many reform efforts have been put forward in past years. However, it is now clear that the previous approach to access to justice problems and solutions, far from succeeding, has produced our present, unsustainable situation.

We need a fresh approach and a new way of thinking. In short, we need a significant shift in culture to achieve meaningful improvement to access to justice in Canada — a new culture of reform. As Lawrence M. Friedman observed, "law reform is doomed to failure if it does not take legal culture into account."[44]

This new culture of reform should be based on six guiding principles. Taken together, these principles spell out the elements of an overriding culture of reform. A new way of thinking, while important, is not enough. We also need innovative ideas, creative solutions and specific goals, as we set out in part 3. A full embrace of a new culture of reform is a precondition for developing those more specific measures.[45]

SIX GUIDING PRINCIPLES FOR CHANGE

Here are six guiding principles that make up this new culture.

1. Put the Public First

We need to change our primary focus. Too often, we focus inward on how the system operates from the point of view of those who work in it. For example, court processes — language, location, operating times, administrative systems, paper and filing requirements, etc. — typically make sense and work for lawyers, judges and court staff. They often do not make sense or do not work for litigants.

The focus must be on the people who need to use the system. This focus must include all people, especially members of immigrant, aboriginal and rural populations and other vulnerable groups. Litigants, and particularly self-represented litigants, are not, as they are too often seen, an inconvenience; they are why the system exists.[46]

Until we involve those who use the system in the reform process, the system will not really work for those who use it. As one court administrator recently commented, we need to "change ... how we do business within the context of courts."[47] Those of us working within the system need to remember that it exists to serve the public. That must be the focus of all reform efforts.

2. Collaborate and Coordinate

We also need to focus on collaboration and coordination. The administration of justice in Canada is fragmented. In fact, it is hard to say that there is a system — as opposed to many systems and parts of systems. Justice services are delivered at various levels in this country — national, provincial and territorial, and often regional, local and sectoral as well.[48]

Within our current constitutional, administrative and sectoral frameworks, much more collaboration and coordination is not only needed but achievable. We can and must improve collaboration and coordination not only across and within jurisdictions, but also across and within all sectors and aspects of the justice system (civil, family, early dispute resolution, courts, tribunals, the Bar, the Bench, court administration, the academy, the public, etc.). We can and must improve collaboration, coordination and service integration with other social service sectors and providers as well.

We are long past the time for reinventing wheels. We can no longer afford to ignore what is going on in different regions and sectors and miss opportunities for sharing and collaboration.[49] Openness, proactivity, collaboration and coordination must animate how we approach improving access to justice at all levels and across all sectors of the system.[50] In sum, we all — those who use the justice system and those who work within the justice community — are in this project together. A just society is in all of our interest.

3. Prevent and Educate

We need to focus not only on resolving disputes but on preventing them as well. Access to justice has often been thought of as access to courts and lawyers.[51] However, we know that everyday legal problems mostly occur outside of formal justice structures.[52] This insight should lead us to fundamentally re-think how we approach legal problems in terms of preventing them from happening where possible, and when they do occur, providing those who experience them with adequate information and resources to deal with them in an efficient and effective way.[53] As the Action Committee's Prevention, Triage and Referral Working Group indicated, "Avoiding problems or the escalation of problems, and/or early resolution of problems is generally cheaper and less disruptive than resolution using the courts. To borrow Richard Susskind's observation, 'it is much less expensive to build a fence at the top of a cliff than to have need of an expensive ambulance at the bottom.'"[54]

4. Simplify, Make Coherent, Proportional and Sustainable

We must work to make things simple, coherent, proportional and sustainable. One aspect of this task, building on the "public first" principle set out above, is the public's understanding of the system. The Canadian Bar Association acknowledged the system's complexity in its 1996 *Systems of Civil Justice Task Force Report*:

> "Many aspects of the civil justice system are difficult to understand for those untrained in the law. Without assistance it is difficult, if not impossible, to gain access to a system one does not comprehend. Barriers to understanding include:
> - unavailability and inaccessibility of legal information;
> - complexity of the law, its vocabulary, procedures and institutions; and
> - linguistic, cultural and communication barriers."[55]

In spite of recent efforts, the civil and family justice system is still too complicated and largely incomprehensible to all but those with legal training. As one participant in a recent access to justice survey of the public put it, we need to "make the whole thing much less complex."[56] Similarly, in a recent study of self-represented litigants, respondents regularly indicated feeling overwhelmed by the complexity of the system. One respondent indicated that the "procedure as I read it sounded easy ... but it was anything but."[57] Another indicated that, as a result of the system's many procedural steps, "I was eaten alive."[58]

Our current formal procedures seem to grow ever more complicated and disproportionate to the needs of the litigants and the matters involved. Everyday legal problems need everyday solutions that are timely, fair and cost-effective. Procedures must be simple and proportional for the entire system to be sustainable. To improve the system, we need a new way of thinking that concentrates on simplicity, coherence, proportionality and sustainability at every stage of the process.

5. Take Action

We need research, thinking and deliberation. But for meaningful change to occur, they are not enough. We also need action. We cannot put off, to another day, formulating and carrying out a specific and effective action plan. There have been many reports and reform initiatives, but the concrete results have been extremely modest. As the Family Justice Working Group indicated, to make a meaningful difference in the lives of the people who rely

on the justice system, we need to move beyond "wise words" and bridge the "implementation gap."[59]

6. Focus On Outcomes

Our final guiding principle calls for a shift in focus from process to outcomes. We must be sure our process is just. But we must not just focus on process. We should not be preoccupied with fair processes for their own sake, but with achieving fair and just **results** for those who use the system. Of course fair process is important. But at the end of the day, what people want most is a safe, healthy and productive life for themselves, their children and their loved ones. In a recent survey of public views about justice, one respondent defined justice as "access to society."[60] According to another respondent: "We're not even talking access to justice ... we're talking access to food, to shelter, to security, to opportunities for ourselves and our kids and until we deal with that, the other stuff doesn't make sense."[61]

In order to make justice more accessible, we must keep in mind that we are trying to improve law and process not for their own sake, but rather for the sake of providing and improving justice in the lives of Canadians. Providing justice — not just in the form of fair and just process but also in the form of fair and just outcomes — must be our primary concern.

(c) Civil Justice Reform — The Toronto Experience[†]

The Honourable Warren K. Winkler, Chief Justice of Ontario

[1] I am very pleased that the University of Ottawa is holding a series of lectures on the important topic of civil procedure, and flattered that the members of the Faculty of Law were so kind as to both name the series in my honour and invite me to deliver the first of the lectures.[1]

[2] J'aimerais remercier sincèrement le Vice-récteur Feldthusen, le Doyen intérimaire Gervais et la Professeure Bailey pour avoir organisé cette conférence.

[3] I propose to make a few comments today about procedural reforms that were introduced almost

three years ago for civil cases in the Superior Court of Justice in the Toronto Region, but before I do so, I would like to say a few words on a more general level about the importance of civil justice reform.

[4] Civil litigation in this province is too expensive and too slow, with the result that many people in Ontario may be denied access to justice. In a recent article in the Toronto Star entitled "Access to justice a 'basic right,'"[2] it was reported that the cost of taking a routine civil case through to a three-day trial in Ontario is about $60,000. This is more than the

† (2007–2008) 39 Ottawa L. Rev. 99–113. (The Warren Winkler Lectures on Civil Justice Reform, delivered at the University of Ottawa's Faculty of Law on September 12, 2007.) [Notes and/or references omitted.] Reproduced with permission.

average Canadian family earns in a year, which means, of course, that the average Canadian family may not be able to afford a simple civil suit, especially if they lose at the end of trial.

[5] None of this is news. Charles Dickens' criticisms of the legal system in Bleak House, which focused in a most pointed way on the costs and delays of civil proceedings, were published almost two centuries ago, and yet they still ring true today. In Ontario as well as across the country, it has been widely acknowledged within the profession for years that there are significant flaws with our civil justice system. Moreover, clients can be short-sighted, lawyers can give bad advice and judges can become too easily frustrated. Even where reasonable clients find themselves in the hands of good lawyers, who appear before the most able judges, lawsuits can take on very nasty lives of their own.

[6] It may be that some of the problems are, at least to a degree, intractable. However, we must also keep in mind that many of the very same processes that drive up costs provide us with assurances that the system is fundamentally fair. We could eliminate all manner of pleadings, oral and documentary discovery, and move each and every case directly to a 15 minute trial, similar to those seen on popular television, but few would argue that the resulting costs savings would justify the damage done to the process. Without meaning to suggest that we could not do better in terms of reducing costs and delay, we should recognize that a just and fair legal system will, by definition, have very real costs associated with it.

[7] Lawyers should, and do, donate their time pro bono for worthy causes and needy clients, and I commend the members of the profession who engage in this form of public service. It is not realistic, however, to expect that charity will, by itself, provide meaningful access to justice for all those who need it. Similarly, it is not realistic to think that we will have universally available legal aid for civil cases any time soon.

[8] I therefore wish to preface my comments with a simple proposition: If one accepts that there will necessarily be costs associated with any justice system worthy of the name, and that funding sources — apart from the clients themselves — are necessarily limited, one would wish to ensure that careful consideration is given to the true cost implications of any proposed reforms, in very practical terms. I will return to this theme at the conclusion of my remarks today.

[9] We should remember that our system does manage to provide meaningful redress for many ordinary Ontarians, in spite of the costs associated with it. Many apparently vulnerable individuals, such as tort victims, wrongfully dismissed employees and others, are routinely able to obtain legal remedies on a cost effective basis. The legislative changes that explicitly allowed lawyers to charge contingency fees[3] has opened the doors of the justice system for many plaintiffs who would otherwise never be able to afford to hire a lawyer, without generating the flood of frivolous cases anticipated by those who opposed permitting such fee arrangements. Similarly, class action legislation[4] in Ontario has allowed plaintiffs who would not ordinarily be able to afford to bring an action to do just that.

[10] Once again, I am not suggesting that the system is perfect; there are many types of cases that are not amenable to contingency fee arrangements or class actions, and even when they are, they are not always fair to the client. My point is merely that it is wrong to think about our civil justice system as a complete failure. Given that the settlement rate for civil lawsuits in Ontario is over 96%, it distorts our analysis somewhat if we focus too closely on the cost associated with the 3% or 4% of cases that go all the way through trial.

[11] We cannot design a process that will make perfect justice available for everyone, at no cost. I am confident, however, that the legal community in Ontario (in which I include not only the bench and bar, but also academic institutions and the government) can achieve a system in which an increasing number of ordinary people can achieve a fair result when resolving their civil disputes, in a cost effective manner. As I have said, in working towards this goal, we should focus not only on the present system's short-comings but also on its successes. For the simple fact is that our justice system is the envy of the world and a model for every free and democratic society.

[12] I turn now to the situation that presented itself in the Toronto Region of the Superior Court in the spring of 2004. I think it is fair to say that the changes to the civil justice system in the Toronto Region of the Superior Court, which were implemented in late 2004, were successful in dealing with the problems that confronted us. My hope is that there are lessons to be learned from the approach which was taken to address the very significant challenges we faced at the time.

[13] The adage that "necessity is the mother of invention" is entirely apt in describing the reforms. By mid-2004, dates for routine motions were being set more than six months out. Long trials (that is, those projected to last more than ten days) were being scheduled more than three years into the future and the waiting times for shorter trials were increasing to over a year. As a consequence of the delays in getting cases on to trial, the number of interlocutory motions was increasing exponentially. In June of that year, it emerged that the Court had not managed to reach some 38 long trials that were to have started that spring on fixed trial dates, because there were no judges to hear the cases. The simplified procedure for claims under $50,000 (a then recent innovation intended to provide affordable, accessible and timely justice for smaller cases) was generating involved, multi-day trials, thereby defeating its very purpose and using up valuable judicial resources in the process. Any sensible observer of the justice system in the Region knew that the end was in sight when the staff at the case management masters office, the nerve centre for civil case management, literally "took the phone off the hook," signifying that the system was hopelessly backlogged.

[14] It was apparent that if a solution was not found and implemented immediately, and the backlog haemorrhaging was not staunched, the Toronto civil lists would implode come September 2004.

[15] The Toronto Region of the Superior Court is the largest civil trial court in Canada. It is composed of more than one hundred judges and masters, who are supported in their work by over five hundred court services employees.

[16] Toronto is the commercial and financial engine of the country, as the home to many head offices, insurance companies, banks, manufacturing concerns and as the primary centre of the Canadian securities industry. The ability to attract and retain business depends in part on access to fair and timely dispute resolution. A properly functioning civil justice system in Toronto is integral to the success of Ontario's economy.

[17] On an individual level, the people of Canada's largest city also require a dynamic and responsive justice system. They are entitled to expect that their legal rights and civil liberties will not be compromised simply because the legal system is too busy to deal with them.

[18] It was unimaginable and unacceptable that the civil justice system could "melt down" for the beginning of a new court year. In order for the Court to meet its obligations as an important part of the economic infrastructure and as one of the province's most important public institutions, a solution had to be found quickly, without alarming Ontarians or sending a wave of panic through business circles.

[19] Although the seriousness and magnitude of the problems were known by those involved, it was another matter to ascertain the root causes of the problems, so that viable solutions could be developed. The problems had to be viewed through the lens of three fundamental principles: Access to justice, judicial economy and proportionality. More to the point, once answers were forthcoming, the solutions had to be capable of speedy implementation.

[20] I had only recently been appointed as the Regional Senior Justice for Toronto, and I began by consulting with as many people as I could in an effort to pinpoint the causes of the problems. Work began in earnest over the July 1st weekend. A small team, comprised of a handful of judges, civil servants and leading lawyers, was put together. It became clear at the outset that the case management system was going to need major surgery. Full case management had been introduced in Toronto only three years previously, with the enactment of Rule 77 of the Rules of Civil Procedure.[5] A great deal of hard work and planning had gone into the introduction of Rule 77, and any major changes were going to require close communication with a number of stakeholders, in order to ensure their support, such as chief justices, the Toronto Region judiciary and masters, bar organizations, mediators and courts services staff.

[21] It also appeared at the outset that the aggressive timeline which was needed to prevent a full-blown crisis made it impossible to effect the solutions by way of amendment to the Rules of Civil Procedure. A decision was taken to introduce the most urgently needed changes by means of a Practice Direction, in which such changes could be mandated and made effective almost immediately. We set a deadline of December 31, 2004 for identifying the causes of the problems, designing the solutions, and drafting, publishing and implementing the Practice Direction. As events unfolded, it was ultimately possible to enact a new rule on an expedited basis. Rule 78 was enacted to codify some of the reforms and on January 1, 2005, sweeping changes were introduced in the civil justice system in the Toronto Region, for the second time in less than four years.

[22] We now have more than two years of experience with this new regime, and while there is unquestionably a great deal of work that remains to be done, the Practice Direction[6] and Rule 78 are widely seen to have brought about vast improvements for those who use, and work in, the civil justice system.

[23] As I mentioned a moment ago, Rule 77 came into effect for all civil cases in Toronto in 2001. In an attempt to address the costs, delays, and backlogs that plagued the system, and thereby acted as barriers to justice, Rule 77 of the Rules of Civil Procedure had been designed so that virtually all of the civil cases would be aggressively and intensively managed by the courts (i.e., "universal case management"). Rule 77 had previously been implemented in Ottawa and Windsor and was generally viewed as a success in those jurisdictions. In the months leading up to its implementation in Toronto, there was great optimism that it would bring meaningful improvements there as well.

[24] As I also mentioned before, however, it was apparent by mid-2004 that the civil justice system in Toronto was lurching towards a crisis, which many judges and lawyers believed had been brought about, at least in part, by the ambitious package of reforms symbolized by Rule 77. We had to figure out what had gone wrong.

[25] As you know, there are a variety of steps which occur in a civil action before the case is actually heard by a trial judge, such as the exchange of pleadings, disclosure of documents, examinations for discovery and pre-trial conferences. Prior to the introduction of case management, the pace and the way in which these steps occurred were determined almost entirely by the parties and their counsel, sometimes with considerable inefficiency and at great cost. In an effort to address this problem, under case management, the courts were given an immediate supervisory role over the progress of cases moving through the system. The various steps prior to trial were to be determined by pre-fixed timetables, and case management judges and masters were to be assigned to individual cases to assist the parties in moving matters along, or in settling or narrowing issues.

[26] The theory was that with early and active intervention by the court, proceedings would become streamlined and judicial resources would be focused where they were needed most. Cases would either settle earlier, or if they were not going to settle, would be brought on for trial more quickly and more efficiently.

[27] Under the Rules of Civil Procedure, case-managed actions began with "early mandatory mediation" at the very outset of the lawsuit. Mediation is an informal process in which a neutral third party helps participants reach their own agreement for resolving their dispute. Unlike a judge or arbitrator, the mediator has no authority to impose a solution. Rather, the mediator's role is to serve as a neutral facilitator, to try to bring the parties to a mutually agreeable compromise. He or she is ordinarily selected by mutual agreement between the parties, as someone in whom they all have confidence. Significantly, for our purposes, mediators are in private practice and are outside the court system, and thus are paid by the parties.

[28] The case management rules prescribed extremely short deadlines for conducting the mediation.[7] However, in practice the parties would frequently not communicate or cooperate in scheduling the mediation session, or could not agree on a mediator, or did not agree about what steps, if any, could or should be taken in advance of the mediation. In serious casualty cases, parties could be required to attend mediation before the plaintiff's injuries had stabilized. The rule was deliberately designed so that the mediation would take place before one party could compel the other to provide any type of disclosure, such as providing copies of their documents or names of witnesses. In cases with multiple defendants, the mediation deadline sometimes expired before all the parties had been served, and thus were even aware of the lawsuit.

[29] As stated, a failure to agree to conduct the mediation within the time limits set out in the rule resulted in court staff assigning a mediator to the case, who was randomly selected from a roster of whichever mediators happened to be available. He or she was ordinarily unknown to the parties and their lawyers, would usually not have any expertise in the subject of the dispute and would be left with the unenviable task of bringing the reluctant parties to the table. Not surprisingly, the vast majority of these forced early mediations did not result in settlement.

[30] The upshot of all of this was that the mediation became an unavoidable, costly and useless obstacle in the path of the party who wanted to move the lawsuit forward (normally the plaintiff). There were countless case conferences in which judges and masters were asked to extend deadlines or otherwise assist parties in cancelling or delaying the mediations.

A body of law developed, as a result of contested motions, about the circumstances in which a mandatory mediation could be deferred, or whether parties could proceed to mediation with a mediator of their choice when they had missed the deadline and the court office had already randomly assigned a stranger from the roster.

[31] Another important feature of case management was the establishment of timetables for the completion of the steps required to advance the proceeding. Under Rule 77, timetables had to be filed within 30 days after the mandatory mediation session if it had not resulted in a settlement of the lawsuit. Thereafter, case conferences were convened, in which judges and masters were asked to fix or vary timetables, where parties could not, or would not, agree on deadlines, or where they later failed to live up to them. Once again, these case conferences ate up costs and slowed cases down, since the booking dates for case conferences stretched further and further into the future because of the backlog of cases.

[32] Time does not permit me to elaborate today about a number of the other aspects of Rule 77, but I would like to mention one final example. As part of the philosophy of case management, trial dates were fixed regardless of whether or not any of the parties had set the action down for trial. As I mentioned a few moments ago, fewer than four percent of the civil cases that are started in Ontario actually go all the way through to trial. Most are either not defended at all, or settle at some stage before trial. Ordinarily, a trial date is assigned only if the case has not settled and one of the parties indicates that he or she is ready for trial and does not want to take any further pre-trial steps (e.g. discoveries). Because the vast majority of cases settle before this happens, trial dates are ordinarily only given out in a small number of cases.

[33] Under Rule 77, a trial date was assigned for every single lawsuit in the system at trial scheduling court (a court that sat regularly simply to set trial dates), even though the majority of the cases were not ready for trial (although they were supposed to be), and would probably never go to trial in any event. It did not take long for the trial schedules to fill up for months and then years into the future, and the waiting times for trial dates mushroomed. As soon as lawyers noticed this, they attempted to secure trial dates years down the road for cases that were not ready to proceed, on the assumption that they would be ready for trial by the time they were reached. Needless to say, as often as not, when the

trial dates were reached, the parties were still not ready to go, and before long, the trial lists were in shambles.

[34] As some lawyers described the process, it was "hurry up and wait" which meant that cases were pushed through on tight timetables, only to languish waiting for trial dates that were three years away, mainly because the ballooned trial list was laden with cases that were not ready for trial. One side effect of this was there were many motions that would not have been brought if trial dates were available on a timely basis.

[35] Notwithstanding its early success in Ottawa and Windsor, universal case management was not workable in Toronto. This was largely due to the volume of cases and relative lack of resources. The bulk of the case management work fell to a handful of case management masters and court administrators, but notwithstanding their Herculean efforts, it soon became apparent that they could not micromanage the almost 20,000 cases filed every year in the Toronto Region, to the extent mandated by Rule 77.

[36] In addition to the problems faced by the Court, the litigants bore the cost of the numerous procedural steps that were added to the civil justice process. As I have said, the various case conferences, filings and mandatory mediations referred to above usually did very little to move the case along, while clients were paying their lawyers for what were frequently premature or unproductive steps.

[37] What I have euphemistically called the "challenges" that we faced in 2004 were not caused solely by Rule 77. The simplified procedure cases that I spoke about before and long trials (those projected to last more than ten days) were also presenting us with great "challenges."

[38] More than 25 percent of the cases commenced each year in Toronto are filed under the simplified procedure available for cases involving less than $50,000. Unfortunately, the provisions of this rule that were designed to keep the pre-trial steps as simple and inexpensive as possible, were making the trials themselves extremely complicated. Because the parties had not had any discoveries before trial, counsel often conducted one during the trial, which consumed excessive amounts of time. More generally, there was a lack of proportionality and trials involving $20,000 or $30,000 were dragging on for four or five days. The judges blamed the lawyers and the lawyers blamed the judges, but no one seemed to be able to stop it.

[39] At the other end of the spectrum, long trials also created their own set of "challenges." Many different types of cases are projected as "long" trials; however, it is important to bear in mind that a significant proportion (approximately two-thirds) are large casualty cases, where plaintiffs are attempting to obtain compensation for serious personal injuries. As I mentioned at the outset, 38 long-trial dates were missed in the spring of 2004. When these cases were adjourned to the fall, it produced a domino effect, since all the long trials that were supposed to start in the fall had to be put off.

[40] As the number of long trials that were not being reached on their appointed dates increased, the settlement rate decreased. When word got around that the Court would be forced to adjourn a fixed trial date, settlement rates took a free fall. This compounded the backlog and brings me to a very important point that applies not just to long trials, but to all cases: Real trial dates lead to settlements.

[41] I begin with the proposition that responsible counsel do not settle their cases until they have considered the issues involved, assessed the strengths and weaknesses of their case and investigated the facts, including facts that may initially be within the exclusive knowledge of the opposite party. I hasten to add that all of this should be proportionate to the amounts of money involved and the seriousness of the issues, and as cost-effective as possible.

[42] My next proposition is that, subject only to investigating the matter in a proportionate and cost-effective way, responsible lawyers settle their cases as early in the life of the file as they can. Unfortunately, for a variety of reasons, the parties will not simultaneously arrive at the moment when they are all ready to settle if left to their own devices.

[43] It is for this reason that I say that real trial dates settle cases. What I mean by this is that the intense preparation that ordinarily takes place immediately before a trial, and the parties' collective realization that they are going to have a result imposed on them by a court if they do not sort the dispute out themselves, leads all parties to focus very attentively on settlement, and to do so at the same time. This is a good thing: There should be a point of reckoning when the parties can make an informed decision about whether or not they wish to settle or proceed to trial. When the trial lists fell apart and the parties knew that their case was not likely to be reached for trial (or that the Court would happily adjourn the case if it was), the day of reckoning — the necessary catalyst for settlement — never arrived.

The settlements of the more intractable cases, which ordinarily take place on the very eve of trial, stopped occurring. The long trial list worked on a fine balance and was judicially staffed based on a known settlement rate for cases. When the settlement rate fell off, there were not enough judges for the cases scheduled to start.

[44] In short, by mid-2004, costs and delays had ballooned for litigants in Toronto. The court system was overburdened with unproductive work tying up valuable resources. While the simplified procedure had proven to be popular, it was not achieving its goal of making civil justice more affordable. Because parties could not get their cases heard, especially if their trial was expected to be lengthy, cases that would ordinarily have been settling were languishing in the system.

[45] Through the summer and early fall of 2004 there were extensive consultations with lawyers, judges, masters and court administrators both inside and outside Toronto. A number of key themes emerged. First, the volume of cases in Toronto had made it impossible to transfer the successes and flexible practices from Ottawa and Windsor to the unique challenges present in the Toronto Region. Successful case management requires a degree of flexibility that cannot be achieved when the court is dealing with vast numbers of cases. Universal case management had to be reworked to apply resources to the cases that "needed" case management. The court-overseen timetabling requirements were unachievable and vast court resources were being eaten up arranging and rearranging lawyers' schedules. The escalation of case conferences was imposing considerable and unnecessary costs on the parties, and draining court resources. The work required of the masters had to be reduced to fit the available personnel. Second, imposing mediation at the very outset of each and every case, before the parties and their counsel were properly informed, was proving to be costly and unproductive. Third, the delays in getting cases on to trial were unacceptable and were creating [their] own host of problems. Fourth, simplified procedures were not working and were tying up critical resources. Finally, Toronto was known as the "motions capital of the world" because [of] the many motions generated by the problems set out above.

[46] I do want to say what, in my view, did not cause the problem. Court staff, judges and in particular the case management masters were more dedicated and diligent than anyone had a right to expect. They were given an impossible task, and worked

under what ultimately proved to be impossible circumstances. Similarly, I do not accept the assertion, advanced in some quarters, that Toronto lawyers are to blame, and that the members of the bar in Toronto work less cooperatively and civilly than lawyers elsewhere in the province. As someone who grew up in Alberta, I can certainly understand that anything that has to do with Toronto is a useful whipping post, but in my experience the negative stereotype about the Toronto Bar has no basis in fact.

[47] Finally, I emphasize that the drafter of Rule 77 had shown great insight about addressing problems in the civil justice system. For the reasons I have already stated, it makes perfect sense for parties to know that real, fixed, trial dates — what I called their day of reckoning — await them. It is reasonable to insist that parties attempt to resolve their case by mediation before they consume the significant public and private resources involved in the conduct of a trial. Moreover, it is in the parties' and the public's interest for the Court to assume some control over pending cases, to ensure that they are not languishing because of inattentive lawyers, or because the case has taken on a nasty life of its own. The theories behind Rule 77 were unassailable, but procedure needed to accommodate the reality of dealing with 20,000 new cases every year.

[48] In countless meetings through September and October, the ad hoc committee turned its attention to the detailed work of figuring out the solutions, which would form the basis of the Practice Direction and later, Rule 78. It soon became clear that it was critically important to ensure that the various individual reforms we were considering could work together as a whole. Further, while the reforms had to set out the basic procedure for the effective management of all of the many cases in the system, it was equally important that there should be a degree of flexibility, in recognition of the fact that the issues, problems and personalities involved in each piece of litigation are different.

[49] After a great deal of coffee and debate, the Practice Direction was finalized and approved by Chief Justice Smith in November 2004, and came into effect on December 31, 2004. Rule 78 came into force shortly thereafter.

[50] Case management was not eliminated. Rather, there was to be "case management as necessary, but not necessarily case management." The reform was to eliminate "universal case management" in Toronto. The goal was to provide "effective, flexible and targeted case management," by only case managing the cases that truly required court intervention. The intention was that there would be a reduction in the number of unnecessary attendances by counsel and thus reduced costs to parties. At the same time, court resources would be freed up to address more substantive issues.

[51] Specifically, case management could be obtained on motion in complex multi-party actions, or where one or more parties were guilty of chronic obstruction. Apart from this, the parties were to be left to run their own lawsuits. Lawsuits were returned to the lawyers to manage and flexibility was to be the touchstone in cases that were to be case managed by the Court.

[52] The other notable aspects of the reforms included discontinuing trial scheduling court, and returning to a system where trial dates would only be given out after one of the parties signified that he or she was ready to proceed to trial. Steps were taken to ensure that trials actually proceeded on their fixed date, and a strict "no adjournment" policy was put in place. The jurisdiction of case management masters was expanded, in order that they could preside at pre-trials in cases involving less than $50,000.

[53] The notion that the parties would run their own cases was subject to an important caveat: Parties or counsel would have to attend Status Hearings if their case appeared to be languishing, and in particular, if the case was not set down for trial within two years of being issued. The procedures governing Status Hearings, which were first introduced in the early 1980s, were modified so that counsel could avoid attending if they took concrete steps to move their action forward after the court office advised them that their delay had not gone unnoticed, and so that case management masters could preside in place of judges.

[54] Further, in an attempt to make pre-trials more meaningful, the requirements as to the information that had to be included in pre-trial briefs was greatly enhanced, so that both the parties and judges would be better prepared to focus on the case at the pre-trial. It was felt that this would increase the rates of settlements which could be achieved at pre-trials, and make trial management more effective in those cases that could not be settled.

[55] The way we dealt with mandatory mediation was as important as any other single reform. There was considerable pressure by the Bar to eliminate mandatory mediation altogether as a costly and ineffective

unnecessary step. This was rejected. Instead, the members of the ad hoc committee were uniformly of the view that the right approach was to insist that the parties engage in mediation at some point before trial, but to extend the timelines so that mediation would occur when it was most likely to be effective. A recommendation of the mediation community was adopted expanding mandatory mediation to include simplified procedure cases, which had been excluded under the former rules. The only expandable resource available to the court system was the outside mediation community and the decision was to capitalize on this valuable resource, not reject it!

[56] The essence is that mediation continues to be mandatory, but the parties should control the timing of such an important event to the extent that this is possible. To ensure that parties do not bypass the step, trial dates are not provided until mediation has been conducted, or at least booked. Mediators know that mediation is about "timing, timing and timing," and the reform in Rules 24.1 and 78 recognizes this truism. Mediation must now, in the words of the practice direction, be conducted "at the earliest stage at which it is likely to be effective," and in any event within 90 days after the case is set down for trial at the latest.[8] In wrongful dismissal and simplified procedure cases, the mediation must take place at the very front end of the lawsuit.

[57] As a further reform, I introduced what is known colloquially as "designated hitter" mediations, which are conducted by handpicked judges with expertise both as mediators and in the area of law involved in the dispute. This is done immediately prior to trial. There are, therefore, three mediations under the present regime: Mandatory mediation, a pre-trial conference and a DH mediation immediately before trial.

[58] The overarching theory of these and the other reforms introduced by Rule 78 and the Practice Direction was to reduce the number of appearances and formal litigation steps as much as possible, and to maximize the effectiveness of those steps that were taken. As stated, the underlying principles are access to justice in the form of shortened delays and reduced costs, the most efficient use of judicial resources, and proportionality and tailor-made case management where needed. Mediation became the centrepiece. Arrangements are underway to conduct a formal study of the results of the reforms over the next several months.

[59] It is nonetheless not too early to declare at least partial victory.

[60] We already know that although the number of civil cases in the system continues to grow, the waiting times for motion dates and trial dates are down. In some cases, such as masters' motions and trials under ten days, the reductions are especially dramatic. Dates for trials under ten days are now available within less than one month in cases of five days or less and available within five months for trials of six to ten days. These cases formerly had a 24-month waiting period. Even for long trials, the waiting time has been reduced from approximately three years to just over 12 months.

[61] Because case management masters have been relieved of the chore of conducting unnecessary case conferences for scheduling matters in routine cases, their time has been freed up to deal with more important practice motions, on a more timely basis, to conduct pre-trials in simplified procedure cases and to conduct Status Hearings. This in turn has freed up more judges to conduct trials, which shortens the waiting times, which leads to earlier negotiated settlements before costs spin out of control. Notably, although early dates are available, there has been a marked reduction in the nature of two-thirds fewer court "events" (which can mean anything from a motion or case conference, to a pre-trial or trial) for each case before trial.

[62] Altogether, the reforms led to a number of changes that improved the court system. Trial scheduling court has been disbanded, removing this time consuming step. Masters have been re-deployed to perform important pre-trials and motions.

[63] Since the timelines have been extended, the success rate for mandatory mediations has almost doubled. Further, it is said that the number of pre-trials in simplified procedure cases has been reduced to about one-third the former number, reflecting the wisdom in extending mediation to those cases. The shortened waiting time for trials has resulted in fewer motions. The bottom line is that as a result of the changes taken globally, more judges have been freed up to handle estates, family and criminal matters which had been suffering from lack of judicial resources, and delays on those lists have been reduced.

[64] Lest anyone think that I am being immodest in declaring at least partial victory, let me repeat what I said before. The reforms were borne of necessity and were the culmination of a great deal of input from a wide variety of people. They were designed by a working group that included representatives of mediators, bar groups, masters, the judiciary and

government court administrators. They were implemented by the assiduous efforts of the court staff, masters and judges of the Superior Court in the Toronto Region. Equally important, the members of the Bar rose to the challenge and, with the assistance of the Law Society of Upper Canada's Continuing Legal Education programmes, are working with the re-designed practices and procedures.

[65] In spite of the work that has gone into these reforms, and although the Bench and Bar have achieved substantial success in Toronto, litigation is nevertheless still beyond the financial means of the average person in Ontario. If we are committed to the rule of law and access to justice, we must redouble our efforts to address cost and delay. When the formal review of the Rule 78 reforms has been completed, I am hopeful that there will be valuable lessons to assist in our continuing effort to introduce constructive reforms to the civil justice system in Ontario.

[66] In the meantime, and in concluding my remarks today, I would like to offer some preliminary observations of what those lessons might be.

[67] First of all, I would begin with the proposition that every step that is added to a proceeding must be presumed to be an impediment to justice, unless the benefits of the proposed added step are empirically demonstrable. Recall[] that the average Canadian family cannot afford unnecessary and costly steps to their already expensive lawsuit.

[68] Early mandatory mediation, detailed mandatory timetables and numerous case conferences may be justifiable on a theoretical basis, but each and every one of these steps costs money, and if the added steps are not in fact moving cases towards resolution, they will drain away resources that litigants could otherwise use on steps that would have greater value in the long run. It was the litigants of modest means — those intended to be the primary beneficiaries of Rule 77 — whose counsel argued most vociferously for the reforms.

[69] It is imperative that when adopting any added procedure, the approach ought to be to add more steps only when they can be justified after rigorous scrutiny of the likely practical results. We must strive to find a balance where we "touch" each file as few times as possible, but make each "touch" of the file as productive as possible in moving the case forward. This should be done with a view to reducing the costs that the parties must bear for multiple attendances and with a view to reducing the depletion of

judicial resources. Under the reforms, the "events" on average have been reduced by more than half.

[70] Secondly, I suggest that we remain ever mindful that procedure should be the servant of substantive justice, and not vice versa. There is the temptation because of our training as judges and lawyers to become focused on procedural points to the exclusion of the substantive rights of parties. At the risk of stating the obvious, process is not an end in itself. If a procedural code or provision is ornate and intricate, the chances are that it will be expensive and cumbersome to administer for both lawyers and courts and that it will thus detract from substantive justice. Keep it simple.

[71] Thirdly, I suggest that mediation has become an integral part of our justice system. This is a good thing, but we must also keep this broad generalization in perspective. For one thing, not every type of case is amenable to mediation. Not every party wants a mediated resolution to his or her dispute. A wasted mediation is an added cost to the litigants and may have other serious negative effects on the case. Even in those cases that are ripe for mediation, the terms of any negotiated settlement will be dictated by the parties' knowledge of what the non-mediated result might look like. Obviously, a party with a strong case on the merits can expect to negotiate a more favourable result than a party with a weak case, which is as it should be.

[72] Quite apart from the merits of a party's case, however, the "non-mediated" result which will drive settlement discussions also refers to process. Parties, and in particular vulnerable parties, will approach negotiations very differently, depending on whether or not a trial is affordable and available without unreasonable delay. There is a risk that the negotiations that take place during mediations, and the terms of any settlement, will become badly lopsided if costs and delays become a disproportionate factor in the mediation dynamic. No party should be forced to accept an unfair settlement at mediation simply because the opponent will be able to grind him or her down and drag a case out so that it takes on Dickensian proportions.

[73] In conclusion, nothing is more effective in the court system than a "day of reckoning" — the prospect of an early and "real" trial date. The very least, and at the same time the most constructive thing that our trial courts can provide to assist parties in resolving their disputes is to ensure that a judge is available to try the case if it cannot be settled, and that a trial date is available within as short a time as

possible after the case is ready for trial. In short, a fair and just system of justice requires a courtroom, a judge and a non-adjournment policy which, in turn, will produce settlements and be less costly to the litigants.

[74] My job today has been easy. I have spoken only in general terms about access to justice, judicial economy and proportionality, all of which are com-plex and difficult subjects. Let's hope that the speak-ers who come after me in this series can contribute to the rigorous debate that is needed to build the civil justice system we would all like to see and strive to create.

[75] Thank you. Merci pour votre attention aujourd'hui.

(d) Access to *Charter* Justice and the Rule of Law†

Carissima Mathen

1. INTRODUCTION

The difficulties experienced by most people in gaining access to the courts are generally acknowledged to be at crisis levels.[1] Numerous judges have expressed frustration at the continuing problems.[2] These diffi-culties are multiplied in constitutional cases. Ideally, courts would recognize that how people get to court is integrally connected to a properly functioning legal system. For the most part, this has not been the case. The current situation is dire, providing little assurance of essential review of laws and government action. This contributes to an overall deficit in state accountability.

This article argues that it is vital to ensure that (a) there is some mechanism by which the constitu-tionality of law and actions can be judged and (b) people have access to legal services. A society which fails in these tasks is little better than a society unbound by constitutional limits — and at risk of los-ing a key determinant of the rule of law.

The article first discusses developments in the law of standing and funding for litigation. The fact that constitutional litigation vindicates fundamental legal and political values warrants a generous approach to both issues. It is through these mecha-nisms that we ensure that the legal system pro-motes and protects such things as the equal protection and benefit of the law, the achievement of social justice and fundamental rights. I conclude by returning more specifically to the rule of law and its implications for access to justice through a discussion of the Supreme Court of Canada's decision in *Chris-tie v. British Columbia (Attorney General)*.[3]

2. STANDING

The standing issue most relevant in *Charter* cases is the ability to litigate in the public interest,[4] a role ordinarily confined to Attorneys General.[5] This role was confirmed in *Alliance for Marriage and Family v. A.A., B.B., C.C. and D.D.*,[6] a 2007 Supreme Court of Canada decision. A.A. *et al.* sought a declaration under Ontario's *Children's Law Reform Act*[7] to recog-nize as a third parent the lesbian partner of D.D.'s biological mother. The Alliance for Marriage and Family intervened against the applicants. After the Ontario Court of Appeal granted the application under its *parens patriae* jurisdiction and the Attorney General of Ontario (which had not participated in that court)[8] declined to pursue an appeal to the Supreme Court of Canada, the Alliance sought to appeal under Rule 18(5).[9] Dismissing the motion, Justice LeBel held that the Alliance was attempting to "substitute itself for the Attorney General in order to bring important legal questions relating to the development and application of the law before this Court".[10] He ruled that it is not open to a pri-vate litigant to "revive litigation in which it ha[s] no personal interest", noting that the Court's "flexibility" had "limits".[11]

Notwithstanding the Court's reasoning, the likeli-hood that an Attorney General will challenge laws

---

† (2008–2009) 25 N.J.C.L. 191 at 191–93, 197–204. [Notes and/or references omitted.] Reproduced with permission.

enacted or relied upon by his or her government is remote. Thus, public interest standing retains great importance. As the Court has noted elsewhere, such litigation can ensure that "ordinary citizens have access to the justice system when they seek to resolve matters of consequence to the community as a whole".[12]

The framework for public interest standing is found in a quartet of cases decided in the 1970s and 1980s.[13] Three criteria are key: (a) there must be a serious issue raised as to the invalidity of the legislation; (b) the litigant must have a genuine interest in the legislation's validity; and (c) there must be no other reasonable or effective manner to bring the issue before the Court.[14]

The *Charter* posed the potential for enormous growth in the Supreme Court's docket including cases initiated by public interest litigants. In an early challenge to aspects of the immigration process, the Court limited the scope of such cases.[15] Though the Court recognized that the test for public interest standing should not be so limited as to render certain areas of the law immune from *Charter* challenge,[16] it was concerned at the prospect of a deluge of "marginal or redundant suits" initiated by well-meaning but misguided public organizations.[17] The Court therefore declined to expand the criteria mentioned above, ruling that the provisions at issue could be challenged by putative immigrants and refugees making a public interest challenge unnecessary.[18]

The most stringent criterion in the standing test is that there must be no other effective means for the issue to come before a court. This factor can be a particularly difficult hurdle in immigration cases. An applicant may be deported or (in cases with greater public appeal) the government may grant individual requests thereby removing the need for a hearing. The continued obstacles to meaningful challenges to immigration law emerged most recently in litigation of the Canadian Council for Refugees (CCR) against the *Safe Third Country Agreement* (STCA). Under the SCTA, refugee claimants entering Canada through U.S. land ports are returned to that country.[19] CCR argued that, in designating the United States as a "safe third country", the Governor in Council exceeded its authority under the *Immigration Act* and violated refugee claimants' *Charter* rights. While CCR was successful in the Federal Court, it lost in the Federal Court of Appeal, *inter alia*, on the basis that it did not have standing to argue the *Charter* issues. The Court noted that a similar claim could be brought by a refugee claimant presenting at a Canadian port of entry. It did not matter that such a lawsuit was extremely unlikely to

occur; so long as a hypothetical plaintiff was identified, it would be inappropriate to grant standing to a public interest litigant. The Supreme Court of Canada refused leave to appeal.[20]

. . . .

3. FUNDING

If standing is the heart of much public law litigation, funding is the lifeblood. It is also under tremendous strain. The lack of a stable source of funding for litigation leads to an *ad hoc* approach to rights advocacy, placing incredible pressure on individual lawyers and groups. It tends to inhibit the development of comprehensive litigation strategies, collaboration and compromise among like-minded interest groups. A lack of funding means that, for the vast majority of people, their ability to seek redress for wrongs done is illusory.

The federal government's decision in 2006 to cancel the Court Challenges Program (CCP), which provided modest funding for a narrow range of *Charter* cases,[40] removed one of the very few stable sources of funding in Canada for constitutional litigation. Though it was limited in scope, the program — perhaps more than any other post-*Charter* initiative — encapsulated the particular nature of the rights project in Canada. It embodied the belief that the protection and promotion of rights is a collective project, not a battle between state and citizen. The program recognized, in a modest but profoundly symbolic way, that we are all part of a rights-respecting culture and that constitutional limits on the state require independent, proactive and effective enforcement.

The program did not just fund litigation; it supported research and analysis on a host of issues important to marginalized communities. Providing opportunities for organizations to develop analytical and strategic approaches to rights advocacy, the CCP showed how the *Charter* and, indeed, constitutionalism itself not only sets limits on state power, but also channels and directs that power in positive ways. It demonstrated that constitutionalism can be a tool to enable the state to do more, not simply an obstacle to be manoeuvred around.

When terminating the program, the government said that it did not make sense to subsidize lawyers to challenge the government's own laws.[41] This statement reveals an impoverished view of rights: an obsession with safeguarding the state's power to enact laws, with minimal or no consideration for the boundaries that properly confine it.

438

One area that illustrates the challenge facing would-be public interest litigants is interim costs. A court may order the government to pay legal costs in advance if the interests of justice require it or if the case is exceptionally important. In *British Columbia (Minister of Forests) v. Okanagan Indian Band*,[42] four Bands claimed the right to log on Crown lands by virtue of Aboriginal title. After the Minister of Forests served the Bands with stop-work orders and commenced proceedings against them, the Bands brought a constitutional challenge to the *Forest Practices Code of British Columbia Act*.[43] In responding to an attempt by the Crown to have the issue remitted for trial, the Bands argued that such action was appropriate only if the Court made an interim costs award. A six–three majority of the Supreme Court upheld the provincial appellate court's decision that interim costs were justified. The trial judge actually supported an interim costs award, but had wrongly permitted that conclusion to be overtaken by irrelevant considerations. The majority noted that the judge found the case to be one of great public importance, raising novel and significant issues the resolution of which was very much in the interests of justice, even going so far as to urge the federal and provincial governments to provide funding.[44] The majority endorsed this view that resolving the issues would be "a major step towards settling the many unresolved problems in the Crown–aboriginal relationship in that province".[45] The circumstances were "special, even extreme".[46]

The following factors would favour (though not mandate) interim costs: (a) the plaintiff's impecuniousness together with an unlikelihood that the case otherwise would proceed; (b) a *prima facie* meritorious claim; and (c) unresolved issues of public importance that transcend the individual interests of the particular litigant.[47] The *Okanagan* factors suggest that allowing a particular case to lapse because of a lack of funds is not in the interests of justice. The Court also specifically acknowledged the role of public interest litigation (indeed, of public law cases in general), noting that society is not served when fiscal concerns deter ordinary citizens from bringing forward constitutional cases. The notion of "public interest" that underlies all constitutional litigation was thus identified as a relevant consideration when making an interim costs award.[48]

A markedly different result occurred in 2007, when a majority of the Court refused to uphold an interim costs award to the Little Sisters Bookstore in its ongoing battle with Canada Customs.[49] When analyzing this decision, one must recall that previous litigation[50] had established systemic discrimination against this bookstore, which served the lesbian and gay community, and had at least suggested bad faith on the state's part (for example, its failure to remove discriminatory criteria[51] from an operations manual after it would have been aware of the inappropriateness).[52] In 2000, the Supreme Court accepted that discrimination had occurred, but declined to impose a direct remedy because the government claimed that the offending aspects of the inspection regime had since been fixed:

> A more structured s. 24(1) remedy might well be helpful but it would serve the interests of none of the parties for this Court to issue a formal declaratory order based on six-year-old evidence supplemented by conflicting oral submissions and speculation on the current state of affairs. The views of the Court on the merits of the appellants' complaints as the situation stood at the end of 1994 are recorded in these reasons ... These findings should provide the appellants with a solid platform from which to launch any further action in the Supreme Court of British Columbia should they consider that further action is necessary.[53]

Believing that it continued to be the subject of disproportionate seizures of its materials, the Little Sisters bookstore launched a new action. Having already spent hundreds of thousands of dollars, the bookstore sought interim costs in the B.C. Supreme Court.[54] That Court separated the case into three parts: a challenge to specific findings of obscenity, a systemic claim against the customs regime and a constitutional question concerning the correct application of obscenity law to gay and lesbian materials. The Court awarded interim costs for the first and second arguments but not for the third. The Court of Appeal set the order aside.

A majority of the Supreme Court of Canada affirmed the Court of Appeal's decision.[55] Essentially the case was reduced to a fact-based dispute over individual publications. The Court simply rejected the claim that *Little Sisters* was about anything more than one bookstore's mistreatment at the hands of Canada Customs. No broader public interest was recognized.

Advance costs are contentious and do not enjoy unqualified support in the legal community.[56] But, if they are to remain a viable choice, it is challenging to think of a *Charter* case in which they would be more justified than *Little Sisters*. Indeed, the strongest advocate for the bookstore was Justice Binnie who, as author of the Court's 2000 decision, declined to award the bookstore a more structured remedy.

Dissenting strongly from the majority in the 2007 decision, he wrote:

> I differ from my colleagues about what is truly at stake in this appeal and this leads to our disagreement about the appropriate outcome. In my view, *Little Sisters No. 1* provides more than "important context" [as my colleagues describe it. The ramifications of that decision go to the heart and soul of the appellant's present application.... This case is not the beginning of a litigation journey. It is 12 years into it ...
>
> The present application for advance costs comes before us precisely because the appellant says that the Minister's assurances proved empty in practice, that the systemic abuses established in the earlier litigation have continued, and that (in its view) Canada Customs has shown itself to be unwilling to administer the Customs legislation fairly and without discrimination. Of course there are two sides to the story. Although for good reason the majority declined to strike down the legislation, it was never doubted that Customs has been given a difficult job to do by Parliament, and that solutions to entrenched problems would take time to put in place. The question of public importance is this: was the Minister as good as his word when his counsel assured the Court that the appropriate reforms had been implemented?[57]

For Justice Binnie, *Little Sisters 2* was an appropriate case for interim costs because to rule otherwise risked rendering the state beyond judicial scrutiny when it could well be operating in disregard of constitutional norms. While the state could vigorously contest such a claim, he suggested that the broader public interest was better served by having the claim ensue — even if paid for by the state — than by allowing the exigencies of protracted litigation to put such action out of reach.

So, while the precedent set by *Okanagan* remains, *Little Sisters 2* does not bode well for the scope of discretionary mechanisms to promote access to justice.

A distinct yet related disappointment emerges in *British Columbia (A.G.) v. Christie*,[58] discussed below.

4. *CHRISTIE*: THE FRAGILITY OF THE RULE OF LAW

Earning no more than $30,000 annually, Dugald Christie ran a law practice in B.C. serving only low-income families ineligible for legal aid. Under the *Social Service Tax Amendment Act (No 2), 1993*,[59] legal services are subject to a 7% tax. Due to his cli-

ents' precarious finances, Christie could not pay the tax owed on those services and had to close his practice. He claimed that the Act was contrary to the rule of law because the legislation, by burdening access to legal counsel, undermined citizens' access to the courts[60] and interfered with citizens' effective use of the courts even if it did not prevent formal access to them.[61] The B.C. Supreme Court agreed that the Act violated indigent citizens' right to access to justice.[62] A majority of the B.C. Court of Appeal dismissed the appeal.[63]

The Supreme Court allowed the government's appeal.[64] Though the Court acknowledged the existence of a constitutional right to access the courts, such a right is not absolute[65] since the *Constitution Act, 1867* grants provincial legislatures "the power to pass laws in relation to the administration of justice".[66] Furthermore, though the Court agreed that the rule of law *might* support a right to assistance of counsel in certain situations, it rejected the idea that it could entail such a right in every case implicating a person's rights and obligations.[67]

In support of his argument that a 7% tax on legal services on its face presents a hurdle for indigent litigants, Christie adduced affidavit evidence. It appears, though, that the Court really wanted to see evidence in favour of the very different argument that such a tax would make the difference between access and lack of access. In the context of this case, such a burden was extremely onerous. The additional evidence that could support this claim would have to show that a sufficient number of lawyers in British Columbia would not and do not lower their fees to accommodate those people who would retain them but for the tax alone; that legal aid does not address the "access deficit" caused by the tax; and that the deficit is not resolved through some other social mechanism.

The success of the case presented depended on the Court's receptiveness to arguments concerning unwritten constitutional principles and to the notion that the rule of law entails a wider right to counsel than that contained in s. 7 of the *Charter*. In previous cases, though, the Court has made it clear that the rule of law imposes few substantive limits on legislative power. In *British Columbia v. Imperial Tobacco Canada Ltd.*,[68] it said that the rule of law embodies three principles: the preclusion of arbitrary exercises of power, the creation and maintenance of an actual order of positive laws, and the expectation that the state–individual relationship will be regulated by law. The conception is highly formalistic, a conclusion supported by the Court's musing in *Imperial Tobacco* that it was "difficult to conceive of how the rule of law could be used as a basis for invalidating legislation ... based on its content".[69]

The first principle articulated in *Imperial Tobacco* might have assisted Christie. If the rule of law first and foremost precludes the "influence of arbitrary power", it is reasonable to ask whether the existing legislative framework — which arguably permits indigent defendants to access the courts only if they happen to find a lawyer willing to provide representation for free or at a substantial discount — truly achieves that goal. Every legal aid system in Canada operates on the assumption that lawyers will "do the right thing" and represent a number of clients on at least a discounted basis. In British Columbia, 97% of the lawyers providing legal aid services in 2005–6 were private, as opposed to staff, lawyers.[70] This means they were under no formal legal obligation to take on legal aid cases.[71] Legal professionals can take pride in the fact that they already do much to help those in need. But the current approach to access to justice institutionalizes a relationship in which lawyers can exercise arbitrary power over lower-class Canadians (even if they exercise it compassionately). Viewed in that light, there may be something to the claim that the existing legislative framework for providing legal representation offends even a deeply formalistic understanding of the rule of law.

Christie raises issues about how unwritten constitutional principles fit alongside written ones. In *Imperial Tobacco*, the Court suggested that where written constitutional provisions protect a value in a certain context and to a certain degree it would hesitate to infer that the rule of law protects that value in other contexts to a greater degree. Thus, inasmuch as s. 11(g) of the *Charter* bars criminal legislation with retroactive application, the rule of law cannot be understood as barring all retroactive legislation.[72] In *Christie*, the Court applied that reasoning. Section 10(b) of the *Charter* protects the right to counsel upon arrest or detention. Section 7 protects the right to counsel in s. 10(b) scenarios as well as state-initiated court proceedings where life, liberty and security of the person are implicated and counsel is necessary for a fair trial. Given the content of these sections, the Court reasoned, the rule of law cannot protect a *general* right to counsel without defeating the *Charter*'s plain meaning.[73]

Now, s. 7 of the *Charter* has been interpreted as both including and *extending* the legal rights enumerated in ss. 8–14.[74] The mere fact that s. 10(b) expressly limits the right to counsel to situations of arrest or detention has not prevented the Supreme Court from finding that s. 7 implicitly guarantees a right to counsel in other contexts, for example, where lack of counsel would put the accused at an unfair risk of suffering a deprivation of security of the person.[75] Yet that understanding of s. 7 appears to make s. 10(b) "redundant" — to defeat the plain meaning of the *Charter*'s text — just as surely as a broad right to counsel read into the rule of law. Put starkly, by interpreting s. 7 in such a way that it effectively swallows s. 10(b), the Court implicitly accepted the possibility that some "larger" constitutional principle — like the rule of law — could swallow s. 7. In *Christie*, it shrank from the consequences of applying that principle to a situation involving socio-economic rights.

The Court's use of *Charter* provisions when interpreting the rule of law illustrates how the *Charter* does not function just as a sword to be used by claimants against the state, but as a shield capable of insulating the state from some constitutional claims. Insofar as the express terms of the *Charter* are used to delimit the scope of rule-of-law challenges, it emerges as a tool by which the Supreme Court can declare certain questions, at least inasmuch as they are framed as *legal* questions, foreclosed by the political decision to protect certain rights in certain terms, to the exclusion of protecting other rights through other terms.

The formalistic understanding of the rule of law articulated in *Christie* is disconcerting. To say that the rule of law does not require legislation to have any particular content is to reinforce the idea that our entrenched civil rights are simply contingent. On the formalist view, the rule of law is fundamentally apolitical and, therefore, has nothing to say about the sort of laws or constitutions a given country should have. A depoliticized understanding of the rule of law may protect judges, as it did in the early days of the *Charter* when the Court was careful to emphasize that it was politicians, and not judges, that made legislation subject to constitutional scrutiny. But it does little to protect anyone else. Those left exposed, those who experience first-hand the gross deficiencies in access to justice that have become endemic in this country, will also experience first-hand just how little work the rule of law does.

5.   CONCLUSION

These are not easy times for would-be *Charter* litigants. Recent failures by organizations seeking to mount systemic challenges to laws and policies that detrimentally affect the most downtrodden in our society reflect a failure of judicial imagination. This failure is an odd contrast with the positively lax approach to standing taken in' *Chaoulli,* a case that articulates classic liberal principles by which the state is rendered less able to deal effectively with pressing social needs. It is hard, at times, to avoid cynicism.

The question of how to fund such challenges is a vexed one. Interim costs remains largely untested in the area of public litigation. However, any approach should be principled and consistent. The differing results in *Okanagan* and *Little Sisters* appear arbitrary.

The state is at the heart of the issues of both funding and standing. The state's limits in acting as guardian of the public interest is apparent when one recognizes that the traditional guardian of that interest — the Attorney General — is institutionally reluc-

tant to challenge laws. Requiring the state to fund some litigation against itself, at times, may be necessary in order to uphold the fundamental values on which our legal system depends. If the government is unwilling to set aside funds for this purpose, and the courts continue to be wary of interim costs, private wealth and fundraising will quickly become the only game in town (supplemented somewhat by *pro bono* litigation). The losers will include not only the most downtrodden who cannot command attention at glittering charity events, but they will also include everyone whose need for the government to do no harm is buttressed by no more than state benevolence and the (occasional, weak) threat of political accountability.

(e) Legal Victory Still Leaves Rosa Becker Out in Cold[†]

William Marsden

Money was the operative word, but revenge was what Rosa Becker really wanted.

Revenge for being tossed out on her fanny by her common-law husband Lothar Pettkus, who showed his appreciation for their 18 years by throwing $3,000 on the floor and suggesting she "get lost."

Rosa thought: That's no way to say goodbye. Not after 18 years (during which she literally cleaned and tied his shoes and ran their business).

So, in 1974, she sued for half of all Pettkus's property, and her revenge turned into one of the most celebrated palimony cases in Canadian history.

In 1980, all nine judges of the Supreme Court of Canada awarded her half of a bee farm the couple built up and half-interest in three properties — setting a legal precedent that the late Chief Bora Laskin believed would settle the matrimonial-property issue.

Her victory was front-page news. Editorials applauded. Her lawyer, Gerald Langlois, predicted a $150,000 settlement for the beekeeping business and other properties. Then the excitement died — and now only law books remember Rosa Becker.

She still has not got her revenge.

Eleven years after she launched her suit and five years after the Supreme Court ruled, she has not received one cent from Lothar Pettkus.

Alone in a 9-room farmhouse in Franklin Centre near Ormstown, where she is paid $3,000 a year plus room and board to clean and cook for a dairy farmer and his farmhand, Becker, 58, reflects on Canadian justice:

"It's weird. I don't understand it."

Lothar Pettkus is 52, 5-foot-11, 200 lbs., strong. He likes hunting moose, is an excellent shot, keeps German shepherds, has thin blond hair, blue eyes.

By his calculation, Rosa Becker has lied 460 times to the Supreme Court of Canada in 1980 and 68 times to the Supreme Court of Ontario during a 1982 trial to divide up the property. He's trying to persuade the Ontario ombudsman to investigate his allegations.

"She was lying so badly that she had the (Supreme Court of Canada) judges convinced that this is the truth and it's definitely not the truth," Pettkus says.

(Judge K.A. Flannigan of the Ontario Supreme Court told Lothar Pettkus at a hearing in 1982:

---

† From *Montreal Gazette* (February 16, 1985) at B5. Material republished with the express permission of Montreal Gazette, a division of Postmedia Network Inc.

"It's the truth because the court found it to be true." But that hasn't stopped Lothar Pettkus.)

Convinced that the courts have been tricked by Rosa and her lawyer and their "lies," he decided that he cannot become a party to the Supreme Court ruling.

"A person who is perjuring herself with her lawyer — I should be party to a criminal act?" he asks rhetorically.

"I am just an innocent citizen sitting back and watching what the law is doing to people like me."

He might prove that, while you can't fight city hall, you sure can fight the Supreme Court of Canada.

Every move Rosa Becker makes, he thwarts, Becker's lawyer Langlois said.

He has exhausted seven lawyers and wielded every available weapon in the justice system to counter the Supreme Court ruling, he said.

Since the Supreme Court judgment, there have been 21 motions, judgments, affidavits, appeals and court orders issued concerning this case and the division of property — and still no money for Rosa Becker.

Court appearances are catfights, with Pettkus at times attempting to retry the case.

At a 1982 hearing into the division of property, Pettkus, between lawyers, represented himself and was questioning Becker about rent received from a West Hawkesbury, Ont., property they owned:

Rosa Becker: In the beginning it was $80 and then it gone up to $100.

Lothar Pettkus: Your honour, that's not true. At the beginning it was $40 and she says April the 14th, this year, that she paid $80. What was the truth now? Tell your honour the truth.

Becker: It was never $40. It was always $80 and then $100 but never $40.

Pettkus: You don't know if it's $80, you don't know if it was $40 and you don't know if it's $100, because you're so confused you can't answer the question proper.

Becker: Can you blame me for being confused after eight years with you in court?

Q: You took me to court.

A: No. I had no choice.

Q: Establish what was paid for in 1980. When you left...

A: I don't care anymore. You want it, shove it, shove it. I'm sick and tired. (Witness leaves courtroom.)

Rosa Becker, small, missing some front teeth, remembers when she first met Lothar Pettkus 30 years ago in the spring of 1955.

It was at a German Club dancehall near the Windsor Hotel. She was 28. He was 22. She earned $28 a week in a lace factory. He earned $75 a week as a garage mechanic.

She thought his tall brushcut made his face "look a mile long." They moved in together. He saved his money. They spent hers.

"Things happen in life that you can't explain and that's one of those things," she said without malice.

He said he "fell into her trap" and stayed for almost 20 years.

In 1960, they bought a 125 acre farm for $5,000, which he paid for out of his savings.

In 1971 and 1973, they purchased properties in East and West Hawkesbury in Ontario, where they moved their beekeeping business.

By that time, they were making as much as $30,000 profit a year. She played a major part in every aspect of the business. Everything was in his name.

But Judge Omer H. Chartrand of the Ontario District Court ruled that Rosa Becker's contribution was in the form of "risk capital invested in the hope of seducing a younger defendant into marriage."

He awarded her 40 empty beehives (which without bees are worthless) and $1,200.

The Court of Appeals ruled in 1978 that Chartrand had undervalued Becker's contributions. It gave her half the assets, valued as of 1974 when the two broke up. The Supreme Court agreed and implied that Chartrand's reference to risk capital "lacked gallantry."

The task then was to evaluate the assets as of 1974, apply interest and give Becker her share.

That process, which normally might take a year, is still not over.

Court judgments so far would put Becker's total claim on Pettkus at about $95,000.

In November 1983, Pettkus offered Becker a deal. He would pay her $46,408.90 if she would allow the Hawkesbury properties to be transferred to Pettkus's wife Monique.

Becker refused because she realized this would leave Pettkus without assets and make it impossible for her to receive the balance owing.

Eric Williams, Pettkus's latest lawyer, points to this offer as an example of Pettkus's willingness to settle. "I'll bet you 99 to one she doesn't get better than that offer," he said, adding that Pettkus has always been willing to settle the matter fairly.

Langlois said he attempted to freeze Lothar Pettkus's bank accounts but found only $12. Pettkus said his wife owns everything now.

Indeed, Monique Pettkus is claiming half her husband's interest in the beekeeping business and the East Hawkesbury property where she and Pettkus live with about 550 beehives. This claim will be fought out in court Feb. 21.

When Langlois tried last fall to seize the beehives, Pettkus's wife went to court and appealed the seizure, claiming that the hives are hers. That trial will be heard in March.

When the bees were seized by the court in November, Pettkus refused to feed them. By the time a court order could be obtained demanding that he feed and maintain the hives (valued at $50 each), most of the bees were dead, Monique told *The Gazette*. Without the bees, the business is worthless.

The only cash available is the $69,000 received from the sale last fall of the two Hawkesbury properties. The money is being held by the court.

By this June, Becker's half with interest will total $32,785.10. But all of that will go to pay her legal fees, which Langlois estimates total about $35,000. She also has to pay half the sheriff, appraisal and real-estate broker fees of about $10,000.

There's a good chance she will get all the $69,000, said Langlois. But it will take a fight, perhaps another year.

"That's the tragedy of this whole thing," Langlois said. "He (Pettkus) is ready to pay whatever amount to whatever lawyers it takes and it's clear that he doesn't intend to pay anything to Rosa Becker.

"She has been given the benefit of these judgments but the law has afforded protection to Pettkus on the realization of the funds."

Williams argues that Becker is trying to get blood out of a stone. "No matter how you cut it, the man is not rich."

Rosa Becker has visions. Ghosts tell her things.

They tell her her lawyer is conspiring with Lothar Pettkus.

"They (the visions) are always true and I know that makes Gerry Langlois uneasy about me," she said.

In 1983, she asked the Law Society of Upper Canada to investigate Langlois. They did and found "absolutely no evidence of professional misconduct."

She has also asked Chief Justice Brian Dickson of the Supreme Court of Canada to intervene on her behalf. He has refused.

"I can understand Rosa's frustration," Langlois said. He knows about her visions.

In December, he sent Rosa Becker a letter suggesting that he withdraw from the file since she has lost confidence in him.

Meanwhile, he is preparing her next court appearance and his bill.

And she's thinking she might take her case to the World Court. Still seeking revenge.

Last month, the Supreme Court of Canada decided that the entire question of division of matrimonial property needed another look. It decided to hear an appeal from Mary Sorochan, 69, of Two Hills, Alberta.

"After 40 years of common-law marriage, she received nothing from her estranged husband, who argued that he owned their 190-hectare farm before she came on the scene.

She wants recognition for her help in maintaining the farm.

IX

The Personnel of Law

Overview of Part IX

Part IX includes articles that discuss several important actors in our legal system: lawyers and paralegals, judges and juries, and law enforcement personnel. It goes beyond simply outlining the roles played by the different actors in the legal system to explore the ways in which these actors are educated and trained and how they are regulated and disciplined. Many of the articles and reports in **Part IX** also critically assess how these actors perform their roles in the legal system.

The articles in **Chapter 22** critically assess a number of issues relevant to the training, work, and regulation of lawyers. These issues include the education of lawyers, the establishment and teaching of ethical principles and standards of practice, the ways in which the business of practising law has changed over time, and the role of law societies in regulating the legal profession. The important issue of the lack of adequate representation of women and racial minorities within the legal profession is also discussed in the chapter.

Chapter 23 addresses the role of the jury in contemporary legal systems. Brooks and Doob outline a number of roles for the jury within modern trials and discuss the role of jury nullification. The excerpt from the *Morgentaler* decision further discusses the role of the jury as "a safety valve" within the Canadian justice system and the limits of jury nullification in the Canadian context. The excerpt from *R. v. Williams* outlines the Supreme Court of Canada's guidelines for addressing concerns of bias within jury pools in Canada. Readers should note the link to Butler's article, in **Chapter 6**, where he makes the controversial case for what he calls "racially based jury nullification". Finally, the article by Morton discusses the importance of ensuring that juries are both impartial and representative of the broader community. In particular, Morton explores the ways courts may ensure that juries include members of minority groups, particularly racial minorities.

Chapter 24 addresses the role of judges in the Canadian legal system. The chapter starts with Justice Kent's discussion of the role of the National Judicial Institute in training judges. Next, the concept of judicial independence, and the restraints it imposes on what judges can do and what they should say in public, is discussed by former Chief Justice Laskin. Chief Justice McLachlin's speech on the relationship between the courts and the media offers perhaps a more contemporary vision of how judges engage with the public. She discusses the importance of the relationship between judges and the media and the role of the media in building public confidence in the judiciary and thereby strengthening the rule of law. The article by Justice Wilson and the excerpt from the *R. v. S. (R.D.)* case both explore the ways in which personal identity and experience may influence judging. The chapter closes with an excerpt from a report of the Canadian Judicial Council that provides an example of the process for disciplining judges, and in extreme cases, dismissing judges for unacceptable conduct.

Finally, **Chapter 25** provides a brief survey of issues relevant to policing in Canada. Rigakos and Leung canvass the different forms of policing and police organizations in Canada. The RCMP Complaints Commission report identifies the need to ensure arm's-length investigation of allegations of police misconduct, and the excerpt from the *Jane Doe* case identifies the very real consequences that arise when police fail to fulfill their roles with the necessary care.

As you read **Part IX**, ask yourself: how do we ensure that the actors in the legal system are performing their roles adequately? Do certain actors have too much power within the system? How much do the personal backgrounds and experiences of legal actors matter in the performance of their duties? How do we ensure that all groups in society are appropriately represented among the various actors in the legal system?

22   Lawyers, Advocates, and Legal Practice

(a)   Legal Education as Training for Hierarchy†

Duncan Kennedy

Law schools are intensely political places despite the fact that they seem intellectually unpretentious, barren of theoretical ambition or practical vision of what social life might be. The trade-school mentality, the endless attention to trees at the expense of forests, the alternating grimness and chumminess of focus on the limited task at hand, all these are only a part of what is going on. The other part is ideological training for willing service in the hierarchies of the corporate welfare state.

To say that law school is ideological is to say that what teachers teach along with basic skills is wrong, is nonsense about what law is and how it works; that the message about the nature of legal competence, and its distribution among students, is wrong, is nonsense; that the ideas about the possibilities of life as a lawyer that students pick up from legal education are wrong, are nonsense. But all this is nonsense with a tilt; it is biased and motivated rather than random error. What it says is that it is natural, efficient, and fair for law firms, the bar as a whole, and the society the bar services to be organized in their actual patterns of hierarchy and domination.

Because students believe what they are told, explicitly and implicitly, about the world they are entering, they behave in ways that fulfill the prophecies the system makes about them and about that world. This is the linkback that completes the system: students do more than accept the way things are, and ideology does more than damp opposition.

Students act affirmatively within the channels cut for them, cutting them deeper, giving the whole a patina of consent, and weaving complicity into everyone's life story.

. . . .

THE FORMAL CURRICULUM: LEGAL RULES AND LEGAL REASONING

The intellectual core of the ideology is the distinction between law and policy. Teachers convince students that legal reasoning exists, and is different from policy analysis, by bullying them into accepting as valid in particular cases arguments about legal correctness that are circular, question-begging, incoherent, or so vague as to be meaningless. Sometimes these are just arguments from authority, with the validity of the authoritative premise put outside discussion by professorial fiat. Sometimes they are policy arguments (e.g., security of transaction, business certainty) that are treated in a particular situation as though they were rules that everyone accepts but that will be ignored in the next case when they would suggest that the decision was wrong. Sometimes they are exercises in doctrinal logic that wouldn't stand up for a minute in a discussion between equals (e.g., the small print in a form contract represents the "will of the parties").

Within a given subfield, the teacher is likely to treat cases in three different ways. There are the cases that present and justify the basic rules and

† From *The Politics of Law: A Progressive Critique* 3rd edition by David Kairys at 54, 60–62, 64–66, 73–75. Copyright © 1998 by David Kairys. Reproduced by permission of Basic Books, a member of the Perseus Books Group.

basic ideas of the field. These are treated as cursory exercises in legal logic. Then there are cases that are anomalous — "outdated" or "wrongly decided" because they don't follow the supposed inner logic of the area. There won't be many of these, but they are important because their treatment persuades students that the technique of legal reasoning is at least minimally independent of the results reached by particular judges and is therefore capable of criticizing as well as legitimating. Finally, there will be an equally small number of peripheral or "cutting-edge" cases the teacher sees as raising policy issues about growth or change in the law. Whereas in discussing the first two kinds of cases the teacher behaves in an authoritarian way supposedly based on his objective knowledge of the technique of legal reasoning, here everything is different. Because we are dealing with "value judgments" that have "political" overtones, the discussion will be much more freewheeling. Rather than every student comment being right or wrong, all student comments get pluralist acceptance, and the teacher will reveal himself to be mildly liberal or conservative rather than merely a legal technician.

The curriculum as a whole has a rather similar structure. It is not really a random assortment of tubs on their own bottoms, a forest of tubs. First, there are contracts, torts, property, criminal law, and civil procedure. The rules in these courses are the ground rules of late-nineteenth-century laissez-faire capitalism. Teachers teach them as though they had an inner logic, as an exercise in legal reasoning, with policy (e.g., commercial certainty in the contracts course) playing a relatively minor role. Then there are second- and third-year courses that expound the moderate reformist program of the New Deal and the administrative structure of the modern regulatory state (with passing reference to the racial egalitarianism of the Warren Court). These courses are more policy oriented than first-year courses, and also much more ad hoc.

Liberal teachers teach students that limited interference with the market makes sense and is as authoritatively grounded in statutes as the ground rules of laissez-faire are grounded in natural law. But each problem is discrete, enormously complicated, and understood in a way that guarantees the practical impotence of the reform program. Conservative teachers teach that much of the reform program is irrational or counter-productive or both, and would have been rolled back long ago were it not for "politics." Finally, there are peripheral subjects, like legal philosophy or legal history, legal process, clinical legal education. These are presented as not truly relevant to the "hard"[,] objective, serious, rigorous analytic core of law; they are a kind of playground or finishing school for learning the social art of self-presentation as a lawyer.

It would be an extraordinary first-year student who could, on his own, develop a theoretically critical attitude toward this system. Entering students just don't know enough to figure out where the teacher is fudging, misrepresenting, or otherwise distorting legal thinking and legal reality. To make matters worse, the most common kind of liberal thinking the student is likely to bring with her is likely to hinder rather than assist in the struggle to maintain some intellectual autonomy from the experience. Most liberal students believe that the liberal program can be reduced to guaranteeing people their rights and to bringing about the triumph of human rights over mere property rights. In this picture, the trouble with the legal system is that it fails to put the state behind the rights of the oppressed, or that the system fails to enforce the rights formally recognized. If one thinks about law this way, one is inescapably dependent on the very techniques of legal reasoning that are being marshalled in defense of the status quo.

This wouldn't be so bad if the problem with legal education were that the teachers *misused* rights reasoning to restrict the range of the rights of the oppressed. But the problem is much deeper than that. Rights discourse is internally inconsistent, vacuous, or circular. Legal thought can generate equally plausible rights justifications for almost any result. Moreover, the discourse of rights imposes constraints on those who use it that make it difficult for it to function effectively as a tool of radical transformation. Rights are by their nature "formal," meaning that they secure to individuals legal protection for as well as from arbitrariness — to speak of rights is precisely *not* to speak of justice between social classes, races, or sexes. Rights discourse, moreover, presupposes or takes for granted that the world is and should be divided between a state sector that enforces rights and a private world of "civil society" in which individuals pursue their diverse goals. This framework is, in itself, a part of the problem rather than of the solution. It makes it difficult even to conceptualize radical proposals such as, for example, decentralized democratic worker control of factories.

Because it is incoherent and manipulable, traditionally individualist, and willfully blind to the realities of *substantive* inequality, rights discourse is a trap. As long as one stays within it, one can produce good pieces of argument about the occasional case on the periphery where everyone recognizes value judgments have to be made. But one is without guidance in deciding what to do about fundamental questions and fated to the gradual loss of confidence in the convincingness of what one has to say in favor of the very results one believes in most passionately.

Left liberal rights analysis submerges the student in legal rhetoric but, because of its inherent vacuousness, can provide no more than an emotional stance against the legal order. It fails liberal students because it offers no base for the mastery of ambivalence. What is needed is to think about law in a way that will allow one to enter into it, to criticize it without utterly rejecting it, and to manipulate it without self-abandonment to *their* system of thinking and doing.

. . . .

INCAPACITATION FOR ALTERNATIVE PRACTICE

Law schools channel their students into jobs in the hierarchy of the bar according to their own standing in the hierarchy of schools. Students confronted with the choice of what to do after they graduate experience themselves as largely helpless: they have no "real" alternative to taking a job in one of the firms that customarily hire from their school. Partly, faculties generate this sense of student helplessness by propagating myths about the character of the different kinds of practice. They extol the forms that are accessible to their students; they subtly denigrate or express envy about the jobs that will be beyond their students' reach; they dismiss as ethically and socially suspect the jobs their students won't have to take.

As for any form of work outside the established system — for example, legal services for the poor and neighborhood law practice — they convey to students that, although morally exalted, the work is hopelessly dull and unchallenging, and that the possibilities of reaching a standard of living appropriate to a lawyer are slim or nonexistent. These messages are just nonsense — the rationalizations of law teachers who long upward, fear status degradation, and above all hate the idea of risk. Legal services practice, for example, is far more intellectually stimulating and demanding, even with a high caseload, than most of what corporate lawyers do. It is also more fun.

Beyond this dimension of professional mythology, law schools act in more concrete ways to guarantee that their students will fit themselves into their appropriate niches in the existing system of practice. First, the actual content of what is taught in a given school will incapacitate students from any other form

of practice than that allotted graduates of that institution. This looks superficially like a rational adaptation to the needs of the market, but it is in fact almost entirely unnecessary. Law schools teach so little, and that so incompetently, that they cannot, as now constituted, prepare students for more than one career at the bar. But the reason for this is that they embed skills training in mystificatory nonsense and devote most of their teaching time to transmitting masses of ill-digested rules. A more rational system would emphasize the way to learn law rather than rules, and skills rather than answers. Student capacities would be more equal as a result, but students would also be radically more flexible in what they could do in practice.

A second incapacitating device is the teaching of doctrine in isolation from practice skills. Students who have no practice skills tend to exaggerate how difficult it is to acquire them. There is a distinct lawyers' mystique of the irrelevance of the "theoretical" material learned in school, and of the crucial importance of abilities that cannot be known or developed until one is out in the "real world" and "in the trenches." Students have little alternative to getting training in this dimension of things after law school. It therefore seems hopelessly impractical to think about setting up your own law firm, and only a little less impractical to go to a small or political or unconventional firm rather than to one of those that offer the standard package of postgraduate education. Law schools are wholly responsible for this situation. They could quite easily revamp their curricula so that any student who wanted it would have a meaningful choice between independence and servility.

A third form of incapacitation is more subtle. Law school, as an extension of the educational system as a whole, teaches students that they are weak, lazy, incompetent, and insecure. And it also teaches them that if they are willing to accept extreme dependency and vulnerability for a probationary term, large institutions will (probably) take care of them almost no matter what. The terms of the bargain are relatively clear. The institution will set limited, defined tasks and specify minimum requirements in their performance. The student/associate has no other responsibilities than performance of those tasks. The institution takes care of all the contingencies of life, both within the law (supervision and backup from other firm members; firm resources and prestige to bail you out if you make a mistake) and in private life (firms offer money but also long-term job security and delicious benefits packages aimed to reduce risks of disaster).

In exchange, you renounce any claim to control your work setting or the actual content of what you do, and agree to show the appropriate form of deference to those above and condescension to those below.

By comparison, the alternatives are risky. Law school does not train you to run a small law business, to realistically assess the outcome of a complex process involving many different actors, or to enjoy the feeling of independence and moral integrity that comes of creating your own job to serve your own goals. It tries to persuade you that you are barely competent to perform the much more limited roles it allows you, and strongly suggests that it is more prudent to kiss the lash than to strike out on your own.

. . . .

For committed liberal students, there is another possibility, which might be called the denunciatory mode. One can take law school work seriously as time serving and do it coldly in that spirit, hate one's fellow students for their surrenders, and focus one's hopes on "not being a lawyer" or on a fantasy of an unproblematically leftist legal job on graduation. This response is hard from the very beginning. If you reject what teachers and the student culture tell you about what the first-year curriculum means and how to enter into learning it, you are adrift as to how to go about becoming minimally competent. You have to develop a theory on your own of what is valid skills training and what is merely indoctrination, and your ambivalent desire to be successful in spite of all is likely to sabotage your independence. As graduation approaches, it becomes clearer that there are precious few unambiguously virtuous law jobs even to apply for, and your situation begins to look more like everyone else's, though perhaps more extreme. Most (by no means all) students who begin with denunciation end by settling for some version of the bargain of public against private life.

I am a good deal more confident about the patterns that I have just described than about the attitudes toward hierarchy that go along with them. My own position in the system of class, sex, and race (as an upper-middle-class white male) and my rank in the professional hierarchy (as a Harvard professor) give me an interest in the perception that hierarchy is both omnipresent and enormously important, even while I am busy condemning it. And there is a problem of imagination that goes beyond that of interest. It is hard for me to know whether I even understand the attitudes toward hierarchy of women and blacks, for example, or of children of working-class parents, or of solo practitioners eking out a living from residential real-estate closings. Members of those groups sometimes suggest that the particularity of their experience of oppression simply cannot be grasped by outsiders, but sometimes that the failure to grasp it is a personal responsibility rather than inevitable. Often it seems to me that all people have at least analogous experiences of the oppressive reality of hierarchy, even those who seem most favored by the system—that the collar feels the same when you get to the end of the rope, whether the rope is ten feet long or fifty. On the other hand, it seems clear that hierarchy creates distances that are never bridged.

It is not uncommon for a person to answer a description of the hierarchy of law firms with a flat denial that the bar is really ranked. Lawyers of lower-middle-class background tend to have far more direct political power in the state governments than "elite" lawyers, even under Republican administrations. Furthermore, every lawyer knows of instances of real friendship, seemingly outside and beyond the distinctions that are supposed to be so important, and can cite examples of lower-middle-class lawyers in upper-middle-class law firms, and vice versa. There are many lawyers who seem to defy hierarchical classification, and law firms and law schools that do likewise, so that one can argue that the hierarchy claim that everyone and everything is ranked breaks down the minute you try to give concrete examples. I have been told often enough that I *may* be right about the pervasiveness of ranking, but that the speaker has never noticed it himself, himself treats all lawyers in the same way, regardless of their class or professional standing, and has never, except in an occasional very bizarre case, found lawyers violating the egalitarian norm.

When the person making these claims is a rich corporate lawyer who was my prep school classmate, I tend to interpret them as a willful denial of the way he is treated and treats others. When the person speaking is someone I perceive as less favored by the system (say, a woman of lower-middle-class origin who went to Brooklyn Law School and now works for a small, struggling downtown law firm), it is harder to know how to react. Maybe I'm just wrong about what it's like out there. Maybe my preoccupation with the horrors of hierarchy is just a way to wring the last ironic drop of pleasure from my own hierarchical superiority. But I don't interpret it that way. The denial of hierarchy is false consciousness. The problem is not whether hierarchy is there, but how to understand it, and what its implications are for political action.

(b) Canadian Legal Ethics: Ready for the Twenty-First Century at Last†

Adam M. Dodek

I. WHAT IS CANADIAN LEGAL ETHICS AND WHY DOES IT MATTER?

.   .   .   .

Given the evolving nature of legal ethics, "Canadian legal ethics" could mean several different things. A strong positivist strain permeates legal ethics in Canada, which views the field as simply encompassing the ethical rules of lawyering, contained for the most part in the CBA's *Code of Professional Conduct*[12] (and its provincial counterparts) as well as in traditional areas of law, such as tort, contract, and agency, among others. While the issues in the codes of conduct provide excellent fodder for analysis and debate, legal ethics consists of much more than "the law governing lawyers."[13] To begin with, the prominence or the relevance of such codes is itself a hotly contested issue in legal ethics, Canadian and otherwise.[14] In addition, many of the codes are silent on some of the most interesting and most debated issues in Canadian legal ethics: lawyers' duties respecting physical evidence of a crime, sex with clients, and corporate fraud, among others. Legal ethics is concerned not only with the positivist inquiry of what is, but very much with the normative inquiry of what ought to be.[15]

Legal ethics consists of "macro-ethics" as well as "micro-ethics." Macro-ethical inquiries address systemic issues within the legal system and the legal profession, such as access to justice, public interest, diversity within the profession, and independence of the bar. Micro-ethics focuses on the ethical issues that confront individuals within the legal system. Micro-ethics — issues such as conflicts of interest, confidentiality, and client perjury — occupy most of the ethical space in discussions about legal ethics, but the macro-ethical issues go to the heart of the legitimacy of the legal profession and the legal system. In addition, legal ethics should be concerned about all of the actors in the legal system: lawyers, judges, clients, self-represented litigants, witnesses, jurors, court administrators, and the media, as well as those outside the formal boundaries of the profession who also provide legal services, such as notaries, immigration consultants, Aboriginal caseworkers, and — dare I suggest — paralegals.[16]

Canadian legal ethics must also attempt to situate ethical issues within a distinctly *Canadian* context.[17] A Canadian scholarship of legal ethics must further seek to identify and articulate uniquely Canadian aspects of our legal system and the practice of lawyering in our country. These distinctions may be structural (such as the impact of federalism, articling, discipline by law societies, and a unitary legal profession, among others) as well as normative or cultural (such as the values of multiculturalism and diversity,[18] or the ethic of "zealous representation.")[19]

One theme of this article is that there are multiple accounts of legal ethics in Canada and that significant disparities exist between them. A public account of Canadian legal ethics emphasizes the issues that the public sees, mostly through reporting in the popular press. The legal profession's account of legal ethics is reflected by the activities of law societies and legal associations, most notably through codes of conduct and discipline, but also through other activities such as task forces, public advocacy, and litigation. Sociological accounts examine what is actually happening within the profession and historical accounts analyze what has happened in the past. We can also conceive of the body of collected academic work on Canadian legal ethics as the scholarly account of the subject. As will be apparent throughout this article, significant gaps exist between the different accounts. In this article, I focus on the accounts of the public and the legal profession and compare their contents to the developing scholarly account of Canadian legal ethics.

.   .   .   .

---

† (2008) 46 Osgoode L.J. 1 at 5–8, 9–20. [Notes and/or references omitted.] Online: <http://papers.ssrn.com/sol3/papers.cfm?abstract_id=1150889>. Reproduced with permission.

II. A BRIEF HISTORY OF CANADIAN LEGAL ETHICS IN THE FIRST DECADE OF THE TWENTY-FIRST CENTURY

Until recently, the Canadian legal academy was not particularly interested in legal ethics. Hutchinson attributes this to the lack of a defining Canadian cultural moment like Watergate "in which lawyers were placed under national scrutiny and obliged to reconsider the legitimacy of their professional practices and norms of conduct."[20] While Hutchinson is correct that there has been no "lawyergate" in Canada to capture the public imagination, the last few years have seen numerous ethical scandals that, cumulatively, seemed capable of exerting some pressure on the legal profession. In this Part, I outline a brief history of Canadian legal ethics in the first decade of this century. For the most part, this history draws heavily on the public account of Canadian legal ethics, but also includes elements from the legal profession's account. The purpose of this section is to discuss examples of lawyers' poor ethical behaviour to which the public has been recently exposed and the legal profession's responses, or lack thereof in some cases, to these and other issues.

For Canadian legal ethics it has been an eventful and challenging decade. The twenty-first century began with the trial of Ken Murray, the lawyer originally retained to defend Canada's notorious murderer, Paul Bernardo. Murray was acquitted, barely, of obstruction of justice in connection with the infamous Bernardo/Homolka videotapes.[21] The Law Society of Upper Canada (LSUC) began a disciplinary investigation into Murray's conduct, but abandoned it in favour of enacting a rule of professional conduct on the issue of lawyers' duties respecting physical evidence of a crime. After releasing a draft rule, the LSUC shelved this project as well. The Murray case thus ended in three negatives: no conviction against Murray, no disciplinary action by the LSUC, and no action by the LSUC to address the issue.[22]

The next big ethical scandal involved law students, rather than lawyers. In 2001, thirty students at the University of Toronto Law School ("U of T" or "Toronto") were caught up in allegations of misrepresenting their grades to prospective summer employers, and twenty-four received sanctions ranging from reprimands to one-year suspensions. The U of T "fake grades scandal" also became an international *cause célèbre* in academic freedom circles because of allegations against a U of T law professor.[23] As might be expected, one of the students sought judicial review and succeeded in having the Dean's deci-

sion against her quashed on jurisdictional grounds.[24] Three years later, another cheating scandal erupted in Toronto, this time at the LSUC's Bar Admission Course. However, while the U of T "fake grades scandal" dragged on for over a year, the Bar Admission Course cheating scandal ended abruptly after a few weeks. When the LSUC made an allegedly secret decision to abandon the investigation,[25] the scandal continued to fester.[26] In between the two Toronto student scandals, the President of the Law Society of British Columbia resigned in 2003, after a conviction for impaired driving, and was subsequently suspended from practice.[27] He would not be the last law society head during the decade forced to resign amidst ethical improprieties.

Lawyers' conduct in the courtroom and in the bedroom dominated ethical discussions at the beginning of this century. Midway through the decade, the CBA embarked on another revision to its Code of Conduct, which had not been overhauled since 1987. The revised CBA Code, based on amendments in 2004 and 2006, is notable mostly for what it did not address, rather than for any ethical boldness. The CBA ducked the Ken Murray problem, took a very modest approach to the issue of dealing with corporate fraud, and rejected a proposed amendment to restrict sexual relations between lawyers and clients,[28] an issue that would resurface sooner rather than later. In 2007, the former Treasurer of the LSUC received a two-month suspension for conflict of interest arising out of a sexual relationship with a client who is now suing him and his law firm.[29] Concerned also with lawyers' misbehaviour in the courtroom, the decade saw the rise of the civility and professionalism movement. Precipitated by the conduct of counsel in several cases,[30] Ontario's Advocate's Society formed a Civility Committee, which produced a Code of Civility[31] that the CBA included as an appendix in its revised Code. Similar concerns motivated the Nova Scotia Barristers' Society to establish a Task Force on Civility.[32] Meanwhile, in British Columbia, solicitor Martin Wirick perpetrated the largest legal fraud in Canadian history, an estimated $50 million, triggering the largest audit and investigation ever undertaken by the Law Society of British Columbia and sending shockwaves throughout the legal profession, as well as the real estate and business communities.[33]

As class action lawsuits began proliferating across the country, the role of lawyers came under scrutiny, especially with regard to fees. Whether it was the $56 million in fees for the settlement of the tainted blood scandal before a single victim was paid, or the $100 million that Regina's Tony Merchant hoped to obtain as part of the record estimated $1.9 billion settlement of residential schools abuse claims, public perception that lawyers put their own interests ahead of those of their clients ran high.[34] Along these lines, concerns about lawyers taking advantage of vulnerable clients led the CBA, the Law Society of Yukon, and the LSUC to each establish guidelines for lawyers acting in Aboriginal residential school abuse cases.[35]

In the courts, the Supreme Court of Canada continued where it left off in *Martin v. Gray* (1990),[36] issuing two decisions, *Neil* (2002)[37] and *Strother* (2007),[38] which helped keep conflict of interest at the top of the legal profession's ethical priority list.[39] On the regulatory front, the Court held that provincial law societies could not prohibit non-lawyers from appearing as counsel before the Immigration and Refugee Board,[40] but that law societies do have the power to regulate Crown prosecutors.[41] In a leading case, the Ontario Court of Appeal held that the Ontario Securities Commission (OSC) could regulate the conduct of lawyers appearing before it.[42] The Supreme Court held that law societies do not have a general duty of care to persons who are defrauded by their lawyers,[43] but also that law societies will not be immunized from liability by ignoring their statutory responsibilities to protect the public.[44] Along these lines, the Court vindicated the Law Society of New Brunswick for meting out the ultimate sanction of disbarment to a lawyer who misled his clients for five years.[45] The Court continued its strong interest in solicitor-client privilege that began in 1999,[46] deciding no fewer than eight cases since then,[47] and elevating that privilege to a constitutional right.[48] The bar across Canada, led by the Federation of Law Societies, exerted tremendous energy and resources to successfully challenge regulations that, among other things, would have required lawyers to report "suspicious transactions" involving $10,000 or more in cash.[49]

In the area of judicial ethics, the Court decided two cases regarding judicial discipline, one involving statements made by a judge in court,[50] and the other concerning attempts to remove a judge because of a later-discovered criminal conviction.[51] The Court dealt with two judicial disqualification cases, both of which arose under unique circumstances and both involving allegations of bias against members of the Court itself. First, in Wewaykum (2003), the losing litigant before the Court was unsuccessful in its attempt to vacate the decision based on the alleged reasonable apprehension of bias arising from Justice Binnie's involvement in the case while holding the position of Associate Deputy Minister of Justice.[52]

Second, in *Mugesera* (2005), lawyer Guy Bertrand made accusations that a Jewish conspiracy had tainted the impartiality of the Court, which the Court found was an "unqualified and abusive attack on the integrity of the Judges of this Court."[53] Bertrand was later formally reprimanded by the Barreau du Quebec.[54]

Over the decade, access to justice was increasingly recognized as an important issue by the courts, the profession, and the media. The Court recognized a doctrine of advance costs but then significantly narrowed it.[55] It unanimously and unceremoniously rejected the constitutional claim for state-funded legal counsel in civil cases,[56] and it forced a representative plaintiff to pay costs likely totaling over one million dollars in an unsuccessful class proceeding.[57] The Court's treatment of access to justice issues was at odds with an increasingly strong *cri de coeur* being heard both within the profession[58] and in the press.[59] The Chief Justice of Canada and other justices and leaders of the bar frequently lament barriers to access to justice for Canadians, but have offered little in the way of solutions. One bright note has been the rise of institutionalized pro bono initiatives, through Pro Bono Law Ontario, Pro Bono Law of British Columbia, and now Pro Bono Law Alberta. Over the decade, the plight of self-represented litigants has increasingly caught the attention of Canada's judges, lawyers, policy-makers, and to some extent, the press.[60]

The years 2006 and 2007 might well be considered the legal profession's *anni horribiles* from the perspective of Canadian legal ethics. With British Columbia still reeling from the Wirick fraud, the Treasurer of the LSUC in Ontario resigned in January 2006 and was ultimately disciplined and suspended for two months in connection with a sexual relationship with a client.[61] In August 2006, legal heavyweight Peter Shoniker pled guilty to money laundering and was sentenced to fifteen months of incarceration.[62] In the spring of 2007, lawyers from Torys LLP were frequently in the news in relation to advice that they gave Conrad Black and other members of Hollinger Inc. regarding non-compete agreements at the center of the Black trial in Chicago. In a deal struck between Torys and the prosecution, the Torys lawyers — not subject to the jurisdiction of the American courts — agreed to testify by recorded videotape in Toronto, with resulting negative press coverage of the lawyers and the law firm.[63] Not to be missed, of course, was the fact that two of the defendants in the Black trial were lawyers: Mark Kipnis and Peter Atkinson (a member of the Ontario bar and a former Torys partner). Rarely mentioned was the fact that Conrad Black is a law graduate (Laval), although not a member of the bar.

In July, lawyers were featured on the cover of *Maclean's* under the headline "Lawyers Are Rats" with titles above various lawyers reading, "I Pad My Bills," "I'm Dishonest," "I sleep with my clients," and "I take bribes" among other things.[64] The cover accompanied an interview with Philip Slayton, ethics columnist for Canadian Lawyer and former law professor, law dean, Bay Street lawyer, and author of *Lawyers Gone Bad: Money, Sex and Madness in Canada's Legal Profession*.[65] The sensationalism of *Maclean's* succeeded in provoking a rash of responses from the organized bar as well as from its individual members.[66] It was likely responsible for temporarily catapulting Slayton's anecdotal collection of lawyer malfeasance onto the bestseller list where it quietly retreated after having wrought havoc on the legal profession for two months.

The year ended with a collective sigh of relief from the legal profession with the Competition Bureau of Canada's report on self-regulated professions, including law.[67] The legal profession had been anxiously awaiting this report, looking over its shoulder at the changes precipitated by similar reports in the United Kingdom and the European Union.[68] On 11 December 2007, the Commissioner released her report amidst minimal fanfare and negligible public interest.[69] While the follow-up remains uncertain, law societies will be able to make small changes in response to the Competition Bureau's report without upsetting the apple cart.

Thus ended the Canadian legal profession's two-year *anni horribiles*, with a whimper not a bang. Somewhat surprisingly, these events appear not to have had much impact on the level of public trust towards lawyers in Canada, which actually went up in 2006 and again in 2007 after a decrease for several years in a row. In 2007, 54 per cent of Canadians said that they trust lawyers, the same level as in 2002. This is a much lower level of trust than that received by perennial favourites — firefighters (97 per cent) and nurses (94 per cent) — but far ahead of politicians (15 per cent) and used car salespersons (12 per cent).[70] While the decade was full of ethical lows and challenges for the Canadian legal profession, Hutchinson's point, first made in 1999, that there has not been a single defining cultural moment for lawyering in Canada, is still the case. Despite the absence of a "lawyergate" that succeeded in capturing the public imagination and spurring an agenda for reform, many of the events described above did have an impact within the profession and the legal academy. Importantly, these events helped stimulate some of the initiatives described in Parts III and IV below, and certainly provided both motivation and opportunities for the scholarship described in the following parts.[71]

(c) Who is Afraid of the Big Bad Social Constructionists? Or Shedding Light on the Unpardonable Whiteness of the Canadian Legal Profession†

Charles C. Smith

I. INTRODUCTION

In 2005, I was asked to participate in a session entitled, "The Implications of 'Bleached-Out' Professionalism for Racialized Lawyers and Communities," which was one of the former Chief Justice of Ontario's forums to discuss contemporary issues within the legal profession.[1] At the time, I remarked that the title of this forum is one of those metaphors that seems easy to grasp. Most of us are aware of efforts within the legal profession, including law schools, law firms, the courts, and so forth, to diversify their representation so that it is more inclusive of the racialized and cultural makeup of the broader society. The record of positive intention has been and continues to be articulated repeatedly in studies, reports, policies and programs that are writ-

† (2008) 45 Alta. L. Rev. 55 at 55–66, 72–73 (Special Issue: Law Society of Alberta 100th Anniversary Conference "Canadian Lawyers in the 21st Century"). [Notes and/or references omitted.] Reproduced with permission.

ten, developed, and implemented by law schools, law societies, legal associations, and law firms. Since the 1993 report of the Task Force on Gender Equality in the Legal Profession, chaired by Bertha Wilson J. (as she then was),[2] a considerable number of these reports and studies have been published.[3]

Over the past eight years I have had the benefit of working in three legal associations on these issues. I have also provided advice and services to several law firms and legal associations. Through all of this, I have gained considerable insight into the challenges related to this topic. This experience has enabled me to research this matter and to develop policies and programs for the Law Society of Upper Canada (LSUC), the Canadian Bar Association (CBA) and, very recently, the Indigenous Bar Association (IBA) where I support their efforts to form a national secretariat to identify, challenge, and eliminate hate and racism in Canada.[4]

It is for these reasons that I questioned the topic of this session. There are two notions which are at issue here. One is that "Bleached-Out Professionalism" suggests eradicating stains or foreign elements in order to return to or "create" a more homogenous, uniform construction. And this is exactly where the second contentious issue emerges. I shall phrase it in the form of a question: Assuming that "bleaching" renders its objects white, when was the legal profession not bleached?[5] Was there ever really a need to "bleach" it? Or would it not be more important to talk about "unbleaching" the profession, particularly now given the challenges faced by Aboriginal peoples and subordinate racialized groups who enter it?

Looking at the faulty metaphor conjures up the great difficulty the legal profession has in talking about race and racism in society generally, and within its ranks in particular. Rather than talk about race and racism directly, problematic metaphors are used. Given the rather undramatic increase in the numbers of Aboriginal lawyers and lawyers from subordinate racialized groups, one would think this issue would be named directly. However, it appears that there is a lack of commitment by the legal profession to produce concrete results aimed at ensuring that the profession reflects the makeup of the Canadian population. For example, a recent article entitled "Reducing the Democratic Deficit: Representation, Diversity and the Canadian Judiciary, or Towards a 'Triple P' Judiciary,"[6] points out the challenges in increasing the racial diversity of the bench. One of the key challenges the authors encountered in doing their research was that there was no information at the federal level about the racialized com-

position of the bench and that the same finding held true for most provinces and territories.[7] Further, neither law societies nor the CBA have canvassed their members to assess their representation based on race or Aboriginal status.

On a related point, Alan J.C. King, Wendy K. Warren, and Sharon R. Miklas note in their recent study of "accessibility" in five Ontario law schools that "[a]dmissions policies that target groups with unique characteristics are not necessarily intended to produce a student body that mirrors the Canadian population."[8] As well, the former Governor General of Canada recently commented on the difficulties in increasing the racial diversity of the legal profession,[9] and the Law Society of British Columbia (LSBC) produced a report on discriminatory barriers faced by Aboriginal law students and lawyers.[10]

In this regard, the legal profession, which may pride itself on being "different" because of its adherence to the rule of law and democratic principle, is really not unlike other professions or the Canadian society at large. Or as Troy Duster wrote in his submission to the Association of American Law Schools (AALS):

> Professions and the institutions which serve them tend to view themselves as having unique traditions, values, skills and missions — even callings. While to some degree this is true, from the perspective of students of higher education, there are strong patterns or parallel trends and forces for a wide range of academic disciplines and professional schools. These parallel experiences and subsequent institutional and organizational dilemmas are particularly salient when we look to the changes that are occurring and have occurred over the last twenty years in institutions of higher education around the shifting demographic composition of undergraduate and graduate student bodies. The experiences of other institutions — both educational and corporate — as they have confronted contested terrain around issues of gender, race, and ethnicity, can help clarify the strategies for addressing these areas of conflict or contest within schools of law.[11]

Evidence indicates the same dilemmas across the legal profession. Finally, one other underlying but critical issue is that the construction of a "bleached" or overwhelmingly white profession requires us to consider the agents behind the bleaching/whiteness. In other words, who is "bleaching" the legal profession? Or keeping it white? Why? How is this being done? And what must be done to change this?

The above discussion is the reason for the title and focus of this article. Given the number of studies, reports, policies, task forces, programs, and so forth, one might expect that the legal profession would be much further along in addressing issues of its racialized composition. One might expect more significant numbers of Aboriginal peoples and individuals from subordinate racialized groups to be studying and practising law, or results that were at least similar to other elite professions, such as medicine, engineering, and the professoriate. Unfortunately, this is not the case. The legal profession, for all its attention to issues of race, lags well behind these other professional fields and so, once again, we are gathered to discuss this fact.

My contention with this subject forms the basis of this article, and in discussing the legal profession, I also contend that it is essential to look at the pathways to it, which requires some discussion on the importance of education and, in particular, legal education.

II.   WHITENESS AND THE LEGAL PROFESSION IN CANADA

Discursive analysis on the education of non-dominant groups and its influence on professional attainment has been emerging over the course of a considerable period of time, particularly that concerning legal education and entry into the practice of law. These matters do not exist in isolation, but rather form part of a social context in which relations between dominant and non-dominant groups are situated, especially in terms of race. This issue has been explored by Aboriginal thinkers and critical race theorists.[12] Many of these authors contend that this relationship is symbiotic and based on an inequitable sharing of resources and power. In particular, Aboriginal peoples and peoples from subordinate racialized groups describe the power imbalance dominating their lives as a centrifugal force placing the pressures of assimilation squarely before them or blocking their access into society's elite professions. Further, as Cornel West notes, these prevailing forces, which are particularly influenced by the regime of law and legal education, have shaped and continue to shape social policy, institutional practices, and community interactions.[13]

In this context, discrimination in education and professional occupations is mirrored and reinforced by discrimination in society through statutes, social policy, institutional practices, or individual and community actions. Such statutes and practices are condoned as acceptable within the social mores of their times and, as such, impact on the abilities of non-

dominant groups to participate in and benefit from the study and practice of law. In examining the whiteness of the legal profession, it is essential to look at the pathways to the practice of law. This means looking at access to a legal education and to those institutions which enable individuals to consider and pursue a legal education and legal practice. In this context, the history of racial discrimination in Canadian educational systems is inescapable.

For example, based on statutes adopted in 1850, such as *The Common Schools Act*[14] in Ontario, separate schools for black children "continued until 1891 in Chatham, 1893 in Sandwich, 1907 in Harrow, 1917 in Amherstburg, and 1965 in North Colchester and Essex counties."[15] Based on statutes dating back to 1833, black children were barred from attending the only public school in Halifax County until 1940, and in 1959, school buses still only stopped in white sections of Hammonds Plains.[16] In 1960, there were seven formal black school districts and three additional exclusively black schools in Nova Scotia.[17] The repeal of the Ontario and Nova Scotia statutes authorizing racial segregation in education did not occur until the mid-1960s. Further, the *Indian Act*[18] had extremely restrictive provisions regarding the education of Aboriginal peoples.

In terms of legal education, W. Wesley Pue summarizes the racist values that contributed to the establishment of common law legal education in Canada. In detailing the history of its development, he writes:

> The period from roughly 1910 to 1920 was important in laying new cultural foundations for modern common law legal education. It produced a melding of persuasive new ideas developed and tested in the USA with longstanding British middle class traditions regarding practical knowledge, honour and authority. For a variety of reasons English Canada's dominant cultural ethos was receptive to influences of both sorts. The conjuncture of industrialisation and westward expansion dominated English Canadian imperial visions.... Challenged by a world of ideas which held no traditions sacrosanct, English élites ... were freed and forced to reconsider their own futures. This reappraisal included fundamental questions about which sorts of institutional arrangements were best suited to the peculiar position of this new, northern, British, and free people.[19]

In this context, Pue describes efforts by the Law Society of Manitoba to stop the development of proprietary schools which:

Judging by U.S.A. experience ... would also almost certainly have opened the door to legal careers for much larger numbers of young men (and women?) of working class or minority ethnic background. This prospect would not have been viewed with equanimity by Manitoba's Anglo élite, who were embedded in a culture which was fiercely pro-British and hierarchical, nativist, even xenophobic.[20]

Pue also notes "the most vigorous proponents of what might be called a 'cultural' agenda in legal education were prominent, energetic, busy, successful practising lawyers. All were either born into the Anglo élite or thoroughly integrated into it. All were active in matters of law society governance or in the activities of bar associations,"[21] and further, that "the cultural assumptions of individuals in that period must be assessed if we are to make any sense of the history of common law legal education in Canada. If we are to understand at all, we have to begin to understand the intellectual climate of the élite, British, Protestant world in which these men lived."[22]

Mirroring Pue's comments, Christopher Moore provides a sense of what the legal profession looked like in the nineteenth and early twentieth centuries. He notes that "[t]he vast majority of nineteenth century Ontario lawyers were English, Scots, or Irish in origin and Protestant in religion, and they tended to take in students of their own class and kind. ... Throughout the nineteenth century, successful families from outside the Anglo-Protestant mainstream were occasionally able to find articling positions for sons inclined to the law."[23]

It was not until 1855 that Robert Sutherland was called to the Bar in Ontario, becoming the first black Canadian lawyer.[24] This was followed by Delos Rogest Davis in 1885.[25] Davis's call to the Bar was not a simple passage but, rather, required a special act of the Ontario Legislature against which the LSUC protested.[26] While information on other black students called to the practice of law is difficult to ascertain, it appears certain that the effects of discrimination in education, combined with racism in society generally, limited the number of black students who entered law school and, further, those who did enter faced barriers in undertaking legal education, particularly in attracting articling positions.[27]

Chinese, Japanese, South Asian, and Aboriginal peoples were prohibited from becoming members of the LSBC until 1947, and until 1948 for people of Japanese descent.[28] Further, until it was amended in 1951, the *Indian Act* required Aboriginal peoples to relinquish their status if they were to pursue higher education.[29] This prevented many Aboriginal peoples from entering university and considering a legal education.

The prevailing presence of social and statutory barriers made it barely possible, and in some cases impossible, for particular groups to receive a legal education in Canada and to enter into legal practice. These barriers have resulted in some communities having few successes in legal education and are a matter of grave concern in terms of efforts to promote equity and diversity in legal education and the legal profession.

III. CONTEMPORARY CHALLENGES AND THE UNPARDONABLE WHITENESS OF BEING

Michael Ornstein has conducted two studies of the demographic makeup of the legal profession.[30] While focusing particularly on Ontario, his research provides insights into the personal characteristics of lawyers across Canada. In both of these studies, Ornstein confirms that the legal profession is predominantly white.[31] This view is also supported by reports by the CBA and the LSBC.[32] Ornstein points out that individuals from subordinate racialized groups and Aboriginal peoples tend to choose professions other than law for their careers. In some cases, the differences are quite significant. For example, in 2001, 3.1 percent of Ontario lawyers were South Asian compared with 9.6 percent of physicians, 7.0 percent of engineers, 4.2 percent of university professors; and 2.1 percent of Ontario lawyers were Chinese compared with 7.7 percent of physicians, 9.6 percent of engineers, and 4.7 percent of university professors.[33] While there is no data examining career choices within these communities, these results are a clear indication of the strong differences in this matter. Ornstein further notes that subordinate racialized groups comprise 25.9 percent of physicians, 27.3 percent of engineers, 15.2 percent of professors, 11.2 percent of high-level managers, and 15.7 percent of middle managers compared to 9.2 percent of lawyers.[34]

The racialized composition of the legal profession has been an issue for some time. Both statistical and anecdotal accounts have been written on this subject and, to date, numerous legal associations have been formed within subordinate racialized communities and amongst Aboriginal lawyers to provide opportunities for them to come together, nurture each other, and support each other's social, cultural, educational, and professional growth and development.[35]

The legal profession is not alone in this dilemma. The experience of Aboriginal lawyers and those from subordinate racialized groups is not much different than that of individuals from these communities working within other professions. For example, in a recent submission to the United Nations International Committee on the Elimination of All Forms of Racial Discrimination, the African Canadian Legal Clinic summarized a number of common issues besetting peoples of African descent and other subordinate racialized groups in terms of equality in employment.[36] This submission describes the numerous reports identifying challenges and barriers to equal employment and provides sociological data identifying the wage and position differential between groups based on race. In presenting this data, the report suggests that such differences are evident even when individuals from subordinate racialized groups have higher educational credentials than their white counterparts.[37]

When it comes to the practice of law, while there may be nuances that are different from other professional fields, clear and compelling explorations demonstrating the commonality of this issue with those of other employment sectors have been addressed in a number of articles.[38] Further, law societies, the CBA, law schools, and law firms have undertaken various initiatives to address this challenge.[39] Unfortunately, the pace of change appears to be very slow and this is particularly a concern in terms of the racial composition of Canada's largest and most prestigious law firms. For example, Michael St. Patrick Baxter suggests, "[h]ere is the reality. Based on the 1997 *Canadian Law List*, there are about 23 Bay Street firms in Toronto. These 23 firms represent a total of about 3,117 lawyers. Of these 3,117 Bay Street lawyers, about 20 are black. This represents six-tenths of 1 percent of the Toronto Bay Street lawyers."[40] This has happened for several reasons: (1) because of the absence of a critical mass of Aboriginal lawyers or lawyers from subordinate racialized groups being within these law firms; (2) large law firms work in ways that are both alien and alienating to individuals from these communities; and (3) the impact of the discriminatory treatment, individual and systemic, that numerous individuals say they have experienced when working in these firms.[41]

As has been noted elsewhere, law schools are "the gatekeepers of legal education.... Ultimately the ethos of the profession is determined by the selection process at law school. In order to ensure that our legal system continues to fulfill its important role in Canadian society it is important that the best can-

didates be chosen."[42] This concern has been quite a focal point in terms of studying the issue of access to legal education and the implications of the deregulation of tuition fees on Aboriginal peoples and individuals from subordinate racialized communities, particularly in terms of the increasing costs of legal education and the potential barriers this may present to these communities. For example, two Ontario law schools approved significant increases to their tuition fees, marking a rise from approximately CDN$2,451 in 1995 to $16,000 for 2003–04 at the University of Toronto, and from $3,228 in 1997 to approximately $8,961 in 2003 at Queen's University.[43] Further, the University of Toronto intends to increase tuition fees until they total $22,000, and Queen's University has projected to increase its fees to $12,856 by 2005.[44]

Concerns regarding the impact of tuition fees on individuals from historically subordinate communities have been addressed by a number of organizations. For example:

- Statistics Canada data indicates that 38.7 percent of youth aged 18–21 years from wealthy families attended university compared to 18.8 percent of youth from poorer families.
- In the report by the Canadian Centre for Policy Alternatives entitled *Missing Pieces V: An Alternative Guide to Canadian Post-Secondary Education*, it is suggested that higher tuition fees result in lower participation rates and that "[r]esearchers at the University of Guelph found that 40% fewer students from low-income families were attending University after tuition fees rose."[45]
- The Canadian Association of University Teachers suggests that, if current trends continue, access to post-secondary education will be increasingly divided along income lines.
- Recent census data indicates that Aboriginal peoples and individuals from subordinate racialized groups tend to fall below the Low-Income Cut Off (LICO) more so than others. The result of this is lowered earnings, leaving these groups less able to support the educational advancement of their children.[46]

The potential impact of increasing law school tuition fees has been explored by the University of Toronto.[47] As the basis for increasing its law school tuition fees to CDN$22,000, the University initiated a study to demonstrate that there would be little, if any, negative impact. This study was completed by the University's Provost and released to its Committee on Academic Policy and Programs of the Governing Council. The points noted immediately above are critical to examining the University of Toronto

Provost's study on accessibility. However, the Provost's study "ignores the well-known history of disparate outcomes in legal practice, including articling, for specific groups and appears to operate on the assumption that once in law school all are equal. This masks deeply entrenched societal and systemic inequalities and evades a critical point on the likely deleterious impact that increasing tuition fees will have."[48]

In terms of first-year students from families with low incomes, the report indicates that in 2002–2003, 17.3 percent of students came from families in the low-income area of less than $60,000, compared to 33 percent of students with family incomes above $90,000, and 33.5 percent of students who did not report their family income.[49] Given that individuals from this latter group do not seek financial assistance, it is likely safe to assume that these individuals are financially well off. As such, this indicates that over 66 percent of students in the Faculty of Law came from families with incomes above $90,000 per year as compared to 17 percent with incomes less than $60,000 per year.[50]

This data supports the concerns expressed earlier, specifically that 38.7 percent of youth aged 18–21 from wealthy families attend university, compared to 18.8 percent of youth from poorer families and, further, that if such trends in increasing tuition fees continue, post-secondary education will be increasingly divided along class lines. Given the intersections between race and family incomes, these divisions will likely be along the lines of race as well.

Following this study, all five law schools in Ontario have examined the issue of accessibility in legal education and the implications/impact of deregulation of tuition fees. There are some startling indicators from this research, including that:

- Aboriginal students comprise 1.3 percent of law school students but make up 3.6 percent of the Ontario population and their numbers have decreased in law school;[51]
- The number of students of African descent have decreased in law school;[52]
- African-Canadian students are nearly twice as likely as their cohorts to leave law school with an accumulated debt of over CDN$70,000 and South Asian students have significant numbers with similar debt loads;[53]
- Choosing a specialization in law affects student course selection and most students prefer civil litigation and commercial law, which are the more financially lucrative areas of practice. This tendency has particular relevance to student interest

in human rights and social justice studies, which has declined from 11 percent to 5.6 percent from first- to third-year students, with only 1.2 percent of recent graduates practising in these areas.[54]

Some of the comments of these students are worth noting. For example:

> With the rising tuition costs, it will be very difficult for other black students like myself to have access to a legal education or to finish the legal education they have already commenced. I am one of five black law students in a class of 180 and I see the numbers going down in the future years because of the high expense incurred to go to law school and the few avenues available which provide financial assistance. (Year 3, Female)[55]
>
> ...
>
> If tuition costs keep going up, First Nations people will not be able to pursue professional careers. As it is now, most Bands will not allow its members to apply to U of T due to high cost. Raising costs will inhibit First Nations People's career choices. (Year 1, Female)[56]

Beyond the direct impact of increasing tuition fees, it is useful to once again review Ornstein's data on the significant earning differential between lawyers based on race. His research indicates that:

- White lawyers between the ages of 25–29 earn approximately CDN$4,000 more per year than lawyers from subordinate racialized groups ($52,000 versus $48,000). This gap increases to approximately $14,000 for lawyers between the ages of 35–39 ($85,000 versus $71,000), and to $39,000 for lawyers between the ages of 40–44 ($97,000 versus $58,000);[57]
- Wage differentials between white lawyers and those from subordinate racialized communities are quite dramatic in the peak earning years of 50–54, with whites earning $70,000 more.[58]

As the CBA article on the University of Toronto study suggests:

> It is essential to highlight these points.... It is rather unusual to approach a study on accessibility and to decontextualize the fundamental issues affecting students, particularly their personal characteristics and how individuals from specific social groups have succeeded in the practice of law. By omitting reference to this information, the Provost study ignores the well-known history of disparate outcomes in legal practice, including articling, for specific groups and appears to operate on the assumption that once in law school all are equal. This masks deeply entrenched societal and systemic inequali-

ties and evades a critical point on the likely deleterious impact that increasing tuition fees will have.[59]

The same might be said of King, Warren, and Miklas's study. Reviewing the earlier comments regarding students who graduate with higher debt loads and limited practice opportunities (Aboriginal peoples, South Asian, and African-Canadians), it is likely that increasing tuition fees will pose significant barriers to their entry and success in the practice of law.

. . . . .

V.   CONCLUSION

While there has been some increase in the racial diversity of law school students and members of the legal profession, this diversity needs to be increased dramatically in order to develop a critical mass of Aboriginal lawyers and lawyers from subordinate racialized groups so that the legal profession will be at the same level of other professions and begin to reflect the makeup of the population.

To achieve this goal, law schools and law firms must demonstrate clear and unequivocal leadership that is measurable and that has specific timelines. The importance of this matter is underscored when considering the social significance of attaining a legal education, a point which is well articulated in the University of Windsor study on law school admissions criteria:

> By necessity, the nature, quality, and effectiveness of the legal system is greatly dependent on the types of individuals who receive a formal legal education. As lawyers, judges, educators, administrators, and legislators, legally trained persons control or materially affect the majority of decision-making and law-enactment processes in society. Law school graduates continue to develop careers in many non-traditional occupations requiring legal expertise; this broadens the profession's sphere of influence. Thus, the legal system, intended for the benefit of all members of society, reflects in some measure the cultural, social, and economic views of the legally trained. To the extent that the legally trained influence the organs of government, access to formal legal education can also be viewed as an important determinant of the political, social, and economic reality. Yet, legal education has traditionally been accessible only to majority social groups in Canada. Therefore, minority perspectives concerning our societal choices may have had only limited influence.[96]

This is what we have to change.

(d)   The Retention of Women in Private Practice Working Group Report — Executive Summary[†]

The Law Society of Upper Canada

I — OVERVIEW

1. Women have been entering the legal profession and private practice in record numbers for at least two decades. However, they have been leaving private practice in droves largely because the legal profession has not effectively adapted to this reality. This report discusses the differences between the legal careers of women and men and outlines business and social reasons for developing strategies to retain women in private practice. It also makes a series of recommendations to promote the advancement of women in the private practice of law.

2. Women's realities, which often include childbirth and taking on a significant share of the family responsibilities, impact on the choices they make in their professional lives. While neither the Law Society nor the profession gen-

---

erally should, nor can, determine the roles women play in their own family relationships, the failure of the profession to adapt to what is not a neutral reality will inevitably affect the quality and competence of the legal services available to the public.

3. The departure of women from private practice means that the legal profession is losing a large component of its best and brightest in core areas of practice. Studies have shown the staggering cost of associate turnover, which is estimated at $315,000 for a four year associate. This cost is equally applicable to associate turnover of men and women, but women are more likely than men to leave their firms before joining the partnership. A shift in thinking is required both on the part of associates and on the part of the employers/firms. This shift would recognize the biological reality of an associate's child bearing years, for which some accommodation is required, the long term nature of a career in private practice and the economic realities of operating a law firm.

4. The legal profession should not assume that change will occur without conscious efforts to create a shift in the legal culture. Law firms have a legal responsibility to provide environments that allow women to advance without barriers based on gender. It is in the public interest for the providers of private legal services to reflect the make up of the society in which we live.

5. We also note that the responsibility to provide leadership in the retention and advancement of women in private practice does not only lie with law firms. Law societies and legal associations have a responsibility to the legal profession and to the public to act as catalysts to influence change and to empower women to take responsibility for their careers and progress.

6. Self-regulation of the legal profession is a privilege and relies on the assumption that the profession is in the best position to set standards and establish ethical rules of conduct for the bar and to regulate lawyers in the best interest of the public. Meeting the public interest requires lawyers to have a sense of professionalism, which includes a sense of integrity, honour, leadership, independence, pride, civility and collegiality.[1] A profession that is representative of the public, and one that provides equal opportunities to men and women serves to enhance the sense of professionalism of our legal profession.

7. In response to the realities outlined above, the Law Society created in 2005 the Retention of Women in Private Practice Working Group (the "Working Group") with a mandate to,
    a. identify best practices in law firms and in sole practice to enhance the retention of women;
    b. determine the role of the Law Society in addressing the issue of retention of women in private practice;
    c. design and implement strategies for medium and large law firms to retain women;
    d. develop strategies to respond to the socio-economic needs of women in small firms and sole practices including the viability of their practices as well as their unique child-care challenges; and
    e. take into account the needs of women from diverse communities.

8. In developing its recommendations, the Working Group considered findings of focus groups conducted with women and interviews conducted with Managing Partners. It also reviewed literature about challenges faced by women in the legal profession, more particularly private practice, and best practices in the legal profession in Ontario, in Canada and in foreign jurisdictions. The Working Group's recommendations aim at allowing women lawyers to make career choices related to their aspirations, may they decide to work as in-house counsel, as government lawyers, in private practice or to stay at home, without being hindered by barriers based on gender.

9. From March to May, 2008, the Law Society embarked on a province-wide consultation to seek the profession's comments on the report and proposed recommendations. The Law Society held meetings in Toronto, Ottawa, Sudbury, Oakville, Kingston, Windsor, Thunder Bay, Orillia, Ajax and London with lawyers, including law firm managing partners and presidents of legal associations. Approximately 900 lawyers and students attended the meetings and the Law Society received more than 55 written submissions.

10. The final consultation attracted a broad spectrum of lawyers, men and women, from all types of practice settings and firm sizes, the government, in-house counsel, articling and law students. Participants included associates, partners and managing partners of all levels of experience and practising in a wide range of areas.

11. Responses to the final consultation were overwhelmingly positive, with some lawyers indicating that they hope this is a first step toward further initiatives. An overview of the final consultation findings is presented in sections VII and VIII of this report. A Final Consultation Report is also available on-line at www.lsuc.on.ca.

II — RESEARCH FINDINGS

12. Studies have identified the following challenges in private practice:
    a. although men and women identify time spent with their family as the aspect of their lives that gives them the most satisfaction, maintaining demanding law careers often [conflicts] with family life and is the most common reason for leaving law practice;
    b. the most immediate issues for women in private practice appear to result from childbirth and parenting responsibilities;
    c. women are particularly affected by the unavailability of support and benefits such as part-time partnerships, part-time employment, predictable hours, job sharing and flexibility in hours;
    d. women in small firms or in sole practices face unique challenges in part because of the lack of income or benefits during leaves and lack of assistance to maintain the practice during absences;
    e. women from Aboriginal, Francophone and/ or equality-seeking communities are often more vulnerable and their experiences and perspectives should be taken into account when developing strategies to retain and advance women in private practice.

13. The Working Group reviewed best practices in Ontario and in other jurisdictions to develop its recommendations. The following conclusions can be drawn from this review:

a. Similar findings are noted in other jurisdictions in Canada and in foreign jurisdictions.
b. Barriers faced by women are systemic and will require organizational and cultural change, along with a focus on the issue if meaningful change is to occur.
c. A number of initiatives designed to assist women would also benefit male lawyers.
d. The experiences and realities of women in larger firms are significantly different than those of women in smaller environments, and therefore recommendations to address challenges faced by women in large and medium firms should be different than those designed to address the needs of women in small firms and sole practices.
e. The recommendations and implementation should take into account the unique challenges faced by women lawyers who are members of Aboriginal, Francophone and/ or equality-seeking communities and their historic under-representation in the legal profession.
f. In the context of large and medium firms, systemic cultural change is necessary and firms will require leadership and commitment from managing partners to implement practices such as the following:
   i. the collection and analysis of law firms' demographic data to assist in the development of strategies based on the firm's needs;
   ii. the adoption, acceptance and effective implementation of maternity/parental leaves and flexible work arrangements;
   iii. programs to assist women to become leaders, both inside and outside their firms, such as effective mentoring programs, gender-based networking opportunities and leadership skills development opportunities.
g. Women in small firms and sole practices are particularly vulnerable because they do not have the financial or human resources to take leaves. The following initiatives would be beneficial:
   i. access to funding to cover some of the expenses of leaves of absences;
   ii. access to practice locums and guidelines to assist in retaining locum lawyers to maintain the practice while on leave;
   iii. access to networking opportunities.

(e) Will the Law Society of Alberta Celebrate Its Bicentenary?†

Harry W. Arthurs

I. INTRODUCTION: THE LINK BETWEEN PROFESSIONAL KNOWLEDGE AND PROFESSIONAL GOVERNANCE

The title of this essay, "Will the Law Society of Alberta Celebrate its Bicentenary?" is intended not as a prediction of impending doom, but rather as an acknowledgment that things change. Things change not only inside the legal profession, but also and especially outside it in society, in the economy, in our political system, and in our natural environment. Those external changes, I will argue, are the primary drivers of internal change. These drivers are so powerful that they are transforming not only legal processes and institutions, not only the profession's clientele and competitive environment, not only the technology and economics of practice, but the very essence of what makes law a profession.[1]

Professions are founded on two premises.[2] The first is that members of the profession know things other people do not. Some of those things they learn from books, others from experience, but always a core body of knowledge is supposedly shared by the members of the profession. Acquiring this body of knowledge is how one gains admission to the profession, and not having a credential which attests to possessing it disqualifies one from doing professional work.[3] The second premise is that their work requires that professionals be allowed to do things forbidden to other people, and vice versa. What can and cannot be done is sometimes laid down by law, sometimes inscribed in formal codes governing professional conduct, and sometimes embedded in cultural practices and traditions. This second premise explains why professions are licensed monopolies and why almost all are at least semi-autonomous and many self-regulating.[4]

Alas, both premises underpinning professionalism have less and less relevance to Canada's legal profession. Lawyers share knowledge less and less with other lawyers, and more and more with people in adjacent lines of work. And lawyers adhere less and less to common codes of conduct, live less and less within a common professional culture, behave more and more like other people, and enjoy dwindling, though still considerable, autonomy.

I am not going to debate whether the decline and fall of legal professionalism might be a good thing or a bad one. Rather I will explain how and why it is happening and sketch out the likely consequences. In each case, I will identify a development out there in the world and then try to show how that development has altered the bar's knowledge base and, ultimately, its political economy, culture, solidarity, autonomy, and governance structures.

II. THE EFFECT OF EXTERNAL CHANGE ON LEGAL ORGANIZATION AND PROFESSIONALISM

I will begin with demographic changes that have occurred since the Law Society of Alberta (LSA) was founded 100 years ago. Canada's population has shifted westwards; it has moved from the countryside to the cities; affluence has increased along with economic inequality; immigration has declined as a percentage of the country's population, but increased in terms of the variety of countries, cultures, and creeds represented amongst our newest communities; the generational balance between young and old has tipped; and, of course, gender roles have been transformed.[5]

These demographic changes have fundamentally altered Canada's political economy and, inevitably, that of the profession as well.[6] Rural societies — like Alberta in 1907 — typically generated little investment capital, supported a short list of businesses, and developed fairly basic forms of social relations and social controls. But greater affluence brings more intense debates over the generation, protection, taxation, and redistribution of wealth; greater inequality and ethno-cultural diversity bring more intense concerns about human rights; urbanization brings greater possibilities for the specialization of economic functions and greater need for and the possibility of the provision of public goods and services; and shifts in the generational balance and in

---

† (2008) 45 Alta. L. Rev. 15–27 (Special Issue: Law Society of Alberta 100th Anniversary Conference "Canadian Lawyers in the 21st Century"). [Notes and/or references omitted.] Reproduced with permission.

gender roles bring new social tensions and generate the need for new institutions to mediate those tensions.[7]

These demographic changes made possible and necessary the development of fields of legal practice that the founding fathers of the LSA would never have been able to imagine: taxation and consumer law, human rights and refugee law, land use and environmental law, labour law, intellectual property law, estate planning, and energy law. These new, specialized fields of practice are defined by new, specialized forms of knowledge. Obviously, that new knowledge is only distantly related to what lawyers knew in 1907.[8] Less obviously, it is almost equally different from what was taught in law schools as recently as, say, 1967 or 1987.[9] Moreover, specialists do not just become immersed in the new knowledge; they tend to abandon the old. Further, the key point: specialists do not simply read different texts and law reports and develop different skill sets and experiential knowledge; they tend also to serve different clienteles, to speak to them in different vernaculars, and to charge fees which are a different order of magnitude from those charged by other lawyers.[10] And finally, a point I will return to below, the trend to specialization in the legal profession has closely tracked the trend to stratification.

And now a paradox: while specialized knowledge is moving lawyers farther and farther away from most of their professional colleagues, it is moving them closer and closer to their "relevant others." If you are an energy lawyer, you will want to walk the walk and talk the talk of the oil and gas industry; if you are a labour lawyer, your "relevant others" are Human Resources managers and union officials; and if you are a tax lawyer, you will be spending a lot of time with accountants. Good lawyering for specialists, then, tends to immerse them in adjacent bodies of non-legal knowledge.

Where do general practitioners fit into this picture? They too deploy specialized knowledge, both legal and non-legal, but its depth and breadth is determined by the modest needs and means of their clientele—typically middle- and working-class individuals, and small- or medium-sized businesses. These clients need wills and divorces; they need to incorporate companies and be helped through routine transactions; they need to collect debts and be defended in lower-level civil, criminal, and regulatory proceedings. But they usually do not need—and often cannot afford—the new legal knowledge dispensed by large law firms with their specialized departments. Consequently, compared to specialists,

the knowledge base of general practitioners more closely resembles that of their predecessors in 1907.

These disparities in knowledge lead to stratification—to the establishment of a pecking order within the legal community.[11] By and large, specialists enjoy higher economic, social, and professional status than general practitioners.[12] There are exceptions: generalists still count for something in small towns, and they may still make their mark in the general legal community, if they are people of unusual character or talents. However, most general practitioners in large cities, like foxes and racoons, survive and prosper in their new habitat by living on the margins. Survival and prosperity usually involve two strategies. First, they must provide efficient legal services at modest prices: this is achieved by routinizing work, delegating it to lay employees, and keeping overheads low. Second, they must exploit their non-legal advantages, such as close affinity with particular client communities, their familiarity as "repeat players" with the bureaucracies of civic governments or lower courts, or their access to financing or other services desired by clients.[13]

So we have specialists, general practitioners, and a variety of lawyers in other settings such as legal clinics, government offices, and corporate law departments. Now come three key points. The first is that these different kinds of lawyers do not simply know different things and serve different clienteles: they work in different practice settings; they receive different psychic and financial rewards; they are shaped by different professional cultures; and they are subject to what amounts de facto to different professional norms and governance structures.[14]

The second point is that while lawyers do move from one elite firm to another, to boutique firms, or to positions as in-house corporate counsel, there is relatively little movement into elite firms from general practice. Those who begin practice in small firms providing routine services for ordinary people are likely to remain in such firms for the rest of their careers.[15]

The third point is that the lawyers who inhabit these different practice roles do not represent a demographic cross-section of the profession. The "typical" lawyer is no longer a white, male, Anglo-Saxon, middle-aged generalist practising in a suburb or small town. There is no longer a "typical" lawyer. With urbanization, immigration, and feminization, the legal profession has indeed become diverse. The problem is that some lawyers are more "diverse" than others. Women remain under-represented in the higher echelons of elite law firms and over-represented in legal clinics, government jobs, and the ranks of in-house counsel. Members of recent immigrant communities are likely to be found most often in small, general practices, or in specialties, like immigration law, which serve their own communities.[16]

To sum up, then, diversity in professional knowledge, experience, culture, and "success" is significantly determined, reinforced, and compounded by diversity in gender, religion, race, and ethnicity. That is what is meant by "stratification."

So far, I have tried to show how demographic change has transformed the economic context of legal practice, which in turn has radically altered — has in fact shattered — the knowledge base of the profession. The fragmentation of knowledge thus reinforces long-standing tendencies to stratification within the profession.

These developments — specialization, stratification, and the transformation of knowledge — are obviously going to have an effect on professional governance. To make a not very bold prediction: we will soon reach the point where a generic law degree will no longer suffice for admission to all kinds of practice; indeed, in some provinces, specialist credentials are already issued to those with practical experience and advanced knowledge of their field.[17] To make a slightly bolder prediction: law societies will have to formally acknowledge that real estate lawyers, those who act for large corporations in merger and acquisitions (M & A) transactions, and criminal lawyers in boutique firms, present quite different governance challenges in terms of enforcing fiduciary duties, requiring pro bono work, paying for malpractice insurance, or maintaining competence through mandatory continuing legal education. Law societies will also have to acknowledge that lawyers who work in large organizations, including large law firms, are usually subject to closer surveillance and sometimes held to higher performance standards by those organizations than by the law society itself. And to make the boldest prediction of all: law societies will ultimately have to acknowledge that the many new sub-professions of law are in any practical sense largely beyond their reach, and that they can best be regulated by bodies whose jurisdictions are defined by the new fault lines of an increasingly disparate and divided profession. Hence my first question: "Will the Law Society of Alberta Celebrate its Bicentenary?"

Now another development which also calls into question the longevity of existing forms of professional governance: the development of national and global markets for all goods and services, including legal services.[18] In 1907, Alberta lawyers would have acted almost exclusively for individuals and local businesses, except for a few who were lucky enough to be retained by the banks, railways, or the government. Today, however, many lawyers in Alberta represent giant national and trans-national companies, or local companies closely linked to them on the food chain.[19] These corporations operate on a scale larger than that of many states: they have complex legal needs; they can pay large fees to specialists to have those needs attended to; and they feel they are best served by lawyers who already have a good knowledge of their business rather than having to educate a new lawyer each time they need one. This logic explains the decline of solo practice and small partnerships that predominated [in] the legal profession from its inception in 1907 until the first wave of large metropolitan and regional firms emerged in the 1960s and 1970s, closely followed by national law firms beginning in the 1980s.[20]

The growth of national law firms, in turn, had a significant impact on provincial and local legal cultures, institutions, and governance arrangements. Because of their large and affluent client base, national law firms could afford to assemble teams of specialists; because of their large revenues, they could afford the most advanced information technology and professional management practices; and because of their contacts outside the province, they were able to acquire knowledge of national, foreign, and international law, which enabled them to corner the market on transactions and disputes requiring such expertise. These advantages allowed them, in effect, to transform the local market for legal services. Local law firms could not compete with them, and consequently, had either to merge with an existing national firm, reinvent themselves as national firms, discover a local niche based on unique local connections or information, or face long-term decline.

The advent of national law firms also raised issues of professional governance. Key members of the firm — often leaders or prospective leaders of the local bar — would migrate across provincial boundaries to wherever they were needed, and sometimes, carried on their practice in more than one province. Provincial law societies could no longer justify the exclusion from practice of these peripatetic but prominent practitioners.[21] Provincial and local bar associations suddenly had to contend with members whose professional contacts and concerns were no longer provincial or local. Local legal cultures, built around shared experiences and values, lost some of their capacity to shape professional behaviour, as key members moved away, or were increasingly influenced by experiences and values shared with their colleagues and counterparts in other jurisdictions.

Even the substance of local law was affected. Provincial law schools could no longer pretend to prepare people only for local practice; they had to design their curricula for graduates who would look for jobs in the new national and international markets for legal talent. Local academics understandably shifted their scholarly focus to issues with national or international salience.[22] Local legislators and regulators suddenly had to contend with lobbying and advocacy by lawyers whose imaginations were no longer dominated by local traditions and expectations, with lawyers who knew how things were done elsewhere, and with clients doing business worldwide, who often resented having to comply with idiosyncratic local regulatory regimes in fields such as securities, pensions, and employment standards.[23]

If I were to end my narrative here, I would have made a strong case that the development of national law firms has put into question the long-term survival of provincial law societies. At the very least I would have demonstrated the necessity of designing new national governance structures to complement, perhaps even eclipse, local governing bodies. However, there is another chapter to the story.

III. GLOBALIZATION AND THE ERODING LOGIC OF LOCAL PROFESSIONAL GOVERNANCE

Globalization has also begun to call into question the future of those very same national law firms or, if not globalization in the broadest sense, then our increasing integration into a North American economic space dominated by the United States. This crucial development I have called "the hollowing out of corporate Canada."[24] Let me first define my terms, and then explain the significance of "hollowing out" for Canada's lawyers and Alberta's in particular. "Hollowing out" has two dimensions. First, significant Canadian corporations, especially in the energy and resource sectors, have been bought out by large firms based in the U.S.[25] Second, other large companies, especially in manufacturing, have been reorganized so that their well-established Canadian subsidiaries enjoy far less functional autonomy than they used to.[26] The result of these two developments is that there are fewer Canadian corporate head offices than previously, and that those which have survived often have less need for high-end legal services than they used to. Moreover, Canadian firms

in the financial services sector, in commercial real estate, advertising, accounting, consulting, and other so-called "business services," also face a loss of clientele, and consequently a diminishing need for lawyers. And even when they do need lawyers — to apply for a trademark, say, or to float an initial public offering of equities — the value-added contributed by their Canadian lawyer has been diminished to the extent that Canadian securities and intellectual property legislation has been brought closely into line with that of the U.S.[27]

To be clear, I am neither attacking nor defending globalization in general, or continental economic integration under the *North American Free Trade Agreement Between the Government of Canada, the Government of Mexico, and the Government of the United States*[28] in particular. Rather, I am offering an hypothesis about the possible effects of our new political economy on the prospects of Canadian lawyers. If my hypothesis proves to be correct, law firms in Calgary, Edmonton, Toronto, and Montreal, which used to provide high-end legal services to important locally-based corporations, will have to start looking elsewhere for clients.

Where might they look? One place, of course, is to the new foreign-based corporations which increasingly dominate some sectors of the Canadian economy. In the short term, this tactic will prove successful. When companies are merged, acquired, or restructured, there is lots of one-off work for corporate, pension, real estate, and securities lawyers.[29] But over time, as the new corporate arrangements are set in place, Canadian lawyers will gradually be replaced on key files by lawyers retained in Chicago or Houston by global head offices located in those cities. Major Canadian law firms may then try to restore their client base by poaching clients from their direct competitors. This strategy again may succeed in the short-term, but in the long-term, as the number and the autonomy of surviving Canadian corporations continues to dwindle, there will be fewer and fewer clients left to poach. A third strategy for national law firms is to reinvent themselves as international firms,[30] or to become the Canadian affiliate of international firms based in New York or London.[31] This is an intriguing possibility, but so far, results have been rather disappointing. Canadian firms can only survive abroad if they can ride the coat-tails of Canadian corporate clients doing business in Shanghai, Frankfurt, or Bangalore. The problem is that not very many Canadian businesses are doing business in such exotic locales. Thus, while a few Canadian law firms have managed to gain a toehold in the U.S., and a few in the United Kingdom and Asia, they seem to have had difficulty in sustaining momentum.

Thus, the hollowing out of corporate Canada may turn out to be the hollowing out of legal Canada as well. This would be a severe disappointment for people who hoped that the emergence of national markets, corporations, and law firms might provide Canada with concentrations of wealth and talent, with economies of scale, and with the new thinking necessary to build a successful economy and a compassionate society. Ironically, however, the demise of corporate Canada and the disappearance of national law firms might leave us back where we began a century ago: with a profession devoted to the simple problems of local clients — not a bad thing in itself, but not a happy prospect for over-invested law firms and ambitious lawyers. If that is the trajectory of Canada's legal professions, it becomes more likely that governing bodies in 2107 will still be provincial. Whether they will also be parochial depends a great deal on the next and final theme I will explore.

IV. HYPHENATED PROFESSIONALISM: THE MOST FUNDAMENTAL CHALLENGE TO PROFESSIONAL GOVERNANCE

That theme involves what I will call "hyphenated professionalism." As I suggested earlier, professionalism involves two main aspects: a unique base of knowledge, and a regulated monopoly over the use of that knowledge. What happens, then, when lay people gain access to knowledge that formerly was exclusively possessed by professionals, and when lawyers lose or surrender their monopoly over the use of such knowledge?

De-professionalization is my first example.[32] Lay people today can acquire legal knowledge which they formerly would have had to buy from a lawyer. Bookstores sell self-help books and the internet has become an infinite font of legal wisdom. Service providers and paralegals incorporate companies, litigate traffic tickets, and represent would-be immigrants and injured workers before specialized tribunals. Law firms and law societies themselves legitimize de-professionalization, if they do not actively promote it, by delegating many legal functions to law clerks and, in Ontario at least, by undertaking to credentialize and regulate them.[33] The net effect is that the legal profession has gradually surrendered its monopoly over many of the tasks that it used to perform or control.

The causes of de-professionalization are pretty obvious: people are more educated than they used to be and have greater confidence in handling their own affairs; many legal procedures have been simplified and standardized to the point where they can be easily mastered by people who lack formal training in law; and information technology has made legal knowledge almost as accessible to lay people as it is to lawyers themselves. And there is one more reason: lawyers are unwilling or unable to deliver certain kinds of standard services at prices that most people can afford. Of course, de-professionalization is fraught with risks. Law clerks, legal agents, service providers, and especially individuals representing themselves can overlook complexities, make mistakes, and exacerbate disputes. On the other hand, they generally do not do so; and lawyers sometimes do.

De-professionalization, whatever its causes and consequences, raises difficult issues for law societies. How can they fight to protect a monopoly over knowledge which clients — the supposed beneficiaries of monopoly — are keen to access directly? How can they insist on the exclusive right of lawyers to deliver certain kinds of services when lawyers retained to deliver those services insist on delegating them to law clerks? And how can the provision of services no longer within the profession's monopoly be regulated to ensure that consumers are protected and unscrupulous service providers are banned from the market?

It would be rash to predict that the profession's monopoly over routine legal procedures and transactions will continue to erode to the point where there is no monopoly left at all. But in the past hundred years, things which were once the staples of legal practice have ceased to be, and the trend seems unlikely to abate.

Indeed, the trend seems likely to move up-market, which brings me to the second of my hyphens, multi-professionalism. As I have already suggested, many legal specialists work in close collaboration with experts in other disciplines. That collaboration is organized either through free-standing, multi-disciplinary practices or, in states which do not permit such practices, through large consulting firms. Indeed, several consulting firms employ so many lawyers that they rank amongst the largest law firms in the world.[34] Sometimes, too, law firms in Canada and elsewhere build up their own in-house consultancies, in which lawyers work alongside economists, planners, other professionals. And sometimes, members of several professions simply work together within the departmental structures of large business corporations.

There is a powerful logic to multi-professional or multi-disciplinary practice.[35] It enhances the likelihood that all relevant skills and knowledge will be mobilized to address the problem at hand; it reduces the likelihood that members of one profession will play a dominant role to the prejudice of another, and ultimately, of the client; it forces all professional participants to rethink the unexplored assumptions of their own discipline or profession in ways which can lead to useful innovation; and of course it can be, should be, more cost-effective for clients.

Professional governing bodies, however, have been reluctant to allow lawyers to participate in multi-disciplinary practices other than those clearly controlled by members of the bar.[36] The ostensible reason is that members of other professions cannot be held to the same high ethical standards as lawyers. While this reasoning is somewhat suspect as a veiled effort at market control, the Enron scandal and others involving the "big five" (or "four" or "three") international consulting firms certainly dampened enthusiasm for multi-professional practices in Canada and elsewhere.

The question is whether the advantages mentioned earlier will ultimately lead to a revival of their credibility and popularity. That is what is going to happen, I believe: multi-disciplinary practices are coming to Canada and the U.S., just as they have come to some European countries, and very recently, to England.[37] Law societies will therefore have to find a way to cope with the new reality that many lawyers will be collaborating more closely with colleagues in other professions than they do with fellow lawyers. Obviously, there are difficulties. At least in the short run, the governing body of each profession will have to restrict its regulatory activities to its own members. And in light of the different histories of the professions, each of the governing bodies is likely to have its own special view of how to regulate honesty, confidentiality, conflicts of interest, and especially, competence. However, sooner, rather than later, we are likely to find that regulation is being exercised by or under the supervision of an umbrella body whose mandate extends to all members of multi-professional or multi-disciplinary practices. In the long run, it seems quite possible that the boundaries amongst the professions will begin to dissolve.

This leads me to my third example of hyphenated professionalism: "post-professionalism."[38] The idea of post-professionalism is pretty simple, but its implications are far-reaching. Essentially, the argument runs, professional boundaries laid down in earlier times no longer have much meaning in the context of our post-industrial, knowledge-based economy. All information, all learning, and all skills relevant to the solution of a given problem should be mobilized for the purpose, and can be mobilized, thanks to new information technologies. However, unlike multi-professional firms, in which each member contributes from within the defined territory of his or her profession, post-professionalism envisages that individual practitioners will be able to do whatever they have the inclination and capacity to do. In a post-professional world, clusters of professions — broadly construed to include all knowledge-based occupations — will dissolve into each other. What post-professional practitioners will have in common is their general knowledge of a social, economic, or technical field, and the ability to recognize its problems, to find solutions, and to know when to seek help from someone with specialized knowledge.

This is not an entirely far-fetched scenario. In fact, it is a reasonably accurate description of the way many lawyers practice today: working far outside the boundaries of their formal legal knowledge; providing strategic advice based on their experience and specialized knowledge of other fields; assembling ad hoc teams of collaborators; and, as suggested earlier, seeing the "client" community as their relevant other, rather than the legal profession. It is also a description of the way in which many students are already pursuing their "legal" educations: taking advanced degrees in other disciplines before or after law school, taking courses in other faculties while studying law, or reading materials from other disciplines as part of their regular law courses.

So legal professionalism is being redefined by three hyphens and three prefixes: de-, multi-, and post-. In each case, a change in the nature, distribution, and deployment of knowledge is detaching lawyers from their familiar, historical roles as advice-givers and advocates who "own" a monopoly over a particular field of human endeavour because they "own" a monopoly over a particular kind of knowledge. Because law societies are mandated to police that monopoly, prevent its abuse, and ensure its use in the public interest, this represents a challenge to their very existence.

V.   CONCLUSION

I have tried to show how developments external to the legal profession are leading to internal changes which are likely to threaten its knowledge base, its monopoly, its governance structures, and perhaps its very existence. I have mentioned three specific examples of such developments: changing demography, globalization, and the dissolution of professional boundaries. I could have mentioned many more: climate change, technology, juridification, the privatization of law production, and new ideas about states and markets come immediately to mind.

Thus the question confronting Canadian lawyers, and their governing bodies, is not simply whether, or even how, law societies will be affected by these transformative developments, it is whether they can survive them at all.

(a) Justice and the Jury†

W. Neil Brooks and Anthony N. Doob

The jury has been described as serving one of two separate functions. It can be seen as an institution designed to ensure the accuracy of fact finding in the adjudication of disputes, applying to the facts of the dispute the law as given by the judge; or it can be seen as an institution which has the right to construe or ignore a relevant rule of law in a case in which its application would not be in accord with the notions of justice and fairness prevailing in the community. After a short review of some of the views taken on each of these sides, we consider the kinds of extra-legal factors that appear to influence jury decisions.

An important function of the legal process is settling controversies by adjudicating competing claims. Characteristically, judicial dispute resolution involves the application of a relevant and fixed rule of law to the factual conflict situation that is found to exist between two contesting parties. To be an effective means of social ordering in a democratic society the application of rules of law must obviously result in decisions that are morally acceptable to the community at large. That is to say, the outcome of adjudication must correspond with shared notions of what is equitable and fair between the parties to the dispute, whether one party is the state and the other a private person, or whether both are private parties.

Rules of law, however, have another important function. They permit social intercourse by serving as guidelines on the basis of which people may plan their affairs, knowing the consequence of different courses of action. To achieve this purpose, rules of law must be formulated at a level of generality that permits each rule to govern the consequence of recurrent factual situations. The necessity on the one hand for general fixed rules of law to regulate social action and the necessity on the other hand for rules that will result in the just resolution of all disputes poses a dilemma for the legal system. A general rule can be formulated that guides behavior and that results in the just resolution of most disputes controlled by it. However, a fact situation will inevitably arise in which, because of the particular equities between the parties to the dispute, a disposition of the case in accord with the relevant rule of law will result in an outcome that does not correspond with the community's notion of fairness, since a judge's decision in a particular case gives rise to a precedent that controls the disposition of all similar cases. Attempts by judges to interpret a general rule of law to reach a just decision in a case in which the equities between the parties are peculiar might cause injustices in future cases: "Hard cases make bad law" is a well known legal adage. A judicial institution that is capable, at least in theory, of resolving the tension between the need for general rules of law and the need to resolve each dispute equitably is the jury.

The proper role of the jury has been the subject of extended and often vigorous debate in legal and political literature. The jury may be seen and defended as fundamentally a political institution which has the right to construe or ignore a relevant rule of law in a case in which its application would not be in accord with the notions of justice and fairness prevailing in the community. This view has been advocated by a number of eminent legal scholars.

Wigmore, the great evidence scholar, urged that the jury's role was to supply "that flexibility of legal rules which is essential to justice and popular contentment" (1929, p. 170). Justice Holmes suggested:

> One reason why I believe in our practice of leaving questions of negligence to the jury is that jurors will introduce into their verdict a certain amount — a very large amount, so far as I have observed — of popular prejudice, and thus keep the administration of the law in accord with the wishes and feelings of the community. (1889, pp. 459–460)

Dean Pound noted that "Jury lawlessness is the great corrective of law in its actual administration" (1910, p. 36). As stated in a Columbia Law Review paper: "Respect for the law is increased when law operates with scrupulous firmness, but with the leaven of charity that is added when the jury acts as the conscience of the community" ("Trial by Jury," 1969, p. 471). The relative importance that is often placed on the jury's role in construing the law in a particular case is illustrated by a statement made in 1789 by Thomas Jefferson: "Were I called upon to decide whether the people had best be omitted in the legislative or judicial departments, I would say it is better to leave them out of the legislative. The execution of the laws is more important than the making of them" (cited in Howe, 1939). Indeed Lord Devlin went so far as to declare: "Each jury is a little parliament. The jury sense is the parliamentary sense" (1956, p. 114).

On the other hand, the jury may be viewed simply as an institution designed to ensure the accuracy of fact finding in the adjudication of disputes, its task being to apply to the facts of the dispute before it, as the jurors find them, the law as given to them by the judge in his instructions. If the general rule of law they are asked to apply appears to result in a harsh or unjust decision in the particular case, that is of no consequence to them in reaching their verdict. Indeed the United States Supreme Court in a case in 1895 (*Sparf & Hansen v. United States*) expressly held that the jury was bound to follow the judge's instructions on the law. The court reasoned that certainty and uniformity in the application of the law was more important than flexibility in individual cases.

Throughout history the legal system has been ambivalent about which of these two roles the jury should assume. When jury trials first emerged in England in the twelfth century, juries were required to apply the law to the facts of the dispute, of which they were assumed to have personal knowledge. If a jury returned a verdict that was found to be wrong they were subject to punishment (Thayer, 1898). However, by the seventeenth century the prevailing view appeared to be that the jury could consider in reaching their verdict the peculiar equities in the case before them. Lord Hale, discussing the function of the jury in 1665, stated, "It is the conscience of the jury that must pronounce the prisoner guilty or not guilty" (cited in Scheflin, 1972). Five years later the judges in Bushnell's Case (1670) held that there was no recourse against the jury for acquitting a person even though the judge or a subsequent jury concluded that the jury's decision was not decided according to the law. Even though it was taken as established that the jury was not accountable for its verdict, and that a verdict of acquittal by the jury was final, several American judges in the middle and late nineteenth century returned to the theoretical position that the jury's only role was to determine the propositions of fact in dispute. The jury, they argued, had no right to refuse to apply the strict letter of the law. These cases are discussed in Howe (1939), in the Yale Law Journal ("The Changing Role," 1964) and in Scheflin (1972). Within the past five years, however, there appears to have been a return to the common law position of the sixteenth century. The decisions in a number of cases, including several Supreme Court of United States decisions have assumed, and several judges have noted, that an important function of the jury is to consider the conscience of the community in reaching its verdict ("Trial by Jury," 1969).

In two states, Indiana and Maryland, the jury's right to nullify the law is given constitutional status, and juries in those states are instructed that they may ignore the strict application of the law. The state of Kansas was considering a constitutional amendment requiring that the following instruction be given to juries:

> It is difficult to draft legal statements that are so exact that they are right for all conceivable circumstances. Accordingly, you are entitled to act upon your conscientious feelings about what is a fair result in this case. (Scheflin, 1972, p. 206)

Whatever role the jury has in theory, in practice it is clear that the jury can ignore the strict application of the law and respond to the unique aspects of each case that comes before it. The jury deliberates in secrecy, they do not give reasons for their verdict, they are in no way accountable for their verdict, their decisions do not establish a precedent that is binding on future cases, and in criminal cases if the jury acquits the accused their decision is final. Indeed the jury's right to determine the facts gives them an almost unlimited discretion in returning whatever verdict they choose. As chief Justice Hughes (cited in Broeder, 1954) in 1931 remarked, "An unscrupulous administrator might be tempted to say, 'Let me find the facts for the people of my country and I care little who lays down the general principles'." Lord Devlin has observed, "I do not mean that they [the jury] often deliberately disregard the law. But if they think it is too stringent, they sometimes take a merciful view of the facts" (1959, p. 21). Indeed the jury's power to ignore the strict application of a relevant rule of law in itself has been construed as the right to do so in certain cases (Kadish and Kadish, 1971).

The jury's right to ignore the law may be supported as an effective means of protecting individuals from the oppressive or unjust use of governmental power. However, whether the rules controlling the jury should permit it wide latitude in deciding a particular case, or indeed if we should retain the jury, because of the need for the exercise of an equitable jurisdiction to mitigate rigid rules in particular cases, depends upon how the jury exercises that function. This empirical question is of overriding importance in the debate on the jury in general. Kalven, co-author of one of the most definitive studies done to date on the jury, has remarked, "Debate about the merits of the jury system should center far more on the value and propriety of the jury's sense of equity, of its modest war with the law, than on its sheer competence" (1964, p. 1702).

Those who oppose the jury on the ground that it is lawless contend that the jury exercises its "equitable" jurisdiction on the basis of prejudices and biases, such as race or physical attractiveness, that are not in accord with acceptable community notions of equity. They argue that jury verdicts result not only in a lack of uniformity in the law but also in malicious decisions and invidious discrimination (Frank, 1949). Those who support the jury and the exercise by it of an equitable jurisdiction, argue that the extra-legal factors that might influence it in reaching its verdict are factors that should be considered by a rational decision maker in reaching a just decision.

STUDIES OF JURY DECISION-MAKING

A few years ago if disputants over the jury were to join on this issue their supporting arguments could only be based on conjecture and isolated personal experiences. In 1954 Broeder observed with respect to the jury's law dispensing function that "we do not know how well it works; the verdict is a seal of secrecy which the law has thus far refused to open" (p. 412). Although the jury's deliberations are still shrouded in secrecy, the use of various methods of empirical research has yielded some data on the extra-legal variables that influence the jury's decision-making process. These studies permit us to draw some tentative conclusions about the basis upon which the jury exercises its equitable jurisdiction.

In the remainder of this paper we will review a few recent studies which illustrate the kinds of extra-legal factors that appear to influence jury decisions. Even this impressionistic review should reveal the direction in which the jury appears to exercise its equitable jurisdiction and thus enable us to draw a tentative conclusion about whether it is a useful social institution for imparting justice into one aspect of societal decision making. But more importantly, it will hopefully illustrate the importance of research on jury decision-making in studying the justice motive (Lerner, 1970; Mysliwiec, 1974).

Common experience suggests that the jury's verdict is likely to be influenced by the personal characteristics of the parties in the dispute, such as their physical attractiveness, character, and race. Empirical studies tend to confirm this commonsense judgment. Efran (1974) found that when subjects were asked to judge a student who was accused of cheating, physically attractive defendants were less likely to be seen as guilty than were unattractive defendants. In this case, attractiveness was manipulated by giving subjects a picture of the hypothetical defendant, one group receiving a photo of an attractive person, the other receiving a photo of an unattractive person. Efran found that students drawn from a similar population generally reported that they did not feel that the defendant's physical attractiveness should influence such decisions. This same bias in favor of physically attractive persons was reflected in a study done by Dion (1972). She found that a transgression by an unattractive child was seen by adults as more serious than was an identical transgression committed by an attractive child.

The attractiveness of a person's personality also affects decisions made by laymen about another's culpability. In a jury simulation experiment, Landy and Aronson (1969) found that on a charge of causing death by criminal negligence the jury recommended a shorter prison term for a defendant who was described as being happily married, regularly employed, and friendly with everyone than they did for a person described as being a janitor, a two-time divorcé, and an ex-convict. Although this was a study in which the simulated jurors were asked to give a judgment about sentencing, it seems likely that the jurors would also consider such facts in deciding on the guilt or innocence of the defendant. Indeed, in view of the danger that if the jury hears about the "bad" character of the accused they might be less careful about determining the certainty of his guilt before convicting, the law tries to keep this information from them. In no Anglo-American jurisdiction can evidence of the accused's bad character be led by the prosecution for the purpose of tending to prove that the accused committed the crime with which he is charged, even though it is sometimes undoubtedly relevant for that purpose.

In apparent conflict with the concern reflected by this rule is the rule whereby if an accused takes the witness stand in his own defense, evidence of his previous criminal convictions can be led by the prosecution. In such a situation, the judge must instruct the jury that this evidence of bad character can be used by them only in evaluating the accused's credibility as a witness. The jury must expressly be told not to infer from the criminal record that the accused is a bad person and therefore is more likely to have committed the crime with which he is charged. Simulations (Doob and Kirshenbaum, 1972; Hans, 1974) and correlational findings from reports of cases (Kalven and Zeisel, 1966) support the conclusion that such instruction is futile. An accused person with previous criminal convictions stands a much greater chance of being convicted of a crime than does a person with no such history.

Race is another personal characteristic that in some jurisdictions has clearly influenced juries in reaching their verdicts. Studies have demonstrated that it is a factor taken into account by the jury in the sentencing process (Bullock, 1961; Thornberry, 1973), and interviews with actual jurors reveal that it is a recurrent topic of conversation throughout their deliberations (Broeder, 1965a).

In criminal cases, the personal characteristics of the victim as well as the accused appear to influence the jury in reaching their verdict. Brooks, Doob, and Kirshenbaum (Note 1), in a jury simulation of a rape case, showed that jurors thought that it was less justified to convict a man of raping a woman who had a history of prostitution than it was to convict a man (on identical evidence) of raping a woman of

chaste character. There was no evidence whatsoever that people thought that the defendant who was accused of raping the prostitute was less likely to have done it; rather it seemed that they simply felt that, given the amount of evidence that existed and the circumstances surrounding the rape, the person ought not to be convicted if the victim were "only" a prostitute. Similarly, Landy and Aronson (1969) found that people recommended longer sentences for someone who had been found guilty of killing (through criminal negligence) a "good" person than they did if the victim were a "bad" person.

The consequence of their decision, although in law irrelevant, is another factor which the jury considers in doing individual justice. In a criminal case, the consequence might be that the defendant will be incarcerated as a result of the decision or, in a few cases, could be executed. Vidmar (1972) and Hester and Smith (1973) have both shown that these consequences do indeed affect jury decision making. Where a jury sees that a consequence might be very severe, they seem less likely to come to a decision that might lead to such a severe result. Similarly, in civil actions the relative ability of the parties to absorb a financial loss is considered by the jury. In cases in which a simulated jury was told that the defendant had liability insurance, the average damages awarded rose considerably. Correspondingly, the jury takes into account any collateral benefits mitigating the loss (Kalven, 1958).

A study based on personal interviews with actual jurors about the deliberation in the jury room revealed that in a civil suit the plaintiff's family responsibilities influenced the jury both in finding liability and in awarding damages (Broeder, 1965b). The government of the province of Prince Edward Island, sensitive to the "deep pocket" philosophy sometimes adopted by jurors in doing individual justice, has recently moved to abolish the jury in civil suits where the government is the defendant (Charlottetown *Guardian*, 1973).

In criminal cases such as assault or various sexual offences, the victim though legally blameless may be partially responsible for the criminal act. The jury, however, is likely to consider the whole situation surrounding the particular crime in coming to a "just" (though not strictly legal) decision. Kalven and Zeisel (1966) found that in cases in which there was some degree of victim precipitation the jury was less likely to convict the accused or at least more likely to convict him of a lesser offense. In the past, a similar result was often revealed by juries in civil cases. Until recently, in many jurisdictions, if the plaintiff contributed to an accident to any degree, he was completely barred from any recovery no matter how negligent the defendant had been in causing the damages. In such cases, rather than bar the plaintiff completely, the jury would take a "merciful view of the facts," and adjust the size of their verdict to correspond to the comparative negligence of the parties (Ulman, 1933).

Kalven and Zeisel (1966) also cite a number of cases where the jury seemed to acquit the defendant because he had suffered enough, even though he might technically be guilty. Thus, for example, it would seem that a jury is less likely to convict a man on a charge of causing death by criminal negligence when it was the defendant's wife who was killed (through his negligence) and the defendant himself was permanently and totally paralyzed in the accident.

Finally, in criminal cases, although only the accused is on trial, the jury in reaching a decision appears to consider whether the state "deserves" to win. If the police have used grossly unfair methods in obtaining evidence against the accused, or if the accused is being singled out for prosecution among many who appear to be equally guilty of the crime, the jury is less likely to convict (Kalven and Zeisel, 1966).

DISCRETION AND EXTRA-LEGAL FACTORS

The argument is often made that to ensure certainty and equal treatment there should be no discretion in the legal process. If injustices result from decisions in particular kinds of cases, then it is the rules of substantive law that should be changed. The rules should not be subverted by ignoring them or by applying them liberally. While many rules of law are in need of reform, it is doubtful whether any system in which fixed rules were applied rigidly, untempered by considerations of justice and fairness in individual cases, could maintain its legitimacy. Kalven has asserted that "we have a sense that many of the jury's most interesting deviations would be exceedingly hard to codify and incorporate by rule" (1964, p. 1071).

The legal system recognizes this need to take into account the peculiar facts of each case. Prosecutors have a broad and largely unreviewable discretion in deciding whether to prosecute a suspected offender. In exercising their discretion, they undoubtedly consider many of the factors reviewed above. Another place in the criminal justice system where most of this kind of information can legally affect the

court's decisions is in the sentencing of a convicted defendant. Indeed, many of the factors that are specifically excluded from the trial of an accused are to be taken into account in determining the proper disposition for a convicted person. Thus such factors as the defendant's criminal record, his standing in the community, his occupational status, etc., often form a critical part of the presentence report on which the judge bases his sentencing decision. The American Law Institute's Model Penal Code states:

> The presentence investigation shall include an analysis of the circumstances attending the commission of the crime, the defendant's history of delinquency or criminality, physical and mental condition, family status and background, economic status, education, occupation and personal habits and any other matters that the probation officer deems relevant or the Court directs to be included. (American Law Institute, 1962, p. 118)

In Canada, recent legislation has given further recognition to the fact that these extra-legal factors should be considered in "doing justice." Where the maximum penalty for a crime is imprisonment of ten years or less, the judge can avoid some of the effects of a guilty verdict by granting an absolute or conditional discharge. The effect of this is that even though the man has been found guilty of a crime, a conviction is not registered. The intent behind the legislation appears to be to encourage a judge to find the defendant guilty or not guilty on the basis of the relevant facts, and then allow himself to be influenced by the totality of the circumstances surrounding the case in his decision to grant or not grant a discharge. (For a more complete description see Greenspan, 1973).

THE JURY'S FUNCTION

The question of whether we should retain the jury because of its ability to dispense justice in individual cases thus depends on the answer to two distinct questions: (a) does the jury exercise discretion in ways that are considered to be just, and (b) in view of the other stages in the legal process where such discretion can be exercised by both the prosecutor and the judge, is there any need for the additional institution of the jury[?] With respect to the first question, it appears, for instance, that in a shoplifting case, if the defendant is a person of some stature and will lose his job if convicted, the jury is likely to find that he has learned his lesson and that the consequences are too serious to warrant conviction. If the prosecutor does not prosecute the ringleader of a gang, but instead calls him as a witness against his underlings, the jury is likely to protest that this is unfair and acquit the accused. If the accused was seriously injured in an accident in which his beloved wife was killed because of his criminal negligence, the jury is likely to find that he has suffered enough. But law dispensing by the jury appears to cut both ways. The fact that minority groups have historically been unfairly subjected to jury lawlessness cannot be doubted. Furthermore, many people would argue that the fact that the accused is a nice fellow, a good looking woman, a cripple, or employed, or that his or her victim is insufferable, should not affect the disposition of the case.

It would appear, not surprisingly, that the jury injects into the legal process notions of fairness that are shared by the average person. However, they are not able to rise above the prejudices and biases held by the same people. Although empirical research is important in demonstrating the subtleties of jury

equity, even when all of the evidence has been collected an important value judgment remains.

If the jury, however, is to perform a function different from that of the prosecutor in exercising his discretion to charge and the judge in exercising his discretion on sentencing, it would appear essential that the jury be representative of the community so that the breadth of community values be represented on the jury. Indeed if the juries were truly representative of the community, perhaps many of the present prejudices that influence the jury would be removed from their deliberations. In this regard, it is interesting that at present a heated battle is being fought over whether the jury should be reduced from the traditional twelve members to six (Note 2). If the jury is reduced in size, then the case for retaining it because of the injection into the legal process of community values would appear to be greatly weakened.

(b) *Morgentaler, Smoling and Scott* v. *The Queen*†

. . . .

Defence Counsel's Address to the Jury

In his concluding remarks to the jury at the trial of the appellants, defence counsel asserted:

> The judge will tell you what the law is. He will tell you about the ingredient of the offence, what the Crown has to prove, what the defences may be or may not be, and you must take the law from him. But I submit to you that it is up to you and you alone to apply the law to this evidence and you have a right to say it shouldn't be applied.

The burden of his argument was that the jury should not apply s. 251 if they thought that it was a bad law, and that, in refusing to apply the law, they could send a signal to Parliament that the law should be changed. Although my disposition of the appeal makes it unnecessary, strictly speaking, to

review Mr. Manning's argument before the jury, I find the argument so troubling that I feel compelled to comment.

It has long been settled in Anglo-Canadian criminal law that in a trial before judge and jury, the judge's role is to state the law and the jury's role is to apply that law to the facts of the case. In *Joshua v. The Queen*, [1955] A.C. 121 at p. 130 (P.C.), Lord Oaksey enunciated the principle succinctly:

> It is a general principle of British law that on a trial by jury it is for the judge to direct the jury on the law and in so far as he thinks necessary on the facts, but the jury, whilst they must take the law from the judge, are the sole judges on the facts.

The jury is one of the great protectors of the citizen because it is composed of 12 persons who collectively express the common sense of the community. But the jury members are not expert in the law, and for that reason they must be guided by the judge on questions of law.

† [1988] 1 S.C.R. 30, 44 D.L.R. 4th. 385 at 417–19.

The contrary principle contended for by Mr. Manning, that a jury may be encouraged to ignore a law it does not like, could lead to gross inequities. One accused could be convicted by a jury who supported the existing law, while another person indicted for the same offence could be acquitted by a jury who, with reformist zeal, wished to express disapproval of the same law. Moreover, a jury could decide that although the law pointed to a conviction, the jury would simply refuse to apply the law to an accused for whom it had sympathy. Alternatively, a jury who feels antipathy towards an accused might convict despite a law which points to acquittal. To give a harsh but I think telling example, a jury fueled by the passions of racism could be told that they need not apply the law against murder to a white man who had killed a black man. Such a possibility need only be stated to reveal the potentially frightening implications of Mr. Manning's assertions. The dangerous argument that a jury may be encouraged to disregard the law was castigated as long ago as 1784 by Lord Mansfield in a criminal libel case, *R. v. Shipley* (1784), 4 Dougl. 73 at pp. 170–1, 99 E.R. 774 at p. 824:

> So the jury who usurp the judicature of law, though they happen to be right, are themselves wrong, because they are right by chance only, and have not taken the constitutional way of deciding the question. It is the duty of the Judge, in all cases of general justice, to tell the jury how to do right, though they have it in their power to do wrong, which is a matter entirely between God and their own consciences.
>
> To be free is to live under a government by law.... Miserable is the condition of individuals, dangerous is the condition of the State, if there is no certain law, or, which is the same thing, no certain administration of law, to protect individuals, or to guard the State.
>
> ...
>
> In opposition to this, what is contended for? — That the law shall be, in every particular cause, what any twelve men, who shall happen to be the jury, shall be inclined to think; liable to no review, and subject to no control, under all the prejudices of the popular cry of the day, and under all the bias of interest in this town, where thousands, more or less, are concerned in the publication of newspapers, paragraphs, and pamphlets. Under such an administration of law, no man could tell, no counsel could advise, whether a paper was or was not punishable.

I can only add my support to that eloquent statement of principle.

It is no doubt true that juries have a *de facto* power to disregard the law as stated to the jury by the judge. We cannot enter the jury room. The jury is never called upon to explain the reasons which lie behind a verdict. It may even be true that in some limited circumstances the private decision of a jury to refuse to apply the law will constitute, in the words of a Law Reform Commission of Canada working paper, "the citizen's ultimate protection against oppressive laws and the oppressive enforcement of the law" (Law Reform Commission of Canada, Working Paper 27, *The Jury in Criminal Trials* (1980)). But recognizing this reality is a far cry from suggesting that counsel may encourage a jury to ignore a law they do not support or to tell a jury that it has a *right* to do so. The difference between accepting the reality of *de facto* discretion in applying the law and elevating such discretion to the level of a right was stated clearly by the United States Court of Appeals, District of Columbia Circuit, in *U.S. v. Dougherty*, 473 F. 2d 1113 (1972), *per* Leventhal J., at p. 1134:

> The jury system has worked out reasonably well overall, providing "play in the joints" that imparts flexibility and avoid[s] undue rigidity. An equilibrium has evolved — an often marvelous balance — with the jury acting as a "safety valve" for exceptional cases, without being a wildcat or runaway institution. There is reason to believe that the simultaneous achievement of modest jury equity and avoidance of intolerable caprice depends on formal instructions that do not expressly delineate a jury charter to carve out its own rules of law.

To accept Mr. Manning's argument that defence counsel should be able to encourage juries to ignore the law would be to disturb the "marvelous balance" of our system of criminal trials before a judge and jury. Such a disturbance would be irresponsible. I agree with the trial judge and with the Court of Appeal that Mr. Manning was quite simply wrong to say to the jury that if they did not like the law they need not enforce it. He should not have done so.

Conclusion

Section [251] of the *Criminal Code* infringes the right to security of the person of many pregnant women. The procedures and administrative structures established in the section to provide for therapeutic abortions do not comply with the principles of fundamental justice. Section 7 of the Charter is infringed and that infringement cannot be saved under s. 1.

(c) *R. v. Williams*†

[McLACHLIN J. for the Court:]

INTRODUCTION

[1] Victor Daniel Williams, an aboriginal, was charged with the robbery of a Victoria pizza parlour in October, 1993. Mr. Williams pleaded not guilty and elected a trial by judge and jury. His defence was that the robbery had been committed by someone else, not him. The issue on this appeal is whether Mr. Williams has the right to question (challenge for cause) potential jurors to determine whether they possess prejudice against aboriginals which might impair their impartiality.

[2] The *Criminal Code*, R.S.C. 1985, c. C-46, s. 638, provides that "an accused is entitled to any number of challenges on the ground that ... a juror is not indifferent between the Queen and the accused," The section confers discretion on the trial judge to permit challenges for cause. The judge should do so where there is a realistic potential of juror partiality. The evidence in this case established widespread racial prejudice against aboriginals. I conclude that in the circumstances of this case, that prejudice established a realistic potential of partiality and that the trial judge should have exercised his discretion to allow the challenge for cause.

HISTORY OF THE PROCEEDINGS

The First Trial

[3] At his first trial, Williams applied to question potential jurors for racial bias under s. 638 of the Code. In support of his application, he filed materials alleging widespread racism against aboriginal people in Canadian society and an affidavit which stated, in part, "[I] hope that the 12 people that try me are not Indian haters." Hutchison J. ruled that Williams had met the threshold test and allowed potential jurors to be asked two questions:

1. Would your ability to judge the evidence in the case without bias, prejudice or partiality be affected by the fact that the person charged is an Indian?

2. Would your ability to judge the evidence in the case without bias, prejudice, or partiality be affected by the fact that the person charged is an Indian and the complainant is white?

On a number of occasions, Hutchison J. allowed additional questions to clarify responses to the first two questions. Forty-three panel members were questioned and 12 were dismissed for risk of bias. The Crown applied for a mistrial on the basis of procedural errors, including use of the same two jurors on all the challenges, coupled with "unfortunate publicity" of the jury selection process. The accused objected, arguing that the Crown was seeking a new trial in order to obtain reversal of the challenge for cause ruling. The trial judge replied that he doubted this would happen, given the case law, and granted the Crown's application for a mistrial.

. . . .

Statutory and Constitutional Provisions

[8] *Criminal Code*, R.S.C., 1985 c. C-46

638.(1) A prosecutor or an accused is entitled to any number of challenges on the ground that

...

(b) a juror is not indifferent between the Queen and the accused;

...

(2) No challenge for cause shall be allowed on a ground not mentioned in subsection (1).

Canadian Charter of Rights and Freedoms

7. Everyone has the right to life, liberty and security of the person and the right not to be deprived thereof except in accordance with the principles of fundamental justice.

11. Any person charged with an offence has the right

...

(d) to be presumed innocent until proven guilty according to law in a fair and public hearing by an independent and impartial tribunal;

15.(1) Every individual is equal before and under the law and has the right to the equal protection and equal benefit of the law without discrimina-

---

† [1998] 1 S.C.R. 1128 at paras. 1–3, 8–13, 15–22, 25, 28–30, 36, 40–42, 52, 55, 58–60.

tion and, in particular, without discrimination based on race, national or ethnic origin, colour, religion, sex, age or mental or physical disability.

ANALYSIS

What Is the Rule?

The Prevailing Canadian Approach to Jury Challenges for Lack of Indifference between the Crown and the Accused

[9] The prosecution and the defence are entitled to challenge potential jurors for cause on the ground that "a juror is not indifferent between the Queen and the accused." Lack of "indifference" may be translated as "partiality," the term used by the Courts below. "Lack of indifference" or "partiality," in turn, refer to the possibility that a juror's knowledge or beliefs may affect the way he or she discharges the jury function in a way that is improper or unfair to the accused. A juror who is partial or "not indifferent" is a juror who is inclined to a certain party or a certain conclusion. The synonyms for "partial" in Burton's Legal Thesaurus (2nd ed. 1992), at p. 374, illustrate the attitudes that may serve to disqualify a juror:

> bigoted, ... discriminatory, favorably disposed, inclined, influenced, ... interested, jaundiced, narrow-minded, one-sided, partisan, predisposed, prejudiced, prepossessed, prone, restricted, ... subjective, swayed, unbalanced, unequal, uneven, unfair, unjust, unjustified, unreasonable.

[10] The predisposed state of mind caught by the term "partial" may arise from a variety of sources. Four classes of potential juror prejudice have been identified — interest, specific, generic and conformity: see Neil Vidmar, "Pretrial prejudice in Canada: a comparative perspective on the criminal jury" (1996), 79 Jud. 249, at p. 252. Interest prejudice arises when jurors may have a direct stake in the trial due to their relationship to the defendant, the victim, witnesses or outcome. Specific prejudice involves attitudes and beliefs about the particular case that may render the juror incapable of deciding guilt or innocence with an impartial mind. These attitudes and beliefs may arise from personal knowledge of the case, publicity through mass media, or public discussion and rumour in the community. Generic prejudice, the class of prejudice at issue on this appeal, arises from stereotypical attitudes about the defendant, victims, witnesses or the nature of the crime itself. Bias against a racial or ethnic group or against persons charged with sex abuse are examples

of generic prejudice. Finally, conformity prejudice arises when the case is of significant interest to the community causing a juror to perceive that there is strong community feeling about a case coupled with an expectation as to the outcome.

[11] Knowledge or bias may affect the trial in different ways. It may incline a juror to believe that the accused is likely to have committed the crime alleged. It may incline a juror to reject or put less weight on the evidence of the accused. Or it may, in a general way, predispose the juror to the Crown, perceived as representative of the "white" majority against the minority-member accused, inclining the juror, for example, to resolve doubts about aspects of the Crown's case more readily: see Sheri Lynn Johnson, "Black Innocence and the White Jury" (1985), 83 Mich. L. Rev. 1611. When these things occur, a juror, however well intentioned, is not indifferent between the Crown and the accused. The juror's own deliberations and the deliberations of other jurors who may be influenced by the juror, risk a verdict that reflects, not the evidence and the law, but juror preconceptions and prejudices. The aim of s. 638 of the Code is to prevent effects like these from contaminating the jury's deliberations and hence the trial: see *R. v. Hubbert* (1975), 29 C.C.C. (2d) 279 (Ont. C.A.). The aim, to put it succinctly, is to ensure a fair trial.

[12] The practical problem is how to ascertain when a potential juror may be partial or "not indifferent" between the Crown and the accused. There are two approaches to this problem. The first approach is that prevailing in the United States. On this approach, every jury panel is suspect. Every candidate for jury duty may be challenged and questioned as to preconceptions and prejudices on any sort of trial. As a result, lengthy trials of jurors before the trial of the accused are routine.

[13] Canada has taken a different approach. In this country, candidates for jury duty are presumed to be indifferent or impartial. Before the Crown or the accused can challenge and question them, they must raise concerns which displace that presumption. Usually this is done by the party seeking the challenge calling evidence substantiating the basis of the concern. Alternatively, where the basis of the concern is "notorious" in the sense of being widely known and accepted, the law of evidence may permit a judge to take judicial notice of it. This might happen, for example, where the basis of the concern is widespread publicity of which the judge and everyone else in the community is aware. The judge has a

wide discretion in controlling the challenge process, to prevent its abuse, to ensure it is fair to the prospective juror as well as the accused, and to prevent the trial from being unnecessarily delayed by unfounded challenges for cause: see Hubbert, *supra*.

. . . .

Identifying Evidentiary Threshold

. . . .

(1) The Assumption that Prejudice Will Be Judicially Cleansed

[20] Underlying the Crown's submissions (as well as the judgments of Esson C.J. and the Court of Appeal) is the assumption that generally jurors will be able to identify and set aside racial prejudice. Only in exceptional cases is there a danger that racial prejudice will affect a juror's impartiality. In contrast, the defence says that jurors may not be able to set aside racial prejudices that fall short of extreme prejudice. Is it correct to assume that jurors who harbour racial prejudices falling short of extreme prejudice will set them aside when asked to serve on a jury? A consideration of the nature of racial prejudice and how it may affect the decision-making process suggests that it is not.

[21] To suggest that all persons who possess racial prejudices will erase those prejudices from the mind when serving as jurors is to underestimate the insidious nature of racial prejudice and the stereotyping that underlies it. As Vidmar, *supra*, points out, racial prejudice interfering with jurors' impartiality is a form of discrimination. It involves making distinctions on the basis of class or category without regard to individual merit. It rests on preconceptions and unchallenged assumptions that unconsciously shape the daily behaviour of individuals. Buried deep in the human psyche, these preconceptions cannot be easily and effectively identified and set aside, even if one wishes to do so. For this reason, it cannot be assumed that judicial directions to act impartially will always effectively counter racial prejudice: see Johnson, *supra*. Doherty J.A. recognized this in *Parks*, *supra*, at p. 371:

> In deciding whether the post-jury selection safeguards against partiality provide a reliable antidote to racial bias, the nature of that bias must be emphasized. For some people, anti-black biases rest on unstated and unchallenged assumptions learned over a lifetime. Those assumptions shape the daily behaviour of individuals, often without any conscious reference to them. In my

opinion, attitudes which are engrained in an individual's subconscious, and reflected in both individual and institutional conduct within the community, will prove more resistant to judicial cleansing than will opinions based on yesterday's news and referable to a specific person or event.

[22] Racial prejudice and its effects are as invasive and elusive as they are corrosive. We should not assume that instructions from the judge or other safeguards will eliminate biases that may be deeply ingrained in the subconscious psyches of jurors. Rather, we should acknowledge the destructive potential of subconscious racial prejudice by recognizing that the post-jury selection safeguards may not suffice. Where doubts are raised, the better policy is to err on the side of caution and permit prejudices to be examined. Only then can we know with any certainty whether they exist and whether they can be set aside or not. It is better to risk allowing what are in fact unnecessary challenges, than to risk prohibiting challenges which are necessary: see *Aldridge* v. *United States*, 283 U.S. 308 (1931), at p. 314, and *Parks*, *supra*.

. . . .

[25] This Court rejected the argument that prejudice based on pre-trial publicity could be cured by the safeguards in the trial process in *Sherratt*, *supra*, at p. 532, per L'Heureux-Dubé J.:

> While it is no doubt true that trial judges have a wide discretion in these matters and that jurors will usually behave in accordance with their oaths, these two principles cannot supersede the right of every accused person to a fair trial, which necessarily includes the empanelling of an impartial jury.

The same may be said of many forms of prejudice based on racial stereotypes. The expectation that jurors usually behave in accordance with their oaths does not obviate the need to permit challenges for cause in circumstances such as the case at bar, where it is established that the community suffers from widespread prejudice against people of the accused's race.

(2) Insistence on the Necessity of a Link Between the Racist Attitude and the Potential for Juror Partiality

. . . .

[28] Racial prejudice against the accused may be detrimental to an accused in a variety of ways. The

link between prejudice and verdict is clearest where there is an "interracial element" to the crime or a perceived link between those of the accused's race and the particular crime. But racial prejudice may play a role in other, less obvious ways. Racist stereotypes may affect how jurors assess the credibility of the accused. Bias can shape the information received during the course of the trial to conform with the bias: see *Parks, supra*, at p. 372. Jurors harbouring racial prejudices may consider those of the accused's race less worthy or perceive a link between those of the accused's race and crime in general. In this manner, subconscious racism may make it easier to conclude that a black or aboriginal accused engaged in the crime regardless of the race of the complainant: see Kent Roach, "Challenges for Cause and Racial Discrimination" (1995), 37 Crim. L.Q. 410, at p. 421.

[29] Again, a prejudiced juror might see the Crown as non-aboriginal or non-black and hence to be favoured over an aboriginal or black accused. The contest at the trial is between the accused and the Crown. Only in a subsidiary sense is it between the accused and another aboriginal. A prejudiced juror might be inclined to favour non-aboriginal Crown witnesses against aboriginal accused. Or a racially prejudiced juror might simply tend to side with the Crown because, consciously or unconsciously, the juror sees the Crown as a defender of majoritarian interests against the minority he or she fears or disfavours. Such feeling might incline the juror to resolve any doubts against the accused.

[30] Ultimately, it is within the discretion of the trial judge to determine whether widespread racial prejudice in the community, absent specific "links" to the trial, is sufficient to give an "air of reality" to the challenge in the particular circumstances of each case. The following excerpt from *Parks, supra*, at pp. 378–79, per Doherty J.A., states the law correctly:

> I am satisfied that in at least some cases involving a black accused there is a realistic possibility that one or more jurors will discriminate against that accused because of his or her colour. In my view, a trial judge, in the proper exercise of his or her discretion, could permit counsel to put the question posed in this case, in any trial held in Metropolitan Toronto involving a black accused. I would go further and hold that it would be the better course to permit that question in all such cases where the accused requests the inquiry.
>
> There will be circumstances in addition to the colour of the accused which will increase the possibility of racially prejudiced verdicts. It is

impossible to provide an exhaustive catalogue of those circumstances. Where they exist, the trial judge must allow counsel to put the question suggested in this case.

. . . .

(4) Impossibility of Proving That Racism in Society Will Lead to Juror Partiality

. . . .

[36] "Concrete" evidence as to whether potential jurors can or cannot set aside their racial prejudices can be obtained only by questioning a juror. If the Canadian system permitted jurors to be questioned after trials as to how and why they made the decisions they did, there might be a prospect of obtaining empirical information on whether racially prejudiced jurors can set aside their prejudices. But s. 649 of the Code forbids this. So, imperfect as it is, the only way we have to test whether racially prejudiced jurors will be able to set aside their prejudices and judge impartially between the Crown and the accused, is by questioning prospective jurors on challenges for cause. In many cases, we can infer from the nature of widespread racial prejudice, that some jurors at least may be influenced by those prejudices in their deliberations. Whether or not this risk will materialize must be left to the triers of impartiality on the challenge for cause. To make it a condition of the right to challenge [for] cause is to require the defence to prove the impossible and to accept that some jurors may be partial.

. . . .

(5) Failure to Read s. 638(1)(b) Purposively

. . . .

[40] This raises the question of what evidentiary standard is appropriate on applications to challenge for cause based on racial prejudice. The appellant appears to accept the standard of widespread racial prejudice in the community. Interveners, however, urge a lower standard. One suggestion is that all aboriginal accused should have the right to challenge for cause. Another is that any accused who is a member of a disadvantaged group under s. 15 of the *Charter* should have the right to challenge for cause. Also possible is a rule which permits challenge for cause whenever there is bias against the accused's

race in the community, even if that bias is not general or widespread.

[41] A rule that accords an automatic right to challenge for cause on the basis that the accused is an aboriginal or member of a group that encounters discrimination conflicts from a methodological point of view with the approach in *Sherratt, supra,* that an accused may challenge for cause only upon establishing that there is a realistic potential for juror partiality. For example, it is difficult to see why women should have an automatic right to challenge for cause merely because they have been held to constitute a disadvantaged group under s. 15 of the *Charter.* Moreover, it is not correct to assume that membership in an aboriginal or minority group always implies a realistic potential for partiality. The relevant community for purposes of the rule is the community from which the jury pool is drawn. That community may or may not harbour prejudices against aboriginals. It likely would not, for example, in a community where aboriginals are in a majority position. That said, absent evidence to the contrary, where widespread prejudice against people of the accused's race is demonstrated at a national or provincial level, it will often be reasonable to infer that such prejudice is replicated at the community level.

[42] On the understanding that the jury pool is representative, one may safely insist that the accused demonstrate widespread or general prejudice against his or her race in the community as a condition of bringing a challenge for cause. It is at this point that bigoted or prejudiced people have the capacity to affect the impartiality of the jury.

. . . .

(7) The Slippery Slope Argument

. . . .

[52] In my view, the rule enunciated by this Court in *Sherratt, supra,* suffices to maintain the right to a fair and impartial trial, without adopting the United States model or a variant on it. Sherratt starts from the presumption that members of the jury pool are capable of serving as impartial jurors. This means that there can be no automatic right to challenge for cause. In order to establish such a right, the accused must show that there is a realistic potential that some members of the jury pool may be biased in a way that may impact negatively on the accused. A realistic potential of racial prejudice can often be demonstrated by establishing widespread prejudice in the community against people of the accused's race. As long as this requirement is in place, the Canadian rule will be much more restrictive than the rule in the United States.

[53] In addition, procedures on challenges for cause can and should be tailored to protect the accused's right to a fair trial by an impartial jury, while also protecting the privacy interests of prospective jurors and avoiding lengthening trials or increasing their cost.

. . . .

[55] At the stage of the actual challenge for cause, the procedure is similarly likely to be summary. The trial judge has a wide discretion in controlling the process to prevent its abuse, to ensure that it is fair to the prospective juror as well as to the accused, and to avoid the trial's being unnecessarily prolonged by challenges for cause: see Hubbert, *supra.* In the case at bar, Hutchison J. at the first trial confined the challenge to two questions, subject to a few tightly controlled subsidiary questions. This is a practice to be emulated. The fear that trials will be lengthened and rendered more costly by upholding the right to challenge for cause where widespread racial prejudice is established is belied by the experience in Ontario since the ruling in *Parks, supra.* The Criminal Lawyers' Association (Ontario), an intervener, advised that in those cases where the matter arises, an average of 35–45 minutes is consumed. The Attorney General for Ontario did not contradict this statement and supports the appellant's position.

. . . .

CONCLUSION

[58] Although they acknowledged the existence of widespread bias against aboriginals, both Esson C.J. and the British Columbia Court of Appeal held that the evidence did not demonstrate a reasonable possibility that prospective jurors would be partial. In my view, there was ample evidence that this widespread prejudice included elements that could have affected the impartiality of jurors. Racism against aboriginals includes stereotypes that relate to credibility, worthiness and criminal propensity. As the Canadian Bar Association stated in Locking up Natives in Canada: A Report of the Committee of the Canadian Bar Association on Imprisonment and Release (1988), at p. 5:

> Put at its baldest, there is an equation of being drunk, Indian and in prison. Like many stereo-

types, this one has a dark underside. It reflects a view of native people as uncivilized and without a coherent social or moral order. The stereotype prevents us from seeing native people as equals.

. . . .

[59] In these circumstances, the trial judge should have allowed the accused to challenge prospective jurors for cause. Notwithstanding the accused's defence that another aboriginal person committed the robbery, juror prejudice could have affected the trial in many other ways. Consequently, there was a realistic potential that some of the jurors might not have been indifferent between the Crown and the accused. The potential for prejudice was increased by the failure of the trial judge to instruct the jury to set aside any racial prejudices that they might have against aboriginals. It cannot be said that the accused had the fair trial by an impartial jury to which he was entitled.

[60] I would allow the appeal and direct a new trial.

(d) Two Conceptions of Representativeness in the Canadian Jury Selection Process: A Case Comment on *R. v. Gayle*†

Emily Morton

I INTRODUCTION

A decade ago, in his dissenting judgment in *R. v. Bain*, Gonthier J. observed that while problems have arisen in the US with the use of peremptory challenges to exclude racial minorities from juries, "Canada has largely been spared of these prosecutorial practices, but if they occur, the common law and the *Charter* offer sufficient protection to the accused...."[1] It was not until the spring of 2001, however, in the case of *R. v. Gayle*,[2] that a Canadian appellate court elaborated on how the *Canadian Charter of Rights and Freedoms*[3] and the common law provide protection against the discriminatory use of peremptory challenges by the prosecution.[4] In that case, Clinton Gayle, a black Jamaican immigrant, appealed his convictions of first-degree murder and attempted murder in the shooting of two white Toronto police officers. Gayle was tried by a jury without any black jurors and argued that the removal of two black prospective jurors from the trial panel by Crown peremptory challenges violated his *Charter* right to a representative jury under s. 11(f), his right to equality under s. 15 and also infringed the two struck jurors's. 15 equality rights.[5]

While Gayle's appeal on these grounds was ultimately dismissed, the Court of Appeal, in *obiter dicta*, indicated that the Crown's use of peremptory challenges may be subject to judicial scrutiny if it is used to eliminate jurors of visible minority groups from the trial panel. This comment analyzes the extent to which the *obiter* commentary in *Gayle* has advanced the jurisprudence regarding the prosecutorial use of peremptory challenges to eliminate prospective jurors belonging to racial minorities. Although Gayle ultimately failed on this ground of appeal, his case may have provided defence counsel with better legal ammunition with which to challenge the prosecutorial use of peremptory challenges. Nevertheless, the Court of Appeal in *Gayle* failed to resolve an important tension that exists in the case law concerning representative trial panels as a goal of the jury selection process. ...

In order to demonstrate both the contributions and the limitations of the *Gayle* decision, it is necessary to trace developments in Canadian jurisprudence regarding the desired characteristics of a jury. In *R. v. Sherratt*, L'Heureux-Dubé J. confirmed that Canadian juries ought to be impartial and representative.[6] More specifically, she wrote,

> [the] perceived importance of the jury and the *Charter* right to a jury trial is meaningless without some guarantee that it will perform its duties impartially and represent, as far as is possible

---

† (2003) 61 U. Toronto Fac. L. Rev. 105 at 106–16, 118–29, 131. [Notes and/or references omitted.] Reproduced with permission.

and appropriate in the circumstances, the larger community ... [W]ithout the two characteristics of impartiality and representativeness, a jury would be unable to perform properly many of the functions that make its existence desirable in the first place.[7]

While it has now become standard for courts to invoke the *desiderata* of representativeness and impartiality in the case law dealing with jury selection,[8] the precise meaning and entailments of these characteristics are in need of clarification. Particularly in light of the Court of Appeal's decision in *Gayle*, there is some confusion in the jurisprudence on jury selection as to what representativeness in the jury selection process actually entails and what relationship it bears to the characteristic of impartiality. In order to demonstrate the extent to which the *Gayle* decision has both advanced and perpetuated the limitations of Canadian jurisprudence dealing with race as an issue in jury selection, this comment sets out two different strands of reasoning as to how impartiality and representativeness are achieved through the jury selection process.

The first and more conventional approach suggests that representativeness is achieved so long as there is no overt exclusion of any group from the initial pool of jurors from which the trial panel is selected. Furthermore, impartiality is achieved so long as no juror selected to sit on the trial panel is shown to be partial or biased in the course of the jury selection process. This critique of discriminatory uses of the peremptory challenge is aligned with equality approaches that seek to redress direct discrimination and so necessarily require a demonstration that the party using the peremptory challenge to strike jurors from minority groups does so with discriminatory intent. The second approach operates from a more substantive and contextualized view of equality and maintains that jury selection procedures should be geared to actively produce substantive representativeness on trial panels, or, at the very least, should discourage practices that have the effect of producing homogenous trial panels.

The aim of this comment is to examine the extent to which the second approach to jury representativeness is recognized by the *Gayle* decision. On one hand, the Court of Appeal in *Gayle* was careful to point out that no accused person is entitled to insist that he or she be tried by a jury that includes one or more individuals who share some personal characteristic, such as race.[9] On the other hand, the Court does not clarify whether the defence must establish that a peremptory challenge by the prosecution was made in bad faith and with the intention of affecting the racial composition, or representativeness, of the jury panel or whether the fact that the use of peremptory challenges merely had the *effect* of undermining substantive representativeness is sufficient to challenge the Crown's use of this discretionary power. Consequently, the *Gayle* decision does not resolve the issue of which of the two accounts of jury representativeness, set out above, should be invoked to resolve the issue of when the use of the peremptory challenge to strike jurors belonging to minority groups should be subject to judicial review. The result is that the *Gayle* decision actually underscores the fact that the precise meaning of the value of representativeness in the Canadian jury selection process remains open for debate.

This comment begins by briefly discussing the procedural history and holdings of the *Gayle* decision itself. In the next section, the conventional approach to jury selection and the discriminatory use of the peremptory challenge is considered, while the "substantive equality" approach to these issues is addressed subsequently. As will be demonstrated, both approaches have found some expression in the pre-*Gayle* jurisprudence surrounding jury selection procedures. In addition, this discussion of the two models will reveal the extent to which the *Gayle* decision itself embraces these two very different conceptions of impartiality and representativeness. ...

II   THE *GAYLE* DECISION

The *Gayle* case marked the first time a Canadian appellate court considered the use of peremptory challenges to impede the selection of racial minorities for jury service. At trial, however, the issue of the use of peremptory challenges to affect the racial composition of the jury was not raised. Of the 91 prospective jurors called at trial, 37 were excused by the trial judge on grounds of personal hardship and 13 were challenged for cause. Of the remaining 41 prospective jurors, 10 were peremptorily challenged by the Crown and 19 by the defence, leaving the 12 that ultimately formed the trial panel.[10]

Crown counsel used peremptory challenges to eliminate two prospective black jurors from the jury. Gayle's trial counsel made no objection to these challenges. The trial record was silent on the racial identity of the two jurors who were challenged in this manner and it was only through affidavit evidence, proffered as fresh evidence on appeal, that the two prospective jurors were identified as black. While the Court of Appeal had no evidence as to the racial composition of the panel from which the jury was selected, it was common ground during the appeal that two of the 12 jurors were members of a visible minority but that none of the 12 jurors was black.[11]

On appeal, Gayle challenged the Crown's use of peremptory challenges on three separate grounds: (1) that the elimination of prospective black jurors violated "[Gayle]'s right to a representative jury, as guaranteed by s. 11(f) of the *Charter*"; (2) that the jury selection process infringed his s. 15 equality rights; and (3) that the s. 15 rights of the prospective jurors who were eliminated from the jury panel were also infringed. Ultimately, the Court of Appeal dismissed this aspect of Gayle's appeal due to the fact that no objection was taken to the Crown's use of peremptory challenges at trial and that there was an incomplete factual record on which to base the appeal.[12] ... Despite the overall failure of this ground of appeal, however, the Court of Appeal did go on to comment, in *obiter*, on whether the Crown's use of peremptory challenges may be reviewed and constrained if this power is used to eliminate visible minority jurors from the trial panel. The Court made this substantive commentary in relation to the first point raised by the appellant — namely, that Gayle's s. 11(1) right to a representative jury was violated as a result of the Crown's use of peremptory challenges. The Court also noted, however, that its comments in the context of the s. 11(f) challenge had equal application to Gayle's argument that his s. 15 equality rights had also been infringed.[13]

To a large extent, the reasons in *Gayle* revolved around the degree to which the Crown's use of the peremptory challenge may be used to undermine the representativeness of the trial panel. Justice Sharpe, writing for the Court, began the discussion by affirming that Canadian law recognizes that representativeness is a crucial characteristic of juries.[14] Immediately after, however, Sharpe J.A. noted that Canadian case law has also made it clear that an accused person does not have the right to insist that he or she be tried by a jury that includes "one or more individuals who share some particular racial, cultural, ethnic, linguistic or other such characteristic."[15] Thus, Sharpe J.A. held that Gayle could not make out a violation of his *Charter* rights to the extent that his challenge was based on the fact that he was tried by a jury that did not include a black juror.

Justice Sharpe then set out what this comment refers to as the "conventional" approach toward (or account of) the role of representativeness in the jury selection process. Again, on this account, the value of representativeness is sufficiently respected once it can be shown that there is no overt discrimination or

exclusion in forming the "array" or the pool of potential jurors from which the trial panel is ultimately selected. However, after noting that this has been the conventional method of considering the issue of representativeness, Sharpe J.A. made the following crucial observation:

> [I]t cannot be the case that concern about the exclusion of jurors on racial grounds is exhausted once an appropriate array of potential jurors has been assembled. The *Charter* right of equality, the right to the benefit of trial by jury and the right to a fair and impartial trial must also be considered in relation to the process that is used to select the jury that will try the case. Just as those *Charter* rights cannot be frustrated or thwarted by the manner in which the array is assembled, nor can they be impeded by shortcomings in the jury selection process.[16]

Justice Sharpe then considered how the value of representativeness is implicated in the prosecution's use of peremptory challenges during the jury selection process. First, Sharpe J.A. noted that the underlying rationale of peremptory challenges (to allow a party to eliminate a juror without having to give reasons, but on the basis of a "hunch") is not necessarily incompatible with the Crown's quasi-judicial role in a criminal trial. Rather, the Crown is obliged to exercise peremptory challenges in a manner that is in keeping with its quasi-judicial role:

> The rationale for peremptory challenges is to foster confidence in the fairness and impartiality of jury trials. The Crown should not be permitted to subvert that rationale by using peremptory challenges to achieve precisely the opposite result.[17]

Thus, the Crown may use peremptory challenges to discharge its responsibility to ensure that the accused is given a fair trial. Importantly, Sharpe J.A. points out that the Crown's use of peremptory challenges can also be used to produce a more representative jury "depending upon both the nature of the community and the accused."[18]

Justice Sharpe then turns to the well-established principle that the Crown must exercise its discretion in conformity with *Charter* principles and values. This principle also constrains the Crown's discretionary power to peremptorily challenge jurors and forms a second basis for judicial scrutiny of the Crown's use of the peremptory challenge. Where this power is used to eliminate minorities, or undermine the representativeness of a trial panel, it is subject to review and constraint. ...

These comments, though made in *obiter*, actually provide the first clear indication in Canadian law of the grounds on which a prosecutor's use of peremptory challenges to eliminate racial minorities from the trial panel may be subject to review. What is most significant about Sharpe J.A.'s comments in this regard is that they explicitly state that the value of representativeness is a concern in the jury selection process itself, as opposed to the conventional view that representativeness is only an issue in determining whether a specific group has been excluded from the initial array of persons from which the trial panel is selected. ...

... It can be argued, therefore, that these aspects of the commentary in *Gayle* attach an independent value to the representativeness of a trial panel that is not present in "conventional" accounts of how the issue of representativeness is dealt with in the jury selection process. Furthermore, if an independent value is being attached by the Court to social diversity, or representativeness, on trial panels then one is left with the question of why that is the case and how far the courts should go in monitoring the use of peremptory challenges in order to achieve substantively representative trial panels. Finally, if one looks behind the idea that substantively representative trial panels are relevant to the fairness of the jury selection process, is it also the case that one should consider the proposition that accused persons have no entitlement to insist they be tried by a jury who share some particular personal characteristic in a different light? These important questions are best examined by setting out the two accounts of the jury selection process in more detail.

III THE CONVENTIONAL ACCOUNT: FORMALLY REPRESENTATIVE JURY SELECTION

i. Overview

As described above, the conventional account of jury selection is that the characteristic of representativeness is guaranteed through provincial legislation that governs the assembly of the array of potential jurors and that impartiality is guaranteed by federal *Criminal Code* provisions governing the in-court selection procedures of the actual trial panel.[21] Provincial statutes set out the sources from which the pool of potential jurors is drawn and representativeness in the initial array is achieved to the extent that no distinctive segment of society is excluded from this initial selection. ...

... Here, representativeness is achieved by random selection from the pool of all competent adult citizens, without deliberate interference in this selection process. If a portion or segment of the community from which the impartial jury is to be drawn is excluded from jury selection, the underlying principle that all citizens are presumed capable of serving as jurors is defeated. Exclusion from the initial array implies that the state has made the determination that those excluded are unfit to try any case.

A corollary of this approach is that if the sources from which the jury panel is selected are representative and there is no deliberate interference with the random selection of jurors from these sources, then there will be no grounds on which to challenge an unrepresentative array of potential jurors. This formalistic approach to challenges to the panel is evidenced by several cases in which it was alleged that the jury lists systematically excluded or caused under-representation of blacks or other racial minorities.[25] The majority of these cases were dismissed on the ground that the mere fact that no racial minorities were summoned did not constitute evidence of partiality.[26]

... It is clear that representativeness is given a very narrow, formal equality-based meaning in this conventional account of jury selection. Representativeness may be challenged on this account only where there is intentional exclusion of a group from the initial pool from which the jury will be selected.

The operation of the criterion of impartiality in this traditional account of the jury selection process also evolves from the formal equality approach. In Canada, potential jurors are presumed to be indifferent or impartial.[29] All prospective jurors, regardless of their background or personal characteristics, are presumed to have an equal capacity for performing their duties in accordance with their oath, weighing the evidence in accordance with judicial instructions, and rendering a verdict with an impartial mind. According to this account, therefore, partiality is not viewed as a function of someone's background or personal characteristics, but as a failure of good will or an inability to set aside biases or prejudices.

Accordingly, the key mechanism by which to displace the presumption of impartiality is the challenge for cause procedure under s. 638(b) of the *Criminal Code*, which gives the prosecutor and the accused the right to an unlimited number of challenges of prospective jurors on the ground that the juror is not "indifferent between the Queen and the accused."[30] In other words, the challenging party must demonstrate a failure of good will or an inability to set aside biases and prejudices. And, while the case of *Williams* relaxed the evidentiary threshold required for initiating this procedure in cases where racial bias and prejudice are a concern, the Supreme Court of Canada has strictly adhered to the principle that jurors are presumptively impartial and that partiality must be proven in order for this presumption to be displaced. This principle that partiality must be specifically proven demonstrates adherence to the formal equality view that partiality is an exercise in bad faith, rather than a result of one's social location, perspective or experiences.

ii. The Role of the Peremptory Challenge in the Conventional Account

At this stage, it is necessary to canvas the justifications for the peremptory challenge based on the assumptions about the meaning of impartiality and representativeness set out above. Section 634 of the *Criminal Code* entitles each party to excuse a certain number of jurors from the array without giving any reasons and, as is noted in *Gayle*, it is the 'very essence' of the peremptory challenge that its exercise requires no justification or explanation. ...

Section 634(1), however, provides that the peremptory challenge may be exercised with or without a challenge for cause procedure. In the absence of a challenge for cause procedure, each side will have only minimal information about each juror[,] including the juror's name, occupation, and address, along with whatever else can be gleaned from a short visual observation of the juror's physical characteristics, dress, and demeanour.[32] In this situation, it is argued that the peremptory challenge enables each side to select a jury that it believes will be most favourable to its position on the basis of its intuition about the possible attitudes or beliefs of the prospective juror. Some commentators maintain that this exercise of the peremptory challenge, in which both sides eliminate those most favourable to the other, will result in a more qualified and impartial jury.[33]

The Court in *Gayle* also adopts this rationale, noting that "[b]y offering each side a limited number of peremptory challenges, the law allows the parties to eliminate **unprovable** but perceived concerns about the propensities of jurors and thereby enhance confidence in the impartiality of the jury and the fairness of the trial."[34] It is not clear, however, how a party can make a meaningful determination on impartiality of a juror based on the limited information it possesses about each prospective juror. Accordingly, other rationales for the peremptory challenge have not focused on its contribution to

enhancing impartiality on the jury, but rather on the utility in providing a party with an opportunity to foster a "good opinion" of the jury. ... Although this rationale for the peremptory challenge applies readily to the defendant, it is unclear whether it applies as readily to the Crown. The Crown and the accused have distinctive roles in the criminal trial process and are subject to different standards when exercising their discretionary powers. On the one hand, the Crown is expected to exercise these powers in keeping with its quasi-judicial role in conducting criminal prosecutions.[36] The accused, on the other hand,

> has a fairly clear and circumscribed role in the trial and in the jury selection process. Nothing more is expected of him or her than trying to avoid conviction and punishment by asserting his or her rights according to law.[37]

On this analysis, as suggested by the Court in *Gayle*, while the peremptory challenge may be extended to the accused so that he or she [] can participate in the construction of a favourable jury, this power is only available to the Crown to the extent that it is used to enhance the jury's impartiality. ...

. . . .

What is interesting about the *Gayle* decision, therefore, is that the Court did not situate its *obiter* comments on the prosecution's use of the peremptory challenge within this formal equality perspective. Rather, the Court structured its reasons around the possibility that the peremptory challenge could be used to undermine representativeness. In addition, the Court chose not to address the issue of whether bad faith on the part of the prosecution must be established in order to successfully challenge the prosecution's use of the peremptory challenge.

. . . .

[T]he entire project of requiring discriminatory intention can be criticized on broader grounds for failing to address what some see as the most troublesome aspect of discrimination resulting from the misuse of peremptory challenges. Because of the low number of racial minorities that will be summoned for jury service, peremptory challenges actually permit the elimination of racial minorities from trial panels altogether. For those who see a need to foster representativeness on trial panels, the question of whether or not a challenger has a discriminatory motivation in striking jurors is irrelevant; the real harm lies in the fact that the substantive representativeness on the trial panel may be undermined. Clearly, this line of argument is quite different from the formal equality approach, insofar as it views the presence of racial minorities on juries as a desirable end in itself. Significantly, as was argued above, the Court in *Gayle* provides qualified approval of the idea that substantive representativeness is an important characteristic of trial panels that is to be a consideration throughout the jury selection process. An alternative approach, which focuses on how jury selection procedures may impact the end result of the composition of the trial panel, therefore, has found its way into the jurisprudence on jury selection. As well, it can be argued that the alternative approach to jury selection builds on a conception of impartiality that is different from the individualistic conception of impartiality set out above. In this account, jury impartiality and jury representativeness are linked.

In what follows, this comment considers how interpretations of the meanings of impartiality and representativeness, distinct from those given above, capture the relationship between the two concepts, leading to an argument for representative trial panels. ...

IV   AN ALTERNATIVE APPROACH: RECONSIDERING IMPARTIALITY AND REPRESENTATIVENESS

i   Two Conceptions of Jury Impartiality

As noted above, there is a legal presumption in Canada that jurors are impartial. This conception of impartiality, however, only captures one of two different interpretations of the root word 'partial' — that is, "[o]ne is partial in the sense of being partial to something [or] liking it. The other is partial in the sense of being only a part."[47] Both are of concern in the jury context. Partiality in the first sense is understood in terms of the potential problem that a juror may favour one side, or a certain outcome, in a given case. In this situation, jurors are presumed to be impartial[,] though the presumption can be displaced through the challenge for cause procedure. Partiality in the second sense reflects the inevitable limitation of one juror's experience, perspective, and perceptions of the evidence. Impartiality in this sense is remedied by ensuring that a diversity of perspectives are engaged in reaching a unanimous decision.

The second sense of the word 'partiality' is relevant when one considers the impartiality of the jury rather than the impartiality of an individual juror. On one hand and according to the conventional approach, the impartiality of the jury is rooted in the presumption that each of its individual members is impartial. On the other hand, the collective decision making aspect of the jury also gives rise to a different understanding of impartiality that inheres in the jury decision-making process. ... This view of impartiality also relates to the unanimous verdict requirement, which is lauded for the thorough examination and weighing of evidence that occurs when all jurors on a trial panel must agree in order to convict or acquit an accused. Indeed, departures from this requirement have been criticized for jeopardizing the impartiality and reliability of the verdict brought about by the collective decision making process of the jury.[50]

While it is uncontroversial to assert that impartiality is considered in both of its senses in the conventional understanding of this desired characteristic of the jury, it is more controversial to suggest that impartiality, in this second sense of 'diffuse impartiality,' bears a significant relation to the characteristic of representativeness.[51] That is, while courts view jury impartiality as inhering in the combination of a diversity of perspectives, diversity is just as easily understood in an individualistic sense — that is, in terms of the pluralism of ideas or life experiences of an individual, regardless of his or her personal characteristics or social group membership. In order to link this second conception of impartiality to representativeness, it is necessary to articulate an independent argument as to how it is that social group diversity may enhance the deliberative aspect of jury impartiality. In what follows, I set out three such arguments.

ii.   The Argument for a Diversity of Perspectives

First, it can be argued that members of different social groups bring to deliberations unique perspectives by virtue of their social group membership. This, for example, is the line of argument adopted by Kim Taylor-Thompson in her critique of the emerging acceptance in the US of non-unanimous verdicts in criminal cases. She claims that this emergent practice threatens the inclusion of the distinctive perspectives of jurors of colour from jury deliberations. Taylor-Thompson writes:

> In the jury room, the juror of color can help to translate experiences for jurors who may otherwise miss the cultural meanings of acts and works ... the juror of color can serve as a jury room interpreter by introducing concepts to the discussion or offering explanations that simply

may not occur to her white counterparts due to different societal experiences ... Particularly, when a trial involves issues of race or a person of color's reactions are at issue in a trial, a juror of color's perceptions may be critical to a determination of truth.[52]

While compelling, this line of argument is subject to the inevitable objection that it operates from a premise of social group essentialism. That is, this argument implies that people belonging to distinctive social groups share an identity of interests or concerns that will be represented in deliberations. This argument also seems to imply that minority jurors will approach their duty as representatives of their social group, rather than judging a case impartially on the basis of the evidence presented at trial and in accordance with their oath.

Both of these objections are reflected in the reasons of the Ontario Court of Appeal and McLachlin J. at the Supreme Court of Canada in *Biddle*. In this case, the appellant was convicted by an all female jury on various charges involving two violent attacks on female victims. The conviction was appealed on the ground that the jury selection process, which involved the empanelling of the all-female jury, created a reasonable apprehension of bias. The Court of Appeal rejected this submission, writing, "it is dangerous and contrary to our concepts of equality and individuality to make findings of partiality on the basis of assumed stereotypical reactions based on gender."[53] While the Court accepted that female jurors may be more inclined to see themselves as victims of the type of assault that occurred in this case, they went on to hold that any reasonable person would feel sympathy for the victims and that any juror would avoid allowing this sympathy to interfere with their obligation to discharge their duty in accordance with their oath.[54] Justice McLachlin, agreeing with the Court of Appeal in *obiter* comments, wrote that she could "see no reason to suppose that an all-woman jury cannot be as impartial as all-male juries have been presumed to be for centuries." Justice McLachlin's comment seems to reflect the latter concern — that is, jurors from different social groups will act as representatives for their social group — by pointing out that we do not impute this attitude to members of historically dominant groups.

... The suggestion that the presence of minority groups on trial panels is important because they are likely to contribute to the deliberative process in a particular way runs up against all sorts of theoretical and normative problems and, in any event, is a dead end as a legal argument.

iii. The Argument for the Presence of Diversity

A second way of expressing the importance of substantive representativeness to the impartiality of the jury is that it enhances the quality of deliberations through the potential transformative effect that diversity may have on the judgment of others. This approach does not necessarily rely on a claim that the perspectives and values of a given juror are determined by their membership in a given social group. Rather than focusing on the racial minority juror as an individual, the focus here shifts to a consideration of the transformative effect that the presence of an individual has on the quality of judgment that emanates from others. The argument can be made that jurors from dominant groups will confront racial biases and prejudices more readily if deliberations are conducted among a racially diverse group. Unconscious stereotypes and prejudices that may have influenced the deliberations of a jury will be checked by the presence of minority jurors — not because minority jurors act as "representatives" of their social group, but because their presence may stem the forwarding of racist considerations by members of dominant groups into the deliberative process.

This second approach may have more viability as a legal argument than the first. While the courts have been resistant to adopting a claim that disadvantaged groups have something distinctive to contribute to deliberation and judgment, they have been much more active in accepting the unconscious effect of bias and prejudice on decision-making processes. For example, the ruling of the Supreme Court of Canada in *Williams* acknowledged the impact that racial prejudice can have on the trial process. This may provide some support for this latter version of why representation may be desirable. In her discussion on how "generic prejudice" may infect the trial process, McLachlin J. wrote:

> It may incline a juror to believe that the accused is likely to have committed the crime alleged. It may incline a juror to reject or put less weight on the evidence of the accused. Or it may, in a general way, predispose the juror to the Crown, perceived as representative of the "white" majority[,] against the minority-member accused ... When these things occur, a juror, however well intentioned, is not indifferent between the Crown and the accused. The juror's own deliberations and the deliberations of other jurors who may be influenced by the juror, risk a verdict that reflects, not the evidence and the law, but juror preconceptions and prejudices.[57]

... [T]there is something unpalatable about this argument, which seems to instrumentalize racial minority jurors by valuing their presence in terms of the effect that it will, arguably, have on the judgment of others. As with the first, this second line of argument presents normative difficulties and is also unlikely to find strong support in the relevant jurisprudence.

iv. The Argument for the Appearance of Diversity

There is a third argument that can be invoked to support the importance of representativeness on trial panels; this argument maintains that representativeness is essential to the *appearance* of impartiality, rather than relying on an independently justified assertion that representativeness and impartiality are interdependent concepts. This argument focuses on the public legitimacy of verdicts, as well as the public's confidence in the fairness and impartiality of the jury system. Courts have long recognized that one of the key functions of the jury system is to instill public confidence in the administration of criminal justice.[58] As Taylor-Thompson puts it, "if decision-makers reflect a fair cross-section of the community, a larger segment of society will likely support their judgment ... As criminal cases continue to track and unearth the depth of ... racial and gender divides, maintaining procedures that emphasize inclusion seems politically advisable."[59] This sentiment finds further support in empirical research revealing a sense on the part of minority groups in Canada that when a member of a racial minority group is on trial, at least some of the jury should be from the same racial minority group as the accused.[60] As well, one finds support for this approach to valuing representativeness in the relevant jurisprudence. This approach is summarized in Gonthier J.'s statement in *Biddle*, where he suggested that "representativeness is a characteristic which furthers the perception of impartiality even if not fully ensuring it."[61] The Ontario Court of Appeal offered an alternative approach in *Church of Scientology of Toronto*, when it argued that "[t]he representative character of the jury also furthers important societal or community interests by instilling confidence in the criminal justice system and acting as a check against oppression."[62] On this approach, representativeness serves an instrumental function of building and maintaining trust in the jury system. Representativeness is not inherently related to the impartiality of jury deliberations, but is fundamental to the public perception of impartiality.

What all of these three arguments have in common is that they view the characteristic of impartiality, and substantive representativeness, as linked. Our ability to translate this theoretical linkage into a legally viable argument depends on how we interpret the existing case law on the characteristic of representativeness in juries. At first glance, it seems as though the weight of judicial opinion favours the conventional understanding of representativeness, exemplified by those cases that view the characteristic of representativeness as meaning the non-exclusion of distinctive social groups from eligibility to serve on a jury. However, as evinced by the *Gayle* decision, there is some recognition in the jurisprudence on the importance of achieving representativeness of actual trial panels, as well as a recognition that this value may have some impact on how the jury selection process is conducted.

v. Jurisprudential Support for Substantive Representativeness on Trial Panels

As Tanovich *et al.* point out, there was some tension among Canadian courts as to the role that representativeness should play in jury selection prior to the *Gayle* decision.[63] Woven into the dominant interpretation is a recognition on the part of the courts that representativeness on trial panels, though not essential, is relevant to and may enhance impartiality. ... This view of the relationship between substantive representativeness and impartiality is also discussed in the *Biddle* case, in which McLachlin and Gonthier JJ. both acknowledged that substantive representativeness, though not an essential or necessary element of a jury, may work to enhance impartiality. Justice Gonthier wrote that "[t]he surest guarantee of jury impartiality consists in the combination of the representativeness with the requirement of a unanimous verdict."[65] Justice Gonthier's endorsement of representativeness is qualified, however, as is evinced by his comment that "representativeness is a characteristic which furthers the *perception* of impartiality even if not fully ensuring it."[66] Furthermore, while holding that substantive representativeness is not a required element in every trial, McLachlin J. nonetheless accepted that this form of representativeness "may provide an extra assurance of impartiality."[67] Thus, while neither Judge envisioned representativeness on juries as a necessary feature of a fair trial, their qualified endorsement of the desirability of substantive representativeness under trial panels is nevertheless distinct from the way in which this characteristic is strictly understood on the conventional approach.

489

. . . .

As was noted above, the merits of substantively representative trial panels were accepted in *Gayle*. The Court affirmed that representativeness does not entail the right of an accused person to a jury that includes one or more individuals who share some personal characteristic, such as race. Specifically, the court suggested that "[i]n the multi-racial society in which we live, the random selection of juries cannot be expected to result in panels that include members having specific racial identities."[72] However, the argument that the issue of representativeness is exhausted once an appropriate array of jurors is assembled was not accepted. Significantly, the Court not only recognized that the jury selection process must strive to attain representativeness, but also grounded this requirement in *Charter* values. Justice Sharpe noted

> that there is a significant body of opinion to the effect that the inappropriate use of peremptory challenges by the Crown has impeded the selection of members of racial minorities for jury service and *undermined public confidence in the jury selection process*.[73]

The common theme running through all of these judgments is that while the accused has no right to a jury that includes one or more jurors sharing some personal characteristic, substantive representativeness is nonetheless an important characteristic which should not be thwarted throughout the jury selection process. The problem, or tension, is clear. It is paradoxical to suggest that substantive representativeness is important while also maintaining that it will never be guaranteed. This tension can be resolved, however, by drawing on the third argument set out above — namely, that substantive representativeness bears no important relation to impartiality in and of itself, but is nevertheless desirable to inspire public confidence in the jury system. Accordingly, the discriminatory use of peremptory challenges is constrained to the extent that it thwarts this goal of the jury selection process.

. . . .

To be certain, the *Gayle* decision does allude to the formal equality approach, insofar as it adopts Trafford J.'s statement from *Brown* that "[t]he application of racial stereotypes, intentionally or unintentionally, is a destructive form of racism that has no part to play in the selection of a jury."[74] While the Court declines to discuss whether a successful challenge to an allegedly discriminatory use of a peremptory challenge requires establishing *mala fides* on the part of the challenger and also declines to discuss the extent to which this practice may engage the equality rights of jurors, there does seem to be a sense that part of the difficulty with this practice lies in the degree to which it applies invidious stereotypes, which are clearly at odds with *Charter* values.

An important contribution of the Court's judgment, however, relates to how the s. 11(f) right to the benefit of trial by jury may constrain the Crown from undermining the substantive *representativeness* of the jury. The Crown, the Court of Appeal seems to indicate, in its quasi-judicial capacity, must only use its peremptory challenge in a manner that is consistent with its responsibility to ensure that the accused is given a fair trial. Part of this responsibility is to ensure that, as far as is possible, a jury is representative of our society.[75] Interestingly, the Court also writes that "[p]eremptory challenges can, in certain circumstances, produce a more representative jury, *depending on both the nature of the community and the accused*."[76] While it would be reading far too much into the statement to suggest that the Court is indicating a possible movement toward Crowns using peremptory challenges to enhance the substantive representativeness of a jury, it does seem to bolster the argument that the Court's main difficulty with the Crown's discriminatory use of the peremptory challenge lies in the potential loss of representativeness on the jury. Furthermore, what is most striking about the Court's remarks on this practice is that it does seem to view the nature of the substantive representativeness of the jury, at least to some extent, as related to the accused himself or herself.

An implication of the Court's comment is that the peremptory challenge may be used to *enhance* substantive representativeness, depending on the nature of the community and the accused. Some commentators believe that certain affirmative approaches may be available in the right case. Professor Aylword suggests a race conscious approach to the use of peremptory challenges, which would recognize the exclusion of blacks from jury service based on their race. Here, an 'asymmetrical' approach would permit a racial minority accused to peremptorily strike white jurors to ensure that at least some racial minorities will be present on the jury, but would prevent prosecutors from striking black jurors on the basis of race.[77] By holding that a representative jury may be a matter of "both the nature of the community and the accused," the *Gayle* decision does seem to create an opening to develop arguments for the adoption of these, albeit limited, affirmative techniques for ensuring the representation of certain groups on trial panels.

. . . .

... Sharpe J.A.'s reference to "the nature of the community and the accused" may be read to provide some guidance as to how the problem of infinite pluralism, cited by McLachlin J. in *Biddle*, can be overcome by positive attempts to ensure a representative jury. That is, representativeness will depend on the particulars of the case at hand. ...

. . . .

V   CONCLUSION

. . . .

As argued in the introduction, the issue of what meaning will be given to the concepts of representativeness and impartiality in jury selection relates to two different visions of what it means to attain equality within the criminal justice system. The first approach balks at the possibility that our institutions of criminal justice could permit direct discrimination against prospective jurors and finds support in a conventional account of the goals and values of the jury selection process. However, this conventional account can be criticized for failing to take into account a different line of reasoning about the discriminatory use of peremptory challenges — namely, that this practice is suspect not only because it discriminates against individual jurors, but also because it jeopardizes the impartiality of the jury by failing to ensure that the jury is substantively representative. While this approach finds some support in more recent judgments that have noted the possible link between impartiality and substantive representativeness, a normatively defensible and legally viable explanation as to how these two characteristics of the jury are actually linked has yet to be articulated. Furthermore, while the least controversial argument seems to be that substantive representativeness is linked only to the *appearance* or *perception* of impartiality in the broader community, even this approach seems to require that, at least in some cases, positive measures are taken to empanel jurors from certain social groups.

. . . .

(a) Embracing Change: How NJI Adapts to the Changing Role of the Judge[†]

Honourable Justice C. Adèle Kent

With the election of President Obama in the United States, everyone is talking about change in the future. The idea of change led me to think about the work of a trial judge in the 15 years that I have sat on the Court of Queen's Bench of Alberta. When I was appointed, the work of a trial judge involved predominantly trials. When a decision had to be made, that is all the judge did. Reasons? Maybe. Other than trial work, from time to time, there was a week of motions court and, every so often, there were some pre-trial conferences — perfunctory meetings to make sure the lawyers were ready for trial. And, unlike today, there were almost always lawyers! On the darker side, judges could say almost anything they wanted to, regardless of whether it was relevant to the issue before them, or how it might affect the sensibilities of those involved in the case.

Today, trials make up a much smaller portion of my work — but how those trials have changed! Jury charges are more complex, and they happen not only at the end of trial, but throughout the trial. Sentencing has become a longer, more involved process. The extent of scientific evidence presented has expanded and requires a careful analysis of its quality. Although the cases we do are structured in the context of an adversarial system, the emphasis is more on settlement than trial. In fact, the demand

for judicial dispute resolution is higher than for trials. And, as for lawyers, much of their work — particularly in the area of family law — is now done with self-represented litigants. Judging today occurs in a more diverse society — one that demands respect from those who judge, not just from those who are being judged.

That is the context within which I think of the National Judicial institute (NJI). The NJI has not only changed dramatically over the past 15 years, but has, in my view, accepted that change is an important principle in creating worthwhile education programs for judges. There are good reasons for this. First, the leaders of the NJI have all been willing to experiment, to consult with judges, and to accept new ideas about the art and craft of judging. Naming names is always dangerous for fear of omitting someone, but the people who have embodied the idea of change include the Executive Directors who have been at the NJI during my judicial career — Dolores M. Hansen, George Thomson, Lynn Smith and Brian Lennox — the Academic and Education Directors, Brettel Dawson and Susan Lightstone, and the many senior advisors with whom I have worked.

The second reason that the NJI has so effectively adapted over the years to the changing role of the judge is because the organization conducts its programs across Canada. Unlike other countries,

---

where judges are sent to the capital city for training at a judicial education institute, when the NJI was established, the model adopted was to take the seminars out to the judges. This allows judges to travel to different parts of the country for seminars, itself a valuable way to learn. It also allows the NJI and, therefore, the judges to make use of the valuable resources available all across the country. For example, as part of the science seminar, *Neuroscience in the Courtroom: What Judges Need to Know*, scheduled to take place in Halifax in 2010, we are organizing a visit to the Brain Repair Centre in Halifax, which studies the brain and recovery of brain function.

So, for all the reasons that judges need to know about the brain — with respect to pain, end of life, memory and so on — leading experts in the field are available within the context of their work. For seminars where it is so important to have input from community leaders, whether it be from the native community, or those involved in addressing domestic violence or poverty, for example, being in the community itself makes the experience authentic. I would suggest that having judicial education seminars move around the country — instead of having a static model — was a brilliant idea. That movement itself encourages change.

The third reason for the effectiveness of the NJI in both leading and embracing change also stems from the way in which programs are developed. I have been fortunate to work on a number of NJI programs, some of which have been a staple of judicial education for years, such as the *Civil Law Seminar*, and some of which are new and developing, like the science programs. One of the fundamental principles of NJI course design is the involvement of judges. Not only does it ensure that the courses are relevant to what the judges are doing, but it also means that judges from across the country and from all levels of court can discuss their work in the context of a particular course. Trends and changes can be more readily identified and incorporated into the courses.

The ability of the NJI to adapt to the changing role of the judge has meant that the array of courses available to judges continues to expand. Two courses come to mind as illustrating not only how broad the range of courses is, but how central they are to effective judging. *Emerging Issues: Judging in the Context of Diverse Faiths and Cultures* was the first in a series of seminars that addressed judging in a diverse society. In addition to featuring compelling lectures on religion and law in Canada by judges and academics, community members addressed the issues that arise as a result of the interface between our legal system and cultures that developed within the context of other legal and cultural systems. At the end of the seminar, it was not hard to see how what we learned would be useful in the courtroom.

As an aside, this seminar is part of the continuing commitment of the NJI to provide courses in contextual judging. When I was appointed, the process of developing judicial education on social context was just beginning. There was significant resistance at that time, in large part, I think, because judges did not understand what social context education entailed. Now, I believe that judges not only accept, but expect to understand the context in which they judge. From time to time, judges may not immediately see how useful this kind of education is, but they understand why it is there.

The second example was the NJI's seminar on sentencing, *Criminal Law Seminar: The Ins and Outs of Sentencing*, which took place a few years ago. As with the course on *Emerging Issues: Judging in the Context of Diverse Faiths and Cultures*, substantive law was presented and applied through small group work. There was more, however. Judges saw the process through the eyes of a victim and through the work of a risk assessment expert.

I began this essay talking about the change that has occurred in the job of judging during my 15 years on the bench. Judging was perhaps simpler 15 years ago, when I was appointed to the bench, but the quality of justice was not of as high a quality as it is today. Despite the complexities that have been added to a judge's role — owing to changing economics, demographics and attitudes about resolving disputes — the fact that Canadian judges are so well equipped to handle those changes is, in large part, due to the effectiveness of the NJI. As I mentioned, I have been involved in the planning process of several NJI courses, which has meant working with many people at the NJI. I note continually the generosity, willingness to volunteer and, quite plainly, the cheerfulness of everyone I work with. That says so much about the organization.

(b) The Meaning and Scope of Judicial Independence†

Bora Laskin

... I hope I do not abuse this privilege if I strike a serious note in this address. It would please me better if I could banter and amuse, which I may assure you is not beyond my capacity. But special reasons, to which I will come shortly, impel me to speak more soberly on a subject of fundamental importance to the judicial office. That subject is the meaning and scope of judicial independence. I would have thought that its meaning would have been well understood over the years in which the Judges have exercised their judicial roles. I would have thought that there was a clear public understanding that Judges cannot be measured in the same way as other holders of public office or any members of the public. In my understanding, and in that of most of the members of the legal profession and members of the Bench, Judges are expected to abstain from participation in political controversy. Obviously, considering the storm that has brewed early this year on the Berger affair, I was somewhat mistaken. The limited public role of the Judge, one perfectly clear to me, seems to have been misunderstood or forgotten, even by lawyers, let alone by members of the press and of the public.

A fundamental principle has pervaded the judicial role since it took root in the reign of Queen Anne. It was established — not without fits and starts — that Judges would no longer hold office at the pleasure of the Crown, at the pleasure of the government. They would have the security of tenure, once assigned to their position, and would hold office during good behaviour to the age of retirement. Their duration in judicial office would no longer depend on governmental whim, and they could be removed only for judicial misbehaviour.

What this imported, as it evolved over the years, was the separation of the executive and the judiciary; no admixture of the one with the other; no mixture of the judiciary in politics or political controversy; correspondingly, no intermeddling of the executive with the judiciary; each branch was to be independent of the other, left alone to carry on its separate duties. For the Judges, they had utmost freedom of speech in the discharge of their judicial functions. Unbelievably, some members of the press and some in public office in this country, seem to think that freedom of speech for the Judges gave them the full scope of participation and comment on current political controversies, on current social and political issues. Was there ever such ignorance of history and of principle?

A Judge, upon appointment — and I am speaking here of appointments which cover all members of our provincial and federal superior courts as well as the Supreme Court of Canada — takes a prescribed oath of office. It is a short oath which is common to all superior court Judges, being as follows:

> I do solemnly and sincerely promise and swear that I will duly and faithfully, and to the best of my skill and knowledge, execute the powers and trust reposed in me as ...
>
> So help me God.

But it is invested with all the authority and surrounded by all the limitations that are imported by the principle of judicial independence and that are spelled out in the *Judges Act*, the federal statute which defines the judicial office.

What does the *Judges Act* say about the judicial office? It says quite clearly that a Judge may not, directly or indirectly, engage in any occupation or business other than his judicial duties. There is a limited exception for him or her to act as commissioner or arbitrator or adjudicator or referee or conciliator or mediator, if so appointed in respect of a federal matter by the federal Government; and similarly, if so appointed by the provincial government in respect of a provincial matter. These are short-term, temporary assignments not intended to give a Judge a regular assignment to carry out a non-judicial role. Two recent illustrations of the distinction may be mentioned. A few years ago, the Government of Canada wished to appoint a Judge as Deputy Minister of an executive department. He was unwilling to accept unless he retained his security as Judge.

---

† An address to the Annual Meeting of the Canadian Bar Association, September 2, 1982, reprinted in F.L. Morton, ed., *Law, Politics and the Judicial Process in Canada* (Calgary: University of Calgary Press, 1985) at 115–20. Reproduced with permission.

The Government was prepared to go along. I felt it my duty as Chief Justice to protest and did so vigorously, pointing out that it was either the one position or the other, but not both.

A Judge who wishes to accept an executive appointment could not remain a Judge at the same time. In the case I mentioned, the Judge put more store on his judicial position than on the proposed executive position. The matter was accordingly dropped. The same thing happened a little later in Ontario when the provincial government wished to appoint an Ontario Supreme Court Judge as Chairman of the provincial Workman's Compensation Board. Again, I protested; if the Judge wished to accept the provincial appointment, he should resign from the Bench; he could not be both Judge and non-judicial or executive functionary. The principle was accepted and the matter was abandoned.

These instances concerned permanent appointments to governmental positions. The authorized exceptions to allow governments to appoint Judges to special assignments as, for example, by order-in-council or by a limited inquiry, do not involve Judges in executive government or in governmental operations. They are asked to perform a particular service, with generally a short-term duration, although some inquiries like the MacKenzie Valley Pipeline and the McDonald Inquiry into the R.C.M.P. did go on for some years.

I am myself not a great supporter of the use of Judges to carry out short-term assignments at the behest of a government, federal or provincial. Apart from anything else, it is not always convenient to spare a particular Judge, given the ever increasing workload of all Courts. Moreover, there is always the likelihood that the Judge will be required to pass on policy, which is not within the scope of the regular judicial function. But I recognize that governments will continue to ask Judges (generally with the consent of their Chief Justice) to perform these limited tasks. The important thing to remember is that these short-term assignments are not intended to establish a career for the Judge in the work he or she carried out. The Judge is expected to make his or her report to the particular government and to regard the assignment as completed without any supplementary comment. Any comment or action is for the government; the Judge himself or herself is *functus*, done with the matter. This has been the general behaviour of Judges who have accepted and carried out special or particular government assignments. Whatever has been the value of the inquiry must rest in what it says — the Judge is certainly not intended to be a protagonist, however enamored he

or she may become of the work. Nor is the Judge intended to make a career of the special assignment.

There has been a large increase in the number of federally-appointed Judges in the last decade. Indeed, there are now 466 superior court Judges throughout Canada and 232 county and district court Judges. I do not take account of provincial court Judges who are appointed by provincial governments. The increase in the number of federally-appointed Judges increased the burden of judicial administration, the need to monitor complaints (which are inevitable, even if in most cases misconceived) and the need also to provide outlets for judicial conferences. It was beyond the capacity of Parliament to provide for these matters and they also raised sensitive matters engaging the independent position of the Judges.

In 1971, a new policy was introduced by Parliament to govern supervision of judicial behaviour or, I should say, alleged misbehaviour....

... The Canadian Judicial Council came into being in October, 1971 and has had a considerable amount of business in the past decade. It has exercised its powers of inquiry and investigation with great care, seeking on the one hand to satisfy complaints against alleged judicial misbehaviour and on the other hand to protect the reputation of the Judge against unfounded allegations. The most common type of complaint received against Judges has to do with objections to their judgments. Laymen have misconceived the role of the Council: it is not a court of appeal to rectify decisions alleged to be in error; for that there are established appeal courts, and the Council repeatedly has to tell complainants that the recourse is an appeal, not an invocation of the powers of the Canadian Judicial Council.

Since the Canadian Judicial Council has a statutory mandate to conduct inquiries into alleged judicial misbehaviour, it can hardly ignore a responsible complaint. In the Berger case, the complaint was made by a long-serving superior court Judge. Was the Canadian Judicial Council to ignore it? At least, it had the obligation to consider whether the complaint merited investigation, that it was not merely frivolous. Those members of the press who became engaged with the complaint in Justice Berger's support seemed entirely ignorant of the mandate of the Canadian Judicial Council. They appeared to be of the view that a Judge's behaviour was for him to measure, that it was not open to the Canadian Judicial Council to investigate, let alone admonish a Judge in respect of a complaint against objectionable behaviour. This was clearly wrong and could have been established by some modest inquiry.

My mention of the Berger case is not to reopen an issue which is closed. It is only to set the record straight on the statutory function and duty of the Canadian Judicial Council, whoever be the subject of a complaint to it. In view of the obvious misunderstanding to which the Berger incident gave rise, it seemed important to me that I, as Chairman, should underline the role and duty of the Canadian Judicial Council, however distasteful it may seem to be to assess the behaviour of a fellow Judge. I would have welcomed, as I always do, the balance provided by the media, by the press, and I regret that it was unfortunate that they did not discharge that responsibility on this occasion.

There was one respect in which members of the press, and indeed some public "bodies" and members of Parliament, showed their ignorance of judicial propriety. It was said that pursuit of the complaint against Justice Berger was an interference with his freedom of speech. Plain nonsense! A Judge has no freedom of speech to address political issues which have nothing to do with his judicial duties. His abstention from political involvement is one of the guarantees of his impartiality, his integrity, his independence. Does it matter that his political intervention supports what many, including the press, think is a desirable stance? Would the same support be offered to a Judge who intervenes in a political matter in an opposite way? Surely there must be one standard, and that is absolute abstention, except possibly where the role of a Court is itself brought into question. Otherwise, a Judge who feels so strongly on political issues that he must speak out is best advised to resign from the Bench. He cannot be allowed to speak from the shelter of a Judgeship.

In the Berger case, the Judge's intervention was on critical political and constitutional issues then under examination by the entire Canadian ministerial establishment. No Judge had a warrant to interfere, in a public way, and his conviction, however well intended, could not justify political intervention simply because he felt himself impelled to speak. To a large degree, Judge Berger was reactivating his McKenzie Valley Pipeline inquiry, a matter which was years behind him and should properly be left dormant for a political decision, if any, and not for his initiative in the midst of a sensitive political controversy.

The Canadian Judicial Council — one member of Parliament accused us of being engaged in a witch hunt — was badly served by those who, obviously, did no homework on the Council's role and on its obligation. There was another matter which seemed rather shabby, also the result of failure to do any homework. It was indicated, quite explicitly in some news quarters, that the Canadian Judicial Council acted because the Prime Minister had complained of the Judge's intrusion into the political sphere when the Prime Minister was giving a press interview in Vancouver. The record on this matter is quite clear. The written complaint against Judge Berger was addressed to me under dates of November 18 and 19, 1981, and delivered to me, from Ottawa, on those days. The next day, November 20, 1981, I sent a memorandum to the Executive Secretary of Council asking that the complaints — there were two successive ones — be referred for consideration by the Executive Committee. So far as the Canadian Judicial Council was concerned, the complaint had become part of our agenda. The interview of the Prime Minister did not take place until November 24, 1981. It is therefore mere mischief making to suggest that the Canadian Judicial Council was moved to action by the Prime Minister.

The Berger inquiry, as I have said, is behind us, and I regret that I found it necessary to say as much as I did about it. However, the Canadian Judicial Council, which does not and cannot reach out publicly to the media, deserves to have its record cleared. This would not have been necessary if we had been better served by the press throughout the whole affair. A matter like the Berger case is not likely to recur; the Canadian Judicial Council has signalled the danger of recommended removal from office if it should recur. As it was, the Council took a placating view and administered an admonishment in the following terms:

1. The Judicial Council is of the opinion that it was an indiscretion on the part of Mr. Justice Berger to express his views as to matters of a political nature, when such matters were in controversy.
2. While the Judicial Council is of the opinion that Mr. Justice Berger's actions were indiscreet, they constitute no basis for a recommendation that he be removed from office.
3. The Judicial Council is of the opinion that members of the judiciary should avoid taking part in controversial political discussions except only in respect of matters that directly affect the operation of the Courts.

In view of the obfuscation that surrounded the Berger case, there are a number of propositions that must be plainly stated. First, however personally compelled a Judge may feel to speak on a political issue, however knowledgeable the Judge may be or think he or she be on such an issue, it is forbidden territory. The Judge must remain and be seen to remain impartial. Compromise which would impair judicial independence and integrity is out, if the Judge is to remain in judicial office. Second, no federally-appointed Judge can claim immunity from examination by the Canadian Judicial Council of complaints (unless obviously frivolous) lodged against the Judge; nor against the decision of the Canadian Judicial Council to investigate the complaints through a formal inquiry. Third, the Canadian Judicial Council is not limited to recommending removal or dismissal; it may attach a reprimand or admonish-

ment without either recommending removal or abandoning the complaint. Only if it gets to removal does it become necessary, in the case of a superior court Judge, to engage the Minister of Justice and Parliament, whose approval on a recommended removal must be sought. Fourth, Judges who are objects or subjects of a complaint are entitled to a fair hearing, to appear before the Council or before an appointed committee or to refuse to appear (as Justice Berger did refuse). Refusal to appear does not paralyse the Council, and did not in the Case under discussion....

(c) The Relationship Between the Courts and the Media†

The Right Honourable Beverley McLachlin, P.C.

Today, I would like to share some thoughts on a topic that I expect is of great interest to us all — the relationship between the courts and the news media. The relationship is not always a comfortable one. Journalists are ever after the "big story". A veteran American court reporter, tongue only partially in cheek, has described his profession thus:

> For the most part we are untrained and deadline crazed, with short attention spans and an inbred preference for heat over light and simplicity over nuance.[1]

By contrast, judges like to think of themselves as "trained" and not overly concerned about deadlines, and possessed of long attention spans, a penchant for nuance, and a confident belief that every word they utter sheds light on the problem at hand, if not on the larger world beyond.

How, one may ask, can such opposites co-exist in a healthy, productive relationship?

My answer is that they can and must, if we want to sustain a society built on the rule of law. Despite occasional discomfort, a free press and an independent judiciary must work together to foster a society committed to the rule of law. The rule of law cannot exist without open justice and deep public confidence in the judiciary and the administration of

justice. And the media is essential to building and maintaining that public confidence.

I will begin by discussing public confidence in the judiciary as a cornerstone of the rule of law. Against that background, I will offer some thoughts on what the legal profession can do to further relationships with the media. Finally, I will discuss some of the challenges that flow from the communications revolution we are currently experiencing.

PUBLIC CONFIDENCE IN THE JUDICIARY

Let me turn to my first proposition — that one of the features of all societies sharing a cultural commitment to the rule of law is public confidence in the justice system and the judiciary. Unless members of the public respect the courts that administer the law, they will not settle their disputes through the courts. They will not obey court orders. Judgments become mere edicts that are, to borrow Shakespeare's words, "like clanging bells, full of sound and fury, but signifying nothing". In his most recent book, *Making Our Democracy Work*, Justice Stephen Breyer of the United States Supreme Court poses a "puzzling question" — why does the public accept

---

† A speech given at Carleton University, Ottawa, Ontario, on January 31, 2012. [Notes and/or references omitted.] Reproduced with permission.

and follow decisions made by the judiciary, a body he describes as "inoffensive, technical, and comparatively powerless." The answer to this question rests in the confidence of the people.

How does one build and maintain this public confidence? Obviously, one must appoint competent judges who observe the highest ethical standards of integrity. One must educate youth and the public generally about the justice system and what judges do. One must ensure that the public has access to justice. But fundamental to maintaining and building confidence in the judiciary is publicizing what judges do.

In the 19th Century, English Philosopher Jeremy Bentham warned against secrecy in the administration of justice:

> Where there is no publicity there is no justice. Publicity is the very soul of justice. It is the keenest spur to exertion and the surest of all guards against improbity. It keeps the judge himself while trying under trial.[2]

Those words still ring true today. In countries sharing the common law tradition, the open courts principle is a fundamental, indeed a constitutional principle.[3] Nonetheless, despite the courts' openness, people may still have little real understanding of how they operate. Most people have neither the time nor the inclination to attend hearings and peruse court records. This is where the media plays a role. Only through the efforts of the press can the vast majority be informed of proceedings before the courts and their judgments.[4] In his book on the U.S. Supreme Court and the press, Joe Mathewson aptly makes this observation:

> When the Court speaks, who listens? Who transmits each new rule of law to the citizenry? Even in the Internet era when the Court posts its opinions promptly on its own Website, both justices and citizens still depend on journalists to get the word out to the broad public. It is still reporters who immediately read the often challenging legal language and make sense of it for lay understanding ...[5]

This places the media in a position of crucial importance, as intermediaries between the legal system and the people it serves. They report on what happens in the courts. And they offer critical reflections on the process.

The duty and right to report includes the right to criticize the way the courts work and the judgments judges render. The right to disagree and criticize is part of the democratic process. It contributes, in the long run, to transparency and to confidence in the judiciary.

This said, we would be naïve not to acknowledge that incomplete, distorted or one-sided press coverage can do lasting damage. Fortunately, the high standards of journalistic ethics in Canada make such incidents rare. The potential for such damage is illustrated by an example from my home province of British Columbia. About 10 years ago, a notorious case involving child pornography went to trial. The defendant, relying on the right to freedom of expression[,] challenged the constitutionality of the prohibition on the possession of child pornography. The trial judge rendered an extremely unpopular decision by striking down the challenged Criminal Code provisions.[6] The media coverage that followed was very disturbing. A number of commentators focussed personally on the judge rather than on the merits of his decision. His intellectual ability was attacked, and he was castigated as a closet paedophile. The vitriol in the press inflamed public passions on a subject that was already very sensitive. The reaction became so extreme that the individual judge received threats and required police protection. Such sensationalization and distortion do little to help people understand the issues or the justice system, and impose serious costs in terms of the security of judges, the independence of the judiciary, and the repute of the judicial system.

So, this is where we stand. The media, reporting accurately and fairly on legal proceedings and judgments, including criticism, even strong criticism, make an invaluable contribution to public confidence in the judiciary and, thus, to the rule of law itself. On the other hand, inaccurate, unfair or sensationalized reportage — fortunately rare in Canada — has the potential to distort the public's view of the justice system and undermine public confidence in the rule of law.

Developing a Positive Relationship with the Media

Faced with this dilemma, we should ask ourselves what we can do [to] encourage media coverage that presents an accurate and fair picture of what happens in the courts — not excluding informed criticism — and thus enhances public confidence in the administration of justice.

First, let me say what, in my opinion, will not work. Restricting access to information and controlling how it may be presented — while sometimes necessary — practiced injudiciously leads the public to infer that the justice system has something to hide. Nor are orders holding reporters in contempt — while occasionally necessary — likely to instil public confidence in the courts. The residual image in the public mind is inevitably that of the bullying judge using state power to punish the valiant reporter. Forgotten is the conduct that made the order necessary.

What then will work? First, instead of viewing the media as the enemy, the justice system should acknowledge the essential role the media plays in informing the public of legal developments. This does not mean that judges or lawyers should condone distortion, inaccuracy and sensationalization. But it does mean that they should promote dialogue with members of the media to the end of ensuring that reporting is accurate, prompt and appropriately complete. There are many ways to do this.

There are many things that courts are doing to help journalists do a better job. Let me list a few of the things we do at the Supreme Court of Canada. We publish statistics on our work, setting out the numbers of applications and judgments, the breakdown by subject matter, and average times taken to deal with the cases heard. Each year, the Chief Justice reports to the bar at the annual CBA conference and follows this with a press conference. From time to time, the Chief Justice gives interviews on how the Court is functioning. Our media relations committee holds yearly meetings with reporters to discuss what is working, and what is not working. Measures such as these attest to the attitude of mutual respect and openness that should prevail between the courts and the press. In our case, they have been much appreciated by the press and have led to improved coverage of the Court and its decisions.

Let me move from "big picture" administrative issues to helping ensure accuracy in the reporting of particular court decisions. Through press officers, summaries of judgments and oral briefings, courts across Canada are helping journalists ensure their reports of cases are complete and accurate. In the long run, public confidence will be undermined if media reports are confusing or misleading. Ensuring accuracy is, of course, the first responsibility of journalists, the vast majority of whom are professional and want nothing more than to "get the story right". However, the law is a complex field. Expert knowledge and years of experience are required to understand its subtleties. And legal language is often difficult for all but the initiated to comprehend.

In the Supreme Court of Canada we try to address the issue of accuracy on a variety of fronts. First, we try to make our judgments as clear as possible. Second, we provide head-notes that summarize the essential points of each decision. Third, the Court's Executive Legal Officer, or ELO, a senior lawyer seconded to the Court for a two year stint, assists journalists by providing briefings on every judgment released by the Court. These briefings are off the record, for information only and not for attribution. The ELO acts as a source of information — not a spokesperson for the Court — and explains the factual and legal background of the case and guides the press through the reasons for judgment. The ELO does not place a "spin" on the judgments. The goal is simply to ensure accuracy by guiding the media through the Court's judgment in as objective a fashion as possible. To help journalists get their stories out in a timely way we have expanded this process to provide lock-ups, where reporters are briefed in advance of the release of a decision. In these and other ways, we try to assist journalists in their job of reporting accurately and completely on judicial decisions.

I have been discussing how courts can help inform the press, (and through the press, the public) on the day-to-day functioning of the courts and the content of judicial decisions. The approach I have discussed is premised on a fundamental principle of great importance — the principle that the courts should be open, subject only to narrow and judicial exceptions.

Of course, not everything can always be disclosed; sometimes the pressing concerns of privacy or security trump openness. Rules of evidence properly curtail what goes into the court record. Publication bans play an essential role in trials of young offenders, sexual offences and some family matters. Restrictions on dissemination, such as sealing orders, may occasionally be necessary.

Concerns of privacy, security and court process may also justify limits on *how* the media go about gathering and transmitting information about judicial proceedings. Electronic media, including television and new web-based media, now represent the primary means by which the vast majority of people receive their news. They constitute uniquely powerful means to provide information to the public about the administration of justice and the decisions of judges and juries. But they also may present risks.

Take, for example, an issue that has been with us for some time — television cameras in the courtroom. In the United States, as you know, television cameras have been allowed in state trial courts for years, (although not in federal courts or in the Supreme Court of the United States). Concerns emerge from this experience. One concern relates to decorum in the court room. The O.J. Simpson murder trial of the mid 1990's, with its media circus atmosphere and around-the-clock coverage[,] did little to foster public confidence in the administration of justice, one might argue. A second concern relates to the privacy of victims and witnesses, who may be transformed from quiet citizens to dinner-table topics overnight. A third concern is that witnesses may be tempted, consciously or unconsciously, to tailor their evidence to what the T.V. audience expects or how they would wish to be seen, corrupting the central truth-finding mission of the trial.

The general practice in Canada is precisely the opposite of that in the United States. Canadian trial courts have not generally permitted their hearings to be broadcast on television, where witnesses are involved. (Recently, while hearing a case concerning the validity of the Canadian *Criminal Code*'s prohibition on polygamy, Chief Justice Baumann of the B.C. Supreme Court permitted the video recording of closing legal arguments[,] which were then streamed to the Internet on a 10 minute delay.)

Before appellate courts in Canada, the practice has been more liberal. The Supreme Court of Canada has permitted television coverage of all its hearings since the mid-1990s. Our courtroom is fitted with fixed cameras that automatically focus on the speaker — whether counsel or a judge — without any disruption. The insomniacs among you will also know that CPAC broadcasts most of the Court's hearings in their entirety. Most of our hearings are now webcast live on the Court's website.

The Supreme Court's experience with television and webcasting has been positive. Live webcasting, in particular, has opened the Court to many citizens across the country. However, this does not mean that other courts ought necessarily to follow our lead. Many of the concerns surrounding the broadcasting of court hearings do not apply to the Supreme Court. We hear no witnesses. With our fixed cameras, there is no possibility of disrupting the decorum of the Court, nor, given the nature of debate before the Court, any real risk of **sensationalization** or trivializing the hearings. From our perspective, which is quite different from that of a trial court, I believe that the broadcasting of our hearings has contributed to public confidence in the Supreme Court of Canada.

THE FUTURE: CHALLENGES POSED BY THE COMMUNICATIONS REVOLUTION

I have been talking about how those involved with the judicial system can constructively work with the media to promote press coverage that is accurate, prompt and appropriately complete in substance and in form. But having urged this course, let me close on a cautionary note. Identifying the media with whom to work and finding effective ways to do this work is about to become much more difficult.

Newspapers, radio and television, despite their importance, are now old technology. Many people today — the young and even the not-so-young — use social media as their main sources of information. Without exaggeration, we are witnessing a profound cultural shift in how people communicate and how information is packaged, disseminated and consumed.

The explosive growth of new media signals a shift in who reports on legal proceedings. Court decisions may no longer be the preserve of trained professional journalists. Anyone with a keyboard and access to a blog can now be a reporter. And who is to say they are not? Some bloggers will be professionals and academics providing thoughtful commentary and analysis. Others will fall short of basic journalistic standards. Will accuracy and fairness be casualties of the social media era? What will be the consequences for public understanding of the administration of justice and confidence in the judiciary? How can a medium such as Twitter inform the public accurately or adequately in 140 characters or less? If witness or juror contamination is a concern with television, is it not even more so with ubiquitous social media accessed or received automatically via a hand-held device?

And overarching all these questions is the essential one — what steps can members of the media or the legal profession take to ensure responsible reporting and its correlative, continued public confidence in the judicial system, in the face of the ever-evolving communications revolution?

Judges in North America are already grappling with some of these questions. Should judges "tweet"? Should they be on Facebook? And other, more complex, queries wait in the wings.

One thing seems to me to be clear. In facing the reality of the modern communications revolution, it is crucial that we understand the technology and how it is being used — something lawyers and judges, often castigated as Luddites, may not find easy. And having understood the new technology and its uses, we must do what we are doing today — discuss, reflect, and share experiences and best practices.

I return to the proposition with which I began: that the relationship between the courts and the media is one of inescapable interdependence. As the late William Brennan Jr. of the United States Supreme Court aptly wrote, there exists:

... a fundamental and necessary interdependence of the Court and the press. The press needs the Court, if only for the simple reason that the Court is the ultimate guardian of the Constitutional rights that support the press. And the Court has a concomitant need for the press, because through the press the Court receives the tacit and accumulated experience of the nation, and — because the judgments of the Court ought also to instruct and inspire — the Court needs the medium of the press to fulfill this task.[7]

Justice Brennan was right: the media and the courts are locked in a mutual, if sometimes uncomfortable embrace. We need each other; our interests are inextricably intertwined. As the media invent and re-invent themselves, so must judicial understanding evolve of how we relate to the media. We must look forward; we dare not hang back. This is our only choice, for what is at stake is nothing less than the rule of law.

(d)   Will Women Judges Really Make a Difference?[†]

Justice Bertha Wilson

When I was appointed to the Supreme Court of Canada in the Spring of 1982 a great many women from all across the country telephoned, cabled or wrote to me rejoicing in my appointment. "Now", they said, "we are represented on Canada's highest court. This is the beginning of a new era for women." So why was I not rejoicing? Why did I not share the tremendous confidence of these women? The reasons form the theme of my lecture this evening.

First of all, of course, came the realization that no-one could live up to the expectations of my well-wishers. I had the sense of being doomed to failure, not because of any excess of humility on my part or any desire to shirk the responsibility of the office, but because I knew from hard experience that the law does not work that way. Change in the law comes slowly and incrementally; that is its nature. It responds to changes in society; it seldom initiates them. And while I was prepared — and, indeed, as a woman judge anxious — to respond to these changes, I wondered to what extent I would be constrained in my attempts to do so by the nature of judicial office itself.

In the literature which is required reading for every newly appointed judge it is repeatedly stated that judges must be both independent and impartial, that these qualities are basic to the proper administration of justice and fundamental to the legitimacy of the judicial role. The judge must not approach his or her task with pre-conceived notions about law or policy, with personal prejudice against parties or issues, or with bias toward a particular outcome of a case. Socrates defined the essential qualities of a judge in the following manner. "Four things belong to a judge; to hear courteously; to answer wisely; to consider soberly and to decide impartially."[1]

In Winters' *Handbook for Judges*,[2] there is a section devoted to the essential qualities of a judge and these are defined as integrity and independence, impartiality, flexibility, creativity, responsibility and common sense. The late Justice Frankfurter was quoted as stating:

> To practise the requisite detachment and to achieve sufficient objectivity no doubt demands of judges the habit of self-discipline and self-criticism, incertitude that one's own views are incontestable and alert tolerance toward views not shared. But these are precisely the presuppositions of our judicial process. They are precisely the qualities society has a right to expect from those entrusted with ... judicial power.[3]

In an article entitled "The Virtue of Impartiality" the late Judge Shientag of the Appellate Division of the New York Supreme Court discusses the difficulty in attaining impartiality and states that the term implies an appreciation and understanding of the differing attitudes and viewpoints of those involved in a controversy.[4] He quotes Lord

---

† From The Fourth Annual Barbara Betcherman Memorial Lecture, Osgoode Hall Law School, February 8, 1990. [Notes and/or references omitted.] Reproduced by permission of the Estate of Hon. Madam Justice Bertha Wilson.

MacMillan's description of the difficulty judges face in this regard:

> The judicial oath of office imposes on the judge a lofty duty of impartiality. But impartiality is not easy of attainment. For a judge does not shed the attributes of common humanity when he assumes the ermine. The ordinary human mind is a mass of prepossessions inherited and acquired, often none the less dangerous because unrecognized by their possessor. Few minds are as neutral as a sheet of plate glass, and indeed a mind of that quality may actually fail in judicial efficiency, for the warmer tints of imagination and sympathy are needed to temper the cold light of reason if human justice is to be done.[5]

And later Lord MacMillan issues the following warning:

> [The judge] must purge his mind not only of partiality to persons, but of partiality to arguments, a much more subtle matter, for every legal mind is apt to have an innate susceptibility to particular classes of arguments.[6]

Many have criticized as totally unreal the concept that judges are somehow super-human, neutral, above politics and unbiased, and are able to completely separate themselves from their personal opinions and pre-dispositions when exercising their judicial function. For example, Lord Justice Scrutton doubted that complete impartiality was possible. He said:

> This is rather difficult to attain in any system. I am not speaking of conscious impartiality; but the habits you are trained in, the people with whom you mix, lead to your having a certain class of ideas of such a nature that, when you have to deal with other ideas, you do not give as sound and accurate judgments as you would wish. This is one of the great difficulties at present with Labour. Labour says: "Where are your impartial Judges? They all move in the same circle as the employers, and they are all educated and nursed in the same ideas as the employers. How can a labour man or a trade unionist get impartial justice?" It is very difficult sometimes to be sure that you have put yourself into a thoroughly impartial position between two disputants, one of your own class and one not of your class. Even in matters outside trade-unionist cases ... it is sometimes difficult to be sure, hard as you have tried, that you have put yourself in a perfectly impartial position between the two litigants.[7]

In his text on *The Politics of the Judiciary*,[8] Professor Griffith caused a furore in legal and judicial circles in the United Kingdom when he questioned whether the English judiciary were capable of impartiality. He stated that for a judge to be completely impartial he or she would have to be like a political, economic and social eunuch and have no interests in the world outside the court. Because this is impossible, Griffith concludes that impartiality is an ideal incapable of realization.[9] He says of the English judiciary:

> These judges have by their education and training and the pursuit of their profession as barristers acquired a strikingly homogeneous collection of attitudes, beliefs, and principles which to them represents the public interest.[10]

The public interest, in other words, is perceived from the viewpoint of their own class. Chief Justice Nemetz has suggested that the views of Professor Griffith may have some validity in Canada too, more particularly, Professor Griffith's view that judicial attitudes towards political and social issues reflect the lack of a proper understanding of the views of labour unions, minorities and the under-privileged.[11]

Judge Rosalie Abella, Chair of the Ontario Law Reform Commission, also doubts that judicial impartiality is a realistic requirement. She emphasizes in her article "The Dynamic Nature of Equality" that "every decision-maker who walks into a court room to hear a case is armed not only with the relevant legal texts but with a set of values, experiences and assumptions that are thoroughly embedded."[12]

Judge Shientag refers to the fact that many judges believe that they have acted with the cold neutrality of an impartial judge when in fact they have completely failed to examine their prejudices and biases. He points out that the partiality and prejudice with which we are concerned is not overt, not something tangible on which the judge can put his or her finger. Yet many judges by failing to appreciate this are lulled into a false sense of security.[13] Judge Shientag emphasizes that progress will only be made when judges recognize this condition as part of the weakness of human nature and then "[h]aving admitted the liability to prejudice, unconscious for the most part, subtle and nebulous at times, the next step is to determine what the judge, with his trained mind, can do to neutralize the incessant play of these obscure yet potent influences."[14] Judge Shientag concludes that "the judge who realizes, before listening to a case, that all men have a natural bias of mind and that thought is apt to be coloured by predilection, is more likely to make a conscientious effort at impartiality and dispassionateness than one who believes that his elevation to the bench makes him at once the dehumanized instrument of infallible logical truth."[15]

But what, you may be asking, has all this got to do with my subject: "Will women judges really make a difference?" Well, I think it has a great deal to do with it and whether you agree with me or not will probably depend on your perception of the degree to which the existing law reflects the judicial neutrality or impartiality we have been discussing. If the existing law can be viewed as the product of judicial neutrality or impartiality, [...] although the judiciary has been very substantially male, then you may conclude that the advent of increased numbers of women judges should make no difference, assuming, that is, that these women judges will bring to bear the same neutrality and impartiality. However, if you conclude that the existing law, in some areas at least, cannot be viewed as the product of judicial neutrality, then your answer may be very different.

Two law professors at New York University, Professor John Johnston and Professor Charles Knapp, have concluded, as a result of their studies of judicial attitudes reflected in the decisions of judges in the United States, that United States judges have succeeded in their conscious efforts to free themselves from habits of stereotypical thought with regard to discrimination based on colour.[16] However, they were unable to reach a similar conclusion with respect to discrimination based on sex and found that American judges had failed to bring to sex discrimination the judicial virtues of detachment, reflection and critical analysis which had served them so well with respect to other areas of discrimination. They state:

> "Sexism" — the making of unjustified (or at least unsupported) assumptions about individual capabilities, interests, goals and social roles solely on the basis of sex differences — is as easily discernible in contemporary judicial opinions as racism ever was.[17]

Professor Norma Wikler, a sociologist at the University of California, has reviewed a number of other studies of judicial attitudes by legal researchers and social scientists and states that these confirm that male judges tend to adhere to traditional values and beliefs about the "natures" of men and women and their proper roles in society. They have found overwhelming evidence that gender-based myths, biases and stereotypes are deeply embedded in the attitudes of many male judges as well as in the law itself. They have concluded that particularly in areas of tort law, criminal law and family law, gender difference has been a significant factor in judicial decision-making. Many have concluded that sexism is

the unarticulated underlying premise of many judgments in these areas and that this is not really surprising having regard to the nature of the society in which the judges themselves have been socialized.[18]

A number of strategies have been tried in the United States for the elimination of gender bias from the courts — legislative reform, enhanced legal representation of women litigants, increased numbers of women lawyers and judges. These measures have been accompanied by an intensive educational program aimed at judges right across the country. Women judges and women lawyers in the United States played a very active role in the creation of this program. They were able to persuade substantial numbers of their male peers that gender bias, like all other forms of bias they had worked so hard to eradicate, violated the core principle of judicial impartiality and neutrality and posed an increasing threat in the seventies and eighties to the maintenance of public confidence in the judiciary.

As might be anticipated, a direct frontal attack on gender bias in the courts and especially the institution of an educational program for judges on this subject[] was highly controversial and would probably have died on the vine but for the support of a substantial number of the country's leading male judges and educators who recognized the profound changes that were taking place in the society[,] including a major redefinition of the roles of men and women.

Professor Wikler has been one of the moving forces behind the United States program to sensitize judges to the problem of gender bias. She reports some modest indicators of success of the program, although she acknowledges that it is too early to assess the long term effects. She reports that requests for speakers and material generated from courses and workshops indicate a growing interest as does also the positive evaluation by judges themselves of the courses presented. Even more gratifying, attorneys practising in States where the program has been actively promoted report a noticeable increase in judicial sensitivity to gender bias. Program materials have been cited in the courts and quoted in the judgments. Judicial Conduct Commissions are disciplining judges for gender biased behaviour such as sexist remarks to women lawyers and litigants and inappropriate comments in rape cases. Professor Wikler concludes that one very important goal has been achieved: gender bias is now a subject which judges and judicial educators think and care about.[19]

Another development in the United States has been the establishment of judicially appointed Task

Forces to investigate the extent to which gender bias exists in the judiciary. The first of these Task Forces was created in New Jersey in 1982 and, as stated by Chief Justice Wilentz, was mandated to "investigate the extent to which gender bias exists in the New Jersey judicial branch, and to develop an educational program to eliminate any such bias".[20] Since 1982 over twenty other States have created Task Forces. Lynn Hecht Schafran, in her article "The Success of the American Program", reports that the Task Forces have significantly enhanced judicial education programs and have created a level of public awareness that generates its own pressures for reform.[21]

Schafran identifies four reasons why a judicially appointed Task Force is important as opposed to other groups outside the court system focussing on particular concerns. The first is that a gender bias Task Force is able to look at a broad range of issues and demonstrate a pattern of gender bias that manifests itself throughout the judicial system. The second reason is credibility. She explains this critical reason in the following manner:

> When a coalition of rape crisis counsellors asserts that rape victims are ill-treated in court, or a women's bar association claims that women attorneys are denied a fair share of appointments to challenging and lucrative civil and criminal cases, these charges are heard as the claims of special interest groups. When a blue ribbon panel appointed by a state's chief justice makes these same charges, people listen. There was little in what the New Jersey and New York Task Forces reported that numerous women's rights organizations and feminists' legal commentators have not been saying for years, but the task force reports twice made the front page of the New York Times.[22]

The third reason relates to the administration of the Task Force. The Chief Justice of the State is in a position to authorize funds, compel co-operation, endorse and propose reforms and ensure their implementation, and support judicial education on the subject. A final reason in favour of the Task Force route to reform is that such a task force brings together judges, lawyers, law professors, and community activists to study an issue which many of them do not initially appreciate is an issue at all. Schafran reports that Task Force members from New Jersey and New York "who start out with no knowledge of gender bias in the courts, or even a conviction that the idea is nonsense, emerge from the data collection process convinced that the problem is real and has deeply serious implications for the administration of justice."[23]

So, where do we stand in Canada on this matter? Well, as you might expect, feminist scholars in Canada have over the past two decades produced a vast quantity of literature on the subject, some of it, in my view, very insightful, very balanced and very useful, and some of it very radical, quite provocative and probably less useful as a result. But all of it, it seems to me, is premised, at least as far as judicial decision-making is concerned, on two basic propositions, one that women view the world and what goes on in it from a different perspective from men, and two that women judges, by bringing to bear that perspective on the cases on which they sit, can play a major role in introducing judicial neutrality and impartiality into the justice system.

Let me say right away from my own experience as a judge of fourteen years' standing, working closely with my male colleagues on the bench, that in my view there are probably whole areas of the law on which there is no uniquely feminine perspective. This is not to say that the development of the law in these areas has not been influenced by the fact that the lawyers and the judges have all been men. But rather that the principles and the underlying premises are so firmly entrenched and, in my opinion, so fundamentally sound that no good would be achieved by attempting to re-invent the wheel, even if the revised version did have a few more spokes in it. I have in mind areas such as the law of contract, the law of real property and the law applicable to corporations. In some other areas of the law, however, I think that a distinctly male perspective is clearly discernible and has resulted in legal principles that are not fundamentally sound and should be revisited as and when the opportunity presents itself. Canadian feminist scholarship has, in my view, done an excellent job of identifying those areas and making suggestions for reform. Some aspects of the criminal law in particular cry out for change since they are based on presuppositions about the nature of women and women's sexuality that in this day and age are little short of ludicrous.

But how do we handle the problem that women judges, just as much as their male counterparts, are subject to the duty of impartiality? As we said at the outset, judges must not approach their task with pre-conceived notions about law and policy. They must approach it with detachment and, as Lord MacMillan said, purge their minds "not only of partiality to persons but of partiality to arguments."[24] Does this then foreclose any kind of "judicial affirmative action" to counteract the influence of the dominant male perspective of the past and establish judicial neutrality through a countervailing female perspective? Is Karen Selick, writing recently in the Lawyers Weekly, correct when she argues that offsetting male bias with female bias would only be compounding the injustice?[25] Does the nature of the judicial process itself present an insuperable hurdle so that the legislatures rather than the courts must be looked to for any significant legal change?

I think in part this may be so. Certainly, the legislature is the more effective instrument for rapid or radical change. But I see no reason why the judiciary cannot exercise some modest degree of creativity in areas where modern insights and life's experience have indicated that the law has gone awry. However, and I think this is extremely important, it will be a Pyrrhic victory for women and for the justice system as a whole if changes in the law come only through the efforts of women lawyers and women judges. The Americans were smart to realize that courses and workshops on gender bias for judges male and female are an essential follow-up to scholarly research and learned writing. In Canada we are just beginning to touch the fringes.

The first national, interdisciplinary conference on the relationship between judicial neutrality and gender equality was held in Banff, Alberta, in May of 1986. At the conference judges, academics, practising lawyers and experts in anthropology, political science, sociology and social welfare examined judicial behaviour in equality related matters. The judicial acceptance of traditional stereotypes concerning women was noted as well as its impact in Canada on important areas of constitutional equality litigation, family law, criminal law, tort law and human rights.[26]

Mr. Justice Rothman of the Quebec Court of Appeal, one of the speakers at the conference, endorsed the approach adopted in the United States to counteract gender bias through nation-wide educational programs for judges and the creation of judicial task forces. In his perception, women face the same kind of discrimination in Canada as they do in the United States and we should be working to change the old attitudes *now*. He suggested that conferences and seminars for newly appointed judges would be a good place to start but, in addition, courses on gender bias should be part of the continuing education programs for judges at all stages of their careers. Justice Rothman added that it is not, however, going to be enough to sensitize judges to equality issues if lawyers are not sensitized to them as well![27]

The Canadian Judicial Council and the Canadian Judicial Centre have both recognized the need for judicial education in this area and will include gender issues in their summer seminars for judges this year. I understand that the Centre hopes to subsequently present the program in a number of locations across the country and the course materials will be available to all Canadian judges. I heartily endorse this initiative. It is, in my view, a significant first step towards the achievement of true judicial neutrality. But it is only a first step and there is a long way to go.

Coming back then to the question whether the appointment of more women judges will make a difference. Because the entry of women into the judiciary is so recent, few studies have been done on the subject. Current statistics, however, show that just over nine percent of federally appointed judges are women[28] and it is reasonable to assume that more and more women will be appointed to the Bench as more and more women become licensed to practise law. Will this growing number of women judges by itself make a difference?

The expectation is that it will; that the mere presence of women on the bench will make a difference. In an article entitled "The Gender of Judges", Suzanna Sherry, an Associate Law Professor at the University of Minnesota, suggests that the mere fact that women are judges serves an educative function and helps to shatter stereotypes about the role of women in society that are held by male judges and lawyers as well as by litigants, jurors and witnesses.[29]

Judge Gladys Kessler, former President of the National Association of Women Judges in the United States, defends the search for competent women appointees to the bench. She says:

> But the ultimate justification for deliberately seeking judges of both sexes and all colors and backgrounds is to keep the public's trust. The public must perceive its judges as fair, impartial and representative of the diversity of those who are being judged.[30]

Justice Wald has expressed similar sentiments. She believes that women judges are indispensable to the public's confidence in the ability of the courts to respond to the legal problems of all classes of citizens.[31]

Diane Martin, a criminal lawyer writing in the Lawyers Weekly, sees another way in which the presence of women on the bench is helpful and constructive. It is easier, she says, for women lawyers to appear as counsel before a woman judge. She says the "difference is that you are 'normal' — you and the judge have certain shared experiences and a shared reality that removes, to a certain extent, the need to 'translate' your submissions into 'man talk' or a context that a male judge will understand."[32] The woman judge does not see you as "out of place" or having "something to prove by appearing in a courtroom arguing a case before her."[33]

For women counsel, appearing in front of a woman judge also decreases the risk of sexist comments and inappropriate efforts at humour. The courtroom treatment of women litigants, witnesses and lawyers was examined by the New Jersey and New York task forces. The New York Task Force found that "[w]omen uniquely, disproportionately, and with unacceptable frequency must endure a climate of condescension, indifference, and hostility".[34] The New Jersey Task Force found strong evidence that women are often treated differently in courtrooms, in judges' chambers and at professional gatherings.[35] As Justice Rothman pointed out at the Banff conference, there is no excuse for a judge allowing himself or anyone else in his courtroom to make unprofessional or inappropriate references to gender. He saw as a possible solution the appointment of more women judges and more courteous and sensitive male judges![36]

Some feminist writers are persuaded that the appointment of more women judges will have an impact on the process of judicial decision-making itself and on the development of the substantive law. As I mentioned earlier, this flows from the belief that women view the world and what goes on in it from a different perspective from men. Some define the difference in perspective solely in terms that women do not accept male perceptions and interpretations of events as the norm or as objective reality. Carol Gilligan, a Professor of Education at Harvard University, sees the difference as going much deeper than that. In her view women think differently from men, particularly in responding to moral dilemmas. They have, she says, different ways of thinking about themselves and their relationships to others.[37]

In her book, *In a Different Voice*,[38] Gilligan analyses data she collected in the form of responses from male and female participants in a number of different studies. These responses, she submits, support her central thesis that women see themselves as essentially connected to others and as members of a community while men see themselves as essentially autonomous and independent of others. Gilligan makes no claim about the origins of the differences she describes. She does, however, use the psychoanalytical work of Dr. Nancy Chodorow as a starting point.[39] Chodorow postulates that gender differences arise from the fact that women do the mothering of children. Because the gender identity of male children is not the same as their mothers, they tend to distance and separate themselves from their mothers' female characteristics in order to develop their masculinity. Female children, on the other hand, define themselves through attachment to their mothers.[40] Masculinity is therefore, according to Gilligan, defined through separation and individualism while femininity is defined through attachment and the formation of relationships. The gender identity of the male, she submits, is threatened by relationships while the gender identity of the female is threatened by separation.[41]

Gilligan's work on conceptions of morality among adults suggests that women's ethical sense is significantly different from men's. Men see moral problems as arising from competing rights; the adversarial process comes easily to them. Women see moral problems as arising from competing obligations, the one to the other, because the important thing is to preserve relationships, to develop an ethic of caring. The goal, according to women's ethical sense, is not seen in terms of winning or losing but rather in terms of achieving an optimum outcome for all individuals involved in the moral dilemma.[42] It is not difficult to see how this contrast in thinking might form the basis of different perceptions of justice.

I think there is merit in Gilligan's analysis. I think it may in part explain the traditional reluctance of courts to get too deeply into the circumstances of a case, their anxiety to reduce the context of the dispute to its bare bones through a complex system of exclusionary evidentiary rules. This is, it seems to me, one of the characteristic features of the adversarial process. We are all familiar with the witness on cross-examination who wants to explain his or her answer, who feels that a simple yes or no is not an adequate response, and who is frustrated and angry at being cut off with a half truth. It is so much easier to come up with a black and white answer if you are unencumbered by a broader context which might prompt you, in Lord MacMillan's words, to temper the cold light of reason with the warmer tints of imagination and sympathy.[43]

It may explain also the hostility of some male judges to permitting intervenors in human rights cases. The main purpose of having intervenors is to broaden the context of the dispute, to show the issue in a larger perspective or as impacting on other groups not directly involved in the litigation at all. But it certainly does complicate the issues to have them presented in polycentric terms.

Professor Patricia Cain of the University of Texas in an article entitled "Good and Bad Bias: A Comment on Feminist Theory and Judging" says:

What we want, it seems to me, are lawyers who can tell their client's story, lawyers who can help judges to see the parties as human beings, and who can help remove the separation between judge and litigant. And, then, what we want from our judges is a special ability to listen with connection before engaging in the separation that accompanies judgment.[44]

Obviously, this is not an easy role for the judge — to enter into the skin of the litigant and make his or her experience part of your experience and only when you have done that, to judge. But I think we have to do it; or at least make an earnest attempt to do it. Whether the criticism of the justice system comes to us through Royal Commissions, through the media or just through our own personal friends, we cannot escape the conclusion that in some respects our existing system of justice has been found wanting. And as Mr. Justice Rothman says — the time to do something about it is *now*.

One of the important conclusions emerging from the Council of Europe's Seminar on Equality between Men and Women held in Strasbourg last November is that the universalist doctrine of Human Rights must include a realistic concept of masculine and feminine humanity regarded as a whole, that human kind *is* dual and must be represented in its dual form if the trap of an asexual abstraction in which "human being" is always declined in the masculine is to be avoided.[45] If women lawyers and women judges through their differing perspectives on life can bring a new humanity to bear on the decision-making process, perhaps they *will* make a difference. Perhaps they will succeed in infusing the law with an understanding of what it means to be fully human.

(e) *R. v. S. (R.D.)*[†]

[GONTHIER J. and La Forest J.:]

[26] I have had the benefit of the reasons of Justice Cory, the joint reasons of Justices L'Heureux-Dubé and McLachlin and the reasons of Justice Major. I agree with Cory J. and L'Heureux-Dubé and McLachlin JJ. as to the disposition of the appeal and with their exposition of the law on bias and impartiality and the relevance of context. However, I am in agreement with and adopt the joint reasons of L'Heureux-Dubé and McLachlin JJ in their treatment of social context and the manner in which it may appropriately enter the decision-making process as well as their assessment of the trial judge's reasons and comments in the present case.

[L'HEUREUX-DUBÉ and McLACHLIN JJ.:]

I. INTRODUCTION

[27] We have read the reasons of our colleague, Justice Cory, and while we agree that this appeal must be allowed, we differ substantially from him in how we reach that outcome. As a result, we find it necessary to write brief concurring reasons.

[28] We endorse Cory J.'s comments on judging in a multicultural society, the importance of perspective and social context in judicial decision-making, and the presumption of judicial integrity. However, we approach the test for reasonable apprehension of bias and its application to the case at bar somewhat differently from our colleague.

[29] In our view, the test for reasonable apprehension of bias established in the jurisprudence is reflective of the reality that while judges can never be neutral, in the sense of purely objective, they can and must strive for impartiality. It therefore recognizes as inevitable and appropriate that the differing experiences of judges assist them in their decision-making process and will be reflected in their judgments, so long as those experiences are relevant to the cases, are not based on inappropriate stereotypes, and do not prevent a fair and just determination of the cases based on the facts in evidence.

---

† [1997] 3 S.C.R. 484 at paras. 60, aff'g (1995) 145 N.S.R. (2d) 284, 418 A.P.R. 284, 102 C.C.C. (3d) 233, 45 C.R. (4th) 361, aff'g [1995] N.S.J. No. 184 (QL).

[30] We find that on the basis of these principles, there is no reasonable apprehension of bias in the case at bar. Like Cory J. we would, therefore, overturn the findings by the Nova Scotia Supreme Court (Trial Division) and the majority of the Nova Scotia Court of Appeal that a reasonable apprehension of bias arises in this case, and restore the acquittal of R.D.S. This said, we disagree with Cory J.'s position that the comments of Judge Sparks were unfortunate, unnecessary, or close to the line. Rather, we find them to reflect an entirely appropriate recognition of the facts in evidence in this case and of the context within which this case arose — a context known to Judge Sparks and to any well-informed member of the community.

II. THE TEST FOR REASONABLE APPREHENSION OF BIAS

[31] The test for reasonable apprehension of bias is that set out by de Grandpré J. in *Committee for Justice and Liberty* v. *National Energy Board*, [1978] 1 S.C.R. 369. Though he wrote dissenting reasons, de Grandpré J.'s articulation of the test for bias was adopted by the majority of the Court, and has been consistently endorsed by this Court in the intervening two decades: see, for example, *Valente* v. *The Queen*, [1985] 2 S.C.R. 673; *R.* v. *Lippé*, [1991] 2 S.C.R. 114; *Ruffo* v. *Conseil de la magistrature*, [1995] 4 S.C.R. 267. De Grandpré J. stated, at pp. 394–95:

> ... the apprehension of bias must be a reasonable one, held by reasonable and right-minded persons, applying themselves to the question and obtaining thereon the required information.... [T]hat test is "what would an informed person, viewing the matter realistically and practically — and having thought the matter through — conclude. Would he think that it is more likely than not that [the decision-maker], whether consciously or unconsciously, would not decide fairly."
>
> The grounds for this apprehension must, however, be substantial and I ... refus[e] to accept the suggestion that the test be related to the "very sensitive or scrupulous conscience".

[32] As Cory J. notes at para. 92, the scope and stringency of the duty of fairness articulated by de Grandpré depends largely on the role and function of the tribunal in question. Although judicial proceedings will generally be bound by the requirements of natural justice to a greater degree than will hearings before administrative tribunals, judicial decision-makers, by virtue of their positions, have nonetheless been granted considerable deference by appellate courts inquiring into the apprehension of bias. This

is because judges "are assumed to be [people] of conscience and intellectual discipline, capable of judging a particular controversy fairly on the basis of its own circumstances": *United States* v. *Morgan*, 313 U.S. 409 (1941), at p. 421. The presumption of impartiality carries considerable weight, for as Blackstone opined at p. 361 in Commentaries on the Laws of England, Book III, cited at footnote 49 in Richard F. Devlin, "We Can't Go On Together with Suspicious Minds: Judicial Bias and Racialized Perspective in R. v. R.D.S." (1995), 18 Dalhousie L.J. 408, at p. 417, "the law will not suppose a possibility of bias or favour in a judge, who is already sworn to administer impartial justice, and whose authority greatly depends upon that presumption and idea". Thus, reviewing courts have been hesitant to make a finding of bias or to perceive a reasonable apprehension of bias on the part of a judge, in the absence of convincing evidence to that effect: *R.* v. *Smith & Whiteway Fisheries Ltd.* (1994), 133 N.S.R. (2d) 50 (C.A.), at pp. 60–61.

[33] Notwithstanding the strong presumption of impartiality that applies to judges, they will nevertheless be held to certain stringent standards regarding bias — "a reasonable apprehension that the judge might not act in an entirely impartial manner is ground for disqualification": *Blanchette* v. *C.I.S. Ltd.*, [1973] S.C.R. 833, at pp. 842–43.

[34] In order to apply this test, it is necessary to distinguish between the impartiality which is required of all judges, and the concept of judicial neutrality. The distinction we would draw is that reflected in the insightful words of Benjamin N. Cardozo in The Nature of the Judicial Process (1921), at pp. 12–13 and 167, where he affirmed the importance of impartiality, while at the same time recognizing the fallacy of judicial neutrality:

> There is in each of us a stream of tendency, whether you choose to call it philosophy or not, which gives coherence and direction to thought and action. Judges cannot escape that current any more than other mortals. All their lives, forces which they do not recognize and cannot name, have been tugging at them — inherited instincts, traditional beliefs, acquired convictions; and the resultant is an outlook on life, a conception of social needs.... In this mental background every problem finds its setting. We may try to see things as objectively as we please. None the less, we can never see them with any eyes except our own.
>
> ...
>
> Deep below consciousness are other forces, the likes and the dislikes, the predilections and

the prejudices, the complex of instincts and emotions and habits and convictions, which make the [person], whether he [or she] be litigant or judge.

[35] Cardozo recognized that objectivity was an impossibility because judges, like all other humans, operate from their own perspectives. As the Canadian Judicial Council noted in Commentaries on Judicial Conduct (1991), at p. 12, "[t]here is no human being who is not the product of every social experience, every process of education, and every human contact". What is possible and desirable, they note, is impartiality:

> ... the wisdom required of a judge is to recognize, consciously allow for, and perhaps to question, all the baggage of past attitudes and sympathies that fellow citizens are free to carry, untested, to the grave.
>
> True impartiality does not require that the judge have no sympathies or opinions; it requires that the judge nevertheless be free to entertain and act upon different points of view with an open mind.

III.   THE REASONABLE PERSON

[36] The presence or absence of an apprehension of bias is evaluated through the eyes of the reasonable, informed, practical and realistic person who considers the matter in some detail (Committee for Justice and Liberty, supra.) The person postulated is not a "very sensitive or scrupulous" person, but rather a right-minded person familiar with the circumstances of the case.

[37] It follows that one must consider the reasonable person's knowledge and understanding of the judicial process and the nature of judging as well as of the community in which the alleged crime occurred.

A.   The Nature of Judging

[38] As discussed above, judges in a bilingual, multiracial and multicultural society will undoubtedly approach the task of judging from their varied perspectives. They will certainly have been shaped by, and have gained insight from, their different experiences, and cannot be expected to divorce themselves from these experiences on the occasion of their appointment to the bench. In fact, such a transformation would deny society the benefit of the valuable knowledge gained by the judiciary while they were members of the Bar. As well, it would preclude the achievement of a diversity of backgrounds in the judiciary. The reasonable person does not expect that

judges will function as neutral ciphers; however, the reasonable person does demand that judges achieve impartiality in their judging.

[39] It is apparent, and a reasonable person would expect, that triers of fact will be properly influenced in their deliberations by their individual perspectives on the world in which the events in dispute in the courtroom took place. Indeed, judges must rely on their background knowledge in fulfilling their adjudicative function. As David M. Paciocco and Lee Stuesser write in their book The Law of Evidence (1996), at p. 277:

> In general, the trier of fact is entitled simply to apply common sense and human experience in determining whether evidence is credible and in deciding what use, if any, to make of it in coming to its finding of fact. [Emphasis in original.]

[40] At the same time, where the matter is one of identifying and applying the law to the findings of fact, it must be the law that governs and not a judge's individual beliefs that may conflict with the law. Further, notwithstanding that their own insights into human nature will properly play a role in making findings of credibility or factual determinations, judges must make those determinations only after being equally open to, and considering the views of, all parties before them. The reasonable person, through whose eyes the apprehension of bias is assessed, expects judges to undertake an open-minded, carefully considered, and dispassionately deliberate investigation of the complicated reality of each case before them.

[41] It is axiomatic that all cases litigated before judges are, to a greater or lesser degree, complex. There is more to a case than who did what to whom, and the questions of fact and law to be determined in any given case do not arise in a vacuum. Rather, they are the consequence of numerous factors, influenced by the innumerable forces which impact on them in a particular context. Judges, acting as finders of fact, must inquire into those forces. In short, they must be aware of the context in which the alleged crime occurred.

[42] Judicial inquiry into the factual, social and psychological context within which litigation arises is not unusual. Rather, a conscious, contextual inquiry has become an accepted step towards judicial impartiality. In that regard, Professor Jennifer Nedelsky's "Embodied Diversity and the Challenges to Law" (1997), 42 McGill L.J. 91, at p. 107, offers the following comment:

What makes it possible for us to genuinely judge, to move beyond our private idiosyncracies and preferences, is our capacity to achieve an "enlargement of mind". We do this by taking different perspectives into account. This is the path out of the blindness of our subjective private conditions. The more views we are able to take into account, the less likely we are to be locked into one perspective.... It is the capacity for "enlargement of mind" that makes autonomous, impartial judgment possible.

[43] Judicial inquiry into context provides the requisite background for the interpretation and the application of the law. For example, in a case involving alleged police misconduct in denying an accused's right to counsel, this Court inquired not simply into whether the accused had been read their *Charter* rights, but also used a contextual approach to ensure that the purpose of the constitutionally protected right was fulfilled: *R. v. Bartle*, [1994] 3 S.C.R. 173. The Court, placing itself in the position of the accused, asked how the accused would have experienced and responded to arrest and detention. Against this background, the Court went on to determine what was required to make the right to counsel truly meaningful. This inquiry provided the Court with a larger picture, which was in turn conducive to a more just determination of the case.

[44] An understanding of the context or background essential to judging may be gained from testimony from expert witnesses in order to put the case in context: *R. v. Lavallee*, [1990] 1 S.C.R. 852, *R. v. Parks* (1993), 15 O.R. (3d) 324 (C.A.), and *Moge v. Moge*, [1992] 3 S.C.R. 813, from academic studies properly placed before the Court; and from the judge's personal understanding and experience of the society in which the judge lives and works. This process of enlargement is not only consistent with impartiality; it may also be seen as its essential precondition.

[45] A reasonable person far from being troubled by this process, would see it as an important aid to judicial impartiality.

B. The Nature of the Community

[46] The reasonable person, identified by de Grandpré J. in Committee for Justice and Liberty, supra, is an informed and right-minded member of the community, a community which, in Canada, supports the fundamental principles entrenched in the Constitution by the Canadian Charter of Rights and Freedoms. Those fundamental principles include the principles of equality set out in s. 15 of the Charter and endorsed in nation-wide quasi-constitutional provincial and federal human rights legislation. The reasonable person must be taken to be aware of the history of discrimination faced by disadvantaged groups in Canadian society protected by the Charter's equality provisions. These are matters of which judicial notice may be taken. In Parks, supra, at p. 342, Doherty J.A., did just this, stating:

> Racism, and in particular anti-black racism, is a part of our community's psyche. A significant segment of our community holds overtly racist views. A much larger segment subconsciously operates on the basis of negative racial stereotypes. Furthermore, our institutions, including the criminal justice system, reflect and perpetuate those negative stereotypes.

[47] The reasonable person is not only a member of the Canadian community, but also, more specifically, is a member of the local communities in which the case at issue arose (in this case, the Nova Scotian and Halifax communities). Such a person must be taken to possess knowledge of the local population and its racial dynamics, including the existence in the community of a history of widespread and systemic discrimination against black and aboriginal people, and high profile clashes between the police and the visible minority population over policing issues: Royal Commission on the Donald Marshall Jr. Prosecution (1989); *R. v. Smith* (1991), 109 N.S.R. (2d) 394 (Co. Ct.). The reasonable person must thus be deemed to be cognizant of the existence of racism in Halifax, Nova Scotia. It follows that judges may take notice of actual racism known to exist in a particular society. Judges have done so with respect to racism in Nova Scotia. In *Nova Scotia (Minister of Community Services) v. S.M.S.* (1992), 110 N.S.R. (2d) 91 (Fam Ct.), it was stated at p. 108:

> [Racism] is a pernicious reality. The issue of racism existing in Nova Scotia has been well documented in the Marshall Inquiry Report (sub. nom. Royal Commission on the Donald Marshall, Jr., Prosecution). A person would have to be stupid, complacent or ignorant not to acknowledge its presence, not only individually, but also systemically and institutionally.

[48] We conclude that the reasonable person contemplated by de Grandpré J., and endorsed by Canadian courts is a person who approaches the question of whether there exists a reasonable apprehension of bias with a complex and contextualized understanding of the issues in the case. The reasonable person understands the impossibility of judicial neu-

trality, but demands judicial impartiality. The reasonable person is cognizant of the racial dynamics in the local community, and, as a member of the Canadian community, is supportive of the principles of equality.

[49] Before concluding that there exists a reasonable apprehension of bias in the conduct of a judge, the reasonable person would require some clear evidence that the judge in question had improperly used his or her perspective in the decision-making process; this flows from the presumption of impartiality of the judiciary. There must be some indication that the judge was not approaching the case with an open mind fair to all parties. Awareness of the context within which a case occurred would not constitute such evidence; on the contrary, such awareness is consistent with the highest tradition of judicial impartiality.

IV. APPLICATION OF THE TEST TO THE FACTS

[50] In assessing whether a reasonable person would perceive the comments of Judge Sparks to give rise to a reasonable apprehension of bias, it is important to bear in mind that the impugned reasons were delivered orally. As Professor Devlin puts it in "We Can't Go On Together with Suspicious Minds: Judicial Bias and Racialized Perspective in R. v. R.D.S.", supra, at p. 414:

> Trial judges have a heavy workload that allows little time for meticulously thought-through reasoning. This is particularly true when decisions are delivered orally immediately after counsel have finished their arguments.

(See also *R. v. Burns*, [1994] 1 S.C.R. 656, at p. 664.)

It follows that for the purposes of this appeal, the oral reasons issued by judge Sparks should be read in their entirety, and the impugned passages should be construed in light of the whole of the trial proceedings and in light of all other portions of the judgment.

[51] Judge Sparks was faced with contradictory testimony from the only two witnesses, the appellant R.D.S., and Constable Stienburg. Both testified as to the events that occurred and were subjected to cross-examination. As trier of fact, Judge Sparks was required to assess their testimony, and to determine whether or not, on the evidence before her, she had a reasonable doubt as to the guilt of the appellant

R.D.S. It is evident in the transcript that Judge Sparks proceeded to do just that.

[52] Judge Sparks briefly summarized the contradictory evidence offered by the two witnesses, and then made several observations about credibility. She noted that R.D.S. testified quite candidly, and with considerable detail. She remarked that contrary to the testimony of Constable Stienburg, it was the evidence of R.D.S. that when he arrived on the scene on his bike, his cousin was handcuffed and not struggling in any way. She found the level of detail that R.D.S. provided to have "a ring of truth", and found him to be "a rather honest young boy". In the end, while Judge Sparks specifically noted that she did not accept all the evidence given by R.D.S., she nevertheless found him to have raised a reasonable doubt by raising queries in her mind as to what actually occurred.

[53] It is important to note that having already found R.D.S. to be credible, and having accepted a sufficient portion of his evidence to leave her with a reasonable doubt as to his guilt, Judge Sparks necessarily disbelieved at least a portion of the conflicting evidence of Constable Stienburg. At that point, Judge Sparks made reference to the submissions of the Crown that "there's absolutely no reason to attack the credibility of the officer", and then addressed herself to why there might, in fact, be a reason to attack the credibility of the officer in this case. It is in this context that Judge Sparks made the statements which have prompted this appeal:

> The Crown says, well, why would the officer say that events occurred the way in which he has relayed them to the Court this morning. I am not saying that the Constable has misled the court, although police officers have been known to do that in the past. I am not saying that the officer overreacted, but certainly police officers do overreact, particularly when they are dealing with non-white groups. That to me indicates a state of mind right there that is questionable. I believe that probably the situation in this particular case is the case of a young police officer who overreacted. I do accept the evidence of [R.D.S.] that he was told to shut up or he would be under arrest. It seems to be in keeping with the prevalent attitude of the day.
>
> At any rate, based upon my comments and based upon all the evidence before the court I have no other choice but to acquit.

[54] These remarks do not support the conclusion that Judge Sparks found Constable Stienburg to have

lied. In fact, Judge Sparks did quite the opposite. She noted firstly, that she was not saying Constable Stienburg had misled the court, although that could be an explanation for his evidence. She then went on to remark that she was not saying that Constable Stienburg had overreacted, though she was alive to that possibility given that it had happened with police officers in the past, and in particular, it had happened when police officers were dealing with non-white groups. Finally, Judge Sparks concluded that, though she was not willing to say that Constable Stienburg did overreact, it was her belief that he probably overreacted. And, in support of that finding, she noted that she accepted the evidence of R.D.S. that "he was told to shut up or he would be under arrest".

[55] At no time did Judge Sparks rule that the probable overreaction by Stienburg was motivated by racism. Rather, she tied her finding of probable overreaction to the evidence that Constable Stienburg had threatened to arrest the appellant R.D.S. for speaking to his cousin. At the same time, there was evidence capable of supporting a finding of racially motivated overreaction. At an earlier point in the proceedings, she had accepted the evidence that the other youth arrested that day[] was handcuffed and thus secured when R.D.S. approached. This constitutes evidence which could lead one to question why it was necessary for both boys to be placed in choke holds by Constable Stienburg, purportedly to secure them. In the face of such evidence, we respectfully disagree with the views of our colleagues Cory and Major JJ. that there was no evidence on which Judge Sparks could have found "racially motivated" overreaction by the police officer.

[56] While it seems clear that Judge Sparks did not in fact relate the officer's probable overreaction to the race of the appellant R.D.S., it should be noted that if Judge Sparks had chosen to attribute the behaviour of Constable Stienburg to the racial dynamics of the situation, she would not necessarily have erred. As a member of the community, it was open to her to take into account the well-known presence of racism in that community and to evaluate the evidence as to what occurred against that background.

[57] That Judge Sparks recognized that police officers sometimes overreact when dealing with non-white groups simply demonstrates that in making her determination in this case, she was alive to the well-known racial dynamics that may exist in interactions between police officers and visible minorities. As found by Freeman J.A. in his dissenting judgment at the Court of Appeal (1995), 145 N.S.R. (2d) 284, at p. 294:

> The case was racially charged, a classic confrontation between a white police officer representing the power of the state and a black youth charged with an offence. Judge Sparks was under a duty to be sensitive to the nuances and implications, and to rely on her own common sense which is necessarily informed by her own experience and understanding.

[58] Given these facts, the question is whether a reasonable and right-minded person, informed of the circumstances of this case, and knowledgeable about the local community and about Canadian Charter values, would perceive that the reasons of Judge Sparks would give rise to a reasonable apprehension of bias. In our view, they would not. The clear evidence of prejudgment required to sustain a reasonable apprehension of bias is nowhere to be found.

[59] Judge Sparks' oral reasons show that she approached the case with an open mind, used her experience and knowledge of the community to achieve an understanding of the reality of the case, and applied the fundamental principle of proof beyond a reasonable doubt. Her comments were based entirely on the case before her, were made after a consideration of the conflicting testimony of the two witnesses and in response to the Crown's submissions, and were entirely supported by the evidence. In alerting herself to the racial dynamic in the case, she was simply engaging in the process of contextualized judging which, in our view, was entirely proper and conducive to a fair and just resolution of the case before her.

V.   CONCLUSION

[60] In the result, we agree with Cory J. as to the disposition of this case. We would allow the appeal, overturn the findings of the Nova Scotia Supreme Court (Trial Division) and the majority of the Nova Scotia Court of Appeal, and restore the acquittal of the appellant R.D.S.

(f)　Re Conduct of Honourable Paul Cosgrove of the Ontario Superior Court of Justice[†]

Canadian Judicial Council

IN THE MATTER OF

Section 65 of the *Judges Act*, R.S., 1985, c. J-1, and of the Inquiry Committee convened by the Canadian Judicial Council to review the conduct of the Honourable Paul Cosgrove of the Ontario Superior Court of Justice:

REPORT OF THE CANADIAN JUDICIAL COUNCIL TO THE MINISTER OF JUSTICE

Pursuant to its mandate under the *Judges Act*, and after inquiring into the conduct of Justice Cosgrove, the Canadian Judicial Council hereby recommends to the Minister of Justice, pursuant to section 65 of the *Judges Act*, that the Honourable Paul Cosgrove be removed from office, for the reasons outlined in this Report.

Presented in Ottawa, 30 March 2009

INTRODUCTION

[1] Public confidence in the judiciary is essential in maintaining the rule of law and preserving the strength of our democratic institutions. All judges have both a personal and collective duty to maintain this confidence by upholding the highest standards of conduct. After inquiring into the conduct of the Honourable Paul Cosgrove, we find that he has failed in the due execution of his office to such an extent that public confidence in his ability to properly discharge his judicial duties in the future cannot be restored. In the result, we conclude that a recommendation be made to the Minister of Justice that Justice Cosgrove be removed from office.

BACKGROUND

[2] On 27 November 2008, we received the *Report to the Canadian Judicial Council of the Inquiry Committee Appointed to Conduct an Investigation Into the Conduct of Mr. Justice Paul Cosgrove, a Justice of the Ontario Superior Court of Justice* (the "Inquiry Committee Report"). This inquiry resulted from the request made by the Attorney General of Ontario on 22 April 2004 pursuant to subsection 63(1) of the *Judges Act*.

[3] From 1997 to 1999, Justice Cosgrove presided over the murder trial of Julia Elliott. A stay of proceedings was granted on 7 September 1999 after Justice Cosgrove concluded that there had been over 150 violations of Ms Elliott's rights under the *Canadian Charter of Rights and Freedoms*. On appeal, the stay of proceedings was set aside, and a new trial was ordered. The Court of Appeal remarked (*R. v. Elliott* (2003), 179 O.A.C. 219, at paragraph 166):

> We conclude this part of our reasons as we began. The evidence does not support most of the findings of Charter breaches by the trial judge. The few Charter breaches that were made out, such as non-disclosure of certain items, were remedied before the trial proper would have commenced had the trial judge not entered the stay of proceedings. The trial judge made numerous legal errors as to the application of the Charter. He made findings of misconduct against Crown counsel and police officers that were unwarranted and unsubstantiated. He misused his powers of contempt and allowed investigations into areas that were extraneous to the real issues in the case.

[4] Following a challenge to the constitutionality of subsection 63(1) of the *Judges Act* by Justice Cosgrove, and subsequent appeals, the Inquiry Committee proceedings resumed on 2 September 2008. The full procedural history of the complaint, the Inquiry, and the related proceedings, is set out in the Inquiry Committee Report at paragraphs 3 to 26.

[5] In its review of the judge's conduct, the Inquiry Committee adopted the reasoning of the Supreme Court of Canada in *Moreau-Bérubé v. New Brunswick (Judicial Council)*, [2002] 1 S.C.R. 249 (paragraph 58):

---

† From Report of the Canadian Judicial Council to the Minister of Justice, presented in Ottawa, March 30, 2009. [Notes and/or references omitted.] Reproduced with permission.

In some cases, however, the actions and expressions of an individual judge trigger concerns about the integrity of the judicial function itself. When a disciplinary process is launched to look at the conduct of an individual judge, it is alleged that an abuse of judicial independence by a judge has threatened the integrity of the judiciary as a whole. The harm alleged is not curable by the appeal process.

[6] The Inquiry Committee found that the judge's conduct included: an inappropriate aligning of the judge with defence counsel giving rise to an apprehension of bias; an abuse of judicial powers by a deliberate, repeated and unwarranted interference in the presentation of the Crown's case; the abuse of judicial powers by inappropriate interference with RCMP activities; the misuse of judicial powers by repeated inappropriate threats of citations for contempt or arrest without foundation; the use of rude, abusive or intemperate language; and the arbitrary quashing of a federal immigration warrant.

[7] The members of the Inquiry Committee then agreed unanimously as follows (paragraph 167):

> In our opinion, the evidence we have characterized as lack of restraint, abuse of judicial independence, or abuse of judicial powers fully warrants a recommendation for removal from office, subject to whatever effect may be given to the judge's statement [of apology] of 10 September 2008.

[8] After considering the judge's statement and the submissions, four out of the five members of the Inquiry Committee concluded as follows (paragraph 189):

> For the reasons given above, the words used and the conduct engaged in by Justice Cosgrove, over a prolonged period of time, constitute a failure in the due exercise of his office by abusing his powers as a judge. They give rise to a reasonable and irremediable apprehension of bias. Regrettably, his statement is insufficient to offset the serious harm done to public confidence in the concept of the judicial role, as described in the Marshall test. He has rendered himself incapable of executing the judicial office.

[9] Chief Justice Allan Wachowich, a member of the Inquiry Committee, indicated in dissenting reasons that while he agreed with the conclusion of the Committee as quoted at paragraph 7 of these reasons, he accepted the view of Independent Counsel, following Justice Cosgrove's apology, that the judge could be strongly admonished and not removed from office.

[10] In accordance with section 9 of the *Canadian Judicial Council Inquiries and Investigations By-Laws*, Justice Cosgrove advised Council that he wished to appear in person to make an oral statement about the Report of the Inquiry Committee. Justice Cosgrove and Independent Counsel provided written submissions for Council's consideration.

[11] At the Council meeting held on 6 March 2009 to consider the Inquiry Committee Report and the response of Council to it, both Justice Cosgrove and his Counsel, Mr Chris Paliare, spoke.

[12] In his statement to Council, Justice Cosgrove confirmed that his personal statement of 10 September 2008 to the Inquiry Committee was intended to be an unqualified recognition of his judicial misconduct and an unqualified apology. He repeated these sentiments in his statement before us. Justice Cosgrove asked that Council, in assessing its recommendation to the Minister of Justice in this matter, take into account his entire judicial career and that the conclusion of the majority of the Inquiry Committee be rejected.

[13] In his submissions on behalf of Justice Cosgrove, Mr Paliare confirmed that the Committee findings of judicial misconduct were not disputed, but asked that Council not recommend to the Minister of Justice that Justice Cosgrove be removed from office. In his submission, the letters of support filed in support of Justice Cosgrove, the opinion expressed by Independent Counsel that a strong admonition was an appropriate sanction, the fact that Justice Cosgrove had sat effectively without incident for 4½ years after the events at issue and, finally, his statement to the Inquiry Committee and his remarks to Council, should lead to the application of a lesser sanction than removal.

[14] Independent Counsel, Mr Earl Cherniak, also spoke. He reiterated his view that "significant weight can be placed on the apology made by Justice Cosgrove" so that a strong admonition was an appropriate outcome in the circumstances, but also noted that both conclusions (removal or a lesser sanction) were open on the evidence. He emphasized that, in the end, the decision was for Council to make and not Independent Counsel.

ISSUES

[15] In discharging our duties pursuant to subsection 65(2) of the *Judges Act*, we must follow a two-stage process, as described in the *Majority Reasons of the*

Canadian Judicial Council In the Matter of an Inquiry into the Conduct Of the Honourable P. Theodore Matlow, 3 December 2008 (see, in particular, paragraph 166). First, we must decide whether or not the judge is "incapacitated or disabled from the due execution of the office of judge" within the meaning of subsection 65(2) of the *Judges Act*. If this question is answered in the affirmative, we must then proceed to the second stage and determine if a recommendation for removal is warranted.

[16] Counsel for Justice Cosgrove, in his written submission, acknowledges that the judge engaged in judicial misconduct and that "it falls within paragraph 65(2)(b) of the *Judges Act*." He also repeated, in relation to the judge's apology, that it "was, and was intended to be, a sincere admission of judicial misconduct."

> Submissions of the Honourable Paul Cosgrove, 26 January 2009, paragraph 107.

[17] Independent Counsel shares this view. He agrees (at paragraph 32 of his written submission) that the misconduct as found by the Inquiry Committee would certainly warrant removal in the absence of a genuine apology: "Independent Counsel was, and is, of the view that, absent Justice Cosgrove's apology, the facts presented to and found by the Inquiry Committee were capable [of] supporting a recommendation for removal to the Minister of Justice."

[18] Given the thorough and cogent analysis of the extensive evidence before the Inquiry Committee, we have no difficulty in agreeing and adopting as our own the conclusions reached by the Committee as expressed in paragraph 167 of its Report. There can be no doubt that Justice Cosgrove engaged in serious judicial misconduct, within the meaning of the *Judges Act*.

[19] Accordingly, it remains for Council to proceed to the second stage and determine if public confidence in the judge's ability to discharge the duties of his office has been undermined to such an extent that a recommendation for removal is warranted. In this regard, we adopt the standard identified by Council in the *Marshall* matter and widely applied in other cases since then:

> Is the conduct alleged so manifestly and profoundly destructive of the concept of the impartiality, integrity, and independence of the judicial role, that public confidence would be sufficiently undermined to render the judge incapable of executing the judicial office?

[20] In order to assess the judge's conduct in relation to this standard, we must answer the following three questions:

1. What is the effect of Justice Cosgrove's statements of apology made before the Inquiry Committee and again before the Council?
2. What is the effect of the views expressed by Independent Counsel regarding removal?
3. What is the effect of taking into account the judge's entire judicial career, character and abilities, as described in the letters of support and submissions from counsel?

[21] We will address each question in turn.

The Apologies

[22] As noted, Justice Cosgrove apologized in person before both the Inquiry Committee and the Canadian Judicial Council. We wish to highlight some key passages from the transcripts of the lengthy hearing before the Inquiry Committee:

> ... I approached each decision I made with an open mind, and I never acted in bad faith, but I now realize that **I made a series of significant errors** that affected the proceedings. ...
>
> ... I made many findings against the Ministry of the Attorney General and its senior representatives, Crown counsel, police officers and public officials that were set aside by the Court of Appeal. **I erred in so doing and I regret those errors**. I regret the effect of my findings on them. ...
>
> ... For the **significant errors** that I have described, I sincerely and unreservedly apologize ...
>
> Finally, I would like to apologize to the family of the victim of this crime who, as a result of **my legal errors**, experienced a significant delay in achieving the closure arrived at by having a criminal prosecution reach its substantive conclusion.
>
> *Transcript of the proceedings before the Inquiry Committee, 10 September 2008, pages 1660 to 1665 — emphasis added*

[23] We also highlight the following passages from the hearing before Council:

> I understood, and I accepted that judgement. Nevertheless, I was sustained by my view that **notwithstanding the errors I had clearly made, those errors had been made in good faith** and what was now obviously a misguided attempt to achieve justice in the case. ...

... Moreover, I would like [to] apologize, again, to the family of the victim of the crime who, **as a result of my errors**, have experienced a significant delay in achieving the closure arrived at by having the criminal prosecution reach its substantive conclusion.

Transcript of proceedings before the Canadian Judicial Council, 6 March 2009, pages 8 and 11-12 — emphasis added

[24] We note that the focus of the apologies appears to be directed more to the "errors" made during the *Elliott* trial and less on a recognition that many of these "errors" were caused by, or constituted in and of themselves, serious misconduct that was damaging both to the administration of justice and the public's confidence in the judiciary. These errors went far beyond the types of errors that can be readily corrected by appellate courts.

[25] As found by the Inquiry Committee, the judge's conduct included: giving rise to an apprehension of bias; repeated and unwarranted interference in the presentation of the Crown's case; inappropriate interference with RCMP activities; inappropriate threats of citations for contempt or arrest without foundation; the use of rude, abusive or intemperate language; and the arbitrary quashing of a federal immigration warrant. These are not mere judicial errors.

[26] Justice Cosgrove made these additional comments before us:

The last thing that I would hope for would be to bring disrespect to this office. I realize that by my actions and my judicial misconduct, I may have done that. I deeply and acutely regret the prospect that my actions may have done damage to this office.

[27] Counsel for Justice Cosgrove argues that the judge's apology was:

... a sincere, complete, and abject apology for acts of judicial misconduct and other acts which may not even amount to judicial misconduct but nevertheless had a significant and troubling effect on the lives of public servants and citizens. It was a promise to do better in the future, which was informed and infused by reference to the canonical works of the CJC.

Submissions on behalf of the Honourable Paul Cosgrove, 26 January 2009, paragraph 100.

[28] Independent Counsel's view is that:

The recognition of errors made by Justice Cosgrove, his apparent understanding and recog-

nition of the impact of his conduct, and the set of full and unreserved apologies he provided led Independent Counsel to the opinion that, in his view, it is unlikely that this conduct will happen again, such that public confidence in the administration of justice could be restored by a pointed and strong admonition.

Submissions of Independent Counsel, February 2009, paragraph 41.

[29] We agree that an apology is an important factor for Council to consider in assessing the future conduct of a judge and, specifically, whether the judge recognizes that they have engaged in misconduct and, further, whether there is a reasonable prospect that the judge will sincerely strive to avoid inappropriate conduct in future.

[30] Justice Cosgrove's apology in this case addresses both of these aspects. Even accepting that the judge's apology was sincere, we must consider an additional — more important — aspect in deciding whether a recommendation for removal is warranted: the effect upon public confidence of the actions of the judge in light of the nature and seriousness of the misconduct.

[31] For Council, therefore, the key question is whether the apology is sufficient to restore public confidence. Even a heartfelt and sincere apology may not be sufficient to alleviate the harm done to public confidence by reason of serious and sustained judicial misconduct. The Supreme Court of Canada in *Moreau-Bérubé* considered the factors that must be considered by a Judicial Council in such circumstances:

[72] The comments of judge Moreau-Bérubé, as well as her apology, are a matter of record. In deciding whether the comments created a reasonable apprehension of bias, the Council applied an objective test, and attempted to ascertain the degree of apprehension that might exist in an ordinary, reasonable person.... In discharging its function, the Council must be acutely sensitive to the requirements of judicial independence, and it must ensure never to kill the expression of unpopular, honestly held views in the context of court proceedings. It must also be equally sensitive to the reasonable expectations of an informed dispassionate public that holders of judicial office will remain at all times worthy of trust, confidence and respect.

[32] Although the New Brunswick Judicial Council in the *Moreau-Bérubé* matter noted that a timely apology had been made, three days after the misconduct, the Supreme Court of Canada did not disturb the

decision of the New Brunswick Judicial Council that, in light of the severity of the judge's misconduct, the application of the identified objective test required the removal of the judge despite the judge's apology.

[33] The Inquiry Committee Report, in Part III, reviews and quotes in some detail the uncontested testimony of four witnesses on the severe effects on them of Justice Cosgrove's conduct in the *Elliott* case (paragraphs 109 to 120). In accepting the uncontradicted evidence as reliable, the Inquiry Committee noted "the credibility of the witnesses was beyond question and they gave compelling evidence" (paragraph 108). We agree.

[34] In this case, it is our conclusion that the misconduct by Justice Cosgrove was so serious and so destructive of public confidence that no apology, no matter its sincerity, can restore public confidence in the judge's future ability to impartially carry out his judicial duties in accordance with the high standards expected of all judges. This was not a single instance of misconduct but, rather, misconduct that was pervasive in both scope and duration.

[35] We endorse the majority's conclusion in regard to the judge's apology (paragraph 187):

> Given the judge's serious misconduct over an extended period of time, this statement, even viewed in its most positive light, cannot serve to restore public confidence in the judge, or in the administration of justice.

[36] In our opinion, the statement made before us by Justice Cosgrove did not add to, or change, the nature and effect of his earlier apology.

[37] It is significant to note that Justice Cosgrove acknowledges that public confidence in his ability to preside [over] certain cases has been seriously shaken. He explains:

> However, under the circumstances, in the event I am assigned to hear cases in the future, it would be inappropriate for me to sit in cases involving the Attorney General of Canada or Her Majesty The Queen in Right of Canada, or the Attorney General of Ontario or Her Majesty The Queen in Right of Ontario, and I would take steps to ensure that that would not occur.
>
> *Transcript of proceedings before the Inquiry Committee, 10 September 2008, page 1667.*

[38] The Inquiry Committee pointed out (at paragraph 188 of its report): "One may well ask what such a direction would say about the ability of the judge to execute his office." We agree. It seems to

us that this concession is a tacit acknowledgement that a significant segment of those persons involved in litigation before the court, including federal and provincial Crown attorneys, may not have confidence in the judge's ability to judge impartially.

Timing of the apology of September 2008

[39] Much has been said about the timing of the apology. At paragraph 113 of his written submission, counsel for Justice Cosgrove argues that "it is difficult to see how Justice Cosgrove's statement could have been given prior to the inquiry. There is no process to do so. Moreover, his statement did not halt the work of the Inquiry Committee, which elected to receive all of the evidence marshal[l]ed by Independent Counsel in order to complete their mandate." Independent Counsel, in his oral submission to the Inquiry Committee, appears to suggest that Justice Cosgrove could not apologize earlier, given his challenge to the constitutionality of the process.

[40] While it is not strictly necessary to address this issue, given the decision just made, we make the following points. It was open to Justice Cosgrove to offer, at any time, an apology about his conduct but he did not. It appears that the judge did not, for years after the fact, appreciate that he had engaged in serious misconduct.

[41] Justice Cosgrove acknowledged his late realization:

> Recently, I began to prepare for the current hearing. My preparation has profoundly affected my appreciation of the circumstance of this case. Both on my own and with my counsel, I have spent literally weeks reviewing the record of the trial proceedings and even reviewing the bench books of the time.
>
> Finally, I have spent days in this room hearing independent counsel reading passages of the evidence from the proceedings.
>
> All of these steps have caused me to relive the trial, but, for the first time, from an entirely different perspective.
>
> *Transcript of proceedings before the Inquiry Committee, 10 September 2008, page 1666.*

[42] The tardiness of the judge's apology reveals both his lack of insight and his lack of appreciation of the impact of his egregious misconduct on public confidence in the judiciary.

[43] It must also be emphasized that the apology was not made any time soon after the constitutional issue was resolved against Justice Cosgrove. In fact, it was only on the seventh day of the eight days of the hearings before the Inquiry Committee that Justice Cosgrove finally tendered his apology. It's not surprising that the Inquiry Committee, after considering all the relevant circumstances, including the timing of Justice Cosgrove's statement, found the apology insufficient to restore public confidence. We agree fully with this conclusion.

Timing of the Attorney General's Request for an Inquiry

[44] Justice Cosgrove's counsel commented on the fact that the Attorney General did not request the commencement of an inquiry until 4 years had passed since the verdict in the *Elliott* matter. In his presentation before us, he argued:

> So if, in fact, there was a concern by the Attorney General about whether or not public confidence could be maintained with respect to Justice Cosgrove sitting, in my respectful view, there was no reason for him not to have written that letter sooner. These two processes could have gone on in parallel, and I simply put that forward to you as yet another factor which demonstrates clearly that Justice Cosgrove can and does have the confidence of the public to continue to sit as a judge.
>
> *Transcript of Council hearing, 6 March 2009,*
> *page 55.*

[45] This interpretation does not take into account the many duties of an Attorney General. Attorneys General have an overall responsibility to administer justice in the public interest. In regard to judicial conduct, Justice Sharlow, in *Attorney General of Canada v. Cosgrove* 2007 FCA 103, commented as follows:

> [35] An important aspect of the traditional constitutional role of the Attorney General of England is to protect the public interest in the administration of justice. In Canada, that role is now shared by all Attorneys General — the provincial Attorneys General within their respective provinces, and the Attorney General of Canada in federal matters.
>
> [36] The public interest in an appropriate procedure for the review of the conduct of judges is an aspect of the public interest in the administration of justice. Therefore, it seems to me to be consistent with Canadian constitutional principles for provincial Attorneys General to play a part in the review of the conduct of judges of the superior courts of their respective provinces.

[46] However, Attorneys General are also responsible for the prosecution of crimes. In discharging this duty, it is well established that Attorneys General must act with the highest standards of fairness. The *Crown Policy Manual* of the Attorney General of Ontario emphasizes that:

> Public confidence in the administration of criminal justice is bolstered by a system where Crown counsel are not only strong and effective advocates for the prosecution, but also Ministers of Justice with a duty to ensure that the criminal justice system operates fairly to all: the accused, victims of crime, and the public.
>
> *"Crown Policy Manual,"*
> *Ministry of the Attorney General of Ontario, 2005*

[47] Given an Attorney General's role and duties, it is understandable that the Attorney General of Ontario at the time did not request that Council commence an inquiry into the conduct of Justice Cosgrove, since the matter giving rise to the complaint was the subject of an appeal by his own Crown counsel. For that reason, we place little weight on the fact that there was a delay between the time of the events in the *Elliott* trial and the time of the request of the Attorney General.

[48] In fact, the Attorney General acted less than 2 months after the appeal period in regard to the decision of the Court of Appeal in *Elliott* lapsed. We find that this timing does not suggest, in any way, that the Attorney General's actions can be characterized as an indication of confidence in the abilities of Justice Cosgrove to properly discharge the duties of his office.

[49] Counsel for Justice Cosgrove also argues that no complaints were made by anyone during the 4½ years in question and that this, therefore, demonstrates continued confidence in Justice Cosgrove. However, the public would not have known of the existence or extent of the judicial misconduct until the time of the decision of the Court of Appeal in *Elliott*. The fact that there was no evidence presented to the Inquiry Committee about subsequent complaints does not lead to the conclusion advanced by Counsel for Justice Cosgrove.

The Views of Independent Counsel Regarding Removal

[50] Counsel for Justice Cosgrove argued that deference should be accorded to the views expressed by Independent Counsel in regard to removal.

[51] Independent Counsel did express his view, in his written submission to Council, that "public confidence in the administration of justice could be restored by a pointed and strong admonition."

[52] However, immediately after Justice Cosgrove made his statement to the Inquiry Committee on 10 September 2008, Independent Counsel had stated:

> I wish to say at the outset that nothing that I am about to say is intended to in any way fetter or interfere with the discretion that this panel has to find, conclude and recommend as you see fit should you see the case differently than I am about to tell you I see it.
>
> As I stated in my opening, my view is that judicial accountability is a matter entirely for the Canadian Judicial Council, including this panel, and not any other body, least of all independent counsel. In my view, that is the constitutional imperative of judicial independence.
>
> *Transcript of proceedings before the Inquiry Committee, 10 September 2008, page 1668.*

[53] At the hearing before us, Independent Counsel emphasized again that it was open to the Inquiry Committee to come to its own view and that both the majority and minority views regarding the judge's removal were defensible.

[54] The mandate of Independent Counsel, it must be remembered, is not that of a lawyer retained to achieve a certain result. His view is but one view, albeit a very important one, arrived at after considering all issues. It cannot be the case that the members of the Inquiry Committee are in a lesser position than Independent Counsel in coming to their own conclusion. Four of the five members of the Inquiry Committee were of the view that public confidence in the judge's ability to discharge his duties impartially could not be restored. We agree. Recommending that the judge be removed from office is a grave duty and, given the principle of judicial independence, one that must ultimately rest with Council.

The Judge's Career, Character and Abilities

[55] Counsel for Justice Cosgrove referred to the many letters of support which in his view are evidence of the judge's character and integrity. As Council stated in its Report to the Minister in the Matlow matter in regard to comparable evidence:

> While the weight to be given to this evidence is admittedly for the inquiry committee, and while

an inquiry committee may elect to give it little weight, still it is an error in principle to simply ignore this kind of evidence for all purposes. In particular, the evidence is relevant to the sanction phase of the proceedings and ought to have been considered in that context.
> *"Majority Reasons of the Canadian Judicial Council In the Matter of an Inquiry into the Conduct Of the Honourable P. Theodore Matlow," 3 December 2008, Paragraph 150*

[56] However, it is clear that the Inquiry Committee considered the letters of support but elected to give them no weight, given that there were unique circumstances before the Inquiry Committee not present in the *Matlow* matter (paragraph 38):

> We mention here also that we are not giving weight to the letters submitted to us on behalf of Justice Cosgrove in our determination of whether his conduct in *Elliott* should lead to a recommendation for removal. One element in some of the letters was that what Justice Cosgrove did in *Elliott* was isolated conduct. The two Court of Appeal decisions, *Perry* and *Lovelace*, might have suggested otherwise. We are leaving both the letters and the two decisions to the side and, as we said, confining our analysis to what happened in *Elliott*.

[57] We are of the view that the opinions of individuals, be they judicial colleagues or otherwise, who do not have the benefit of the evidentiary record and a complete knowledge and appreciation of the issues before Council, will generally be of little assistance in determining whether public confidence has been undermined to such an extent as to render a judge incapable of discharging the duties of their office. In this particular instance, we accord little weight to the letters of support. They may provide insight into the judge's character and work ethic, but they do not address the decisive issue before us, namely the damage done to public confidence by virtue of the judge's judicial misconduct. This is an issue that rightly rests with the Inquiry Committee and Council itself.

THE ISSUE OF INCOMPETENCE

[58] While not required to do so, we wish to make some observations about the issue of incompetence.

[59] The Inquiry Committee expressed the view that some of Justice Cosgrove's conduct demonstrated incompetence. They also expressed the view (at paragraph 151) that "such pervasive incompetence is of grave concern and is bound to undermine public confidence in the administration of justice." We agree.

[60] However, the Inquiry Committee was ultimately of the opinion that (paragraph 152):

> ... [W]e consider that the public interest concern against removal for incompetence as expressed by Professor Shetreet should be given primacy. Protecting the judicial independence of all judges is more important than sanctioning the troubling incompetence of one.

[61] This perspective would appear to be based on the idea that since judicial independence protects a judge, after the fact, from having to justify or explain their decision, there should be no scrutiny of the judge's competence in arriving at a particular decision. However, we note the countervailing view, as indicated by Professor Shetreet, that incompetence could be grounds for removal in certain serious cases.

[62] In light of our earlier conclusion, we need not address whether incompetence could justify removal from office. The *Judges Act* refers in section 65 to a judge who "has become incapacitated or disabled" (in the French version "*est inapte*"). We are of the view that whether incompetence can be a ground for removal from office, in any given case, would best be dealt with another day, when the issue is more directly raised.

DECISION

[63] We agree with the conclusions reached by the majority of the members of the Inquiry Committee, as outlined in paragraph 189 of their report, which we now repeat:

> For the reasons given above, the words used and the conduct engaged in by Justice Cosgrove, over a prolonged period of time, constitute a failure in the due exercise of his office by abusing his powers as a judge. They give rise to a reasonable and irremediable apprehension of bias. Regrettably, his statement is insufficient to offset the serious harm done to public confidence in the concept of the judicial role, as described in the Marshall test. He has rendered himself incapable of executing the judicial office.

[64] We find that Justice Cosgrove has failed in the execution of the duties of his judicial office and that public confidence in his ability to discharge those duties in future has been irrevocably lost. We find that there is no alternative measure to removal that would be sufficient to restore public confidence in the judge in this case. Therefore, we hereby recommend to the Minister of Justice, in accordance with section 65 of the *Judges Act*, that Justice Cosgrove be removed from office.

Law Enforcement Personnel

(a) Plural Policing: A Comparative Perspective — Canada†

George S. Rigakos and Cherie Leung

This chapter deals with the structure of contemporary Canadian policing by examining the variable roles of both public-sector and commercial security provision in the last three decades. It covers core municipal, provincial, and federal public policing as well as other quasi-public and ancillary state regulatory inspectorates and the rapid growth of private policing bodies especially in large metropolitan areas. The general approach is to provide a concise overview of the state of contemporary Canadian policy and to identify current large-scale demographic trends that are indicative of the future direction of public and private security provision in this country.

STATE POLICING

One of Canada's unique features is its identification with its federal police as a national symbol of sovereignty. The Royal Canadian Mounted Police (RCMP), affectionately known as the 'Mounties,' are perhaps internationally the most widely recognized police agency in their unique red tunic, Strathcona boots, and wide-brimmed hats. The RCMP's 'great march west,' their storied civilizing effect during the Klondike gold rush, and their reputation for 'always getting their man' is an embedded part of the Canadian national identity (e.g. Horrall 1973; Macleod 1976). While the RCMP are a federal, centralized, quasi-military constabulary, they are also responsible for local municipal and provincial policing through contractual relationships with regional municipalities,

provinces, and federal territories except in Québec and Ontario (who maintain their own provincial services: the Ontario Provincial Police and Sûreté du Québec). Of course, the RCMP still maintain primary responsibility for federal issues such as co-ordinating with Interpol, maintaining a centralized national police criminal database, national security and terrorism, co-ordinating efforts in drug trafficking, organized crime, and security for major international events.

When one includes specialized aboriginal policing, there are generally four levels of public policing in Canada: municipal, provincial, federal, and First Nations. The five largest Canadian police forces, the RCMP, Metropolitan Toronto Police, OPP, Sûreté du Québec, and the Montréal Urban Community Police, are thus alternately federal, municipal or provincial and account for over 60 percent of all Canadian police officers. First Nations policing is governed by an assortment of direct policing agreements between aboriginal communities across Canada and the RCMP, the OPP, or the Sûreté du Québec.[1] In certain instances, stand-alone First Nations police services have responsibility for policing their own communities and in others the community uses tribal police or band constables pursuant to the Indian Act. The latter band constables may enforce band bylaws but are not fully sworn constables. Bayley (1985: 57) adeptly describes the existing configuration of Canadian public policing as a *decentralized–co-ordinated–multiple* system because 'in any

---

† From Trevor Jones and Time Newburn (eds.), Plural Policing: A Comparative Perspective (New York: Routledge, 2006) 126–38. [Notes and/or references omitted.] Copyright c2006 Routlege, reproduced with permission of Taylor & Francis Books UK.

one place policing is overwhelmingly the responsibility of a single force — though that force may be variously national, provincial, or municipal.' When a contracted provincial force (or the RCMP) is removed, another fills its place with limited jurisdictional overlap. There is thus a great degree of variation across Canada when one looks at the number of police officers employed in the 581 Canadian municipal police services. For example, as of 1997, 196 municipal forces were RCMP contracts and 36 others were OPP contracts (Swol 1999: 13) while Canada's three federal territories (Yukon, Northwest, and Nunavut) had no municipal police whatsoever.

Municipal police services, therefore, vary greatly in size and operating expenditures — from Canada's largest municipal force, the Metropolitan Toronto Police Service with an annual operating budget of over $635 million to RCMP detachments such as Qualicum Beach, British Columbia at $389,689. The RCMP is thus a federal service but more than half of its officers provide policing services to provinces, territories or municipalities under contract to these levels of government. Overall, in 2001, total policing expenditures in Canada totaled $7.3 billion which represents an increase of 6.9 percent from 2000.

In constant dollars, expenditures are up 4.2 percent, the fifth year in a row that costs have increased (Canadian Center for Justice Statistics 2002:57). While costs have been rising, public police demographics suggest that there has been an overall decrease in the number of uniformed public police officers relative to the Canadian population since the 1950s. It is difficult, indeed, to get an accurate count of state-sponsored policing given the wide host of other public servants who conduct regulatory and enforcement functions (Jones and Newburn 1999) (such as social housing special constables, railway and other transit police, wildlife, game and park wardens, Competition Bureau investigators, etc.,) but the statistics compiled by the federal government focus on the defensible barometer of uniformed public police officers per the defensible barometer of uniformed public police officers at the provincial, federal, and municipal levels. The largest rise in police officers per population took place after the 1960s. In 1960 there were fewer than 145 police officers per 100,000 population but by the mid-1970s this had risen to 200 police per 100,000 population, peaking in 1991 at 203. By 2000, however that number had dropped to 182 police per 100,000 population (Canadian Center for Justice Statistics 2001: 40–1) reflecting the recent belief that public policing has not kept pace with the Canadian population. The cost of public policing has thus risen while the number of uniformed police officers per capita has been declining in recent years, creating an emerging perception that the Canadian public is paying more for less. Between the 1988–89 fiscal year and the 1994–5 fiscal year, the cost for public police services per Canadian rose from $163 to $198 while controlling for inflation (Rigakos 2000b: 176).

The increased cost of public policing has long been considered to be a key factor behind the expansion of private security (Spitzer and Scull 1977) although, in the Canadian context, there has been no direct empirical support to substantiate this claim (Rigakos 2000b). This issue, among others, will be explored in a more substantive manner when considering private security later in this chapter. Canadian public police unionization since the late 1970s has surely contributed to higher wages through nationally coordinated collective bargaining teams. In addition, it is important to reflect on two recent developments that bear directly on the increasing per capita cost of public police: the drive toward regionalization, and state investment in policing in the aftermath of the terrorist attacks in New York City on 11 September 2001.

Given Canada's contract-based policing arrangements between municipalities and either provincial services or the RCMP, it is not surprising to see a movement towards the amalgamation of smaller forces as a third option. One of the most significant developments in Canadian policing over the last three decades has been a general move towards larger regional or provincially contracted detachments in lieu of smaller local policing units. This process accelerated in the 1990s as the conservative provincial government in Ontario, in keeping with their wide-ranging neo-liberal initiatives, passed legislation that amended the Police Services Act in favor of 'equitable police financing.' Whereas the provincial government historically subsidized smaller town policing, amendments pursuant to Bill 105 created new regional authorities that were responsible for the full costs of their own policing. The process of regionalization was already under way: from 1962 to 1996, 153 police services were amalgamated into 11 regional police services providing policing to over 60 percent of Ontario's population. After legislative changes introduced by the Conservative government, the Ontario Provincial Police went from providing 35 police service contracts in 1998 to 92 contracts with full cost recovery in 2002. The OPP managed to cut the number of subsidized contracts in the same period from 576 to 199. The provincial government also made it possible for municipalities to contract from more than one service in any given jurisdiction.

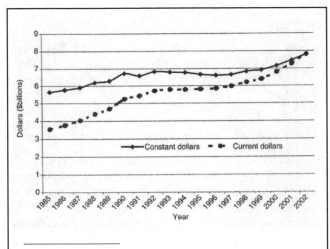

Figure 7.1. Current and constant dollar spending on policing, Canada, 1985–2002.
Source: Police Administration Survey, Canadian Centre for Justice Statistics

The main benefactors seem to be the OPP who contracted their specialized services such as emergency dispatch and detective work on top of local regional or municipal police patrol. Thus, as of 2003, the OPP was servicing 54 specialized contracts and providing quotes for an additional 24 municipalities (OPP 2003). This development lends itself to the possible long-term displacement of the dominant single-jurisdiction, single-police service model in Canada. In fact, the Quinte West police transition board entertained bids from private security companies for tertiary policing responsibilities to supplement the eventual creation of a regional police service (Rigakos 2002).

The federal government has for some time adopted a similar service delivery philosophy for the RCMP. From 1928 to 1966, the Solicitor General paid for 60 percent of local or provincial policing contracted with the RCMP. This federal share dropped slowly to 30 percent by 1990 and the long-term goal of the RCMP contract policing unit is 100 percent cost recovery. Thus, all expansions must be cost-neutral to the federal government. So, while the RCMP increased by five the number of its municipal contracts in British Columbia between 1997 to 2002, the municipal share of police expenditures also rose from 82.4 percent to 87.2 percent in the same five-year period (Canadian Center for Justice Statistics 1998: 18; Canadian Centre for Justice Statistics 2003: 23).

For both federal and provincial governments, the monetary incentive to divest policing responsibility to local regions and municipalities is rather transparent. But the move toward regional police services was also seen as essential for 'effective and efficient' policing. Despite this rationalization rhetoric there is actually contrary empirical evidence suggesting larger regional forces are no better or more effective than smaller, local police services based on measures such as clearance rates, and cost per officer (Lithopoulos and Rigakos forthcoming).

In the five years after 2005 federal expenditures on policing can be expected to increase due to the federal government's investment in the national security of Canadians following the terrorist attack in the United States on September 11, 2001. An immediate $280 million Anti-Terrorism Plan was announced in October 2001. Two months later, a new federal budget allocated $7.7 billion over five years for initiatives aimed at terrorism, including $1.6 billion for strengthened intelligence and policing. The funds are slated to enhance information-sharing capabilities among policing services and intelligence and national security agencies, as well as increase the number of police and intelligence officers and better equip them for response and prevention to terrorist activity (Canadian Center for Justice Statistics 2002: 21). By the time these initiatives are fully implemented they may have some effect on public police employment and expenditure statistics in Canada, including the police–citizen ratio.

OTHER STATE AND QUASI-STATE POLICING BODIES

There are myriad regulatory personnel involved in policing functions on behalf of Canada's three levels of government. These range from Canada's 400-plus park wardens, to tax investigators, to campus security, to military police, and the quasi-public Corps of Commissionaires, Canada's railway police, special constables who guard legislative assemblies, etc. Indeed, it would be impossible to cover even a representative minority of all of these various regulatory organizations. Instead, in this section we examine more closely three selected policing organizations that are of particular interest, playing as they do a prominent role in quasi-public policing in Canada.

The Corps of Commissionaires

The Corps of Commissionaires can trace their roots to 1859 and to Captain Edward Walter, who was concerned with the difficult transition of war veterans back into civilian life after the Crimean war. In 1915, the Governor General suggested that an organization similar to the British Corps of Commissionaires be formed in Canada after World War I. In 1925, the Canadian Corps of Commissionaires came into existence through a Federal Charter under a Letters Patent issued by the government.

Today, the Corps of Commissionaires is a private not-for-profit organization employing over 18,000 former members of the Armed Forces, the RCMP, and other organizations.[2] Some divisions of the Corps also recruit graduates with recognized law and security college qualifications, which has been somewhat controversial among executives in the private security industry. The Corps offers security services to businesses, industries, homeowners and provincial governments but its main client is the federal government through its role of guarding federal facilities and buildings. In 1945, the Corps of Commissionaires approached the Secretary of the Treasury Board for special dispensation. They argued that after the Second World War the number of security contracts filled by the Corps had been decreasing while the number of veterans available for work had increased. This resulted in the rather unique Treasury Board position that all federal departments, boards and commissions give first consideration to the Corps for all security service contracts. This has come to be known as the *right of first refusal* which means that all federal government security contracts are offered first to the Corps of Commissionaires. The Corps may choose to accept or reject contracts based on the availability of personnel. The right of first refusal was re-examined in 1996 and reinstated for another five years. In 2000, the Auditor General of Canada examined the policy and the right of first refusal was reinstated for another five years.

The Corps of Commissionaires is therefore in a rather ambiguous market position. Executives from security companies believe that the right of first refusal stunts competition and drives down market prices because members of the Corps are subsidized by their own federal and/or military pension plans. This allows the Corps of Commissionaires to accept contracts at very low rates. Indeed, the Corps of Commissionaires has more than doubled in size since 1961, from 5,211 officers gradually increasing to 11,217 officers in 1998 (see Figure 7.2). Proponents of the Corps argue that the agency fulfills a very important public function by providing employment to veterans. Moreover, the availability of the Corps allows the federal government to keep its security costs down all the while employing well-trained and certified security personnel who are also military pensioners. As it stands, the Corps of Commissionaires accepts about 80 percent of the right of first

Figure 7.2: Corps of Commissionaires, Canada, 1961–1999.
Source: Compiled b George S. Rigakos, Minutes of Meeting (Annual)

refusal contracts it is offered by the federal government. The Corps of Commissionaires is also typically the security service of preference by other jurisdictions such as small municipalities that contract with it for municipal bylaw enforcement. Another source of discontent among some security executives is that the Corps of Commissionaires has started an ancillary branch known as 'Corps 2' that competes alongside other private-contract security providers and employs non-veteran staff. The Corps' right of first refusal is once again under review by the Treasury Board. The federal government is a major employer of contract security services and a change of policy would have serious implications for the configuration of private security provision in Canada.

The Canadian Air Transport Security Authority (CATSA)

Unlike the Corps of Commissionaires, the Canadian Air Transport Security Authority (CATSA) has a very recent history, being established on 1 April 2002 in response to the terrorist attacks of 11 September 2001.[3] The new federal authority is also a not-for-profit Crown corporation but is responsible for key aviation issues pursuant to the new Canadian Air Transport Security Authority Act. CATSA is part of a $2.2 billion federal initiative for aviation security.

CATSA officers, in their distinct security uniforms, are deployed in airports across Canada. They are responsible for screening passengers and baggage, patrolling restricted areas, enforcing pass systems and overseeing the program of RCMP officers on board aircraft. To most Canadians, CATSA would appear to be a large, federal, uniformed security agency and this is intended. The 'common look and feel, including the new CATSA logo and uniform worn by screening officers' conveys the image of 'consistent service to travelers' and is aimed at contributing to 'a greater sense of professionalism among screening officers' (CATSA 2004: 21). In terms of who actually services the public, however, very little has changed. While CATSA sets minimum standards and requirements for screening officers, this task is still contracted out to private security providers. Whereas the mish-mash of uniforms that dominated airports across Canada (Rigakos 2000a: 145) seems to have become more homogenized, CATSA screening officers are nonetheless contracted security personnel from a variety of competing regional providers. In many cases, screening officers simply switched their company uniforms for CATSA uniforms. CATSA has, however, improved working conditions for screening officers by introducing minimum wages, the latest in screening technology, and improved training and the potential for career development which has purportedly resulted in lower turnover rates (CATSA 2004: 36). Alongside CATSA personnel, the Corps of Commissionaires still patrols airport parking lots and entranceways, issuing parking notices and enforcing municipal bylaws.

BIAs and Paid Duty Policing

The proliferation of Business Improvement Areas or Associations (BIAs) across North America has had particular effects on policing. BIAs concern themselves with improving the area around storefronts including lighting, pedestrian walkways, general beautification and promotional activities for merchants. A BIA allows local businesses to join together and organize, finance and carry out physical improvements and promote economic development in their district. The BIA reports to the local municipality which approves the budget of the association. According to the Ontario Business Improvement Association there are over 230 BIAs operating in the province.[4] In British Columbia there are another 53 BIAs in operation.[5] Canadian police researchers have pointed out how these BIAs have used private security to patrol high-traffic public areas and act as 'ambassadors' to shoppers and tourists (Murphy and Clarke 2002). The use of private security to patrol public streets is becoming increasingly common in Canada. In Halifax, the Spring Garden merchant district is patrolled by private security alongside the local municipal Halifax Police. In Gastown and the west end of Vancouver, BIAs employ uniformed ambassadors to direct tourists, issue parking notices, and move along undesirables. The Downtown Vancouver Business Improvement Association (DVBIA) meets regularly with the Vancouver public police to co-ordinate security efforts with its private security officers. Indeed, the DVBIA is perhaps the first Canadian BIA to have a full-time Crime Prevention Officer on its Board of Directors.

While the DVBIA utilizes private security guards to patrol public streets, the Yonge-Dundas BIA (YDBIA) in the heart of Toronto's merchant district employs paid duty Metropolitan Toronto Police officers. The YDBIA had difficulty with the high turnover of extra-duty police officers who patrolled the large downtown tract that includes over 1,400 businesses. In order to make sure its concerns were being met, the YDBIA Operations Manager insisted that police officers would file reports and conduct targeted runs on their patrols by visiting local merchants and asking them if there are any crime problems. This is probably the first instance in which public police officers are required to file shift reports summarizing their activities with a private client. The occurrence reports contain directions for officers including what stores they are to visit and a notification that failure to submit the reports will mean that they will not get paid. It is perhaps fitting that this development should take place in the heart of Toronto, where Shearing and Stenning first identified the rise of 'mass private property' (Shearing and Stenning 1983). Whereas the large tracts of feudal-like policing arrangements described by Shearing and Stenning increased the privatization of indoor spaces[6] such as large retail malls, thereby squeezing out the public police, here we have the mall literally being turned inside out in the same neighborhood and the police themselves being privatized.[7] In order to solidify their status to make arrests on behalf of merchants that line the YDBIA, the Metropolitan Toronto Police required that merchants fill out a Trespass to Property Act consent form allowing them to act as agents of the property owner for enforcing trespass-related issues. That downtown merchants would pool their resources together and insist that public police officers patrol their public storefronts and report in their association directly is truly revolutionary in the history of Canadian policing, albeit now common course for private security.

The interchangeability, overlapping jurisdiction, and cross-fertilization of public and private policing is thus perhaps most evident in the recent evolution of BIAs in Canada.

PRIVATE SECURITY

Ascertaining the relative size of the private security industry is no easy task in most national contexts (de Waard 1999; Jones and Newburn 1995). The generally accepted (conservative) estimate of the ratio of private security agents to public police officers in Canada is 2:1 (Swol 1999) despite more recent statistics that grossly under-count the industry based on national labor force estimates (Sanders 2003). It appears that the private security industry in Canada began to overtake the public police somewhere in the late sixties to early seventies (Rigakos 2000b) and that with the gradual decline of public police officers per 100,000 population, the private security industry has continued to increase the gap (see Figure 7.3). As might be imagined, the breadth of private security provision in this country is vast. Companies offer services ranging from forensic investigations to bodyguard services and access control. Although mass private property — especially with the development of large retail spaces — has dramatically affected delivery of security, Canada has not experienced the rapid growth of gated residential communities seen in the United States (Blakely and Snyder 1997).

Current oversight structures for the private security industry are in the hands of provincial registrars.

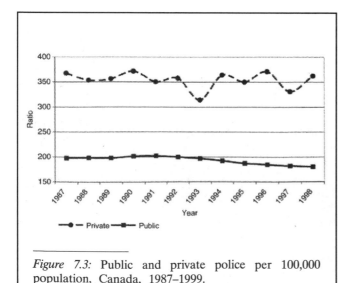

Figure 7.3: Public and private police per 100,000 population, Canada, 1987–1999.
Sources: Swol, 1999; CCJS, 2000.

With the exception of British Columbia and Newfoundland, there are no minimum training standards for security guards across Canada. Moreover, only contract private security personnel are required by law to pass background criminal history checks and the proprietary security sector is entirely unregulated. There has been a recent whirlwind of activity in Canada around regulating the private security industry including national radio documentaries, television specials, an international conference, and an imminent Report to Parliament on the relationship between public police and private security by the Law Commission of Canada. In the province of Ontario, a recent coroner's inquest into the death of Patrick Shand (a black shoplifter who died while being handcuffed and arrested by security agents in a Toronto Mall) resulted in recommendations that the private security industry be regulated, minimum training standards be set, and that the in-house security sector be brought into account. Given academic and policy concerns about the rise of the private security sector it would appear that changes are on the horizon, albeit 30 years overdue.

There is some comparative demographic information about the public police and private security industry in Canada. Women seem to be better represented in the private security industry on the whole depending on the type of work and company. Sanders (2003) reports that between 1991 to 2000 approximately 20 percent of security employees in Canada were female. In 1993, Erickson found that 34 percent of security guards in Toronto were women (Erickson 1993). However, in Rigakos' study of a private 'law enforcement company' that engaged in high-risk 'parapolicing' he found that only 8 percent of the workforce were women (Rigakos 2002: 85). There have been concerted efforts to increase recruitment and retention of female constables. Services such as day care and targeted recruiting have resulted in the gradual increase of women from 0.6 percent in 1962 to 12.2 percent in 1998 in public police services (Swol 1999: 8).

The percentage of Canadian-born security officers employed by contract firms has been reported at 57 percent in Ontario for 1980 (Shearing *et al.* 1980: 141), 44 percent in Toronto for 1993 (Erickson 1993: 15), and 23 percent for Rigakos' parapolic in 2002 (Rigakos 2002: 85). Comparatively, in 1998 only 7.6 percent of uniformed Metropolitan Toronto Police officers were members of visible minority groups (Rigakos 2002: 94). According to Statistics Canada, as of 1999, visible minorities accounted for 10 percent of the Canadian labor force, but only 3 percent of Canadian police officers. Aboriginal persons were

2 percent of the Canadian labor force but accounted for 3 percent of police officers (Swol 1999: 9).

CONCLUSIONS: PUBLIC AND PRIVATE POLICING IN CANADA AT THE CROSSROADS

The state of Canadian public and private policing is at a crossroads. The state was becoming increasingly involved in the use, management, and possible regulation of the private security sector even before the terrorist attack on New York City on 11 September 2001. Moreover, the interchangeable use of private security or paid duty public policing on public streets on behalf of BIAs is creating an atmosphere of increased competition and commodification (Loader 1999; Rigakos 2002) both between public police services, as in the case of regionalization and municipal sub-contracting, as well as between private security agencies and the public police. When the Yonge–Dundas BIA insisted that paid duty police officers report directly to the operations manager through shift reports it was under the auspices of a threat to move to private security. When the police transition board in Quinte West entertained bids for the policing contract under a new regional governance structure forced upon it by provincial neoliberal policies, the board listened to proposals from local town police, proposed regional forces, the Ontario Provincial Police, and even private security companies to perform 'tertiary policing' duties.

Radical proposals have been floated that would allow current regional Police Service Boards to contract with and license special constabularies and private security companies to perform ancillary policing tasks (CAPB, 2002). These newly constituted boards would be in charge of public security and have a dedicated budget aside from funds earmarked for the public regional or municipal force aimed at subsidized local initiatives for securing communities. As a mechanism for recovering 'the public good' (Loader and Walker 2001) in Canadian private policing, proposals from all quarters including academics, policy-makers, police associations, and security executives themselves have called for an oversight system that includes civilians on provincial licensing, regulatory, and enforcement commissions.

This chapter has only highlighted a few areas where the confluence and confusion about public and private policing in Canada are apparent. In the next few years many of the proposals alluded to above may be either ignored or acted upon by provincial and federal policy-makers. It remains to be seen whether or not market principles alone will dictate the future of security provision in this country or whether the state will reimpose itself to reclaim policing as public good.

(b) Police Investigating Police — Executive Summary†

Commission for Public Complaints Against the RCMP

The RCMP currently investigates its own members for statutory offences. At issue is whether or not an organization whose members' actions have resulted in serious injury or death should be the very same organization then charged with the responsibility to investigate the incident (with the prospect of laying criminal charges).

Investigations of RCMP members resulting from a number of high profile cases including that of Ian Bush, who was shot and killed by an RCMP member in 2005, to the 2007 death of Robert Dziekanski at the Vancouver International Airport (following the RCMP use of the conducted energy weapon), have brought the issue of police investigating police to front of mind domestically and internationally.

These cases raise a fundamental question. Can the current process of the RCMP investigating itself legitimately engender confidence in the transparency, impartiality and integrity of the criminal investigation and its outcome?

---

† Source "Executive Summary", *Police Investigating Police: Final Report*, pages iii–xvi, Commission for Public Complaints Against the RCMP, August 11, 2009. [Notes and/or references omitted.] Reproduced with permission of the Civilian Review and Complaints Commission for the RCMP, 2015.

The Chair of the Commission for Public Complaints Against the RCMP (CPC) set out to answer this and other questions by launching a public interest investigation on November 28, 2007, to assess the adequacy of how the RCMP investigates its own members, specifically in cases where member action resulted in serious injury or death.[1]

WHAT IS CURRENTLY GUIDING RCMP MEMBER INVESTIGATIONS?

An important part of the CPC assessment involved determining exactly how the RCMP is currently managing its own member investigations. To develop this baseline knowledge, the CPC looked at all legislation, policies and procedures currently guiding member investigations at the national and divisional (provincial)[2] level.

No specific requirements exist under the Criminal Code regarding how an investigation into police officers should be handled. And while specific reference to how police should investigate police is also absent from the *Royal Canadian Mounted Police Act (RCMP Act)*, there are a number of features of the *RCMP Act* that warrant special attention.

The first is section 37 of the *RCMP Act* which outlines eight guidelines for the appropriate behaviour expected of RCMP members at all times. This section legislates the imperative need for members, as representatives of the RCMP, to act respectfully, dutifully and free from conflict of interest, specifically requiring members to "avoid any actual, apparent or potential conflict of interests" (s. 37(d)). A second legislative feature is the Commissioner's Standing Orders (Public Complaints) (s. 9), which states: "A member shall not investigate a complaint where that member may be in a conflict of interest situation." Of particular concern is the fact that the term "conflict of interest" is not defined further in either the *RCMP Act* or the Commissioner's Standing Orders. Public and stakeholder criticism remains largely focused on the very issue that the nature of police investigating police creates a significant conflict of interest, or at the least the perception of one (particularly in cases of serious injury or death).

Of additional concern is subsection I.2.b of the Commissioner's Standing Orders, which states: "If, as a result of an investigation, a member is believed to have committed a statutory offence: 1. it is within RCMP primary jurisdiction, <u>take the same action as you would for any other person</u>." This passage is also found in the RCMP's *National Investigation Guidelines* (F.1.a) and repeated further in some divisional policies.

While the intention of the RCMP requesting that member investigations[3] be handled like any other investigation may be an honourable one (meaning without bias), the very nature of an investigation by one police officer into another is fundamentally different from the police investigating a member of the public for the exact same crime. Police are held to higher account by the very nature of the work they do. Like other professions that directly impact the safety and welfare of those they serve, there is a public expectation requiring that a higher standard of behaviour be upheld. By exposing the police thinking that investigations into its own members should be handled like any other investigation, we begin to identify the root philosophy guiding individual member behaviour.

It is therefore the CPC's contention that criminal investigations into RCMP members should **not** be treated the same as any other criminal investigation.

Given the absence of direction prescribed in legislation regarding how members should investigate other members, the adequacy of RCMP policy to ensure impartiality, transparency and rigour in the process becomes all the more paramount. Results of the CPC's policy analysis revealed inconsistencies in content and application across RCMP divisions. While the RCMP has developed a number of policies relating to how criminal investigations should be undertaken generally, very few policies address the issue of RCMP member-committed offences specifically. This is a serious concern.

The sheer volume and variety of RCMP policies with implications for the issue of police investigating police is overwhelmingly large (e.g. hundreds of pages of policy relevant to the PIP were reviewed for this report alone). This policy "overload" poses a great threat to the RCMP's operational effectiveness. The very nature of front-line policing requires that direction be provided in a format that is clear, concise and easy to access. As previously stated in other CPC reports, law drives policy, which drives training, which directly influences member behaviour.

Inconsistencies across divisions demonstrate the absence of clear guidance on the issue. In some policies at both the national and divisional level, involvement of an independent investigator or an external police force is mandatory; in others, it is left to the discretion of the officer in charge. Only three RCMP divisions currently have memoranda of agreement in place with the involvement of external police forces for the purpose of member investigations in specific cases. Similarly, only three divisional policies dictate the appointment of an independent investigator in cases of member-committed offences. Some divisional policies do not address the issue of officer-committed violations and the pursuant investigations at all. The scope of policy varies as well — while most national policies are limited to cases of serious injury or death, many divisional policies encompass all statutory violations.

While a new proposed RCMP national policy, *External Investigations or Review*, takes active steps towards providing consolidated guidance in relation to member investigations, the content remains vague and far too much discretion remains with the divisions (divisional Commanding Officers, Officers in Charge or Criminal Operations Officers) to determine an appropriate response.

CPC ASSESSMENT OF THE HANDLING OF RCMP MEMBER INVESTIGATIONS

With this baseline understanding of the current handling and procedures guiding member investigations, the CPC then requested that the RCMP divisions identify all files related to criminal investigations of RCMP members by other RCMP members between April 1, 2002 and March 31, 2007 involving assault causing bodily harm; sexual assault; and death, including death caused by operating a personal motor vehicle (PMV).

The retrieval of member investigation cases from the RCMP revealed critical issues in the RCMP's administrative handling and management of these types of investigations. RCMP national and divisional headquarters do not have any centralized tracking or monitoring capacity for member investigations. As such, most divisions generated relevant files for the CPC public interest investigation by searching through divisional records housed at their respective headquarters using key word searches. Some divisions were better able to narrow the scope of their search to fit the parameters of the review through effective record-keeping processes making for easier retrieval, while other divisions did not have the same capacity. Overall, the lack of national and divisional data collection — or monitoring capacity — for member investigations (combined with varied divisional RCMP record-keeping and retrieval methods on this issue) demonstrates a lack of attention being placed on member investigations.

Bearing these challenges in mind, the CPC reviewed all RCMP files received in order to determine which ones were relevant to the parameters of the public interest investigation. Approximately 150 of the 600 RCMP cases provided were deemed relevant to the parameters of the public interest investigation. Recognizing that it would be prohibitive to review *all* relevant cases, they were further reduced to a sample size of 28 cases representative of each of the three categories (14 assault causing bodily harm cases; eight sexual assault cases; and six death cases).

It is important to note that, as per the map outlined in the *CPC Data at a Glance* section, the RCMP's Central Region was not represented in the random sample because no cases were identified by Quebec (C) Division; Ontario (O) Division; and HQ (A) Division that fit the parameters of the Chair-initiated complaint. Furthermore, no files were identified by Nova Scotia (H) Division, and Prince Edward Island (L) Division. And while a small number of files were initially identified by the RCMP for New Brunswick (J) Division and Yukon Territory (M) Division, these files did not meet the CPC criteria and were therefore excluded. Of concern to the CPC is the absence of any cases identified by the bulk of the Maritime Provinces given the RCMP's contract policing role there.

With all relevant material identified, the CPC Review Team investigators analyzed all files and written material provided by the RCMP to assess the appropriate handling of each case against the established CPC criteria and terms of reference (specifically: line management, level of response, timeliness, member conduct, and compliance with policy). After completing a comprehensive file review of the 28 cases, the CPC Review Team investigators then recommended that full-field reviews be undertaken for a select number of cases. Overall, eight cases were selected for full-field review. Field interviews were conducted in various divisions and detachments. In total, 31 members were interviewed regarding the files selected for in-depth review. Thirteen civilians were asked to be interviewed for the purposes of this report but refused or did not respond to our request for an interview. One comment from a family member associated to one file stated: "It won't do any good. [The RCMP members involved] have all been promoted and transferred out."

CPC ASSESSMENT OF RCMP HANDLING OF MEMBER INVESTIGATIONS

The criteria used to assess each of the 28 cases and the resultant findings are outlined in detail in chapter 5 of this report. Below are some highlights of the CPC findings.

As per the complaint parameters, the CPC investigators assessed 28 cases in order to determine how appropriately each RCMP member investigation was handled against five key criteria: conduct, policy compliance, timeliness, line management and level of response.

Overall, **RCMP member conduct was deemed highly appropriate in 100% of the cases reviewed.** The CPC found that the RCMP investigators charged with the task of investigating another member acted professionally and free from bias.

The CPC investigators also concluded that **RCMP member policy compliance was appropriate in 93% of the cases. Only two minor policy violations were found.** It is important to note that this criterion sought only to determine how well members followed policy in place at the time of each investigation, and did not seek to assess the adequacy of these policies (this issue was assessed separately, as outlined previously).

The timeliness of member investigations was also deemed overall appropriate 82% of the time. Of the 28 cases reviewed, 60% were completed in six months or less. However, 19% of these cases took over one year to complete, thereby potentially excluding members from internal disciplinary processes, if required. Specific concerns were also raised around the handling of historical cases which took considerably longer to investigate (one historical case still remained ongoing after 28 months at the time of publication).

The two criteria the CPC investigators found of greatest concern were the RCMP's handling of the investigations in relation to **line management (which looked at any actual/perceived conflict of interest[,] appropriate management structure and reporting relationships)** and **level of response (which looked at how appropriate and proportionate the RCMP response was to the gravity of the incident).** Given the fact that these two criteria specifically relate to the process of *how* member investigations are handled, this analysis further helps to illustrate the fact that **CPC concerns relate largely to the current RCMP process (which is flawed) and not individual RCMP member action.**

Of particular concern to the CPC is the RCMP's line management, which was deemed to be appropriate in only 32% of the cases. Sixty-eight percent of the cases reviewed were deemed to be handled either partially or entirely inappropriately. Of particular concern was the fact that **25% of primary investigators identified themselves as per-**

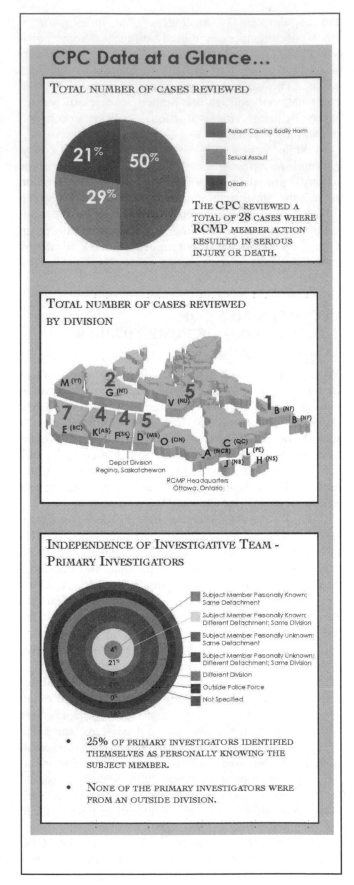

sonally knowing the subject member. Another critical concern is the fact that **in 60% of the cases reviewed, a single investigator was assigned** to investigate another member, thereby placing the integrity of the investigation at risk for potential conflict of interest or perception of bias.

Further, **in 32% of the cases, the primary investigator assigned was of the same or lower rank as the subject member**, thereby creating the potential for intimidation. Recommendations to address these concerns are outlined in greater detail in chapter 7, *CPC Recommended Model for RCMP Member Investigations*.

Of equal concern to the CPC is the 68% of cases deemed to be partially or entirely inappropriate for level of response. Of particular concern was the fact that **interviews with subject members and witness officers were conducted by a lone investigator in 17 of the 28 cases**, again creating the potential for intimidation or a conflict of interest.

It is important to note that while no specific conflicts of interest were noted in these particular cases, the practice of single-member interviews was deemed to be inappropriate.

CPC investigators also found a significant disparity in the qualifications of the investigators (including primary investigators) assigned to member investigations.

In addition, the complete **absence of reassignment of duties or adjustment of workload** for members assigned to investigators undertaking member investigations was also noted as a serious concern impacting the integrity and timeliness of member investigations undertaken. The call for an administrative review of member investigations was also found to be inconsistently applied across the country (an administrative review was only called for in four of the 28 cases).

Recommendations to address these concerns are outlined in greater detail in chapter 7, *CPC Recommended Model for RCMP Member Investigations*.

WHAT WE CAN LEARN FROM OTHER MODELS

Overall, an analysis of 14 different domestic and international police review agencies[4] was undertaken in an effort to determine how other jurisdictions handle allegations of police misconduct. Three types of models were identified based on the level of civilian involvement in the investigation: (1) Dependent Model, (2) Interdependent Model and (3) Independent Model.

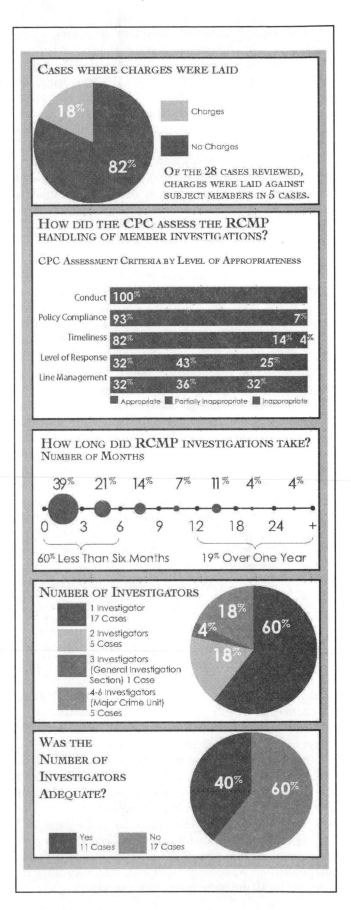

531

The **dependent model** essentially represents more traditional "police investigation of police." There is no civilian involvement in the criminal investigation and, therefore, there is a total dependence on the police for the handling of criminal investigations. There are two subcategories to this model: (1.1) police investigating police and (1.2) police investigating another police force.

In the police investigating police subcategory, the police service is fully responsible for the criminal investigation and administration of public complaints alleging criminal offences. The review body in question does not conduct criminal investigations, but it may recognize complaints regarding service, internal discipline or public trust.

The second sub-category involves "police investigating *another* police force" in specific cases so that the police service does not investigate its own members in instances of serious injury or death. In three selected Canadian provinces, formal memoranda of agreement exist between the local police and the RCMP that allow an outside police force to handle the investigations of the RCMP member(s).

The **interdependent model** introduces civilian involvement into the criminal investigation to varying degrees. There are also two sub-types to this model: (2.1) civilian observation and (2.2) hybrid investigation.

In the first sub-type of the interdependent model, a civilian observer is assigned to the police investigation to ensure that the latter is conducted with impartiality. The hybrid investigation comprises mostly of a civilian review body whose involvement in the investigation goes beyond the role of mere overseer. In this model, the police force may be engaged in some form of collaboration with the review body, although the latter may have the ability to conduct the investigation entirely on its own.

Examples of the interdependent model, which introduces civilian involvement into the police criminal investigation, are found in British Columbia, Saskatchewan, Alberta, Yukon, New Zealand, United Kingdom and South Australia.

The **independent model** is embodied by a totally independent criminal investigation with no police involvement. The review body composed of civilians undertakes independent criminal investigation and may have the authority to make binding findings and lay charges. Ontario's Special Investigations Unit, the Independent Police Review Authority in Chicago and the Police Ombudsman for Northern Ireland are representative of this model. The key advantage of an independent review body is that it offers an appearance of total independence and objectivity.

For Canada, there is no single model that can be applied in its current form and expected to function effectively without taking into account the particular characteristics of our country and the size and scope (municipal, provincial, federal, territorial and First Nations) of the policing activities undertaken by the RCMP. The size of the territory and sheer vastness of the country, coupled with budget realities, must be considered. Valuable lessons were learned from our domestic and foreign counterparts in the development of the CPC's approach for the RCMP in the Canadian context, outlined next.

CPC'S RECOMMENDED MODEL FOR HANDLING OF RCMP MEMBER INVESTIGATIONS

The CPC's recommended option underlines the importance of police in the process (as part of the solution), while also recognizing that an enhanced degree of civilian engagement in the criminal investigation process is fundamental to ensure its impartiality and integrity. To that end, the CPC recommends shifting from the current "dependent model" towards the "interdependent model."

The recommended "interdependent model" rests between the basic dependent model and the full-featured interdependent model:

Overall, the CPC believes that a criminal investigation resulting from member conduct is unlike *any other* criminal investigation and accordingly must be handled procedurally very differently. Therefore, to help transition the RCMP from its current "dependent (police investigating police) model" to the "interdependent model" (involving an enhanced CPC role in the context of RCMP member investigations), a number of legislative, structural, and policy changes are recommended.

RECOMMENDED LEGISLATIVE CHANGES

To effectively enhance review capacity, legislative changes should be considered to provide the new RCMP Review Body the authority to:

- **Refer an RCMP member investigation** to another police force or to another criminal investigative body in Canada.

- Grant the RCMP Review Body the authority to **monitor any criminal investigation** relating to a member of the RCMP, where it deems it appropriate to do so. This would therefore extend the RCMP Review Body's ability to deploy the observer to an RCMP member investigation being undertaken by an external police service and/or provincial criminal investigative body. While permission from the investigating body would be required to embed the observer, the authority would at least provide the RCMP Review Body with the power where granted permission to observe.

- **Undertake joint investigations** with like-mandated bodies. The amendment could allow the new RCMP Review Body to "conduct a joint investigation, review, inquiry, audit or hearing with another body in Canada that has powers, duties and functions that are similar to the RCMP Review Body's, including provincial criminal investigative bodies." This would allow the new RCMP Review Body to undertake investigations with new criminal investigative bodies (like the Alberta Serious Incident Response Team) as they emerge across the country.

Other recommended legislative changes should include:

- The RCMP Commissioner revise the current version of his Standing Orders to direct handling of member investigations, as per the recommendations herein (specify that member investigations are not to be handled like any other criminal investigation and a better definition of the term "conflict of interest" should be included).

RECOMMENDED STRUCTURAL CHANGES FOR THE RCMP

- Create the position of National RCMP Member Investigation Registrar to manage, track, train, promote and advise on all issues related to member investigations. The National Registrar would be responsible to:
  - Create an RCMP National Registry for all police investigating police data (especially for serious injury, sexual assault, and death cases) with timely sharing of data with the CPC.

- Create and manage an RCMP Police Investigating Police Advisory Group to help determine actions to be taken in sensitive cases.
- Monitor effective compliance with policy and enforce compliance where necessary (e.g. consultation with Crown re: laying of charges mandatory).
- Create and oversee a specialized unit with expertise on the handling of RCMP historical cases to be consulted — or deployed — where necessary.
- Create a mobile critical incident member investigation team (with a CPC civilian observer embedded) that can be deployed where both the RCMP National Registrar and the CPC Chair jointly determined it necessary to do so (a pool of qualified senior investigators placed on standby that can be deployed quickly).

RECOMMENDED RCMP POLICY AND PROCEDURAL CHANGES

There are certain instances where the RCMP should *not* investigate itself. Below is a chart that delineates that as the seriousness of the member-involved offence increases, a corresponding degree of independence and impartiality in that member investigation is required. The chart below highlights the CPC's contention that as the seriousness of the offence alleged against a member rises, the discretion for the RCMP to respond as it deems appropriate must be removed and **mandatory** requirements inserted in its place. [See Chart on next page.]

RECOMMENDED POLICY CHANGES FOR THE RCMP

The CPC's policy analysis revealed that RCMP policies, while voluminous, are inconsistent and do not adequately address the handling of member investigations. Criminal investigations into members should not be treated the same as any other criminal investigation. To address the current void in effective and consistent policies and procedures related to the handling of member investigations, the CPC recommends the following key changes:

- Criminal investigations of RCMP members into allegations of serious injury, sexual assault or death in hardship or remote postings must be consistent with all other member investigation protocols, no exception.
- An administrative review is mandatory for all member investigations.

Recommended RCMP Response to Member Investigations

Type of offence defined	Member offence (by level of seriousness)	Current RCMP handling	Recommended RCMP handling of member investigation
MANDATORY RCMP ACTION WITH CPC ROLE			
Indictable offences[5] An offence which, in Canada, is more serious than those which can proceed by summary conviction. In many regards, this is the Canadian equivalent to the USA felony. Murder and treason are examples of crimes committed in Canada which would be indictable offences. These crimes are usually tried by federally-appointed judges and carry heavy sentences.	**Death** Criminal Negligence causing Death (s. 220 CCC)	Discretionary at RCMP Division level	**RCMP Mandatory Action:** • CPC to refer all death cases to external police service or provincial criminal investigative body (no RCMP member involvement) • Divisional MOUs activated • CPC Observer embedded
	Serious Injury & Sexual Assault Assault with Weapon or Assault Causing Bodily Harm (s. 267 CCC) Sexual Assault (s. 272 CCC)	Discretionary at RCMP Division level	**RCMP Mandatory Action:** CPC and National Registrar to determine appropriate response from options below for serious injury/sexual assault cases: • Referral to external police service or to provincial investigative body through MOU[6] • Deployment of RCMP HQ mobile critical incident member investigation team • CPC Observer embedded
DISCRETION RETAINED BY THE RCMP			
Hybrid Offences Dual Procedure Offences which Crown can elect to proceed with an indictable offence or a summary conviction.	**Assault** (s. 265 CCC)	Discretionary at RCMP Division level	**RCMP HQ National Registrar retains discretion to determine appropriate response.**
Summary Conviction In Canada, a less serious offence than indictable offences for which both the procedure and punishment tends to be less onerous.	**Example:** Theft under $5,000	Discretionary at RCMP Division level	**RCMP HQ National Registrar retains discretion to determine appropriate response.** • Recommended CPC standard policies and procedures are followed (outlined next).

(Right margin vertical labels: MANDATORY / DISCRETIONARY)

• **The RCMP establish formalized MOUs for** *every* **RCMP division to ensure the mandatory referral of member investigations to an external police service is consistent and documented.** At present, only New Brunswick (J) Division, Nova Scotia (H) Division and Newfoundland (B) Division have formalized MOUs in place. These existing MOUs should be revised as per the CPC's recommendations to reflect new processes.

Where it is deemed appropriate for the RCMP to handle its own member investigation or where an RCMP member forms part of the investigative team (led by an external police force), the following policy recommendations would apply.

• **Create an RCMP integrated manual** to specifically address procedures for investigations undertaken by the RCMP into one of its own members. This integrated manual should have links to any additional relevant policies for ease of reference. Key features to be included in the integrated manual: CPC recommended investigative team structure:

• Qualified primary investigator at least one rank higher than that of subject member;
  ○ A minimum of two members required for every member [investigation] (including for subject and witness officer interviews);
  ○ Minimum mandatory qualifications of investigative team;
  ○ Workload of members assigned to member investigations reassigned or adjusted to prioritize member investigation accordingly;
  ○ Timely completion of investigation preferably six months and not recommended to exceed one year;
  ○ Assign liaison position to member of investigative team to ensure timely and effective communication with public, family and subject member;
  ○ Self-identification of knowledge of subject member mandatory;
  ○ Use of the probe[7] in lower-end investigations.

CPC OVERALL CONCLUSION

To answer the question raised at the outset, *"Can the current process of the RCMP investigating itself legitimately engender confidence in the transparency and integrity of the criminal investigation and its outcome?"* The informed CPC answer is that it cannot. To address this, the CPC has recommended legislative, policy, procedural and structural proposals for changes, including an enhanced civilian presence during the investigative process to protect against any real or perceived conflicts of interest involving RCMP member investigations. It is important to note that the RCMP recommendations specifically related to structure, procedure and policy do not rely on any legislative enhancements and can be implemented immediately.

(c) *Doe v. Metropolitan Toronto (Municipality) Commissioners of Police*†

[MacFARLAND J.:]

[1] Jane Doe was raped and otherwise sexually assaulted at knifepoint in her own bed in the early morning hours of August 24, 1986 by a stranger subsequently identified as Paul Douglas Callow. Ms. Doe then lived in a second-floor apartment at 88 Wellesley Street East, in the City of Toronto; her apartment had a balcony which was used by the rapist to gain access to her premises. At the time, Ms. Doe was the fifth known victim of Callow who would become known as "the balcony rapist".

[2] Ms. Doe brings a suit against the Metropolitan Toronto Police Force (hereafter referred to as MTPF) on two bases; firstly she suggests that the MTPF conducted a negligent investigation in relation to the balcony rapist and failed to warn women whom they knew to be potential targets of Callow of the fact that they were at risk. She says, as the result of such conduct, Callow was not apprehended as early as he might otherwise have been and she was denied the opportunity, had she known the risk she faced, to take any specific measures to protect herself from attack. Secondly, she said that the MTPF being a public body having the statutory duty to protect the public from criminal activity, must exercise that duty in accordance with the *Canadian Charter of Rights and Freedoms* and may not act in a way that is discriminatory because of gender. She says the police must act constitutionally, they did not do so in this case and as the result, her rights under ss. 15 and 7 of the *Charter* have been breached. She seeks damages against the MTPF under both heads of her claim.

[3] The trial of this action took place over approximately eight weeks; some 30 witnesses were called and voluminous documentary evidence filed. Counsel have filed lengthy written argument and had two days in which to give an oral outline of their written submissions.

· · · ·

CONCLUSIONS
Competency of the Investigation

[137] It is suggested that the investigation into the balcony rapist was slipshod and incompetent. The plaintiff has criticized the documentary productions of the defendant and suggested they are incomplete. Professor Hodgson testified that every step in an investigation should be recorded on supplementary occurrence reports. In this way he said anyone picking up the file could be reasonably informed on the status of the investigation. While that may be the ideal I accept that it is not the reality. Often steps taken and information gathered were recorded on supplementary reports but often they were not. Officers differ in their manner and method of note and record-keeping. I accept that there were numerous documents created in relation to this investigation which unfortunately were destroyed before the litigation was commenced.

---

† 39 O.R. (3d) 487, [1998] O.J. No. 2681 (Ont. Ct. (General Division)) at paras. 1–3, 137–79, 214–20, 253–55.

[138] I am not persuaded on the evidence that Callow would have been identified and apprehended any earlier because of documentary deficiencies.

[139] I am satisfied that the officers ultimately assigned to this investigation had too many other urgent assignments ongoing at the same time which prevented them from devoting the necessary attention which this investigation required. At the critical time much of their energy and attention was directed to other matters — often for days at a time. They had no back-up, no one else directly responsible for this investigation when they were otherwise engaged.

[140] While it is true that there was no evidence called in relation to what other demands there may have been on the MTPF for manpower at this time, one must bear in mind that it is the evidence of the police that sexual assault is a very serious crime second only to homicide and then consider the resources made available in the Annex Rapist investigation in his same division only a month or two before.

[141] While the plaintiff submits that I must infer that Callow would have been apprehended sooner had greater resources been devoted to this investigation earlier on the theory — the sooner a job is started the sooner it is finished — I cannot agree with. While one may say in that event Callow might have been apprehended sooner, it is to my mind equally probable that he might not have been.

[142] I am compelled, however, to conclude that the only difference between the Annex Rapist investigation and this investigation was the level of violence in addition to the rape itself. Dawson Davidson also physically beat many of his victims in addition to sexually assaulting them.

[143] As this is the only real distinguishing factor between the two investigations I must conclude that it was this factor — the lack of additional violence — which resulted in this investigation being essentially on the back burner in so far as resources were concerned. The sense of urgency which drove the Dawson Davidson investigation was markedly absent from this investigation. I can only conclude because Callow's victims were "merely raped" by a "gentleman rapist" — according to the Oliver Zink Rape Cookbook definition — this case did not have the urgency of the other.

Decision Not to Warn

[144] As I have said, Sgts. Cameron and Derry determined that this investigation would be "low key" compared to the investigation conducted into the "Annex Rapist" and no warning would be given to the women they knew to be at risk for fear of displacing the rapist leaving him free to re-offend elsewhere undetected.

[145] I am not persuaded that their professed reason for not warning women is the real reason no warning was issued.

[146] Firstly, there is evidence that the Annex Rapist, Dawson Davidson, did not flee to Vancouver because of the media attention paid to his crimes and/or the obvious increased police presence in the neighbourhood. Indeed, much of the coverage occurred after Davidson had already left Toronto.

[147] Additionally P.C. Gary Ellis, who had assisted in the Dawson Davidson investigation at one point, actually telephoned Callow's ex-wife directly when he learned of Callow's existence and record from probation officer Alton. Police Constable Ellis worked out of the same 52 Division as Sgts. Cameron and Derry and would have, presumably, been aware of any discussions in relation to the fear of displacing Callow — by media attention or knocking on his door for the purpose of giving a warning about sexual assaults — yet he phoned directly to Callow's wife without even hesitating it seems.

[148] There was, I find, no "policy" not to issue warnings to potential victims in these cases — clearly warnings had been given in the Dawson Davidson Annex Rapist investigation — warnings [...] which incidentally all defence expert witnesses agreed were appropriate in the circumstances.

[149] I find that the real reason a warning was not given in the circumstances of this case was because Sgts. Cameron and Derry believed that women living in the area would become hysterical and panic and their investigation would thereby be jeopardized. In addition, they were not motivated by any sense of urgency because Callow's attacks were not seen as "violent" as Dawson Davidson's by comparison had been.

[150] I am satisfied on the evidence that a meaningful warning could and should have been given to the women who were at particular risk. That warning could have been by way of a canvass of their apartments, by a media blitz — by holding widely publicized public meetings or any one or combination of these methods. Such warning should have alerted the particular women at risk, and advised them of suggested precautions they might take to protect themselves. The defence experts, with the exception of

Mr. Piers, agreed that a warning could have been given without compromising the investigation on the facts of the case.

[151] Even the experienced defence expert witnesses Det. Inspector Kevin Rossmo and former FBI special agent McCrary agreed that as Det. Inspector Rossmo said:

> The police have a responsibility to release a balanced volume of information to protect the community. ... where that balance is will depend on the particular facts of the case.

[152] In my view it has been conceded in this case clearly and unequivocally by the Chief of Police at the time, Jack Marks, that no warning was given in this case and one ought to have been. His public response to the proposals of the group known as Women against Violence against Women in the aftermath of this investigation presented to the Board of Commissioners of Police could not in my view be any clearer when he said:

> I would concede that for a variety of reasons unique to the Church/Wellesley investigation, no press release in the nature of a general warning was issued and acknowledged that one should have been. This is not only a matter for concern and regret, but action has already been taken to prevent a similar breakdown from occurring in the future. Specifically, the Sexual Assault Coordinator who monitors all of these offences has been directed to ensure that members of the public are informed about such matters which may affect their safety. These warnings will be directed toward all potential victims with special attention given to members of the public who have been identified as most at risk, e.g. as in the case at hand, women living in high-rise buildings in the downtown area would be targeted as a high risk group and requiring extra efforts to bring the potential risk to their attention.

[153] I accept and agree entirely with these remarks.

[154] I must confess I was taken aback at the suggestion of Det. Sgt. Robin Breen who authored these remarks for the Chief when he suggested, I think, that in effect what it says is not what it says. The remarks were not intended to mean that the police felt a warning ought to have been given but rather were merely an invitation to get this group — known as WAVAW — to the discussion table.

[155] His evidence was pure double-talk as far as I am concerned and simply made no sense.

[156] It seems the MTPF has been trying to back away from these words of their then Chief ever since they were stated. The Chief's statement was an appropriate one in the circumstances and it is to his credit in my view, that he made the statement when and as he did.

[157] There are three other factors which have influenced my decision that a warning ought to have been given.

- the fact that Sgts. Cameron and Derry thought it appropriate to warn S.G. and M.L., that they may be potential targets of the balcony rapist after they reported break-ins to their apartments in their absence.
- the fact that Dawson Davidson had been arrested in July 1986 received considerable publicity. Women living in the general vicinity may have felt some relief knowing that a serial rapist had been apprehended and let down their guard somewhat completely unaware that another serial rapist was on the loose in their neighbourhood.
- the fact that Sgt. Hughes in his memo to his superior Staff Sgt. Hein — both of 52 Division — dated July 29, 1986 thought that building superintendents should have been contacted and told to advise "trusted tenants" especially single women to be aware of the occurrences and to advise police of any person they felt may be suspect.

[158] I am satisfied on Ms. Doe's evidence that if she had been aware a serial rapist was in her neighbourhood raping women whose apartments he accessed via their balconies she would have taken steps to protect herself and that most probably those steps would have prevented her from being raped.

[159] Section 57 of the *Police Act*, R.S.O. 1980, c. 381 (the governing statute at the time these events occurred), provides:

> 57. ... members of police forces ... are charged with the duty of preserving the peace, preventing robberies and other crimes ...

[160] The police are statutorily obligated to prevent crime and at common law they owe a duty to protect life and property. As Schroeder J.A. stated in *Schacht v. R.*, [1973] 1 O.R. 221 at pp. 231–32, 30 D.L.R. (3d) 641:

> The duties which I would lay upon them stem not only from the relevant statutes to which reference has been made, but from the common law, which recognizes the existence of a broad conventional or customary duty in the established

constabulary as an arm of the State to protect the life, limb and property of the subject.

[161] In my view, the police failed utterly in their duty to protect these women and the plaintiff in particular from the serial rapist the police knew to be in their midst by failing to warn so that they may have had the opportunity to take steps to protect themselves.

[162] It is no answer for the police to say women are always at risk and as an urban adult living in downtown Toronto they have an obligation to look out for themselves. Women generally do, every day of their lives, conduct themselves and their lives in such a way as to avoid the general pervasive threat of male violence which exists in our society. Here police were aware of a specific threat or risk to a specific group of women and they did nothing to warn those women of the danger they were in, nor did they take any measures to protect them.

Discrimination

[163] The plaintiff's argument is not simply that she has been discriminated against, because she is a woman, by individual officers in the investigation of her specific complaint, but that systemic discrimination existed within the MTPF in 1986 which impacted adversely on all women and, specifically, those who were survivors of sexual assault who came into contact with the MTPF — a class of persons of which the plaintiff was one. She says, in effect, the sexist stereotypical views held by the MTPF informed the investigation of this serial rapist and caused that investigation to be conducted incompetently and in such a way that the plaintiff has been denied the equal protection and equal benefit of law guaranteed to her by s. 15(1) of the *Charter*.

[164] The MTPF has since at least 1975 been aware of the problems it has in relation to the investigation of sexual assaults.

[165] Among those problems:

- survivors of sexual assault are not treated sensitively;
- lack of effective training for officers engaged in the investigation of sexual assault including a lack of understanding of rape trauma syndrome and the needs of survivors;
- lack of co-ordination of sexual assault investigations;
- some officers not suited by personality/attitude to investigation of sexual assault;

- too many investigators coming into contact with victims;
- lack of experienced investigators investigating sexual assault;
- lack of supervision of those conducting sexual assault investigations.

[166] The force has conceded in public documents as well as in internal documents at least since 1975, that it has difficulties in these areas, that it will take immediate steps to remedy these shortcomings — yet the problems continued through to 1987 and beyond.

[167] It seemed in that period that the public and persons who had brought their concerns in these areas to the attention of police were being publicly assured the problems would be eliminated, yet within the force the status quo remained pretty much as it had always been.

[168] Every police officer who testified agreed that sexual assault is a serious crime, second only to homicide. Yet, I cannot help but ask rhetorically — do they really believe that especially when one reviews their record in this area? It seems to me it was, as the plaintiff suggests, largely an effort in impression management rather than an indication of any genuine commitment for change.

[169] Former Chief of Police, Jack Marks, said that he would not have stood for problems like those outlined above continuing in the homicide squad for example. He said, assuming he were aware of the problems, that he would "root them out" and "correct" them — yet these problems were allowed to continue over at least the better part of two decades in relation to the investigation of sexual assaults. Although the MTPF say they took the crime of sexual assault seriously in 1985–86 I must conclude, on the evidence before me, that they did not.

[170] The rape trauma syndrome was clearly not understood by too many officers who were charged with the responsibility of investigating sexual assaults — others, including even some who had taken the sexual assault investigators course, adhered to rape myths. Examples can clearly be seen in this investigation — for example, Sgt. Duggan's occurrence reports in relation to the B.K. investigation — clearly "slanted toward disbelieving the victim", to quote Margo Pulford. It is obvious to anyone that Sgt. Duggan was strongly influenced by the fact that a bowl of potato chips on the bed where the rape occurred apparently remained undisturbed. He concluded there had been no struggle and hence no forced sexual intercourse. His denial in this regard is

simply incredible in the face of his own written record. Other examples are set out above as quoted from Det. Sgt. Boyd's report and her comment that these problems existed in every station in every division in the force.

[171] The protocol established by the force, AP No. 22, as it was designated, for the investigation of sexual assaults was often not followed and when it was not there is no evidence that any senior officer or supervisor followed up.

[172] The problems continued and because among adults, women are overwhelmingly the victims of sexual assault, they are and were disproportionately impacted by the resulting poor quality of investigation. The result is that women are discriminated against and their right to equal protection and benefit of the law is thereby compromised as the result.

[173] In my view the conduct of this investigation and the failure to warn in particular, was motivated and informed by the adherence to rape myths as well as sexist stereotypical reasoning about rape, about women and about women who are raped. The plaintiff therefore has been discriminated against by reason of her gender and as the result the plaintiff's rights to equal protection and equal benefit of the law were compromised.

Security of the Person

[174] I am satisfied that the defendants deprived the plaintiff of her right to security of the person by subjecting her to the very real risk of attack by a serial rapist — a risk of which they were aware but about which they quite deliberately failed to inform the plaintiff or any women living in the Church/Wellesley area at the time save only S.G. and M.L. and where in the face of that knowledge and their belief that the rapist would certainly attack again, they additionally failed to take any steps to protect the plaintiff or other women like her. Clearly the rape of the plaintiff constituted a deprivation of her security of the person. As Madam Justice Wilson stated in *Singh v. Canada (Minister of Employment & Immigration)*, [1985] 1 S.C.R. 177 at p. 207, 17 D.L.R. (4th) 422:

> ... "security of the person" must encompass freedom from the threat of physical punishment or suffering as well as freedom from such punishment itself.

[175] As I have indicated, because the defendants exercised their discretion in the investigation of this case in a discriminatory and negligent way as I have detailed above, their exercise of discretion was thereby contrary to the principle of fundamental justice.

[176] Section 1 of the *Charter* has no application in circumstances because the conduct of police in issue here is not "prescribed by law" within the meaning the jurisprudence has ascribed to that phrase.

[177] Here the plaintiff's *Charter* rights have been infringed by police conduct — not a legislative enactment or a common law rule.

[178] In any event the defendants made no effort in evidence to satisfy the requirements of s. 1 and demonstrate a s. 1 defence — they simply denied the plaintiff's rights which were infringed. I have found differently.

[179] In view of my findings the plaintiff is entitled under s. 24 to a remedy.

· · · ·

Damages

[214] Ms. Doe precisely detailed the events of the early morning hours of August 24, 1986 in her evidence. It was obvious to everyone that giving this evidence was a difficult and painful process for her. Her attacker was armed with a knife and had concealed his identity with a mask he had fashioned and wore. The attack was terrifying and she feared for her life.

[215] Following her call to 911 a number of police officers arrived at her apartment and over the next hours she was obliged to repeat the details of her attack to a number of officers.

[216] She was taken to hospital for forensic testing by ambulance — an intrusive and painful process.

[217] This attack by a stranger in her own bed in her home has had a profound and lasting effect on Ms. Doe as she stated in her evidence:

> ... my life was shattered as a result of the rape, and I experienced it literally as being shattered for at least two to three years ...

[218] Some of the complaints include:

* difficulty sleeping;
* recurrent intrusive nightmares;
* panic attacks and nausea;
* lack of self-confidence;
* emotional detachment from friends;

- inability to socialize where strangers may be present;
- fear of men in general which impacted on everyday life, *i.e.*, stopped using TTC at night;
- no enjoyment of life.

[219] Although Ms. Doe had suffered from depression prior to August 24, 1986, this condition was greatly exacerbated as the result of the rape.

[220] On the evidence there can be no question but that the plaintiff suffered serious post-traumatic stress immediately following the rape and she continues to this day to exhibit symptoms which are consistent in post-traumatic stress disorder — at the time of trial some 11 years after her attack.

· · · ·

Special Damages

· · · ·

[253] I should add that the Chief of Police is responsible to see the members of his force carry out their duties properly and will be vicariously liable when they fail to do so as will the Board of Commissioners of Police which is charged with the overall responsibility of policing and maintaining law and order within the Municipality of Metropolitan Toronto (as it then was).

[241] In conclusion the plaintiff shall have judgment against the defendants in the following amounts:

General Damages	$175,000.00
Special Damages to date	$ 37,301.58
Future Costs	$ 8,062.74
Total	$220,364.32

together with an amount which represents the present value of a sum required to produce $2,000 annually for a period of 15 years and a declaration that the defendants did in 1986 violate Ms. Doe's s. 7 and s. 15(1) rights under the *Canadian Charter of Rights and Freedoms*.

[252] Matters of prejudgment interest and costs to be addressed at a future date to be agreed upon among counsel and the court and arranged through the trial co-ordinator's office.

Judgment accordingly.

X

Law and Social Transformation

Overview of Part X

The articles included in **Part X** consider the role of law as an agent of, and a response to, social change. It considers both the theoretical and practical potential of law and also the various limits of law in this regard.

Chapter 26 includes a series of articles that discuss the potential for the *Canadian Charter of Rights and Freedoms* to act as a catalyst of social change. Knopff and Morton present a critique that focuses on the ways in which the *Charter* enhances the policy-making role of judges at the expense of legislators. They contend that the *Charter* has done little to improve the freedoms enjoyed by most Canadians and only solidified the power of "an elite" that stand to benefit most from the expansion of judicial power. Justice Abella counters that the legislators themselves entrenched the *Charter* and in so doing entrusted the courts with the role of protecting the public interest. When judges strike down legislation that violates the *Charter*, judges reinforce democracy rather than undermine it. All branches of government, she stresses, are responsible for the "delivery of justice", though each in its own way.

Finally, Arbour and Lafontaine consider the achievements of *Charter* litigation in the first 25 years since entrenchment in an international context. They identify a number of ways to improve the interaction between international legal norms and our domestic human rights system and identify key challenges for rights protection in Canada.

As you read these different perspectives, consider how you would evaluate the impact of the *Charter*. Has it changed the values or behaviour of Canadians, or even the way we identify as Canadian? Has it changed the way governments operate, or the relationship between government and individuals? Does the *Charter* give too much power to judges? Does it distract from, or does it provoke, political action? On balance, has the *Charter* been a positive or negative influence on Canadian society?

The articles in **Chapter 27** provide a broader, more theoretical perspective on the relationship between law and social change. The selections by Brickey and Comack and by Bowles and Gintis again highlight some of the internal inconsistencies of law and discuss the potential to harness law as a mechanism for not only resisting but, more importantly, *challenging* dominant social interests

and existing inequalities and injustices. In their article, Sullivan and Tifft investigate the ways in which native conceptions of restorative justice may effectively challenge traditional conceptions of law and justice and bring about meaningful social change.

The final two articles in the chapter explore the potential of law to affect social change through two very different legal processes of reconciliation. The article by LeMon focuses on the gacaca court system in a post-genocide "transitional" Rwanda. Established as a central mechanism to achieve both "justice" and "reconciliation", LeMon underscores the numerous reasons why the gacaca court system has largely failed to achieve either. The article that follows, by Stanton, introduces readers to Canada's Truth and Reconciliation Commission (TRC) established to address the legacy of the Indian Residential Schools (IRS) system. Echoing many of the pointed criticisms made by Dickson and Malette in **Chapter 18**, Stanton draws clear connections between the gross mistreatment of Canada's First Nations in the IRS system, past political failures to take responsibility for the destructive consequences of the IRS system, and the ongoing challenges faced by Indigenous communities. She argues that the impetus for the TRC was not a popular acknowledgment — nor a "groundswell of concern" for survivors — by average Canadians, but rather a calculated response on the part of the government to minimize the escalating costs of related litigation, and a basic acknowledgement that current legal mechanisms to address the issue were wholly inadequate for everyone involved. The article by Stanton highlights for readers the relative advantage and potential challenges of establishing a TRC in the Canadian context (cf. "transitional societies" like South Africa) and asks us to consider whether meaningful reconciliation, or broad transformation on a societal level, might be possible through processes like the TRC.

The articles in this final section further challenge readers to rethink the composition and role of law; to see law as much more than a narrow instrument to secure or stabilize an existing order — or orders — within society. How can law or legal processes promote, or even stifle, meaningful social change? In what ways might such changes occur given that — as we have seen throughout preceding chapters — law is not only a set of formal rules, and not only an extensive framework for understanding and ordering the world and our relationships with others, but also a critical part of our identity (e.g. citizenship). One might argue that law can never disentangle itself from the question of social transformation because it is, at its core, a basic statement about how society *ought* to be — both now and in the future. Is law then inescapably a discourse of social transformation and change?

(a)   Ardour in the Court†

Rainer Knopff and F.L. Morton

The Charter has done less to enhance your rights than to increase the policy-making power of judges

In 1992, former chief justice Antonio Lamer described the adoption of the Charter of Rights as "a revolution on the scale of the introduction of the metric system, the great medical discoveries of Louis Pasteur, and the invention of penicillin and the laser." Five years later, Mr. Lamer thanked "God for the Charter," adding that people "just don't have these rights." Life without the Charter, presumably, would be as bad as life before antibiotics.

We agree that the Charter has wrought a revolution but, contrary to the penicillin analogy, its effect hasn't been akin to saving and improving the lives of untold millions. Can anyone who remembers pre-1982 Canada seriously believe that the Charter has enriched and improved our lives to that extent?

Do we have dramatically improved freedom of speech? Well, okay, we are freer to collect kiddie porn.

Is freedom of religion much better protected? Maybe, but mainly in the sense of more freedom from religion, especially Christianity, which is increasingly seen as disqualifying any policy position with which it is associated.

Are we significantly less likely to convict the innocent? Probably not, though we may be more likely to let the guilty go free.

Are we more equal? Not if one is to believe equality rights advocates, who never tire of pointing out growing disparities.

The pre-Charter world was far from perfect, but it was hardly the Dark Age implied by Mr. Lamer's revolutionary rhetoric. Nor is the post-Charter world remarkably better. There have been changes, but inflationary "rights talk" notwithstanding, they have mainly been shifts in the policy balance on matters of ongoing reasonable disagreement.

The Charter's main revolutionary effect has not been to improve society but to enhance the political and policy influence of judges, to give them more power over the matters of reasonable disagreement that legislatures used to settle.

The judges themselves have admitted as much. Mr. Lamer, for example, has "no doubt" that the judiciary has been "drawn into the political arena to a degree unknown prior to 1982," and that it is often called upon "to make what used to be a political call." Similarly, the late Justice John Sopinka admitted that in "deciding a Charter case, the court is in a sense legislating." When York University's Ian Greene and several colleagues interviewed many of Canada's appellate court judges, virtually all of them admitted to a new lawmaking role. Earlier this week, Chief Justice Beverley McLachlin associated a "litigation explosion" with the advent of the Charter of Rights, indicating just how extensive the new policymaking role has become.

When so-called "court bashers" challenge this transfer of political power to unelected officials, the judges often reverse course insisting that there is no revolution after all. Judges have always enjoyed a degree of policymaking discretion, they contend, and have exercised that discretion in applying the consti-

---

† From *The Globe and Mail* (April 7, 2000) A17. Reproduced with permission of the authors.

tutional law of federalism. The Charter, far from effecting a revolutionary change, now appears as just a minor extension of well-established practice.

Unfortunately, this dodge doesn't work. While it is certainly true that federalism jurisprudence also involves judicial policymaking, deciding under the Charter whether government as such may (or must) do something goes far beyond deciding which government may do it. As Ian Hunter has aptly put it, "It may be true that elephants and chipmunks are both mammals, but to fail to acknowledge the difference between them is wilful deception."

Another response to the court bashers is to claim that judges are merely discharging duties imposed on them by the Canadian people when the Charter was democratically adopted. They are simply applying the Charter. However, this legalistic view of judging cannot be reconciled with whatever meaning the judges choose. "We have lots of discretion," Justice Claire L'Heureux-Dubé told the Canadian Bar Association last August. "So put yourself in where there is nothing else to go on." In other words, judges drive the Charter, not vice versa.

Judges do not drive the Charter alone, however. When Justice L'Heureux-Dubé admits to putting herself into the Charter, she is following the lead of countless activist commentators who insist, for example, that "the shaping of the Charter will be an intensely political process, far more responsive to public pressure than to constitutional law," or that litigating "law reform is part of an ideological battle." Groups such as LEAF (the Legal Education and Action Fund) have mounted fully self-conscious campaigns of "influencing the influencers," by "flooding the law reviews" with advice on just how judges should put themselves into the Charter.

Without the constant barrage of such activist scholarship, Justice L'Heureux-Dubé's unabashed put-yourself-in statement would be inconceivable, as would her remark in another speech that she is an "equality person" who will "do any thing I can to achieve it [equality]." Anything? Judges from earlier eras would never have so blatantly treated law as the vehicle for a political agenda.

Like the Charter itself, in other words, judges are as much a means as a cause of the Charter revolution. While judges are in the vanguard of the revolution, they are being pushed as much as they lead. They are being pushed by what we call the "Court Party," a loose constellation of interests that assiduously promote judicial power because they stand to benefit from it.

Today's Court Party, we contend, is a party of elites. It is dominated by the chattering classes. The Charter revolution it promotes is a revolution from the top, part of what Christopher Lasch — turning Ortega y Gassett on his head — has christened the "revolt of the elites."

Despite the rhetorical evasions, the revolution in judicial power is now widely conceded — even, as we have seen, by judges in their more candid moments. The Charter itself, however, is not so much the cause of the revolution as the means through which it is carried out. The Declaration of Independence did not cause the American Revolution, nor the Declaration of the Rights of Man the French Revolution. A revolution cannot occur without leaders and the support of interested classes. The Charter Revolution and the Court Party explains the political economy and sociology of the Charter revolution.

(b) The Case for a Strong Court†

Judge Rosalie Abella

The judiciary is accountable to the public interest, not public opinion, says Judge Rosalie Abella

Democracy is not — and never was — just about the wishes of the majority. What pumps oxygen no less

forcefully through vibrant democratic veins is the protection of rights, through the courts, notwithstanding the wishes of the majority. It is this second, crucial aspect of democratic values that has been submerged by the [recent] swirling discourse [about the role of judges in enforcing rights].

† From *The Globe and Mail* (April 13, 2000) A15. Adapted from the keynote address at the Constitutional Law Conference on April 7, 2000 at Osgoode Hall Law School. Reproduced with permission.

I think it is fair to say that until 1981, when the Charter was donated to the British North America Act by the federal government, no one ever accused the Canadian judiciary of aggressive rights protection. In fact, many of us, reared on the constitutional diet of division-of-powers jurisprudence, looked wistfully at the wide selection on the constitutional menu available to American judges. With rare exceptions, the Canadian Supreme Court not only shared the apparent inhibitions of its American and British counterparts about welcoming rights into the judicial fold, they remained reluctant at least a generation longer.

By the time I graduated from law school in 1970, the perception was that the Supreme Court was the place that decided constitutional issues such as whether Persons in the British North [America] Act included women and whether egg marketing boards were a provincial or a federal undertaking.

Then, in 1978, just before we got a Charter, the Supreme Court in Rathwell v. Rathwell reversed a decision it had made only five years earlier in Murdoch v. Murdoch, thereby rewriting the archaic matrimonial property regime we had been subject to for over 100 years. No longer equitable, said the court. Time to adjust to a new appreciation about the role played by husbands and wives in a marriage. Time, in short, to create a new social contract. The public cheered. The media cheered. Within months, practically every province had amended its family property laws accordingly.

Then we got the Charter of Rights and Freedoms. To the Constitution's division of powers, it added rights: civil rights, such as the freedoms of religion, association and expression; the right to counsel; and the right to security of a person. And human rights, such as equality, linguistic rights, aboriginal rights and multiculturalism. What Canada got with the Charter was a dramatic package of guaranteed rights, subject only to those reasonable limits that were demonstrably justified in a free and democratic society; a package assembled by the legislature, which in turn, it bears repeating, assigned to the courts the duty to decide whether its laws, policies or practices met the constitutional standards set out in the Charter.

In the first decade of Charter adjudication, the Supreme Court was energetic. It struck down Sabbatarian and sign laws, said equality meant more than treating people the same, and decriminalized abortion. It ventured fearlessly into the overgrown fields of the law and cut a wide path for other courts to follow. Again the public cheered. Even the media cheered. It was clear that the 1960s and 1970s had generated a public thirst for rights protection,

and Charter adjudication in the Supreme Court in the 1980s was beginning to quench that thirst.

With the arrival of the 1990s, a few abrupt voices were heard to challenge the Supreme Court, voices in large part belonging to those whose psychological security or territorial hegemony were at risk from the Charter's reach. As the decade advanced, so did the courage and insistence of these New Inhibitors, most of whom appeared to congregate at one end of the ideological spectrum. While their articulated target was the Supreme Court of Canada, their real target was the way the Charter was transforming their traditional expectations and entitlements.

They made their arguments skillfully. In essence, they turned the good news of constitutionalized rights, the mark of a secure and mature democracy, into the bad news of judicial autocracy, the mark of a debilitated and devalued legislature. They called minorities seeking the right to be free from discrimination "special interest groups seeking to jump the queue." They called efforts to reverse discrimination "reverse discrimination."

They pretended that concepts or words in the Charter such as freedom, equality and justice had no pre-existing political aspect and bemoaned the politicization of the judiciary. They trumpeted the rights of the majority and ignored the fact that minorities are people who want rights, too. They said courts should only interpret, not make law, thereby ignoring the entire history of common law. They called advocates for equality, human rights, and the Charter "biased" and defenders of the status quo "impartial." They urged the courts to defer to legislation, unless, ironically, they disagreed with the legislation. They said judges are not accountable because they are not elected, yet held them to negative account for every expanded right. They claimed a monopoly on truth, frequently used invectives to assert it, then accused their detractors of personalizing the debate.

The essence of their message was that there is an anti-democratic, socially hazardous turbulence in the air, most notably during judicial flights. And while it is a message that has every right to be heard, it is not the whole story. The whole story is that the Charter does not represent heterodoxy about democracy, but rather its finest manifestation. People elect legislators who enact the laws they think the majority of their constituents want them to enact, and appoint judges who are expected to be independent from those legislators and impartial in determining whether the legislature's actions meet constitutional standards.

When legislatures elected by majorities enact laws such as the Charter, the majority is presumed to agree with that legislature's decision to entrench rights and extend a constitutionally guaranteed invitation to the courts to intervene when legislative conduct is not demonstrably justified in a democratic society.

In enforcing the Charter, therefore, the courts are not trespassing on legislative authority, they are fulfilling their assigned democratic duty to prevent legislative trespass on constitutional rights.

While all branches of government are responsible for the delivery of justice, they respond to different imperatives. Legislators, our elected proxies, consult constituents, fellow parliamentarians, and available research until the public's opinions are sufficiently digestible to be swallowed by a parliamentary majority. And if they cannot be made sufficiently palatable, they are starved for want of political nourishment.

This is the dilemma all legislators face — they are elected to implement the public will, the public will is often difficult to ascertain or implement, and they are therefore left to implement only those constituency concerns that can survive the gauntlet of the prevailing partisan ideology. At the end of any given parliamentary session, many public concerns [lie] scattered of necessity on the cutting-room floor, awaiting either wider public endorsement or a newly elected partisan ideology.

The judiciary has a different relationship with the public. It is accountable less to the public's opinions and more to the public interest. It discharges that accountability by being principled, independent, and impartial. Of all the public institutions responsible for delivering justice, the judiciary is the only one for whom justice is the exclusive mandate. This means that while legislatures respond of necessity to the urgings of the public, however we define it, judges, on the other hand, serve only justice. As Lillian Hellman once said: "I will not cut my conscience to fit this year's fashions."

This means that the occasional judgment will collide with some public expectations, which will, inevitably, create controversy. But judgments that are controversial are not thereby illegitimate or undemocratic; they are, in fact, democracy at work.

This defence of constitutional rights does not mean that there are no outstanding issues. There are several to discuss: public information about who judges are and how they are appointed; the interrelationship between courts and legislatures, including the reminder that the notwithstanding clause gives legislatures the final say; when to read in corrective words to effect constitutional compliance and when to leave corrective compliance to the legislature; the tension between those who think the rights stage is overpopulated and those who are in the wings waiting to join the cast; whether labels such as progressive, conservative, activist, restraint, or politicization really contribute to a thoughtful analysis of judicial behaviour; whether the search for consensus is replacing compassion and courage as the defining justice objective and, as a corollary, whether the proposition that entitlement should be a matter of timing can ever be consistent with the fact that rights are guaranteed now.

All of these are issues that we are, and should be, talking about. It is a conversation I hope we will keep constructive, rigorous, and continuous.

(c) Beyond Self-congratulation: The *Charter* at 25 in an International Perspective†

Louise Arbour and Fannie Lafontaine

I. INTRODUCTION

[1] When celebrating the coming into force of an instrument aimed at protecting fundamental human rights, we are unavoidably torn between the desire to rejoice at the immense progress made because of the instrument and the disturbing awareness of the extent of the efforts required for what has yet to be accomplished. This is exactly as it should be. For anniversaries to be meaningful, one must be able to both take note of the successes of the past and commit to meeting the challenges of the future.

† (2007) 45 Osgoode Hall L.J. 239–75 at paras. 1–25, 47–70. [Notes and/or references omitted.] Reproduced with permission.

[2] There is little room for progress while indulging in selfrighteousness and self-congratulation, an endearing tendency Canadians seem to have when nurturing their national self-image as humanitarian, pro-human rights, and internationalist.

[3] On this important occasion — the 25th Anniversary of the *Canadian Charter of Rights and Freedoms*[1] — this article will situate the Canadian human rights evolution in an international context. There, it should be noted that in 2008 we celebrate the 60th anniversary of the *Universal Declaration of Human Rights*,[2] a fundamental document which marked the international community's commitment to a new relationship between the state and the individual. The *Universal Declaration* sparked the steady and accelerating development of the field relating to persons as new subjects of international law.

[4] We will reflect on the influence that the "rights revolution"[3] at the international level continues to have on the *Charter*. In an era of globalization, how has the *Charter* contributed to the integration of universal values in Canada? How has the *Charter* accompanied the changing self-identification process of an internationalized Canada, strongly influenced socially, economically, and politically by its position in the global arena and increasingly identifying itself as a people of peoples, a people whose unity is built on recognizing the distinct identity not only of its founding peoples, but also of its first peoples and of its new members of various origins? We propose to look first at the context of the *Charter*'s adoption and the characteristics that make it an agent of positive social change. Second, we will discuss three areas where interaction between international legal values and our domestic human rights system can be rendered more effective. We will conclude by discussing briefly two key challenges for ensuring meaningful rights protection in Canada.

II. THE *CHARTER*: A DOMESTIC INSTRUMENT WITH AN INTERNATIONAL PURPOSE AND STATURE

A. 1982: Impetus for an Entrenched *Charter* of Rights: The Rise of Rights and the Rise of Law

[5] The *Charter* is situated in a post-war momentum at the international level that saw a proliferation of national and international rights-protection instruments, starting with the *Universal Declaration*. In powerful and somewhat symbolic language, the *Universal Declaration* expresses its repulsion at the excesses and barbarity of war, genocide, and fascism. Meanwhile, national contexts saw the emergence of new democracies, which functioned with a new understanding of the relationship between the state and the individual, and which were characterized by the establishment of structures for effective rights protection.[4]

[6] Through legislation such as the *Canadian Bill of Rights*[5] and provincial human rights codes, Canada was part of the post-Second World War move for rights development even before the enactment of the *Charter*; however, the evolution of human rights law had become stagnant. In many areas, notably in the field of equality rights, we were at a standstill. The establishment of the *Charter* marked a significant move from parliamentary to constitutional democracy and a desire to prevent, by empowering disadvantaged and minority groups, a possible rupture of the country's fabric and unity — a threat which, two years after Quebec's first referendum on sovereignty-association in 1980, deeply influenced the political climate in Canada. While the text is distinctive in ways that characterize Canada's particular historical and political features, the drafting of the *Charter* was heavily influenced by international rights-protection instruments. One of its primary purposes was to bring Canada into compliance with international law.[6]

[7] The connection between domestic efforts worldwide to move to new rights-based democracies and similar developments at the supranational level sparked the will and the need to draw on international human rights instruments, as well as to undertake comparative research in other jurisdictions. Canada drew from others' experiences, as others drew from ours. This trend illustrates the progressively more porous boundaries between domestic constitutional law, foreign law, and international human rights law, as well as the globalization of human rights and of jurisprudence. In a world where countries are increasingly linked by commonly agreed standards, the "rights practice and interpretation in one country rapidly spread to another," as Michael Ignatieff has put it.[7] Canada has become an exporter of its homemade human rights system and solutions, and a growing importer of international and foreign human rights experiences and standards. As Ignatieff rightly points out, "the world is interested in us because we have the world's problems — how to make a multi-cultural, multi-ethnic, multi-national, multi-lingual state cohere in an age of rights."[8] For the same reasons, we should therefore be interested in the world.

[8] The adoption of the *Charter* also took place in a period of sharp increase in the use of legislation to effect social changes.[9] Notably coinciding with the development of human rights law at the international level, post-Second World War legislation focused on the needs of groups previously not protected or outrightly disadvantaged by law, and was designed to "promote social change on behalf of the 'have-nots.'"[10] Many parallel developments in Canada affirmed the positive role of the law in the accomplishment of social change. In the 1970s, the establishment of law reform commissions in Canada showed the importance of the process of reform through the legal system and the possibility of using the law to affect positively the lives of ordinary citizens. Arguably, the pre-*Charter* law-based initiatives aimed at social change — such as the law reform commissions — as well as the development of federal and provincial human rights legislation and specialized agencies and tribunals — including the *Canadian Bill of Rights* and its disappointing performance — contributed significantly to a political climate open to an entrenched rights document and, later, to a judicial climate receptive to generous interpretations of the *Charter* guarantees.[11]

[9] The *Charter* is thus Canada's response to various trends that developed worldwide after the Second World War. Fundamentally, it is an internationally oriented document that found its own ways to respond to the country's specificities. Let us now see how (or whether) the *Charter* has been a catalyst for positive social change in the country and which of its features allowed it to play that role.

B. The *Charter* as a Catalyst for Positive Social Change in Canada: The Rise of Democracy and of Judicial Review

[10] If the patriation of the *Constitution*[12] represented for some an expression of self-determination by the country, the *Charter* represented a broader agreement as a statement of the fundamental values that the country would endeavour to defend.[13] These include the right to participate in the democratic process, freedom of expression, freedom of religion, liberty, equality, linguistic rights, Aboriginal rights, and more. In the twenty-five years since its adoption, we have seen a growing resolve from citizens and civil society organizations to meet the challenge of building a more just, more democratic, and more humane country, and world, according to the principles of the *Charter*. The *Charter* represented a local translation of internationally recognized minimal common denominators. It permitted rights-holders to assert ownership of these rights and it allowed those tasked to protect or interpret these rights to consider them as our homemade response to discrimination, unfairness, or abuse.

[11] The *Charter* has clearly been a catalyst for positive social change in Canada, in line with similar developments at the international level triggered by the post-war rights revolution. At the same time, some features of the *Charter* mark a distinctively Canadian approach, and have contributed greatly to the social change it has stimulated in the last twenty-five years. Indeed, although the normative content is very much in line with international standards — with some notable exceptions such as the absence of property rights — the implementation structure of the *Charter* is truly imaginative, and has contributed greatly to its early and lasting impact.

[12] Strikingly, the *Charter* begins by articulating the framework for the outer limits of the exercise of rights. Section 1 was the result of difficult compromises that led to a political agreement on a constitutionally entrenched rights document. The early jurisprudential development of the section 1 limitations framework proved critical in the evolution of the broader rights jurisprudence. Hesitance and false starts at that stage could have paralyzed the generous expression of substantive rights. Moreover, section 33, also the result of compromise, was a sort of political trump card negotiated in as a safety net. Though it has proven to be a more theoretical than real impediment to rights protection, it has preserved a notional preference for the tyranny of the majority over the potential tyranny of the judiciary.

[13] The three-year moratorium on equality rights also proved farsighted. It allowed judges to flex their intellectual muscles and express a newfound boldness in the familiar terrain of criminal procedure and fair trial standards, a field in which they had always been somewhat willing to stand up to parliaments for the protection of the vulnerable. Those early but easier decisions enabled them to tackle the more challenging section 15 issues that involved the kind of social engineering that judges were traditionally hesitant to embark upon. On the strength of this work on legal rights and section 1, truly progressive development of human rights law became possible. It is far from certain that we would be where we are today if the first *Charter* challenges had called on courts to expand the enumerated list in section 15 or had impeached formal equality. The notable contributions of the

Court Challenges Program, as well as those of the Women's Legal Education and Action Fund (LEAF) and others, led the way for the evolution of the *Charter* as a solid instrument of social progress in Canada.

[14] Apart from these features of the *Charter*'s structure and the particularities of its early implementation, we can safely say that the driving force of the development of human rights law in Canada has been judicial review. Many early landmark cases became solid pillars for meaningful judicial development of substantive human rights. In that regard, none was probably more significant, then and now, than the *B.C. Motor Vehicle Reference*,[14] for moving the courts from procedural to substantive rights. But we should not disregard process altogether. In fact, the criminal procedure and evidence litigation, like judicial review on federalism grounds, was a common feature of our pre-*Charter* legal system, and a proxy for a true "rights" debate.[15]

[15] The *Charter* has expanded the field and depth of judicial intervention, thereby opening the door to an appearance of activism or increased politicization. In reality, however, the *Charter* has not fundamentally altered the methods used for judicial review. The constitutional power of the courts, criticized by some as undemocratic, represents in our view a fundamentally democratic choice: that of articulating the constraints under which the majority can impose its will and the limits to its potential override of protected interests. Judicial review is therefore a democratic choice to be governed by the rule of law.[16] That choice effectively provides a megaphone to the voices of those who may not or cannot be heard in the other democratic institutions. Lacking a broad political base and faced with a lack of good faith or will by governments to negotiate on sensitive issues, many groups have chosen the courts as a forum of choice for the advancement of their rights. The land claims of indigenous peoples and the quest for equality for sexual minorities are good examples.

[16] Our understanding of democracy has evolved, again in line with similar developments at the international level since the Second World War.[17] The constitutionalization of rights has accompanied this evolving conception of democracy, and so has the legitimate demand on courts to check, against the fundamental rights on which we founded our democracy, the inevitable inclinations of the majority to exclude the unpopular or the uninvited. Of course, the judiciary's influence on the development of the law has not taken place in isolation. The particulari-

ties of the *Charter*, notably its limitation and override clauses, call for the active role of the other branches of the government and allow for the aptly named "dialogue" between the judges and the legislatures.[18] The *Charter* has also contributed to the development of a rights consciousness at the administrative level; while some see this as a layer of protection for legislation to comply with *Charter* rights,[19] others claim that it legalizes politics and grants unprecedented powers to lawyers within the governance structure.[20]

[17] This article does not discuss the interaction between the various branches of government for effective rights protection in Canada. Rather, it will contrast the advances made possible by the adjudicative power of our courts with the non-adjudicative international framework. A mere quarter century has assured the irreversible impact of human rights in Canada; similar progress in the non-coercive international setting has taken some sixty years.

[18] The structure established by the *Charter* highlights the essential nature of judicial review as a feature of effective rights protection, a feature that is missing in many countries that work under the same substantive standards, but with less successful implementation. The same is true of the international arena. Indeed, the development of international human rights law is somewhat limited by the absence of binding jurisprudence. The reporting system to the treaty bodies[21] has proved to be a useful mechanism for the improvement of states' compliance with international standards. If nothing else, this mechanism stimulates discussion and requires states to justify their human rights performance or lack thereof. Decisions on individual complaints have also proved valuable and have allowed for increased dialogue between states and the international bodies, though the individual complaints mechanism remains underutilized.[22] However, it is clear that the binding nature of decisions by domestic courts, or by regional human rights courts such as the European Court of Human Rights[23] and the InterAmerican Court of Human Rights,[24] allows for a more sustained and rigorous development of the law.[25]

[19] That said, the dialogue provoked by the reporting process at the international level is very useful. In addition to a government's own report, the treaty bodies may receive information on that country's human rights situation from other sources, including non-governmental organizations (NGOs), United Nations agencies, other intergovernmental organizations, academic institutions, and the press. Even

accounting for generous intervention access, this inclusive process is very different from the judicial model, where the court must decide specific issues relating generally to the situation of only one group or individual, despite the broader impact of the resulting judgement. The international process, with its more consensual and consultative nature, may have contributed to the development of certain rights at the international level that have suffered from a lack of judicial recognition in domestic courts. Economic, social, and cultural rights, for example, are significantly more advanced at the international level than in Canada.[26]

[20] The *Charter* and the considerable impact of judicial review on the development of human rights law may have obscured the relevance and usefulness of parallel processes of consultation and dialogue on human rights issues, like the ones that the Law Reform Commission of Canada (LRCC) had successfully conducted in the past. In this regard, it is noteworthy that much of the LRCC's reform agenda became law, not through Parliament, but through the courts. Though some issues advanced via the *Charter*, many rights-related issues would have arisen in the courts regardless. Developments in the law of evidence were strongly influenced by the LRCC, including common law developments on the inadmissibility of illegally obtained evidence, which was evolving rapidly before section 24(2) of the *Charter* provided a constitutional remedy.

[21] Though the *Charter* has raised rights consciousness, Canada still lacks an entity tasked to evaluate human rights compliance. The federal human rights commission has a limited mandate, and Senate and Parliament standing committees, as well as administrative sensitivity, can only fulfill part of this task. Commissions of inquiry exist somewhere between courts and other oversight mechanisms, and have played a crucial role on many important human rights issues, but they remain ad hoc initiatives. Countries such as Australia, New Zealand, and the United Kingdom — where courts cannot invalidate legislation for violation of human rights — usually, perhaps consequentially, have effective mechanisms to ensure that bills conform to rights guarantees.[27] However, there is no reason not to have strong judicial oversight and strong institutional mechanisms to ensure legislative compliance. Improving those mechanisms would bring Canada to a privileged position for the advancement of human rights.

III. IMPLEMENTATION OF UNIVERSAL VALUES AND INVOLVEMENT IN REGIONAL AND INTERNATIONAL PROTECTION SYSTEMS

[22] Of course, Canada is not isolated from the phenomenon of globalization, and this cannot but impact on how we take into account and integrate international norms in our response to domestic challenges. More than a decade ago, Justice La Forest put it aptly in stating that human rights principles "are applied consistently, with an international vision and on the basis of international experience. Thus our courts — and many other national courts — are truly becoming international courts in many areas involving the rule of law."[28] Courts are increasingly opening themselves to the persuasion of international law in shaping Canadian domestic law. Professor William Schabas has noted that the *Charter* forced courts to open up to international law and, in doing so, to set an example for other constitutional courts. In 2000, he predicted: "A quarter century from now, we may speak of this as the dawn of judicial globalization."[29] It is unquestionable that the judicial globalization process is well in motion, and from a Canadian perspective it was sparked by a quarter century of *Charter* jurisprudence.[30]

[23] This reality is not restricted to Canadian courts, but has impregnated various layers of society. For instance, Parliamentary and Senate Committees discuss international human rights law and apply it to issues before them. Canadian NGOs dedicate significant time and resources to influence international human rights law, as well as domestic law, with the help of the international standards, both in Canada and in multilateral forums. Individuals also frequently use international remedies available to them, the most popular being the use of "communications" to the UN Human Rights Committee, but also to the UN Committee Against Torture and, though underutilized, to the Inter-American Commission on Human Rights for breaches of the *American Declaration of the Rights and Duties of Man*.[31]

[24] This dynamism and internationalism is beneficial both for Canada, which receives the by-products of the creativity it engenders, as well as for the community of states, which profits from Canada's vibrant experience of rights protection in a diverse environment. This demonstrates that true universality can accommodate domestic specificities and the uniqueness of each different system and culture.

551

[25] This irreversible internationalization process influences and guides the way human rights evolve in Canada. Let us briefly touch upon three different areas where this is particularly the case: a) the use of international law in defining the content and possible limitations of *Charter* rights; b) the increased necessity for a better implementation of international human rights obligations and interaction with international bodies; and c) the appropriateness of Canada's full integration to the Americas' human rights system.

. . . .

IV. LIVING UP TO THE PROMISE OF THE "LIVING TREE" METAPHOR: SOME CRITICAL CHALLENGES AHEAD FOR RIGHTS PROTECTION IN CANADA

> Legal historians tend to concentrate on change and innovation. They wish to explain why an innovation occurred when it did. But to understand law and society one must also explain why a legal change did not occur when society changed, or when perceptions about the quality of the law changed.[82]

[47] Alan Watson's comments highlight the complexity of the relationship between law and social change. While we are quick to explain how the *Charter* has made our society evolve (we think readily of progressive changes with respect to the rights of same-sex partners, or of linguistic minorities, or in checking the abuse of police powers, for instance), we are hesitant to identify how and why the *Charter* has failed to prompt social change where it arguably should have. We can celebrate the social achievements of the *Charter* and still acknowledge that it has not yet brought Canada where it committed itself to be, in critical areas such as the protection of economic and social rights and access to justice for all. The protection of other human rights is far from fully secured, and these are but two of the numerous challenges ahead. We should not be complacent about the rights of vulnerable groups or decrease our efforts to ensure their effective protection and promotion, particularly as concerning the rights of women, of Aboriginal peoples, and of visible minorities. Any step backwards in the protection of these rights, and others, would be a blow to the credibility of the *Charter*.

[48] Let us further note that the *Charter* cannot be the sole legal tool for social change. Legislative action in many fields is essential to attain various societal goals and achieve social justice. However, it is our view that the *Charter* is equipped to protect broader interests and values than the purely "negative" rights designed to protect individuals from state interference. The current individual-rights focus given to the *Charter* has limited communal or collective gains. The *Charter* is, and must be able, to offer effective tools for redressing social injustice.

A. Poverty, and Economic, Social, and Cultural Rights Generally

[49] As was emphasised with particular vigour on International Human Rights Day in December 2006,[83] dedicated to the fight against poverty, poverty is frequently both a cause and a consequence of human rights violations. All human rights — freedom of speech and the right to vote, but also to food, work, housing, and health — are jeopardized for the poor, because destitution and exclusion are intertwined with discrimination and unequal access to resources and opportunities. However, poverty is often perceived as a regrettable but accidental condition, or as an inevitable consequence of decisions and events occurring elsewhere, or even as the sole responsibility of those who suffer it. Various factors compound these misconceptions, including the fact that governments often see claims by the poor as stemming more from necessity alone than from enforceable legal entitlements. In addition, there is an overemphasis on civil and political rights, notably in western countries, to the detriment of economic, cultural, and social rights, which the west perceives as "second tier" rights. These "second tier" entitlements are seen as mere privileges, which can be claimed only after fundamental freedoms and civil and political rights have been established and secured, and when countries are strong enough, economically, to address these issues. We agree with Professor Lucie Lamarche that the effects of globalization on vulnerable groups in industrialized economies can be countered by reclaiming international economic rights as human rights in local struggles linked to the deleterious effects of globalization.[84]

[50] In Canada, social and economic rights have failed to be appropriately recognized as rights, and continue, in our view, to be inadequately protected. This accounts for poverty and inequities that are incompatible with the level of social justice that is within our reach. We do not intend here to argue the entire case for economic and social rights to be fully protected as rights in Canada. The High Com-

missioner has discussed this failure,[85] and frequently stated, at the international level, that human rights are indivisible, and that the western countries' historical hesitation to provide equal protection to economic and social rights is unjustified.[86] International monitoring bodies have often criticized Canada on its economic and social rights record,[87] and have noted, among other things, that, sadly, "poverty rates remain very high among disadvantaged and marginalized individuals and groups such as Aboriginal peoples, African Canadians, immigrants, persons with disabilities, youth, low-income women and single mothers."[88]

[51] As Ignatieff correctly points out, it is a major limitation of the rights discourse in Canada — as in other western countries — that it has focused on justice for ethnic, linguistic, and cultural minorities, and for women and persons with disabilities, without sufficient concern for the economic and social inequality resulting from capitalism. Indeed, Ignatieff suggests that the prevailing rights discourse diverts political attention from these inequalities.[89]

[52] While the current rights discourse in Canada does not adequately recognize social, economic, and cultural rights, a lack of capacity is not the problem. Rather, this reflects a choice, one that should be reversed. In fact, if courts and parliaments have been hesitant to recognize economic and social rights, it is not for a lack of discussion on these issues or a shortage of such claims being brought forward.[90] The "rights talk" in Canada is slowly but steadily putting economic and social rights at the forefront and advocating to have them recognized both by parliaments and by courts.

[53] Economic and social rights are arguably better protected elsewhere than in the *Charter* — for instance in provincial human rights legislation. The *Quebec Charter of Rights and Freedoms*[91] guarantees a whole range of economic, social, and cultural rights and prohibits discrimination based on social condition; the New Brunswick Human Rights Act[92] also prohibits discrimination based on social condition.[93] However, in addition to the Supreme Court's narrow view of the *Charter* protections of equality, life, and security, *Gosselin v. Quebec*[94] showed the limitations of internationally-protected rights that are not given the constitutional (or quasi-constitutional) status that allows courts to strike down laws that conflict with them. Chief Justice McLachlin, speaking for the majority, had this to say on the inherent value of these rights in the *Quebec Charter*:

These may be symbolic, in that they cannot ground the invalidation of other laws or an action in damages. But there is a remedy for breaches of the social and economic rights set out in Chapter IV of the *Quebec Charter*: where these rights are violated, a court of competent jurisdiction can declare that this is so.[95]

[54] Justice Bastarache (dissenting), with whom Justice Arbour (as she then was) agreed on this issue, said:

[E]ven though the section does not provide for financial redress from the government in this case, the section is not without value. Indeed it is not uncommon for governments to outline non-judiciable rights in human rights Charters. Courts are not the only institutions mandated to enforce constitutional documents. Legislatures also have a duty to uphold them. If, in this case, the court cannot force the government to change the law by virtue of s. 45, the *Quebec Charter* still has moral and political force.[96]

In separate dissenting reasons, Justice Arbour added:

The right that is provided for in s. 45, while not enforceable here, stands nevertheless as a strong political and moral benchmark in Quebec society and a reminder of the most fundamental requirements of that province's social compact. In that sense, its symbolic and political force cannot be underestimated.[97]

[55] While all of this is indeed correct legally, it highlights that the "symbolic," "moral," and "political" force of rights that are not truly enforceable does not give, in many instances, concrete remedies to the aggrieved right-holder. This shows the potential of judicial review as a driving force for the evolution of law in a democratic rights-based society. The Commission des droits de la personne et des droits de la jeunesse du Québec[98] and others have strongly argued, notably on the occasion of the 25th anniversary of the *Quebec Charter*, for a revision that would raise economic and social rights to the same level of protection as that afforded to other rights. This initiative should be supported.

[56] For several years now, many have argued that "social condition" should be added to the prohibited grounds of discrimination in the federal *Canadian Human Rights Act*.[99] Such a change was recommended, inter alia, by the *Canadian Human Rights Act* Review Panel in its June 2000 report,[100] as well as by the CESCR, notably in its December 1998 concluding observations on Canada's Third Report under the *ICESCR*.[101] Poverty has long been recog-

nized as a contributing factor in the discrimination suffered by disadvantaged social groups. Regardless of such an addition in the federal legislation, it is striking that the courts have been somewhat daring in recognizing nonenumerated "analogous" grounds under section 15 of the Charter on certain issues, such as sexual orientation, but timid and even cold-footed on others, such as poverty or social condition. In our view, this reflects an unjustified belief that social and economic rights are values dependent on the market or on governmental policy, not legal rights worthy of constitutional protection.

[57] Whichever avenue Canada takes to ensure full protection of economic and social rights, whether through a constitutional amendment, a more progressive interpretation of the current *Charter* text, a modification of other (federal and provincial) human rights instruments, or otherwise, this is the next step which must be taken if Canada wants to ensure that the most disadvantaged members of society will truly benefit from the immense promise of the *Charter*. As one author put it five years ago, on the 20th anniversary of the *Charter* — and we believe it more acutely now — social and economic rights are the "next frontier" of *Charter* rights protection.[102]

[58] It is high time to guarantee claimants access to the courts to articulate the full scope of these rights and secure their enforcement, in the same way that the contours of the civil and political rights took shape in the early years of the *Charter*. Rights are not just about protection against abusive or unjustified interference by the state. The role of the state has evolved and it has become central for human dignity and security to be fulfilled through a system of public policy and legislation aimed at protecting the individual and his or her family from want and need. This is indeed what is suggested by the *Universal Declaration*: a state both respectful of individual freedoms and responsible through positive action for the preservation of human dignity and legitimate expectations of social justice. The duality of roles for the state that is mandated by international human rights law needs to be integrated into our understanding of the *Charter*.

[59] Many modern constitutions have strived to attain that balance. The South African Constitution is one of the most progressive and modern constitutions in the world, with one of the most comprehensive bills of rights. It contains rights of access to housing, health care, social assistance, and education.[103] Some of these social and economic rights are qualified in that they require the state to take rea-

sonable steps, according to its available resources, to realize the rights progressively. Even so, the Constitutional Court has handed down some groundbreaking decisions in which, for instance, it declared the government's housing policy invalid,[104] and found that the state was not fulfilling its constitutional duty to provide access to health care because it had failed to take adequate steps to prevent the mother to child transmission of HIV.[105] Other high courts in many other countries, including India and Argentina, have taken progressive stances on economic and social rights.

[60] Meanwhile, it is incongruous for Canada to afford constitutional protection to some rights and allow others to be claimed only as reasonable limits to the exercise of other rights. Section 1 is indeed often said to set out collective values, including social justice, against which individual rights are to be balanced. Courts in Canada have looked at international human rights instruments for indications as to the criteria that may be invoked in section 1 analyses,[106] including the rights contained in the *ICESCR*.[107] Nevertheless, to selectively recognize and ensure the protection of some rights while not affording the same protection to others is at odds with the principles of international human rights law that embrace all human rights, be they civil, social, economic, cultural, or political in nature. There is no valid reason to claim that economic and social rights can be adequately addressed by deference to government's policy concerning social justice at the justification stage, rather than to recognize these rights as justiciable.

[61] At the international level, there is encouraging movement towards the adoption of a protocol to permit individual petitions alleging violations of the *ICESCR*,[108] which could have great, and positive, domestic impact in Canada. If and when ratified by Canada, this new instrument would provide Canadians with a forum of choice to claim their internationally-protected economic, social, and cultural rights, a particularly valuable remedy considering the unavailability of any such domestic legal avenues.

B. Access to Justice

[62] As was noted above, perhaps the most enduring impact of the *Charter* on our society and legal system is how it has been at the vanguard of social change in the country, aided in that by the vigorous judicial review it has prompted.

[63] Individuals and groups have turned to the courts to remedy violations of their rights or to artic-

ulate those rights. This could not have happened unless those who had succeeded had access to the courts. Though the "rights revolution" would not have happened without rightsholders' access to justice, there is no constitutionally protected general right to access to justice. The Supreme Court recently held that there is no general right to be represented by a lawyer in court or tribunal proceedings where a person's legal rights and obligations are at stake.[109]

[64] The *Charter* may not have always translated to concrete and substantive improvements in the lives of the most disadvantaged. Yet, the *Charter* has created a culture of expectations, perhaps even of entitlements. Individuals and groups turn to the *Charter*, and thus to the courts, to challenge discriminatory practices and other violations of their rights. In that context, the Canadian Bar Association's position that "access to justice is the biggest challenge facing our justice system at this time" is particularly acute.[110] Chief Justice McLachlin has also highlighted on numerous occasions the importance of access to justice for all Canadians. To protect the integrity of our legal system, and of the constitution that supports it, it is essential that everyone in Canada have access to the courts.

[65] Cuts in financial support to legal aid services across the country prevent, in many cases, the exercise of rights protected by the *Charter*, and lead to situations where poor people, in particular poor single women, who are denied benefits and services to which they are entitled under law, cannot access the available remedies.[111] Furthermore, the cancellation of the Court Challenges Program,[112] a program that had proved a significant ally to equality in the country and been hailed as uniquely Canadian, was a hard blow for access to justice. Many had identified the program as central to the rights revolution that occurred in the country.

[66] Critics of the program and of the power of judicial review more generally are quick to condemn the "interest group litigation"[113] that the *Charter* might have prompted. There is some truth to the myth that rights-advancing litigation has evolved with the *Charter*.[114] However, we must remember that the very people some discount as merely selfindulgent "interest groups" are called "human rights defenders" at the international level, and benefit from international protection.[115] We should be very careful about dismissing those who strive to advance human rights causes through legally available means.

[67] With the winding up of the Court Challenges Program, the serious obstacles facing legal aid programs, and the high bar imposed on litigants for obtaining interim costs in *Charter* litigation,[116] it may be a good time for the legal profession to unite on the issue of access to justice. Given the economic deterrent inherent in the current litigation system and the lack of access to funding, it is essential to find ways to ensure that the *Charter* is still seen as, and made to be, accessible to all.

[68] It is through the ingenuity of litigants that the protection of human rights in Canada has progressed this far. There is no reason to disempower them in the face of the challenges that lie ahead, be it on environmental issues, minority protection, the reach of equality, or the ever-present security concerns.

V. CONCLUSION

[69] Central to the position of the *Charter* in Canadian federalism is the idea, perhaps counterintuitive, that the greatest protection for individual rights and freedoms comes in large, pluralistic environments. Conversely, the greater danger comes from small, homogeneous communities that lack the imagination and the means to deal effectively with the competing individual claims from within, specially the claims that question the apparent homogeneity.

[70] This also speaks loudly in favour of strong regional and international human rights protection systems, as they serve to push back narrow national horizons to put in full view the claims and aspirations of the whole of the human race.

(a) The Role of Law in Social Transformation: Is a Jurisprudence of Insurgency Possible?†

Stephen Brickey and Elizabeth Comack

Contemporary Marxist theorizing on law has produced a number of different ways of conceptualizing the class character of law within a capitalist society. The main focus of these approaches has largely been on the role of law in maintaining and reproducing an unequal, exploitative system. As a consequence, the issue, even the possibility of using law as a mechanism for securing substantial social change has been downplayed and, in some cases, precluded.

The purpose of this paper is to argue for a rethinking of law, especially in terms of its potential as an agent for social transformation. The discussion will be divided into two main sections. The first involves theoretical considerations. Problems encountered with existing approaches to law *vis-à-vis* their implications for change will be examined and the direction in which a theoretical reformulation might proceed will be outlined. The second involves practical considerations. Here the focus will be on the kinds of legal strategies and particular forms and conditions of law that could be extended or developed in order to move in the direction of a socialist society.

. . . .

Toward a Theoretical Reformulation

It is not our intention to deny the insights to be gained from current Marxist theorizing on law. Much has been accomplished, for example, in the way of clarifying the class character of law under capitalism. Nor is it our intention to deny the significance of law as a mechanism of class domination. In this regard, we would agree with writers like Picciotto that the rule of law — to the extent that it has bourgeois limitations and characteristics — must and should be transcended. The question remains, however, as to *how* that is to be accomplished. Neither instrumentalism nor structuralism offers much hope for law as a mechanism for social transformation. Even those writers who are sensitive to the changing forms of state and law under advanced capitalism offer little guidance in the way of concrete strategies or proposals for bringing about substantive change.[20] As a result, we are left with the uneasy feeling that social transformation must await the 'revolution,' but are given no real indication as to how that will be possible.

In contrast, we would argue that law offers an important (although by no means the sole) source for realizing substantive social change. Implicit in this position is a particular conception of law. As opposed to instrumentalism, we take law to have a distinctly social character; that is, more than just a 'tool' or an external set of rules imposed on individuals, law emerges out of distinct social and historical conditions. In contrast to the structuralist tendency toward 'overdetermination,' we would suggest that emphasis be placed on the role of social actors in the constitution and reproduction of legal order. Fol-

† (1987) 2 C.J.L.S. 97 at 97, 102–14. [Notes and/or references omitted.] Reproduced with the permission of Cambridge University Press.

lowing this, the legal sphere can be viewed as an arena of struggle which engages individuals of different classes and political positions.

We would also argue that there are some very good reasons for not abandoning the law. First, if we turn our backs on law, then, as Young suggests, we are left in a position whereby we are denied *any* of the protections afforded by the law — however limited they may be.[21]

Second, although several writers have objected to the discourse of rights as an inappropriate form for generating liberating practices,[22] the fact remains that the very terms of political argument and debate in advanced capitalist societies are unavoidably legalistic. As Hunt remarks:

> All political issues involve, usually quite directly, appeals to rights; whether it be the 'right to work' or 'the right to a fair profit,' 'a woman's right to choose' or 'the right to life,' politics and political demands invoke appeals to rights, or to the analogous language of 'freedom.' So persistent is this appeal to rights that it makes little or no sense to dismiss this reality as some on the left seek to do, by arguing that "rights" are merely ideological masks disguising naked interests.[23]

In this respect, despite its 'bourgeois character,' rights discourse at the very least offers the potential of facilitating the mobilization of political action among subordinate groups.

Third, the tendency for those on the left to deny the possibility of 'legal justice' has left the door wide open for other interpretations. As a result, the right has been given relatively free [rein] in defining the terms and parameters of 'law and order' issues. The increasing prominence of right wing law and order campaigns, coupled with the emergence of the new law and order state,[24] with its reduction of welfare services and legal encroachments on civil liberties and legal rights, only showcases the need to mount a defense and extension of existing rights and liberties.[25] Indeed, if (as the structuralists suggest) 'crime control' and related issues are an important source of legitimation for the status quo, then there is all the more reason to formulate a Marxist dialectical position which justifies the defense of legal rights and civil liberties.

Finally, to view the law as irrelevant in the attempt to secure social transformation denies the significance of the rights struggles of women, Natives, youth, prisoners and other subordinated segments of society. It promotes a narrow conception of class struggle in that, as Sumner notes, it excises the class character of these conflicts and reduces the struggle of the working class to the economic claims of an urban, white, male labour aristocracy.[26] In effect, it amounts to the 'colonization' of subordinate fractions of the working class by a dominant fraction. Not to give significance to these types of rights struggles also suggests that social transformation may result in a classless society, but it would still be sexist, racist and ageist.[27]

The question remains, then, as [in] what direction theoretical reformulation should proceed in order to fashion an approach which incorporates, rather than abandons, law as a potential agent for social transformation?

If the law is too narrowly conceived as simply a mechanism of class rule, then it can be easily dismissed as a 'fraud'; as an empty set of guarantees of equity and fairness that have somehow been sold to an unwitting public. Such a narrow conception of law misses some important considerations, not the least of which is that justice *is* often seen to be done. In order to maintain the appearance of equity and fairness, the law must live up to its own claims. As Thompson notes:

> If the law is evidently partial and unjust, then it will mask nothing, legitimate nothing, contribute nothing to any class's hegemony. The essential precondition for the effectiveness of law, in its function as ideology, is that it shall display an independence from gross manipulation and shall seem to be just. It cannot seem to be so without upholding its own logic and criteria of equity; indeed, on occasion, by actually *being* just.[28]

Mandel offers further clarification in the distinction he makes between two opposing senses of the rule of law. The first, which he labels 'democratic,' is essentially the one invoked by Thompson. It "stresses the inhibitions placed on official power ... by clear rules strictly adhered to ... [rules which] contribute in content to real equality and freedom."[29] The second, which Mandel labels the "juridical," is best described by Pashukanis's analysis of the legal form under capitalism.[30] It "stresses those characteristic features which work to strengthen the *status quo* of unequal social power...."[31] One of the main insights to be gained from this distinction is that there is an inherent *tension* built into the law. This tension is further reflected in the fact that law is *both* a means of coercive and ideological domination; of force *and* consent. As an ideological form, the law acts as a legitimizer of capitalist social relations — it presents those relations in a certain light. Yet, at one and the same time, it too must be legitimized. The law requires an ideological base without which it is simply 'naked power.'[32]

In order to win the consent of the dominated classes to the capitalist order — in order to mediate class relations — the law has to take into account interests other than those of the dominant class. In this sense, "law is not simply imposed upon people, but is also a *product* and *object of* and provides an arena which circumscribes class (and other types of) struggle."[33] Indeed, the rights enshrined in law (universal suffrage, right to form a union, right to strike and so on) were not simply handed down by a benevolent state, but were the outcome of progressive struggles by the subordinate classes.

Thus, as Thompson and others have shown, if the law is to be a legitimizer of capitalist social relations, then the rhetoric and rules of law must be more than 'sham.' Law must provide some protection against the arbitrary use of state power. It must live up to its own claims of equity and fairness. While one need not go so far as to suggest, as Thompson does,[34] that the rule of law is an 'unqualified good' that should be defended at all costs (especially given its 'juridical' sense), the recognition of the tension built into law does open up a number of theoretical possibilities concerning its implications for social transformation. Specifically, law is no longer viewed exclusively as a weapon of class rule, as an abstract, homogeneous entity whose functions can be generalized across different historical periods and circumstances. Instead, the function of law can differ, depending upon the relative strength of social forces that struggle around and within the legal order. Such an assertion involves working at a different level of abstraction than most structuralist accounts.

As Hall and Scraton note, if we rely on Marx's writings in *Capital*, which discuss the 'laws of motion' of a capitalist economy at a very high and abstract level (generalizing these laws across historical periods and societies), then law will be assigned a more 'fixed' and determined role within capitalism.[35] If, however, we rely on the more historical writings of Marx, in which he takes account of the whole social formation — including its political, legal and ideological aspects — then the role of law is treated more problematically.[36] This latter viewpoint allows us to break with the notion of a 'necessary' or 'functional' fit between law and the economic interests of capital. Instead we are left with a very contradictory picture. To quote Hall and Scraton:

> There is no historical guarantee that capital must prevail, and no certainty that it can prevail on its own terms, outside the limits imposed by contestation and struggle. The outcomes of par-

ticular struggles, sometimes waged within and about the law, sometimes against it, will have real and pertinent effects on how particular historical struggles develop. Law, in this sense, is constitutive of (i.e., it creates) the very conditions of historical development and struggle, and does not merely reflect them.[37]

What we would advocate, therefore, is a theoretical approach to law that moves beyond both a narrow conception of the relations between base and superstructure, and the more fixed and deterministic view of law as operating to the permanent advantage of capital. Such an approach must be materialist and dialectical. It must also be sensitive to the historically specific and contradictory nature of the bourgeois legal form and the system in which it operates.

An appropriate starting point for such an approach is the Marxist conception of social formation. 'Social formation' connotes that certain elements and forms of politics, culture and law are organic to a particular mode of production at a given phase of its development. Without their establishment and maintenance, such a mode of production cannot survive.[38] Once established, however, a capitalist mode of production generates its own internal contradictions. These contradictions will be expressed not only in the economic form (at the point of production), but also in the forms of politics, culture and law which correspond to it. Moreover, these internal contradictions will generate particular legal forms of resistance, which will emerge alongside economic, political and cultural forms. To quote Sumner: "Like feudalism, capitalism must breed its successor in legal forms ... before it leaves the scene."[39] As such, the task — both theoretical and practical — is to determine what forms and principles of law we should develop and extend *now* as a precondition for a socialist transformation.

A general strategy for realizing this task is the development of what Tigar and Levy refer to as a "jurisprudence of insurgency."[40] Jurisprudence can be defined as a "process by which legal ideology is created and elaborated." Following this, "jurisprudence of insurgency" can be used to refer to "a certain kind of jurisprudential activity in which a group challenging the prevailing system of social relations no longer seeks to reform it but rather to overthrow it and replace it with another."[41]

If capitalist legality contains the seeds of a socialist legality, then one step toward the development of a jurisprudence of insurgency would be to explore the limits of the dominant legal ideology in order to gauge how much can be accomplished within those limits.[42] This would involve, as Tigar and Levy note, the use of the assumptions of the governing class to one's own advantage. In short, given the tension built into law, the aim would be to grasp the contradictions inherent in the bourgeois legal form — to work *through* law — in order to alter the very nature of that legal form. Rather than dismissing the rule of law, therefore, we need to consider what effect pushing the 'democratic' sense of the rule of law to its full limit and extent would have on undermining the social relations of capitalism. It is this kind of strategy that we will explore in the remainder of this paper.

PRACTICAL CONSIDERATIONS

In approaching the task of assessing the role of law in social transformation, we start from the premise, documented in Tigar and Levy's analysis of European society between the eleventh and nineteenth centuries, that legal change did not simply go through a single stage of transformation in the movement from feudalism to capitalism. Rather, the process was one of an increasing number of small, incremental legal changes that gave increasing power and legitimacy to the fledgling capitalist class. Consistent with this premise, we do not expect law to be either the vanguard or the consequence of the transformation from capitalist to socialist society. We would argue, instead, that it will be one of many strategic areas where existing tension within the system can be used to push the contradictions that result from the structure of capitalism.

Before delineating those legal activities that best represent a jurisprudence of insurgency, we readily admit the difficulty in attempting to predict what will be the most 'progressive' avenues of legal reform. The advantage of retrospective analysis — like that conducted by Tigar and Levy — is that one can discern the significance of small legal changes over historical periods by examining the diverse consequences these changes had over time. When trying to forecast how current legal changes may facilitate future substantive changes in society, one is blind to all of the potential consequences these changes may produce. If, however, historical analysis has any value, it is in the extent to which it enables us to make prescriptive statements, even tentative ones, on how to transform the existing system.

The central issue to be addressed is one of specifying the criteria by which legal reforms are to be evaluated. More specifically, what kinds of legal reform could be defined as insurgent in terms of their orientation or consequence? How do we distinguish, for example, between reforms which aim only for a greater participation of individuals within the capitalist order (i.e., demanding a "bigger share" of the capitalist pie) from those which aim to transform the very basis of that order?[43]

Structuralists have premised their scepticism about law on the observation that equality is limited to the legal sphere (i.e., it does not extend to the economic sphere of capitalist society). It is in this respect that principles like "equality of all before the law" or "blind justice" are viewed as a major source of legitimation for the system of structured or economic inequality. However, several writers have argued that this position with its ritual invocation of the Anatole France quote, lets the law off too lightly since the law is applied in anything but an equal manner.[44] This recognition of the inequalities in the legal order has led to a number of suggestions for reform.

Mandel, for example, in his analysis of Canadian sentencing law, notes that a central feature of sentencing practices is the recognition of varying punishment according to the offender's 'character,' in particular, the offender's relation to the productive apparatus.[45] By taking into account such factors as educational attainment, employment record and one's "good standing in the community" in the determination of sentence, the law operates to the advantage of one class over another. High status offenders, by virtue of their class position, are perceived as requiring (even deserving) less punishment to ensure their continued conformity. Hence, by varying punishment according to class, the law has the net effect of preserving the status quo of inequality, dominance and subordination. In light of this analysis, Mandel suggests that if sentencing was based solely on the utilitarian principle of general deterrence, that is, the protection of individuals from the harmful effects of crime at the least social cost, punishment would then be based entirely on the conduct sought to be prevented, and not on the "character" (i.e., class) of the offender.

What would be the effect of such a reform? Mandel suggests that it would represent a move in the direction of the 'neutral' state which liberals claim exists in modern democratic societies, that is, the system would be more 'just' in the sense that punishment would no longer vary by class. In this respect, such a reform strategy is laudable to the extent that it would mitigate the unequal treatment to which members of the subordinate classes are subjected by the legal system.

Yet, what of the structuralist argument that equality in sentencing practices would only reinforce the system of economic inequality and hence further legitimate that system? On the one hand, removing the class-based nature of punishment (i.e., viewing dominant class members as 'deserving' of lesser punishment) would eliminate one of the means by which class relations are strengthened and reinforced by the legal order. On the other hand, not taking class differences into account could be viewed as a way of ignoring and/or denying the class differences that do exist.[46] Although punishment would no longer vary by class, crime would continue to vary by class. In this respect Mandel's reform proposal has its advantages, but it is limited.[47] It would only take us part way toward the development of a 'jurisprudence of insurgency.' Such a reform is not insurgent to the extent that it fails to call into question class relations.

Other writers have focused their attention on the content of law.[48] While the criminal law defines certain acts as 'socially injurious' or 'harmful,' it does not tend to define other acts — which are potentially more serious and harmful — as criminal and hence worthy of severe sanctions. For instance, violence against individuals occurs regularly in the workplace of capitalist societies. This typically takes the form of unsafe or hazardous working conditions, exposure to carcinogenic substances and the like. The result has been the loss of life and health for a substantial number of workers. Yet, while such occurrences meet the requirements normally associated with crime (for example, the intentional failure to provide safety equipment or the flagrant violation of safety regulations by owners in order to cut costs and increase profits), they are seldom defined or sanctioned as such. Reiman, therefore, has suggested that the criminal law be redrawn to more accurately reflect the real dangers that individuals pose to society:

Avoidable acts where the actor had reason to know that his or her acts were likely to lead to someone's death should be counted as forms of murder. Avoidable acts where the actor had reason to believe that his or her acts were likely to lead to someone's injury should be counted as forms of assault and battery. Acts that illegitimately deprive people of their money or possessions should be treated as forms of theft regardless of the color of the thief's collar. Crime in the suites should be prosecuted and punished as vigorously as crime in the streets.[49]

Glasbeek and Rowland have taken this issue one step further.[50] They suggest that there already exist provisions in the criminal law which, although not initially designed for the purpose, could be applied to employer violations of workplace health and safety.[51] This approach is essentially one which advocates the use of criminal law as a vehicle for highlighting the class conflicts inherent in the productive process. By criminalizing employer practices which result in worker injury and death, the severity of the problem would be reinforced. In effect, the strategy proposed by Glasbeek and Rowland is one which aims at using the assumptions of the governing class to the advantage of the working class. To quote the authors:

Because of the assumptions of the liberal state, the ideology of law requires it to claim that it punishes behaviour which has been judged unacceptable by society no matter who the perpetrator of the offensive behaviour is. It will be interesting to see how the administrators of the legal justice system respond when it is argued that entrepreneurs offend against the criminal process in much the same way as do robbers of private property and people.[52]

In this respect, such a reform strategy would advance the development of a jurisprudence of insurgency in that it endeavours to push the rule of law to its full limit and extent. Defining the violence which occurs in the workplace of capitalist societies as criminal would have the potential of not only holding employers more accountable for their actions but raising the consciousness of workers as well.

On another level a jurisprudence of insurgency must also be capable of addressing the *manner* in which legal issues are handled by the courts. To elaborate, the law adheres to the principle of 'blind justice.' In so doing, it responds not to the "why" of an act, but to whether or not the act was committed. The race, class or sex of the accused is deemed irrelevant, as the primary criterion for judging cases is the empirical question of whether a formally proscribed act was committed. In short, the issue becomes a matter of "legally relevant facts" and, in the process of resolving this issue, the case is both *individualized* and *depoliticized*. As Grau explains:

Cases are tried only between legal parties with defined legal interests that conflict over narrowly drawn legal issues. Collective needs are denied. The specificity of the rights and the narrowness of the legal issues combine to preclude the introduction of broader, though relevant, social questions. This restriction effectively depoliticizes the case.[53]

This feature of the legal order contributes to one of the main legitimizing effects of the rule of law, that is, the idea that society is composed, almost exclusively, of individuals and not groups, aggregates or classes. Equally significant is the related belief that legal struggles and political struggles are separate and distinct activities. We would argue, therefore, that a jurisprudence of insurgency must alter this artificial distinction between legal and political issues. This will encompass a two-sided dialectical process. The one side involves attempting to bring the collective nature of the problem into the legal arena while the other side involves broadening the definition of the situation to encompass the political nature of the problem.

"Collectivizing" and "Politicizing" Legal Battles

One way in which the law is being pushed to deal with problems that are more than individual concerns is the strategic use of law by groups to address collective problems. Historically, the labour movement was one of the first to view the problems of workers as a condition common to all individuals whose work placed them in a subordinated position to capital. Because of the blatant nature of this subordination and the fact that workers could readily interact with other co-workers who were experiencing the same consequences of subordination, craft workers were quicker than other groups to approach their problems as collective in nature.

Before describing how some collectivities are currently attempting to use the law and assessing the insurgent nature of these efforts, it is important to note the dynamic interplay that appears to exist between groups defining their problems as collective problems and the concomitant recognition of the political nature of their problems. The consistency with which groups redefine their problems as political issues suggests that politicization is a typical — if not inevitable — consequence of recognizing the collective nature of the problem. By the very act of sharing their problem with others in a similar condition, people come to realize that approaching the problem as a narrow legal issue is unrealistic and often ineffective.

Of greater significance, however, is the tendency for groups not to rely solely on the courts to resolve their problems. By recognizing the political nature of their problems, activist groups also attempt to put pressure directly on the state by engaging in legislative and lobbying activities, which has traditionally been the almost exclusive domain of the major economic interests in society. The use of lobbying by farmworkers, tenants, environmental groups, women, Indians, the handicapped and the elderly is an indication of the extent to which collectivities are broadening the scope of their struggles beyond the traditional locus of the courts.

Although the lobbying efforts of the above groups may not be successful, they are an indication of how the groups view their difficulties as political problems and not simply legal problems. Billings describes this difference in her assessment on the use of advocacy by women's organizations:

> More and more, therefore, lobbying ... has become a familiar tool of the women's movement. Although largely unproductive in proportion to the amount of energy [expended], *lobbying has at least familiarized women with the corridors of power,* created networks across the country and ... created lengthy policy agendas that are agreed to nation-wide as the action priorities.[54]

Although we will argue that the strategies utilized by some groups are more "insurgent" than other strategies, it is important to recognize that the very act of subordinate groups approaching the law as a collective is of value to the extent that it results in politicizing the manner in which the problem is defined.

Collectivities Using the Law

There appears to be a growing awareness among activist groups of the limitations and constraints of approaching the law as individuals. One way in which groups have attempted to increase their power in using the law is to develop strategies that increase the chances that cases heard before the courts represent the collective interests of the group (given the structural limitation that these collective interests must be fought on an individual basis since collectivities are not recognized as legal actors). Some of these strategies continue to use the courts as the arena for battle but expand the techniques by which groups gain access to the courts. The methods used include class action suits, test cases, judicial reviews, standing as *amicus curiae* and private prosecutions.[55]

There are a number of current examples of individuals in Canada forming groups with the sole purpose of fighting legal issues from a collective rather than an individual base. One of the most recent examples of this is the organization of women fighting for a range of issues that address the many consequences of the systemic subordination of women in capitalist society. These issues include affirmative action, equal pay for work of equal value, the handling of sexual offenses by the criminal justice system and the way in which wife battering is dealt with by the police and the courts. One of the consequences of women defining the legal battle as a collective battle is the shift in strategies that will increase the ability of women to influence the types of cases that should be emphasized in the legal arena. A report by the Canadian Advisory Council on the Status of Women, for example, suggests taking a systematic approach to litigation that would further the collective interests of women. The approach would involve the following four steps:

1. defining a goal in terms of the desired principle of law to be established;
2. plotting how the principle of law can be established from case to case in incremental, logical and clear steps;
3. selecting winnable cases suitable for each stage taken to achieve the goal;
4. consolidating wins at each stage by bringing similar cases to create a cluster of cases in support of the principle established.[56]

It is true that some of the above issues (such as affirmative action) simply strive for women to gain a larger piece of the pie within the existing system. Nonetheless, their importance is in the fact that the state is being asked to recognize that it is *not* the problem of a few individuals but a condition of a large segment of the population that has been adversely affected by the economic system. This demand for the recognition of problems as more than individual problems is also evident in the development of anti-poverty organizations, Indian groups fighting for aboriginal land claims and victims' groups demanding greater participation in the criminal justice system. The presumption that legal battles, particularly those in the area of civil law, are exclusively conflicts between individuals and the state or individuals against corporations is becoming less and less tenable.

Although the above strategies used by groups in approaching the law have a number of advantages over traditional approaches, the fact that the law forces these groups to fight their battles through cases of specific individuals in court limits the ability to use the law to redress collective problems. As long as the state is allowed to approach problems of inequality on an individual, case by case basis, there is little likelihood of the law being an effective tool for redressing the collective problems of subordinate groups.

Collective Rights

We would argue that one way in which the law could be used to promote substantive change is to have collectivities recognized as legal actors in society. In other words, to establish the legal principle that, in addition to individual rights in law, there are or should be collective rights that would acknowledge the existence of subordinate groups and provide them, analogically, with the same rights and freedoms that individuals currently have, in principle if not in practice. The recognition of collective rights enables groups to move away from the narrowly defined manner in which current legal ideology defines conflicts in society.

One subject which immediately comes to mind when discussing collective rights is the *Canadian Charter of Rights and Freedoms*. The passage of the *Constitution Act, 1982* has been lauded by some commentators as a means of providing the legal rights and guarantees that would mitigate against the discrimination of minorities in Canada. However, as Rush[57] has argued, while the *Charter* protects individual rights, collective rights are either ill-protected or disregarded altogether.[58] Rush suggests two ways in which collective rights can be perceived constitutionally:

> First, collective rights are those rights which accrue to individuals because of their placement or membership in an identifiable group. In this sense, the realization of the right for each individual depends on its realisation for everyone in the group. These are the rights of cultural communities, ethnic and minority groups.... Second, collective rights are also rights which accrue to groups as groups. These include: the right of Indian people to title to and jurisdiction over their aboriginal land; and the right of women to affirmative action programmes in the workplace.[59]

Following this, Rush notes that "working class rights," full aboriginal rights and the rights of women have not been recognized.[60] In this regard, we would argue, alongside Rush, that continued pressure from working people, women, and ethnic and minority groups for greater recognition of collective rights in the *Charter* is needed.

It should be noted that not every instance of the demand for, or recognition of, collective rights represents explicit insurgent activity. For example, the current legislation in Canada regarding hate literature gives groups the legal ability to prohibit the broadcast or publication of material that has the express purpose of producing hatred toward the group. It is the collective analogy to the law of libel that affords an individual the right to protection from malicious material. While this law recognizes the existence of groups as legal actors, there is nothing within the law that directly addresses the relationship of groups to the state or to the economic base of the system. Similarly, what has historically been recognized as the collective right of management to determine the conditions of work, rates of productivity and the like would obviously fall outside the boundaries of a jurisprudence of insurgency. What this highlights is the need to question "collective right to what?" and establish the criteria and principles on which collective rights should be based.

Legal Recognition of Structural Inequality

To what extent is the demand for collective rights and the politicization of collectivities in their legal struggles indicative of a jurisprudence of insurgency? We would argue that, in addition to the obvious value of individuals no longer viewing their problems as isolated, non-political problems, there has been limited success by collectivities in demanding that the legal system *not* approach all citizens as equals. That is, groups are contending that it is unjust to start from the premise that all individuals are equal legally.

The current emphasis on affirmative action programs by the government could be interpreted as a recognition by the state that there is *structural* and *systemic* inequality in capitalist society. Women, minority groups, the handicapped and other groups who have been at the economic margins have been successful in getting the state at least to acknowledge the problem (even if the remedies to the problem have not been forthcoming). In a similar manner, the current efforts to establish the principle of equal-pay-for-work-of-equal-value is an attempt to pressure the government to acknowledge the structural inequality that has resulted from a segmented labour market.

Both affirmative action and the principle of equal-pay-for-work-of-equal-value are *potentially* insurgent because they use a contradiction within legal ideology to push the law and the state past the limits established by the legal system. By groups bringing public attention to the inconsistency that the law is premised on all citizens being equal, yet large segments of the society have been placed in a position of structural inequality, the state is placed in a position of either admitting that all citizens are not equal

or making adjustments to provide greater equality. Although the state may attempt to coopt movement toward greater equality, the public focus on the contradiction requires that the state take some form of ameliorative action.

CONCLUSION

The purpose of this paper has been to open up debate on and interest in the role of law in social transformation. If one accepts that a socialist society is not going to emerge in a full-blown manner, then one must assess how the existing system — including law — can be used to push capitalist society along the path toward socialism. The jurisprudence of insurgency is based on the idea that to abandon law as an agent of change is to negate one method that can be used to challenge the present system. The insurgent role of law is to identify the existing contradictions within legal ideology and to use those contradictions to pit that ideology against itself.

Although it has been argued in this paper that the area of collective rights is one avenue that has the potential of bringing the issue of systemic inequality to the forefront, it must also be admitted that the demand for collective rights has the potential of producing divisions within the working class. These divisions are most likely to occur where some segments of the working class perceive a threat from the collective rights won by other segments of that class. A current example of this is affirmative action policy and the negative reaction to this initiative by individuals who do not fit into one of the target groups identified in the policy. The nature of this conflict is often expressed in the form of collective rights versus individual rights. While there will undoubtedly be instances where collective and individual rights will come into conflict, one should also note that capitalists have in the past facilitated this view of the inherent incompatibility of collective rights and individual rights to suit their own interests.[61]

It must also be admitted that there is a danger in groups using the law in the attempt to achieve their aims. Chief among these dangers is the likelihood that groups will start to define their struggles as ones to be fought exclusively within the legal arena. The consequence of this is that a loss in the courts is seen as the end of the struggle.[62] Several authors have written on the difficulties encountered when a group places all of its energies in legal struggles. In fact, Glasbeek has taken the position that groups should avoid using the *Charter* as a political tool.[63] While recognizing the difficulties in using law in a progressive manner, we would continue to argue, for the reasons stated earlier, that the law should not be abandoned as an arena for social struggle.[64]

Finally, a jurisprudence of insurgency has implications for the role that social scientists and legal practitioners play in legal struggles. For the social scientist, perhaps the most important role is to perform the task originally explicated by C. Wright Mills: to demonstrate the linkage between private troubles and public issues.[65] Applying Mills's dictum to the area of law, the task of the social scientist is to show the commonality of individuals' legal problems and the commonality of interests individuals have in collectively addressing these problems.

For the legal practitioner, the traditional approach to the practice of law and the lawyer-client relationship would be inadequate in developing collective struggles in law. In an article written on the subject of poverty law, Wexler describes the inadequacies of approaching social problems from a narrow legal perspective and suggests that conventional legal training does not equip lawyers for the problems that are systemic in nature:

> Traditional practice hurts poor people by isolating them from each other, and fails to meet their need for a lawyer by completely misunderstanding that need. Poor people have few individual legal problems in the traditional sense; their problems are the product of poverty, and are common to all poor people.... In this setting the object of practicing poverty law must be to organize poor people, rather than to solve their legal problems. The proper job for a poor people's lawyer is helping poor people to organize themselves to change things so that either no one is poor or (less radically) so that poverty does not entail misery.[66]

By defining legal problems in a larger economic and social context, the lawyer is more likely to adopt an approach to litigation and other legal activities that would best benefit the group. Just as importantly, a lawyer who views the problem in the above manner will, one hopes, also see the value of other kinds of insurgent activities that fall outside of the traditional boundaries of adversarial law, such as confrontations, rent strikes, boycotts and other actions that, while not always legal, can produce effective results for economically subordinate groups.

(b)   Structure: The Mosaic of Dominion†

Samuel Bowles and Herbert Gintis

Power may be wielded in numerous ways. Historically, armed force has been a central pillar of power, as liberal theory rightly stresses. But the arsenal of domination goes beyond the gun. Control of the tools with which we produce our livelihood and the words that give our lives and loyalties their meanings have been no less central to the exercise of power.

Debates among Marxian and liberal theorists concerning the roots of domination have tended to adopt an impoverished conception of power. The liberal concern with the despotic state is matched in its narrowness by the Marxian concern with class domination. Each ignores the undeniable insights of the other; both give scant theoretical attention to forms of power that cannot be reduced to either state despotism and class. The most ubiquitous of these excluded forms of power is the domination of women by men.

Equally important, the grand debates between the liberal and Marxian political traditions skirt a central concern of democratic theory, the relationship between power and freedom. Democracy promises the collective accountability of power, but it promises another, more constructive concept as well; namely, the ability of people to effectively carry out their individual and common projects unencumbered by arbitrary constraint. For the liberal, this positive side of power — agency — is rendered minimally, as political liberty and the freedom to contract with whomever one pleases. Both of these liberal forms of freedom represent the absence of constraint rather than personal or collective empowerment. They are,

---

† From Samuel Bowles and Herbert Gintis, *Democracy and Capitalism* (New York: Basic Books Inc., 1987) at 92–98. Copyright © 1987 Samuel Bowles. Reprinted by permission of Basic Books, a member of the Perseus Books Group.

in [Isaiah] Berlin's apt terminology, "negative freedoms." For the classical Marxist, agency is the ability of an emerging class to carry out a historic project dictated by the onward march of the productive forces of society. Neither the liberal nor the Marxian definition encompasses the vision of people and of a people free to be the architects of their own personal and social histories.

We will address the problems raised for democratic theory by these partial conceptions of power in this chapter and in chapter 5, which considers the question of the individual and agency. Here we will develop a conception of power, the structures of social domination, and the resistance to domination capable of understanding the historical dynamics of diverse forms of power — patriarchal, state, class, or other. We will analyze the reproduction of patriarchal domination both as a central issue of democracy in its own right and as an illustration of our approach.

. . . .

The underlying logic of our argument contrasts in two important ways with dominant conceptions in social theory. First, though we affirm that historical change is structured, systematic, and hence understandable in more than simply empirical terms, we reject the notion that either stability or change obeys a single logic, whether of enlightenment, modernization, or the advance of productive capacities. Underlying this denial is our second fundamental commitment, a rejection of the concept of power as unitary; it is the notion that power emanates from a single source in society that provides the bedrock of what might be called the unitary conception of history.

We believe that an alternative conception of power, social structure, and history can make better sense of the historical clash of rights in liberal democratic capitalism and the political nature of the economy. The next two sections develop such a conception of power, in terms of the following five propositions.

First, power is heterogeneous, wielding a variety of weapons, yielding to a host of counterpressures, and obeying no single logic. Here we focus on the distinct forms of domination and solidarity based on class, state, and gender.

Second, power is not an amorphous constraint on action but rather a structure of rules empowering and restraining actors in varying degrees. These distinct sets of rules may be embodied in concrete institutions (for example, the World Bank), in linguistic convention (as in the generic term *man*), in unwritten custom (for example, primogeniture), in legal practice (as in the formal recognition of collective bargaining for wages), and, as we have seen, in more general conceptions of property and personal rights.

Third, the perpetuation of any power structure is generally problematic. Further, a structure of power is secured or toppled not only by history-making collective struggles, but more prosaically by a complex society-wide web of everyday individual action and compliance.

Fourth, distinct structures of power — be they the liberal democratic state, the patriarchal family, the capitalist economy, or other — are not merely juxtaposed, they are bound together in a common process of social reproduction. Each one may contribute to the survival of another; or they may foster mutually corrosive and subversive impulses.

And fifth, because people's lives are generally governed by more than one distinct power structure — for example one may be a worker, a wife, and a citizen — we experience power as heterogeneous, and are often able to bring the experiences within one system of power to bear in the pursuit of our projects within another. The clash of rights, based on impressive ability of elites and democratic movements alike to extend rights from one sphere of society to others, is the most important historical example of this transportation of practices from one social realm to another.

We refer to our approach as a historical-structural model of power. As we deny the usefulness of a general theory of power and its reproduction, we will seek to develop these five propositions in a particular historical setting; that is, the liberal capitalist nations of Europe and North America over the past two centuries.[1]

A POLITICAL CONCEPTION OF FAMILY, STATE, AND ECONOMY

It has become fashionable, in reacting against the traditional unitary conception of power, to profess a richly textured alternative notion — an idea of power as likely to be illuminated by the study of words and symbols as of armaments and property. Michel Foucault, for instance, writes:

> The analysis made in terms of power, must not assume that the sovereignty of the state, the form of the law or the overall unity of a domination are given at the outset.... Power is everywhere....[2]

This acute and welcome sensitivity to the ubiquity of power, however, can easily slip into treating power *per se* as domination, and replacing a critique of domination with a diffuse critique of authority of no particular use to democratic social movements. Thus Thomas Wartenberg notes, in a perceptive analysis of Foucault's attempt at deconstructing power, that

> at the political level, this problem asserts itself in Foucault's failure to distinguish different types of repressive societies.... Though all social systems do exist by means of a structuring of human beings to meet the needs of that system, we need to have a way to talk about how much pain such structuring inflicts upon the creatures for whom it exists.[3]

We also need, we might add, a way to talk about the *structure* of power in order to assess its *accountability*.

Our conception of power is at once a theory of domination and a theory of structural change flowing from collective resistance to domination. It is at the same time a structural theory and a theory of social action. Marx, in criticizing Ludwig Feuerbach, lamented the fact that materialist thought tended to denigrate action in favor of structure: "Hence it happened that the active side, in contradistinction to materialism, was developed by the idealism."[4] Analogously, structural theories of power often support a conception either of unquestioned, monolithic, uncontested domination or of the mechanistic inevitability of the collapse of domination.* The commonplace observation that structures do not reproduce or destroy themselves but are perpetuated or overturned by *what people do* finds no place in most structural theories. The active side of power is more fully developed by theories of choice.

Theories of choice, however — for reasons we will address in the next chapter — generally fail to provide an adequate account of the forms of collective action central to an active and historical conception of power. By developing the relationship between domination and solidarity, we seek to avoid both the individualism of choice theories and the presumption of a pregiven logic of either stability or crisis in structural theories. More positively, we will embrace the fundamental tenet of structural theories — that individual action is highly regulated — in a framework that insists that the historical dynamics of the structures regulating choice are themselves the result, however indirect and unintended, of individual action.

Vertical relationships of superior to subordinate, of employer to worker, of man to woman, of despot to subject, of white to black, provide the raw materials with which people construct the corresponding horizontal structures of social bonding — class consciousness, democratic nationalism, racial unity, and the like. (This rudimentary statement of the conditions of collective action simply generalizes Marx's insight that the structure of exploitation might provide the conditions for the unification of the exploited. We will turn to this issue in some detail in chapter 6.) These structures of social bonding allow people to forge from their individual experiences of oppression (and those of other people) an ensemble of cultural and organizational tools upon which collective action may be based.

The active side of power surely includes the exercise of domination by the powerful and the complicity of the oppressed in their oppression. But it also includes revolutionary collective action: forging communicative and organizational tools of bonding from the cacophony of discourses to which the mosaic of domination gives rise, and putting these tools to use in transforming structures of power. The clash of rights in liberal democratic capitalism, in particular, has seen both the collective action of the dispossessed in pitting personal rights against the privileges of wealth, race, and gender as well as the counterstrategies of the privileged in shoring up patriarchal rights, property rights, and "skin privilege."

Recognition of the heterogeneity of power invites a more searching analysis of the way in which distinct spheres of social life regulate social action in such a manner as to produce systems of domination *and* the possibility of their elimination.

Power is the capacity to render social action effective. It is coextensive with neither the state, nor with physical force, nor with face-to-face command.[5] Power may be exercised through the ability to overcome the resistance of others — as in Max Weber's conception — but it may equally be exercised through the ability to avoid resistance, either through control over which issues become contestable or through influence over others' wants, sentiments, desires, or, more generally, objectives.[6]

.   .   .   .

We focus on three general forms of the asymmetrical exercise of power: domination through the monopoly of the means of coercion, through the exercise of property rights, and through the operation of gender-based privilege. These are certainly not the only forms of domination observed in modern society. Race, ethnicity, religion, language, and region, among others, have served as major bases of social oppression and *loci* of bitter conflict. We focus on these three forms of domination not because other forms are less general, affecting particular liberal democratic capitalist societies in widely differing degrees and in quite distinct manners.*

Each of these three forms of domination may be considered to be a means of regulating social action. Thus, in three distinct ways, action is structured by a specific set of rules of the game: (a) the forms and rewards of participation of individuals in a practice are socially regulated; (b) the range of feasible alternative forms of practice are socially delimited; and (c) the potential effectiveness of distinct types of practice are socially mediated.

(c) Introduction: The Healing Dimension of Restorative Justice — A one-world body†

Dennis Sullivan and Larry Tifft

THE ESSENCE OF RESTORATIVE JUSTICE

When members of the Navajo Nation try to explain why people harm others, they say that a person who does harm to another 'acts as if he [sic] has no relatives' (Yazzie 1998: 126; see Kaplan and Johnson 1964: 216–17). That is, the offending person has become so disconnected from the world around him, so disengaged from the world around him, so disengaged from the people he lives and works with each day, that his acts no longer have a personal foundation.

To remedy harm situations when they do occur, to help those affected by a harm to begin upon the path of healing, historically the Navajo have taken steps that are consistent with their views on the 'causes' of harm. They call upon the relatives of the person responsible for the harm (as well as those of the person harmed) to come forth and help their kin re-connect with the community they live in or, as happens in the case of some, become connected to that community for the very first time.

The Navajo call this process of connection and re-connection 'peacemaking'. It is a form of restorative justice an essential part of which is community members assembling to 'talk things out' so that harmony might be restored to relationships that have been set on end. It is the same kind of process that South Africans embraced with their Truth and Reconciliation Commission in 1995 in an effort to heal from the human rights violations that occurred during apartheid (Skelton and Frank 2001).

On the best of days these processes, and all other forms of restorative justice, enable those responsible for a harm-done to work through their twisted logic and excuses — what Robert Yazzie (1998), former Chief Justice of the Navaho Nation Court, used to refer to in good Navajo vernacular as 'fuzzy thinking' (125; see also Zion 1997). The hope is that those responsible for a harm will be able to acknowledge to the community and perhaps to the person(s) they harmed what they did and in some way make amends, to 'make things right.' As anyone who has begun to familiarize him- or herself with the meaning of restorative justice knows, those affected by the harm in question seek to reach an agreement whereby the needs of the person(s) harmed, the victims/survivors, are taken into account to the fullest extent possible.

The Navajo peacemaking process is a quintessential form of restorative justice because it involves the community in restoring people and groups to well-being in a needs-meeting way: that is, the needs of everyone in the healing process are of paramount concern (Sullivan and Tifft 2005). Such a perspective or way of thinking derives from long-held indigenous customs in which kin, members of an immediate family, community, or nation seek to meet the needs of all involved in a harm situation. They know that, if a wrong is not righted in ways that take into account the needs of those who have been affected, the community will eat away at itself (Sather 2004).

Such an ethic is strange to so many of us in our post-modern world because it harkens back to a time when people saw their lives 'bound up together in ... one common life. The members of one kindred looked on themselves as one living whole, a single animated mass of blood, flesh, and bones, of which no member could be touched without all the members suffering' (Smith 1907: 273–4). In other words, when one person suffers a harm, all suffer from the harm to one degree or other. And all are responsible for making things right in such situations because all are in some way responsible for that harm occurring in the first place, being a co-creator (whether actively or passively, directly or indirectly) of that 'single animated mass of blood, flesh, and bones.'

This is very powerful medicine and in part explains why restorative justice is at its core a form of insurgency and subversive in nature. That is, it is a process that competes with the state's way of doing business not only in ways to respond to harm (non-violently, restoratively) but also in defining what harms we need to give attention to in the first place. Restorative justice sees the pain and suffering of all as worthy of our collective attention while the state discriminates between those worthy of the community's attention and those not. It is easy to see how such differing views contain the seeds of ideological and administrative dissension and why restorative justice is seen by the state as subversive, as an act of insurgency that must be put down, contained, co-opted, or modified in some other way to meet the state's ideological and administrative requirements.

With respect to the process of 'making things right,' the greatest hope of restorative justice advocates is that those who have been traumatized by a harm will want to participate in the process by telling their story as well as by listening to the story of the person who has harmed them so as to gain a better sense of who that person is (Mike *et al.* 2003). In this way the person harmed and their kin are more likely to develop some degree of compassion and empathy for the harming person and those who care for her/him, and are more likely to set aside feelings of anger, vengeance, and loss. We know, however, that this cannot be anything other than a voluntary process for those who have been harmed (Achilles 2004: 72), for sometimes their greatest need and that of their family is to keep as much distance between themselves and those responsible for the harm. So victim needs/wishes are paramount and must be respected at all times (Achilles 2004: 70; Amstutz 2004; Strang 2004).

While persons harmed may be receptive to participating in a victim–offender encounter and to accepting a genuine apology when offered, and occasionally come to forgive the person who harmed them, they should always receive, before deciding whether to participate in a restorative process, direct assurances from the community that they will not be re-victimized and that steps will be taken to ensure that other members of the community will be less likely to suffer as they have (McCold 2003: 96). Therefore, as members of this community, we must rally to support those harmed by providing the short- and long-term care they require even in cases when no one has been identified as the offending person (Achilles 2004: 71). Such support might come in the form of emergency medical, legal, counselling, victim compensation, and financial recovery services but it also might come in the form of challenge to the structural inequalities in our communities that prevent us from attending to the needs of those harmed in the way they expressed them (Thomson 2004).

What is distinctive about restorative justice as a response to harm, then, is that it is a process that belongs to relatives, to the community at large (Mika 2002) and that, when they become involved in the healing process, they develop greater competency not only in resolving community conflicts themselves but also in defining those acts they wish to pay especial attention to (Johnstone 2002; Bush and Folger 1994). As might be expected, the development of such competencies does not occur *sua sponte* but requires conscious and deliberate reflection on the part of people about what kind of restorative justice encounter — be it a conference or circle experience — will best meet the needs of all involved (Bush and Folger 1994). By fostering such active participation, restorative justice empowers people in a world in which globalization increasingly excludes them from the definition and correction of what ails them (Garland 2001). And understandably so, for once community members commit themselves to developing competencies based in restorative principles, they are more likely to engage in effecting cultural and social change so as to prevent structural harms from occurring in the first place.

BARRIERS TO RESTORATIVE JUSTICE PROCESSES

As might be imagined, there are all sorts of ideological, political, social, and psychological barriers that can insert themselves into the restorative justice venture at any point (Zehr and Toews 2004). Indeed, one of the glaring ironies of restorative justice is that its wide array of programs are dependent upon the state for their funding, development, assessment, and continuation. As a result, many restorative programs quickly find themselves narrowed in focus and scope, soon evolving into little more than correctional alternatives such as probation and other forms of community supervision. Indeed, we see in such cases the restorative process become overwhelmingly 'offender-centered' with the 'offender's' liability becoming the event around which the justice system convenes to deliberate (Roche 2003: 143). Why, when this is the focus of justice, would anyone desire to work toward developing restorative, community competencies and toward fostering greater access to supportive 're-integrative' resources [since] the justice process is all about the state being harmed and state officials exacting retribution for the collective (Zehr and Mika 1998)?

But those who seek to encourage and/or regain interpersonal harmony restoratively know that it is not the state that has been physically harmed when interpersonal violence takes place, but persons; it is not the law that needs to be restored, but people's lives (Zehr 1990). We cannot call any correctional process restorative, therefore, if, in its defense of the state, it helps re-establish or reaffirms power-based, hierarchical, non-participatory, need-depriving relationships (Tifft and Sullivan 1980: 57). One of the competencies that restorative justice fosters is learning which questions to ask about the value or morality of social arrangements that manufacture and maintain structural inequities in societies, that are the root of most interpersonal crime, and that compete with restorative processes as an appropriate (healing) response to such crime (Lemonne 2003; Pavlich 2004).

When we look at the many ways that we might opt to relate to young people who grow up within non-participatory, needs-denying arrangements, restorative justice continually presents us with difficult moral choices (see Paul Goodman 1961; Sullivan 1982). For example, do we wish that young persons who harm others be deterred from undertaking 'irrational,' unlawful actions and treated/rehabilitated so they might be adjusted to the exploited, development-thwarted life-positions in the social hierarchies they come from? Or perhaps we wish that these young persons be shamed and reintegrated into structurally and spiritually violent life conditions and strife-torn, dead neighbourhoods and 'communities'? In other words, is it our wish that these young people become designated surrogates for the state's usurped responsibility for moral condemnation?

These are not rhetorical questions without consequence for, when we respond to them affirmatively, we insult those who have been harmed. We not only re-victimize them by not taking their suffering and needs into account but also lose an opportunity to commit ourselves to the restorative justice directive to create a more civil, participatory society (Braithwaite and Strang 2001), one with more competent individuals and communities. Lost is the opportunity that restorative justice offers as a philosophy of justice to facilitate a more inclusive society, one in which our prevailing concern is meeting everyone's needs (Sullivan and Tifft 2004, 2001, 2005; Tifft and Sullivan 2005), developing their talents and gifts, and thus greatly decreasing all forms of social harms and non-responsiveness (Pepinsky 1991). Also lost is 'the potential of restorative justice to transform entire legal systems, our family lives, our conduct in the workplace, our practice of politics' (Braithwaite 2003: 1; also see Sullivan and Tifft 2004 and the discussion in Johnstone 2004). When we set forth this larger, transformative vision of restorative justice, it is not surprising that many of its advocates come to see the restorative justice they practice (oftentimes begrudgingly) as the functional equivalent of an individual-offender-focused accountability process (see Bazemore 1996 regarding these paradigms). When we assess the needs of the young people we mentioned earlier within such a framework, restorative justice processes become 'programs' that fail to take these young persons seriously and to provide them with an environment for positive moral growth, a vocation, a connection to their relatives (Bazemore 1996).

RESTORATIVE JUSTICE AND COMMUNITY

The Navajo peacemaking process, though it might not meet all of the desired dimensions of the full restorative/transformative processes we alluded to, is a quintessential form of restorative justice because it involves the community in restoring persons and groups of people to well-being in a needs-meeting way. That is, the needs of everyone involved are of paramount concern (Sullivan and Tifft 2005). Such a perspective or way of thinking derives from long-held, pre-state, indigenous customs in which kin, members of an immediate family, community, or nation of people collaborate to meet the needs of all in daily life including in situations when someone was harmed. These relationships are of a continuous nature and, if not attended to, jeopardize the health and well-being of the community, even its collective survival. That is, if essential needs are not met, and if a 'wrong' is not righted in ways that take into account the needs of those who have been affected, the community loses its competencies to evolve successfully (Sather 2004; Piercy 1976; Kropotkin 1913).

In other forums and venues we have written extensively about the relationship between this needs-based perspective and personal and collective restoration (Sullivan and Tifft 2005). It is a perspective that repeatedly calls attention to our connectedness as relatives. In terms of needs it says that, when someone's essential needs are not met or when someone violates another's needs causing harm, all suffer from this harm to one degree or other (Gil 1999). And all have a responsibility to ensure that a restorative response is made, for all are additionally harmed when this situation is not addressed and things 'made right.' Again, 'made right,' especially in repetitive harm situations, requires social change, requires attention to how social life is organized, for clearly some persons' needs and freedoms have been thwarted. In such situations we recognize that we are all responsible for creating the contexts in which some persons' needs are (oftentimes with regularity) not met. And it is with this insight that we acknowledge that we are all responsible for making things right because we are all the co-creators of how we organize our collective social life and relate with one another. This perspective or re-conceptualization of restorative justice is one of immense human compassion and accountability. Making such a restorative response, a response that is simultaneously concerned with the personal empowerment and growth of each and the collective well-being of all, is powerful medicine. It explains why restorative justice is at its core subversive and a form of insurgency.

RESTORATIVE JUSTICE AS INSURGENCY

Restorative justice is a form of insurgency because it 'competes with' the state (and power-based social arrangements generally) in how it responds to interpersonal or intergroup conflicts and how it defines what harms the human community should give restorative attention to in the first place. But restorative justice is also subversive because it challenges, both conceptually and in practice, social arrangements and processes that thwart human development and prevent human needs from being met. As we mentioned earlier, it reflects a vision of social life that sees the pain and suffering of all as worthy of

the community's attention while the state and power-based institutions discriminate between those worthy of attention and those not. In its transformative dimensions restorative justice exposes the nature of power-based orders (disorders) as they manifest themselves in the home, the school, the workplace, and in societies throughout the world. And the measure restorative justice advocates use to assess the quality or value of social institutions in our globalizing world order is the extent to which they foster the full development of each and every person's human potential, meet each and every person's essential needs (Chomsky 2003). Are they organized to foster human development and meet the needs of all or of some at the expense and exclusion of others? Here we are introduced to the economics or political economy of restorative justice which many advocates of the process refuse to acknowledge as relevant to both its practices and theory (Sullivan and Tifft 1998).

But once we acknowledge the importance of understanding the political economy of restorative justice — how human relationships work and are enhanced or diminished — we find ourselves squarely situated in the realms of social and distributive justice, of visions of what kind of world we wish to live in, or must have, if we are to become a one-world (self-restoring) body. In puzzlement we have asked over and over how scholars and practitioners of restorative justice can speak of its various practices as responses to interpersonal harm without asking at the same time about the nature of the social conditions which the participants in a conference or circle come from and to which they return after the conference. Imagine for a moment holding a conference to address an instance or pattern of physical wife-battering. Would we call a restorative justice encounter successful that concluded with the persons involved returning home to resume a relationship in which one person was perceived as an object, an inferior, to be used in meeting the needs and desires of the other? That is, a relationship in which one person's life plan or existence is perceived as more important than the others, in which the more powerful person relies on tyrannical decision-making patterns to uphold his power and his needs-meeting while the voice of his 'partner' was silenced? Clearly such an encounter would not be considered successful for these are not social conditions for relating as intimates (relatives). They not only stimulate harms such as battering but themselves constitute structural battering or violence (Tifft 1993).

Imagine as well holding a conference to address an instance of physical battery/robbery between two strangers — a young man throwing an elderly man to the ground and taking his wallet and watch at a bus stop. Would we call a restorative justice conference successful that concluded with these persons returning to their neighborhoods that are without the resources to meet their respective needs? Of course not. Such 'killed neighborhoods,' as Nils Christie (1993) has described them, do not have the resources to help the elderly man ease his trauma or meet his need to have his trust in others revitalized, nor to help him physically recover from bodily injuries while paying his medical expenses. Such neighborhoods are without the resources to help the young man deal with his on-going trauma of being perceived as one of an economically produced 'army of superfluous workers,' with his need to belong to a real community where he is respected and acknowledged as being human: that is, viewed as worthy of attention in the first place going unrecognized. In such neighborhoods he will not be offered an opportunity to develop his human competencies and gifts, to channel his energy in ways that open him up to others, and to receive a livable wage. Yet these are the social conditions within which far too many young men and women grow up and suffer throughout their formative years and even later, the social conditions of having no 'relatives.'

Finally, imagine holding a series of truth and reconciliation hearings to acknowledge a pattern of gross human rights violations and attempting to make things right through a public airing and discussion of the impact of the harms on people's lives and the society as a whole (Walgrave 2003). Would such hearings be considered successful if they concluded with the persons involved returning home in largely segregated neighborhoods or in separate geographic regions of a nation-state to continue to relate as they had, with ethnic, tribal, or inter-nation-state hatred and gross stratification arrangements remaining intact, if only in less institutionalized and legal forms? Would such a series of processes be considered restorative if few acknowledgements were generated, if no reparations were forthcoming, or if a new nation-state administration instituted only slightly different modes of stratification and retribution? Restorative justice is a form of insurgency because it demands that we explore how the groups or nation-states involved are able to deny their responsibilities for such atrocities or, if they do acknowledge them, can go on without making things right, without reparation of a nature that supports those harmed [to] recover their dignity and cultural autonomy (Friedrichs 2002; Friedrichs and Friedrichs 2002).

(d) Rwanda's Troubled Gacaca Courts†

Christopher J. Le Mon

Many countries emerging from periods of mass violence or dictatorship have recognized the limits inherent in criminal prosecutions. In such cases, transitioning societies have decided that criminal trials simply cannot address the wide scope of the crimes committed, bring to justice the large number of perpetrators, or promote the country's need for reconciliation. As a result, these transitioning societies have chosen to prosecute only the most senior perpetrators of past violence, and have created alternative justice mechanisms such as truth commissions or lustration programs to address the crimes committed by lower-level actors. Rwanda, however, has differed in its response to the mass atrocities of its recent past.

From April to July 1994, Rwanda's ethnic Tutsis and moderate Hutus were targeted for extinction in a genocide that had been planned for years. At least 800,000 people were killed in the violence that ensued. The number of people suspected of taking part in the killings was staggering: state authorities have estimated that more than 761,000 persons, or slightly less than half the adult male Hutu population of Rwanda in 1994, ultimately would be accused of crimes related to the genocide.[1]

After the violence subsided, Rwanda's government, like others emerging from periods of atrocity or repression, had numerous goals: to rebuild the country, establish a historical record of the genocide, ensure that those who committed crimes did not

† (2007) 14:2 Human Rights Brief 16. [Notes and/or references omitted.] Reproduced with permission.

escape with impunity, impart to survivors and victims that justice was being done, and reintegrate the vast numbers of perpetrators into their communities without provoking retributive violence against them. Like many transitioning societies, however, Rwanda's courts were in shambles, and prosecution and imprisonment of all perpetrators seemed an impossible task.[2] But while many other countries responded to similar dilemmas by devising alternatives to widespread prosecutions, Rwanda embraced a model centered on criminal prosecution. In an attempt to overcome its institutional incapacities and the logistical hurdles involved in such an endeavor, the government took a traditional Rwandan mechanism, known as gacaca, and transformed it into a system of informal criminal courts, which it called gacaca courts.

The details of Rwanda's gacaca court system have been explored at length by other authors, and so I recount them only briefly here.[3] Historically, a gacaca was a community-based informal arbitration convened by the parties to a civil dispute; its legitimacy was founded upon the willing participation of the parties and the community. The parties typically chose a respected person to serve as a neutral arbiter, and the outcome was limited to resolution of the minor dispute at hand. Gacaca had as its goal the achievement of a settlement that was accepted by both parties to the dispute, and the restoration of tranquility within the community.

Yet the gacaca courts established to try perpetrators of the 1994 genocide bear sharp contrast to this traditional Rwandan conciliation institution for which they are named. Gacaca courts are state-sanctioned criminal tribunals created by statute, whose legitimacy is derived from their status as governmental institutions. Their stated functions are to punish crimes committed during the genocide, establish a truthful history of that period, eliminate a "culture of impunity" within Rwanda, and reconcile Rwandans with each other.[4] Their mandate empowers them as the courts of first instance for cases ranging from theft or destruction of property through homicide. Judges for gacaca courts are chosen by community election; they are given minimal training in criminal law, serve without pay, and may impose sentences ranging up to 30 years' imprisonment. Each adult Rwandan not accused of involvement in crimes during the genocide is tasked with taking part in the gacaca court proceedings as a type of co-prosecutor and witness.

Most commentary on Rwanda's gacaca courts can be roughly grouped into three categories. The most critical measures the gacaca court process against objective international human rights standards, and finds it to be sorely lacking. Meanwhile,

the panglossian position celebrates gacaca courts as a novel new direction in transitional justice, one that couples traditional local institutions with more modern judicial practices, and will be responsible for transformative democratic change in Rwanda. The middle position accepts both the former criticism, and, drawing somewhat on the latter applause, concludes that given the resource limitations and the political and social conditions in post-genocide Rwanda, genocide trials by gacaca courts were the best possible mechanism for attempting to achieve Rwanda's transitional justice goals. Although commentators espousing either the critical or panglossian positions take the time to challenge the other, little attention has been devoted to questioning the moderate position, namely that Rwanda could not have done any better, given its social and political situation.

By relying on gacaca courts, Rwanda sought to pursue a comprehensive prosecution strategy and set out to try every person who took part in the genocide. But for the hundreds of thousands of accused perpetrators, the Rwandan government has lowered its standards of justice in the name of expediting trials and convictions. And in pursuing prosecutions of questionable fairness, the government may also have sacrificed the possibility of societal reconciliation and risked unleashing another cycle of violence in a country that has yet to recover from the genocide.

TACKLING CORRUPTION WITHIN GACACA COURTS

Early on, many Rwandans believed that the gacaca court system could serve as an effective transitional justice mechanism for their troubled country. During an 18-month pilot phase that established a mere 750 gacaca courts across the country, more than 2000 defendants pleaded guilty, and during the first nine months of nationwide gacaca court trials, nearly 6000 defendants were convicted. For comparison, a total of just over 7000 were tried by Rwandan criminal courts from 1996 to 2002.[5] However, even in the initial stages of this process, not everyone believed the gacaca courts would be fair; more than 10,000 Rwandans fled the country in anticipation of gacaca court inquiries, fearing "false accusations and unfair trials."[6] Unfortunately, many of these fears were quickly realized.

Troubles began with the first phase of the gacaca trials. At this stage, cell-level gacaca courts were tasked with classifying the crimes of which defendants stood accused. Category One crimes include the planning or organization of killings, as well as the commission of sexual crimes such as rape. Rwanda's ordinary criminal courts retain jurisdiction over these Category One offenses, which carry with them penalties ranging from 25 years imprisonment to capital punishment. By contrast, murder, complicity in murder, and causing bodily injury are classified as Category Two offenses, while property crimes fall under Category Three. These Category Two and Three crimes are tried before gacaca courts, with the possibility of more lenient punishment — including community service and credit for pretrial detention. Moreover, a defendant in Rwanda's judicial system faces an agonizing wait before the beginning of an ordinary criminal trial; because gacaca court trials for most defendants would begin far sooner than trial by the ordinary criminal courts, defendants who are prosecuted in the gacaca courts likely face shorter overall terms of imprisonment (including pretrial detention) regardless of the verdict. For a criminal defendant, then, categorization is critical.

Soon after the gacaca courts' inception, the media began uncovering incidents of gacaca court judges being bribed by defendants in order to ensure that the defendants' cases were not classified as Category One, and thus making certain that defendants would appear before gacaca courts rather than ordinary criminal courts.[7] Further, since gacaca proceedings began in mid-2006, corruption scandals have only continued, further marring public support for these courts. Under the law establishing the gacaca courts, judges (who number approximately 200,000) serve without pay, thus raising their susceptibility to corruption. Although no comprehensive statistics are available to establish the exact number of gacaca court judges accused of bribery or removed from their positions, news articles from the Rwandan media announce with unfortunate regularity such occurrences.[8]

Perhaps more important than the number of gacaca court judges sacked for corruption, however, is the public perception of judicial wrongdoing. Given the prevalence of media reports citing such bribery, and their geographical distribution, many people believe that there is a widespread problem of corruption among gacaca court officials. Public statements by the administrative head of the gacaca courts confirm that the Rwandan government itself recognizes the seriousness of the bribery issue.[9]

VIOLENCE AND THREATS OF VIOLENCE DETERRING WITNESSES

Even more concerning than corruption scandals is the increase in violence toward genocide survivors who are called as witnesses in gacaca court trials, and toward gacaca court officials themselves. Sadly, a number of witnesses and gacaca court officials have been killed across the country, often in a brutal manner echoing the savagery that marked the 1994 genocide. In one chilling case, the president of a gacaca court in Gisanza cell was murdered, with her body "hacked into pieces" and her "eyes plucked out."[10]

A recent report by a respected Rwandan human rights organization concludes that gacaca court witnesses suffer harassment and intimidation, and lack physical security.[11] In the second half of 2006 alone, at least 40 gacaca court witnesses were victims of murder or attempted murder.[12] According to another Rwandan NGO that tracks reprisals, this figure represents a severe rise in the level of violence against gacaca court witnesses. One witness had her house set on fire while her family slept inside; they narrowly escaped.[13] Another witness, an 80 year-old widow, survived after she, her daughter, and her grandchildren were attacked with a machete.[14] Although these egregious incidents of violence were reported, it seems likely that many other attacks have not found their way into the media.

Clearly, attacks against witnesses are aimed at discouraging or punishing testimony before the gacaca courts. Threats of violence have had a chilling effect on witness testimony, and thus on the ability of gacaca courts both to establish a historical record of the genocide and to signal an end to impunity. Entire communities of survivors have refused to testify after suffering harassment and threats, afraid to risk their lives after receiving no action or reassurance of safety from police or other state authorities.[15] In a cruel twist of fate, at least one gacaca court conducted its proceedings at the precise site where remains of genocide victims had been hastily buried in 1994, though as a result of threats from a perpetrator's family, "no member of the 450 families in the three villages came up to reveal the information."[16]

The pattern of violence surrounding the gacaca courts is not lost on Rwandan citizens. As an opinion piece in Rwanda's leading daily newspaper noted, "[o]ne may wonder why all the deaths today are associated with either Gacaca leaders or genocide survivors."[17] The violence against gacaca court officials and witnesses preparing to testify in genocide trials before the gacaca courts has become so severe that Rwandan president Paul Kagame and other senior government officials have highlighted it as a rising concern, urging Rwandans to take steps to prevent it.[18] But in spite of such calls for solidarity with survivors and victims, the reactions to these killings and acts of intimidation offer further evidence of the continuing divide within Rwanda; while victims and survivors have spoken out against these serious problems, persons who have been accused of crimes, or who fear being so accused, have remained silent even when present at the murder of gacaca court witnesses.[19]

PUBLIC PARTICIPATION EVAPORATING

In another ominous sign for gacaca courts, public participation in these proceedings is on the decline. Penal Reform International has reported that although attendance at gacaca court proceedings has remained high (likely in part due to the fact that absence is punishable by law), participation has markedly decreased since the proceedings began.[20] Avocats Sans Frontières, a Belgian human rights NGO, seconded this observation, noting that "attendees, often numerous, only participated minimally in the proceedings."[21] From this, Human Rights Watch has concluded that gacaca courts "were supposed to draw their legitimacy from popular participation, but many Rwandans did not trust them and boycotted the sessions."[22] As one goal of the gacaca courts is to create among the citizenry an established truth of what occurred during the genocide, this marked decline in public participation bodes poorly for the effectiveness of this justice strategy.

The reasons for the decline in public participation are varied. As noted above, these include the fear of violence against participants, and the perception that gacaca court judges are corrupt. In addition, tens of thousands of gacaca court judges have been accused of participating themselves in crimes during the genocide; no doubt the suspected culpability of those intended to sit in judgment has discouraged or intimidated potential witnesses.[23]

With Rwandan citizens increasingly detached from the process of rendering justice in gacaca courts, the country seems close to a dangerous abandonment by would-be participants of the goals of the gacaca courts process. If this continues, many survivors will not testify about their experiences, and perpetrators may not be convicted of all the crimes they committed. As Penal Reform International concludes,

"a meaningful participation of the population is the only way to know the truth about the genocide intimately and also to give full meaning to a process where the final objective is to lead to the reconciliation of Rwandans."[24] In the absence of meaningful public participation in the gacaca proceedings, it will also prove impossible to establish a historical record of the genocide, conduct fair trials, or impart to survivors and victims that justice has been done.[25]

FAILURE TO PROVIDE RECONCILIATION

Another of the gacaca courts' goals, namely societal reconciliation, is proving elusive as well. In particular, the refusal of the gacaca courts to investigate crimes committed by Rwandan Patriotic Army (RPA) forces (who were led by Rwanda's current president Paul Kagame)[26] against Hutu civilians, or reprisal attacks after the genocide, have led many Hutus to question the stated goal of reconciliation.[27] Instead of healing the rift between Hutus and Tutsis, the operation of the gacaca courts is threatening to reinforce it by affirming group personas of victim and perpetrator, innocent and guilty.

In part, it is the gacaca courts' structure, which pits the population against the perpetrators, that makes them unlikely to be able to effect societal reconciliation. Even traditional criminal trials, which by their adversarial nature focus on determining individual guilt rather than establishing a comprehensive historical truth, focus on retribution and deterrence at the expense of reconciliation. If ordinary criminal prosecutions do not constitute a justice strategy conducive to reconciliation, gacaca court trials, which are administered by minimally-trained civilians without significant organization or legal rules, are even less likely to do so.

Even the official explanation by the Rwandan government of the reconciliatory effect of the gacaca courts fails to convince, reading more like a chance for participatory popular punishment, rather than an opportunity to bring together perpetrators, victims, and survivors. In one official document, the government has explained:

> The Gacaca Courts system will allow the population of the same Cell, the same Sector to work together in order to judge those who have participated in the genocide, identify the victims and rehabilitate the innocents. The Gacaca Courts system will thus become the basis of collaboration and unity ...[28]

To the extent, however, that gacaca court proceedings assign collective guilt to Hutus by ignoring crimes committed by the RPA, and permit primarily Tutsi survivors to stand in judgment of primarily Hutu perpetrators, gacaca courts will hinder reconciliation within the country. As William Schabas has noted, "[r]ather than resolve the outstanding cases ... the initial gacaca [court] hearings appear to have opened a Pandora's box."[29]

NO ROOM FOR CRITICISM

Given these concerns, the absence of political space for criticism of the gacaca courts is disconcerting. When a member of Rwanda's senate misspoke in response to a legal question about the powers of the gacaca courts, his statement was made out to be "a scandalous attack on Gacaca courts." Three commissions of inquiry were opened, and the senator faced severe pressure to resign from office.[30] Because of incidents like this, many Rwandans have been too intimidated to challenge gacaca courts.

The Rwandan government has itself undermined its policy of national unity, at times having accused those who have spoken out against gacaca courts of harboring a "genocidal ideology."[31] One local government official, who accused Rwandans that failed to attend gacaca court proceedings of having "genocide and ethnic ideologies," threatened that their continuing failure to attend would be "seriously punished." Illustratively, the citizens were undertaking a boycott of the local gacaca court based on allegations that the judges had been soliciting bribes from criminal defendants.[32]

Human rights groups have also been forced to suspend their operations, sometimes permanently, after questioning aspects of the gacaca court process. Human Rights Watch has noted that "as high-level [Rwandan government] officials focused on 'genocidal ideology' in speeches and ceremonies, Rwandan and international NGOs tailored their activities to avoid confrontation with authorities. Human rights organizations ... avoided taking stands likely to draw official ire."[33] Unfortunately, this government crackdown on criticism has served to silence those best positioned to speak frankly about the gacaca process.

Ordinary citizens have suffered from the government's conflation of criticism regarding gacaca courts and disloyalty to the state, as well, and sadly there are signs that this climate of intolerance for criticism may be undermining the very participation upon which the legitimacy of the gacaca courts depends. As such, gacaca courts have not led to the sort of "democratic dialogue" between the governed and the government that they might otherwise have fostered.[34]

CONCLUSION

Torn between the need to reconcile a deeply divided population and the duty, both moral and legal, to punish those who sought to eradicate an entire people, Rwanda's attempt at combining criminal justice and community reconciliation might have provided a "third way" for societies in transition. As it has been implemented, however, the gacaca court system — fraught with corruption and violence, and insulated from much-needed change by a government that brooks no criticism — is quickly proving that in seeking to achieve both justice and reconciliation, the gacaca courts may very well achieve neither.

Sadly, the net effect of the gacaca courts on the development of open discussion in Rwanda has been nil to negative; not only has their operation not resulted in a free dialogue between the government and the population, they instead have provided another basis for the government to accuse critics and dissenters of possessing a "divisive ideology."[35] So long as this intolerance for criticism remains, the public disaffection with the gacaca courts will result not in needed policy shifts, but instead in decreasing participation and abandonment of the noble goals that the gacaca courts set out to accomplish. Unfortunately, the establishment of the gacaca court system may foreclose the possibility of other transitional justice institutions, such as a truth commission, that could help the country to achieve reconciliation.

Ultimately, then, the gacaca courts likely will be unable to achieve their stated goals of psychologically rebuilding Rwanda, establishing a historical record of the genocide, avoiding impunity, showing that justice is being done, and reintegrating hundreds of thousands of perpetrators into their communities without provoking retributive violence. By themselves, the gacaca courts today seem to be offering only popular punishment — and "popular" only in the sense that it is carried out by members of the population, not in that it enjoys broad approval. Yet the gacaca courts are a reality, and the Rwandan government seems unlikely to significantly alter their operation, even in the face of obvious deficiencies.

If Rwanda is to break the cycle of violence and vengeance that has plagued it since independence, it must find a new way to achieve reconciliation between perpetrators and victims who must live side by side in a densely-populated territory. If the current relative peace is to be sustained, the government must accept that the impartial rule of law, and not draconian treatment of policy critics, can best prevent the escalation of grievance into violence. If the goals of justice and reconciliation are not met, Rwandans will live daily with the risk that another tragic collective bloodletting may follow.

(e) Canada's Truth and Reconciliation Commission: Settling the Past?[†]

Kim Stanton

The Indian Residential Schools (IRS) system[1] has been referred to as "Canada's greatest national shame".[2] The IRS system is now the subject of the Canadian Truth and Reconciliation Commission (TRC). Unlike other truth commissions that have been created due to regime change, where a majority of citizens sought a truth-seeking process, Canada's TRC arose as a result of protracted litigation by survivors of the IRS system against the government and churches that ran the schools. This article reviews the genesis of TRC in a legal settlement agreement, along with some of the challenges this origin entails.

For over a century, the Canadian government sought to assimilate Indigenous children into the non-Indigenous culture by promoting and then requiring their attendance at church-run schools. The first Indian residential schools opened in the 1880s in western Canada and eventually, they operated in every province and territory except Prince Edward Island, New Brunswick and Newfoundland. The system was at its height in the 1920s with compulsory attendance under the *Indian Act* and over 80 schools in operation.[3] Most Indian Residential Schools were run by entities of the Catholic church,[4] with others run by the Anglican, Presbyterian, Methodist and later the United churches.

Children were separated from their families and communities and sent far away to schools where they were forbidden to speak their languages, practice their spirituality or express their cultures. The impacts of this policy as manifested through IRS have echoed down the generations. Indigenous people who never attended an IRS have nonetheless suffered from the harms inflicted there due to the interruption of traditional cultural transmission and parenting skills, the loss of skills enabling traditional life on the land, the pathologies and dysfunction now endemic in many Indigenous communities and the loss of language, culture and spirituality. It is only in the last few years that the government has acknowledged that its assimilation policy was harmful.[5] It has done so only in response to overwhelming legal pressure.

While it is true that there were caring individuals among the teachers and workers at some of the schools, and some children did receive an education, the dominant narrative of the schools reveals the violence inherent in the policy behind the IRS system: to "kill the Indian [to] save the man".[6] Those that escaped physical or sexual abuse still suffered the loneliness of separation from family, the confusion of being taught their culture was inferior, and the loss of their language and spirituality. Eventually the government concluded that the schools were not successful tools of assimilation. The government withdrew from its partnership with the churches in 1969, at which time it took over the IRS and began to transfer control to Indian bands. The majority of residential schools were closed by the mid-1980s, with a few remaining until the last closure in 1996.

Despite earlier press reports[7] and several criminal investigations by police in the late 1980s,[8] the IRS issue did not garner national attention until 1990, when Chief Phil Fontaine went public with his experience of IRS abuse,[9] opening the door for other survivors to begin sharing their experiences. The extent of the IRS legacy became better known with the establishment of the Royal Commission on Aboriginal Peoples (RCAP).[10] RCAP was established in 1991, and during the course of 178 days of public

---

† (2011) 2:3 The International Indigenous Policy Journal (www.iipj.org). [Notes and/or references omitted.] Reproduced with permission.

hearings in 96 communities, many survivors of the schools gave emotional and troubling testimony recounting the abuses they had suffered, thus bringing wider attention to the IRS legacy. In 1996, RCAP made its recommendation calling for a public inquiry into IRS. No public inquiry was established in response to that recommendation. The federal government made what it called a Statement of Reconciliation.[11] Minister of Indian Affairs Jane Stewart made the statement but for many, it fell short of an apology.[12] The Native Women's Association of Canada formally refused to accept the Statement as an apology, and the Inuit Tapirisat of Canada found the Statement to be incomplete.[13] Indeed, the word "apology" did not appear in the statement. Observers suggest that the government did not issue a full apology for fear it would be viewed as an admission of liability that would weaken its legal position in the various court claims being brought by IRS survivors.[14]

In the late 1990s, the failure of the government to adequately respond to RCAP, and in particular, to adequately address the recommendations on IRS, created enormous frustration amongst survivors and dashed any hopes of a political resolution to the issue.[15] This frustration with the lack of a political response prompted IRS survivors to turn to legal responses in an effort to seek redress in the courts for the harms they suffered, a strategy that ultimately led to a negotiated solution.[16] The legal mechanisms survivors turned to included criminal prosecution, civil litigation, and Alternative Dispute Resolution. Criminal prosecution resulted in some retributive justice with respect to a few individual aging perpetrators of sexual abuse, but could not address systemic issues and harms of IRS. Civil litigation also resulted in some damage awards for a few survivors, but the process was lengthy and again the harms acknowledged by the courts were limited. Alternative Dispute Resolution (ADR) was an attempt to remedy the difficulties of the civil litigation system but it too ultimately failed to fulfill the goal of having a streamlined and effective process to address survivors' needs. Thus, each mechanism offered a measure of assistance in bringing the IRS legacy to public attention, but each mechanism failed to adequately address the historical injustices created by the IRS system.

In 1997 Phil Fontaine was elected National Chief of the Assembly of First Nations and commenced negotiations with the churches and the federal government for a settlement for IRS survivors. Settlement discussions began to be impacted when the courts started to decide some of the first IRS civil cases, apportioning liability between the government and the churches.[17] Following the launch of multiple class action lawsuits,[18] a consensus developed around the Assembly of First Nations' recommendations in its 2004 report which called for a lump sum reparations payment, additional compensation for specific abuses, expedited payments for the sick and elderly, and a truth-sharing and reconciliation process.[19] In November 2005, the parties reached an Agreement in Principle that was finalized in May 2006,[20] and approved by the courts later in the year.[21] The Settlement Agreement came into effect 19 September 2007. By the time of the Settlement Agreement, 14,903 survivors had filed claims against the government. Only 2,805 claims had been resolved through litigation or the ADR process, with damage awards upwards of $110 million.[22]

The IRS Settlement Agreement is the largest class action settlement in Canadian history[23] and has well over 100 signatories. The Settlement Agreement sets aside $1.9 billion for the approximately 80,000 living survivors of the IRS schools.[24] The Settlement Agreement comprises several mechanisms of redress for survivors of IRS, including a Common Experience Payment,[25] an Independent Assessment Process,[26] a fund for commemorative projects,[27] and a fund for healing projects.[28] Finally, the Settlement Agreement provides for the establishment of the Truth and Reconciliation Commission.

The TRC is like other truth and reconciliation commissions in that it is an official, temporary, non-judicial fact-finding body set up to investigate a pattern of abuses of human rights committed over a number of years.[29] That is, it is a government-sponsored commission, with a five-year mandate, intended to investigate the IRS system and its legacy. Like other truth commissions, the TRC mandate includes the creation of a historical record and the making of recommendations. However, aside from the unique mandate and structure that reflect the national context in which the TRC is taking place, the TRC is distinctive in that it is the only truth commission to be created out of litigation. In other contexts in which truth commissions have arisen, they have been instigated by a new regime to look into the abuses of a past regime, as in Argentina, Peru and Chile. Occasionally, a truth commission arises as part of a peace accord brokered between parties to a conflict, as in El Salvador, Guatemala and Sierra Leone. In Canada, the TRC is a result of negotiations between multiple parties of class action lawsuits. This means that the TRC will be faced with the need to prompt Canadians to invest in and take ownership of a process that they did not instigate. That is, the TRC was not created out of a groundswell of concern about IRS survivors by the public; rather it was agreed to by their government's legal advisers in order to settle costly litigation. Were it not for the enormous financial cost to the government of continuing to defend against the class actions, the TRC would not exist in Canada.

As adverted to above, one of the reasons that people sought a truth commission in Canada was that the usual legal mechanisms had proven to be inadequate. In response to survivor experiences with the criminal and civil litigation processes, it appears from Schedule N that the Settlement Agreement negotiators sought to establish a body that would not mimic a legal proceeding such as a trial. Schedule N specifies the powers, duties and procedures of the TRC, including receiving statements.[30] The Schedule also sets out what the TRC may not do in pursuit of its mandate; it shall not hold formal hearings, have subpoena powers, or name names, as discussed below. The TRC's responsibilities with respect to methodology and procedure are enumerated.[31] The factors the TRC must take into account in exercising its duties are set out, including a direction that the commissioners: "shall not hold formal hearings, nor act as a public inquiry, nor conduct a formal legal process".[32] With this wording, the negotiators of the Settlement Agreement likely were trying to stress their intention for the TRC not to duplicate criminal or civil court proceedings or the Independent Assessment Process. Nor is the TRC to repeat the perceived difficulties encountered with public inquiries in the past, where adversarial processes overtook the substance of the inquiry. This section of the mandate can be read as eschewing a formal legal process for the TRC, and by formal, it seems to refer to adversarial processes.

The guiding principles state at the outset of the mandate that the TRC will focus on being victim-centred, and respect the health and safety of participants. These aspects acknowledge that previous legal mechanisms have caused grief and pain to survivors, and attempt to avoid duplication of that occurrence.[33] The TRC was sought as a mechanism that would operate in a non-adversarial manner. In other contexts, truth commissions have been expected to be less 'lawyer-driven' than other legal mechanisms.[34] While all truth commissions do involve lawyers in their activities to varying degrees, the idea that negotiators in Canada gleaned from international examples is to emphasize the focus on victims, and reduce the focus on the skill of legal counsel to shape the information gained. This reduced focus on legal personnel arose because sometimes truth commissions

are established in environments where the legal system may be in disarray, with few lawyers and judges left in a country (either alive, or who are not part of the prior regime). It may also be because the number of violations is so large that the prosecutorial system is overwhelmed and another mechanism is necessary to seek accountability. A truth commission may also be sought in order to elicit truth-telling in an environment where the adversarial approach of a trial, with its tools such as cross-examination, would be inappropriate.

In Canada, where the government and the churches have acknowledged that abuses occurred and that the IRS system was harmful, the evidence that is presented to the TRC is not for the purposes of convincing the Commissioners that the abuses occurred. The TRC is occurring separately from the reparations process and other elements of the Settlement Agreement. The purpose of having the TRC as a separate body allows for a focus on its distinctive goals: acknowledging and witnessing the IRS experience, promoting awareness of the IRS system and its impacts, and creating a public record of the IRS legacy.[35] These goals suggest a desire for a less adversarial process than the court process.

Alleged perpetrators have no incentive to participate in the TRC but perhaps they may be more willing to engage in the process if they know that they will not be subject to any legal proceedings as a result of their participation. A truth commission is intended to promote public accountability and combat impunity for human rights violations, so a refusal to name names where there is clear evidence of culpability may attract criticism. On the other hand, while most truth commissions have the power to name perpetrators, few have done so.[36] And in the Canadian context, the institutional nature of the main "perpetrators" — the government and the churches — alters the dynamic. Many of the people who staffed the schools or directed government IRS policy are dead, thus there will be more participation of present day government and church institutional representatives than of individuals who were directly involved with the IRS. As parties to the Settlement Agreement, there is an expectation that the institutions will participate in the TRC process. Given that most of their representatives will not themselves have been perpetrators of specific abuses, it is perhaps not surprising that the TRC has neither subpoena power nor the power to name names, two commonly allocated powers for truth commissions.

Aside from the frustrations of the lack of a political response to the IRS legacy and the dissatisfaction with the other legal mechanisms available, a further reason that survivors sought a truth commission in the IRS negotiations was the widespread ignorance amongst non-Indigenous Canadians about the IRS system and its profound and continuing effect on Indigenous communities. The advantage of a truth commission for combating such ignorance is the ability to create an incontrovertible historical record and enable significant public education. The TRC is tasked with creating a record of the IRS system and its impacts.

However, while gaining the truth about IRS for non-Indigenous people may be educational, it may be re-traumatizing for survivors.[37] In addition, the truth will be different for each person depending on their experiences. Some survivors and church or government representatives will resist the idea that the IRS system was wholly negative, preferring to focus on the fact that some children did receive an education and that some survivors look back to their teachers with fondness.[38] Still, the truth that the IRS system existed and that it has been largely devastating for Indigenous peoples is already known to Indigenous peoples, but this truth is not well known to the majority of Canadians:

> Consensus that residential school experience was injurious in itself, not just in instances of physical and sexual abuse, is shared by only a small proportion of Canadian citizens, in contrast to the view of most First Nations, Inuit and Métis people.[39]

There are significant gaps between the knowledge and understanding of the IRS system that many non-Indigenous people may be expected to have as compared to that of many Indigenous people.[40] These gaps arise from longstanding beliefs about the history and intentions of government policy, and the legacies of such policies such as cycles of dependency and negative social indicators.[41] In other contexts, truth commissions have attempted to create a more complete historical record of a tragic period in a state's history by rounding out the state's version of events with information gained from investigation, records and testimony.

As with other truth commissions, it is not that the TRC is likely to expose facts that were previously unknown; rather, it will "make an indispensable contribution in acknowledging these facts".[42] In Canada, the factual truth about IRS may be publicly available, but that truth is still resisted in the dominant narrative. This dominant narrative says that the schools were created and run with the best intentions and that in hindsight some of the methods used and some of the individuals involved may have

been overly harsh or abusive. At variance with that narrative is a conflicting account that views the schools as one attempt at obliterating the Indigenous cultures in what is now Canada.[43] Some view the IRS system as only one component of a larger colonial project that is embodied in many aspects of the *Indian Act*.[44] However, non-Indigenous Canadians will largely be unaware of the systemic aspect of the IRS legacy.[45] In the Canadian case, the fact that the government has issued an unequivocal apology may help to refute the myth held by many non-Indigenous Canadians that IRS was akin to a bad boarding school, where individual teachers were abusive. The apology acknowledged that IRS was intended to force assimilation of Indigenous children — "to kill the Indian in the child".[46] The importance of the work the TRC must do, at the outset, to address these differing narratives cannot be underestimated if the reconciliation aspect of the mandate is to have any chance of success.

Canadians may find that a commission addressing the legacy of residential schools provides a manageable way to learn about and understand the larger causes of the colonial policy under which IRS was created. Still, given that the TRC will not be able to identify perpetrators in its report, the truth it tells about IRS will necessarily be incomplete. The TRC report will therefore need to address the broader truth about the IRS system itself, identifying the structures and institutions that created and perpetuated the toll upon Indigenous peoples. The ability to focus on the larger picture can then be a strength of the TRC.

One of the most important things a truth commission can do is to engage the wider public with its work. The utility of the commission is lessened if it compiles a history that is destined to silently land on a library shelf.[47] A commission must create a narrative that may form the basis of national reconciliation, but the commission must first "manage to penetrate the collective consciousness of the people."[48] How can this be achieved? Hayner and Freeman set out factors that are likely to improve the chances of a truth commission being effective. In particular, they note the importance of public support for the establishment of a truth commission; the presence of a vigorous and engaged civil society (and in particular of strong victims' groups, human rights groups, religious leaders and intellectuals); widespread social identification with the victims of the abuses; vocal and independent media; and persistent international attention and pressure.[49] The Canadian TRC has not yet attained all of these factors. It is unclear how wide public support was for its establishment since the Canadian public at large was not formally consulted in the IRS negotiations. While Canada has strong civil society organizations, there is not yet any organized coalition (outside the parties to the Settlement Agreement) vocally supporting the TRC's work. There has been some positive media coverage but the TRC is yet to be ubiquitous in the press, either domestic or international.[50] Certainly with a country as large as Canada, the media will be an important tool in engaging those who are unable to participate in the TRC's national events because the events are distant from where they live.

An unusual aspect of this TRC is that its mandate does not direct that it will hold hearings. Rather, Schedule N refers to receiving "statements", holding "sessions", "consultations" and "public events".[51] As noted above, the mandate states that the TRC: "shall not hold formal hearings".[52] While this is no doubt in part to protect the privacy of survivors, it also shields the government and churches from scrutiny by the public. It means that the TRC will not hold an activity that is virtually a hallmark of truth commissions elsewhere. This aspect of the TRC's mandate must be explained to and by the media for the public to understand, since most people associate truth commissions with the South African TRC, which held public hearings, and people may thus reasonably expect a truth commission to hold hearings.[53]

Other truth commissions have held institutional hearings to focus on the issues arising in certain sectors of the public service or society at large. For instance, South Africa had hearings on the legal profession and the judiciary, while Ghana had institutional hearings with respect to the security sector, media, prisons, as well as the legal profession and the judiciary.[54] The purpose is to reveal the structural and institutional nature of the human rights violations that occurred in order to recommend ways in which to prevent future recurrences, regardless of the individuals who may be in charge of or working for those institutions. It is not clear if the TRC will hold any such hearings, yet institutional hearings with respect to government policy in different areas of Indigenous people's lives may be useful and important for preventing recurrences of abuses such as IRS.[55] There is no requirement for a report at the end of the five-year mandate of the TRC, but such a report would be useful in order for the TRC to have the opportunity to assess the material it has reviewed and heard to identify structural or systemic issues. Both institutional hearings and a final report are vehicles with important potential for public education by the TRC.

The mandate as set out in Schedule N of the Settlement Agreement frames the TRC as part of a process of "rebuilding and renewing ... the relationship between Aboriginal and non-Aboriginal Canadians", requiring "commitment from ... the people of Canada". In order to work toward reconciliation of the Canadian society as a whole, there needs to be active, sustained and significant outreach to civil society beyond the parties to the Settlement Agreement. Such processes of dialogue and consultation help to generate awareness and then cultivate ownership of the national reconciliation process.

While the Canadian TRC is a result of a legal settlement that includes parties that represent some components of civil society, they are by no means broadly representative of Canadian society as a whole. Although some of the major Aboriginal organizations are involved in the TRC process, not all Aboriginal organizations are parties to the Settlement Agreement. Large swaths of the non-Indigenous public have no involvement in the TRC so far. Involving the broader public will be easier if civil society organizations, beyond the parties to the Settlement Agreement, get involved and support the work of the TRC. This could be instigated by outreach from the TRC itself, but given its limited resources, it would be useful if the parties to the Settlement Agreement could take the initiative. Church groups and survivor groups could collaborate and contact other civil society organizations to form a broad-based coalition to support and to increase awareness of the TRC's work.

In Canada, Indigenous legal institutions and systems have often been ignored and devalued. The TRC must proceed with an acute awareness of this history and adopt the advice of RCAP on the concept of respecting the systems of traditions of the peoples whom it hopes to reconcile. As Llewellyn observes, the TRC's mandate does not provide much detail with respect to the reconciliation aspect of its work.[56] The mandate refers to healing the relationship between peoples.[57] In the transitional justice context, mechanisms such as apologies, commemoration, reparations, and truth commissions are viewed as means for achieving societal reconciliation. Reconciliation is a multifaceted process and often, as with South Africa, truth commissions are expected to engage several of these mechanisms in an effort to achieve societal healing. Canada's TRC is not asked to do all the work of redress because the elements of commemoration and reparations are structured as different parts of the Settlement Agreement. This means that the focus of the TRC's work need not be to determine the compensation that survivors should receive or to duplicate the commemorative work that is already being done by the Aboriginal Healing Foundation, a body created in response to RCAP's recommendations on IRS.[58]

An additional element critical to the reconciliation process that the TRC does not have to address is that of an apology. The TRC was inaugurated on 1 June 2008. Although not part of the Settlement Agreement, on 11 June 2008, the government gave its long-awaited apology to survivors of the IRS.[59] The Prime Minister gave this apology in the House of Commons. The leaders of the other federal parties represented in Parliament also gave an apology. The leaders of five national Aboriginal organizations responded from the floor of the House. The apology received a generally positive response from survivors and the public and marked a rare moment of awareness in the general Canadian population.[60] The apology also provided the TRC with a good start: the government acknowledged the truth of the IRS system's harms, enabling the TRC to commence its work without having to convince the country that the IRS legacy existed.

Truth commissions are often expected to make recommendations with respect to appropriate reparations for the victims such as compensation that may enable the victims to improve their quality of life. These recommendations are adopted to varying degrees by the state. In the Canadian context, the reparations have already been determined in large part through the Common Experience Payment and Independent Assessment Process. What if the TRC makes determinations that go far beyond what the reparative mechanisms of the Settlement Agreement encompass? What can be the response to the TRC's findings if the apology and reparations have already been meted out? These are challenges that may arise given the ambitious structure of the Settlement Agreement. It is too early to tell whether these matters will arise, but they are possibilities that the TRC can contemplate in determining its process.

The fact that the IRS negotiators decided to have a TRC in addition to and separate from these other aspects of the settlement suggests that there is something to be gained from having the TRC process itself. That is, something is expected from the TRC that is different from the usual truth commission results of making recommendations for commemoration, apology and reparation. There is something about the *process* itself that is valued here; something unique to the Canadian context. It remains to be seen if separating the truth-seeking process from the reparations process is an appropriate way of proceeding. Again, this is one of the rea-

sons why it will be so important for the TRC to actively educate the public as to its operations and goals.

How well a truth commission educates the public about its work will determine its ability to garner public support. A high level of public support can bolster a commission's credibility and thus its reputation, which can in turn smooth the way for the commission to access information and address the needs of victims. Also important for maintaining its own credibility is a truth commission's management of public expectations about its work. This is another task that does not appear in any written mandate for a truth and reconciliation commission. The TRC will need to be extremely conscious of the expectations that it may arouse in survivors of IRS. These expectations will be of an order entirely different [from] and more complex than those of the non-Indigenous public. Truth commissions have often raised expectations of victims that there will be some resolution to their situation because the very existence of a commission suggests that its presence will make a difference.[61] Expectations may be even higher when the commission seeks not just truth but also reconciliation as a central goal.

Another challenge for the TRC relates to the likelihood that most of the testimony it receives will come from survivors. This may create the appearance that the TRC will rely upon the survivors to do the work to be reconciled or perhaps reintegrated (or "conciled"/integrated) into Canadian society. The TRC must be careful not to reinforce the idea rejected by RCAP: that the government avoided responsibility by expecting IRS survivors to do the work to heal themselves.[62] The means of reconciliation include truth telling, acknowledgement of past wrongs, reparations for the victims, addressing the structural causes of the wrongs, and a rebalancing between societal groups to prevent the harms recurring. The TRC must find a way to include the non-Indigenous public such that they acknowledge the IRS system is everyone's problem to address. The reconciliation process must be framed by the TRC as a mutual process to be engaged in by Indigenous and non-Indigenous peoples alike; it should not be a one-sided process.

While the Settlement Agreement negotiators emphatically sought to distinguish the TRC from the South African version,[63] it is important to glean from the comparative experience some realistic guidance about what this TRC can achieve. Not all truth commissions have framed their goal as reconciliation of the country, but "[t]hose that have — including South Africa's TRC and the National Commission on Truth and Reconciliation in Chile — have found it to be a very difficult mission."[64] Reconciliation may or may not occur on an individual or national level; calling the exercise "truth and reconciliation" sets up both concepts as a goal, but no one can declare a person or nation to be reconciled. In addition, it is possible that truth (a slippery concept at the best of times) and reconciliation will be viewed completely differently depending upon who is asked. Some may see that these objectives have been achieved while others will dispute that perception. The latter may be concerned that those in power have appeared to support reconciliation for their own political purposes.

Further, the term "reconciliation" implies that the parties were once whole, experienced a rift, and now must be made whole again. But in colonial settings, this is not the case. The relationship between Indigenous and settler peoples in Canada was one of nations encountering nations, where one gradually oppressed and marginalized the other. Indigenous peoples never agreed to the denial of their sovereignty, cultures or identities.[65] Thus, in the Canadian context, reconciliation must refer to "transformative" as opposed to "restorative" reconciliation.[66] One commentator notes that reconciliation on a national level must be at least in part a political process that includes acknowledgement of political and legal rights of Indigenous peoples.[67] This highlights the difficulty with public expectations that can be created when a body called a "truth and *reconciliation*" commission is created. The TRC cannot reasonably be expected to reconcile on its own the entire relationship between Indigenous and non-Indigenous peoples in Canada. On the face of it, the TRC's mandate is limited to the IRS system: to create a historical record of the IRS system and to educate the public about the IRS legacy.

In Canada, continued power imbalances will make it difficult for a reconciliation process to truly take root.[68] When he was Lieutenant Governor of Ontario, James Bartleman, a member of the Chippewas of Mnjikaning First Nation, warned that unless Canadian society as a whole signals that it is serious about according equal economic and social rights to Indigenous Canadians, the TRC's Commissioners will find that "they have been shod with shoes of clay. There can be no true reconciliation and Canada cannot claim it is a just and equal society unless economic and social equality is accorded to Aboriginal people."[69]

How can the TRC contribute to a broader sense of reconciliation in a society that is only prepared to address these power imbalances in an incremental way?[70] Castellano recalls the observation in RCAP's report that in the search for reconciliation between peoples, the leadership of public institutions in adopting a more respectful stance is extremely important.[71] The fact that the mandate does not provide much detail does offer an opportunity for the TRC to broadly interpret its possibilities. While the TRC must exercise caution with respect to what it can reasonably accomplish in the five years it has been granted, perhaps the IRS system can be a springboard for the exploration of broader issues in Indigenous/non-Indigenous relations in Canada. After all, there is a distinction to be made in the TRC's mandate — the TRC is expected to address the IRS *system*, but it is also expected to address the IRS *legacy*. The IRS system is something that can be quantified with respect to how many schools, where they were in operation, for how long, and under what government directives. The IRS legacy is a much more amorphous question. The TRC can complete an effective historical study of the IRS system while exploring broader political questions in its discussion of the IRS legacy. This may include situating the IRS legacy within colonialism, making connections between IRS and socioeconomic conditions for Indigenous communities, consideration of the levels of violence, criminalization, marginalization and discrimination experienced by Indigenous people, or a myriad of other possible avenues of investigation.

Gonzales lists advantages Canada has compared to other states in holding a truth commission, including the government's apology, the presence of "sophisticated advocacy institutions" that have assisted survivors, and the Settlement Agreement on reparations and truth-telling.[72] He states that unlike most societies seeking to inaugurate a truth commission, Canada is not emerging from a period of prolonged or significant violence that has left legal and governance institutions in disarray.[73] Nonetheless, even if Canada does have certain advantages compared to other countries establishing truth commissions, it has some challenges ahead: "Multiple violations of the human dignity of Aboriginal peoples over generations and their relative powerlessness in the face of public institutions have created distrust that public dialogue can bring about change."[74]

Canada has a comparatively privileged opportunity to make considered decisions with respect to institutional design of mechanisms to address deep societal problems. It has a functioning parliament and justice system, a constitution that includes a *Charter of Rights and Freedoms*, an independent judiciary, thousands of trained legal professionals, an active civil society and a rights-conscious culture. These factors can facilitate a process that is responsive to survivors of historical injustice. However, it was a legal settlement agreement that produced the TRC in Canada. Survivors called for the truth commission after years of seeking redress through other legal mechanisms; a truth commission was not the government's choice of how to proceed.[75] Other established democracies that are faced with addressing historical injustices might glean from the Canadian process that a truth commission process may have stronger prospects if it arises from a societal decision, rather than as a result of a settlement of litigation. The survivors sought a legal mechanism other than those that have been tried so far in Canada to address the legacy of IRS. In its mandate, the TRC is designed to fulfill the goals of the parties. However, while the TRC may fulfill some of the needs expressed by survivors for a reconciliation process, given the negligible involvement of the non-Indigenous public, it is hard to say whether reconciliation on a broader societal level can be initiated.